The C++ Standard Library
Second Edition

The C++ Standard Library

A Tutorial and Reference

Second Edition

Nicolai M. Josuttis

✦✦Addison-Wesley

Upper Saddle River, NJ • Boston • Indianapolis • San Francisco
New York • Toronto • Montreal • London • Munich • Paris • Madrid
Capetown • Sydney • Tokyo • Singapore • Mexico City

Many of the designations used by manufacturers and sellers to distinguish their products are claimed as trademarks. Where those designations appear in this book, and the publisher was aware of a trademark claim, the designations have been printed with initial capital letters or in all capitals.

The author and publisher have taken care in the preparation of this book, but make no expressed or implied warranty of any kind and assume no responsibility for errors or omissions. No liability is assumed for incidental or consequential damages in connection with or arising out of the use of the information or programs contained herein.

The publisher offers excellent discounts on this book when ordered in quantity for bulk purchases or special sales, which may include electronic versions and/or custom covers and content particular to your business, training goals, marketing focus, and branding interests. For more information, please contact:

U.S. Corporate and Government Sales
(800) 382-3419
corpsales@pearsontechgroup.com

For sales outside the United States, please contact:
International Sales
international@pearson.com

Visit us on the Web: informit.com/aw

Library of Congress Cataloging-in-Publication Data

Josuttis, Nicolai M.
   The C++ standard library : a tutorial and reference / Nicolai M. Josuttis.—2nd ed.
      p.   cm.
   Includes bibliographical references and index.
   ISBN 978-0-321-62321-8 (hardcover : alk. paper)
   1. C++ (Computer program language) I. Title.
   QA76.73.C153J69 2012
   005.13'3-dc23

                                                        2011045071

This book was typeset by the author using the LaTeX document processing system.

ISBN-13: 978-0-321-62321-8
ISBN-10:   0-321-62321-5

Text printed in the United States on recycled paper at Edwards Brothers in Ann Arbor, Michigan.
First printing, March 2012

To those who care
for people and mankind

Contents

Preface to the Second Edition

I never thought that the first edition of this book would sell so long. But now, after twelve years, it's time for a new edition that covers C++11, the new C++ standard.

Note that this means more than simply adding new libraries. C++ has changed. Almost all typical applications of parts of the library look a bit different now. This is not the result of a huge language change. It's the result of many minor changes, such as using rvalue references and move semantics, range-based `for` loops, `auto`, and new template features. Thus, besides presenting new libraries and supplementary features of existing libraries, almost all of the examples in this book were rewritten at least partially. Nevertheless, to support programmers who still use "old" C++ environments, this book will describe differences between C++ versions whenever they appear.

I learned C++11 the hard way. Because I didn't follow the standardization as it was happening I started to look at C++11 about two years ago. I really had trouble understanding it. But the people on the standardization committee helped me to describe and present the new features as they are intended to be used now.

Note, finally, that this book now has a problem: Although the book's size grew from about 800 to more than 1,100 pages, I still can't present the C++ standard library as a whole. The library part of the new C++11 standard alone now has about 750 pages, written in very condensed form without much explanation. For this reason, I had to decide which features to describe and in how much detail. Again, many people in the C++ community helped me to make this decision. The intent was to concentrate on what the average application programmer needs. For some missing parts, I provide a supplementary chapter on the Web site of this book, `http://www.cppstdlib.com`, but you still will find details not mentioned here in the standard.

The art of teaching is not the art of presenting everything. It's the art of separating the wheat from the chaff so that you get the most out of it. May the exercise succeed.

Acknowledgments for the Second Edition

This book presents ideas, concepts, solutions, and examples from many sources. Over the past several years, the C++ community introduced many ideas, concepts, proposals, and enhancements to C++ that became part of C++11. Thus, again I'd like to thank all the people who helped and supported me while preparing this new edition.

First, I'd like to thank everyone in the C++ community and on the C++ standardization committee. Besides all the work to add new language and library features, they had a hard time explaining everything to me, but they did so with patience and enthusiasm.

Scott Meyers and Anthony Williams allowed me to use their teaching material and book manuscripts so that I could find many useful examples not yet publicly available.

I'd also like to thank everyone who reviewed this book and gave valuable feedback and clarifications: Dave Abrahams, Alberto Ganesh Barbati, Pete Becker, Thomas Becker, Hans Boehm, Walter E. Brown, Paolo Carlini, Lawrence Crowl, Beman Dawes, Doug Gregor, David Grigsby, Pablo Halpern, Howard Hinnant, John Lakos, Bronek Kozicki, Dietmar Kühl, Daniel Krügler, Mat Marcus, Jens Maurer, Alisdair Meredith, Bartosz Milewski, P. J. Plauger, Tobias Schüle, Peter Sommerlad, Jonathan Wakely, and Anthony Williams.

There is one person who did an especially outstanding job. Whenever I had a question, Daniel Krügler answered almost immediately with incredible accurateness and knowledge. Everyone in the standardization process know that he treats everybody this way. Without him, both the C++ standard and this book would not have the quality they have now.

Many thanks to my editor Peter Gordon, Kim Boedigheimer, John Fuller, and Anna Popick from Addison-Wesley. Besides their support, they found the right balance between patience and pressure. The copy editor Evelyn Pyle and the proofreader Diane Freed did an incredible job translating my German English into American English. In addition, thanks to Frank Mittelbach for solving my LATEX issues.

Last but not least, all my thanks go to Jutta Eckstein. Jutta has the wonderful ability to force and support people in their ideals, ideas, and goals. While most people experience this only when working with her, I have the honor to benefit in my day-to-day life.

Preface to the First Edition

In the beginning, I only planned to write a small German book (400 pages or so) about the C++ standard library. That was in 1993. Now, in 1999 you see the result — a book in English with more than 800 pages of facts, figures, and examples. My goal is to describe the C++ standard library so that all (or almost all) your programming questions are answered before you think of the question. Note, however, that this is not a complete description of all aspects of the C++ standard library. Instead, I present the most important topics necessary for learning and programming in C++ by using its standard library.

Each topic is described based on the general concepts; this discussion then leads to the specific details needed to support everyday programming tasks. Specific code examples are provided to help you understand the concepts and the details.

That's it — in a nutshell. I hope you get as much pleasure from reading this book as I did from writing it. Enjoy!

Acknowledgments for the First Edition

This book presents ideas, concepts, solutions, and examples from many sources. In a way it does not seem fair that my name is the only name on the cover. Thus, I'd like to thank all the people and companies who helped and supported me during the past few years.

First, I'd like to thank Dietmar Kühl. Dietmar is an expert on C++, especially on input/output streams and internationalization (he implemented an I/O stream library just for fun). He not only translated major parts of this book from German to English, he also wrote sections of this book using his expertise. In addition, he provided me with invaluable feedback over the years.

Second, I'd like to thank all the reviewers and everyone else who gave me their opinion. These people endow the book with a quality it would never have had without their input. (Because the list is extensive, please forgive me for any oversight.) The reviewers for the English version of this book included Chuck Allison, Greg Comeau, James A. Crotinger, Gabriel Dos Reis, Alan Ezust, Nathan Myers, Werner Mossner, Todd Veldhuizen, Chichiang Wan, Judy Ward, and Thomas Wikehult. The German reviewers included Ralf Boecker, Dirk Herrmann, Dietmar Kühl, Edda Lörke, Herbert Scheubner, Dominik Strasser, and Martin Weitzel. Additional input was provided by Matt Austern, Valentin Bonnard, Greg Colvin, Beman Dawes, Bill Gibbons, Lois Goldthwaite, Andrew Koenig, Steve Rumsby, Bjarne Stroustrup, and David Vandevoorde.

Special thanks to Dave Abrahams, Janet Cocker, Catherine Ohala, and Maureen Willard who reviewed and edited the whole book very carefully. Their feedback was an incredible contribution to the quality of this book.

A special thanks goes to my "personal living dictionary" — Herb Sutter — the author of the famous "Guru of the Week" (a regular series of C++ programming problems that is published on the `comp.lang.c++.moderated` Internet newsgroup).

I'd also like to thank all the people and companies who gave me the opportunity to test my examples on different platforms with different compilers. Many thanks to Steve Adamczyk, Mike Anderson, and John Spicer from EDG for their great compiler and their support. It was a big help during the standardization process and the writing of this book. Many thanks to P. J. Plauger and Dinkumware, Ltd, for their early standard-conforming implementation of the C++ standard library. Many thanks to Andreas Hommel and Metrowerks for an evaluative version of their CodeWarrior Programming Environment. Many thanks to all the developers of the free GNU and egcs compilers. Many thanks to Microsoft for an evaluative version of Visual C++. Many thanks to Roland Hartinger from Siemens Nixdorf Informations Systems AG for a test version of their C++ compiler. Many thanks to Topjects GmbH for an evaluative version of the ObjectSpace library implementation.

Many thanks to everyone from Addison Wesley Longman who worked with me. Among others this includes Janet Cocker, Mike Hendrickson, Debbie Lafferty, Marina Lang, Chanda Leary, Catherine Ohala, Marty Rabinowitz, Susanne Spitzer, and Maureen Willard. It was fun.

In addition, I'd like to thank the people at BREDEX GmbH and all the people in the C++ community, particularly those involved with the standardization process, for their support and patience (sometimes I ask really silly questions).

Last but not least, many thanks and kisses for my family: Ulli, Lucas, Anica, and Frederic. I definitely did not have enough time for them due to the writing of this book.

Have fun and be human!

Chapter 1

About This Book

1.1 Why This Book

Soon after its introduction, C++ became a de facto standard in object-oriented programming. This led to the goal of standardization. Only by having a standard could programs be written that would run on different platforms — from PCs to mainframes. Furthermore, a standard *library* would enable programmers to use general components and a higher level of abstraction without losing portability rather than having to develop all code from scratch.

Now, with the second standard, called C++11 (see Section 2.1, page 7, for the detailed history of C++ standards), we have a huge C++ standard library whose specification requires more than double the size of the core language features. The library enables the use of

- Input/output (I/O) classes
- String types and regular expressions
- Various data structures, such as dynamic arrays, linked lists, binary trees, and hash tables
- Various algorithms, such as a variety of sorting algorithms
- Classes for multithreading and concurrency
- Classes for internationalization support
- Numeric classes
- Plenty of utilities

However, the library is not self-explanatory. To use these components and to benefit from their power, you need an introduction that explains the concepts and the important details instead of simply listing the classes and their functions. This book is written exactly for that purpose. First, it introduces the library and all its components from a conceptual point of view. Next, the book describes the details needed for practical programming. Examples are included to demonstrate the exact use of the components. Thus, this book is a detailed introduction to the C++ library for both the beginner and the practicing programmer. Armed with the data provided herein, you should be able to take full advantage of the C++ standard library.

Caveat: I don't promise that everything described is easy and self-explanatory. The library provides a lot of flexibility, but flexibility for nontrivial purposes has a price. The library has traps and pitfalls, which I point out when we encounter them and suggest ways of avoiding them.

1.2 Before Reading This Book

To get the most from this book, you should already know C++. (The book describes the standard components of C++ but not the language itself.) You should be familiar with the concepts of classes, inheritance, templates, exception handling, and namespaces. However, you don't have to know all the minor details about the language. The important details are described in the book; the minor details about the language are more important for people who want to implement the library rather than to use it.

Note that the language has changed during the standardization of C++11, just as it changed during the standardization of C++98, so your knowledge might not be up-to-date. Chapter 3 provides a brief overview of and introduction to the latest language features that are important for using the C++11 library. Many of the new library features use these new language features, so you should read Chapter 3 to review all the new features of C++. But I will also refer to that chapter when libraries use new language features.

1.3 Style and Structure of the Book

The C++ standard library provides components that are somewhat, but not totally, independent of one another, so there is no easy way to describe each part without mentioning others. I considered various approaches for presenting the contents of this book. One was on the order of the C++ standard. However, this is not the best way to explain the components of the C++ standard library from scratch. Another approach was to start with an overview of all components, followed by chapters that provided more details. Alternatively, I could have sorted the components, trying to find an order that had a minimum of cross-references to other sections. My solution was to use a mixture of all three approaches. I start with a brief introduction of the general concepts and the utilities that the library uses. Then, I describe all the components, each in one or more chapters. The first component is the standard template library (STL). There is no doubt that the STL is the most powerful, most complex, and most exciting part of the library. Its design influences other components heavily. Then, I describe the more self-explanatory components, such as special containers, strings, and regular expressions. The next component discussed is one you probably know and use already: the IOStream library. That component is followed by a discussion of internationalization, which had some influence on the IOStream library. Finally, I describe the library parts dealing with numerics, concurrency, and allocators.

Each component description begins with the component's purpose, design, and some examples. Next, a detailed description begins with various ways to use the component, as well as any traps and pitfalls associated with it. The description usually ends with a reference section, in which you can find the exact signature and definition of a component's classes and its functions.

List of Contents

The first five chapters introduce this book and the C++ standard library in general:

- **Chapter 1: About This Book** introduces the book's subject and describes its contents.
- **Chapter 2: Introduction to C++ and the Standard Library** provides a brief overview of the history of the C++ standard library and the context of its standardization and introduces the concept of complexity.
- **Chapter 3: New Language Features** provides an overview of the new language features you should know to read this book and to use the C++ standard library.
- **Chapter 4: General Concepts** describes the fundamental library concepts that you need to understand to work with all the components. In particular, the chapter introduces the namespace std, the format of header files, and the general support of error and exception handling.
- **Chapter 5: Utilities** describes several small utilities provided for the user of the library and for the library itself. In particular, the chapter describes classes pair<> and tuple<>, smart pointers, numeric limits, type traits and type utilities, auxiliary functions, class ratio<>, clocks and timers, and available C functions.

Chapters 6 through 11 describe all aspects of the STL:

- **Chapter 6: The Standard Template Library** presents a detailed introduction to the concept of the STL, which provides container classes and algorithms that are used to process collections of data. The chapter explains step-by-step the concept, the problems, and the special programming techniques of the STL, as well as the roles of its parts.
- **Chapter 7: STL Containers** explains the concepts and describes the abilities of the STL's container classes. The chapter describes arrays, vectors, deques, lists, forward lists, sets, maps, and unordered containers with their common abilities, differences, specific benefits, and drawbacks and provides typical examples.
- **Chapter 8: STL Container Members in Detail** lists and describes all container members (types and operations) in the form of a handy reference.
- **Chapter 9: STL Iterators** explains the various iterator categories, the auxiliary functions for iterators, and the iterator adapters, such as stream iterators, reverse iterators, insert iterators, and move iterators.
- **Chapter 10: STL Function Objects and Using Lambdas** details the STL's function object classes, including lambdas, and how to use them to define the behavior of containers and algorithms.
- **Chapter 11: STL Algorithms** lists and describes the STL's algorithms. After a brief introduction and comparison of the algorithms, each algorithm is described in detail, followed by one or more example programs.

Chapters 12 through 14 describe "simple" individual standard classes of the C++ standard library:

- **Chapter 12: Special Containers** describes the container adapters for queues and stacks, as well as the class bitset, which manages a bitfield with an arbitrary number of bits or flags.
- **Chapter 13: Strings** describes the string types of the C++ standard library (yes, there are more than one). The standard provides strings as "kind of" fundamental data types with the ability to use different types of characters.

- **Chapter 14: Regular Expressions** describes the interface to deal with regular expressions, which can be used to search and replace characters and substrings.

Chapters 15 and 16 deal with the two closely related subjects of I/O and internationalization:

- **Chapter 15: Input/Output Using Stream Classes** covers the standardized form of the commonly known IOStream library. The chapter also describes details that are typically not so well known but that may be important to programmers, such as the correct way to define and integrate special I/O channels.

- **Chapter 16: Internationalization** covers the concepts and classes for the internationalization of programs, such as the handling of different character sets and the use of different formats for floating-point numbers and dates.

The remaining chapters cover numerics, concurrency, and allocators:

- **Chapter 17: Numerics** describes the numeric components of the C++ standard library: in particular, classes for random numbers and distributions, types for complex numbers, and some numeric C functions.

- **Chapter 18: Concurrency** describes the features provided by the C++ standard library to enable and support concurrency and multithreading.

- **Chapter 19: Allocators** describes the concept of different memory models in the C++ standard library.

The book concludes with a **bibliography** and an **index**.

Due to the size of this book I had to move material that is not so relevant for the average application programmer but should be covered to a **supplementary chapter** provided on the Web site of this book: `http::/www.cppstdlib.com`. That material includes:

- Details of bitsets (introduced in Section 12.5)
- Class `valarray<>` (very briefly introduced in Section 17.4)
- Details of allocators (introduced in Chapter 19)

1.4   How to Read This Book

This book is both an introductory user's guide and a structured reference manual about the C++ standard library. The individual components of the C++ standard library are somewhat independent of one another, so after reading Chapters 2 through 5 you could read the chapters that discuss the individual components in any order. Bear in mind that Chapters 6 through 11 all describe the same component. To understand the other STL chapters, you should start with the introduction to the STL in Chapter 6.

If you are a C++ programmer who wants to know, in general, the concepts and all parts of the library, you could simply read the book from beginning to end. However, you should skip the reference sections. To program with certain components of the C++ standard library, the best way to find something is to use the index, which I have tried to make comprehensive enough to save you time when you are looking for something.

In my experience, the best way to learn something new is to look at examples. Therefore, you'll find a lot of examples throughout the book. They may be a few lines of code or complete programs.

In the latter case, you'll find the name of the file containing the program as the first comment line. You can find the files on the Internet at the Web site of the book: `http://www.cppstdlib.com`.

1.5 State of the Art

The C++11 standard was completed while I was writing this book. Please bear in mind that some compilers might not yet conform to the standard. This will most likely change in the near future. As a consequence, you might discover that not all things covered in this book work as described on your system, and you may have to change example programs to fit your specific environment.

1.6 Example Code and Additional Information

You can access all example programs and acquire more information about this book and the C++ standard library from my Web site: `http://www.cppstdlib.com`. Also, you can find a lot of additional information about this topic on the Internet. See the bibliography, which is also provided on the Web site, for some of them.

1.7 Feedback

I welcome your feedback (good and bad) on this book. I tried to prepare it carefully; however, I'm human, and at some point I have to stop writing and tweaking. So, you may find some errors, inconsistencies, or subjects that could be described better. Your feedback will give me the chance to improve later editions.

The best way to reach me is by email. However, to avoid spam problems, I haven't included an email address inside this book. (I had to stop using the email address I put in the first edition after I started getting thousands of spam emails per day.) Please refer to the book's Web site, `http://www.cppstdlib.com`, to get an email address for feedback.

Many thanks.

Chapter 2

Introduction to C++ and the Standard Library

In this chapter, I discuss the history and different versions of C++ and introduce the *Big-O notation*, which is used to specify the performance and scalability of library operations.

2.1 History of the C++ Standards

The standardization of C++ was started in 1989 by the International Organization for Standardization (ISO), which is a group of national standards organizations, such as ANSI in the United States. To date, this work has resulted in four milestones, which are more or less C++ standards available on different platforms throughout the world:

1. **C++98**, approved in 1998, was the first C++ standard. Its official title is *Information Technology — Programming Languages — C++*, and its document number is ISO/IEC 14882:1998.

2. **C++03**, a so-called "technical corrigendum" ("TC"), contains minor bug fixes to C++98. Its document number is ISO/IEC 14882:2003. Thus, both C++98 and C++03 refer to the "first C++ standard."

3. **TR1** contains library extensions for the first standard. Its official title is *Information Technology — Programming Languages — Technical Report on C++ Library Extensions*, and its document number is ISO/IEC TR 19768:2007. The extensions specified here were all part of a namespace `std::tr1`.

4. **C++11**, approved in 2011, is the second C++ standard. C++11 has significant improvements in both the language and the library, for which the extensions of TR1 have become part of namespace `std`). The official title is again *Information Technology — Programming Languages — C++*, but a new document number is used: ISO/IEC 14882:2011.

This books covers C++11, which long had the working title "C++0x," with the expectation that it would be done no later than 2009.[1] So, both C++11 and C++0x mean the same thing. Throughout the book, I use the term C++11.

Because some platforms and environments still do not support all of C++11 (both language features and libraries), I mention whether a feature or behavior is available only since C++11.

2.1.1   Common Questions about the C++11 Standard

Where Is the Standard Available?

The latest freely available draft of the C++11 standard is available as document N3242 (see [*C++Std2011Draft*]). While that draft should be adequate for most users and programmers, those who need the real standard have to pay ISO or a national body a price for it.

Why Did the Standardization Take So Long?

You may wonder why the standardization process for both standards took 10 years or more and why it is still not perfect. Note, however, that the standard is the result of many people and companies suggesting improvements and extensions, discussing them with others, waiting for implementations to test them, and solving all problems caused by the intersection of all the features. Nobody was working as a full-time employee for the new C++ standard. The standard is not the result of a company with a big budget and a lot of time. Standards organizations pay nothing or almost nothing to the people who work on developing standards. So, if a participant doesn't work for a company that has a special interest in the standard, the work is done for fun. Thank goodness a lot of dedicated people had the time and the money to do just that. Between 50 and 100 people regularly met about three times a year for a week to discuss all topics and finish the task and used email throughout the rest of the year. As a result, you won't get anything perfect or consistently designed. The result is usable in practice but is not perfect (nothing ever is).

The description of the standard library took up about 50% of the first standard, and that increased to 65% in the second standard. (With C++11, the number of pages covering the library rose from about 350 to about 750 pages.)

Note that the standard has various sources. In fact, any company or country or even individuals could propose new features and extensions, which then had to get accepted by the whole standardization organization. In principle, nothing was designed from scratch.[2] Thus, the result is not very homogeneous. You will find different design principles for different components. A good example is the difference between the string class and the STL, which is a framework for data structures and algorithms:

- String classes are designed as a safe and convenient component. Thus, they provide an almost self-explanatory interface and check for many errors in the interface.

---

[1] The usual joke here is that x finally became a hexadecimal b.

[2] You may wonder why the standardization process did not design a new library from scratch. The major purpose of standardization is not to invent or to develop something; it is to harmonize an existing practice.

- The STL was designed to combine different data structures with different algorithms while achieving the best performance. Thus, the STL is not very convenient and is not required to check for many logical errors. To benefit from the powerful framework and great performance of the STL, you must know the concepts and apply them carefully.

Both of these components are part of the same library. They were harmonized a bit, but they still follow their individual, fundamental design philosophies.

Nevertheless, another goal of C++11 was to simplify things. For this reason, a lot of proposals were introduced in C++11 to solve problems, inconsistencies, and other flaws people found in practice. For example, the way to initialize values and objects was harmonized with C++11. Also, the more or less broken smart pointer class `auto_ptr` was replaced by multiple improved smart pointer classes, previously matured in Boost, a Web site dedicated to free peer-reviewed portable C++ source libraries (see [*Boost*]) to gain practical experience before being included in a new standard or another technical corrigendum.

Is This the Last C++ Standard?

C++11 is not the end of the road. People already have bug fixes, additional requirements, and proposals for new features. Thus, there will probably be another "technical corrigendum" with fixes of bugs and inconsistencies, and sooner or later, there might be a "TR2" and/or a third standard.

2.1.2 Compatibility between C++98 and C++11

A design goal of C++11 was that it remain backward compatible with C++98. In principle, everything that compiled with C++98 or C++03 should compile with C++11. However, there are some exceptions. For example, variables cannot have the name of newly introduced keywords anymore.

If code should work with different C++ versions but benefit from the improvements of C++11, if available, you can evaluate the predefined macro `__cplusplus`. For C++11, the following definition holds when compiling a C++ translation unit:

```
#define __cplusplus 201103L
```

By contrast, with both C++98 and C++03, it was:

```
#define __cplusplus 199711L
```

Note, however, that compiler vendors sometimes provide different values here.

Note that backward compatibility applies only to the source code. Binary compatibility is not guaranteed, which leads to problems, especially when an existing operation got a new return type, because overloading by the return type only is not allowed (for example, this applies to some STL algorithms and to some member functions of STL containers). So, compiling all parts, including the libraries, of a C++98 program using a C++11 compiler should usually work. Linking code compiled using a C++11 compiler with code compiled using a C++98 compiler might fail.

2.2   Complexity and Big-O Notation

For certain parts of the C++ standard library — especially for the STL — the performance of algorithms and member functions was considered carefully. Thus, the standard requires a certain *complexity* of them. Computer scientists use a specialized notation to express the relative complexity of an algorithm. Using this measure, one can quickly categorize the relative runtime of an algorithm, as well as perform qualitative comparisons between algorithms. This measure is called *Big-O notation*.

Big-O notation expresses the runtime of an algorithm as a function of a given input of size n. For example, if the runtime grows linearly with the number of elements — doubling the input doubles the runtime — the complexity is $O(n)$. If the runtime is independent of the input, the complexity is $O(1)$. Table 2.1 lists typical values of complexity and their Big-O notation.

Type	Notation	Meaning
Constant	$O(1)$	The runtime is independent of the number of elements.
Logarithmic	$O(log(n))$	The runtime grows logarithmically with respect to the number of elements.
Linear	$O(n)$	The runtime grows linearly (with the same factor) as the number of elements grows.
n-log-n	$O(n * log(n))$	The runtime grows as a product of linear and logarithmic complexity.
Quadratic	$O(n^2)$	The runtime grows quadratically with respect to the number of elements.

Table 2.1. Typical Values of Complexity

It is important to observe that Big-O notation hides factors with smaller exponents, such as constant factors. In particular, it doesn't matter how long an algorithm takes. Any two linear algorithms are considered equally acceptable by this measure. There may even be some situations in which the constant is so huge in a linear algorithm that even an exponential algorithm with a small constant would be preferable in practice. This is a valid criticism of Big-O notation. Just be aware that it is only a rule of thumb; the algorithm with optimal complexity is not necessarily the best one.

Table 2.2 lists all the categories of complexity with a certain number of elements to give you a feel of how fast the runtime grows with respect to the number of elements. As you can see, with a small number of elements, the running times don't differ much. Here, constant factors that are hidden by Big-O notation may have a big influence. However, the more elements you have, the bigger the differences in the running times, so constant factors become meaningless. Remember to "think big" when you consider complexity.

Some complexity definitions in the C++ reference manual are specified as *amortized*. This means that the operations *in the long term* behave as described. However, a single operation may take longer than specified. For example, if you append elements to a dynamic array, the runtime depends on whether the array has enough memory for one more element. If there is enough memory, the complexity is constant because inserting a new last element always takes the same time. However, if there is not enough memory, the complexity is linear because, depending on the number of elements, you have to allocate new memory and copy all elements. Reallocations are rather rare, so any

Complexity		Number of Elements							
Type	**Notation**	**1**	**2**	**5**	**10**	**50**	**100**	**1,000**	**10,000**
Constant	O(1)	1	1	1	1	1	1	1	1
Logarithmic	O($log(n)$)	1	2	3	4	6	7	10	13
Linear	O(n)	1	2	5	10	50	100	1,000	10,000
n-log-n	O($n * log(n)$)	1	4	15	40	300	700	10,000	130,000
Quadratic	O(n^2)	1	4	25	100	2,500	10,000	1,000,000	100,000,000

Table 2.2. Runtime with Respect to the Complexity and the Number of Elements

sufficiently long sequence of that operation behaves as if each operation has constant complexity. Thus, the complexity of the insertion is "amortized" constant time.

Chapter 3

New Language Features

The core language and the library of C++ are usually standardized in parallel. In this way, the library can benefit from improvements in the language, and the language can benefit from experiences of library implementation. As a result, a C++ standard library always uses specific language features, which might not be available with previous versions of the standard.

Thus, C++11 is not the same language as C++98/C++03, and C++98/C++03 differs from C++ before it was standardized. If you didn't follow its evolution, you may be surprised by the new language features the library uses. This chapter gives you a brief overview of the new features of C++11, which are important for the design, understanding, or application of the C++11 standard library. The end of this chapter covers some of the features that were available before C++11 but are still not widely known.

While I was writing this book (in 2010 and 2011), not all compilers were able to provide all the new language features of C++11. I expect that this will soon change because all major C++ compiler vendors were part of the standardization process. But for some period of time, you may be restricted in your use of the library. Throughout the book I'll use footnotes to mention any restrictions that are typical and important.

3.1 New C++11 Language Features

3.1.1 Important Minor Syntax Cleanups

First, I'd like to introduce two new features of C++11 that are minor but important for your day-to-day programming.

Spaces in Template Expressions

The requirement to put a space between two closing template expressions has gone:

```
vector<list<int> >;      // OK in each C++ version
vector<list<int>>;       // OK since C++11
```

Throughout the book (as in real code) you will find both forms.

`nullptr` and `std::nullptr_t`

C++11 lets you use `nullptr` instead of 0 or NULL to specify that a pointer refers to no value (which differs from having an undefined value). This new feature especially helps to avoid mistakes that occurred when a null pointer was interpreted as an integral value. For example:

```
void f(int);
void f(void*);

f(0);           // calls f(int)
f(NULL);        // calls f(int) if NULL is 0, ambiguous otherwise
f(nullptr);     // calls f(void*)
```

`nullptr` is a new keyword. It automatically converts into each pointer type but not to any integral type. It has type `std::nullptr_t`, defined in `<cstddef>` (see Section 5.8.1, page 161), so you can now even overload operations for the case that a null pointer is passed. Note that `std::nullptr_t` counts as a fundamental data type (see Section 5.4.2, page 127).

3.1.2 Automatic Type Deduction with `auto`

With C++11, you can declare a variable or an object without specifying its specific type by using `auto`.[1] For example:

```
auto i = 42;     // i has type int
double f();
auto d = f();    // d has type double
```

The type of a variable declared with `auto` is deduced from its initializer. Thus, an initialization is required:

```
auto i;          // ERROR: can't deduce the type of i
```

Additional qualifiers are allowed. For example:

```
static auto vat = 0.19;
```

Using `auto` is especially useful where the type is a pretty long and/or complicated expression. For example:

```
vector<string> v;
...
auto pos = v.begin();    // pos has type vector<string>::iterator

auto l = [] (int x) -> bool {    // l has the type of a lambda
            ...,                 // taking an int and returning a bool
         };
```

The latter is an object, representing a lambda, which is introduced in Section 3.1.10, page 28.

---

[1] Note that `auto` is an old keyword of C. As the counterpart of `static`, declaring a variable as local, it was never used, because not specifying something as static implicitly declared it as `auto`.

3.1.3 Uniform Initialization and Initializer Lists

Before C++11, programmers, especially novices, could easily become confused by the question of how to initialize a variable or an object. Initialization could happen with parentheses, braces, and/or assignment operators.

For this reason, C++11 introduced the concept of uniform initialization, which means that for any initialization, you can use one common syntax. This syntax uses braces, so the following is possible now:

```
int values[] { 1, 2, 3 };
std::vector<int> v { 2, 3, 5, 7, 11, 13, 17 };
std::vector<std::string> cities {
    "Berlin", "New York", "London", "Braunschweig", "Cairo", "Cologne"
};
std::complex<double> c{4.0,3.0};    // equivalent to c(4.0,3.0)
```

An initializer list forces so-called *value initialization*, which means that even local variables of fundamental data types, which usually have an undefined initial value, are initialized by zero (or `nullptr`, if it is a pointer):

```
int i;         // i has undefined value
int j{};       // j is initialized by 0
int* p;        // p has undefined value
int* q{};      // q is initialized by nullptr
```

Note, however, that *narrowing* initializations — those that reduce precision or where the supplied value gets modified — are not possible with braces. For example:

```
int x1(5.3);                      // OK, but OUCH: x1 becomes 5
int x2 = 5.3;                     // OK, but OUCH: x2 becomes 5
int x3{5.0};                      // ERROR: narrowing
int x4 = {5.3};                   // ERROR: narrowing
char c1{7};                       // OK: even though 7 is an int, this is not narrowing
char c2{99999};                   // ERROR: narrowing (if 99999 doesn't fit into a char)
std::vector<int> v1 { 1, 2, 4, 5 };     // OK
std::vector<int> v2 { 1, 2.3, 4, 5.6 };  // ERROR: narrowing doubles to ints
```

As you can see, to check whether narrowing applies, even the current values might be considered, if available at compile time. As Bjarne Stroustrup writes in [*Stroustrup:FAQ*] regarding this example: "The way C++11 avoids a lot of incompatibilities is by relying on the actual values of initializers (such as 7 in the example above) when it can (and not just type) when deciding what is a narrowing conversion. If a value can be represented exactly as the target type, the conversion is not narrowing. Note that floating-point to integer conversions are always considered narrowing — even 7.0 to 7."

To support the concept of initializer lists for user-defined types, C++11 provides the class template `std::initializer_list<>`. It can be used to support initializations by a list of values or in any other place where you want to process just a list of values. For example:

```
void print (std::initializer_list<int> vals)
{
    for (auto p=vals.begin(); p!=vals.end(); ++p) {   // process a list of values
        std::cout << *p << "\n";
    }
}
```

```
print ({12,3,5,7,11,13,17});   // pass a list of values to print()
```

When there are constructors for both a specific number of arguments and an initializer list, the
version with the initializer list is preferred:

```
class P
{
  public:
    P(int,int);
    P(std::initializer_list<int>);
};
```

```
P p(77,5);          // calls P::P(int,int)
P q{77,5};          // calls P::P(initializer_list)
P r{77,5,42};       // calls P::P(initializer_list)
P s = {77,5};       // calls P::P(initializer_list)
```

Without the constructor for the initializer list, the constructor taking two ints would be called to
initialize q and s, while the initialization of r would be invalid.

Because of initializer lists, explicit now also becomes relevant for constructors taking more
than one argument. So, you can now disable automatic type conversions from multiple values, which
is also used when an initialization uses the = syntax:

```
class P
{
  public:
    P(int a, int b) {
        ...
    }
    explicit P(int a, int b, int c) {
        ...
    }
};
```

```
P x(77,5);        // OK
P y{77,5};        // OK
P z {77,5,42};    // OK
P v = {77,5};     // OK (implicit type conversion allowed)
P w = {77,5,42};  // ERROR due to explicit (no implicit type conversion allowed)
```

```
void fp(const P&);
```

```
fp({47,11});        // OK, implicit conversion of {47,11} into P
fp({47,11,3});      // ERROR due to explicit
fp(P{47,11});       // OK, explicit conversion of {47,11} into P
fp(P{47,11,3});     // OK, explicit conversion of {47,11,3} into P
```

In the same manner, an `explicit` constructor taking an initializer list disables implicit conversions for initializer lists with zero, one, or more initial values.

3.1.4 Range-Based `for` Loops

C++11 introduces a new form of `for` loop, which iterates over all elements of a given range, array, or collection. It's what in other programming languages would be called a *foreach* loop. The general syntax is as follows:

```
for ( decl : coll ) {
    statement
}
```

where *decl* is the declaration of each element of the passed collection *coll* and for which the statements specified are called. For example, the following calls for each value of the passed initializer list the specified statement, which writes it on a line to the standard output `cout`:

```
for ( int i : { 2, 3, 5, 7, 9, 13, 17, 19 } ) {
    std::cout << i << std::endl;
}
```

To multiply each element `elem` of a vector `vec` by 3 you can program as follows:

```
std::vector<double> vec;
...
for ( auto& elem : vec ) {
    elem *= 3;
}
```

Here, declaring `elem` as a reference is important because otherwise the statements in the body of the `for` loop act on a local copy of the elements in the vector (which sometimes also might be useful).

This means that to avoid calling the copy constructor and the destructor for each element, you should usually declare the current element to be a constant reference. Thus, a generic function to print all elements of a collection should be implemented as follows:

```
template <typename T>
void printElements (const T& coll)
{
    for (const auto& elem : coll) {
        std::cout << elem << std::endl;
    }
}
```

Here, the range-based `for` statement is equivalent to the following:

```
{
    for (auto _pos=coll.begin(); _pos != coll.end(); ++_pos ) {
        const auto& elem = *_pos;
        std::cout << elem << std::endl;
    }
}
```

In general, a range-based `for` loop declared as

```
for ( decl : coll ) {
    statement
}
```

is equivalent to the following, if *coll* provides `begin()` and `end()` members:

```
{
    for (auto _pos=coll.begin(), _end=coll.end(); _pos!=_end; ++_pos ) {
        decl = *_pos;
        statement
    }
}
```

or, if that doesn't match, to the following by using a global `begin()` and `end()` taking *coll* as argument:

```
{
    for (auto _pos=begin(coll), _end=end(coll); _pos!=_end; ++_pos ) {
        decl = *_pos;
        statement
    }
}
```

As a result, you can use range-based `for` loops even for initializer lists because the class template `std::initializer_list<>` provides `begin()` and `end()` members.

In addition, there is a rule that allows you to use ordinary C-style arrays of known size. For example:

```
int array[] = { 1, 2, 3, 4, 5 };

long sum=0;        // process sum of all elements
for (int x : array) {
    sum += x;
}

for (auto elem : { sum, sum*2, sum*4 } ) {  // print some multiples of sum
    std::cout << elem << std::endl;
}
```

has the following output:

```
15
30
60
```

Note that no explicit type conversions are possible when elements are initialized as *decl* inside the for loop. Thus, the following does not compile:

```
class C
{
  public:
    explicit C(const std::string& s);   // explicit(!) type conversion from strings
    ...
};

std::vector<std::string> vs;
for (const C& elem : vs) {   // ERROR, no conversion from string to C defined
    std::cout << elem << std::endl;
}
```

3.1.5 Move Semantics and Rvalue References

One of the most important new features of C++11 is the support of move semantics. This feature goes further into the major design goal of C++ to avoid unnecessary copies and temporaries.

This new feature is so complex that I recommend using a more detailed introduction to this topic, but I will try to give a brief introduction and summary here.[2]

Consider the following code example:

```
void createAndInsert (std::set<X>& coll)
{
    X x;  // create an object of type X
    ...
    coll.insert(x);   // insert it into the passed collection
}
```

Here, we insert a new object into a collection, which provides a member function that creates an internal copy of the passed element:

```
namespace std {
    template <typename T, ...> class set {
      public:
        ... insert (const T& v);   // copy value of v
```

___

[2] This introduction is based on [*Abrahams:RValues*] (with friendly permission by Dave Abrahams), on [*Becker:RValues*] (with friendly permission by Thomas Becker), and some emails exchanged with Daniel Krügler, Dietmar Kühl, and Jens Maurer.

```
        ...
    };
}
```

This behavior is useful because the collection provides value semantics and the ability to insert temporary objects or objects that are used and modified after being inserted:

```
X x;
coll.insert(x);        // inserts copy of x

...

coll.insert(x+x);      // inserts copy of temporary rvalue

...

coll.insert(x);        // inserts copy of x (although x is not used any longer)
```

However, for the last two insertions of x, it would be great to specify a behavior that the passed values (the result of x+x and x) are no longer used by the caller so that `coll` internally could avoid creating a copy and somehow *move* the contents of them into its new elements. Especially when copying x is expensive — for example, if it is a large collection of strings — this could become a big performance improvement.

Since C++11, such a behavior is possible. The programmer, however, has to specify that a move is possible unless a temporary is used. Although a compiler might find this out in trivial cases, allowing the programmer to perform this task lets this feature be used in all cases, where logically appropriate. The preceding code simply has to get modified as follows:

```
X x;
coll.insert(x);        // inserts copy of x (OK, x is still used)

...

coll.insert(x+x);      // moves (or copies) contents of temporary rvalue

...

coll.insert(std::move(x));    // moves (or copies) contents of x into coll
```

With `std::move()`, declared in `<utility>`, x can be *moved* instead of being copied. However, `std::move()` doesn't itself do any moving, but merely converts its argument into a so-called *rvalue reference*, which is a type declared with two ampersands: X&&. This new type stands for rvalues (anonymous temporaries that can appear only on the right-hand side of an assignment) that can be modified. The contract is that this is a (temporary) object that is not needed any longer so that you can *steal* its contents and/or its resources.

Now, the collection can provide an overloaded version of `insert()`, which deals with these rvalue references:

```
namespace std {
    template <typename T, ...> class set {
      public:
        ... insert (const T& x);    // for lvalues: copies the value
        ... insert (T&& x);         // for rvalues: moves the value

        ...
    };
}
```

The version for rvalue references can now be optimized so that its implementation *steals* the contents of x. To do that, however, we need the help of the type of x, because only the type of x has access to its internals. So, for example, you could use internal arrays and pointers of x to initialize the inserted element, which would be a huge performance improvement if class x is itself a complex type, where you had to copy element-by-element instead. To initialize the new internal element, we simply call a so-called *move constructor* of class X, which *steals* the value of the passed argument to initialize a new object. All complex types should — and in the C++ standard library will — provide such a special constructor, which moves the contents of an existing element to a new element:

```
class X {
  public:
    X (const X& lvalue);   // copy constructor
    X (X&& rvalue);        // move constructor
    ...
};
```

For example, the move constructor for strings typically just assigns the existing internal character array to the new object instead of creating a new array and copying all elements. The same applies to all collection classes: Instead of creating a copy of all elements, you just assign the internal memory to the new object. If no move constructor is provided, the copy constructor will be used.

In addition, you have to ensure that any modification — especially a destruction — of the passed object, where the value was *stolen* from, doesn't impact the state of the new object that now owns the value. Thus, you usually have to clear the contents of the passed argument (for example, by assigning nullptr to its internal member referring to its elements).

Clearing the contents of an object for which move semantics were called is, strictly speaking, not required, but not doing so makes the whole mechanism almost useless. In fact, for the classes of the C++ standard library in general, it is guaranteed that after a move, the objects are in a *valid but unspecified* state. That is, you can assign new values afterward, but the current value is not defined. For STL containers, it is guaranteed that containers where the value was moved from are empty afterward.

In the same way, any nontrivial class should provide both a copy assignment and a move assignment operator:

```
class X {
  public:
    X& operator= (const X& lvalue);  // copy assignment operator
    X& operator= (X&& rvalue);       // move assignment operator
    ...
};
```

For strings and collections these operators could be implemented by simply swapping the internal contents and resources. However, you should also clear the contents of *this because this object might hold resources, such as locks, for which it is better to release them sooner. Again, the move semantics don't require that, but it is a quality of move support that, for example, is provided by the container classes of the C++ standard library.

Finally, note the following two remarks about this feature: (1) overloading rules for rvalue and lvalue references and (2) returning rvalue references.

Overloading Rules for Rvalue and Lvalue References

The overloading rules for rvalues and lvalues are as follows:[3]

- If you implement only

      void foo(X&);

  without `void foo(X&&)`, the behavior is as in C++98: `foo()` can be called for lvalues but not for rvalues.
- If you implement

      void foo(const X&);

  without `void foo(X&&)`, the behavior is as in C++98: `foo()` can be called for rvalues and for lvalues.
- If you implement

      void foo(X&);
      void foo(X&&);

  or

      void foo(const X&);
      void foo(X&&);

  you can distinguish between dealing with rvalues and lvalues. The version for rvalues is allowed to and should provide move semantics. Thus, it can *steal* the internal state and resources of the passed argument.
- If you implement

      void foo(X&&);

  but neither `void foo(X&)` nor `void foo(const X&)`, `foo()` can be called on rvalues, but trying to call it on an lvalue will trigger a compile error. Thus, only move semantics are provided here. This ability is used inside the library: for example, by unique pointers (see Section 5.2.5, page 98), file streams (see Section 15.9.2, page 795), or string streams (see Section 15.10.2, page 806),

This means that if a class does not provide move semantics and has only the usual copy constructor and copy assignment operator, these will be called for rvalue references. Thus, `std::move()` means to call move semantics, if provided, and copy semantics otherwise.

Returning Rvalue References

You don't have to and should not `move()` return values. According to the language rules, the standard specifies that for the following code:[4]

```
X foo ()
{
    X x;
    ...
```

---

[3] Thanks to Thomas Becker for providing this wording.

[4] Thanks to Dave Abrahams for providing this wording.

```
        return x;
    }
```

the following behavior is guaranteed:

- If X has an accessible copy or move constructor, the compiler may choose to elide the copy. This is the so-called *(named) return value optimization ((N)RVO)*, which was specified even before C++11 and is supported by most compilers.
- Otherwise, if X has a move constructor, x is moved.
- Otherwise, if X has a copy constructor, x is copied.
- Otherwise, a compile-time error is emitted.

Note also that returning an rvalue reference is an error if the returned object is a local nonstatic object:

```
X&& foo ()
{
    X x;
    ...
    return x;   // ERROR: returns reference to nonexisting object
}
```

An rvalue reference is a reference, and returning it while referring to a local object means that you return a reference to an object that doesn't exist any more. Whether std::move() is used doesn't matter.

3.1.6   New String Literals

Since C++11, you can define raw string and multibyte/wide-character string literals.

Raw String Literals

Such a raw string allows one to define a character sequence by writing exactly its contents as a raw character sequence. Thus, you save a lot of escapes necessary to mask special characters.

A raw string starts with R" (and ends with) ". The string might contain line breaks. For example, an ordinary string literal representing two backslashes and an n would be defined as an ordinary string literal as follows:

```
"\\\\n"
```

and as a raw string literal as follows:

```
R"(\\n)"
```

To be able to have) " inside the raw string, you can use a delimiter. Thus, the complete syntax of a raw string is R"*delim*(...)*delim*", where *delim* is a character sequence of at most 16 basic characters except the backslash, whitespaces, and parentheses.

For example, the raw string literal

```
R"nc(a\
     b\nc()"
     )nc";
```

is equivalent to the following ordinary string literal:

```
"a\\\n     b\\nc()\"\n     "
```

Thus, the string contains an a, a backslash, a newline character, some spaces, a b, a backslash, an n, a c, a double quote character, a newline character, and some spaces.

Raw string literals are especially useful when defining regular expressions. See Chapter 14 for details.

Encoded String Literals

By using an *encoding prefix*, you can define a special character encoding for string literals. The following encoding prefixes are defined:

- **u8** defines a UTF-8 encoding. A UTF-8 string literal is initialized with the given characters as encoded in UTF-8. The characters have type const char.
- **u** defines a string literal with characters of type char16_t.
- **U** defines a string literal with characters of type char32_t.
- **L** defines a wide string literal with characters of type wchar_t.

For example:

```
L"hello"    // defines "hello" as wchar_t string literal
```

The initial R of a raw string can be preceded by an encoding prefix.

See Chapter 16 for details about using different encodings for internationalization.

3.1.7   Keyword `noexcept`

C++11 provides the keyword noexcept. It can be used to specify that a function cannot throw — or is not prepared to throw. For example:

```
void foo () noexcept;
```

declares that foo() won't throw. If an exception is not handled locally inside foo() — thus, if foo() throws — the program is terminated, calling std::terminate(), which by default calls std::abort() (see Section 5.8.2, page 162).

noexcept targets a lot of problems (empty) exception specifications have. To quote from [*N3051:DeprExcSpec*] (with friendly permission by Doug Gregor):

- *Runtime checking*: C++ exception specifications are checked at runtime rather than at compile time, so they offer no programmer guarantees that all exceptions have been handled. The runtime failure mode (calling std::unexpected()) does not lend itself to recovery.
- *Runtime overhead*: Runtime checking requires the compiler to produce additional code that also hampers optimizations.

- *Unusable in generic code*: Within generic code, it is not generally possible to know what types of exceptions may be thrown from operations on template arguments, so a precise exception specification cannot be written.

In practice, only two forms of exception-throwing guarantees are useful: An operation might throw an exception (any exception) or an operation will never throw any exception. The former is expressed by omitting the exception-specification entirely, while the latter can be expressed as `throw()` but rarely is, due to performance considerations.

Especially because `noexcept` does not require stack unwinding, programmers can now express the nothrow guarantee without additional overhead. As a result, the use of exception specifications is deprecated since C++11.

You can even specify a condition under which a function throws no exception. For example, for any type *Type*, the global `swap()` usually is defined as follows:

```
void swap (Type& x, Type& y) noexcept(noexcept(x.swap(y)))
{
    x.swap(y);
}
```

Here, inside `noexcept(...)`, you can specify a Boolean condition under which no exception gets thrown: Specifying `noexcept` without condition is a short form of specifying `noexcept(true)`.

In this case, the condition is `noexcept(x.swap(y))`. Here, the *operator* `noexcept` is used, which yields `true` if an evaluated expression, which is specified within parentheses, can't throw an exception. Thus, the global `swap()` specifies that it does not throw an exception if the member function `swap()` called for the first argument does not throw.

As another example, the move assignment operator for value pairs is declared as follows:

```
pair& operator= (pair&& p)
        noexcept(is_nothrow_move_assignable<T1>::value &&
                 is_nothrow_move_assignable<T2>::value);
```

Here, the `is_nothrow_move_assignable` type trait is used, which checks whether for the passed type, a move assignment that does not throw is possible (see Section 5.4.2, page 127).

According to [*N3279:LibNoexcept*], `noexcept` was introduced inside the library with the following conservative approach (words and phrases in *italics* are quoted literally):

- *Each library function ... that ... cannot throw* and does not specify any undefined behavior — for example, caused by a broken precondition — *should be marked as unconditionally* `noexcept`.
- *If a library swap function, move constructor, or move assignment operator ... can be proven not to throw by applying the* `noexcept` *operator, it should be marked as conditionally* `noexcept`. *No other function should use a conditional* `noexcept` *specification.*
- *No library destructor should throw. It must use the implicitly supplied (nonthrowing) exception specification.*
- *Library functions designed for compatibility with C code ... may be marked as unconditionally* `noexcept`.

Note that `noexcept` was deliberately not applied to any C++ function having a precondition that, if violated, could result in undefined behavior. This allows library implementations to provide a "safe mode" throwing a "precondition violation" exception in the event of misuse.

Throughout this book I usually skip `noexcept` specifications to improve readability and save space.

3.1.8 Keyword `constexpr`

Since C++11, `constexpr` can be used to enable that expressions be evaluated at compile time. For example:

```
constexpr int square (int x)
{
    return x * x;
}
float a[square(9)];   // OK since C++11: a has 81 elements
```

This keyword fixes a problem C++98 had when using numeric limits (see Section 5.3, page 115). Before C++11, an expression such as

```
std::numeric_limits<short>::max()
```

could not be used as an integral constant, although it was functionally equivalent to the macro `INT_MAX`. Now, with C++11, such an expression is declared as `constexpr` so that, for example, you can use it to declare arrays or in compile-time computations (metaprogramming):

```
std::array<float,std::numeric_limits<short>::max()> a;
```

Throughout this book I usually skip `constexpr` specifications to improve readability and save space.

3.1.9 New Template Features

Variadic Templates

Since C++11, templates can have parameters that accept a variable number of template arguments. This ability is called *variadic templates*. For example, you can use the following to call `print()` for a variable number of arguments of different types:

```
void print ()
{
}

template <typename T, typename... Types>
void print (const T& firstArg, const Types&... args)
{
    std::cout << firstArg << std::endl;   // print first argument
    print(args...);                       // call print() for remaining arguments
}
```

If one or more arguments are passed, the function template is used, which by specifying the first argument separately allows the first argument to print and then recursively calls `print()` for the remaining arguments. To end the recursion, the non-template overload of `print()` is provided.

For example, an input such as

```
print (7.5, "hello", std::bitset<16>(377), 42);
```

would output the following (see Section 12.5.1, page 652 for details of bitsets):

```
7.5
hello
0000000101111001
42
```

Note that it is currently under discussion whether the following example also is valid. The reason is that formally for a single argument the variadic form is ambiguous with the nonvariadic form for a single argument; however, compilers usually accept this code:

```
template <typename T>
void print (const T& arg)
{
    std::cout << arg << std::endl;
}

template <typename T, typename... Types>
void print (const T& firstArg, const Types&... args)
{
    std::cout << firstArg << std::endl;   // print first argument
    print(args...);                       // call print() for remaining arguments
}
```

Inside variadic templates, `sizeof...(args)` yields the number of arguments.

Class `std::tuple<>` makes heavy use of this feature (see Section 5.1.2, page 68).

Alias Templates (Template Typedef)

Since C++11, template (partial) type definitions also are supported. However, because all approaches with the `typename` keyword failed for some reason, the keyword `using` was introduced here, and the term *alias template* is used for it. For example, after

```
template <typename T>
using Vec = std::vector<T,MyAlloc<T>>;   // standard vector using own allocator
```

the term

```
Vec<int> coll;
```

is equivalent to

```
std::vector<int,MyAlloc<int>> coll;
```

See Section 5.2.5, page 108, for another example.

Other New Template Features

Since C++11, function templates (see Section 3.2, page 34) may have default template arguments. In addition, local types can be used now as template arguments, and functions with internal linkage can now be used as arguments to nontype templates of function pointers or function references.

3.1.10   Lambdas

C++11 introduced *lambdas*, allowing the definition of inline functionality, which can be used as a parameter or a local object.

Lambdas change the way the C++ standard library is used. For example, Section 6.9, page 229, and Section 10.3, page 499, discuss how to use lambdas with STL algorithms and containers. Section 18.1.2, page 958, demonstrates how to use lambdas to define code that can run concurrently.

Syntax of Lambdas

A lambda is a definition of functionality that can be defined inside statements and expressions. Thus, you can use a lambda as an inline function.

The minimal lambda function has no parameters and simply does something. For example:

```
[] {
    std::cout << "hello lambda" << std::endl;
}
```

You can call it directly:

```
[] {
    std::cout << "hello lambda" << std::endl;
} ();            // prints ''hello lambda''
```

or pass it to objects to get called:

```
auto l = [] {
            std::cout << "hello lambda" << std::endl;
        };
...
l();            // prints ''hello lambda''
```

As you can see, a lambda is always introduced by a so-called *lambda introducer:* brackets within which you can specify a so-called *capture* to access nonstatic outside objects inside the lambda. When there is no need to have access to outside data, the brackets are just empty, as is the case here. Static objects such as std::cout can be used.

Between the lambda introducer and the lambda body, you can specify parameters, mutable, an exception specification, attribute specifiers, and the return type. All of them are optional, but if one of them occurs, the parentheses for the parameters are mandatory. Thus, the syntax of a lambda is either

```
        [...]   {...}
```

or

```
        [...]   (...)   mutableopt throwSpecopt ->retTypeopt {...}
```

A lambda can have parameters specified in parentheses, just like any other function:

```
auto l = [] (const std::string& s) {
            std::cout << s << std::endl;
        };
l("hello lambda");      // prints ''hello lambda''
```

Note, however, that lambdas can't be templates. You always have to specify all types.

A lambda can also return something. Without any specific definition of the return type, it is deduced from the return value. For example, the return type of the following lambda is `int`:

```
[] {
    return 42;
}
```

To specify a return type, you can use the new syntax C++ also provides for ordinary functions (see Section 3.1.12, page 32). For example, the following lambda returns `42.0`:

```
[] () -> double {
    return 42;
}
```

In this case, you have to specify the return type after the parentheses for the arguments, which are required then, and the characters "->."

Between the parameters and the return specification or body, you can also specify an exception specification like you can do for functions. However, as for functions exception specifications are deprecated now (see Section 3.1.7, page 24).

Captures (Access to Outer Scope)

Inside the lambda introducer (brackets at the beginning of a lambda), you can specify a *capture* to access data of outer scope that is not passed as an argument:

- `[=]` means that the outer scope is passed to the lambda by value. Thus, you can read but not modify all data that was readable where the lambda was defined.
- `[&]` means that the outer scope is passed to the lambda by reference. Thus, you have write access to all data that was valid when the lambda was defined, provided that you had write access there.

You can also specify individually for each object that inside the lambda you have access to it by value or by reference. So, you can limit the access and mix different kinds of access. For example, the following statements:

```
int x=0;
int y=42;
auto qqq = [x, &y] {
                std::cout << "x: " << x << std::endl;
                std::cout << "y: " << y << std::endl;
                ++y;  // OK
            };
x = y = 77;
qqq();
qqq();
std::cout << "final y: " << y << std::endl;
```

produce the following output:

```
x: 0
y: 77
x: 0
y: 78
final y: 79
```

Because x gets copied by value, you are not allowed to modify it inside the lambda; calling ++x
inside the lambda would not compile. Because y is passed by reference, you have write access to it
and are affected by any value change; so calling the lambda twice increments the assigned value 77.

Instead of [x, &y], you could also have specified [=, &y] to pass y by reference and all other
objects by value.

To have a mixture of passing by value and passing by reference, you can declare the lambda as
mutable. In that case, objects are passed by value, but inside the function object defined by the
lambda, you have write access to the passed value. For example:

```
int id = 0;
auto f = [id] () mutable {
            std::cout << "id: " << id << std::endl;
            ++id;       // OK
          };
id = 42;
f();
f();
f();
std::cout << id << std::endl;
```

has the following output:

```
id: 0
id: 1
id: 2
42
```

You can consider the behavior of the lambda to be like the following function object (see Section 6.10, page 233):

```
class {
  private:
    int id;   // copy of outside id
  public:
    void operator() () {
            std::cout << "id: " << id << std::endl;
            ++id;       // OK
    }
};
```

Due to `mutable`, operator `()` is defined as a nonconstant member function, which means that write access to `id` is possible. So, with `mutable`, a lambda becomes stateful even if the state is passed by value. Without `mutable`, which is the usual case, operator `()` becomes a constant member function so that you only have read access to objects that were passed by value. See Section 10.3.2, page 501, for another example of using `mutable` with lambdas, which also discusses possible problems.

Type of Lambdas

The type of a lambda is an anonymous function object (or functor) that is unique for each lambda expression. Thus, to declare objects of that type, you need templates or `auto`. If you need the type, you can use `decltype()` (see Section 3.1.11, page 32), which is, for example, required to pass a lambda as hash function or ordering or sorting criterion to associative or unordered containers. See Section 6.9, page 232, and Section 7.9.7, page 379, for details.

Alternatively, you can use the `std::function<>` class template, provided by the C++ standard library, to specify a general type for functional programming (see Section 5.4.4, page 133). That class template provides the only way to specify the return type of a function returning a lambda:

```
// lang/lambda1.cpp

#include<functional>
#include<iostream>

std::function<int(int,int)> returnLambda ()
{
    return [] (int x, int y) {
               return x*y;
           };
}

int main()
{
    auto lf = returnLambda();
    std::cout << lf(6,7) << std::endl;
}
```

The output of the program is (of course):

```
42
```

3.1.11   Keyword `decltype`

By using the new `decltype` keyword, you can let the compiler find out the type of an expression. This is the realization of the often requested `typeof` feature. However, the existing `typeof` implementations were inconsistent and incomplete, so C++11 introduced a new keyword. For example:

```
std::map<std::string,float> coll;
decltype(coll)::value_type elem;
```

One application of `decltype` is to declare return types (see below). Another is to use it in metaprogramming (see Section 5.4.1, page 125) or to pass the type of a lambda (see Section 10.3.4, page 504).

3.1.12   New Function Declaration Syntax

Sometimes, the return type of a function depends on an expression processed with the arguments. However, something like

```
template <typename T1, typename T2>
decltype(x+y) add(T1 x, T2 y);
```

was not possible before C++11, because the return expression uses objects not introduced or in scope yet.

But with C++11, you can alternatively declare the return type of a function behind the parameter list:

```
template <typename T1, typename T2>
auto add(T1 x, T2 y) -> decltype(x+y);
```

This uses the same syntax as for lambdas to declare return types (see Section 3.1.10, page 28).

3.1.13   Scoped Enumerations

C++11 allows the definition of *scoped enumerations* — also called *strong enumerations*, or *enumeration classes* — which are a cleaner implementation of enumeration values (*enumerators*) in C++. For example:

```
enum class Salutation : char { mr, ms, co, none };
```

The important point is to specify keyword `class` behind `enum`.

Scoped enumerations have the following advantages:

- Implicit conversions to and from `int` are not possible.
- Values like `mr` are not part of the scope where the enumeration is declared. You have to use `Salutation::mr` instead.
- You can explicitly define the underlying type (`char` here) and have a guaranteed size (if you skip ": char" here, `int` is the default).
- Forward declarations of the enumeration type are possible, which eliminates the need to recompile compilation units for new enumerations values if only the type is used.

Note that with the type trait `std::underlying_type`, you can evaluate the underlying type of an enumeration type (see Section 5.4.2, page 130).

As an example, error condition values of standard exceptions are *scoped enumerators* (see Section 4.3.2, page 45).

3.1.14 New Fundamental Data Types

The following new fundamental data types are defined in C++11:

- `char16_t` and `char32_t` (see Section 16.1.3, page 852)
- `long long` and `unsigned long long`
- `std::nullptr_t` (see Section 3.1.1, page 14)

3.2 Old "New" Language Features

Although C++98 is more than 10 years old now, programmers still can be surprised by some of the language features. Some of those are presented in this section.

Nontype Template Parameters

In addition to type parameters, it is also possible to use nontype parameters. A nontype parameter is then considered part of the type. For example, for the standard class `bitset<>` (see Section 12.5, page 650), you can pass the number of bits as the template argument. The following statements define two bitfields: one with 32 bits and one with 50 bits:

```
bitset<32> flags32;      // bitset with 32 bits
bitset<50> flags50;      // bitset with 50 bits
```

These bitsets have different types because they use different template arguments. Thus, you can't assign or compare them unless a corresponding type conversion is provided.

Default Template Parameters

Class templates may have default arguments. For example, the following declaration allows one to declare objects of class `MyClass` with one or two template arguments:

```
template <typename T, typename container = vector<T>>
class MyClass;
```

If you pass only one argument, the default parameter is used as the second argument:

```
MyClass<int> x1;          // equivalent to: MyClass<int,vector<int>>
```

Note that default template arguments may be defined in terms of previous arguments.

Keyword `typename`

The keyword `typename` was introduced to specify that the identifier that follows is a type. Consider the following example:

```
template <typename T>
class MyClass {
    typename T::SubType * ptr;
    ...
};
```

Here, `typename` is used to clarify that SubType is a type defined within class T. Thus, `ptr` is a pointer to the type T::SubType. Without `typename`, SubType would be considered a static member, and thus

```
T::SubType * ptr
```

would be a multiplication of value SubType of type T with `ptr`.

According to the qualification of SubType being a type, any type that is used in place of T must provide an inner type SubType. For example, the use of type Q as a template argument is possible only if type Q has an inner type definition for SubType:

```
class Q {
    typedef int SubType;
    ...
};
```

```
MyClass<Q> x;      // OK
```

In this case, the `ptr` member of `MyClass<Q>` would be a pointer to type `int`. However, the subtype could also be an abstract data type, such as a class:

```
class Q {
    class SubType;
    ...
};
```

Note that `typename` is always necessary to qualify an identifier of a template as being a type, even if an interpretation that is not a type would make no sense. Thus, the general rule in C++ is that any identifier of a template is considered to be a value except if it is qualified by `typename`.

Apart from this, `typename` can also be used instead of `class` in a template declaration:

```
template <typename T> class MyClass;
```

Member Templates

Member functions of classes may be templates. However, member templates may not be virtual. For example:

```
class MyClass {
    ...
    template <typename T>
    void f(T);
};
```

Here, `MyClass::f` declares a set of member functions for parameters of any type. You can pass any argument as long as its type provides all operations used by `f()`.

This feature is often used to support automatic type conversions for members in class templates. For example, in the following definition, the argument x of `assign()` must have exactly the same type as the object it is called for:

```
template <typename T>
class MyClass {
  private:
    T value;
  public:
    void assign (const MyClass<T>& x) {  // x must have same type as *this
        value = x.value;
    }
    ...
};
```

It would be an error to use different template types for the objects of the `assign()` operation even if an automatic type conversion from one type to the other is provided:

```
void f()
{
    MyClass<double> d;
    MyClass<int> i;

    d.assign(d);    // OK
    d.assign(i);    // ERROR: i is MyClass<int>
                    //        but MyClass<double> is required
}
```

By providing a different template type for the member function, you relax the rule of exact match. The member function template argument may have any template type, then, as long as the types are assignable:

```
template <typename T>
class MyClass {
  private:
    T value;
  public:
    template <typename X>                   // member template
    void assign (const MyClass<X>& x) {     // allows different template types
        value = x.getValue();
    }
```

```
        T getValue () const {
            return value;
        }
        ...
    };

    void f()
    {
        MyClass<double> d;
        MyClass<int> i;

        d.assign(d);    // OK
        d.assign(i);    // OK (int is assignable to double)
    }
```

Note that the argument x of `assign()` now differs from the type of `*this`. Thus, you can't access private and protected members of `MyClass<>` directly. Instead, you have to use something like `getValue()` in this example.

A special form of a member template is a *template constructor*. Template constructors are usually provided to enable implicit type conversions when objects are copied. Note that a template constructor does not suppress the implicit declaration of the copy constructor. If the type matches exactly, the implicit copy constructor is generated and called. For example:

```
    template <typename T>
    class MyClass {
      public:
        // copy constructor with implicit type conversion
        // - does not suppress implicit copy constructor
        template <typename U>
        MyClass (const MyClass<U>& x);
        ...
    };

    void f()
    {
        MyClass<double> xd;
        ...
        MyClass<double> xd2(xd);    // calls implicitly generated copy constructor
        MyClass<int> xi(xd);        // calls template constructor
        ...
    }
```

Here, the type of xd2 is the same as the type of xd and so is initialized via the implicitly generated copy constructor. The type of xi differs from the type of xd and so is initialized by using the template constructor. Thus, if you implement a template constructor, don't forget to provide a default constructor if its default behavior does not fit your needs. See Section 5.1.1, page 60, for another example of member templates.

Nested Class Templates

Nested classes may also be templates:

```
template <typename T>
class MyClass {
    ...
    template <typename T2>
    class NestedClass;
    ...
};
```

3.2.1 Explicit Initialization for Fundamental Types

If you use the syntax of an explicit constructor call without arguments, fundamental types are initialized with zero:

```
int i1;                   // undefined value
int i2 = int();           // initialized with zero
int i3{};                 // initialized with zero (since C++11)
```

This feature enables you to write template code that ensures that values of any type have a certain default value. For example, in the following function, the initialization guarantees that x is initialized with zero for fundamental types:

```
template <typename T>
void f()
{
    T x = T();
    ...
}
```

If a template forces the initialization with zero, its value is so-called *zero initialized*. Otherwise it's *default initialized*.

3.2.2 Definition of `main()`

I'd also like to clarify an important, often misunderstood, aspect of the core language: namely, the only correct and portable versions of main(). According to the C++ standard, only two definitions of main() are portable:

```
int main()
{
    ...
}
```

and

```
int main (int argc, char* argv[])
{
    ...
}
```

where `argv` (the array of command-line arguments) might also be defined as `char**`. Note that the return type `int` is required.

You may, but are not required to, end `main()` with a `return` statement. Unlike C, C++ defines an implicit

```
return 0;
```

at the end of `main()`. This means that every program that leaves `main()` without a `return` statement is successful. Any value other than 0 represents a kind of failure (see Section 5.8.2, page 162, for predefined values). Therefore, my examples in this book have no `return` statement at the end of `main()`.

To end a C++ program without returning from `main()`, you usually should call `exit()`, `quick_exit()` (since C++11), or `terminate()`. See Section 5.8.2, page 162, for details.

Chapter 4

General Concepts

This chapter describes the fundamental C++ standard library concepts that you need to work with all or most components:

- The namespace `std`
- The names and formats of header files
- The general concept of error and exception handling
- Callable objects
- Basic concepts about concurrency and multithreading
- A brief introduction to allocators

4.1 Namespace `std`

If you use different modules and/or libraries, you always have the potential for name clashes. This is because modules and libraries might use the same identifier for different things. This problem was solved by the introduction of *namespaces* to C++. A namespace is a certain scope for identifiers. Unlike a class, a namespace is open for extensions that might occur at any source. Thus, you could use a namespace to define components that are distributed over several physical modules. A typical example of such a component is the C++ standard library, so it follows that it uses a namespace.

In fact, all identifiers of the C++ standard library are defined in a namespace called `std`. With C++11, this also applies to identifiers that were introduced with TR1 and had namespace `std::tr1` there (see Section 2.1, page 7). In addition, namespace `posix` is reserved now, although it is not used by the C++ standard library.

Note that the following namespaces nested within `std` are used inside the C++ standard library:

- `std::rel_ops` (see Section 5.5.3, page 138)
- `std::chrono` (see Section 5.7.1, page 144)
- `std::placeholders` (see Section 6.10.3, page 243)
- `std::regex_constants` (see Section 14.6, page 732)
- `std::this_thread` (see Section 18.3.7, page 981)

According to the concept of namespaces, you have three options when using an identifier of the C++ standard library:

1. You can qualify the identifier directly. For example, you can write `std::ostream` instead of `ostream`. A complete statement might look like this:

   ```
   std::cout << std::hex << 3.4 << std::endl;
   ```

2. You can use a *using declaration*. For example, the following code fragment introduces the local ability to skip `std::` for cout and endl:

   ```
   using std::cout;
   using std::endl;
   ```

   Thus, the example in option 1 could be written like this:

   ```
   cout << std::hex << 3.4 << endl;
   ```

3. You can use a *using directive*. This is the easiest option. By using a using directive for namespace `std`, all identifiers of the namespace `std` are available as if they had been declared globally. Thus, the statement

   ```
   using namespace std;
   ```

   allows you to write

   ```
   cout << hex << 3.4 << endl;
   ```

   Note that in complex code, this might lead to accidental name clashes or, worse, to different behavior due to some obscure overloading rules. You should never use a using directive when the context is not clear, such as in header files.

The examples in this book are quite small, so for my own convenience, I usually use using directives throughout this book in complete example programs.

4.2   Header Files

The use of namespace `std` for all identifiers of the C++ standard library was introduced during the standardization process. This change is not backward compatible to old header files, in which identifiers of the C++ standard library are declared in the global scope. In addition, some interfaces of classes changed during the standardization process (however, the goal was to stay backward compatible if possible). So, a new style for the names of standard header files was introduced, thus allowing vendors to stay backward compatible by providing the old header files.

The definition of new names for the standard header files was a good opportunity to standardize the extensions of header files. Previously, several extensions for header files were used; for example, `.h`, `.hpp`, and `.hxx`. However, the new standard extension for header files might be a surprise: Standard headers no longer have extensions. Hence, `include` statements for standard header files look like this:

```
#include <iostream>
#include <string>
```

This convention also applies to header files assumed from the C standard. C header files now have the new prefix c instead of the old extension `.h`:

```
#include <cstdlib>        // was: <stdlib.h>
#include <cstring>        // was: <string.h>
```

Inside these header files, all identifiers are declared in namespace `std`.

One advantage of this naming scheme is that you can distinguish the old string header for `char*` C functions from the new string header for the standard C++ class `string`:

```
#include <string>         // C++ class string
#include <cstring>        // char* functions from C
```

The new naming scheme of header files does not necessarily mean that the filenames of standard header files have no extensions from the point of view of the operating system. How `include` statements for standard header files are handled is implementation defined. C++ systems might add an extension or even use built-in declarations without reading a file. In practice, however, most systems simply include the header from a file that has exactly the same name as used in the `include` statement. So, in most systems, C++ *standard* header files simply have no extension. In general, it is still a good idea to use a certain extension for your own header files to help identify them in a file system.

To maintain compatibility with C, the "old" standard C header files are still available. So if necessary, you can still use, for example:

```
#include <stdlib.h>
```

In this case, the identifiers are declared in both the global scope and namespace `std`. In fact, these headers behave as if they declare all identifiers in namespace `std`, followed by an explicit using declaration.

For the C++ header files in the "old" format, such as `<iostream.h>`, there is no specification in the standard. Hence, they are not supported. In practice, most vendors will probably provide them to enable backward compatibility. Note that there were more changes in the headers than just the introduction of namespace `std`. In general, you should either use the old names of header files or switch to the new standardized names.

4.3   Error and Exception Handling

The C++ standard library is heterogeneous. It contains software from diverse sources that have different styles of design and implementation. Error and exception handling is a typical example of these differences. Parts of the library, such as string classes, support detailed error handling, checking for every possible problem that might occur and throwing an exception if there is an error. Other parts, such as the STL and valarrays, prefer speed over safety, so they rarely check for logical errors and throw exceptions only if runtime errors occur.

4.3.1   Standard Exception Classes

All exceptions thrown by the language or the library are derived from the base class `exception`, defined in `<exception>`. This class is the root of several standard exception classes, which form a hierarchy, as shown in Figure 4.1. These standard exception classes can be divided into three groups:

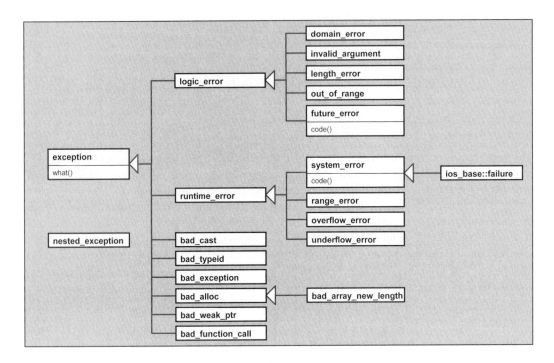

Figure 4.1. Hierarchy of Standard Exceptions

1. Language support
2. Logic errors
3. Runtime errors

Logic errors usually can be avoided because the reason is inside the scope of a program, such as a precondition violation. Runtime exceptions are caused by a reason that is outside the scope of the program, such as not enough resources.

Exception Classes for Language Support

Exceptions for language support are used by language features. So in a way they are part of the core language rather than the library. These exceptions are thrown when the following operations fail:

- An exception of class `bad_cast`, defined in `<typeinfo>`, is thrown by the `dynamic_cast` operator if a type conversion on a reference fails at runtime.
- An exception of class `bad_typeid`, defined in `<typeinfo>`, is thrown by the `typeid` operator for runtime type identification. If the argument to `typeid` is zero or the null pointer, this exception gets thrown.
- An exception of class `bad_exception`, defined in `<exception>`, is used to handle unexpected exceptions. It can be thrown by the function `unexpected()`, which is called if a function throws an exception that is not listed in an exception specification Note, however, that the use of exception specifications is deprecated since C++11 (see Section 3.1.7, page 24).

These exceptions might also be thrown by library functions. For example, `bad_cast` might be thrown by `use_facet<>` if a facet is not available in a locale (see Section 16.2.2, page 864).

Exception Classes for Logic Errors

Exception classes for logic errors are usually derived from class `logic_error`. Logic errors are errors that, at least in theory, could be avoided by the program; for example, by performing additional tests of function arguments. Examples of such errors are a violation of logical preconditions or a class invariant. The C++ standard library provides the following classes for logic errors:

- An exception of class `invalid_argument` is used to report invalid arguments, such as when a bitset (array of bits) is initialized with a `char` other than `'0'` or `'1'`.
- An exception of class `length_error` is used to report an attempt to do something that exceeds a maximum allowable size, such as appending too many characters to a string.
- An exception of class `out_of_range` is used to report that an argument value is not in the expected range, such as when a wrong index is used in an array-like collection or string.
- An exception of class `domain_error` is used to report a domain error.
- Since C++11, an exception of class `future_error` is used to report logical errors when using asynchronous system calls (see Chapter 18). Note that runtime errors in this domain are raised via class `system_error`.

In general, classes for logic errors are defined in `<stdexcept>`. However, class `future_error` is defined in `<future>`.

Exception Classes for Runtime Errors

Exceptions derived from `runtime_error` are provided to report events that are beyond the scope of a program and are not easily avoidable. The C++ standard library provides the following classes for runtime errors:

- An exception of class `range_error` is used to report a range error in internal computations. In the C++ standard library, the exception can occur since C++11 in conversions between wide strings and byte strings (see Section 16.4.4, page 901).
- An exception of class `overflow_error` is used to report an arithmetic overflow. In the C++ standard library the exception can occur if a bitset is converted into an integral value (see Section 12.5.1, page 652).
- An exception of class `underflow_error` is used to report an arithmetic underflow.
- Since C++11, an exception of class `system_error` is used to report errors caused by the underlying operating system. In the C++ standard library, this exception can be thrown in the context of concurrency, such as class `thread`, classes to control data races, and `async()` (see Chapter 18).
- An exception of class `bad_alloc`, defined in `<new>`, is thrown whenever the global operator `new` fails, except when the `nothrow` version of `new` is used. This is probably the most important runtime exception because it might occur at any time in any nontrivial program.

  Since C++11, `bad_array_new_length`, derived from `bad_alloc`, will be thrown by `new` if the size passed to `new` is less than zero or such that the size of the allocated object would exceed the implementation-defined limit (that is, if it's a logic error rather than a runtime error).

- An exception of class `bad_weak_ptr`, defined in `<memory>`, is thrown whenever the creation of a weak pointer out of a shared pointer fails. See Section 5.2.2, page 89, for details.
- An exception of class `bad_function_call`, defined in `<functional>`, is thrown whenever a `function` wrapper object gets invoked but has no target. See Section 5.4.4, page 133, for details.

In addition, for the I/O part of the library, a special exception class called `ios_base::failure` is provided in `<ios>`. An exception of this class may be thrown when a stream changes its state due to an error or end-of-file. Since C++11, this class is derived from `system_error`; before C++11, it was directly derived from class `exception`. The exact behavior of this exception class is described in Section 15.4.4, page 762.

Conceptionally, `bad_alloc` can be considered a system error. However, for historical reasons and because of its importance, implementations are encouraged to throw a `bad_alloc` rather than a `system_error` exception if an error represents an out-of-memory condition.

In general, classes for runtime errors are defined in `<stdexcept>`. Class `system_error`, however, is defined in `<system_error>`.

Exceptions Thrown by the Standard Library

As the previous description shows, almost all exception classes can be thrown by the C++ standard library. In particular, `bad_alloc` exceptions can be thrown whenever storage is allocated.

In addition, because library features might use code provided by the application programmer, functions might throw any exception indirectly.

Any implementation of the standard library might also offer additional exception classes either as siblings or as derived classes. However, the use of these nonstandard classes makes code nonportable because you could not use another implementation of the standard library without breaking your code. So, you should always use only the standard exception classes.

Header Files for Exception Classes

The exception classes are defined in many different header files. Thus, to be able to deal with all exceptions the library might throw, you have to include:

```
#include <exception>       // for classes exception and bad_exception
#include <stdexcept>       // for most logic and runtime error classes
#include <system_error>    // for system errors (since C++11)
#include <new>             // for out-of-memory exceptions
#include <ios>             // for I/O exceptions
#include <future>          // for errors with async() and futures (since C++11)
#include <typeinfo>        // for bad_cast and bad_typeid
```

4.3.2 Members of Exception Classes

To handle an exception in a `catch` clause, you may use the interface provided by the exception classes. For all classes, `what()` is provided; for some classes, `code()` also is provided.

The Member `what()`

For all standard exception classes, only one member can be used to get additional information besides the type itself: the virtual member function `what()`, which returns a null-terminated byte string:

```
namespace std {
    class exception {
      public:
        virtual const char* what() const noexcept;
        ...
    };
}
```

The content of the string returned by `what()` is implementation defined. Note that the string might be a null-terminated multibyte string that is suitable to convert and display as `wstring` (see Section 13.2.1, page 664). The C-string returned by `what()` is valid until the exception object from which it is obtained gets destroyed or a new value is assigned to the exception object.

Error Codes versus Error Conditions

For the exception classes `system_error` and `future_error`, there is an additional member to get details about the exception. However, before going into details, we have to introduce the difference between error codes and error conditions:

- **Error codes** are light-weight objects that encapsulate error code values that might be implementation-specific. However, some error codes also are standardized.
- **Error conditions** are objects that provide portable abstractions of error descriptions.

Depending on the context, for exceptions the C++ standard library sometimes specifies error code and sometimes error conditions. In fact:

- Class `std::errc` provides *error conditions* for `std::system_error` exceptions corresponding to standard system error numbers defined in `<cerrno>` or `<errno.h>`.
- Class `std::io_errc` provides an *error code* for `std::ios_base::failure` exceptions thrown by stream classes since C++11 (see Section 15.4.4, page 762).
- Class `std::future_errc` provides *error codes* for `std::future_error` exceptions thrown by the concurrency library (see Chapter 18).

Tables 4.1 and 4.2 list the error condition values that are specified by the C++ standard library for `system_error` exceptions. These are *scoped enumerators* (see Section 3.1.13, page 32), so the prefix `std::errc::` has to be used. The values of these conditions are required to have the corresponding `errno` value defined in `<cerrno>` or `<errno.h>` This is *not* the error code; the error codes usually will be implementation-specific.

Error Condition	Enum Value
address_family_not_supported	EAFNOSUPPORT
address_in_use	EADDRINUSE
address_not_available	EADDRNOTAVAIL
already_connected	EISCONN
argument_list_too_long	E2BIG
argument_out_of_domain	EDOM
bad_address	EFAULT
bad_file_descriptor	EBADF
bad_message	EBADMSG
broken_pipe	EPIPE
connection_aborted	ECONNABORTED
connection_already_in_progress	EALREADY
connection_refused	ECONNREFUSED
connection_reset	ECONNRESET
cross_device_link	EXDEV
destination_address_required	EDESTADDRREQ
device_or_resource_busy	EBUSY
directory_not_empty	ENOTEMPTY
executable_format_error	ENOEXEC
file_exists	EEXIST
file_too_large	EFBIG
filename_too_long	ENAMETOOLONG
function_not_supported	ENOSYS
host_unreachable	EHOSTUNREACH
identifier_removed	EIDRM
illegal_byte_sequence	EILSEQ
inappropriate_io_control_operation	ENOTTY
interrupted	EINTR
invalid_argument	EINVAL
invalid_seek	ESPIPE
io_error	EIO
is_a_directory	EISDIR
message_size	EMSGSIZE
network_down	ENETDOWN
network_reset	ENETRESET
network_unreachable	ENETUNREACH
no_buffer_space	ENOBUFS
no_child_process	ECHILD
no_link	ENOLINK
no_lock_available	ENOLCK
no_message_available	ENODATA
no_message	ENOMSG
no_protocol_option	ENOPROTOOPT
no_space_on_device	ENOSPC
no_stream_resources	ENOSR
no_such_device_or_address	ENXIO
no_such_device	ENODEV
no_such_file_or_directory	ENOENT
no_such_process	ESRCH
not_a_directory	ENOTDIR
not_a_socket	ENOTSOCK

Table 4.1. Error Conditions of system_errors, *Part 1*

Error Condition	Enum Value
not_a_stream	ENOSTR
not_connected	ENOTCONN
not_enough_memory	ENOMEM
not_supported	ENOTSUP
operation_canceled	ECANCELED
operation_in_progress	EINPROGRESS
operation_not_permitted	EPERM
operation_not_supported	EOPNOTSUPP
operation_would_block	EWOULDBLOCK
owner_dead	EOWNERDEAD
permission_denied	EACCES
protocol_error	EPROTO
protocol_not_supported	EPROTONOSUPPORT
read_only_file_system	EROFS
resource_deadlock_would_occur	EDEADLK
resource_unavailable_try_again	EAGAIN
result_out_of_range	ERANGE
state_not_recoverable	ENOTRECOVERABLE
stream_timeout	ETIME
text_file_busy	ETXTBSY
timed_out	ETIMEDOUT
too_many_files_open_in_system	ENFILE
too_many_files_open	EMFILE
too_many_links	EMLINK
too_many_symbolic_link_levels	ELOOP
value_too_large	EOVERFLOW
wrong_protocol_type	EPROTOTYPE

Table 4.2. Error Conditions of `system_errors`*, Part 2*

Table 4.3 lists the error code values that are specified by the C++ standard library for exceptions of type `future_errc`. These are *scoped enumerators* (see Section 3.1.13, page 32), so the prefix `std::future_errc::` has to be used.[1]

The only error code specified for `ios_base::failure` exceptions is `std::io_errc::stream`.

Error Code	Meaning
broken_promise	shared state abandoned
future_already_retrieved	get_future() already called
promise_already_satisfied	Shared state already has a value/exception or already invoked
no_state	No shared state

Table 4.3. Error Codes of `future_errors`

---

[1] Note that in the C++11 standard, the error codes of future errors are defined explicitly with `future_errc::broken_promise` having the value 0. But because error code 0 usually stands for "no error," this was a design mistake. The fix is that all future error code values are now defined to be implementation-specific.

Dealing with Error Codes and Error Conditions

For error codes and error conditions, two different types are provided by the C++ standard library: class `std::error_code` and class `std::error_condition`. This might lead to the impression that dealing with errors is pretty complicated. However, the library is designed so that you can always compare error codes with error conditions using both the objects or enumeration values. For example, for any error object ec of type `std::error_code` or `std::error_condition` the following is possible:

```
if (ec == std::errc::invalid_argument) {    // check for specific error condition
    ...
}
if (ec == std::future_errc::no_state) {     // check for specific error code
    ...
}
```

Thus, when dealing with errors only to check for specific error codes or conditions, the difference between codes and conditions doesn't matter.

To be able to deal with error codes and error conditions, class `std::system_error`, including its derived class `std::ios_base::failure`, and class `std::_future_error` provide the additional nonvirtual member function `code()` returning an object of class `std::error_code`:[2]

```
namespace std {
    class system_error : public runtime_error {
      public:
        virtual const char* what() const noexcept;
        const error_code& code() const noexcept;
        ...
    };

    class future_error : public logic_error {
      public:
        virtual const char* what() const noexcept;
        const error_code& code() const noexcept;
        ...
    };
}
```

Class `error_code` then provides member functions to get some details of the error:

```
namespace std {
    class error_code {
      public:
```

---

[2] Strictly speaking, these declarations are in different header files, and `what()` is not declared as virtual here but derives its virtuality from its base class.

```
        const error_category& category() const noexcept;
        int                   value() const noexcept;
        string                message() const;
        explicit operator bool() const noexcept;
        error_condition       default_error_condition() const noexcept;
        ...
    };
}
```

This interface is driven by the following design:

- Different libraries might use the same integral values for different error codes. So, each error has
  a category and a value. Only inside a category is each value distinct and has a clear specified
  meaning.
- `message()` yields a corresponding message, which usually is part of what `what()` yields in
  general for all exceptions, although this is not required.
- `operator bool()` yields whether an error code is set (0 is the value that stands for "no error").
  When exceptions are caught, this operator usually should yield `true`.
- `default_error_condition()` returns the corresponding `error_condition`, again providing
  `category()`, `value()`, `message()`, and `operator bool()`:

```
    namespace std {
        class error_condition {
          public:
            const error_category& category() const noexcept;
            int                   value() const noexcept;
            string                message() const;
            explicit operator bool() const noexcept;
            ...
        };
    }
```

Class `std::error_category` provides the following interface:

```
    namespace std {
        class error_category {
          public:
            virtual const char*     name() const noexcept = 0;
            virtual string          message (int ev) const = 0;
            virtual error_condition default_error_condition (int ev)
                                                            const noexcept;
            bool operator == (const error_category& rhs) const noexcept;
            bool operator != (const error_category& rhs) const noexcept;
            ...
        };
    }
```

Here, `name()` yields the name of the category. `message()` and `default_error_condition()` return the message and the default error condition according to the passed value (this is what the corresponding `error_code` member functions call). Operators `==` and `!=` allow you to compare error categories.

The following category names are defined by the C++ standard library:

- `"iostream"` for I/O stream exceptions of type `ios_base::failure`
- `"generic"` for system exceptions of type `system_error`, where the value corresponds to a POSIX errno value
- `"system"` for system exceptions of type `system_error`, where the value does not correspond to a POSIX errno value
- `"future"` for exceptions of type `future_error`

For each category, global functions are provided that return the category:[3]

```
const error_category& generic_category() noexcept;   // in <system_errror>
const error_category& system_category() noexcept;    // in <system_error>
const error_category& iostream_category();           // in <ios>
const error_category& future_category() noexcept;    // in <future>
```

Thus, for an error code object e, you can also call the following to find out whether it is an I/O failure:

```
if (e.code().category() == std::iostream_category())
```

The following code demonstrates how to use a generic function to process (here, print) different exceptions:

```
// util/exception.hpp

#include <exception>
#include <system_error>
#include <future>
#include <iostream>

template <typename T>
void processCodeException (const T& e)
{
    using namespace std;
    auto c = e.code();
    cerr << "- category:     " << c.category().name() << endl;
    cerr << "- value:        " << c.value() << endl;
    cerr << "- msg:          " << c.message() << endl;
    cerr << "- def category: "
         << c.default_error_condition().category().name() << endl;
```

---

[3] It's probably an oversight that `iostream_category()` is not declared with `noexcept`.

```
        cerr << "- def value:    "
             << c.default_error_condition().value() << endl;
        cerr << "- def msg:      "
             << c.default_error_condition().message() << endl;
}

void processException()
{
    using namespace std;
    try {
        throw;   // rethrow exception to deal with it here
    }
    catch (const ios_base::failure& e) {
        cerr << "I/O EXCEPTION: " << e.what() << endl;
        processCodeException(e);
    }
    catch (const system_error& e) {
        cerr << "SYSTEM EXCEPTION: " << e.what() << endl;
        processCodeException(e);
    }
    catch (const future_error& e) {
        cerr << "FUTURE EXCEPTION: " << e.what() << endl;
        processCodeException(e);
    }
    catch (const bad_alloc& e) {
        cerr << "BAD ALLOC EXCEPTION: " << e.what() << endl;
    }
    catch (const exception& e) {
        cerr << "EXCEPTION: " << e.what() << endl;
    }
    catch (...) {
        cerr << "EXCEPTION (unknown)" << endl;
    }
}
```

This allows to handle exceptions as follows:

```
try {
    ...
}
catch (...) {
    processException();
}
```

Other Members

The remaining members of the standard exception classes create, copy, assign, and destroy exception objects.

Note that besides `what()` and `code()`, for any of the standard exception classes, no additional member is provided that describes the kind of exception. For example, there is no portable way to find out the context of an exception or the faulty index of a range error. Thus, a portable evaluation of an exception could print only the message returned from `what()`:

```cpp
try {
    ...
}
catch (const std::exception& error) {
    // print implementation-defined error message
    std::cerr << error.what() << std::endl;
    ...
}
```

The only other possible evaluation might be an interpretation of the exact type of the exception. For example, when a `bad_alloc` exception is thrown, a program might try to get more memory.

4.3.3 Passing Exceptions with Class `exception_ptr`

Since C++11, the C++ standard library provides the ability to store exceptions into objects of type `exception_ptr` to process them later or in other contexts:

```cpp
#include <exception>

std::exception_ptr eptr;      // object to hold exceptions (or nullptr)

void foo ()
{
    try {
        throw ...;
    }
    catch (...) {
        eptr = std::current_exception();   // save exception for later processing
    }
}

void bar ()
{
    if (eptr != nullptr) {
        std::rethrow_exception(eptr);      // process saved exception
    }
}
```

current_exception() returns an exception_ptr object that refers to the currently handled exception The value returned by current_exception() is valid as long as an exception_ptr refers to it. rethrow_exception() rethrows the stored exception so that bar() behaves as the initial exception thrown in foo() would have occured inside bar().

This feature is especially useful to pass exception between threads (see Section 18.2.1, page 964).

4.3.4 Throwing Standard Exceptions

You can throw standard exceptions inside your own library or program. All logic error and runtime error standard exception classes that provide the what() interface have only a constructor for std::string and (since C++11) for const char*. The value passed here will become the description returned by what(). For example, the class logic_error is defined as follows:

```
namespace std {
    class logic_error : public exception {
      public:
        explicit logic_error (const string& whatString);
        explicit logic_error (const char*  whatString);  // since C++11
        ...
    };
}
```

Class std::system_error provides the ability to create an exception object by passing an error code, a what() string, and an optional category:

```
namespace std {
    class system_error : public runtime_error {
      public:
        system_error (error_code ec, const string& what_arg);
        system_error (error_code ec, const char* what_arg);
        system_error (error_code ec);
        system_error (int ev, const error_category& ecat,
                      const string& what_arg);
        system_error (int ev, const error_category& ecat,
                      const char* what_arg);
        ...
    };
}
```

To provide an error_code object, make_error_code() convenience functions are provided that take only the error code value.

Class std::ios_base::failure provides constructors taking a what() string and (since C++11) an optional error_code object. Class std::future_error provides only a constructor taking a single error_code object.

Thus, throwing a standard exception is pretty easy:

```
throw std::out_of_range ("out_of_range (somewhere, somehow)");

throw
    std::system_error (std::make_error_code(std::errc::invalid_argument),
                       "argument ... is not valid");
```

You can't throw exceptions of the base class `exception` and any exception class that is provided for language support (`bad_cast`, `bad_typeid`, `bad_exception`).

4.3.5 Deriving from Standard Exception Classes

Another possibility for using the standard exception classes in your code is to define a special exception class derived directly or indirectly from class `exception`. To do this, you must ensure that the `what()` mechanism or `code()` mechanism works, which is possible because `what()` is virtual. For an example, see class `Stack` in Section 12.1.3, page 635.

4.4 Callable Objects

At different places, the C++ standard library uses the term *callable object*, which means objects that somehow can be used to call some functionality:

- A function, where additional *args* are passed to as arguments
- A pointer to a member function, which is called for the object passed as the first additional argument (must be reference or pointer) and gets the remaining arguments as member function parameters
- A function object (operator () for a passed object), where additional *args* are passed as arguments
- A lambda (see Section 3.1.10, page 28), which strictly speaking is a kind of function object

For example:

```
void func (int x, int y);

auto l = [] (int x, int y) {
            ...
        };

class C {
  public:
    void operator () (int x, int y) const;
    void memfunc (int x, int y) const;
};
```

```
int main()
{
    C c;
    std::shared_ptr<C> sp(new C);

    // bind() uses callable objects to bind arguments:
    std::bind(func,77,33)();           // calls: func(77,33)
    std::bind(l,77,33)();              // calls: l(77,33
    std::bind(C(),77,33)();            // calls: C::operator()(77,33)
    std::bind(&C::memfunc,c,77,33)();  // calls: c.memfunc(77,33)
    std::bind(&C::memfunc,sp,77,33)(); // calls: sp->memfunc(77,33)

    // async() uses callable objects to start (background) tasks:
    std::async(func,42,77);            // calls: func(42,77)
    std::async(l,42,77);               // calls: l(42,77)
    std::async(c,42,77);               // calls: c.operator()(42,77)
    std::async(&C::memfunc,&c,42,77);  // calls: c.memfunc(42,77)
    std::async(&C::memfunc,sp,42,77);  // calls: sp->memfunc(42,77)
}
```

As you can see, even smart pointers (see Section 5.2, page 76) can be used to pass an object a member function is called for. See Section 10.2.2, page 487, for details about std::bind() and Section 18.1, page 946, for details about std::async().

To declare *callable objects*, in general class std::function<> can be used (see Section 5.4.4, page 133).

4.5   Concurrency and Multithreading

Before C++11, there was no support for concurrency in the language and the C++ standard library, although implementations were free to give some guarantees. With C++11, this has changed. Both the core language and the library got improvements to support concurrent programming.

The following apply in the core language, for example:

- We now have a memory model, which guarantees that updates on two different objects used by two different threads are independent of each other. Before C++11, there was no guarantee that writing a char in one thread could not interfere with writing *another* char in another thread (see section "The memory model" in [*Stroustrup:C++0x*]).

- A new keyword, thread_local, was introduced for defining thread-specific variables and objects.

In the library, we got the following:

- Some guarantees regarding thread safety

- Supporting classes and functions for concurrency (starting and synchronizing multiple threads)

The supporting classes and functions are discussed in Chapter 18. The guarantees are discussed throughout the book. However, I want to give an overview of the general guarantees here.

The General Concurrency Guarantees of the C++ Standard Library

The general constraints the C++ standard library provides regarding concurrency and multithreading since C++11 are as follows:

- In general, sharing a library object by multiple threads — where at least one thread modifies the object — might result in undefined behavior. To quote the standard: *"Modifying an object of a standard library type that is shared between threads risks undefined behavior unless objects of that type are explicitly specified as being sharable without data races or the user supplies a locking mechanism."*
- Especially during the construction of an object in one thread, using that object in another thread results in undefined behavior. Similarly, destructing an object in one thread while using it in another thread results in undefined behavior. Note that this applies even to objects that are provided for thread synchronization.

The most important places where concurrent access to library objects *is* supported are as follows:

- For STL containers (see Chapter 7) and container adapters (see Chapter 12), the following guarantees are given:
  - Concurrent read-only access is possible. This explicitly implies calling the nonconstant member functions `begin()`, `end()`, `rbegin()`, `rend()`, `front()`, `back()`, `data()`, `find()`, `lower_bound()`, `upper_bound()`, `equal_range()`, `at()`, and except for associative containers, operator `[]` as well as access by iterators, if they do not modify the containers.
  - Concurrent access to *different elements* of the same container is possible (except for class `vector<bool>`). Thus, different threads might concurrently read and/or write different elements of the same container. For example, each thread might process something and store the result in "its" element of a shared vector.
- For formatted input and output to a standard stream, which is synchronized with C I/O (see Section 15.14.1, page 845), concurrent access is possible, although it might result in interleaved characters. This by default applies to `std::cin`, `std::cout`, `std::cerr`. However, for string streams, file streams, or stream buffers, concurrent access results in undefined behavior.
- Concurrent calls of `atexit()` and `at_quick_exit()` (see Section 5.8.2, page 162) are synchronized. The same applies to functions that set or get the new, terminate, or unexpected handler (`set_new_handler()`, `set_unexpected()`, `set_terminate()` and the corresponding getters). Also, `getenv()` is synchronized.
- For all member functions of the default allocator (see Chapter 19) except destructors, concurrent access is synchronized.

Note also that the library guarantees that the C++ standard library has no "hidden" side effects that break concurrent access to different objects. Thus, the C++ standard library

- Does not access reachable objects other than those required for a specific operation,
- Is not allowed to internally introduce shared static objects without synchronization,
- Allows implementations to parallelize operations only if there are no visible side effects for the programmer. However, see Section 18.4.2, page 983.

4.6 Allocators

In several places, the C++ standard library uses special objects to handle the allocation and deallocation of memory. Such objects are called *allocators*. They represent a special memory model and are
used as an abstraction to translate the *need* to use memory into a raw *call* for memory. The use of
different allocator objects at the same time allows you to use different memory models in a program.

Originally, allocators were introduced as part of the STL to handle the nasty problem of different
pointer types on PCs (such as near, far, and huge pointers). Now, allocators serve as a base for
technical solutions that use certain memory models, such as shared memory, garbage collection, and
object-oriented databases, without changing the interfaces. However, this use is relatively new and
not yet widely adopted (this will probably change).

The C++ standard library defines a *default allocator* as follows:

```
namespace std {
    template <typename T>
    class allocator;
}
```

The default allocator is used as the default value everywhere an allocator can be used as an argument. It does the usual calls for memory allocation and deallocation; that is, it calls the new and
delete operators. However, when or how often these operators are called is unspecified. Thus, an
implementation of the default allocator might, for example, cache the allocated memory internally.

The default allocator is used in most programs. However, other libraries sometimes provide allocators to fit certain needs. In such cases, you must simply pass them as arguments. Only occasionally
does it make sense to program allocators. In practice, the default allocator is typically used. The
discussion of allocators is deferred until Chapter 19, which covers in detail not only allocators but
also their interfaces.

Chapter 5

Utilities

This chapter describes the general utilities of the C++ standard library. These utilities are small and simple classes, types, or functions that perform frequently needed tasks:

- Class pair<> and class tuple<>
- Smart pointer classes (class shared_ptr<> and class unique_ptr)
- Numeric limits[1]
- Type traits and type utilities
- Auxiliary functions (for example, min(), max(), and swap())
- Class ratio<>[1]
- Clocks and timers
- Some important C functions

Most, but not all, of these utilities are described in clause 20, "General Utilities," of the C++ standard. The rest are described along with more major components of the library either because they are used primarily with that particular component or due to historical reasons. For example, some general auxiliary functions are defined as part of the <algorithm> header, although they are not algorithms in the sense of the STL (which is described in Chapter 6).

Several of these utilities are also used within the C++ standard library. For example, type pair<> is used whenever two values need to be treated as a single unit — for example, if a function has to return two values or when elements of containers are key/value pairs — and type traits are used wherever complicated type conversions are necessary.

---

[1] One could argue that numeric limits and class ratio<> should be part of Chapter 17, which covers numerics, but these classes are used in some other parts of the library, so I decided to describe them here.

5.1 Pairs and Tuples

In C++98, the first version of the C++ standard library, a simple class was provided to handle value pairs of different types without having to define a specific class. The C++98 class was used when a value pair was returned by standard functions and the container elements were key/value pairs.

TR1 introduced a tuple class, which extended this concept for an arbitrary but still limited number of elements. Implementations did portably allow tuples with up to ten elements of different types.

With C++11, the tuple class was reimplemented by using the concept of variadic templates (see Section 3.1.9, page 26). Now, there is a standard tuple class for a heterogeneous collection of any size. In addition, class `pair` is still provided for two elements and can be used in combination with a two-element tuple.

However, the `pair` class of C++11 was also extended a lot, which to some extent demonstrates the enhancements that C++ as a language and its library received with C++11.

5.1.1 Pairs

The class `pair` treats two values as a single unit. This class is used in several places within the C++ standard library. In particular, the container classes `map`, `multimap`, `unordered_map`, and `unordered_multimap` use `pairs` to manage their elements, which are key/value pairs (see Section 7.8, page 331). Other examples of the use of `pairs` are functions that return two values, such as `minmax()` (see Section 5.5.1, page 134).

The structure `pair` is defined in `<utility>` and provides the operations listed in Table 5.1. In principle, you can create, copy/assign/swap, and compare a `pair<>`. In addition, there are type definitions for `first_type` and `second_type`, representing the types of the first and second values.

Element Access

To process the values of the `pair` direct access to the corresponding members is provided. In fact, the type is declared as `struct` instead of `class` so that all members are public:

```
namespace std {
    template <typename T1, typename T2>
    struct pair {
        // member
        T1 first;
        T2 second;
        ...
    };
}
```

Operation	Effect
`pair<T1,T2> p`	Default constructor; creates a pair of values of types T1 and T2, initialized with their default constructors
`pair<T1,T2> p(val1,val1)`	Creates a pair of values of types T1 and T2, initialized with *val1* and *val1*
`pair<T1,T2> p(rv1,rv2)`	Creates a pair of values of types T1 and T2, move initialized with *rv1* and *rv2*
`pair<T1,T2> p(piecewise_ construct, t1,t2)`	Creates a pair of values of types T1 and T2, initialized by the elements of the tuples *t1* and *t2*
`pair<T1,T2> p(p2)`	Copy constructor; creates p as copy of *p2*
`pair<T1,T2> p(rv)`	Move constructor; moves the contents of *rv* to p (implicit type conversions are possible)
`p = p2`	Assigns the values of *p2* to *p* (implicit type conversions are possible since C++11)
`p = rv`	Move assigns the values of *rv* to *p* (provided since C++11; implicit type conversions are possible)
`p.first`	Yields the first value inside the pair (direct member access)
`p.second`	Yields the second value inside the pair (direct member access)
`get<0>(p)`	Equivalent to `p.first` (since C++11)
`get<1>(p)`	Equivalent to `p.second` (since C++11)
`p1 == p2`	Returns whether *p1* is equal to *p2* (equivalent to `p1.first==p2.first && p1.second==p2.second`)
`p1 != p2`	Returns whether *p1* is not equal to *p2* (`!(p1==p2)`)
`p1 < p2`	Returns whether *p1* is less than *p2* (compares `first` or if equal `second` of both values)
`p1 > p2`	Returns whether *p1* is greater than *p2* (`p2<p1`)
`p1 <= p2`	Returns whether *p1* is less than or equal to *p2* (`!(p2<p1)`)
`p1 >= p2`	Returns whether *p1* is greater than or equal to *p2* (`!(p1<p2)`)
`p1.swap(p2)`	Swaps the data of *p1* and *p2* (since C++11)
`swap(p1,p2)`	Same (as global function) (since C++11)
`make_pair(val1,val2)`	Returns a pair with types and values of *val1* and *val2*

Table 5.1. Operations of `pairs`

For example, to implement a generic function template that writes a value pair to a stream, you have to program:[2]

---

[2] Note that this output operator does not work where *ADL* (*argument-dependent lookup*) does not work (see Section 15.11.1, page 812, for details).

```
// generic output operator for pairs (limited solution)
template <typename T1, typename T2>
std::ostream& operator << (std::ostream& strm,
                           const std::pair<T1,T2>& p)
{
    return strm << "[" << p.first << "," << p.second << "]";
}
```

In addition, a tuple-like interface (see Section 5.1.2, page 68) is available since C++11. Thus, you can use `tuple_size<>::value` to yield the number of elements and `tuple_element<>::type` to yield the type of a specific element, and you can use `get()` to gain access to `first` or `second`:

```
typedef std::pair<int,float> IntFloatPair;
IntFloatPair p(42,3.14);
```

```
std::get<0>(p)                                // yields p.first
std::get<1>(p)                                // yields p.second
std::tuple_size<IntFloatPair>::value          // yields 2
std::tuple_element<0,IntFloatPair>::type      // yields int
```

Constructors and Assignment Operators

The default constructor creates a value pair with values that are initialized by the default constructor of their type. Because of language rules, an explicit call of a default constructor also initializes fundamental data types, such as `int`. Thus, the declaration

```
std::pair<int,float> p;    // initialize p.first and p.second with zero
```

initializes the values of p by using `int()` and `float()`, which yield zero in both cases. See Section 3.2.1, page 37, for a description of the rules for explicit initialization for fundamental types.

The copy constructor is provided with both versions for a pair of the same types and as member template, which is used when implicit type conversions are necessary. If the types match, the normal implicitly generated copy constructor is called.[3] For example:

```
void f(std::pair<int,const char*>);
void g(std::pair<const int,std::string>);
...
void foo() {
    std::pair<int,const char*> p(42,"hello");
    f(p);     // OK: calls implicitly generated copy constructor
    g(p);     // OK: calls template constructor
}
```

---

[3] A template constructor does not hide the implicitly generated copy constructor. See Section 3.2, page 36, for more details about this topic.

Since C++11, a `pair<>` using a type that has only a nonconstant copy constructor will no longer compile:[4]

```
class A
{
  public:
    ...
    A(A&);    // copy constructor with nonconstant reference
    ...
};
```

```
std::pair<A,int> p;    // Error since C++11
```

Since C++11, the assignment operator is also provided as a member template so that implicit type conversions are possible. In addition, move semantics — moving the first and second elements — are supported.

Piecewise Construction

Class `pair<>` provides three constructors to initialize the `first` and `second` members with initial values:

```
namespace std {
    template <typename T1, typename T2>
    struct pair {
        ...
        pair(const T1& x, const T2& y);
        template<typename U, typename V> pair(U&& x, V&& y);
        template <typename... Args1, typename... Args2>
          pair(piecewise_construct_t,
               tuple<Args1...> first_args,
               tuple<Args2...> second_args);
        ...
    };
}
```

The first two of these constructors provide the usual behavior: passing one argument for `first` and one for `second`, including support of move semantics and implicit type conversions. However, the third constructor is something special. It allows passing two tuples — objects of a variable number of elements of different types (see Section 5.1.2, page 68) — but processes them in a different way. Normally, by passing one or two tuples, the first two constructors would allow initializing a pair, where `first` and/or `second` are tuples. But the third constructor uses the tuples to pass their *elements* to the constructors of `first` and `second`. To force this behavior, you have to pass `std::piecewise_construct` as an additional first argument. For example:

---

[4] Thanks to Daniel Krügler for pointing this out.

```cpp
// util/pair1.cpp

#include <iostream>
#include <utility>
#include <tuple>
using namespace std;

class Foo {
  public:
    Foo (tuple<int, float>) {
        cout << "Foo::Foo(tuple)" << endl;
    }
    template <typename... Args>
    Foo (Args... args) {
        cout << "Foo::Foo(args...)" << endl;
    }
};

int main()
{
    // create tuple t:
    tuple<int,float> t(1,2.22);

    // pass the tuple as a whole to the constructor of Foo:
    pair<int,Foo> p1 (42, t);

    // pass the elements of the tuple to the constructor of Foo:
    pair<int,Foo> p2 (piecewise_construct, make_tuple(42), t);
}
```

The program has the following output:

```
Foo::Foo(tuple)
Foo::Foo(args...)
```

Only where `std::piecewise_construct` is passed as the first argument is class Foo forced to use a constructor that takes the *elements* of the tuple (an `int` and a `float`) rather than a tuple as a whole. This means that in this example, the varargs constructor of Foo is called. If provided, a constructor `Foo::Foo(int,float)` would be called.

As you can see, both arguments have to be a tuple to force this behavior. Therefore, the first argument, 42, is explicitly converted into a tuple, using `make_tuple()` (you could instead pass `std::tuple(42)`).

Note that this form of initialization is required to `emplace()` a new element into an (unordered) map or multimap (see Section 7.8.2, page 341, and Section 7.9.3, page 373).

Convenience Function `make_pair()`

The `make_pair()` function template enables you to create a value pair without writing the types explicitly.[5] For example, instead of

```
std::pair<int,char>(42,'@')
```

you can write the following:

```
std::make_pair(42,'@')
```

Before C++11, the function was simply declared and defined as follows:

```
namespace std {
    // create value pair only by providing the values
    template <template T1, template T2>
    pair<T1,T2> make_pair (const T1& x, const T2& y) {
        return pair<T1,T2>(x,y);
    }
}
```

However, since C++11, things have become more complicated because this class also deals with move semantics in a useful way. So, since C++11, the C++ standard library states that `make_pair()` is declared as:

```
namespace std {
    // create value pair only by providing the values
    template <template T1, template T2>
    pair<V1,V2> make_pair (T1&& x, T2&& y);
}
```

where the details of the returned values and their types `V1` and `V2` depend on the types of `x` and `y`. Without going into details, the standard now specifies that `make_pair()` uses move semantics if possible and copy semantics otherwise. In addition, it "decays" the arguments so that the expression `make_pair("a","xy")` yields a `pair<const char*,const char*>` instead of a `pair<const char[2],const char[3]>` (see Section 5.4.2, page 132).

The `make_pair()` function makes it convenient to pass two values of a pair directly to a function that requires a pair as its argument. Consider the following example:

```
void f(std::pair<int,const char*>);
void g(std::pair<const int,std::string>);
...
void foo() {
    f(std::make_pair(42,"empty"));   // pass two values as pair
    g(std::make_pair(42,"chair"));   // pass two values as pair with type conversions
}
```

---

[5] Using `make_pair()` should cost no runtime. The compiler should always optimize any implied overhead.

As the example shows, `make_pair()` works even when the types do not match exactly, because the template constructor provides implicit type conversion. When you program by using maps or multimaps, you often need this ability (see Section 7.8.2, page 341).

Note that since C++11, you can, alternatively, use initializer lists:

```
f({42,"empty"});    // pass two values as pair
g({42,"chair"});    // pass two values as pair with type conversions
```

However, an expression that has the explicit type description has an advantage because the resulting type of the pair is not derived from the values. For example, the expression

```
std::pair<int,float>(42,7.77)
```

does *not* yield the same as

```
std::make_pair(42,7.77)
```

The latter creates a pair that has `double` as the type for the second value (unqualified floating literals have type `double`). The exact type may be important when overloaded functions or templates are used. These functions or templates might, for example, provide versions for both `float` and `double` to improve efficiency.

With the new semantic of C++11, you can influence the type `make_pair()` yields by forcing either move or reference semantics. For move semantics, you simply use `std::move()` to declare that the passed argument is no longer used:

```
std::string s, t;
...
auto p = std::make_pair(std::move(s),std::move(t));
...   // s and t are no longer used
```

To force reference semantics, you have to use `ref()`, which forces a reference type, or `cref()`, which forces a constant reference type (both provided by `<functional>`; see Section 5.4.3, page 132). For example, in the following statements, a pair refers to an `int` twice so that, finally, `i` has the value 2:

```
#include <utility>
#include <functional>
#include <iostream>

int i = 0;
auto p = std::make_pair(std::ref(i),std::ref(i));   // creates pair<int&,int&>
++p.first;                                           // increments i
++p.second;                                          // increments i again
std::cout << "i: " << i << std::endl;                // prints i: 2
```

Since C++11, you can also use the `tie()` interface, defined in `<tuple>`, to extract values out of a pair:

```
#include <utility>
#include <tuple>
#include <iostream>

std::pair<char,char> p=std::make_pair('x','y');   // pair of two chars

char c;
std::tie(std::ignore,c) = p;   // extract second value into c (ignore first one)
```

In fact, here the pair p is assigned to a tuple, where the second value is a reference to c (see Section 5.1.2, page 70, for details).

Pair Comparisons

For the comparison of two pairs, the C++ standard library provides the usual comparison operators. Two value pairs are equal if both values are equal:

```
namespace std {
    template <typename T1, typename T2>
    bool operator== (const pair<T1,T2>& x, const pair<T1,T2>& y) {
        return x.first == y.first && x.second == y.second;
    }
}
```

In a comparison of pairs, the first value has higher priority. Thus, if the first values of two pairs differ, the result of their comparison is used as the result of the overall comparison of the pairs. If the members first are equal, the comparison of the members second yields the overall result:

```
namespace std {
    template <typename T1, typename T2>
    bool operator< (const pair<T1,T2>& x, const pair<T1,T2>& y) {
        return x.first < y.first ||
                (!(y.first < x.first) && x.second < y.second);
    }
}
```

The other comparison operators are defined accordingly.

Examples of Pair Usage

The C++ standard library uses pairs a lot. For example, the (unordered) map and multimap containers use pair as a type to manage their elements, which are key/value pairs. See Section 7.8, page 331, for a general description of maps and multimaps, and in particular Section 6.2.2, page 179, for an example that shows the usage of type pair.

Objects of type pair are also used inside the C++ standard library in functions that return two values (see Section 7.7.2, page 323, for an example).

5.1.2   Tuples

Tuples were introduced in TR1 to extend the concept of `pairs` to an arbitrary number of elements. That is, tuples represent a heterogeneous list of elements for which the types are specified or deduced at compile time.

However, with TR1 using the language features of C++98, it was not possible to define a template for a variable number of elements. For this reason, implementations had to specify all possible numbers of elements a tuple could have. The recommendation in TR1 was to support at least ten arguments, which meant that tuples were usually defined as follows, although some implementations did provide more template parameters:

```
template <typename T0 = ..., typename T1 = ..., typename T2 = ...,
          typename T3 = ..., typename T4 = ..., typename T5 = ...,
          typename T6 = ..., typename T7 = ..., typename T8 = ...,
          typename T9 = ...>
class tuple;
```

That is, class `tuple` has at least ten template parameters of different types, with an implementation-specific default value used to give unused tuple elements a default type with no abilities. This was in fact an emulation of variadic templates, which in practice, however, was quite cumbersome and very limited.

With C++11, variadic templates were introduced to enable templates to accept an arbitrary number of template arguments (see Section 3.1.9, page 26). As a consequence, the declaration for class `tuple`, which happens in `<tuple>`, is now reduced to the following:

```
namespace std {
  template <typename... Types>
  class tuple;
}
```

Tuple Operations

In principle, the tuple interface is very straightforward:

- You can create a tuple by declaring it either explicitly or implicitly with the convenience function `make_tuple()`.
- You can access elements with the `get<>()` function template.

Here is a basic example of this interface:

```
// util/tuple1.cpp

#include <tuple>
#include <iostream>
#include <complex>
#include <string>
using namespace std;
```

```
int main()
{
    // create a four-element tuple
    // - elements are initialized with default value (0 for fundamental types)
    tuple<string,int,int,complex<double>> t;

    // create and initialize a tuple explicitly
    tuple<int,float,string> t1(41,6.3,"nico");

    // "iterate" over elements:
    cout << get<0>(t1) << " ";
    cout << get<1>(t1) << " ";
    cout << get<2>(t1) << " ";
    cout << endl;

    // create tuple with make_tuple()
    // - auto declares t2 with type of right-hand side
    // - thus, type of t2 is tuple
    auto t2 = make_tuple(22,44,"nico");

    // assign second value in t2 to t1
    get<1>(t1) = get<1>(t2);

    // comparison and assignment
    // - including type conversion from tuple<int,int,const char*>
    //   to tuple<int,float,string>
    if (t1 < t2) {   // compares value for value
        t1 = t2;     // OK, assigns value for value
    }
}
```

The following statement creates a heterogeneous four-element tuple:

```
tuple<string,int,int,complex<double>> t;
```

The values are initialized with their default constructors. Fundamental types are initialized with 0 (this guarantee applies only since C++11).

The statement

```
tuple<int,float,string> t1(41,6.3,"nico");
```

creates and initializes a heterogeneous three-element tuple.

Alternatively, you can use `make_tuple()` to create a tuple in which the types are automatically derived from the initial values. For example, you can use the following to create and initialize a tuple of the corresponding types `int`, `int`, and `const char*`.[6]

```
make_tuple(22,44,"nico")
```

Note that a tuple type can be a reference. For example:

```
string s;
tuple<string&> t(s);    // first element of tuple t refers to s

get<0>(t) = "hello";    // assigns "hello" to s
```

A tuple is no ordinary container class where you can iterate over the elements. Instead, for element access, member templates are provided so that you have to know the index of elements you want to access at compile time. For example, you get access to the first element of tuple `t1` as follows:

```
get<0>(t1)
```

Passing an index at runtime is not possible:

```
int i;
get<i>(t1)      // compile-time error: i is no compile-time value
```

The good news is that it is also a compile-time error to pass an invalid index:

```
get<3>(t1)      // compile-time error if t1 has only three elements
```

In addition, tuples provide the usual copy, assignment, and comparison operations. For all of them, implicit type conversions are possible (because member templates are used), but the number of elements must match. Tuples are equal if all elements are equal. To check whether a container is less than another container, a lexicographical comparison is done (see Section 11.5.4, page 548).

Table 5.2 lists all operations provided for tuples.

Convenience Functions `make_tuple()` and `tie()`

The convenience function `make_tuple()` creates a tuple of values without explicitly specifying their types. For example, the expression

```
make_tuple(22,44,"nico")
```

creates and initializes a tuple of the corresponding types `int`, `int`, and `const char*`.

By using the special `reference_wrapper<>` function object and its convenience functions `ref()` and `cref()` (all available since C++11 in `<functional>`; see Section 5.4.3, page 132) you can influence the type that `make_tuple()` yields. For example, the following expression yields a tuple with a reference to variable/object x:

```
string s;
make_tuple(ref(s))      // yields type tuple<string&>, where the element refers to s
```

---

[6] The type of "nico" is `const char[5]`, but it *decays* to `const char*` using the type trait `std::decay()` (see Section 5.4.2, page 132).

Operation	Effect
`tuple<T1,T2,...,Tn> t`	Creates a tuple with *n* elements of the specified types, initialized with their default constructors (0 for fundamental types)
`tuple<T1,T2,...,Tn>` `t(v1,v2,...,vn)`	Creates a tuple with *n* elements of the specified types, initialized with the specified values
`tuple<T1,T2> t(p)`	Creates a tuple with two elements of the specified type, initialized with the values of the passed `pair` *p* (*p*s types must match)
`t = t2`	Assigns the values of *t2* to *t*
`t = p`	Assigns a `pair` *p* to a tuple with two elements (the types of the pair *p* must match)
`t1 == t2`	Returns whether *t1* is equal to *t2* (true if a comparison with == of all elements yields `true`)
`t1 != t2`	Returns whether *t1* is not equal to *t2* (`!(t1==t2)`)
`t1 < t2`	Returns whether *t1* is less than T*It2* (uses lexicographical comparison)
`t1 > t2`	Returns whether *t1* is greater than *t2* (*t2<t1*)
`t1 <= t2`	Returns whether *t1* is less than or equal to *t2* (`!(t2<t1)`)
`t1 >= t2`	Returns whether *t1* is greater than or equal to *t2* (`!(t1<t2)`)
`t1.swap(t2)`	Swaps the data of *t1* and *t2* (since C++11)
`swap(t1,t2)`	Same (as global function) (since C++11)
`make_tuple(v1,v2,...)`	Creates a tuple with types and values of all passed values, and allows extracting values out of a tuple
`tie(ref1,ref2,...)`	Creates a tuple of references, which allows extracting (individual) values out of a tuple

Table 5.2. Operations of `tuples`

This can be important if you want to modify an existing value via a tuple:

```
std::string s;
```

```
auto x = std::make_tuple(s);      // x is of type tuple<string>
std::get<0>(x) = "my value";      // modifies x but not s
```

```
auto y = std::make_tuple(ref(s)); // y is of type tuple<string&>, thus y refers to s
std::get<0>(y) = "my value";      // modifies y
```

By using references with `make_tuple()`, you can extract values of a tuple back to some other variables. Consider the following example:

```
std::tuple <int,float,std::string> t(77,1.1,"more light");
int i;
float f;
std::string s;
// assign values of t to i, f, and s:
std::make_tuple(std::ref(i),std::ref(f),std::ref(s)) = t;
```

To make the use of references in tuples even more convenient, the use of `tie()` creates a tuple of references:

```
std::tuple <int,float,std::string> t(77,1.1,"more light");
int i;
float f;
std::string s;
std::tie(i,f,s) = t;   // assigns values of t to i, f, and s
```

Here, `std::tie(i,f,s)` creates a tuple with references to i, f, and s, so the assignment of t assigns the elements in t to i, f, and s.

The use of `std::ignore` allows ignoring tuple elements while parsing with `tie()`. This can be used to extract tuple values partially:

```
std::tuple <int,float,std::string> t(77,1.1,"more light");
int i;
std::string s;
std::tie(i,std::ignore,s) = t;   // assigns first and third value of t to i and s
```

Tuples and Initializer Lists

The constructor taking a variable number of arguments to initialize a tuple is declared as `explicit`:

```
namespace std {
    template <typename... Types>
    class tuple {
      public:
        explicit tuple(const Types&...);
        template <typename... UTypes> explicit tuple(UTypes&&...);
        ...
    };
}
```

The reason is to avoid having single values implicitly converted into a tuple with one element:

```
template <typename... Args>
void foo (const std::tuple<Args...> t);
```

```
foo(42);                 // ERROR: explicit conversion to tuple<> required
foo(make_tuple(42));   // OK
```

This situation, however, has consequences when using initializer lists to define values of a tuple. For example, you can't use the assignment syntax to initialize a tuple because that is considered to be an implicit conversion:

```
std::tuple<int,double> t1(42,3.14);       // OK, old syntax
std::tuple<int,double> t2{42,3.14};       // OK, new syntax
std::tuple<int,double> t3 = {42,3.14};  // ERROR
```

In addition, you can't pass an initializer list where a tuple is expected:

```
std::vector<std::tuple<int,float>> v { {1,1.0}, {2,2.0} };   // ERROR

std::tuple<int,int,int> foo() {
    return { 1, 2, 3 };   // ERROR
}
```

Note that it works for pair<>s and containers (except array<>s):

```
std::vector<std::pair<int,float>> v1 { {1,1.0}, {2,2.0} };   // OK
std::vector<std::vector<float>>   v2 { {1,1.0}, {2,2.0} };   // OK

std::vector<int> foo2() {
    return { 1, 2, 3 };   // OK
}
```

But for tuples, you have to explicitly convert the initial values into a tuple (for example, by using make_tuple()):

```
std::vector<std::tuple<int,float>> v { std::make_tuple(1,1.0),
                                       std::make_tuple(2,2.0) };   // OK

std::tuple<int,int,int> foo() {
    return std::make_tuple(1,2,3);   // OK
}
```

Additional Tuple Features

For tuples, some additional helpers are declared, especially to support generic programming:

- tuple_size<*tupletype*>::value yields the number of elements.
- tuple_element<*idx*, *tupletype*>::type yields the type of the element with index *idx* (this is the type get() returns).
- tuple_cat() concatenates multiple tuples into one tuple.

The use of tuple_size<> and tuple_element<> shows the following example:

```
typename std::tuple<int,float,std::string> TupleType;

std::tuple_size<TupleType>::value        // yields 3
std::tuple_element<1,TupleType>::type    // yields float
```

You can use tuple_cat() to concatenate all forms of tuples, including pair<>s:

```
int n;
auto tt = std::tuple_cat (std::make_tuple(42,7.7,"hello"),
                          std::tie(n));
```

Here, tt becomes a tuple with all elements of the passed tuples, including the fact that the last element is a reference to n.

5.1.3   I/O for Tuples

The `tuple` class was first made public in the Boost library (see [*Boost*]). There, `tuple` had an
interface to write values to output streams, but there is no support for this in the C++ standard
library. With the following header file, you can print any tuple with the standard output operator
`<<`:[7]

```
// util/printtuple.hpp

#include <tuple>
#include <iostream>

// helper: print element with index IDX of tuple with MAX elements
template <int IDX, int MAX, typename... Args>
struct PRINT_TUPLE {
    static void print (std::ostream& strm, const std::tuple<Args...>& t) {
      strm << std::get<IDX>(t) << (IDX+1==MAX ? "" : ",");
      PRINT_TUPLE<IDX+1,MAX,Args...>::print(strm,t);
    }
};

// partial specialization to end the recursion
template <int MAX, typename... Args>
struct PRINT_TUPLE<MAX,MAX,Args...> {
    static void print (std::ostream& strm, const std::tuple<Args...>& t) {
    }
};

// output operator for tuples
template <typename... Args>
std::ostream& operator << (std::ostream& strm,
                           const std::tuple<Args...>& t)
{
    strm << "[";
    PRINT_TUPLE<0,sizeof...(Args),Args...>::print(strm,t);
    return strm << "]";
}
```

This code makes heavy use of template metaprogramming to recursively iterate at compile time over
the elements of a tuple. Each call of `PRINT_TUPLE<>::print()` prints one element and calls the

---

[7] Note that this output operator does not work where *ADL* (*argument-dependent lookup*) does not work (see
Section 15.11.1, page 812, for details).

same function for the next element. A partial specialization, where the current index IDX and the number of elements in the tuple MAX are equal, ends this recursion. For example, the program

```
// util/tuple2.cpp

#include "printtuple.hpp"
#include <tuple>
#include <iostream>
#include <string>
using namespace std;

int main()
{
    tuple <int,float,string> t(77,1.1,"more light");
    cout << "io: " << t << endl;
}
```

has the following output:

```
io: [77,1.1,more light]
```

Here, the output expression

```
cout << t
```

calls

```
PRINT_TUPLE<0,3,Args...>::print(cout,t);
```

5.1.4   Conversions between `tuples` and `pairs`

As listed in Table 5.2 on page 71, you can initialize a two-element tuple with a pair. Also, you can assign a pair to a two-element tuple.

Note that pair<> provides a special constructor to use tuples to initialize its elements. See Section 5.1.1, page 63, for details. Note also that other types might provide a tuple-like interface. In fact, class pair<> (see Section 5.1.1, page 62) and class array<> (see Section 7.2.5, page 268) do.

5.2 Smart Pointers

Since C, we know that pointers are important but are a source of trouble. One reason to use pointers is to have reference semantics outside the usual boundaries of scope. However, it can be very tricky to ensure that their lifetime and the lifetime of the objects they refer to match, especially when multiple pointers refer to the same object. For example, to have the same object in multiple collections (see Chapter 7), you have to pass a pointer into each collection, and ideally there should be no problems when one of the pointers gets destroyed (no "dangling pointers" or multiple deletions of the referenced object) and when the last reference to an object gets destroyed (no "resource leaks").

A usual approach to avoid these kinds of problems is to use "smart pointers." They are "smart" in the sense that they support programmers in avoiding problems such as those just described. For example, a smart pointer can be so smart that it "knows" whether it is the last pointer to an object and uses this knowledge to delete an associated object only when it, as "last owner" of an object, gets destroyed.

Note, however, that it is not sufficient to provide only one smart pointer class. Smart pointers can be smart about different aspects and might fulfill different priorities, because you might pay a price for the smartness. Note that with a specific smart pointer, it's still possible to misuse a pointer or to program erroneous behavior.

Since C++11, the C++ standard library provides two types of smart pointer:

1. Class `shared_ptr` for a pointer that implements the concept of *shared ownership*. Multiple smart pointers can refer to the same object so that the object and its associated resources get released whenever the last reference to it gets destroyed. To perform this task in more complicated scenarios, helper classes, such as `weak_ptr`, `bad_weak_ptr`, and `enable_shared_from_this`, are provided.

2. Class `unique_ptr` for a pointer that implements the concept of *exclusive ownership* or *strict ownership*. This pointer ensures that only one smart pointer can refer to this object at a time. However, you can transfer ownership. This pointer is especially useful for avoiding resource leaks, such as missing calls of `delete` after or while an object gets created with `new` and an exception occurred.

Historically, C++98 had only one smart pointer class provided by the C++ standard library, class `auto_ptr<>`, which was designed to perform the task that `unique_ptr` now provides. However, due to missing language features, such as move semantics for constructors and assignment operators and other flaws, this class turned out to be difficult to understand and error prone. So, after class `shared_ptr` was introduced with TR1 and class `unique_ptr` was introduced with C++11, class `auto_ptr` officially became deprecated with C++11, which means that you should not use it unless you have old existing code to compile.

All smart pointer classes are defined in the `<memory>` header file.

5.2.1 Class `shared_ptr`

Almost every nontrivial program needs the ability to use or deal with objects at multiple places at the same time. Thus, you have to "refer" to an object from multiple places in your program. Although the language provides references and pointers, this is not enough, because you often have to ensure that when the last reference to an object gets deleted, the object itself gets deleted, which might require some cleanup operations, such as freeing memory or releasing a resource.

So we need a semantics of "cleanup when the object is nowhere used anymore." Class `shared_ptr` provides this semantics of *shared ownership*. Thus, multiple `shared_ptrs` are able to share, or "own," the same object. The last owner of the object is responsible for destroying it and cleaning up all resources associated with it.

By default, the cleanup is a call of `delete`, assuming that the object was created with `new`. But you can (and often must) define other ways to clean up objects. You can define your own *destruction policy*. For example, if your object is an array allocated with `new[]`, you have to define that the cleanup performs a `delete[]`. Other examples are the deletion of associated resources, such as handles, locks, associated temporary files, and so on.

To summarize, the goal of `shared_ptrs` is to automatically release resources associated with objects when those objects are no longer needed (but not before).

Using Class `shared_ptr`

You can use a `shared_ptr` just as you would any other pointer. Thus, you can assign, copy, and compare shared pointers, as well as use operators `*` and `->`, to access the object the pointer refers to. Consider the following example:

```
// util/sharedptr1.cpp

#include <iostream>
#include <string>
#include <vector>
#include <memory>
using namespace std;

int main()
{
    // two shared pointers representing two persons by their name
    shared_ptr<string> pNico(new string("nico"));
    shared_ptr<string> pJutta(new string("jutta"));

    // capitalize person names
    (*pNico)[0] = 'N';
    pJutta->replace(0,1,"J");

    // put them multiple times in a container
    vector<shared_ptr<string>> whoMadeCoffee;
    whoMadeCoffee.push_back(pJutta);
    whoMadeCoffee.push_back(pJutta);
    whoMadeCoffee.push_back(pNico);
    whoMadeCoffee.push_back(pJutta);
    whoMadeCoffee.push_back(pNico);
```

```
// print all elements
for (auto ptr : whoMadeCoffee) {
    cout << *ptr << "  ";
}
cout << endl;

// overwrite a name again
*pNico = "Nicolai";

// print all elements again
for (auto ptr : whoMadeCoffee) {
    cout << *ptr << "  ";
}
cout << endl;

// print some internal data
cout << "use_count: " << whoMadeCoffee[0].use_count() << endl;
}
```

After including <memory>, where shared_ptr class is defined, two shared_ptrs representing
pointers to strings are declared and initialized:

```
shared_ptr<string> pNico(new string("nico"));
shared_ptr<string> pJutta(new string("jutta"));
```

Note that because the constructor taking a pointer as single argument is explicit, you can't use the
assignment notation here because that is considered to be an implicit conversion. However, the new
initialization syntax is also possible:

```
shared_ptr<string> pNico = new string("nico");   // ERROR
shared_ptr<string> pNico{new string("nico")};    // OK
```

You can also use the convenience function make_shared() here:

```
shared_ptr<string> pNico = make_shared<string>("nico");
shared_ptr<string> pJutta = make_shared<string>("jutta");
```

This way of creation is faster and safer because it uses one instead of two allocations: one for the
object and one for the shared data the shared pointer uses to control the object (see Section 5.2.4,
page 95, for details).

Alternatively, you can declare the shared pointer first and assign a new pointer later on. However,
you can't use the assignment operator; you have to use reset() instead:

```
shared_ptr<string> pNico4;
pNico4 = new string("nico");   // ERROR: no assignment for ordinary pointers
pNico4.reset(new string("nico"));   // OK
```

The following two lines demonstrate that using shared pointers is just like using ordinary pointers:

```
(*pNico)[0] = 'N';
pJutta->replace(0,1,"J");
```

With operator *, you yield the object pNico refers to to assign a capital 'N' to its first character. With operator ->, you get access to a member of the object pJutta refers to. Thus, here the member function replace() allows you to replace substrings (see Section 13.3.7, page 706).

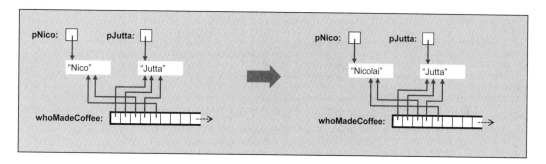

Figure 5.1. Using shared_ptrs

Next we insert both pointers multiple times into a container of type vector<> (see Section 7.3, page 270). The container usually creates its own copy of the elements passed, so we would insert copies of strings if we inserted the strings directly. However, because we pass pointers to the strings, these pointers are copied, so the container now contains multiple references to the same object. This means that if we modify the objects, all occurrences of this object in the container get modified. Thus, after replacing the value of the string pNico

```
*pNico = "Nicolai";
```

all occurrences of this object now refer to the new value, as you can see in Figure 5.1 and according to the corresponding output of the program:

```
Jutta   Jutta   Nico   Jutta   Nico
Jutta   Jutta   Nicolai   Jutta   Nicolai
use_count: 4
```

The last row of the output is the result of calling use_count() for the first shared pointer in the vector. use_count() yields the current number of owners an object referred to by shared pointers has. As you can see, we have four owners of the object referred to by the first element in the vector: pJutta and the three copies of it inserted into the container.

At the end of the program, when the last owner of a string gets destroyed, the shared pointer calls delete for the object it refers to. Such a deletion does not necessarily have to happen at the end of the scope. For example, assigning the nullptr (see Section 3.1.1, page 14) to pNico or resizing the vector so that it contains only the first two elements would delete the last owner of the string initialized with nico.

Defining a Deleter

We can declare our own deleter, which, for example, prints a message before it deletes the referenced object:

```
shared_ptr<string> pNico(new string("nico"),
                         [](string* p) {
                             cout << "delete " << *p << endl;
                             delete p;
                         });
```

```
...
pNico = nullptr;              // pNico does not refer to the string any longer
whoMadeCoffee.resize(2);  // all copies of the string in pNico are destroyed
```

Here, we pass a lambda (see Section 3.1.10, page 28) as the second argument to the constructor of a shared_ptr. Having pNico declared that way, the lambda function gets called when the last owner of a string gets destroyed. So the preceding program with this modification would print

```
delete Nicolai
```

when resize() gets called after all statements as discussed before. The effect would be the same if we first changed the size of the vector and then assigned nullptr or another object to pNico.

For another example application of shared_ptr<>, see how elements can be shared by two containers in Section 7.11, page 388.

Dealing with Arrays

Note that the default deleter provided by shared_ptr calls delete, not delete[]. This means that the default deleter is appropriate only if a shared pointer owns a single object created with new. Unfortunately, creating a shared_ptr for an array is possible but wrong:

```
std::shared_ptr<int> p(new int[10]);    // ERROR, but compiles
```

So, if you use new[] to create an array of objects you have to define your own deleter. You can do that by passing a function, function object, or lambda, which calls delete[] for the passed ordinary pointer. For example:

```
std::shared_ptr<int> p(new int[10],
                       [](int* p) {
                           delete[] p;
                       });
```

You can also use a helper officially provided for unique_ptr, which calls delete[] as deleter (see Section 5.2.5, page 106):

```
std::shared_ptr<int> p(new int[10],
                       std::default_delete<int[]>());
```

Note, however, that shared_ptr and unique_ptr deal with deleters in slightly different ways. For example, unique_ptrs provide the ability to own an array simply by passing the corresponding element type as template argument, whereas for shared_ptrs this is not possible:

```
std::unique_ptr<int[]> p(new int[10]);   // OK
std::shared_ptr<int[]> p(new int[10]);   // ERROR: does not compile
```

In addition, for unique_ptrs, you have to specify a second template argument to specify your own deleter:

```
std::unique_ptr<int,void(*)(int*)> p(new int[10],
                                     [](int* p) {
                                         delete[] p;
                                     });
```

Note also that shared_ptr does not provide an operator []. For unique_ptr, a partial specialization for arrays exists, which provides operator [] instead of operators * and ->. The reason for this difference is that unique_ptr is optimized for performance and flexibility. See Section 5.2.8, page 114, for details.

Dealing with Other Destruction Policies

When the cleanup after the last owning shared pointer is something other than deleting memory, you have to specify your own deleter. You can understand this to specify your own *destruction policy*.

As a first example, suppose that we want to ensure that a temporary file gets removed when the last reference to it gets destroyed. This is how it could be done:

```
// util/sharedptr2.cpp

#include <string>
#include <fstream>    // for ofstream
#include <memory>     // for shared_ptr
#include <cstdio>     // for remove()

class FileDeleter
{
  private:
    std::string filename;
  public:
    FileDeleter (const std::string& fn)
     : filename(fn) {
    }
    void operator () (std::ofstream* fp) {
        fp->close();                      // close file
        std::remove(filename.c_str());    // delete file
    }
};

int main()
{
    // create and open temporary file:
```

```
    std::shared_ptr<std::ofstream> fp(new std::ofstream("tmpfile.txt"),
                                  FileDeleter("tmpfile.txt"));

    ...

}
```

Here, we initialize a shared_ptr with a newly created output file (see Section 15.9, page 791). The passed FileDeleter ensures that this files gets closed and deleted with the standard C function remove(), provided in <cstdio> when the last copy of this shared pointer loses the ownership of this output stream. Because remove() needs the filename, we pass this as an argument to the constructor of FileDeleter.

Our second example demonstrates how to use shared_ptrs to deal with shared memory:[8]

```
// util/sharedptr3.cpp

#include <memory>       // for shared_ptr
#include <sys/mman.h>   // for shared memory
#include <fcntl.h>
#include <unistd.h>
#include <cstring>      // for strerror()
#include <cerrno>       // for errno
#include <string>
#include <iostream>

class SharedMemoryDetacher
{
  public:
    void operator () (int* p) {
        std::cout << "unlink /tmp1234" << std::endl;
        if (shm_unlink("/tmp1234") != 0) {
            std::cerr << "OOPS: shm_unlink() failed" << std::endl;
        }
    }
};

std::shared_ptr<int> getSharedIntMemory (int num)
{
    void* mem;
    int shmfd = shm_open("/tmp1234", O_CREAT|O_RDWR, S_IRWXU|S_IRWXG);
    if (shmfd < 0) {
        throw std::string(strerror(errno));
    }
```

---

[8] There are multiple system-dependent ways to deal with shared memory. Here, the standard POSIX way with shm_open() and mmap() is used, which requires shm_unlink() to be called to release the (persistent) shared memory.

```
    if (ftruncate(shmfd, num*sizeof(int)) == -1) {
        throw std::string(strerror(errno));
    }
    mem = mmap(nullptr, num*sizeof(int), PROT_READ | PROT_WRITE,
               MAP_SHARED, shmfd, 0);
    if (mem == MAP_FAILED) {
        throw std::string(strerror(errno));
    }
    return std::shared_ptr<int>(static_cast<int*>(mem),
                                SharedMemoryDetacher());
}

int main()
{
    // get and attach shared memory for 100 ints:
    std::shared_ptr<int> smp(getSharedIntMemory(100));

    // init the shared memory
    for (int i=0; i<100; ++i) {
        smp.get()[i] = i*42;
    }

    // deal with shared memory somewhere else:
    ...
    std::cout << "<return>" << std::endl;
    std::cin.get();

    // release shared memory here:
    smp.reset();
    ...
}
```

First, a deleter SharedMemoryDetacher is defined to detach shared memory. The deleter releases the shared memory, which getSharedIntMemory() gets and attaches. To ensure that the deleter is called when the last use of the shared memory is over, it is passed when getSharedIntMemory() creates a shared_ptr for the attached memory:

```
    return std::shared_ptr<int>(static_cast<int*>(mem),
                                SharedMemoryDetacher());   // calls shmdt()
```

Alternatively, you could use a lambda here (skipping prefix std::):

```
    return shared_ptr<int>(static_cast<int*>(mem),
                           [](int* p) {
                               cout << "unlink /tmp1234" << endl;
```

```
                    if (shm_unlink("/tmp1234") != 0) {
                        cerr << "OOPS: shm_unlink() failed"
                             << endl;
                    }
                });
```

Note that the passed deleter is not allowed to throw exceptions. Therefore, we only write an error message to std::cerr here.

Because the signature of shm_unlink() already fits, you could even use shm_unlink() directly as deleter if you don't want to check its return value:

```
    return std::shared_ptr<int>(static_cast<int*>(mem),
                                shm_unlink);
```

Note that shared_ptrs provide only operators * and ->. Pointer arithmetic and operator [ ] are not provided. Thus, to access the memory, you have to use get(), which yields the internal pointer wrapped by shared_ptr to provide the full pointer semantics:

```
    smp.get()[i] = i*42;
```

Thus, get() provides an alternative of calling:

```
    (&*smp)[i] = i*42;
```

For both examples, another possible implementation technique is probably cleaner than this: Just create a new class, where the constructor does the initial stuff and the destructor does the cleanup. You can then just use shared_ptrs to manage objects of this class created with new. The benefit is that you can define a more intuitive interface, such as an operator [ ] for an object representing shared memory. However, you should then carefully think about copy and assignment operations; if in doubt, disable them.

5.2.2   Class weak_ptr

The major reason to use shared_ptrs is to avoid taking care of the resources a pointer refers to. As written, shared_ptrs are provided to automatically release resources associated with objects no longer needed.

However, under certain circumstances, this behavior doesn't work or is not what is intended:

- One example is cyclic references. If two objects refer to each other using shared_ptrs, and you want to release the objects and their associated resource if no other references to these objects exist, shared_ptr won't release the data, because the use_count() of each object is still 1. You might want to use ordinary pointers in this situation, but doing so requires explicitly caring for and managing the release of associated resources.

- Another example occurs when you explicitly want to share but not own an object. Thus, you have the semantics that the lifetime of a reference to an object outlives the object it refers to. Here, shared_ptrs would never release the object, and ordinary pointers might not notice that the object they refer to is not valid anymore, which introduces the risk of accessing released data.

For both cases, class `weak_ptr` is provided, which allows sharing but not owning an object. This class requires a shared pointer to get created. Whenever the last shared pointer owning the object loses its ownership, any weak pointer automatically becomes empty. Thus, besides default and copy constructors, class `weak_ptr` provides only a constructor taking a `shared_ptr`.

You can't use operators * and -> to access a referenced object of a `weak_ptr` directly. Instead, you have to create a shared pointer out of it. This makes sense for two reasons:

1. Creating a shared pointer out of a weak pointer checks whether there is (still) an associated object. If not, this operation will throw an exception or create an empty shared pointer (what exactly happens depends on the operation used).

2. While dealing with the referenced object, the shared pointer can't get released.

As a consequence, class `weak_ptr` provides only a small number of operations: Just enough to create, copy, and assign a weak pointer and convert it into a shared pointer or check whether it refers to an object.

Using Class `weak_ptr`

Consider the following example:

```
// util/weakptr1.cpp

#include <iostream>
#include <string>
#include <vector>
#include <memory>
using namespace std;

class Person {
  public:
    string name;
    shared_ptr<Person> mother;
    shared_ptr<Person> father;
    vector<shared_ptr<Person>> kids;

    Person (const string& n,
            shared_ptr<Person> m = nullptr,
            shared_ptr<Person> f = nullptr)
     : name(n), mother(m), father(f) {
    }

    ~Person() {
      cout << "delete " << name << endl;
    }
};
```

```cpp
shared_ptr<Person> initFamily (const string& name)
{
    shared_ptr<Person> mom(new Person(name+"'s mom"));
    shared_ptr<Person> dad(new Person(name+"'s dad"));
    shared_ptr<Person> kid(new Person(name,mom,dad));
    mom->kids.push_back(kid);
    dad->kids.push_back(kid);
    return kid;
}

int main()
{
    shared_ptr<Person> p = initFamily("nico");

    cout << "nico's family exists" << endl;
    cout << "- nico is shared " << p.use_count() << " times" << endl;
    cout << "- name of 1st kid of nico's mom: "
         << p->mother->kids[0]->name << endl;

    p = initFamily("jim");
    cout << "jim's family exists" << endl;
}
```

Here, a class Person has a name and optional references to other Persons, namely, the parents (mother and father) and the kids (a vector; see Section 7.3, page 270).

First, initFamily() creates three Persons: mom, dad, and kid, initialized with corresponding names based on the passed argument. In addition, kid is initialized with the parents, and for both parents, kid is inserted in the list of kids. Finally, initFamily() returns the kid. Figure 5.2 shows the resulting situation at the end of initFamily() and after calling and assigning the result to p.

As you can see, p is our last handle into the family created. Internally, however, each object has references from the kid to each parent and backwards. So, for example, nico was shared three times before p gets a new value. Now, if we release our last handle to the family — either by assigning a new person or nullptr to p or by leaving the scope of p at the end of main() — none of the Persons gets released, because each still has at least one shared pointer referring to it. As a result, the destructor of each Person, which would print "delete *name*," never gets called:

```
nico's family exists
- nico shared 3 times
- name of 1st kid of nicos mom: nico
jim's family exists
```

Using weak_ptrs instead helps here. For example, we can declare kids to be a vector of weak_ptrs:

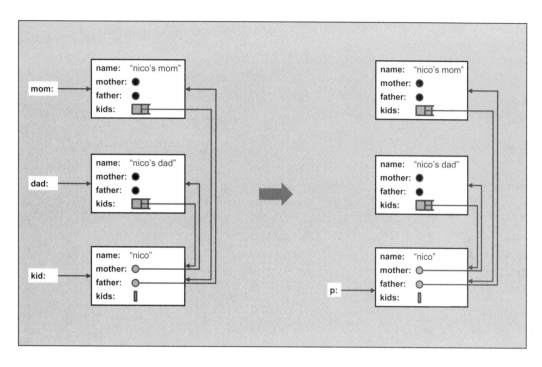

Figure 5.2. A Family Using `shared_ptrs` *Only*

```
// util/weakptr2.cpp
...
class Person {
  public:
    string name;
    shared_ptr<Person> mother;
    shared_ptr<Person> father;
    vector<weak_ptr<Person>> kids;   // weak pointer !!!
    Person (const string& n,
            shared_ptr<Person> m = nullptr,
            shared_ptr<Person> f = nullptr)
        : name(n), mother(m), father(f) {
    }
    ~Person() {
      cout << "delete " << name << endl;
    }
};
...
```

By doing so, we can break the cycle of shared pointers so that in one direction (from kid to parent) a shared pointer is used, whereas from a parent to the kids, weak pointers are used (the dashed line in Figure 5.3).

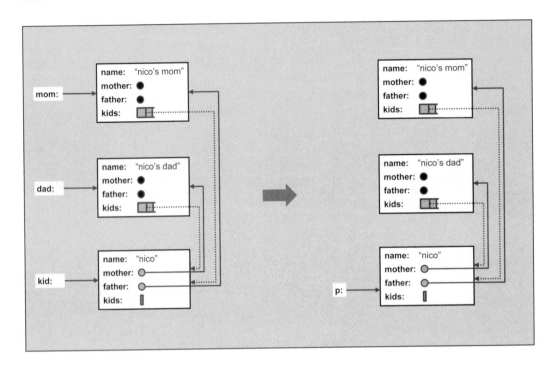

Figure 5.3. A Family Using `shared_ptrs` *and* `weak_ptrs`

As a result, the program now has the following output:

```
nico's family exists
- nico shared 1 times
- name of 1st kid of nicos mom: nico
delete nico
delete nico's dad
delete nico's mom
jim's family exists
delete jim
delete jim's dad
delete jim's mom
```

As soon as we lose our handle into a family created — either by assigning a new value to p or by leaving main() — the kid's object of the family loses its last owner (use_count() yielded 1 before), which has the effect that both parents lose their last owner. So all objects, initially created by new, are deleted now so that their destructors get called.

Note that by using weak pointers, we had to slightly modify the way we access the object referred to via a weak pointer. Instead of calling

```
p->mother->kids[0]->name
```

we now have to insert lock() into the expression

```
p->mother->kids[0].lock()->name
```

which yields a `shared_ptr` out of the `weak_ptr` the vector of `kids` contains. If this modification is not possible — for example, because the last owner of the object released the object in the meantime — `lock()` yields an empty `shared_ptr`. In that case, calling operator `*` or `->` would cause undefined behavior.

If you are not sure that the object behind a weak pointer still exists, you have several options:

1. You can call `expired()`, which returns `true` if the `weak_ptr` doesn't share an object any longer. This option is equivalent to checking whether `use_count()` is equal to 0 but might be faster.

2. You can explicitly convert a `weak_ptr` into a `shared_ptr` by using a corresponding `shared_ptr` constructor. If there is no valid referenced object, this constructor will throw a `bad_weak_ptr` exception. This is an exception of a class derived from `std::exception`, where `what()` yields `"bad_weak_ptr"`.[9] See Section 4.3.1, page 43, for details about all standard exceptions.

3. You can call `use_count()` to ask for the number of owners the associated object has. If the return value is 0, there is no valid object any longer. Note, however, that you should usually call `use_count()` only for debugging purposes; the C++ standard library explicitly states: "`use_count()` is not necessarily efficient."

For example:

```
try {
    shared_ptr<string> sp(new string("hi"));    // create shared pointer
    weak_ptr<string> wp = sp;                    // create weak pointer out of it
    sp.reset();                                  // release object of shared pointer
    cout << wp.use_count() << endl;              // prints: 0
    cout << boolalpha << wp.expired() << endl;   // prints: true
    shared_ptr<string> p(wp);                    // throws std::bad_weak_ptr
}
catch (const std::exception& e) {
    cerr << "exception: " << e.what() << endl;   // prints: bad_weak_ptr
}
```

5.2.3 Misusing Shared Pointers

Although `shared_ptrs` improve program safety, because in general resources associated with objects are automatically released, problems are possible when objects are no longer in use. One problem just discussed is "dangling pointers" caused by cyclic dependencies.

As another problem, you have to ensure that only one group of shared pointers owns an object. The following code will not work:

---

[9] For exceptions, the return value of `what()` is usually implementation specific. However, the standard specifies to yield `"bad_weak_ptr"` here. Nevertheless, implementations might not follow this advice; for example, GCC 4.6.1 returned `"std::bad_weak_ptr"`.

```
int* p = new int;
shared_ptr<int> sp1(p);
shared_ptr<int> sp2(p);          // ERROR: two shared pointers manage allocated int
```

The problem is that both sp1 and sp2 would release the associated resource (call delete) when they lose their ownership of p. In general, having two owning groups means that the release of the associated resource is performed twice whenever the last owner of each group loses the ownership or gets destroyed. For this reason, you should always directly initialize a smart pointer the moment you create the object with its associated resource:

```
shared_ptr<int> sp1(new int);
shared_ptr<int> sp2(sp1);        // OK
```

This problem might also occur indirectly. In the example just introduced, suppose that we want to introduce a member function for a Person that creates both the reference from a kid to the parent and a corresponding reference back:

```
shared_ptr<Person> mom(new Person(name+"'s mom"));
shared_ptr<Person> dad(new Person(name+"'s dad"));
shared_ptr<Person> kid(new Person(name));
kid->setParentsAndTheirKids(mom,dad);
```

Here is a naive implementation of setParentsAndTheirKids():

```
class Person {
  public:
    ...
    void setParentsAndTheirKids (shared_ptr<Person> m = nullptr,
                                 shared_ptr<Person> f = nullptr) {
        mother = m;
        father = f;
        if (m != nullptr) {
            m->kids.push_back(shared_ptr<Person>(this));  // ERROR
        }
        if (f != nullptr) {
            f->kids.push_back(shared_ptr<Person>(this));  // ERROR
        }
    }
    ...
};
```

The problem is the creation of a shared pointer out of this. We do that because we want to set the kids of members mother and father. But to do that, we need a shared pointer to the kid, which we don't have at hand. However, creating a new shared pointer out of this doesn't solve the issue, because we then open a new group of owners.

One way to deal with this problem is to pass the shared pointer to the kid as a third argument. But the C++ standard library provides another option: class std::enable_shared_from_this<>.

You can use class std::enable_shared_from_this<> to derive your class, representing objects managed by shared pointers, with your class name passed as template argument. Doing so al-

lows you to use a derived member function `shared_from_this()` to create a correct `shared_ptr`
out of `this`:

```
class Person : public std::enable_shared_from_this<Person> {
  public:
    ...
    void setParentsAndTheirKids (shared_ptr<Person> m = nullptr,
                                 shared_ptr<Person> f = nullptr) {
        mother = m;
        father = f;
        if (m != nullptr) {
            m->kids.push_back(shared_from_this());   // OK
        }
        if (f != nullptr) {
            f->kids.push_back(shared_from_this());   // OK
        }
    }
    ...
};
```

You find the whole resulting program in *util/enableshared1.cpp*.

Note that you can't call `shared_from_this()` inside the constructor (well, you can, but the
result is a runtime error):

```
class Person : public std::enable_shared_from_this<Person> {
  public:
    ...
    Person (const string& n,
            shared_ptr<Person> m = nullptr,
            shared_ptr<Person> f = nullptr)
     : name(n), mother(m), father(f) {
        if (m != nullptr) {
            m->kids.push_back(shared_from_this());   // ERROR
        }
        if (f != nullptr) {
            f->kids.push_back(shared_from_this());   // ERROR
        }
    }
    ...
};
```

The problem is that `shared_ptr` stores itself in a private member of Person's base class,
`enable_shared_from_this<>`, *at the end* of the construction of the Person.

So, there is absolutely no way to create cyclic references of shared pointers during the construction of the object that initializes the shared pointer. You have to do it in two steps — one way or the
other.

5.2.4   Shared and Weak Pointers in Detail

Let's summarize and present the whole interface that shared and weak pointers provide.

Class `shared_ptr` in Detail

As introduced in Section 5.2.1, page 76, class `shared_ptr` provides the concept of a smart pointer
with shared ownership semantics. Whenever the last owner of a shared pointer gets destroyed, the
associated object gets deleted (or the associated resources are cleaned up).

Class `shared_ptr<>` is templatized for the type of the object the initial pointer refers to:

```
namespace std {
    template <typename T>
    class shared_ptr
    {
      public:
        typedef T element_type;
        ...
    };
}
```

The element type might be `void`, which means that the shared pointer shares ownership of an object
with an unspecified type, like `void*` does.

An *empty* `shared_ptr` does not share ownership of an object, so `use_count()` yields 0. Note,
however, that due to one special constructor, the shared pointer still might refer to an object.

Tables 5.3 and 5.4 list all operations provided for shared pointers.

Whenever ownership is transferred to a shared pointer that already owned another object, the
deleter for the previously owned object gets called if that shared pointer was the last owner. The same
applies if a shared pointer gets a new value either by assigning a new value or by calling `reset()`:
If the shared pointer previously owned an object and was the last owner, the corresponding deleter
(or `delete`) gets called for the object. Note again that the passed deleter shall not throw.

The shared pointers might use different object types, provided that there is an implicit pointer
conversion. For this reason, constructors, assignment operators, and `reset()` are member templates,
whereas comparison operators are templatized for different types.

All comparison operators compare the raw pointers the shared pointers internally use (i.e., they
call the same operator for the values returned by `get()`). They all have overloads for `nullptr` as
argument. Thus, you can check whether there is a valid pointer or even whether the raw pointer is
less than or greater than `nullptr`.

The constructor taking a `weak_ptr` argument throws `bad_weak_ptr` (see Section 5.2.2, page 89)
if the weak pointer is empty (`expired()` yields `true`).

Operation	Effect
`shared_ptr<T> ` *sp*	Default constructor; creates an empty shared pointer, using the default deleter (calling `delete`)
`shared_ptr<T> ` *sp(ptr)*	Creates a shared pointer owning **ptr*, using the default deleter (calling `delete`)
`shared_ptr<T> ` *sp(ptr,del)*	Creates a shared pointer owning **ptr*, using *del* as deleter
`shared_ptr<T> ` *sp(ptr,del,ac)*	Creates a shared pointer owning **ptr*, using *del* as deleter and *ac* as allocator
`shared_ptr<T> ` *sp(*`nullptr`*)*	Creates an empty shared pointer, using the default deleter (calling `delete`)
`shared_ptr<T> ` *sp(*`nullptr`*,del)*	Creates an empty shared pointer, using *del* as deleter
`shared_ptr<T> ` *sp(*`nullptr`, *del,ac)*	Creates an empty shared pointer, using *del* as deleter and *ac* as allocator
`shared_ptr<T> ` *sp(sp2)*	Creates a shared pointer sharing ownership with *sp2*
`shared_ptr<T> ` *sp(*`move`*(sp2))*	Creates a shared pointer owning the pointer previously owned by *sp2* (*sp2* is empty afterward)
`shared_ptr<T> ` *sp(sp2,ptr)*	Alias constructor; creates a shared pointer sharing ownership of *sp2* but referring to **ptr*
`shared_ptr<T> ` *sp(wp)*	Creates a shared pointer out of a weak pointer *wp*
`shared_ptr<T> ` *sp(*`move`*(up))*	Creates a shared pointer out of a `unique_ptr` *up*
`shared_ptr<T> ` *sp(*`move`*(ap))*	Creates a shared pointer out of an `auto_ptr` *ap*
sp.`~shared_ptr()`	Destructor; calls the deleter if *sp* owns an object
sp `=` *sp2*	Assignment (*sp* shares ownership with *sp2* afterward, giving up ownership of the object previously owned)
sp `= move(`*sp2*`)`	Move assignment (*sp2* transfers ownership to *sp*)
sp `= move(`*up*`)`	Assigns `unique_ptr` *up* (*up* transfers ownership to *sp*)
sp `= move(`*ap*`)`	Assigns `auto_ptr` *ap* (*ap* transfers ownership to *sp*)
sp1.`swap(`*sp2*`)`	Swaps pointers and deleters of *sp1* and *sp2*
`swap(`*sp1,sp2*`)`	Swaps pointers and deleters of *sp1* and *sp2*
sp.`reset()`	Gives up ownership and reinitializes the shared pointer as being empty
sp.`reset(`*ptr*`)`	Gives up ownership and reinitializes the shared pointer owning **ptr*, using the default deleter (calling `delete`)
sp.`reset(`*ptr,del*`)`	Gives up ownership and reinitializes the shared pointer owning **ptr*, using *del* as deleter
sp.`reset(`*ptr,del,ac*`)`	Gives up ownership and reinitializes the shared pointer owning **ptr*, using *del* as deleter and *ac* as allocator
`make_shared(`...`)`	Creates a shared pointer for a new object initialized by the passed arguments
`allocate_shared(`*ac*,...`)`	Creates a shared pointer for a new object initialized by the passed arguments, using allocator *ac*

Table 5.3. Operations of `shared_ptrs`, *Part 1*

Operation	Effect
sp.get()	Returns the stored pointer (usually the address of the owned object or nullptr if none)
*sp	Returns the owned object (undefined behavior if none)
sp->...	Provides member access for the owned object (undefined behavior if none)
sp.use_count()	Returns the number of shared owners (including *sp*) or 0 if the shared pointer is empty
sp.unique()	Returns whether *sp* is the only owner (equivalent to *sp*.use_count()==1 but might be faster)
if (*sp*)	Operator bool(); yields whether sp is empty
sp1 == *sp2*	Calls == for the stored pointers (nullptr is possible)
sp1 != *sp2*	Calls != for the stored pointers (nullptr is possible)
sp1 < *sp2*	Calls < for the stored pointers (nullptr is possible)
sp1 <= *sp2*	Calls <= for the stored pointers (nullptr is possible)
sp1 > *sp2*	Calls > for the stored pointers (nullptr is possible)
sp1 >= *sp2*	Calls >= for the stored pointers (nullptr is possible)
static_pointer_cast(*sp*)	static_cast<> semantic for *sp*
dynamic_pointer_cast(*sp*)	dynamic_cast<> semantic for *sp*
const_pointer_cast(*sp*)	const_cast<> semantic for *sp*
get_deleter(*sp*)	Returns the address of the deleter, if any, or nullptr otherwise
strm << *sp*	Calls the output operator for its raw pointer (is equal to *strm*<<*sp*.get())
sp.owner_before(*sp2*)	Provides a strict weak ordering with another shared pointer
sp.owner_before(*wp*)	Provides a strict weak ordering with a weak pointer

Table 5.4. Operations of shared_ptrs, *Part 2*

get_deleter() yields a pointer to the function defined as a deleter, if any, or nullptr otherwise. The pointer is valid as long as a shared pointer owns that deleter. To get the deleter, however, you have to pass its type as a template argument. For example:

```
auto del = [] (int* p) {
                delete p;
            };
std::shared_ptr<int>  p(new int, del);
decltype(del)* pd = std::get_deleter<decltype(del)>(p);
```

Note that shared pointers do not provide a release() operation to give up ownership and return the control of an object back to the caller. The reason is that other shared pointers might still own the object.

More Sophisticated `shared_ptr` Operations

A few operations are provided that might not be obvious. Most of them were motivated and introduced with [*N2351:SharedPtr*].

The constructor taking another shared pointer and an additional raw pointer is the so-called *aliasing constructor*, which allows you to capture the fact that one object owns another. For example:

```
struct X
{
    int a;
};
shared_ptr<X> px(new X);
shared_ptr<int> pi(px, &px->a);
```

The object of type X "owns" its member a, so to create a shared pointer to a, you need to keep the surrounding object alive by attaching to its reference count by means of the aliasing constructor. Other, more complex, examples exist, such as referring to a container element or to a shared library symbol.[10]

Note that, as a consequence, the programmer has to ensure that the lifetimes of both objects match. Otherwise, dangling pointers or resource leaks might occur. For example:

```
shared_ptr<X> sp1(new X);
shared_ptr<X> sp2(sp1,new X);    // ERROR: delete for this X will never be called

sp1.reset();                     // deletes first X; makes sp1 empty
shared_ptr<X> sp3(sp1,new X);    // use_count()==0, but get()!=nullptr
```

Both `make_shared()` and `allocate_shared()` are provided to optimize the creation of a shared object and its associated control block (for example, maintaining the use count). Note that

```
shared_ptr<X>(new X(...))
```

performs two allocations: one for X and one for the control block used, for example, by the shared pointer to manage its use count. Using

```
make_shared<X>(...)
```

instead is considerably faster, performing only one allocation, and safer because a situation where the allocation of X succeeds but the allocation of the control block fails cannot occur. `allocate_shared()` allows passing your own allocator as first argument here.

The cast operators allow casting a pointer to a different type. The semantic is the same as the corresponding operators, and the result is another shared pointer of a different type. Note that using the ordinary cast operators is not possible, because it results in undefined behavior:

```
shared_ptr<void> sp(new int);    // shared pointer holds a void* internally
...
shared_ptr<int>(static_cast<int*>(sp.get()))    // ERROR: undefined behavior
static_pointer_cast<int*>(sp)                    // OK
```

---

[10] Thanks to Peter Dimov for pointing this out.

Class `weak_ptr` in Detail

As introduced in Section 5.2.2, page 84, class `weak_ptr` is a helper of class `shared_ptr` to share an object without owing it. Its `use_count()` returns the number of `shared_ptr` owners of an object, for which the `weak_ptr`s sharing the object do not count. Also, a `weak_ptr` can be empty, which is the case if it is not initialized by a `shared_ptr` or if the last owner of the corresponding object was deleted. Class `weak_ptr<>` is also templatized for the type of the object the initial pointer refers to:

```
namespace std {
    template <typename T>
    class weak_ptr
    {
      public:
        typedef T element_type;
        ...
    };
}
```

Table 5.5 lists all operations provided for weak pointers.

The default constructor creates an empty weak pointer, which means that `expired()` yields `true`. Because `lock()` yields a shared pointer, the use count of the object increments for the lifetime of the shared pointer. This is the only way to deal with the object a weak pointer shares.

Thread-Safe Shared Pointer Interface

In general, shared pointers are not thread safe. Thus, to avoid undefined behavior due to data races (see Section 18.4.1, page 982), you have to use techniques, such as mutexes or locks, when shared pointers refer to the same object in multiple threads. However, reading the use count while another thread modifies it does not introduce a data race, although the value might not be up-to-date. In fact, one thread might check a use count while another thread might manipulate it. See Chapter 18 for details.

Corresponding to the atomic C-style interface for ordinary pointers (see Section 18.7.3, page 1019), overloaded versions for shared pointers are provided, which allow dealing with shared pointers concurrently. Note that concurrent access to the *pointers*, not to the values they refer to, is meant.

For example:[11]

```
std::shared_ptr<X> global;   // initially nullptr

void foo()
{
    std::shared_ptr<X> local{new X};
    ...
    std::atomic_store(&global,local);
}
```

---

[11] Thanks to Anthony Williams for providing this example.

Operation	Effect
`weak_ptr<T> wp`	Default constructor; creates an empty weak pointer
`weak_ptr<T> wp(sp)`	Creates a weak pointer sharing ownership of the pointer owned by *sp*
`weak_ptr<T> wp(wp2)`	Creates a weak pointer sharing ownership of the pointer owned by *wp2*
`wp.~weak_ptr()`	Destructor; destroys the weak pointer but has no effect on the object owned
`wp = wp2`	Assignment (*wp* shares ownership of *wp2* afterward, giving up ownership of the object previously owned)
`wp = sp`	Assigns shared pointer *sp* (*wp* shares ownership of *sp* afterward, giving up ownership of the object previously owned)
`wp.swap(wp2)`	Swaps the pointers of *wp* and *wp2*
`swap(wp1,wp2)`	Swaps the pointers of *wp1* and *wp2*
`wp.reset()`	Gives up ownership of owned object, if any, and reinitializes as empty weak pointer
`wp.use_count()`	Returns the number of shared owners (`shared_ptrs` owning the object) or 0 if the weak pointer is empty
`wp.expired()`	Returns whether *wp* is empty (equivalent to `wp.use_count()==0` but might be faster)
`wp.lock()`	Returns a shared pointer sharing ownership of the pointer owned by the weak pointer (or an empty shared pointer if none)
`wp.owner_before(wp2)`	Provides a strict weak ordering with another weak pointer
`wp.owner_before(sp)`	Provides a strict weak ordering with a shared pointer

Table 5.5. Operations of `weak_ptrs`

Table 5.6 lists the high-level interface. A corresponding low-level interface (see Section 18.7.4, page 1019) is also provided.

Operation	Effect
`atomic_is_lock_free(&sp)`	Returns `true` if the atomic interface to *sp* is lock free
`atomic_load(&sp)`	Returns *sp*
`atomic_store(&sp,sp2)`	Assigns *sp2* to *sp*
`atomic_exchange(&sp,sp2)`	Exchange values of *sp* and *sp2*

Table 5.6. High-Level Atomic Operations of `shared_ptr`

5.2.5 Class `unique_ptr`

The `unique_ptr` type, provided by the C++ standard library since C++11, is a kind of a smart pointer that helps to avoid resource leaks when exceptions are thrown. In general, this smart pointer implements the concept of *exclusive ownership*, which means that it ensures that an object and its associated resources are "owned" only by one pointer at a time. When this owner gets destroyed or becomes empty or starts to own another object, the object previously owned also gets destroyed, and any associated resources are released.

Class `unique_ptr` succeeds class `auto_ptr`, which was originally introduced with C++98 but is deprecated now (see Section 5.2.7, page 113). Class `unique_ptr` provides a simple and clearer interface, making it less error prone than `auto_pointers` have been.

Purpose of Class `unique_ptr`

Functions often operate in the following way:[12]

1. Acquire some resources.
2. Perform some operations.
3. Free the acquired resources.

If bound to local objects, the resources acquired on entry get freed automatically on function exit because the destructors of those local objects are called. But if resources are acquired explicitly and are not bound to any object, they must be freed explicitly. Resources are typically managed explicitly when pointers are used.

A typical example of using pointers in this way is the use of `new` and `delete` to create and destroy an object:

```
void f()
{
    ClassA* ptr = new ClassA;     // create an object explicitly
    ...                           // perform some operations
    delete ptr;                   // clean up (destroy the object explicitly)
}
```

This function is a source of trouble. One obvious problem is that the deletion of the object might be forgotten, especially if you have `return` statements inside the function. There also is a less obvious danger that an exception might occur. Such an exception would exit the function immediately, without calling the `delete` statement at the end of the function. The result would be a memory leak or, more generally, a resource leak.

---

[12] This motivation, originally written for class `auto_ptr`, is adapted, with permission, from Scott Meyers' book *More Effective C++*. The general technique was originally presented by Bjarne Stroustrup as the "resource allocation is initialization" idiom in his books *The C++ Programming Language, 2nd edition* and *The Design and Evolution of C++*.

Avoiding such a resource leak usually requires that a function catch all exceptions. For example:

```
void f()
{
    ClassA* ptr = new ClassA;      // create an object explicitly

    try {
        ...                         // perform some operations
    }
    catch (...) {                   // for any exception
        delete ptr;                 // - clean up
        throw;                      // - rethrow the exception
    }

    delete ptr;                     // clean up on normal end
}
```

To handle the deletion of this object properly in the event of an exception, the code gets more complicated and redundant. If a second object is handled in this way, or if more than one `catch` clause is used, the problem gets worse. This is bad programming style and should be avoided because it is complex and error prone.

A smart pointer can help here. The smart pointer can free the data to which it points whenever the pointer itself gets destroyed. Furthermore, because it is a local variable, the pointer gets destroyed automatically when the function is exited, regardless of whether the exit is normal or is due to an exception. The class `unique_ptr` was designed to be such a smart pointer.

A `unique_ptr` is a pointer that serves as a unique *owner* of the object to which it refers. As a result, an object gets destroyed automatically when its `unique_ptr` gets destroyed. A requirement of a `unique_ptr` is that its object have only one owner.

Here is the previous example rewritten to use a `unique_ptr`:

```
// header file for unique_ptr
#include <memory>

void f()
{
    // create and initialize an unique_ptr
    std::unique<ClassA> ptr(new ClassA);

    ...                                         // perform some operations
}
```

That's all. The `delete` statement and the `catch` clause are no longer necessary.

Using a `unique_ptr`

A `unique_ptr` has much the same interface as an ordinary pointer; that is, operator `*` dereferences the object to which it points, whereas operator `->` provides access to a member if the object is a class or a structure:

```
// create and initialize (pointer to) string:
std::unique_ptr<std::string> up(new std::string("nico"));
```

```
(*up)[0] = 'N';                    // replace first character
up->append("lai");                 // append some characters
std::cout << *up << std::endl;  // print whole string
```

However, no pointer arithmetic, such as `++`, is defined (this counts as an advantage because pointer arithmetic is a source of trouble).

Note that class `unique_ptr<>` does not allow you to initialize an object with an ordinary pointer by using the assignment syntax. Thus, you must initialize the `unique_ptr` directly, by using its value:

```
std::unique_ptr<int> up = new int;     // ERROR
std::unique_ptr<int> up(new int);      // OK
```

A `unique_ptr` does not have to own an object, so it can be *empty*.[13] This is, for example, the case when it is initialized with the default constructor:

```
std::unique_ptr<std::string> up;
```

You can also assign the `nullptr` or call `reset()` :

```
up = nullptr;
up.reset();
```

In addition, you can call `release()`, which yields the object a `unique_ptr` owned, and gives up ownership so that the caller is responsible for its object now:

```
std::unique_ptr<std::string> up(new std::string("nico"));
...
std::string* sp = up.release();   // up loses ownership
```

You can check whether a unique pointer owns an object by calling operator `bool()`:

```
if (up) {       // if up is not empty
    std::cout << *up << std::endl;
}
```

Instead, you can also compare the unique pointer with `nullptr` or query the raw pointer inside the `unique_ptr`, which yields `nullptr` if the `unique_ptr` doesn't own any object:

```
if (up != nullptr)              // if up is not empty

if (up.get() != nullptr)        // if up is not empty
```

---

[13] Although the C++ standard library does define the term *empty* only for shared pointers, I don't see any reason not to do that in general.

Transfer of Ownership by `unique_ptr`

A `unique_ptr` provides the semantics of exclusive ownership. However, it's up to the programmer to ensure that no two unique pointers are initialized by the same pointer:

```
std::string* sp = new std::string("hello");
std::unique_ptr<std::string> up1(sp);
std::unique_ptr<std::string> up2(sp);    // ERROR: up1 and up2 own same data
```

Unfortunately, this is a runtime error, so the programmer has to avoid such a mistake.

This leads to the question of how the copy constructor and the assignment operator of `unique_ptrs` operate. The answer is simple: You can't copy or assign a unique pointer if you use the ordinary copy semantics. However, you can use the move semantics provided since C++11 (see Section 3.1.5, page 19). In that case, the constructor or assignment operator *transfers* the ownership to another unique pointer.[14]

Consider, for example, the following use of the copy constructor:

```
// initialize a unique_ptr with a new object
std::unique_ptr<ClassA> up1(new ClassA);

// copy the unique_ptr
std::unique_ptr<ClassA> up2(up1);    // ERROR: not possible

// transfer ownership of the unique_ptr
std::unique_ptr<ClassA> up3(std::move(up1));    // OK
```

After the first statement, up1 owns the object that was created with the `new` operator. The second, which tries to call the copy constructor, is a compile-time error because up2 can't become another owner of that object. Only one owner at a time is allowed. However, with the third statement, we transfer ownership from up1 to up3. So afterward, up3 owns the object created with `new`, and up1 no longer owns the object. The object created by `new ClassA` gets deleted exactly once: when up3 gets destroyed.

The assignment operator behaves similarly:

```
// initialize a unique_ptr with a new object
std::unique_ptr<ClassA> up1(new ClassA);
std::unique_ptr<ClassA> up2;    // create another unique_ptr

up2 = up1;                      // ERROR: not possible

up2 = std::move(up1);           // assign the unique_ptr
                                // - transfers ownership from up1 to up2
```

Here, the move assignment transfers ownership from up1 to up2. As a result, up2 owns the object previously owned by up1.

---

[14] Here is the major difference with `auto_ptr`, which did transfer the ownership with the ordinary copy semantics, resulting in a source of trouble and confusion.

If up2 owned an object before an assignment, `delete` is called for that object:

```
// initialize a unique_ptr with a new object
std::unique_ptr<ClassA> up1(new ClassA);
// initialize another unique_ptr with a new object
std::unique_ptr<ClassA> up2(new ClassA);

up2 = std::move(up1);        // move assign the unique_ptr
                             // - delete object owned by up2
                             // - transfer ownership from up1 to up2
```

A `unique_ptr` that loses the ownership of an object without getting a new ownership refers to no object.

To assign a new value to a `unique_ptr`, this new value must also be a `unique_ptr`. You can't assign an ordinary pointer:

```
std::unique_ptr<ClassA> ptr;               // create a unique_ptr

ptr = new ClassA;                          // ERROR
ptr = std::unique_ptr<ClassA>(new ClassA); // OK, delete old object
                                           //     and own new
```

Assigning `nullptr` is also possible, which has the same effect as calling `reset()`:

```
up = nullptr;   // deletes the associated object, if any
```

Source and Sink

The transfer of ownership implies a special use for `unique_ptrs`; that is, functions can use them to transfer ownership to other functions. This can occur in two ways:

1. A function can behave as a *sink* of data. This happens if a `unique_ptr` is passed as an argument to the function by rvalue reference created with `std::move()`. In this case, the parameter of the called function gets ownership of the `unique_ptr`. Thus, if the function does not transfer it again, the object gets deleted on function exit:

   ```
   void sink(std::unique_ptr<ClassA> up)      // sink() gets ownership
   {
       ...
   }

   std::unique_ptr<ClassA> up(new ClassA);
   ...
   sink(std::move(up));       // up loses ownership
   ...
   ```

2. A function can behave as a *source* of data. When a `unique_ptr` is returned, ownership of
    the returned value gets transferred to the calling context. The following example shows this
    technique:[15]

    ```cpp
    std::unique_ptr<ClassA> source()
    {
        std::unique_ptr<ClassA> ptr(new ClassA);  // ptr owns the new object
        ...
        return ptr;                 // transfer ownership to calling function
    }

    void g()
    {
        std::unique_ptr<ClassA> p;

        for (int i=0; i<10; ++i) {
            p = source();      // p gets ownership of the returned object
                               // (previously returned object of f() gets deleted)
            ...
        }
    }  // last-owned object of p gets deleted
    ```

Each time `source()` is called, it creates an object with `new` and returns the object, along with
its ownership, to the caller. The assignment of the return value to p transfers ownership to p.
In the second and additional passes through the loop, the assignment to p deletes the object that
p owned previously. Leaving `g()`, and thus destroying p, results in the destruction of the last
object owned by p. In any case, no resource leak is possible. Even if an exception is thrown, any
`unique_ptr` that owns data ensures that this data is deleted.

The reason that no `std::move()` is necessary in the return statement of `source()` is that
according to the language rules of C++11, the compiler will try a move automatically (see Section 3.1.5, page 22).

`unique_ptr`s as Members

By using `unique_ptr`s within a class, you can also avoid resource leaks. If you use a `unique_ptr`
instead of an ordinary pointer, you no longer need a destructor because the object gets deleted with
the deletion of the member. In addition, a `unique_ptr` helps to avoid resource leaks caused by
exceptions thrown during the initialization of an object. Note that destructors are called only if any
construction is completed. So, if an exception occurs inside a constructor, destructors are called
only for objects that have been fully constructed. This can result in resource leaks for classes with
multiple raw pointers if during the construction the first `new` was successful but the second was not.
For example:

---

[15] If you assume to declare the return type as rvalue reference, don't do that; doing so would return a dangling
pointer (see Section 3.1.5, page 22).

```
class ClassB {
  private:
    ClassA* ptr1;          // pointer members
    ClassA* ptr2;
  public:
    // constructor that initializes the pointers
    // - will cause resource leak if second new throws
    ClassB (int val1, int val2)
      : ptr1(new ClassA(val1)), ptr2(new ClassA(val2)) {
    }

    // copy constructor
    // - might cause resource leak if second new throws
    ClassB (const ClassB& x)
      : ptr1(new ClassA(*x.ptr1)), ptr2(new ClassA(*x.ptr2)) {
    }

    // assignment operator
    const ClassB& operator= (const ClassB& x) {
      *ptr1 = *x.ptr1;
      *ptr2 = *x.ptr2;
      return *this;
    }

    ~ClassB () {
      delete ptr1;
      delete ptr2;
    }
    ...
};
```

To avoid such a possible resource leak, you can simply use unique_ptrs:

```
class ClassB {
  private:
    std::unique_ptr<ClassA> ptr1;          // unique_ptr members
    std::unique_ptr<ClassA> ptr2;
  public:
    // constructor that initializes the unique_ptrs
    // - no resource leak possible
    ClassB (int val1, int val2)
      : ptr1(new ClassA(val1)), ptr2(new ClassA(val2)) {
    }
```

```
// copy constructor
// - no resource leak possible
ClassB (const ClassB& x)
 : ptr1(new ClassA(*x.ptr1)), ptr2(new ClassA(*x.ptr2)) {
}

// assignment operator
const ClassB& operator= (const ClassB& x) {
    *ptr1 = *x.ptr1;
    *ptr2 = *x.ptr2;
    return *this;
}

// no destructor necessary
// (default destructor lets ptr1 and ptr2 delete their objects)
    ...
};
```

Note, first, that you can skip the destructor now because `unique_ptr` does the job for you. You also have to implement the copy constructor and assignment operator. By default, both would try to copy or assign the members, which isn't possible. If you don't provide them, `ClassB` also would provide only move semantics.

Dealing with Arrays

By default, `unique_ptrs` call `delete` for an object they own if they lose ownership (because they are destroyed, get a new object assigned, or become empty). Unfortunately, due to the language rules derived from C, C++ can't differentiate between the type of a pointer to one object and an array of objects. However, according to language rules for arrays, operator `delete[]` rather than `delete` has to get called. So, the following is possible but wrong:

```
std::unique_ptr<std::string> up(new std::string[10]);   // runtime ERROR
```

Now, you might assume that as for class `shared_ptr` (see Section 5.2.1, page 80), you have to define your own deleter to deal with arrays. But this is not necessary.

Fortunately, the C++ standard library provides a partial specialization of class `unique_ptr` for arrays, which calls `delete[]` for the referenced object when the pointer loses the ownership to it. So, you simply have to declare:

```
std::unique_ptr<std::string[]> up(new std::string[10]);   // OK
```

Note, however, that this partial specialization offers a slightly different interface. Instead of operators `*` and `->`, operator `[]` is provided to access one of the objects inside the referenced array:

```
std::unique_ptr<std::string[]> up(new std::string[10]);   // OK
    ...
std::cout << *up << std::endl;     // ERROR: * not defined for arrays
std::cout << up[0] << std::endl;   // OK
```

As usual, it's up to the programmer to ensure that the index is valid. Using an invalid index results in undefined behavior.

Note also that this class does not allow getting initialized by an array of a derived type. This reflects that fact that polymorphism does not work for plain arrays.

Class `default_delete<>`

Let's look a bit into the declaration of class `unique_ptr`. Conceptionally, this class is declared as follows:[16]

```
namespace std {
    // primary template:
    template <typename T, typename D = default_delete<T>>
    class unique_ptr
    {
      public:
        ...
        T& operator*() const;
        T* operator->() const noexcept;
        ...
    };

    // partial specialization for arrays:
    template<typename T, typename D>
    class unique_ptr<T[], D>
    {
      public:
        ...
        T& operator[](size_t i) const;
        ...
    }
}
```

Here, we can see that there is a special version of `unique_ptr` to deal with arrays. That version provides operator `[]` instead of operators `*` and `->` to deal with arrays rather than single objects. But both use class `std::default_delete<>` as deleter, which itself is specialized to call `delete[]` instead of `delete` for arrays:

```
namespace std {
    // primary template:
    template <typename T> class default_delete {
      public:
        void operator()(T* p) const;  // calls delete p
```

---

[16] In the C++ standard library, class `unique_ptr` is actually more complicated because some template magic is used to specify the exact return type for operators `*` and `->`.

```
            ...
        };

        // partial specialization for arrays:
        template <typename T> class default_delete<T[]> {
          public:
            void operator()(T* p) const;   // calls delete[] p
            ...
        };
    }
```

Note that default template arguments automatically also apply to partial specializations.

Deleters for Other Associated Resources

When the object you refer to requires something other than calling `delete` or `delete[]`, you have to specify your own deleter. Note, however, that the approach to defining a deleter differs slightly from that for `shared_ptrs`. You have to specify the type of the deleter as second template argument. That type can be a reference to a function, function pointer, or function object (see Section 6.10, page 233). If a function object is used, its "function call operator" () should be declared to take a pointer to the object.

For example, the following code prints an additional message before deleting an object with `delete`:

```
class ClassADeleter
{
  public:
    void operator () (ClassA* p) {
        std::cout << "call delete for ClassA object" << std::endl;
        delete p;
    }
};
...
```

```
std::unique_ptr<ClassA,ClassADeleter> up(new ClassA());
```

To specify a function or a lambda, you have to either declare the type of the deleter as `void(*)(T*)` or `std::function<void(T*)>` or use `decltype` (see Section 3.1.11, page 32). For example, to use your own deleter for an array of `int`s specified as a lambda, this looks as follows:

```
std::unique_ptr<int,void(*)(int*)> up(new int[10],
                                      [](int* p) {
                                          ...
                                          delete[] p;
                                      });
```

or

```
std::unique_ptr<int,std::function<void(int*)>> up(new int[10],
                                                  [](int* p) {
                                                      ...
                                                      delete[] p;
                                                  });
```

or

```
auto l = [](int* p) {
              ...
              delete[] p;
         };
std::unique_ptr<int,decltype(l)>> up(new int[10], l);
```

To avoid having to specify the *type* of the deleter when passing a function pointer or a lambda, you could also use an alias template, a language feature provided since C++11 (see Section 3.1.9, page 27):

```
template <typename T>
using uniquePtr = std::unique_ptr<T,void(*)(T*)>;    // alias template
...

uniquePtr<int> up(new int[10], [](int* p) {          // used here
                                   ...
                                   delete[] p;
                               });
```

This way, you would have more or less the same interface to specify deleters as for shared_ptrs.

Here is a complete example of using your own deleter:

```
// util/uniqueptr1.cpp

#include <iostream>
#include <string>
#include <memory>      // for unique_ptr
#include <dirent.h>    // for opendir(), ...
#include <cstring>     // for strerror()
#include <cerrno>      // for errno
using namespace std;

class DirCloser
{
  public:
    void operator () (DIR* dp) {
        if (closedir(dp) != 0) {
            std::cerr << "OOPS: closedir() failed" << std::endl;
        }
    }
};
```

```
int main()
{
    // open current directory:
    unique_ptr<DIR,DirCloser> pDir(opendir("."));

    // process each directory entry:
    struct dirent *dp;
    while ((dp = readdir(pDir.get())) != nullptr) {
        string filename(dp->d_name);
        cout << "process " << filename << endl;
        ...
    }
}
```

Here, inside main(), we deal with the entries of the current directory, using the standard POSIX interface of opendir(), readdir(), and closedir(). To ensure that in any case the directory opened is closed by closedir(), we define a unique_ptr, which causes the DirCloser to be called whenever the handle referring to the opened directory gets destroyed. As for shared pointers, deleters for unique pointers may not throw. For this reason, we print only an error message here.

Another advantage of using a unique_ptr is that no copies are possible. Note that readdir() is not stateless, so it's a good idea to ensure that while using a handle to deal with a directory, a copy of the handle can't modify its state.

If you don't want to process the return value of closedir(), you could also pass closedir() directly as a function pointer, specifying that the deleter is a function pointer. But beware: The often recommended declaration

```
unique_ptr<DIR,int(*)(DIR*)> pDir(opendir("."),
                                  closedir);  // might not work
```

is not guaranteed to be portable, because closedir has extern "C" linkage, so in C++ code, this is not guaranteed to be convertible into int(*)(DIR*). For portable code, you would need an intermediate type definition like this:[17]

```
extern "C" typedef int(*DIRDeleter)(DIR*);
unique_ptr<DIR, DIRDeleter> pDir(opendir("."),
                                 closedir);  // OK
```

Note that closedir() returns an int, so we have to specify int(*)(DIR*) as the type of the deleter. Note, however, that a call through a function pointer is an indirect call, which is harder to optimize away.

See Section 15.12.3, page 822, for another example of using your own unique_ptr deleter to restore a redirected output buffer.

---

[17] Thanks to Daniel Krügler for pointing this out.

5.2.6 Class `unique_ptr` in Detail

As introduced in Section 5.2.5, page 98, class `unique_ptr` provides the concept of a smart pointer with *exclusive ownership* semantics. Once a unique pointer has exclusive control, you cannot (accidentally) create a situation in which multiple pointers own the associated object. The major goal is to ensure that with the end of the pointer's lifetime, the associated object gets deleted (or its resource gets cleaned up). This especially helps to provide exception safety. In contrast to shared pointers, a minimum space and time overhead is the focus of this class.

Class `unique_ptr<>` is templatized for the type of the object the initial pointer refers to and its deleter:

```
namespace std {
    template <typename T, typename D = default_delete<T>>
    class unique_ptr
    {
      public:
        typedef ... pointer;   // may be D::pointer
        typedef T element_type;
        typedef D deleter_type;
        ...
    };
}
```

A partial specialization for arrays is provided (note that by language rules, it has the same default deleter, which is `default_delete<T[]>` then):

```
namespace std {
    template <typename T, typename D>
    class unique_ptr<T[], D>
    {
      public:
        typedef ... pointer;   // may be D::pointer
        typedef T element_type;
        typedef D deleter_type;
        ...
    };
}
```

The element type T might be `void` so that the unique pointer owns an object with an unspecified type, like `void*` does. Note also that a type `pointer` is defined, which is not necessarily defined as `T*`. If the deleter D has a `pointer` typedef, this type will be used instead. In such a case, the template parameter T has only the effect of a type tag, because there is no member as part of class `unique_ptr<>` that depends on T; everything depends on `pointer`. The advantage is that a `unique_ptr` can thus hold other smart pointers.

If a `unique_ptr` is *empty*, it does not own an object, so `get()` returns the `nullptr`.

Table 5.7 lists all operations provided for unique pointers.

Operation	Effect
`unique_ptr<...>` *up*	Default constructor; creates an empty unique pointer, using an instance of the default/passed deleter type as deleter
`unique_ptr<T>` *up*`(nullptr)`	Creates an empty unique pointer, using an instance of the default/passed deleter type as deleter
`unique_ptr<...>` *up*(*ptr*)	Creates a unique pointer owning *∗ptr*, using an instance of the default/passed deleter type as deleter
`unique_ptr<...>` *up*(*ptr*, *del*)	Creates a unique pointer owning *∗ptr*, using *del* as deleter
`unique_ptr<T>` *up*(move(*up2*))	Creates a unique pointer owning the pointer previously owned by *up2* (*up2* is empty afterward)
`unique_ptr<T>` *up*(move(*ap*))	Creates a unique pointer owning the pointer previously owned by the `auto_ptr` *ap* (*ap* is empty afterward)
up.~`unique_ptr()`	Destructor; calls the deleter for an owned object
up = move(*up2*)	Move assignment (*up2* transfers ownership to *up*)
up = `nullptr`	Calls the deleter for an owned object and makes *up* empty (equivalent to *up*.`reset()`)
up1.`swap`(*up2*)	Swaps pointers and deleters of *up1* and *up2*
`swap`(*up1*, *up2*)	Swaps pointers and deleters of *up1* and *up2*
up.`reset()`	Calls the deleter for an owned object and makes *up* empty (equivalent to *up*=`nullptr`)
up.`reset`(*ptr*)	Calls the deleter for an owned object and reinitializes the shared pointer to own *∗ptr*
up.`release()`	Gives up ownership back to the caller (returns owned object without calling the deleter)
up.`get()`	Returns the stored pointer (the address of the object owned or `nullptr` if none)
∗up	Single objects only; returns the owned object (undefined behavior if none)
up->...	Single objects only; provides member access for the owned object (undefined behavior if none)
up[*idx*]	Array objects only; returns the element with index *idx* of the stored array (undefined behavior if none)
`if (`*up*`)`	Operator `bool()`; yields whether *up* is empty
up1 == *up2*	Calls == for the stored pointers (`nullptr` is possible)
up1 != *up2*	Calls != for the stored pointers (`nullptr` is possible)
up1 < *up2*	Calls < for the stored pointers (`nullptr` is possible)
up1 <= *up2*	Calls <= for the stored pointers (`nullptr` is possible)
up1 > *up2*	Calls > for the stored pointers (`nullptr` is possible)
up1 >= *up2*	Calls >= for the stored pointers (`nullptr` is possible)
up.`get_deleter()`	Returns a reference of the deleter

Table 5.7. Operations of `unique_ptrs`

The constructor taking a pointer and a deleter as arguments is overloaded for different types, so
the following behavior is specified:

```
D d;                                        // instance of the deleter type
unique_ptr<int, D> p1(new int, D());    // D must be MoveConstructible
unique_ptr<int, D> p2(new int, d);      // D must be CopyConstructible
unique_ptr<int, D&> p3(new int, d);     // p3 holds a reference to d
unique_ptr<int, const D&> p4(new int, D()); // Error: rvalue deleter object
                                            // can't have reference deleter type
```

For single objects, the move constructor and the assignment operator are member templates, so a
type conversion is possible. All comparison operators are templatized for different element and
deleter types.

All comparison operators compare the raw pointers the shared pointers internally use (call the
same operator for the values returned by `get()`). They all have overloads for `nullptr` as argument.
Thus, you can check whether there is a valid pointer or even if the raw pointer is less than or greater
than `nullptr`.

The specialization for array types has the following differences compared to the single-object
interface:

- Instead of operators `*` and `->`, operator `[]` is provided.
- The default deleter calls `delete[]` rather than just `delete`.
- Conversions between different types are not supported. Pointers to derived element types are
  especially not possible.

Note that the deleter interface differs from class `shared_ptr` (see Section 5.2.1, page 80, for details).
However, as for shared pointers, deleters shall not throw.

5.2.7 Class `auto_ptr`

Unlike C++11, the C++98 standard library provided only one smart pointer class, `auto_ptr`, which is deprecated since C++11. Its goal was to provide the semantics that `unique_ptr` now does. However, class `auto_ptr` introduced a few problems:

- At the time of its design, the language had no move semantics for constructors and assignment operators. However, the goal was still to provide the semantics of ownership transfer. As a result, copy and assignment operators got a move semantic, which could cause serious trouble, especially when passing an `auto_ptr` as argument.

- There was no semantic of a *deleter*, so you could use it only to deal with single objects allocated with `new`.

- Because this was initially the only smart pointer provided by the C++ standard library, it was often misused, especially assuming that it provided the semantics of *shared ownership* as class `shared_ptr` does now.

Regarding the danger of unintended loss of ownership, consider the following example, consisting of a naive implementation of a function that prints the object to which an `auto_ptr` refers:

```
// this is a bad example
template <typename T>
void bad_print(std::auto_ptr<T> p)     // p gets ownership of passed argument
{
    // does p own an object ?
    if (p.get() == NULL) {
        std::cout << "NULL";
    }
    else {
        std::cout << *p;
    }
}                      // Oops, exiting deletes the object to which p refers
```

Whenever an `auto_ptr` is passed to this implementation of `bad_print()`, the objects it owns, if any, are deleted. The reason is that the ownership of the `auto_ptr` that is passed as an argument is passed to the parameter p, and p deletes the object it owns on function exit. This is probably not the programmer's intention and would result in fatal runtime errors:

```
std::auto_ptr<int> p(new int);
*p = 42;           // change value to which p refers
bad_print(p);      // Oops, deletes the memory to which p refers
*p = 18;           // RUNTIME ERROR
```

That behavior especially applies when passing an `auto_ptr` to a container. With `unique_ptr`, such a mistake is no longer possible, because you explicitly would have to pass the argument with `std::move()`.

5.2.8   Final Words on Smart Pointers

As we have seen, C++11 provides two concepts of a smart pointer:

1. `shared_ptr` for shared ownership
2. `unique_ptr` for exclusive ownership

The latter replaces the old `auto_ptr` of C++98, which is deprecated now.

Performance Issues

You might wonder why the C++ standard library not only provides one smart pointer class with shared ownership semantics because this also avoids resource leaks or transfers ownership. The answer has to do with the performance impact of shared pointers.

Class `shared_ptr` is implemented with a nonintrusive (noninvasive) approach, which means that objects managed by this class don't have to fulfill a specific requirement, such as a common base class. The big advantage is that this concept can be applied to any type, including fundamental data types. The price is that a `shared_ptr` object internally needs multiple members: an ordinary pointer to the referenced object and a reference counter shared by all shared pointers that refer to the same object. Because weak pointers might refer to a shared object, you even need another counter. (Even if no more shared pointer uses an object, you need the counter until all weak pointers end referring to it; otherwise, you can't guarantee that they return a `use_count()` of 0.)[18]

Thus, shared and weak pointers internally need additional helper objects, to which internal pointers refer, which means that a couple of specific optimizations are not possible (including empty base class optimizations, which would allow elimination of any memory overhead).

Unique pointers do not require any of this overhead. Their "smartness" is based on special constructors and special destructors and the elimination of copy semantics. With a stateless or empty deleter a unique pointer should consume the same amount of memory as a native pointer, and there should be no runtime overhead compared to using native pointers and doing the deletes manually. However, to avoid the introduction of unnecessary overhead, you should use function objects (including lambdas) for deleters to allow the best optimizations with, ideally, zero overhead.

Usage Issues

Smart pointers are not perfect, and you still have to know which problems they solve and which problems remain. For example, for any smart pointer class, you should never create multiple smart pointers out of the same ordinary pointer.

See Section 7.11, page 388, for an example of using shared pointers in multiple STL containers.

Classes `shared_ptr` and `unique_ptr` provide different approaches to deal with arrays and deleters. Class `unique_ptr` has a partial specialization for arrays, which provides a different interface. It is more flexible and provides less performance overhead but might require a bit more work to use it.

Finally, note that in general, smart pointers are not thread safe, although some guarantees apply. See Section 5.2.4, page 96, for details.

---

[18] Thanks to Howard Hinnant for pointing this out.

5.3   Numeric Limits

Numeric types in general have platform-dependent limits. The C++ standard library provides these limits in the template `numeric_limits`. These numeric limits replace and supplement the ordinary preprocessor C constants, which are still available for integer types in `<climits>` and `<limits.h>` and for floating-point types in `<cfloat>` and `<float.h>`. The new concept of numeric limits has two advantages: First, it offers more type safety. Second, it enables a programmer to write templates that evaluate these limits.

The numeric limits are discussed in the rest of this section. Note, however, that it is always better to write platform-independent code by using the minimum guaranteed precision of the types. These minimum values are provided in Table 5.8.[19]

Type	Minimum Size
`char`	1 byte (8 bits)
`short int`	2 bytes
`int`	2 bytes
`long int`	4 bytes
`long long int`	8 bytes
`float`	4 bytes
`double`	8 bytes
`long double`	8 bytes

Table 5.8. Minimum Size of Built-In Types

Class `numeric_limits<>`

You usually use templates to implement something once for any type. However, you can also use templates to provide a common interface that is implemented for each type, where it is useful. You can do this by providing specializations of a general template. A typical example of this technique is `numeric_limits`, which works as follows:

- A general template provides the default numeric values for any type:

```
namespace std {
    // general numeric limits as default for any type
    template <typename T>
    class numeric_limits {
      public:
        // by default no specialization for any type T exists
        static constexpr bool is_specialized = false;
```

---

[19] Note that "bytes" means an octet with 8 bits. Strictly speaking, it is possible that even a `long int` has one byte with at least 32 bits.

```
        ...    // other members are meaningless for the general template
    };
}
```

This general template of the numeric limits says that no numeric limits are available for type T. This is done by setting the member `is_specialized` to `false`.

- Specializations of the template define the numeric limits for each numeric type as follows:

```
namespace std {
    // numeric limits for int
    // - implementation defined
    template<> class numeric_limits<int> {
      public:
        // yes, a specialization for numeric limits of int does exist
        static constexpr bool is_specialized = true;

        static constexpr int min() noexcept {
            return -2147483648;
        }
        static constexpr int max() noexcept {
            return 2147483647;
        }
        static constexpr int digits = 31;
        ...
    };
}
```

Here, `is_specialized` is set to `true`, and all other members have the values of the numeric limits for the particular type.

The general `numeric_limits` template and its standard specializations are provided in the header file `<limits>`. The specializations are provided for any fundamental type that can represent numeric values: `bool`, `char`, `signed char`, `unsigned char`, `char16_t`, `char32_t`, `wchar_t`, `short`, `unsigned short`, `int`, `unsigned int`, `long`, `unsigned long`, `long long`, `unsigned long long`, `float`, `double`, and `long double`.[20] They can be supplemented easily for user-defined numeric types.

Tables 5.9 and 5.10 list all members of the class `numeric_limits<>` and their meanings. Applicable corresponding C constants for these members, defined in `<climits>`, `<limits.h>`, `<cfloat>`, and `<float.h>`, are also given.

---

[20] The specializations for `char16_t`, `char32_t`, `long long`, and `unsigned long long` are provided since C++11.

Member	Meaning	C Constants
is_specialized	Type has specialization for numeric limits	
is_signed	Type is signed	
is_integer	Type is integer	
is_exact	Calculations produce no rounding errors (true for all integer types)	
is_bounded	The set of values representable is finite (true for all built-in types)	
is_modulo	Adding two positive numbers may wrap to a lesser result	
is_iec559	Conforms to standards IEC 559 and IEEE 754	
min()	Minimum finite value (minimum positive normalized value for floating-point types with denormalization; meaningful if is_bounded||!is_signed)	INT_MIN,FLT_MIN, CHAR_MIN,...
max()	Maximum finite value (meaningful if is_bounded)	INT_MAX,FLT_MAX,...
lowest()	Maximum negative finite value (meaningful if is_bounded; since C++11)	
digits	Character/integer: number of bits, excluding sign (binary digits)	CHAR_BIT
	Floating point: number of radix digits in the mantissa	FLT_MANT_DIG,...
digits10	Number of decimal digits (meaningful if is_bounded)	FLT_DIG,...
max_digits10	Number of required decimal digits to ensure that values that differ are always differentiated (meaningful for all floating-point types; since C++11)	
radix	Integer: base of the representation (almost always 2)	
	Floating point: base of the exponent representation	FLT_RADIX
min_exponent	Minimum negative integer exponent for base radix	FLT_MIN_EXP,...
max_exponent	Maximum positive integer exponent for base radix	FLT_MAX_EXP,...
min_exponent10	Minimum negative integer exponent for base 10	FLT_MIN_10_EXP,...
max_exponent10	Maximum positive integer exponent for base 10	FLT_MAX_10_EXP,...
epsilon()	Difference of 1 and least value greater than 1	FLT_EPSILON,...
round_style	Rounding style (see page 119)	
round_error()	Measure of the maximum rounding error (according to standard ISO/IEC 10967-1)	
has_infinity	Type has representation for positive infinity	
infinity()	Representation of positive infinity, if available	
has_quiet_NaN	Type has representation for nonsignaling "Not a Number"	
quiet_NaN()	Representation of quiet "Not a Number," if available	

Table 5.9. Members of Class numeric_limits<>, *Part 1*

Member	Meaning	C Constants
has_signaling_NaN	Type has representation for signaling "Not a Number"	
signaling_NaN()	Representation of signaling "Not a Number," if available	
has_denorm	Whether type allows denormalized values (variable numbers of exponent bits; see page 119)	
has_denorm_loss	Loss of accuracy is detected as a denormalization loss rather than as an inexact result	
denorm_min()	Minimum positive denormalized value	
traps	Trapping is implemented	
tinyness_before	Tinyness is detected before rounding	

Table 5.10. Members of Class numeric_limits<>, *Part 2*

The following is a possible full specialization of the numeric limits for type float, which is platform dependent and shows the exact signatures of the members:

```
namespace std {
    template<> class numeric_limits<float> {
      public:
        // yes, a specialization for numeric limits of float does exist
        static constexpr bool is_specialized = true;

        inline constexpr float min() noexcept {
            return 1.17549435E-38F;
        }
        inline constexpr float max() noexcept {
            return 3.40282347E+38F;
        }
        inline constexpr float lowest() noexcept {
            return -3.40282347E+38F;
        }

        static constexpr int digits = 24;
        static constexpr int digits10 = 6;
        static constexpr int max_digits10 = 9;

        static constexpr bool is_signed = true;
        static constexpr bool is_integer = false;
        static constexpr bool is_exact = false;
        static constexpr bool is_bounded = true;
        static constexpr bool is_modulo = false;
        static constexpr bool is_iec559 = true;
```

```
        static constexpr int radix = 2;

        inline constexpr float epsilon() noexcept {
            return 1.19209290E-07F;
        }

        static constexpr float_round_style round_style
            = round_to_nearest;
        inline constexpr float round_error() noexcept {
            return 0.5F;
        }

        static constexpr int min_exponent = -125;
        static constexpr int max_exponent = +128;
        static constexpr int min_exponent10 = -37;
        static constexpr int max_exponent10 = +38;

        static constexpr bool has_infinity = true;
        inline constexpr float infinity() noexcept { return ...; }
        static constexpr bool has_quiet_NaN = true;
        inline constexpr float quiet_NaN() noexcept { return ...; }
        static constexpr bool has_signaling_NaN = true;
        inline constexpr float signaling_NaN() noexcept { return ...; }
        static constexpr float_denorm_style has_denorm = denorm_absent;
        static constexpr bool has_denorm_loss = false;
        inline constexpr float denorm_min() noexcept { return min(); }

        static constexpr bool traps = true;
        static constexpr bool tinyness_before = true;
    };
}
```

Note that since C++11, all members are declared as constexpr (see Section 3.1.8, page 26). For example, you can use max() at places where compile-time expressions are required:

```
    static const int ERROR_VALUE = std::numeric_limits<int>::max();
    float a[std::numeric_limits<short>::max()];
```

Before C++11, all nonfunction members were constant and static, so their values could be determined at compile time. However, function members were static only, so the preceding expressions were not possible. Also note that before C++11, lowest() and max_digits10 were not provided and that empty exception specifications instead of noexcept (see Section 3.1.7, page 24) were used.

The values of round_style are shown in Table 5.11. The values of has_denorm are shown in Table 5.12. Unfortunately, the member has_denorm is not called denorm_style. This happened because during the standardization process, there was a late change from a Boolean to an enumerative value. However, you can use the has_denorm member as a Boolean value because the standard

Round Style	Meaning
round_toward_zero	Rounds toward zero
round_to_nearest	Rounds to the nearest representable value
round_toward_infinity	Rounds toward positive infinity
round_toward_neg_infinity	Rounds toward negative infinity
round_indeterminate	Indeterminable

Table 5.11. Round Style of numeric_limits<>

Denorm Style	Meaning
denorm_absent	The type does not allow denormalized values
denorm_present	The type allows denormalized values to the nearest representable value
denorm_indeterminate	Indeterminable

Table 5.12. Denormalization Style of numeric_limits<>

guarantees that denorm_absent is 0, which is equivalent to false, whereas denorm_present is 1 and denorm_indeterminate is -1, both of which are equivalent to true. Thus, you can consider has_denorm a Boolean indication of whether the type may allow denormalized values.

Example of Using numeric_limits<>

The following example shows possible uses of some numeric limits, such as the maximum values for certain types and determining whether char is signed:

```
// util/limits1.cpp

#include <iostream>
#include <limits>
#include <string>
using namespace std;

int main()
{
    // use textual representation for bool
    cout << boolalpha;

    // print maximum of integral types
    cout << "max(short): " << numeric_limits<short>::max() << endl;
    cout << "max(int):   " << numeric_limits<int>::max() << endl;
    cout << "max(long):  " << numeric_limits<long>::max() << endl;
    cout << endl;
```

```
// print maximum of floating-point types
cout << "max(float):       "
     << numeric_limits<float>::max() << endl;
cout << "max(double):      "
     << numeric_limits<double>::max() << endl;
cout << "max(long double): "
     << numeric_limits<long double>::max() << endl;
cout << endl;

// print whether char is signed
cout << "is_signed(char): "
     << numeric_limits<char>::is_signed << endl;
cout << endl;

// print whether numeric limits for type string exist
cout << "is_specialized(string): "
     << numeric_limits<string>::is_specialized << endl;
}
```

The output of this program is platform dependent. Here is a possible output of the program:

```
max(short): 32767
max(int):   2147483647
max(long):  2147483647

max(float):        3.40282e+38
max(double):       1.79769e+308
max(long double):  1.79769e+308

is_signed(char): false

is_specialized(string): false
```

The last line shows that no numeric limits are defined for the type string. This makes sense because strings are not numeric values. However, this example shows that you can query for any arbitrary type whether or not it has numeric limits defined.

5.4 Type Traits and Type Utilities

Almost everything in the C++ standard library is template based. To support the programming of templates, sometimes called *metaprogramming*, template utilities are provided to help both programmers and library implementers.

Type traits, which were introduced with TR1 and extended with C++11, provide a mechanism to define behavior depending on types. They can be used to optimize code for types that provide special abilities.

Other utilities, such as reference and function wrappers, might also be helpful.

5.4.1 Purpose of Type Traits

A type trait provides a way to deal with the properties of a type. It is a template, which at compile time yields a specific type or value based on one or more passed template arguments, which are usually types.

Consider the following example:

```
template <typename T>
void foo (const T& val)
{
    if (std::is_pointer<T>::value) {
        std::cout << "foo() called for a pointer" << std::endl;
    }
    else {
        std::cout << "foo() called for a value" << std::endl;
    }
    ...
}
```

Here, the trait `std::is_pointer`, defined in `<type_traits>`, is used to check whether type T is a pointer type. In fact, `is_pointer<>` yields either a type `true_type` or a type `false_type`, for which `::value` either yields `true` or `false`. As a consequence, `foo()` will output

```
foo() called for a pointer
```

if the passed parameter `val` is a pointer.

Note, however, that you can't do something like:

```
template <typename T>
void foo (const T& val)
{
    std::cout << (std::is_pointer<T>::value ? *val : val)
              << std::endl;
}
```

The reason is that code is generated for both `*val` and `val`. Even when passing an `int` so that the expression `is_pointer<T>::value` yields `false` at compile time, the code expands to:

```
cout << (false ? *val : val) << endl;
```

And this won't compile, because *val is an invalid expression for ints.

But you can do the following:

```
// foo() implementation for pointer types:
template <typename T>
void foo_impl (const T& val, std::true_type)
{
    std::cout << "foo() called for pointer to " << *val
              << std::endl;
}


// foo() implementation for non-pointer types:
template <typename T>
void foo_impl (const T& val, std::false_type)
{
    std::cout << "foo() called for value to " << val
              << std::endl;
}


template <typename T>
void foo (const T& val)
{
    foo_impl (val, std::is_pointer<T>());
}
```

Here, inside foo(), the expression

```
std::is_pointer<T>()
```

at compile time yields std::true_type or std::false_type, which defines which of the provided foo_impl() overloads gets instantiated.

Why is that better than providing two overloads of foo(): one for ordinary types and one for pointer types?

```
template <typename T>
void foo (const T& val);            // general implementation


template <typename T>
void foo<T*> (const T& val);   // partial specialization for pointers
```

One answer is that sometimes, too many overloads are necessary. In general, the power of type traits comes more from the fact that they are *building blocks* for generic code, which can be demonstrated by two examples.

Flexible Overloading for Integral Types

In [*Becker:LibExt*], Pete Becker gives a nice example, which I modified slightly here. Suppose that you have a function foo() that should be implemented differently for integral and floating-point type arguments. The usual approach would be to overload this function for all available integral and floating-point types:[21]

```
void foo (short);                  // provide integral version
void foo (unsigned short);
void foo (int);
...
void foo (float);                  // provide floating-point version
void foo (double);
void foo (long double);
```

This repetition is not only tedious but also introduces the problem that it might not work for new integral or floating-point types, either provided by the standard, such as long long, or provided as user-defined types.

With the type traits, you can provide the following instead:

```
template <typename T>
void foo_impl (T val, true_type);   // provide integral version

template <typename T>
void foo_impl (T val, false_type);    // provide floating-point version

template <typename T>
void foo (T val)
{
    foo_impl (val, std::is_integral<T>());
}
```

Thus, you provide two implementations — one for integral and one for floating-point types — and choose the right implementation according to what std::is_integral<> yields for the type.

Processing the Common Type

Another example for the usability of type traits is the need to process the "common type" of two or more types. This is a type I could use to deal with the values of two different types, provided there is a common type. For example, it would be an appropriate type of the minimum or the sum of two values of different type. Otherwise, if I want to implement a function that yields the minimum of two values of different types, which return type should it have:

```
template <typename T1, typename T2>
??? min (const T1& x, const T2& y);
```

----

[21] According to the C++ standard, the term *integral type* includes bool and character types, but that's not meant here.

Using the type traits, you can simply use the `std::common_type<>` to declare this type:

```
template <typename T1, typename T2>
typename std::common_type<T1,T2>::type min (const T1& x, const T2& y);
```

For example, the expression `std::common_type<T1,T2>::type` yields `int` if both arguments are `int`, `long`, if one is `int` and the other is `long`, or `std::string` if one is a string and the other is a string literal (type `const char*`).

How does it do that? Well, it simply uses the rules implemented for operator `?:`, which has to yield one result type based on the types of both operands. In fact, `std::common_type<>` is implemented as follows:

```
template <typename T1, typename T2>
struct common_type<T1,T2> {
    typedef decltype(true ? declval<T1>() : declval<T2>()) type;
};
```

where `decltype` is a new keyword in C++11 (see Section 3.1.11, page 32) to yield the type of an expression, and `declval<>` is an auxiliary trait to provide a declared value of the passed type without evaluating it (generating an rvalue reference for it).

Thus, when operator `?:` is able to find a common type, `common_type<>` will yield it. If not, you can still provide an overload of `common_type<>` (this, for example, is used by the chrono library to be able to combine durations; see Section 5.7.2, page 145).

5.4.2 Type Traits in Detail

The type traits are usually defined in `<type_traits>`.

(Unary) Type Predicates

As introduced in Section 5.4.1, page 122, the type predicates yield `std::true_type` if a specific property applies and `std::false_type` if not. These types are specialization of the helper `std::integral_constant`, so their corresponding `value` members yield `true` or `false`:

```
namespace std {
    template <typename T, T val>
    struct integral_constant {
        static constexpr T value = val;
        typedef T value_type;
        typedef integral_constant<T,v> type;
        constexpr operator value_type() {
            return value;
        }
    };
    typedef integral_constant<bool,true>  true_type;
    typedef integral_constant<bool,false> false_type;
}
```

Trait	Effect
`is_void<T>`	Type `void`
`is_integral<T>`	Integral type (including `bool`, `char`, `char16_t`, `char32_t`, `wchar_t`)
`is_floating_point<T>`	Floating-point type (`float`, `double`, `long double`)
`is_arithmetic<T>`	Integral (including `bool` and characters) or floating-point type
`is_signed<T>`	Signed arithmetic type
`is_unsigned<T>`	Unsigned arithmetic type
`is_const<T>`	`const` qualified
`is_volatile<T>`	`volatile` qualified
`is_array<T>`	Ordinary array type (not type `std::array`)
`is_enum<T>`	Enumeration type
`is_union<T>`	Union type
`is_class<T>`	Class/struct type but not a union type
`is_function<T>`	Function type
`is_reference<T>`	Lvalue or rvalue reference
`is_lvalue_reference<T>`	Lvalue reference
`is_rvalue_reference<T>`	Rvalue reference
`is_pointer<T>`	Pointer type (including function pointer but not pointer to nonstatic member)
`is_member_pointer<T>`	Pointer to nonstatic member
`is_member_object_pointer<T>`	Pointer to a nonstatic data member
`is_member_function_pointer<T>`	Pointer to a nonstatic member function
`is_fundamental<T>`	`void`, integral (including `bool` and characters), floating-point, or `std::nullptr_t`
`is_scalar<T>`	Integral (including `bool` and characters), floating-point, enumeration, pointer, member pointer, `std::nullptr_t`
`is_object<T>`	Any type except `void`, function, or reference
`is_compound<T>`	Array, enumeration, union, class, function, reference, or pointer
`is_trivial<T>`	Scalar, trivial class, or arrays of these types
`is_trivially_copyable<T>`	Scalar, trivially copyable class, or arrays of these types
`is_standard_layout<T>`	Scalar, standard layout class, or arrays of these types
`is_pod<T>`	Plain old data type (type where `memcpy()` works to copy objects)
`is_literal_type<T>`	Scalar, reference, class, or arrays of these types

Table 5.13. Traits to Check Type Properties

Table 5.13 lists the type predicates provided for all types. Table 5.14 lists the traits that clarify details of class types.

Trait	Effect
`is_empty<T>`	Class with no members, virtual member functions, or virtual base classes
`is_polymorphic<T>`	Class with a (derived) virtual member function
`is_abstract<T>`	Abstract class (at least one pure virtual function)
`has_virtual_destructor<T>`	Class with virtual destructor
`is_default_constructible<T>`	Class enables default construction
`is_copy_constructible<T>`	Class enables copy construction
`is_move_constructible<T>`	Class enables move construction
`is_copy_assignable<T>`	Class enables copy assignment
`is_move_assignable<T>`	Class enables move assignment
`is_destructible<T>`	Class with callable destructor (not deleted, protected, or private)
`is_trivially_default_constructible<T>`	Class enables trivial default construction
`is_trivially_copy_constructible<T>`	Class enables trivial copy construction
`is_trivially_move_constructible<T>`	Class enables trivial move construction
`is_trivially_copy_assignable<T>`	Class enables trivial copy assignment
`is_trivially_move_assignable<T>`	Class with trivial move assignment
`is_trivially_destructible<T>`	Class with trivial callable destructor
`is_nothrow_default_constructible<T>`	Class enables default construction that doesn't throw
`is_nothrow_copy_constructible<T>`	Class enables copy construction that doesn't throw
`is_nothrow_move_constructible<T>`	Class enables move construction that doesn't throw
`is_nothrow_copy_assignable<T>`	Class enables copy assignment that doesn't throw
`is_nothrow_move_assignable<T>`	Class enables move assignment that doesn't throw
`is_nothrow_destructible<T>`	Class with callable destructor that doesn't throw

Table 5.14. Traits to Check Type Properties of Class Types

Note that `bool` and all character types (`char`, `char16_t`, `char32_t`, and `wchar_t`) count as integral types and that type `std::nullptr_t` (see Section 3.1.1, page 14) counts as a fundamental data type.

Most, but not all, of these traits are unary. That is, they use one template argument. For example, `is_const<>` checks whether the passed type is `const`:

```
is_const<int>::value                   // false
is_const<const volatile int>::value    // true
```

```
is_const<int* const>::value        // true
is_const<const int*>::value        // false
is_const<const int&>::value        // false
is_const<int[3]>::value            // false
is_const<const int[3]>::value      // true
is_const<int[]>::value             // false
is_const<const int[]>::value       // true
```

Note that a nonconstant pointer or reference to a constant type is not constant, whereas an ordinary array of constant elements is.[22]

Note that the traits checking for copy and move semantics only check whether the corresponding expressions are possible. For example, a type with a copy constructor with constant argument but no move constructor is still move constructible.

The is_nothrow... type traits are especially used to formulate noexcept specifications (see Section 3.1.7, page 24).

Traits for Type Relations

Table 5.15 lists the type traits that allow checking relations between types. This includes checking which constructors and assignment operators are provided for class types.

Trait	Effect
is_same<*T1*,*T2*>	*T1* and *T2* are the same types (including const/volatile qualifiers)
is_base_of<*T*,*D*>	Type *T* is base class of type *D*
is_convertible<*T*,*T2*>	Type *T* is convertible into type *T2*
is_constructible<*T*,*Args*...>	Can initialize type *T* with types *Args*
is_trivially_constructible<*T*,*Args*...>	Can trivially initialize type *T* with types *Args*
is_nothrow_constructible<*T*,*Args*...>	Initializing type *T* with types *Args* doesn't throw
is_assignable<*T*,*T2*>	Can assign type *T2* to type *T*
is_trivially_assignable<*T*,*T2*>	Can trivially assign type *T2* to type *T*
is_nothrow_assignable<*T*,*T2*>	Assigning type *T2* to type *T* doesn't throw
uses_allocator<*T*,*Alloc*>	*Alloc* is convertible into *T*::allocator_type

Table 5.15. Traits to Check Type Relations

---

[22] Whether this is correct is currently an issue to decide in the core language group.

Note that a type like `int` represents an lvalue or an rvalue. Because you can't assign

```
42 = 77;
```

`is_assignable<>` for a nonclass type as first type always yields `false_type`. For class types, however, passing their ordinary type as first type is fine because there is a funny old rule that you can invoke member functions of rvalues of class types.[23] For example:

```
is_assignable<int,int>::value                   // false
is_assignable<int&,int>::value                  // true
is_assignable<int&&,int>::value                 // false
is_assignable<long&,int>::value                 // true
is_assignable<int&,void*>::value                // false
is_assignable<void*,int>::value                 // false
is_assignable<const char*,std::string>::value   // false
is_assignable<std::string,const char*>::value   // true
```

Trait `is_constructible<>` yields, for example, the following:

```
is_constructible<int>::value                          // true
is_constructible<int,int>::value                      // true
is_constructible<long,int>::value                     // true
is_constructible<int,void*>::value                    // false
is_constructible<void*,int>::value                    // false
is_constructible<const char*,std::string>::value      // false
is_constructible<std::string,const char*>::value      // true
is_constructible<std::string,const char*,int,int>::value // true
```

`std::uses_allocator<>` is defined in `<memory>` (see Section 19.1, page 1024).

Type Modifiers

The traits listed in Table 5.16 allow you to modify types.

All modifying traits add a type property, provided it doesn't exist yet, or remove a property provided it exists already. For example, type `int` might only be extended:

```
typedef int T;
add_const<T>::type                // const int
add_lvalue_reference<T>::type     // int&
add_rvalue_reference<T>::type     // int&&
add_pointer<T>::type              // int*
make_signed<T>::type              // int
make_unsigned<T>::type            // unsigned int
remove_const<T>::type             // int
remove_reference<T>::type         // int
remove_pointer<T>::type           // int
```

---

[23] Thanks to Daniel Krügler for pointing this out.

Trait	Effect
remove_const<*T*>	Corresponding type without const
remove_volatile<*T*>	Corresponding type without volatile
remove_cv<*T*>	Corresponding type without const and volatile
add_const<*T*>	Corresponding const type
add_volatile<*T*>	Corresponding volatile type
add_cv<*T*>	Corresponding const volatile type
make_signed<*T*>	Corresponding signed nonreference type
make_unsigned<*T*>	Corresponding unsigned nonreference type
remove_reference<*T*>	Corresponding nonreference type
add_lvalue_reference<*T*>	Corresponding lvalue reference type (rvalues become lvalues)
add_rvalue_reference<*T*>	Corresponding rvalue reference type (lvalues remain lvalues)
remove_pointer<*T*>	Referred type for pointers (same type otherwise)
add_pointer<*T*>	Type of pointer to corresponding nonreference type

Table 5.16. Traits for Type Modifications

whereas type const int& might be reduced and/or extended:

```
typedef const int& T;
add_const<T>::type                    // const int&
add_lvalue_reference<T>::type         // const int&
add_rvalue_reference<T>::type         // const int& (yes, lvalue remains lvalue)
add_pointer<T>::type                  // const int*
make_signed<T>::type                  // undefined behavior
make_unsigned<T>::type                // undefined behavior
remove_const<T>::type                 // const int&
remove_reference<T>::type             // const int
remove_pointer<T>::type               // const int&
```

Note again that a reference to a constant type is not constant, so you can't remove constness there. Note that add_pointer<> implies the application of remove_reference<>. However, make_signed<> and make_unsigned<> require that the arguments be either integral or enumeration types, except bool, so passing references results in undefined behavior.

Note that add_lvalue_reference<> converts an rvalue reference into an lvalue reference, whereas add_rvalue_reference<> does *not* convert an lvalue reference into an rvalue reference (the type remains as it was). Thus, to convert an lvalue into a rvalue reference, you have to call:

```
add_rvalue_reference<remove_reference<T>::type>::type
```

Other Type Traits

Table 5.17 lists all remaining type traits. They query special properties, check type relations, or provide more complicated type transformations.

Trait	Effect
rank<*T*>	Number of dimensions of an array type (or 0)
extent<*T*,*I*=0>	Extent of dimension *I* (or 0)
remove_extent<*T*>	Element types for arrays (same type otherwise)
remove_all_extents<*T*>	Element type for multidimensional arrays (same type otherwise)
underlying_type<*T*>	Underlying type of an enumeration type (see Section 3.1.13, page 32)
decay<*T*>	Transfers to corresponding "by-value" type
enable_if<*B*,*T*=void>	Yields type *T* only if bool *B* is true
conditional<*B*,*T*,*F*>	Yields type *T* if bool *B* is true and type *F* otherwise
common_type<*T1*,...>	Common type of all passed types
result_of<*F*,*ArgTypes*>	Type of calling *F* with argument types *ArgTypes*
alignment_of<*T*>	Equivalent to alignof(*T*)
aligned_storage<*Len*>	Type of *Len* bytes with default alignment
aligned_storage<*Len*,*Align*>	Type of *Len* bytes aligned according to a divisor of size_t *Align*
aligned_union<*Len*,*Types*...>	Type of *Len* bytes aligned for a union of *Types*...

Table 5.17. Other Type Traits

The traits that deal with rank s and extent s allow you to deal with (multidimensional) arrays. For example:

```
rank<int>::value              // 0
rank<int[]>::value            // 1
rank<int[5]>::value           // 1
rank<int[][7]>::value         // 2
rank<int[5][7]>::value        // 2

extent<int>::value            // 0
extent<int[]>::value          // 0
extent<int[5]>::value         // 5
extent<int[][7]>::value       // 0
extent<int[5][7]>::value      // 5
extent<int[][7],1>::value     // 7
extent<int[5][7],1>::value    // 7
extent<int[5][7],2>::value    // 0

remove_extent<int>::type      // int
remove_extent<int[]>::type    // int
remove_extent<int[5]>::type   // int
remove_extent<int[][7]>::type // int[7]
remove_extent<int[5][7]>::type // int[7]

remove_all_extents<int>::type // int
```

```
remove_all_extents<int[]>::type        // int
remove_all_extents<int[5]>::type       // int
remove_all_extents<int[][7]>::type     // int
remove_all_extents<int[5][7]>::type    // int
```

Trait `decay<>` provides the ability to convert a type T into its corresponding type when this type is passed by value. Thus, it converts array and function types into pointers as well as lvalues into rvalues, including removing `const` and `volatile`. See Section 5.1.1, page 65, for an example of its use.

As introduced in Section 5.4.1, page 124, `common_type<>` provides a common type for all passed types (may be one, two, or more type arguments).

5.4.3 Reference Wrappers

Class `std::reference_wrapper<>`, declared in `<functional>`, is used primarily to "feed" references to function templates that take their parameter by value. For a given type T, this class provides `ref()` for an implicit conversion to `T&` and `cref()` for an implicit conversion to `const T&`, which usually allows function templates to work on references without specialization.

For example, after a declaration such as

```
template <typename T>
void foo (T val);
```

by calling

```
int x;
foo (std::ref(x));
```

T becomes `int&`, whereas by calling

```
int x;
foo (std::cref(x));
```

T becomes `const int&`.

This feature is used by the C++ standard library at various places. For example:

- `make_pair()` uses this to be able to create a `pair<>` of references (see Section 5.1.1, page 66).
- `make_tuple()` uses this to be able to create a `tuple<>` of references (see Section 5.1.2, page 70).
- Binders use this to be able to bind references (see Section 10.2.2, page 491).
- Threads use this to pass arguments by reference (see Section 18.2.2, page 971).

Note also that class `reference_wrapper` allows you to use references as first-class objects, such as element type in arrays or STL containers:

```
std::vector<MyClass&> coll;                              // Error
std::vector<std::reference_wrapper<MyClass>> coll;       // OK
```

See Section 7.11, page 391, for details.

5.4.4 Function Type Wrappers

Class `std::function<>`, declared in `<functional>`, provides polymorphic wrappers that generalize the notion of a function pointer. This class allows you to use *callable objects* (functions, member functions, function objects, and lambdas; see Section 4.4, page 54) as first-class objects.

For example:

```
void func (int x, int y);
```

```
// initialize collections of tasks:
std::vector<std::function<void(int,int)>> tasks;
tasks.push_back(func);
tasks.push_back([] (int x, int y) {
                    ...
                });
```

```
// call each task:
for (std::function<void(int,int)> f : tasks) {
    f(33,66);
}
```

When member functions are used, the object they are called for has to be the first argument:

```
class C {
  public:
    void memfunc (int x, int y) const;
};
```

```
std::function<void(const C&,int,int)> mf;
mf = &C::memfunc;
mf(C(),42,77);
```

Another application of this is to declare functions that return lambdas (see Section 3.1.10, page 31).

Note that performing a function call without having a *target* to call throws an exception of type `std::bad_function_call` (see Section 4.3.1, page 43):

```
std::function<void(int,int)> f;
f(33,66);   // throws std::bad_function_call
```

5.5   Auxiliary Functions

The C++ standard library provides some small auxiliary functions that process minimum and maximum, swap values, or provide supplementary comparison operators.

5.5.1   Processing the Minimum and Maximum

Table 5.18 lists the utility functions `<algorithm>` provides to process the minimum and/or maximum of two or more values. All `minmax()` functions and all function for initializer lists are provided since C++11.

Operation	Effect
`min(`*a*`,`*b*`)`	Returns the minimum of *a* and *b*, comparing with <
`min(`*a*`,`*b*`,`*cmp*`)`	Returns the minimum of *a* and *b*, comparing with *cmp*
`min(`*initlist*`)`	Returns the minimum in *initlist*, comparing with <
`min(`*initlist*`,`*cmp*`)`	Returns the minimum in *initlist*, comparing with *cmp*
`max(`*a*`,`*b*`)`	Returns the maximum of *a* and *b*, comparing with <
`max(`*a*`,`*b*`,`*cmp*`)`	Returns the maximum of *a* and *b*, comparing with *cmp*
`max(`*initlist*`)`	Returns the maximum in *initlist*, comparing with <
`max(`*initlist*`,`*cmp*`)`	Returns the maximum in *initlist*, comparing with *cmp*
`minmax(`*a*`,`*b*`)`	Returns the minimum and maximum of *a* and *b*, comparing with <
`minmax(`*a*`,`*b*`,`*cmp*`)`	Returns the minimum and maximum of *a* and *b*, comparing with *cmp*
`minmax(`*initlist*`)`	Returns the minimum and maximum of *initlist* comparing with <
`minmax(`*initlist*`,`*cmp*`)`	Returns the minimum and maximum of *initlist* comparing with *cmp*

Table 5.18. Operations to Process Minimum and Maximum

The function `minmax()` returns a `pair<>` (see Section 5.1.1, page 60), where the first value is the minimum, and the second value is the maximum.

For the versions with two arguments, `min()` and `max()` return the first element if both values are equal. For initializer lists, `min()` and `max()` return the first of multiple minimum or maximum elements. `minmax()` returns the pair of a and b for two equal arguments and the first minimum but the last maximum element for an initializer list. However, it is probably a good programming style not to rely on this.

Note that the versions taking two values return a reference; the versions taking initializer lists return copies of the values:

```
namespace std {
    template <typename T>
      const T& min (const T& a, const T& b);
    template <typename T>
      T min (initializer_list<T> initlist);
    ...
}
```

The reason is that for an initializer list, you need an internal temporary, so returning a reference would return a dangling reference.

Both functions are also provided with the comparison criterion as an additional argument:

```
namespace std {
    template <typename T, typename Compare>
      const T& min (const T& a, const T& b, Compare cmp);
    template <typename T, typename Compare>
      T min (initializer_list<T> initlist, Compare cmp);
    ...
}
```

The comparison argument might be a function or a function object (see Section 6.10, page 233) that compares both arguments and returns whether the first is less than the second in some particular order.

The following example shows how to use the maximum function by passing a special comparison function as an argument:

```
// util/minmax1.cpp

#include <algorithm>

// function that compares two pointers by comparing the values to which they point
bool int_ptr_less (int* a, int* b)
{
    return *a < *b;
}

int main()
{
    int x = 17;
    int y = 42;
    int z = 33;
    int* px = &x;
    int* py = &y;
    int* pz = &z;

    // call max() with special comparison function
    int* pmax = std::max (px, py, int_ptr_less);

    // call minmax() for initializer list with special comparison function
    std::pair<int*,int*> extremes = std::minmax ({px, py, pz},
                                                 int_ptr_less);
    ...
}
```

Alternatively, you could use new language features, such as a lambda, to specify the comparison criterion and `auto` to avoid the explicit declaration of the return value:

```
auto extremes = std::minmax ({px, py, pz}, [](int*a, int*b) {
                                              return *a < *b;
                            });
```

Note that the definitions of `min()` and `max()` require that both types match. Thus, you can't call them for objects of different types:

```
int i;
long l;
...
std::max(i,l);          // ERROR: argument types don't match
std::max({i,l});        // ERROR: argument types don't match
```

However, you could qualify explicitly the type of your template arguments (and thus the return type):

```
std::max<long>(i,l);      // OK
std::max<long>({i,l});    // OK
```

5.5.2 Swapping Two Values

The function `swap()` is provided to swap the values of two objects. The general implementation of `swap()` is defined in `<utility>` as follows:[24]

```
namespace std {
    template <typename T>
    inline void swap(T& a, T& b) ... {
        T tmp(std::move(a));
        a = std::move(b);
        b = std::move(tmp);
    }
}
```

Thus, internally, the values are moved or move assigned (see Section 3.1.5, page 19, for details of move semantics). Before C++11, the values were assigned or copied.

By using this function, you can have two arbitrary variables x and y swap their values by calling

```
std::swap(x,y);
```

Of course, this call is possible only if move or copy semantics are provided by the parameter type.

Note that `swap()` provides an exception specification (that's why ... is used in the previous declarations). The exception specification for the general `swap()` is:[25]

---

[24] Before C++11, `swap()` was defined in `<algorithm>`.

[25] See Section 3.1.7, page 24, for details about `noexcept` and Section 5.4.2, page 127, for the type traits used here.

```
noexcept(is_nothrow_move_constructible<T>::value &&
         is_nothrow_move_assignable<T>::value)
```

Since C++11, the C++ standard library also provides an overload for arrays:

```
namespace std {
  template <typename T, size_t N>
  void swap (T (&a)[N], T (&b)[N])
            noexcept(noexcept(swap(*a,*b)));
}
```

The big advantage of using `swap()` is that it enables you to provide special implementations for more complex types by using template specialization or function overloading. These special implementations might save time by swapping internal members rather than by assigning the objects. This is the case, for example, for all standard containers (see Section 7.1.2, page 258) and strings (see Section 13.2.8, page 674). For example, a `swap()` implementation for a simple container that has only an array and the number of elements as members could look like this:

```
class MyContainer {
  private:
    int* elems;        // dynamic array of elements
    int  numElems;     // number of elements
  public:
    ...
    // implementation of swap()
    void swap(MyContainer& x) {
        std::swap(elems,x.elems);
        std::swap(numElems,x.numElems);
    }
    ...
};


// overloaded global swap() for this type
inline void swap (MyContainer& c1, MyContainer& c2)
                 noexcept(noexcept(c1.swap(c2)))
{
    c1.swap(c2);      // calls implementation of swap()
}
```

So, calling `swap()` instead of swapping the values directly might result in substantial performance improvements. You should always offer a specialization of `swap()` for your own types if doing so has performance advantages.

Note that both types have to match:

```
int i;
long l;
std::swap(i,l);           // ERROR: argument types don't match
```

```
int a1[10];
int a3[11];
std::swap(a1,a3);      // ERROR: arrays have different types (different sizes)
```

5.5.3 Supplementary Comparison Operators

Four function templates define the comparison operators !=, >, <=, and >= by calling the operators == and <. These functions are declared in <utility> and are usually defined as follows:

```
namespace std {
    namespace rel_ops {
        template <typename T>
        inline bool operator!= (const T& x, const T& y) {
            return !(x == y);
        }
        template <typename T>
        inline bool operator> (const T& x, const T& y) {
            return y < x;
        }
        template <typename T>
        inline bool operator<= (const T& x, const T& y) {
            return !(y < x);
        }
        template <typename T>
        inline bool operator>= (const T& x, const T& y) {
            return !(x < y);
        }
    }
}
```

To use these functions, you need only define operators < and ==. Using namespace std::rel_ops defines the other comparison operators automatically. For example:

```
#include <utility>

class X {
  public:
    bool operator== (const X& x) const;
    bool operator< (const X& x) const;
    ...
};
```

```
void foo()
{
    using namespace std::rel_ops;      // make !=, >, etc., available
    X x1, x2;
    ...
    if (x1 != x2) {      // OK
        ...
    }
    if (x1 > x2) {      // OK
        ...
    }
}
```

These operators are defined in a subnamespace of `std`, called `rel_ops`. They are in a separate namespace so that user-defined relational operators in the global namespace won't clash even if all identifiers of namespace `std` become global by using a general using directive:

```
using namespace std;               // operators are not in global scope
```

On the other hand, users who want to get their hands on them explicitly can implement the following without having to rely on lookup rules to find them implicitly:

```
using namespace std::rel_ops;      // operators are in global scope
```

Some implementations define the operators by using two different argument types:

```
namespace std {
    namespace rel_ops {
        template <typename T1, typename T2>
        inline bool operator!=(const T1& x, const T2& y) {
            return !(x == y);
        }
        ...
    }
}
```

The advantage of such an implementation is that the types of the operands may differ, provided the types are comparable. But note that this kind of implementation is not provided by the C++ standard library. Thus, taking advantage of it makes code nonportable.

5.6   Compile-Time Fractional Arithmetic with Class `ratio<>`

Since C++11, the C++ standard library provides an interface to specify compile-time fractions and to perform compile-time arithmetic with them. To quote [*N2661:Chrono*] (with minor modifications):[26]

> *The ratio utility is a general purpose utility inspired by Walter E. Brown allowing one to easily and safely compute rational values at compile time. The* ratio *class catches all errors (such as divide by zero and overflow) at compile time. It is used in the duration and time_point libraries [see Section 5.7, page 143] to efficiently create units of time. It can also be used in other "quantity" libraries (both standard-defined and user-defined), or anywhere there is a rational constant which is known at compile time. The use of this utility can greatly reduce the chances of runtime overflow because a ratio and any ratios resulting from ratio arithmetic are always reduced to lowest terms.*

The ratio utility is provided in `<ratio>`, with class `ratio<>` defined as follows:

```
namespace std {
    template <intmax_t N, intmax_t D = 1>
    class ratio {
      public:
        typedef ratio<num,den> type;
        static constexpr intmax_t num;
        static constexpr intmax_t den;
    };
}
```

`intmax_t` designates a signed integer type capable of representing any value of any signed integer type. It is defined in `<cstdint>` or `<stdint.h>` with at least 64 bits. Numerator and denominator are both public and are automatically reduced to the lowest terms. For example:

```
// util/ratio1.cpp

#include <ratio>
#include <iostream>
using namespace std;

int main()
{
    typedef ratio<5,3> FiveThirds;
    cout << FiveThirds::num << "/" << FiveThirds::den << endl;
```

---

[26] Thanks to Walter E. Brown, Howard Hinnant, Jeff Garland, and Marc Paterno for their friendly permission to quote [*N2661:Chrono*] here and in the following section covering the chrono library.

```
    typedef ratio<25,15> AlsoFiveThirds;
    cout << AlsoFiveThirds::num << "/" << AlsoFiveThirds::den << endl;

    ratio<42,42> one;
    cout << one.num << "/" << one.den << endl;

    ratio<0> zero;
    cout << zero.num << "/" << zero.den << endl;

    typedef ratio<7,-3> Neg;
    cout << Neg::num << "/" << Neg::den << endl;
}
```

The program has the following output:

```
5/3
5/3
1/1
0/1
-7/3
```

Table 5.19 lists the compile-time operations defined for ratio types. The four basic arithmetic compile-time operations +, -, *, and / are defined as `ratio_add`, `ratio_subtract`, `ratio_multiply`, and `ratio_divide`. The resulting type is a `ratio<>`, so the static member type yields the corresponding type. For example, the following expression yields `std::ratio<13,21>` (computed as $\frac{6}{21} + \frac{7}{21}$):

```
std::ratio_add<std::ratio<2,7>,std::ratio<2,6>>::type
```

Operation	Meaning	Result
`ratio_add`	Reduced sum of ratios	`ratio<>`
`ratio_subtract`	Reduced difference of ratios	`ratio<>`
`ratio_multiply`	Reduced product of ratios	`ratio<>`
`ratio_divide`	Reduced quotient of ratios	`ratio<>`
`ratio_equal`	Checks for ==	`true_type` or `false_type`
`ratio_not_equal`	Checks for !=	`true_type` or `false_type`
`ratio_less`	Checks for <	`true_type` or `false_type`
`ratio_less_equal`	Checks for <=	`true_type` or `false_type`
`ratio_greater`	Checks for >	`true_type` or `false_type`
`ratio_greater_equal`	Checks for >=	`true_type` or `false_type`

Table 5.19. Operations of `ratio<>` Types

In addition, you can compare two ratio types with `ratio_equal`, `ratio_not_equal`, `ratio_less`, `ratio_less_equal`, `ratio_greater`, or `ratio_greater_equal`. As with type traits, the resulting type is derived from `true_type` or `false_type` (see Section 5.4.2, page 125), so its member value yields `true` or `false`:

```
ratio_equal<ratio<5,3>,ratio<25,15>>::value    // yields true
```

As written, class `ratio` catches all errors, such as divide by zero and overflow, at compile time. For example,

```
ratio_multiply<ratio<1,numeric_limits<long long>::max()>,
               ratio<1,2>>::type
```

won't compile, because $\frac{1}{max}$ times $\frac{1}{2}$ results in an overflow, with the resulting value of the denominator exceeding the limit of its type.

Similarly, the following expression won't compile, because this is a division by zero:

```
ratio_divide<fiveThirds,zero>::type
```

Note, however, that the following expression will compile because the invalid value is detected when member type, num, or den are evaluated:

```
ratio_divide<fiveThirds,zero>
```

Name	Unit
yocto	$\frac{1}{1,000,000,000,000,000,000,000,000}$ (optional)
zepto	$\frac{1}{1,000,000,000,000,000,000,000}$ (optional)
atto	$\frac{1}{1,000,000,000,000,000,000}$
femto	$\frac{1}{1,000,000,000,000,000}$
pico	$\frac{1}{1,000,000,000,000}$
nano	$\frac{1}{1,000,000,000}$
micro	$\frac{1}{1,000,000}$
milli	$\frac{1}{1,000}$
centi	$\frac{1}{100}$
deci	$\frac{1}{10}$
deca	10
hecto	100
kilo	$1,000$
mega	$1,000,000$
giga	$1,000,000,000$
tera	$1,000,000,000,000$
peta	$1,000,000,000,000,000$
exa	$1,000,000,000,000,000,000$
zetta	$1,000,000,000,000,000,000,000$ (optional)
yotta	$1,000,000,000,000,000,000,000,000$ (optional)

Table 5.20. Predefined `ratio` *Units*

Predefined ratios make it more convenient to specify large or very small numbers (see Table 5.20). They allow you to specify large numbers without the inconvenient and error-prone listing of zeros. For example,

```
std::nano
```

is equivalent to

```
std::ratio<1,1000000000LL>
```

which makes it more convenient to specify, for example, nanoseconds (see Section 5.7.2, page 145). The units marked as "optional" are defined only if they are representable by `intmax_t`.

5.7 Clocks and Timers

One of the most obvious libraries a programming language should have is one to deal with date and time. However, experience shows that such a library is harder to design than it sounds. The problem is the amount of flexibility and precision the library should provide. In fact, in the past, the interfaces to system time provided by C and POSIX switched from seconds to milliseconds, then to microseconds, and finally to nanoseconds. The problem was that for each switch, a new interface was provided. For this reason, a precision-neutral library was proposed for C++11. This library is usually called the *chrono library* because its features are defined in `<chrono>`.

In addition, the C++ standard library provides the basic C and POSIX interfaces to deal with calendar time. Finally, you can use the thread library, provided since C++11, to wait for a thread or the program (the main thread) for a period of time.

5.7.1 Overview of the Chrono Library

The chrono library was designed to be able to deal with the fact that timers and clocks might be different on different systems and improve over time in precision. To avoid having to introduce a new time type every 10 years or so — as happened with the POSIX time libraries, for example — the goal was to provide a precision-neutral concept by separating duration and point of time ("timepoint") from specific clocks. As a result, the core of the chrono library consists of the following types or concepts, which serve as abstract mechanisms to specify and deal with points in and durations of time:

- A **duration** of time is defined as a specific number of ticks over a time unit. One example is a duration such as "3 minutes" (3 ticks of a "minute"). Other examples are "42 milliseconds" or "86,400 seconds," which represents the duration of 1 day. This concept also allows specifying something like "1.5 times a third of a second," where 1.5 is the number of ticks and "a third of a second" the time unit used.
- A **timepoint** is defined as combination of a duration and a beginning of time (the so-called **epoch**). A typical example is a timepoint that represents "New Year's Midnight 2000," which is described as "1,262,300,400 seconds since January 1, 1970" (this day is the epoch of the system clock of UNIX and POSIX systems).

- The concept of a timepoint, however, is parametrized by a **clock**, which is the object that defines the epoch of a timepoint. Thus, different clocks have different epochs. In general, operations dealing with multiple timepoints, such as processing the duration/difference between two timepoints, require using the same epoch/clock. A clock also provides a convenience function to yield the timepoint of *now*.

In other words, timepoint is defined as a duration before or after an epoch, which is defined by a clock (see Figure 5.4).

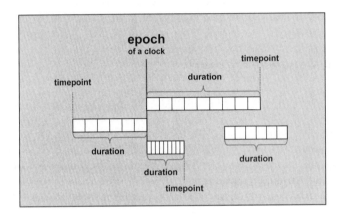

Figure 5.4. Epoch, Durations, and Timepoints

For more details about the motivation and design of these classes, see [*N2661:Chrono*].[27] Let's look into these types and concepts in detail.

Note that all identifiers of the chrono library are defined in namespace std::chrono.

5.7.2 Durations

A duration is a combination of a **value** representing the number of ticks and a **fraction** representing the unit in seconds. Class ratio is used to specify the fraction (see Section 5.6, page 140). For example:

```
std::chrono::duration<int>                    twentySeconds(20);
std::chrono::duration<double,std::ratio<60>>  halfAMinute(0.5);
std::chrono::duration<long,std::ratio<1,1000>> oneMillisecond(1);
```

Here, the first template argument defines the type of the ticks, and the optional second template argument defines the unit type in seconds. Thus, the first line uses seconds as unit type, the second line uses minutes ("$\frac{60}{1}$ seconds"), and the third line uses milliseconds ("$\frac{1}{1000}$ of a second").

For more convenience, the C++ standard library provides the following type definitions:

---

[27] I use some quotes of [*N2661:Chrono*] in this book with friendly permission by the authors.

```
namespace std {
  namespace chrono {
    typedef duration<signed int-type >= 64 bits,nano>        nanoseconds;
    typedef duration<signed int-type >= 55 bits,micro>       microseconds;
    typedef duration<signed int-type >= 45 bits,milli>       milliseconds;
    typedef duration<signed int-type >= 35 bits>             seconds;
    typedef duration<signed int-type >= 29 bits,ratio<60>>   minutes;
    typedef duration<signed int-type >= 23 bits,ratio<3600>> hours;
  }
}
```

With them, you can easily specify typical time periods:

```
std::chrono::seconds      twentySeconds(20);
std::chrono::hours        aDay(24);
std::chrono::milliseconds oneMillisecond(1);
```

Arithmetic Duration Operations

You can compute with durations in the expected way (see Table 5.21):

- You can process the sum, difference, product, or quotient of two durations.
- You can add or subtract ticks or other durations.
- You can compare two durations.

The important point here is that the unit type of two durations involved in such an operation might be different. Due to a provided overloading of common_type<> (see Section 5.4.1, page 124) for durations, the resulting duration will have a unit that is the greatest common divisor of the units of both operands.

For example, after

```
chrono::seconds      d1(42);     // 42 seconds
chrono::milliseconds d2(10);     // 10 milliseconds
```

the expression

```
d1 - d2
```

yields a duration of 41,990 ticks of unit type milliseconds ($\frac{1}{1000}$ seconds).

Or, more generally, after

```
chrono::duration<int,ratio<1,3>> d1(1);     // 1 tick of 1/3 second
chrono::duration<int,ratio<1,5>> d2(1);     // 1 tick of 1/5 second
```

the expression

```
d1 + d2
```

yields 8 ticks of $\frac{1}{15}$ second and

```
d1 < d2
```

yields false. In both cases, d1 gets expanded to 5 ticks of $\frac{1}{15}$ second, and d2 gets expanded to 3 ticks of $\frac{1}{15}$ second. So the sum of 3 and 5 is 8, and 5 is not less than 3.

Operation	Effect
d1 + *d2*	Process sum of durations *d1* and *d2*
d1 − *d2*	Process difference of durations *d1* and *d2*
d * *val*	Return result of *val* times duration *d*
val * *d*	Return result of *val* times duration *d*
d / *val*	Return of the duration *d* divided by value *val*
d1 / *d2*	Compute factor between durations *d1* and *d2*
d % *val*	Result of duration *d* modulo value *val*
d % *d2*	Result of duration *d* modulo the value of *d2*
d1 == *d2*	Return whether duration *d1* is equal to duration *d2*
d1 != *d2*	Return whether duration *d1* differs from duration *d2*
d1 < *d2*	Return whether duration *d1* is shorter than duration *d2*
d1 <= *d2*	Return whether duration *d1* is not longer than duration *d2*
d1 > *d2*	Return whether duration *d1* is longer than duration *d2*
d1 <= *d2*	Return whether duration *d1* is not shorter than duration *d2*
++*d*	Increment duration *d* by 1 tick
d++	Increment duration *d* by 1 tick
−−*d*	Decrement duration *d* by 1 tick
d−−	Decrement duration *d* by 1 tick
d += *d1*	Extend the duration *d* by the duration *d1*
d −= *d1*	Shorten the duration *d* by the duration *d1*
d *= *val*	Multiply the duration *d* by *val*
d /= *val*	Divide the duration *d* by *val*
d %= *val*	Process duration *d* modulo *val*
d %= *d2*	Process duration *d* modulo the value of *d2*

Table 5.21. Arithmetic Operations of `durations`

You can also convert durations into durations of different units, as long as there is an implicit type conversion. Thus, you can convert hours into seconds but not the other way around. For example:

```
std::chrono::seconds twentySeconds(20);    // 20 seconds
std::chrono::hours    aDay(24);            // 24 hours

std::chrono::milliseconds ms;              // 0 milliseconds
ms += twentySeconds + aDay;                // 86,400,000 milliseconds
--ms;                                      // 86,399,999 milliseconds
ms *= 2;                                   // 172,839,998 milliseconds
std::cout << ms.count() << " ms" << std::endl;
std::cout << std::chrono::nanoseconds(ms).count() << " ns" << std::endl;
```

These conversions result in the following output:

```
172839998 ms
172839998000000 ns
```

Other Duration Operations

In the preceding example, we use the member `count()` to yield the current number of ticks, which is one of the other operations provided for durations. Table 5.22 lists all operations, members, and types available for durations besides the arithmetic operations of Table 5.21. Note that the default constructor default-initializes (see Section 3.2.1, page 37) its value, which means that for fundamental representation types, the initial value is undefined.

Operation	Effect
`duration d`	Default constructor; creates duration (default-initialized)
`duration d(d2)`	Copy constructor; copies duration (*d2* might have a different unit type)
`duration d(val)`	Creates duration of *val* ticks of *d*s unit type
`d = d2`	Assigns duration *d2* to *d* (implicit conversion possible)
`d.count()`	Returns ticks of the duration *d*
`duration_cast<D>(d)`	Returns duration *d* explicitly converted into type *D*
`duration::zero()`	Yields duration of zero length
`duration::max()`	Yields maximum possible duration of this type
`duration::min()`	Yields minimum possible duration of this type
`duration::rep`	Yields the type of the ticks
`duration::period`	Yields the type of the unit type

Table 5.22. Other Operations and Types of durations

You can use these members to define a convenience function for the output operator `<<` for durations:[28]

```
template <typename V, typename R>
ostream& operator << (ostream& s, const chrono::duration<V,R>& d)
{
    s << "[" << d.count() << " of " << R::num << "/"
                                    << R::den << "]";
    return s;
}
```

Here, after printing the number of ticks with `count()`, we print the numerator and denominator of the unit type used, which is a `ratio` processed at compile time (see Section 5.6, page 140). For example,

```
std::chrono::milliseconds d(42);
std::cout << d << std::endl;
```

will then print:

```
[42 of 1/1000]
```

---

[28] Note that this output operator does not work where *ADL (argument-dependent lookup)* does not work (see Section 15.11.1, page 812, for details).

As we have seen, implicit conversions to a more precise unit type are always possible. However, conversions to a coarser unit type are not, because you might lose information. For example, when converting an integral value of 42,010 milliseconds into seconds, the resulting integral value, 42, means that the precision of having a duration of 10 milliseconds over 42 seconds gets lost. But you can still explicitly force such a conversion with a duration_cast. For example:

```
std::chrono::seconds sec(55);
std::chrono::minutes m1 = sec;          // ERROR
std::chrono::minutes m2 =
   std::chrono::duration_cast<std::chrono::minutes>(sec);   // OK
```

As another example, converting a duration with a floating-point tick type also requires an explicit cast to convert it into an integral duration type:

```
std::chrono::duration<double,std::ratio<60>> halfMin(0.5);
std::chrono::seconds s1 = halfMin;       // ERROR
std::chrono::seconds s2 =
   std::chrono::duration_cast<std::chrono::seconds>(halfMin);   // OK
```

A typical example is code that segments a duration into different units. For example, the following code segments a duration of milliseconds into the corresponding hours, minutes, seconds, and milliseconds (to output the first line starting with raw: we use the output operator just defined):

```
using namespace std;
using namespace std::chrono;
milliseconds ms(7255042);

// split into hours, minutes, seconds, and milliseconds
hours    hh = duration_cast<hours>(ms);
minutes mm = duration_cast<minutes>(ms % chrono::hours(1));
seconds ss = duration_cast<seconds>(ms % chrono::minutes(1));
milliseconds msec
            = duration_cast<milliseconds>(ms % chrono::seconds(1));

// and print durations and values:
cout << "raw: " << hh << "::" << mm << "::"
                << ss << "::" << msec << endl;
cout << "     " << setfill('0') << setw(2) << hh.count() << "::"
                               << setw(2) << mm.count() << "::"
                               << setw(2) << ss.count() << "::"
                               << setw(3) << msec.count() << endl;
```

Here, the cast

```
std::chrono::duration_cast<std::chrono::hours>(ms)
```

converts the milliseconds into hours, where the values are truncated, not rounded. Thanks to the modulo operator %, for which you can even pass a duration as second argument, you can easily process the remaining milliseconds with `ms % std::chrono::hours(1)`, which is then converted into minutes. Thus, the output of this code will be as follows:

```
raw: [2 of 3600/1]::[0 of 60/1]::[55 of 1/1]::[42 of 1/1000]
     02::00::55::042
```

Finally, class `duration` provides three static functions: `zero()`, which yields a duration of 0 seconds, as well as `min()` and `max()`, which yield the minimum and maximum value a duration can have.

5.7.3 Clocks and Timepoints

The relationships between timepoints and clocks are a bit tricky:

- A **clock** defines an epoch and a tick period. For example, a clock might tick in milliseconds since the UNIX epoch (January 1, 1970) or tick in nanoseconds since the start of the program. In addition, a clock provides a type for any timepoint specified according to this clock.

  The interface of a clock provides a function `now()` to yield an object for the current point in time.

- A **timepoint** represents a specific point in time by associating a positive or negative duration to a given clock. Thus, if the duration is "10 days" and the associated clock has the epoch of January 1, 1970, the timepoint represents January 11, 1970.

  The interface of a timepoint provides the ability to yield the epoch, minimum and maximum timepoints according to the clock, and timepoint arithmetic.

Clocks

Table 5.23 lists the type definitions and static members required for each clock.

Operation	Effect
`clock::duration`	Yields the duration type of the clock
`clock::rep`	Yields the type of the ticks (equivalent to `clock::duration::rep`)
`clock::period`	Yields the type of the unit type (equivalent to `clock::duration::period`)
`clock::time_point`	Yields the timepoint type of the clock
`clock::is_steady`	Yields `true` if the clock is steady
`clock::now()`	Yields a `time_point` for the current point in time

Table 5.23. Operations and Types of Clocks

The C++ standard library provides three clocks, which provide this interface:

1. The **system_clock** represents timepoints associated with the usual real-time clock of the current system. This clock also provides convenience functions `to_time_t()` and `from_time_t()`

to convert between any timepoint and the C system time type `time_t`, which means that you can convert into and from calendar times (see Section 5.7.4, page 158).

2. The **steady_clock** gives the guarantee that it never gets adjusted.[29] Thus, timepoint values never decrease as the physical time advances, and they advance at a steady rate relative to real time.

3. The **high_resolution_clock** represents a clock with the shortest tick period possible on the current system.

Note that the standard does not provide requirements for the precision, the epoch, and the range (minimum and maximum timepoints) of these clocks. For example, your system clock might have the UNIX epoch (January 1, 1970) as epoch, but this is not guaranteed. If you require a specific epoch or care for timepoints that might not be covered by the clock, you have to use convenience functions to find it out.

For example, the following function prints the properties of a clock:

```
// util/clock.hpp

#include <chrono>
#include <iostream>
#include <iomanip>

template <typename C>
void printClockData ()
{
    using namespace std;

    cout << "- precision: ";
    // if time unit is less or equal one millisecond
    typedef typename C::period P;    // type of time unit
    if (ratio_less_equal<P,milli>::value) {
        // convert to and print as milliseconds
        typedef typename ratio_multiply<P,kilo>::type TT;
        cout << fixed << double(TT::num)/TT::den
             << " milliseconds" << endl;
    }
    else {
        // print as seconds
        cout << fixed << double(P::num)/P::den << " seconds" << endl;
    }
    cout << "- is_steady: " << boolalpha << C::is_steady << endl;
}
```

We can call this function for the various clocks provided by the C++ standard library:

---

[29] The steady_clock was initially proposed as monotonic_clock.

```
// util/clock1.cpp

#include <chrono>
#include "clock.hpp"

int main()
{
    std::cout << "system_clock: " << std::endl;
    printClockData<std::chrono::system_clock>();
    std::cout << "\nhigh_resolution_clock: " << std::endl;
    printClockData<std::chrono::high_resolution_clock>();
    std::cout << "\nsteady_clock: " << std::endl;
    printClockData<std::chrono::steady_clock>();
}
```

The program might, for example, have the following output:

```
system_clock:
- precision: 0.000100 milliseconds
- is_steady: false

high_resolution_clock:
- precision: 0.000100 milliseconds
- is_steady: true

steady_clock:
- precision: 1.000000 milliseconds
- is_steady: true
```

Here, for example, the system and the high-resolution clock have the same precision of 100 nanoseconds, whereas the steady clock uses milliseconds. You can also see that both the steady clock and high-resolution clock can't be adjusted. Note, however, that this might be very different on other systems. For example, the high-resolution clock might be the same as the system clock.

The `steady_clock` is important to compare or compute the difference of two times in your program, where you processed the current point in time. For example, after

```
auto system_start = chrono::system_clock::now();
```

a condition to check whether the program runs more than one minute:

```
if (chrono::system_clock::now() > system_start + minutes(1))
```

might not work, because if the clock was adjusted in the meantime, the comparison might yield `false`, although the program did run more than a minute. Similarly, processing the elapsed time of a program:

```
auto diff = chrono::system_clock::now() - system_start;
auto sec = chrono::duration_cast<chrono::seconds>(diff);
cout << "this program runs:  " << s.count() << " seconds" << endl;
```

might print a negative duration if the clock was adjusted in the meantime. For the same reason, using timers with other than the `steady_clock` might change their duration when the system clock gets adjusted (see Section 5.7.5, page 160, for details).

Timepoints

With any of these clocks — or even with user-defined clocks — you can deal with timepoints. Class `time_point` provides the corresponding interface, parametrized by a clock:

```
namespace std {
  namespace chrono {
    template <typename Clock,
              typename Duration = typename Clock::duration>
      class time_point;
  }
}
```

Four specific timepoints play a special role:

1. The **epoch**, which the default constructor of class `time_point` yields for each clock.
2. The **current time**, which the static member function `now()` of each clock yields (see Section 5.7.3, page 149).
3. The **minimum timepoint**, which the static member function `min()` of class `time_point` yields for each clock.
4. The **maximum timepoint**, which the static member function `max()` of class `time_point` yields for each clock.

For example, the following program assigns these timepoints to `tp` and prints them converted into a calendar notation:

```
// util/chrono1.cpp

#include <chrono>
#include <ctime>
#include <string>
#include <iostream>

std::string asString (const std::chrono::system_clock::time_point& tp)
{
    // convert to system time:
    std::time_t t = std::chrono::system_clock::to_time_t(tp);
    std::string ts = std::ctime(&t);        // convert to calendar time
    ts.resize(ts.size()-1);                 // skip trailing newline
    return ts;
}

int main()
{
```

```
    // print the epoch of this system clock:
    std::chrono::system_clock::time_point tp;
    std::cout << "epoch: " << asString(tp) << std::endl;

    // print current time:
    tp = std::chrono::system_clock::now();
    std::cout << "now:   " << asString(tp) << std::endl;

    // print minimum time of this system clock:
    tp = std::chrono::system_clock::time_point::min();
    std::cout << "min:   " << asString(tp) << std::endl;

    // print maximum time of this system clock:
    tp = std::chrono::system_clock::time_point::max();
    std::cout << "max:   " << asString(tp) << std::endl;
}
```

After including `<chrono>`, we first declare a convenience function `asString()`, which converts a timepoint of the system clock into the corresponding calendar time. With

```
    std::time_t t = std::chrono::system_clock::to_time_t(tp);
```

we use the static convenience function `to_time_t()`, which converts a timepoint into an object of the traditional time type of C and POSIX, type `time_t`, which usually represents the number of seconds since the UNIX epoch, January 1, 1970 (see Section 5.7.4, page 157). Then,

```
    std::string ts = std::ctime(&t);
```

uses `ctime()` to convert this into a calendar notation, for which

```
    ts.resize(ts.size()-1);
```

removes the trailing newline character.

Note that `ctime()` takes the local time zone into account, which has consequences we will discuss shortly. Note also that this convenience function probably will work only for `system_clocks`, the only clocks that provide an interface for conversions to and from `time_t`. For other clocks, such an interface might also work but is not portable, because the other clocks are not required to have epoch of the system time as their internal epoch.

Note also that the output format for timepoints might better get localized by using the `time_put` facet. See Section 16.4.3, page 884, for details, and page 886 for an example.

Inside `main()`, the type of `tp`, declared as

```
    std::chrono::system_clock::time_point
```

is equivalent to:[30]

```
    std::chrono::time_point<std::chrono::system_clock>
```

---

[30] According to the standard, a `system_clock::time_point` could also be identical to `time_point<C2,system_clock::duration>`, where C2 is a different clock but has the same epoch as `system_clock`.

Thus, `tp` is declared as the timepoint of the `system_clock`. Having the clock as template argument ensures that only timepoint arithmetic with the same clock (epoch) is possible.

The program might have the following output:

```
epoch: Thu Jan  1 01:00:00 1970
now:   Sun Jul 24 19:40:46 2011
min:   Sat Mar  5 18:27:38 1904
max:   Mon Oct 29 07:32:22 2035
```

Thus, the default constructor, which yields the epoch, creates a timepoint, which `asString()` converts into

```
Thu Jan  1 01:00:00 1970
```

Note that it's 1 o'clock rather than midnight. This may look a bit surprising, but remember that the conversion to the calendar time with `ctime()` inside `asString()` takes the time zone into account. Thus, the UNIX epoch used here — which, again, is not always guaranteed to be the epoch of the system time — started at 00:00 in Greenwich, UK. In my time zone, Germany, it was 1 a.m. at that moment, so in my time zone the epoch started at 1 a.m. on January 1, 1970. Accordingly, if you start this program, your output is probably different, according to your time zone, even if your system uses the same epoch in its system clock.

To have the universal time (UTC) instead, you should use the following conversion rather than calling `ctime()`, which is a shortcut for `asctime(localtime(...))` (see Section 5.7.4, page 157):

```
std::string ts = std::asctime(gmtime(&t));
```

In that case, the output of the program would be:

```
epoch: Thu Jan  1 00:00:00 1970
now:   Sun Jul 24 17:40:46 2011
min:   Sat Mar  5 17:27:38 1904
max:   Mon Oct 29 06:32:22 2035
```

Yes, here, the difference is 2 hours for `now()`, because this timepoint is when summertime is used, which leads to a 2-hour difference to UTC in Germany.

In general, `time_point` objects have only one member, the duration, which is relative to the epoch of the associated clock. The timepoint value can be requested by `time_since_epoch()`. For timepoint arithmetic, any useful combination of a timepoint and another timepoint or duration is provided (see Table 5.24).

Although the interface uses class `ratio` (see Section 5.6, page 140), which ensures that overflows by the duration units yield a compile-time error, overflows on the duration values are possible. Consider the following example:

```
// util/chrono2.cpp

#include <chrono>
#include <ctime>
#include <iostream>
#include <string>
using namespace std;
```

Operation	Yields	Effect
timepoint t	*timepoint*	Default constructor; creates a timepoint representing the epoch
timepoint t(*tp2*)	*timepoint*	Creates a timepoint equivalent to *tp2* (the duration unit might be finer grained)
timepoint t(*d*)	*timepoint*	Creates a timepoint having duration *d* after the epoch
time_point_cast<*C*,*D*>(*tp*)	*timepoint*	Converts *tp* into a timepoint with clock *C* and duration *D* (which might be more coarse grained)
tp += *d*	*timepoint*	Adds duration *d* to the current timepoint *tp*
tp -= *d*	*timepoint*	Subtracts duration *d* from the current timepoint *tp*
tp + *d*	*timepoint*	Returns a new timepoint of *tp* with duration *d* added
d + *tp*	*timepoint*	Returns a new timepoint of *tp* with duration *d* added
tp - *d*	*timepoint*	Returns a new timepoint of *tp* with duration *d* subtracted
tp1 - *tp2*	*duration*	Returns the duration between timepoints *tp1* and *tp2*
tp1 == *tp2*	bool	Returns whether timepoint *tp1* is equal to timepoint *tp2*
tp1 != *tp2*	bool	Returns whether timepoint *tp1* differs from timepoint *tp2*
tp1 < *tp2*	bool	Returns whether timepoint *tp1* is before timepoint *tp2*
tp1 <= *tp2*	bool	Returns whether timepoint *tp1* is not after timepoint *tp2*
tp1 > *tp2*	bool	Returns whether timepoint *tp1* is after timepoint *tp2*
tp1 >= *tp2*	bool	Returns whether timepoint *tp1* is not before timepoint *tp2*
tp.time_since_epoch()	*duration*	Returns the duration between the epoch and timepoint *tp*
timepoint::min()	*timepoint*	Returns the first possible timepoint of type *timepoint*
timepoint::max()	*timepoint*	Returns the last possible timepoint of type *timepoint*

Table 5.24. Operations of time_points

```
string asString (const chrono::system_clock::time_point& tp)
{
    time_t t = chrono::system_clock::to_time_t(tp);  // convert to system time
    string ts = ctime(&t);                           // convert to calendar time
    ts.resize(ts.size()-1);                          // skip trailing newline
    return ts;
}

int main()
{
    // define type for durations that represent day(s):
    typedef chrono::duration<int,ratio<3600*24>> Days;

    // process the epoch of this system clock
    chrono::time_point<chrono::system_clock> tp;
    cout << "epoch:    " << asString(tp) << endl;

    // add one day, 23 hours, and 55 minutes
    tp += Days(1) + chrono::hours(23) + chrono::minutes(55);
    cout << "later:    " << asString(tp) << endl;

    // process difference from epoch in minutes and days:
    auto diff = tp - chrono::system_clock::time_point();
    cout << "diff:     "
         << chrono::duration_cast<chrono::minutes>(diff).count()
         << " minute(s)" << endl;
    Days days = chrono::duration_cast<Days>(diff);
    cout << "diff:     " << days.count() << " day(s)" << endl;

    // subtract one year (hoping it is valid and not a leap year)
    tp -= chrono::hours(24*365);
    cout << "-1 year:  " << asString(tp) << endl;

    // subtract 50 years (hoping it is valid and ignoring leap years)
    tp -= chrono::duration<int,ratio<3600*24*365>>(50);
    cout << "-50 years: " << asString(tp) << endl;

    // subtract 50 years (hoping it is valid and ignoring leap years)
    tp -= chrono::duration<int,ratio<3600*24*365>>(50);
    cout << "-50 years: " << asString(tp) << endl;
}
```

First, expressions, such as

```
tp = tp + Days(1) + chrono::hours(23) + chrono::minutes(55);
```

or

```
tp -= chrono::hours(24*365);
```

allow adjusting timepoints by using timepoint arithmetic.

Because the precision of the system clock usually is better than minutes and days, you have to explicitly cast the difference between two timepoints to become days:

```
auto diff = tp - chrono::system_clock::time_point();
Days days = chrono::duration_cast<Days>(diff);
```

Note, however, that these operation do not check whether a combination performs an overflow. On my system, the output of the program is as follows:

```
epoch:      Thu Jan  1 01:00:00 1970
later:      Sat Jan  3 00:55:00 1970
diff:       2875 minute(s)
diff:       1 day(s)
-1 year:    Fri Jan  3 00:55:00 1969
-50 years:  Thu Jan 16 00:55:00 1919
-50 years:  Sat Mar  5 07:23:16 2005
```

You can see the following:

- The cast uses `static_cast<>` for the destination unit, which for ordinary integral unit types means that values are truncated instead of rounded. For this reason, a duration of 47 hours and 55 minutes converts into 1 day.

- Subtracting 50 years of 365 days does not take leap years into account, so the resulting day is January 16 instead of January 3.

- When deducting another 50 years the timepoint goes below the minimum timepoint, which is March 5, 1904 on my system (see Section 5.7.3, page 152), so the result is the year 2005. No error processing is required by the C++ standard library in this case.

This demonstrates that chrono is a duration and a timepoint but not a date/time library. You can compute with durations and timepoints but still have to take epoch, minimum and maximum timepoints, leap years, and leap seconds into account.

5.7.4 Date and Time Functions by C and POSIX

The C++ standard library also provides the standard C and POSIX interfaces to deal with date and time. In `<ctime>`, the macros, types, and functions of `<time.h>` are available in namespace `std`. The types and functions are listed in Table 5.25. In addition, the macro `CLOCKS_PER_SEC` defines the unit type of `clock()` (which returns the elapsed CPU time in $\frac{1}{CLOCKS\_PER\_SEC}$ seconds). See Section 16.4.3, page 884, for some more details and examples using these time functions and types.

Identifier	Meaning
clock_t	Type of numeric values of elapsed CPU time returned by clock()
time_t	Type of numeric values representing timepoints
struct tm	Type of "broken down" calendar time
clock()	Yields the elapsed CPU time in $\frac{1}{CLOCKS\_PER\_SEC}$ seconds
time()	Yields the current time as numeric value
difftime()	Yields the difference of two time_t in seconds as double
localtime()	Converts a time_t into a struct tm taking time zone into account
gmtime()	Converts a time_t into a struct tm not taking time zone into account
asctime()	Converts a struct tm into a standard calendar time string
strftime()	Converts a struct tm into a user-defined calendar time string
ctime()	Converts a time_t into a standard calendar time string taking time zone into account (shortcut for asctime(localtime(t)))
mktime()	Converts a struct tm into a time_t and queries weekday and day of the year

Table 5.25. Definitions in <ctime>

Note that time_t usually is just the number of seconds since the UNIX epoch, which is January 1, 1970. However, according to the C and C++ standard, this is not guaranteed.

Conversions between Timepoints and Calendar Time

The convenience function to transfer a timepoint to a calendar time string was already discussed in Section 5.7.3, page 153. Here is a header file that also allows converting calendar times into timepoints:

```
// util/timepoint.hpp

#include <chrono>
#include <ctime>
#include <string>

// convert timepoint of system clock to calendar time string
inline
std::string asString (const std::chrono::system_clock::time_point& tp)
{
    // convert to system time:
    std::time_t t = std::chrono::system_clock::to_time_t(tp);
    std::string ts = ctime(&t);     // convert to calendar time
    ts.resize(ts.size()-1);         // skip trailing newline
    return ts;
}
```

```
// convert calendar time to timepoint of system clock
inline
std::chrono::system_clock::time_point
makeTimePoint (int year, int mon, int day,
               int hour, int min, int sec=0)
{
    struct std::tm t;
    t.tm_sec = sec;        // second of minute (0 .. 59 and 60 for leap seconds)
    t.tm_min = min;        // minute of hour (0 .. 59)
    t.tm_hour = hour;      // hour of day (0 .. 23)
    t.tm_mday = day;       // day of month (0 .. 31)
    t.tm_mon = mon-1;      // month of year (0 .. 11)
    t.tm_year = year-1900; // year since 1900
    t.tm_isdst = -1;       // determine whether daylight saving time
    std::time_t tt = std::mktime(&t);
    if (tt == -1) {
        throw "no valid system time";
    }
    return std::chrono::system_clock::from_time_t(tt);
}
```

The following program demonstrates these convenience functions:

```
// util/timepoint1.cpp

#include <chrono>
#include <iostream>
#include "timepoint.hpp"

int main()
{
    auto tp1 = makeTimePoint(2010,01,01,00,00);
    std::cout << asString(tp1) << std::endl;

    auto tp2 = makeTimePoint(2011,05,23,13,44);
    std::cout << asString(tp2) << std::endl;
}
```

The program has the following output:

```
Fri Jan  1 00:00:00 2010
Mon May 23 13:44:00 2011
```

Note again that both makeTimePoint() and asString() take the local time zone into account. For this reason, the date passed to makeTimePoint() matches the output with asString(). Also, it doesn't matter whether daylight saving time is used (passing a negative value to t.tm_isdst in `makeTimePoint()` causes `mktime()` to attempt to determine whether daylight saving time is in effect for the specified time).

Again, to let `asString()` use the universal time UTC instead, use `asctime(gmtime(...))` rather than `ctime(...)`. For `mktime()`, there is no specified way to use UTC, so `makeTimePoint()` always takes the current time zone into account.

Section 16.4.3, page 884, demonstrates how to use locales to internationalize the reading and writing of time data.

5.7.5 Blocking with Timers

Durations and timepoints can be used to block threads or programs (i.e., the main thread). These blocks can be conditionless or can be used to specify a maximum duration when waiting for a lock, a condition variable, or another thread to end (see Chapter 18):

- `sleep_for()` and `sleep_until()` are provided by `this_thread` to block threads (see Section 18.3.7, page 981).
- `try_lock_for()` and `try_lock_until()` are provided to specify a maximum interval when waiting for a mutex (see Section 18.5.1, page 994).
- `wait_for()` and `wait_until()` are provided to specify a maximum interval when waiting for a condition variable or a future (see Section 18.1.1, page 953 or Section 18.6.4, page 1010).

All the blocking functions that end with ..._for() use a duration, whereas all functions that end with ..._until() use a timepoint as argument. For example,

```
this_thread::sleep_for(chrono::seconds(10));
```

blocks the current thread, which might be the main thread, for 10 seconds, whereas

```
this_thread::sleep_until(chrono::system_clock::now()
                         + chrono::seconds(10));
```

blocks the current thread until the system clock has reached a timepoint 10 seconds later than now.

Although these calls look the same, they are not! For all ..._until() functions, where you pass a timepoint, time adjustments might have an effect. If, during the 10 seconds after calling `sleep_until()`, the system clock gets adjusted, the timeout will be adjusted accordingly. If, for example, we wind the system clock back 1 hour, the program will block for 60 minutes and 10 seconds. If, for example, we adjust the clock forward for more than 10 seconds, the timer will end immediately.

If you use a ..._for() function, such as `sleep_for()`, where you pass a duration, or if you use the `steady_clock`, adjustments of the system clock *usually* will have no effect on the duration of timers. However, on hardware where a steady clock is not available, and thus the platform gives no chance to count seconds independently of a possibly adjusted system time, time adjustments can also impact the ..._for() functions.

All these timers do not guarantee to be exact. For any timer, there will be a delay because the system only periodically checks for expired timers, and the handling of timers and interrupts takes some time. Thus, durations of timers will take their specified time plus a period that depends on the quality of implementation and the current situation.

5.8   Header Files `<cstddef>`, `<cstdlib>`, and `<cstring>`

The following header files compatible with C are often used in C++ programs: `<cstddef>`, `<cstdlib>`, and `<cstring>`. They are the C++ versions of the C header files `<stddef.h>`, `<stdlib.h>`, and `<string.h>` and they define some common constants, macros, types, and functions.

5.8.1   Definitions in `<cstddef>`

Identifier	Meaning
NULL	Pointer value for "not defined" or "no value"
nullptr_t	Type of `nullptr` (since C++11)
size_t	Unsigned type for size units, such as number of elements
ptrdiff_t	Signed type for differences of pointer
max_align_t	Type with maximum alignment in all contexts (since C++11)
offsetof(*type*, *mem*)	Offset of a member *mem* in a structure or union *type*

Table 5.26. Definitions in `<cstddef>`

Table 5.26 shows the definitions of the `<cstddef>` header file. Before C++11, NULL was often used to indicate that a pointer points to nothing. Since C++11, `nullptr` is provided for this semantics (see Section 3.1.1, page 14).

Note that NULL in C++ is guaranteed to be simply the value 0 (either as an `int` or as a `long`). In C, NULL is often defined as `(void*)0`. However, this is incorrect in C++, which requires that the type of NULL be an integer type. Otherwise, you could not assign NULL to a pointer. This is because in C++ there is no automatic conversion from `void*` to any other type. Since C++11, you should use `nullptr` instead (see Section 3.1.1, page 14).[31] Note also that NULL is also defined in the header files `<cstdio>`, `<cstdlib>`, `<cstring>`, `<ctime>`, `<cwchar>`, and `<clocale>`.

---

[31] Due to the mess with the type of NULL, several people and style guides recommend not using NULL in C++. Instead, 0 or a special user-defined constant, such as NIL, might work better. Fortunately, this problem is solved with `nullptr`.

5.8.2   Definitions in `<cstdlib>`

Table 5.27 shows the most important definitions of the `<cstdlib>` header file. The two constants
`EXIT_SUCCESS` and `EXIT_FAILURE` are defined as arguments for `exit()` and can also be used as a
return value in `main()`.

Definition	Meaning
`EXIT_SUCCESS`	Indicates a normal end of the program
`EXIT_FAILURE`	Indicates an abnormal end of the program
`exit (int` *status*`)`	Exit program (cleans up static objects)
`quick_exit (int` *status*`)`	Exit program with cleanup according to `at_quick_exit()` (since C++11)
`_Exit (int` *status*`)`	Exit program with no cleanup (since C++11)
`abort()`	Abort program (might force a crash on some systems)
`atexit (void (*`*func*`)())`	Call *func* on exit
`at_quick_exit (void (*`*func*`)())`	Call *func* on `quick_exit()` (since C++11)

Table 5.27. Definitions in `<cstdlib>`

The functions that are registered by `atexit()` are called at normal program termination in reverse
order of their registration. It doesn't matter whether the program exits due to a call of `exit()` or the
end of `main()`. No arguments are passed.

The `exit()` and `abort()` functions are provided to terminate a program in any function without
going back to `main()`:

- `exit()` destroys all static objects, flushes all buffers, closes all I/O channels, and terminates
  the program, including calling `atexit()` functions. If functions passed to `atexit()` throw
  exceptions, `terminate()` is called.

- `abort()` terminates a program immediately with no cleanup.

Neither of these functions destroys local objects, because no stack unwinding occurs. To ensure
that the destructors of all local objects are called, you should use exceptions or the ordinary return
mechanism to return to and exit `main()`.

Since C++11, the `quick_exit()` semantics provided does not destroy objects but calls functions registered by calls to `at_quick_exit()` in the reverse order of their registration and calls
`_Exit()`, which terminates the program then without any destruction or cleanup.[32] This means that
`quick_exit()` and `_Exit()` do not flush standard file buffers (standard output and error output).

The usual way for C++ to abort programs — which is an unexpected end in contrast to an expected end signaling an error — is to call `std::terminate()`, which by default calls `abort()`.
This is done, for example, if a destructor or a function declared with `noexcept` (see Section 3.1.7,
page 24) throws.

---

[32] This feature was introduced to avoid the risk that detached threads access global/static objects (see Section 18.2.1, page 967).

5.8.3 Definitions in `<cstring>`

Table 5.28 shows the most important definitions of the `<cstring>` header file: the low-level functions to set, copy, and move memory. One application of these functions is character traits (see Section 16.1.4, page 855).

Definition	Meaning
`memchr (const void* ` *ptr*`, int ` *c*`, size_t ` *len*`)`	Finds character *c* in first *len* bytes of *ptr*
`memcmp (const void* ` *ptr1*`, const void* ` *ptr2*`,` `        size_t ` *len*`)`	Compares *len* bytes of *ptr1* and *ptr2*
`memcpy (void* ` *toPtr*`, const void* ` *fromPtr*`,` `        size_t ` *len*`)`	Copies *len* bytes of *fromPtr* to *toPtr*
`memmove (void* ` *toPtr*`, const void* ` *fromPtr*`,` `         size_t ` *len*`)`	Copies *len* bytes of *fromPtr* to *toPtr* (areas may overlap)
`memset (void* ` *ptr*`, int ` *c*`, size_t ` *len*`)`	Assigns character *c* to first *len* bytes of *ptr*

Table 5.28. Definitions in `<cstring>`

Chapter 6

The Standard Template Library

The heart of the C++ standard library — the part that influenced its overall architecture — is the *standard template library* (*STL*). The STL is a generic library that provides solutions to managing collections of data with modern and efficient algorithms. It allows programmers to benefit from innovations in the area of data structures and algorithms without needing to learn how they work.

From the programmer's point of view, the STL provides a bunch of collection classes that meet various needs, together with several algorithms that operate on them. All components of the STL are templates, so they can be used for arbitrary element types. But the STL does even more: It provides a framework for supplying other collection classes or algorithms for which existing collection classes and algorithms work. All in all, the STL gives C++ a new level of abstraction. Forget programming dynamic arrays, linked lists, binary trees, or hash tables; forget programming different search algorithms. To use the appropriate kind of collection, you simply define the appropriate container and call the corresponding member functions and algorithms to process the data.

The STL's flexibility, however, has a price, chief of which is that it is not self-explanatory. Therefore, the subject of the STL fills several chapters in this book. This chapter introduces the general concept of the STL and explains the programming techniques needed to use it. The first examples show how to use the STL and what to consider while doing so. Chapters 7 through 11 discuss the components of the STL (containers, iterators, function objects, and algorithms) in detail and present several more examples.

6.1 STL Components

The STL is based on the cooperation of various well-structured components, key of which are containers, iterators, and algorithms:

- **Containers** are used to manage collections of objects of a certain kind. Every kind of container has its own advantages and disadvantages, so having different container types reflects different requirements for collections in programs. The containers may be implemented as arrays or as linked lists, or they may have a special key for every element.

- **Iterators** are used to step through the elements of collections of objects. These collections may be containers or subsets of containers. The major advantage of iterators is that they offer a small but common interface for any arbitrary container type. For example, one operation of this interface lets the iterator step to the next element in the collection. This is done independently of the internal structure of the collection. Regardless of whether the collection is an array, a tree, or a hash table, it works. This is because every container class provides its own iterator type that simply "does the right thing" because it knows the internal structure of its container.

  The interface for iterators is almost the same as for ordinary pointers. To increment an iterator, you call operator ++. To access the value of an iterator, you use operator *. So, you might consider an iterator a kind of a smart pointer that translates the call "go to the next element" into whatever is appropriate.

- **Algorithms** are used to process the elements of collections. For example, algorithms can search, sort, modify, or simply use the elements for various purposes. Algorithms use iterators. Thus, because the iterator interface for iterators is common for all container types, an algorithm has to be written only once to work with arbitrary containers.

  To give algorithms more flexibility, you can supply certain auxiliary functions called by the algorithms. Thus, you can use a general algorithm to suit your needs even if that need is very special or complex. For example, you can provide your own search criterion or a special operation to combine elements. Especially since C++11, with the introduction of lambdas, you can easily specify almost any kind of functionality while running over the elements of a container.

The concept of the STL is based on a separation of data and operations. The data is managed by container classes, and the operations are defined by configurable algorithms. Iterators are the glue between these two components. They let any algorithm interact with any container (Figure 6.1).

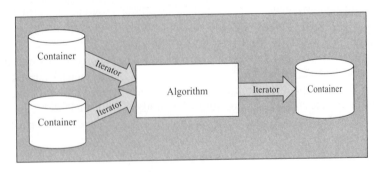

Figure 6.1. STL Components

In a way, the STL concept contradicts the original idea of object-oriented programming: The STL *separates* data and algorithms rather than combining them. However, the reason for doing so is very important. In principle, you can combine every kind of container with every kind of algorithm, so the result is a very flexible but still rather small framework.

One fundamental aspect of the STL is that all components work with arbitrary types. As the name "standard template library" indicates, all components are templates for any type, provided that type is able to perform the required operations. Thus, the STL is a good example of the concept of *generic programming*. Containers and algorithms are generic for arbitrary types and classes, respectively.

The STL provides even more generic components. By using certain *adapters* and *function objects* (or *functors*), you can supplement, constrain, or configure the algorithms and the interfaces for special needs. However, I'm jumping the gun. First, I want to explain the concept step-by-step by using examples. This is probably the best way to understand and become familiar with the STL.

6.2   Containers

Container classes, or *containers* for short, manage a collection of elements. To meet different needs, the STL provides different kinds of containers, as shown in Figure 6.2.

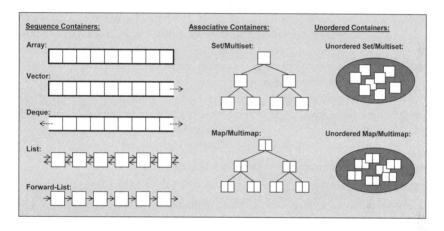

Figure 6.2. STL Container Types

There are three general kinds of containers:

1. **Sequence containers** are *ordered collections* in which every element has a certain position. This position depends on the time and place of the insertion, but it is independent of the value of the element. For example, if you put six elements into an ordered collection by appending each element at the end of the collection, these elements are in the exact order in which you put them. The STL contains five predefined sequence container classes: `array`, `vector`, `deque`, `list`, and `forward_list`.[1]

2. **Associative containers** are *sorted collections* in which the position of an element depends on its value (or key, if it's a key/value pair) due to a certain sorting criterion. If you put six elements into a collection, their value determines their order. The order of insertion doesn't matter. The STL contains four predefined associative container classes: `set`, `multiset`, `map`, and `multimap`.

3. **Unordered (associative) containers** are *unordered collections* in which the position of an element doesn't matter. The only important question is whether a specific element is in such a collection. Neither the order of insertion nor the value of the inserted element has an influ-

---

[1] Class `array` was added with TR1; `forward_list` was added with C++11.

ence on the position of the element, and the position might change over the lifetime of the container. Thus, if you put six elements into a collection, their order is undefined and might change over time. The STL contains four predefined unordered container classes: `unordered_set`, `unordered_multiset`, `unordered_map`, and `unordered_multimap`.

Unordered containers were introduced with TR1 and created a bit of confusion in container terminology. Officially, unordered containers are categorized as "unordered associative containers." For this reason, it's a bit unclear, what is meant by "associative container": Is it a general term of (ordered) associative containers and unordered associative containers, or is it the counterpart of unordered containers? The answer often depends on the context. Throughout this book, I mean the "old" sorted associative containers when I use the term "associative containers" and use the term "unordered containers" without "associative" in the middle.

The three container categories introduced here are just logical categories according to the way the order of elements is defined. According to this point of view, an associative container can be considered a special kind of sequence container because sorted collections have the additional ability to be ordered according to a sorting criterion. You might expect this, especially if you have used other libraries of collection classes, such as those in Smalltalk or the NIHCL,[2] in which sorted collections are derived from ordered collections. However, the STL collection types are completely distinct from one another and have very different implementations that are not derived from one another. As we will see:

- Sequence containers are usually implemented as arrays or linked lists.
- Associative containers are usually implemented as binary trees.
- Unordered containers are usually implemented as hash tables.

Strictly speaking, the particular implementation of any container is not defined by the C++ standard library. However, the behavior and complexity specified by the standard do not leave much room for variation. So, in practice, the implementations differ only in minor details.

When choosing the right container, abilities other than the order of elements might be taken into account. In fact, the automatic sorting of elements in associative containers does *not* mean that those containers are especially designed for sorting elements. You can also sort the elements of a sequence container. The key advantage of automatic sorting is better performance when you search elements. In particular, you can always use a binary search, which results in logarithmic complexity rather than linear complexity. For example, this means that for a search in a collection of 1,000 elements, you need, on average, only 10 instead of 500 comparisons (see Section 2.2, page 10). Thus, automatic sorting is only a (useful) "side effect" of the implementation of an associative container, designed to enable better performance.

The following subsections discuss the container classes in detail: how containers are typically implemented and the benefits and drawbacks this introduces. Chapter 7 covers the exact behavior of the container classes, describing their common and individual abilities and member functions in detail. Section 7.12, page 392, discusses in detail when to use which container.

---

[2] The National Institutes of Health's Class Library was one of the first class libraries in C++.

6.2.1   Sequence Containers

The following sequence containers are predefined in the STL:
- Arrays (a class called `array`)
- Vectors
- Deques
- Lists (singly and doubly linked)

We start with the discussion of vectors because `arrays` came later, with TR1, into the C++ standard and have some special properties that are not common for STL containers in general.

Vectors

A vector manages its elements in a dynamic array. It enables random access, which means that you can access each element directly with the corresponding index. Appending and removing elements at the end of the array is very fast.[3] However, inserting an element in the middle or at the beginning of the array takes time because all the following elements have to be moved to make room for it while maintaining the order.

The following example defines a vector for integer values, inserts six elements, and prints the elements of the vector:

```
// stl/vector1.cpp

#include <vector>
#include <iostream>
using namespace std;

int main()
{
    vector<int> coll;       // vector container for integer elements

    // append elements with values 1 to 6
    for (int i=1; i<=6; ++i) {
        coll.push_back(i);
    }

    // print all elements followed by a space
    for (int i=0; i<coll.size(); ++i) {
        cout << coll[i] << ' ';
    }
    cout << endl;
}
```

---

[3] Strictly speaking, appending elements is *amortized* very fast. An individual append may be slow when a vector has to reallocate new memory and to copy existing elements into the new memory. However, because such reallocations are rather rare, the operation is very fast in the long term. See Section 2.2, page 10, for a discussion of complexity.

The header file for vectors is included with

```
#include <vector>
```

The following declaration creates a vector for elements of type `int`:

```
vector<int> coll;
```

The vector is not initialized by any value, so the default constructor creates it as an empty collection. The `push_back()` function appends an element to the container:

```
coll.push_back(i);
```

This member function is provided for all sequence containers, where appending an element is possible and reasonably fast.

The `size()` member function returns the number of elements of a container:

```
for (int i=0; i<coll.size(); ++i) {
    ...
}
```

`size()` is provided for any container class except singly linked lists (class `forward_list`).

By using the subscript operator `[ ]`, you can access a single element of a vector:

```
cout << coll[i] << ' ';
```

Here, the elements are written to the standard output, so the output of the whole program is as follows:

```
1 2 3 4 5 6
```

Deques

The term *deque* (it rhymes with "check"[4]) is an abbreviation for "double-ended queue." It is a dynamic array that is implemented so that it can grow in both directions. Thus, inserting elements at the end *and* at the beginning is fast. However, inserting elements in the middle takes time because elements must be moved.

The following example declares a deque for floating-point values, inserts elements from 1.1 to 6.6 at the front of the container, and prints all elements of the deque:

```
// stl/deque1.cpp

#include <deque>
#include <iostream>
using namespace std;

int main()
{
    deque<float> coll;       // deque container for floating-point elements
```

---

[4] It is only a mere accident that "deque" also sounds like "hack" :-) .

```
    // insert elements from 1.1 to 6.6 each at the front
    for (int i=1; i<=6; ++i) {
        coll.push_front(i*1.1);        // insert at the front
    }

    // print all elements followed by a space
    for (int i=0; i<coll.size(); ++i) {
        cout << coll[i] << ' ';
    }
    cout << endl;
}
```

In this example, the header file for deques is included with

```
    #include <deque>
```

The following declaration creates an empty collection of floating-point values:

```
    deque<float> coll;
```

Here, the `push_front()` member function is used to insert elements:

```
    coll.push_front(i*1.1);
```

`push_front()` inserts an element at the front of the collection. This kind of insertion results in a reverse order of the elements because each element gets inserted in front of the previous inserted elements. Thus, the output of the program is as follows:

```
    6.6 5.5 4.4 3.3 2.2 1.1
```

You could also insert elements in a deque by using the `push_back()` member function. The `push_front()` function, however, is not provided for vectors, because it would have a bad runtime for vectors (if you insert an element at the front of a vector, all elements have to be moved). Usually, the STL containers provide only those special member functions that in general have "good" performance, where "good" normally means constant or logarithmic complexity. This prevents a programmer from calling a function that might cause bad performance.

Nevertheless, it *is* possible to insert an element at the beginning of a vector — as it is possible to insert an element in the middle of both vectors and deques — by using a general insert function we will come to later.

Arrays

An array (an object of class `array`)[5] manages its elements in an array of fixed size (sometimes called a "static array" or "C array"). Thus, you can't change the number of elements but only their values. Consequently, you have to specify its size at creation time. An array also enables random access, which means that you can access each element directly with the corresponding index.

The following example defines an array for string values:

---

[5] Class `array<>` was introduced with TR1.

```cpp
// stl/array1.cpp

#include <array>
#include <string>
#include <iostream>
using namespace std;

int main()
{
    // array container of 5 string elements:
    array<string,5> coll = { "hello", "world" };

    // print each element with its index on a line
    for (int i=0; i<coll.size(); ++i) {
        cout << i << ": " << coll[i] << endl;
    }
}
```

The header file for arrays is included with

```cpp
#include <array>
```

The following declaration creates an array for five elements of type `string`:

```cpp
array<string,5> coll
```

By default, these elements are initialized with the default constructor of the element's type. This means that for fundamental data types, the initial value is undefined.

However, in this program, an initializer list (see Section 3.1.3, page 15) is used, which allows initializing class objects at creation time by a list of values. Since C++11, such a way of initialization is provided by every container, so we could also use it for vectors and deques. In that case, for fundamental data types *zero initialization* is used, which means that fundamental data types are guaranteed to be initialized with 0 (see Section 3.2.1, page 37).

Here, by using `size()` and the subscript operator `[]`, all elements are written with their index line-by-line to the standard output. The output of the whole program is as follows:

```
0: hello
1: world
2:
3:
4:
```

As you can see, the program outputs five lines, because we have an array with five strings defined. According to the initializer list, the first two elements were initialized with "hello" and "world", and the remaining elements have their default value, which is the empty string.

Note that the number of elements is a part of the type of an array. Thus, `array<int,5>` and `array<int,10>` are two different types, and you can't assign or compare them as a whole.

Lists

Historically, we had only one list class in C++11. However, since C++11, two different list containers are provided by the STL: class list<> and class forward_list<>. Thus, the term *list* might refer to the specific class or be a general term for both list classes. However, to some extent, a forward list is just a restricted list and, in practice, this difference is not so important. So, when I use the term *list* I usually mean class list<>, which nevertheless often implies that abilities also apply to class forward_list<>. For specifics of class forward_list<>, I use the term *forward list*. So, this subsection discusses "ordinary" lists, which have been part of the STL since the beginning.

A list<> is implemented as a doubly linked list of elements. This means each element in the list has its own segment of memory and refers to its predecessor and its successor.

Lists do not provide random access. For example, to access the tenth element, you must navigate the first nine elements by following the chain of their links. However, a step to the next or previous element is possible in constant time. Thus, the general access to an arbitrary element takes linear time because the average distance is proportional to the number of elements. This is a lot worse than the amortized constant time provided by vectors and deques.

The advantage of a list is that the insertion or removal of an element is fast at any position. Only the links must be changed. This implies that moving an element in the middle of a list is very fast compared to moving an element in a vector or a deque.

The following example creates an empty list of characters, inserts all characters from 'a' to 'z', and prints all elements:

```cpp
// stl/list1.cpp

#include <list>
#include <iostream>
using namespace std;

int main()
{
    list<char> coll;          // list container for character elements

    // append elements from 'a' to 'z'
    for (char c='a'; c<='z'; ++c) {
        coll.push_back(c);
    }

    // print all elements:
    // - use range-based for loop
    for (auto elem : coll) {
        cout << elem << ' ';
    }
    cout << endl;
}
```

As usual, the header file for lists, `<list>`, is used to define a collection of type `list` for character values:

```
list<char> coll;
```

To print all elements, a range-based `for` loop is used, which is available since C++11 and allows performing statements with each element (see Section 3.1.4, page 17). A direct element access by using operator `[]` is not provided for lists. This is because lists don't provide random access, and so an operator `[]` would have bad performance.

Inside the loop, `auto` is used to declare the type of the `coll` element currently being processed. Thus, the type of `elem` is automatically deduced as `char` because `coll` is a collection of `char`s (see Section 3.1.2, page 14, for details of type deduction with `auto`). Instead, you could also explicitly declare the type of `elem`:

```
for (char elem : coll) {
    ...
}
```

Note that `elem` is always a copy of the element currently processed. Thus, you can modify it, but this would have an effect only for the statements called for this element. Inside `coll`, nothing gets modified. To modify the elements in the passed collection, you have to declare `elem` to be a nonconstant reference:

```
for (auto& elem : coll) {
    ...      // any modification of elem modifies the current element in coll
}
```

As for function parameters, you should generally use a constant reference to avoid a copy operation. Thus, the following function template outputs all elements of a passed container:

```
template <typename T>
void printElements (const T& coll)
{
    for (const auto& elem : coll) {
        std::cout << elem << std::endl;
    }
}
```

Before C++11, you had to use iterators to access all elements. Iterators are introduced later, so you will find a corresponding example in Section 6.3, page 189.

However, another way to "print" all elements before C++11 (without using iterators) is to print and remove the first element while there are elements in the list:

```
// stl/list2.cpp

#include <list>
#include <iostream>
using namespace std;

int main()
{
```

```
list<char> coll;        // list container for character elements

// append elements from 'a' to 'z'
for (char c='a'; c<='z'; ++c) {
    coll.push_back(c);
}

// print all elements
// - while there are elements
// - print and remove the first element
while (! coll.empty()) {
    cout << coll.front() << ' ';
    coll.pop_front();
}
cout << endl;
}
```

The `empty()` member function returns whether the container has no elements. The loop continues as long as it returns `false` (that is, the container contains elements):

```
while (! coll.empty()) {
    ...
}
```

Inside the loop, the `front()` member function returns the first element:

```
cout << coll.front() << ' ';
```

The `pop_front()` function removes the first element:

```
coll.pop_front();
```

Note that `pop_front()` does not return the element it removed. Thus, you can't combine the previous two statements into one.

The output of the program depends on the character set in use. For the ASCII character set, it is as follows:[6]

```
a b c d e f g h i j k l m n o p q r s t u v w x y z
```

Forward Lists

Since C++11, the C++ standard library provides an additional list container: a forward list. A `forward_list<>` is implemented as a *singly* linked list of elements. As in an ordinary `list`, each element has its own segment of memory, but to save memory the element refers only to its successor.

---

[6] For other character sets, the output may contain characters that aren't letters, or it may even be empty (if `'z'` is not greater than `'a'`).

As a consequence, a forward list is in principle just a limited list, where all operations that move backward or that would cause a performance penalty are not supported. For this reason, member functions such as `push_back()` and even `size()` are not provided.

In practice, this limitation is even more awkward than it sounds. One problem is that you can't search for an element and then delete it or insert another element in front of it. The reason is that to delete an element, you have to be at the position of the preceding element, because that is the element that gets manipulated to get a new successor. As a consequence, forward lists provide special member functions, discussed in Section 7.6.2, page 305.

Here is a small example of forward lists:

```
// stl/forwardlist1.cpp

#include <forward_list>
#include <iostream>
using namespace std;

int main()
{
    // create forward-list container for some prime numbers
    forward_list<long> coll = { 2, 3, 5, 7, 11, 13, 17 };

    // resize two times
    // - note: poor performance
    coll.resize(9);
    coll.resize(10,99);

    // print all elements:
    for (auto elem : coll) {
        cout << elem << ' ';
    }
    cout << endl;
}
```

As usual, the header file for forward lists, `<forward_list>`, is used to be able to define a collection of type `forward_list` for long integer values, initialized by some prime numbers:

```
    forward_list<long> coll = { 2, 3, 5, 7, 11, 13, 17 };
```

Then `resize()` is used to change the number of elements. If the size grows, you can pass an additional parameter to specify the value of the new elements. Otherwise, the default value (zero for fundamental types) is used. Note that calling `resize()` is really an expensive operation here. It has linear complexity because to reach the end, you have to go element-by-element through the whole list. But this is one of the operations almost all sequence containers provide, ignoring possible bad performance (only `arrays` do not provide `resize()`, because their size is constant).

As for lists, we use a range-based `for` loop to print all elements. The output is as follows:

```
    2 3 5 7 11 13 17 0 0 99
```

6.2.2 Associative Containers

Associative containers sort their elements automatically according to a certain ordering criterion. The elements can be either values of any type or key/value pairs. For key/value pairs, each key, which might be of any type, maps to an associated value, which might be of any type. The criterion to sort the elements takes the form of a function that compares either the value or, if it's a key/value pair, the key. By default, the containers compare the elements or the keys with operator <. However, you can supply your own comparison function to define another ordering criterion.

Associative containers are typically implemented as binary trees. Thus, every element (every node) has one parent and two children. All ancestors to the left have lesser values; all ancestors to the right have greater values. The associative containers differ in the kinds of elements they support and how they handle duplicates.

The major advantage of associative containers is that finding an element with a specific value is rather fast because it has logarithmic complexity (in all sequence containers, you have linear complexity). Thus, when using associative containers, with 1,000 elements you have 10 instead of 500 comparisons on average. However, a drawback is that you can't modify values directly, because doing so would corrupt the automatic sorting of the elements.

The following associative containers are predefined in the STL:

- A **set** is a collection in which elements are sorted according to their own values. Each element may occur only once, so duplicates are not allowed.
- A **multiset** is the same as a set except that duplicates are allowed. Thus, a multiset may contain multiple elements that have the same value.
- A **map** contains elements that are key/value pairs. Each element has a key that is the basis for the sorting criterion and a value. Each key may occur only once, so duplicate keys are not allowed. A map can also be used as an *associative array*, an array that has an arbitrary index type (see Section 6.2.4, page 185, for details).
- A **multimap** is the same as a map except that duplicates are allowed. Thus, a multimap may contain multiple elements that have the same key. A multimap can also be used as *dictionary* (See Section 7.8.5, page 348, for an example).

All these associative container classes have an optional template argument for the sorting criterion. The default sorting criterion is the operator <. The sorting criterion is also used as the test for equivalence;[7] that is, two elements are duplicates if neither of their values/keys is less than the other.

You can consider a set as a special kind of map, in which the value is identical to the key. In fact, all these associative container types are usually implemented by using the same basic implementation of a binary tree.

Examples of Using Sets and Multisets

Here is a first example, using a multiset:

---

[7] Note that I use the term *equivalent* here, not *equal*, which usually implies using operator == for the element as a whole.

```cpp
// stl/multiset1.cpp

#include <set>
#include <string>
#include <iostream>
using namespace std;

int main()
{
    multiset<string> cities {
        "Braunschweig", "Hanover", "Frankfurt", "New York",
        "Chicago", "Toronto", "Paris", "Frankfurt"
    };

    // print each element:
    for (const auto& elem : cities) {
        cout << elem << "  ";
    }
    cout << endl;

    // insert additional values:
    cities.insert( {"London", "Munich", "Hanover", "Braunschweig"} );

    // print each element:
    for (const auto& elem : cities) {
        cout << elem << "  ";
    }
    cout << endl;
}
```

After declaring the set types in the header file `<set>`, we can declare `cities` being a multiset of strings:

```cpp
multiset<string> cities
```

With the declaration, a couple of elements are passed for initialization and later inserted using an initializer list (see Section 3.1.3, page 15). To print all the elements, we use a range-based `for` loop (see Section 3.1.4, page 17). Note that we declare the elements to be `const auto&`, which means that we derive the type of the elements from the container (see Section 3.1.2, page 14) and avoid having to create a copy for each element the body of the loop is called for.

Internally, all the elements are sorted, so the first output is as follows:

```
Braunschweig  Chicago  Frankfurt  Frankfurt  Hanover  New York
    Paris  Toronto
```

The second output is:

Braunschweig Braunschweig Chicago Frankfurt Frankfurt Hanover
Hanover London Munich New York Paris Toronto

As you can see, because we use a multiset rather than a set, duplicates are allowed. If we had declared a set instead of a multiset, each value would be printed only once. If we were to use an unordered multiset, the order of the elements would be undefined (see Section 6.2.3, page 182).

Examples of Using Maps and Multimaps

The following example demonstrates the use of maps and multimaps:

```
// stl/multimap1.cpp

#include <map>
#include <string>
#include <iostream>
using namespace std;

int main()
{
    multimap<int,string> coll;           // container for int/string values

    // insert some elements in arbitrary order
    // - a value with key 1 gets inserted twice
    coll = { {5,"tagged"},
             {2,"a"},
             {1,"this"},
             {4,"of"},
             {6,"strings"},
             {1,"is"},
             {3,"multimap"} };

    // print all element values
    // - element member second is the value
    for (auto elem : coll) {
        cout << elem.second << ' ';
    }
    cout << endl;
}
```

After including <map>, a map with elements that have an int as the key and a string as value gets declared:

```
    multimap<int,string> coll;
```

Because the elements of maps and multimaps are key/value pairs, the declaration, the insertion, and the access to elements are a bit different:

- First, to initialize (or assign or insert) elements, you have to pass key/value pairs, which is done here by assigning nested initializer lists. The inner lists define the key and the value of each element; the outer list groups all these elements. Thus, {5,"tagged"} specifies the first element inserted.

- When processing the elements, you again have to deal with key/value pairs. In fact, the type of an element is pair<const *key*,*value*> (type pair is introduced in Section 5.1.1, page 60). The key is constant because any modification of its value would break the order of the elements, which are automatically sorted by the container. Because pairs don't have an output operator, you can't print them as a whole. Instead, you must access the members of the pair structure, which are called first and second.

  Thus, the following expression yields the second part of the key/value pair, which is the value of the multimap element:

  ```
  elem.second
  ```

  Similarly, the following expression yields the first part of the key/value pair, which is the key of the multimap element:

  ```
  elem.first
  ```

As a result, the program has the following output:

```
this is a multimap of tagged strings
```

Before C++11, there was no clear guarantee for the order of equivalent elements (elements having an equal key). So, until C++11, the order of "this" and "is" might be the other way around. C++11 guarantees that newly inserted elements are inserted at the end of equivalent elements that multisets and multimaps already contain. In addition, the order of equivalent elements is guaranteed to remain stable if insert(), emplace(), or erase() is called.

Other Examples for Associative Containers

Section 6.2.4, page 185, gives an example for using a map, which can be used as a so-called *associative array*.

Section 7.7 discusses sets and multisets in detail, with additional examples. Section 7.8 discusses maps and multimaps in detail, with additional examples.

Multimaps can also be used as *dictionaries*. See Section 7.8.5, page 348, for an example.

6.2.3 Unordered Containers

In unordered containers, elements have no defined order. Thus, if you insert three elements, they might have any order when you iterate over all the elements in the container. If you insert a fourth element, the order of the elements previously inserted might change. The only important fact is that a specific element is *somewhere* in the container. Even when you have two containers with equal elements inside, the order might be different. Think of it as like a bag.

Unordered containers are typically implemented as a hash table (Figure 6.3). Thus, internally, the container is an array of linked lists. Using a *hash function*, the position of an element in the array gets processed. The goal is that each element has its own position so that you have fast access to

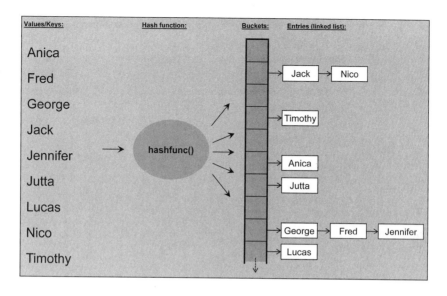

Figure 6.3. Unordered Containers Are Hash Tables

each element, provided that the hash function is fast. But because such a fast perfect hash function is not always possible or might require that the array consumes a huge amount of memory, multiple elements might have the same position. For this reason, the elements in the array are linked lists so that you can store more than one element at each array position.

The major advantage of unordered containers is that finding an element with a specific value is even faster than for associative containers. In fact, the use of unordered containers provides amortized constant complexity, provided that you have a good hash function. However, providing a good hash function is not easy (see Section 7.9.2, page 363), and you might need a lot of memory for the buckets.

According to associative containers, the following unordered containers are predefined in the STL:

- An **unordered set** is a collection of unordered elements, where each element may occur only once. Thus, duplicates are not allowed.

- An **unordered multiset** is the same as an unordered set except that duplicates are allowed. Thus, an unordered multiset may contain multiple elements that have the same value.

- An **unordered map** contains elements that are key/value pairs. Each key may occur only once, so duplicate keys are not allowed. An unordered map can also be used as an *associative array*, an array that has an arbitrary index type (see Section 6.2.4, page 185, for details).

- An **unordered multimap** is the same as an unordered map except that duplicates are allowed. Thus, an unordered multimap may contain multiple elements that have the same key. An unordered multimap can also be used as *dictionary* (see Section 7.9.7, page 383, for an example).

All these unordered container classes have a couple of optional template arguments to specify a hash function and an equivalence criterion. The equivalence criterion is used to find specific values and to identify duplicates. The default equivalence criterion is the operator ==.

You can consider an unordered set as a special kind of unordered map, in which the value is identical to the key. In fact, all these unordered container types are usually implemented by using the same basic implementation of a hash table.

Examples of Using Unordered Sets and Multisets

Here is a first example, using an unordered multiset of strings:

```cpp
// stl/unordmultiset1.cpp

#include <unordered_set>
#include <string>
#include <iostream>
using namespace std;

int main()
{
    unordered_multiset<string> cities {
        "Braunschweig", "Hanover", "Frankfurt", "New York",
        "Chicago", "Toronto", "Paris", "Frankfurt"
    };

    // print each element:
    for (const auto& elem : cities) {
        cout << elem << "  ";
    }
    cout << endl;

    // insert additional values:
    cities.insert( {"London", "Munich", "Hanover", "Braunschweig"} );

    // print each element:
    for (const auto& elem : cities) {
        cout << elem << "  ";
    }
    cout << endl;
}
```

After including the required header file

```cpp
#include <unordered_set>
```

we can declare and initialize an unordered set of strings:

```cpp
unordered_multiset<string> cities { ... };
```

Now, if we print all elements, the order might be different because the order is undefined. The only guarantee is that duplicates, which are possible because a *multi*set is used, are grouped together in the order of their insertion. Thus, a possible output might be:

```
Paris  Toronto  Chicago  New York  Frankfurt  Frankfurt  Hanover
    Braunschweig
```

Any insertion can change this order. In fact, any operation that causes rehashing can change this order. So, after inserting a couple more values, the output might be as follows:

```
London  Hanover  Hanover  Frankfurt  Frankfurt  New York  Chicago
    Munich  Braunschweig  Braunschweig  Toronto  Paris
```

What happens depends on the rehashing policy, which can be influenced in part by the programmer. For example, you can reserve enough room so that rehashing won't happen up to a specific number of elements. In addition, to ensure that you can delete elements while processing all elements, the standard guarantees that deleting elements does not cause a rehashing. But an insertion after a deletion might cause rehashing. For details, see Section 7.9, page 355.

In general, associative and unordered containers provide the same interface. Only declarations might differ, and unordered containers provide special member functions to influence the internal behavior or to inspect the current state. Thus, in the example presented here, only the header files and types differ from the corresponding example using an ordinary multiset, which was introduced in Section 6.2.2, page 177.

Again, before C++11, you needed iterators to access the elements. See Section 6.3.1, page 193, for an example.

Examples of Using Unordered Maps and Multimaps

The example presented for multimaps on page 179 also works for an unordered multimap if you replace `map` by `unordered_map` in the include directive and `multimap` by `unordered_multimap` in the declaration of the container:

```
#include <unordered_map>
...
unordered_multimap<int,string> coll;
...
```

The only difference is that the order of the elements is undefined. However, on most platforms, the elements will still be sorted because as a default hash function, the modulo operator is used. Thus, a sorted order is also a valid undefined order. However, that's not guaranteed, and if you add more elements, the order will be different.

Here is another example using an unordered map. In this case, we use an unordered map where the keys are strings and the values are doubles:

```
// stl/unordmap1.cpp

#include <unordered_map>
#include <string>
```

```
#include <iostream>
using namespace std;

int main()
{
    unordered_map<string,double> coll { { "tim", 9.9 },
                                        { "struppi", 11.77 }
                                      };

    // square the value of each element:
    for (pair<const string,double>& elem : coll) {
        elem.second *= elem.second;
    }

    // print each element (key and value):
    for (const auto& elem : coll) {
        cout << elem.first << ": " << elem.second << endl;
    }
}
```

After the usual includes for maps, strings, and iostreams, an unordered map is declared and initialized by two elements. Here, we use nested initializer lists so that

```
{ "tim", 9.9 }
```

and

```
{ "struppi", 11.77 }
```

are the two elements used to initialize the map.

Next, we square the value of each element:

```
for (pair<const string,double>& elem : coll) {
    elem.second *= elem.second;
}
```

Here again, you can see the internal type of the elements, which is a pair<> (see Section 5.1.1, page 60) of constant strings and doubles. Thus, we could not modify the key member first in the element:

```
for (pair<const string,double>& elem : coll) {
    elem.first = ...;     // ERROR: keys of a map are constant
}
```

As usual since C++11, we don't have to specify the type of the elements explicitly, because in a range-based for loop, it is deduced from the container. For this reason, the second loop, which outputs all elements, uses auto. In fact, by declaring elem as const auto&, we avoid having copies created:

```
for (const auto& elem : coll) {
    cout << elem.first << ": " << elem.second << endl;
}
```

As a result, one *possible* output of the program is as follows:

```
struppi: 138.533
tim: 98.01
```

This order is not guaranteed, because the actual order is undefined. If we used an ordinary `map` instead, the order of the elements would be guaranteed to print the element with key `"struppi"` before the element with key `"tim"`, because the map sorts the elements according to the key, and the string `"struppi"` is less than `"tim"`. See Section 7.8.5, page 345, for a corresponding example using a map and also using algorithms and lambdas instead of range-based `for` loops.

Other Examples for Unordered Containers

The classes for unordered containers provide a couple of additional optional template arguments, such as the hash function and the equivalence comparison. A default hash function is provided for fundamental types and strings, but we would have to declare our own hash function for other types. This is discussed in Section 7.9.2, page 363.

The next section gives an example for using a map as a so-called *associative array*. Section 7.9 discusses unordered containers in detail, with additional examples. Unordered multimaps can also be used as *dictionaries* (see Section 7.9.7, page 383, for an example).

6.2.4 Associative Arrays

Both maps and unordered maps are collections of key/value pairs with unique keys. Such a collection can also be thought of as an *associative array*, an array whose index is not an integer value. As a consequence, both containers provide the subscript operator `[ ]`.

Consider the following example:

```
// stl/assoarray1.cpp

#include <unordered_map>
#include <string>
#include <iostream>
using namespace std;

int main()
{
    // type of the container:
    // - unordered_map: elements are key/value pairs
    // - string: keys have type string
    // - float: values have type float
    unordered_map<string,float> coll;
```

```
    // insert some elements into the collection
    // - using the syntax of an associative array
    coll["VAT1"] = 0.16;
    coll["VAT2"] = 0.07;
    coll["Pi"] = 3.1415;
    coll["an arbitrary number"] = 4983.223;
    coll["Null"] = 0;

    // change value
    coll["VAT1"] += 0.03;

    // print difference of VAT values
    cout << "VAT difference: " << coll["VAT1"] - coll["VAT2"] << endl;
}
```

The declaration of the container type must specify both the type of the key and the type of the value:

```
    unordered_map<string,float> coll;
```

This means that the keys are strings and the associated values are floating-point values.

According to the concept of associative arrays, you can access elements by using the subscript operator `[]`. Note, however, that the subscript operator does not behave like the usual subscript operator for arrays: Not having an element for an index is *not* an error. A new index (or key) is taken as a reason to create and insert a new map element that has the index as the key. Thus, you can't have an invalid index.

Therefore, in this example, the statement

```
    coll["VAT1"] = 0.16;
```

creates a new element, which has the key `"VAT1"` and the value `0.16`.

In fact, the following expression creates a new element that has the key `"VAT1"` and is initialized with its default value (using the default constructor or 0 for fundamental data types):

```
    coll["VAT1"]
```

The whole expression yields access to the value of this new element, so the assignment operator assigns `0.16` then.

Since C++11, you can, alternatively, use `at()` to access values of elements while passing the key. In this case, a key not found results in an `out_of_range` exception:

```
    coll.at("VAT1") = 0.16;       // out_of_range exception if no element found
```

With expressions such as

```
    coll["VAT1"] += 0.03;
```

or

```
    coll["VAT1"] - coll["VAT2"]
```

you gain read and write access to the value of these elements. Thus, the output of the program is as follows:

```
VAT difference: 0.12
```

As usual, the difference between using an unordered map and a map is that the elements in an unordered map have arbitrary order, whereas the elements in a map are sorted. But because the complexity for element access is amortized constant for unordered maps rather than logarithmic for maps, you should usually prefer unordered maps over maps unless you need the sorting or can't use an unordered map because your environment does not support features of C++11. In that case, you simply have to change the type of the container: remove the "unordered_" in both the include directive and the container declaration.

Section 7.8.3, page 343, and Section 7.9.5, page 374, discuss maps and unordered_maps as associative arrays in more detail.

6.2.5 Other Containers

Strings

You can also use strings as STL containers. By *strings*, I mean objects of the C++ string classes (basic_string<>, string, and wstring), which are introduced in Chapter 13. Strings are similar to vectors but have characters as elements. Section 13.2.14, page 684, provides details.

Ordinary C-Style Arrays

Another kind of container is a type of the core C and C++ language rather than a class: an ordinary array ("C-style array") that has a declared fixed size or a dynamic size managed by malloc() and realloc(). However, such ordinary arrays are not STL containers, because they don't provide member functions, such as size() and empty(). Nevertheless, the STL's design allows you to call algorithms for them.

The use of ordinary arrays is nothing new. What is new is using algorithms for them. This is explained in Section 7.10.2, page 386.

In C++, it is no longer necessary to program C-style arrays directly. Vectors and arrays provide all properties of ordinary C-style arrays but with a safer and more convenient interface. See Section 7.2.3, page 267, and Section 7.3.3, page 278, for details.

User-Defined Containers

In principle, you can give any container-like object a corresponding STL interface to be able to iterate through elements or provide standard operations to manipulate its content. For example, you might introduce a class that represents a directory where you can iterate over the files as elements and manipulate them. The best candidates for STL-container-like interfaces are the common container operations introduced in Section 7.1, page 254.

However, some container-like objects do not fit into the concept of the STL. For example, the fact that STL containers have a begin and an end makes it hard for circular container types, such as a ring buffer, to fit into the STL framework.

6.2.6   Container Adapters

In addition to the fundamental container classes, the C++ standard library provides so-called *container adapters*, which are predefined containers that provide a restricted interface to meet special needs. These container adapters are implemented by using the fundamental container classes. The predefined container adapters are as follows:

- A **stack** (the name says it all) manages its elements by the LIFO (last-in-first-out) policy.
- A **queue** manages its elements by the FIFO (first-in-first-out) policy. That is, it is an ordinary buffer.
- A **priority queue** is a container in which the elements may have different priorities. The priority is based on a sorting criterion that the programmer may provide (by default, operator < is used). A priority queue is, in effect, a buffer in which the next element is always one having the highest priority inside the queue. If more than one element has the highest priority, the order of these elements is undefined.

Container adapters are historically part of the STL. However, from a programmer's viewpoint, they are just special container classes that use the general framework of the containers, iterators, and algorithms provided by the STL. Therefore, container adapters are described apart from the STL core in Chapter 12.

6.3   Iterators

Since C++11, we can process all elements by using a range-based `for` loop. However, to find an element, we don't want to process all elements. Instead, we have to iterate over all elements until we find what we are searching for. In addition, we probably want to be able to store this position somewhere, for example, to continue with the iteration or some other processing later on. Thus, we need a concept of an object that represents positions of elements in a container. This concept exists. Objects that fulfill this concept are called **iterators**. In fact, as we will see, range-based `for` loops are a convenience interface to this concept. That is, they internally use iterator objects that iterate over all elements.

An iterator is an object that can iterate over elements (navigate from element to element). These elements may be all or a subset of the elements of an STL container. An iterator represents a certain position in a container. The following fundamental operations define the behavior of an iterator:

- **Operator** ``*`` returns the element of the current position. If the elements have members, you can use operator ``->`` to access those members directly from the iterator.
- **Operator** ``++`` lets the iterator step forward to the next element. Most iterators also allow stepping backward by using operator ``--``.
- **Operators** ``==`` and ``!=`` return whether two iterators represent the same position.
- **Operator** ``=`` assigns an iterator (the position of the element to which it refers).

These operations provide exactly the interface of ordinary pointers in C and C++ when these pointers are used to iterate over the elements of an ordinary array. The difference is that iterators may be *smart pointers* — pointers that iterate over more complicated data structures of containers. The internal behavior of iterators depends on the data structure over which they iterate. Hence, each container type supplies its own kind of iterator. As a result, iterators share the same interface but have different types. This leads directly to the concept of generic programming: Operations use the same interface but different types, so you can use templates to formulate generic operations that work with arbitrary types that satisfy the interface.

All container classes provide the same basic member functions that enable them to use iterators to navigate over their elements. The most important of these functions are as follows:

- **begin()** returns an iterator that represents the beginning of the elements in the container. The beginning is the position of the first element, if any.

- **end()** returns an iterator that represents the end of the elements in the container. The end is the position *behind* the last element. Such an iterator is also called a *past-the-end iterator*.

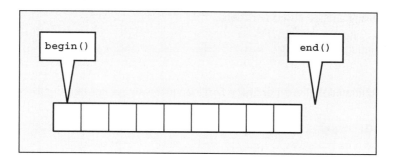

Figure 6.4. begin() *and* end() *for Containers*

Thus, begin() and end() define a *half-open range* that includes the first element but excludes the last (Figure 6.4). A half-open range has two advantages:

1. You have a simple end criterion for loops that iterate over the elements: They simply continue as long as end() is not reached.

2. It avoids special handling for empty ranges. For empty ranges, begin() is equal to end().

The following example demonstrating the use of iterators prints all elements of a list container (it is the iterator-based version of the first list example in Section 6.2.1, page 173):

```
// stl/list1old.cpp

#include <list>
#include <iostream>
using namespace std;

int main()
{
    list<char> coll;        // list container for character elements

    // append elements from 'a' to 'z'
    for (char c='a'; c<='z'; ++c) {
        coll.push_back(c);
    }
```

```
// print all elements:
// - iterate over all elements
list<char>::const_iterator pos;
for (pos = coll.begin(); pos != coll.end(); ++pos) {
    cout << *pos << ' ';
}
cout << endl;
}
```

Again, after the list is created and filled with the characters 'a' through 'z', we print all elements. But instead of using a range-based for loop:

```
for (auto elem : coll) {
    cout << elem << ' ';
}
```

all elements are printed within an ordinary for loop using an iterator iterating over all elements of the container:

```
list<char>::const_iterator pos;
for (pos = coll.begin(); pos != coll.end(); ++pos) {
    cout << *pos << ' ';
}
```

The iterator pos is declared just before the loop. Its type is the iterator type for constant element access of its container class:

```
list<char>::const_iterator pos;
```

In fact, every container defines two iterator types:

1. *container*::iterator is provided to iterate over elements in read/write mode.
2. *container*::const_iterator is provided to iterate over elements in read-only mode.

For example, in class list, the definitions might look like the following:

```
namespace std {
    template <typename T>
    class list {
      public:
        typedef ... iterator;
        typedef ... const_iterator;
        ...
    };
}
```

The exact type of iterator and const_iterator is implementation defined.

Inside the for loop, the iterator pos first gets initialized with the position of the first element:

```
pos = coll.begin()
```

The loop continues as long as pos has not reached the end of the container elements:

```
pos != coll.end()
```

Here, pos is compared with a so-called past-the-end iterator, which represents the position right behind the last element. While the loop runs the increment operator, ++pos navigates the iterator pos to the next element.

All in all, pos iterates from the first element, element-by-element, until it reaches the end (Figure 6.5). If the container has no elements, the loop does not run, because coll.begin() would equal coll.end().

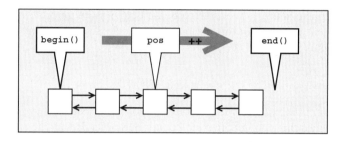

Figure 6.5. Iterator pos *Iterating over Elements of a List*

In the body of the loop, the expression *pos represents the current element. In this example, it is written to the standard output cout, followed by a space character. You can't modify the elements, because a const_iterator is used. Thus, from the iterator's point of view, the elements are constant. However, if you use a nonconstant iterator and the type of the elements is nonconstant, you can change the values. For example:

```
// make all characters in the list uppercase
list<char>::iterator pos;
for (pos = coll.begin(); pos != coll.end(); ++pos) {
    *pos = toupper(*pos);
}
```

If we use iterators to iterate over the elements of (unordered) maps and multimaps, pos would again refer to key/value pairs. Thus, the expression

```
pos->second
```

would yield the second part of the key/value pair, which is the value of the element, whereas

```
pos->first
```

would yield its (constant) key.

++pos versus pos++

Note that the preincrement operator (prefix ++) is used here to move the iterator to the next element. The reason is that it might have better performance than the postincrement operator. The latter internally involves a temporary object because it must return the old position of the iterator. For this reason, it generally is better to prefer ++pos over pos++. Thus, you should avoid the following version:

```
for (pos = coll.begin(); pos != coll.end(); pos++) {
                                            ^^^^^    // OK, but slightly slower

    ...
}
```

These kinds of performance improvements almost always don't matter. So, don't interpret this recommendation to mean that you should do everything to avoid even the smallest performance penalties. Readable and maintainable programs are far more important than optimized performance. The important point here is that in this case, you don't pay a price for preferring the preincrement over the postincrement version. For this reason, it is a good advice to prefer the preincrement and predecrement operators in general.

cbegin() and cend()

Since C++11, we can use the keyword auto (see Section 3.1.2, page 14) to specify the exact type of the iterator (provided that you initialize the iterator during its declaration so that its type can be derived from the initial value). Thus, by initializing the iterator directly with begin(), you can use auto to declare its type:

```
for (auto pos = coll.begin(); pos != coll.end(); ++pos) {
    cout << *pos << ' ';
}
```

As you can see, one advantage of using auto is that the code is more condensed. Without auto, declaring the iterator inside the loop looks as follows:

```
for (list<char>::const_iterator pos = coll.begin();
     pos != coll.end();
     ++pos) {
    cout << *pos << ' ';
}
```

The other advantage is that the loop is robust for such code modifications as changing the type of the container. However, the drawback is that the iterator loses its constness, which might raise the risk of unintended assignments. With

```
auto pos = coll.begin()
```

pos becomes a nonconstant iterator because begin() returns an object of type *cont*::iterator. To ensure that constant iterators are still used, cbegin() and cend() are provided as container functions since C++11. They return an object of type *cont*::const_iterator.

To summarize the improvements, since C++11, a loop that allows iterating over all the elements of a container without using a range-based for loop might look as follows:

```
for (auto pos = coll.cbegin(); pos != coll.cend(); ++pos) {

    ...
}
```

Range-Based `for` Loops versus Iterators

Having introduced iterators, we can explain the exact behavior of range-based `for` loops. For containers, in fact, a range-based `for` loop is nothing but a convenience interface, which is defined to iterate over all elements of the passed range/collection. Within each loop body, the actual element is initialized by the value the current iterator refers to.

Thus,

```
for (type elem : coll) {
    ...
}
```

is interpreted as

```
for (auto pos=coll.begin(), end=coll.end(); pos!=end; ++pos) {
    type elem = *pos;
    ...
}
```

Now we can understand why we should declare `elem` to be a constant reference to avoid unnecessary copies. Otherwise, `elem` will be initialized as a copy of *pos. See Section 3.1.4, page 17, for details.

6.3.1 Further Examples of Using Associative and Unordered Containers

Having introduced iterators, we can present some example programs using associative containers without using such language features of C++11 as range-based `for` loops, `auto`, and initializer lists. In addition, the features used here can also be useful with C++11 for some special requirements.

Using Sets before C++11

The first example shows how to insert elements into a set and use iterators to print them if C++11 features are not available:

```
// stl/set1.cpp

#include <set>
#include <iostream>

int main()
{
    // type of the collection
    typedef std::set<int> IntSet;

    IntSet coll;            // set container for int values
```

```
// insert elements from 1 to 6 in arbitrary order
// - note that there are two calls of insert() with value 1
coll.insert(3);
coll.insert(1);
coll.insert(5);
coll.insert(4);
coll.insert(1);
coll.insert(6);
coll.insert(2);

// print all elements
// - iterate over all elements
IntSet::const_iterator pos;
for (pos = coll.begin(); pos != coll.end(); ++pos) {
    std::cout << *pos << ' ';
}
std::cout << std::endl;
}
```

As usual, the `include` directive defines all necessary types and operations of sets:

```
#include <set>
```

The type of the container is used in several places, so first, a shorter type name gets defined:

```
typedef set<int> IntSet;
```

This statement defines type `IntSet` as a set for elements of type `int`. This type uses the default sorting criterion, which sorts the elements by using operator <, so the elements are sorted in ascending order. To sort in descending order or use a completely different sorting criterion, you can pass it as a second template parameter. For example, the following statement defines a set type that sorts the elements in descending order:

```
typedef set<int,greater<int>> IntSet;
```

`greater<>` is a predefined function object discussed in Section 6.10.2, page 239. For a sorting criterion that uses only part of the data of an object, such as the ID, see Section 10.1.1, page 476.

All associative containers provide an `insert()` member function to insert a new element:

```
coll.insert(3);
coll.insert(1);
...
```

Since C++11, we can simply call:

```
coll.insert ( { 3, 1, 5, 4, 1, 6, 2 } );
```

Each inserted element receives the correct position automatically according to the sorting criterion. You can't use the `push_back()` or `push_front()` functions provided for sequence containers. They make no sense here, because you can't specify the position of the new element.

After all values are inserted in any order, the state of the container is as shown in Figure 6.6. The elements are sorted into the internal tree structure of the container, so the value of the left child of an element is always less, with respect to the current sorting criterion, and the value of the right child of an element is always greater. Duplicates are not allowed in a set, so the container contains the value 1 only once.

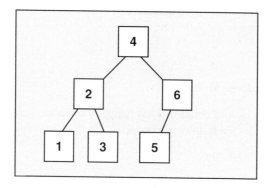

Figure 6.6. A Set of Six Elements

To print the elements of the container, you use the same loop as in the previous list example. An iterator iterates over all elements and prints them:

```
IntSet::const_iterator pos;
for (pos = coll.begin(); pos != coll.end(); ++pos) {
    cout << *pos << ' ';
}
```

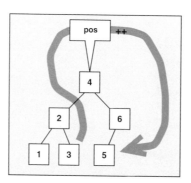

Figure 6.7. Iterator pos *Iterating over Elements of a Set*

Because it is defined by the container, the iterator does the right thing, even if the internal structure of the container is more complicated. For example, if the iterator refers to the third element, operator ++ moves to the fourth element at the top. After the next call of operator ++, the iterator refers to the fifth element at the bottom (Figure 6.7). The output of the program is as follows:

```
1 2 3 4 5 6
```

To use a multiset rather than a set, you need only change the type of the container; the header file remains the same:

```
typedef multiset<int> IntSet;
```

A multiset allows duplicates, so it would contain two elements that have value 1. Thus, the output of the program would change to the following:

```
1 1 2 3 4 5 6
```

Details of Using an Unordered Multiset

As another example, let's look in detail at what happens when we iterate over all elements of an unordered multiset. Consider the following example:

```
// stl/unordmultiset2.cpp

#include <unordered_set>
#include <iostream>

int main()
{
    // unordered multiset container for int values
    std::unordered_multiset<int> coll;

    // insert some elements
    coll.insert({1,3,5,7,11,13,17,19,23,27,1});

    // print all elements
    for (auto elem : coll) {
        std::cout << elem << ' ';
    }
    std::cout << std::endl;

    // insert one more element
    coll.insert(25);

    // print all elements again
    for (auto elem : coll) {
        std::cout << elem << ' ';
    }
    std::cout << std::endl;
}
```

The order of the elements is undefined. It depends on the internal layout of the hash table and its hashing function. Even when the elements are inserted in sorted order, they have an arbitrary order inside the container.[8] Adding one more element might change the order of all existing elements. Thus, one of the possible outputs of this program is as follows:

```
11 23 1 1 13 3 27 5 17 7 19
23 1 1 25 3 27 5 7 11 13 17 19
```

As you can see, the order is indeed undefined, but might differ if you run this example on your platform. Adding just one element might change the whole order. However, it is guaranteed that elements with equal values are adjacent to each other.

When iterating over all elements to print them:

```
for (auto elem : coll) {
    std::cout << elem << ' ';
}
```

this is equivalent to the following:

```
for (auto pos = coll.begin(); pos != coll.end(); ++pos) {
    auto elem = *pos;
    std::cout << elem << ' ';
}
```

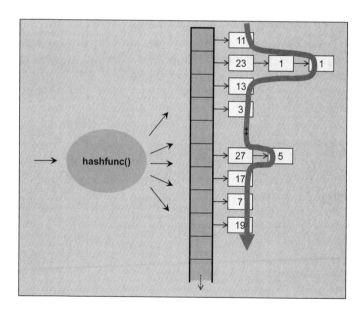

Figure 6.8. Iterator pos *Iterating over Elements of an Unordered Multiset*

---

[8] Note that the order might also be sorted because this is one possible arbitrary order. In fact, if you insert 1, 2, 3, 4, and 5, this will typically be the case.

Again, the internal iterator `pos` internally used in the `for` loop has a type provided by the container so that it "knows" how to iterate over all the elements. So, with this output, the internal state of the unordered multiset might look like Figure 6.8 when the iterator is used to print all the elements the first time.

When not allowing duplicates by switching to an unordered set:

```
std::unordered_set<int> coll;
```

the output might look as follows:

```
11 23 1 13 3 27 5 17 7 19
11 23 1 13 25 3 27 5 17 7 19
```

6.3.2 Iterator Categories

In addition to their fundamental operations, iterators can have capabilities that depend on the internal structure of the container type. As usual, the STL provides only those operations that have good performance. For example, if containers have random access, such as vectors or deques, their iterators are also able to perform random-access operations, such as positioning the iterator directly at the fifth element.

Iterators are subdivided into *categories* based on their general abilities. The iterators of the predefined container classes belong to one of the following three categories:

1. **Forward iterator**s are able to iterate only forward, using the increment operator. The iterators of the class `forward_list` are forward iterators. The iterators of the container classes `unordered_set`, `unordered_multiset`, `unordered_map`, and `unordered_multimap` are "at least" forward iterators (libraries are allowed to provide bidirectional iterators instead, see Section 7.9.1, page 357).

2. **Bidirectional iterator**s are able to iterate in two directions: forward, by using the increment operator, and backward, by using the decrement operator. The iterators of the container classes `list`, `set`, `multiset`, `map`, and `multimap` are bidirectional iterators.

3. **Random-access iterator**s have all the properties of bidirectional iterators. In addition, they can perform random access. In particular, they provide operators for *iterator arithmetic* (in accordance with *pointer arithmetic* of an ordinary pointer). You can add and subtract offsets, process differences, and compare iterators by using relational operators, such as < and >. The iterators of the container classes `vector`, `deque`, `array`, and iterators of strings are random-access iterators.

In addition, two other iterator categories are defined:

• **Input iterator**s are able to read/process some values while iterating forward. Input stream iterators are an example of such iterators (see Section 6.5.2, page 212).

• **Output iterator**s are able to write some values while iterating forward. Inserters (Section 6.5.1, page 210) and output stream iterators (see Section 6.5.2, page 212) are examples of such iterators.

Section 9.2, page 433, discusses all iterator categories in detail.

To write generic code that is as independent of the container type as possible, you should not use special operations for random-access iterators. For example, the following loop works with any container:

```
for (auto pos = coll.begin(); pos != coll.end(); ++pos) {
    ...
}
```

However, the following does *not* work with all containers:

```
for (auto pos = coll.begin(); pos < coll.end(); ++pos) {
    ...
}
```

The only difference is the use of operator < instead of operator != in the condition of the loop. Operator < is provided only for random-access iterators, so this loop does not work with lists, sets, and maps. To write generic code for arbitrary containers, you should use operator != rather than operator <. However, doing so might lead to code that is less safe. The reason is that you may not recognize that pos gets a position behind end() (see Section 6.12, page 245, for more details about possible errors when using the STL). It's up to you to decide which version to use. It might be a question of the context or even of taste.

To avoid misunderstanding, note that I am talking about "categories," *not* "classes." A category defines only the abilities of iterators. The type doesn't matter. The generic concept of the STL works with *pure abstraction*: anything that *behaves* like a bidirectional iterator *is* a bidirectional iterator.

6.4 Algorithms

The STL provides several standard algorithms for processing elements of collections. These algorithms offer general fundamental services, such as searching, sorting, copying, reordering, modifying, and numeric processing.

Algorithms are not member functions of the container classes but instead are global functions that operate with iterators. This has an important advantage: Instead of each algorithm being implemented for each container type, all are implemented only once for any container type. The algorithm might even operate on elements of different container types. You can also use the algorithms for user-defined container types. All in all, this concept reduces the amount of code and increases the power and the flexibility of the library.

Note that this is not an object-oriented programming paradigm; it is a generic functional programming paradigm. Instead of data and operations being unified, as in object-oriented programming, they are separated into distinct parts that can interact via a certain interface. However, this concept also has its price: First, the usage is not intuitive. Second, some combinations of data structures and algorithms might not work. Even worse, a combination of a container type and an algorithm might be possible but not useful (for example, it may lead to bad performance). Thus, it is important to learn the concepts and the pitfalls of the STL to benefit from it without abusing it. I provide examples and more details about this throughout the rest of this chapter.

Let's start with a simple example of the use of STL algorithms. The following program shows some algorithms and their usage:

```
// stl/algo1.cpp

#include <algorithm>
#include <vector>
#include <iostream>
using namespace std;

int main()
{
    // create vector with elements from 1 to 6 in arbitrary order
    vector<int> coll = { 2, 5, 4, 1, 6, 3 };

    // find and print minimum and maximum elements
    auto minpos = min_element(coll.cbegin(),coll.cend());
    cout << "min: "  << *minpos << endl;
    auto maxpos = max_element(coll.cbegin(),coll.cend());
    cout << "max: "  << *maxpos << endl;

    // sort all elements
    sort (coll.begin(), coll.end());

    // find the first element with value 3
    // - no cbegin()/cend() because later we modify the elements pos3 refers to
    auto pos3 = find (coll.begin(), coll.end(),   // range
                      3);                         // value

    // reverse the order of the found element with value 3 and all following elements
    reverse (pos3, coll.end());

    // print all elements
    for (auto elem : coll) {
        cout << elem << ' ';
    }
    cout << endl;
}
```

To be able to call the algorithms, you must include the header file `<algorithm>` (some algorithms need special header files, see Section 11.1, page 505):

```
#include <algorithm>
```

The first two algorithms, `min_element()` and `max_element()`, are called with two parameters that define the range of the processed elements. To process all elements of a container, you simply use `cbegin()` and `cend()` or `begin()` and `end()`, respectively. Both algorithms return an iterator for the position of the element found. Thus, in the statement

```
    auto minpos = min_element(coll.cbegin(),coll.cend());
```

the `min_element()` algorithm returns the position of the minimum element. (If there is more than one minimum element, the algorithm returns the first.) The next statement prints the element the iterator refers to:

```
cout << "min: " << *minpos << endl;
```

Of course, you could do both in one statement:

```
cout << *min_element(coll.cbegin(),coll.cend()) << endl;
```

The next algorithm, `sort()`, as the name indicates, sorts the elements of the range defined by the two arguments. As usual, you could pass an optional sorting criterion. The default sorting criterion is operator <. Thus, in this example, all elements of the container are sorted in ascending order:

```
sort (coll.begin(), coll.end());
```

Thus, afterward, the vector contains the elements in this order:

```
1 2 3 4 5 6
```

Note that you can't use `cbegin()` and `cend()` here, because `sort()` modifies the values of the elements, which is not possible for `const_iterators`.

The `find()` algorithm searches for a value inside the given range. In this example, this algorithm searches for the first element that is equal to the value 3 in the whole container:

```
auto pos3 = find (coll.begin(), coll.end(),   // range
                  3);                          // value
```

If the `find()` algorithm is successful, it returns the iterator position of the element found. If the algorithm fails, it returns the end of the range passed as second argument, which is the past-the-end iterator of `coll` here. In this example, the value 3 is found as the third element, so afterward, `pos3` refers to the third element of `coll`.

The last algorithm called in the example is `reverse()`, which reverses the elements of the passed range. Here, the third element that was found by the `find()` algorithm and the past-the-end iterator are passed as arguments:

```
reverse (pos3, coll.end());
```

This call reverses the order of the third element up to the last one. Because this is a modification, we have to use a nonconstant iterator here, which explains why we called `find()` with `begin()` and `end()` instead of `cbegin()` and `cend()`. Otherwise, `pos3` would be a `const_iterator`, which would result in an error when passing it to `reverse()`.

The output of the program is as follows:

```
min: 1
max: 6
1 2 6 5 4 3
```

Note that a couple of features of C++11 are used in this example. If you have a platform that doesn't support all features of C++11, the same program might look as follows:

```cpp
// stl/algo1old.cpp

#include <algorithm>
#include <vector>
#include <iostream>
using namespace std;

int main()
{
    // create vector with elements from 1 to 6 in arbitrary order
    vector<int> coll;
    coll.push_back(2);
    coll.push_back(5);
    coll.push_back(4);
    coll.push_back(1);
    coll.push_back(6);
    coll.push_back(3);

    // find and print minimum and maximum elements
    vector<int>::const_iterator minpos = min_element(coll.begin(),
                                                      coll.end());

    cout << "min: "   << *minpos << endl;
    vector<int>::const_iterator maxpos = max_element(coll.begin(),
                                                     coll.end());

    cout << "max: "   << *maxpos << endl;

    // sort all elements
    sort (coll.begin(), coll.end());

    // find the first element with value 3
    vector<int>::iterator pos3;
    pos3 = find (coll.begin(), coll.end(),   // range
                 3);                         // value

    // reverse the order of the found element with value 3 and all following elements
    reverse (pos3, coll.end());

    // print all elements
    vector<int>::const_iterator pos;
    for (pos=coll.begin(); pos!=coll.end(); ++pos) {
        cout << *pos << ' ';
    }
    cout << endl;
}
```

The differences are as follows:

- No initializer list can be used to initialize the vector.
- Members `cbegin()` and `cend()` are not provided, so you have to use `begin()` and `end()` instead. But you can still use `const_iterators`.
- Instead of using `auto`, you always have to declare the iterators explicitly.
- Instead of range-based `for` loops, you have to use iterators to output each element.

6.4.1 Ranges

All algorithms process one or more *ranges* of elements. Such a range might, but is not required to, embrace all elements of a container. Therefore, to be able to handle subsets of container elements, you pass the beginning and the end of the range as two separate arguments rather than the whole collection as one argument.

This interface is flexible but dangerous. The caller must ensure that the first and second arguments define a *valid* range. A range is valid if the end of the range is *reachable* from the beginning by iterating through the elements. This means that it is up to the programmer to ensure that both iterators belong to the same container and that the beginning is not behind the end. Otherwise, the behavior is undefined, and endless loops or forbidden memory access may result. In this respect, iterators are just as unsafe as ordinary pointers. But undefined behavior also means that an implementation of the STL is free to find such kinds of errors and handle them accordingly. The following paragraphs show that ensuring that ranges are valid is not always as easy as it sounds. See Section 6.12, page 245, for more details about the pitfalls and safe versions of the STL.

Every algorithm processes *half-open* ranges. Thus, a range is defined so that it includes the position used as the beginning of the range but excludes the position used as the end. This concept is often described by using the traditional mathematical notations for half-open ranges:

$[begin,end)$

or

$[begin,end[$

In this book, I use the first alternative.

The half-open-range concept has the advantages that it is simple and avoids special handling for empty collections (see Section 6.3, page 189). However, it also has some disadvantages. Consider the following example:

```
// stl/find1.cpp

#include <algorithm>
#include <list>
#include <iostream>
using namespace std;

int main()
{
    list<int> coll;
```

```
// insert elements from 20 to 40
for (int i=20; i<=40; ++i) {
    coll.push_back(i);
}

// find position of element with value 3
// - there is none, so pos3 gets coll.end()
auto pos3 = find (coll.begin(), coll.end(),    // range
                  3);                          // value

// reverse the order of elements between found element and the end
// - because pos3 is coll.end() it reverses an empty range
reverse (pos3, coll.end());

// find positions of values 25 and 35
list<int>::iterator pos25, pos35;
pos25 = find (coll.begin(), coll.end(),    // range
              25);                         // value
pos35 = find (coll.begin(), coll.end(),    // range
              35);                         // value

// print the maximum of the corresponding range
// - note: including pos25 but excluding pos35
cout << "max: " << *max_element (pos25, pos35) << endl;

// process the elements including the last position
cout << "max: " << *max_element (pos25, ++pos35) << endl;
}
```

In this example, the collection is initialized with integral values from 20 to 40. When the search for an element with the value 3 fails, find() returns the end of the processed range (coll.end() in this example) and assigns it to pos3. Using that return value as the beginning of the range in the following call of reverse() poses no problem, because it results in the following call:

```
reverse (coll.end(), coll.end());
```

This is simply a call to reverse an empty range. Thus, it is an operation that has no effect (a so-called "no-op").

However, if find() is used to find the first and the last elements of a subset, you should consider that passing these iterator positions as a range will exclude the last element. So, the first call of max_element()

```
max_element (pos25, pos35)
```

finds 34 and not 35:

```
max: 34
```

To process the last element, you have to pass the position that is one past the last element:

```
max_element (pos25, ++pos35)
```

Doing this yields the correct result:

```
max: 35
```

Note that this example uses a list as the container. Thus, you must use operator ++ to get the position that is behind pos35. If you have random-access iterators, as with vectors and deques, you also could use the expression pos35 + 1 because random-access iterators allow *iterator arithmetic* (see Section 6.3.2, page 198, and Section 9.2.5, page 438, for details).

Of course, you could use pos25 and pos35 to find something in that subrange. Again, to search including pos35, you have to pass the position after pos35. For example:

```
// increment pos35 to search with its value included
++pos35;
pos30 = find(pos25,pos35,     // range
             30);             // value
if (pos30 == pos35) {
    cout << "30 is NOT in the subrange" << endl;
}
else {
    cout << "30 is in the subrange" << endl;
}
```

All the examples in this section work only because you know that pos25 is in front of pos35. Otherwise, [pos25,pos35) would not be a valid range. If you are not sure which element is in front, things get more complicated, and undefined behavior may easily occur.

Suppose that you don't know whether the element having value 25 is in front of the element having value 35. It might even be possible that one or both values are not present. By using random-access iterators, you can call operator < to check this:

```
if (pos25 < pos35) {
    // only [pos25,pos35) is valid

    ...
}
else if (pos35 < pos25) {
    // only [pos35,pos25) is valid

    ...
}
else {
    // both are equal, so both must be end()

    ...
}
```

However, without random-access iterators, you have no simple, fast way to find out which iterator is in front. You can only search for one iterator in the range of the beginning to the other iterator or in the range of the other iterator to the end. In this case, you should change your algorithm as follows: Instead of searching for both values in the whole source range, you should try to find out, while searching for them, which value comes first. For example:

```
pos25 = find (coll.begin(), coll.end(),      // range
                25);                          // value
pos35 = find (coll.begin(), pos25,           // range
                35);                          // value
if (pos25 != coll.end() && pos35 != pos25) {
    // pos35 is in front of pos25
    // so, only [pos35,pos25) is valid
    ...
}
else {
    pos35 = find (pos25, coll.end(),         // range
                    35);                      // value
    if (pos35 != coll.end()) {
        // pos25 is in front of pos35
        // so, only [pos25,pos35) is valid
        ...
    }
    else {
        // 25 and/or 35 not found
        ...
    }
}
```

In contrast to the previous version, you don't search for 35 in the full range of all elements of coll. Instead, you first search for it from the beginning to pos25. Then, if it's not found, you search for it in the part that contains the remaining elements after pos25. As a result, you know which iterator position comes first and which subrange is valid.

This implementation is not very efficient. A more efficient way to find the first element that has either value 25 or value 35 is to search exactly for that. You could do this by using find_if() and passing a lambda (see Section 3.1.10, page 28), defining the criterion that is evaluated with each element in coll:

```
pos = find_if (coll.begin(), coll.end(),   // range
                [] (int i) {                // criterion
                    return i == 25 || i == 35;
                });
if (pos == coll.end()) {
    // no element with value 25 or 35 found
    ...
}
else if (*pos == 25) {
```

```
        // element with value 25 comes first
        pos25 = pos;
        pos35 = find (++pos, coll.end(),        // range
                      35);                       // value
        ...
    }
    else {
        // element with value 35 comes first
        pos35 = pos;
        pos25 = find (++pos, coll.end(),        // range
                      25);                       // value
        ...
    }
```

Here, the special lambda expression

```
    [] (int i) {
        return i == 25 || i == 35;
    }
```

is used as a criterion that allows a search of the first element that has either value 25 or value 35. The use of lambdas in the STL is introduced in Section 6.9, page 229, and discussed in detail in Section 10.3, page 499.

6.4.2 Handling Multiple Ranges

Several algorithms process more than one range. In this case, you usually must define both the beginning and the end only for the first range. For all other ranges, you need to pass only their beginnings. The ends of the other ranges follow from the number of elements in the first range. For example, the following call of equal() compares all elements of the collection coll1 element-by-element with the elements of coll2, beginning with its first element:

```
    if (equal (coll1.begin(), coll1.end(),   // first range
               coll2.begin())) {             // second range
        ...
    }
```

Thus, the number of elements of coll2 that are compared with the elements of coll1 is specified indirectly by the number of elements in coll1 (see Figure 6.9).

This leads to an important consequence: **When you call algorithms for multiple ranges, make sure that the second and additional ranges have at least as many elements as the first range.** In particular, make sure that destination ranges are big enough for algorithms that write to collections.

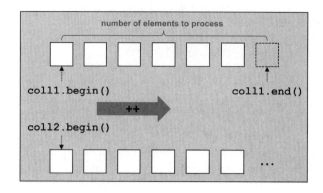

Figure 6.9. Algorithm Iterating over Two Ranges

Consider the following program:

```
// stl/copybug.cpp

#include <algorithm>
#include <list>
#include <vector>
using namespace std;

int main()
{
    list<int>   coll1 = { 1, 2, 3, 4, 5, 6, 7, 8, 9 };
    vector<int> coll2;

    // RUNTIME ERROR:
    // - overwrites nonexisting elements in the destination
    copy (coll1.cbegin(), coll1.cend(),    // source
          coll2.begin());                  // destination
    ...
}
```

Here, the copy() algorithm is called. It simply copies all elements of the first range into the destination range. As usual, the beginning and the end are defined for the first range, whereas only the beginning is specified for the second range. However, the algorithm overwrites rather than inserts. So, the algorithm *requires* that the destination has enough elements to be overwritten. If there is not enough room, as in this case, the result is undefined behavior. In practice, this often means that you overwrite whatever comes after the coll2.end(). If you're in luck, you'll get a crash, so at least you'll know that you did something wrong. However, you can force your luck by using a safe version of the STL for which the undefined behavior is defined as leading to a certain error-handling procedure (see Section 6.12.1, page 247).

To avoid these errors, you can (1) ensure that the destination has enough elements on entry, or (2) use *insert iterators*. Insert iterators are covered in Section 6.5.1, page 210. I'll first explain how to modify the destination so that it is big enough on entry.

To make the destination big enough, you must either create it with the correct size or change its size explicitly. Both alternatives apply only to some sequence containers (`vector`, `deque`, `list`, and `forward_list`). However, this is not really a problem for other containers, because associative and unordered containers cannot be used as a destination for overwriting algorithms (Section 6.7.2, page 221, explains why). The following program shows how to increase the size of containers:

```
// stl/copy1.cpp

#include <algorithm>
#include <list>
#include <vector>
#include <deque>
using namespace std;

int main()
{
    list<int>   coll1 = { 1, 2, 3, 4, 5, 6, 7, 8, 9 };
    vector<int> coll2;

    // resize destination to have enough room for the overwriting algorithm
    coll2.resize (coll1.size());

    // copy elements from first into second collection
    // - overwrites existing elements in destination
    copy (coll1.cbegin(), coll1.cend(),    // source
          coll2.begin());                  // destination

    // create third collection with enough room
    // - initial size is passed as parameter
    deque<int> coll3(coll1.size());

    // copy elements from first into third collection
    copy (coll1.cbegin(), coll1.cend(),    // source
          coll3.begin());                  // destination
}
```

Here, `resize()` is used to change the number of elements in the existing container `coll2`:

```
    coll2.resize (coll1.size());
```

Later, coll3 is initialized with a special initial size so that it has enough room for all elements of coll1:

```
deque<int> coll3(coll1.size());
```

Note that both resizing and initializing the size create new elements. These elements are initialized by their default constructor because no arguments are passed to them. You can pass an additional argument both for the constructor and for resize() to initialize the new elements.

6.5   Iterator Adapters

Iterators are *pure abstractions*: Anything that *behaves* like an iterator *is* an iterator. For this reason, you can write classes that have the interface of iterators but do something completely different. The C++ standard library provides several predefined special iterators: *iterator adapters*. They are more than auxiliary classes; they give the whole concept a lot more power.

The following subsections introduce the following iterator adapters:

1. Insert iterators
2. Stream iterators
3. Reverse iterators
4. Move iterators (since C++11)

Section 9.4, page 448, covers them in detail.

6.5.1   Insert Iterators

Insert iterators, or *inserters*, are used to let algorithms operate in insert mode rather than in overwrite mode. In particular, inserters solve the problem of algorithms that write to a destination that does not have enough room: They let the destination grow accordingly.

Insert iterators redefine their interface internally as follows:

* If you assign a value to their element, they insert that value into the collection to which they belong. Three different insert iterators have different abilities with regard to where the elements are inserted — at the front, at the end, or at a given position.
* A call to step forward is a no-op.

With this interface, they fall under the category of output iterators, which are able to write/assign values only while iterating forward (see Section 9.2, page 433, for details of iterator categories).

Consider the following example:

```
// stl/copy2.cpp

#include <algorithm>
#include <iterator>
#include <list>
#include <vector>
#include <deque>
```

```
#include <set>
#include <iostream>
using namespace std;

int main()
{
    list<int> coll1 = { 1, 2, 3, 4, 5, 6, 7, 8, 9 };

    // copy the elements of coll1 into coll2 by appending them
    vector<int> coll2;
    copy (coll1.cbegin(), coll1.cend(),      // source
          back_inserter(coll2));             // destination

    // copy the elements of coll1 into coll3 by inserting them at the front
    // - reverses the order of the elements
    deque<int> coll3;
    copy (coll1.cbegin(), coll1.cend(),      // source
          front_inserter(coll3));            // destination

    // copy elements of coll1 into coll4
    // - only inserter that works for associative collections
    set<int> coll4;
    copy (coll1.cbegin(), coll1.cend(),      // source
          inserter(coll4,coll4.begin()));    // destination
}
```

This example uses all three predefined insert iterators:

1. **Back inserters** insert the elements at the back of their container (appends them) by calling `push_back()`. For example, with the following statement, all elements of `coll1` are appended into `coll2`:

```
copy (coll1.cbegin(), coll1.cend(),      // source
      back_inserter(coll2));             // destination
```

Of course, back inserters can be used only for containers that provide `push_back()` as a member function. In the C++ standard library, these containers are `vector`, `deque`, `list`, and strings.

2. **Front inserters** insert the elements at the front of their container by calling `push_front()`. For example, with the following statement, all elements of `coll1` are inserted into `coll3`:

```
copy (coll1.cbegin(), coll1.cend(),      // source
      front_inserter(coll3));            // destination
```

Note that this kind of insertion reverses the order of the inserted elements. If you insert 1 at the front and then 2 at the front, the 1 is after the 2.

Front inserters can be used only for containers that provide `push_front()` as a member function. In the C++ standard library, these containers are `deque`, `list`, and `forward_list`.

3. **General inserters**, or simply *inserters*, insert elements directly in front of the position that is passed as the second argument of its initialization. A general inserter calls the `insert()` member function with the new value and the new position as arguments. Note that all predefined containers except `array` and `forward_list` have such an `insert()` member function. Thus, this is the only predefined inserter for associative and unordered containers.

But wait a moment. Passing a position to insert a new element doesn't sound useful for associative and unordered containers, does it? Within associative containers, the position depends on the *value* of the elements, and in unordered containers the position of an element is undefined. The solution is simple: For associative and unordered containers, the position is taken as a *hint* to start the search for the correct position. However, the containers are free to ignore it. Section 9.6, page 471, describes a user-defined inserter that is more useful for associative and unordered containers.

Table 6.1 lists the functionality of insert iterators. Additional details are described in Section 9.4.2, page 454.

Expression	Kind of Inserter
`back_inserter`(*container*)	Appends in the same order by using `push_back`(*val*)
`front_inserter`(*container*)	Inserts at the front in reverse order by using `push_front`(*val*)
`inserter`(*container*,*pos*)	Inserts at *pos* (in the same order) by using `insert`(*pos*,*val*)

Table 6.1. Predefined Insert Iterators

6.5.2   Stream Iterators

Stream iterators read from or write to a stream.[9] Thus, they provide an abstraction that lets the input from the keyboard behave as a collection from which you can read. Similarly, you can redirect the output of an algorithm directly into a file or onto the screen.

The following example is typical for the power of the whole STL. Compared with ordinary C or C++, the example does a lot of complex processing by using only a few statements:

```
// stl/ioiter1.cpp

#include <iterator>
#include <algorithm>
#include <vector>
#include <string>
#include <iostream>
using namespace std;
```

---

[9] A stream is an object that represents I/O channels (see Chapter 15).

```
int main()
{
    vector<string> coll;

    // read all words from the standard input
    // - source: all strings until end-of-file (or error)
    // - destination: coll (inserting)
    copy (istream_iterator<string>(cin),       // start of source
          istream_iterator<string>(),          // end of source
          back_inserter(coll));                // destination

    // sort elements
    sort (coll.begin(), coll.end());

    // print all elements without duplicates
    // - source: coll
    // - destination: standard output (with newline between elements)
    unique_copy (coll.cbegin(), coll.cend(),                    // source
                 ostream_iterator<string>(cout,"\n"));  // destination
}
```

The program has only three statements that read all words from the standard input and print a sorted list of them. Let's consider the three statements step-by-step. In the statement

```
copy (istream_iterator<string>(cin),
      istream_iterator<string>(),
      back_inserter(coll));
```

two input stream iterators are used:

1. The expression

   ```
   istream_iterator<string>(cin)
   ```

   creates a stream iterator that reads from the standard input stream cin. The template argument string specifies that the stream iterator reads elements of this type (string types are covered in Chapter 13). These elements are read with the usual input operator >>. Thus, each time the algorithm wants to process the next element, the istream iterator transforms that desire into a call of

   ```
   cin >> string
   ```

   The input operator for strings usually reads one word separated by whitespaces (see Section 13.2.10, page 677), so the algorithm reads word by word.

2. The expression

   ```
   istream_iterator<string>()
   ```

   calls the default constructor of istream iterators that creates a so-called *end-of-stream iterator*. It represents a stream from which you can no longer read.

As usual, the `copy()` algorithm operates as long as the (incremented) first argument differs from the second argument. The end-of-stream iterator is used as the *end of the range,* so the algorithm reads all strings from `cin` until it can no longer read any more (owing to end-of-stream or an error). To summarize, the source of the algorithm is "all words read from `cin`." These words are copied by inserting them into `coll` with the help of a back inserter.

The `sort()` algorithm sorts all elements:

```
sort (coll.begin(), coll.end());
```

Finally, the statement

```
unique_copy (coll.cbegin(), coll.cend(),
             ostream_iterator<string>(cout,"\n"));
```

copies all elements from the collection into the destination `cout`. During this process, the `unique_copy()` algorithm eliminates adjacent duplicate values. The expression

```
ostream_iterator<string>(cout,"\n")
```

creates an output stream iterator that writes `strings` to `cout` by calling operator `<<` for each element. The second argument behind `cout` is optional and serves as a separator between the elements. In this example, it is a newline character, so every element is written on a separate line.

All components of the program are templates, so you can change the program easily to sort other value types, such as integers or more complex objects. Section 9.4.3, page 460, explains more and gives more examples about iostream iterators.

In this example, one declaration and three statements were used to sort all words read from standard input. However, you could do the same by using only one declaration and one statement. See Section 1, page 394, for an example.

6.5.3 Reverse Iterators

Reverse iterators let algorithms operate backward by switching the call of an increment operator internally into a call of the decrement operator, and vice versa. All containers with bidirectional iterators or random-access iterators (all sequence containers except `forward_list` and all associative containers) can create reverse iterators via their member functions `rbegin()` and `rend()`. Since C++11, the corresponding member functions returning read-only iterators, `crbegin()` and `crend()`, are also provided.

For `forward_lists` and unordered containers, no backward-iteration interface (`rbegin()`, `rend()`, etc.) is provided. The reason is that the implementation requires only singly linked lists to go through the elements.

Consider the following example:

```
// stl/reviter1.cpp

#include <iterator>
#include <algorithm>
#include <vector>
#include <iostream>
using namespace std;

int main()
{
    vector<int> coll;

    // insert elements from 1 to 9
    for (int i=1; i<=9; ++i) {
        coll.push_back(i);
    }

    // print all element in reverse order
    copy (coll.crbegin(), coll.crend(),        // source
          ostream_iterator<int>(cout," "));    // destination
    cout << endl;
}
```

The following expression returns a read-only reverse iterator for `coll`:

```
coll.crbegin()
```

This iterator may be used as the beginning of a reverse iteration over the elements of the collection. The iterator's position is the last element of the collection. Thus, the following expression returns the value of the last element:

```
*coll.crbegin()
```

Accordingly, the following expression returns for `coll` a reverse iterator that may be used as the end of a reverse iteration.

```
coll.crend()
```

As usual for ranges, the iterator's position is past the end of the range but from the opposite direction; that is, it is the position *before* the first element in the collection.

Again, you should never use operator * (or operator ->) for a position that does not represent a valid element. Thus, the expression

```
*coll.crend()
```

is as undefined as `*coll.end()` or `*coll.cend()`.

The advantage of using reverse iterators is that all algorithms are able to operate in the opposite direction without special code. A step to the next element with operator ++ is redefined into a step backward with operator `--`. For example, in this case, `copy()` iterates over the elements of `coll` from the last to the first element. So, the output of the program is as follows:

```
9 8 7 6 5 4 3 2 1
```

You can also switch "normal" iterators into reverse iterators, and vice versa. However, the referenced value of an iterator changes in doing so. This and other details about reverse iterators are covered in Section 9.4.1, page 448.

6.5.4 Move Iterators

Move iterators are provided since C++11. They convert any access to the underlying element into a move operation. As a result, they allow moving elements from one container into another either in constructors or while applying algorithms. See Section 9.4.4, page 466, for details.

6.6   User-Defined Generic Functions

The STL is an extensible framework. This means you can write your own functions and algorithms to process elements of collections. Of course, these operations may also be generic. However, to declare a valid iterator in these operations, you must use the type of the container, which is different for each container type. To facilitate the writing of generic functions, each container type provides some internal type definitions. Consider the following example:

```cpp
// stl/print.hpp

#include <iostream>
#include <string>

// PRINT_ELEMENTS()
// - prints optional string optstr followed by
// - all elements of the collection coll
// - in one line, separated by spaces
template <typename T>
inline void PRINT_ELEMENTS (const T& coll,
                            const std::string& optstr="")
{
    std::cout << optstr;
    for (const auto&  elem : coll) {
        std::cout << elem << ' ';
    }
    std::cout << std::endl;
}
```

This example defines a generic function that prints an optional string followed by all elements of the passed container.

Before C++11, the loop over the elements had to look as follows:

```
typename T::const_iterator pos;
for (pos=coll.begin(); pos!=coll.end(); ++pos) {
    std::cout << *pos << ' ';
}
```

Here, pos is declared as having the iterator type of the passed container type. Note that typename is necessary here to specify that const_iterator is a type and not a static member of type T (see the introduction of typename in Section 3.2, page 34).

In addition to iterator and const_iterator, containers provide other types to facilitate the writing of generic functions. For example, they provide the type of the elements to enable the handling of temporary copies of elements. See Section 9.5.1, page 468, for details.

The optional second argument of PRINT_ELEMENTS is a string that is used as a prefix before all elements are written. Thus, by using PRINT_ELEMENTS(), you could comment or introduce the output like this:

```
PRINT_ELEMENTS (coll, "all elements: ");
```

I introduced this function here because I use it often in the rest of the book to print all elements of containers by using a simple call.

6.7 Manipulating Algorithms

So far, I have introduced the whole concept of the STL as a framework: Containers represent different concepts to manage collections of data. Algorithms are provided to perform read and write operations on these collections. Iterators are the glue between containers and algorithms. Provided by the containers, iterators allow you to iterate over all elements in different orders and in special modes, such as an appending mode.

Now, however, it's time for the "BUT" of the STL framework: In practice, there are some limits and workarounds you should know. Many of these have to do with modifications.

Several algorithms modify destination ranges. In particular, those algorithms may remove elements. If this happens, special aspects apply, which are explained in this section. These aspects are surprising and show the price of the STL concept that separates containers and algorithms with great flexibility.

6.7.1 "Removing" Elements

The remove() algorithm removes elements from a range. However, using this algorithm for all elements of a container operates in a surprising way. Consider the following example:

```
// stl/remove1.cpp

#include <algorithm>
#include <iterator>
#include <list>
#include <iostream>
using namespace std;

int main()
{
    list<int> coll;

    // insert elements from 6 to 1 and 1 to 6
    for (int i=1; i<=6; ++i) {
        coll.push_front(i);
        coll.push_back(i);
    }

    // print all elements of the collection
    cout << "pre:  ";
    copy (coll.cbegin(), coll.cend(),            // source
          ostream_iterator<int>(cout," "));      // destination
    cout << endl;

    // remove all elements with value 3
    remove (coll.begin(), coll.end(),            // range
            3);                                  // value

    // print all elements of the collection
    cout << "post: ";
    copy (coll.cbegin(), coll.cend(),            // source
          ostream_iterator<int>(cout," "));      // destination
    cout << endl;
}
```

Someone without deeper knowledge reading this program would expect that all elements with value 3 are removed from the collection. However, the output of the program is as follows:

```
pre:  6 5 4 3 2 1 1 2 3 4 5 6
post: 6 5 4 2 1 1 2 4 5 6 5 6
```

Thus, `remove()` did not change the number of elements in the collection for which it was called. The `cend()` member function returns the old end — as would `end()` — whereas `size()` returns the old number of elements. However, something has changed: The elements changed their order as if the elements had been removed. Each element with value 3 was overwritten by the following elements (see Figure 6.10). At the end of the collection, the old elements that were not overwritten by the algorithm remain unchanged. Logically, these elements no longer belong to the collection.

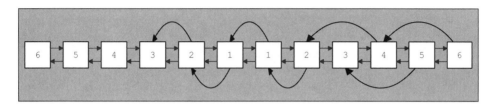

Figure 6.10. How `remove()` *Operates*

However, the algorithm does return the new logical end. By using the algorithm, you can access the resulting range, reduce the size of the collection, or process the number of removed elements. Consider the following modified version of the example:

```
// stl/remove2.cpp

#include <algorithm>
#include <iterator>
#include <list>
#include <iostream>
using namespace std;

int main()
{
    list<int> coll;

    // insert elements from 6 to 1 and 1 to 6
    for (int i=1; i<=6; ++i) {
        coll.push_front(i);
        coll.push_back(i);
    }

    // print all elements of the collection
    copy (coll.cbegin(), coll.cend(),
          ostream_iterator<int>(cout," "));
    cout << endl;

    // remove all elements with value 3
    // - retain new end
```

```
list<int>::iterator end = remove (coll.begin(), coll.end(),
                                  3);

// print resulting elements of the collection
copy (coll.begin(), end,
      ostream_iterator<int>(cout," "));
cout << endl;

// print number of removed elements
cout << "number of removed elements: "
     << distance(end,coll.end()) << endl;

// remove "removed" elements
coll.erase (end, coll.end());

// print all elements of the modified collection
copy (coll.cbegin(), coll.cend(),
      ostream_iterator<int>(cout," "));
cout << endl;
}
```

In this version, the return value of `remove()` is assigned to the iterator end:

```
list<int>::iterator end = remove (coll.begin(), coll.end(),
                                  3);
```

This is the new logical end of the modified collection after the elements are "removed." You can use this return value as the new end for further operations:

```
copy (coll.begin(), end,
      ostream_iterator<int>(cout," "));
```

Note that you have to use `begin()` here rather than `cbegin()` because end is defined a nonconstant iterator, and the begin and end of a range have to get specified by the same types.

Another possibility is to process the number of "removed" elements by processing the distance between the "logical" and the real end of the collection:

```
cout << "number of removed elements: "
     << distance(end,coll.end()) << endl;
```

Here, a special auxiliary function for iterators, `distance()`, is used. It returns the distance between two iterators. If the iterators were random-access iterators, you could process the difference directly with operator −. However, the container is a list, so it provides only bidirectional iterators. See Section 9.3.3, page 445, for details about `distance()`.

If you really want to remove the "removed" elements, you must call an appropriate member function of the container. To do this, containers provide the `erase()` member function, which removes all elements of the range that is specified by its arguments:

```
coll.erase (end, coll.end());
```

Here is the output of the whole program:

```
6 5 4 3 2 1 1 2 3 4 5 6
6 5 4 2 1 1 2 4 5 6
number of removed elements: 2
6 5 4 2 1 1 2 4 5 6
```

If you really want to remove elements in one statement, you can call the following statement:

```
coll.erase (remove(coll.begin(),coll.end(),
                    3),
            coll.end());
```

Why don't algorithms call `erase()` by themselves? This question highlights the price of the flexibility of the STL. The STL separates data structures and algorithms by using iterators as the interface. However, iterators are an abstraction to represent a position in a container. In general, iterators do *not* know their containers. Thus, the algorithms, which use the iterators to access the elements of the container, can't call any member function for it.

This design has important consequences because it allows algorithms to operate on ranges that are different from "all elements of a container." For example, the range might be a subset of all elements of a collection. The range might even be a container that provides no `erase()` member function (an array is an example of such a container). So, to make algorithms as flexible as possible, there are good reasons not to require that iterators know their container.

Note that often it is not necessary to remove the "removed" elements. Often, it is no problem to use the returned new logical end instead of the real end of the container. In particular, you can call all algorithms with the new logical end.

6.7.2 Manipulating Associative and Unordered Containers

Manipulation algorithms — those that remove elements and those that reorder or modify elements — have another problem when you try to use them with associative or unordered containers: Associative and unordered containers can't be used as a destination. The reason is simple: If they would work for associative or unordered containers, modifying algorithms could change the value or position of elements, thereby violating the order maintained by the container (sorted for associative containers or according to the hash function for unordered containers). In order to avoid compromising the internal order, every iterator for an associative and unordered container is declared as an iterator for a constant value or key. Thus, manipulating elements of or in associative and unordered containers results in a failure at compile time. [10]

This problem also prevents you from calling removing algorithms for associative containers, because these algorithms manipulate elements implicitly. The values of "removed" elements are overwritten by the following elements that are not removed.

Now the question arises: How does one remove elements in associative containers? Well, the answer is simple: Call their member functions! Every associative and unordered container provides

---

[10] Unfortunately, some systems provide really bad error handling. You see that something went wrong but have problems finding out why.

member functions to remove elements. For example, you can call the member function `erase()` to remove elements:

```cpp
// stl/remove3.cpp

#include <set>
#include <algorithm>
#include <iterator>
#include <iostream>
using namespace std;

int main()
{
    // unordered set with elements from 1 to 9
    set<int> coll = { 1, 2, 3, 4, 5, 6, 7, 8, 9 };

    // print all elements of the collection
    copy (coll.cbegin(), coll.cend(),
          ostream_iterator<int>(cout," "));
    cout << endl;

    // Remove all elements with value 3
    // - algorithm remove() does not work
    // - instead member function erase() works
    int num = coll.erase(3);

    // print number of removed elements
    cout << "number of removed elements: " << num << endl;

    // print all elements of the modified collection
    copy (coll.cbegin(), coll.cend(),
          ostream_iterator<int>(cout," "));
    cout << endl;
}
```

Note that containers provide different `erase()` member functions. Only the form that gets the value of the element(s) to remove as a single argument returns the number of removed elements (see Section 8.7.3, page 418). Of course, when duplicates are not allowed, the return value can only be 0 or 1, as is the case for `sets`, `maps`, `unordered_sets`, and `unordered_maps`.

The output of the program is as follows:

```
1 2 3 4 5 6 7 8 9
number of removed elements: 1
1 2 4 5 6 7 8 9
```

6.7.3   Algorithms versus Member Functions

Even if you are able to use an algorithm, it might be a bad idea to do so. A container might have member functions that provide much better performance.

Calling `remove()` for elements of a list is a good example of this. If you call `remove()` for elements of a list, the algorithm doesn't know that it is operating on a list and thus does what it does for any container: reorder the elements by changing their values. If, for example, the algorithm removes the first element, all the following elements are assigned to their previous elements. This behavior contradicts the main advantage of lists: the ability to insert, move, and remove elements by modifying the links instead of the values.

To avoid bad performance, lists provide special member functions for all manipulating algorithms. You should always prefer them. Furthermore, these member functions really remove "removed" elements, as this example shows:

```
// stl/remove4.cpp

#include <list>
#include <algorithm>
using namespace std;

int main()
{
    list<int> coll;

    // insert elements from 6 to 1 and 1 to 6
    for (int i=1; i<=6; ++i) {
        coll.push_front(i);
        coll.push_back(i);
    }

    // remove all elements with value 3 (poor performance)
    coll.erase (remove(coll.begin(),coll.end(),
                       3),
                coll.end());

    // remove all elements with value 4 (good performance)
    coll.remove (4);
}
```

You should always prefer a member function over an algorithm if good performance is the goal. The problem is, you have to know that a member function exists that has significantly better performance for a certain container. No warning or error message appears if you use the `remove()` algorithm for a list. However, if you prefer a member function in these cases, you have to change the code when you switch to another container type. In the reference sections of algorithms (Chapter 11), I mention whether a member function exists that provides better performance than an algorithm.

6.8   Functions as Algorithm Arguments

To increase their flexibility and power, several algorithms allow the passing of user-defined auxiliary functions. These functions are called internally by the algorithms.

6.8.1   Using Functions as Algorithm Arguments

The simplest example is the `for_each()` algorithm, which calls a user-defined function for each element of the specified range. Consider the following example:

```
// stl/foreach1.cpp

#include <vector>
#include <algorithm>
#include <iostream>
using namespace std;

// function that prints the passed argument
void print (int elem)
{
    cout << elem << ' ';
}

int main()
{
    vector<int> coll;

    // insert elements from 1 to 9
    for (int i=1; i<=9; ++i) {
        coll.push_back(i);
    }

    // print all elements
    for_each (coll.cbegin(), coll.cend(),   // range
              print);                       // operation
    cout << endl;
}
```

The `for_each()` algorithm calls the passed `print()` function for every element in the range `[coll.cbegin(),coll.cend())`. Thus, the output of the program is as follows:

```
1 2 3 4 5 6 7 8 9
```

Algorithms use auxiliary functions in several variants: some optional, some mandatory. In particular, you can use auxiliary functions to specify a search criterion or a sorting criterion or to define a manipulation while transferring elements from one collection to another.

Here is another example program:

```cpp
// stl/transform1.cpp

#include <set>
#include <vector>
#include <algorithm>
#include <iterator>
#include <iostream>
#include "print.hpp"

int square (int value)
{
    return value*value;
}

int main()
{
    std::set<int>    coll1;
    std::vector<int> coll2;

    // insert elements from 1 to 9 into coll1
    for (int i=1; i<=9; ++i) {
        coll1.insert(i);
    }
    PRINT_ELEMENTS(coll1,"initialized: ");

    // transform each element from coll1 to coll2
    // - square transformed values
    std::transform (coll1.cbegin(),coll1.cend(),    // source
                    std::back_inserter(coll2),       // destination
                    square);                         // operation

    PRINT_ELEMENTS(coll2,"squared:     ");
}
```

In this example, `square()` is used to square each element of `coll1` while it is transformed to `coll2` (Figure 6.11). The program has the following output:

```
initialized: 1 2 3 4 5 6 7 8 9
squared:     1 4 9 16 25 36 49 64 81
```

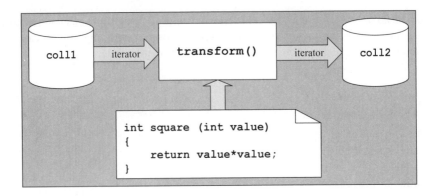

Figure 6.11. How `transform()` *Operates*

6.8.2 Predicates

A *predicate* is a special kind of auxiliary function. Predicates return a Boolean value and are often used to specify a sorting or a search criterion. Depending on their purpose, predicates are unary or binary.

Not every unary or binary function that returns a Boolean value is a valid predicate. In addition, the STL requires that predicates be stateless, meaning that they should always yield the same result for the same value. This rules out functions that modify their internal state when they are called. See Section 10.1.4, page 483, for details.

Unary Predicates

Unary predicates check a specific property of a single argument. A typical example is a function that is used as a search criterion to find the first prime number:

```
// stl/prime1.cpp

#include <list>
#include <algorithm>
#include <iostream>
#include <cstdlib>        // for abs()
using namespace std;

// predicate, which returns whether an integer is a prime number
bool isPrime (int number)
{
    // ignore negative sign
    number = abs(number);

    // 0 and 1 are no prime numbers
    if (number == 0 || number == 1) {
```

```
            return false;
        }

        // find divisor that divides without a remainder
        int divisor;
        for (divisor = number/2; number%divisor != 0; --divisor) {
            ;
        }

        // if no divisor greater than 1 is found, it is a prime number
        return divisor == 1;
    }

    int main()
    {
        list<int> coll;

        // insert elements from 24 to 30
        for (int i=24; i<=30; ++i) {
            coll.push_back(i);
        }

        // search for prime number
        auto pos = find_if (coll.cbegin(), coll.cend(),    // range
                            isPrime);                       // predicate
        if (pos != coll.end()) {
            // found
            cout << *pos << " is first prime number found" << endl;
        }
        else {
            // not found
            cout << "no prime number found" << endl;
        }
    }
```

In this example, the find_if() algorithm is used to search for the first element of the given range for which the passed unary predicate yields true. Here, the predicate is the isPrime() function, which checks whether a number is a prime number. By using this predicate, the algorithm returns the first prime number in the given range. If it does not find any element that matches the predicate, the algorithm returns the end of the range (its second argument). This is checked after the call. The collection in this example has a prime number between 24 and 30, so the output of the program is as follows:

```
29 is first prime number found
```

Binary Predicates

Binary predicates typically compare a specific property of two arguments. For example, to sort elements according to your own criterion, you could provide it as a simple predicate function. This might be necessary because the elements do not provide operator < or because you wish to use a different criterion.

The following example sorts elements of a deque by the first name and last name of a person:

```
// stl/sort1.cpp

#include <algorithm>
#include <deque>
#include <string>
#include <iostream>
using namespace std;

class Person {
  public:
    string firstname() const;
    string lastname() const;
    ...
};

// binary function predicate:
// - returns whether a person is less than another person
bool personSortCriterion (const Person& p1, const Person& p2)
{
    // a person is less than another person
    // - if the last name is less
    // - if the last name is equal and the first name is less
    return p1.lastname()<p2.lastname() ||
           (p1.lastname()==p2.lastname() &&
            p1.firstname()<p2.firstname());
}

int main()
{
    deque<Person> coll;
    ...

    sort(coll.begin(),coll.end(),       // range
         personSortCriterion);          // sort criterion
    ...
}
```

Note that you can also implement a sorting criterion as a function object. This kind of implementation has the advantage that the criterion is a type, which you could use, for example, to declare sets that use this criterion for sorting its elements. See Section 10.1.1, page 476, for such an implementation of this sorting criterion.

6.9 Using Lambdas

Lambdas, introduced with C++11, define a way to specify functional behavior inside an expression or statement (see Section 3.1.10, page 28). As a consequence, you can define objects that represent functional behavior and pass these objects as inline argument to algorithms to be used as predicates or for other purposes.

For example, in the following statement:

```
// transform all elements to the power of 3
std::transform (coll.begin(), coll.end(),     // source
                coll.begin(),                 // destination
                [](double d) {                // lambda as function object
                    return d*d*d;
                });
```

the expression

```
[](double d) { return d*d*d; }
```

defines a lambda expression, which represents a function object that returns a `double` raised to the power of 3. As you can see, this provides the ability to specify the functional behavior passed to `transform()` directly where it is called.

The Benefit of Lambdas

Using lambdas to specify behavior inside the STL framework solves a lot of drawbacks of previous attempts. Suppose that you search in a collection for the first element with a value that is between x and y:

```
// stl/lambda1.cpp

#include <algorithm>
#include <deque>
#include <iostream>
using namespace std;

int main()
{
    deque<int> coll = { 1, 3, 19, 5, 13, 7, 11, 2, 17 };
```

```
    int x = 5;
    int y = 12;
    auto pos = find_if (coll.cbegin(), coll.cend(),   // range
                        [=](int i) {                   // search criterion
                            return i > x && i < y;
                        });
    cout << "first elem >5 and <12: " << *pos << endl;
}
```

When calling find_if(), you pass the corresponding predicate inline as the third argument:

```
auto pos = find_if (coll.cbegin(), coll.cend(),
                    [=](int i) {
                        return i > x && i < y;
                    });
```

The lambda is just a function object taking an integer i and returning whether it is greater than x and less than y:

```
[=](int i) {
    return i > x && i < y;
}
```

By specifying = as a *capture* inside [=], you pass the symbols, which are valid where the lambda gets declared, *by value* into the body of the lambda. Thus, inside the lambda, you have read access to the variables x and y declared in main(). With [&], you could even pass the values by reference so that inside the lambda, you could modify their values (see Section 3.1.10, page 29, for more details about captures).

Now compare this way to search for "the first element >5 and <12" with the other approaches provided by C++ before lambdas were introduced:

- In contrast to using handwritten loops:

```
// find first element > x and < y
vector<int>::iterator pos;
for (pos = coll.begin() ; pos != coll.end(); ++pos) {
    if (*pos > x && *pos < y) {
        break; // the loop
    }
}
```

you benefit from using predefined algorithms and avoid a more or less ugly break.

- In contrast to using a self-written function predicate:

```
bool pred (int i)
{
    return i > x && i < y;
}
...
```

```
pos = find_if (coll.begin(), coll.end(),        // range
               pred);                            // search criterion
```

you don't have the problem that the details of the behavior are written somewhere else and you have to scroll up to find out what `find_if()` exactly is looking for, unless you have and trust a corresponding comment. In addition, C++ compilers optimize lambdas better than they do ordinary functions.

What's more, access to x and y becomes really ugly in this scenario. The usual solution before C++11 to use a function object (see Section 6.10, page 233) demonstrates the whole ugliness of this approach:

```
class Pred
{
  private:
    int x;
    int y;
  public:
    Pred (int xx, int yy) : x(xx), y(yy) {
    }
    bool operator() (int i) const {
        return i > x && i < y;
    }
};
...
pos = find_if (coll.begin(), coll.end(),        // range
               Pred(x,y));                       // search criterion
```

- In contrast to using binders (introduced in Section 6.10.3, page 241):

```
pos = find_if (coll.begin(), coll.end(),        // range
               bind(logical_and<bool>(),         // search criterion
                    bind(greater<int>(),_1,x),
                    bind(less<int>(),_1,y)));
```

you don't have problems understanding the expression defined here.

To summarize, lambdas provide the first convenient, readable, fast, and maintainable approach to use STL algorithms.

Using Lambdas as Sorting Criterion

As another example, let's use a lambda expression to define the criterion when sorting a vector of Persons (see Section 6.8.2, page 228, for a corresponding program that uses a function to define the sorting criterion):

```
// stl/sort2.cpp

#include <algorithm>
#include <deque>
```

```cpp
#include <string>
#include <iostream>
using namespace std;

class Person {
  public:
    string firstname() const;
    string lastname() const;
    ...
};

int main()
{
    deque<Person> coll;
    ...

    // sort Persons according to lastname (and firstname):
    sort(coll.begin(),coll.end(),                    // range
        [] (const Person& p1, const Person& p2) { // sort criterion
              return p1.lastname()<p2.lastname() ||
                     (p1.lastname()==p2.lastname() &&
                      p1.firstname()<p2.firstname());
        });
    ...
}
```

Limits of Lambdas

However, lambdas are not better in every case. Consider, for example, using a lambda to specify the sorting criterion for associative containers:

```cpp
auto cmp = [] (const Person&  p1, const Person&  p2) {
                return p1.lastname()<p2.lastname() ||
                       (p1.lastname()==p2.lastname()&&
                        p1.firstname()<p2.firstname());
           };
...
std::set<Person,decltype(cmp)> coll(cmp);
```

Because you need the type of the lambda for the declaration of the set, decltype (see Section 3.1.11, page 32) must be used, which yields the type of a lambda object, such as cmp. Note that you also have to pass the lambda object to the constructor of coll; otherwise, coll would call the default constructor for the sorting criterion passed, and by rule lambdas have no default constructor and no assignment operator.[11] So, for a sorting criterion, a class defining the function objects might still be more intuitive.

Another problem of lambdas is that they can't have an internal state held over multiple calls of a lambda. If you need such a state, you have declare an object or variable in the outer scope and pass it by-reference with a capture into the lambda. In contrast, function objects allow you to encapsulate an internal state (see Section 10.3.2, page 500, for more details and examples).

Nevertheless, you can also use lambdas to specify a hash function and/or equivalence criterion of unordered containers. See Section 7.9.7, page 379, for an example.

6.10   Function Objects

Functional arguments for algorithms don't have to be functions. As seen with lambdas, functional arguments can be objects that behave like functions. Such an object is called a *function object*, or *functor*.[12] Instead of using a lambda, you can define a function object as an object of a class that provides a *function call operator*. This was possible even before C++11.

6.10.1   Definition of Function Objects

Function objects are another example of the power of generic programming and the concept of pure abstraction. You could say that anything that *behaves* like a function *is* a function. So, if you define an object that behaves as a function, it can be used like a function.

So, what is the behavior of a function? A functional behavior is something that you can call by using parentheses and passing arguments. For example:

```
function(arg1,arg2);    // a function call
```

If you want objects to behave this way, you have to make it possible to "call" them by using parentheses and passing arguments. Yes, that's possible (rarely are things not possible in C++). All you have to do is define operator () with the appropriate parameter types:

```
class X {
  public:
    // define "function call" operator:
    return-value operator() (arguments) const;
    ...
};
```

---

[11] Thanks to Alisdair Meredith for pointing this out.

[12] Since C++11, the standard uses the term *function object* for every object that can be used as a function call. Thus, function pointers, objects of classes with operator () or with a conversion to a pointer to function, and lambdas are function objects. Here in this book, however, I use the term for objects of classes with operator () defined.

Now you can use objects of this class to behave like a function that you can call:

```
X fo;
...
fo(arg1,arg2);                    // call operator () for function object fo
```

The call is equivalent to:

```
fo.operator()(arg1,arg2);  // call operator () for function object fo
```

The following is a complete example. This is the function object version of a previous example (see Section 6.8.1, page 224) that did the same with an ordinary function:

```
// stl/foreach2.cpp

#include <vector>
#include <algorithm>
#include <iostream>
using namespace std;

// simple function object that prints the passed argument
class PrintInt {
  public:
    void operator() (int elem) const {
        cout << elem << ' ';
    }
};

int main()
{
    vector<int> coll;

    // insert elements from 1 to 9
    for (int i=1; i<=9; ++i) {
        coll.push_back(i);
    }

    // print all elements
    for_each (coll.cbegin(), coll.cend(),   // range
              PrintInt());                  // operation
    cout << endl;
}
```

The class PrintInt defines objects for which you can call operator () with an int argument. The expression

```
PrintInt()
```

in the statement

```
for_each (coll.cbegin(), coll.cend(),
          PrintInt());
```

creates a temporary object of this class, which is passed to the `for_each()` algorithm as an argument. The `for_each()` algorithm is written like this:

```
namespace std {
    template <typename Iterator, typename Operation>
    Operation for_each (Iterator act, Iterator end, Operation op)
    {
        while (act != end) {      // as long as not reached the end
            op(*act);             // - call op() for actual element
            ++act;                // - move iterator to the next element
        }
        return op;
    }
}
```

`for_each()` uses the temporary function object `op` to call `op(*act)` for each element `act`. If op is an ordinary function, `for_each()` simply calls it with `*act` as an argument. If op is a function object, `for_each()` calls its operator () with `*act` as an argument. Thus, in this example program, `for_each()` calls:

```
PrintInt::operator()(*act)
```

You may be wondering what all this is good for. You might even think that function objects look strange, nasty, or nonsensical. It is true that they do complicate code. However, function objects are more than functions, and they have some advantages:

1. **Function objects are "functions with state."** Objects that behave like pointers are smart pointers. This is similarly true for objects that behave like functions: They can be "smart functions" because they may have abilities beyond operator (). Function objects may have other member functions and attributes. This means that function objects have a state. In fact, the same functionality, represented by two different function objects of the same type, may have different states at the same time. This is not possible for ordinary functions. Another advantage of function objects is that you can initialize them at runtime before you use/call them.

2. **Each function object has its own type.** Ordinary functions have different types only when their signatures differ. However, function objects can have different types even when their signatures are the same. In fact, each functional behavior defined by a function object has its own type. This is a significant improvement for generic programming using templates because you can pass functional behavior as a template parameter. Doing so enables containers of different types to use the same kind of function object as a sorting criterion, ensuring that you don't assign, combine, or compare collections that have different sorting criteria. You can even design hierarchies of function objects so that you can, for example, have different, special kinds of one general criterion.

3. **Function objects are usually faster than ordinary functions.** The concept of templates usually allows better optimization because more details are defined at compile time. Thus, passing function objects instead of ordinary functions often results in better performance.

In the rest of this subsection, I present some examples that demonstrate how function objects can be "smarter" than ordinary functions. Chapter 10, which deals only with function objects, provides more examples and details. In particular, Chapter 10 shows how to benefit from the ability to pass functional behavior as a template parameter.

Suppose that you want to add a certain value to all elements of a collection. If you know the value you want to add at compile time, you could use an ordinary function:

```
void add10 (int& elem)
{
    elem += 10;
}


void f1()
{
    vector<int> coll;

    ...


    for_each (coll.begin(), coll.end(),      // range
              add10);                        // operation
}
```

If you need different values that are known at compile time, you could use a template instead:

```
template <int theValue>
void add (int& elem)
{
    elem += theValue;
}


void f1()
{
    vector<int> coll;

    ...


    for_each (coll.begin(), coll.end(),      // range
              add<10>);                      // operation
}
```

If you process the value to add at runtime, things get complicated. You must pass that value to the function before the function is called. This normally results in a global variable that is used both by the function that calls the algorithm and by the function that is called by the algorithm to add that value. This is messy style.

If you need such a function twice, with two different values to add, and if both values are processed at runtime, you can't achieve this with one ordinary function. You must either pass a tag or write two different functions. Did you ever copy the definition of a function because it had a static variable to keep its state and you needed the same function with another state at the same time? This is exactly the same type of problem.

With function objects, you can write a "smarter" function that behaves in the desired way. Because it may have a state, the object can be initialized by the correct value. Here is a complete example:[13]

```
// stl/add1.cpp

#include <list>
#include <algorithm>
#include <iostream>
#include "print.hpp"
using namespace std;

// function object that adds the value with which it is initialized
class AddValue {
  private:
    int theValue;      // the value to add
  public:
    // constructor initializes the value to add
    AddValue(int v) : theValue(v) {
    }

    // the "function call" for the element adds the value
    void operator() (int& elem) const {
        elem += theValue;
    }
};

int main()
{
    list<int> coll;

    // insert elements from 1 to 9
    for (int i=1; i<=9; ++i) {
        coll.push_back(i);
    }

    PRINT_ELEMENTS(coll,"initialized:                     ");

    // add value 10 to each element
```

---

[13] The auxiliary function PRINT_ELEMENTS() was introduced in Section 6.6, page 216.

```
        for_each (coll.begin(), coll.end(),    // range
                AddValue(10));                  // operation

    PRINT_ELEMENTS(coll,"after adding 10:                    ");

    // add value of first element to each element
    for_each (coll.begin(), coll.end(),    // range
            AddValue(*coll.begin()));       // operation

    PRINT_ELEMENTS(coll,"after adding first element: ");
}
```

After the initialization, the collection contains the values 1 to 9:

```
    initialized:              1 2 3 4 5 6 7 8 9
```

The first call of `for_each()` adds 10 to each value:

```
    for_each (coll.begin(), coll.end(),    // range
            AddValue(10));                  // operation
```

Here, the expression `AddValue(10)` creates an object of type `AddValue` that is initialized with the value 10. The constructor of `AddValue` stores this value as the member `theValue`. Inside `for_each()`, "`()`" is called for each element of `coll`. Again, this is a call of operator `()` for the passed temporary function object of type `AddValue`. The actual element is passed as an argument. The function object adds its value 10 to each element. The elements then have the following values:

```
    after adding 10:          11 12 13 14 15 16 17 18 19
```

The second call of `for_each()` uses the same functionality to add the value of the first element to each element. This call initializes a temporary function object of type `AddValue` with the first element of the collection:

```
    AddValue(*coll.begin())
```

The output is then as follows:

```
    after adding first element: 22 23 24 25 26 27 28 29 30
```

See Section 11.4, page 520, for a modified version of this example, in which the `AddValue` function object type is a template for the type of value to add.

With this technique, two different function objects can solve the problem of having a function with two states at the same time. For example, you could simply declare two function objects and use them independently:

```
    AddValue addx(x);      // function object that adds value x
    AddValue addy(y);      // function object that adds value y

    for_each (coll.begin(),coll.end(),      // add value x to each element
            addx);
    ...
```

```
for_each (coll.begin(),coll.end(),     // add value y to each element
          addy);
...
for_each (coll.begin(),coll.end(),     // add value x to each element
          addx);
```

Similarly, you can provide additional member functions to query or to change the state of the function object during its lifetime. See Section 10.1.3, page 482, for a good example.

Note that for some algorithms, the C++ standard library does not specify how often function objects are called for each element, and it might happen that different copies of the function object are passed to the elements. This might have some nasty consequences if you use function objects as predicates. Section 10.1.4, page 483, covers this issue.

6.10.2 Predefined Function Objects

The C++ standard library contains several predefined function objects that cover fundamental operations. By using them, you don't have to write your own function objects in several cases. A typical example is a function object used as a sorting criterion. The default sorting criterion for operator < is the predefined sorting criterion less<>. Thus, if you declare

```
set<int> coll;
```

it is expanded to

```
set<int,less<int>> coll;     // sort elements with <
```

From there, it is easy to sort elements in the opposite order:

```
set<int,greater<int>> coll;  // sort elements with >
```

Another place to apply predefined function objects are algorithms. Consider the following example:

```
// stl/fo1.cpp

#include <deque>
#include <algorithm>
#include <functional>
#include <iostream>
#include "print.hpp"
using namespace std;

int main()
{
    deque<int> coll = { 1, 2, 3, 5, 7, 11, 13, 17, 19 };

    PRINT_ELEMENTS(coll,"initialized: ");

    // negate all values in coll
```

```
      transform (coll.cbegin(),coll.cend(),       // source
                 coll.begin(),                     // destination
                 negate<int>());                   // operation
      PRINT_ELEMENTS(coll,"negated:      ");

      // square all values in coll
      transform (coll.cbegin(),coll.cend(),       // first source
                 coll.cbegin(),                    // second source
                 coll.begin(),                     // destination
                 multiplies<int>());               // operation
      PRINT_ELEMENTS(coll,"squared:      ");
  }
```

First, the header for the predefined function objects is included: `<functional>`

```
  #include <functional>
```

Then, two predefined function objects are used to negate and square the elements in `coll`. In

```
      transform (coll.cbegin(), coll.cend(),   // source
                 coll.begin(),                 // destination
                 negate<int>());               // operation
```

the expression

```
  negate<int>()
```

creates a function object of the predefined class template `negate<>` that simply returns the negated element of type `int` for which it is called. The `transform()` algorithm uses that operation to transform all elements of the first collection into the second collection. If source and destination are equal, as in this case, the returned negated elements overwrite themselves. Thus, the statement negates each element in the collection.

Similarly, the function object `multiplies` is used to square all elements in `coll`:

```
      transform (coll.cbegin(), coll.cend(),   // first source
                 coll.cbegin(),                // second source
                 coll.begin(),                 // destination
                 multiplies<int>());           // operation
```

Here, another form of the `transform()` algorithm combines elements of two collections by using the specified operation and writes the resulting elements into the third collection. Again, all collections are the same, so each element gets multiplied by itself, and the result overwrites the old value.

Thus, the program has the following output:

```
  initialized: 1 2 3 5 7 11 13 17 19
  negated:     -1 -2 -3 -5 -7 -11 -13 -17 -19
  squared:     1 4 9 25 49 121 169 289 361
```

6.10.3 Binders

You can use special *function adapters*, or so-called *binders*, to combine predefined function objects with other values or use special cases. Here is a complete example:

```cpp
// stl/bind1.cpp

#include <set>
#include <deque>
#include <algorithm>
#include <iterator>
#include <functional>
#include <iostream>
#include "print.hpp"
using namespace std;
using namespace std::placeholders;

int main()
{
    set<int,greater<int>> coll1 = { 1, 2, 3, 4, 5, 6, 7, 8, 9 };
    deque<int> coll2;

    // Note: due to the sorting criterion greater<>() elements have reverse order:
    PRINT_ELEMENTS(coll1,"initialized: ");

    // transform all elements into coll2 by multiplying them with 10
    transform (coll1.cbegin(),coll1.cend(),        // source
               back_inserter(coll2),               // destination
               bind(multiplies<int>(),_1,10));     // operation
    PRINT_ELEMENTS(coll2,"transformed: ");

    // replace value equal to 70 with 42
    replace_if (coll2.begin(),coll2.end(),         // range
                bind(equal_to<int>(),_1,70),       // replace criterion
                42);                               // new value
    PRINT_ELEMENTS(coll2,"replaced:    ");

    // remove all elements with values between 50 and 80
    coll2.erase(remove_if(coll2.begin(),coll2.end(),
                          bind(logical_and<bool>(),
                               bind(greater_equal<int>(),_1,50),
                               bind(less_equal<int>(),_1,80))),
                coll2.end());
    PRINT_ELEMENTS(coll2,"removed:     ");
}
```

Here, the statement

```
transform (coll1.cbegin(),coll1.cend(),          // source
           back_inserter(coll2),                 // destination
           bind(multiplies<int>(),_1,10));       // operation
```

transforms all elements of `coll1` into `coll2` (inserting) while multiplying each element by 10. To define the corresponding operation, `bind()` is used, which allows you to compose high-level function objects out of low-level function objects and placeholders, which are numeric identifiers that start with an underscore. By specifying

```
bind(multiplies<int>(),_1,10)
```

you define a function object that multiplies a first passed argument with 10.

You could also use such a function object to multiply any value by 10. For example, the following statements write 990 to the standard output:

```
auto f = bind(multiplies<int>(),_1,10);
cout << f(99) << endl;
```

This function object is passed to `transform()`, which is expecting as its fourth argument an operation that takes one argument; namely, the actual element. As a consequence, `transform()` calls "multiply by 10" for each actual element and inserts the result into `coll2`, which means that afterward `coll2` contains all values of `coll1` multiplied by 10.

Similarly, in

```
replace_if (coll2.begin(),coll2.end(),           // range
            bind(equal_to<int>(),_1,70),         // replace criterion
            42);                                 // new value
```

the following expression is used as a criterion to specify the elements that are replaced by 42:

```
bind(equal_to<int>(),_1,70)
```

Here, `bind()` calls the binary predicate `equal_to` with the passed first parameter as first argument and 70 as second argument. Thus, the function object specified via `bind()` yields `true` if a passed argument (element of `coll2`) is equal to 70. As a result, the whole statement replaces each value equal to 70 by 42.

The last example uses a combination of binders, where

```
bind(logical_and<bool>(),
     bind(greater_equal<int>(),_1,50),
     bind(less_equal<int>(),_1,80))
```

specifies for a parameter x the unary predicate "x>=50&&x<=80." This example demonstrates that you can use nested `bind()` expressions to describe even more complicated predicates and function objects. In this case, `remove_if()` uses the function object to remove all values between 50 and 80 out of the collection. In fact, `remove_if()` changes only the order and returns the new end, whereas `coll2.erase()` deletes the "removed" elements out of `coll2` (see Section 6.7.1, page 218, for details).

The output of the whole program is as follows:

```
initialized:  9 8 7 6 5 4 3 2 1
transformed:  90 80 70 60 50 40 30 20 10
replaced:     90 80 42 60 50 40 30 20 10
removed:      90 42 40 30 20 10
```

Note that the placeholders have their own namespace: `std::placeholders`. For this reason, a corresponding using directive is placed at the beginning to be able to write _1 or _2 for a first or second parameter of binders. Without any using directive, the last combination of binders would have to be specified as follows:

```
std::bind(std::logical_and<bool>(),
     std::bind(std::greater_equal<int>(),std::placeholders::_1,50),
     std::bind(std::less_equal<int>(),std::placeholders::_1,80))
```

This kind of programming results in *functional composition*. What is interesting is that all these function objects are usually declared inline. Thus, you use a function-like notation or abstraction, but you get good performance.

There are other ways to define function objects. For example, to call a member function for each element of a collection, you can specify the following:

```
for_each (coll.cbegin(), coll.cend(),   // range
          bind(&Person::save,_1));      // operation: Person::save(elem)
```

The function object `bind` binds a specified member function to call it for every element, which is passed here with placeholder `_1`. Thus, for each element of the collection `coll`, the member function `save()` of class `Person` is called. Of course, this works only if the elements have type `Person` or a type derived from `Person`.

Section 10.2, page 486, lists and discusses in more detail all predefined function objects, function adapters, and aspects of functional composition. Also given there is an explanation of how you can write your own function objects.

Before TR1, there were other binders and adapters for functional composition, such as `bind1st()`, `bind2nd()`, `ptr_fun()`, `mem_fun()`, and `mem_fun_ref()`, but they have been deprecated with C++11. See Section 10.2.4, page 497, for details.

6.10.4 Function Objects and Binders versus Lambdas

Lambdas are a kind of implicitly defined function object. Thus, as written in Section 6.9, page 230, lambdas usually provide the more intuitive approach to defining functional behavior of STL algorithms. In addition, lambdas should be as fast as function objects.

However, there are also some drawbacks to lambdas:

- You can't have a hidden internal state of such a function object. Instead, all data that defines a state is defined by the caller and passed as a capture.
- The advantage of specifying the functional behavior where it is needed partially goes away when it is needed at multiple places. You can define a lambda and assign it to an `auto` object then (see Section 6.9, page 232), but whether this is more readable than directly defining a function object is probably a matter of taste.

6.11   Container Elements

Elements of containers must meet certain requirements because containers handle them in a special way. In this section, I describe these requirements and discuss the consequences of the fact that containers make copies of their elements internally.

6.11.1   Requirements for Container Elements

Containers, iterators, and algorithms of the STL are templates. Thus, they can process both predefined or user-defined types. However, because of the operations that are called, some requirements apply. The elements of STL containers must meet the following three fundamental requirements:

1. An element must be *copyable* or *movable*. Thus, an element type implicitly or explicitly has to provide a copy or move constructor.

    A generated copy should be equivalent to the source. This means that any test for equality returns that both are equal and that both source and copy behave the same.

2. An element must be *(move) assignable* by the assignment operator. Containers and algorithms use assignment operators to overwrite old elements with new elements.

3. An element must be *destroyable* by a destructor. Containers destroy their internal copies of elements when these elements are removed from the container. Thus, the destructor must not be private. Also, as usual in C++, a destructor must not throw; otherwise, all bets are off.

These three operations are generated implicitly for any class. Thus, a class meets the requirements automatically, provided that no special versions of these operations are defined and no special members disable the sanity of those operations.

Elements might also have to meet the following requirements:

- For some member functions of sequence containers, the *default constructor* must be available. For example, it is possible to create a nonempty container or increase the number of elements with no hint of the values those new elements should have. These elements are created without any arguments by calling the default constructor of their type.

- For several operations, the *test of equality* with operator == must be defined and is especially needed when elements are searched. For unordered containers, however, you can provide your own definition of equivalence if the elements do not support operator == (see Section 7.9.7, page 379).

- For associative containers, the operations of the *sorting criterion* must be provided by the elements. By default, this is the operator <, which is called by the less<> function object.

- For unordered containers, a *hash function* and an *equivalence criterion* must be provided for the elements. See Section 7.9.2, page 363, for details.

6.11.2 Value Semantics or Reference Semantics

Usually, all containers create internal copies of their elements and return copies of those elements. This means that container elements are equal but not identical to the objects you put into the container. If you modify objects as elements of the container, you modify a copy, not the original object.

Copying values means that the STL containers provide *value semantics*. The containers contain the values of the objects you insert rather than the objects themselves. In practice, however, you may also need *reference semantics*. This means that the containers contain references to the objects that are their elements.

The approach of the STL to support only value semantics has both strengths and weaknesses. Its strengths are that

- Copying elements is simple.
- References are error prone. You must ensure that references don't refer to objects that no longer exist. You also have to manage circular references, which might occur.

Its weaknesses are as follows:

- Copying elements might result in bad performance or may not even be possible.
- Managing the same object in several containers at the same time is not possible.

In practice, you need both approaches; you need copies that are independent of the original data (value semantics) and copies that still refer to the original data and get modified accordingly (reference semantics). Unfortunately, there is no support for reference semantics in the C++ standard library. However, you can implement reference semantics in terms of value semantics.

The obvious approach to implementing reference semantics is to use pointers as elements.[14] However, ordinary pointers have the usual problems. For example, objects to which they refer may no longer exist, and comparisons may not work as desired because pointers instead of the objects are compared. Thus, you should be very careful when you use ordinary pointers as container elements.

A better approach is to use a kind of *smart pointer*: objects that have a pointer-like interface but that do some additional checking or processing internally. Since TR1, in fact, the C++ standard library provides class `shared_ptr` for smart pointers that can share the same object (see Section 5.2.1, page 76). In addition, you could use class `std::reference_wrapper<>` (see Section 5.4.3, page 132) to let STL containers hold references. Section 7.11, page 388, provides examples for both approaches.

6.12 Errors and Exceptions inside the STL

Errors happen. They might be logical errors caused by the program (the programmer) or runtime errors caused by the context or the environment of a program (such as low memory). Both kinds of errors may be handled by exceptions. This section discusses how errors and exceptions are handled inside the STL.

---

[14] C programmers might recognize the use of pointers to get reference semantics. In C, function arguments are able to get passed only by value, so you need pointers to enable a call-by-reference.

6.12.1   Error Handling

The design goal of the STL was the best performance rather than the highest security. Error checking wastes time, so almost none is done. This is fine if you can program without making any errors but can be a catastrophe if you can't. Before the STL was adopted into the C++ standard library, discussions were held about whether to introduce more error checking. The majority decided not to, for two reasons:

1. Error checking reduces performance, and speed is still a general goal of programs. As mentioned, good performance was one of the design goals of the STL.

2. If you prefer safety over speed, you can still get it, either by adding wrappers or by using special versions of the STL. But when error checking is built into all basic operations, you can't program to avoid error checking to get better performance For example, when every subscript operation checks whether a range is valid, you can't write your own subscripts without checking. However, it is possible the other way around.

As a consequence, error checking is possible but usually not required inside the STL.

The C++ standard library states that any STL use that violates preconditions results in undefined behavior. Thus, if indexes, iterators, or ranges are not valid, the result is undefined. If you do not use a safe version of the STL, undefined memory access typically results, which causes some nasty side effects or even a crash. In this sense, the STL is as error prone as pointers are in C. Finding such errors could be very hard, especially without a safe version of the STL.

In particular, the use of the STL requires that the following be met:

- Iterators must be valid. For example, they must be initialized before they are used. Note that iterators may become invalid as a side effect of other operations. In particular, iterators become invalid
  - for vectors and deques, if elements are inserted or deleted or reallocation takes place, and
  - for unordered containers, if rehashing takes place (which also might be the result of an insertion).

- Iterators that refer to the past-the-end position have no element to which to refer. Thus, calling operator * or operator -> is not allowed. This is especially true for the return values of the end(), cend(), and rend() container member functions.

- Ranges must be valid:
  - Both iterators that specify a range must refer to the same container.
  - The second iterator must be reachable from the first iterator.

- If more than one source range is used, the second and later ranges usually must have at least as many elements as the first one.

- Destination ranges must have enough elements that can be overwritten; otherwise, insert iterators must be used.

The following example shows some possible errors:

```
// stl/iterbug.cpp

#include <vector>
#include <algorithm>
using namespace std;

int main()
{
    vector<int> coll1;       // empty collection
    vector<int> coll2;       // empty collection

    // RUNTIME ERROR:
    // - beginning is behind the end of the range
    vector<int>::iterator pos = coll1.begin();
    reverse (++pos, coll1.end());

    // insert elements from 1 to 9 into coll1
    for (int i=1; i<=9; ++i) {
        coll1.push_back (i);
    }

    // RUNTIME ERROR:
    // - overwriting nonexisting elements
    copy (coll1.cbegin(), coll1.cend(),   // source
          coll2.begin());                 // destination

    // RUNTIME ERROR:
    // - collections mistaken
    // - cbegin() and cend() refer to different collections
    copy (coll1.cbegin(), coll2.cend(),   // source
          coll1.end());                   // destination
}
```

Note that because these errors occur at runtime, not at compile time, they cause undefined behavior.

There are many ways to make mistakes when using the STL, and the STL is not required to protect you from yourself. Thus, it is a good idea to use a "safe" STL, at least during software development. A first version of a safe STL was introduced by Cay Horstmann (see [*SafeSTL*]). Another example is the "STLport," which is available for free for almost any platform at [*STLport*]. In addition, library vendors now provide flags to enable a "safer" mode, which especially should be enabled during development.[15]

---

[15] For example, gcc provides the -D_GLIBCXX_DEBUG option for that.

6.12.2 Exception Handling

The STL almost never checks for logical errors. Therefore, almost no exceptions are generated by the STL itself owing to a logical problem. In fact, there are only two function calls for which the standard requires that it might cause an exception directly: the `at()` member function, which is the checked version of the subscript operator, and `reserve()` if the passed size of elements exceeds `max_size()`. Other than that, the standard requires that only the usual standard exceptions may occur, such as `bad_alloc` for lack of memory or exceptions of user-defined operations.

When are exceptions generated, and what happens to STL components when they are? For a long time during the standardization process of C++98, there was no defined behavior about this. In fact, every exception resulted in undefined behavior. Even the destruction of an STL container resulted in undefined behavior if an exception was thrown during one of its operations. Thus, the STL was useless when you needed guaranteed and defined behavior, because it was not even possible to unwind the stack.

How to handle exceptions was one of the last topics addressed during the standardization process of C++98. Finding a good solution was not easy, and it took a long time for the following reasons:

1. It was very difficult to determine the degree of safety the C++ standard library should provide. You might argue that it is always best to provide as much safety as possible. For example, you could say that the insertion of a new element at any position in a vector ought to either succeed or have no effect. Ordinarily, an exception might occur while copying later elements into the next position to make room for the new element, from which a full recovery is impossible. To achieve the stated goal, the insert operation would need to be implemented to copy *every* element of the vector into new storage, which would have a serious impact on performance. If good performance is a design goal, as is the case for the STL, you can't provide perfect exception handling in all cases. You have to find a compromise that meets both needs.

2. There is no doubt that it is better to have guaranteed, defined behavior for exceptions without a significant performance penalty instead of the risk that exceptions might crash your system. However, there was a concern that the presence of code to handle exceptions could adversely affect performance. This would contradict the design goal of achieving the best possible performance. During the standardization of C++98, compiler writers stated that, in principle, exception handling can be implemented without any significant performance overhead. However, it turned out that exception specifications could cause performance penalties, so they were replaced by `noexcept` with C++11 (see Section 3.1.7, page 24).

As a result of these discussions, the C++ standard library since C++98 gives the following *basic guarantee* for exception safety:[16] The C++ standard library will not leak resources or violate container invariants in the face of exceptions.

Unfortunately, this is not enough for many purposes. Often, you need a stronger guarantee that specifies that an operation has no effect if an exception is thrown. Such operations can be considered to be *atomic* with respect to exceptions. Or, to use terms from database programming, you could say that these operations support *commit-or-rollback* behavior or are *transaction safe*.

---

[16] Many thanks to Dave Abrahams and Greg Colvin for their work on exception safety in the C++ standard library and for the feedback they gave me about this topic.

Regarding this stronger guarantee, the C++ standard library now guarantees the following:

- In general, no `erase()`, `clear()`, `pop_back()`, `pop_front()`, or `swap()` function throws an exception. Also, no copy constructor or assignment operator of a returned iterator throws an exception.

- For all *node-based containers* (lists, forward lists, sets, multisets, maps, and multimaps), including the *unordered containers*, any failure to construct a node simply leaves the container as it was. Furthermore, removing a node can't fail, provided that destructors don't throw. However, for multiple-element insert operations of associative containers, the need to keep elements sorted makes full recovery from throws impractical. Thus, all single-element insert operations of associative and unordered containers support commit-or-rollback behavior, provided that the hash function for unordered containers does not throw. That is, the single-element insert operations either succeed or have no effect. In addition, it is guaranteed that all erase operations for both single and multiple elements always succeed, provided that the container's compare or hash function does not throw.

  For lists, even multiple-element insert operations are transaction safe. In fact, all list operations except `remove()`, `remove_if()`, `merge()`, `sort()`, and `unique()` either succeed or have no effect. For some of the exceptional operations, the C++ standard library provides conditional guarantees. Thus, if you need a transaction-safe container, you should use a list.

  For forward lists, `insert_after()`, `emplace_after()`, and `push_front()` are transaction safe.[17]

- All *array-based containers* (`arrays`, `vectors`, and `deques`) do not fully recover when an element gets inserted. To do this, they would have to copy all subsequent elements before any insert operation, and handling full recovery for all copy operations would take quite a lot of time. However, push and pop operations that operate at the end do not require that existing elements get copied. If they throw, it is guaranteed that they have no effect. Furthermore, if elements have a type with copy operations (copy constructor and assignment operator) that do not throw, every container operation for these elements either succeeds or has no effect.

Note that all these guarantees are based on the requirement that destructors never throw, which should always be the case in C++. The C++ standard library makes this promise, and so must the application programmer.

If you need a container with full commit-or-rollback ability, you should use either a list (without calling or special handling for `remove()`, `remove_if()`, `merge()`, `sort()`, and `unique()`) or an associative/unordered container (without calling their multiple-element insert operations). This avoids having to make copies before a modifying operation to ensure that no data gets lost. Note that making copies of a container could be very expensive.

If you can't use a node-based container and need the full commit-or-rollback ability, you have to provide wrappers for each critical operation. For example, the following function would almost safely insert a value in any container at a certain position:

---

[17] The C++11 standard does not say this for `emplace_after()` and `push_front()`, which likely is a defect.

```
template <typename T, typename Cont, typename Iter>
void insert (Cont& coll, const Iter& pos, const T& value)
{
    Cont tmp(coll);                 // copy container and all elements
    try {
        coll.insert(pos,value);     // try to modify the copy
    }
    catch (...) {                   // in case of an exception
        coll.swap(tmp);             // - restore original container
        throw;                      // - and rethrow the exception
    }
}
```

Note that I wrote "almost," because this function still is not perfect: the `swap()` operation throws when, for associative containers, copying the comparison criterion throws. You see, handling exceptions perfectly is not easy.

6.13   Extending the STL

The STL is designed as a framework that may be extended in almost any direction.

6.13.1   Integrating Additional Types

You can supply your own containers, iterators, algorithms, or function objects, provided that they meet certain requirements. In fact, the C++ standard library lacks some useful extensions. This happened because at some point, the committee had to stop introducing new features and concentrate on perfecting the existing parts; otherwise, the job would never have been completed. That was the reason, for example, that hash tables were not part of C++98.

Useful extensions can be iterators (see Section 9.6, page 471, or Section 14.3, page 726), containers (see Section 7.10, page 385), and algorithms (for example, see Section 7.6.2, page 308, or Section 9.5.1, page 468). Note that all these extensions follow the principle of generic programming:

- Anything that *behaves* like a container *is* a container.
- Anything that *behaves* like an iterator *is* an iterator.

Thus, whenever you have a container-like class, you can integrate it into the framework of the STL by providing the corresponding interface (`begin()`, `end()`, some type definitions, etc.). If you can't add members to such a class, you can still provide a wrapper class that provides corresponding iterators.

Note, however, that some container-like objects do not fit into the concept of the STL. For example, the fact that STL containers have a begin and an end makes it hard for circular container types, such as a ring buffer, to fit in the STL framework.

Section 7.1.2, page 254, lists all common container operations and marks those that are required for STL containers. Note, however, that this doesn't mean that you have to fit in the STL framework only if you meet *all* these requirements. It might often be enough to fulfill requirements only partially so that some but not all behavior might work. Even some standard STL containers violate STL container requirements. For example, `forward_lists` do not provide `size()`, and `arrays` do not fulfill the general requirement that an STL container initialized with the default constructor is empty.

6.13.2 Deriving from STL Types

Another question is whether you can extend the behavior of STL types by deriving from them and adding behavior. However, usually that's not possible. For performance reasons, all the STL classes have no virtual functions and are therefore not provided for polymorphism through public inheritance. To add new behavior for containers, you should define a new class that internally uses STL classes or derives privately from them.

Chapter 7

STL Containers

Continuing the discussion begun in Chapter 6, this chapter discusses STL containers in detail. The chapter starts with an overview of the general abilities and operations of all container classes, with each container class explained in detail. The explanation includes a description of their internal data structures, their operations, and their performance. It also shows how to use the various operations and gives examples if the usage is not trivial. Examples are given showing the typical use of each container. The chapter then discusses the interesting question of when to use which container. By comparing the general abilities, advantages, and disadvantages of all container types, the chapter shows you how to find the best container to meet your needs.

The chapter is supplemented by Chapter 8, which explains all container members, types, and operations in detail.

The C++ standard library provides some special container classes, the so-called *container adapters* (stack, queue, priority queue). In addition, a few classes provide a container-like interface (for example, strings, bitsets, and valarrays). All these classes are covered separately.[1] Container adapters and bitsets are covered in Chapter 12. The STL interface of strings is covered in Section 13.2.14, page 684. Valarrays are described in Section 17.4, page 943.

---

[1] Historically, container adapters are part of the STL. However, from a conceptual perspective, they are not part of the STL framework but rather "only" use the STL.

7.1   Common Container Abilities and Operations

7.1.1   Container Abilities

This section covers the common abilities of STL container classes. Most of these abilities are requirements that, in general, every STL container should meet. The three core abilities are as follows:

1. All containers provide value rather than reference semantics. Containers copy and/or move elements internally when they are inserted rather than managing references to them. Thus, ideally, each element of an STL container must be able to be copied and moved. If objects you want to store don't have a public copy constructor, or if copying is not useful — because, for example, it takes too much time or elements must be part of multiple containers — you might use only move operations, or the container elements must be pointers or pointer objects that refer to these objects. Section 7.11, page 388, provides an example for using shared pointers to get reference semantics.

2. The elements inside a container have a specific order. Each container type provides operations that return iterators to iterate over the elements. This is the key interface of the STL algorithms. Thus, if you iterate multiple times over the elements, you will find the same order, provided that you don't insert or delete elements. This applies even to "unordered containers," as long as you don't call operations that add or delete elements or force an internal reorganization.

3. In general, operations are not "safe" in the sense that they check for every possible error. The caller must ensure that the parameters of the operations meet the requirements these operations have. Violating these requirements, such as using an invalid index, results in undefined behavior, which means that anything can happen.

   Usually, the STL does *not* throw exceptions by itself. If user-defined operations called by the STL containers do throw, the behavior differs. See Section 6.12.2, page 248, for details.

7.1.2   Container Operations

The standard specifies a list of common container requirements that shall apply to all STL containers. However, due to the variety of containers provided with C++11, there might be exceptions so that some containers even don't fulfill all general container requirements, and that there are additional operations provided by all containers. Tables 7.1 and 7.2 list the operations that are common to (almost) all containers. Column "**Req**" signs operations that are part of the general container requirements. The following subsections explore some of these common operations.

Initialization

Every container class provides a default constructor, a copy constructor, and a destructor. You can also initialize a container with elements of a given range and, since C++11, with an initializer list.

Operation	Req	Effect
ContType c	Yes	Default constructor; creates an empty container without any element (`array<>` gets default elements)
ContType c(c2)	Yes	Copy constructor; creates a new container as a copy of *c2* (all elements are copied)
ContType c = c2	Yes	Copy constructor; creates a new container as a copy of *c2* (all elements are copied)
ContType c(rv)	Yes	Move constructor; creates a new container, taking the contents of the rvalue *rv* (since C++11; not for `array<>`)
ContType c = rv	Yes	Move constructor; creates a new container, taking the contents of the rvalue *rv* (since C++11; not for `array<>`)
ContType c(beg,end)	–	Creates a container and initializes it with copies of all elements of [*beg,end*) (not for `array<>`)
ContType c(initlist)	–	Creates a container and initializes it with copies of the values of the initializer list *initlist* (since C++11; not for `array<>`)
ContType c = initlist	–	Creates a container and initializes it with copies of the values of the initializer list *initlist* (since C++11)
c.~*ContType*()	Yes	Deletes all elements and frees the memory, if possible
c.empty()	Yes	Returns whether the container is empty (equivalent to `size()==0` but might be faster)
c.size()	Yes	Returns the current number of elements (not for `forward_list<>`)
c.max_size()	Yes	Returns the maximum number of elements possible
c1 == c2	Yes	Returns whether *c1* is equal to *c2*
c1 != c2	Yes	Returns whether *c1* is not equal to *c2* (equivalent to `!(c1==c2)`)
c1 < c2	–	Returns whether *c1* is less than *c2* (not for unordered containers)
c1 > c2	–	Returns whether *c1* is greater than *c2* (equivalent to *c2*<*c1*; not for unordered containers)
c1 <= c2	–	Returns whether *c1* is less than or equal to *c2* (equivalent to `!(c2<c1)`; not for unordered containers)
c1 >= c2	–	Returns whether *c1* is greater than or equal to *c2* (equivalent to `!(c1<c2)`; not for unordered containers)
c = c2	Yes	Assigns all elements of *c2* to c
c = rv	Yes	Move assigns all elements of the rvalue *rv* to c (since C++11; not for `array<>`)
c = initlist	–	Assigns all elements of the initializer list *initlist* (since C++11; not for `array<>`)
c1.swap(c2)	Yes	Swaps the data of *c1* and *c2*
swap(c1,c2)	Yes	Swaps the data of *c1* and *c2*

Table 7.1. Common Operations of (Almost All) Container Classes, Part 1

Operation	Req	Effect
`c.begin()`	Yes	Returns an iterator for the first element
`c.end()`	Yes	Returns an iterator for the position after the last element
`c.cbegin()`	Yes	Returns a constant iterator for the first element (since C++11)
`c.cend()`	Yes	Returns a constant iterator for the position after the last element (since C++11)
`c.clear()`	–	Removes all elements (empties the container; not for `array<>`)

Table 7.2. Common Operations of (Almost All) Container Classes, Part 2

The constructor for an initializer list (see Section 3.1.3, page 15) provides a convenient way to specify initial values. This is especially useful to initialize constant containers:

```
// initialize a vector with some specific values (since C++11)
const std::vector<int> v1 = { 1, 2, 3, 5, 7, 11, 13, 17, 21 };
```

```
// same with different syntax
const std::vector<int> v2 { 1, 2, 3, 5, 7, 11, 13, 17, 21 };
```

```
// initialize an unordered set with "hello" and two empty strings
std::unordered_set<std::string> w = { "hello", std::string(), "" };
```

Some special rules apply to the use of initializer lists for `array<>` containers (see Section 7.2.1, page 262, for details).

The constructor for a given range provides the ability to initialize the container with elements of another container, with a C-style array, or from standard input. This constructor is a member template (see Section 3.2, page 34), so not only the container but also the type of the elements may differ, provided that there is an automatic conversion from the source element type to the destination element type. For example:

- You can initialize a container with the elements of another container:
  ```
  std::list<int> l;          // l is a linked list of ints
  ...
  // copy all elements of the list as floats into a vector
  std::vector<float> c(l.begin(),l.end());
  ```
  Since C++11, you can also move the elements here, using a move iterator (see Section 9.4.4, page 466):
  ```
  std::list<std::string> l;   // l is a linked list of strings
  ...
  // move all elements of the list into a vector
  std::vector<std::string> c(std::make_move_iterator(l.begin()),
                             std::make_move_iterator(l.end()));
  ```

- You can initialize a container with the elements of an ordinary C-style array:

  ```
  int carray[] = { 2, 3, 17, 33, 45, 77 };
  ...
  ```

  // copy all elements of the C-style array into a set
  ```
  std::set<int> c(std::begin(carray),std::end(carray));
  ```
  `std::begin()` and `std::end()` for C-style arrays are defined since C++11 in `<iterator>`. Note that before C++11, you had to call:
  ```
  std::set<int> c(carray,carray+sizeof(carray)/sizeof(carray[0]));
  ```

- You can initialize a container from standard input:

  // read all integer elements of the deque from standard input
  ```
  std::deque<int> c{std::istream_iterator<int>(std::cin),
                    std::istream_iterator<int>()};
  ```
  Note that you should use the new uniform initialization syntax with brackets (see Section 3.1.3, page 15). Otherwise, you need extra parentheses around the initializer arguments here:

  // read all integer elements of the deque from standard input
  ```
  std::deque<int> c((std::istream_iterator<int>(std::cin)),
                    (std::istream_iterator<int>()));
  ```
  The reason is that without the extra parentheses, you specify something very different, so you will probably get some strange warnings or errors in following statements. Consider writing the statement without extra parentheses:
  ```
  std::deque<int> c(std::istream_iterator<int>(std::cin),
                    std::istream_iterator<int>());
  ```
  In this case, c declares a *function* having deque<int> as return type. Its first parameter is of type `istream_iterator<int>` with the name cin, and its second unnamed parameter is of type "function taking no arguments returning `istream_iterator<int>`." This construct is valid syntactically as either a declaration or an expression. So, according to language rules, it is treated as a declaration. The extra parentheses force the initializer not to match the syntax of a declaration.[2]

In principle, these techniques are also provided to assign or to insert elements from another range. However, for those operations, the exact interfaces either differ due to additional arguments or are not provided for all container classes.

Finally, since C++11, you can use a move constructor (see Section 3.1.5, page 21) to initialize a container (for array<>, it is implicitly defined):

```
std::vector<int> v1;
...
```

// move contents of v1 into v2, state of v1 undefined afterward
```
std::vector<int> v2 = std::move(v1);
```

As a result, the newly created container has the elements of the container used for initialization, whereas the contents of the container used for the initialization is unspecified afterward. This constructor provides significant performance improvements because internally, the elements are moved

---

[2] Thanks to John H. Spicer from EDG for this explanation.

by switching some pointers instead of copying element by element. So whenever you no longer need a container, which gets copied, you should use the move constructor.

Assignments and `swap()`

If you assign containers, you copy all elements of the source container and remove all old elements in the destination container. Thus, assignment of containers is relatively expensive.

Since C++11, you can use the move assignment semantics instead (see Section 3.1.5, page 21). All containers provide move assignment operators (`array<>` implicitly again), declared for rvalues, which internally just swap pointers to the memory of values rather than copying all values. The exact behavior is not specified, but the guarantee of constant complexity for this operation leads to an implementation like this. The C++ standard library simply specifies that after a move assignment, the container on the left-hand side of the assignment has the elements that the container on the right-hand side of the assignment had before. The contents of the container on the right-hand side are undefined afterward:

```
std::vector<int> v1;
std::vector<int> v2;
...
// move contents of v1 into v2, state of v1 undefined afterward
v2 = std::move(v1);
```

So, for performance reasons, you should use this way of assignment if after an assignment, the contents of the container on the right-hand side are no longer used.

In addition and since C++98, all containers provide a `swap()` member function to swap contents of two containers. In fact, it swaps only some internal pointers that refer to the data (elements, allocator, sorting criterion, if any). So, `swap()` is guaranteed to have only constant complexity, not the linear complexity of a copy assignment. Iterators and references to elements of a container follow swapped elements. So, after `swap()`, iterators and references still refer to the elements they referred to before, which, however, are in a different container then.

Note that for containers of type `array<>`, the behavior of `swap()` is slightly different. Because you can't internally just swap pointers, `swap()` has linear complexity, and iterators and references refer to the same container but different elements afterward.

Size Operations

For (almost) all container classes, three size operations are provided:

1. **empty()** returns whether the number of elements is zero (`begin()==end()`). You should prefer it over `size()==0`, because it might be implemented more efficiently than `size()`, and `size()` is not provided for forward lists.

2. **size()** returns the current number of elements of the container. This operation is not provided for `forward_list<>` because it couldn't have constant complexity there.

3. **max_size()** returns the maximum number of elements a container might contain. This value is implementation defined. For example, a vector typically contains all elements in a single block

of memory, so there might be relevant restrictions on PCs. Otherwise, `max_size()` is usually the maximum value of the type of the index.

Comparisons

For all but unordered containers, the usual comparison operators ==, !=, <, <=, >, and >= are defined according to the following three rules:

1. Both containers must have the same type.
2. Two containers are equal if their elements are equal and have the same order. To check equality of elements, operator == is used.
3. To check whether a container is less than another container, a lexicographical comparison is done (see Section 11.5.4, page 548).

For unordered containers, only the operators == and != are defined. They return `true` when each element in one container has an equal element in the other container. The order doesn't matter (that's why they are unordered containers).

Because the operators <, <=, >, and >= are not provided for unordered container, only the operators == and != are a common container requirement. Before C++11 all comparison operators were required. Since C++11 there is an table of "optional container requirements" that covers the remaining four comparison operators.

To compare containers with different types, you must use the comparing algorithms of Section 11.5.4, page 542.

Element Access

All containers provide an iterator interface, which means that range-based `for` loops are supported (see Section 3.1.4, page 17). Thus, the easiest way to get access to all elements since C++11 is as follows:

```
for (const auto& elem : coll) {
    std::cout << elem << std::endl;
}
```

To be able to manipulate the elements, you should skip the `const`:

```
for (auto& elem : coll) {
    elem = ...;
}
```

To operate with positions (for example, to be able to insert, delete, or move elements around), you can always use iterators yielded by `cbegin()` and `cend()` for read-only access:

```
for (auto pos=coll.cbegin(); pos!=coll.cend(); ++pos) {
    std::cout << *pos << std::endl;
}
```

and iterators yielded by `begin()` and `end()` for write access:

```
for (auto pos=coll.begin(); pos!=coll.end(); ++pos) {
    *pos = ...;
}
```

Before C++11, you had to, and still can, declare the type of the iterator explicitly for read access:

```
colltype::const_iterator pos;
for (pos=coll.begin(); pos!=coll.end(); ++pos) {
    ...;
}
```

or for write access

```
colltype::iterator pos;
for (pos=coll.begin(); pos!=coll.end(); ++pos) {
    ...;
}
```

All containers except vectors and deques guarantee that iterators and references to elements remain valid if other elements are deleted. For vectors, only the elements before the point of erase remain valid.

If you remove all elements by using clear(), for vectors, deques, and strings any *past-the-end iterator* returned by end() or cend() may become invalid.

If you insert elements, only lists, forward lists, and associative containers guarantee that iterators and references to elements remain valid. For vectors, this guarantee is given if insertions don't exceed the capacity. For unordered containers, that guarantee is given to references in general but to iterators only when no rehashing happens, which is guaranteed as long as with insertions the number of resulting elements is less than the bucket count times the maximum load factor.

7.1.3   Container Types

All containers provide common type definitions, which are listed in Table 7.3.

Type	Req	Effect
size_type	Yes	Unsigned integral type for size values
difference_type	Yes	Signed integral type for difference values
value_type	Yes	Type of the elements
reference	Yes	Type of element references
const_reference	Yes	Type of constant element references
iterator	Yes	Type of iterators
const_iterator	Yes	Type of iterators to read-only elements
pointer	–	Type of pointers to elements (since C++11)
const_pointer	–	Type of pointers to read-only elements (since C++11)

Table 7.3. Common Types Defined by All Container Classes

7.2 Arrays

An array — an instance of the container class `array<>` — models a static array. It wraps an ordinary static C-style array providing the interface of an STL container (Figure 7.1). Conceptionally, an array is a sequence of elements with constant size. Thus, you can neither add nor remove elements to change the size. Only a replacement of element values is possible.

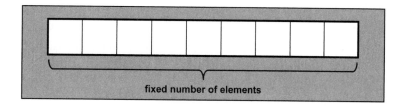

Figure 7.1. Structure of an Array

Class `array<>`, introduced to the C++ standard library with TR1, results from a useful wrapper class for ordinary C-style arrays Bjarne Stroustrup introduced in his book [*Stroustrup:C++*]. It is safer and has no worse performance than an ordinary array.

To use an array, you must include the header file `<array>`:

```
#include <array>
```

There, the type is defined as a class template inside namespace `std`:

```
namespace std {
    template <typename T, size_t N>
    class array;
}
```

The elements of an array may have any type `T`.

The second template parameter specifies the number of elements the array has throughout its lifetime. Thus, `size()` always yields `N`.

Allocator support is not provided.

7.2.1 Abilities of Arrays

Arrays copy their elements into their internal static C-style array. The elements always have a certain order. Thus, arrays are a kind of *ordered collection*. Arrays provide *random access*. Thus, you can access every element directly in constant time, provided that you know its position. The iterators are random-access iterators, so you can use any algorithm of the STL.

If you need a sequence with a fixed number of elements, class `array<>` has the best performance because memory is allocated on the stack (if possible), reallocation never happens, and you have random access.

Initialization

Regarding initialization, class `array<>` has some unique semantics. As a first example, the default constructor does not create an empty container, because the number of elements in the container is always constant according to the second template parameter throughout its lifetime.

Note that `array<>` is the only container whose elements are *default initialized* when nothing is passed to initialize the elements. This means that for fundamental types, the initial value might be undefined rather than zero (see Section 3.2.1, page 37). For example:

```
std::array<int,4> x;          // OOPS: elements of x have undefined value
```

You can provide an empty initializer list instead. In that case, all values are guaranteed to be value initialized, which has the effect that elements of fundamental types are *zero initialized*:

```
std::array<int,4> x = {};     // OK: all elements of x have value 0 (int())
```

The reason is that although `array<>` seems to provide a constructor for initializer lists, it does not. Instead, `array<>` fulfills the requirements of an aggregate.[3] Therefore, even before C++11, you could use an initializer list to initialize an array when it got created:

```
std::array<int,5> coll = { 42, 377, 611, 21, 44 };
```

The elements in the initializer list must have the same type, or there must be a type conversion to the element type of the array defined.

If an initializer list does not have enough elements, the elements in the array are initialized via the default constructor of the element type. In this case, it is guaranteed that for fundamental data types the elements are zero initialized. For example:

```
std::array<int,10> c2 = { 42 }; // one element with value 42
                                // followed by 9 elements with value 0
```

If the number of elements in the initializer lists is higher than the size of the array, the expression is ill-formed:

```
std::array<int,5> c3 = { 1, 2, 3, 4, 5, 6 };  // ERROR: too many values
```

Because no constructors or assignment operators for initializer lists are provided, initializing an array during its declaration is the only way to use initializer lists. For this reason, you also can't use the parenthesis syntax to specify initial values (which differs from other container types):

```
std::array<int,5> a({ 1, 2, 3, 4, 5, 6 });  // ERROR
std::vector<int>  v({ 1, 2, 3, 4, 5, 6 });  // OK
```

Class `array<>` being an aggregate also means that the member that holds all the elements is public. However, its name is not specified in the standard; thus, any direct access to the public member that holds all elements results in undefined behavior and is definitely not portable.

---

[3] An aggregate is an array or a class with no user-provided constructors, no private or protected nonstatic data members, no base classes, and no virtual functions.

swap() and Move Semantics

As for all other containers, array<> provides swap() operations. Thus, you can swap elements with a container of the same type (same element type and same number of elements). Note, however, that an array<> can't simply swap pointers internally. For this reason, swap() has linear complexity and the effect that iterators and references don't swap containers with their elements. So, iterators and references refer to the same container but different elements afterward.

You can use move semantics, which are implicitly provided for arrays. For example:[4]

```
std::array<std::string,10>  as1, as2;
...
as1 = std::move(as2);
```

Size

It is possible to specify a size of 0, which is an array with no elements. In that case, begin() and end(), cbegin() and cend(), and the corresponding reverse iterators still yield the same unique value. However, the return value of front() and back() is undefined:

```
std::array<Elem,0> coll;                 // array with no elements

std::sort(coll.begin(),coll.end());      // OK (but has no effect)

coll[5] = elem;                          // RUNTIME ERROR ⇒ undefined behavior
std::cout << coll.front();               // RUNTIME ERROR ⇒ undefined behavior
```

For data(), the return value is unspecified, which means that you can pass the return value to other places as long as you don't dereference it.

7.2.2 Array Operations

Create, Copy, and Destroy

Table 7.4 lists the constructors and destructors for arrays. Because class array<> is an aggregate, these constructors are only implicitly defined. You can create arrays with and without elements for initialization. The default constructor default initializes the elements, which means that the value of fundamental types is undefined. If you use an initializer list but do not pass enough elements, the remaining elements are created with their default constructor (0 for fundamental types). See Section 7.1.2, page 254, for some remarks about possible initialization sources.

Again, note that unlike with other containers, you can't use the parenthesis syntax with initializer lists:

```
std::array<int,5> a({ 1, 2, 3, 4, 5 });  // ERROR
```

---

[4] Thanks to Daniel Krügler for providing this example.

Operation	Effect
`array<Elem,N> c`	Default constructor; creates an array with default-initialized elements
`array<Elem,N> c(c2)`	Copy constructor; creates a copy of another array of the same type (all elements are copied)
`array<Elem,N> c = c2`	Copy constructor; creates a copy of another array of the same type (all elements are copied)
`array<Elem,N> c(rv)`	Move constructor; creates a new array taking the contents of the rvalue *rv* (since C++11)
`array<Elem,N> c = rv`	Move constructor; creates a new array, taking the contents of the rvalue *rv* (since C++11)
`array<Elem,N> c = initlist`	Creates an array initialized with the elements of the initializer list

Table 7.4. Constructors of Class `array<>`

Nonmodifying Operations

Table 7.5 lists all nonmodifying operations of arrays. See the additional remarks in Section 7.1.2, page 254.

Operation	Effect
`c.empty()`	Returns whether the container is empty (equivalent to `size()==0` but might be faster)
`c.size()`	Returns the current number of elements
`c.max_size()`	Returns the maximum number of elements possible
`c1 == c2`	Returns whether *c1* is equal to *c2* (calls == for the elements)
`c1 != c2`	Returns whether *c1* is not equal to *c2* (equivalent to `!(c1==c2)`)
`c1 < c2`	Returns whether *c1* is less than *c2*
`c1 > c2`	Returns whether *c1* is greater than *c2* (equivalent to `c2<c1`)
`c1 <= c2`	Returns whether *c1* is less than or equal to *c2* (equivalent to `!(c2<c1)`)
`c1 >= c2`	Returns whether *c1* is greater than or equal to *c2* (equivalent to `!(c1<c2)`)

Table 7.5. Nonmodifying Operations of Class `array<>`

Assignments

Table 7.6 lists the ways to assign new values. Besides the assignment operator, you can use only `fill()` to assign a new value to each element, or `swap()` to swap values with another array. For operator = and `swap()`, both arrays have to have the same type, which means that both element type and size have to be the same.

Operation	Effect
c = c2	Assigns all elements of *c2* to *c*
c = *rv*	Move assigns all elements of the rvalue *rv* to *c* (since C++11)
c.fill(*val*)	Assigns *val* to each element in array *c*
c1.swap(c2)	Swaps the data of *c1* and *c2*
swap(c1,c2)	Swaps the data of *c1* and *c2*

Table 7.6. Assignment Operations of Class array<>

Note that swap() can't guarantee constant complexity for arrays, because it is not possible to exchange some pointers internally (see Section 7.2.1, page 263). Instead, as with the algorithm swap_ranges() (see Section 11.6.4, page 566), for both arrays involved, all elements get new values assigned.

Internally, all these operations call the assignment operator of the element type.

Element Access

To access all elements of an array, you must use range-based for loops (see Section 3.1.4, page 17), specific operations, or iterators. In addition, a tuple interface is provided, so you can also use get<>() to access a specific element (see Section 7.2.5, page 268, for details). Table 7.7 shows all array operations for direct element access. As usual in C and C++, the first element has index 0, and the last element has index size()-1. Thus, the *n*th element has index *n*-1. For nonconstant arrays, these operations return a reference to the element. Thus, you could modify an element by using one of these operations, provided it is not forbidden for other reasons.

Operation	Effect
c[*idx*]	Returns the element with index *idx* (*no* range checking)
c.at(*idx*)	Returns the element with index *idx* (throws range-error exception if *idx* is out of range)
c.front()	Returns the first element (*no* check whether a first element exists)
c.back()	Returns the last element (*no* check whether a last element exists)

Table 7.7. Direct Element Access of Class array<>

The most important issue for the caller is whether these operations perform range checking. Only at() performs range checking. If the index is out of range, at() throws an out_of_range exception (see Section 4.3, page 41). All other functions do *not* check. A range error results in undefined behavior. Calling operator [], front(), and back() for an empty array<> always results in undefined behavior. Note however that it is only empty if declared to have a size of 0:

```
std::array<Elem,4> coll;        // only four elements!

coll[5] = elem;                 // RUNTIME ERROR ⇒ undefined behavior
std::cout << coll.front();      // OK (coll has 4 element after construction)
```

```
std::array<Elem,0> coll2;        // always empty
std::cout << coll2.front();      // RUNTIME ERROR ⇒ undefined behavior
```

So, in doubt you must ensure that the index for operator [ ] is valid or use at():

```
template <typename C>
void foo (C& coll)
{
    if (coll.size() > 5) {
        coll[5] = ...;           // OK
    }

    coll.at(5) = ...;            // throws out_of_range exception
}
```

Note that this code is OK only in single-threaded environments. In multithreaded contexts, you need synchronization mechanisms to prevent coll from being modified between the check for its size and the access to the element (see Section 18.4.3, page 984, for details).

Iterator Functions

Arrays provide the usual operations to get iterators (Table 7.8). Array iterators are random-access iterators (see Section 9.2, page 433, for a discussion of iterator categories). Thus, in principle, you could use all algorithms of the STL.

Operation	Effect
c.begin()	Returns a random-access iterator for the first element
c.end()	Returns a random-access iterator for the position after the last element
c.cbegin()	Returns a constant random-access iterator for the first element (since C++11)
c.cend()	Returns a constant random-access iterator for the position after the last element (since C++11)
c.rbegin()	Returns a reverse iterator for the first element of a reverse iteration
c.rend()	Returns a reverse iterator for the position after the last element of a reverse iteration
c.crbegin()	Returns a constant reverse iterator for the first element of a reverse iteration (since C++11)
c.crend()	Returns a constant reverse iterator for the position after the last element of a reverse iteration (since C++11)

Table 7.8. Iterator Operations of Class array<>

The exact type of these iterators is implementation defined. For arrays, however, the iterators returned by begin(), cbegin(), end(), and cend() are often ordinary pointers, which is fine because an array<> internally uses a C-style array for the elements and ordinary pointers provide the interface of random-access iterators. However, you can't count on the fact that the iterators are ordinary pointers. For example, if a safe version of the STL that checks range errors and other potential problems is used, the iterator type is usually an auxiliary class. See Section 9.2.6, page 440, for a nasty difference between iterators implemented as pointers and iterators implemented as classes.

Iterators remain valid as long as the array remains valid. However, unlike for all other containers, `swap()` assigns new values to the elements that iterators, references, and pointers refer to.

7.2.3 Using `arrays` as C-Style Arrays

As for class `vector<>`, the C++ standard library guarantees that the elements of an `array<>` are in contiguous memory. Thus, you can expect that for any valid index `i` in array `a`, the following yields true:

```
&a[i] == &a[0] + i
```

This guarantee has some important consequences. It simply means that you can use an `array<>` wherever you can use an ordinary C-style array. For example, you can use an array to hold data of ordinary C-strings of type `char*` or `const char*`:

```
std::array<char,41> a;            // create static array of 41 chars

strcpy(&a[0],"hello, world");     // copy a C-string into the array
printf("%s\n", &a[0]);            // print contents of the array as C-string
```

Note, however, that you don't have to use the expression `&a[0]` to get direct access to the elements in the array, because the member function `data()` is provided for this purpose:

```
std::array<char,41> a;            // create static array of 41 chars

strcpy(a.data(),"hello, world");  // copy a C-string into the array
printf("%s\n", a.data());         // print contents of the array as C-string
```

Of course, you have to be careful when you use an `array<>` in this way (just as you always have to be careful when using ordinary C-style arrays and pointers). For example, you have to ensure that the size of the array is big enough to copy some data into it and that you have an `'\0'` element at the end if you use the contents as a C-string. However, this example shows that whenever you need an array of type T for any reason, such as for an existing C library, you can use an `array<>` (or `vector<>`) and use `data()` where the ordinary C-style interface is required.

Note that you must not pass an iterator as the address of the first element. Iterators of class `array<>` have an implementation-specific type, which may be totally different from an ordinary pointer:

```
printf("%s\n", a.begin());        // ERROR (might work, but not portable)
printf("%s\n", a.data());         // OK
```

7.2.4   Exception Handling

Arrays provide only minimal support for logical error checking. The only member function for which the standard requires that it may throw an exception is at(), which is the safe version of the subscript operator (see Section 7.2.2, page 265).

For functions called by an array (functions for the element type or functions that are user-supplied) no special guarantees are generally given (because you can't insert or delete elements, exceptions might occur only if you copy, move, or assign values). Note especially that swap() might throw because it performs an element-wise swap, which might throw.

See Section 6.12.2, page 248, for a general discussion of exception handling in the STL.

7.2.5   Tuple Interface

Arrays provide the tuple interface (see Section 5.1.2, page 68). Thus, you can use the expressions tuple_size<>::value to yield the number of elements, tuple_element<>::type to yield the type of a specific element, and get() to gain access to a specific element. For example:

```
typedef std::array<std::string,5> FiveStrings;

FiveStrings a = { "hello", "nico", "how", "are", "you" };

std::tuple_size<FiveStrings>::value          // yields 5
std::tuple_element<1,FiveStrings>::type      // yields std::string
std::get<1>(a)                               // yields std::string("nico")
```

7.2.6   Examples of Using Arrays

The following example shows a simple use of class array<>:

```
// cont/array1.cpp

#include <array>
#include <algorithm>
#include <functional>
#include <numeric>
#include "print.hpp"
using namespace std;

int main()
{
    // create array with 10 ints
    array<int,10> a = { 11, 22, 33, 44 };

    PRINT_ELEMENTS(a);
```

```
    // modify last two elements
    a.back() = 9999999;
    a[a.size()-2] = 42;
    PRINT_ELEMENTS(a);

    // process sum of all elements
    cout << "sum: "
         << accumulate(a.begin(),a.end(),0)
         << endl;

    // negate all elements
    transform(a.begin(),a.end(),      // source
              a.begin(),              // destination
              negate<int>());         // operation
    PRINT_ELEMENTS(a);
}
```

As you can see, you can use the general container interface operations (operator =, size(), and operator [ ]) to manipulate the container directly. Because member functions such as begin() and end() for iterator access are also provided, you can also use different operations that call begin() and end(), such as modifying and nonmodifying algorithms and the auxiliary function PRINT_ELEMENTS(), which is introduced in Section 6.6, page 216.

The output of the program is as follows:

```
11 22 33 44 0 0 0 0 0 0
11 22 33 44 0 0 0 0 42 9999999
sum: 10000151
-11 -22 -33 -44 0 0 0 0 -42 -9999999
```

7.3   Vectors

A vector models a dynamic array. Thus, a vector is an abstraction that manages its elements with a dynamic C-style array (Figure 7.2). However, the standard does not specify that the implementation uses a dynamic array. Rather, this follows from the constraints and specification of the complexity of its operation.

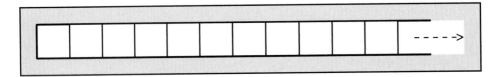

Figure 7.2. Structure of a Vector

To use a vector, you must include the header file `<vector>`:

```
#include <vector>
```

There, the type is defined as a class template inside namespace `std`:

```
namespace std {
    template <typename T,
                typename Allocator = allocator<T> >
    class vector;
}
```

The elements of a vector may have any type T. The optional second template parameter defines the memory model (see Chapter 19). The default memory model is the model `allocator`, which is provided by the C++ standard library.

7.3.1   Abilities of Vectors

A vector copies its elements into its internal dynamic array. The elements always have a certain order. Thus, a vector is a kind of *ordered collection*. A vector provides *random access*. Thus, you can access every element directly in constant time, provided that you know its position. The iterators are random-access iterators, so you can use any algorithm of the STL.

Vectors provide good performance if you append or delete elements at the end. If you insert or delete in the middle or at the beginning, performance gets worse. This is because every element behind has to be moved to another position. In fact, the assignment operator would be called for every following element.

Size and Capacity

Part of the way in which vectors give good performance is by allocating more memory than they need to contain all their elements. To use vectors effectively and correctly, you should understand how size and capacity cooperate in a vector.

Vectors provide the usual size operations `size()`, `empty()`, and `max_size()` (see Section 7.1.2, page 254). An additional "size" operation is the `capacity()` function, which returns the number of elements a vector could contain in its actual memory. If you exceed the `capacity()`, the vector has to reallocate its internal memory.

The capacity of a vector is important for two reasons:

1. Reallocation invalidates all references, pointers, and iterators for elements of the vector.
2. Reallocation takes time.

Thus, if a program manages pointers, references, or iterators into a vector, or if speed is a goal, it is important to take the capacity into account.

To avoid reallocation, you can use `reserve()` to ensure a certain capacity before you really need it. In this way, you can ensure that references remain valid as long as the capacity is not exceeded:

```
std::vector<int> v;      // create an empty vector
v.reserve(80);           // reserve memory for 80 elements
```

Another way to avoid reallocation is to initialize a vector with enough elements by passing additional arguments to the constructor. For example, if you pass a numeric value as parameter, it is taken as the starting size of the vector:

```
std::vector<T> v(5);     // creates a vector and initializes it with five values
                         // (calls five times the default constructor of type T)
```

Of course, the type of the elements must provide a default constructor for this ability. For fundamental types, zero initialization (see Section 3.2.1, page 37) is guaranteed. But note that for complex types, even if a default constructor is provided, the initialization takes time. If the only reason for initialization is to reserve memory, you should use `reserve()`.

The concept of capacity for vectors is similar to that for strings (see Section 13.2.5, page 669), with one big difference: Unlike for strings, it is not possible to call `reserve()` for vectors to shrink the capacity. Calling `reserve()` with an argument that is less than the current capacity is a no-op. Furthermore, how to reach an optimal performance regarding speed and memory use is implementation defined. Thus, implementations might increase capacity in larger steps. In fact, to avoid internal fragmentation, many implementations allocate a whole block of memory (such as 2K) the first time you insert anything if you don't call `reserve()` first yourself. This can waste a lot of memory if you have many vectors with only a few small elements.

Because the capacity of vectors never shrinks, it is guaranteed that references, pointers, and iterators remain valid even when elements are deleted, provided that they refer to a position before the manipulated elements. However, insertions invalidate all references, pointers, and iterators when the capacity gets exceeded.

C++11 introduced a new member function for vectors: a nonbinding request to shrink the capacity to fit the current number of elements:

```
v.shrink_to_fit();       // request to shrink memory (since C++11)
```

This request is nonbinding to allow latitude for implementation-specific optimizations. Thus, you cannot expect that afterward `v.capacity==v.size()` yields `true`.

Before C++11, there you could shrink the capacity only indirectly: Swapping the contents with another vector swaps the capacity. The following function shrinks the capacity while preserving the elements:

```
template <typename T>
void shrinkCapacity(std::vector<T>& v)
{
    std::vector<T> tmp(v);       // copy elements into a new vector
    v.swap(tmp);                 // swap internal vector data
}
```

You could even shrink the capacity without calling this function by calling the following statement:[5]

// shrink capacity of vector v for type T
```
std::vector<T>(v).swap(v);
```

However, note that after `swap()`, all references, pointers, and iterators swap their containers. They still refer to the elements to which they referred on entry. Thus, `shrinkCapacity()` invalidates all references, pointers, and iterators. The same is true for `shrink_to_fit()`.

Operation	Effect
`vector<Elem> c`	Default constructor; creates an empty vector without any elements
`vector<Elem> c(c2)`	Copy constructor; creates a new vector as a copy of *c2* (all elements are copied)
`vector<Elem> c = c2`	Copy constructor; creates a new vector as a copy of *c2* (all elements are copied)
`vector<Elem> c(rv)`	Move constructor; creates a new vector, taking the contents of the rvalue *rv* (since C++11)
`vector<Elem> c = rv`	Move constructor; creates a new vector, taking the contents of the rvalue *rv* (since C++11)
`vector<Elem> c(n)`	Creates a vector with *n* elements created by the default constructor
`vector<Elem> c(n,elem)`	Creates a vector initialized with *n* copies of element *elem*
`vector<Elem> c(beg,end)`	Creates a vector initialized with the elements of the range [*beg*,*end*)
`vector<Elem> c(initlist)`	Creates a vector initialized with the elements of initializer list *initlist* (since C++11)
`vector<Elem> c = initlist`	Creates a vector initialized with the elements of initializer list *initlist* (since C++11)
`c.~vector()`	Destroys all elements and frees the memory

Table 7.9. Constructors and Destructor of Vectors

---

[5] You (or your compiler) might consider this statement as being incorrect because it calls a nonconstant member function for a temporary value. However, standard C++ allows you to call a nonconstant member function for temporary values.

7.3.2   Vector Operations

Create, Copy, and Destroy

Table 7.9 lists the constructors and destructors for vectors. You can create vectors with and without elements for initialization. If you pass only the size, the elements are created with their default constructor. Note that an explicit call of the default constructor also initializes fundamental types, such as `int`, with zero (see Section 3.2.1, page 37). See Section 7.1.2, page 254, for some remarks about possible initialization sources.

Nonmodifying Operations

Table 7.10 lists all nonmodifying operations of vectors.[6] See additional remarks in Section 7.1.2, page 254, and Section 7.3.1, page 270.

Operation	Effect
`c.empty()`	Returns whether the container is empty (equivalent to `size()==0` but might be faster)
`c.size()`	Returns the current number of elements
`c.max_size()`	Returns the maximum number of elements possible
`c.capacity()`	Returns the maximum possible number of elements without reallocation
`c.reserve(`*num*`)`	Enlarges capacity, if not enough yet[6]
`c.shrink_to_fit()`	Request to reduce capacity to fit number of elements (since C++11)[6]
`c1 == c2`	Returns whether c_1 is equal to c_2 (calls == for the elements)
`c1 != c2`	Returns whether c_1 is not equal to c_2 (equivalent to `!(c1==c2)`)
`c1 < c2`	Returns whether c_1 is less than c_2
`c1 > c2`	Returns whether c_1 is greater than c_2 (equivalent to $c_2 < c_1$)
`c1 <= c2`	Returns whether c_1 is less than or equal to c_2 (equivalent to `!(c2<c1)`)
`c1 >= c2`	Returns whether c_1 is greater than or equal to c_2 (equivalent to `!(c1<c2)`)

Table 7.10. Nonmodifying Operations of Vectors

Assignments

Table 7.11 lists the ways to assign new elements while removing all ordinary elements. The set of `assign()` functions matches the set of constructors. You can use different sources for assignments

---

[6] `reserve()` and `shrink_to_fit()` manipulate the vector because they invalidate references, pointers, and iterators to elements. However, they are mentioned here because they do not manipulate the logical contents of the container.

Operation	Effect
c = c2	Assigns all elements of *c2* to *c*
c = *rv*	Move assigns all elements of the rvalue *rv* to *c* (since C++11)
c = *initlist*	Assigns all elements of the initializer list *initlist* to *c* (since C++11)
c.assign(*n*,*elem*)	Assigns *n* copies of element *elem*
c.assign(*beg*,*end*)	Assigns the elements of the range [*beg*,*end*)
c.assign(*initlist*)	Assigns all the elements of the initializer list *initlist*
c1.swap(c2)	Swaps the data of *c1* and *c2*
swap(c1,c2)	Swaps the data of *c1* and *c2*

Table 7.11. Assignment Operations of Vectors

(containers, arrays, standard input) similar to those described for constructors (see Section 7.1.2, page 254). All assignment operations call the default constructor, copy constructor, assignment operator, and/or destructor of the element type, depending on how the number of elements changes. For example:

```
std::list<Elem> l;
std::vector<Elem> coll;

...
// make coll be a copy of the contents of l
coll.assign(l.begin(),l.end());
```

Element Access

To access all elements of a vector, you must use range-based for loops (see Section 3.1.4, page 17), specific operations, or iterators. Table 7.12 shows all vector operations for direct element access. As usual in C and C++, the first element has index 0, and the last element has index size()-1. Thus, the *n*th element has index *n*-1. For nonconstant vectors, these operations return a reference to the element. Thus, you could modify an element by using one of these operations, provided it is not forbidden for other reasons.

Operation	Effect
c[*idx*]	Returns the element with index *idx* (*no* range checking)
c.at(*idx*)	Returns the element with index *idx* (throws range-error exception if *idx* is out of range)
c.front()	Returns the first element (*no* check whether a first element exists)
c.back()	Returns the last element (*no* check whether a last element exists)

Table 7.12. Direct Element Access of Vectors

The most important issue for the caller is whether these operations perform range checking. Only at() performs range checking. If the index is out of range, at() throws an out_of_range exception (see Section 4.3, page 41). All other functions do *not* check. A range error results in undefined behavior. Calling operator [], `front()`, and `back()` for an empty container always results in undefined behavior:

```
std::vector<Elem> coll;          // empty!

coll[5] = elem;                  // RUNTIME ERROR ⇒ undefined behavior
std::cout << coll.front();       // RUNTIME ERROR ⇒ undefined behavior
```

So, you must ensure that the index for operator [] is valid and that the container is not empty when either `front()` or `back()` is called:

```
std::vector<Elem> coll;          // empty!

if (coll.size() > 5) {
    coll[5] = elem;              // OK
}
if (!coll.empty()) {
    cout << coll.front();        // OK
}
coll.at(5) = elem;               // throws out_of_range exception
```

Note that this code is OK only in single-threaded environments. In multithreaded contexts, you need synchronization mechanisms to ensure that `coll` is not modified between the check for its size and the access to the element (see Section 18.4.3, page 984, for details).

Iterator Functions

Vectors provide the usual operations to get iterators (Table 7.13). Vector iterators are random-access iterators (see Section 9.2, page 433, for a discussion of iterator categories). Thus, in principle you could use all algorithms of the STL.

The exact type of these iterators is implementation defined. For vectors, however, the iterators returned by `begin()`, `cbegin()`, `end()`, and `cend()` are often ordinary pointers, which is fine because vectors usually use a C-style array for the elements and ordinary pointers provide the interface of random-access iterators. However, you can't count on the fact that the iterators are ordinary pointers. For example, if a safe version of the STL that checks range errors and other potential problems is used, the iterator type is usually an auxiliary class. See Section 9.2.6, page 440, for a nasty difference between iterators implemented as pointers and iterators implemented as classes.

Iterators remain valid until an element with a smaller index gets inserted or removed or until reallocation occurs and capacity changes (see Section 7.3.1, page 270).

Inserting and Removing Elements

Table 7.14 shows the operations provided for vectors to insert or to remove elements. As usual when using the STL, you must ensure that the arguments are valid. Iterators must refer to valid positions, and the beginning of a range must have a position that is not behind the end.

Operation	Effect
c.begin()	Returns a random-access iterator for the first element
c.end()	Returns a random-access iterator for the position after the last element
c.cbegin()	Returns a constant random-access iterator for the first element (since C++11)
c.cend()	Returns a constant random-access iterator for the position after the last element (since C++11)
c.rbegin()	Returns a reverse iterator for the first element of a reverse iteration
c.rend()	Returns a reverse iterator for the position after the last element of a reverse iteration
c.crbegin()	Returns a constant reverse iterator for the first element of a reverse iteration (since C++11)
c.crend()	Returns a constant reverse iterator for the position after the last element of a reverse iteration (since C++11)

Table 7.13. Iterator Operations of Vectors

As usual, it is up to the programmer to ensure that the container is not empty when pop_back() is called. For example:

```
std::vector<Elem> coll;              // empty!

coll.pop_back();                     // RUNTIME ERROR ⇒ undefined behavior

if (!coll.empty()) {
    coll.pop_back();                 // OK
}
```

However, note that in a multithreaded context you have to ensure that coll doesn't get modified between the check for being empty and pop_back() (see Section 18.4.3, page 984).

Regarding performance, you should consider that inserting and removing happens faster when

- Elements are inserted or removed at the end.
- The capacity is large enough on entry.
- Multiple elements are inserted by a single call rather than by multiple calls.

Inserting or removing elements invalidates references, pointers, and iterators that refer to the following elements. An insertion that causes reallocation invalidates all references, iterators, and pointers.

Vectors provide no operation to remove elements directly that have a certain value. You must use an algorithm to do this. For example, the following statement removes all elements that have the value val:

```
std::vector<Elem> coll;
...
// remove all elements with value val
coll.erase(remove(coll.begin(),coll.end(),
                   val),
           coll.end());
```

This statement is explained in Section 6.7.1, page 218.

Operation	Effect
c.push_back(*elem*)	Appends a copy of *elem* at the end
c.pop_back()	Removes the last element (does not return it)
c.insert(*pos*,*elem*)	Inserts a copy of *elem* before iterator position *pos* and returns the position of the new element
c.insert(*pos*,*n*,*elem*)	Inserts *n* copies of *elem* before iterator position *pos* and returns the position of the first new element (or *pos* if there is no new element)
c.insert(*pos*,*beg*,*end*)	Inserts a copy of all elements of the range [*beg*,*end*) before iterator position *pos* and returns the position of the first new element (or pos if there is no new element)
c.insert(*pos*,*initlist*)	Inserts a copy of all elements of the initializer list *initlist* before iterator position *pos* and returns the position of the first new element (or *pos* if there is no new element; since C++11)
c.emplace(*pos*,*args*...)	Inserts a copy of an element initialized with *args* before iterator position *pos* and returns the position of the new element (since C++11)
c.emplace_back(*args*...)	Appends a copy of an element initialized with *args* at the end (returns nothing; since C++11)
c.erase(*pos*)	Removes the element at iterator position *pos* and returns the position of the next element
c.erase(*beg*,*end*)	Removes all elements of the range [*beg*,*end*) and returns the position of the next element
c.resize(*num*)	Changes the number of elements to *num* (if size() grows new elements are created by their default constructor)
c.resize(*num*,*elem*)	Changes the number of elements to *num* (if size() grows new elements are copies of *elem*)
c.clear()	Removes all elements (empties the container)

Table 7.14. Insert and Remove Operations of Vectors

To remove only the first element that has a certain value, you must use the following statements:

```
std::vector<Elem> coll;
...
// remove first element with value val
std::vector<Elem>::iterator pos;
pos = find(coll.begin(),coll.end(),
           val);
if (pos != coll.end()) {
    coll.erase(pos);
}
```

7.3.3 Using Vectors as C-Style Arrays

As for class `array<>`, the C++ standard library guarantees that the elements of a vector are in contiguous memory. Thus, you can expect that for any valid index i in vector v, the following yields true:

```
&v[i] == &v[0] + i
```

This guarantee has some important consequences. It simply means that you can use a vector in all cases in which you could use a dynamic array. For example, you can use a vector to hold data of ordinary C-strings of type `char*` or `const char*`:

```
std::vector<char> v;               // create vector as dynamic array of chars

v.resize(41);                      // make room for 41 characters (including '\0')
strcpy(&v[0],"hello, world");      // copy a C-string into the vector
printf("%s\n", &v[0]);             // print contents of the vector as C-string
```

Note, however, that since C++11, you don't have to use the expression `&a[0]` to get direct access to the elements in the vector, because the member function `data()` is provided for this purpose:

```
std::vector<char,41> v;            // create static array of 41 chars

strcpy(v.data(),"hello, world");   // copy a C-string into the array
printf("%s\n", v.data());          // print contents of the array as C-string
```

Of course, you have to be careful when you use a vector in this way (just as you always have to be careful when using ordinary C-style arrays and pointers). For example, you have to ensure that the size of the vector is big enough to copy some data into it and that you have an '\0' element at the end if you use the contents as a C-string. However, this example shows that whenever you need an array of type T for any reason, such as for an existing C library, you can use a `vector<T>` and pass the address of the first element.

Note that you must not pass an iterator as the address of the first element. Iterators of vectors have an implementation-specific type, which may be totally different from an ordinary pointer:

```
printf("%s\n", v.begin());         // ERROR (might work, but not portable)
printf("%s\n", v.data());          // OK (since C++11)
printf("%s\n", &v[0]);             // OK, but data() is better
```

7.3.4 Exception Handling

Vectors provide only minimal support for logical error checking. The only member function for which the standard requires that it may throw an exception is `at()`, which is the safe version of the subscript operator (see Section 7.3.2, page 274). In addition, the standard requires that only the usual standard exceptions may occur, such as `bad_alloc` for a lack of memory or exceptions of user-defined operations.

If functions called by a vector (functions for the element type or functions that are user-supplied) throw exceptions, the C++ standard library provides the following guarantees:

1. If an element gets inserted with `push_back()` and an exception occurs, this function has no effect.
2. `insert()`, `emplace()`, `emplace_back()`, and `push_back()` either succeed or have no effect, provided that the copy/move operations (constructors and assignment operators) of the elements do not throw.
3. `pop_back()` does not throw any exceptions.
4. `erase()` does not throw if the copy/move operations (constructors and assignment operators) of the elements do not throw.
5. `swap()` and `clear()` do not throw.
6. If elements are used that never throw exceptions on copy/move operations (constructors and assignment operators), every operation is either successful or has no effect. Such elements might be "plain old data" (POD). POD describes types that use no special C++ feature. For example, every ordinary C structure is POD.

All these guarantees are based on the requirements that destructors don't throw. See Section 6.12.2, page 248, for a general discussion of exception handling in the STL.

7.3.5   Examples of Using Vectors

The following example shows a simple use of vectors:

```cpp
// cont/vector1.cpp

#include <vector>
#include <iostream>
#include <string>
#include <algorithm>
#include <iterator>
using namespace std;

int main()
{
    // create empty vector for strings
    vector<string> sentence;

    // reserve memory for five elements to avoid reallocation
    sentence.reserve(5);

    // append some elements
    sentence.push_back("Hello,");
    sentence.insert(sentence.end(),{"how","are","you","?"});

    // print elements separated with spaces
    copy (sentence.cbegin(), sentence.cend(),
          ostream_iterator<string>(cout," "));
```

```
        cout << endl;

        // print "technical data"
        cout << " max_size(): " << sentence.max_size() << endl;
        cout << " size():     " << sentence.size()     << endl;
        cout << " capacity(): " << sentence.capacity() << endl;

        // swap second and fourth element
        swap (sentence[1], sentence[3]);

        // insert element "always" before element "?"
        sentence.insert (find(sentence.begin(),sentence.end(),"?"),
                         "always");

        // assign "!" to the last element
        sentence.back() = "!";

        // print elements separated with spaces
        copy (sentence.cbegin(), sentence.cend(),
              ostream_iterator<string>(cout," "));
        cout << endl;

        // print some "technical data" again
        cout << " size():     " << sentence.size()     << endl;
        cout << " capacity(): " << sentence.capacity() << endl;

        // delete last two elements
        sentence.pop_back();
        sentence.pop_back();
        // shrink capacity (since C++11)
        sentence.shrink_to_fit();

        // print some "technical data" again
        cout << " size():     " << sentence.size()     << endl;
        cout << " capacity(): " << sentence.capacity() << endl;
    }
```

The output of the program might look like this:

```
    Hello, how are you ?
      max_size(): 1073741823
      size():     5
      capacity(): 5
```

```
Hello, you are how always !
   size():     6
   capacity(): 10
   size():     4
   capacity(): 4
```

Note my use of the word *might*. The values of `max_size()` and `capacity()` are unspecified and might vary from platform to platform. Here, for example, you can see that the implementation seems to double the capacity if the capacity no longer fits and not necessarily shrinks if there is a request to do so.

7.3.6 Class `vector<bool>`

For Boolean elements, the C++ standard library provides a specialization of `vector<>`. The goal is to have a version that is optimized to use less size than a usual implementation of `vector<>` for type `bool`. Such a usual implementation would reserve at least 1 byte for each element. The `vector<bool>` specialization usually uses internally only 1 bit for an element, so it is typically eight times smaller. But such an optimization also has a snag: In C++, the smallest addressable value must have a size of at least 1 byte. Thus, such a specialization of a vector needs special handling for references and iterators.

As a result, a `vector<bool>` does not meet all requirements of other vectors. For example, a `vector<bool>::reference` is not a true lvalue and `vector<bool>::iterator` is not a random-access iterator. Therefore, template code might work for vectors of any type except `bool`. In addition, `vector<bool>` might perform worse than normal implementations, because element operations have to be transformed into bit operations. However, how `vector<bool>` is implemented is implementation specific. Thus, the performance (speed and memory) might differ.

Note that class `vector<bool>` is more than a specialization of `vector<>` for `bool`. It also provides some special bit operations. You can handle bits or flags in a more convenient way.

`vector<bool>` has a dynamic size, so you can consider it a bitfield with dynamic size. Thus, you can add and remove bits. If you need a bitfield with static size, you should use `bitset` rather than a `vector<bool>`. Class `bitset` is covered in Section 12.5, page 650.

The additional operations of `vector<bool>` are shown in Table 7.15.

Operation	Effect
`c.flip()`	Negates all Boolean elements (complement of all bits)
`c[idx].flip()`	Negates the Boolean element with index *idx* (complement of a single bit)
`c[idx] = val`	Assigns *val* to the Boolean element with index *idx* (assignment to a single bit)
`c[idx1] = c[idx2]`	Assigns the value of the element with index *idx2* to the element with index *idx1*

Table 7.15. Special Operations of `vector<bool>`

The operation `flip()`, which processes the complement, can be called for all bits and a single bit of the vector. The latter is remarkable because you might expect the operator `[ ]` to return a `bool` and that calling `flip()` for such a fundamental type is not possible. Here, the class `vector<bool>` uses a common trick, called a *proxy*:[7] For `vector<bool>`, the return type of the subscript operator (and other operators that return an element) is an auxiliary class. If you need the return value to be `bool`, an automatic type conversion is used. For other operations, the member functions are provided. The relevant part of the declaration of `vector<bool>` looks like this:

```
namespace std {
    template <typename Allocator> class vector<bool,Allocator> {
      public:
        // auxiliary proxy type for element modifications:
        class reference {
            ...
          public:
            reference& operator= (const bool) noexcept;      // assignments
            reference& operator= (const reference&) noexcept;
            operator bool() const noexcept;      // automatic type conversion to bool
            void flip() noexcept;                 // bit complement
        };
        ...


        // operations for element access return reference proxy instead of bool:
        reference operator[](size_type idx);
        reference at(size_type idx);
        reference front();
        reference back();
        ...
    };
}
```

As you can see, all member functions for element access return type `reference`. Thus, you could program something like the following statements:

```
c.front().flip();        // negate first Boolean element
c[5] = c.back();         // assign last element to element with index 5
```

As usual, to avoid undefined behavior, the caller must ensure that the first, sixth, and last elements exist here.

Note that the internal proxy type `reference` is used only for nonconstant containers of type `vector<bool>`. The constant member functions for element access return values of type `const_reference`, which is a type definition for `bool`.

---

[7] A proxy allows you to keep control where usually no control is provided. This is often used to get more security. In this case, the proxy maintains control to allow certain operations, although, in principle, the return value behaves as `bool`.

7.4 Deques

A deque (pronounced "deck") is very similar to a vector. It manages its elements with a dynamic array, provides random access, and has almost the same interface as a vector. The difference is that with a deque, the dynamic array is open at both ends. Thus, a deque is fast for insertions and deletions at both the end and the beginning (Figure 7.3).

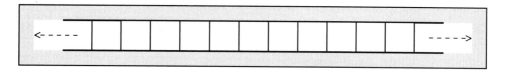

Figure 7.3. Logical Structure of a Deque

To provide this ability, the deque is typically implemented as a bunch of individual blocks, with the first block growing in one direction and the last block growing in the opposite direction (Figure 7.4).

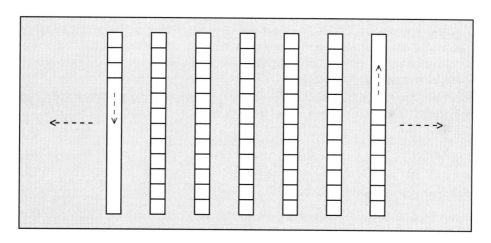

Figure 7.4. Internal Structure of a Deque

To use a deque, you must include the header file <deque>:

```
#include <deque>
```

There, the type is defined as a class template inside namespace std:

```
namespace std {
    template <typename T,
              typename Allocator = allocator<T> >
    class deque;
}
```

As with all sequence containers, the type of the elements is passed as a first template parameter. The optional second template argument is the memory model, with `allocator` as the default (see Chapter 19).

7.4.1   Abilities of Deques

The abilities of deques differ from those of vectors as follows:

- Inserting and removing elements is fast at both the beginning and the end (for vectors, it is fast only at the end). These operations are done in amortized constant time.
- The internal structure has one more indirection to access the elements, so with deques, element access and iterator movement are usually a bit slower.
- Iterators must be smart pointers of a special type rather than ordinary pointers because they must jump between different blocks.
- In systems that have size limitations for blocks of memory (for example, some PC systems), a deque might contain more elements because it uses more than one block of memory. Thus, `max_size()` might be larger for deques.
- Deques provide no support to control the capacity and the moment of reallocation. In particular, any insertion or deletion of elements other than at the beginning or end invalidates all pointers, references, and iterators that refer to elements of the deque. However, reallocation may perform better than for vectors because according to their typical internal structure, deques don't have to copy all elements on reallocation.
- Blocks of memory might get freed when they are no longer used, so the memory size of a deque might shrink (however, whether and how this happens is implementation specific).

The following features of vectors apply also to deques:

- Inserting and deleting elements in the middle is relatively slow because all elements up to either end may be moved to make room or to fill a gap.
- Iterators are random-access iterators.

In summary, you should prefer a deque if the following are true:

- You insert and remove elements at both ends (this is the classic case for a queue).
- You don't refer to elements of the container.
- It is important that the container frees memory when it is no longer used (however, the standard does not guarantee that this happens).

The interface of vectors and deques is almost the same, so trying both is very easy when no special feature of a vector or a deque is necessary.

7.4.2   Deque Operations

Tables 7.16 through 7.18 list all operations provided for deques.[8]

Operation	Effect
`deque<Elem> c`	Default constructor; creates an empty deque without any elements
`deque<Elem> c(c2)`	Copy constructor; creates a new deque as a copy of *c2* (all elements are copied)
`deque<Elem> c = c2`	Copy constructor; creates a new deque as a copy of *c2* (all elements are copied)
`deque<Elem> c(rv)`	Move constructor; creates a new deque, taking the contents of the rvalue *rv* (since C++11)
`deque<Elem> c = rv`	Move constructor; creates a new deque, taking the contents of the rvalue *rv* (since C++11)
`deque<Elem> c(n)`	Creates a deque with *n* elements created by the default constructor
`deque<Elem> c(n,elem)`	Creates a deque initialized with *n* copies of element *elem*
`deque<Elem> c(beg,end)`	Creates a deque initialized with the elements of the range [*beg,end*)
`deque<Elem> c(initlist)`	Creates a deque initialized with the elements of initializer list *initlist* (since C++11)
`deque<Elem> c = initlist`	Creates a deque initialized with the elements of initializer list *initlist* (since C++11)
`c.~deque()`	Destroys all elements and frees the memory

Table 7.16. Constructors and Destructor of Deques

Deque operations differ from vector operations in only two ways:

1. Deques do not provide the functions for capacity (`capacity()` and `reserve()`).
2. Deques do provide direct functions to insert and to delete the first element (`push_front()` and `pop_front()`).

Because the other operations are the same, they are not explained again here. See Section 7.3.2, page 273, for a description of them.

Note, however, that `shrink_to_fit()` was added with C++11 as nonbinding request to shrink the internal memory to fit the number of elements. You might argue that `shrink_to_fit()` makes no sense for deques because they are allowed to free blocks of memory. However, the memory that contains all the pointers to the blocks of memory usually does not shrink, which might change with this call.

---

[8] `shrink_to_fit()` manipulates the deque because it invalidates references, pointers, and iterators to elements. However, it is listed as a nonmodifying operation because it does not manipulate the logical contents of the container.

Operation	Effect
`c.empty()`	Returns whether the container is empty (equivalent to `size()==0` but might be faster)
`c.size()`	Returns the current number of elements
`c.max_size()`	Returns the maximum number of elements possible
`c.shrink_to_fit()`	Request to reduce capacity to fit number of elements (since C++11)[8]
`c1 == c2`	Returns whether `c1` is equal to `c2` (calls `==` for the elements)
`c1 != c2`	Returns whether `c1` is not equal to `c2` (equivalent to `!(c1==c2)`)
`c1 < c2`	Returns whether `c1` is less than `c2`
`c1 > c2`	Returns whether `c1` is greater than `c2` (equivalent to `c2<c1`)
`c1 <= c2`	Returns whether `c1` is less than or equal to `c2` (equivalent to `!(c2<c1)`)
`c1 >= c2`	Returns whether `c1` is greater than or equal to `c2` (equivalent to `!(c1<c2)`)
`c[idx]`	Returns the element with index *idx* (*no* range checking)
`c.at(idx)`	Returns the element with index *idx* (throws range-error exception if *idx* is out of range)
`c.front()`	Returns the first element (*no* check whether a first element exists)
`c.back()`	Returns the last element (*no* check whether a last element exists)
`c.begin()`	Returns a random-access iterator for the first element
`c.end()`	Returns a random-access iterator for the position after the last element
`c.cbegin()`	Returns a constant random-access iterator for the first element (since C++11)
`c.cend()`	Returns a constant random-access iterator for the position after the last element (since C++11)
`c.rbegin()`	Returns a reverse iterator for the first element of a reverse iteration
`c.rend()`	Returns a reverse iterator for the position after the last element of a reverse iteration
`c.crbegin()`	Returns a constant reverse iterator for the first element of a reverse iteration (since C++11)
`c.crend()`	Returns a constant reverse iterator for the position after the last element of a reverse iteration (since C++11)

Table 7.17. Nonmodifying Operations of Deques

In addition, note that you still must consider the following:

1. No member functions for element access (except `at()`) check whether an index or an iterator is valid.

2. An insertion or deletion of elements might cause a reallocation. Thus, any insertion or deletion invalidates all pointers, references, and iterators that refer to other elements of the deque. The exception is when elements are inserted at the front or the back. In this case, references and pointers to elements stay valid, but iterators don't.

Operation	Effect
c = *c2*	Assigns all elements of *c2* to *c*
c = *rv*	Move assigns all elements of the rvalue *rv* to *c* (since C++11)
c = *initlist*	Assigns all elements of the initializer list *initlist* to *c* (since C++11)
c.assign(*n*,*elem*)	Assigns *n* copies of element *elem*
c.assign(*beg*,*end*)	Assigns the elements of the range [*beg*,*end*)
c.assign(*initlist*)	Assigns all the elements of the initializer list *initlist*
c1.swap(*c2*)	Swaps the data of *c1* and *c2*
swap(*c1*,*c2*)	Swaps the data of *c1* and *c2*
c.push_back(*elem*)	Appends a copy of *elem* at the end
c.pop_back()	Removes the last element (does not return it)
c.push_front(*elem*)	Inserts a copy of *elem* at the beginning
c.pop_front()	Removes the first element (does not return it)
c.insert(*pos*,*elem*)	Inserts a copy of *elem* before iterator position *pos* and returns the position of the new element
c.insert(*pos*,*n*,*elem*)	Inserts *n* copies of *elem* before iterator position *pos* and returns the position of the first new element (or *pos* if there is no new element)
c.insert(*pos*,*beg*,*end*)	Inserts a copy of all elements of the range [*beg*,*end*) before iterator position *pos* and returns the position of the first new element (or pos if there is no new element)
c.insert(*pos*,*initlist*)	Inserts a copy of all elements of the initializer list *initlist* before iterator position *pos* and returns the position of the first new element (or *pos* if there is no new element; since C++11)
c.emplace(*pos*,*args*...)	Inserts a copy of an element initialized with *args* before iterator position *pos* and returns the position of the new element (since C++11)
c.emplace_back(*args*...)	Appends a copy of an element initialized with *args* at the end (returns nothing; since C++11)
c.emplace_front(*args*...)	Inserts a copy of an element initialized with *args* at the beginning (returns nothing; since C++11)
c.erase(*pos*)	Removes the element at iterator position *pos* and returns the position of the next element
c.erase(*beg*,*end*)	Removes all elements of the range [*beg*,*end*) and returns the position of the next element
c.resize(*num*)	Changes the number of elements to *num* (if size() grows new elements are created by their default constructor)
c.resize(*num*,*elem*)	Changes the number of elements to *num* (if size() grows new elements are copies of *elem*)
c.clear()	Removes all elements (empties the container)

Table 7.18. Modifying Operations of Deques

7.4.3   Exception Handling

In principle, deques provide the same support for exception handing that vectors do (see Section 7.3.4, page 278). The additional operations push_front() and pop_front() behave according to push_back() and pop_back(), respectively. Thus, the C++ standard library provides the following behavior:

- If an element gets inserted with push_back() or push_front() and an exception occurs, these functions have no effect.
- Neither pop_back() nor pop_front() throws any exceptions.

See Section 6.12.2, page 248, for a general discussion of exception handling in the STL.

7.4.4   Examples of Using Deques

The following program shows the abilities of deques:

```cpp
// cont/deque1.cpp

#include <iostream>
#include <deque>
#include <string>
#include <algorithm>
#include <iterator>
using namespace std;

int main()
{
    // create empty deque of strings
    deque<string> coll;

    // insert several elements
    coll.assign (3, string("string"));
    coll.push_back ("last string");
    coll.push_front ("first string");

    // print elements separated by newlines
    copy (coll.cbegin(), coll.cend(),
          ostream_iterator<string>(cout,"\n"));
    cout << endl;

    // remove first and last element
    coll.pop_front();
    coll.pop_back();
```

```
// insert ''another'' into every element but the first
for (unsigned i=1; i<coll.size(); ++i) {
    coll[i] = "another " + coll[i];
}

// change size to four elements
coll.resize (4, "resized string");

// print elements separated by newlines
copy (coll.cbegin(), coll.cend(),
      ostream_iterator<string>(cout,"\n"));
}
```

The program has the following output:

```
first string
string
string
string
last string

string
another string
another string
resized string
```

7.5   Lists

A list (an instance of the container class `list<>`) manages its elements as a doubly linked list (Figure 7.5). As usual, the C++ standard library does not specify the kind of the implementation, but it follows from the list's name, constraints, and specifications.

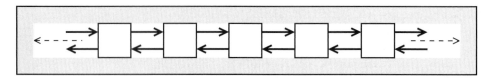

Figure 7.5. Structure of a List

To use a list, you must include the header file `<list>`:

```
#include <list>
```

There, the type is defined as a class template inside namespace `std`:

```
namespace std {
    template <typename T,
              typename Allocator = allocator<T> >
    class list;
}
```

The elements of a list may have any type T. The optional second template parameter defines the memory model (see Chapter 19). The default memory model is the model `allocator`, which is provided by the C++ standard library.

7.5.1   Abilities of Lists

The internal structure of a list is totally different from that of an `array`, a vector, or a deque. The list object itself provides two pointers, the so-called *anchors*, which refer to the first and last elements. Each element has pointers to the previous and next elements (or back to the anchor). To insert a new element, you just manipulate the corresponding pointers (see Figure 7.6).

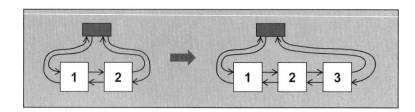

Figure 7.6. Internal Structure of a List when Appending a Value

Thus, a list differs in several major ways from arrays, vectors, and deques:

- A list does not provide random access. For example, to access the fifth element, you must navigate the first four elements, following the chain of links. Thus, accessing an arbitrary element using a list is slow. However, you can navigate through the list from both end. So accessing both the first and the last elements is fast.

- Inserting and removing elements is fast at each position (provided you are there), and not only at one or both ends. You can always insert and delete an element in constant time, because no other elements have to be moved. Internally, only some pointer values are manipulated.

- Inserting and deleting elements does not invalidate pointers, references, and iterators to other elements.

- A list supports exception handling in such a way that almost every operation succeeds or is a no-op. Thus, you can't get into an intermediate state in which only half of the operation is complete.

The member functions provided for lists reflect these differences from arrays, vectors, and deques as follows:

- Lists provide front(), push_front(), and pop_front(), as well as back(), push_back(), and pop_back().

- Lists provide neither a subscript operator nor at(), because no random access is provided.

- Lists don't provide operations for capacity or reallocation, because neither is needed. Each element has its own memory that stays valid until the element is deleted.

- Lists provide many special member functions for moving and removing elements. These member functions are faster versions of general algorithms that have the same names. They are faster because they only redirect pointers rather than copy and move the values.

7.5.2 List Operations

Create, Copy, and Destroy

The ability to create, copy, and destroy lists is the same as it is for every sequence container. See Table 7.19 for the list operations that do this. See also Section 7.1.2, page 254, for some remarks about possible initialization sources.

Nonmodifying Operations

Lists provide the usual operations for size and comparisons. See Table 7.20 for a list and Section 7.1.2, page 254, for details.

Assignments

Lists also provide the usual assignment operations for sequence containers (Table 7.21). As usual, the insert operations match the constructors to provide different sources for initialization (see Section 7.1.2, page 254, for details).

Operation	Effect
`list<Elem> c`	Default constructor; creates an empty list without any elements
`list<Elem> c(c2)`	Copy constructor; creates a new list as a copy of *c2* (all elements are copied)
`list<Elem> c = c2`	Copy constructor; creates a new list as a copy of *c2* (all elements are copied)
`list<Elem> c(rv)`	Move constructor; creates a new list, taking the contents of the rvalue *rv* (since C++11)
`list<Elem> c = rv`	Move constructor; creates a new list, taking the contents of the rvalue *rv* (since C++11)
`list<Elem> c(n)`	Creates a list with *n* elements created by the default constructor
`list<Elem> c(n,elem)`	Creates a list initialized with *n* copies of element *elem*
`list<Elem> c(beg,end)`	Creates a list initialized with the elements of the range [*beg,end*)
`list<Elem> c(initlist)`	Creates a list initialized with the elements of initializer list *initlist* (since C++11)
`list<Elem> c = initlist`	Creates a list initialized with the elements of initializer list *initlist* (since C++11)
`c.~list()`	Destroys all elements and frees the memory

Table 7.19. Constructors and Destructor of Lists

Operation	Effect
`c.empty()`	Returns whether the container is empty (equivalent to `size()==0` but might be faster)
`c.size()`	Returns the current number of elements
`c.max_size()`	Returns the maximum number of elements possible
`c1 == c2`	Returns whether *c1* is equal to *c2* (calls == for the elements)
`c1 != c2`	Returns whether *c1* is not equal to *c2* (equivalent to `!(c1==c2)`)
`c1 < c2`	Returns whether *c1* is less than *c2*
`c1 > c2`	Returns whether *c1* is greater than *c2* (equivalent to *c2<c1*)
`c1 <= c2`	Returns whether *c1* is less than or equal to *c2* (equivalent to `!(c2<c1)`)
`c1 >= c2`	Returns whether *c1* is greater than or equal to *c2* (equivalent to `!(c1<c2)`)

Table 7.20. Nonmodifying Operations of Lists

Element Access

To access all elements of a list, you must use range-based `for` loops (see Section 3.1.4, page 17), specific operations, or iterators. Because it does not have random access, a list provides only `front()` and `back()` for accessing elements directly (Table 7.22).

Operation	Effect
c = c2	Assigns all elements of *c2* to *c*
c = *rv*	Move assigns all elements of the rvalue *rv* to *c* (since C++11)
c = *initlist*	Assigns all elements of the initializer list *initlist* to *c* (since C++11)
c.assign(*n*,*elem*)	Assigns *n* copies of element *elem*
c.assign(*beg*,*end*)	Assigns the elements of the range [*beg*,*end*)
c.assign(*initlist*)	Assigns all the elements of the initializer list *initlist*
c1.swap(c2)	Swaps the data of *c1* and *c2*
swap(c1,c2)	Swaps the data of *c1* and *c2*

Table 7.21. Assignment Operations of Lists

Operation	Effect
c.front()	Returns the first element (*no* check whether a first element exists)
c.back()	Returns the last element (*no* check whether a last element exists)

Table 7.22. Direct Element Access of Lists

As usual, these operations do *not* check whether the container is empty. If the container is empty, calling these operations results in undefined behavior. Thus, the caller must ensure that the container contains at least one element. For example:

```
std::list<Elem> coll;              // empty!

std::cout << coll.front();         // RUNTIME ERROR ⇒ undefined behavior

if (!coll.empty()) {
    std::cout << coll.back();     // OK
}
```

Note that this code is OK only in single-threaded environments. In multithreaded contexts, you need synchronization mechanisms to ensure that coll is not modified between the check for its size and the access to the element (see Section 18.4.3, page 984, for details).

Iterator Functions

To access all elements of a list, you must use iterators. Lists provide the usual iterator functions (Table 7.23). However, because a list has no random access, these iterators are only bidirectional. Thus, you can't call algorithms that require random-access iterators. All algorithms that manipulate the order of elements a lot, especially sorting algorithms, are in this category. However, for sorting the elements, lists provide the special member function sort() (see Section 8.8.1, page 422).

Operation	Effect
c.begin()	Returns a bidirectional iterator for the first element
c.end()	Returns a bidirectional iterator for the position after the last element
c.cbegin()	Returns a constant bidirectional iterator for the first element (since C++11)
c.cend()	Returns a constant bidirectional iterator for the position after the last element (since C++11)
c.rbegin()	Returns a reverse iterator for the first element of a reverse iteration
c.rend()	Returns a reverse iterator for the position after the last element of a reverse iteration
c.crbegin()	Returns a constant reverse iterator for the first element of a reverse iteration (since C++11)
c.crend()	Returns a constant reverse iterator for the position after the last element of a reverse iteration (since C++11)

Table 7.23. Iterator Operations of Lists

Inserting and Removing Elements

Table 7.24 shows the operations provided for lists to insert and to remove elements. Lists provide all functions of deques, supplemented by special implementations of the `remove()` and `remove_if()` algorithms.

As usual when using the STL, you must ensure that the arguments are valid. Iterators must refer to valid positions, and the beginning of a range must have a position that is not behind the end.

Inserting and removing is faster if, when working with multiple elements, you use a single call for all elements rather than multiple calls.

For removing elements, lists provide special implementations of the `remove()` algorithms (see Section 11.7.1, page 575). These member functions are faster than the `remove()` algorithms because they manipulate only internal pointers rather than the elements. So, unlike with vectors or deques, you should call `remove()` as a member function and not as an algorithm (see Section 7.3.2, page 276, for details). To remove all elements that have a certain value, you can do the following (see Section 6.7.3, page 223, for further details):

```
std::list<Elem> coll;

...
// remove all elements with value val
coll.remove(val);
```

However, to remove only the first occurrence of a value, you must use an algorithm such as that mentioned for vectors in Section 7.3.2, page 277.

You can use `remove_if()` to define the criterion for the removal of the elements by a function or a function object. `remove_if()` removes each element for which calling the passed operation yields `true`. An example of the use of `remove_if()` is a statement to remove all elements that have an even value:

Operation	Effect
c.push_back(*elem*)	Appends a copy of *elem* at the end
c.pop_back()	Removes the last element (does not return it)
c.push_front(*elem*)	Inserts a copy of *elem* at the beginning
c.pop_front()	Removes the first element (does not return it)
c.insert(*pos*,*elem*)	Inserts a copy of *elem* before iterator position *pos* and returns the position of the new element
c.insert(*pos*,*n*,*elem*)	Inserts *n* copies of *elem* before iterator position *pos* and returns the position of the first new element (or *pos* if there is no new element)
c.insert(*pos*,*beg*,*end*)	Inserts a copy of all elements of the range [*beg*,*end*) before iterator position *pos* and returns the position of the first new element (or pos if there is no new element)
c.insert(*pos*,*initlist*)	Inserts a copy of all elements of the initializer list *initlist* before iterator position *pos* and returns the position of the first new element (or *pos* if there is no new element; since C++11)
c.emplace(*pos*,*args*...)	Inserts a copy of an element initialized with *args* before iterator position *pos* and returns the position of the new element (since C++11)
c.emplace_back(*args*...)	Appends a copy of an element initialized with *args* at the end (returns nothing; since C++11)
c.emplace_front(*args*...)	Inserts a copy of an element initialized with *args* at the beginning (returns nothing; since C++11)
c.erase(*pos*)	Removes the element at iterator position *pos* and returns the position of the next element
c.erase(*beg*,*end*)	Removes all elements of the range [*beg*,*end*) and returns the position of the next element
c.remove(val)	Removes all elements with value val
c.remove_if(*op*)	Removes all elements for which *op*(elem) yields true
c.resize(*num*)	Changes the number of elements to *num* (if size() grows new elements are created by their default constructor)
c.resize(*num*,*elem*)	Changes the number of elements to *num* (if size() grows new elements are copies of *elem*)
c.clear()	Removes all elements (empties the container)

Table 7.24. Insert and Remove Operations of Lists

```
// remove all even elements
coll.remove_if ([] (int i) {
                return i % 2 == 0;
            });
```

Here, a lambda is used to find out which elements to remove. Because the lambda returns, whether a passed element is even, the statement as a whole removes all even elements. See Section 11.7.1, page 575, for additional examples of `remove()` and `remove_if()`.

The following operations do not invalidate iterators and references to other members: `insert()`, `emplace()`, `emplace...()`, `push_front()`, `push_back()`, `pop_front()`, `pop_back()`, and `erase()`.

Splice Functions and Functions to Change the Order of Elements

Linked lists have the advantage that you can remove and insert elements at any position in constant time. If you move elements from one container to another, this advantage doubles in that you need only redirect some internal pointers (Figure 7.7).

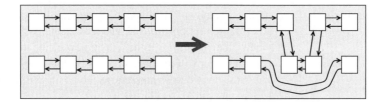

Figure 7.7. Splice Operations to Change the Order of List Elements

To support this ability, lists provide not only `remove()` but also additional modifying member functions to change the order of and relink elements and ranges. You can call these operations to move elements inside a single list or between two lists, provided that the lists have the same type. Table 7.25 lists these functions. They are covered in detail in Section 8.8, page 420, with examples on page 298.

7.5.3   Exception Handling

Lists have the best support of exception safety of the standard containers in the STL. Almost all list operations will either succeed or have no effect. The only operations that don't give this guarantee in the face of exceptions are assignment operations and the member function `sort()` (they give the usual "basic guarantee" that they will not leak resources or violate container invariants in the face of exceptions). `merge()`, `remove()`, `remove_if()`, and `unique()` give guarantees under the condition that comparing the elements (using operator `==` or the predicate) doesn't throw. Thus, to use a term from database programming, you could say that lists are *transaction safe*, provided that you don't call assignment operations or `sort()` and that you ensure that comparing elements doesn't throw. Table 7.26 lists all operations that give special guarantees in the face of exceptions. See Section 6.12.2, page 248, for a general discussion of exception handling in the STL.

Operation	Effect
c.unique()	Removes duplicates of consecutive elements with the same value
c.unique(*op*)	Removes duplicates of consecutive elements, for which *op*() yields true
c.splice(*pos*,*c2*)	Moves all elements of *c2* to c in front of the iterator position *pos*
c.splice(*pos*,*c2*,*c2pos*)	Moves the element at *c2pos* in *c2* in front of *pos* of list c (c and *c2* may be identical)
c.splice(*pos*,*c2*, *c2beg*,*c2end*)	Moves all elements of the range [*c2beg*,*c2end*) in *c2* in front of *pos* of list c (c and *c2* may be identical)
c.sort()	Sorts all elements with operator <
c.sort(*op*)	Sorts all elements with *op*()
c.merge(*c2*)	Assuming that both containers contain the elements sorted, moves all elements of *c2* into c so that all elements are merged and still sorted
c.merge(*c2*,*op*)	Assuming that both containers contain the elements sorted due to the sorting criterion *op*(), moves all elements of *c2* into c so that all elements are merged and still sorted according to *op*()
c.reverse()	Reverses the order of all elements

Table 7.25. Special Modifying Operations for Lists

Operation	Guarantee
push_back()	Either succeeds or has no effect
push_front()	Either succeeds or has no effect
insert()	Either succeeds or has no effect
pop_back()	Doesn't throw
pop_front()	Doesn't throw
erase()	Doesn't throw
clear()	Doesn't throw
resize()	Either succeeds or has no effect
remove()	Doesn't throw if comparing the elements doesn't throw
remove_if()	Doesn't throw if the predicate doesn't throw
unique()	Doesn't throw if comparing the elements doesn't throw
splice()	Doesn't throw
merge()	Either succeeds or has no effect if comparing the elements doesn't throw
reverse()	Doesn't throw
swap()	Doesn't throw

Table 7.26. List Operations with Special Guarantees in Face of Exceptions

7.5.4   Examples of Using Lists

The following example in particular shows the use of the special member functions for lists:

```cpp
// cont/list1.cpp

#include <list>
#include <iostream>
#include <algorithm>
#include <iterator>
using namespace std;

void printLists (const list<int>& l1, const list<int>& l2)
{
    cout << "list1: ";
    copy (l1.cbegin(), l1.cend(), ostream_iterator<int>(cout," "));
    cout << endl << "list2: ";
    copy (l2.cbegin(), l2.cend(), ostream_iterator<int>(cout," "));
    cout << endl << endl;
}

int main()
{
    // create two empty lists
    list<int> list1, list2;

    // fill both lists with elements
    for (int i=0; i<6; ++i) {
        list1.push_back(i);
        list2.push_front(i);
    }
    printLists(list1, list2);

    // insert all elements of list1 before the first element with value 3 of list2
    // - find() returns an iterator to the first element with value 3
    list2.splice(find(list2.begin(),list2.end(),   // destination position
                      3),
                 list1);                            // source list
    printLists(list1, list2);

    // move first element of list2 to the end
    list2.splice(list2.end(),           // destination position
                 list2,                 // source list
                 list2.begin());        // source position
```

```
    printLists(list1, list2);

    // sort second list, assign to list1 and remove duplicates
    list2.sort();
    list1 = list2;
    list2.unique();
    printLists(list1, list2);

    // merge both sorted lists into the first list
    list1.merge(list2);
    printLists(list1, list2);
}
```

The program has the following output:

```
list1: 0 1 2 3 4 5
list2: 5 4 3 2 1 0

list1:
list2: 5 4 0 1 2 3 4 5 3 2 1 0

list1:
list2: 4 0 1 2 3 4 5 3 2 1 0 5

list1: 0 0 1 1 2 2 3 3 4 4 5 5
list2: 0 1 2 3 4 5

list1: 0 0 0 1 1 1 2 2 2 3 3 3 4 4 4 5 5 5
list2:
```

See Section 7.6.4, page 312, for a corresponding example using a forward list.

7.6   Forward Lists

A forward list (an instance of the container class `forward_list<>`), which was introduced with C++11, manages its elements as a singly linked list (Figure 7.8). As usual, the C++ standard library does not specify the kind of the implementation, but it follows from the forward list's name, constraints, and specifications.

Figure 7.8. Structure of a Forward List

To use a forward list, you must include the header file `<forward_list>`:

```
#include <forward_list>
```

There, the type is defined as a class template inside namespace `std`:

```
namespace std {
    template <typename T,
              typename Allocator = allocator<T> >
    class forward_list;
}
```

The elements of a forward list may have any type T. The optional second template parameter defines the memory model (see Chapter 19). The default memory model is the model `allocator`, which is provided by the C++ standard library.

7.6.1   Abilities of Forward Lists

Conceptionally, a forward list is a list (object of class `list<>`) restricted such that it is not able to iterate backward. It provides no functionality that is not also provided by lists. As benefits, it uses less memory and provides slightly better runtime behavior. The standard states: "*It is intended that* `forward_list` *have zero space or time overhead relative to a hand-written C-style singly linked list. Features that would conflict with that goal have been omitted.*"

Forward lists have the following limitations compared to lists:

- A forward list provides only forward iterators, not bidirectional iterators. As a consequence, no reverse iterator support is provided, which means that types, such as `reverse_iterator`, and member functions, such as `rbegin()`, `rend()`, `crbegin()`, and `crend()`, are not provided.
- A forward list does not provide a `size()` member function. This is a consequence of omitting features that create time or space overhead relative to a handwritten singly linked list.
- The anchor of a forward list has no pointer to the last element. For this reason, a forward list does not provide the special member functions to deal with the last element, `back()`, `push_back()`, and `pop_back()`.

- For all member functions that modify forward lists in a way that elements are inserted or deleted at a specific position, special versions for forward lists are provided. The reason is that you have to pass the position of the element *before* the first element that gets manipulated, because there you have to assign a new successor element. Because you can't navigate backwards (at least not in constant time), for all these member functions you have to pass the position of the preceding element. Because of this difference, these member functions have a _after suffix in their name. For example, instead of `insert()`, `insert_after()` is provided, which inserts new elements after the element passed as first argument; that is, it *appends* an element at that position.

- For this reason, forward lists provide `before_begin()` and `cbefore_begin()`, which yield the position of a virtual element before the first element (technically speaking, the anchor of the linked list), which can be used to let built-in algorithms ending with _after exchange even the first element.

The decision not to provide `size()` might be especially surprising because `size()` is one of the operations required for all STL containers (see Section 7.1.2, page 254). Here, you can see the consequences of the design goal to have "zero space or time overhead relative to a hand-written C-style singly linked list." The alternative would have been either to compute the size each time `size()` is called, which would have linear complexity, or to provide an additional field in the `forward_list` object for the size, which is updated with each and every operation that changes the number of elements. As the design paper for the forward list, [*N2543:FwdList*], mentions: "It's a cost that all users would have to pay for, whether they need this feature or not." So, if you need the size, either track it outside the `forward_list` or use a `list` instead.

Other than these differences, forward lists behave just like lists:

- A forward list does not provide random access. For example, to access the fifth element, you must navigate the first four elements, following the chain of links. Thus, using a forward list to access an arbitrary element is slow.

- Inserting and removing elements is fast at each position, if you are there. You can always insert and delete an element in constant time, because no other elements have to be moved. Internally, only some pointer values are manipulated.

- Inserting and deleting elements does not invalidate iterators, references, and pointers to other elements.

- A forward list supports exception handling in such a way that almost every operation succeeds or is a no-op. Thus, you can't get into an intermediate state in which only half of the operation is complete.

- Forward lists provide many special member functions for moving and removing elements. These member functions are faster versions of general algorithms, because they only redirect pointers rather than copy and move the values. However, when element positions are involved, you have to pass the preceding position, and the member function has the suffix _after in its name.

7.6.2   Forward List Operations

Create, Copy, and Destroy

The ability to create, copy, and destroy forward lists is the same as it is for every sequence container. See Table 7.27 for the forward list operations that do this. See also Section 7.1.2, page 254, for some remarks about possible initialization sources.

Operation	Effect
`forward list<Elem> c`	Default constructor; creates an empty forward list without any elements
`forward list<Elem> c(c2)`	Copy constructor; creates a new forward list as a copy of *c2* (all elements are copied)
`forward list<Elem> c = c2`	Copy constructor; creates a new forward list as a copy of *c2* (all elements are copied)
`forward list<Elem> c(rv)`	Move constructor; creates a new forward list, taking the contents of the rvalue *rv* (since C++11)
`forward list<Elem> c = rv`	Move constructor; creates a new forward list, taking the contents of the rvalue *rv* (since C++11)
`forward list<Elem> c(n)`	Creates a forward list with *n* elements created by the default constructor
`forward list<Elem> c(n,elem)`	Creates a forward list initialized with *n* copies of element *elem*
`forward list<Elem> c(beg,end)`	Creates a forward list initialized with the elements of the range [*beg,end*)
`forward list<Elem> c(initlist)`	Creates a forward list initialized with the elements of initializer list *initlist* (since C++11)
`forward list<Elem> c = initlist`	Creates a forward list initialized with the elements of initializer list *initlist* (since C++11)
`c.~forward list()`	Destroys all elements and frees the memory

Table 7.27. Constructors and Destructor of Forward Lists

Nonmodifying Operations

With one exception, forward lists provide the usual operations for size and comparisons: Forward lists provide no `size()` operation. The reason is that it is not possible to store or compute the current number of elements in constant time. And to make the fact visible that `size()` is an expensive operation, it is not provided. If you have to compute the number of elements, you can use `distance()` (see Section 9.3.3, page 445):

```
#include <forward_list>
#include <iterator>
```

```
std::forward_list<int> l;
...
std::cout << "l.size(): " << std::distance(l.begin(),l.end())
          << std::endl;
```

But note that `distance()` is a call with linear complexity here.

See Table 7.28 for a complete list of the nonmodifying operations of forward lists and Section 7.1.2, page 254, for more details about the other operations.

Operation	Effect
`c.empty()`	Returns whether the container is empty
`c.max_size()`	Returns the maximum number of elements possible
`c1 == c2`	Returns whether $c1$ is equal to $c2$ (calls == for the elements)
`c1 != c2`	Returns whether $c1$ is not equal to $c2$ (equivalent to `!(c1==c2)`)
`c1 < c2`	Returns whether $c1$ is less than $c2$
`c1 > c2`	Returns whether $c1$ is greater than $c2$ (equivalent to `c2<c1`)
`c1 <= c2`	Returns whether $c1$ is less than or equal to $c2$ (equivalent to `!(c2<c1)`)
`c1 >= c2`	Returns whether $c1$ is greater than or equal to $c2$ (equivalent to `!(c1<c2)`)

Table 7.28. Nonmodifying Operations of Forward Lists

Assignments

Forward lists also provide the usual assignment operations for sequence containers (Table 7.29). As usual, the insert operations match the constructors to provide different sources for initialization (see Section 7.1.2, page 254, for details).

Operation	Effect
`c = c2`	Assigns all elements of $c2$ to c
`c = rv`	Move assigns all elements of the rvalue *rv* to c (since C++11)
`c = initlist`	Assigns all elements of the initializer list *initlist* to c (since C++11)
`c.assign(n,elem)`	Assigns n copies of element *elem*
`c.assign(beg,end)`	Assigns the elements of the range $[beg,end)$
`c.assign(initlist)`	Assigns all the elements of the initializer list *initlist*
`c1.swap(c2)`	Swaps the data of $c1$ and $c2$
`swap(c1,c2)`	Swaps the data of $c1$ and $c2$

Table 7.29. Assignment Operations of Forward Lists

Element Access

To access all elements of a forward list, you must use range-based `for` loops (see Section 3.1.4, page 17), specific operations, or iterators. In contrast to lists, the only element you can access directly is the first element, if any. For this reason, only `front()` is provided to access elements directly (Table 7.30).

Operation	Effect
`c.front()`	Returns the first element (*no* check whether a first element exists)

Table 7.30. Direct Element Access of Forward Lists

As usual, this operation does *not* check whether the container is empty. If the container is empty, calling `front()` results in undefined behavior. In addition, in multithreaded contexts, you need synchronization mechanisms to ensure that `coll` is not modified between the check for its size and the access to an element (see Section 18.4.3, page 984).

Iterator Functions

To access all elements of a forward list, you must use iterators. However, because you can traverse elements only in forward order, the iterators are forward iterators, and no support for reverse iterators is provided (Table 7.31).

Thus, you can't call algorithms that require bidirectional iterators or random-access iterators. All algorithms that manipulate the order of elements a lot, especially sorting algorithms, are in this category. However, for sorting the elements, forward lists provide the special member function `sort()` (see Section 8.8.1, page 422).

In addition, `before_begin()` and `cbefore_begin()` are provided to yield the position of a virtual element before the first element, which is necessary to be able to modify the next element even if the next element is the first element.

Operation	Effect
`c.begin()`	Returns a bidirectional iterator for the first element
`c.end()`	Returns a bidirectional iterator for the position after the last element
`c.cbegin()`	Returns a constant bidirectional iterator for the first element (since C++11)
`c.cend()`	Returns a constant bidirectional iterator for the position after the last element (since C++11)
`c.before_begin()`	Returns a forward iterator for the position before the first element
`c.cbefore_begin()`	Returns a constant forward iterator for the position before the first element

Table 7.31. Iterator Operations of Forward Lists

Note that `before_begin()` and `cbefore_begin()` do not represent a valid position of a forward list. Therefore, dereferencing these positions results in undefined behavior. Thus, using any ordinary algorithm with `before_begin()` as first argument passed results in a runtime error:

```
// RUNTIME ERROR: before_begin() is only valid with ..._after() operations
std::copy (fwlist.before_begin(), fwlist.end(),
           ...);
```

Besides copying and assignments, the only valid operations for return values of `before_begin()` are ++, ==, and !=.

Inserting and Removing Elements

Table 7.32 shows the operations provided for forward lists to insert and to remove elements. Due to the nature of lists in general and forward lists in particular, we have to discuss them in detail.

First, the usual general hints apply:

- As usual when using the STL, you must ensure that the arguments are valid. Iterators must refer to valid positions, and the beginning of a range must have a position that is not behind the end.
- Inserting and removing is faster if, when working with multiple elements, you use a single call for all elements rather than multiple calls.

Then, as for lists, forward lists provide special implementations of the `remove()` algorithms (see Section 11.7.1, page 575). These member functions are faster than the `remove()` algorithms because they manipulate only internal pointers rather than the elements. For more details, see the description of these operations for lists in Section 7.5.2, page 294.

Note that for all the insert, emplace, and erase member functions provided for forward lists, you have a problem: They usually get a position of an element, where you have to insert a new element or must delete. But this requires a modification of the *preceding* element, because there the pointer to the next element has to get modified. For lists, you can just go backward to the previous element to manipulate it, but for forward lists, you can't. For this reason, the member functions behave differently than for lists, which is reflected by the name of the member functions. All end with `_after`, which means that they insert a new element *after* the one passed (i.e., they *append*) or delete the element *after* the element passed.

In combination with `before_begin()` to ensure that the first element is covered, when you use these member functions, a typical access of forward lists is as follows (see Figure 7.9):

```
std::forward_list<int> fwlist = { 1, 2, 3 };

// insert 77, 88, and 99 at the beginning:
fwlist.insert_after (fwlist.before_begin(),      // position
                     { 77, 88, 99 } );           // values
```

Note that calling an `_after` member function with `end()` or `cend()` results in undefined behavior because to append a new element at the end of a forward list, you have to pass the position of the last element (or `before_begin()` if none):

```
// RUNTIME ERROR: appending element after end is undefined behavior
fwlist.insert_after(fwlist.end(),9999);
```

Operation	Effect
c.push_front(*elem*)	Inserts a copy of *elem* at the beginning
c.pop_front()	Removes the first element (does not return it)
c.insert_after(*pos*,*elem*)	Inserts a copy of *elem* after iterator position *pos* and returns the position of the new element
c.insert_after(*pos*,*n*,*elem*)	Inserts *n* copies of *elem* after iterator position *pos* and returns the position of the first new element (or pos if there is no new element)
c.insert_after(*pos*,*beg*,*end*)	Inserts a copy of all elements of the range [*beg*,*end*) after iterator position *pos* and returns the position of the first new element (or *pos* if there is no new element)
c.insert_after(*pos*,*initlist*)	Inserts a copy of all elements of the initializer list *initlist* after iterator position *pos* and returns the position of the first new element (or *pos* if there is no new element)
c.emplace_after(*pos*,*args...*)	Inserts a copy of an element initialized with *args* after iterator position *pos* and returns the position of the new element (since C++11)
c.emplace_front(*args...*)	Inserts a copy of an element initialized with *args* at the beginning (returns nothing; since C++11)
c.erase_after(*pos*)	Removes the element after iterator position *pos* (returns nothing)
c.erase_after(*beg*,*end*)	Removes all elements of the range [*beg*,*end*) (returns nothing)
c.remove(*val*)	Removes all elements with value *val*
c.remove_if(*op*)	Removes all elements for which *op*(*elem*) yields true
c.resize(*num*)	Changes the number of elements to *num* (if size() grows new elements are created by their default constructor)
c.resize(*num*,*elem*)	Changes the number of elements to *num* (if size() grows new elements are copies of *elem*)
c.clear()	Removes all elements (empties the container)

Table 7.32. Insert and Remove Operations of Forward Lists

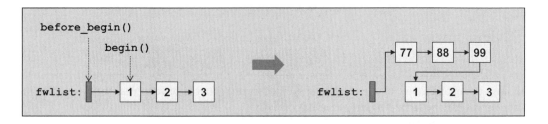

Figure 7.9. Inserting Elements at the Beginning of a Forward List

Find and Remove or Insert

The drawbacks of having a singly linked list, where you can only traverse forward, gets even worse when trying to find an element to insert or delete something there. The problem is that when you find the element, you are too far, because to insert or delete something there you have to manipulate the element before the element you are searching for. For this reason, you have to find an element by determining whether the *next* element fits a specific criterion. For example:

```
// cont/forwardlistfind1.cpp

#include <forward_list>
#include "print.hpp"
using namespace std;

int main()
{
    forward_list<int> list = { 1, 2, 3, 4, 5, 97, 98, 99 };

    // find the position before the first even element
    auto posBefore = list.before_begin();
    for (auto pos=list.begin(); pos!=list.end(); ++pos, ++posBefore) {
        if (*pos % 2 == 0) {
            break;  // element found
        }
    }

    // and insert a new element in front of the first even element
    list.insert_after(posBefore,42);
    PRINT_ELEMENTS(list);
}
```

Here, pos iterates over the list to find a specific element, whereas posBefore is always before pos to be able to return the position of the element before the element searched for (see Figure 7.10). So, the program has the following output:

```
1 42 2 3 4 5 97 98 99
```

Alternatively, you can use the next() convenience function for iterators, which is available since C++11 (see Section 9.3.2, page 443):

```
#include <iterator>
...
auto posBefore = list.before_begin();
for ( ; next(posBefore)!=list.end(); ++posBefore) {
    if (*next(posBefore) % 2 == 0) {
        break;  // element found
    }
}
```

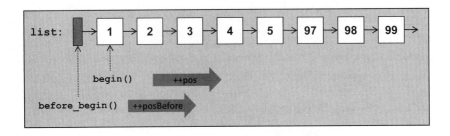

Figure 7.10. Searching for a Position to Insert or Delete

If this is something you need more often, you might define your own algorithms to find a position before the element that has a specific value or fulfills a specific condition:

```
// cont/findbefore.hpp

template <typename InputIterator, typename Tp>
inline InputIterator
find_before (InputIterator first, InputIterator last, const Tp& val)
{
    if (first==last) {
        return first;
    }
    InputIterator next(first);
    ++next;
    while (next!=last && !(*next==val)) {
        ++next;
        ++first;
    }
    return first;
}


template <typename InputIterator, typename Pred>
inline InputIterator
find_before_if (InputIterator first, InputIterator last, Pred pred)
{
    if (first==last) {
        return first;
    }
    InputIterator next(first);
    ++next;
    while (next!=last && !pred(*next)) {
        ++next;
        ++first;
    }
    return first;
}
```

With these algorithms, you can use lambdas to find the corresponding position (for the complete example, see *cont/fwlistfind2.cpp*):

```
// find the position before the first even element
auto posBefore = find_before_if (list.before_begin(), list.end(),
                                 [] (int i) {
                                     return i%2==0;
                                 });
// and insert a new element in front of it
list.insert_after(posBefore,42);
```

You have to call `find_before_if()` with the position returned by `before_begin()`. Otherwise, you skip the first element. To avoid undefined behavior if you pass `begin()`, the algorithms first check whether the beginning of the range is equal to the end. A better approach would have been to let forward lists provide corresponding member functions, but this is, unfortunately, not the case.

Splice Functions and Functions to Change the Order of Elements

As with lists, forward lists have the advantage that you can remove and insert elements at any position in constant time. If you move elements from one container to another, this advantage doubles in that you need to redirect only some internal pointers. For this reason, forward lists provide almost the same member functions to splice lists or to change the order of elements. You can call these operations to move elements inside a single list or between two lists, provided that the lists have the same type. The only difference from lists is that `splice_after()` is provided instead of `splice()`, because the position of the element in front of the element where the splice applies is passed.

Table 7.33 lists these functions. They are covered in detail in Section 8.8, page 420. The following program demonstrates how to use the splice functions for forward lists. Here the first element with value 3 in the forward list `l1` is moved before the first element with value 99 in `l2`:

```
// cont/forwardlistsplice1.cpp

#include <forward_list>
#include "print.hpp"
using namespace std;

int main()
{
    forward_list<int> l1 = { 1, 2, 3, 4, 5 };
    forward_list<int> l2 = { 97, 98, 99 };

    // find 3 in l1
    auto pos1=l1.before_begin();
    for (auto pb1=l1.begin(); pb1 != l1.end(); ++pb1, ++pos1) {
        if (*pb1 == 3) {
            break;  // found
        }
    }
```

```
// find 99 in l2
auto pos2=l2.before_begin();
for (auto pb2=l2.begin(); pb2 != l2.end(); ++pb2, ++pos2) {
    if (*pb2 == 99) {
        break;    // found
    }
}


// splice 3 from l1 to l2 before 99
l1.splice_after(pos2, l2,    // destination
                pos1);       // source

PRINT_ELEMENTS(l1,"l1: ");
PRINT_ELEMENTS(l2,"l2: ");
}
```

Operation	Effect
c.unique()	Removes duplicates of consecutive elements with the same value
c.unique(op)	Removes duplicates of consecutive elements, for which op() yields true
c.splice_after(pos,c2)	Moves all elements of c2 to c right behind the iterator position pos
c.splice_after(pos,c2,c2pos)	Moves the element behind c2pos in c2 right after pos of forward list c (c and c2 may be identical)
c.splice_after(pos,c2, c2beg,c2end)	Moves all elements between c2beg and c2end (both not included) in c2 right after pos of forward list c (c and c2 may be identical)
c.sort()	Sorts all elements with operator <
c.sort(op)	Sorts all elements with op()
c.merge(c2)	Assuming that both containers contain the elements sorted, moves all elements of c2 into c so that all elements are merged and still sorted
c.merge(c2,op)	Assuming that both containers contain the elements sorted by the sorting criterion op(), moves all elements of c2 into c so that all elements are merged and still sorted according to op()
c.reverse()	Reverses the order of all elements

Table 7.33. Special Modifying Operations for Forward Lists

First, in l1 we search for the position before the first element with value 3. Then, in l2 we search for the position before the first element with value 99. Finally, with both positions splice_after() is called, which just modifies the internal pointers in the lists (see Figure 7.11).

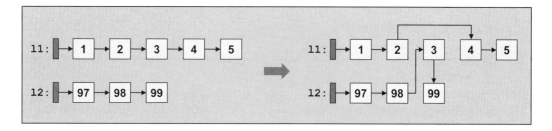

Figure 7.11. Effect of splice_after() *with Forward Lists*

Again, with our find_before() algorithms, the code looks a lot simpler:

```
// splice 3 from l1 to l2 before 99
l1.splice_after(l2.find_before(99), l2,    // destination
                l1.find_before(3));        // source
```

Note that source and destination for splice operations might be the same. Thus, you can move elements inside a forward list. However, note that calling splice_after() with end() results in undefined behavior, as all _after functions do with end():

```
// RUNTIME ERROR: move first element to the end is not possible that way
fwlist.splice_after(fwlist.end(),      // destination position
                    fwlist,            // source list
                    fwlist.begin());   // source position
```

7.6.3 Exception Handling

Forward lists give the same guarantees that lists give regarding exception handling, provided that the corresponding member function is available. See Section 7.5.3, page 296, for details.

7.6.4 Examples of Using Forward Lists

The following example shows the use of the special member functions for forward lists:

```
// cont/forwardlist1.cpp

#include <forward_list>
#include <iostream>
#include <algorithm>
#include <iterator>
#include <string>
using namespace std;

void printLists (const string& s, const forward_list<int>& l1,
                                  const forward_list<int>& l2)
{
    cout << s << endl;
    cout << " list1: ";
    copy (l1.cbegin(), l1.cend(), ostream_iterator<int>(cout," "));
    cout << endl << " list2: ";
    copy (l2.cbegin(), l2.cend(), ostream_iterator<int>(cout," "));
    cout << endl;
}

int main()
{
    // create two forward lists
    forward_list<int> list1 = { 1, 2, 3, 4 };
    forward_list<int> list2 = { 77, 88, 99 };
    printLists ("initial:", list1, list2);

    // insert six new element at the beginning of list2
    list2.insert_after(list2.before_begin(),99);
    list2.push_front(10);
    list2.insert_after(list2.before_begin(), {10,11,12,13} );
    printLists ("6 new elems:", list1, list2);

    // insert all elements of list2 at the beginning of list1
    list1.insert_after(list1.before_begin(),
                       list2.begin(),list2.end());
    printLists ("list2 into list1:", list1, list2);

    // delete second element and elements after element with value 99
    list2.erase_after(list2.begin());
```

```
        list2.erase_after(find(list2.begin(),list2.end(),
                            99),
                          list2.end());
        printLists ("delete 2nd and after 99:", list1, list2);

        // sort list1, assign it to list2, and remove duplicates
        list1.sort();
        list2 = list1;
        list2.unique();
        printLists ("sorted and unique:", list1, list2);

        // merge both sorted lists into list1
        list1.merge(list2);
        printLists ("merged:", list1, list2);
    }
```

The program has the following output:

```
    initial:
     list1: 1 2 3 4
     list2: 77 88 99
    6 new elems:
     list1: 1 2 3 4
     list2: 10 11 12 13 10 99 77 88 99
    list2 into list1:
     list1: 10 11 12 13 10 99 77 88 99 1 2 3 4
     list2: 10 11 12 13 10 99 77 88 99
    delete 2nd and after 99:
     list1: 10 11 12 13 10 99 77 88 99 1 2 3 4
     list2: 10 12 13 10 99
    sorted and unique:
     list1: 1 2 3 4 10 10 11 12 13 77 88 99 99
     list2: 1 2 3 4 10 11 12 13 77 88 99
    merged:
     list1: 1 1 2 2 3 3 4 4 10 10 10 11 11 12 12 13 13 77 77 88 88 99 99 99
     list2:
```

See Section 7.5.4, page 298, for a corresponding example using a list.

7.7   Sets and Multisets

Set and multiset containers sort their elements automatically according to a certain sorting criterion. The difference between the two types of containers is that multisets allow duplicates, whereas sets do not (see Figure 7.12 and the earlier discussion on this topic in Chapter 6).

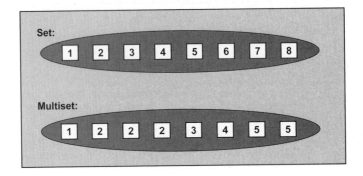

Figure 7.12. Sets and Multisets

To use a set or a multiset, you must include the header file <set>:

```
#include <set>
```

There, the types are defined as class templates inside namespace std:

```
namespace std {
    template <typename T,
              typename Compare = less<T>,
              typename Allocator = allocator<T> >
        class set;

    template <typename T,
              typename Compare = less<T>,
              typename Allocator = allocator<T> >
        class multiset;
}
```

The elements of a set or a multiset may have any type T that is comparable according to the sorting criterion. The optional second template argument defines the sorting criterion. If a special sorting criterion is not passed, the default criterion less is used. The function object less sorts the elements by comparing them with operator < (see Section 10.2.1, page 487, for details about less). The optional third template parameter defines the memory model (see Chapter 19). The default memory model is the model allocator, which is provided by the C++ standard library.

The sorting criterion must define *strict weak ordering*, which is defined by the following four properties:

1. It has to be **antisymmetric**.
   This means that for operator <: If x < y is true, then y < x is false.
   This means that for a predicate op(): If op(x,y) is true, then op(y,x) is false.

2. It has to be **transitive**.
   This means that for operator <: If x < y is true and y < z is true, then x < z is true.
   This means that for a predicate op(): If op(x,y) is true and op(y,z) is true, then op(x,z) is true.

3. It has to be **irreflexive**.
   This means that for operator <: x < x is always false.
   This means that for a predicate op(): op(x,x) is always false.

4. It has to have **transitivity of equivalence**, which means roughly: If a is equivalent to b and b is equivalent to c, then a is equivalent to c.
   This means that for operator <: If !(a<b) && !(b<a) is true and !(b<c) && !(c<b) is true then !(a<c) && !(c<a) is true.
   This means that for a predicate op(): If op(a,b), op(b,a), op(b,c), and op(c,b) all yield false, then op(a,c) and op(c,a) yield false.

Note that this means that you have to distinguish between less and equal. A criterion such as operator <= does not fulfill this requirement.

Based on these properties, the sorting criterion is also used to check equivalence. That is, two elements are considered to be duplicates if neither is less than the other (or if both op(x,y) and op(y,x) are false).

For multisets, the order of equivalent elements is random but stable. Thus, insertions and erasures preserve the relative ordering of equivalent elements (guaranteed since C++11).

7.7.1 Abilities of Sets and Multisets

Like all standardized associative container classes, sets and multisets are usually implemented as balanced binary trees (Figure 7.13). The standard does not specify this, but it follows from the complexity of set and multiset operations.[9]

The major advantage of automatic sorting is that a binary tree performs well when elements with a certain value are searched. In fact, search functions have logarithmic complexity. For example, to search for an element in a set or a multiset of 1,000 elements, a tree search performed by a member function needs, on average, one-fiftieth of the comparisons of a linear search (which is performed by a search algorithm that iterates over all elements). See Section 2.2, page 10, for more details about complexity.

However, automatic sorting also imposes an important constraint on sets and multisets: You may *not* change the value of an element directly, because doing so might compromise the correct order.

---

[9] In fact, sets and multisets are typically implemented as *red-black trees*, which are good for both changing the number of elements and searching for elements. They guarantee at most two internal relinks on insertions and that the longest path is at most twice as long as the shortest path to a leaf.

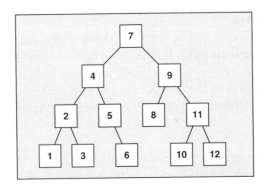

Figure 7.13. Internal Structure of Sets and Multisets

Therefore, to modify the value of an element, you must remove the element having the old value and insert a new element that has the new value. The interface reflects this behavior:

- Sets and multisets don't provide operations for direct element access.
- Indirect access via iterators has the constraint that, from the iterator's point of view, the element value is constant.

7.7.2   Set and Multiset Operations

Create, Copy, and Destroy

Table 7.34 lists the constructors and destructors of sets and multisets.

You can define the sorting criterion in two ways:

1. **As a template parameter.** For example:
   ```
   std::set<int,std::greater<int>> coll;
   ```
   In this case, the sorting criterion is part of the type. Thus, the type system ensures that only containers with the same sorting criterion can be combined. This is the usual way to specify the sorting criterion. To be more precise, the second parameter is the *type* of the sorting criterion. The concrete sorting criterion is the function object that gets created with the container. To do this, the constructor of the container calls the default constructor of the type of the sorting criterion. See Section 10.1.1, page 476, for an example that uses a user-defined sorting criterion.

2. **As a constructor parameter.** In this case, you might have a type for several sorting criteria that allows having different initial values or states. This is useful when processing the sorting criterion at runtime and when sorting criteria are needed that are different but of the same data type. See Section 7.7.5, page 328, for a complete example.

If no special sorting criterion is passed, the default sorting criterion, function object less<>, is used, which sorts the elements by using operator <.

Note that the sorting criterion is also used to check for equivalence of two elements in the same container (i.e., to find duplicates). Thus, when the default sorting criterion is used, the check for equivalence of two elements looks like this:

```
if (! (elem1<elem2 || elem2<elem1))
```

Operation	Effect
set c	Default constructor; creates an empty set/multiset without any elements
set c(*op*)	Creates an empty set/multiset that uses *op* as the sorting criterion
set c(*c2*)	Copy constructor; creates a copy of another set/multiset of the same type (all elements are copied)
set c = *c2*	Copy constructor; creates a copy of another set/multiset of the same type (all elements are copied)
set c(*rv*)	Move constructor; creates a new set/multiset of the same type, taking the contents of the rvalue *rv* (since C++11)
set c = *rv*	Move constructor; creates a new set/multiset of the same type, taking the contents of the rvalue *rv* (since C++11)
set c(*beg*,*end*)	Creates a set/multiset initialized by the elements of the range [*beg*,*end*)
set c(*beg*,*end*,*op*)	Creates a set/multiset with the sorting criterion *op* initialized by the elements of the range [*beg*,*end*)
set c(*initlist*)	Creates a set/multiset initialized with the elements of initializer list *initlist* (since C++11)
set c = *initlist*	Creates a set/multiset initialized with the elements of initializer list *initlist* (since C++11)
c.˜*set*()	Destroys all elements and frees the memory

Here, *set* may be one of the following types:

set	Effect
set<*Elem*>	A set that by default sorts with less<> (operator <)
set<*Elem*,*Op*>	A set that by default sorts with Op
multiset<*Elem*>	A multiset that by default sorts with less<> (operator <)
multiset<*Elem*,*Op*>	A multiset that by default sorts with Op

Table 7.34. Constructors and Destructors of Sets and Multisets

This has three advantages:

1. You need to pass only one argument as the sorting criterion.
2. You don't have to provide operator == for the element type.
3. You can have contrary definitions between equivalence and equality (however, this might be a source of confusion).

Checking for equivalence in this way takes a bit more time because two comparisons might be necessary to evaluate the previous expression. Note, however, that if the result of the first comparison yields true, the second comparison is not evaluated.

Note also that if two containers are compared by operator ==, the elements in both containers are compared using their operator ==, which means that operator == has to be provided for the element type.

The constructor for the beginning and the end of a range could be used to initialize the container with elements from containers that have other types, from arrays, or from the standard input. See Section 7.1.2, page 254, for details.

Nonmodifying Operations

Sets and multisets provide the usual nonmodifying operations to query the size and to make comparisons (Table 7.35).

Operation	Effect
`c.key_comp()`	Returns the comparison criterion
`c.value_comp()`	Returns the comparison criterion for values as a whole (same as `key_comp()`)
`c.empty()`	Returns whether the container is empty (equivalent to `size()==0` but might be faster)
`c.size()`	Returns the current number of elements
`c.max_size()`	Returns the maximum number of elements possible
`c1 == c2`	Returns whether `c1` is equal to `c2` (calls == for the elements)
`c1 != c2`	Returns whether `c1` is not equal to `c2` (equivalent to `!(c1==c2)`)
`c1 < c2`	Returns whether `c1` is less than `c2`
`c1 > c2`	Returns whether `c1` is greater than `c2` (equivalent to `c2<c1`)
`c1 <= c2`	Returns whether `c1` is less than or equal to `c2` (equivalent to `!(c2<c1)`)
`c1 >= c2`	Returns whether `c1` is greater than or equal to `c2` (equivalent to `!(c1<c2)`)

Table 7.35. Nonmodifying Operations of Sets and Multisets

Comparisons are provided only for containers of the same type. Thus, the elements *and* the sorting criterion must have the same types; otherwise, a type error occurs at compile time. For example:

```
std::set<float> c1;          // sorting criterion: std::less<>
std::set<float,std::greater<float> > c2;
...
if (c1 == c2) {              // ERROR: different types
    ...
}
```

The check whether a container is less than another container is done by a lexicographical comparison (see Section 11.5.4, page 548). To compare containers of different types (different sorting criteria), you must use the comparing algorithms in Section 11.5.4, page 542.

Special Search Operations

Because they are optimized for fast searching of elements, sets and multisets provide special search functions (Table 7.36). These functions are special versions of general algorithms that have the same name. You should always prefer the optimized versions for sets and multisets to achieve logarithmic complexity instead of the linear complexity of the general algorithms. For example, a search of a collection of 1,000 elements requires on average only 10 comparisons instead of 500 (see Section 2.2, page 10).

Operation	Effect
`c.count(`*val*`)`	Returns the number of elements with value *val*
`c.find(`*val*`)`	Returns the position of the first element with value *val* (or `end()` if none found)
`c.lower_bound(`*val*`)`	Returns the first position, where *val* would get inserted (the first element >= *val*)
`c.upper_bound(`*val*`)`	Returns the last position, where *val* would get inserted (the first element > *val*)
`c.equal_range(`*val*`)`	Returns a range with all elements with a value equal to *val* (i.e., the first and last position, where *val* would get inserted)

Table 7.36. Special Search Operations of Sets and Multisets

The `find()` member function searches the first element that has the value that was passed as the argument and returns its iterator position. If no such element is found, `find()` returns `end()` of the container.

`lower_bound()` and `upper_bound()` return the first and last position, respectively, at which an element with the passed value would be inserted. In other words, `lower_bound()` returns the position of the first element that has the same or a greater value than the argument, whereas `upper_bound()` returns the position of the first element with a greater value. `equal_range()` returns both return values of `lower_bound()` and `upper_bound()` as a `pair` (type `pair` is introduced in Section 5.1.1, page 60). Thus, `equal_range()` returns the range of elements that have the same value as the argument. If `lower_bound()` or the first value of `equal_range()` is equal to `upper_bound()` or the second value of `equal_range()`, no elements with the same value exist in the set or multiset. Naturally, the range of elements having the same values could contain at most one element in a set.

The following example shows how to use `lower_bound()`, `upper_bound()`, and `equal_range()`:

```
// cont/setrange1.cpp

#include <iostream>
#include <set>
using namespace std;
```

```
int main ()
{
    set<int> c;

    c.insert(1);
    c.insert(2);
    c.insert(4);
    c.insert(5);
    c.insert(6);

    cout << "lower_bound(3): " << *c.lower_bound(3) << endl;
    cout << "upper_bound(3): " << *c.upper_bound(3) << endl;
    cout << "equal_range(3): " << *c.equal_range(3).first << " "
                               << *c.equal_range(3).second << endl;
    cout << endl;
    cout << "lower_bound(5): " << *c.lower_bound(5) << endl;
    cout << "upper_bound(5): " << *c.upper_bound(5) << endl;
    cout << "equal_range(5): " << *c.equal_range(5).first << " "
                               << *c.equal_range(5).second << endl;
}
```

The output of the program is as follows:

```
lower_bound(3): 4
upper_bound(3): 4
equal_range(3): 4 4

lower_bound(5): 5
upper_bound(5): 6
equal_range(5): 5 6
```

If you use a multiset instead of a set, the program has the same output.

Assignments

As listed in Table 7.37, Sets and multisets provide only the fundamental assignment operations that all containers provide (see Section 7.1.2, page 258).

For these operations, both containers must have the same type. In particular, the type of the comparison criteria must be the same, although the comparison criteria themselves may be different. See Section 7.7.5, page 328, for an example of different sorting criteria that have the same type. If the criteria are different, they will also get assigned or swapped.

Operation	Effect
c = c2	Assigns all elements of *c2* to *c*
c = rv	Move assigns all elements of the rvalue *rv* to *c* (since C++11)
c = *initlist*	Assigns all elements of the initializer list *initlist* to *c* (since C++11)
c1.swap(c2)	Swaps the data of *c1* and *c2*
swap(c1,c2)	Swaps the data of *c1* and *c2*

Table 7.37. Assignment Operations of Sets and Multisets

Iterator Functions

Sets and multisets do not provide direct element access, so you have to use range-based `for` loops (see Section 3.1.4, page 17) or iterators. Sets and multisets provide the usual member functions for iterators (Table 7.38).

Operation	Effect
c.begin()	Returns a bidirectional iterator for the first element
c.end()	Returns a bidirectional iterator for the position after the last element
c.cbegin()	Returns a constant bidirectional iterator for the first element (since C++11)
c.cend()	Returns a constant bidirectional iterator for the position after the last element (since C++11)
c.rbegin()	Returns a reverse iterator for the first element of a reverse iteration
c.rend()	Returns a reverse iterator for the position after the last element of a reverse iteration
c.crbegin()	Returns a constant reverse iterator for the first element of a reverse iteration (since C++11)
c.crend()	Returns a constant reverse iterator for the position after the last element of a reverse iteration (since C++11)

Table 7.38. Iterator Operations of Sets and Multisets

As with all associative container classes, the iterators are bidirectional iterators (see Section 9.2.4, page 437). Thus, you can't use them in algorithms that are provided only for random-access iterators, such as algorithms for sorting or random shuffling.

More important is the constraint that, from an iterator's point of view, all elements are considered constant. This is necessary to ensure that you can't compromise the order of the elements by changing their values. However, as a result, you can't call any modifying algorithm on the elements of a set or a multiset. For example, you can't call the `remove()` algorithm, because it "removes" by overwriting "removed" elements with the following elements (see Section 6.7.2, page 221, for a detailed discussion of this problem). To remove elements in sets and multisets, you can use only member functions provided by the container.

Inserting and Removing Elements

Table 7.39 shows the operations provided for sets and multisets to insert and remove elements.

Operation	Effect
c.insert(*val*)	Inserts a copy of *val* and returns the position of the new element and, for sets, whether it succeeded
c.insert(*pos*,*val*)	Inserts a copy of *val* and returns the position of the new element (*pos* is used as a hint pointing to where the insert should start the search)
c.insert(*beg*,*end*)	Inserts a copy of all elements of the range [*beg*,*end*) (returns nothing)
c.insert(*initlist*)	Inserts a copy of all elements in the initializer list *initlist* (returns nothing; since C++11)
c.emplace(*args*...)	Inserts a copy of an element initialized with *args* and returns the position of the new element and, for sets, whether it succeeded (since C++11)
c.emplace_hint(*pos*,*args*...)	Inserts a copy of an element initialized with *args* and returns the position of the new element (*pos* is used as a hint pointing to where the insert should start the search)
c.erase(*val*)	Removes all elements equal to *val* and returns the number of removed elements
c.erase(*pos*)	Removes the element at iterator position *pos* and returns the following position (returned nothing before C++11)
c.erase(*beg*,*end*)	Removes all elements of the range [*beg*,*end*) and returns the following position (returned nothing before C++11)
c.clear()	Removes all elements (empties the container)

Table 7.39. Insert and Remove Operations of Sets and Multisets

As usual when using the STL, you must ensure that the arguments are valid. Iterators must refer to valid positions, and the beginning of a range must have a position that is not behind the end.

Inserting and removing is faster if, when working with multiple elements, you use a single call for all elements rather than multiple calls.

For multisets, since C++11 it is guaranteed that insert(), emplace(), and erase() preserve the relative ordering of equivalent elements, and that inserted elements are placed at the end of existing equivalent values.

Note that the return types of the inserting functions insert() and emplace() differ as follows:

- **Sets** provide the following interface:[10]

```
pair<iterator,bool>    insert (const value_type& val);
iterator               insert (const_iterator posHint,
                                 const value_type& val);
template <typename... Args>
 pair<iterator, bool> emplace (Args&&... args);
template <typename... Args>
 iterator              emplace_hint (const_iterator posHint,
                                      Args&&... args);
```

- **Multisets** provide the following interface:[10]

```
iterator               insert (const value_type& val);
iterator               insert (const_iterator posHint,
                                 const value_type& val);
template <typename... Args>
 iterator              emplace (Args&&... args);
template <typename... Args>
 iterator              emplace_hint (const_iterator posHint,
                                      Args&&... args);
```

The difference in return types results because multisets allow duplicates, whereas sets do not. Thus, the insertion of an element might fail for a set if it already contains an element with the same value. Therefore, the return type for a set returns two values by using a `pair` structure (`pair` is discussed in Section 5.1.1, page 60):

1. The member `second` of the `pair` structure returns whether the insertion was successful.
2. The member `first` of the `pair` structure returns the position of the newly inserted element or the position of the still existing element.

In all other cases, the functions return the position of the new element or of the existing element if the set already contains an element with the same value.

The following example shows how to use this interface to insert a new element into a set. It tries to insert the element with value 3.3 into the set c:

```
std::set<double> c;
...
if (c.insert(3.3).second) {
    std::cout << "3.3 inserted" << std::endl;
}
else {
    std::cout << "3.3 already exists" << std::endl;
}
```

If you also want to process the new or old positions, the code gets more complicated:

---

[10] Before C++11, only `insert()` was provided, and *posHint* had type `iterator` instead of `const_iterator`.

```
// insert value and process return value
auto status = c.insert(value);
if (status.second) {
    std::cout << value << " inserted as element "
}
else {
    std::cout << value << " already exists as element "
}
std::cout << std::distance(c.begin(),status.first) + 1 << std::endl;
```

The output of two calls of this sequence might be as follows:

```
8.9 inserted as element 4
7.7 already exists as element 3
```

In this example, the type of status is as follows:

```
std::pair<std::set<float>::iterator,bool>
```

Note that the return types of the insert functions with an additional position parameter don't differ. These functions return a single iterator for both sets and multisets. However, these functions have the same effect as the functions without the position parameter. They differ only in their performance. You can pass an iterator position, but this position is processed as a hint to optimize performance. In fact, if the element gets inserted right after the position that is passed as the first argument, the time complexity changes from logarithmic to amortized constant (complexity is discussed in Section 2.2, page 10). The fact that the return type for the insert functions with the additional position hint doesn't have the same difference as the insert functions without the position hint ensures that you have one insert function that has the same interface for all container types. In fact, this interface is used by general inserters. See Section 9.4.2, especially page 458, for details about inserters.

To remove an element that has a certain value, you simply call erase():

```
std::set<Elem> coll;

...

// remove all elements with passed value
coll.erase(value);
```

Note that this member function has a different name than remove() provided for lists (see Section 7.5.2, page 294, for a discussion of remove()). It behaves differently in that it returns the number of removed elements. When called for sets, it returns only 0 or 1.

If a multiset contains duplicates, you can't use erase() to remove only the first element of these duplicates. Instead, you can code as follows:

```
std::multiset<Elem> coll;

...

// remove first element with passed value
std::multiset<Elem>::iterator pos;
pos = coll.find(value);
if (pos != coll.end()) {
    coll.erase(pos);
}
```

Because it is faster, you should use the member function `find()` instead of the `find()` algorithm here.

Note that before C++11, the `erase()` functions of associative containers returned nothing (had return type `void`). The reason was performance. It might cost time to find and return the successor in an associative container, because the container is implemented as a binary tree. However, this greatly complicated code where you erase elements while iterating over them (see Section 7.8.2, page 342).

Note also that for sets that use iterators as elements, calling `erase()` might be ambiguous now. For this reason, C++11 gets fixed to provide overloads for both `erase(iterator)` and `erase(const_iterator)`.

For multisets, all `insert()`, `emplace()`, and `erase()` operations preserve the relative order of equivalent elements. Since C++11, calling `insert(val)` or `emplace(args...)` guarantees that the new element is inserted at the end of the range of equivalent elements.

7.7.3 Exception Handling

Sets and multisets are node-based containers, so any failure to construct a node simply leaves the container as it was. Furthermore, because destructors in general don't throw, removing a node can't fail.

However, for multiple-element insert operations, the need to keep elements sorted makes full recovery from throws impractical. Thus, all single-element insert operations support commit-or-rollback behavior. That is, they either succeed or have no effect. In addition, it is guaranteed that all multiple-element delete operations always succeed or have no effect, provided that the comparison criterion does not throw. If copying/assigning the comparison criterion may throw, `swap()` may throw.

See Section 6.12.2, page 248, for a general discussion of exception handling in the STL.

7.7.4 Examples of Using Sets and Multisets

The following program demonstrates some abilities of sets:

```
// cont/set1.cpp

#include <iostream>
#include <set>
#include <algorithm>
#include <iterator>
using namespace std;

int main()
{
    // type of the collection:
    // - no duplicates
    // - elements are integral values
```

```
// - descending order
set<int,greater<int>> coll1;

// insert elements in random order using different member functions
coll1.insert({4,3,5,1,6,2});
coll1.insert(5);

// print all elements
for (int elem : coll1) {
    cout << elem << ' ';
}
cout << endl;

// insert 4 again and process return value
auto status = coll1.insert(4);
if (status.second) {
    cout << "4 inserted as element "
         << distance(coll1.begin(),status.first) + 1 << endl;
}
else {
    cout << "4 already exists" << endl;
}

// assign elements to another set with ascending order
set<int> coll2(coll1.cbegin(),coll1.cend());

// print all elements of the copy using stream iterators
copy (coll2.cbegin(), coll2.cend(),
      ostream_iterator<int>(cout," "));
cout << endl;

// remove all elements up to element with value 3
coll2.erase (coll2.begin(), coll2.find(3));

// remove all elements with value 5
int num;
num = coll2.erase (5);
cout << num << " element(s) removed" << endl;

// print all elements
copy (coll2.cbegin(), coll2.cend(),
      ostream_iterator<int>(cout," "));
cout << endl;
}
```

At first, an empty set is created and several elements are inserted by using different overloads of insert():

```
set<int,greater<int>> coll1;

coll1.insert({4,3,5,1,6,2});
coll1.insert(5);
```

Note that the element with value 5 is inserted twice. However, the second insertion is ignored because sets do not allow duplicates.

After printing all elements, the program tries again to insert the element 4. This time, it processes the return values of insert() as discussed in Section 7.7.2, page 323.

The statement

```
set<int> coll2(coll1.cbegin(),coll1.cend());
```

creates a new set of ints with ascending order and initializes it with the elements of the old set.

Both containers have different sorting criteria, so their types differ, and you can't assign or compare them directly. However, you can use algorithms, which in general are able to handle different container types as long as the element types are equal or convertible.

The following statement removes all elements up to the element with value 3:

```
coll2.erase (coll2.begin(), coll2.find(3));
```

Note that the element with value 3 is the end of the range, so it is not removed.

Finally, all elements with value 5 are removed:

```
int num;
num = coll2.erase (5);
cout << num << " element(s) removed" << endl;
```

The output of the whole program is as follows:

```
6 5 4 3 2 1
4 already exists
1 2 3 4 5 6
1 element(s) removed
3 4 6
```

For multisets, the same program (provided in *cont/multiset1.cpp*) looks a bit different and produces different results. First, in all cases type set has to get replaced by multiset (the header file remains the same):

```
multiset<int,greater<int>> coll1;
    ...
multiset<int> coll2(coll1.cbegin(),coll1.cend());
```

In addition, the processing of the return value of insert() looks different. Sets allow no duplicates, so insert() returns both the new position of the inserted element and whether the insertion was successful:

```
auto status = coll1.insert(4);
if (status.second) {
    cout << "4 inserted as element "
         << distance(coll1.begin(),status.first) + 1 << endl;
}
else {
    cout << "4 already exists" << endl;
}
```

For multisets, insert() only returns the new position (because multisets may contain duplicates, the insertion can fail only if an exception gets thrown):

```
auto ipos = coll1.insert(4);
cout << "4 inserted as element "
     << distance(coll1.begin(),ipos) + 1 << endl;
```

The output of the program changes as follows:

```
6 5 4 3 2 1
4 already exists
1 2 3 4 5 6
1 element(s) removed
3 4 6
```

7.7.5 Example of Specifying the Sorting Criterion at Runtime

Normally, you define the sorting criterion as part of the type, by either passing it as a second template argument or using the default sorting criterion less<>. Sometimes, however, you must process the sorting criterion at runtime, or you may need different sorting criteria with the same data type. In such cases, you need a special type for the sorting criterion: one that lets you pass your sorting details at runtime. The following example program demonstrates how to do this:[11]

```
// cont/setcmp1.cpp

#include <iostream>
#include <set>
#include "print.hpp"
using namespace std;

// type for runtime sorting criterion
class RuntimeCmp {
  public:
    enum cmp_mode {normal, reverse};
```

---

[11] Thanks to Daniel Krügler for details of this example.

```
    private:
      cmp_mode mode;
    public:
      // constructor for sorting criterion
      // - default criterion uses value normal
      RuntimeCmp (cmp_mode m=normal) : mode(m) {
      }
      // comparison of elements
      // - member function for any element type
      template <typename T>
      bool operator() (const T& t1, const T& t2) const {
          return mode==normal ?   t1<t2
                                :   t2<t1;
      }
      // comparison of sorting criteria
      bool operator== (const RuntimeCmp& rc) const {
          return mode == rc.mode;
      }
};

// type of a set that uses this sorting criterion
typedef set<int,RuntimeCmp> IntSet;

int main()
{
    // create, fill, and print set with normal element order
    // - uses default sorting criterion
    IntSet coll1 = { 4, 7, 5, 1, 6, 2, 5 };
    PRINT_ELEMENTS (coll1, "coll1: ");

    // create sorting criterion with reverse element order
    RuntimeCmp reverse_order(RuntimeCmp::reverse);

    // create, fill, and print set with reverse element order
    IntSet coll2(reverse_order);
    coll2 = { 4, 7, 5, 1, 6, 2, 5 };
    PRINT_ELEMENTS (coll2, "coll2: ");

    // assign elements AND sorting criterion
    coll1 = coll2;
    coll1.insert(3);
    PRINT_ELEMENTS (coll1, "coll1: ");
```

```
// just to make sure...
if (coll1.value_comp() == coll2.value_comp()) {
    cout << "coll1 and coll2 have the same sorting criterion"
        << endl;
}
else {
    cout << "coll1 and coll2 have a different sorting criterion"
        << endl;
}
}
```

In this program, the class `RuntimeCmp` provides the general ability to specify, at runtime, the sorting criterion for any type. Its default constructor sorts in ascending order, using the default value `normal`. It also is possible to pass `RuntimeCmp::reverse` to sort in descending order.

The output of the program is as follows:

```
coll1: 1 2 4 5 6 7
coll2: 7 6 5 4 2 1
coll1: 7 6 5 4 3 2 1
coll1 and coll2 have the same sorting criterion
```

Note that `coll1` and `coll2` have the same type, which is not the case when passing `less<>` and `greater<>` as sorting criteria. Note also that the assignment operator assigns the elements *and* the sorting criterion; otherwise, an assignment would be an easy way to compromise the sorting criterion.

7.8   Maps and Multimaps

Maps and multimaps are containers that manage key/value pairs as elements. These containers sort their elements automatically, according to a certain sorting criterion that is used for the key. The difference between the two is that multimaps allow duplicates, whereas maps do not (Figure 7.14).

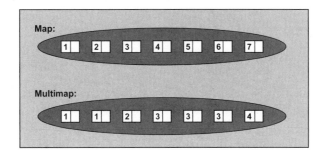

Figure 7.14. Maps and Multimaps

To use a map or a multimap, you must include the header file <map>:

```
#include <map>
```

There, the types are defined as class templates inside namespace std:

```
namespace std {
    template <typename Key, typename T,
             typename Compare = less<Key>,
             typename Allocator = allocator<pair<const Key,T> > >
        class map;

    template <typename Key, typename T,
             typename Compare = less<Key>,
             typename Allocator = allocator<pair<const Key,T> > >
        class multimap;
}
```

The first template parameter is the type of the element's key, and the second template parameter is the type of the element's associated value. The elements of a map or a multimap may have any types Key and T that meet the following two requirements:

1. Both key and value must be copyable or movable.

2. The key must be comparable with the sorting criterion.

Note that the element type (value_type) is a pair <const *Key*, *T*>.

The optional third template parameter defines the sorting criterion. As for sets, this sorting criterion must define a "strict weak ordering" (see Section 7.7, page 314). The elements are sorted according to their keys, so the value doesn't matter for the order of the elements. The sorting criterion is also used to check for equivalence; that is, two elements are equal if neither key is less than the other.

If a special sorting criterion is not passed, the default criterion less<> is used. The function object less<> sorts the elements by comparing them with operator < (see Section 10.2.1, page 487, for details about less).

For multimaps, the order of elements with equivalent keys is random but stable. Thus, insertions and erasures preserve the relative ordering of equivalent elements (guaranteed since C++11).

The optional fourth template parameter defines the memory model (see Chapter 19). The default memory model is the model allocator, which is provided by the C++ standard library.

7.8.1   Abilities of Maps and Multimaps

Like all standardized associative container classes, maps and multimaps are usually implemented as balanced binary trees (Figure 7.15). The standard does not specify this, but it follows from the complexity of the map and multimap operations. In fact, sets, multisets, maps, and multimaps typically use the same internal data type. So, you could consider sets and multisets as special maps and multimaps, respectively, for which the value and the key of the elements are the same objects. Thus, maps and multimaps have all the abilities and operations of sets and multisets. Some minor differences exist, however. First, their elements are key/value pairs. In addition, maps can be used as associative arrays.

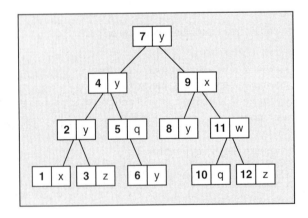

Figure 7.15. Internal Structure of Maps and Multimaps

Maps and multimaps sort their elements automatically, according to the element's keys, and so have good performance when searching for elements that have a certain key. Searching for elements that have a certain value promotes bad performance. Automatic sorting imposes an important constraint on maps and multimaps: You may *not* change the key of an element directly, because doing so might compromise the correct order. To modify the key of an element, you must remove the element that has the old key and insert a new element that has the new key and the old value (see Section 7.8.2, page 339, for details). As a consequence, from the iterator's point of view, the element's key is constant. However, a direct modification of the value of the element is still possible, provided that the type of the value is not constant.

7.8.2   Map and Multimap Operations

Create, Copy, and Destroy

Table 7.40 lists the constructors and destructors of maps and multimaps.

Operation	Effect
map c	Default constructor; creates an empty map/multimap without any elements
map c(*op*)	Creates an empty map/multimap that uses *op* as the sorting criterion
map c(*c2*)	Copy constructor; creates a copy of another map/multimap of the same type (all elements are copied)
map c = *c2*	Copy constructor; creates a copy of another map/multimap of the same type (all elements are copied)
map c(*rv*)	Move constructor; creates a new map/multimap of the same type, taking the contents of the rvalue *rv* (since C++11)
map c = *rv*	Move constructor; creates a new map/multimap of the same type, taking the contents of the rvalue *rv* (since C++11)
map c(*beg*,*end*)	Creates a map/multimap initialized by the elements of the range [*beg*,*end*)
map c(*beg*,*end*,*op*)	Creates a map/multimap with the sorting criterion *op* initialized by the elements of the range [*beg*,*end*)
map c(*initlist*)	Creates a map/multimap initialized with the elements of initializer list *initlist* (since C++11)
map c = *initlist*	Creates a map/multimap initialized with the elements of initializer list *initlist* (since C++11)
c.~*map*()	Destroys all elements and frees the memory

Here, *map* may be one of the following types:

map	Effect
map<*Key*,*Val*>	A map that by default sorts keys with less<> (operator <)
map<*Key*,*Val*,*Op*>	A map that by default sorts keys with *Op*
multimap<*Key*,*Val*>	A multimap that by default sorts keys with less<> (operator <)
multimap<*Key*,*Val*,*Op*>	A multimap that by default sorts keys with *Op*

Table 7.40. Constructors and Destructors of Maps and Multimaps

You can define the sorting criterion in two ways:

1. **As a template parameter.** For example:

   ```
   std::map<float,std::string,std::greater<float>> coll;
   ```

   In this case, the sorting criterion is part of the type. Thus, the type system ensures that only containers with the same sorting criterion can be combined. This is the usual way to specify the sorting criterion. To be more precise, the third parameter is the *type* of the sorting criterion. The concrete sorting criterion is the function object that gets created with the container. To do this, the constructor of the container calls the default constructor of the type of the sorting criterion. See Section 10.1.1, page 476, for an example that uses a user-defined sorting criterion.

2. **As a constructor parameter.** In this case, you might have a type for several sorting criteria, and the initial value or state of the sorting criteria might differ. This is useful when processing the sorting criterion at runtime or when sorting criteria are needed that are different but of the same data type. A typical example is specifying the sorting criterion for string keys at runtime. See Section 7.8.6, for a complete example.

If no special sorting criterion is passed, the default sorting criterion, function object less<>, is used, which sorts the elements according to their key by using operator <. Again, the sorting criterion is also used to check for equivalence of two elements in the same container (i.e., to find duplicates). Only to compare two containers is operator == required.

You might prefer a type definition to avoid the boring repetition of the type whenever it is used:

```
typedef std::map<std::string,float,std::greater<std::string>>
        StringFloatMap;

...

StringFloatMap coll;
```

The constructor for the beginning and the end of a range could be used to initialize the container with elements from containers that have other types, from arrays, or from the standard input. See Section 7.1.2, page 254, for details. However, the elements are key/value pairs, so you must ensure that the elements from the source range have or are convertible into type pair<*key*, *value*>.

Nonmodifying and Special Search Operations

Maps and multimaps provide the usual nonmodifying operations: those that query size aspects and make comparisons (Table 7.41).

Comparisons are provided only for containers of the same type. Thus, the key, the value, and the sorting criterion must be of the same type. Otherwise, a type error occurs at compile time. For example:

```
std::map<float,std::string> c1;          // sorting criterion: less<>
std::map<float,std::string,std::greater<float> > c2;

...

if (c1 == c2) {                          // ERROR: different types

    ...

}
```

Operation	Effect
`c.key_comp()`	Returns the comparison criterion
`c.value_comp()`	Returns the comparison criterion for values as a whole (an object that compares the key in a key/value pair)
`c.empty()`	Returns whether the container is empty (equivalent to `size()==0` but might be faster)
`c.size()`	Returns the current number of elements
`c.max_size()`	Returns the maximum number of elements possible
`c1 == c2`	Returns whether $c1$ is equal to $c2$ (calls == for the elements)
`c1 != c2`	Returns whether $c1$ is not equal to $c2$ (equivalent to `!(c1==c2)`)
`c1 < c2`	Returns whether $c1$ is less than $c2$
`c1 > c2`	Returns whether $c1$ is greater than $c2$ (equivalent to $c2<c1$)
`c1 <= c2`	Returns whether $c1$ is less than or equal to $c2$ (equivalent to `!(c2<c1)`)
`c1 >= c2`	Returns whether $c1$ is greater than or equal to $c2$ (equivalent to `!(c1<c2)`)

Table 7.41. Nonmodifying Operations of Maps and Multimaps

Checking whether a container is less than another container is done by a lexicographical comparison (see Section 11.5.4, page 548). To compare containers of different types (different sorting criterion), you must use the comparing algorithms of Section 11.5.4, page 542.

Special Search Operations

As for sets and multisets, maps and multimaps provide special search member functions that perform better because of their internal tree structure (Table 7.42).

Operation	Effect
`c.count(val)`	Returns the number of elements with key *val*
`c.find(val)`	Returns the position of the first element with key *val* (or `end()` if none found)
`c.lower_bound(val)`	Returns the first position where an element with key *val* would get inserted (the first element with a key >= *val*)
`c.upper_bound(val)`	Returns the last position where an element with key *val* would get inserted (the first element with a key > *val*)
`c.equal_range(val)`	Returns a range with all elements with a key equal to *val* (i.e., the first and last positions, where an element with key *val* would get inserted)

Table 7.42. Special Search Operations of Maps and Multimaps

The `find()` member function searches for the first element that has the appropriate key and returns its iterator position. If no such element is found, `find()` returns `end()` of the container. You can't use the `find()` member function to search for an element that has a certain value. Instead, you have to use a general algorithm, such as the `find_if()` algorithm, or program an explicit loop. Here is an example of a simple loop that does something with each element that has a certain value:

```
std::multimap<std::string,float> coll;
...
// do something with all elements having a certain value
std::multimap<std::string,float>::iterator pos;
for (pos = coll.begin(); pos != coll.end(); ++pos) {
    if (pos->second == value) {
        do_something();
    }
}
```

Be careful when you want to use such a loop to remove elements. It might happen that you saw off the branch on which you are sitting. See Section 7.8.2, page 342, for details about this issue.

Using the `find_if()` algorithm to search for an element that has a certain value is even more complicated than writing a loop, because you have to provide a function object that compares the value of an element with a certain value. See Section 7.8.5, page 350, for an example.

The `lower_bound()`, `upper_bound()`, and `equal_range()` functions behave as they do for sets (see Section 7.7.2, page 319), except that the elements are key/value pairs.

Assignments

As listed in Table 7.43, maps and multimaps provide only the fundamental assignment operations that all containers provide (see Section 7.1.2, page 258).

Operation	Effect
`c = c2`	Assigns all elements of *c2* to *c*
`c = rv`	Move assigns all elements of the rvalue *rv* to *c* (since C++11)
`c = initlist`	Assigns all elements of the initializer list *initlist* to *c* (since C++11)
`c1.swap(c2)`	Swaps the data of *c1* and *c2*
`swap(c1,c2)`	Swaps the data of *c1* and *c2*

Table 7.43. Assignment Operations of Maps and Multimaps

For these operations, both containers must have the same type. In particular, the type of the comparison criteria must be the same, although the comparison criteria themselves may be different. See Section 7.8.6, page 351, for an example of different sorting criteria that have the same type. If the criteria are different, they also get assigned or swapped.

Iterator Functions and Element Access

Maps and multimaps do not provide direct element access, so the usual way to access elements is via range-based `for` loops (see Section 3.1.4, page 17) or iterators. An exception to that rule is that maps provide `at()` and the subscript operator to access elements directly (see Section 7.8.3, page 343). Table 7.44 lists the usual member functions for iterators that maps and multimaps provide.

Operation	Effect
`c.begin()`	Returns a bidirectional iterator for the first element
`c.end()`	Returns a bidirectional iterator for the position after the last element
`c.cbegin()`	Returns a constant bidirectional iterator for the first element (since C++11)
`c.cend()`	Returns a constant bidirectional iterator for the position after the last element (since C++11)
`c.rbegin()`	Returns a reverse iterator for the first element of a reverse iteration
`c.rend()`	Returns a reverse iterator for the position after the last element of a reverse iteration
`c.crbegin()`	Returns a constant reverse iterator for the first element of a reverse iteration (since C++11)
`c.crend()`	Returns a constant reverse iterator for the position after the last element of a reverse iteration (since C++11)

Table 7.44. Iterator Operations of Maps and Multimaps

As for all associative container classes, the iterators are bidirectional (see Section 9.2.4, page 437). Thus, you can't use them in algorithms that are provided only for random-access iterators, such as algorithms for sorting or random shuffling.

More important is the constraint that the key of all elements inside a map and a multimap is considered to be constant. Thus, the type of the elements is `pair<const Key, T>`. This is necessary to ensure that you can't compromise the order of the elements by changing their keys. However, you can't call any modifying algorithm if the destination is a map or a multimap. For example, you can't call the `remove()` algorithm, because it "removes" by overwriting "removed" elements with the following elements (see Section 6.7.2, page 221, for a detailed discussion of this problem). To remove elements in maps and multimaps, you can use only member functions provided by the container.

The following is an example of element access via use range-based `for` loops:

```cpp
std::map<std::string,float> coll;
...
for (auto elem& : coll) {
    std::cout << "key: "   << elem.first  << "\t"
              << "value: " << elem.second << std::endl;
}
```

Inside the loop, `elem` becomes a reference referring to the actual element of the container `coll` currently processed. Thus. `elem` has type `pair<const std::string,float>`. The expression `elem.first` yields the key of the actual element, whereas the expression `elem.second` yields the value of the actual element.

The corresponding code using iterators, which has to be used before C++11, looks as follows:

```
std::map<std::string,float> coll;

...

std::map<std::string,float>::iterator pos;
for (pos = coll.begin(); pos != coll.end(); ++pos) {
    std::cout << "key: "   << pos->first  << "\t"
                << "value: " << pos->second << std::endl;
}
```

Here, the iterator pos iterates through the sequence of pairs of const `string` and `float`, and you have to use operator `->` to access key and value of the actual element.[12]

Trying to change the value of the key results in an error:

```
elem.first = "hello";     // ERROR at compile time
pos->first = "hello";     // ERROR at compile time
```

However, changing the value of the element is no problem, as long as `elem` is declared as a nonconstant reference and the type of the value is not constant:

```
elem.second = 13.5;     // OK
pos->second = 13.5;     // OK
```

If you use algorithms and lambdas to operate with the elements of a map, you explicitly have to declare the element type:

```
std::map<std::string,float> coll;

...

// add 10 to the value of each element:
std::for_each (coll.begin(), coll.end(),
                    [] (std::pair<const std::string,float>& elem) {
                        elem.second += 10;
                    });
```

Instead of using the following:

```
std::pair<const std::string,float>
```

you could use

```
std::map<std::string,float>::value_type
```

or

```
decltype(coll)::value_type
```

to declare the type of an element. See Section 7.8.5, page 345, for a complete example.

To change the key of an element, you have only one choice: You must replace the old element with a new element that has the same value. Here is a generic function that does this:

---

[12] `pos->first` is a shortcut for `(*pos).first`.

```
// cont/newkey.hpp

namespace MyLib {
    template <typename Cont>
    inline
    bool replace_key (Cont& c,
                      const typename Cont::key_type& old_key,
                      const typename Cont::key_type& new_key)
    {
        typename Cont::iterator pos;
        pos = c.find(old_key);
        if (pos != c.end()) {
            // insert new element with value of old element
            c.insert(typename Cont::value_type(new_key,
                                               pos->second));
            // remove old element
            c.erase(pos);
            return true;
        }
        else {
            // key not found
            return false;
        }
    }
}
```

The `insert()` and `erase()` member functions are discussed in the next subsection.

To use this generic function, you simply pass the container, the old key, and the new key. For example:

```
std::map<std::string,float> coll;
...
MyLib::replace_key(coll,"old key","new key");
```

It works the same way for multimaps.

Note that maps provide a more convenient way to modify the key of an element. Instead of calling `replace_key()`, you can simply write the following:

```
// insert new element with value of old element
coll["new_key"] = coll["old_key"];
// remove old element
coll.erase("old_key");
```

See Section 7.8.3, page 343, for details about the use of the subscript operator with maps.

Inserting and Removing Elements

Operation	Effect
c.insert(*val*)	Inserts a copy of *val* and returns the position of the new element and, for maps, whether it succeeded
c.insert(*pos*,*val*)	Inserts a copy of *val* and returns the position of the new element (*pos* is used as a hint pointing to where the insert should start the search)
c.insert(*beg*,*end*)	Inserts a copy of all elements of the range [*beg,end*) (returns nothing)
c.insert(*initlist*)	Inserts a copy of all elements in the initializer list *initlist* (returns nothing; since C++11)
c.emplace(*args*...)	Inserts a copy of an element initialized with *args* and returns the position of the new element and, for maps, whether it succeeded (since C++11)
c.emplace_hint(*pos*,*args*...)	Inserts a copy of an element initialized with *args* and returns the position of the new element (*pos* is used as a hint pointing to where the insert should start the search)
c.erase(*val*)	Removes all elements equal to *val* and returns the number of removed elements
c.erase(*pos*)	Removes the element at iterator position *pos* and returns the following position (returned nothing before C++11)
c.erase(*beg*,*end*)	Removes all elements of the range [*beg,end*) and returns the following position (returned nothing before C++11)
c.clear()	Removes all elements (empties the container)

Table 7.45. Insert and Remove Operations of Maps and Multimaps

Table 7.45 shows the operations provided for maps and multimaps to insert and remove elements. The remarks in Section 7.7.2, page 322, regarding sets and multisets apply here. In particular, the return types of these operations have the same differences as they do for sets and multisets. However, note that the elements here are key/value pairs. So, the use is getting a bit more complicated.

For multimaps, since C++11 it is guaranteed that insert(), emplace(), and erase() preserve the relative ordering of equivalent elements, and that inserted elements are placed at the end of existing equivalent values.

To insert a key/value pair, you must keep in mind that inside maps and multimaps, the key is considered to be constant. You must provide either the correct type or you need to provide implicit or explicit type conversions.

Since C++11, the most convenient way to insert elements is to pass them as an initializer list, where the first entry is the key and the second entry is the value:

```
std::map<std::string,float> coll;

...

coll.insert({"otto",22.3});
```

Alternatively, there are three other ways to pass a value into a map or a multimap:

1. **Use `value_type`.** To avoid implicit type conversion, you could pass the correct type explicitly by using `value_type`, which is provided as a type definition by the container type. For example:

   ```
   std::map<std::string,float> coll;
   ...
   coll.insert(std::map<std::string,float>::value_type("otto",
                                                        22.3));
   ```

   or

   ```
   coll.insert(decltype(coll)::value_type("otto",22.3));
   ```

2. **Use `pair<>`.** Another way is to use pair<> directly. For example:

   ```
   std::map<std::string,float> coll;
   ...
   // use implicit conversion:
   coll.insert(std::pair<std::string,float>("otto",22.3));
   // use no implicit conversion:
   coll.insert(std::pair<const std::string,float>("otto",22.3));
   ```

   In the first `insert()` statement, the type is not quite right, so it is converted into the real element type. For this to happen, the `insert()` member function is defined as a member template (see Section 3.2, page 34).

3. **Use `make_pair()`.** Probably the most convenient way before C++11 was to use make_pair(), which produces a pair object that contains the two values passed as arguments (see Section 5.1.1, page 65):

   ```
   std::map<std::string,float> coll;
   ...
   coll.insert(std::make_pair("otto",22.3));
   ```

   Again, the necessary type conversions are performed by the `insert()` member template.

Here is a simple example of the insertion of an element into a map that also checks whether the insertion was successful:

```
std::map<std::string,float> coll;
...
if (coll.insert(std::make_pair("otto",22.3)).second) {
    std::cout << "OK, could insert otto/22.3" << std::endl;
}
else {
    std::cout << "OOPS, could not insert otto/22.3 "
              << "(key otto already exists)" << std::endl;
}
```

See Section 7.7.2, page 322, for a discussion about the return values of the `insert()` functions and more examples that also apply to maps. Note, again, that maps provide operator `[]` and `at()` as another convenient way to insert (and set) elements with the subscript operator (see Section 7.8.3, page 343).

When using `emplace()` to insert a new element by passing the values for its construction, you have to pass two lists of arguments: one for the key and one for the element. The most convenient way to do this is as follows:

```
std::map<std::string,std::complex<float>> m;
```

```
m.emplace(std::piecewise_construct,      // pass tuple elements as arguments
          std::make_tuple("hello"),      // elements for the key
          std::make_tuple(3.4,7.8));     // elements for the value
```

See Section 5.1.1, page 63, for details of piecewise construction of pairs.

To remove an element that has a certain value, you simply call `erase()`:

```
std::map<std::string,float> coll;
...
// remove all elements with the passed key
coll.erase(key);
```

This version of `erase()` returns the number of removed elements. When called for maps, the return value of `erase()` can only be 0 or 1.

If a multimap contains duplicates and you want to remove only the first element of these duplicates, you can't use `erase()`. Instead, you could code as follows:

```
std::multimap<std::string,float> coll;
...
// remove first element with passed key
auto pos = coll.find(key);
if (pos != coll.end()) {
    coll.erase(pos);
}
```

You should use the member function `find()` instead of the `find()` algorithm here because it is faster (see an example with the `find()` algorithm in Section 7.3.2, page 277). However, you can't use the `find()` member functions to remove elements that have a certain value instead of a certain key. See Section 7.8.2, page 335, for a detailed discussion of this topic.

When removing elements, be careful not to saw off the branch on which you are sitting. There is a big danger that you will remove an element to which your iterator is referring. For example:

```
std::map<std::string,float> coll;
...
for (auto pos = coll.begin(); pos != coll.end(); ++pos) {
    if (pos->second == value) {
        coll.erase(pos);                        // RUNTIME ERROR !!!
    }
}
```

Calling `erase()` for the element to which you are referring with pos invalidates pos as an iterator of `coll`. Thus, if you use pos after removing its element without any reinitialization, all bets are off. In fact, calling ++pos results in undefined behavior.

Since C++11, a solution is easy because `erase()` always returns the value of the following element:

```
std::map<std::string,float> coll;
...
for (auto pos = coll.begin(); pos != coll.end(); ) {
    if (pos->second == value) {
        pos = coll.erase(pos);   // possible only since C++11
    }
    else {
        ++pos;
    }
}
```

Unfortunately, before C++11, it was a design decision not to return the following position, because if not needed, it costs unnecessary time. However, this made programming tasks like this error prone and complicated and even more costly in terms of time. Here is an example of the correct way to remove elements to which an iterator refers before C++11:

```
typedef std::map<std::string,float> StringFloatMap;
StringFloatMap coll;
StringFloatMap::iterator pos;
...
// remove all elements having a certain value
for (pos = coll.begin(); pos != coll.end(); ) {
    if (pos->second == value) {
        coll.erase(pos++);
    }
    else {
        ++pos;
    }
}
```

Note that pos++ increments pos so that it refers to the next element but yields a copy of its original value. Thus, pos doesn't refer to the element that is removed when `erase()` is called.

Note also that for sets that use iterators as elements, calling `erase()` might be ambiguous now. For this reason, C++11 gets fixed to provide overloads for both `erase(iterator)` and `erase(const_iterator)`.

For multimaps, all `insert()`, `emplace()`, and `erase()` operations preserve the relative order of equivalent elements. Since C++11, calling `insert(`*val*`)` or `emplace(`*args...*`)` guarantees that the new element is inserted at the end of the range of equivalent elements.

7.8.3 Using Maps as Associative Arrays

Associative containers don't typically provide abilities for direct element access. Instead, you must use iterators. For maps, as well as for unordered maps (see Section 7.9, page 355), however, there is an exception to this rule. Nonconstant maps provide a subscript operator for direct element access. In addition, since C++11, a corresponding member function at() is provided for constant and nonconstant maps (see Table 7.46).

Operation	Effect
c[*key*]	Inserts an element with *key*, if it does not yet exist, and returns a reference to the value of the element with *key* (only for nonconstant maps)
c.at(*key*)	Returns a reference to the value of the element with *key* (since C++11)

Table 7.46. Direct Element Access of Maps

at() yields the value of the element with the passed key and throws an exception object of type out_of_range if no such element is present.

For operator [], the index also is the key that is used to identify the element. This means that for operator [], the index may have any type rather than only an integral type. Such an interface is the interface of a so-called *associative array*.

For operator [], the type of the index is not the only difference from ordinary arrays. In addition, you can't have a wrong index. If you use a key as the index for which no element yet exists, a new element gets inserted into the map automatically. The value of the new element is initialized by the default constructor of its type. Thus, to use this feature, you can't use a value type that has no default constructor. Note that the fundamental data types provide a default constructor that initializes their values to zero (see Section 3.2.1, page 37).

This behavior of an associative array has both advantages and disadvantages:

- The advantage is that you can insert new elements into a map with a more convenient interface. For example:

      ```
      std::map<std::string,float> coll;      // empty collection
      ```

      ```
      // insert "otto"/7.7 as key/value pair
      // - first it inserts "otto"/float()
      // - then it assigns 7.7
      coll["otto"] = 7.7;
      ```

  The statement

      ```
      coll["otto"] = 7.7;
      ```

  is processed here as follows:

  1. Process coll["otto"] expression:
     - If an element with key "otto" exists, the expression returns the value of the element by reference.
     - If, as in this example, no element with key "otto" exists, the expression inserts a new element automatically, with "otto" as key and the value of the default constructor of the value type as the element value. It then returns a reference to that new value of the new element.
  2. Assign value 7.7:
     - The second part of the statement assigns 7.7 to the value of the new or existing element.

  The map then contains an element with key "otto" and value 7.7.

- The disadvantage is that you might insert new elements by accident or mistake. For example, the following statement does something you probably hadn't intended or expected:

  ```
  std::cout << coll["ottto"];
  ```

  It inserts a new element with key "ottto" and prints its value, which is 0 by default. However, it should have generated an error message telling you that you wrote "otto" incorrectly.

  Note, too, that this way of inserting elements is slower than the usual way for maps, which is described in Section 7.8.2, page 340. The reason is that the new value is first initialized by the default value of its type, which is then overwritten by the correct value.

See Section 6.2.4, page 185, and Section 7.8.5, page 346, for some example code.

7.8.4 Exception Handling

Maps and multimaps provide the same behavior as sets and multisets with respect to exception safety. This behavior is mentioned in Section 7.7.3, page 325.

7.8.5 Examples of Using Maps and Multimaps

Using Algorithms and Lambdas with a Map/Multimap

Section 6.2.3, page 183, introduced an example for an unordered multimap, which could also be used with an ordinary (sorting) map or multimap. Here is a corresponding example using a map. This program also demonstrates how to use algorithms and lambdas instead of range-based `for` loops:

```cpp
// cont/map1.cpp

#include <map>
#include <string>
#include <iostream>
#include <algorithm>
using namespace std;

int main()
{
    map<string,double> coll { { "tim", 9.9 },
                              { "struppi", 11.77 }
                            } ;

    // square the value of each element:
    for_each (coll.begin(), coll.end(),
            [] (pair<const string,double>& elem) {
                elem.second *= elem.second;
            });
```

```
// print each element:
for_each (coll.begin(), coll.end(),
          [] (const map<string,double>::value_type& elem) {
              cout << elem.first << ": " << elem.second << endl;
          });
}
```

As you can see, for a map, `for_each()` is called twice: once to square each element and once to print each element. In the first call, the type of an element is declared explicitly; in the second call, `value_type` is used. In the first call, the element is passed by reference to be able to modify its value; in the second call, a constant reference is used to avoid unnecessary copies.

The program has the following output:

```
struppi: 138.533
tim: 98.01
```

Using a Map as an Associative Array

The following example shows the use of a map as an associative array. The map is used as a stock chart. The elements of the map are pairs in which the key is the name of the stock and the value is its price:

```
// cont/map2.cpp

#include <map>
#include <string>
#include <iostream>
#include <iomanip>
using namespace std;

int main()
{
    // create map / associative array
    // - keys are strings
    // - values are floats
    typedef map<string,float> StringFloatMap;

    StringFloatMap stocks;          // create empty container

    // insert some elements
    stocks["BASF"] = 369.50;
    stocks["VW"] = 413.50;
    stocks["Daimler"] = 819.00;
    stocks["BMW"] = 834.00;
    stocks["Siemens"] = 842.20;
```

```
// print all elements
StringFloatMap::iterator pos;
cout << left;   // left-adjust values
for (pos = stocks.begin(); pos != stocks.end(); ++pos) {
    cout << "stock: " << setw(12) << pos->first
         << "price: " << pos->second << endl;
}
cout << endl;

// boom (all prices doubled)
for (pos = stocks.begin(); pos != stocks.end(); ++pos) {
    pos->second *= 2;
}

// print all elements
for (pos = stocks.begin(); pos != stocks.end(); ++pos) {
    cout << "stock: " << setw(12) << pos->first
         << "price: " << pos->second << endl;
}
cout << endl;

// rename key from "VW" to "Volkswagen"
// - provided only by exchanging element
stocks["Volkswagen"] = stocks["VW"];
stocks.erase("VW");

// print all elements
for (pos = stocks.begin(); pos != stocks.end(); ++pos) {
    cout << "stock: " << setw(12) << pos->first
         << "price: " << pos->second << endl;
}
}
```

The program has the following output:

```
stock: BASF        price: 369.5
stock: BMW         price: 834
stock: Daimler     price: 819
stock: Siemens     price: 842.2
stock: VW          price: 413.5

stock: BASF        price: 739
stock: BMW         price: 1668
stock: Daimler     price: 1638
```

```
stock: Siemens      price: 1684.4
stock: VW           price: 827

stock: BASF         price: 739
stock: BMW          price: 1668
stock: Daimler      price: 1638
stock: Siemens      price: 1684.4
stock: Volkswagen   price: 827
```

Using a Multimap as a Dictionary

The following example shows how to use a multimap as a dictionary:

```cpp
// cont/multimap1.cpp

#include <map>
#include <string>
#include <iostream>
#include <iomanip>
using namespace std;

int main()
{
    // create multimap as string/string dictionary
    multimap<string,string> dict;

    // insert some elements in random order
    dict.insert ( { {"day","Tag"}, {"strange","fremd"},
                    {"car","Auto"}, {"smart","elegant"},
                    {"trait","Merkmal"}, {"strange","seltsam"},
                    {"smart","raffiniert"}, {"smart","klug"},
                    {"clever","raffiniert"} } );

    // print all elements
    cout.setf (ios::left, ios::adjustfield);
    cout << ' ' << setw(10) << "english "
         << "german " << endl;
    cout << setfill('-') << setw(20) << ""
         << setfill(' ') << endl;
    for ( const auto& elem : dict ) {
        cout << ' ' << setw(10) << elem.first
             << elem.second << endl;
    }
    cout << endl;
```

```
        // print all values for key "smart"
        string word("smart");
        cout << word << ": " << endl;
        for (auto pos = dict.lower_bound(word);
             pos != dict.upper_bound(word);
             ++pos) {
            cout << "    " << pos->second << endl;
        }

        // print all keys for value "raffiniert"
        word = ("raffiniert");
        cout << word << ": " << endl;
        for (const auto& elem : dict) {
            if (elem.second == word) {
                cout << "    " << elem.first << endl;
            }
        }
    }
```

The program has the following output:

```
    english    german
    --------------------

    car        Auto
    clever     raffiniert
    day        Tag
    smart      elegant
    smart      raffiniert
    smart      klug
    strange    fremd
    strange    seltsam
    trait      Merkmal

smart:
    elegant
    raffiniert
    klug
raffiniert:
    clever
    smart
```

See a corresponding example that uses an unordered multimap as a dictionary in Section 7.9.7, page 383.

Finding Elements with Certain Values

The following example shows how to use the global find_if() algorithm to find an element with a certain value (in contrast to finding a key with a certain value):

```cpp
// cont/mapfind1.cpp

#include <map>
#include <iostream>
#include <algorithm>
#include <utility>
using namespace std;

int main()
{
    // map with floats as key and value
    // - initializing keys and values are automatically converted to float
    map<float,float> coll = { {1,7}, {2,4}, {3,2}, {4,3},
                              {5,6}, {6,1}, {7,3} };

    // search an element with key 3.0 (logarithmic complexity)
    auto posKey = coll.find(3.0);
    if (posKey != coll.end()) {
        cout << "key 3.0 found ("
             << posKey->first << ":"
             << posKey->second << ")" << endl;
    }

    // search an element with value 3.0 (linear complexity)
    auto posVal = find_if(coll.begin(),coll.end(),
                          [] (const pair<float,float>& elem) {
                              return elem.second == 3.0;
                          });
    if (posVal != coll.end()) {
        cout << "value 3.0 found ("
             << posVal->first << ":"
             << posVal->second << ")" << endl;
    }
}
```

The output of the program is as follows:

```
key 3.0 found (3:2)
value 3.0 found (4:3)
```

7.8.6   Example with Maps, Strings, and Sorting Criterion at Runtime

The example here is for advanced programmers rather than STL beginners. You can take it as an example of both the power and the problems of the STL. In particular, this example demonstrates the following techniques:

- How to use maps, including the associative array interface
- How to write and use function objects
- How to define a sorting criterion at runtime
- How to compare strings in a case-insensitive way

```cpp
// cont/mapcmp1.cpp

#include <iostream>
#include <iomanip>
#include <map>
#include <string>
#include <algorithm>
#include <cctype>
using namespace std;

// function object to compare strings
// - allows you to set the comparison criterion at runtime
// - allows you to compare case insensitive
class RuntimeStringCmp {
  public:
    // constants for the comparison criterion
    enum cmp_mode {normal, nocase};
  private:
    // actual comparison mode
    const cmp_mode mode;

    // auxiliary function to compare case insensitive
    static bool nocase_compare (char c1, char c2) {
        return toupper(c1) < toupper(c2);
    }
  public:
    // constructor: initializes the comparison criterion
    RuntimeStringCmp (cmp_mode m=normal) : mode(m) {
    }

    // the comparison
    bool operator() (const string& s1, const string& s2) const {
```

```
            if (mode == normal) {
                return s1<s2;
            }
            else {
                return lexicographical_compare (s1.begin(), s1.end(),
                                                s2.begin(), s2.end(),
                                                nocase_compare);
            }
        }
    }
};

// container type:
// - map with
//     - string keys
//     - string values
//     - the special comparison object type
typedef map<string,string,RuntimeStringCmp> StringStringMap;

// function that fills and prints such containers
void fillAndPrint(StringStringMap& coll);

int main()
{
    // create a container with the default comparison criterion
    StringStringMap coll1;
    fillAndPrint(coll1);

    // create an object for case-insensitive comparisons
    RuntimeStringCmp ignorecase(RuntimeStringCmp::nocase);

    // create a container with the case-insensitive comparisons criterion
    StringStringMap coll2(ignorecase);
    fillAndPrint(coll2);
}

void fillAndPrint(StringStringMap& coll)
{
    // insert elements in random order
    coll["Deutschland"] = "Germany";
    coll["deutsch"] = "German";
    coll["Haken"] = "snag";
    coll["arbeiten"] = "work";
    coll["Hund"] = "dog";
```

```
    coll["gehen"] = "go";
    coll["Unternehmen"] = "enterprise";
    coll["unternehmen"] = "undertake";
    coll["gehen"] = "walk";
    coll["Bestatter"] = "undertaker";

    // print elements
    cout.setf(ios::left, ios::adjustfield);
    for (const auto& elem : coll) {
        cout << setw(15) << elem.first << " "
             << elem.second << endl;
    }
    cout << endl;
}
```

In the program, `main()` creates two containers and calls `fillAndPrint()` for them, which fills these containers with the same elements and prints their contents. However, the containers have two different sorting criteria:

1. `coll1` uses the default function object of type `RuntimeStringCmp`, which compares the elements by using operator `<`.

2. `coll2` uses a function object of type `RuntimeStringCmp`, which is initialized by value `nocase` of class `RuntimeStringCmp`. `nocase` forces this function object to sort strings in a case-insensitive way.

The program has the following output:

```
Bestatter       undertaker
Deutschland     Germany
Haken           snag
Hund            dog
Unternehmen     enterprise
arbeiten        work
deutsch         German
gehen           walk
unternehmen     undertake

arbeiten        work
Bestatter       undertaker
deutsch         German
Deutschland     Germany
gehen           walk
Haken           snag
Hund            dog
Unternehmen     undertake
```

The first block of the output prints the contents of the first container that compares with operator <. The output starts with all uppercase keys, followed by all lowercase keys.

The second block prints all case-insensitive items, so the order changed. But note that the second block has one item less because the uppercase word "Unternehmen" is, from a case-insensitive point of view, equal to the lowercase word "unternehmen,"[13] and we use a map that does not allow duplicates according to its comparison criterion. Unfortunately the result is a mess because the German key, initialized by is the translation for "enterprise," got the value "undertake." So a multimap should probably be used here. Doing so makes sense because a multimap is the typical container for dictionaries.

---

[13] In German, all nouns are written with an initial capital letter, whereas all verbs are written in lowercase letters.

7.9 Unordered Containers

The hash table, one important data structure for collections, was not part of the first version of the C++ standard library. They were not part of the original STL and the committee decided that the proposal for their inclusion in C++98 came too late. (At some point you have to stop introducing features and focus on the details. Otherwise, you never finish the work.) However, with TR1, containers with the characteristics of hash tables finally came into the standard.

Nevertheless, even before TR1, several implementations of hash tables were available in the C++ community. Libraries typically provided four kinds of hash tables: `hash_set`, `hash_multiset`, `hash_map`, and `hash_multimap`. However, those hash tables have been implemented slightly differently. With TR1, a consolidated group of hash table-based containers was introduced. The features provided for the standardized classes combined existing implementations and didn't match any of them completely. To avoid name clashes, therefore, different class names were chosen. The decision was to provide all the existing associative containers with the prefix `unordered_`. This also demonstrates the most important difference between ordinary and the new associative containers: With the hash table-based implementations, the elements have no defined order. See [*N1456:HashTable*] for details about the design decisions for all the unordered containers.

Strictly speaking, the C++ standard library calls unordered containers "unordered associative containers." However, I will just use "unordered containers" when I refer to them. With "associative containers," I still refer to the "old" associative containers, which are provided since C++98 and implemented as binary trees (set, multiset, map, and multimap).

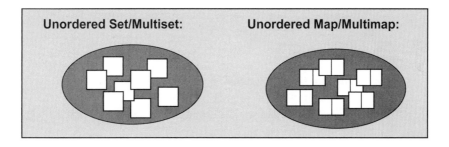

Figure 7.16. Unordered Containers

Conceptionally, unordered containers contain all the elements you insert in an arbitrary order (see Figure 7.16). That is, you can consider the container to be a bag: you can put in elements, but when you open the bag to do something with all the elements, you access them in a random order. So, in contrast with (multi)sets and (multi)maps, there is no sorting criterion; in contrast with sequence containers, you have no semantics to put an element into a specific position.

As with associative containers, the individual classes differ as follows:

- Unordered sets and multisets store single values of a specific type, whereas in unordered maps and multimaps, the elements are key/value pairs, where the key is used to store and find a specific element, including its associated value.
- Unordered sets and maps allow no duplicates, whereas unordered multisets and multimaps do.

To use an unordered set or multiset, you must include the header file `<unordered_set>`. To use an unordered map or multimap, you must include the header file `<unordered_map>`:

```
#include <unordered_set>
#include <unordered_map>
```

There, the types are defined as class templates inside namespace std:

```
namespace std {
    template <typename T,
             typename Hash = hash<T>,
             typename EqPred = equal_to<T>,
             typename Allocator = allocator<T> >
        class unordered_set;

    template <typename T,
             typename Hash = hash<T>,
             typename EqPred = equal_to<T>,
             typename Allocator = allocator<T> >
        class unordered_multiset;

    template <typename Key, typename T,
             typename Hash = hash<T>,
             typename EqPred = equal_to<T>,
             typename Allocator = allocator<pair<const Key, T> > >
        class unordered_map;

    template <typename Key, typename T,
             typename Hash = hash<T>,
             typename EqPred = equal_to<T>,
             typename Allocator = allocator<pair<const Key, T> > >
        class unordered_multimap;
}
```

The elements of an unordered set or multiset may have any type T that is comparable.

For unordered maps and multimaps, the first template parameter is the type of the element's key, and the second template parameter is the type of the element's associated value. The elements of an unordered map or an unordered multimap may have any types Key and T that meet the following two requirements:

1. Both key and value must be copyable or movable.
2. The key must be comparable with the equivalence criterion.

Note that the element type (`value_type`) is a pair<const *Key,T*>.

The optional second/third template parameter defines the hash function. If a special hash function is not passed, the default hash function hash<> is used, which is provided as a function object in `<functional>` for all integral types, all floating-point types, pointers, strings, and some special types.[14] For all other value types, you must pass your own hash function, which is explained in Section 7.9.2, page 363, and Section 7.9.7, page 377.

The optional third/fourth template parameter defines an equivalence criterion: a predicate that is used to find elements. It should return whether two values are equal. If a special compare criterion is not passed, the default criterion `equal_to<>` is used, which compares the elements by comparing them with operator == (see Section 10.2.1, page 487, for details about `equal_to<>`).

The optional fourth/fifth template parameter defines the memory model (see Chapter 19). The default memory model is the model `allocator`, which is provided by the C++ standard library.

7.9.1 Abilities of Unordered Containers

All standardized unordered container classes are implemented as hash tables, which nonetheless still have a variety of implementation options. As usual, the C++ standard library does not specify all these implementation details to allow a variety of possible implementation options, but a few of the specified abilities of unordered containers are based on the following assumptions (see [*N1456:HashTable*]):

- The hash tables use the "chaining" approach, whereby a hash code is associated with a linked list. (This technique, also called "open hashing" or "closed addressing," should not be confused with "open addressing" or "closed hashing.")
- Whether these linked lists are singly or doubly linked is open to the implementers. For this reason, the standard guarantees only that the iterators are "at least" forward iterators.
- Various implementation strategies are possible for rehashing:
  - With the traditional approach, a complete reorganization of the internal data happens from time to time as a result of a single insert or erase operation.
  - With incremental hashing, a resizing of the number of bucket or slots is performed gradually, which is especially useful in real-time environments, where the price of enlarging a hash table all at once can be too high.

Unordered containers allow both strategies and give no guarantee that conflicts with either of them.

Figure 7.17 shows the typical internal layout of an unordered set or multiset according to the minimal guarantees given by the C++ standard library. For each value to store, the hash function maps it to a bucket (slot) in the hash table. Each bucket manages a singly linked list containing all the elements for which the hash function yields the same value.

Figure 7.18 shows the typical internal layout of an unordered map or multimap according to the minimal guarantees given by the C++ standard library. For each element to store, which is a key/value pair, the hash function maps the value of the key to a bucket (slot) in the hash table. Each bucket manages a singly linked list containing all the elements for which the hash function yields the same value.

The major advantage of using a hash table internally is its incredible running-time behavior. Assuming that the hashing strategy is well chosen and well implemented, you can guarantee amor-

---

[14] `error_code`, `thread::id`, `bitset<>`, and `vector<bool>`

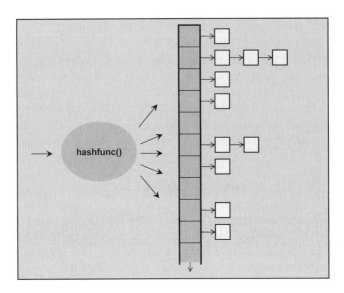

Figure 7.17. Internal Structure of Unordered Sets and Multisets

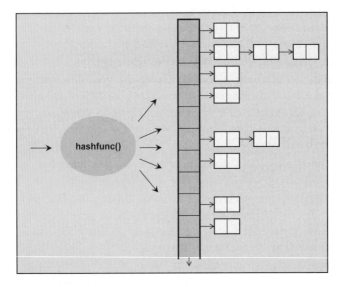

Figure 7.18. Internal Structure of Unordered Maps and Multimaps

tized constant time for insertions, deletions, and element search ("amortized" because the occasional rehashing happens that occurs can be a large operation with a linear complexity).

The expected behavior of nearly all the operations on unordered containers, including copy construction and assignment, element insertion and lookup, and equivalence comparison, depends on the quality of the hash function. If the hash function generates equal values for different elements, which also happens if an unordered container that allows duplicates is populated with equivalent values or keys, any hash table operation results in poor runtime performance. This is a fault not so much of the data structure itself but rather of its use by unenlightened clients.

Unordered containers also have some disadvantages over ordinary associative containers:

- Unordered containers don't provide operators <, >, <=, and >= to order multiple instances of these containers. However, == and != are provided (since C++11).
- lower_bound() and upper_bound() are not provided.
- Because the iterators are guaranteed only to be forward iterators, reverse iterators, including rbegin(), rend(), crbegin(), and crend(), are not supported, and you can't use algorithms that require bidirectional iterators, or at least this is not portable.

Because the (key) value of an element specifies its position — in this case, its bucket entry — you are *not* allowed to modify the (key) value of an element directly. Therefore, much as with associative containers, to modify the value of an element, you must remove the element that has the old value and insert a new element that has the new value. The interface reflects this behavior:

- Unordered containers don't provide operations for direct element access.
- Indirect access via iterators has the constraint that, from the iterator's point of view, the element's (key) value is constant.

As a programmer, you can specify parameters that influence the behavior of the hash table:

- You can specify the minimum number of buckets.
- You can (and sometimes have to) provide your own hash function.
- You can (and sometimes have to) provide your own equivalence criterion: a predicate that is used to find the right element among all entries in the bucket lists.
- You can specify a maximum load factor, which leads to automatic rehashing when it is exceeded.
- You can force rehashing.

But you can't influence the following behavior:

- The growth factor, which is the factor automatic rehashing uses to grow or shrink the list of buckets
- The minimum load factor, which is used to force rehashing when the number of elements in the container shrinks

Note that rehashing is possible only after a call to insert(), rehash(), reserve(), or clear(). This is a consequence of the guarantee that erase() never invalidates iterators, references, and pointers to the elements. Thus, if you delete hundreds of elements, the bucket size will not change. But if you insert one element afterward, the bucket size might shrink.

Also note that in containers that support equivalent keys — unordered multisets and multimaps — elements with equivalent keys are adjacent to each other when iterating over the elements of the container. Rehashing and other operations that internally change the order of elements preserve the relative order of elements with equivalent keys.

7.9.2   Creating and Controlling Unordered Containers

Hash tables are pretty complicated data structures. For this reason, you have a lot of abilities to define or query their behavior.

Create, Copy, and Destroy

Table 7.47 lists the constructors and destructors of unordered associative containers. Table 7.48 lists the types *Unord* that can be used with these constructors and destructors.

Operation	Effect
Unord c	Default constructor; creates an empty unordered container without any elements
Unord c(*bnum*)	Creates an empty unordered container that internally uses at least *bnum* buckets
Unord c(*bnum*,*hf*)	Creates an empty unordered container that internally uses at least *bnum* buckets and *hf* as hash function
Unord c(*bnum*,*hf*,*cmp*)	Creates an empty unordered container that internally uses at least *bnum* buckets, *hf* as hash function, and *cmp* as predicate to identify equal values
Unord c(*c2*)	Copy constructor; creates a copy of another unordered container of the same type (all elements are copied)
Unord c = c2	Copy constructor; creates a copy of another unordered container of the same type (all elements are copied)
Unord c(*rv*)	Move constructor; creates an unordered container, taking the contents of the rvalue *rv* (since C++11)
Unord c = *rv*	Move constructor; creates an unordered container, taking the contents of the rvalue *rv* (since C++11)
Unord c(*beg*,*end*)	Creates an unordered container initialized by the elements of the range [*beg*,*end*)
Unord c(*beg*,*end*,*bnum*)	Creates an unordered container initialized by the elements of the range [*beg*,*end*) that internally uses at least bnum buckets
Unord c(*beg*,*end*,*bnum*,*hf*)	Creates an unordered container initialized by the elements of the range [*beg*,*end*) that internally uses at least *bnum* buckets and *hf* as hash function
Unord c(*beg*,*end*,*bnum*,*hf*,*cmp*)	Creates an unordered container initialized by the elements of the range [*beg*,*end*) that internally uses at least *bnum* buckets, *hf* as hash function, and *cmp* as predicate to identify equal values
Unord c(*initlist*)	Creates an unordered unordered container initialized by the elements of the initializer list *initlist*
Unord c = *initlist*	Creates an unordered unordered container initialized by the elements of the initializer list *initlist*
c.~*Unord*()	Destroys all elements and frees the memory

Table 7.47. Constructors and Destructors of Unordered Containers

Unord	Effect
unordered_set<*Elem*>	An unordered set that by default hashes with hash<> and compares equal_to<> (operator ==)
unordered_set<*Elem,Hash*>	An unordered set that by default hashes with *Hash* and compares equal_to<> (operator ==)
unordered_set<*Elem,Hash,Cmp*>	An unordered set that by default hashes with *Hash* and compares with *Cmp*
unordered_multiset<*Elem*>	An unordered multiset that by default hashes with hash<> and compares equal_to<> (operator ==)
unordered_multiset<*Elem,Hash*>	An unordered multiset that by default hashes with *Hash* and compares equal_to<> (operator ==)
unordered_multiset<*Elem,Hash,Cmp*>	An unordered multiset that by default hashes with *Hash* and compares with *Cmp*
unordered_map<*Key,T*>	An unordered map that by default hashes with hash<> and compares equal_to<> (operator ==)
unordered_map<*Key,T,Hash*>	An unordered map that by default hashes with *Hash* and compares equal_to<> (operator ==)
unordered_map<*Key,T,Hash,Cmp*>	An unordered map that by default hashes with *Hash* and compares with *Cmp*
unordered_multimap<*Key,T*>	An unordered multimap that by default hashes with hash<> and compares equal_to<> (operator ==)
unordered_multimap<*Key,T,Hash*>	An unordered multimap that by default hashes with *Hash* and compares equal_to<> (operator ==)
unordered_multimap<*Key,T,Hash,Cmp*>	An unordered multimap that by default hashes with *Hash* and compares with *Cmp*

*Table 7.48. Possible Types **Unord** of Unordered Containers*

For the construction, you have multiple abilities to pass arguments. On one hand, you can pass values as initial elements:

- An existing container of the same type (copy constructor)
- All elements of a range [begin,end)
- All elements of an initializer list

On the other hand, you can pass arguments that influence the behavior of the unordered container:

- The hash function (either as template or as constructor argument)
- The equivalence criterion (either as template or as constructor argument)
- The initial number of buckets (as constructor argument)

Note that you can't specify the maximum load factor as part of the type or via a constructor argument, although this is something you might often want to set initially. To specify the maximum load factor, you have to call a member function right after construction (see Table 7.49):

```
std::unordered_set<std::string> coll;
coll.max_load_factor(0.7);
```

The argument for `max_load_factor()` has to be a `float`. In general, a value between 0.7 and 0.8 provides a good compromise between speed and memory consumption. Note that the default maximum load factor is 1.0, which means that, usually, collisions apply before rehash happens. For this reason, if speed is an issue, you should always explicitly set the maximum load factor.

Layout Operations

Unordered containers also provide operations to query and influence the internal layout. Table 7.49 lists these operations.

Operation	Effect
`c.hash_function()`	Returns the hash function
`c.key_eq()`	Returns the equivalence predicate
`c.bucket_count()`	Returns the current number of buckets
`c.max_bucket_count()`	Returns the maximum number of buckets possible
`c.load_factor()`	Returns the current load factor
`c.max_load_factor()`	Returns the current maximum load factor
`c.max_load_factor(`*val*`)`	Sets the maximum load factor to *val*
`c.rehash(`*bnum*`)`	Rehashes the container so that it has a bucket size of at least *bnum*
`c.reserve(`*num*`)`	Rehashes the container so that is has space for at least *num* elements (since C++11)

Table 7.49. Layout Operations of Unordered Containers

Besides `max_load_factor()`, the member functions `rehash()` and `reserve()` are important. They provide the functionality to rehash an unordered container (i.e., change the number of buckets) with a slightly different interface: Originally, with TR1, only `rehash()` was provided, which is a request to provide a hash table with a bucket size of at least the size passed. The problem was that with this interface, you still had to take the maximum load factor into account. If the maximum load factor is 0.7 and you want to be prepared for 100 elements, you have to divide 100 by 0.7 to compute the size that does not cause rehashing as long as no more than 100 elements have been inserted. That is, you have to pass 143 to `rehash()` to avoid further rehashing for up to 100 elements. With `reserve()`, this computing is done internally, so you can simply pass the number of elements the hash table should be prepared for:

```
coll.rehash(100);   // prepare for 100/max_load_factor() elements
coll.reserve(100);  // prepare for 100 elements (since C++11)
```

With `bucket_count()`, you can query the number of buckets an unordered container currently has. This value can be used for a number of member functions that provide a "bucket interface" you can use to inspect the exact internal state of an unordered container. See Section 7.9.4, page 374, for more details about and Section 7.9.7, page 380, for an example of inspecting the internal layout of an unordered container with the bucket interface.

Providing Your Own Hash Function

All hash tables use a hash function, which maps the values of the elements that you put into the container to a specific bucket. The goal is that two equal values always yield the same bucket index, whereas for different values, different bucket entries ideally should be processed. For any range of passed values, the hash function should provide a good distribution of hash values.

The hash function has to be a function or a function object that takes a value of the element type as parameter and returns a value of type `std::size_t`. Thus, the current number of buckets is not taken into account. Mapping the return value to the range of valid bucket indexes is done internally in the container. Thus, your goal is to provide a function that maps the different element values equally distributed in the range $[0,\texttt{size\_t})$.

Here is an example of how to provide your own hash function:

```
#include <functional>

class Customer {
    ...
};

class CustomerHash
{
  public:
    std::size_t operator() (const Customer& c) const {
        return ...
    }
};

std::unordered_set<Customer,CustomerHash> custset;
```

Here, `CustomerHash` is a function object that defines the hash function for class `Customer`.

Instead of passing a function object to the type of the container, you can also pass a hash function as construction argument. Note, however, that the template type for the hash function must be set accordingly:

```
std::size_t customer_hash_func (const Customer& c)
{
    return ...
};

std::unordered_set<Customer,std::size_t(*)(const Customer&)>
      custset(20,customer_hash_func);
```

Here, `customer_hash_func()` is passed as second constructor argument with its type "pointer to a function taking a `Customer` and returning a `std::size_t`" passed as second template argument.

If a special hash function is not passed, the default hash function `hash<>` is used, which is provided as a function object in `<functional>` for "common" types: all integral types, all floating-point types, pointers, strings, and some special types.[15] For all other types, you have to provide your own hash function.

Providing a good hash function is trickier than it sounds. As a rule of thumb, you might use the default hash functions to specify your own hash functions. A naive approach would be to simply add all hash values for those attributes that are relevant for the hash function. For example:

```
class CustomerHash
{
  public:
    std::size_t operator() (const Customer& c) const {
        return std::hash<std::string>()(c.fname) +
               std::hash<std::string>()(c.lname) +
               std::hash<long>()(c.no);
    }
};
```

Here, the hash value returned is just the sum of the hash value for the `Customer`'s attributes `fname`, `lname`, and `no`. If the predefined hash functions for the types of these attributes work fine for the given values, the result is the sum of three values in the range $[0,$ `std::size_t`$)$. According to the common overflow rules, the resulting value should then also be reasonably well distributed.

Note, however, that experts will claim that this is still a poor hash function and that providing a good hash function can be very tricky. In addition, providing such a hash function doesn't seem as easy as it should be.

A better approach is the following, which uses a hash function provided by Boost (see [*Boost*]) and a more convenient interface:

```
// cont/hashval.hpp

#include <functional>

// from boost (functional/hash):
// see http://www.boost.org/doc/libs/1_35_0/doc/html/hash/combine.html
template <typename T>
inline void hash_combine (std::size_t& seed, const T& val)
{
    seed ^= std::hash<T>()(val) + 0x9e3779b9 + (seed<<6) + (seed>>2);
}
```

---

[15] `error_code`, `thread::id`, `bitset<>`, and `vector<bool>`

```
// auxiliary generic functions to create a hash value using a seed
template <typename T>
inline void hash_val (std::size_t& seed, const T& val)
{
    hash_combine(seed,val);
}
template <typename T, typename... Types>
inline void hash_val (std::size_t& seed,
                      const T& val, const Types&... args)
{
    hash_combine(seed,val);
    hash_val(seed,args...);
}
```

```
// auxiliary generic function to create a hash value out of a heterogeneous list of arguments
template <typename... Types>
inline std::size_t hash_val (const Types&... args)
{
    std::size_t seed = 0;
    hash_val (seed, args...);
    return seed;
}
```

A convenience function implemented using variadic templates (see Section 3.1.9, page 26) allows calling hash_val() with an arbitrary number of elements of any type to process a hash value out of all these values. For example:

```
class CustomerHash
{
  public:
    std::size_t operator() (const Customer& c) const {
        return hash_val(c.fname,c.lname,c.no);
    }
};
```

Internally, hash_combine() is called, which some experience has shown to be a good candidate for a generic hash function (see [*HoadZobel:HashCombine*]).

Especially when the input values to the hash function have specific constraints, you might want to provide your own specific hash function. In any case, to verify the effect of your own hash function, you may use the bucket interface (see Section 7.9.7, page 380).

See Section 7.9.7, page 377, for some complete examples about how to specify your own hash function. You can also use lambdas to specify the hash function (see Section 7.9.7, page 379, for details and an example).

Providing Your Own Equivalence Criterion

As the third/fourth template parameter of the unordered container types, you can pass the equivalence criterion, a predicate that is used to find equal values in the same bucket. The default predicate is `equal_to<>`, which compares the elements with operator `==`. For this reason, the most convenient approach to providing a valid equivalence criterion is to provide operator `==` for your own type if it is not predefined either as member or as global function. For example:

```
class Customer {
   ...
};
bool operator == (const Customer& c1, const Customer& c2) {
   ...
}


std::unordered_multiset<Customer,CustomerHash> custmset;
std::unordered_map<Customer,String,CustomerHash> custmap;
```

Instead, however, you can also provide your own equivalence criterion as the following example demonstrates:

```
#include <functional>

class Customer {
   ...
};

class CustomerEqual
{
  public:
    bool operator() (const Customer& c1, Customer& c2) const {
       return ...
    }
};


std::unordered_set<Customer,CustomerHash,CustomerEqual> custset;
std::unordered_multimap<Customer,String,
                        CustomerHash,CustomerEqual> custmmap;
```

Here, for type `Customer`, a function object is defined in which you have to implement `operator()` so that it compares two elements (or two keys for maps) and returns a Boolean value indicating whether they are equal.

See Section 7.9.7, page 377, for a complete example about how to provide your own equivalence criterion (and hash function). Again, you can also use lambdas to specify the equivalence criterion (see Section 7.9.7, page 379, for details and an example).

Whenever values are considered to be equal according to the current equivalence criterion, they should also yield the same hash values according to the current hash function. For this reason, an unordered container that is instantiated with a nondefault equivalence predicate usually needs a nondefault hash function as well.

7.9.3   Other Operations for Unordered Containers

The remaining operations for unordered containers are more or less the same as for associative containers.

Nonmodifying Operations

Unordered containers provide the nonmodifying operations listed in Table 7.50.

Operation	Effect
`c.empty()`	Returns whether the container is empty (equivalent to `size()==0` but might be faster)
`c.size()`	Returns the current number of elements
`c.max_size()`	Returns the maximum number of elements possible
`c1 == c2`	Returns whether `c1` is equal to `c2`
`c1 != c2`	Returns whether `c1` is not equal to `c2` (equivalent to `!(c1==c2)`)

Table 7.50. Nonmodifying Operations of Unordered Containers

Note again that for comparisons, only operators == and != are provided for unordered containers.[16] In worst-case scenarios, they might, however, provide quadratic complexity.

Special Search Operations

Unordered containers are optimized for fast searching of elements. To benefit from this behavior, the containers provide special search functions (see Table 7.51). These functions are special versions of general algorithms that have the same name. You should always prefer the optimized versions for unordered containers to achieve constant complexity instead of the linear complexity of the general algorithms, provided that the hash values are evenly distributed. For example, a search in a collection of 1,000 elements requires on average only 1 comparison instead of 10 for associative containers and 500 for sequence containers (see Section 2.2, page 10).

See Section 7.7.2, page 319, for a detailed description of these member functions, including an example program that demonstrates their application.

---

[16] Operators == and != are not provided for unordered containers with TR1.

Operation	Effect
c.count(*val*)	Returns the number of elements with value *val*
c.find(*val*)	Returns the position of the first element with value *val* (or end() if none found)
c.equal_range(*val*)	Returns a range with all elements with a value equal to *val* (i.e., the first and last positions, where val would get inserted)

Table 7.51. Special Search Operations of Unordered Containers

Assignments

As listed in Table 7.52, unordered containers provide only the fundamental assignment operations that all containers provide (see Section 7.1.2, page 258).

Operation	Effect
c = c2	Assigns all elements of *c2* to *c*
c = *rv*	Move assigns all elements of the rvalue *rv* to *c* (since C++11)
c = *initlist*	Assigns all elements of the initializer list *initlist* to *c* (since C++11)
c1.swap(c2)	Swaps the data of *c1* and *c2*
swap(c1, c2)	Swaps the data of *c1* and *c2*

Table 7.52. Assignment Operations of Unordered Containers

For these operations, both containers must have the same type. In particular, the type of the hash functions and the equivalence criteria must be the same, although the functions themselves may be different. If the functions are different, they will also get assigned or swapped.

Iterator Functions and Element Access

Unordered containers do not provide direct element access, so you have to use range-based for loops (see Section 3.1.4, page 17) or iterators. Because the iterators are guaranteed to be only forward iterators (see Section 9.2.3, page 436), no support for bidirectional iterators or random-access iterators is provided (Table 7.53). Thus, you can't use them in algorithms that are provided for bidirectional iterators or random-access iterators only, such as algorithms for sorting or random shuffling.

For unordered (multi)sets, all elements are considered constant from an iterator's point of view. For unordered (multi)maps, the key of all elements is considered to be constant. This is necessary to ensure that you can't compromise the position of the elements by changing their values. Although there is no specific order, the value defines the bucket position according to the current hash function. For this reason, you can't call any modifying algorithm on the elements. For example, you can't call the remove() algorithm, because it "removes" by overwriting "removed" elements with the following elements (see Section 6.7.2, page 221, for a detailed discussion of this problem). To

Operation	Effect
`c.begin()`	Returns a forward iterator for the first element
`c.end()`	Returns a forward iterator for the position after the last element
`c.cbegin()`	Returns a constant forward iterator for the first element (since C++11)
`c.cend()`	Returns a constant forward iterator for the position after the last element (since C++11)
`c.rbegin()`	Returns a reverse iterator for the first element of a reverse iteration
`c.rend()`	Returns a reverse iterator for the position after the last element of a reverse iteration
`c.crbegin()`	Returns a constant reverse iterator for the first element of a reverse iteration (since C++11)
`c.crend()`	Returns a constant reverse iterator for the position after the last element of a reverse iteration (since C++11)

Table 7.53. Iterator Operations of Unordered Containers

remove elements in unordered sets and multisets, you can use only member functions provided by the container.

In correspondence to maps and multimaps, the type of the elements of unordered maps and multimap is pair<const Key, T>, which means that you need `first` and `second` to access the key and the value of an element (see Section 7.8.2, page 337 for details):

```
std::unordered_map<std::string,float> coll;
...
for (auto elem& : coll) {
    std::cout << "key: "   << elem.first  << "\t"
              << "value: " << elem.second << std::endl;
}
...
for (auto pos = coll.begin(); pos != coll.end(); ++pos) {
    std::cout << "key: "   << pos->first  << "\t"
              << "value: " << pos->second << std::endl;
}
```

Trying to change the value of the key results in an error:

```
elem.first = "hello";     // ERROR at compile time
pos->first = "hello";     // ERROR at compile time
```

However, changing the value of the element is no problem, as long as `elem` is a nonconstant reference and the type of the value is not constant:

```
elem.second = 13.5;       // OK
pos->second = 13.5;       // OK
```

If you use algorithms and lambdas to operate on the elements of a map, you explicitly have to declare the element type:

```
std::unordered_map<std::string,int> coll;
...
// add 10 to the value of each element:
std::for_each (coll.begin(), coll.end(),
               [] (pair<const std::string,int>& elem) {
                   elem.second += 10;
               });
```

Instead of using the following:

```
pair<const std::string,int>
```

you could also use

```
unordered_map<std::string,int>::value_type
```

or

```
decltype(coll)::value_type
```

to declare the type of an element. See Section 7.8.5, page 345, for a complete example with maps that also works with unordered maps.

To change the key of an element, you have only one choice: You must replace the old element with a new element that has the same value. This is described for maps in Section 7.8.2, page 339.

Note that unordered maps can also be used as associative arrays, so you can use the subscript operator to access elements. See Section 7.9.5, page 374, for details.

Note also that there is an additional iterator interface to iterate over the buckets of an unordered container. See Section 7.9.7, page 380, for details.

Inserting and Removing Elements

Table 7.54 shows the operations provided for unordered containers to insert and remove elements.

As usual when using the STL, you must ensure that the arguments are valid. Iterators must refer to valid positions, and the beginning of a range must have a position that is not behind the end.

In general, erasing functions do not invalidate iterators and references to other elements. However, the `insert()` and `emplace()` members may invalidate all iterators when rehashing happens, whereas references to elements always remain valid. Rehashing happens when, because of an insertion, the number of resulting elements is equal to or exceeds the bucket count times the maximum load factor (i.e., when the guarantee given by the maximum load factor would be broken). The `insert()` and `emplace()` members do not affect the validity of references to container elements.

Inserting and removing is faster if, when working with multiple elements, you use a single call for all elements rather than multiple calls. Note, however, that the exception guarantees are reduced for multi-element operations (see Section 7.9.6, page 375).

Note that the return types of the inserting functions `insert()` and `emplace()` differ as follows:

Operation	Effect
c.insert(*val*)	Inserts a copy of *val* and returns the position of the new element and, for unordered containers, whether it succeeded
c.insert(*pos*,*val*)	Inserts a copy of *val* and returns the position of the new element (*pos* is used as a hint pointing to where the insert should start the search)
c.insert(*beg*,*end*)	Inserts a copy of all elements of the range [*beg*,*end*) (returns nothing)
c.insert(*initlist*)	Inserts a copy of all elements in the initializer list *initlist* (returns nothing; since C++11)
c.emplace(*args*...)	Inserts a copy of an element initialized with *args* and returns the position of the new element and, for unordered containers, whether it succeeded (since C++11)
c.emplace_hint(*pos*,*args*...)	Inserts a copy of an element initialized with *args* and returns the position of the new element (*pos* is used as a hint pointing to where the insert should start the search)
c.erase(*val*)	Removes all elements equal to *val* and returns the number of removed elements
c.erase(*pos*)	Removes the element at iterator position *pos* and returns the following position (returned nothing before C++11)
c.erase(*beg*,*end*)	Removes all elements of the range [*beg*,*end*) and returns the following position (returned nothing before C++11)
c.clear()	Removes all elements (empties the container)

Table 7.54. Insert and Remove Operations of Unordered Containers

- **Unordered sets** provide the following interface:
  ```
  pair<iterator,bool> insert(const value_type& val);
  iterator            insert(iterator posHint,
                             const value_type& val);
  template <typename... Args>
  pair<iterator,bool> emplace(Args&&... args);
  template <typename... Args>
  iterator            emplace_hint(const_iterator posHint,
                                   Args&&... args);
  ```
- **Unordered multisets** provide the following interface:
  ```
  iterator            insert(const value_type& val);
  iterator            insert(iterator posHint,
                             const value_type& val);
  template <typename... Args>
  iterator            emplace(Args&&... args);
  ```

```
template <typename... Args>
iterator                emplace_hint(const_iterator posHint,
                                     Args&&... args);
```

The difference in return types results because unordered multisets and multimaps allow duplicates, whereas unordered sets and maps do not. Thus, the insertion of an element might fail for an unordered set if it already contains an element with the same value. Therefore, the return type for a set returns two values by using a `pair` structure (pair is discussed in Section 5.1.1, page 60):

1. The member `second` of the `pair` structure returns whether the insertion was successful.
2. The member `first` of the `pair` structure returns the position of the newly inserted element or the position of the still existing element.

In all other cases, the functions return the position of the new element or of the existing element if the unordered set already contains an element with the same value. See Section 7.7.2, page 323, for some examples about these interfaces.

For unordered maps and multimaps, to insert a key/value pair, you must keep in mind that inside, the key is considered to be constant. You must provide either the correct type or implicit or explicit type conversions.

Since C++11, the most convenient way to insert elements is to pass them as an initializer list, where the first entry is the key and the second entry is the value:

```
std::unordered_map<std::string,float> coll;
...
coll.insert({"otto",22.3});
```

Alternatively, there are also the three other ways to pass a value into an unordered map or multimap that were introduced for maps and multimaps already (see Section 7.8.2, page 341, for details):

1. Use **value_type**:
   ```
   std::unordered_map<std::string,float> coll;
   ...
   coll.insert(std::unordered_map<std::string,float>::value_type
                   ("otto",22.3));
   coll.insert(decltype(coll)::value_type("otto",22.3));
   ```

2. Use **pair<>**:
   ```
   std::unordered_map<std::string,float> coll;
   ...
   coll.insert(std::pair<std::string,float>("otto",22.3));
   coll.insert(std::pair<const std::string,float>("otto",22.3));
   ```

3. Use **make_pair()**:
   ```
   std::unordered_map<std::string,float> coll;
   ...
   coll.insert(std::make_pair("otto",22.3));
   ```

Here is a simple example of the insertion of an element into an unordered map that also checks whether the insertion was successful:

```
std::unordered_map<std::string,float> coll;
...
if (coll.insert(std::make_pair("otto",22.3)).second) {
    std::cout << "OK, could insert otto/22.3" << std::endl;
}
else {
    std::cout << "Oops, could not insert otto/22.3 "
              << "(key otto already exists)" << std::endl;
}
```

Note again that when using `emplace()` to insert a new element by passing the values for its construction, you have to pass two lists of arguments: one for the key and one for the element. The most convenient way to do this is as follows:

```
std::unordered_map<std::string,std::complex<float>> m;
```

```
m.emplace(std::piecewise_construct,       // pass tuple elements as arguments
          std::make_tuple("hello"),       // elements for the key
          std::make_tuple(3.4,7.8));      // elements for the value
```

See Section 5.1.1, page 63, for details of piecewise construction of pairs.

Note again that unordered maps provide another convenient way to insert and set elements with the subscript operator (see Section 7.9.5, page 374).

To remove an element that has a certain value, you simply call `erase()`:

```
std::unordered_set<Elem> coll;
...
// remove all elements with passed value
coll.erase(value);
```

Note that this member function has a different name than `remove()` provided for lists (see Section 7.5.2, page 294, for a discussion of `remove()`). It behaves differently because it returns the number of removed elements. When called for unordered maps, it returns only 0 or 1.

If an unordered multiset or multimap contains duplicates and you want to remove only the first element of these duplicates, you can't use `erase()`. Instead, you can code as follows:

```
std::unordered_multimap<Key,T> coll;
...
// remove first element with passed value
auto pos = coll.find(value);
if (pos != coll.end()) {
    coll.erase(pos);
}
```

You should use the member function `find()` here because it is faster than the `find()` algorithm (see the example in Section 7.3.2, page 277).

When removing elements, be careful not to saw off the branch on which you are sitting. See Section 7.8.2, page 342, for a detailed description of this problem.

7.9.4   The Bucket Interface

It is possible to access the individual buckets with a specific bucket interface to expose the internal state of the whole hash table. Table 7.55 shows the operations provided to directly access buckets.

Operation	Effect
c.bucket_count()	Returns the current number of buckets
c.bucket(*val*)	Returns the index of the bucket in which *val* would/could be found
c.bucket_size(*buckidx*)	Returns the number of elements in the bucket with index *buckidx*
c.begin(*buckidx*)	Returns a forward iterator for the first element of the bucket with index *buckidx*
c.end(*buckidx*)	Returns a forward iterator for the position after the last element of the bucket with index *buckidx*
c.cbegin(*buckidx*)	Returns a constant forward iterator for the first element of the bucket with index *buckidx*
c.cend(*buckidx*)	Returns a constant forward iterator for the position after the last element of the bucket with index *buckidx*

Table 7.55. Bucket Interface Operations of Unordered Sets and Multisets

See Section 7.9.7, page 380, for an example of how to use the bucket interface to inspect the internal layout of an unordered container.

7.9.5   Using Unordered Maps as Associative Arrays

As with maps, unordered maps provide a subscript operator for direct element access and a corresponding member function at() (see Table 7.56).

Operation	Effect
c[*key*]	Inserts an element with *key*, if it does not yet exist, and returns a reference to the value of the element with *key* (only for nonconstant unordered maps)
c.at(*key*)	Returns a reference to the value of the element with *key* (since C++11)

Table 7.56. Direct Element Access of Unordered Maps

at() yields the value of the element with the passed key and throws an exception object of type out_of_range if no such element is present.

For operator [], the index also is the key used to identify the element. This means that for operator [], the index may have any type rather than only an integral type. Such an interface is the interface of a so-called *associative array*.

For operator [], the type of the index is not the only difference from ordinary C-style arrays. In addition, you can't have a wrong index. If you use a key as the index for which no element yet exists, a new element gets inserted into the map automatically. The value of the new element is initialized by the default constructor of its type. Thus, to use this feature, you can't use a value type that has no default constructor. Note that the fundamental data types provide a default constructor that initializes their values to zero (see Section 3.2.1, page 37).

See Section 7.8.3, page 344, for a detailed discussion of the advantages and disadvantages this container interface provides. See Section 6.2.4, page 185, and Section 7.8.5, page 346, for some example code (partially using maps, which provide the same interface).

7.9.6 Exception Handling

Unordered containers are node-based containers, so any failure to construct a node simply leaves the container as it was. However, the fact that a rehashing may occur comes into account. For this reason, the following guarantees apply to all unordered containers:

- Single-element insertions have the commit-or-rollback behavior, provided that the hash and equivalence functions don't throw. Thus, if they don't throw, the operations either succeed or have no effect.
- `erase()` does not throw an exception, provided that the hash function and the equivalence criterion don't throw, which is the case for the default functions.
- No `clear()` function throws an exception.
- No `swap()` function throws an exception, provided that the copy constructor or the copy assignment operator of the hash or equivalence functions don't throw.
- `rehash()` has the commit-or-rollback behavior, provided that the hash and equivalence functions don't throw. Thus, if they don't throw, the operations either succeed or have no effect.

See Section 6.12.2, page 248, for a general discussion of exception handling in the STL.

7.9.7 Examples of Using Unordered Containers

The following program demonstrates the fundamental abilities of unordered containers, using an unordered set:

```
// cont/unordset1.cpp

#include <unordered_set>
#include <numeric>
#include "print.hpp"
using namespace std;

int main()
{
    // create and initialize unordered set
    unordered_set<int> coll = { 1,2,3,5,7,11,13,17,19,77 };

    // print elements
    // - elements are in arbitrary order
```

```
    PRINT_ELEMENTS(coll);

    // insert some additional elements
    // - might cause rehashing and create different order
    coll.insert({-7,17,33,-11,17,19,1,13});
    PRINT_ELEMENTS(coll);

    // remove element with specific value
    coll.erase(33);

    // insert sum of all existing values
    coll.insert(accumulate(coll.begin(),coll.end(),0));
    PRINT_ELEMENTS(coll);

    // check if value 19 is in the set
    if (coll.find(19) != coll.end()) {
        cout << "19 is available" << endl;
    }

    // remove all negative values
    unordered_set<int>::iterator pos;
    for (pos=coll.begin(); pos!= coll.end(); ) {
        if (*pos < 0) {
            pos = coll.erase(pos);
        }
        else {
            ++pos;
        }
    }
    PRINT_ELEMENTS(coll);
}
```

As long as you only insert, erase, and find elements with a specific value, unordered containers provide the best running-time behavior because all these operations have amortized constant complexity. However, you can't make any assumption about the order of the elements. For example, the program might have the following output:

```
77 11 1 13 2 3 5 17 7 19
-11 1 2 3 -7 5 7 77 33 11 13 17 19
-11 1 2 3 -7 5 7 77 11 13 17 19 137
19 is available
1 2 3 5 7 77 11 13 17 19 137
```

For anything else – for example, to accumulate the values in the container or find and remove all negative values — you have to iterate over all elements (either directly with iterators or indirectly using a range-based for loop).

When using an unordered multiset rather than an unordered set, duplicates are allowed. For example, the following program:

```cpp
// cont/unordmultiset1.cpp

#include <unordered_set>
#include "print.hpp"
using namespace std;

int main()
{
    // create and initialize, expand, and print unordered multiset
    unordered_multiset<int> coll = { 1,2,3,5,7,11,13,17,19,77 };
    coll.insert({-7,17,33,-11,17,19,1,13});
    PRINT_ELEMENTS(coll);

    // remove all elements with specific value
    coll.erase(17);

    // remove one of the elements with specific value
    auto pos = coll.find(13);
    if (pos != coll.end()) {
        coll.erase(pos);
    }
    PRINT_ELEMENTS(coll);
}
```

might have the following output:

```
33 19 19 17 17 17 77 11 7 -7 5 3 13 13 2 -11 1 1
33 19 19 77 11 7 -7 5 3 13 2 -11 1 1
```

Example of Providing Your Own Hash Function and Equivalence Criterion

The following example shows how to define and specify a hash function and an equivalence criterion for a type Customer, which is used as element type of an unordered set:

```cpp
// cont/hashfunc1.cpp

#include <unordered_set>
#include <string>
#include <iostream>
#include "hashval.hpp"
#include "print.hpp"
```

```cpp
using namespace std;

class Customer {
  private:
    string fname;
    string lname;
    long   no;
  public:
    Customer (const string& fn, const string& ln, long n)
      : fname(fn), lname(ln), no(n) {}
    friend ostream& operator << (ostream& strm, const Customer& c) {
        return strm << "[" << c.fname << "," << c.lname << ","
                    << c.no << "]";
    }
    friend class CustomerHash;
    friend class CustomerEqual;
};

class CustomerHash
{
  public:
    std::size_t operator() (const Customer& c) const {
        return hash_val(c.fname,c.lname,c.no);
    }
};

class CustomerEqual
{
  public:
    bool operator() (const Customer& c1, Customer& c2) const {
        return c1.no == c2.no;
    }
};

int main()
{
    // unordered set with own hash function and equivalence criterion
    unordered_set<Customer,CustomerHash,CustomerEqual> custset;

    custset.insert(Customer("nico","josuttis",42));
    PRINT_ELEMENTS(custset);

}
```

The program has the following output:

```
[nico,josuttis,42]
```

Here, the `hash_val()` convenience function for an arbitrary number of elements of different types introduced in Section 7.9.2, page 364, is used.

As you can see, the equivalence function does not necessarily have to evaluate the same values as the hash function. However, as written, it should be guaranteed that values that are equal according the equivalence criterion yield the same hash value (which indirectly is the case here assuming that customer numbers are unique).

Without specifying an equivalence function, the declaration of `custset` would be:

```
std::unordered_set<Customer,CustomerHash> custset;
```

and operator `==` would be used as equivalence criterion, which you had to define for `Customers` instead.

You could also use an ordinary function as hash function. But in that case you have to pass the function as constructor argument, which means that you also have to pass the initial bucket count and specify the corresponding function pointer as second template parameter (see Section 7.9.2, page 363, for details).

Using Lambdas as Hash Function and Equivalence Criterion

You can even use lambdas to specify the hash function and/or the equivalence criterion. For example:

```cpp
// cont/hashfunc2.cpp

#include <string>
#include <iostream>
#include <unordered_set>
#include "hashval.hpp"
#include "print.hpp"
using namespace std;

class Customer {
  private:
    string fname;
    string lname;
    long   no;
  public:
    Customer (const string& fn, const string& ln, long n)
      : fname(fn), lname(ln), no(n) {
    }
    string firstname() const {
        return fname;
    };
```

```
        string lastname() const {
            return lname;
        };
        long number() const {
            return no;
        };
        friend ostream& operator << (ostream& strm, const Customer& c) {
            return strm << "[" << c.fname << "," << c.lname << ","
                            << c.no << "]";
        }
    };

    int main()
    {
        // lambda for user-defined hash function
        auto hash = [] (const Customer& c) {
            return hash_val(c.firstname(),c.lastname(),c.number());
        };

        // lambda for user-defined equality criterion
        auto eq = [] (const Customer& c1, Customer& c2) {
            return c1.number() == c2.number();
        };

        // create unordered set with user-defined behavior
        unordered_set<Customer,
                        decltype(hash),decltype(eq)> custset(10,hash,eq);

        custset.insert(Customer("nico","josuttis",42));
        PRINT_ELEMENTS(custset);

    }
```

Note that you have to use `decltype` to yield the type of the lambda to be able to pass it as template argument to the declaration of the unordered container. The reason is that for lambdas, no default constructor and assignment operator are defined. Therefore, you also have to pass the lambdas to the constructor. This is possible only as second and third arguments. Thus, you have to specify the initial bucket size 10 in this case.

Example of Using the Bucket Interface

The following example demonstrates an application of the bucket interface provided to inspect the internal state of an unordered container (see Section 7.9.4, page 374). In `printHashTableState()`, the whole state, including the detailed layout of an unordered container, is printed:

```cpp
// cont/buckets.hpp

#include <iostream>
#include <iomanip>
#include <utility>
#include <iterator>
#include <typeinfo>

// generic output for pairs (map elements)
template <typename T1, typename T2>
std::ostream& operator << (std::ostream& strm, const std::pair<T1,T2>& p)
{
    return strm << "[" << p.first << "," << p.second << "]";
}


template <typename T>
void printHashTableState (const T& cont)
{
    // basic layout data:
    std::cout << "size:           " << cont.size() << "\n";
    std::cout << "buckets:        " << cont.bucket_count() << "\n";
    std::cout << "load factor:    " << cont.load_factor() << "\n";
    std::cout << "max load factor: " << cont.max_load_factor() << "\n";

    // iterator category:
    if (typeid(typename std::iterator_traits
                        <typename T::iterator>::iterator_category)
          == typeid(std::bidirectional_iterator_tag)) {
        std::cout << "chaining style:  doubly-linked" << "\n";
    }
    else {
        std::cout << "chaining style:  singly-linked" << "\n";
    }

    // elements per bucket:
    std::cout << "data: " << "\n";
    for (auto idx=0; idx != cont.bucket_count(); ++idx) {
        std::cout << " b[" << std::setw(2) << idx << "]: ";
        for (auto pos=cont.begin(idx); pos != cont.end(idx); ++pos) {
            std::cout << *pos << " ";
        }
        std::cout << "\n";
    }
    std::cout << std::endl;
}
```

For example, you can use this header file to print the internal layout of an unordered set:

// cont/unordinspect1.cpp

```
#include <unordered_set>
#include <iostream>
#include "buckets.hpp"

int main()
{
    // create and initialize an unordered set
    std::unordered_set<int> intset = { 1,2,3,5,7,11,13,17,19 };
    printHashTableState(intset);

    // insert some additional values (might cause rehashing)
    intset.insert({-7,17,33,4});
    printHashTableState(intset);
}
```

Comparing the first and second call of `printHashTableState()`, the program might have the following output (details depend on the concrete layout and rehashing strategy of the standard library used):

```
size:           9                    size:           12
buckets:        11                   buckets:        23
load factor:    0.818182             load factor:    0.521739
max load factor: 1                   max load factor: 1
chaining style: singly-linked        chaining style: singly-linked
data:                                data:
 b[ 0]: 11                            b[ 0]:
 b[ 1]: 1                             b[ 1]: 1
 b[ 2]: 13 2                          b[ 2]: 2
 b[ 3]: 3                             b[ 3]: 3
 b[ 4]:                               b[ 4]: 4
 b[ 5]: 5                             b[ 5]: 5 -7
 b[ 6]: 17                            b[ 6]:
 b[ 7]: 7                             b[ 7]: 7
 b[ 8]: 19                            b[ 8]:
 b[ 9]:                               b[ 9]:
 b[10]:                               b[10]: 33
                                      b[11]: 11
                                      b[12]:
                                      b[13]: 13
                                      b[14]:
                                      b[15]:
                                      b[16]:
                                      b[17]: 17
                                      b[18]:
                                      b[19]: 19
                                      b[20]:
                                      b[21]:
                                      b[22]:
```

As another example for the application of the bucket interface, the following program creates a dictionary of string values mapped to other string values (compare this example with a corresponding version for maps in Section 7.8.5, page 348):

```cpp
// cont/unordmultimap1.cpp

#include <unordered_map>
#include <string>
#include <iostream>
#include <utility>
#include "buckets.hpp"
using namespace std;

int main()
{
    // create and initialize an unordered multimap as dictionary
    std::unordered_multimap<string,string> dict = {
                    {"day","Tag"},
                    {"strange","fremd"},
                    {"car","Auto"},
                    {"smart","elegant"},
                    {"trait","Merkmal"},
                    {"strange","seltsam"}
    };
    printHashTableState(dict);

    // insert some additional values (might cause rehashing)
    dict.insert({{"smart","raffiniert"},
                {"smart","klug"},
                {"clever","raffiniert"}
                });
    printHashTableState(dict);

    // modify maximum load factor (might cause rehashing)
    dict.max_load_factor(0.7);
    printHashTableState(dict);
}
```

Again, the output of this program is implementation specific. For example, the output of this program might be as follows (slightly modified to fit the page width):

```
size:                6          size:                9          size:                9
buckets:             7          buckets:             11         buckets:             17
current load factor: 0.857143   current load factor: 0.818182   current load factor: 0.529412
max load factor:     1          max load factor:     1          max load factor:     0.7
chaining style:      singly     chaining style:      singly     chaining style:      singly
data:                           data:                           data:
 b[ 0]: [day,Tag]                b[ 0]: [smart,elegant]          b[ 0]:
 b[ 1]: [car,Auto]                      [smart,raffiniert]       b[ 1]:
 b[ 2]:                                 [smart,klug]             b[ 2]:
 b[ 3]: [smart,elegant]          b[ 1]:                          b[ 3]:
 b[ 4]:                          b[ 2]:                          b[ 4]: [car,Auto]
 b[ 5]: [trait,Merkmal]          b[ 3]:                          b[ 5]:
 b[ 6]: [strange,fremd]          b[ 4]:                          b[ 6]: [smart,elegant]
        [strange,seltsam]        b[ 5]: [clever,raffiniert]             [smart,raffiniert]
                                 b[ 6]: [strange,fremd]                 [smart,klug]
                                        [strange,seltsam]        b[ 7]:
                                 b[ 7]:                          b[ 8]: [day,Tag]
                                 b[ 8]:                          b[ 9]: [clever,raffiniert]
                                 b[ 9]: [trait,Merkmal] [car,Auto] b[10]:
                                 b[10]: [day,Tag]                 b[11]: [trait,Merkmal]
                                                                 b[12]:
                                                                 b[13]:
                                                                 b[14]:
                                                                 b[15]: [strange,fremd]
                                                                        [strange,seltsam]
                                                                 b[16]:
```

Whereas on another platform the output of this program might be as follows (again, slightly modified to fit the page width):

```
size:                6          size:                9          size:                9
buckets:             11         buckets:             11         buckets:             13
current load factor: 0.545455   current load factor: 0.818182   current load factor: 0.692308
max load factor:     1          max load factor:     1          max load factor:     0.7
chaining style:      singly     chaining style:      singly     chaining style:      singly
data:                           data:                           data:
 b[ 0]:                          b[ 0]:                          b[ 0]:
 b[ 1]:                          b[ 1]:                          b[ 1]: [day,Tag]
 b[ 2]: [trait,Merkmal]          b[ 2]: [clever,raffiniert]      b[ 2]:
        [car,Auto]                      [trait,Merkmal]          b[ 3]:
 b[ 3]: [day,Tag]                       [car,Auto]               b[ 4]: [smart,elegant]
 b[ 4]:                          b[ 3]: [day,Tag]                       [smart,raffiniert]
 b[ 5]:                          b[ 4]:                                 [smart,klug]
 b[ 6]:                          b[ 5]:                                 [car,Auto]
 b[ 7]:                          b[ 6]:                          b[ 5]:
 b[ 8]: [smart,elegant]          b[ 7]:                          b[ 6]:
 b[ 9]: [strange,seltsam]        b[ 8]: [smart,elegant]          b[ 7]:
        [strange,fremd]                 [smart,raffiniert]       b[ 8]:
 b[10]:                                 [smart,klug]             b[ 9]: [clever,raffiniert]
                                 b[ 9]: [strange,seltsam]        b[10]: [strange,seltsam]
                                        [strange,fremd]                 [strange,fremd]
                                 b[10]:                          b[11]:
                                                                 b[12]: [trait,Merkmal]
                                                                        [clever,raffiniert]
```

Note that in any case rehashing preserves the relative ordering of equivalent elements. However, the order of equivalent elements might not match the order of their insertion.

7.10   Other STL Containers

The STL is a framework. In addition to the standard container classes, the STL allows you to use other data structures as containers. You can use strings or ordinary arrays as STL containers, or you can write and use special containers that meet special needs. Doing so has the advantage that you can benefit from algorithms, such as sorting or merging, for your own type. Such a framework is a good example of the *Open Closed Principle*: *open* to extension; *closed* to modification.[17]

There are three different approaches to making containers "STL-able":

1. **The invasive approach.**[18] You simply provide the interface that an STL container requires. In particular, you need the usual member functions of containers, such as begin() and end(). This approach is invasive because it requires that a container be written in a certain way.

2. **The noninvasive approach.**[18] You write or provide special iterators that are used as an interface between the algorithms and special containers. This approach is noninvasive. All it requires is the ability to step through all the elements of a container, an ability that any container provides in some way.

3. **The wrapper approach.** Combining the two previous approaches, you write a wrapper class that encapsulates any data structure with an STL container-like interface.

This subsection first discusses strings as a standard container, which is an example of the invasive approach. It then covers an important standard container that uses the noninvasive approach: ordinary C-style arrays. However, you can also use the wrapper approach to access data of an ordinary array.

Whoever wants to write an STL container might also support the ability to get parametrized on different allocators. The C++ standard library provides some special functions and classes for programming with allocators and uninitialized memory. See Section 19.3, page 1026, for details.

7.10.1   Strings as STL Containers

The string classes of the C++ standard library (introduced and discussed in Chapter 13) are an example of the invasive approach of writing STL containers. Strings can be considered containers of characters. The characters inside the string build a sequence over which you can iterate to process the individual characters. Thus, the standard string classes provide the container interface of the STL. They provide the begin() and end() member functions, which return random-access iterators to iterate over a string. The string classes also provide some operations for iterators and iterator adapters. For example, push_back() is provided to enable the use of back inserters.

Note that string processing from the STL's point of view is a bit unusual. Normally you process strings as a whole object (you pass, copy, or assign strings). However, when individual character processing is of interest, the ability to use STL algorithms might be helpful. For example, you could read the characters with istream iterators, or you could transform string characters by making them

---

[17] I first heard of the *Open Closed Principle* from Robert C. Martin, who himself heard it from Bertrand Meyer.

[18] Instead of *invasive* and *noninvasive*, the terms *intrusive* and *nonintrusive* are sometimes used.

uppercase or lowercase. In addition, by using STL algorithms you can use a special comparison criterion for strings. The standard string interface does not provide that ability.

Section 13.2.14, page 684, discusses the STL aspects of strings in more detail and gives examples.

7.10.2 Ordinary C-Style Arrays as STL Containers

You can use ordinary C-style arrays as STL containers. However, ordinary C-style arrays are not classes, so they don't provide member functions such as begin() and end(), and you can't define member functions for them. Here, either the noninvasive approach or the wrapper approach must be used.

Using the noninvasive approach is simple. You need only objects that are able to iterate over the elements of an array by using the STL iterator interface. Such iterators already exist: ordinary pointers. An STL design decision was to use the pointer interface for iterators so that you could use ordinary pointers as iterators. This again shows the generic concept of pure abstraction: Anything that *behaves* like an iterator *is* an iterator. In fact, pointers are random-access iterators (see Section 9.2.5, page 438). The following example demonstrates how to use C-style arrays as STL containers since C++11:

```
// cont/cstylearray1.cpp

#include <iterator>
#include <vector>
#include <iostream>

int main()
{
    int vals[] = { 33, 67, -4, 13, 5, 2 };

    // use begin() and end() for ordinary C arrays
    std::vector<int> v(std::begin(vals), std::end(vals));

    // use global begin() and end() for containers:
    std::copy (std::begin(v), std::end(v),
               std::ostream_iterator<int>(std::cout," "));
    std::cout << std::endl;
}
```

Here, we use a helper function defined in <iterator> and every container header, which allows using a global begin() and end() for ordinary C-style arrays. As you can see, for any ordinary C-style array, vals std::begin() and std::end() yield the corresponding begin and end to use it in the STL framework:

```
int vals[] = { 33, 67, -4, 13, 5, 2 };
```

```
std::begin(vals)        // yields vals
std::end(vals)          // yields vals+NumOfElementsIn(vals)
```

These functions are also overloaded, so you can use STL containers or all classes that provide begin() and end() as member functions:

```
std::vector<int> v;
```

```
std::begin(v)           // yields v.begin()
std::end(v)             // yields v.end()
```

The output of the program is as follows:

```
33 67 -4 13 5 2
```

Before C++11, you had to pass the raw pointers to the algorithms because begin() and end() were not globally provided. For example:

```
// cont/cstylearray1old.cpp

#include <iostream>
#include <algorithm>
#include <functional>
#include <iterator>
using namespace std;

int main()
{
    int coll[] = { 5, 6, 2, 4, 1, 3 };

    // square all elements
    transform (coll, coll+6,        // first source
               coll,                // second source
               coll,                // destination
               multiplies<int>());  // operation

    // sort beginning with the second element
    sort (coll+1, coll+6);

    // print all elements
    copy (coll, coll+6,
          ostream_iterator<int>(cout," "));
    cout << endl;
}
```

You had to be careful to pass the correct end of the array, as is done here by using `coll+6`. And, as usual, you have to make sure that the end of the range is the position after the last element.

The output of the program is as follows:

```
25 1 4 9 16 36
```

Additional examples for the use of ordinary C-style arrays are in Section 11.7.2, page 579, and in Section 11.10.2, page 620.

7.11   Implementing Reference Semantics

In general, STL container classes provide value semantics and not reference semantics. Thus, the containers create internal copies of the elements they contain and return copies of those elements. Section 6.11.2, page 245, discusses the pros and cons of this approach and touches on its consequences. To summarize, if you want reference semantics in STL containers — whether because copying elements is expensive or because identical elements will be shared by different collections — you should use a smart pointer class that avoids possible errors. In addition, using a reference wrapper is possible.

Using Shared Pointers

As introduced in Section 5.2, page 76, the C++ standard library provides different smart pointer classes. For sharing objects between different containers, class `shared_ptr<>` is the appropriate smart pointer class. Using it for this purpose looks as follows:

```
// cont/refsem1.cpp

#include <iostream>
#include <string>
#include <set>
#include <deque>
#include <algorithm>
#include <memory>

class Item {
  private:
    std::string name;
    float   price;
  public:
    Item (const std::string& n, float p = 0) : name(n), price(p) {
    }
    std::string getName () const {
        return name;
    }
}
```

```cpp
        void setName (const std::string& n) {
            name = n;
        }
        float getPrice () const {
            return price;
        }
        float setPrice (float p) {
            price = p;
        }
};

template <typename Coll>
void printItems (const std::string& msg, const Coll& coll)
{
    std::cout << msg << std::endl;
    for (const auto& elem : coll) {
        std::cout << ' ' << elem->getName() << ": "
                          << elem->getPrice() << std::endl;
    }
}

int main()
{
    using namespace std;

    // two different collections sharing Items
    typedef shared_ptr<Item> ItemPtr;
    set<ItemPtr> allItems;
    deque<ItemPtr> bestsellers;

    // insert objects into the collections
    // - bestsellers are in both collections
    bestsellers = { ItemPtr(new Item("Kong Yize",20.10)),
                    ItemPtr(new Item("A Midsummer Night's Dream",14.99)),
                    ItemPtr(new Item("The Maltese Falcon",9.88)) };
    allItems = { ItemPtr(new Item("Water",0.44)),
                 ItemPtr(new Item("Pizza",2.22)) };
    allItems.insert(bestsellers.begin(),bestsellers.end());

    // print contents of both collections
    printItems ("bestsellers:", bestsellers);
    printItems ("all:", allItems);
    cout << endl;
```

```
// double price of bestsellers
for_each (bestsellers.begin(), bestsellers.end(),
          [] (shared_ptr<Item>& elem) {
              elem->setPrice(elem->getPrice() * 2);
          });

// replace second bestseller by first item with name "Pizza"
bestsellers[1] = *(find_if(allItems.begin(),allItems.end(),
                           [] (shared_ptr<Item> elem) {
                               return elem->getName() == "Pizza";
                           }));

// set price of first bestseller
bestsellers[0]->setPrice(44.77);

// print contents of both collections
printItems ("bestsellers:", bestsellers);
printItems ("all:", allItems);
}
```

The program has the following output:

```
bestsellers:
 Kong Yize: 20.1
 A Midsummer Night's Dream: 14.99
 The Maltese Falcon: 9.88
all:
 Kong Yize: 20.1
 A Midsummer Night's Dream: 14.99
 The Maltese Falcon: 9.88
 Water: 0.44
 Pizza: 2.22

bestsellers:
 Kong Yize: 44.77
 Pizza: 2.22
 The Maltese Falcon: 19.76
all:
 Kong Yize: 44.77
 A Midsummer Night's Dream: 29.98
 The Maltese Falcon: 19.76
 Water: 0.44
 Pizza: 2.22
```

Note that using `shared_ptr<>` makes things significantly more complicated. For example, `find()` for sets, which looks for elements that have an equal value, will now compare the internal pointers returned by `new`:

```
allItems.find(ItemPtr(new Item("Pizza",2.22)))    // can't be successful
```

So, you have to use the `find_if()` algorithm here.

If you call an auxiliary function that saves one element of the collections (an `ItemPtr`) somewhere else, the value to which it refers stays valid even if the collections get destroyed or all their elements are removed.

Using the Reference Wrapper

If it is guaranteed that the elements referred to in a container exist as long as the container exists, another approach is possible: using class `reference_wrapper<>` (see Section 5.4.3, page 132). For example, the following is possible, using class `Item` as introduced in the previous example:

```
std::vector<std::reference_wrapper<Item>> books;   // elements are references

Item f("Faust",12.99);
books.push_back(f);        // insert book by reference

// print books:
for (const auto& book : books) {
    std::cout << book.get().getName() << ": "
              << book.get().getPrice() << std::endl;
}

f.setPrice(9.99);     // modify book outside the containers
std::cout << books[0].get().getPrice() << std::endl; // print price of first book

// print books using type of the elements (no get() necessary):
for (const Item& book : books) {
    std::cout << book.getName() << ": " << book.getPrice() << std::endl;
}
```

The advantage is that no pointer syntax is required. This, however, is also a risk because it's not obvious that references are used here.

Note that the following declaration isn't possible:

```
vector<Item&> books;
```

Note also that class `reference_wrapper<>` provides a conversion operator to `T&` so that the range-based `for` loop can be declared dealing with elements of type `Item&`. However, for a direct call of a member function for the first element, `get()` is necessary.

The program has following output (see `cont/refwrap1.cpp` for the complete example):

```
Faust: 12.99
9.99
Faust: 9.99
```

7.12   When to Use Which Container

The C++ standard library provides different container types with different abilities. The question now is: When do you use which container type? Table 7.57 provides an overview. However, it contains general statements that might not fit in reality. For example, if you manage only a few elements, you can ignore the complexity because short element processing with linear complexity is better than long element processing with logarithmic complexity (in practice, "few" might become very large here).

As a supplement to the table, the following rules of thumb might help:

- By default, you should use a vector. It has the simplest internal data structure and provides random access. Thus, data access is convenient and flexible, and data processing is often fast enough.

- If you insert and/or remove elements often at the beginning and the end of a sequence, you should use a deque. You should also use a deque if it is important that the amount of internal memory used by the container shrinks when elements are removed. Also, because a vector usually uses one block of memory for its elements, a deque might be able to contain more elements because it uses several blocks.

- If you insert, remove, and move elements often in the middle of a container, consider using a list. Lists provide special member functions to move elements from one container to another in constant time. Note, however, that because a list provides no random access, you might suffer significant performance penalties on access to elements inside the list if you have only the beginning of the list.

  Like all node-based containers, a list doesn't invalidate iterators that refer to elements, as long as those elements are part of the container. Vectors invalidate all their iterators, pointers, and references whenever they exceed their capacity and part of their iterators, pointers, and references on insertions and deletions. Deques invalidate iterators, pointers, and references when they change their size, respectively.

- If you need a container that handles exceptions so that each operation either succeeds or has no effect, you should use either a list (without calling assignment operations and `sort()` and, if comparing the elements may throw, without calling `merge()`, `remove()`, `remove_if()`, and `unique()`; see Section 7.5.3, page 296) or an associative/unordered container (without calling the multiple-element insert operations and, if copying/assigning the comparison criterion may throw, without calling `swap()` or `erase()`). See Section 6.12.2, page 248, for a general discussion of exception handling in the STL.

- If you often need to search for elements according to a certain criterion, use an unordered set or multiset that hashes according to this criterion. However, hash containers have no ordering, so if you need to rely on element order, you should use a set or a multiset that sorts elements according to the search criterion.

- To process key/value pairs, use an unordered (multi)map or, if the element order matters, a (multi)map.

- If you need an associative array, use an unordered map or, if the element order matters, a map.

- If you need a dictionary, use an unordered multimap or, if the element order matters, a multimap.

	Array	Vector	Deque	List	Forward List	Associative Containers	Unordered Containers
Available since	TR1	C++98	C++98	C++98	C++11	C++98	TR1
Typical internal data structure	Static array	Dynamic array	Array of arrays	Doubly linked list	Singly linked list	Binary tree	Hash table
Element type	Value	Value	Value	Value	Value	Set: value Map: key/value	Set: value Map: key/value
Duplicates allowed	Yes	Yes	Yes	Yes	Yes	Only multiset or multimap	Only multiset or multimap
Iterator category	Random access	Random access	Random access	Bidirectional	Forward	Bidirectional (element/key constant)	Forward (element/key constant)
Growing/shrinking	Never	Yes	At both ends	Everywhere	Everywhere	Everywhere	Everywhere
Random access available	Yes	Yes	Yes	No	No	No	Almost
Search/find elements	Slow	Slow	Slow	Very slow	Very slow	Fast	Very fast
Inserting/removing invalidates iterators	—	On reallocation	Always	Never	Never	Never	On rehashing
Inserting/removing references, pointers	—	On reallocation	Always	Never	Never	Never	Never
Allows memory reservation	—	Yes	No	—	—	—	Yes (buckets)
Frees memory for removed elements	—	Only with shrink_to_fit()	Sometimes	Always	Always	Always	Sometimes
Transaction safe (success or no effect)	No	Push/pop at the end	Push/pop at the beginning and the end	All insertions and all erasures	All insertions and all erasures	Single-element insertions and all erasures if comparing doesn't throw	Single-element insertions and all erasures if hashing and comparing don't throw

Table 7.57. Overview of Container Abilities

A problem that is not easy to solve is how to sort objects according to two different sorting criteria. For example, you might have to keep elements in an order provided by the user while providing search capabilities according to another criterion. As in databases, you need fast access about two or more different criteria. In this case, you could probably use two sets or two maps that share the same objects with different sorting criteria. However, having objects in two collections is a special issue, covered in Section 7.11, page 388.

The automatic sorting of associative containers does not mean that these containers perform better when sorting is needed. This is because an associative container sorts each time a new element gets inserted. An often faster way is to use a sequence container and to sort all elements after they are all inserted, by using one of the several sort algorithms (see Section 11.2.2, page 511).

The following two simple programs sort all strings read from the standard input and print them without duplicates, by using two different containers:

1. Using a **set**:

```
// cont/sortset.cpp

#include <iostream>
#include <string>
#include <algorithm>
#include <iterator>
#include <set>
using namespace std;

int main()
{
    // create a string set
    // - initialized by all words from standard input
    set<string> coll((istream_iterator<string>(cin)),
                      istream_iterator<string>());

    // print all elements
    copy (coll.cbegin(), coll.cend(),
          ostream_iterator<string>(cout, "\n"));
}
```

2. Using a **vector**:

```
// cont/sortvec.cpp

#include <iostream>
#include <string>
#include <algorithm>
#include <iterator>
#include <vector>
```

```
using namespace std;

int main()
{
    // create a string vector
    // - initialized by all words from standard input
    vector<string> coll((istream_iterator<string>(cin)),
                         istream_iterator<string>());

    // sort elements
    sort (coll.begin(), coll.end());

    // print all elements ignoring subsequent duplicates
    unique_copy (coll.cbegin(), coll.cend(),
                 ostream_iterator<string>(cout, "\n"));
}
```

When I tried both programs with about 350,000 strings on one system, the vector version was approximately 10% faster. Inserting a call of `reserve()` made the vector version 5% faster. Allowing duplicates — using a `multiset` instead of a `set` and calling `copy()` instead of `unique_copy()`, respectively — changed things dramatically: The vector version was more than 40% faster. However, on another system, the vector versions were up to 50% slower. These measurements are not representative, but they show that it is often worth trying different ways of processing elements.

In practice, predicting which container type is the best is often difficult. The big advantage of the STL is that you can try different versions without much effort. The major work — implementing the different data structures and algorithms — is done. You have only to combine them in a way that is best for you.

Chapter 8
STL Container Members in Detail

This chapter discusses in detail all the operations that STL containers provide. The types and members are grouped by functionality. For each type and operation, this chapter describes the signature, the behavior, and the container types that provide it. Possible containers types are array, vector, deque, list, forward list, set, multiset, map, multimap, unordered set, unordered multiset, unordered map, unordered multimap, and string. In the following sections, *container* means the container type that provides the member.

8.1   Type Definitions

container::**value_type**
- The type of elements.
- For (unordered) sets and multisets, it is constant.
- For (unordered) maps and multimaps, it is pair `<const` *key-type*, *mapped-type*`>`.
- Provided by array, vector, deque, list, forward list, set, multiset, map, multimap, unordered set, unordered multiset, unordered map, unordered multimap, string.

container::**reference**
- The type of element references.
- Typically: *container*::`value_type&`.
- For `vector<bool>`, it is an auxiliary class (see Section 7.3.6, page 282).
- Provided by array, vector, deque, list, forward list, set, multiset, map, multimap, unordered set, unordered multiset, unordered map, unordered multimap, string.

container::**const_reference**
- The type of read-only element references.
- Typically: const *container*::`value_type&`.
- For `vector<bool>`, it is bool.
- Provided by array, vector, deque, list, forward list, set, multiset, map, multimap, unordered map, unordered multimap, string.

container::**iterator**

- The type of iterators.
- Provided by array, vector, deque, list, forward list, set, multiset, map, multimap, unordered set, unordered multiset, unordered map, unordered multimap, string.

container::**const_iterator**

- The type of read-only iterators.
- Provided by array, vector, deque, list, forward list, set, multiset, map, multimap, unordered set, unordered multiset, unordered map, unordered multimap, string.

container::**reverse_iterator**

- The type of reverse iterators.
- Provided by array, vector, deque, list, set, multiset, map, multimap, string.

container::**const_reverse_iterator**

- The type of read-only reverse iterators.
- Provided by array, vector, deque, list, set, multiset, map, multimap, string.

container::**pointer**

- The type of pointers to elements.
- Provided by array, vector, deque, list, forward list, set, multiset, map, multimap, unordered set, unordered multiset, unordered map, unordered multimap, string.

container::**const_pointer**

- The type of read-only pointers to elements.
- Provided by array, vector, deque, list, forward list, set, multiset, map, multimap, unordered set, unordered multiset, unordered map, unordered multimap, string.

container::**size_type**

- The unsigned integral type for size values.
- Provided by array, vector, deque, list, forward list, set, multiset, map, multimap, unordered set, unordered multiset, unordered map, unordered multimap, string.

container::**difference_type**

- The signed integral type for difference values.
- Provided by array, vector, deque, list, forward list, set, multiset, map, multimap, unordered set, unordered multiset, unordered map, unordered multimap, string.

container::**key_type**

- The type of the key of the elements for associative and unordered containers.
- For (unordered) sets and multisets, it is equivalent to `value_type`.
- Provided by set, multiset, map, multimap, unordered set, unordered multiset, unordered map, unordered multimap.

container::**mapped_type**

- The type of the value part of the elements of associative and unordered containers.
- Provided by map, multimap, unordered map, unordered multimap.

container::**key_compare**

- The type of the comparison criterion of associative containers.
- Provided by set, multiset, map, multimap.

container::**value_compare**

- The type of the comparison criterion for the whole element type.
- For sets and multisets, it is equivalent to `key_compare`.
- For maps and multimaps, it is an auxiliary class for a comparison criterion that compares only the key part of two elements.
- Provided by set, multiset, map, multimap.

container::**hasher**

- The type of the hashing function of unordered containers.
- Provided by unordered set, unordered multiset, unordered map, unordered multimap.

container::**key_equal**

- The type of the equality predicate of unordered containers.
- Provided by unordered set, unordered multiset, unordered map, unordered multimap.

container::**local_iterator**

- The type of the bucket iterators of unordered containers.
- Available since C++11.
- Provided by unordered set, unordered multiset, unordered map, unordered multimap.

container::**const_local_iterator**

- The type of read-only bucket iterators of unordered containers.
- Available since C++11.
- Provided by unordered set, unordered multiset, unordered map, unordered multimap.

In addition, type `allocator_type` is provided for all containers except arrays (see Section 8.10.1, page 430).

8.2 Create, Copy, and Destroy Operations

Containers provide the following constructors and destructors. In addition, most constructors allow you to pass an allocator as an additional argument, covered in Section 8.10, page 430. See Section 7.1.2, page 254, for a general discussion about initializing containers.

container::*container* ()

- The default constructor.
- Creates a new empty container.
- For arrays, the operation is implicitly defined and creates a nonempty container where the elements might have undefined values (see Section 7.2.1, page 262).
- Provided by array, vector, deque, list, forward list, set, multiset, map, multimap, unordered set, unordered multiset, unordered map, unordered multimap, string.

explicit *container*::*container* (const CompFunc& *cmpPred*)

- Creates a new empty container with *cmpPred* used as the sorting criterion (see Section 7.7.5, page 328, and Section 7.8.6, page 351, for examples).
- The sorting criterion must define a *strict weak ordering* (see Section 7.7, page 314).
- Provided by set, multiset, map, multimap.

explicit *container*::*container* (size_type *bnum*)

explicit *container*::*container* (size_type *bnum*, const Hasher& *hasher*)

explicit *container*::*container* (size_type *bnum*, const Hasher& *hasher*,
                                 const KeyEqual& *eqPred*)

- Create a new empty container with at least *bnum* buckets, *hasher* used as hashing function, and *eqPred* used as criterion to identify equal values.
- If *eqPred* is not passed, the default equivalence criterion of the container type is used (see Section 7.9.2, page 366, for details).
- If *hasher* is not passed, the default hashing function of the container type is used (see Section 7.9.2, page 363, for details).
- Provided by unordered set, unordered multiset, unordered map, unordered multimap.

container::*container* (*initializer-list*)

- Creates a new container that is initialized by the elements of *initializer-list*.
- For arrays, the operation is implicitly defined (see Section 7.2.1, page 262).
- Available since C++11.
- Provided by array, vector, deque, list, forward list, set, multiset, map, multimap, unordered set, unordered multiset, unordered map, unordered multimap, string.

container::*container* (*initializer-list*, const CompFunc& *cmpPred*)

- Creates a container that has the sorting criterion *cmpPred* and is initialized by the elements of *initializer-list*.
- The sorting criterion must define a *strict weak ordering* (see Section 7.7, page 314).
- Available since C++11.
- Provided by set, multiset, map, multimap.

container::*container* (*initializer-list*, size_type *bnum*)
container::*container* (*initializer-list*, size_type *bnum*,
                  const Hasher& *hasher*)
container::*container* (*initializer-list*, size_type *bnum*,
                  const Hasher& *hasher*, const KeyEqual& *eqPred*)

- Create a container with at least *bnum* buckets, *hasher* used as hashing function, and *eqPred* used as criterion to identify equal values, initialized by the elements of *initializer-list*.
- If *eqPred* is not passed, the default equivalence criterion of the container type is used (see Section 7.9.2, page 366, for details).
- If *hasher* is not passed, the default hashing function of the container type is used (see Section 7.9.2, page 363, for details).
- Provided by unordered set, unordered multiset, unordered map, unordered multimap.

container::*container* (const *container*& *c*)

- The copy constructor.
- Creates a new container as a copy of the existing container *c*.
- Calls the copy constructor for every element in *c*.
- For arrays, the operation is implicitly defined.
- Provided by array, vector, deque, list, forward list, set, multiset, map, multimap, unordered set, unordered multiset, unordered map, unordered multimap, string.

container::*container* (*container*&& *c*)

- The move constructor.
- Creates a new container initialized with the elements of the existing container *c*.
- After this call, c is valid but has an unspecified value.
- For arrays, the operation is implicitly defined.
- Available since C++11.
- Provided by array, vector, deque, list, forward list, set, multiset, map, multimap, unordered set, unordered multiset, unordered map, unordered multimap, string.

explicit *container*::*container* (size_type *num*)

- Creates a container with *num* elements.
- The elements are created by their default constructor.
- Provided by vector, deque, list, forward list.

container::*container* (size_type *num*, const T& *value*)

- Creates a container with *num* elements.
- The elements are created as copies of *value*.
- T is the type of the container elements.
- For strings, *value* is not passed by reference.
- Provided by vector, deque, list, forward list, string.

container::*container* (InputIterator *beg*, InputIterator *end*)

- Creates a container initialized by all elements of the range [*beg,end*).
- This function is a member template (see Section 3.2, page 34). Thus, the elements of the source range may have any type convertible into the element type of the container.
- See Section 7.1.2, page 256, for examples and a discussion of a problem resulting from the fact that this is a member function.
- Provided by vector, deque, list, forward list, set, multiset, map, multimap, unordered set, unordered multiset, unordered map, unordered multimap, string.

container::*container* (InputIterator *beg*, InputIterator *end*,
                    const CompFunc& *cmpPred*)

- Creates a container that has the sorting criterion *cmpPred* and is initialized by all elements of the range [*beg,end*).
- This function is a member template (see Section 3.2, page 34). Thus, the elements of the source range may have any type convertible into the element type of the container.
- The sorting criterion must define a *strict weak ordering* (see Section 7.7, page 314).
- Provided by set, multiset, map, multimap.

container::*container* (InputIterator *beg*, InputIterator *end*, size_type *bnum*)

container::*container* (InputIterator *beg*, InputIterator *end*, size_type *bnum*,
                    const Hasher& *hasher*)

container::*container* (InputIterator *beg*, InputIterator *end*, size_type *bnum*,
                    const Hasher& *hasher*, const KeyEqual& *eqPred*)

- Create a container with at least *bnum* buckets, *hasher* used as hashing function, and *eqPred* used as criterion to identify equal values, which is initialized by all elements of the range [*beg,end*).
- If *eqPred* is not passed, the default equivalence criterion of the container type is used (see Section 7.9.2, page 366, for details).
- If *hasher* is not passed, the default hashing function of the container type is used (see Section 7.9.2, page 363, for details).
- Provided by unordered set, unordered multiset, unordered map, unordered multimap.

container::~*container* ()

- The destructor.
- Removes all elements and frees the memory.
- Calls the destructor for every element.
- Provided by array, vector, deque, list, forward list, set, multiset, map, multimap, unordered set, unordered multiset, unordered map, unordered multimap, string.

8.3 Nonmodifying Operations

8.3.1 Size Operations

bool *container*::**empty** () const

- Returns whether the container is empty (contains no elements).
- It is equivalent to begin()==end() but may be faster.
- Complexity: constant.
- Provided by array, vector, deque, list, forward list, set, multiset, map, multimap, unordered set, unordered multiset, unordered map, unordered multimap, string.

size_type *container*::**size** () const

- Returns the current number of elements.
- To check whether the container is empty (contains no elements), you should use empty(), which may be faster.
- Complexity: constant.
- Provided by array, vector, deque, list, set, multiset, map, multimap, unordered set, unordered multiset, unordered map, unordered multimap, string.

size_type *container*::**max_size** () const

- Returns the maximum number of elements a container may contain.
- This is a technical value that may depend on the memory model of the container. In particular, because vectors usually use one memory segment, this value may be less for them than for other containers.
- Complexity: constant.
- Provided by array, vector, deque, list, forward list, set, multiset, map, multimap, unordered set, unordered multiset, unordered map, unordered multimap, string.

8.3.2   Comparison Operations

```
bool operator == (const container& c1, const container& c2)
bool operator != (const container& c1, const container& c2)
```

- Returns whether the two containers are (not) equal.
- Two containers are equal if they have the same number of elements and contain the same elements (for all comparisons of two corresponding elements, operator == has to yield `true`). Except for unordered containers, equal elements have to have the same order.
- Complexity: linear, in general. For unordered containers, quadratic in the worst case.
- Provided by array, vector, deque, list, forward list, set, multiset, map, multimap, unordered set, unordered multiset, unordered map, unordered multimap, string.

```
bool operator <  (const container& c1, const container& c2)
bool operator <= (const container& c1, const container& c2)
bool operator >  (const container& c1, const container& c2)
bool operator >= (const container& c1, const container& c2)
```

- Returns the result of the comparison of two containers of same type.
- To check whether a container is less than another container, the containers are compared lexicographically (see the description of the `lexicographical_compare()` algorithm in Section 11.5.4, page 548).
- Complexity: linear.
- Provided by array, vector, deque, list, forward list, set, multiset, map, multimap, string.

8.3.3   Nonmodifying Operations for Associative and Unordered Containers

The member functions mentioned here are special implementations of corresponding STL algorithms discussed in Section 11.5, page 524, and Section 11.9, page 596. These member functions provide better performance because they rely on the fact that the elements of associative containers are sorted and, in fact, they provide logarithmic complexity instead of linear complexity. For example, to search for one of 1,000 elements, no more than ten comparisons on average are needed (see Section 2.2, page 10).

```
size_type container::count (const T& value) const
```

- Returns the number of elements that are equivalent to *value*.
- This is the special version of the count() algorithm discussed in Section 11.5.1, page 524.
- T is the type of the sorted value:
  - For sets and multisets, it is the type of the elements.
  - For maps and multimaps, it is the type of the keys.
- Complexity: logarithmic.
- Provided by set, multiset, map, multimap, unordered set, unordered multiset, unordered map, unordered multimap.

```
iterator container::find (const T& value)
const_iterator container::find (const T& value) const
```

- Return the position of the first element that has a value equivalent to *value*.
- Return `end()` if no element is found.
- These are the special versions of the `find()` algorithm discussed in Section 11.5.3, page 528.
- T is the type of the sorted value:
  - For sets and multisets, it is the type of the elements.
  - For maps and multimaps, it is the type of the keys.
- Complexity: logarithmic for associative containers and constant for unordered containers, provided that a good hash function is used.
- Provided by set, multiset, map, multimap, unordered set, unordered multiset, unordered map, unordered multimap.

```
iterator container::lower_bound (const T& value)
const_iterator container::lower_bound (const T& value) const
```

- Return the first position where a copy of *value* would get inserted according to the sorting criterion.
- Return `end()` if no such element is found.
- The return value is the position of the first element that has a value equal to or greater than *value* (which might be `end()`).
- These are the special versions of the `lower_bound()` algorithm discussed in Section 11.10.1, page 611.
- T is the type of the sorted value:
  - For sets and multisets, it is the type of the elements.
  - For maps and multimaps, it is the type of the keys.
- Complexity: logarithmic.
- Provided by set, multiset, map, multimap.

```
iterator container::upper_bound (const T& value)
const_iterator container::upper_bound (const T& value) const
```

- Return the last position where a copy of *value* would get inserted according to the sorting criterion.
- Return `end()` if no such element is found.
- The return value is the position of the first element that has a value greater than *value* (which might be `end()`).
- These are the special versions of the `upper_bound()` algorithm discussed in Section 11.10.1, page 611.
- T is the type of the sorted value:
  - For sets and multisets, it is the type of the elements.
  - For maps and multimaps, it is the type of the keys.
- Complexity: logarithmic.
- Provided by set, multiset, map, multimap.

```
pair<iterator,iterator> container::equal_range (const T& value)
pair<const_iterator,const_iterator>
                    container::equal_range (const T& value) const
```

- Return a pair with the first and last positions where a copy of *value* would get inserted according to the sorting criterion.
- The return value is the range of elements equal to *value*.
- They are equivalent to:
  ```
  make_pair(lower_bound(value),upper_bound(value))
  ```
- These are the special versions of the equal_range() algorithm discussed in Section 11.10.1, page 613.
- T is the type of the sorted value:
  - For sets and multisets, it is the type of the elements.
  - For maps and multimaps, it is the type of the keys.
- Complexity: logarithmic.
- Provided by set, multiset, map, multimap, unordered set, unordered multiset, unordered map, unordered multimap.

8.4 Assignments

container& **container**::**operator =** (const *container&* *c*)

- Copy assignment operator.
- Assigns all elements of *c*; that is, it replaces all existing elements with copies of the elements of *c*.
- The operator may call the assignment operator for elements that have been overwritten, the copy constructor for appended elements, and the destructor of the element type for removed elements.
- Provided by array, vector, deque, list, forward list, set, multiset, map, multimap, unordered set, unordered multiset, unordered map, unordered multimap, string.

container& **container**::**operator =** (*container&&* *c*)

- Move assignment operator.
- Moves all elements of *c* to *this; that is, it replaces all existing elements with the elements of *c*.
- After this call, c is valid but has an unspecified value.
- Available since C++11.
- Provided by vector, deque, list, forward list, set, multiset, map, multimap, unordered set, unordered multiset, unordered map, unordered multimap, string.

container& ***container*** : : **operator =** (*initializer-list*)

- Assigns all elements of *initializer-list*; that is, it replaces all existing elements with copies of the passed elements.
- The operator may call the assignment operator for elements that have been overwritten, the copy constructor for appended elements, and the destructor of the element type for removed elements.
- Available since C++11.
- Provided by vector, deque, list, forward list, set, multiset, map, multimap, unordered set, unordered multiset, unordered map, unordered multimap, string.

void ***container*** : : **assign** (*initializer-list*)

- Assigns all elements of the *initializer-list*; that is, it replaces all existing elements with copies of the passed elements.
- Available since C++11.
- Provided by vector, deque, list, forward list, string.

void ***array*** : : **fill** (const T& *value*)

- Assigns *value* to all elements; that is, it replaces all existing elements with copies of the *value*.
- Available since C++11.
- Provided by array.

void ***container*** : : **assign** (size_type *num*, const T& *value*)

- Assigns *num* occurrences of *value*; that is, it replaces all existing elements by *num* copies of *value*.
- T has to be the element type.
- Provided by vector, deque, list, forward list, string.

void ***container*** : : **assign** (InputIterator *beg*, InputIterator *end*)

- Assigns all elements of the range [*beg,end*); that is, it replaces all existing elements with copies of the elements of [*beg,end*).
- This function is a member template (see Section 3.2, page 34). Thus, the elements of the source range may have any type convertible into the element type of the container.
- Provided by vector, deque, list, forward list, string.

void ***container*** : : **swap** (*container&* *c*)
void **swap** (*container&* *c1*, *container&* *c2*)

- Swap the contents with *c* or between *c1* and *c2*, respectively.
- Both swap:
  - The container's elements
  - Their sorting criterion, equivalence predicate, and hash function object, if any.
  The references, pointers, and iterators referring to elements swap their containers, because they still refer to the same swapped elements afterward.

- Arrays can't internally just swap pointers. Thus, swap() has linear complexity, and iterators and references refer to the same container but different elements afterward.

- For associative containers, the function may throw only if copying or assigning the comparison criterion may throw. For unordered containers, the function may throw only if the equivalence predicate or the hash function object may throw. For all other containers, the function does not throw.

- Complexity: constant, in general. For arrays it is linear.

- Due to its complexity, you should always prefer swap() over a copy assignment when you no longer need the assigned object (see Section 7.1.2, page 258).

- Provided by array, vector, deque, list, forward list, set, multiset, map, multimap, unordered set, unordered multiset, unordered map, unordered multimap, string.

8.5 Direct Element Access

reference *container*::**at** (size_type *idx*)

const_reference *container*::**at** (size_type *idx*) const

- Return the element with the index *idx* (the first element has index 0).

- Passing an invalid index (less than 0 or equal to size() or greater than size()) throws an out_of_range exception.

- The returned reference may get invalidated due to later modifications or reallocations.

- If you are sure that the index is valid, you can use operator [ ], which is faster.

- Provided by array, vector, deque, string.

T& *map*::**operator at** (const key_type& *key*)

const T& *map*::**operator at** (const key_type& *key*) const

- Return the corresponding value to *key* in a map.

- Throw an out_of_range exception if no element with a key equal to *key* exists.

- Available since C++11.

- Provided by map, unordered map.

reference *container*::**operator [ ]** (size_type *idx*)

const_reference *container*::**operator [ ]** (size_type *idx*) const

- Both return the element with the index *idx* (the first element has index 0).

- Passing an invalid index (less than 0 or equal to size() or greater than size()) results in undefined behavior. Thus, the caller must ensure that the index is valid; otherwise, at() should be used.

- The returned reference may get invalidated due to later modifications or reallocations.

- Provided by array, vector, deque, string.

T& *map*::**operator [ ]** (const key_type& *key*)

T& *map*::**operator [ ]** (key_type&& *key*)

- Operator [ ] for associative arrays.
- Return the corresponding value to *key* in a map.
- If no element with a key equal to *key* exists, these operations *create* a new element automatically with this key (copied or moved) and a value that is initialized by the default constructor of the value type. Thus, you can't have an invalid index (only wrong behavior). See Section 6.2.4, page 185, and Section 7.8.3, page 344, for details.
- With the second form, the state of *key* is undefined afterward (this form provides move semantics for the case that the key doesn't exist yet).
- The first form is equivalent to:
  (*((insert(make_pair(*key*,T())))).first)).second
- The second form is available since C++11.
- Provided by map, unordered map.

reference *container*::**front** ()

const_reference *container*::**front** () const

- Both return the first element (the element with index 0).
- The caller must ensure that the container contains an element (size()>0); otherwise, the behavior is undefined.
- For strings, it is provided since C++11.
- Provided by array, vector, deque, list, forward list, string.

reference *container*::**back** ()

const_reference *container*::**back** () const

- Both return the last element (the element with index size()-1).
- The caller must ensure that the container contains an element (size()>0); otherwise, the behavior is undefined.
- For strings, it is provided since C++11.
- Provided by array, vector, deque, list, string.

T* *container*::**data** ()

const T* *container*::**data** () const

- Both return an ordinary C-style array with all elements (that is, a pointer to the first element).
- This function is provided to pass the elements of the array to C-style interfaces.
- For strings, only the second form is provided.
- For arrays and vectors, available since C++11.
- Provided by array, vector, string.

8.6   Operations to Generate Iterators

The following member functions return iterators to iterate over the elements of the containers. Table 8.1 lists the iterator category (see Section 9.2, page 433) according to the various container types.

Container	Iterator Category
Array	Random access
Vector	Random access
Deque	Random access
List	Bidirectional
Forward list	Forward
Set	Bidirectional; element is constant
Multiset	Bidirectional; element is constant
Map	Bidirectional; key is constant
Multimap	Bidirectional; key is constant
Unordered set	Forward; element is constant
Unordered multiset	Forward; element is constant
Unordered map	Forward; key is constant
Unordered multimap	Forward; key is constant
String	Random access

Table 8.1. Required Iterator Categories of Container Types

```
iterator container::begin ()
const_iterator container::begin () const
const_iterator container::cbegin () const
```

- Return an iterator for the beginning of the container (the position of the first element).
- If the container is empty, the calls are equivalent to *container*::end() or *container*::cend(), respectively.
- Note that unordered containers also provide begin() and cbegin() for a numeric argument to provide the bucket interface (see Section 8.9.3, page 429, for details).
- cbegin() is available since C++11.
- Provided by array, vector, deque, list, forward list, set, multiset, map, multimap, unordered set, unordered multiset, unordered map, unordered multimap, string.

```
iterator container::end ()
const_iterator container::end () const
const_iterator container::cend () const
```

- Return an iterator for the end of the container (the position after the last element).

- If the container is empty, the calls are equivalent to *container*::begin() or *container*::cbegin(), respectively.
- Note that unordered containers also provide begin() and cbegin() for a numeric argument to provide the bucket interface (see Section 8.9.3, page 430, for details).
- cend() is available since C++11.
- Provided by array, vector, deque, list, forward list, set, multiset, map, multimap, unordered set, unordered multiset, unordered map, unordered multimap, string.

reverse_iterator *container*::**rbegin** ()

const_reverse_iterator *container*::**rbegin** () const

const_reverse_iterator *container*::**crbegin** () const

- Return a reverse iterator for the beginning of a reverse iteration over the elements of the container (the position of the last element).
- If the container is empty, the calls are equivalent to *container*::rend() or *container*::crend(), respectively.
- For details about reverse iterators, see Section 9.4.1, page 448.
- crbegin() is available since C++11.
- Provided by array, vector, deque, list, set, multiset, map, multimap, string.

reverse_iterator *container*::**rend** ()

const_reverse_iterator *container*::**rend** () const

const_reverse_iterator *container*::**crend** () const

- Return a reverse iterator for the end of a reverse iteration over the elements of the container (the position before the first element).
- If the container is empty, the calls are equivalent to *container*::rbegin() or *container*::crbegin(), respectively.
- For details about reverse iterators, see Section 9.4.1, page 448.
- crend() is available since C++11.
- Provided by array, vector, deque, list, set, multiset, map, multimap, string.

8.7   Inserting and Removing Elements

8.7.1   Inserting Single Elements

iterator *container*::**insert** (const T& *value*)

iterator *container*::**insert** (T&& *value*)

pair<iterator,bool> *container*::**insert** (const T& *value*)

pair<iterator,bool> *container*::**insert** (T&& *value*)

- Insert *value* into an associative or unordered container.
- The first and third forms copy *value*.
- The second and fourth forms move *value* to the container so that the value of *value* is unspecified afterward.
- Containers that allow duplicates, (unordered) multisets and multimaps, have the first and second signatures. They return the position of the new element. Since C++11, newly inserted elements are guaranteed to be placed at the end of existing equivalent values.
- Containers that do not allow duplicates, (unordered) sets and maps, have the second and fourth signature. If they can't insert the value because an element with an equal value or key exists, they return the position of the existing element and `false`. If they can insert the value, they return the position of the new element and `true`.
- T is the type of the container elements. Thus, for (unordered) maps and multimaps, it is a key/value pair.
- For map, multimap, unordered map, and unordered multimap, the corresponding form with move semantic is a member template (see Section 3.2, page 34). Thus, *value* may have any type convertible into the value type (key/value pair) of the container. This was introduced to allow you to pass two strings so that the first one gets converted into a constant string (which is the key type).
- The functions either succeed or have no effect, provided that for unordered containers the hash function does not throw.
- For all containers, references to existing elements remain valid. For associative containers, all iterators to existing elements remain valid. For unordered containers, iterators to existing elements remain valid if no rehashing is forced (if the number of resulting elements is equal to or greater than the bucket count times the maximum load factor).
- The second and fourth forms are available since C++11.
- Provided by set, multiset, map, multimap, unordered set, unordered multiset, unordered map, unordered multimap.

iterator *container*::**emplace** (*args*)

pair<iterator,bool> *container*::**emplace** (*args*)

- Insert a new element initialized by *args* into an associative or unordered container.
- Containers that allow duplicates (ordered and unordered multisets and multimaps) have the first signature. They return the position of the new element. It is guaranteed that newly inserted elements are placed at the end of existing equivalent values.
- Containers that do not allow duplicates (ordered and unordered sets and maps) have the second signature. If they can't insert the value because an element with an equal value or key exists, they return the position of the existing element and `false`. If they can insert the value, they return the position of the new element and `true`.
- The function either succeeds or has no effect, provided that for unordered containers the hash function does not throw.

- For all containers, references to existing elements remain valid. For associative containers, all iterators to existing elements remain valid. For unordered containers, iterators to existing elements remain valid if no rehashing is forced (if the number of resulting elements is equal to or greater than the bucket count times the maximum load factor).
- Note that for sequence containers, the same signature is possible, where the first argument is processed as the position where the new element gets inserted (see Section 8.7.1, page 414).
- Note that to emplace new key/value pairs for (unordered) maps and multimaps, you have to use piecewise construction (see Section 7.8.2, page 341, for details).
- Available since C++11.
- Provided by set, multiset, map, multimap, unordered set, unordered multiset, unordered map, unordered multimap.

```
iterator container::insert (const_iterator pos, const T& value)
iterator container::insert (const_iterator pos, T&& value)
```

- Insert *value* at the position of iterator *pos*.
- The first form copies *value*.
- The second form moves *value* to the container so that the value of *value* is unspecified afterward.
- Return the position of the new element.
- If the container does not allow duplicates (set, map, unordered set, unordered map) and already contains an element equal to (the key of) *value*, the call has no effect, and the return value is the position of the existing element.
- For associative and unordered containers, the position is used only as a hint pointing to where the insert should start to search. If *value* is inserted right at *pos*, the function has amortized constant complexity; otherwise, it has logarithmic complexity.
- For vectors, this operation invalidates iterators and references to other elements if reallocation happens (the new number of elements exceeds the previous capacity).
- For deques, this operation invalidates iterators and references to other elements.
- T is the type of the container elements. Thus, for (unordered) maps and multimaps, it is a key/value pair.
- For map, multimap, unordered map, and unordered multimap, the second form with move semantics is a member template (see Section 3.2, page 34). Thus, *value* may have any type convertible into the value type (key/value pair) of the container. This was introduced to allow passing two strings so that the first one gets converted into a constant string (which is the key type).
- For strings, *value* is passed by value.
- For vectors and deques, if the copy/move operations (constructor and assignment operator) of the elements don't throw, the function either succeeds or has no effect. For unordered containers, the function either succeeds or has no effect if the hash function does not throw. For all other standard containers, the function either succeeds or has no effect.
- The second form is available since C++11. Before C++11, type iterator was used instead of const_iterator.
- Provided by vector, deque, list, set, multiset, map, multimap, unordered set, unordered multiset, unordered map, unordered multimap, string.

iterator *container*::**emplace** (const_iterator *pos*, *args*)

- Inserts a new element initialized by *args* at the position of iterator *pos*.
- Returns the position of the new element.
- For vectors, this operation invalidates iterators and references to other elements if reallocation happens (the new number of elements exceeds the previous capacity).
- For deques, this operation invalidates iterators and references to other elements.
- T is the type of the container elements.
- For vectors and deques, if the copy operations (copy constructor and assignment operator) of the elements don't throw, the function either succeeds or has no effect. For all other standard containers, the function either succeeds or has no effect.
- For associative containers, the same signature is possible, where *pos* is processed as first argument for the new element (see Section 8.7.1, page 412).
- The function either succeeds or has no effect, provided that for unordered containers the hash function does not throw.
- Available since C++11.
- Provided by vector, deque, list.

iterator *container*::**emplace_hint** (const_iterator *pos*, *args*)

- Inserts a new element initialized by *args* at the position of iterator *pos*.
- Returns the position of the new element.
- If the container does not allow duplicates (set, map, unordered set, unordered map) and already contains an element equal to (the key of) *value*, the call has no effect, and the return value is the position of the existing element.
- The position is used only as a hint, pointing to where the insert should start to search. If the new element is inserted at *pos*, the function has amortized constant complexity; otherwise, it has logarithmic complexity.
- T is the type of the container elements. Thus, for (unordered) maps and multimaps, it is a key/value pair.
- The function either succeeds or has no effect, provided that for unordered containers the hash function does not throw.
- Available since C++11.
- Provided by set, multiset, map, multimap, unordered set, unordered multiset, unordered map, unordered multimap.

void *container*::**push_front** (const T& *value*)

void *container*::**push_front** (T&& *value*)

- Insert *value* as the new first element.
- The first form copies *value*.
- The second form, which is available since C++11, moves *value* to the container, so the state of *value* is undefined afterward.
- T is the type of the container elements.

- Both forms are equivalent to insert(begin(),*value*).
- For deques, this operation invalidates iterators to other elements. References to other elements remain valid.
- This function either succeeds or has no effect.[1]
- Provided by deque, list, forward list.

void *container*::**emplace_front** (*args*)

- Inserts a new first element, which is initialized by the argument list *args*.
- Thus, for the element type there must be a callable constructor for *args*.
- For deques, this operation invalidates iterators to other elements. References to other elements remain valid.
- This function either succeeds or has no effect.
- Available since C++11.
- Provided by deque, list, forward list.

void *container*::**push_back** (const T& *value*)
void *container*::**push_back** (T&& *value*)

- Append *value* as the new last element.
- The first form copies *value*.
- The second form, which is available since C++11, moves *value* to the container, so the state of *value* is undefined afterward.
- T is the type of the container elements.
- Both forms are equivalent to insert(end(),*value*).
- For vectors, this operation invalidates iterators and references to other elements if reallocation happens (the new number of elements exceeds the previous capacity).
- For deques, this operation invalidates iterators to other elements. References to other elements remain valid.
- For strings, *value* is passed by value.
- For vectors and deques, this function either succeeds or has no effect, provided that the copy/move constructor does not throw. For lists, this function either succeeds or has no effect.
- Provided by vector, deque, list, string.

void *container*::**emplace_back** (*args*)

- Appends a new last element, which is initialized by the argument list *args*.
- Thus, for the element type, there must be a callable constructor for *args*.
- For vectors, this operation invalidates iterators and references to other elements if reallocation happens (the new number of elements exceeds the previous capacity).

---

[1] For forward lists, the standard currently does not say this, which likely is a defect.

- For deques, this operation invalidates iterators to other elements. References to other elements remain valid.
- This function either succeeds or has no effect, provided that for vectors and deques the copy/move constructor does not throw.
- Available since C++11.
- Provided by vector, deque, list.

8.7.2   Inserting Multiple Elements

void *container*::**insert** (*initializer-list*)

- Inserts copies of the elements of *initializer-list* into an associative container.
- For all containers, references to existing elements remain valid. For associative containers, all iterators to existing elements remain valid. For unordered containers, iterators to existing elements remain valid if no rehashing is forced (if the number of resulting elements is equal to or greater than the bucket count times the maximum load factor).
- Available since C++11.
- Provided by set, multiset, map, multimap, unordered set, unordered multiset, unordered map, unordered multimap.

iterator *container*::**insert** (const_iterator *pos*, *initializer-list*)

- Inserts copies of the elements of *initializer-list* at the position of iterator *pos*.
- Returns the position of the first inserted element or *pos* if *initializer-list* is empty.
- For vectors, this operation invalidates iterators and references to other elements if reallocation happens (the new number of elements exceeds the previous capacity).
- For deques, this operation invalidates iterators and references to other elements.
- For lists, the function either succeeds or has no effect.
- Available since C++11.
- Provided by vector, deque, list, string.

iterator *container*::**insert** (const_iterator *pos*,
                                   size_type *num*, const T& *value*)

- Inserts *num* copies of *value* at the position of iterator *pos*.
- Returns the position of the first inserted element or *pos* if *num*==0 (before C++11. nothing was returned).
- For vectors, this operation invalidates iterators and references to other elements if reallocation happens (the new number of elements exceeds the previous capacity).
- For deques, this operation invalidates iterators and references to other elements.
- T is the type of the container elements. Thus, for maps and multimaps, it is a key/value pair.
- For strings, *value* is passed by value.

- For vectors and deques, if the copy/move operations (constructor and assignment operator) of the elements don't throw, the function either succeeds or has no effect. For lists, the function either succeeds or has no effect.
- Before C++11, type `iterator` was used instead of `const_iterator` and the return type was `void`.
- Provided by vector, deque, list, string.

void *container*::**insert** (InputIterator *beg*, InputIterator *end*)

- Inserts copies of all elements of the range [*beg*,*end*) into the associative container.
- This function is a member template (see Section 3.2, page 34). Thus, the elements of the source range may have any type convertible into the element type of the container.
- For all containers, references to existing elements remain valid. For associative containers, all iterators to existing elements remain valid. For unordered containers, iterators to existing elements remain valid if no rehashing is forced (if the number of resulting elements is equal to or greater than the bucket count times the maximum load factor).
- The function either succeeds or has no effect, provided that for unordered containers the hash function does not throw.
- Provided by set, multiset, map, multimap, unordered set, unordered multiset, unordered map, unordered multimap.

iterator *container*::**insert** (const_iterator *pos*,
                           InputIterator *beg*, InputIterator *end*)

- Inserts copies of all elements of the range [*beg*,*end*) at the position of iterator *pos*.
- Returns the position of the first inserted element or *pos* if *beg*==*end* (before C++11, nothing was returned).
- This function is a member template (see Section 3.2, page 34). Thus, the elements of the source range may have any type convertible into the element type of the container.
- For vectors, this operation invalidates iterators and references to other elements if reallocation happens (the new number of elements exceeds the previous capacity).
- For vectors and deques, this operation might invalidate iterators and references to other elements.
- For lists, the function either succeeds or has no effect.
- Before C++11, type `iterator` was used instead of `const_iterator` and the return type was `void`.
- Provided by vector, deque, list, string.

8.7.3 Removing Elements

size_type *container*::**erase** (const T& *value*)

- Removes all elements equivalent to *value* from an associative or unordered container.
- Returns the number of removed elements.

- Calls the destructors of the removed elements.
- T is the type of the sorted value:
  - For (unordered) sets and multisets, it is the type of the elements.
  - For (unordered) maps and multimaps, it is the type of the keys.
- The function does not invalidate iterators and references to other elements.
- The function may throw if the comparison test or hash function object throws.
- Provided by set, multiset, map, multimap, unordered set, unordered multiset, unordered map, unordered multimap.
- For (forward) lists, `remove()` provides the same functionality (see Section 8.8.1, page 420). For other containers, the `remove()` algorithm can be used (see Section 11.7.1, page 575).

iterator *container*::**erase** (const_iterator *pos*)

- Removes the element at the position of iterator *pos*.
- Returns the position of the following element (or `end()`).
- Calls the destructor of the removed element.
- The caller must ensure that the iterator *pos* is valid. For example:
    ```
    coll.erase(coll.end());   // ERROR ⇒ undefined behavior
    ```
- For vectors and deques, this operation might invalidate iterators and references to other elements. For all other containers, iterators and references to other elements remain valid.
- For vectors, deques, and lists, the function does not throw. For associative and unordered containers, the function may throw if the comparison test or hash function object throws.
- Before C++11, the return type was `void` for associative containers, and type `iterator` was used instead of `const_iterator`.
- For sets that use iterators as elements, calling `erase()` might be ambiguous since C++11. For this reason, C++11 currently gets fixed to provide overloads for both `erase(iterator)` and `erase(const_iterator)`.
- Provided by vector, deque, list, set, multiset, map, multimap, unordered set, unordered multiset, unordered map, unordered multimap, string.

iterator *container*::**erase** (const_iterator *beg*, const_iterator *end*)

- Removes the elements of the range [*beg*,*end*).
- Returns the position of the element that was behind the last removed element on entry (or `end()`).
- As always for ranges, all elements, including *beg* but excluding *end*, are removed.
- Calls the destructors of the removed elements.
- The caller must ensure that *beg* and *end* define a valid range that is part of the container.
- For vectors and deques, this operation might invalidate iterators and references to other elements. For all other containers, iterators and references to other elements remain valid.
- For vectors, deques, and lists the function does not throw. For associative and unordered containers, the function may throw if the comparison test or hash function object throws.
- Before C++11, the return type was `void` for associative containers and type `iterator` was used instead of `const_iterator`.

- Provided by vector, deque, list, set, multiset, map, multimap, unordered set, unordered multiset, unordered map, unordered multimap, string.

`void` *container*::**pop_front** `()`

- Removes the first element of the container.
- Is equivalent to
     container`.erase(`*container*`.begin())`
  or for forward lists, to
     container`.erase_after(`*container*`.before_begin())`
- If the container is empty, the behavior is undefined. Thus, the caller must ensure that the container contains at least one element (`!empty()`).
- The function does not throw.
- Iterators and references to other elements remain valid.
- Provided by deque, list, forward list.

`void` *container*::**pop_back** `()`

- Removes the last element of the container.
- Is equivalent to
     container`.erase(prev(`*container*`.end()))`
- If the container is empty, the behavior is undefined. Thus, the caller must ensure that the container contains at least one element (`!empty()`).
- The function does not throw.
- Iterators and references to other elements remain valid.
- For strings, it is provided since C++11.
- Provided by vector, deque, list, string.

`void` *container*::**clear** `()`

- Removes all elements (empties the container).
- Calls the destructors of the removed elements.
- Invalidates all iterators and references to elements of the container.
- For vectors, deques, and strings, it even invalidates any past-the-end-iterator, which was returned by `end()` or `cend()`.
- The function does not throw (before C++11, for vectors and deques, the function could throw if the copy constructor or assignment operator throws).
- Provided by vector, deque, list, forward list, set, multiset, map, multimap, unordered set, unordered multiset, unordered map, unordered multimap, string.

8.7.4   Resizing

void *container*::**resize** (size_type *num*)

void *container*::**resize** (size_type *num*, const T& *value*)

- Change the number of elements to *num*.
- If size() is *num* on entry, they have no effect.
- If *num* is greater than size() on entry, additional elements are created and appended to the end of the container. The first form creates the new elements by calling their default constructor; the second form creates the new elements as copies of *value*.
- If *num* is less than size() on entry, elements are removed at the end to get the new size. In this case, they call the destructor of the removed elements.
- For vectors and deques, this operation might invalidate iterators and references to other elements. For all other containers, iterators and references to other elements remain valid.
- For vectors and deques, these functions either succeed or have no effect, provided that the constructor or the assignment operator of the elements doesn't throw. For lists and forward lists, the functions either succeed or have no effect.
- Before C++11, *value* was passed by value.
- For strings, *value* is passed by value.
- Provided by vector, deque, list, forward list, string.

8.8   Special Member Functions for Lists and Forward Lists

8.8.1   Special Member Functions for Lists (and Forward Lists)

void *list*::**remove** (const T& *value*)

void *list*::**remove_if** (UnaryPredicate *op*)

- remove() removes all elements with value value.
- remove_if() removes all elements for which the unary predicate

     op(*elem*)

  yields true.
- Note that *op* should not change its state during a function call. See Section 10.1.4, page 483, for details.
- Both call the destructors of the removed elements.
- The order of the remaining arguments remains stable.
- This is the special version of the remove() algorithm, which is discussed in Section 11.7.1, page 575.

- T is the type of the container elements.
- For further details and examples, see Section 7.5.2, page 294.
- The functions may throw only if the comparison of the elements may throw.
- Provided by list, forward list.

void *list*::**unique** ()

void *list*::**unique** (BinaryPredicate *op*)

- Remove subsequent duplicates of (forward) list elements so that the value of each element is different from that of the following element.
- The first form removes all elements for which the previous values are equal.
- The second form removes all elements that follow an element *e* and for which the binary predicate
  $$op(elem,e)$$
  yields true. In other words, the predicate is not used to compare an element with its predecessor; the element is compared with the previous element that was not removed.
- Note that *op* should not change its state during a function call. See Section 10.1.4, page 483, for details.
- Both call the destructors of the removed elements.
- These are the special versions of the unique() algorithms (see Section 11.7.2, page 578).
- The functions do not throw if the comparisons of the elements do not throw.
- Provided by list, forward list.

void *list*::**splice** (const_iterator *pos*, list& *source*)

void *list*::**splice** (const_iterator *pos*, list&& *source*)

- Move all elements of the list *source* into *this and insert them at the position of iterator *pos*.
- After the call, *source* is empty.
- If *source* and *this are identical, the behavior is undefined. Thus, the caller must ensure that *source* is a different list. To move elements inside the same list, you must use the following forms of splice().
- The caller must ensure that *pos* is a valid position of *this; otherwise, the behavior is undefined.
- Pointers, iterators, and references to members of *source* remain valid. Thus, they belong to this afterward.
- This function does not throw.
- The second form is available since C++11. Before C++11, type iterator was used instead of const_iterator.
- Provided by list.

void *list*::**splice** (const_iterator *pos*, list& *source*, const_iterator *sourcePos*)

void *list*::**splice** (const_iterator *pos*, list&& *source*, const_iterator *sourcePos*)

- Move the element at the position *sourcePos* of the list *source* into *this and insert it at the position of iterator *pos*.
- *source* and *this may be identical. In this case, the element is moved inside the list.

- If *source* is a different list, it contains one element less after the operation.
- The caller must ensure that *pos* is a valid position of `*this`, that *sourcePos* is a valid iterator of *source*, and that *sourcePos* is not *source*.`end()`; otherwise, the behavior is undefined.
- Pointers, iterators, and references to members of *source* remain valid. Thus, they belong to `this` afterward.
- This function does not throw.
- The second form is available since C++11. Before C++11, type `iterator` was used instead of `const_iterator`.
- Provided by list.

void *list*::**splice** (`const_iterator` *pos*, `list&` *source*,
                      `const_iterator` *sourceBeg*, `const_iterator` *sourceEnd*)

void *list*::**splice** (`const_iterator` *pos*, `list&&` *source*,
                      `const_iterator` *sourceBeg*, `const_iterator` *sourceEnd*)

- Move the elements of the range [*sourceBeg*,*sourceEnd*) of the list *source* to `*this` and insert them at the position of iterator *pos*.
- *source* and `*this` may be identical. In this case, *pos* must not be part of the moved range, and the elements are moved inside the list.
- If *source* is a different list, it contains fewer elements after the operation.
- The caller must ensure that *pos* is a valid position of `*this` and that *sourceBeg* and *sourceEnd* define a valid range that is part of *source*; otherwise, the behavior is undefined.
- Pointers, iterators, and references to members of *source* remain valid. Thus, they belong to `this` afterward.
- This function does not throw.
- The second form is available since C++11. Before C++11, type `iterator` was used instead of `const_iterator`.
- Provided by list.

void *list*::**sort** ()

void *list*::**sort** (`CompFunc` *cmpPred*)

- Sort the elements.
- The first form sorts all elements with operator <.
- The second form sorts all elements by calling *cmpPred* to compare two elements:
       op(*elem1*,*elem2*)
- The order of elements that have an equal value remains stable unless an exception is thrown.
- These are the special versions of the `sort()` and `stable_sort()` algorithms (see Section 11.9.1, page 596).
- Provided by list, forward list.

void *list*::**merge** (*list& source*)

void *list*::**merge** (*list&& source*)

void *list*::**merge** (*list& source,* CompFunc *cmpPred*)

void *list*::**merge** (*list&& source,* CompFunc *cmpPred*)

- Merge all elements of the (forward) list *source* into *this.
- After the call, *source* is empty.
- The first two forms use operator < as the sorting criterion.
- The last two forms use *cmpPred* as the optional sorting criterion and to compare two elements:
    cmpPred(*elem*,*sourceElem*)
- The order of elements that have an equivalent value remains stable.
- If *this and *source* are sorted on entry according to the sorting criterion < or *cmpPred*, the resulting (forward) list is also sorted and equivalent elements of *this precede equivalent elements of *source*. Strictly speaking, the standard requires that both (forward) lists be sorted on entry. In practice, however, merging is also possible for unsorted lists. However, you should check this before you rely on it.
- This is the special version of the merge() algorithm (see Section 11.10.2, page 614).
- If the comparisons of the elements do not throw, the functions either succeed or have no effect.
- Provided by list, forward list.

void *list*::**reverse** ()

- Reverses the order of the elements in a (forward) list.
- This is the special version of the reverse() algorithm (see Section 11.8.1, page 583).
- This function does not throw.
- Provided by list, forward list.

8.8.2 Special Member Functions for Forward Lists Only

iterator *forwardlist*::**before_begin** ()

const_iterator *forwardlist*::**before_begin** () const

const_iterator *forwardlist*::**cbefore_begin** () const

- Return an iterator for the the position before the first element.
- Because you can't iterate backward, this member function allows you to yield the position to insert a new or delete the first element.
- Provided by forward list.

iterator *forwardlist*::**insert_after** (const_iterator *pos,* const T& *value*)

iterator *forwardlist*::**insert_after** (const_iterator *pos,* T&& *value*)

- Insert *value* right after the position of iterator *pos*.
- The first form copies *value*.

- The second form moves *value* to the container, so the state of *value* is undefined afterward.
- Return the position of the new element.
- The function either succeeds or has no effect.
- Passing `end()` or `cend()` of a container as *pos* results in undefined behavior.
- Provided by forward list.

iterator *forwardlist*::**emplace_after** (const_iterator *pos*, *args*)

- Inserts a new element initialized by *args* right after the position of iterator *pos*.
- Returns the position of the new element.
- The function either succeeds or has no effect.[2]
- Passing `end()` or `cend()` of a container as *pos* results in undefined behavior.
- Provided by forward list.

iterator *forwardlist*::**insert_after** (const_iterator *pos*,
                                            size_type *num*, const T& *value*)

- Inserts *num* copies of *value* right behind the position of iterator *pos*.
- Returns the position of the last inserted element or *pos* if *num*==0.
- The function either succeeds or has no effect.
- Passing `end()` or `cend()` of a container as *pos* results in undefined behavior.
- Provided by forward list.

iterator *forwardlist*::**insert_after** (const_iterator *pos*, *initializer-list*)

- Inserts copies of the elements of *initializer-list* right after the position of iterator *pos*.
- Returns the position of the last inserted element or *pos* if *initializer-list* is empty.
- The function either succeeds or has no effect.
- Passing `end()` or `cend()` of a container as *pos* results in undefined behavior.
- Available since C++11. forward list.

iterator *forwardlist*::**insert_after** (const_iterator *pos*,
                                            InputIterator *beg*, InputIterator *end*)

- Inserts copies of all elements of the range [*beg,end*) right after the position of iterator *pos*.
- Returns the position of the last inserted element or *pos* if *beg*==*end*.
- This function is a member template (see Section 3.2, page 34). Thus, the elements of the source range may have any type convertible into the element type of the container.
- The function either succeeds or has no effect.
- Passing `end()` or `cend()` of a container as *pos* results in undefined behavior.
- Provided by forward list.

---

[2] Currently, the standard does not say this, which likely is a defect.

iterator *forwardlist*::**erase_after** (const_iterator *pos*)

- Removes the element right after the position of iterator *pos*.
- Returns the position of the following element (or `end()`).
- Calls the destructor of the removed element.
- Iterators and references to other elements remain valid.
- The caller must ensure that the iterator *pos* is valid, which excludes to pass `end()` and the position before `end()`.
- The function does not throw.
- Passing `end()` or `cend()` of a container as *pos* results in undefined behavior.
- Provided by forward list.

void *forwardlist*::**erase_after** (const_iterator *beg*, const_iterator *end*)

- Removes the elements of the range (*beg*,*end*). Note that this is *not* a half-open range, because it excludes both *beg* and *end*. [*beg*,*end*]. For example:

      coll.erase(coll.before_begin(),coll.end());   *// OK: erases all elements*

- Returns *end*.
- Calls the destructors of the removed elements.
- The caller must ensure that *beg* and *end* define a valid range that is part of the container.
- The function does not throw.
- Iterators and references to other elements remain valid.
- Provided by forward list.

void *forwardlist*::**splice_after** (const_iterator *pos*, *forwardlist&* *source*)

void *forwardlist*::**splice_after** (const_iterator *pos*, *forwardlist&&* *source*)

- Move all elements of *source* into `*this` and insert them at the position right after iterator *pos*.
- After the call, *source* is empty.
- If *source* and `*this` are identical, the behavior is undefined. Thus, the caller must ensure that *source* is a different list. To move elements inside the same list, you must use the following forms of `splice_after()`.
- The caller must ensure that *pos* is a valid position of `*this`; otherwise, the behavior is undefined.
- Pointers, iterators, and references to members of *source* remain valid. Thus, they belong to `this` afterward.
- This function does not throw.
- Passing `end()` or `cend()` of a container as *pos* results in undefined behavior.
- Provided by forward list.

void *forwardlist*::**splice_after** (const_iterator *pos*,
                                      forwardlist& *source*, const_iterator *sourcePos*)

void *forwardlist*::**splice_after** (const_iterator *pos*,
                                      forwardlist&& *source*, const_iterator *sourcePos*)

- Move the element right after the position *sourcePos* of the list *source* into *this and insert it at the position right after iterator *pos*.
- *source* and *this may be identical. In this case, the element is moved inside the list.
- If *source* is a different list, it contains one element less after the operation.
- The caller must ensure that *pos* is a valid position of *this, that *sourcePos* is a valid iterator of *source*, and that *sourcePos* is not *source*.end(); otherwise, the behavior is undefined.
- Pointers, iterators, and references to members of *source* remain valid. Thus, they belong to this afterward.
- This function does not throw.
- Passing end() or cend() of a container as *pos* results in undefined behavior.
- Provided by forward list.

void *forwardlist*::**splice_after** (const_iterator *pos*, *forwardlist*& *source*,
                                      const_iterator *sourceBeg*,
                                      const_iterator *sourceEnd*)

void *forwardlist*::**splice_after** (const_iterator *pos*, *forwardlist*&& *source*,
                                      const_iterator *sourceBeg*,
                                      const_iterator *sourceEnd*)

- Move the elements of the range (*sourceBeg*,*sourceEnd*) of the list *source* to *this and insert them at the position right after iterator *pos*. Note that the last two arguments are *not* a half-open range, because it excludes both *beg* and *end*. For example, the following call moves all elements of coll2 to the beginning of coll:
    ```
    coll.splice_after(coll.before_begin(), coll2,
                      coll2.before_begin(), coll2.end());
    ```
- *source* and *this may be identical. In this case, *pos* must not be part of the moved range, and the elements are moved inside the list.
- If *source* is a different list, it contains fewer elements after the operation.
- The caller must ensure that *pos* is a valid position of *this and that *sourceBeg* and *sourceEnd* define a valid range that is part of *source*; otherwise, the behavior is undefined.
- Pointers, iterators, and references to members of *source* remain valid. Thus, they belong to this afterward.
- This function does not throw.
- Passing end() or cend() of a container as *pos* results in undefined behavior.
- Provided by forward list.

8.9 Container Policy Interfaces

8.9.1 Nonmodifying Policy Functions

size_type *container*::**capacity** () const

- Returns the number of elements the container may contain without reallocation.
- Provided by vector, string.

value_compare *container*::**value_comp** () const

- Returns the object that is used as the comparison criterion of associative containers for values as a whole.
- For sets and multisets, it is equivalent to key_comp().
- For maps and multimaps, it is an auxiliary class for a comparison criterion that compares only the key part of the key/value pair.
- Provided by set, multiset, map, multimap.

key_compare *container*::**key_comp** () const

- Returns the comparison criterion of associative containers.
- Provided by set, multiset, map, multimap.

key_equal *container*::**key_eq** () const

- Returns the equivalence criterion of unordered containers.
- Provided by unordered set, unordered multiset, unordered map, unordered multimap.

hasher *container*::**hash_function** () const

- Returns the hash function of unordered containers.
- Provided by unordered set, unordered multiset, unordered map, unordered multimap.

float *container*::**load_factor** () const

- Returns the current average number of elements per bucket of an unordered container.
- Provided by unordered set, unordered multiset, unordered map, unordered multimap.

float *container*::**max_load_factor** () const

- Returns the maximum load factor of an unordered container. The container automatically re-hashes (increases the number of buckets as necessary) to keep its load factor below or equal to this number.
- Note that the default is 1.0, which usually should be modified (see Section 7.9.2, page 362).
- Provided by unordered set, unordered multiset, unordered map, unordered multimap.

8.9.2   Modifying Policy Functions

void *container*::**reserve** (size_type *num*)

- Reserves internal memory for at least *num* elements.
- For vectors, this call can only increase the capacity. Thus, it has no effect if *num* is less than or equal to the actual capacity. To shrink the capacity of vectors, see shrink_to_fit() on page 428 and the example in Section 7.3.1, page 271.
- For unordered containers
    - This call is equivalent to rehash(ceil(*num/max_load_factor*)) (ceil() yields the round-up value).
    - This operation invalidates iterators, changes ordering between elements, and changes the buckets the elements appear in. The operation does not invalidate pointers or references to elements.
- For strings, *num* is optional (default: 0), and the call is a nonbinding shrink request if *num* is less than the actual capacity.
- This operation might invalidate iterators and (for vectors and strings) references and pointers to elements. However, it is guaranteed that no reallocation takes place during insertions that happen after a call to reserve() until the time when an insertion would make the size greater than num. Thus, reserve() can increase speed and help to keep references, pointers, and iterators valid (see Section 7.3.1, page 271, for details).
- Throws length_error (see Section 4.3.1, page 43) if *num*>max_size() or an appropriate exception if the memory allocation fails.
- Available for unordered containers since C++11.
- Provided by vector, unordered set, unordered multiset, unordered map, unordered multimap, string.

void *container*::**shrink_to_fit** ()

- Shrinks the internal memory to fit the exact number of elements.
- This call is a nonbinding request, which means that implementations can ignore this call to allow latitude for implementation-specific optimizations. Thus, it is not guaranteed that afterward capacity() == size() yields true.
- This operation might invalidate references, pointers, and iterators to elements.
- Available since C++11. To shrink the capacity of vectors before C++11, see Section 7.3.1, page 271, for an example.
- Provided by vector, deque, string.

void *container*::**rehash** (size_type *bnum*)

- Changes the number of buckets of an unordered container to at least *bnum*.
- This operation invalidates iterators, changes ordering between elements, and changes the buckets the elements appear in. The operation does not invalidate pointers or references to elements.

- If an exception is thrown other than by the container's hash or comparison function, the operation has no effect.
- For unordered multisets and multimaps, rehashing preserves the relative ordering of equivalent elements.
- Provided by unordered set, unordered multiset, unordered map, unordered multimap.

void *container*::**max_load_factor** (float *loadFactor*)

- Sets the maximum load factor of an unordered container to *loadFactor*.
- *loadFactor* is taken as a hint so that implementations are free to adjust this value according to their internal layout philosophy.
- This operation might cause a rehashing, which invalidates iterators, changes ordering between elements, and changes the buckets the elements appear in. The operation does not invalidate pointers or references to elements.
- Provided by unordered set, unordered multiset, unordered map, unordered multimap.

8.9.3   Bucket Interface for Unordered Containers

size_type *container*::**bucket_count** () const

- Returns the current number of buckets of an unordered container.
- Provided by unordered set, unordered multiset, unordered map, unordered multimap.

size_type *container*::**max_bucket_count** () const

- Returns the maximum possible number of buckets of an unordered container.
- Provided by unordered set, unordered multiset, unordered map, unordered multimap.

size_type *container*::**bucket** (const key_type *key*) const

- Returns the index of the bucket in which elements with a key equivalent to *key* would be found, if any such element existed.
- The return value is in the range [0,bucket_count()).
- The return value is undefined if bucket_count() is zero.
- Provided by unordered set, unordered multiset, unordered map, unordered multimap.

size_type *container*::**bucket_size** (size_type *bucketIdx*) const

- Returns the number of elements in the bucket with index *bucketIdx*.
- If *bucketIdx* is not a valid index in the range [0,bucket_count()), the effect is undefined.
- Provided by unordered set, unordered multiset, unordered map, unordered multimap.

local_iterator *container*::**begin** (size_type *bucketIdx*)

const_local_iterator *container*::**begin** (size_type *bucketIdx*) const

const_local_iterator *container*::**cbegin** (size_type *bucketIdx*) const

- All three return an iterator for the beginning of all elements (the position of the first element) of the bucket with index *bucketIdx*.
- If the bucket is empty, the calls are equivalent to *container*::end(*bucketIdx*) or *container*::cend(*bucketIdx*), respectively.
- If *bucketIdx* is not a valid index in the range [0,bucket_count()), the effect is undefined.
- Provided by unordered set, unordered multiset, unordered map, unordered multimap.

```
local_iterator container::end (size_type bucketIdx)
const_local_iterator container::end (size_type bucketIdx) const
const_local_iterator container::cend (size_type bucketIdx) const
```

- All three return an iterator for the end of all elements (the position after the last element) of the bucket with index *bucketIdx*.
- If the bucket is empty, the calls are equivalent to *container*::begin(*bucketIdx*) or *container*::cbegin(*bucketIdx*), respectively.
- If *bucketIdx* is not a valid index in the range [0,bucket_count()), the effect is undefined.
- Provided by unordered set, unordered multiset, unordered map, unordered multimap.

8.10   Allocator Support

All STL containers can be used with a special memory model that is defined by an allocator object (see Chapter 19 for details). This section describes the members for allocator support.

8.10.1   Fundamental Allocator Members

container::**allocator_type**
- The type of the allocator.
- Provided by vector, deque, list, forward list, set, multiset, map, multimap, unordered set, unordered multiset, unordered map, unordered multimap, string.

```
allocator_type container::get_allocator () const
```
- Returns the memory model of the container.
- Provided by vector, deque, list, forward list, set, multiset, map, multimap, unordered set, unordered multiset, unordered map, unordered multimap, string.

8.10.2   Constructors with Optional Allocator Parameters

```
explicit container::container (const Allocator& alloc)
```
- Creates a new empty container that uses the memory model *alloc*.

- Provided by vector, deque, list, forward list, set, multiset, map, multimap, unordered set, unordered multiset, unordered map, unordered multimap, string.

container::*container* (const CompFunc& *cmpPred*, const Allocator& *alloc*)

- Creates a new empty container, with *cmpPred* used as the sorting criterion and *alloc* used as memory model.
- The sorting criterion must define a *strict weak ordering* (see Section 7.7, page 314).
- Provided by set, multiset, map, multimap.

container::*container* (size_type *bnum*, const Hasher& *hasher*,
                         const KeyEqual& *eqPred*, const Allocator& *alloc*)

- Creates a new empty container with at least *bnum* buckets, with *hasher* used as hashing function, *eqPred* used as criterion to identify equal values, and *alloc* used as memory model.
- Provided by unordered set, unordered multiset, unordered map, unordered multimap.

container::*container* (*initializer-list*, const Allocator& *alloc*)

- Creates a new container that uses the memory model *alloc* and is initialized by the elements of *initializer-list*.
- Available since C++11.
- Provided by vector, deque, list, forward list, string.

container::*container* (*initializer-list*, const CompFunc& *cmpPred*,
                         const Allocator& *alloc*)

- Creates a container that has the sorting criterion *cmpPred*, uses the memory model *alloc*, and is initialized by the elements of *initializer-list*.
- The sorting criterion must define a *strict weak ordering* (see Section 7.7, page 314).
- Available since C++11.
- Provided by set, multiset, map, multimap.

container::*container* (*initializer-list*, size_type *bnum*, const Hasher& *hasher*,
                         const KeyEqual& *eqPred* const Allocator& *alloc*)

- Creates a container with at least *bnum* buckets, *hasher* used as hashing function, *eqPred* used as criterion to identify equal values, and *alloc* used as memory model, which is initialized by the elements of *initializer-list*.
- Provided by unordered set, unordered multiset, unordered map, unordered multimap.

container::*container* (const *container*& *c*, const Allocator& *alloc*)
container::*container* (*container*&& *c*, const Allocator& *alloc*)

- Create a new container that uses the memory model *alloc* and is initialized with copied/moved elements of the existing container *c*.
- Call the copy/move constructor for every element in *c*.

- For the second form, after this call, c is valid but has an unspecified value.
- Available since C++11.
- Provided by vector, deque, list, forward list, set, multiset, map, multimap, unordered set, unordered multiset, unordered map, unordered multimap, string.

container::*container* (size_type *num*, const T& *value*, const Allocator& *alloc*)

- Creates a container with *num* elements and hat uses the memory model *alloc*.
- The elements are created as copies of *value*.
- T is the type of the container elements. Note that for strings, *value* is passed by value.
- Provided by vector, deque, list, forward list, string.

container::*container* (InputIterator *beg*, InputIterator *end*,
            const Allocator& *alloc*)

- Creates a container that is initialized by all elements of the range [*beg,end*) and uses the memory model *alloc*.
- This function is a member template (see Section 3.2, page 34). Thus, the elements of the source range may have any type convertible into the element type of the container.
- Provided by vector, deque, list, forward list, string.

container::*container* (InputIterator *beg*, InputIterator *end*,
            const CompFunc& *cmpPred*, const Allocator& *alloc*)

- Creates a container that has the sorting criterion *cmpPred*, is initialized by all elements of the range [*beg,end*), and uses the memory model *alloc*.
- This function is a member template (see Section 3.2, page 34). Thus, the elements of the source range may have any type convertible into the element type of the container.
- The sorting criterion must define a *strict weak ordering* (see Section 7.7, page 314).
- Provided by set, multiset, map, multimap.

container::*container* (InputIterator *beg*, InputIterator *end*,
            size_type *bnum*, const Hasher& *hasher*,
            const KeyEqual& *eqPred*, const Allocator& *alloc*)

- Creates a container with at least *bnum* buckets, *hasher* used as hashing function, *eqPred* used as criterion to identify equal values, and *alloc* used as memory model, which is initialized by all elements of the range [*beg,end*).
- Provided by unordered set, unordered multiset, unordered map, unordered multimap.

Chapter 9

STL Iterators

This chapter describes iterators in detail. It covers iterator categories, iterator-specific operations, iterator adapters, and user-defined iterators.

9.1 Header Files for Iterators

All containers define their own iterator types, so you don't need a special header file for using iterators of containers. However, several definitions for special iterators, such as reverse iterators, and some auxiliary iterator functions are introduced by the `<iterator>` header file. Some implementations include this header file for any container to define its reverse iterator types. This, however, is not portable. Thus, when you need more than ordinary container iterators and their type, you should include this header.

9.2 Iterator Categories

Iterators are objects that can iterate over elements of a sequence via a common interface that is adapted from ordinary pointers (see Section 6.3, page 188). Iterators follow the concept of pure abstraction: Anything that *behaves* like an iterator *is* an iterator. However, iterators have different abilities. These abilities are important because some algorithms require special iterator abilities. For example, sorting algorithms require iterators that can perform random access because otherwise, the runtime would be poor. For this reason, iterators have different categories (Figure 9.1). The abilities of these categories are listed in Table 9.1 and discussed in the following subsections.

Reading iterators that can also write are called *mutable* iterators (for example, *mutable forward iterator*).

9.2.1 Output Iterators

Output iterators can only step forward with write access. Thus, you can assign new values only element-by-element. You can't use an output iterator to iterate twice over the same range. In fact, it

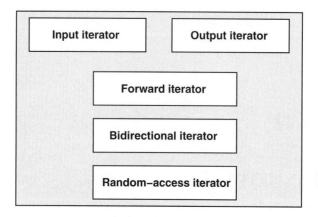

Figure 9.1. Iterator Categories

Iterator Category	Ability	Providers
Output iterator	Writes forward	Ostream, inserter
Input iterator	Reads forward once	Istream
Forward iterator	Reads forward	Forward list, unordered containers
Bidirectional iterator	Reads forward and backward	List, set, multiset, map, multimap
Random-access iterator	Reads with random access	Array, vector, deque, string, C-style array

Table 9.1. Abilities of Iterator Categories

is even not guaranteed that you can assign a value twice without incrementing the iterator. The goal is to write a value into a "black hole" in the following way:

```
while (...) {
    *pos = ...;         // assign a value
    ++pos;              // advance (prepare for the next assignment)
}
```

Table 9.2 lists the valid operations for output iterators. The only valid use of operator * is on the left side of an assignment statement.

No comparison operations are required for output iterators. You can't check whether an output iterator is valid or whether a "writing" was successful. You can only write, and write, and write values. Usually, the end of a writing is defined by an additional requirement for specific output iterators.

Expression	Effect
iter = val	Writes *val* to where the iterator refers
++*iter*	Steps forward (returns new position)
iter++	Steps forward (returns old position)
TYPE(iter)	Copies iterator (copy constructor)

Table 9.2. Operations of Output Iterators

Often, iterators can read and write values. For this reason, all reading iterators might have the additional ability to write. In that case, they are called *mutable* iterators.

A typical example of a pure output iterator is one that writes to the standard output (for example, to the screen or a printer). If you use two output iterators to write to the screen, the second word follows the first rather than overwriting it. Inserters are another typical example of output iterators. Inserters are iterators that insert values into containers. If you assign a value, you insert it. If you then write a second value, you don't overwrite the first value; you just also insert it. Inserters are discussed in Section 9.4.2, page 454.

All `const_iterators` provided by containers and their member functions `cbegin()` and `cend()` are not output iterators, because they don't allow you to write to where the iterator refers.

9.2.2 Input Iterators

Input iterators can only step forward element-by-element with read access. Thus, they return values element-wise. Table 9.3 lists the operations of input iterators.

Expression	Effect
iter	Provides read access to the actual element
iter ->*member*	Provides read access to a member of the actual element
++*iter*	Steps forward (returns new position)
iter++	Steps forward
iter1 == *iter2*	Returns whether two iterators are equal
iter1 != *iter2*	Returns whether two iterators are not equal
TYPE(iter)	Copies iterator (copy constructor)

Table 9.3. Operations of Input Iterators

Input iterators can read elements only once. Thus, if you copy an input iterator and let the original and the copy read forward, they might iterate over different values.

All iterators that refer to values to process have the abilities of input iterators. Usually, however, they can have more. A typical example of a pure input iterator is one that reads from the standard input, which is typically the keyboard. The same value can't be read twice. Once a word is read from an input stream, the next read access returns another word.

For input iterators, operators == and != are provided only to check whether an iterator is equal to a *past-the-end iterator*. This is required because operations that deal with input iterators usually do the following:

InputIterator pos, end;

```
while (pos != end) {
    ...  // read-only access using *pos
    ++pos;
}
```

There is no guarantee that two different iterators that are both not *past-the-end iterators* compare unequal if they refer to different positions. (This requirement is introduced with forward iterators.)

Note also that for input iterators it is not required that the postincrement operator *iter++* returns something. Usually, however, it returns the old position.

You should always prefer the preincrement operator over the postincrement operator because it might perform better. This is because the preincrement operator does not have to return an old value that must be stored in a temporary object. So, for any iterator pos (and any abstract data type), you should prefer

    ++pos   // OK and fast

rather than

    pos++   // OK, but not so fast

The same applies to decrement operators, as long as they are defined (they aren't for input iterators).

9.2.3   Forward Iterators

Forward iterators are input iterators that provide additional guarantees while reading forward. Table 9.4 summarizes the operations of forward iterators.

Expression	Effect
iter	Provides access to the actual element
iter->member	Provides access to a member of the actual element
++iter	Steps forward (returns new position)
iter++	Steps forward (returns old position)
iter1 == *iter2*	Returns whether two iterators are equal
iter1 != *iter2*	Returns whether two iterators are not equal
TYPE()	Creates iterator (default constructor)
TYPE(iter)	Copies iterator (copy constructor)
iter1 = *iter2*	Assigns an iterator

Table 9.4. Operations of Forward Iterators

Unlike for input iterators, it is guaranteed that for two forward iterators that refer to the same element, operator == yields `true` and that they will refer to the same value after both are incremented. For example:

ForwardIterator `pos1, pos2;`

```
pos1 = pos2 = begin;   // both iterators refer to the same element
if (pos1 != end) {
    ++pos1;                        // pos1 is one element ahead
    while (pos1 != end) {
        if (*pos1 == *pos2) {
            ...  // process adjacent duplicates
            ++pos1;
            ++pos2;
    }
}
```

Forward iterators are provided by the following objects and types:

- Class `<forward_list<>`
- Unordered containers

However, for unordered containers, libraries are allowed to provide bidirectional iterators instead (see Section 7.9.1, page 357).

A forward iterator that fulfills the requirements of an output iterator is a *mutable* forward iterator, which can be used for both reading and writing.

9.2.4 Bidirectional Iterators

Bidirectional iterators are forward iterators that provide the additional ability to iterate backward over the elements. Thus, they provide the decrement operator to step backward (Table 9.5).

Expression	Effect
--iter	Steps backward (returns new position)
iter--	Steps backward (returns old position)

Table 9.5. Additional Operations of Bidirectional Iterators

Bidirectional iterators are provided by the following objects and types:

- Class `list<>`
- Associative containers

A bidirectional iterator that fulfills the requirements of an output iterator is a *mutable* bidirectional iterator, which can be used for both reading and writing.

9.2.5 Random-Access Iterators

Random-access iterators provide all the abilities of bidirectional iterators plus random access. Thus, they provide operators for *iterator arithmetic* (in accordance with the *pointer arithmetic* of ordinary pointers). That is, they can add and subtract offsets, process differences, and compare iterators with relational operators, such as < and >. Table 9.6 lists the additional operations of random-access iterators.

Expression	Effect
iter [*n*]	Provides access to the element that has index *n*
iter+=*n*	Steps *n* elements forward (or backward, if *n* is negative)
iter-=*n*	Steps *n* elements backward (or forward, if *n* is negative)
iter+*n*	Returns the iterator of the *n*th next element
n+*iter*	Returns the iterator of the *n*th next element
iter-*n*	Returns the iterator of the *n*th previous element
iter1-*iter2*	Returns the distance between *iter1* and *iter2*
iter1<*iter2*	Returns whether *iter1* is before *iter2*
iter1>*iter2*	Returns whether *iter1* is after *iter2*
iter1<=*iter2*	Returns whether *iter1* is not after *iter2*
iter1>=*iter2*	Returns whether *iter1* is not before *iter2*

Table 9.6. Additional Operations of Random-Access Iterators

Random-access iterators are provided by the following objects and types:
- Containers with random access (`array`, `vector`, `deque`)
- Strings (`string`, `wstring`)
- Ordinary C-style arrays (pointers)

The following program shows the special abilities of random-access iterators:

```
// iter/itercategory1.cpp

#include <vector>
#include <iostream>
using namespace std;

int main()
{
    vector<int> coll;

    // insert elements from -3 to 9
    for (int i=-3; i<=9; ++i) {
        coll.push_back (i);
    }
```

```
// print number of elements by processing the distance between beginning and end
// - NOTE: uses operator - for iterators
cout << "number/distance: " << coll.end()-coll.begin() << endl;

// print all elements
// - NOTE: uses operator < instead of operator !=
vector<int>::iterator pos;
for (pos=coll.begin(); pos<coll.end(); ++pos) {
    cout << *pos << ' ';
}
cout << endl;

// print all elements
// - NOTE: uses operator [] instead of operator *
for (int i=0; i<coll.size(); ++i) {
    cout << coll.begin()[i] << ' ';
}
cout << endl;

// print every second element
// - NOTE: uses operator +=
for (pos = coll.begin(); pos < coll.end()-1; pos += 2) {
    cout << *pos << ' ';
}
cout << endl;
}
```

The output of the program is as follows:

```
number/distance: 13
-3 -2 -1 0 1 2 3 4 5 6 7 8 9
-3 -2 -1 0 1 2 3 4 5 6 7 8 9
-3 -1 1 3 5 7
```

This example won't work with (forward) lists, (unordered) sets, and (unordered) maps, because all operations marked with "*NOTE:*" are provided only for random-access iterators. In particular, keep in mind that you can use operator < as an end criterion in loops for random-access iterators only.

Note that in the last loop the following expression requires that `coll` contains at least one element:

```
pos < coll.end()-1
```

If the collection was empty, `coll.end()-1` would be the position before `coll.begin()`. The comparison might still work, but, strictly speaking, moving an iterator to before the beginning results in undefined behavior. Similarly, the expression `pos += 2` might result in undefined behavior if it moves the iterator beyond the `end()` of the collection. Therefore, changing the final loop to the following is very dangerous because it results in undefined behavior if the collection contains an odd number of elements (Figure 9.2):

```
for (pos = coll.begin(); pos < coll.end(); pos += 2) {
    cout << *pos << ' ';
}
```

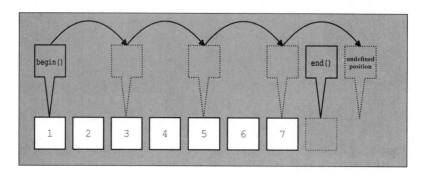

Figure 9.2. Incrementing Iterators by More than One Element

A random-access iterator that fulfills the requirements of an output iterator is a *mutable* random-access iterator, which can be used for both reading and writing.

9.2.6 The Increment and Decrement Problem of Vector Iterators

The use of the increment and decrement operators of iterators includes a strange problem. In general, you can increment and decrement temporary iterators. However, for arrays, vectors, and strings, this might not compile on some platforms. Consider the following example:

```
std::vector<int> coll;
...
// sort, starting with the second element
// - NONPORTABLE version
if (coll.size() > 1) {
    std::sort(++coll.begin(), coll.end());
}
```

Depending on the platform, the compilation of ++coll.begin() might fail. However, if you use, for example, a deque rather than a vector, the compilation always succeeds.

The reason for this strange problem lies in the fact that iterators of vectors, arrays, and strings might be implemented as ordinary pointers. And for all fundamental data types, such as pointers, you are not allowed to modify temporary values. For structures and classes, however, doing so is allowed. Thus, if the iterator is implemented as an ordinary pointer, the compilation fails; if implemented as a class, it succeeds.

As a consequence, the preceding code always works with all containers except `arrays`, vectors, and strings, because you can't implement iterators as ordinary pointers for them. But for `arrays`, vectors, and strings, whether the code works depends on the implementation. Often, ordinary pointers are used. But if, for example, you use a "safe version" of the STL (as is more and more the case), the iterators are implemented as classes.

To make your code portable, the utility function `next()` is provided since C++11 (see Section 9.3.2, page 443), so you can write:

```cpp
std::vector<int> coll;
...
// sort, starting with the second element
// - PORTABLE version since C++11
if (coll.size() > 1) {
    std::sort(std::next(coll.begin()), coll.end());
}
```

Before C++11, you had to use an auxiliary object instead:

```cpp
std::vector<int> coll;
...
// sort, starting with the second element
// - PORTABLE version before C++11
if (coll.size() > 1) {
    std::vector<int>::iterator beg = coll.begin();
    std::sort(++beg, coll.end());
}
```

The problem is not as bad as it sounds. You can't get unexpected behavior, because the problem is detected at compile time. But it is tricky enough to spend time solving it.

9.3 Auxiliary Iterator Functions

The C++ standard library provides some auxiliary functions for dealing with iterators: `advance()`, `next()`, `prev()`, `distance()`, and `iter_swap()`. The first four give all iterators some abilities usually provided only for random-access iterators: to step more than one element forward (or backward) and to process the difference between iterators. The last auxiliary function allows you to swap the values of two iterators.

9.3.1 `advance()`

The function `advance()` increments the position of an iterator passed as the argument. Thus, the function lets the iterator step forward (or backward) more than one element:

```
#include <iterator>
void advance (InputIterator& pos, Dist n)
```

- Lets the input iterator *pos* step *n* elements forward (or backward).

- For bidirectional and random-access iterators, *n* may be negative to step backward.

- Dist is a template type. Normally, it must be an integral type because operations such as <, ++, --, and comparisons with 0 are called.

- Note that advance() does *not* check whether it crosses the end() of a sequence (it can't check because iterators in general do not know the containers on which they operate). Thus, calling this function might result in undefined behavior because calling operator ++ for the end of a sequence is not defined.

Due to the use of iterator traits (see Section 9.5, page 466), the function always uses the best implementation, depending on the iterator category. For random-access iterators, it simply calls *pos+=n*. Thus, for such iterators, advance() has constant complexity. For all other iterators, it calls *++pos* *n* times (or *--pos* if *n* is negative). Thus, for all other iterator categories, advance() has linear complexity.

To be able to change container and iterator types, you should use advance() rather than operator +=. In doing so, however, be aware that you risk unintended worse performance. The reason is that you don't recognize that the performance is worsening when you use other containers that don't provide random-access iterators (bad runtime is the reason why operator += is provided only for random-access iterators). Note also that advance() does not return anything. Operator += returns the new position, so it might be part of a larger expression. Here is an example of the use of advance():

```
// iter/advance1.cpp

#include <iterator>
#include <iostream>
#include <list>
#include <algorithm>
using namespace std;

int main()
{
    list<int> coll;

    // insert elements from 1 to 9
    for (int i=1; i<=9; ++i) {
        coll.push_back(i);
    }

    list<int>::iterator pos = coll.begin();
```

```
// print actual element
cout << *pos << endl;

// step three elements forward
advance (pos, 3);

// print actual element
cout << *pos << endl;

// step one element backward
advance (pos, -1);

// print actual element
cout << *pos << endl;
}
```

In this program, `advance()` lets the iterator pos step three elements forward and one element backward. Thus, the output is as follows:

```
1
4
3
```

Another way to use `advance()` is to ignore some input for iterators that read from an input stream. See the example in Section 9.4.3, page 465.

9.3.2 `next()` and `prev()`

Since C++11, two additional helper functions allow you to move to following or previous iterator positions.

```
#include <iterator>
```

ForwardIterator **next** (ForwardIterator *pos*)

ForwardIterator **next** (ForwardIterator *pos*, *Dist n*)

- Yields the position the forward iterator *pos* would have if moved forward 1 or *n* positions.
- For bidirectional and random-access iterators, *n* may be negative to yield previous positions.
- Dist is type `std::iterator_traits<ForwardIterator>::difference_type`.
- Calls `advance`(*pos,n*) for an internal temporary object.
- Note that `next()` does *not* check whether it crosses the `end()` of a sequence. Thus, it is up to the caller to ensure that the result is valid.

```
#include <iterator>
BidirectionalIterator prev (BidirectionalIterator pos)
BidirectionalIterator prev (BidirectionalIterator pos, Dist n)
```

- Yields the position the bidirectional iterator *pos* would have if moved backward 1 or *n* positions.
- *n* may be negative to yield following positions.
- Dist is type. std::iterator_traits<BidirectionalIterator>::difference_type.
- Calls advance (*pos*,-*n*) for an internal temporary object.
- Note that prev() does *not* check whether it crosses the begin() of a sequence. Thus, it is up to the caller to ensure that the result is valid.

This allows, for example, running over a collection while checking values of the next element:

```
auto pos = coll.begin();
while (pos != coll.end() && std::next(pos) != coll.end()) {
    ...
    ++pos;
}
```

Doing so especially helps because forward and bidirectional iterators do not provide operators + and -. Otherwise, you always need a temporary:

```
auto pos = coll.begin();
auto nextPos = pos;
++nextPos;
while (pos != coll.end() && nextPos != coll.end()) {
    ...
    ++pos;
    ++nextPos;
}
```

or have to restrict code to random-access iterators only:

```
auto pos = coll.begin();
while (pos != coll.end() && pos+1 != coll.end()) {
    ...
    ++pos;
}
```

Don't forget to ensure that there is a valid position before you use it (for this reason, we first check whether pos is equal to coll.end() before we check the next position).

Another application of next() and prev() is to avoid expressions, such as ++coll.begin(), to deal with the second element of a collection. The problem is that using ++coll.begin() instead of std::next(coll.begin()) might not compile (see Section 9.2.6, page 440, for details).

A third application of next() is to work with forward_lists and before_begin() (see Section 7.6.2, page 307, for an example).

9.3.3 `distance()`

The `distance()` function is provided to process the difference between two iterators:

```
#include <iterator>
```
Dist **distance** (InputIterator *pos1*, InputIterator *pos2*)

- Returns the distance between the input iterators *pos1* and *pos2*.
- Both iterators have to refer to elements of the same container.
- If the iterators are not random-access iterators, *pos2* must be reachable from *pos1*; that is, it must have the same position or a later position.
- The return type, *Dist*, is the difference type according to the iterator type:
  ```
  iterator_traits<InputIterator>::difference_type
  ```
  See Section 9.5, page 466, for details.

By using iterator tags, this function uses the best implementation according to the iterator category. For random-access iterators, this function simply returns *pos2−pos1*. Thus, for such iterators, `distance()` has constant complexity. For all other iterator categories, *pos1* is incremented until it reaches *pos2* and the number of increments is returned. Thus, for all other iterator categories, `distance()` has linear complexity. Therefore, `distance()` has bad performance for other than random-access iterators. You should consider avoiding it.

The implementation of `distance()` is described in Section 9.5.1, page 470. The following example demonstrates its use:

```
// iter/distance1.cpp

#include <iterator>
#include <iostream>
#include <list>
#include <algorithm>
using namespace std;

int main()
{
    list<int> coll;

    // insert elements from -3 to 9
    for (int i=-3; i<=9; ++i) {
        coll.push_back(i);
    }

    // search element with value 5
    list<int>::iterator pos;
    pos = find (coll.begin(), coll.end(),     // range
                5);                           // value
```

```
    if (pos != coll.end()) {
        // process and print difference from the beginning
        cout << "difference between beginning and 5: "
             << distance(coll.begin(),pos) << endl;
    }
    else {
        cout << "5 not found" << endl;
    }
}
```

After `find()` assigns the position of the element with value 5 to pos, `distance()` uses this position to process the difference between this position and the beginning. The output of the program is as follows:

```
difference between beginning and 5: 8
```

To be able to change iterator and container types, you should use `distance()` instead of operator `-`. However, if you use `distance()`, you don't recognize that the performance is getting worse when you switch from random-access iterators to other iterators.

To process the difference between two iterators that are not random-access iterators, you must be careful. The first iterator must refer to an element that is not after the element of the second iterator. Otherwise, the behavior is undefined. If you don't know which iterator position comes first, you have to process the distance between both iterators to the beginning of the container and process the difference of these distances. However, you must then know to which container the iterators refer. Otherwise, you have no chance of processing the difference of the two iterators without running into undefined behavior. See the remarks about subranges in Section 6.4.1, page 205, for additional aspects of this problem.

9.3.4 `iter_swap()`

This simple auxiliary function is provided to swap the values to which two iterators refer:

```
#include <algorithm>
```
void **iter_swap** (ForwardIterator1 *pos1*, ForwardIterator2 *pos2*)

- Swaps the values to which iterators *pos1* and *pos2* refer.
- The iterators don't need to have the same type. However, the values must be assignable.

Here is a simple example (function PRINT_ELEMENTS() is introduced in Section 6.6, page 216):

```
// iter/iterswap1.cpp

#include <iostream>
#include <list>
#include <algorithm>
#include <iterator>
```

```
#include "print.hpp"
using namespace std;

int main()
{
    list<int> coll;

    // insert elements from 1 to 9
    for (int i=1; i<=9; ++i) {
        coll.push_back(i);
    }

    PRINT_ELEMENTS(coll);

    // swap first and second value
    iter_swap (coll.begin(), next(coll.begin()));

    PRINT_ELEMENTS(coll);

    // swap first and last value
    iter_swap (coll.begin(), prev(coll.end()));

    PRINT_ELEMENTS(coll);
}
```

The output of the program is as follows:

```
1 2 3 4 5 6 7 8 9
2 1 3 4 5 6 7 8 9
9 1 3 4 5 6 7 8 2
```

Note that `next()` and `prev()` are provided since C++11, and that using operators `++` and `--` instead might not compile for each container:

```
vector<int> coll;
...
iter_swap (coll.begin(), ++coll.begin());    // ERROR: might not compile
...
iter_swap (coll.begin(), --coll.end());      // ERROR: might not compile
```

See Section 9.2.6, page 440, for details about this problem.

9.4   Iterator Adapters

This section covers iterator adapters provided by the C++ standard library. These special iterators allow algorithms to operate in reverse, in insert mode, and with streams.

9.4.1   Reverse Iterators

Reverse iterators redefine increment and decrement operators so that they behave in reverse. Thus, if you use these iterators instead of ordinary iterators, algorithms process elements in reverse order. Most container classes — all except forward lists and unordered containers — as well as strings provide the ability to use reverse iterators to iterate over their elements. Consider the following example:

```
// iter/reviter1.cpp

#include <iostream>
#include <list>
#include <algorithm>
using namespace std;

void print (int elem)
{
    cout << elem << ' ';
}

int main()
{
    // create list with elements from 1 to 9
    list<int> coll = { 1, 2, 3, 4, 5, 6, 7, 8, 9 };

    // print all elements in normal order
    for_each (coll.begin(), coll.end(),      // range
              print);                        // operation
    cout << endl;

    // print all elements in reverse order
    for_each (coll.rbegin(), coll.rend(),    // range
              print);                        // operations
    cout << endl;
}
```

The rbegin() and rend() member functions return a reverse iterator. According to begin() and end(), these iterators define the elements to process as a half-open range. However, they operate in a reverse direction:

- **rbegin()** returns the position of the first element of a reverse iteration. Thus, it returns the position of the last element.
- **rend()** returns the position after the last element of a reverse iteration. Thus, it returns the position *before* the first element.

Thus, the output of the program is as follows:

```
1 2 3 4 5 6 7 8 9
9 8 7 6 5 4 3 2 1
```

Since C++11, corresponding `crbegin()` and `crend()` member functions are provided, which return read-only reverse iterators. Because we only read the elements, they could (and should) be used in this example:

```
// print all elements in reverse order
for_each (coll.crbegin(), coll.crend(),   // range
          print);                          // operations
```

Iterators and Reverse Iterators

You can convert normal iterators into reverse iterators. Naturally, the iterators must be bidirectional iterators, but note that the logical position of an iterator is moved during the conversion. Consider the following program:

```
// iter/reviter2.cpp

#include <iterator>
#include <iostream>
#include <vector>
#include <algorithm>
using namespace std;

int main()
{
    // create list with elements from 1 to 9
    vector<int> coll = { 1, 2, 3, 4, 5, 6, 7, 8, 9 };

    // find position of element with value 5
    vector<int>::const_iterator pos;
    pos = find (coll.cbegin(), coll.cend(),
                5);

    // print value to which iterator pos refers
    cout << "pos:  " << *pos << endl;

    // convert iterator to reverse iterator rpos
    vector<int>::const_reverse_iterator rpos(pos);
```

```
    // print value to which reverse iterator rpos refers
    cout << "rpos: " << *rpos << endl;
}
```

This program has the following output:

```
pos:  5
rpos: 4
```

Thus, if you print the value of an iterator and convert the iterator into a reverse iterator, the value has changed. This is not a bug; it's a feature! This behavior is a consequence of the fact that ranges are half open. To specify all elements of a container, you must use the position after the last argument. However, for a reverse iterator, this is the position before the first element. Unfortunately, such a position may not exist. Containers are not required to guarantee that the position before their first element is valid. Consider that ordinary strings and arrays might also be containers, and the language does not guarantee that arrays don't start at address zero.

As a result, the designers of reverse iterators use a trick: They "physically" reverse the "half-open principle." Physically, in a range defined by reverse iterators, the beginning is *not* included, whereas the end *is*. However, logically, they behave as usual. Thus, there is a distinction between the physical position that defines the element to which the iterator refers and the logical position that defines the value to which the iterator refers (Figure 9.3). The question is, what happens on a conversion from an iterator to a reverse iterator? Does the iterator keep its logical position (the value) or its physical position (the element)? As the previous example shows, the latter is the case. Thus, the value is moved to the previous element (Figure 9.4).

Figure 9.3. Position and Value of Reverse Iterators

You can't understand this decision? Well, it has its advantages: You have nothing to do when you convert a range that is specified by two iterators rather than a single iterator. All elements remain valid. Consider the following example:

```
// iter/reviter3.cpp

#include <iterator>
#include <iostream>
#include <deque>
```

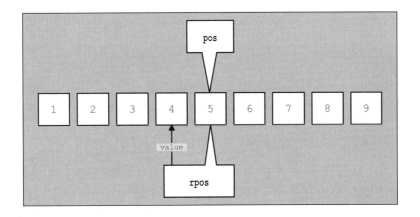

Figure 9.4. Conversion between Iterator pos *and Reverse Iterator* rpos

```cpp
#include <algorithm>
using namespace std;

void print (int elem)
{
    cout << elem << ' ';
}

int main()
{
    // create deque with elements from 1 to 9
    deque<int> coll = { 1, 2, 3, 4, 5, 6, 7, 8, 9 };

    // find position of element with value 2
    deque<int>::const_iterator pos1;
    pos1 = find (coll.cbegin(), coll.cend(),   // range
                 2);                           // value

    // find position of element with value 7
    deque<int>::const_iterator pos2;
    pos2 = find (coll.cbegin(), coll.cend(),   // range
                 7);                           // value

    // print all elements in range [pos1,pos2)
    for_each (pos1, pos2,        // range
              print);            // operation
    cout << endl;
```

```
        // convert iterators to reverse iterators
        deque<int>::const_reverse_iterator rpos1(pos1);
        deque<int>::const_reverse_iterator rpos2(pos2);

        // print all elements in range [pos1,pos2) in reverse order
        for_each (rpos2, rpos1,     // range
                  print);           // operation
        cout << endl;
    }
```

The iterators pos1 and pos2 specify the half-open range, including the element with value 2 but excluding the element with value 7. When the iterators describing that range are converted into reverse iterators, the range remains valid and can be processed in reverse order. Thus, the output of the program is as follows:

```
2 3 4 5 6
6 5 4 3 2
```

Thus, rbegin() is simply:

```
container::reverse_iterator(end())
```

and rend() is simply:

```
container::reverse_iterator(begin())
```

Of course, constant iterators are converted into type const_reverse_iterator.

Converting Reverse Iterators Back Using base()

You can convert reverse iterators back into normal iterators. To do this, reverse iterators provide the base() member function:

```
namespace std {
    template <typename Iterator>
    class reverse_iterator ... {
        ...
        Iterator base() const;
        ...
    };
}
```

Here is an example of the use of base():

```
// iter/reviter4.cpp

#include <iterator>
#include <iostream>
```

```cpp
#include <list>
#include <algorithm>
using namespace std;

int main()
{
    // create list with elements from 1 to 9
    list<int> coll = { 1, 2, 3, 4, 5, 6, 7, 8, 9 };

    // find position of element with value 5
    list<int>::const_iterator pos;
    pos = find (coll.cbegin(), coll.cend(),    // range
                5);                            // value

    // print value of the element
    cout << "pos:    " << *pos << endl;

    // convert iterator to reverse iterator
    list<int>::const_reverse_iterator rpos(pos);

    // print value of the element to which the reverse iterator refers
    cout << "rpos:   " << *rpos << endl;

    // convert reverse iterator back to normal iterator
    list<int>::const_iterator rrpos;
    rrpos = rpos.base();

    // print value of the element to which the normal iterator refers
    cout << "rrpos: " << *rrpos << endl;
}
```

The program has the following output:

```
pos:    5
rpos:   4
rrpos: 5
```

Thus, the conversion with `base()`

```
*rpos.base()
```

is equivalent to the conversion in a reverse iterator. That is, the physical position (the element of the iterator) is retained, but the logical position (the value of the element) is moved. See Section 11.5.3, page 539. for another example of the use of `base()`.

9.4.2   Insert Iterators

Insert iterators, also called *inserters*, are iterator adapters that transform an assignment of a new value into an insertion of that new value. By using insert iterators, algorithms can insert rather than overwrite. All insert iterators are in the output-iterator category. Thus, they provide only the ability to assign new values (see Section 9.2.1, page 433).

Functionality of Insert Iterators

Usually, an algorithm assigns values to a destination iterator. For example, consider the `copy()` algorithm (described in Section 11.6.1, page 557):

```
namespace std {
    template <typename InputIterator, typename OutputIterator>
    OutputIterator copy (InputIterator from_pos,    // beginning of source
                         InputIterator from_end,    // end of source
                         OutputIterator to_pos)     // beginning of dest.
    {
        while (from_pos != from_end) {
            *to_pos = *from_pos;    // copy values
            ++from_pos;             // increment iterators
            ++to_pos;
        }
        return to_pos;
    }
}
```

The loop runs until the actual position of the source iterator has reached the end. Inside the loop, the source iterator, `from_pos`, is assigned to the destination iterator, `to_pos`, and both iterators get incremented.

The interesting part is the assignment of the new value:

`*to_pos = ` *value*

An insert iterator transforms such an assignment into an insertion. However, two operations are involved: First, operator `*` returns the current element of the iterator; second, operator `=` assigns the new value. Implementations of insert iterators usually use the following two-step trick:

1. Operator `*` is implemented as a no-op that simply returns `*this`. Thus, for insert iterators, `*pos` is equivalent to `pos`.
2. The assignment operator is implemented so that it gets transferred into an insertion. In fact, the insert iterator calls the `push_back()`, `push_front()`, or `insert()` member function of the container.

Thus, for insert iterators, you could write pos=*value* instead of *pos=*value* to insert a new value. However, I'm talking about implementation details of input iterators. The correct expression to assign a new value is *pos=*value*.

Similarly, the increment operator is implemented as a no-op that simply returns `*this`. Thus, you can't modify the position of an insert iterator. Table 9.7 lists all operations of insert iterators.

Expression	Effect
iter	No-op (returns *iter*)
iter = *value*	Inserts *value*
++*iter*	No-op (returns *iter*)
iter++	No-op (returns *iter*)

Table 9.7. Operations of Insert Iterators

Kinds of Insert Iterators

The C++ standard library provides three kinds of insert iterators: back inserters, front inserters, and general inserters. They differ in their handling of the position at which to insert a value. In fact, each uses a different member function, which it calls for the container to which it belongs. Thus, an insert iterator must be always initialized with its container.

Each kind of insert iterator has a convenience function for its creation and initialization. Table 9.8 lists the kinds of insert iterators and their abilities.

Name	Class	Called Function	Creation
Back inserter	`back_insert_iterator`	push_back(*value*)	`back_inserter`(*cont*)
Front inserter	`front_insert_iterator`	push_front(*value*)	`front_inserter`(*cont*)
General inserter	`insert_iterator`	insert(*pos*,*value*)	`inserter`(*cont*,*pos*)

Table 9.8. Kinds of Insert Iterators

Of course, the container must provide the member function that the insert iterator calls; otherwise, that kind of insert iterator can't be used. For this reason, back inserters are available only for vectors, deques, lists, and strings; front inserters are available only for deques and lists.

Back Inserters

A *back inserter*, or *back insert iterator*, appends a value at the end of a container by calling the push_back() member function (see Section 8.7.1, page 415, for details about push_back()). push_back() is available only for vectors, deques, lists, and strings, so these are the only containers in the C++ standard library for which back inserters are usable.

A back inserter must be initialized with its container at creation time. The back_inserter() function provides a convenient way of doing this. The following example demonstrates the use of back inserters:

```
// iter/backinserter1.cpp

#include <vector>
#include <algorithm>
#include <iterator>
#include "print.hpp"
using namespace std;
```

```
int main()
{
    vector<int> coll;

    // create back inserter for coll
    // - inconvenient way
    back_insert_iterator<vector<int> > iter(coll);

    // insert elements with the usual iterator interface
    *iter = 1;
    iter++;
    *iter = 2;
    iter++;
    *iter = 3;
    PRINT_ELEMENTS(coll);

    // create back inserter and insert elements
    // - convenient way
    back_inserter(coll) = 44;
    back_inserter(coll) = 55;
    PRINT_ELEMENTS(coll);

    // use back inserter to append all elements again
    // - reserve enough memory to avoid reallocation
    coll.reserve(2*coll.size());
    copy (coll.begin(), coll.end(),        // source
          back_inserter(coll));            // destination
    PRINT_ELEMENTS(coll);
}
```

The output of the program is as follows:

```
1 2 3
1 2 3 44 55
1 2 3 44 55 1 2 3 44 55
```

Note that you must not forget to reserve enough space before calling copy(). The reason is that the back inserter inserts elements, which might invalidate all other iterators referring to the same vector. Thus, if not enough space is reserved, the algorithm invalidates the passed source iterators while running.

Strings also provide an STL container interface, including push_back(). Therefore, you could use back inserters to append characters in a string. See Section 13.2.14, page 688, for an example.

Front Inserters

A *front inserter*, or *front insert iterator*, inserts a value at the beginning of a container by calling the push_front() member function (see Section 8.7.1, page 414, for details about push_front()). push_front() is available only for deques, lists, and forward lists, so these are the only containers in the C++ standard library for which front inserters are usable.

A front inserter must be initialized with its container at creation time. The front_inserter() function provides a convenient way of doing this. The following example demonstrates the use of front inserters:

```cpp
// iter/frontinserter1.cpp

#include <list>
#include <algorithm>
#include <iterator>
#include "print.hpp"
using namespace std;

int main()
{
    list<int> coll;

    // create front inserter for coll
    // - inconvenient way
    front_insert_iterator<list<int> > iter(coll);

    // insert elements with the usual iterator interface
    *iter = 1;
    iter++;
    *iter = 2;
    iter++;
    *iter = 3;

    PRINT_ELEMENTS(coll);

    // create front inserter and insert elements
    // - convenient way
    front_inserter(coll) = 44;
    front_inserter(coll) = 55;

    PRINT_ELEMENTS(coll);
```

```
// use front inserter to insert all elements again
copy (coll.begin(), coll.end(),      // source
      front_inserter(coll));         // destination

PRINT_ELEMENTS(coll);
}
```

The output of the program is as follows:

```
3 2 1
55 44 3 2 1
1 2 3 44 55 55 44 3 2 1
```

Note that the front inserter inserts multiple elements in reverse order. This happens because it always inserts the next element in front of the previous one.

General Inserters

A *general inserter*, or *general insert iterator*,[1] is initialized with two values: the container and the position that is used for the insertions. Using both, a general inserter calls the `insert()` member function with the specified position as argument. The `inserter()` function provides a convenient way of creating and initializing a general inserter.

A general inserter is available for all standard containers except arrays and forward lists, because these containers provide the needed `insert()` member function (see Section 8.7.1, page 413). However, for associative and unordered containers, the position is used only as a hint, because the value of the element defines the correct position. See Section 8.7.1, page 413, for details.

After an insertion, the general inserter gets the position of the new inserted element. In particular, the following statements are called:

> *pos* = *container*.`insert`(*pos*, *value*) ;
> ++*pos*;

The assignment of the return value of `insert()` ensures that the iterator's position is always valid. Without the assignment of the new position for deques, vectors, and strings, the general inserter would invalidate itself. The reason is that each insertion does, or at least might, invalidate all iterators that refer to the container.

The following example demonstrates the use of general inserters:

```
// iter/inserter1.cpp

#include <set>
#include <list>
```

---

[1] A general inserter is often simply called an *insert iterator*, or *inserter*. This means that the words *insert iterator* and *inserter* have different meanings: They are a general term for all kinds of insert iterators and are also used as names for a special insert iterator that inserts at a specified position rather than in the front or in the back. To avoid this ambiguity, I use the term *general inserter* in this book.

```cpp
#include <algorithm>
#include <iterator>
#include "print.hpp"
using namespace std;

int main()
{
    set<int> coll;

    // create insert iterator for coll
    // - inconvenient way
    insert_iterator<set<int> > iter(coll,coll.begin());

    // insert elements with the usual iterator interface
    *iter = 1;
    iter++;
    *iter = 2;
    iter++;
    *iter = 3;

    PRINT_ELEMENTS(coll,"set:   ");

    // create inserter and insert elements
    // - convenient way
    inserter(coll,coll.end()) = 44;
    inserter(coll,coll.end()) = 55;

    PRINT_ELEMENTS(coll,"set:   ");

    // use inserter to insert all elements into a list
    list<int> coll2;
    copy (coll.begin(), coll.end(),        // source
          inserter(coll2,coll2.begin()));  // destination

    PRINT_ELEMENTS(coll2,"list: ");

    // use inserter to reinsert all elements into the list before the second element
    copy (coll.begin(), coll.end(),          // source
          inserter(coll2,++coll2.begin()));  // destination

    PRINT_ELEMENTS(coll2,"list: ");
}
```

The output of the program is as follows:

```
set:  1 2 3
set:  1 2 3 44 55
list: 1 2 3 44 55
list: 1 1 2 3 44 55 2 3 44 55
```

The calls of copy() demonstrate that the general inserter maintains the order of the elements. The second call of copy() uses a certain position inside the range that is passed as argument.

A User-Defined Inserter for Associative Containers

As mentioned previously, for associative containers, the position argument of general inserters is used only as a hint. This hint might help to improve speed but also might cause bad performance. For example, if the inserted elements are in reverse order, the hint may slow down programs a bit because the search for the correct insertion point always starts at a wrong position. Thus, a bad hint might even be worse than no hint. This is a good example of the need for supplementation of the C++ standard library. See Section 9.6, page 471, for such an extension.

9.4.3 Stream Iterators

A *stream iterator* is an iterator adapter that allows you to use a stream as a source or destination of algorithms. In particular, an istream iterator can be used to read elements from an input stream, and an ostream iterator can be used to write values to an output stream.

A special form of a stream iterator is a *stream buffer iterator*, which can be used to read from or write to a stream buffer directly. Stream buffer iterators are discussed in Section 15.13.2, page 828.

Ostream Iterators

Ostream iterators write assigned values to an output stream. By using ostream iterators, algorithms can write directly to streams. The implementation of an ostream iterator uses the same concept as the implementation of insert iterators (see Section 9.4.2, page 454). The only difference is that they transform the assignment of a new value into an output operation by using operator <<. Thus, algorithms can write directly to streams by using the usual iterator interface. Table 9.9 lists the operations of ostream iterators.

When the ostream iterator is created, you must pass the output stream on which the values are written. An optional string can be passed, written as a separator between single values. Without the delimiter, the elements directly follow each other.

Ostream iterators are defined for a certain element type T:

```
namespace std {
    template <typename T,
              typename charT = char,
              typename traits = char_traits<charT> >
    class ostream_iterator;
}
```

Expression	**Effect**
`ostream_iterator<`*T*`>(`*ostream*`)`	Creates an ostream iterator for *ostream*
`ostream_iterator<`*T*`>(`*ostream*,*delim*`)`	Creates an ostream iterator for *ostream*, with the string *delim* as the delimiter between the values (note that *delim* has type `const char*`)
*iter	No-op (returns *iter*)
iter = value	Writes *value* to *ostream*: *ostream<<value* (followed by *delim*, if set)
++iter	No-op (returns *iter*)
iter++	No-op (returns *iter*)

Table 9.9. Operations of ostream Iterators

The optional second and third template arguments specify the type of stream that is used (see Section 15.2.1, page 749, for their meaning).[2]

The following example demonstrates the use of ostream iterators:

```
// iter/ostreamiter1.cpp

#include <iostream>
#include <vector>
#include <algorithm>
#include <iterator>
using namespace std;

int main()
{
    // create ostream iterator for stream cout
    // - values are separated by a newline character
    ostream_iterator<int> intWriter(cout,"\n");

    // write elements with the usual iterator interface
    *intWriter = 42;
    intWriter++;
    *intWriter = 77;
    intWriter++;
    *intWriter = -5;

    // create collection with elements from 1 to 9
    vector<int> coll = { 1, 2, 3, 4, 5, 6, 7, 8, 9 };
```

[2] In older systems, the optional template arguments for the stream type are missing.

```
// write all elements without any delimiter
copy (coll.cbegin(), coll.cend(),
      ostream_iterator<int>(cout));
cout << endl;

// write all elements with " < " as delimiter
copy (coll.cbegin(), coll.cend(),
      ostream_iterator<int>(cout," < "));
cout << endl;
}
```

The output of the program is as follows:

```
42
77
-5
123456789
1 < 2 < 3 < 4 < 5 < 6 < 7 < 8 < 9 <
```

Note that the delimiter has type `const char*`. Thus, if you pass an object of type `string`, you must call its member function `c_str()` (see Section 13.3.6, page 700) to get the correct type. For example:

```
string delim;
...
ostream_iterator<int>(cout,delim.c_str());
```

Istream Iterators

Istream iterators are the counterparts of ostream iterators. An istream iterator reads elements from an input stream. By using istream iterators, algorithms can read from streams directly. However, istream iterators are a bit more complicated than ostream iterators (as usual, reading is more complicated than writing).

At creation time, the istream iterator is initialized by the input stream from which it reads. Then, by using the usual interface of input iterators (see Section 9.2.2, page 435), the istream iterator reads element-by-element, using operator `>>`. However, reading might fail (due to end-of-file or an error), and source ranges of algorithms need an "end position." To handle both problems, you can use an *end-of-stream iterator*, which is created with the default constructor for istream iterators. If a read fails, every istream iterator becomes an end-of-stream iterator. Thus, after any read access, you should compare an istream iterator with an end-of-stream iterator to check whether the iterator has a valid value. Table 9.10 lists all operations of istream iterators.

Expression	Effect
istream_iterator<*T*>()	Creates an end-of-stream iterator
istream_iterator<*T*>(*istream*)	Creates an istream iterator for *istream* (and might read the first value)
*iter	Returns the value, read before (reads first value if not done by the constructor)
iter->member	Returns a member, if any, of the actual value, read before
++iter	Reads next value and returns its position
iter++	Reads next value but returns an iterator for the previous value
iter1 == *iter2*	Tests *iter1* and *iter2* for equality
iter1 != *iter2*	Tests *iter1* and *iter2* for inequality

Table 9.10. Operations of istream Iterators

Note that the constructor of an istream iterator opens the stream and usually reads the first element. Otherwise, it could not return the first element when operator * is called after the initialization. However, implementations may defer the first read until the first call of operator *. So, you should not define an istream iterator before you need it.

Istream iterators are defined for a certain element type T:

```
namespace std {
    template <typename T,
              typename charT = char,
              typename traits = char_traits<charT>,
              typename Distance = ptrdiff_t>
    class istream_iterator;
}
```

The optional second and third template arguments specify the type of stream that is used (see Section 15.2.1, page 749, for their meaning). The optional fourth template argument specifies the difference type for the iterators.[3]

Two istream iterators are equal if

- both are end-of-stream iterators and thus can no longer read, or
- both can read and use the same stream.

---

[3] In older systems without default template parameters, the optional fourth template argument is required as the second argument, and the arguments for the stream type are missing.

The following example demonstrates the operations provided for istream iterators:

```
// iter/istreamiter1.cpp

#include <iostream>
#include <iterator>
using namespace std;

int main()
{
    // create istream iterator that reads integers from cin
    istream_iterator<int> intReader(cin);

    // create end-of-stream iterator
    istream_iterator<int> intReaderEOF;

    // while able to read tokens with istream iterator
    // - write them twice
    while (intReader != intReaderEOF) {
        cout << "once:        " << *intReader << endl;
        cout << "once again: " << *intReader << endl;
        ++intReader;
    }
}
```

If you start the program with the following input:

```
1 2 3 f 4
```

the output of the program is as follows:

```
once:        1
once again: 1
once:        2
once again: 2
once:        3
once again: 3
```

As you can see, the input of character f ends the program. Due to a format error, the stream is no longer in a good state. Therefore, the istream iterator intReader is equal to the end-of-stream iterator intReaderEOF. So, the condition of the loop yields false.

Example of Stream Iterators and `advance()`

The following example uses both kinds of stream iterators and the `advance()` helper function:

```cpp
// iter/advance2.cpp

#include <iterator>
#include <iostream>
#include <string>
#include <algorithm>
using namespace std;

int main()
{
    istream_iterator<string> cinPos(cin);
    ostream_iterator<string> coutPos(cout," ");

    // while input is not at the end of the file
    // - write every third string
    while (cinPos != istream_iterator<string>()) {
        // ignore the following two strings
        advance (cinPos, 2);

        // read and write the third string
        if (cinPos != istream_iterator<string>()) {
            *coutPos++ = *cinPos++;
        }
    }
    cout << endl;
}
```

The `advance()` iterator function is provided to advance the iterator to another position (see Section 9.3.1, page 441). Used with istream iterators, `advance()` skips input tokens. For example, if you have the following input:[4]

```
No one objects if you are doing
a good programming job for
someone whom you respect.
```

the output is as follows:

```
objects are good for you
```

---

[4] Thanks to Andrew Koenig for the nice input of this example.

Don't forget to check whether the istream iterator is still valid after calling advance() and before accessing its value with *cinPos. Calling operator * for an end-of-stream iterator results in undefined behavior.

For other examples that demonstrate how algorithms use stream iterators to read from and write to streams, see Section 6.5.2, page 212; Section 11.6.1, page 560; and Section 11.7.2, page 582.

9.4.4 Move Iterators

Since C++11, an iterator adapter is provided that converts any access to the underlying element into a move operation. For example:

```
std::list<std::string> s;
...
std::vector<string> v1(s.begin(), s.end());              // copy strings into v1

std::vector<string> v2(make_move_iterator(s.begin()),   // move strings into v2
                       make_move_iterator(s.end()));
```

One application of these iterators is to let algorithms move instead of copy elements from one range into another. However, note that in general, the move() algorithm also does that (see Section 11.6.2, page 561).

In general, using a move iterator in algorithms only makes sense when the algorithm transfers elements of a source range to a destination range. In addition, you have to ensure that each element is accessed only once. Otherwise, the contents would be moved more than once, which would result in undefined behavior.

Note that the only iterator category that guarantees that elements are read or processed only once is the input iterator category (see Section 9.2.2, page 435). Thus, using move iterators usually makes sense only when an algorithm has a source where the input iterator category is required and a destination that uses the output iterator category. The only exception is for_each(), which can be used to process the moved elements of the passed range (for example, to move them into a new container).

9.5 Iterator Traits

The various iterator categories (see Section 9.2, page 433) represent special iterator abilities. It might be useful or even necessary to be able to overload behavior for different iterator categories. By using iterator tags and iterator traits (both provided in <iterator>), such an overloading can be performed.

For each iterator category, the C++ standard library provides an *iterator tag* that can be used as a "label" for iterators:

```
namespace std {
    struct output_iterator_tag {
    };
    struct input_iterator_tag {
    };
    struct forward_iterator_tag
      : public input_iterator_tag {
    };
    struct bidirectional_iterator_tag
      : public forward_iterator_tag {
    };
    struct random_access_iterator_tag
      : public bidirectional_iterator_tag {
    };
}
```

Note that inheritance is used. So, for example, any forward iterator *is a* kind of input iterator. However, note that the tag for forward iterators is derived only from the tag for input iterators, not from the tag for output iterators. Thus, any forward iterator *is not a* kind of output iterator. Only a *mutable* forward iterator also fulfills the requirements of output iterators (see Section 9.2, page 433), but no specific category exists for this.

If you write generic code, you might not be interested only in the iterator category. For example, you may need the type of the elements to which the iterator refers. Therefore, the C++ standard library provides a special template structure to define the *iterator traits*. This structure contains all relevant information about an iterator and is used as a common interface for all the type definitions an iterator should have (the category, the type of the elements, and so on):

```
namespace std {
    template <typename T>
    struct iterator_traits {
        typedef typename T::iterator_category  iterator_category;
        typedef typename T::value_type         value_type;
        typedef typename T::difference_type    difference_type;
        typedef typename T::pointer            pointer;
        typedef typename T::reference          reference;
    };
}
```

In this template, T stands for the type of the iterator. Thus, you can write code that, for any iterator, uses its category, the type of its elements, and so on. For example, the following expression yields the value type of iterator type T:

```
typename std::iterator_traits<T>::value_type
```

This structure has two advantages:

1. It ensures that an iterator provides all type definitions.
2. It can be (partially) specialized for (sets of) special iterators.

The latter is done for ordinary pointers that also can be used as iterators:

```
namespace std {
    template <typename T>
    struct iterator_traits<T*> {
        typedef T                             value_type;
        typedef ptrdiff_t                     difference_type;
        typedef random_access_iterator_tag    iterator_category;
        typedef T*                            pointer;
        typedef T&                            reference;
    };
}
```

Thus, for any type "pointer to T," it is defined as having the random-access iterator category. A corresponding partial specialization exists for constant pointers (const T*).

Note that output iterators can be used only to write something. Thus, in the case of an output iterator, value_type, difference_type, pointer, and reference may be defined as void.

9.5.1 Writing Generic Functions for Iterators

Using iterator traits, you can write generic functions that derive type definitions or use different implementation code depending on the iterator category.

Using Iterator Types

A simple example of the use of iterator traits is an algorithm that needs a temporary variable for the elements. Such a temporary value is declared simply like this:

```
typename std::iterator_traits<T>::value_type tmp;
```

where T is the type of the iterator.

Another example is an algorithm that shifts elements cyclically:

```
template <typename ForwardIterator>
void shift_left (ForwardIterator beg, ForwardIterator end)
{
    // temporary variable for first element
    typedef typename
      std::iterator_traits<ForwardIterator>::value_type value_type;

    if (beg != end) {
        // save value of first element
        value_type tmp(*beg);

        // shift following values
        ...
    }
}
```

Using Iterator Categories

To use different implementations for different iterator categories you must follow these two steps:

1. Let your function template call another function with the iterator category as an additional argument. For example:

```
template <typename Iterator>
inline void foo (Iterator beg, Iterator end)
{
    foo (beg, end,
         std::iterator_traits<Iterator>::iterator_category());
}
```

2. Implement that other function for any iterator category that provides a special implementation that is not derived from another iterator category. For example:

```
// foo() for bidirectional iterators
template <typename BiIterator>
void foo (BiIterator beg, BiIterator end,
          std::bidirectional_iterator_tag)
{
    ...
}
```

```
// foo() for random-access iterators
template <typename RaIterator>
void foo (RaIterator beg, RaIterator end,
          std::random_access_iterator_tag)
{
    ...
}
```

The version for random-access iterators could, for example, use random-access operations, whereas the version for bidirectional iterators would not. Due to the hierarchy of iterator tags (see Section 9.5, page 466), you could provide one implementation for more than one iterator category.

Implementation of `distance()`

An example of following those two steps is the implementation of the auxiliary `distance()` iterator function, which returns the distance between two iterator positions and their elements (see Section 9.3.3, page 445). The implementation for random-access iterators uses only the operator –. For all other iterator categories, the number of increments to reach the end of the range is returned:

```
// general distance()
template <typename Iterator>
typename std::iterator_traits<Iterator>::difference_type
distance (Iterator pos1, Iterator pos2)
{
    return distance (pos1, pos2,
                     std::iterator_traits<Iterator>
                          ::iterator_category());
}


// distance() for random-access iterators
template <typename RaIterator>
typename std::iterator_traits<RaIterator>::difference_type
distance (RaIterator pos1, RaIterator pos2,
          std::random_access_iterator_tag)
{
    return pos2 - pos1;
}


// distance() for input, forward, and bidirectional iterators
template <typename InIterator>
typename std::iterator_traits<InIterator>::difference_type
distance (InIterator pos1, InIterator pos2,
          std::input_iterator_tag)
{
    typename std::iterator_traits<InIterator>::difference_type d;
    for (d=0; pos1 != pos2; ++pos1, ++d) {
        ;
    }
    return d;
}
```

The difference type of the iterator is used as the return type. Note that the second version uses the tag for input iterators, so this implementation is also used by forward and bidirectional iterators because their tags are derived from `input_iterator_tag`.

9.6 Writing User-Defined Iterators

Let's write an iterator. As mentioned in the previous section, you need iterator traits provided for the user-defined iterator. You can provide them in one of two ways:

1. Provide the necessary five type definitions for the general `iterator_traits` structure (see Section 9.5, page 467).

2. Provide a (partial) specialization of the `iterator_traits` structure.

For the first way, the C++ standard library provides a special base class, `iterator<>`, that does the type definitions. You need only pass the types:

```
class MyIterator
  : public std::iterator <std::bidirectional_iterator_tag,
                          type, std::ptrdiff_t, type*, type&> {
    ...
};
```

The first template parameter defines the iterator category, the second defines the element type *type*, the third defines the difference type, the fourth defines the pointer type, and the fifth defines the reference type. The last three arguments are optional and have the default values `ptrdiff_t`, *type**, and *type&*. Thus, often it is enough to use the following definition:

```
class MyIterator
  : public std::iterator <std::bidirectional_iterator_tag, type> {
    ...
};
```

The following example demonstrates how to write a user-defined iterator. It is an insert iterator for associative and unordered containers. Unlike insert iterators of the C++ standard library (see Section 9.4.2, page 454), no insert position is used.

Here is the implementation of the iterator class:

```
// iter/assoiter.hpp

#include <iterator>

// class template for insert iterator for associative and unordered containers
template <typename Container>
class asso_insert_iterator
  : public std::iterator <std::output_iterator_tag,
                          typename Container::value_type>
{
  protected:
    Container& container;      // container in which elements are inserted

  public:
    // constructor
    explicit asso_insert_iterator (Container& c) : container(c) {
    }
```

```cpp
    // assignment operator
    // - inserts a value into the container
    asso_insert_iterator<Container>&
    operator= (const typename Container::value_type& value) {
        container.insert(value);
        return *this;
    }


    // dereferencing is a no-op that returns the iterator itself
    asso_insert_iterator<Container>& operator* () {
        return *this;
    }


    // increment operation is a no-op that returns the iterator itself
    asso_insert_iterator<Container>& operator++ () {
        return *this;
    }
    asso_insert_iterator<Container>& operator++ (int) {
        return *this;
    }
};


// convenience function to create the inserter
template <typename Container>
inline asso_insert_iterator<Container> asso_inserter (Container& c)
{
    return asso_insert_iterator<Container>(c);
}
```

The asso_insert_iterator class is derived from the iterator class, where corresponding types are defined. The first template argument passed is output_iterator_tag to specify the iterator category. The second argument is the type of the values the iterator refers to, which is the value_type of the container. Because output iterators can be used only to write something, this type definition is not necessary, so you can pass void here. However, passing the value type as demonstrated here works for any iterator category.

At creation time the iterator stores its container in its container member. Any value that gets assigned is inserted into the container by insert(). Operators * and ++ are no-ops that simply return the iterator itself. Thus, the iterator maintains control. If the usual iterator interface

```cpp
    *pos = value
```

is used, the *pos expression returns *this, to which the new value is assigned. That assignment is transferred into a call of insert(value) for the container.

After the definition of the inserter class, the usual convenient function `asso_inserter` is defined as a convenience function to create and initialize an inserter. The following program uses such an inserter to insert some elements into an unordered set:

```cpp
// iter/assoiter1.cpp

#include <iostream>
#include <unordered_set>
#include <vector>
#include <algorithm>
#include "print.hpp"
#include "assoiter.hpp"

int main()
{
    std::unordered_set<int> coll;

    // create inserter for coll
    // - inconvenient way
    asso_insert_iterator<decltype(coll)> iter(coll);

    // insert elements with the usual iterator interface
    *iter = 1;
    iter++;
    *iter = 2;
    iter++;
    *iter = 3;

    PRINT_ELEMENTS(coll);

    // create inserter for coll and insert elements
    // - convenient way
    asso_inserter(coll) = 44;
    asso_inserter(coll) = 55;

    PRINT_ELEMENTS(coll);

    // use inserter with an algorithm
    std::vector<int> vals = { 33, 67, -4, 13, 5, 2 };
    std::copy (vals.begin(), vals.end(),        // source
               asso_inserter(coll));            // destination

    PRINT_ELEMENTS(coll);
}
```

The normal application of the `asso_inserter` demonstrates the `copy()` call:

```
std::copy (vals.begin(), vals.end(),        // source
           asso_inserter(coll));            // destination
```

Here, `asso_inserter(coll)` creates an inserter that inserts any argument passed into `coll`, calling `coll.insert(val)`.

The other statements demonstrate the behavior of the inserter in detail. The output of the program is as follows:

```
1 2 3
55 44 1 2 3
-4 33 55 44 67 1 13 2 3 5
```

Note that this iterator could also be used by associative containers. Thus, if you replace `unordered_set` by `set` in both the include directive and the declaration of `coll`, the program would still work (although the elements in the container would be sorted then).

Chapter 10

STL Function Objects and Using Lambdas

This chapter discusses in detail the features to pass specific functionality to algorithms and member functions, *function objects*, or *functors* for short (introduced in Section 6.10, page 233). It covers the full set of predefined function objects and function adapters and binders and the concept of functional composition, provides examples of self-written function objects, and presents details about the application of lambdas (introduced in Section 3.1.10, page 28, and Section 6.9, page 229).

As a consequence, you will learn details and surprising behavior of the algorithms `remove_if()` and `for_each()`.

10.1   The Concept of Function Objects

A function object, or *functor*, is an object that has operator () defined so that in the following example

   FunctionObjectType `fo;`

   ...

   `fo(...);`

the expression `fo()` is a call of operator () for the function object `fo` instead of a call of the function `fo()`. At first, you could consider a function object as an ordinary function that is written in a more complicated way. Instead of writing all the function statements inside the function body:

```
void fo() {
     statements
}
```

you write them inside the body of operator () of the function object class:

```
class FunctionObjectType {
  public:
    void operator() () {
        statements
    }
};
```

This kind of definition is more complicated but has three important advantages:

1. A function object might be smarter because it may have a state (associated members that influence the behavior of the function object). In fact, you can have two instances of the same function object class, which may have different states at the same time. This is not possible for ordinary functions.

2. Each function object has its own type. Thus, you can pass the type of a function object to a template to specify a certain behavior, and you have the advantage that container types with different function objects differ.

3. A function object is usually faster than a function pointer.

See Section 6.10.1, page 235, for more details about these advantages and an example that shows how function objects can be smarter than ordinary functions.

In the next two subsections, I present two other examples that go into more detail about function objects. The first example demonstrates how to benefit from the fact that each function object usually has its own type. The second example demonstrates how to benefit from the state of function objects and leads to an interesting property of the `for_each()` algorithm, which is covered in Section 10.1.3, page 482.

10.1.1   Function Objects as Sorting Criteria

Programmers often need a sorted collection of elements that have a special class (for example, a collection of Persons). However, you either don't want to or can't use the usual operator < to sort the objects. Instead, you sort the objects according to a special sorting criterion based on some member function. In this regard, a function object can help. Consider the following example:

```
// fo/sort1.cpp

#include <iostream>
#include <string>
#include <set>
#include <algorithm>
using namespace std;

class Person {
  public:
    string firstname() const;
    string lastname() const;
    ...
};
```

```cpp
// class for function predicate
// - operator () returns whether a person is less than another person
class PersonSortCriterion {
  public:
    bool operator() (const Person& p1, const Person& p2) const {
        // a person is less than another person
        // - if the last name is less
        // - if the last name is equal and the first name is less
        return p1.lastname()<p2.lastname() ||
               (p1.lastname()==p2.lastname() &&
                p1.firstname()<p2.firstname());
    }
};

int main()
{
    // create a set with special sorting criterion
    set<Person,PersonSortCriterion> coll;
    ...

    // do something with the elements
    for (auto pos = coll.begin(); pos != coll.end(); ++pos) {
        ...
    }
    ...
}
```

The set `coll` uses the special sorting criterion `PersonSortCriterion`, which is defined as a function object class. `PersonSortCriterion` defines operator () in such a way that it compares two Persons according to their last names and, if they are equal, to their first names. The constructor of `coll` creates an instance of class `PersonSortCriterion` automatically so that the elements are sorted according to this sorting criterion.

Note that the sorting criterion `PersonSortCriterion` is a *type*. Thus, you can use it as a template argument for the set. This would not be possible if you implement the sorting criterion as a plain function (as was done in Section 6.8.2, page 228).

All sets with this sorting criterion have their own type. You can't combine or assign a set that has a "normal" or another user-defined sorting criterion. Thus, you can't compromise the automatic sorting of the set by any operation; however, you can design function objects that represent different sorting criteria with the same type (see Section 7.8.6, page 351).

10.1.2   Function Objects with Internal State

The following example shows how function objects can be used to behave as a function that may
have more than one state at the same time:

```cpp
// fo/sequence1.cpp

#include <iostream>
#include <list>
#include <algorithm>
#include <iterator>
#include "print.hpp"
using namespace std;

class IntSequence {
  private:
    int value;
  public:
    IntSequence (int initialValue)    // constructor
     : value(initialValue) {
    }

    int operator() () {               // "function call"
        return ++value;
    }
};

int main()
{
    list<int> coll;

    // insert values from 1 to 9
    generate_n (back_inserter(coll),  // start
                9,                     // number of elements
                IntSequence(1));       // generates values, starting with 1

    PRINT_ELEMENTS(coll);

    // replace second to last element but one with values starting at 42
    generate (next(coll.begin()),      // start
              prev(coll.end()),        // end
              IntSequence(42));        // generates values, starting with 42

    PRINT_ELEMENTS(coll);
}
```

In this example, the function object `IntSequence` generates a sequence of integral values. Each time operator `()` is called, it returns its actual value and increments it. You can pass the start value as a constructor argument.

Two such function objects are then used by the `generate()` and `generate_n()` algorithms, which use generated values to write them into a collection: The expression

```
IntSequence(1)
```

in the statement

```
generate_n (back_inserter(coll),
            9,
            IntSequence(1));
```

creates such a function object initialized with 1. The `generate_n()` algorithm uses it nine times to write an element, so it generates values 1 to 9. Similarly, the expression

```
IntSequence(42)
```

generates a sequence beginning with value 42. The `generate()` algorithm replaces the elements beginning with the second up to the last but one.[1] The output of the program is as follows:

```
2 3 4 5 6 7 8 9 10
2 43 44 45 46 47 48 49 10
```

Using other versions of operator `()`, you can easily produce more complicated sequences.

By default, function objects are passed by value rather than by reference. Thus, the algorithm does not change the state of the function object. For example, the following code generates the sequence starting with value 1 twice:

```
IntSequence seq(1);     // integral sequence starting with value 1

// insert sequence beginning with 1
generate_n (back_inserter(coll), 9, seq);

// insert sequence beginning with 1 again
generate_n (back_inserter(coll), 9, seq);
```

Passing function objects by value instead of by reference has the advantage that you can pass constant and temporary expressions. Otherwise, passing `IntSequence(1)` would not be possible.

The disadvantage of passing the function object by value is that you can't benefit from modifications of the state of the function objects. Algorithms can modify the state of the function objects, but you can't access and process their final states, because they make internal copies of the function objects. However, access to the final state might be necessary, so the question is how to get a "result" from an algorithm.

There are three ways to get a "result" or "feedback" from function objects passed to algorithms:

---

[1] `std::next()` and `std::prev()` are provided since C++11 (see Section 9.3.2, page 443). Note that using `++coll.begin()` and `--coll.end()` might not always compile (see Section 9.2.6, page 440).

1. You can keep the state externally and let the function object refer to it.
2. You can pass the function objects by reference.
3. You can use the return value of the `for_each()` algorithm.

The last option is discussed in the next subsection.

    To pass a function object by reference, you simply have to qualify the call of the algorithm so that the function object type is a reference.[2] For example:

```cpp
// fo/sequence2.cpp

#include <iostream>
#include <list>
#include <algorithm>
#include <iterator>
#include "print.hpp"
using namespace std;

class IntSequence {
  private:
    int value;
  public:
    // constructor
    IntSequence (int initialValue)
     : value(initialValue) {
    }

    // ''function call''
    int operator() () {
        return ++value;
    }
};

int main()
{
    list<int> coll;
    IntSequence seq(1);        // integral sequence starting with 1

    // insert values from 1 to 4
    // - pass function object by reference
    //   so that it will continue with 5
    generate_n<back_insert_iterator<list<int>>,
               int, IntSequence&>(back_inserter(coll),     // start
                                  4,          // number of elements
```

---

[2] Thanks to Philip Köster for pointing this out.

```
                                       seq);      // generates values
        PRINT_ELEMENTS(coll);

        // insert values from 42 to 45
        generate_n (back_inserter(coll),     // start
                    4,                        // number of elements
                    IntSequence(42));         // generates values
        PRINT_ELEMENTS(coll);

        // continue with first sequence
        // - pass function object by value
        //   so that it will continue with 5 again
        generate_n (back_inserter(coll),     // start
                    4,                        // number of elements
                    seq);                     // generates values
        PRINT_ELEMENTS(coll);

        // continue with first sequence again
        generate_n (back_inserter(coll),     // start
                    4,                        // number of elements
                    seq);                     // generates values
        PRINT_ELEMENTS(coll);
    }
```

The program has the following output:

```
    2 3 4 5
    2 3 4 5 43 44 45 46
    2 3 4 5 43 44 45 46 6 7 8 9
    2 3 4 5 43 44 45 46 6 7 8 9 6 7 8 9
```

In the first call of generate_n(), the function object seq is passed by reference. To do this, the template arguments are qualified explicitly:

```
    generate_n<back_insert_iterator<list<int>>,
               int, IntSequence&>(back_inserter(coll),     // start
                                  4,                        // number of elements
                                  seq);                     // generates values
```

As a result, the internal value of seq is modified after the call, and the second use of seq by the third call of generate_n() continues the sequence of the first call. However, this call passes seq by value:

```
    generate_n (back_inserter(coll),     // start
                4,                        // number of elements
                seq);                     // generates values
```

Thus, the call does not change the state of seq. As a result, the last call of generate_n() continues the sequence with value 5 again.

10.1.3   The Return Value of `for_each()`

The effort involved with passing a function object by reference in order to access its final state is not necessary if you use the `for_each()` algorithm. `for_each()` has the unique ability to return its function object (no other algorithm can do this). Thus, you can query the state of your function object by checking the return value of `for_each()`.

The following program is a nice example of the use of the return value of `for_each()`. It shows how to process the mean value of a sequence:

```cpp
// fo/foreach3.cpp

#include <iostream>
#include <vector>
#include <algorithm>
using namespace std;

// function object to process the mean value
class MeanValue {
  private:
    long num;      // number of elements
    long sum;      // sum of all element values
  public:
    // constructor
    MeanValue () : num(0), sum(0) {
    }

    // "function call"
    // - process one more element of the sequence
    void operator() (int elem) {
        ++num;            // increment count
        sum += elem;      // add value
    }

    // return mean value
    double value () {
        return static_cast<double>(sum) / static_cast<double>(num);
    }
};

int main()
{
    vector<int> coll = { 1, 2, 3, 4, 5, 6, 7, 8 };
```

```
                // process and print mean value
                MeanValue mv = for_each (coll.begin(), coll.end(),   // range
                                         MeanValue());               // operation
                cout << "mean value: " << mv.value() << endl;
            }
```

The expression

```
    MeanValue()
```

creates a function object that counts the number of elements and processes the sum of all element values. By passing the function object to `for_each()`, it is called for each element of the container `coll`:

```
    MeanValue mv = for_each (coll.begin(), coll.end(),
                             MeanValue());
```

The function object is returned and assigned to `mv`, so you can query its state after the statement by calling: `mv.value()`. Therefore, the program has the following output:

```
    mean value: 4.5
```

You could even make the class `MeanValue` a bit smarter by defining an automatic type conversion to `double`. You could then use the mean value that is processed by `for_each()` directly. See Section 11.4, page 522, for such an example.

Note that lambdas provide a more convenient way to specify this behavior (see Section 10.3.2, page 500, for a corresponding example). However, that does not mean that lambdas are always better than function objects. Function objects are more convenient when their type is required, such as for a declaration of a hash function, sorting, or equivalence criterion of associative or unordered containers. The fact that a function object is usually globally introduced helps to provide them in header files or libraries, whereas lambdas are better for specific behavior specified locally.

10.1.4   Predicates versus Function Objects

Predicates are functions or function objects that return a Boolean value (a value that is convertible into `bool`). However, not every function that returns a Boolean value is a valid predicate for the STL. This may lead to surprising behavior. Consider the following example:

```
    // fo/removeif1.cpp

    #include <iostream>
    #include <list>
    #include <algorithm>
    #include "print.hpp"
    using namespace std;
```

```
class Nth {        // function object that returns true for the nth call
  private:
    int nth;         // call for which to return true
    int count;       // call counter
  public:
    Nth (int n) : nth(n), count(0) {
    }
    bool operator() (int) {
        return ++count == nth;
    }
};

int main()
{
    list<int> coll = { 1, 2, 3, 4, 5, 6, 7, 8, 9, 10 };
    PRINT_ELEMENTS(coll,"coll:          ");

    // remove third element
    list<int>::iterator pos;
    pos = remove_if(coll.begin(),coll.end(),    // range
                    Nth(3));                     // remove criterion
    coll.erase(pos,coll.end());

    PRINT_ELEMENTS(coll,"3rd removed: ");
}
```

This program defines a function object Nth that yields true for the *n*th call. However, when passing it to remove_if(), an algorithm that removes all elements for which a unary predicate yields true (see Section 11.7.1, page 575), the result is a big surprise:[3]

```
coll:          1 2 3 4 5 6 7 8 9 10
3rd removed: 1 2 4 5 7 8 9 10
```

Two elements, the third and sixth elements, are removed. This happens because the usual implementation of the algorithm copies the predicate internally during the algorithm:

```
template <typename ForwIter, typename Predicate>
ForwIter std::remove_if(ForwIter beg, ForwIter end,
                        Predicate op)
{
    beg = find_if(beg, end, op);
```

---

[3] At least this is the output of gcc 4.5 and Visual C++ 2010, but other platforms might result in a different output; see the following discussion.

```
        if (beg == end) {
            return beg;
        }
        else {
            ForwIter next = beg;
            return remove_copy_if(++next, end, beg, op);
        }
    }
```

The algorithm uses `find_if()` to find the first element that should be removed. However, the algorithm then uses a copy of the passed predicate op to process the remaining elements, if any. Here, `Nth` in its original state is used again and also removes the third element of the remaining elements, which is in fact the sixth element.

This behavior is not a bug. The standard does not specify how often a predicate might be copied internally by an algorithm. Thus, to get the guaranteed behavior of the C++ standard library, you should not pass a function object for which the behavior depends on how often it is copied or called. Thus, if you call a unary predicate for two arguments and both arguments are equal, the predicate should always yield the same result.

In other words: **A predicate should always be stateless**. That is, a predicate should not change its state due to a call, and a copy of a predicate should have the same state as the original. To ensure that you can't change the state of a predicate due to a function call, you should declare operator () as a constant member function.

It is possible to avoid this surprising behavior and to guarantee that this algorithm works as expected even for a function object such as `Nth`, without any performance penalties. You could implement `remove_if()` in such a way that the call of `find_if()` is replaced by its contents:

```
    template <typename ForwIter, typename Predicate>
    ForwIter std::remove_if(ForwIter beg, ForwIter end,
                            Predicate op)
    {
        while (beg != end && !op(*beg)) {
            ++beg;
        }
        if (beg == end) {
            return beg;
        }
        else {
            ForwIter next = beg;
            return remove_copy_if(++next, end, beg, op);
        }
    }
```

So, it might be a good idea to change the implementation of `remove_if()` or submit a change request to the implementer of the library. To my knowledge, this problem arises in current implementations only with the `remove_if()` algorithm. If you use `remove_copy_if()`, all works as expected. (Whether the C++ standard library should guarantee the expected behavior in cases such as those presented in this example was under discussion but never changed.) However, for portability, you should never rely on this implementation detail. You should always declare the function call operator of predicates as being a constant member function.

Note that with lambdas, you can share the state among all copies of the function object, so this problem doesn't apply. See Section 10.3.2, page 501, for details.

10.2   Predefined Function Objects and Binders

As mentioned in Section 6.10.2, page 239, the C++ standard library provides many predefined function objects and binders that allow you to compose them into more sophisticated function objects. This ability, called *functional composition*, requires fundamental function objects and adapters, which are both presented here. To use these function objects and binders, you must include the header file `<functional>`:

```
#include <functional>
```

10.2.1   Predefined Function Objects

Table 10.1 lists all predefined function objects (`bit_and`, `bit_or`, and `bit_xor` are available since C++11).

Expression	Effect
negate<*type*>()	– *param*
plus<*type*>()	*param1* + *param2*
minus<*type*>()	*param1* – *param2*
multiplies<*type*>()	*param1* * *param2*
divides<*type*>()	*param1* / *param2*
modulus<*type*>()	*param1* % *param2*
equal_to<*type*>()	*param1* == *param2*
not_equal_to<*type*>()	*param1* != *param2*
less<*type*>()	*param1* < *param2*
greater<*type*>()	*param1* > *param2*
less_equal<*type*>()	*param1* <= *param2*
greater_equal<*type*>()	*param1* >= *param2*
logical_not<*type*>()	! *param*
logical_and<*type*>()	*param1* && *param2*
logical_or<*type*>()	*param1* || *param2*
bit_and<*type*>()	*param1* & *param2*
bit_or<*type*>()	*param1* | *param2*
bit_xor<*type*>()	*param1* ^ *param2*

Table 10.1. Predefined Function Objects

less<> is the default criterion whenever objects are sorted or compared by sorting functions and associative containers. Thus, default sorting operations always produce an ascending order (*element* < *nextElement*). equal_to<> is the default equivalence criterion for unordered containers.

To compare internationalized strings, the C++ standard library provides the ability to use locale objects as function objects so that they can be used as a sorting criterion for strings (see Section 16.3, page 868, for details).

10.2.2 Function Adapters and Binders

A function adapter is a function object that enables the composition of function objects with each other, with certain values, or with special functions (according to the composite pattern in [*GoF:DesignPatterns*]). However, over time, the way function objects are composed changed. In fact, all such features that were provided for C++98 are deprecated since C++11, which introduced more convenient and more flexible adapters. Here, I first present the current way to compose function objects. In Section 10.2.4, page 497, I give a very brief overview of the deprecated features.

Table 10.2 lists the function adapters provided by the C++ standard library since C++11.

Expression	Effect
bind(*op*,*args...*)	Binds *args* to *op*
mem_fn(*op*)	Calls *op*() as a member function for an object or pointer to object
not1(*op*)	Unary negation: !*op*(*param*)
not2(*op*)	Binary negation: !*op*(*param1*,*param2*)

Table 10.2. Predefined Function Adapters

The most important adapter is bind(). It allows you to:

- Adapt and compose new function objects out of existing or predefined function objects
- Call global functions
- Call member functions for objects, pointers to objects, and smart pointers to objects

The bind() Adapter

In general, bind() binds parameters for *callable objects* (see Section 4.4, page 54). Thus, if a function, member function, function object, or lambda requires some parameters, you can bind them to specific or passed arguments. Specific arguments you simply name. For passed arguments, you can use the predefined *placeholders* _1, _2, ... defined in namespace std::placeholders.

A typical application of binders is to specify parameters when using the predefined function objects provided by the C++ standard library (see Section 10.2.1, page 486). For example:

```cpp
// fo/bind1.cpp

#include <functional>
#include <iostream>

int main()
{
    auto plus10 = std::bind(std::plus<int>(),
                            std::placeholders::_1,
                            10);
    std::cout << "+10:    " << plus10(7) << std::endl;

    auto plus10times2 = std::bind(std::multiplies<int>(),
                                  std::bind(std::plus<int>(),
                                            std::placeholders::_1,
                                            10),
                                  2);
    std::cout << "+10 *2: " << plus10times2(7) << std::endl;

    auto pow3 = std::bind(std::multiplies<int>(),
                          std::bind(std::multiplies<int>(),
                                    std::placeholders::_1,
                                    std::placeholders::_1),
                          std::placeholders::_1);
    std::cout << "x*x*x:  " << pow3(7) << std::endl;

    auto inversDivide = std::bind(std::divides<double>(),
                                  std::placeholders::_2,
                                  std::placeholders::_1);
    std::cout << "invdiv: " << inversDivide(49,7) << std::endl;
}
```

Here, four different binders that represent function objects are defined. For example, plus10, defined as

```cpp
std::bind(std::plus<int>(),
          std::placeholders::_1,
          10)
```

represents a function object, which internally calls plus<> (i.e., operator +), with a placeholder _1
as first parameter/operand and 10 as second parameter/operand. The placeholder _1 represents the
first argument passed to the expression as a whole. Thus, for any argument passed to this expression,
this function object yields the value of that argument +10.

    To avoid the tedious repetition of the namespace placeholders, you can use a corresponding
using directive. Thus, with two using directives, you condense the whole statement:

```
using namespace std;
using namespace std::placeholders;
```

```
bind (plus<int>(), _1, 10)        // param1+10
```

The binder can also be called directly. For example,

```
std::cout << std::bind(std::plus<int>(),_1,10)(32) << std::endl;
```

will write 42 to standard output and, if you pass this function object to an algorithm, the algorithm can apply it to every element the algorithms operates with. For example:

```
// add 10 to each element
std::transform (coll.begin(), coll.end(),        // source
                coll.begin(),                    // destination
                std::bind(std::plus<int>(),_1,10)); // operation
```

In the same way, you can define a binder that represents a sorting criterion. For example, to find the first element that is greater than 42, you bind `greater<>` with the passed argument as first and 42 as second operator:

```
// find first element >42
auto pos = std::find_if (coll.begin(),coll.end(),
                std::bind(std::greater<int>(),_1,42))
```

Note that you always have to specify the argument type of the predefined function object used. If the type doesn't match, a type conversion is forced, or the expression results in a compile-time error.

The remaining statements in this example program demonstrate that you can nest binders to compose even more complicated function objects. For example, the following expression defines a function object that adds 10 to the passed argument and then multiplies it by 2 (namespaces omitted):

```
bind(multiplies<int>(),                  // (param1+10)*2
        bind(plus<int>(),_1,
                10),
        2);
```

As you can see, the expressions are evaluated from the inside to the outside.

Similarly, we can raise a value to the power of 3 by combining two `multiplies<>` objects with three placeholders for the argument passed:

```
bind(multiplies<int>(),                  // (param1*param1)*param1
        bind(multiplies<int>(),_1,
                _1),
        _1);
```

The final expression defines a function object, where the arguments for a division are swapped. Thus, it divides the second argument by the first argument:

```
bind(divides<double>(),_2,               // param2/param1
                _1);
```

Thus, the example program as a whole has the following output:

```
+10:     17
+10 *2:  34
x*x*x:   343
invdiv:  0.142857
```

Section 6.10.3, page 241, offers some other examples of the use of binders. Section 10.3.1, page 499, provides the same functionality using lambdas.

Calling Global Functions

The following example demonstrates how `bind()` can be used to call global functions (see Section 10.3.3, page 502, for a version with lambdas):

```cpp
// fo/compose3.cpp

#include <iostream>
#include <algorithm>
#include <functional>
#include <locale>
#include <string>
using namespace std;
using namespace std::placeholders;

char myToupper (char c)
{
    std::locale loc;
    return std::use_facet<std::ctype<char> >(loc).toupper(c);
}

int main()
{
    string s("Internationalization");
    string sub("Nation");

    // search substring case insensitive
    string::iterator pos;
    pos = search (s.begin(),s.end(),          // string to search in
                  sub.begin(),sub.end(),      // substring to search
                  bind(equal_to<char>(),      // compar. criterion
                       bind(myToupper,_1),
                       bind(myToupper,_2)));
    if (pos != s.end()) {
        cout << "\"" << sub << "\" is part of \"" << s << "\""
             << endl;
    }
}
```

Here, we use the `search()` algorithm to check whether `sub` is a substring in `s`, when case sensitivity doesn't matter. With

```
bind(equal_to<char>(),
     bind(myToupper,_1),
     bind(myToupper,_2)));
```

we create a function object calling:

myToupper(*param1*)==myToupper(*param2*)

where `myToupper()` is our own convenience function to convert the characters of the strings into uppercase (see Section 16.4.4, page 891, for details).

Note that `bind()` internally copies passed arguments. To let the function object use a reference to a passed argument, use `ref()` or `cref()` (see Section 5.4.3, page 132). For example:

```
void incr (int& i)
{
    ++i;
}

int i=0;
bind(incr,i)();      // increments a copy of i, no effect for i
bind(incr,ref(i))(); // increments i
```

Calling Member Functions

The following program demonstrates how `bind()` can be used to call member functions (see Section 10.3.3, page 503, for a version with lambdas):

```
// fo/bind2.cpp

#include <functional>
#include <algorithm>
#include <vector>
#include <iostream>
#include <string>
using namespace std;
using namespace std::placeholders;

class Person {
  private:
    string name;
  public:
    Person (const string& n) : name(n) {
    }
    void print () const {
        cout << name << endl;
    }
```

```cpp
        void print2 (const string& prefix) const {
            cout << prefix << name << endl;
        }
        ...
    };

    int main()
    {
        vector<Person> coll
                = { Person("Tick"), Person("Trick"), Person("Track") };

        // call member function print() for each person
        for_each (coll.begin(), coll.end(),
                  bind(&Person::print,_1));
        cout << endl;

        // call member function print2() with additional argument for each person
        for_each (coll.begin(), coll.end(),
                  bind(&Person::print2,_1,"Person: "));
        cout << endl;

        // call print2() for temporary Person
        bind(&Person::print2,_1,"This is: ")(Person("nico"));
    }
```

Here,

```cpp
    bind(&Person::print,_1)
```

defines a function object that calls *param1*.`print()` for a passed `Person`. That is, because the first argument is a member function, the next argument defines the object for which this member function gets called.

Any additional argument is passed to the member function. That means:

```cpp
    bind(&Person::print2,_1,"Person: ")
```

defines a function object that calls *param1*.`print2("Person:  ")` for any passed `Person`.

Here, the passed objects are the members of `coll`, but in principle, you can pass objects directly. For example:

```cpp
    Person n("nico");
    bind(&Person::print2,_1,"This is: ")(n);
```

calls `n.print2("This is:  ")`.

The output of the program is as follows:

```
Tick
Trick
Track

Person: Tick
Person: Trick
Person: Track

This is: nico
```

Note that you can also pass pointers to objects and even smart pointers to `bind()`:

```
std::vector<Person*> cp;
...

std::for_each (cp.begin(), cp.end(),
               std::bind(&Person::print,
                         std::placeholders::_1));

std::vector<std::shared_ptr<Person>> sp;
...

std::for_each (sp.begin(), sp.end(),
               std::bind(&Person::print,
                         std::placeholders::_1));
```

Note that you can also call modifying member functions:

```
class Person {
  public:
    ...
    void setName (const std::string& n) {
        name = n;
    }
};

std::vector<Person> coll;
...
std::for_each (coll.begin(), coll.end(),         // give all Persons same name
               std::bind(&Person::setName,
                         std::placeholders::_1,
                         "Paul"));
```

Calling virtual member functions also works. If a method of the base class is bound and the object is of a derived class, the correct virtual function of the derived class gets called.

The `mem_fn()` Adapter

For member functions, you can also use the `mem_fn()` adapter, whereby you can skip the placeholder for the object the member function is called for:

```
std::for_each (coll.begin(), coll.end(),
               std::mem_fn(&Person::print));
```

Thus, `mem_fn()` simply calls an initialized member function for a passed argument while additional arguments are passed as parameters to the member function:

```
std::mem_fn(&Person::print)(n);              // calls n.print()
std::mem_fn(&Person::print2)(n,"Person: ");  // calls n.print2("Person: ")
```

However, to bind an additional argument to the function object, you again have to use `bind()`:

```
std::for_each (coll.begin(), coll.end(),
               std::bind(std::mem_fn(&Person::print2),
               std::placeholders::_1,
               "Person: "));
```

Binding to Data Members

You can also bind to data members. Consider the following example (namespaces omitted):[4]

```
map<string,int> coll;      // map of int values associated to strings
...
// accumulate all values (member second of the elements)
int sum
  = accumulate (coll.begin(), coll.end(),
                0,
                bind(plus<int>(),
                    _1,
                    bind(&map<string,int>::value_type::second,
                        _2)));
```

Here, `accumulate()` is called, which uses a binary predicate to sum up all values of all elements (see Section 11.11.1, page 623). However, because we use a map, where the elements are key/value pairs, to gain access to an element's value

```
bind(&map<string,int>::value_type::second,_2)
```

binds the passed second argument of each call of the predicate to its member `second`.

Adapters `not1()` and `not2()`

The adapters `not1()` and `not2()` can be considered as almost deprecated.[5] The only way to use them is to negate the meaning of predefined function objects. For example:

---

[4] This example is based on code taken from [*Karlsson:Boost*], page 260, with friendly permission by the author.

[5] In fact, they were close to being deprecated with C++11, see [*N3198:DeprAdapt*]

```
std::sort (coll.begin(), coll.end(),
           std::not2(std::less<int>()));
```

This looks more convenient than:

```
std::sort (coll.begin(), coll.end(),
           std::bind(std::logical_not<bool>(),
                     std::bind(std::less<int>(),_1,_2)));
```

However, there is no real real-world scenario for not1() and not2() because you can simply use another predefined function object here:

```
std::sort (coll.begin(), coll.end(),
           std::greater_equal<int>());
```

More important, note that calling not2() with less<> is wrong anyway. You probably meant to change the sorting from ascending to descending. But the negation of < is >=, not >. In fact, greater_equal<> even leads to undefined behavior because sort() requires a *strict weak ordering*, which < provides, but >= does not provide because it violates the requirement to be antisymmetric (see Section 7.7, page 314). Thus, you either pass

```
greater<int>()
```

or swap the order of arguments by passing

```
bind(less<int>(),_2,_1)
```

See Section 10.2.4, page 497, for other examples using not1() and not2() with deprecated function adapters.

10.2.3   User-Defined Function Objects for Function Adapters

You can also use binders for your user-defined function objects. The following example shows a complete definition for a function object that processes the first argument raised to the power of the second argument:

```
// fo/fopow.hpp

#include <cmath>

template <typename T1, typename T2>
struct fopow
{
    T1 operator() (T1 base, T2 exp) const {
        return std::pow(base,exp);
    }
};
```

Note that the first argument and the return value have the same type, T1, whereas the exponent may have a different type T2.

The following program shows how to use the user-defined function object `fopow<>()`. In particular, it uses `fopow<>()` with the `bind()` function adapters:

```
// fo/fopow1.cpp

#include <iostream>
#include <vector>
#include <algorithm>
#include <iterator>
#include <functional>
#include "fopow.hpp"
using namespace std;
using namespace std::placeholders;

int main()
{
    vector<int> coll = { 1, 2, 3, 4, 5, 6, 7, 8, 9 };

    // print 3 raised to the power of all elements
    transform (coll.begin(), coll.end(),             // source
               ostream_iterator<float>(cout," "),    // destination
               bind(fopow<float,int>(),3,_1));        // operation
    cout << endl;

    // print all elements raised to the power of 3
    transform (coll.begin(), coll.end(),             // source
               ostream_iterator<float>(cout," "),    // destination
               bind(fopow<float,int>(),_1,3));        // operation
    cout << endl;
}
```

The program has the following output:

```
3 9 27 81 243 729 2187 6561 19683
1 8 27 64 125 216 343 512 729
```

Note that `fopow<>()` is realized for types `float` and `int`. If you use `int` for both base and exponent, you'd call `pow()` with two arguments of type `int`, but this isn't portable, because according to the standard, `pow()` is overloaded for more than one but not all fundamental types:

```
transform (coll.begin(), coll.end(),
           ostream_iterator<int>(cout," "),
           bind1st(fopow<int,int>(),3));     // ERROR: ambiguous
```

See Section 17.3, page 942, for details about this problem.

10.2.4   Deprecated Function Adapters

Table 10.3 lists the predefined function adapter classes that were provided by the C++ standard library before C++11 and are deprecated now.[6] Just in case you encounter the deprecated stuff, here are some brief examples of how to use them.

Expression	Effect
bind1st(*op*,*arg*)	Calls *op*(*arg*,*param*)
bind2nd(*op*,*arg*)	Calls *op*(*param*,*arg*)
ptr_fun(*op*)	Calls *op(*param*) or *op(*param1*,*param2*)
mem_fun(*op*)	Calls *op*() as a member function for a pointer to an object
mem_fun_ref(*op*)	Calls *op*() as a member function for an object
not1(*op*)	Unary negation: !*op*(*param*)
not2(*op*)	Binary negation: !*op*(*param1*,*param2*)

Table 10.3. Deprecated Predefined Function Adapters

Note that these adapters required certain type definitions in the functions objects used. To define these types, the C++ standard library provides special base classes for function adapters: std::unary_function<> and std::binary_function<>. These classes also are deprecated now.

Both bind1st() and bind2nd() operate like bind(), with fixed positions that a parameter is bound to. For example:

```
// find first element >42
std::find_if (coll.begin(),coll.end(),          // range
              std::bind2nd(std::greater<int>(),42))   // criterion
```

However, bind1st() and bind2nd() can't be used to compose binders out of binders or pass ordinary functions directly.

not1() and not2() are "almost deprecated" because they are useful only with the other deprecated function adapters. For example:

```
std::find_if (coll.begin(), coll.end(),
              std::not1(std::bind2nd(std::modulus<int>(),2)));
```

finds the position of the first even int (%2 yields 0 for even values, which not1() negates into true). However, this looks more convenient than using the new binders:

```
std::find_if (coll.begin(), coll.end(),
              std::bind(std::logical_not<bool>(),
                        std::bind(std::modulus<int>(),
                                  std::placeholders::_1,
                                  2)));
```

---

[6] Although not1() and not2() are not officially deprecated, you need the other deprecated function adapters for real-world usage.

Being able to use a lambda is really an improvement here:

```
std::find_if (coll.begin(), coll.end(),
              [](int elem){
                  return elem%2==0;
              });
```

`ptr_fun()` was provided to be able to call ordinary functions. For example, suppose that you have a global function, which checks something for each parameter:

```
bool check(int elem);
```

To find the first element for which the check does not succeed, you could call the following statement:

```
std::find_if (coll.begin(), coll.end(),          // range
              std::not1(std::ptr_fun(check)));    // search criterion
```

The second form of `ptr_fun()` was used when you had a global function for two parameters and, for example, you wanted to use it as a unary function:

```
// find first string that is not empty
std::find_if (coll.begin(), coll.end(),
              std::bind2nd(std::ptr_fun(std::strcmp),""));
```

Here, the `strcmp()` C function is used to compare each element with the empty C-string. If both strings match, `strcmp()` returns 0, which is equivalent to `false`. So, this call of `find_if()` returns the position of the first element that is not the empty string.

Both `mem_fun()` and `mem_fun_ref()` were provided to define function objects that call member functions.[7] For example:

```
class Person {
  public:
    void print () const;
    ...
};
```

```
const std::vector<Person> coll;
```

```
...
// call member function print() for each person
std::for_each (coll.begin(), coll.end(),
               std::mem_fun_ref(&Person::print));
```

Note that the member functions called by `mem_fun_ref()` and `mem_fun()` and passed as arguments to `bind1st()` or `bind2nd()` must be *constant* member functions.

---

[7] These member function adapters use the auxiliary classes `mem_fun_t`, `mem_fun_ref_t`, `const_mem_fun_t`, `const_mem_fun_ref_t`, `mem_fun1_t`, `mem_fun1_ref_t`, `const_mem_fun1_t`, and `const_mem_fun1_ref_t`.

10.3 Using Lambdas

As introduced in Section 3.1.10, page 28, lambdas were introduced with C++11. They provide
a powerful and very convenient way to provide local functionality, especially to specify details of
algorithms and member functions. Although lambdas are a language feature, their use is so important
for the C++ standard library that I will go into a couple of details here.

As introduced in Section 6.9, page 229, lambdas provide significant improvements for C++ when
using the STL because now you have an intuitive, readable way to pass individual behavior to algorithms and container member functions. If you need specific behavior passed to an algorithm, just
specify it like any other function right there where you need it.

The best way to demonstrate the use of lambdas is by example, especially when comparing
corresponding code not using lambdas. In the following subsections, I provide some examples of
functionality introduced before with other function objects and adapters, such as bind().

10.3.1 Lambdas versus Binders

Take, for example, *fo/bind1.cpp*, which is presented in Section 10.2.2, page 488. When lambdas
are used, the corresponding code looks as follows:

```
// fo/lambda1.cpp

#include <iostream>

int main()
{
    auto plus10 = [] (int i) {
                     return i+10;
                  };
    std::cout << "+10:    " << plus10(7) << std::endl;

    auto plus10times2 = [] (int i) {
                           return (i+10)*2;
                        };
    std::cout << "+10 *2: " << plus10times2(7) << std::endl;

    auto pow3 = [] (int i) {
                   return i*i*i;
                };
    std::cout << "x*x*x:  " << pow3(7) << std::endl;

    auto inversDivide = [] (double d1, double d2) {
                           return d2/d1;
                        };
    std::cout << "invdiv: " << inversDivide(49,7) << std::endl;
}
```

Just to compare one function object declaration: Declaring to "add 10 and multiply by 2" looks with binders as follows:

```
auto plus10times2 = std::bind(std::multiplies<int>(),
                              std::bind(std::plus<int>(),
                                        std::placeholders::_1,
                                        10),
                      2);
```

The same functionality defined with lambdas looks as follows:

```
auto plus10times2 = [] (int i) {
                        return (i+10)*2;
                    };
```

10.3.2 Lambdas versus Stateful Function Objects

Let's now replace a custom function object by a lambda. Consider the example to process the mean value of elements in Section 10.1.3, page 482. A version with lambdas looks as follows:

```
// fo/lambda2.cpp

#include <iostream>
#include <vector>
#include <algorithm>
using namespace std;

int main()
{
    vector<int> coll = { 1, 2, 3, 4, 5, 6, 7, 8 };

    // process and print mean value
    long sum = 0;
    for_each (coll.begin(), coll.end(),   // range
              [&sum] (int elem) {
                  sum += elem;
              });
    double mv = static_cast<double>(sum)/static_cast<double>(coll.size());
    cout << "mean value: " << mv << endl;
}
```

Here, instead of the need to define a class for the function object passed, you simply pass the required functionality. However, the state of the calculation is held outside the lambda in sum, so you ultimately have to use sum to compute the mean value.

With a function object, this state (sum) is entirely encapsulated, and we can provide additional member functions to deal with the state (such as to process the mean value out of sum).

```
MeanValue mv = for_each (coll.begin(), coll.end(),    // range
                          MeanValue());               // operation
cout << "mean value: " << mv.value() << endl;
```

So, from a calling point of view, you can consider the user-defined function object as being more condensed and less error-prone than the lambda version presented here.

When dealing with state, you should also be careful when using `mutable`. Consider the example introduced in Section 10.1.4, page 483, in which your search criterion is a stateful function object searching for the third element. A corresponding version using lambdas should, strictly speaking, pass the internal counter, which represents its state, by value because the counter is not needed outside the algorithm called. By using `mutable`, you could provide write access to this state then for all "function calls":

```
// fo/lambda3.cpp

#include <iostream>
#include <list>
#include <algorithm>
#include "print.hpp"
using namespace std;

int main()
{
    list<int> coll = { 1, 2, 3, 4, 5, 6, 7, 8, 9, 10 };
    PRINT_ELEMENTS(coll,"coll:         ");

    // remove third element
    list<int>::iterator pos;
    int count=0;        // call counter
    pos = remove_if(coll.begin(),coll.end(),     // range
                    [count] (int) mutable {    // remove criterion
                        return ++count == 3;
                    });
    coll.erase(pos,coll.end());

    PRINT_ELEMENTS(coll,"3rd removed: ");
}
```

However, as described in Section 10.1.4, page 483, you can then run into the problem that two elements, the third and the sixth, get removed, which results in the following output:

```
coll:         1 2 3 4 5 6 7 8 9 10
3rd removed: 1 2 4 5 7 8 9 10
```

Again, the reason for this output is that the lambda object gets copied by the `remove_if()` algorithm while it is running, so two lambda objects exist that both remove the third element. Thus, the state gets duplicated.

If you pass the argument by reference and don't use `mutable`, the behavior is as expected, because both lambda objects internally used by `remove_if()` share the same state. Thus, with the following:

```
int count=0;          // call counter
pos = remove_if(coll.begin(),coll.end(),   // range
                [&count] (int) {           // remove criterion
                    return ++count == 3;
                });
```

the output is:

```
coll:          1 2 3 4 5 6 7 8 9 10
3rd removed: 1 2 4 5 6 7 8 9 10
```

10.3.3   Lambdas Calling Global and Member Functions

Of course, any lambda can call other functions, so the lambda version of *fo/compose3.cpp* in Section 10.2.2, page 490, looks as follows:

```
// fo/lambda4.cpp

#include <iostream>
#include <algorithm>
#include <locale>
#include <string>
using namespace std;

char myToupper (char c)
{
    std::locale loc;
    return std::use_facet<std::ctype<char> >(loc).toupper(c);
}

int main()
{
    string s("Internationalization");
    string sub("Nation");

    // search substring case insensitive
    string::iterator pos;
    pos = search (s.begin(),s.end(),            // string to search in
                  sub.begin(),sub.end(),        // substring to search
                  [] (char c1, char c2) {       // compar. criterion
                      return myToupper(c1)==myToupper(c2);
                  });
```

```
        if (pos != s.end()) {
            cout << "\"" << sub << "\" is part of \"" << s << "\""
                 << endl;
        }
    }
```

Of course, you can call member functions the same way (compare with Section 10.2.2, page 491):

```
// fo/lambda5.cpp

#include <functional>
#include <algorithm>
#include <vector>
#include <iostream>
#include <string>
using namespace std;
using namespace std::placeholders;

class Person {
  private:
    string name;
  public:
    Person (const string& n) : name(n) {
    }
    void print () const {
        cout << name << endl;
    }
    void print2 (const string& prefix) const {
        cout << prefix << name << endl;
    }
    ...
};

int main()
{
    vector<Person> coll
            = { Person("Tick"), Person("Trick"), Person("Track") };

    // call member function print() for each person
    for_each (coll.begin(), coll.end(),
              [] (const Person& p) {
                  p.print();
              });
    cout << endl;
```

```
// call member function print2() with additional argument for each person
for_each (coll.begin(), coll.end(),
          [] (const Person& p) {
              p.print2("Person: ");
          });
}
```

10.3.4 Lambdas as Hash Function, Sorting, or Equivalence Criterion

As mentioned before, you can also use lambdas as hash functions, ordering, or sorting criteria. For example:

```
class Person {
    ...
};

auto hash = [] (const Person& p) {
    ...
};
auto eq = [] (const Person& p1, Person& p2) {
    ...
};

// create unordered set with user-defined behavior
unordered_set<Person,decltype(hash),decltype(eq)> pset(10,hash,eq);
```

Note again that you have to use `decltype` to pass the type of the lambda to the `unordered_set` because it creates its own instance of them. In addition, you have to pass a hash function and equivalence criterion to the constructor because otherwise, the constructor calls the default constructor for the hash function and equivalence criterion, which is not defined for lambdas.

Due to these inconveniences, specifying a class for the function objects here can be considered as being more readable and even more convenient. So when state is involved, lambdas are not always better.

See Section 7.9.7, page 379, for a complete example of how to use lambdas to specify a hash function and an equivalence criterion for unordered containers.

Chapter 11
STL Algorithms

This chapter describes all the algorithms of the C++ standard library. It begins with an overview of the algorithms and some general remarks about them. The chapter then presents the exact signature of each algorithm and one or more examples of its use.

11.1 Algorithm Header Files

To use the algorithms of the C++ standard library, you must include the header file `<algorithm>`:

```
#include <algorithm>
```

This header file also includes some auxiliary functions: `min()`, `max()`, and `minmax()` were presented in Section 5.5.1, page 134. The `iter_swap()` iterator function was discussed in Section 9.3.4, page 446.

Some of the STL algorithms are provided for numeric processing. Thus, they are defined in `<numeric>`:

```
#include <numeric>
```

In general, Chapter 17 discusses the numeric components of the C++ standard library. However, I decided to discuss the numeric algorithms here because, in my opinion, the fact that they are STL algorithms is more important than the fact that they are used for numeric processing.

When you use algorithms, you often also need function objects and function adapters. These were described in Chapter 10 and are defined in `<functional>`:

```
#include <functional>
```

11.2 Algorithm Overview

This section presents an overview of all the C++ standard library algorithms to give you an idea of their abilities and to be better able to find the best algorithm to solve a certain problem.

11.2.1   A Brief Introduction

Algorithms were introduced in Chapter 6 along with the STL. In particular, Section 6.4, page 199, and Section 6.7, page 217, discuss the role of algorithms and some important constraints about their use. All STL algorithms process one or more iterator ranges. The first range is usually specified by its beginning and its end. For additional ranges, you generally need to pass only the beginning because the end follows from the number of elements of the first range. The caller must ensure that the ranges are valid. That is, the beginning must refer to a previous or the same element of the same container as the end. Additional ranges must have enough elements.

Algorithms work in overwrite mode rather than in insert mode. Thus, the caller must ensure that destination ranges have enough elements. You can use special insert iterators (see Section 9.4.2, page 454) to switch from overwrite to insert mode.

To increase their flexibility and power, several algorithms allow the user to pass user-defined operations, which they call internally. These operations might be ordinary functions or function objects. If these functions return a Boolean value, they are called *predicates*. You can use predicates for the following tasks:

- You can pass a function, a function object, or a lambda that specifies a unary predicate as the search criterion for a search algorithm. The unary predicate is used to check whether an element fits the criterion. For example, you could search the first element that is less than 50.

- You can pass a function, a function object, or a lambda that specifies a binary predicate as the sorting criterion for a sort algorithm. The binary predicate is used to compare two elements. For example, you could pass a criterion that lets objects that represent a person sort according to the person's last name (see Section 10.1.1, page 476, for an example).

- You can pass a unary predicate as the criterion that specifies for which elements an operation should apply. For example, you could specify that only elements with an odd value should be removed.

- You can specify the numeric operation of numeric algorithms. For example, you could use `accumulate()`, which normally processes the sum of elements, to process the product of all elements.

Note that predicates should not modify their state due to a function call (see Section 10.1.4, page 483).

See Section 6.8, page 224, Section 6.9, page 229, Section 6.10, page 233, and Chapter 10 for examples and details about functions, function objects, and lambdas that are used as algorithm parameters.

11.2.2   Classification of Algorithms

Different algorithms meet different needs and so can be classified by their main purposes. For example, some algorithms operate as read only, some modify elements, and some change the order of elements. This subsection gives you a brief idea of the functionality of each algorithm and in which aspect it differs from similar algorithms.

The name of an algorithm gives you a first impression of its purpose. The designers of the STL introduced two special suffixes:

1. **The `_if` suffix** is used when you can call two forms of an algorithm that have the same number of parameters either by passing a value or by passing a function or function object. In this case, the version without the suffix is used for values, and the version with the `_if` suffix is used for functions and function objects. For example, `find()` searches for an element that has a certain value, whereas `find_if()` searches for an element that meets the criterion passed as a function, a function object, or a lambda.

   However, not all algorithms that have a parameter for functions and function objects have the `_if` suffix. When the function or function-object version of an algorithm has an additional argument, it has the same name. For example, `min_element()` called with two arguments returns the minimum element in the range according to a comparison with operator <. If you pass a third element, it is used as the comparison criterion.

2. **The `_copy` suffix** is used as an indication that elements are not only manipulated but also copied into a destination range. For example, `reverse()` reverses the order of elements inside a range, whereas `reverse_copy()` copies the elements into another range in reverse order.

The following subsections and sections describe the algorithms according to the following classification:

- Nonmodifying algorithms
- Modifying algorithms
- Removing algorithms
- Mutating algorithms
- Sorting algorithms
- Sorted-range algorithms
- Numeric algorithms

Algorithms belonging to more than one category are described in the category I consider to be the most important.

Nonmodifying Algorithms

Nonmodifying algorithms change neither the order nor the value of the elements they process. These algorithms operate with input and forward iterators; therefore, you can call them for all standard containers. Table 11.1 lists the nonmodifying algorithms of the C++ standard library. See page 515 for nonmodifying algorithms that are provided especially for sorted input ranges.

Historically, one of the most important algorithms was `for_each()`. `for_each()` calls an operation provided by the caller for each element. That operation is usually used to process each element of the range individually. For example, you can pass `for_each()` a function that prints each element or calls a modifying operation for each element. Note, however, that since C++11, the range-based `for` loop provides this behavior more conveniently and more naturally (see Section 3.1.4, page 17, and Section 6.2.1, page 174). Thus, `for_each()` might lose its importance over time.

Several of the nonmodifying algorithms perform searching. Unfortunately, the naming scheme of searching algorithms is a mess. In addition, the naming schemes of searching algorithms and searching string functions differ (Table 11.2). As is often the case, there are historical reasons for this. First, the STL and string classes were designed independently. Second, the `find_end()`,

Name	Effect	Page
for_each()	Performs an operation for each element	519
count()	Returns the number of elements	524
count_if()	Returns the number of elements that match a criterion	524
min_element()	Returns the element with the smallest value	526
max_element()	Returns the element with the largest value	526
minmax_element()	Returns the elements with the smallest and largest value (since C++11)	526
find()	Searches for the first element with the passed value	528
find_if()	Searches for the first element that matches a criterion	528
find_if_not()	Searches for the first element that matches a criterion not (since C++11)	528
search_n()	Searches for the first *n* consecutive elements with certain properties	531
search()	Searches for the first occurrence of a subrange	534
find_end()	Searches for the last occurrence of a subrange	537
find_first_of()	Searches the first of several possible elements	539
adjacent_find()	Searches for two adjacent elements that are equal (by some criterion)	540
equal()	Returns whether two ranges are equal	542
is_permutation()	Returns whether two unordered ranges contain equal elements (since C++11)	544
mismatch()	Returns the first elements of two sequences that differ	546
lexicographical... _compare()	Returns whether a range is lexicographically less than another range	548
is_sorted()	Returns whether the elements in a range are sorted (since C++11)	550
is_sorted_until()	Returns the first unsorted element in a range (since C++11)	550
is_partitioned()	Returns whether the elements in a range are partitioned in two groups according to a criterion (since C++11)	552
partition_point()	Returns the partitioning element for a range partitioned into elements fulfilling and elements not fulfilling a predicate (since C++11)	552
is_heap()	Returns whether the elements in a range are sorted as a heap (since C++11)	554
is_heap_until()	Returns the first element in a range not sorted as a heap (since C++11)	554
all_of()	Returns whether all elements match a criterion (since C++11)	555
any_of()	Returns whether at least one element matches a criterion (since C++11)	555
none_of()	Returns whether none of the elements matches a criterion (since C++11)	555

Table 11.1. Nonmodifying Algorithms

Search for	String Function	STL Algorithm
First occurrence of one element	`find()`	`find()`
Last occurrence of one element	`rfind()`	`find()` with reverse iterators
First occurrence of a subrange	`find()`	`search()`
Last occurrence of a subrange	`rfind()`	`find_end()`
First occurrence of several elements	`find_first_of()`	`find_first_of()`
Last occurrence of several elements	`find_last_of()`	`find_first_of()` with reverse iterators
First occurrence of *n* consecutive elements		`search_n()`

Table 11.2. Comparison of Searching String Operations and Algorithms

`find_first_of()`, and `search_n()` algorithms were not part of the original STL. So, for example, the name `find_end()` instead of `search_end()` was chosen by accident (it is easy to forget aspects of the whole picture, such as consistency, when you are caught up in the details). Also by accident, a form of `search_n()` breaks the general concept of the original STL. See Section 11.5.3, page 532, for a description of this problem.

Modifying Algorithms

Modifying algorithms change the value of elements. Such algorithms might modify the elements of a range directly or modify them while they are being copied into another range. If elements are copied into a destination range, the source range is not changed. Table 11.3 lists the modifying algorithms of the C++ standard library.

The fundamental modifying algorithms are `for_each()` (again) and `transform()`. You can use both to modify elements of a sequence. However, their behavior differs as follows:

- **for_each()** accepts an operation that modifies its argument. Thus, the argument has to be passed by reference. For example:

  ```
  void square (int& elem)        // call-by-reference
  {
      elem = elem * elem;        // assign processed value directly
  }
  ...
  for_each(coll.begin(),coll.end(),      // range
           square);                      // operation
  ```

- **transform()** uses an operation that returns the modified argument. The trick is that it can be used to assign the result to the original element. For example:

  ```
  int square (int elem)          // call-by-value
  {
      return elem * elem;        // return processed value
  }
  ```

Name	Effect	Page
for_each()	Performs an operation for each element	519
copy()	Copies a range starting with the first element	557
copy_if()	Copies elements that match a criterion (since C++11)	557
copy_n()	Copies *n* elements (since C++11)	557
copy_backward()	Copies a range starting with the last element	561
move()	Moves elements of a range starting with the first element (since C++11)	557
move_backward()	Moves elements of a range starting with the last element (since C++11)	561
transform()	Modifies (and copies) elements; combines elements of two ranges	563 564
merge()	Merges two ranges	614
swap_ranges()	Swaps elements of two ranges	566
fill()	Replaces each element with a given value	568
fill_n()	Replaces *n* elements with a given value	568
generate()	Replaces each element with the result of an operation	569
generate_n()	Replaces *n* elements with the result of an operation	569
iota()	Replaces each element with a sequence of incremented values (since C++11)	571
replace()	Replaces elements that have a special value with another value	571
replace_if()	Replaces elements that match a criterion with another value	571
replace_copy()	Replaces elements that have a special value while copying the whole range	573
replace_copy_if()	Replaces elements that match a criterion while copying the whole range	573

Table 11.3. Modifying Algorithms

```
    ...
    transform (coll.cbegin(), coll.cend(),    // source range
               coll.begin(),                   // destination range
               square);                        // operation
```

Using `transform()` is a bit slower because it returns and assigns the result instead of modifying the element directly. However, it is more flexible because it can also be used to modify elements while they are being copied into a different destination sequence. Another version of `transform()` can process and combine elements of two source ranges.

Strictly speaking, `merge()` does not necessarily have to be part of the list of modifying algorithms, because it requires that its input ranges be sorted. So, it should be part of the algorithms for sorted ranges (see page 515). In practice, however, `merge()` also merges the elements of unsorted ranges. Of course, then the result is unsorted. Nevertheless, to be safe, you should call `merge()` only for sorted ranges.

Note that elements of associative and unordered containers are constant to ensure that you can't compromise the sorted order of the elements due to an element modification. Therefore, you can't use these containers as a destination for modifying algorithms.

In addition to these modifying algorithms, the C++ standard library provides modifying algorithms for sorted ranges. See page 515 for details.

Removing Algorithms

Removing algorithms are a special form of modifying algorithms. They can remove the elements either in a single range or while these elements are being copied into another range. As with modifying algorithms, you can't use an associative or unordered container as a destination, because the elements of these containers are considered to be constant. Table 11.4 lists the removing algorithms of the C++ standard library.

Name	Effect	Page
`remove()`	Removes elements with a given value	575
`remove_if()`	Removes elements that match a given criterion	575
`remove_copy()`	Copies elements that do not match a given value	577
`remove_copy_if()`	Copies elements that do not match a given criterion	577
`unique()`	Removes adjacent duplicates (elements that are equal to their predecessor)	578
`unique_copy()`	Copies elements while removing adjacent duplicates	580

Table 11.4. Removing Algorithms

Note that these algorithms remove elements logically only by overwriting them with the following elements that were not removed. Thus, removing algorithms do not change the number of elements in the ranges on which they operate. Instead, they return the position of the new "end" of the range. It's up to the caller to use that new end, such as to remove the elements physically. See Section 6.7.1, page 218, for a detailed discussion of this behavior.

Mutating Algorithms

Mutating algorithms are algorithms that change the order of elements (and not their values) by assigning and swapping their values. Table 11.5 lists the mutating algorithms of the C++ standard library. As with modifying algorithms, you can't use an associative or unordered container as a destination, because the elements of these containers are considered to be constant.

Sorting Algorithms

Sorting algorithms are a special kind of mutating algorithm because they also change the order of the elements. However, sorting is more complicated and therefore usually takes more time than

Name	Effect	Page
reverse()	Reverses the order of the elements	583
reverse_copy()	Copies the elements while reversing their order	583
rotate()	Rotates the order of the elements	584
rotate_copy()	Copies the elements while rotating their order	585
next_permutation()	Permutates the order of the elements	587
prev_permutation()	Permutates the order of the elements	587
shuffle()	Brings the elements into a random order (since C++11)	589
random_shuffle()	Brings the elements into a random order	589
partition()	Changes the order of the elements so that elements that match a criterion are at the front	592
stable_partition()	Same as partition() but preserves the relative order of matching and nonmatching elements	592
partition_copy()	Copies the elements while changing the order so that elements that match a criterion are at the front	594

Table 11.5. Mutating Algorithms

simple mutating operations. In fact, these algorithms usually have worse than linear complexity[1] and require random-access iterators (for the destination). Table 11.6 lists the sorting algorithms. Table 11.7 lists the corresponding algorithms that allow checking whether a sequence is (partially) sorted.

Time often is critical for sorting algorithms. Therefore, the C++ standard library provides more than one sorting algorithm. The algorithms use different ways of sorting, and some algorithms don't sort all elements. For example, nth_element() stops when the *n*th element of the sequence is correct according to the sorting criterion. For the other elements, it guarantees only that the previous elements have a lesser or equal value and that the following elements have a greater or equal value. To sort all elements of a sequence, you should consider the following algorithms:

- **sort()**, based historically on *quicksort*. Thus, this algorithm guarantees a good runtime ($n * log(n)$ complexity) on average but may have a very bad runtime (quadratic complexity) in the worst case:

  ```
  // sort all elements
  // - best n*log(n) complexity on average
  // - n*n complexity in worst case
  sort (coll.begin(), coll.end());
  ```

  If avoiding the worst-case behavior is important, you should use another algorithm, such as partial_sort() or stable_sort().

- **partial_sort()**, based historically on *heapsort*. Thus, it guarantees $n * log(n)$ complexity in any case. However, in most circumstances, heapsort is slower than quicksort by a factor of two to five. So, if sort() is implemented as quicksort and partial_sort() is implemented

---

[1] See Section 2.2, page 10, for an introduction to and a discussion of complexity.

Name	Effect	Page
sort()	Sorts all elements	596
stable_sort()	Sorts while preserving order of equal elements	596
partial_sort()	Sorts until the first *n* elements are correct	599
partial_sort_copy()	Copies elements in sorted order	600
nth_element()	Sorts according to the *n*th position	602
partition()	Changes the order of the elements so that elements that match a criterion are at the beginning	592
stable_partition()	Same as partition() but preserves the relative order of matching and nonmatching elements	592
partition_copy()	Copies the elements while changing the order so that elements that match a criterion are at the beginning	594
make_heap()	Converts a range into a heap	604
push_heap()	Adds an element to a heap	605
pop_heap()	Removes an element from a heap	605
sort_heap()	Sorts the heap (it is no longer a heap after the call)	605

Table 11.6. Sorting Algorithms

Name	Effect	Page
is_sorted()	Returns whether the elements in a range are sorted (since C++11)	550
is_sorted_until()	Returns the first unsorted element in a range (since C++11)	550
is_partitioned()	Returns whether the elements in a range are partitioned in two groups according to a criterion (since C++11)	552
partition_point()	Returns the partitioning element for a range partitioned into elements fulfilling and elements not fulfilling a predicate (since C++11)	552
is_heap()	Returns whether the elements in a range are sorted as a heap (since C++11)	554
is_heap_until()	Returns the first element in a range not sorted as a heap (since C++11)	554

Table 11.7. Algorithms Checking for Sortings

as heapsort, partial_sort() has the better complexity, but sort() has the better runtime in most cases. The advantage of partial_sort() is that it guarantees $n * log(n)$ complexity in any case, so it never reaches quadratic complexity.

In addition, partial_sort() has the special ability to stop sorting when only the first *n* elements need to be sorted. To sort all the elements, you have to pass the end of the sequence as second and last argument:

```
// sort all elements
// - always n*log(n) complexity
// - but usually twice as long as sort()
partial_sort (coll.begin(), coll.end(), coll.end());
```

- **stable_sort()**, based historically on *mergesort*. It sorts all the elements:
  ```
  // sort all elements
  // - n*log(n) or n*log(n)*log(n) complexity
  stable_sort (coll.begin(), coll.end());
  ```
  However, it needs enough additional memory to have $n * log(n)$ complexity. Otherwise, it has $n * log(n) * log(n)$ complexity. The advantage of stable_sort() is that it preserves the order of equal elements.

Now you have a brief idea of which sorting algorithm might best meet your needs. But the story doesn't end here. The standard guarantees complexity but not how it is implemented. This is an advantage in that an implementation could benefit from algorithm innovations and use a better way of sorting without breaking the standard. For example, the sort() algorithm in the SGI implementation of the STL is implemented by using *introsort*. Introsort is a new algorithm that, by default, operates like quicksort but switches to heapsort when it is going to have quadratic complexity. The disadvantage of the fact that the standard does not guarantee exact complexity is that an implementation could use a standard-conforming, but very bad, algorithm. For example, using heapsort to implement sort() would be standard conforming. Of course, you simply could test which algorithm fits best, but be aware that measurements might not be portable.

There are even more algorithms to sort elements. For example, the heap algorithms are provided to call the functions that implement a heap directly (a heap can be considered as a binary tree implemented as sequential collection). The heap algorithms are provided and used as the base for efficient implementations of priority queues (see Section 12.3, page 641). You can use them to sort all elements of a collection by calling them as follows:

```
// sort all elements
// - n+n*log(n) complexity
make_heap (coll.begin(), coll.end());
sort_heap (coll.begin(), coll.end());
```

See Section 11.9.4, page 604, for details about heaps and heap algorithms.

The nth_element() algorithms are provided if you need only the *n*th sorted element or the set of the *n* highest or *n* lowest elements (not sorted). Thus, nth_element() is a way to split elements into two subsets according to a sorting criterion. However, you could also use partition() or stable_partition() to do this. The differences are as follows:

- For **nth_element()**, you pass the number of elements you want to have in the first part (and therefore also in the second part). For example:
  ```
  // move the four lowest elements to the front
  nth_element (coll.begin(),        // beginning of range
               coll.begin()+3,      // position between first and second part
               coll.end());         // end of range
  ```

However, after the call, you don't know the exact criterion that is the difference between the first and the second parts. Both parts may, in fact, have elements with the same value as the *n*th element.

- For **partition()**, you pass the exact sorting criterion that serves as the difference between the first and the second parts. For example:

```
// move all elements less than seven to the front
vector<int>::iterator pos;
pos = partition (coll1.begin(), coll1.end(),     // range
                [](int elem){                    // criterion
                    return elem<7;
                });
```

Here, after the call, you don't know how many elements are owned by the first and the second parts. The return value pos refers to the first element of the second part that contains all elements that don't match the criterion, if any.

- **stable_partition()** behaves similarly to partition() but has an additional ability. It guarantees that the order of the elements in both parts remains stable according to their relative positions to the other elements in the same part.

You can always pass the sorting criterion to all sorting algorithms as an optional argument. The default sorting argument is the function object less<>, so that elements are sorted in ascending order according to their values. Note that the sorting criterion has to define a *strict weak ordering* on the values. A criterion, where values are compared as equal or less, such as operator <=, does not fit this requirement. See Section 7.7, page 314, for details.

As with modifying algorithms, you can't use an associative container as a destination, because the elements of the associative containers are considered to be constant.

Lists and forward lists do not provide random-access iterators, so you can't call sorting algorithms for them either. However, both provide a member function sort() to sort their elements; see Section 8.8.1, page 422.

Sorted-Range Algorithms

Sorted-range algorithms require that the ranges on which they operate be sorted according to their sorting criterion. Table 11.8 lists all C++ standard library algorithms that are especially written for sorted ranges. As for associative containers, these algorithms have the advantage of a better complexity.

The first five sorted-range algorithms in Table 11.8 are nonmodifying, searching only according to their purpose. The other algorithms combine two sorted input ranges and write the result to a destination range. In general, the result of these algorithms is also sorted.

Numeric Algorithms

These algorithms combine numeric elements in different ways. Table 11.9 lists the numeric algorithms of the C++ standard library. If you understand the names, you get an idea of the purpose of the algorithms. However, these algorithms are more flexible and more powerful than they may seem at first. For example, by default, accumulate() processes the sum of all elements. When you use

Name	Effect	Page
binary_search()	Returns whether the range contains an element	608
includes()	Returns whether each element of a range is also an element of another range	609
lower_bound()	Finds the first element greater than or equal to a given value	611
upper_bound()	Finds the first element greater than a given value	611
equal_range()	Returns the range of elements equal to a given value	613
merge()	Merges the elements of two ranges	614
set_union()	Processes the sorted union of two ranges	616
set_intersection()	Processes the sorted intersection of two ranges	617
set_difference()	Processes a sorted range that contains all elements of a range that are not part of another range	618
set_symmetric_difference()	Processes a sorted range that contains all elements that are in exactly one of two ranges	619
inplace_merge()	Merges two consecutive sorted ranges	622
partition_point()	Returns the partitioning element for a range partitioned into elements fulfilling and elements not fulfilling a predicate (since C++11)	552

Table 11.8. Algorithms for Sorted Ranges

Name	Effect	Page
accumulate()	Combines all element values (processes sum, product, and so forth)	623
inner_product()	Combines all elements of two ranges	625
adjacent_difference()	Combines each element with its predecessor	628
partial_sum()	Combines each element with all its predecessors	627

Table 11.9. Numeric Algorithms

strings as elements, you concatenate them by using this algorithm. When you switch from operator + to operator *, you get the product of all elements. As another example, you should know that adjacent_difference() and partial_sum() transfer a range of absolute values into a range of relative values and vice versa.

Both accumulate() and inner_product() process and return a single value without modifying the ranges. The other algorithms write the results to a destination range that has the same number of elements as the source range.

11.3   Auxiliary Functions

The rest of this chapter discusses the algorithms in detail and includes at least one example of each algorithm. To simplify the examples, I use some auxiliary functions so that you can concentrate on the essence of the examples:

```cpp
// algo/algostuff.hpp

#ifndef ALGOSTUFF_HPP
#define ALGOSTUFF_HPP

#include <array>
#include <vector>
#include <deque>
#include <list>
#include <forward_list>
#include <set>
#include <map>
#include <unordered_set>
#include <unordered_map>
#include <algorithm>
#include <iterator>
#include <functional>
#include <numeric>
#include <iostream>
#include <string>

// INSERT_ELEMENTS (collection, first, last)
// - fill values from first to last into the collection
// - NOTE: NO half-open range
template <typename T>
inline void INSERT_ELEMENTS (T& coll, int first, int last)
{
    for (int i=first; i<=last; ++i) {
        coll.insert(coll.end(),i);
    }
}


// PRINT_ELEMENTS()
// - prints optional string optcstr followed by
// - all elements of the collection coll
// - separated by spaces
template <typename T>
```

```cpp
inline void PRINT_ELEMENTS (const T& coll,
                            const std::string& optcstr="")
{
    std::cout << optcstr;
    for (auto elem : coll) {
        std::cout << elem << ' ';
    }
    std::cout << std::endl;
}


// PRINT_MAPPED_ELEMENTS()
// - prints optional string optcstr followed by
// - all elements of the key/value collection coll
// - separated by spaces
template <typename T>
inline void PRINT_MAPPED_ELEMENTS (const T& coll,
                                   const std::string& optcstr="")
{
    std::cout << optcstr;
    for (auto elem : coll) {
        std::cout << '[' << elem.first
                  << ',' << elem.second << "] ";
    }
    std::cout << std::endl;
}


#endif /*ALGOSTUFF_HPP*/
```

First, `algostuff.hpp` includes all header files that may be necessary to implement the examples, so the program doesn't have to do it. Second, it defines three auxiliary functions:[2]

1. `INSERT_ELEMENTS()` inserts elements into the container that is passed as the first argument. These elements get the values from the value passed as the second argument up to the value passed as the third argument. Both argument values are included, so this is *not* a half-open range.

2. `PRINT_ELEMENTS()` prints all elements of the container that is passed as the first argument, separated by spaces. You can pass a second argument optionally for a string that is used as a prefix in front of the elements (see Section 6.6, page 216).

3. `PRINT_MAPPED_ELEMENTS()` is the same for containers with a key/value pair: map, multimap, unordered map, and unordered multimap.

---

[2] Since C++11, `PRINT_MAPPED_ELEMENTS()` could also be defined as partial specialization of `PRINT_ELEMENTS()`. However, to avoid requiring too many new language features, both functions are defined separately.

11.4 The `for_each()` Algorithm

The `for_each()` algorithm is very flexible because it allows you to access, process, and modify each element in many different ways. Note, however, that since C++11, the range-based `for` loop provides this behavior more conveniently and more naturally (see Section 3.1.4, page 17, and Section 6.2.1, page 174). Thus, `for_each()` might lose its importance over time.

`UnaryProc`
for_each (InputIterator *beg*, InputIterator *end*, UnaryProc *op*)

- Calls

    op(*elem*)

    for each element in the range [*beg*,*end*).
- Returns the (internally modified) copy of *op*. Since C++11, the returned *op* is moved.
- *op* might modify the elements. However, see Section 11.2.2, page 509, for a comparison with the `transform()` algorithm, which is able to do the same thing in a slightly different way.
- Any return value of *op* is ignored.
- See Section 6.10.1, page 235, for the implementation of the `for_each()` algorithm.
- Complexity: linear (*numElems* calls of *op*()).

The following example of `for_each()` passes each element to a lambda that prints the passed element. Thus, the call prints each element:

```cpp
// algo/foreach1.cpp

#include "algostuff.hpp"
using namespace std;

int main()
{
    vector<int> coll;

    INSERT_ELEMENTS(coll,1,9);

    // call print() for each element
    for_each (coll.cbegin(), coll.cend(),   // range
              [](int elem){                  // operation
                  cout << elem << ' ';
              });
    cout << endl;
}
```

The program has the following output:

```
1 2 3 4 5 6 7 8 9
```

Instead of a lambda, you could also pass an ordinary function, which is called for each element:

```
void print (int elem)
{
    cout << elem << ' ';
}
...
for_each (coll.cbegin(), coll.cend(),   // range
          print);                        // operation
```

But note again that since C++11, using a range-based for loop is often more convenient:

```
for (auto elem : coll) {
    cout << elem << ' ';
}
```

The following example demonstrates how to modify each element:

```
// algo/foreach2.cpp

#include "algostuff.hpp"
using namespace std;

int main()
{
    vector<int> coll;

    INSERT_ELEMENTS(coll,1,9);

    // add 10 to each element
    for_each (coll.begin(), coll.end(),        // range
              [](int& elem){                   // operation
                  elem += 10;
              });
    PRINT_ELEMENTS(coll);

    // add value of first element to each element
    for_each (coll.begin(), coll.end(),        // range
              [=](int& elem){                  // operation
                  elem += *coll.begin();
              });
    PRINT_ELEMENTS(coll);
}
```

The program has the following output:

```
11 12 13 14 15 16 17 18 19
22 23 24 25 26 27 28 29 30
```

As you can see, you have to declare the elem to be a reference in order to modify it and to define a capture, such as [=], to be able to add a copy of the first element:

```
for_each (coll.begin(), coll.end(),        // range
          [=](int& elem){                  // operation
              elem += *coll.begin();
          });
```

If instead you passed a reference to the first element with the second call of for_each():

```
for_each (coll.begin(), coll.end(),        // range
          [&](int& elem){                  // operation
              elem += *coll.begin();
          });
```

the value to add would change while the elements are processed, which would result in the following output:

```
11 12 13 14 15 16 17 18 19
22 34 35 36 37 38 39 40 41
```

You could also define an ordinary function object:

```
// function object that adds the value with which it is initialized
template <typename T>
class AddValue {
  private:
    T theValue;      // value to add
  public:
    // constructor initializes the value to add
    AddValue (const T& v) : theValue(v) {
    }

    // the function call for the element adds the value
    void operator() (T& elem) const {
        elem += theValue;
    }
};
```

and pass it to for_each():

```
for_each (coll.begin(), coll.end(),          // range
          AddValue<int>(10));                // operation
...
for_each (coll.begin(), coll.end(),          // range
          AddValue<int>(*coll.begin()));     // operation
```

The AddValue<> class defines function objects that add a value to each element that is passed to the constructor. See Section 6.10.1, page 237, for more details about this example.

Note also that you can do the same by using the transform() algorithm (see Section 11.6.3, page 563) in the following way:

```
// add 10 to each element
transform (coll.cbegin(), coll.cend(),        // source range
           coll.begin(),                      // destination range
           [](int elem){                      // operation
               return elem + 10;
           });

...


// add value of first element to each element
transform (coll.cbegin(), coll.cend(),        // source range
           coll.begin(),                      // destination range
           [=](int elem){                     // operation
               return elem + *coll.begin();
           });
```

See Section 11.2.2, page 509, for a general comparison between for_each() and transform().

A third example demonstrates how to use the return value of the for_each() algorithm. Because for_each() has the special property that it returns its operation, you can process and return a result inside the operation:

```
// algo/foreach3.cpp

#include "algostuff.hpp"
using namespace std;

// function object to process the mean value
class MeanValue {
  private:
    long num;      // number of elements
    long sum;      // sum of all element values
  public:
    // constructor
    MeanValue () : num(0), sum(0) {
    }

    // function call
    // - process one more element of the sequence
    void operator() (int elem) {
        num++;              // increment count
        sum += elem;        // add value
    }
```

```
        // return mean value (implicit type conversion)
        operator double() {
            return static_cast<double>(sum) / static_cast<double>(num);
        }
};

int main()
{
    vector<int> coll;

    INSERT_ELEMENTS(coll,1,8);

    // process and print mean value
    double mv = for_each (coll.begin(), coll.end(),   // range
                          MeanValue());               // operation
    cout << "mean value: " << mv << endl;
}
```

The program has the following output:

```
mean value: 4.5
```

You could also use a lambda and pass the value to return by reference. However, in this scenario, a lambda is not necessarily better, because a function object really encapsulates both sum as internal state and the final division of dividing the sum by the number of elements. See Section 10.1.3, page 482, for details.

11.5   Nonmodifying Algorithms

The algorithms presented in this section enable you to access elements without modifying their values or changing their order.

11.5.1   Counting Elements

difference_type
count (InputIterator *beg*, InputIterator *end*, const T& *value*)

difference_type
count_if (InputIterator *beg*, InputIterator *end*, UnaryPredicate *op*)

- The first form counts the elements in the range [*beg*,*end*) that are equal to value *value*.
- The second form counts the elements in the range [*beg*,*end*) for which the unary predicate
    op(*elem*)
  yields true.
- The type of the return value, *difference_type*, is the difference type of the iterator:
    typename iterator_traits<InputIterator>::difference_type
  (Section 9.5, page 466, introduces iterator traits.)
- Note that *op* should not change its state during a function call. See Section 10.1.4, page 483, for details.
- *op* should not modify the passed arguments.
- Associative and unordered containers provide a similar member function, count(), to count the number of elements that have a certain value as key (see Section 8.3.3, page 404).
- Complexity: linear (*numElems* comparisons or calls of *op*(), respectively).

The following example counts elements according to various criteria:

```
// algo/count1.cpp

#include "algostuff.hpp"
using namespace std;

int main()
{
    vector<int> coll;
    int num;
    INSERT_ELEMENTS(coll,1,9);
    PRINT_ELEMENTS(coll,"coll: ");

    // count elements with value 4
    num = count (coll.cbegin(), coll.cend(),    // range
                 4);                            // value
    cout << "number of elements equal to 4:    " << num << endl;
```

```
// count elements with even value
num = count_if (coll.cbegin(), coll.cend(),   // range
                [](int elem){                  // criterion
                    return elem%2==0;
                });
cout << "number of elements with even value: " << num << endl;

// count elements that are greater than value 4
num = count_if (coll.cbegin(), coll.cend(),   // range
                [](int elem){                  // criterion
                    return elem>4;
                });
cout << "number of elements greater than 4:  " << num << endl;
}
```

The program has the following output:

```
coll: 1 2 3 4 5 6 7 8 9
number of elements equal to 4:     1
number of elements with even value: 4
number of elements greater than 4:  5
```

Instead of using a lambda, which checks whether the element is even, you could use binders like the following expression:

```
std::bind(std::logical_not<bool>(),
        std::bind(std::modulus<int>(),std::placeholders::_1,2)));
```

or even the deprecated expression:

```
std::not1(std::bind2nd(std::modulus<int>(),2))
```

See Section 10.2.4, page 497, for more details regarding these expressions.

11.5.2   Minimum and Maximum

```
ForwardIterator
min_element (ForwardIterator beg, ForwardIterator end)

ForwardIterator
min_element (ForwardIterator beg, ForwardIterator end, CompFunc op)

ForwardIterator
max_element (ForwardIterator beg, ForwardIterator end)

ForwardIterator
max_element (ForwardIterator beg, ForwardIterator end, CompFunc op)
```

```
pair<ForwardIterator,ForwardIterator>
```
minmax_element (ForwardIterator *beg*, ForwardIterator *end*)

```
pair<ForwardIterator,ForwardIterator>
```
minmax_element (ForwardIterator *beg*, ForwardIterator *end*, CompFunc *op*)

- These algorithms return the position of the minimum, the maximum element, or a pair of the minimum and the maximum element in the range [*beg*,*end*].
- The versions without *op* compare the elements with operator <.
- *op* is used to compare two elements:
  > *op* (*elem1* , *elem2*)

  It should return true when the first element is less than the second element.
- If more than one minimum or maximum element exists, min_element() and max_element() return the first found; minmax_element() returns the first minimum but the last maximum element, so max_element() and minmax_element() don't yield the same maximum element.
- If the range is empty, the algorithms return *beg* or a pair<*beg*,*beg*>.
- *op* should not modify the passed arguments.
- Complexity: linear (*numElems*-1 comparisons or calls of *op*(), respectively, for min_element() and max_element() and $\frac{3}{2}$ (*numElems*-1) comparisons or calls of *op*(), respectively, for minmax_element()).

The following program prints the minimum and the maximum of the elements in coll, using min_element() and max_element(), as well as minmax_element(), and, by using absLess(), prints the minimum and the maximum of the absolute values:

```cpp
// algo/minmax1.cpp

#include <cstdlib>
#include "algostuff.hpp"
using namespace std;

bool absLess (int elem1, int elem2)
{
    return abs(elem1) < abs(elem2);
}

int main()
{
    deque<int> coll;

    INSERT_ELEMENTS(coll,2,6);
    INSERT_ELEMENTS(coll,-3,6);

    PRINT_ELEMENTS(coll);
```

```
// process and print minimum and maximum
cout << "minimum: "
     << *min_element(coll.cbegin(),coll.cend())
     << endl;
cout << "maximum: "
     << *max_element(coll.cbegin(),coll.cend())
     << endl;

// print min and max and their distance using minmax_element()
auto mm = minmax_element(coll.cbegin(),coll.cend());
cout << "min: " << *(mm.first) << endl;       // print minimum
cout << "max: " << *(mm.second) << endl;      // print maximum
cout << "distance: " << distance(mm.first,mm.second) << endl;

// process and print minimum and maximum of absolute values
cout << "minimum of absolute values: "
     << *min_element(coll.cbegin(),coll.cend(),
                     absLess)
     << endl;
cout << "maximum of absolute values: "
     << *max_element(coll.cbegin(),coll.cend(),
                     absLess)
     << endl;
}
```

The program has the following output:

```
2 3 4 5 6 -3 -2 -1 0 1 2 3 4 5 6
minimum: -3
maximum: 6
min: -3
max: 6
distance: 9
minimum of absolute values: 0
maximum of absolute values: 6
```

Note that the algorithms return the *position* of the maximum or minimum element, respectively. Thus, you must use the unary operator * to print their values:

```
auto mm = minmax_element(coll.begin(),coll.end());
cout << "min: " << *(mm.first) << endl;
cout << "max: " << *(mm.second) << endl;
```

Note also that `minmax_element()` yields the last maximum, so the distance (see Section 9.3.3, page 445) is 9. By using `max_element()`, the distance would be −1.

11.5.3 Searching Elements

Search First Matching Element

```
InputIterator
```
find (InputIterator *beg*, InputIterator *end*, const T& *value*)

```
InputIterator
```
find_if (InputIterator *beg*, InputIterator *end*, UnaryPredicate *op*)

```
InputIterator
```
find_if_not (InputIterator *beg*, InputIterator *end*, UnaryPredicate *op*)

- The first form returns the position of the first element in the range [*beg*,*end*) that has a value equal to *value*.
- The second form returns the position of the first element in the range [*beg*,*end*) for which the unary predicate
  > *op*(*elem*)

  yields true.
- The third form (available since C++11) returns the position of the first element in the range [*beg*,*end*) for which the unary predicate
  > *op*(*elem*)

  yields false.
- All algorithms return *end* if no matching elements are found.
- Note that *op* should not change its state during a function call. See Section 10.1.4, page 483, for details.
- *op* should not modify the passed arguments.
- If the range is sorted, you should use the lower_bound(), upper_bound(), equal_range(), or binary_search() algorithms (see Section 11.10, page 608).
- Associative and unordered containers provide an equivalent member function, find() (see Section 8.3.3, page 405), which has a better complexity (logarithmic for associative and even constant for unordered containers).
- Complexity: linear (at most, *numElems* comparisons or calls of *op*(), respectively).

The following example demonstrates how to use find() to find a subrange starting with the first element with value 4 and ending after the second 4, if any:

```
// algo/find1.cpp

#include "algostuff.hpp"
using namespace std;

int main()
{
    list<int> coll;
```

```
    INSERT_ELEMENTS(coll,1,9);
    INSERT_ELEMENTS(coll,1,9);

    PRINT_ELEMENTS(coll,"coll: ");

    // find first element with value 4
    list<int>::iterator pos1;
    pos1 = find (coll.begin(), coll.end(),    // range
                 4);                          // value

    // find second element with value 4
    // - note: continue the search behind the first 4 (if any)
    list<int>::iterator pos2;
    if (pos1 != coll.end()) {
        pos2 = find (++pos1, coll.end(),      // range
                     4);                      // value
    }

    // print all elements from first to second 4 (both included)
    // - note: now we need the position of the first 4 again (if any)
    if (pos1!=coll.end() && pos2!=coll.end()) {
        copy (--pos1, ++pos2,
              ostream_iterator<int>(cout," "));
        cout << endl;
    }
}
```

To find the second 4, you must increment the position of the first 4. However, incrementing the `end()` of a collection results in undefined behavior. Thus, if you are not sure, you should check the return value of `find()` before you increment it. The program has the following output:

```
coll: 1 2 3 4 5 6 7 8 9 1 2 3 4 5 6 7 8 9
4 5 6 7 8 9 1 2 3 4
```

You can call `find()` twice for the same range but with two different values. However, you have to be careful to use the results as the beginning and the end of a subrange of elements; otherwise, the subrange might not be valid. See Section 6.4.1, page 203, for a discussion of possible problems and for an example.

The following example demonstrates how to use `find_if()` and `find_if_not()` to find elements according to very different search criteria:

```
// algo/find2.cpp

#include "algostuff.hpp"
using namespace std;
using namespace std::placeholders;
```

```cpp
int main()
{
    vector<int> coll;
    vector<int>::iterator pos;

    INSERT_ELEMENTS(coll,1,9);
    PRINT_ELEMENTS(coll,"coll: ");

    // find first element greater than 3
    pos = find_if (coll.begin(), coll.end(),     // range
                   bind(greater<int>(),_1,3));   // criterion

    // print its position
    cout << "the "
         << distance(coll.begin(),pos) + 1
         << ". element is the first greater than 3" << endl;

    // find first element divisible by 3
    pos = find_if (coll.begin(), coll.end(),
                   [](int elem){
                       return elem%3==0;
                   });

    // print its position
    cout << "the "
         << distance(coll.begin(),pos) + 1
         << ". element is the first divisible by 3" << endl;

    // find first element not <5
    pos = find_if_not (coll.begin(), coll.end(),
                       bind(less<int>(),_1,5));
    cout << "first value >=5: " << *pos << endl;
}
```

The first call of find_if() uses a simple function object combined with the bind adapter (see Section 10.2.2, page 487) to search for the first element that is greater than 3. The second call uses a lambda to find the first element that is divisible by 3 without remainder.

The program has the following output:

```
coll: 1 2 3 4 5 6 7 8 9
the 4. element is the first greater than 3
the 3. element is the first divisible by 3
first value >=5: 5
```

See Section 6.8.2, page 226, for an example that lets find_if() find the first prime number.

Search First *n* Matching Consecutive Elements

```
ForwardIterator
search_n (ForwardIterator beg, ForwardIterator end,
         Size count, const T& value)

ForwardIterator
search_n (ForwardIterator beg, ForwardIterator end,
         Size count, const T& value, BinaryPredicate op)
```

- The first form returns the position of the first of *count* consecutive elements in the range [*beg,end*) that all have a value equal to *value*.

- The second form returns the position of the first of *count* consecutive elements in the range [*beg,end*) for which the binary predicate

  $$op(elem,value)$$

  yields true (*value* is the passed fourth argument).

- Both forms return *end* if no matching elements are found.

- Note that *op* should not change its state during a function call. See Section 10.1.4, page 483, for details.

- *op* should not modify the passed arguments.

- These algorithms were not part of the original STL and were not introduced very carefully. The fact that the second form uses a binary predicate instead of a unary predicate breaks the consistency of the original STL. See the remarks on page 532.

- Complexity: linear (at most, *numElems*count* comparisons or calls of *op*(), respectively).

The following example searches for consecutive elements that have a value equal to 7 or an odd value:

```cpp
// algo/searchn1.cpp

#include "algostuff.hpp"
using namespace std;

int main()
{
    deque<int> coll;

    coll = { 1, 2, 7, 7, 6, 3, 9, 5, 7, 7, 7, 3, 6 };
    PRINT_ELEMENTS(coll);

    // find three consecutive elements with value 7
    deque<int>::iterator pos;
    pos = search_n (coll.begin(), coll.end(),    // range
                    3,                           // count
                    7);                          // value
```

```
    // print result
    if (pos != coll.end()) {
        cout << "three consecutive elements with value 7 "
             << "start with " << distance(coll.begin(),pos) +1
             << ". element" << endl;
    }
    else {
        cout << "no four consecutive elements with value 7 found"
             << endl;
    }


    // find four consecutive odd elements
    pos = search_n (coll.begin(), coll.end(),    // range
                    4,                           // count
                    0,                           // value
                    [](int elem, int value){     // criterion
                        return elem%2==1;
                    });

    // print result
    if (pos != coll.end()) {
        cout << "first four consecutive odd elements are: ";
        for (int i=0; i<4; ++i, ++pos) {
            cout << *pos << ' ';
        }
    }
    else {
        cout << "no four consecutive elements with value > 3 found";
    }
    cout << endl;
}
```

The program has the following output:

```
1 2 7 7 6 3 9 5 7 7 7 3 6
three consecutive elements with value 7 start with 9. element
first four consecutive odd elements are: 3 9 5 7
```

There is a nasty problem with the second form of search_n(). Consider the second call of search_n():

```
pos = search_n (coll.begin(), coll.end(),    // range
                4,                           // count
                0,                           // value
```

```
        [](int elem, int value){       // criterion
            return elem%2==1;
        });
```

This kind of searching for elements that match a special criterion does not conform to the rest of the STL. Following the usual concepts of the STL, the call should be as follows:

```
pos = search_n_if (coll.begin(), coll.end(),   // range
                   4,                            // count
                   [](int elem){                 // criterion
                       return elem%2==1;
                   });
```

However, the algorithm requires a unary predicate, which gets the value passed as fourth argument to search_n() as second parameter.

Unfortunately, nobody noticed this inconsistency when these new algorithms were introduced to the C++98 standard (they were not part of the original STL). At first, it seemed that the version with four arguments is more convenient because you could implement something like:

```
// find four consecutive elements with value greater than 3
pos = search_n (coll.begin(), coll.end(),   // range
                4,                            // count
                3,                            // value
                greater<int>());              // criterion
```

However, as our example demonstrates, it requires a binary predicate even if you need only a unary predicate.

The consequence is that if you have an ordinary unary predicate, such as

```
bool isPrime (int elem);
```

you either have to change the signature of your function or write a simple wrapper:

```
bool binaryIsPrime (int elem1, int) {
    return isPrime(elem1);
}
...
pos = search_n (coll.begin(), coll.end(),   // range
                4,                            // count
                0,                            // required dummy value
                binaryIsPrime);               // binary criterion
```

Search First Subrange

```
ForwardIterator1
```
search (ForwardIterator1 *beg*, ForwardIterator1 *end*,
        ForwardIterator2 *searchBeg*, ForwardIterator2 *searchEnd*)

```
ForwardIterator1
```
search (ForwardIterator1 *beg*, ForwardIterator1 *end*,
        ForwardIterator2 *searchBeg*, ForwardIterator2 *searchEnd*,
        BinaryPredicate *op*)

- Both forms return the position of the first element of the first subrange matching the range [*searchBeg,searchEnd*) in the range [*beg,end*).
- In the first form, the elements of the subrange have to be equal to the elements of the whole range.
- In the second form, for every comparison between elements, the call of the binary predicate
        op(*elem*,*searchElem*)
  has to yield true.
- Both forms return *end* if no matching elements are found.
- Note that *op* should not change its state during a function call. See Section 10.1.4, page 483, for details.
- *op* should not modify the passed arguments.
- See Section 6.4.1, page 203, for a discussion of how to find a subrange for which you know only the first and the last elements.
- Complexity: linear (at most, *numElems*numSearchElems* comparisons or calls of *op*(), respectively).

The following example demonstrates how to find a sequence as the first subrange of another sequence (compare with the example of find_end() on page 537):

```cpp
// algo/search1.cpp

#include "algostuff.hpp"
using namespace std;

int main()
{
    deque<int> coll;
    list<int> subcoll;

    INSERT_ELEMENTS(coll,1,7);
    INSERT_ELEMENTS(coll,1,7);
    INSERT_ELEMENTS(subcoll,3,6);

    PRINT_ELEMENTS(coll,    "coll:    ");
    PRINT_ELEMENTS(subcoll,"subcoll: ");
```

```
// search first occurrence of subcoll in coll
deque<int>::iterator pos;
pos = search (coll.begin(), coll.end(),          // range
              subcoll.begin(), subcoll.end());   // subrange

// loop while subcoll found as subrange of coll
while (pos != coll.end()) {
    // print position of first element
    cout << "subcoll found starting with element "
         << distance(coll.begin(),pos) + 1
         << endl;

    // search next occurrence of subcoll
    ++pos;
    pos = search (pos, coll.end(),                  // range
                  subcoll.begin(), subcoll.end());  // subrange
}
}
```

The program has the following output:

```
coll:     1 2 3 4 5 6 7 1 2 3 4 5 6 7
subcoll: 3 4 5 6
subcoll found starting with element 3
subcoll found starting with element 10
```

The next example demonstrates how to use the second form of the search() algorithm to find a subsequence that matches a more complicated criterion. Here, the subsequence *even, odd, and even value* is searched:

```
// algo/search2.cpp

#include "algostuff.hpp"
using namespace std;

// checks whether an element is even or odd
bool checkEven (int elem, bool even)
{
    if (even) {
        return elem % 2 == 0;
    }
    else {
        return elem % 2 == 1;
    }
}
```

```
int main()
{
    vector<int> coll;

    INSERT_ELEMENTS(coll,1,9);
    PRINT_ELEMENTS(coll,"coll: ");

    // arguments for checkEven()
    // - check for: "even odd even"
    bool checkEvenArgs[3] = { true, false, true };

    // search first subrange in coll
    vector<int>::iterator pos;
    pos = search (coll.begin(), coll.end(),         // range
                  checkEvenArgs, checkEvenArgs+3,   // subrange values
                  checkEven);                       // subrange criterion

    // loop while subrange found
    while (pos != coll.end()) {
        // print position of first element
        cout << "subrange found starting with element "
             << distance(coll.begin(),pos) + 1
             << endl;

        // search next subrange in coll
        pos = search (++pos, coll.end(),                // range
                      checkEvenArgs, checkEvenArgs+3,   // subr. values
                      checkEven);                       // subr. criterion
    }
}
```

The program has the following output:

```
coll: 1 2 3 4 5 6 7 8 9
subrange found starting with element 2
subrange found starting with element 4
subrange found starting with element 6
```

Search Last Subrange

```
ForwardIterator1
```
find_end (ForwardIterator1 *beg*, ForwardIterator1 *end*,
              ForwardIterator2 *searchBeg*, ForwardIterator2 *searchEnd*)

```
ForwardIterator1
```
find_end (ForwardIterator1 *beg*, ForwardIterator1 *end*,
              ForwardIterator2 *searchBeg*, ForwardIterator2 *searchEnd*,
              BinaryPredicate *op*)

- Both forms return the position of the first element of the last subrange matching the range [*searchBeg,searchEnd*) in the range [*beg,end*).
- In the first form, the elements of the subrange have to be equal to the elements of the whole range.
- In the second form, for every comparison between elements, the call of the binary predicate
      op(*elem*,*searchElem*)
  has to yield true.
- Both forms return *end* if no matching elements are found.
- Note that *op* should not change its state during a function call. See Section 10.1.4, page 483, for details.
- *op* should not modify the passed arguments.
- See Section 6.4.1, page 203, for a discussion of how to find a subrange for which you know only the first and the last elements.
- These algorithms were not part of the original STL. Unfortunately, they were called find_end() instead of search_end(), which would be more consistent, because the algorithm used to search the first subrange is called search().
- Complexity: linear (at most, *numElems*∗*numSearchElems* comparisons or calls of *op*(), respectively).

The following example demonstrates how to find a sequence as the last subrange of another sequence (compare with the example of search() on page 534):

```cpp
// algo/findend1.cpp

#include "algostuff.hpp"
using namespace std;

int main()
{
    deque<int> coll;
    list<int> subcoll;

    INSERT_ELEMENTS(coll,1,7);
    INSERT_ELEMENTS(coll,1,7);
```

```
INSERT_ELEMENTS(subcoll,3,6);

PRINT_ELEMENTS(coll,    "coll:     ");
PRINT_ELEMENTS(subcoll,"subcoll: ");

// search last occurrence of subcoll in coll
deque<int>::iterator pos;
pos = find_end (coll.begin(), coll.end(),           // range
                  subcoll.begin(), subcoll.end());  // subrange

// loop while subcoll found as subrange of coll
deque<int>::iterator end(coll.end());
while (pos != end) {
    // print position of first element
    cout << "subcoll found starting with element "
        << distance(coll.begin(),pos) + 1
        << endl;

    // search next occurrence of subcoll
    end = pos;
    pos = find_end (coll.begin(), end,               // range
                  subcoll.begin(), subcoll.end()); // subrange
}
}
```

The program has the following output:

```
coll:    1 2 3 4 5 6 7 1 2 3 4 5 6 7
subcoll: 3 4 5 6
subcoll found starting with element 10
subcoll found starting with element 3
```

For the second form of this algorithm, see the second example of search() on page 535. You can use find_end() in a similar manner.

Search First of Several Possible Elements

```
InputIterator
find_first_of (InputIterator beg, InputIterator end,
               ForwardIterator searchBeg, ForwardIterator searchEnd)
```

```
InputIterator
find_first_of (InputIterator beg, InputIterator end,
               ForwardIterator searchBeg, ForwardIterator searchEnd,
               BinaryPredicate op)
```

- The first form returns the position of the first element in the range [*beg,end*) that is also in the range [*searchBeg,searchEnd*).
- The second form returns the position of the first element in the range [*beg,end*) for which any call

    op(*elem*,*searchElem*)

  with all elements of [*searchBeg,searchEnd*) yields `true`.
- Both forms return *end* if no matching elements are found.
- Note that *op* should not change its state during a function call. See Section 10.1.4, page 483, for details.
- *op* should not modify the passed arguments.
- By using reverse iterators, you can find the last of several possible values.
- These algorithms were not part of the original STL.
- Before C++11, these algorithms required forward iterators instead of input iterators for the range [*beg,end*).
- Complexity: linear (at most, *numElems*∗*numSearchElems* comparisons or calls of *op*(), respectively).

The following example demonstrates the use of `find_first_of()`:

```
// algo/findof1.cpp

#include "algostuff.hpp"
using namespace std;

int main()
{
    vector<int> coll;
    list<int> searchcoll;

    INSERT_ELEMENTS(coll,1,11);
    INSERT_ELEMENTS(searchcoll,3,5);

    PRINT_ELEMENTS(coll,      "coll:       ");
    PRINT_ELEMENTS(searchcoll,"searchcoll: ");

    // search first occurrence of an element of searchcoll in coll
    vector<int>::iterator pos;
    pos = find_first_of (coll.begin(), coll.end(),      // range
                         searchcoll.begin(),    // beginning of search set
                         searchcoll.end());     // end of search set
```

```
        cout << "first element of searchcoll in coll is element "
             << distance(coll.begin(),pos) + 1
             << endl;

        // search last occurrence of an element of searchcoll in coll
        vector<int>::reverse_iterator rpos;
        rpos = find_first_of (coll.rbegin(), coll.rend(),   // range
                              searchcoll.begin(),   // beginning of search set
                              searchcoll.end());   // end of search set
        cout << "last element of searchcoll in coll is element "
             << distance(coll.begin(),rpos.base())
             << endl;
    }
```

The second call uses reverse iterators to find the last element that has a value equal to one element in `searchcoll`. To print the position of the element, `base()` is called to transform the reverse iterator into an iterator. Thus, you can process the distance from the beginning. Normally, you would have to add 1 to the result of `distance()` because the first element has distance 0 but actually is element 1. However, because `base()` moves the position of the value to which it refers, you have the same effect (see Section 9.4.1, page 452, for the description of `base()`).

The program has the following output:

```
coll:       1 2 3 4 5 6 7 8 9 10 11
searchcoll: 3 4 5
first element of searchcoll in coll is element 3
last element of searchcoll in coll is element 5
```

Search Two Adjacent, Equal Elements

```
ForwardIterator
```
adjacent_find (ForwardIterator *beg*, ForwardIterator *end*)

```
ForwardIterator
```
adjacent_find (ForwardIterator *beg*, ForwardIterator *end*,
                BinaryPredicate *op*)

- The first form returns the first element in the range [*beg*,*end*) that has a value equal to the value of the following element.
- The second form returns the first element in the range [*beg*,*end*) for which the binary predicate
      op(*elem*,*nextElem*)
  yields true.
- Both forms return *end* if no matching elements are found.
- Note that *op* should not change its state during a function call. See Section 10.1.4, page 483, for details.

- *op* should not modify the passed arguments.
- Complexity: linear (at most, *numElems* comparisons or calls of *op()*, respectively).

The following program demonstrates both forms of `adjacent_find()`:

```
// algo/adjacentfind1.cpp

#include "algostuff.hpp"
using namespace std;

// return whether the second object has double the value of the first
bool doubled (int elem1, int elem2)
{
    return elem1 * 2 == elem2;
}

int main()
{
    vector<int> coll;

    coll.push_back(1);
    coll.push_back(3);
    coll.push_back(2);
    coll.push_back(4);
    coll.push_back(5);
    coll.push_back(5);
    coll.push_back(0);

    PRINT_ELEMENTS(coll,"coll: ");

    // search first two elements with equal value
    vector<int>::iterator pos;
    pos = adjacent_find (coll.begin(), coll.end());

    if (pos != coll.end()) {
        cout << "first two elements with equal value have position "
             << distance(coll.begin(),pos) + 1
             << endl;
    }

    // search first two elements for which the second has double the value of the first
    pos = adjacent_find (coll.begin(), coll.end(),    // range
                         doubled);                    // criterion

    if (pos != coll.end()) {
```

```
        cout << "first two elements with second value twice the "
             << "first have pos. "
             << distance(coll.begin(),pos) + 1
             << endl;
    }
}
```

The first call of `adjacent_find()` searches for equal values. The second form uses `doubled()` to find the first element for which the successor has the double value. The program has the following output:

```
coll: 1 3 2 4 5 5 0
first two elements with equal value have position 5
first two elements with second value twice the first have pos. 3
```

11.5.4 Comparing Ranges

Testing Equality

```
bool
equal (InputIterator1 beg, InputIterator1 end,
       InputIterator2 cmpBeg)
```

```
bool
equal (InputIterator1 beg, InputIterator1 end,
       InputIterator2 cmpBeg,
       BinaryPredicate op)
```

- The first form returns whether the elements in the range [*beg*,*end*) are equal to the elements in the range starting with *cmpBeg*.
- The second form returns whether each call of the binary predicate
      op(*elem*,*cmpElem*)
  with the corresponding elements in the range [*beg*,*end*) and in the range starting with *cmpBeg* yields true.
- Note that *op* should not change its state during a function call. See Section 10.1.4, page 483, for details.
- *op* should not modify the passed arguments.
- The caller must ensure that the range starting with *cmpBeg* contains enough elements.
- To determine the details of any differences, you should use the `mismatch()` algorithm (see page 546).
- To determine whether two sequences contain the same elements in different order, algorithm `is_permutation()` is provided since C++11 (see page 544).
- Complexity: linear (at most, *numElems* comparisons or calls of *op*(), respectively).

The following example demonstrates both forms of equal(). The first call checks whether the elements have values with equal elements. The second call uses an auxiliary predicate function to check whether the elements of both collections have corresponding even and odd elements:

```cpp
// algo/equal1.cpp

#include "algostuff.hpp"
using namespace std;

bool bothEvenOrOdd (int elem1, int elem2)
{
    return elem1 % 2 == elem2 % 2;
}

int main()
{
    vector<int> coll1;
    list<int> coll2;

    INSERT_ELEMENTS(coll1,1,7);
    INSERT_ELEMENTS(coll2,3,9);

    PRINT_ELEMENTS(coll1,"coll1: ");
    PRINT_ELEMENTS(coll2,"coll2: ");

    // check whether both collections are equal
    if (equal (coll1.begin(), coll1.end(),    // first range
               coll2.begin())) {              // second range
        cout << "coll1 == coll2" << endl;
    }
    else {
        cout << "coll1 != coll2" << endl;
    }

    // check for corresponding even and odd elements
    if (equal (coll1.begin(), coll1.end(),    // first range
               coll2.begin(),                 // second range
               bothEvenOrOdd)) {              // comparison criterion
        cout << "even and odd elements correspond" << endl;
    }
    else {
        cout << "even and odd elements do not correspond" << endl;
    }
}
```

The program has the following output:

```
coll1: 1 2 3 4 5 6 7
coll2: 3 4 5 6 7 8 9
coll1 != coll2
even and odd elements correspond
```

Testing for Unordered Equality

```
bool
```
is_permutation (ForwardIterator1 *beg1*, ForwardIterator1 *end1*,
                  ForwardIterator2 *beg2*)

```
bool
```
is_permutation (ForwardIterator1 *beg1*, ForwardIterator1 *end1*,
                  ForwardIterator2 *beg2*,
                  CompFunc *op*)

- Both forms return whether the elements in the range [*beg1*,*end1*) are a permutation of the elements in the range starting with *beg2*; that is, whether they return equal elements in whatever order.
- The first form compares the elements by using operator ==.
- The second form compares the elements by using the binary predicate
    op(*elem1*,*elem2*)
  which should return `true` when *elem1* is equal to *elem2*.
- Note that *op* should not change its state during a function call. See Section 10.1.4, page 483, for details.
- *op* should not modify the passed arguments.
- All Iterators must have the same value type.
- These algorithms are available since C++11.
- Complexity: at worst quadratic (*numElems1* comparisons or calls of *op*(), if all elements are equal and have the same order).

The following example demonstrates the use of an unordered comparison:

```
// algo/ispermutation1.cpp

#include "algostuff.hpp"
using namespace std;

bool bothEvenOrOdd (int elem1, int elem2)
{
    return elem1 % 2 == elem2 % 2;
}
```

```
int main()
{
    vector<int> coll1;
    list<int> coll2;
    deque<int> coll3;

    coll1 = { 1, 1, 2, 3, 4, 5, 6, 7, 8, 9 };
    coll2 = { 1, 9, 8, 7, 6, 5, 4, 3, 2, 1 };
    coll3 = { 11, 12, 13, 19, 18, 17, 16, 15, 14, 11 };

    PRINT_ELEMENTS(coll1,"coll1: ");
    PRINT_ELEMENTS(coll2,"coll2: ");
    PRINT_ELEMENTS(coll3,"coll3: ");

    // check whether both collections have equal elements in any order
    if (is_permutation (coll1.cbegin(), coll1.cend(), //first range
                        coll2.cbegin())) {            // second range
        cout << "coll1 and coll2 have equal elements" << endl;
    }
    else {
        cout << "coll1 and coll2 don't have equal elements" << endl;
    }

    // check for corresponding number of even and odd elements
    if (is_permutation (coll1.cbegin(), coll1.cend(), //first range
                        coll3.cbegin(),               // second range
                        bothEvenOrOdd)) {             // comparison criterion
        cout << "numbers of even and odd elements match" << endl;
    }
    else {
        cout << "numbers of even and odd elements don't match" << endl;
    }
}
```

The program has the following output:

```
coll1: 1 1 2 3 4 5 6 7 8 9
coll2: 1 9 8 7 6 5 4 3 2 1
coll3: 11 12 13 19 18 17 16 15 14 11
coll1 and coll2 have equal elements
numbers of even and odd elements match
```

Search the First Difference

```
pair<InputIterator1,InputIterator2>
mismatch (InputIterator1 beg, InputIterator1 end,
          InputIterator2 cmpBeg)

pair<InputIterator1,InputIterator2>
mismatch (InputIterator1 beg, InputIterator1 end,
          InputIterator2 cmpBeg,
          BinaryPredicate op)
```

- The first form returns the first two corresponding elements of range [*beg,end*) and the range starting with *cmpBeg* that differ.
- The second form returns the first two corresponding elements of range [*beg,end*) and the range starting with *cmpBeg* for which the binary predicate
    op(*elem*,*cmpElem*)
  yields `false`.
- If no difference is found, a `pair<>` of *end* and the corresponding element of the second range is returned. Note that this does not mean that both sequences are equal, because the second sequence might contain more elements.
- Note that *op* should not change its state during a function call. See Section 10.1.4, page 483, for details.
- *op* should not modify the passed arguments.
- The caller must ensure that the range starting with *cmpBeg* contains enough elements.
- To check whether two ranges are equal, you should use algorithm `equal()` (see Section 11.5.4, page 542).
- Complexity: linear (at most, *numElems* comparisons or calls of *op*(), respectively).

The following example demonstrates both forms of `mismatch()`:

```
// algo/mismatch1.cpp

#include "algostuff.hpp"
using namespace std;

int main()
{
    vector<int> coll1 = { 1, 2, 3, 4, 5, 6 };
    list<int>   coll2 = { 1, 2, 4, 8, 16, 3 };

    PRINT_ELEMENTS(coll1,"coll1: ");
    PRINT_ELEMENTS(coll2,"coll2: ");
```

```
// find first mismatch
auto values = mismatch (coll1.cbegin(), coll1.cend(),    // first range
                        coll2.cbegin());                 // second range
if (values.first == coll1.end()) {
    cout << "no mismatch" << endl;
}
else {
    cout << "first mismatch: "
         << *values.first  << " and "
         << *values.second << endl;
}


// find first position where the element of coll1 is not
// less than the corresponding element of coll2
values = mismatch (coll1.cbegin(), coll1.cend(),    // first range
                   coll2.cbegin(),                  // second range
                   less_equal<int>());              // criterion
if (values.first == coll1.end()) {
    cout << "always less-or-equal" << endl;
}
else {
    cout << "not less-or-equal: "
         << *values.first  << " and "
         << *values.second << endl;
}
}
```

The first call of `mismatch()` searches for the first corresponding elements that are not equal. The return type is:

```
pair<vector<int>::const_iterator,list<int>::const_iterator>
```

By checking whether the first element in the returned pair equals the end of the passed range, we check whether a mismatch exists. In that case, the values of the corresponding elements are written to standard output.

The second call searches for the first pair of elements in which the element of the first collection is greater than the corresponding element of the second collection and returns these elements. The program has the following output:

```
coll1: 1 2 3 4 5 6
coll2: 1 2 4 8 16 3
first mismatch: 3 and 4
not less-or-equal: 6 and 3
```

Testing for "Less Than"

```
bool
lexicographical_compare (InputIterator1 beg1, InputIterator1 end1,
                         InputIterator2 beg2, InputIterator2 end2)

bool
lexicographical_compare (InputIterator1 beg1, InputIterator1 end1,
                         InputIterator2 beg2, InputIterator2 end2,
                         CompFunc op)
```

- Both forms return whether the elements in the range [*beg1*,*end1*) are "lexicographically less than" the elements in the range [*beg2*,*end2*).
- The first form compares the elements by using operator <.
- The second form compares the elements by using the binary predicate
    op(*elem1*,*elem2*)
  which should return `true` when *elem1* is less than *elem2*.
- *Lexicographical comparison* means that sequences are compared element-by-element until any of the following occurs:
    - When two elements are not equal, the result of their comparison is the result of the whole comparison.
    - When one sequence has no more elements, the sequence that has no more elements is less than the other. Thus, the comparison yields `true` if the first sequence is the one that has no more elements.
    - When both sequences have no more elements, both sequences are equal, and the result of the comparison is `false`.
- Note that *op* should not change its state during a function call. See Section 10.1.4, page 483, for details.
- *op* should not modify the passed arguments.
- Complexity: linear (at most, min(*numElems1*,*numElems2*) comparisons or calls of *op*(), respectively).

The following example demonstrates the use of a lexicographical sorting of collections:

```
// algo/lexicocmp1.cpp

#include "algostuff.hpp"
using namespace std;

void printCollection (const list<int>& l)
{
    PRINT_ELEMENTS(l);
}
```

```
bool lessForCollection (const list<int>& l1, const list<int>& l2)
{
    return lexicographical_compare
                (l1.cbegin(), l1.cend(),     // first range
                 l2.cbegin(), l2.cend());    // second range
}

int main()
{
    list<int> c1, c2, c3, c4;

    // fill all collections with the same starting values
    INSERT_ELEMENTS(c1,1,5);
    c4 = c3 = c2 = c1;

    // and now some differences
    c1.push_back(7);
    c3.push_back(2);
    c3.push_back(0);
    c4.push_back(2);

    // create collection of collections
    vector<list<int>> cc;
    cc.insert ( cc.begin(), { c1, c2, c3, c4, c3, c1, c4, c2 } );

    // print all collections
    for_each (cc.cbegin(), cc.cend(),
            printCollection);
    cout << endl;

    // sort collection lexicographically
    sort (cc.begin(), cc.end(),      // range
        lessForCollection);          // sorting criterion

    // print all collections again
    for_each (cc.cbegin(), cc.cend(),
            printCollection);
}
```

The vector cc is initialized with several collections (all lists). The call of sort() uses the binary predicate lessForCollection() to compare two collections (see Section 11.9.1, page 596, for a description of sort()). In lessForCollection(), the lexicographical_compare() algorithm is used to compare the collections lexicographically.

The program has the following output:

```
1 2 3 4 5 7
1 2 3 4 5
1 2 3 4 5 2 0
1 2 3 4 5 2
1 2 3 4 5 2 0
1 2 3 4 5 7
1 2 3 4 5 2
1 2 3 4 5

1 2 3 4 5
1 2 3 4 5
1 2 3 4 5 2
1 2 3 4 5 2
1 2 3 4 5 2 0
1 2 3 4 5 2 0
1 2 3 4 5 7
1 2 3 4 5 7
```

11.5.5 Predicates for Ranges

The following algorithms were introduced with C++11 to check a specific condition for a given range.

Check for (Partial) Sorting

```
bool
```
is_sorted (ForwardIterator *beg*, ForwardIterator *end*)

```
bool
```
is_sorted (ForwardIterator *beg*, ForwardIterator *end*, BinaryPredicate *op*)

```
ForwardIterator
```
is_sorted_until (ForwardIterator *beg*, ForwardIterator *end*)

```
ForwardIterator
```
is_sorted_until (ForwardIterator *beg*, ForwardIterator *end*, BinaryPredicate *op*)

- `is_sorted()` returns whether the elements in the range [*beg,end*) are sorted.
- `is_sorted()_until` returns the position of the first element in the range [*beg,end*), which breaks the sorting of this range, or *end* if none.

- The first and third forms use operator < to compare elements. The second and fourth forms use the binary predicate

    op(*elem1*,*elem2*)

  which should return `true` if *elem1* is "less than" *elem2*.
- If the range is empty or has only one element, the algorithms return `true` or *end*, respectively.
- Note that *op* should not change its state during a function call. See Section 10.1.4, page 483, for details.
- *op* should not modify the passed arguments.
- These algorithms are available since C++11.
- Complexity: linear (at most *numElems*−1 calls of < or *op*()).

The following program demonstrates the use of these algorithms:

```cpp
// algo/issorted1.cpp

#include "algostuff.hpp"
using namespace std;

int main()
{
    vector<int> coll1 = { 1, 1, 2, 3, 4, 5, 6, 7, 8, 9 };
    PRINT_ELEMENTS(coll1,"coll1: ");

    // check whether coll1 is sorted
    if (is_sorted (coll1.begin(), coll1.end())) {
        cout << "coll1 is sorted" << endl;
    }
    else {
        cout << "coll1 is not sorted" << endl;
    }

    map<int,string> coll2;
    coll2 = { {1,"Bill"}, {2,"Jim"}, {3,"Nico"}, {4,"Liu"}, {5,"Ai"} };
    PRINT_MAPPED_ELEMENTS(coll2,"coll2: ");

    // define predicate to compare names
    auto compareName = [](const pair<int,string>& e1,
                          const pair<int,string>& e2){
                            return e1.second<e2.second;
                      };

    // check whether the names in coll2 are sorted
    if (is_sorted (coll2.cbegin(), coll2.cend(),
                   compareName)) {
        cout << "names in coll2 are sorted" << endl;
    }
```

```
        else {
            cout << "names in coll2 are not sorted" << endl;
        }

        // print first unsorted name
        auto pos = is_sorted_until (coll2.cbegin(), coll2.cend(),
                                    compareName);
        if (pos != coll2.end()) {
            cout << "first unsorted name: " << pos->second << endl;
        }
    }
```

The program has the following output:
```
coll1: 1 1 2 3 4 5 6 7 8 9
coll1 is sorted
coll2: [1,Bill] [2,Jim] [3,Nico] [4,Liu] [5,Ai]
names in coll2 are not sorted
first unsorted name: Liu
```

Note that is_sorted_until() returns the position of the first unsorted element as an iterator, so we have to call pos->second to access the name (the value of the key/value pair).

Check for Being Partitioned

```
bool
```
is_partitioned (InputIterator *beg*, InputIterator *end*, UnaryPredicate *op*)

```
ForwardIterator
```
partition_point (ForwardIterator *beg*, ForwardIterator *end*, BinaryPredicate *op*)

- is_partitioned() returns whether the elements in the range [*beg,end*) are partitions, so all the elements fulfilling the predicate *op*() are positioned before all elements that do not fulfill it.
- partition_point() returns the position of the first element in the *partitioned* range [*beg,end*). Thus, for [*beg,end*), is_partitioned() has to yield true on entry.
- The algorithms use the binary predicate
  op(*elem1*, *elem2*)
  which should return true if *elem1* is "less than" *elem2*.
- If the range is empty, partition_point() returns *end*.
- Note that *op* should not change its state during a function call. See Section 10.1.4, page 483, for details.
- *op* should not modify the passed arguments.

- These algorithms are available since C++11.
- Complexity:
  - is_partitioned(): linear (at most *numElems* calls of *op*()).
  - partition_point(): logarithmic for random-access iterators and linear otherwise (in any case, at most log(*numElems*) calls of *op*()).

The following program demonstrates the use of these algorithms:

```
// algo/ispartitioned1.cpp

#include "algostuff.hpp"
using namespace std;

int main()
{
    vector<int> coll = { 5, 3, 9, 1, 3, 4, 8, 2, 6 };
    PRINT_ELEMENTS(coll,"coll: ");

    // define predicate: check whether element is odd:
    auto isOdd = [](int elem) {
                    return elem%2==1;
                 };

    // check whether coll is partitioned in odd and even elements
    if (is_partitioned (coll.cbegin(), coll.cend(),   // range
                        isOdd)) {                      // predicate
        cout << "coll is partitioned" << endl;

        // find first even element:
        auto pos = partition_point (coll.cbegin(),coll.cend(),
                                    isOdd);
        cout << "first even element: " << *pos << endl;
    }
    else {
        cout << "coll is not partitioned" << endl;
    }
}
```

The program has the following output:

```
coll: 5 3 9 1 3 4 8 2 6
coll is partitioned
first even element: 4
```

Check for Being a Heap (Maximum Element First)

```
bool
```
is_heap (RandomAccessIterator *beg*, RandomAccessIterator *end*)

```
bool
```
is_heap (RandomAccessIterator *beg*, RandomAccessIterator *end*, BinaryPredicate *op*)


```
RandomAccessIterator
```
is_heap_until (RandomAccessIterator *beg*, RandomAccessIterator *end*)

```
RandomAccessIterator
```
is_heap_until (RandomAccessIterator *beg*, RandomAccessIterator *end*,
                 BinaryPredicate *op*)

- is_heap() returns whether the elements in the range [*beg,end*) are a heap (see Section 11.9.4, page 604), which means that *beg* is (one of) the maximum element(s).
- is_heap()_until returns the position of the first element in the range [*beg,end*) that breaks the sorting as a heap (is larger than the first element) or *end* if none.
- The first and third forms use operator < to compare elements. The second and fourth forms use the binary predicate
    op(*elem1*,*elem2*)
  which should return true if *elem1* is "less than" *elem2*.
- If the range is empty or has only one element, the algorithms return true or *end*, respectively.
- Note that *op* should not change its state during a function call. See Section 10.1.4, page 483, for details.
- *op* should not modify the passed arguments.
- These algorithms are available since C++11.
- Complexity: linear (at most *numElems*-1 calls of < or *op*()).

The following demonstrates the use of these algorithms:

```cpp
// algo/isheap1.cpp

#include "algostuff.hpp"
using namespace std;

int main()
{
    vector<int> coll1 = { 9, 8, 7, 7, 7, 5, 4, 2, 1 };
    vector<int> coll2 = { 5, 3, 2, 1, 4, 7, 9, 8, 6 };
    PRINT_ELEMENTS(coll1,"coll1: ");
    PRINT_ELEMENTS(coll2,"coll2: ");
```

```
// check whether the collections are heaps
cout << boolalpha << "coll1 is heap: "
     << is_heap (coll1.cbegin(), coll1.cend()) << endl;
cout << "coll2 is heap: "
     << is_heap (coll2.cbegin(), coll2.cend()) << endl;

// print the first element that is not a heap in coll2
auto pos = is_heap_until (coll2.cbegin(), coll2.cend());
if (pos != coll2.end()) {
    cout << "first non-heap element: " << *pos << endl;
}
}
```

The program has the following output:

```
coll1: 9 8 7 7 7 5 4 2 1
coll2: 5 3 2 1 4 7 9 8 6
coll1 is heap: true
coll2 is heap: false
first non-heap element: 4
```

All, Any, or None

```
bool
all_of (InputIterator beg, InputIterator end, UnaryPredicate op)

bool
any_of (InputIterator beg, InputIterator end, UnaryPredicate op)

bool
none_of (InputIterator beg, InputIterator end, UnaryPredicate op)
```

- These algorithms return whether for all, any (at least one), or none of the elements in the range [*beg,end*), the unary predicate
    op(*elem*)
  yields true.
- If the range is empty, all_of() and none_of() return true, whereas any_of() returns false.
- Note that *op* should not change its state during a function call. See Section 10.1.4, page 483, for details.
- *op* should not modify the passed arguments.
- These algorithms are available since C++11.
- Complexity: linear (at most *numElems* calls of *op*()).

The following demonstrates the use of these algorithms:

```
// algo/allanynone1.cpp

#include "algostuff.hpp"
using namespace std;

int main()
{
    vector<int> coll;
    vector<int>::iterator pos;

    INSERT_ELEMENTS(coll,1,9);
    PRINT_ELEMENTS(coll,"coll: ");

    // define an object for the predicate (using a lambda)
    auto isEven = [](int elem) {
                        return elem%2==0;
                  };

    // print whether all, any, or none of the elements are/is even
    cout << boolalpha << "all even?:   "
         << all_of(coll.cbegin(),coll.cend(), isEven) << endl;
    cout << "any even?:   "
         << any_of(coll.cbegin(),coll.cend(), isEven) << endl;
    cout << "none even?: "
         << none_of(coll.cbegin(),coll.cend(), isEven) << endl;
}
```

The program has the following output:

```
coll: 1 2 3 4 5 6 7 8 9
all even?:   false
any even?:   true
none even?: false
```

11.6   Modifying Algorithms

This section describes algorithms that modify the elements of a range. There are two ways to modify elements:

1. Modify them directly while iterating through a sequence.
2. Modify them while copying them from a source range to a destination range.

Several modifying algorithms provide both ways of modifying the elements of a range. In this case, the name of the latter uses the _copy suffix.

You can't use an associative or unordered container as a destination range, because the elements in these containers are constant. If you could, it would be possible to compromise the automatic sorting or the hash based position, respectively.

All algorithms that have a separate destination range return the position after the last copied element of that range.

11.6.1   Copying Elements

```
OutputIterator
copy (InputIterator sourceBeg, InputIterator sourceEnd,
       OutputIterator destBeg)


OutputIterator
copy_if (InputIterator sourceBeg, InputIterator sourceEnd,
          OutputIterator destBeg,
          UnaryPredicate op)


OutputIterator
copy_n (InputIterator sourceBeg,
          Size num,
          OutputIterator destBeg)


BidirectionalIterator2
copy_backward (BidirectionalIterator1 sourceBeg,
                 BidirectionalIterator1 sourceEnd,
                 BidirectionalIterator2 destEnd)
```

- All algorithms copy all elements of a source range ([*sourceBeg,sourceEnd*) or *num* elements starting with *sourceBeg*) into the destination range starting with *destBeg* or ending with *destEnd*, respectively.

- They return the position after the last copied element in the destination range (the first element that is not overwritten).

- For copy(), *destBeg* should not be part of [*sourceBeg,sourceEnd*). For copy_if(), source and destination ranges should not overlap. For copy_backward(), *destEnd* should not be part of (*sourceBeg,sourceEnd*].

- copy() iterates forward through the sequence, whereas copy_backward() iterates backward. This difference matters only if the source and destination ranges overlap.
    - To copy a subrange to the front, use copy(). Thus, for copy(), *destBeg* should have a position in front of *sourceBeg*.
    - To copy a subrange to the back, use copy_backward(). Thus, for copy_backward(), *destEnd* should have a position after *sourceEnd*.

  So, whenever the third argument is an element of the source range specified by the first two arguments, use the other algorithm. Note that switching to the other algorithm means that you switch from passing the beginning of the destination range to passing the end. See page 559 for an example that demonstrates the differences.
- The caller must ensure that the destination range is big enough or that insert iterators are used.
- See Section 9.4.2, page 454, for the implementation of the copy() algorithm.
- Since C++11, if the source elements are no longer used, you should prefer move() over copy() and move_backward() over and copy_backward() (see Section 11.6.2, page 561).
- Before C++11, no copy_if() and copy_n() algorithms were provided. To copy only those elements meeting a certain criterion, you had to use remove_copy_if() (see Section 11.7.1, page 577) with a negated predicate.
- Use reverse_copy() to reverse the order of the elements during the copy (see Section 11.8.1, page 583). Note that reverse_copy() may be slightly more efficient than using copy() with reverse iterators.
- To assign all elements of a container, use the assignment operator if the containers have the same type (see Section 8.4, page 406) or the assign() member function if the containers have different types (see Section 8.4, page 407).
- To remove elements while they are being copied, use remove_copy() and remove_copy_if() (see Section 11.7.1, page 577).
- To modify elements while they are being copied, use transform() (see Section 11.6.3, page 563) or replace_copy() (see Section 11.6.6, page 573).
- Use partition_copy() (see Section 11.8.6, page 594) to copy elements into two destination ranges: one fulfilling and one not fulfilling a predicate.
- Complexity: linear (*numElems* assignments).

The following example shows some simple calls of copy() (see Section 11.6.2, page 562, for a corresponding version using move() when possible):

```
// algo/copy1.cpp

#include "algostuff.hpp"
using namespace std;

int main()
{
    vector<string> coll1 = { "Hello", "this", "is", "an", "example" };
    list<string> coll2;
```

```
    // copy elements of coll1 into coll2
    // - use back inserter to insert instead of overwrite
    copy (coll1.cbegin(), coll1.cend(),         // source range
          back_inserter(coll2));                // destination range

    // print elements of coll2
    // - copy elements to cout using an ostream iterator
    copy (coll2.cbegin(), coll2.cend(),         // source range
          ostream_iterator<string>(cout," "));  // destination range
    cout << endl;

    // copy elements of coll1 into coll2 in reverse order
    // - now overwriting
    copy (coll1.crbegin(), coll1.crend(),       // source range
          coll2.begin());                       // destination range

    // print elements of coll2 again
    copy (coll2.cbegin(), coll2.cend(),         // source range
          ostream_iterator<string>(cout," "));  // destination range
    cout << endl;
}
```

In this example, back inserters (see Section 9.4.2, page 455) are used to insert the elements into the destination range. Without using inserters, copy() would overwrite the empty collection coll2, resulting in undefined behavior. Similarly, the example uses ostream iterators (see Section 9.4.3, page 460) to use standard output as the destination. The program has the following output:

```
Hello this is an example
example an is this Hello
```

The following example demonstrates the difference between copy() and copy_backward():

```
// algo/copy2.cpp

#include "algostuff.hpp"
using namespace std;

int main()
{
    // initialize source collection with ".........abcdef.........."
    vector<char> source(10,'.');
    for (int c='a'; c<='f'; c++) {
        source.push_back(c);
    }
    source.insert(source.end(),10,'.');
    PRINT_ELEMENTS(source,"source: ");
```

```
// copy all letters three elements in front of the 'a'
vector<char> c1(source.cbegin(),source.cend());
copy (c1.cbegin()+10, c1.cbegin()+16,              // source range
        c1.begin()+7);                             // destination range
PRINT_ELEMENTS(c1,"c1:       ");

// copy all letters three elements behind the 'f'
vector<char> c2(source.cbegin(),source.cend());
copy_backward (c2.cbegin()+10, c2.cbegin()+16,     // source range
                c2.begin()+19);                    // destination range
PRINT_ELEMENTS(c2,"c2:       ");
}
```

Note that in both calls of copy() and copy_backward(), the third argument is not part of the source range. The program has the following output:

```
source: . . . . . . . . . . a b c d e f . . . . . . . . . .
c1:       . . . . . . . a b c d e f d e f . . . . . . . . .
c2:       . . . . . . . . . . a b c a b c d e f . . . . . .
```

A third example demonstrates how to use copy() as a data filter between standard input and standard output. The program reads strings and prints them, each on one line:

```
// algo/copy3.cpp

#include <iostream>
#include <algorithm>
#include <iterator>
#include <string>
using namespace std;

int main()
{
    copy (istream_iterator<string>(cin),           // beginning of source
          istream_iterator<string>(),              // end of source
          ostream_iterator<string>(cout,"\n"));    // destination
}
```

11.6.2 Moving Elements

```
OutputIterator
move (InputIterator sourceBeg, InputIterator sourceEnd,
     OutputIterator destBeg)
```

```
BidirectionalIterator2
move_backward (BidirectionalIterator1 sourceBeg,
               BidirectionalIterator1 sourceEnd,
               BidirectionalIterator2 destEnd)
```

- Both algorithms move all elements of the source range [*sourceBeg,sourceEnd*) into the destination range starting with *destBeg* or ending with *destEnd*, respectively.
- Call for each element:
    destElem=std::move(*sourceElem*)
  Thus, if the element type provides move semantics, the value of the source elements becomes undefined, so the source element should no longer be used except to reinitialize or assign a new value to it. Otherwise, the elements are copied as with copy() or copy_backward() (see Section 11.6.1, page 557).
- They return the position after the last copied element in the destination range (the first element that is not overwritten).
- For move(), *destBeg* should not be part of [*sourceBeg,sourceEnd*). For move_backward(), *destEnd* should not be part of (*sourceBeg,sourceEnd*].
- move() iterates forward through the sequence, whereas move_backward() iterates backward. This difference matters only if the source and destination ranges overlap.
    - To move a subrange to the front, use move(). Thus, for move(), *destBeg* should have a position in front of *sourceBeg*.
    - To move a subrange to the back, use move_backward(). Thus, for move_backward(), *destEnd* should have a position after *sourceEnd*.
  So, whenever the third argument is an element of the source range specified by the first two arguments, use the other algorithm. Note that switching to the other algorithm means that you switch from passing the beginning of the destination range to passing the end. See Section 11.6.1, page 559, for an example that demonstrates the differences for the corresponding copy algorithms.
- The caller must ensure that the destination range is big enough or that insert iterators are used.
- These algorithms are available since C++11.
- Complexity: linear (*numElems* move assignments).

The following example demonstrates some simple calls of move(). It is the improved example of *algo/copy1.cpp* (see Section 11.6.1, page 558), using move() instead of copy() whenever possible:

```cpp
// algo/move1.cpp

#include "algostuff.hpp"
using namespace std;

int main()
{
    vector<string> coll1 = { "Hello", "this", "is", "an", "example" };
    list<string> coll2;

    // copy elements of coll1 into coll2
    // - use back inserter to insert instead of overwrite
    // - use copy() because the elements in coll1 are used again
    copy (coll1.cbegin(), coll1.cend(),          // source range
          back_inserter(coll2));                 // destination range

    // print elements of coll2
    // - copy elements to cout using an ostream iterator
    // - use move() because these elements in coll2 are not used again
    move (coll2.cbegin(), coll2.cend(),          // source range
          ostream_iterator<string>(cout," "));   // destination range
    cout << endl;

    // copy elements of coll1 into coll2 in reverse order
    // - now overwriting (coll2.size() still fits)
    // - use move() because the elements in coll1 are not used again
    move (coll1.crbegin(), coll1.crend(),        // source range
          coll2.begin());                        // destination range

    // print elements of coll2 again
    // - use move() because the elements in coll2 are not used again
    move (coll2.cbegin(), coll2.cend(),          // source range
          ostream_iterator<string>(cout," "));   // destination range
    cout << endl;
}
```

Note that the elements in coll2 have an undefined state after their first output because move() is used. However, coll2 still has the size of 5 elements, so we can overwrite these elements with the second call of move(). The program has the following output:

```
Hello this is an example
example an is this Hello
```

11.6.3 Transforming and Combining Elements

The `transform()` algorithms provide two abilities:

1. The first form has four arguments. It transforms elements from a source to a destination range. Thus, this form copies and modifies elements in one step.

2. The second form has five arguments. It combines elements from two source sequences and writes the results to a destination range.

Transforming Elements

```
OutputIterator
transform (InputIterator sourceBeg, InputIterator sourceEnd,
           OutputIterator destBeg,
           UnaryFunc op)
```

- Calls

    op(elem)

  for each element in the source range [*sourceBeg,sourceEnd*) and writes each result of *op* to the destination range starting with *destBeg*:

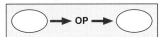

- Returns the position after the last transformed element in the destination range (the first element that is not overwritten with a result).

- The caller must ensure that the destination range is big enough or that insert iterators are used.

- *sourceBeg* and *destBeg* may be identical. Thus, as with `for_each()`, you can use this algorithm to modify elements inside a sequence. See the comparison with the `for_each()` algorithm (Section 11.2.2, page 509) for this kind of use.

- To replace elements matching a criterion with a particular value, use the `replace()` algorithms (see Section 11.6.6, page 571).

- Complexity: linear (*numElems* calls of *op()*).

The following program demonstrates how to use this kind of `transform()`:

```cpp
// algo/transform1.cpp

#include "algostuff.hpp"
using namespace std;
using namespace std::placeholders;

int main()
{
    vector<int> coll1;
    list<int> coll2;
```

```
    INSERT_ELEMENTS(coll1,1,9);
    PRINT_ELEMENTS(coll1,"coll1:    ");

    // negate all elements in coll1
    transform (coll1.cbegin(), coll1.cend(),    // source range
               coll1.begin(),                   // destination range
               negate<int>());                  // operation
    PRINT_ELEMENTS(coll1,"negated: ");

    // transform elements of coll1 into coll2 with ten times their value
    transform (coll1.cbegin(), coll1.cend(),    // source range
               back_inserter(coll2),            // destination range
               bind(multiplies<int>(),_1,10));  // operation
    PRINT_ELEMENTS(coll2,"coll2:    ");

    // print coll2 negatively and in reverse order
    transform (coll2.crbegin(), coll2.crend(),  // source range
               ostream_iterator<int>(cout," "), // destination range
               [](int elem){                    // operation
                   return -elem;
               });
    cout << endl;
}
```

The program has the following output:

```
coll1:    1 2 3 4 5 6 7 8 9
negated: -1 -2 -3 -4 -5 -6 -7 -8 -9
coll2:    -10 -20 -30 -40 -50 -60 -70 -80 -90
90 80 70 60 50 40 30 20 10
```

Combining Elements of Two Sequences

```
OutputIterator
transform (InputIterator1 source1Beg, InputIterator1 source1End,
           InputIterator2 source2Beg,
           OutputIterator destBeg,
           BinaryFunc op)
```

- Calls

    op(source1Elem,source2Elem)

    for all corresponding elements from the first source range [*source1Beg,source1End*) and the second source range starting with *source2Beg* and writes each result to the destination range starting with *destBeg*:

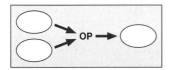

- Returns the position after the last transformed element in the destination range (the first element that is not overwritten with a result).
- The caller must ensure that the second source range is big enough (has at least as many elements as the source range).
- The caller must ensure that the destination range is big enough or that insert iterators are used.
- *source1Beg*, *source2Beg*, and *destBeg* may be identical. Thus, you can process the results of elements that are combined with themselves, and you can overwrite the elements of a source with the results.
- Complexity: linear (*numElems* calls of *op*()).

The following program demonstrates how to use this form of `transform()`:

```
// algo/transform2.cpp

#include "algostuff.hpp"
using namespace std;

int main()
{
    vector<int> coll1;
    list<int> coll2;

    INSERT_ELEMENTS(coll1,1,9);
    PRINT_ELEMENTS(coll1,"coll1:    ");

    // square each element
    transform (coll1.cbegin(), coll1.cend(),    // first source range
               coll1.cbegin(),                  // second source range
               coll1.begin(),                   // destination range
               multiplies<int>());              // operation
    PRINT_ELEMENTS(coll1,"squared: ");

    // add each element traversed forward with each element traversed backward
    // and insert result into coll2
    transform (coll1.cbegin(), coll1.cend(),    // first source range
               coll1.crbegin(),                 // second source range
               back_inserter(coll2),            // destination range
               plus<int>());                    // operation
    PRINT_ELEMENTS(coll2,"coll2:    ");
```

```
    // print differences of two corresponding elements
    cout << "diff:     ";
    transform (coll1.cbegin(), coll1.cend(),    // first source range
               coll2.cbegin(),                  // second source range
               ostream_iterator<int>(cout, " "), // destination range
               minus<int>());                   // operation
    cout << endl;
}
```

The program has the following output:

```
coll1:    1 2 3 4 5 6 7 8 9
squared: 1 4 9 16 25 36 49 64 81
coll2:    82 68 58 52 50 52 58 68 82
diff:     -81 -64 -49 -36 -25 -16 -9 -4 -1
```

11.6.4   Swapping Elements

```
ForwardIterator2
swap_ranges (ForwardIterator1 beg1, ForwardIterator1 end1,
             ForwardIterator2 beg2)
```

- Swaps the elements in the range [*beg1,end1*) with the corresponding elements starting with *beg2*.
- Returns the position after the last swapped element in the second range.
- The caller must ensure that the second range is big enough.
- Both ranges must not overlap.
- To swap all elements of a container of the same type, use its `swap()` member function because the member function usually has constant complexity (see Section 8.4, page 407).
- Complexity: linear (*numElems* swap operations).

The following example demonstrates how to use `swap_ranges()`:

```
// algo/swapranges1.cpp

#include "algostuff.hpp"
using namespace std;

int main()
{
    vector<int> coll1;
    deque<int> coll2;

    INSERT_ELEMENTS(coll1,1,9);
    INSERT_ELEMENTS(coll2,11,23);
```

```
        PRINT_ELEMENTS(coll1,"coll1: ");
        PRINT_ELEMENTS(coll2,"coll2: ");

        // swap elements of coll1 with corresponding elements of coll2
        deque<int>::iterator pos;
        pos = swap_ranges (coll1.begin(), coll1.end(),    // first range
                           coll2.begin());                // second range

        PRINT_ELEMENTS(coll1,"\ncoll1: ");
        PRINT_ELEMENTS(coll2,"coll2: ");
        if (pos != coll2.end()) {
            cout << "first element not modified: "
                 << *pos << endl;
        }

        // mirror first three with last three elements in coll2
        swap_ranges (coll2.begin(), coll2.begin()+3,      // first range
                     coll2.rbegin());                     // second range

        PRINT_ELEMENTS(coll2,"\ncoll2: ");
    }
```

The first call of `swap_ranges()` swaps the elements of `coll1` with the corresponding elements of `coll2`. The remaining elements of `coll2` are not modified. The `swap_ranges()` algorithm returns the position of the first element not modified. The second call swaps the first and the last three elements of `coll2`. One of the iterators is a reverse iterator, so the elements are mirrored (swapped from outside to inside). The program has the following output:

```
    coll1: 1 2 3 4 5 6 7 8 9
    coll2: 11 12 13 14 15 16 17 18 19 20 21 22 23

    coll1: 11 12 13 14 15 16 17 18 19
    coll2: 1 2 3 4 5 6 7 8 9 20 21 22 23
    first element not modified: 20

    coll2: 23 22 21 4 5 6 7 8 9 20 3 2 1
```

11.6.5   Assigning New Values

Assigning the Same Value

```
void
fill (ForwardIterator beg, ForwardIterator end,
      const T& newValue)
```

```
void
fill_n (OutputIterator beg, Size num,
         const T& newValue)
```

- `fill()` assigns *newValue* to each element in the range [*beg,end*).
- `fill_n()` assigns *newValue* to the first *num* elements in the range starting with *beg*. If num is negative, `fill_n()` does nothing (specified only since C++11).
- The caller must ensure that the destination range is big enough or that insert iterators are used.
- Since C++11, `fill_n()` returns the position after the last modified element (*beg+num*) or *beg* if *num* is negative (before C++11, `fill_n()` had return type `void`).
- Complexity: linear (*numElems*, *num*, or 0 assignments).

The following program demonstrates the use of `fill()` and `fill_n()`:

```cpp
// algo/fill1.cpp

#include "algostuff.hpp"
using namespace std;

int main()
{
    // print ten times 7.7
    fill_n(ostream_iterator<float>(cout, " "),  // beginning of destination
           10,                                   // count
           7.7);                                 // new value
    cout << endl;

    list<string> coll;

    // insert "hello" nine times
    fill_n(back_inserter(coll),        // beginning of destination
           9,                          // count
           "hello");                   // new value
    PRINT_ELEMENTS(coll,"coll: ");

    // overwrite all elements with "again"
    fill(coll.begin(), coll.end(),     // destination
         "again");                     // new value
```

```
    PRINT_ELEMENTS(coll,"coll: ");

    // replace all but two elements with "hi"
    fill_n(coll.begin(),              // beginning of destination
           coll.size()-2,             // count
           "hi");                     // new value
    PRINT_ELEMENTS(coll,"coll: ");

    // replace the second and up to the last element but one with "hmmm"
    list<string>::iterator pos1, pos2;
    pos1 = coll.begin();
    pos2 = coll.end();
    fill (++pos1, --pos2,             // destination
          "hmmm");                    // new value
    PRINT_ELEMENTS(coll,"coll: ");
}
```

The first call shows how to use `fill_n()` to print a certain number of values. The other calls of `fill()` and `fill_n()` insert and replace values in a list of strings. The program has the following output:

```
7.7 7.7 7.7 7.7 7.7 7.7 7.7 7.7 7.7 7.7
coll: hello hello hello hello hello hello hello hello hello
coll: again again again again again again again again again
coll: hi hi hi hi hi hi hi again again
coll: hi hmmm hmmm hmmm hmmm hmmm hmmm hmmm again
```

Assigning Generated Values

```
void
generate (ForwardIterator beg, ForwardIterator end,
          Func op)

void
generate_n (OutputIterator beg, Size num,
            Func op)
```

- `generate()` assigns the values that are generated by a call of
     `op()`
  to each element in the range [*beg,end*).
- `generate_n()` assigns the values that are generated by a call of
     `op()`
  to the first *num* elements in the range starting with *beg*. If num is negative, `generate_n()` does nothing (specified only since C++11).

- The caller must ensure that the destination range is big enough or that insert iterators are used.
- Since C++11, generate_n() returns the position after the last modified element (*beg+num*) or *beg* if *num* is negative (before C++11, generate_n() had return type void).
- Complexity: linear (*numElems*, *num*, or 0 calls of *op*() and assignments).

The following program demonstrates how to use generate() and generate_n() to insert or assign some random numbers:

```cpp
// algo/generate1.cpp

#include <cstdlib>
#include "algostuff.hpp"
using namespace std;

int main()
{
    list<int> coll;

    // insert five random numbers
    generate_n (back_inserter(coll),    // beginning of destination range
                5,                       // count
                rand);                   // new value generator
    PRINT_ELEMENTS(coll);

    // overwrite with five new random numbers
    generate (coll.begin(), coll.end(),  // destination range
              rand);                     // new value generator
    PRINT_ELEMENTS(coll);
}
```

The rand() function is described in Section 17.3, page 942. The program might have the following output:

```
1481765933 1085377743 1270216262 1191391529 812669700
553475508 445349752 1344887256 730417256 1812158119
```

The output is platform dependent because the random-number sequence that rand() generates is not standardized.

See Section 10.1.2, page 478, for an example that demonstrates how to use generate() with function objects so that it generates a sequence of numbers.

Assigning Sequence of Increments Values

```
void
iota (ForwardIterator beg, ForwardIterator end,
      T startValue)
```

- assigns *startValue*, *startValue*+1, *startValue*+2, and so on.
- Provided since C++11.
- Complexity: linear (*numElems* assignments and increments).

The following program demonstrates how to use `iota()`:

```cpp
// algo/iota1.cpp

#include "algostuff.hpp"
using namespace std;

int main()
{
    array<int,10> coll;

    iota (coll.begin(), coll.end(),   // destination range
          42);                        // start value

    PRINT_ELEMENTS(coll,"coll: ");
}
```

The program has the following output:

```
coll: 42 43 44 45 46 47 48 49 50 51
```

11.6.6   Replacing Elements

Replacing Values Inside a Sequence

```
void
replace (ForwardIterator beg, ForwardIterator end,
         const T& oldValue, const T& newValue)
```

```
void
replace_if (ForwardIterator beg, ForwardIterator end,
            UnaryPredicate op, const T& newValue)
```

- `replace()` replaces each element in the range [*beg*,*end*) that is equal to *oldValue* with *newValue*.

- replace_if() replaces each element in the range [*beg,end*) for which the unary predicate
     op(elem)
  yields true with *newValue*.
- Note that *op* should not change its state during a function call. See Section 10.1.4, page 483, for details.
- Complexity: linear (*numElems* comparisons or calls of *op()*, respectively).

The following program demonstrates some examples of the use of replace() and replace_if():

```cpp
// algo/replace1.cpp

#include "algostuff.hpp"
using namespace std;

int main()
{
    list<int> coll;

    INSERT_ELEMENTS(coll,2,7);
    INSERT_ELEMENTS(coll,4,9);
    PRINT_ELEMENTS(coll,"coll: ");

    // replace all elements with value 6 with 42
    replace (coll.begin(), coll.end(),      // range
             6,                             // old value
             42);                           // new value
    PRINT_ELEMENTS(coll,"coll: ");

    // replace all elements with value less than 5 with 0
    replace_if (coll.begin(), coll.end(),   // range
                [] (int elem){              // criterion for replacement
                    return elem<5;
                },
                0);                         // new value
    PRINT_ELEMENTS(coll,"coll: ");
}
```

The program has the following output:

```
coll: 2 3 4 5 6 7 4 5 6 7 8 9
coll: 2 3 4 5 42 7 4 5 42 7 8 9
coll: 0 0 0 5 42 7 0 5 42 7 8 9
```

Copying and Replacing Elements

```
OutputIterator
replace_copy (InputIterator sourceBeg, InputIterator sourceEnd,
              OutputIterator destBeg,
              const T& oldValue, const T& newValue)
```

```
OutputIterator
replace_copy_if (InputIterator sourceBeg, InputIterator sourceEnd,
                 OutputIterator destBeg,
                 UnaryPredicate op, const T& newValue)
```

- `replace_copy()` is a combination of `copy()` and `replace()`. It replaces each element in the source range [*sourceBeg,sourceEnd*) that is equal to *oldValue* with *newValue* while the elements are copied into the destination range starting with *destBeg*.

- `replace_copy_if()` is a combination of `copy()` and `replace_if()`. It replaces each element in the source range [*sourceBeg,sourceEnd*) for which the unary predicate
  op(*elem*)
  yields `true` with *newValue* while the elements are copied into the destination range starting with *destBeg*.

- Both algorithms return the position after the last copied element in the destination range (the first element that is not overwritten).

- Note that *op* should not change its state during a function call. See Section 10.1.4, page 483, for details.

- The caller must ensure that the destination range is big enough or that insert iterators are used.

- Complexity: linear (*numElems* comparisons or calls of *op*() and assignments, respectively).

The following program demonstrates how to use `replace_copy()` and `replace_copy_if()`:

```
// algo/replace2.cpp

#include "algostuff.hpp"
using namespace std;
using namespace std::placeholders;

int main()
{
    list<int> coll;

    INSERT_ELEMENTS(coll,2,6);
    INSERT_ELEMENTS(coll,4,9);
    PRINT_ELEMENTS(coll);

    // print all elements with value 5 replaced with 55
```

```
        replace_copy(coll.cbegin(), coll.cend(),        // source
                    ostream_iterator<int>(cout," "),    // destination
                    5,                                   // old value
                    55);                                 // new value
        cout << endl;

        // print all elements with a value less than 5 replaced with 42
        replace_copy_if(coll.cbegin(), coll.cend(),      // source
                    ostream_iterator<int>(cout," "),     // destination
                    bind(less<int>(),_1,5),              // replacement criterion
                    42);                                 // new value
        cout << endl;

        // print each element while each odd element is replaced with 0
        replace_copy_if(coll.cbegin(), coll.cend(),      // source
                    ostream_iterator<int>(cout," "),     // destination
                    [](int elem){                        // replacement criterion
                        return elem%2==1;
                    },
                    0);                                  // new value
        cout << endl;
    }
```

The program has the following output:

```
2 3 4 5 6 4 5 6 7 8 9
2 3 4 55 6 4 55 6 7 8 9
42 42 42 5 6 42 5 6 7 8 9
2 0 4 0 6 4 0 6 0 8 0
```

11.7 Removing Algorithms

The following algorithms remove elements from a range according to their value or to a criterion. These algorithms, however, *cannot* change the number of elements. The algorithms move logically only by overwriting "removed" elements with the following elements that were not removed. They return the new logical end of the range (the position after the last element not removed). See Section 6.7.1, page 218, for details.

11.7.1 Removing Certain Values

Removing Elements in a Sequence

```
ForwardIterator
remove (ForwardIterator beg, ForwardIterator end,
         const T& value)
```

```
ForwardIterator
remove_if (ForwardIterator beg, ForwardIterator end,
            UnaryPredicate op)
```

- `remove()` removes each element in the range [*beg*,*end*) that is equal to *value*.
- `remove_if()` removes each element in the range [*beg*,*end*) for which the unary predicate

  op(*elem*)

  yields `true`.
- Both algorithms return the logical new end of the modified sequence (the position after the last element not removed).
- The algorithms overwrite "removed" elements by the following elements that were not removed.
- The order of elements that were not removed remains stable.
- It is up to the caller, after calling this algorithm, to use the returned new logical end instead of the original end *end* (see Section 6.7.1, page 218, for more details).
- Note that *op* should not change its state during a function call. See Section 10.1.4, page 483, for details.
- Note that `remove_if()` usually copies the unary predicate inside the algorithm and uses it twice. This may lead to problems if the predicate changes its state due to the function call. See Section 10.1.4, page 483, for details.
- Due to modifications, you can't use these algorithms for an associative or unordered container (see Section 6.7.2, page 221). However, these containers provide a similar member function, `erase()` (see Section 8.7.3, page 417).
- Lists provide an equivalent member function, `remove()`, which offers better performance because it relinks pointers instead of assigning element values (see Section 8.8.1, page 420).
- Complexity: linear (*numElems* comparisons or calls of *op*(), respectively).

The following program demonstrates how to use `remove()` and `remove_if()`:

```cpp
// algo/remove1.cpp

#include "algostuff.hpp"
using namespace std;

int main()
{
    vector<int> coll;

    INSERT_ELEMENTS(coll,2,6);
    INSERT_ELEMENTS(coll,4,9);
    INSERT_ELEMENTS(coll,1,7);
    PRINT_ELEMENTS(coll,"coll:                ");

    // remove all elements with value 5
    vector<int>::iterator pos;
    pos = remove(coll.begin(), coll.end(),      // range
                 5);                            // value to remove

    PRINT_ELEMENTS(coll,"size not changed:   ");

    // erase the "removed" elements in the container
    coll.erase(pos, coll.end());
    PRINT_ELEMENTS(coll,"size changed:       ");

    // remove all elements less than 4
    coll.erase(remove_if(coll.begin(), coll.end(), // range
                         [](int elem){             // remove criterion
                             return elem<4;
                         }),
               coll.end());
    PRINT_ELEMENTS(coll,"<4 removed:         ");
}
```

The program has the following output:

```
coll:               2 3 4 5 6 4 5 6 7 8 9 1 2 3 4 5 6 7
size not changed:   2 3 4 6 4 6 7 8 9 1 2 3 4 6 7 5 6 7
size changed:       2 3 4 6 4 6 7 8 9 1 2 3 4 6 7
<4 removed:         4 6 4 6 7 8 9 4 6 7
```

Removing Elements While Copying

```
OutputIterator
remove_copy (InputIterator sourceBeg, InputIterator sourceEnd,
            OutputIterator destBeg,
            const T& value)
```

```
OutputIterator
remove_copy_if (InputIterator sourceBeg, InputIterator sourceEnd,
                OutputIterator destBeg,
                UnaryPredicate op)
```

- `remove_copy()` is a combination of `copy()` and `remove()`. It copies each element in the source range [*sourceBeg,sourceEnd*) that is not equal to *value* into the destination range starting with *destBeg*.

- `remove_copy_if()` is a combination of `copy()` and `remove_if()`. It copies each element in the source range [*sourceBeg,sourceEnd*) for which the unary predicate
    op(*elem*)
  yields `false` into the destination range starting with *destBeg*.

- Both algorithms return the position after the last copied element in the destination range (the first element that is not overwritten).

- Note that *op* should not change its state during a function call. See Section 10.1.4, page 483, for details.

- The caller must ensure that the destination range is big enough or that insert iterators are used.

- Use `partition_copy()` (see Section 11.8.6, page 594), to copy elements into two destination ranges: one fulfilling and one non fulfilling a predicate (available since C++11).

- Complexity: linear (*numElems* comparisons or calls of *op*() and assignments, respectively).

The following program demonstrates how to use `remove_copy()` and `remove_copy_if()`:

```cpp
// algo/remove2.cpp

#include "algostuff.hpp"
using namespace std;
using namespace std::placeholders;

int main()
{
    list<int> coll1;

    INSERT_ELEMENTS(coll1,1,6);
    INSERT_ELEMENTS(coll1,1,9);
    PRINT_ELEMENTS(coll1);
```

```
// print elements without those having the value 3
remove_copy(coll1.cbegin(), coll1.cend(),        // source
            ostream_iterator<int>(cout," "),     // destination
            3);                                   // removed value
cout << endl;

// print elements without those having a value greater than 4
remove_copy_if(coll1.cbegin(), coll1.cend(),     // source
               ostream_iterator<int>(cout," "),  // destination
               [](int elem){           // criterion for elements NOT copied
                   return elem>4;
               });
cout << endl;

// copy all elements not less than 4 into a multiset
multiset<int> coll2;
remove_copy_if(coll1.cbegin(), coll1.cend(),     // source
               inserter(coll2,coll2.end()),      // destination
               bind(less<int>(),_1,4));          // elements NOT copied
PRINT_ELEMENTS(coll2);
}
```

The program has the following output:

```
1 2 3 4 5 6 1 2 3 4 5 6 7 8 9
1 2 4 5 6 1 2 4 5 6 7 8 9
1 2 3 4 1 2 3 4
4 4 5 5 6 6 7 8 9
```

11.7.2   Removing Duplicates

Removing Consecutive Duplicates

```
ForwardIterator
unique (ForwardIterator beg, ForwardIterator end)
```

```
ForwardIterator
unique (ForwardIterator beg, ForwardIterator end,
        BinaryPredicate op)
```

- Both forms collapse consecutive equal elements by removing the following duplicates.
- The first form removes from the range [beg,end) all elements that are equal to the previous elements. Thus, only when the elements in the sequence are sorted, or at least when all elements of the same value are adjacent, does it remove all duplicates.

- The second form removes all elements that follow an element *e* and for which the binary predicate

    op(*e*,*elem*)

  yields `true`. In other words, the predicate is not used to compare an element with its predecessor; the element is compared with the previous element that was not removed (see the following examples).
- Both forms return the logical new end of the modified sequence (the position after the last element not removed).
- The algorithms overwrite "removed" elements by the following elements that were not removed.
- The order of elements that were not removed remains stable.
- It is up to the caller, after calling this algorithm, to use the returned new logical end instead of the original end *end* (see Section 6.7.1, page 218, for more details).
- Note that *op* should not change its state during a function call. See Section 10.1.4, page 483, for details.
- Due to modifications, you can't use these algorithms for an associative or unordered container (see Section 6.7.2, page 221).
- Lists provide an equivalent member function, `unique()`, which offers better performance because it relinks pointers instead of assigning element values (see Section 8.8.1, page 421).
- Complexity: linear (*numElems* comparisons or calls of *op*(), respectively).

The following program demonstrates how to use `unique()`:

```
// algo/unique1.cpp

#include "algostuff.hpp"
using namespace std;

int main()
{
    // source data
    int source[] = { 1, 4, 4, 6, 1, 2, 2, 3, 1, 6, 6, 6, 5, 7,
                     5, 4, 4 };
    list<int> coll;

    // initialize coll with elements from source
    copy (begin(source), end(source),        // source
          back_inserter(coll));               // destination
    PRINT_ELEMENTS(coll);

    // remove consecutive duplicates
    auto pos = unique (coll.begin(), coll.end());
```

```
    // print elements not removed
    // - use new logical end
    copy (coll.begin(), pos,                         // source
            ostream_iterator<int>(cout," "));        // destination
    cout << "\n\n";

    // reinitialize coll with elements from source
    copy (begin(source), end(source),                // source
            coll.begin());                           // destination
    PRINT_ELEMENTS(coll);

    // remove elements if there was a previous greater element
    coll.erase (unique (coll.begin(), coll.end(),
                        greater<int>()),
                coll.end());
    PRINT_ELEMENTS(coll);
}
```

The program has the following output:

```
1 4 4 6 1 2 2 3 1 6 6 6 5 7 5 4 4
1 4 6 1 2 3 1 6 5 7 5 4

1 4 4 6 1 2 2 3 1 6 6 6 5 7 5 4 4
1 4 4 6 6 6 6 7
```

The first call of `unique()` removes consecutive duplicates. The second call shows the behavior of the second form and removes all the consecutive following elements of an element for which the comparison with `greater` yields `true`. For example, the first 6 is greater than the following 1, 2, 2, 3, and 1, so all these elements are removed. In other words, the predicate is not used to compare an element with its predecessor; the element is compared with the previous element that was not removed (see the following description of `unique_copy()` for another example).

Removing Duplicates While Copying

```
OutputIterator
```
unique_copy (InputIterator *sourceBeg*, InputIterator *sourceEnd*,
            OutputIterator *destBeg*)

```
OutputIterator
```
unique_copy (InputIterator *sourceBeg*, InputIterator *sourceEnd*,
            OutputIterator *destBeg*,
            BinaryPredicate *op*)

- Both forms are a combination of copy() and unique().
- They copy all elements of the source range [*sourceBeg,sourceEnd*) that are no duplicates of their previous elements into the destination range starting with *destBeg*.
- Both forms return the position after the last copied element in the destination range (the first element that is not overwritten).
- The caller must ensure that the destination range is big enough or that insert iterators are used.
- Complexity: linear (*numElems* comparisons or calls of *op*() and assignments, respectively).

The following program demonstrates how to use unique_copy():

```cpp
// algo/unique2.cpp

#include "algostuff.hpp"
using namespace std;

bool differenceOne (int elem1, int elem2)
{
    return elem1 + 1 == elem2 || elem1 - 1 == elem2;
}

int main()
{
    // source data
    int source[] = { 1, 4, 4, 6, 1, 2, 2, 3, 1, 6, 6, 6, 5, 7,
                     5, 4, 4 };

    // initialize coll with elements from source
    list<int> coll;
    copy(begin(source), end(source),              // source
         back_inserter(coll));                    // destination
    PRINT_ELEMENTS(coll);

    // print elements with consecutive duplicates removed
    unique_copy(coll.cbegin(), coll.cend(),       // source
                ostream_iterator<int>(cout," "));  // destination
    cout << endl;

    // print elements without consecutive entries that differ by one
    unique_copy(coll.cbegin(), coll.cend(),       // source
                ostream_iterator<int>(cout," "),  // destination
                differenceOne);                   // duplicates criterion
    cout << endl;
}
```

The program has the following output:

```
1 4 4 6 1 2 2 3 1 6 6 6 5 7 5 4 4
1 4 6 1 2 3 1 6 5 7 5 4
1 4 4 6 1 3 1 6 6 6 4 4
```

Note that the second call of `unique_copy()` does not remove the elements that differ by 1 from their predecessor by one. Instead, it removes all elements that differ by 1 from their previous element *that is not removed.* For example, after the three occurrences of 6, the following 5, 7, and 5 differ by 1 compared with 6, so they are removed. However, the following two occurrences of 4 remain in the sequence because compared with 6, the difference is not 1.

Another example compresses sequences of spaces:

```
// algo/unique3.cpp

#include <iostream>
#include <algorithm>
#include <iterator>
using namespace std;

bool bothSpaces (char elem1, char elem2)
{
    return elem1 == ' ' && elem2 == ' ';
}

int main()
{
    // don't skip leading whitespaces by default
    cin.unsetf(ios::skipws);

    // copy standard input to standard output
    // - while compressing spaces
    unique_copy(istream_iterator<char>(cin),     // beginning of source: cin
                istream_iterator<char>(),        // end of source: end-of-file
                ostream_iterator<char>(cout),    // destination: cout
                bothSpaces);                      // duplicate criterion
}
```

With the input of

```
Hello, here are   sometimes more  and sometimes fewer    spaces.
```

this example produces the following output:

```
Hello, here are sometimes more and sometimes fewer spaces.
```

11.8   Mutating Algorithms

Mutating algorithms change the order of elements but not their values. Because elements of associative and unordered containers have an order defined by the container, you can't use these algorithms as a destination for mutating algorithms.

11.8.1   Reversing the Order of Elements

```
void
reverse (BidirectionalIterator beg, BidirectionalIterator end)
```

```
OutputIterator
reverse_copy (BidirectionalIterator sourceBeg, BidirectionalIterator sourceEnd,
              OutputIterator destBeg)
```

- reverse() reverses the order of the elements inside the range [beg,end).
- reverse_copy() reverses the order of the elements while copying them from the source range [sourceBeg,sourceEnd) to the destination range starting with destBeg.
- reverse_copy() returns the position after the last copied element in the destination range (the first element that is not overwritten).
- The caller must ensure that the destination range is big enough or that insert iterators are used.
- Lists provide an equivalent member function, reverse(), which offers better performance because it relinks pointers instead of assigning element values (see Section 8.8.1, page 423).
- Complexity: linear (numElems/2 swaps or numElems assignments, respectively).

The following program demonstrates how to use reverse() and reverse_copy():

```
// algo/reverse1.cpp

#include "algostuff.hpp"
using namespace std;

int main()
{
    vector<int> coll;

    INSERT_ELEMENTS(coll,1,9);
    PRINT_ELEMENTS(coll,"coll: ");

    // reverse order of elements
    reverse (coll.begin(), coll.end());
    PRINT_ELEMENTS(coll,"coll: ");
```

```
// reverse order from second to last element but one
reverse (coll.begin()+1, coll.end()-1);
PRINT_ELEMENTS(coll,"coll: ");

// print all of them in reverse order
reverse_copy (coll.cbegin(), coll.cend(),          // source
              ostream_iterator<int>(cout," "));    // destination
cout << endl;
}
```

The program has the following output:

```
coll: 1 2 3 4 5 6 7 8 9
coll: 9 8 7 6 5 4 3 2 1
coll: 9 2 3 4 5 6 7 8 1
1 8 7 6 5 4 3 2 9
```

11.8.2   Rotating Elements

Rotating Elements inside a Sequence

ForwardIterator
rotate (ForwardIterator *beg*, ForwardIterator *newBeg*, ForwardIterator *end*)

- Rotates elements in the range [*beg*,*end*) so that *newBeg* is the new first element after the call.
- Since C++11, returns *beg*+(*end*−*newbeg*), which is the new position of the first element. Before C++11, the return type was void.
- The caller must ensure that *newBeg* is a valid position in the range [*beg*,*end*); otherwise, the call results in undefined behavior.
- Complexity: linear (at most, *numElems* swaps).

The following program demonstrates how to use rotate():

```
// algo/rotate1.cpp

#include "algostuff.hpp"
using namespace std;

int main()
{
    vector<int> coll;

    INSERT_ELEMENTS(coll,1,9);
    PRINT_ELEMENTS(coll,"coll:          ");
```

```
        // rotate one element to the left
        rotate (coll.begin(),        // beginning of range
                coll.begin() + 1,    // new first element
                coll.end());         // end of range
        PRINT_ELEMENTS(coll,"one left:  ");

        // rotate two elements to the right
        rotate (coll.begin(),        // beginning of range
                coll.end() - 2,      // new first element
                coll.end());         // end of range
        PRINT_ELEMENTS(coll,"two right: ");

        // rotate so that element with value 4 is the beginning
        rotate (coll.begin(),                          // beginning of range
                find(coll.begin(),coll.end(),4),       // new first element
                coll.end());                           // end of range
        PRINT_ELEMENTS(coll,"4 first:   ");
    }
```

As the example shows, you can rotate to the left with a positive offset for the beginning and rotate to the right with a negative offset to the end. However, adding the offset to the iterator is possible only when you have random-access iterators, as you have for vectors. Without such iterators, you must use `advance()` (see the example of `rotate_copy()` on page 586).

The program has the following output:

```
coll:      1 2 3 4 5 6 7 8 9
one left:  2 3 4 5 6 7 8 9 1
two right: 9 1 2 3 4 5 6 7 8
4 first:   4 5 6 7 8 9 1 2 3
```

Rotating Elements While Copying

`OutputIterator`
rotate_copy (ForwardIterator *sourceBeg*, ForwardIterator *newBeg*,
              ForwardIterator *sourceEnd*,
              OutputIterator *destBeg*)

- Is a combination of `copy()` and `rotate()`.
- Copies the elements of the source range [*sourceBeg*,*sourceEnd*) into the destination range starting with *destBeg* in rotated order so that **newBeg* is the new first element.
- Returns *destBeg*+(*sourceEnd*−*sourceBeg*), which is the position after the last copied element in the destination range.
- The caller must ensure that *newBeg* is an element in the range [*beg*,*end*); otherwise, the call results in undefined behavior.

- The caller must ensure that the destination range is big enough or that insert iterators are used.
- The source and destination ranges should not overlap.
- Complexity: linear (*numElems* assignments).

The following program demonstrates how to use `rotate_copy()`:

```
// algo/rotate2.cpp

#include "algostuff.hpp"
using namespace std;

int main()
{
    set<int> coll;

    INSERT_ELEMENTS(coll,1,9);
    PRINT_ELEMENTS(coll);

    // print elements rotated one element to the left
    set<int>::const_iterator pos = next(coll.cbegin());
    rotate_copy(coll.cbegin(),                      // beginning of source
                pos,                                // new first element
                coll.cend(),                        // end of source
                ostream_iterator<int>(cout," "));   // destination
    cout << endl;

    // print elements rotated two elements to the right
    pos = coll.cend();
    advance(pos,-2);
    rotate_copy(coll.cbegin(),                      // beginning of source
                pos,                                // new first element
                coll.cend(),                        // end of source
                ostream_iterator<int>(cout," "));   // destination
    cout << endl;

    // print elements rotated so that element with value 4 is the beginning
    rotate_copy(coll.cbegin(),                      // beginning of source
                coll.find(4),                       // new first element
                coll.cend(),                        // end of source
                ostream_iterator<int>(cout," "));   // destination
    cout << endl;
}
```

Unlike the previous example of `rotate()` (see Section 11.8.2, page 584), here a set is used instead of a vector. This has two consequences:

1. You must use `advance()` (see Section 9.3.1, page 441) or `next()` (see Section 9.3.2, page 443) to change the value of the iterator, because bidirectional iterators do not provide operator +.

2. You should use the `find()` member function instead of the `find()` algorithm, because the former has better performance.

The program has the following output:

```
1 2 3 4 5 6 7 8 9
2 3 4 5 6 7 8 9 1
8 9 1 2 3 4 5 6 7
4 5 6 7 8 9 1 2 3
```

11.8.3 Permuting Elements

bool
next_permutation (BidirectionalIterator *beg*, BidirectionalIterator *end*)

bool
next_permutation (BidirectionalIterator *beg*, BidirectionalIterator *end*,
                    BinaryPredicate *op*)

bool
prev_permutation (BidirectionalIterator *beg*, BidirectionalIterator *end*)

bool
prev_permutation (BidirectionalIterator *beg*, BidirectionalIterator *end*,
                    BinaryPredicate *op*)

- `next_permutation()` changes the order of the elements in [*beg*,*end*) according to the next permutation.

- `prev_permutation()` changes the order of the elements in [*beg*,*end*) according to the previous permutation.

- The first forms compare the elements by using operator <.

- The second forms compare the elements by using the binary predicate
    op(*elem1*,*elem2*)
which should return `true` if *elem1* is "less than" *elem2*.

- Both algorithms return `false` if the elements got the "normal" (lexicographical) order: that is, ascending order for `next_permutation()` and descending order for `prev_permutation()`. So, to run through all permutations, you have to sort all elements (ascending or descending), and start a loop that calls `next_permutation()` or `prev_permutation()` as long as these algorithms return `true`.[3] See Section 11.5.4, page 548, for an explanation of lexicographical sorting.

- Complexity: linear (at most, *numElems*/2 swaps).

---

[3] `next_permutation()` and `prev_permutation()` could also be used to sort elements in a range. You just call them for a range as long as they return `true`. However, doing so would produce really bad performance.

The following example demonstrates how `next_permutation()` and `prev_permutation()` run through all permutations of the elements:

```
// algo/permutation1.cpp

#include "algostuff.hpp"
using namespace std;

int main()
{
    vector<int> coll;
    INSERT_ELEMENTS(coll,1,3);
    PRINT_ELEMENTS(coll,"on entry:  ");

    // permute elements until they are sorted
    // - runs through all permutations because the elements are sorted now
    while (next_permutation(coll.begin(),coll.end())) {
        PRINT_ELEMENTS(coll," ");
    }
    PRINT_ELEMENTS(coll,"afterward: ");

    // permute until descending sorted
    // - this is the next permutation after ascending sorting
    // - so the loop ends immediately
    while (prev_permutation(coll.begin(),coll.end())) {
        PRINT_ELEMENTS(coll," ");
    }
    PRINT_ELEMENTS(coll,"now:       ");

    // permute elements until they are sorted in descending order
    // - runs through all permutations because the elements are sorted in descending order now
    while (prev_permutation(coll.begin(),coll.end())) {
        PRINT_ELEMENTS(coll," ");
    }
    PRINT_ELEMENTS(coll,"afterward: ");
}
```

The program has the following output:

```
on entry:  1 2 3
  1 3 2
  2 1 3
  2 3 1
  3 1 2
  3 2 1
```

```
afterward: 1 2 3
now:       3 2 1
  3 1 2
  2 3 1
  2 1 3
  1 3 2
  1 2 3
afterward: 3 2 1
```

11.8.4 Shuffling Elements

Shuffling Using the Random-Number Library

```
void
shuffle (RandomAccessIterator beg, RandomAccessIterator end,
       UniformRandomNumberGenerator&& eng)
```

```
void
random_shuffle (RandomAccessIterator beg, RandomAccessIterator end)
```

```
void
random_shuffle (RandomAccessIterator beg, RandomAccessIterator end,
               RandomFunc&& op)
```

- The first form, available since C++11, shuffles the order of the elements in the range [*beg,end*), using an *engine eng* as introduced by the random numbers and distributions library (see Section 17.1.2, page 912).
- The second form shuffles the order of the elements in the range [*beg,end*), using an implementation-defined uniform distribution random-number generator, such as the C function `rand()`.
- The third form shuffles the order of the elements in the range [*beg,end*), using *op*. *op* is called with an integral value of `difference_type` of the iterator:
    op(*max*)
  which should return a random number greater than or equal to zero and less than *max*. Thus, it should not return *max* itself.
- For `shuffle()`, you should not pass an engine just temporarily created. See Section 17.1.1, page 911, for details.
- Before C++11, *op* was declared as `RandomFunc&`, so you couldn't pass a temporary value or an ordinary function.
- Complexity: linear (*numElems*-1 swaps).

Note that old global C functions, such as `rand()`, store their local states in a static variable. However, this has some disadvantages: For example, the random-number generator is inherently thread unsafe, and you can't have two independent streams of random numbers. Therefore, function objects provide a better solution by encapsulating their local states as one or more member variables. For this reason, the algorithms change the state of the passed generator while generating a new random number.

The following example demonstrates how to shuffle elements by calling `random_shuffle()` without passing a random-number generator or by using `shuffle()`:

```cpp
// algo/shuffle1.cpp

#include <cstdlib>
#include "algostuff.hpp"
using namespace std;

int main()
{
    vector<int> coll;

    INSERT_ELEMENTS(coll,1,9);
    PRINT_ELEMENTS(coll,"coll:       ");

    // shuffle all elements randomly
    random_shuffle (coll.begin(), coll.end());

    PRINT_ELEMENTS(coll,"shuffled: ");

    // sort them again
    sort (coll.begin(), coll.end());
    PRINT_ELEMENTS(coll,"sorted:   ");

    // shuffle elements with default engine
    default_random_engine dre;
    shuffle (coll.begin(), coll.end(),   // range
             dre);                       // random-number generator

    PRINT_ELEMENTS(coll,"shuffled: ");
}
```

A possible (but not portable) output of the program is as follows:

```
coll:     1 2 3 4 5 6 7 8 9
shuffled: 8 2 4 9 5 7 3 6 1
sorted:   1 2 3 4 5 6 7 8 9
shuffled: 8 7 5 6 2 4 9 3 1
```

See Section 17.1, page 907, for details about engines you can pass to `shuffle()`.

The following example demonstrates how to shuffle elements by using your own random-number generator passed to `random_shuffle()`:

```cpp
// algo/randomshuffle1.cpp

#include <cstdlib>
#include "algostuff.hpp"
using namespace std;

class MyRandom {
  public:
    ptrdiff_t operator() (ptrdiff_t max) {
        double tmp;
        tmp = static_cast<double>(rand())
                / static_cast<double>(RAND_MAX);
        return static_cast<ptrdiff_t>(tmp * max);
    }
};

int main()
{
    vector<int> coll;

    INSERT_ELEMENTS(coll,1,9);
    PRINT_ELEMENTS(coll,"coll:      ");

    // shuffle elements with self-written random-number generator
    MyRandom rd;
    random_shuffle (coll.begin(), coll.end(),    // range
                       rd);                       // random-number generator

    PRINT_ELEMENTS(coll,"shuffled: ");
}
```

The call of random() uses the self-written random-number generator rd(), an object of the auxiliary function object class MyRandom, which uses a random-number algorithm that often is better than the usual direct call of rand().[4] Note that before C++11, you couldn't pass a temporary object as random-number generator:

```cpp
random_shuffle (coll.begin(), coll.end(),
                   MyRandom());                   // ERROR before C++11
```

Again, a possible but not portable output of the program is as follows:

```
coll:      1 2 3 4 5 6 7 8 9
shuffled: 1 8 6 2 4 9 3 7 5
```

See Section 17.1.1, page 912, for some general comments about the use of rand().

---

[4] The way MyRandom generates random numbers is introduced and described in [*Stroustrup:C++*].

11.8.5   Moving Elements to the Front

ForwardIterator
partition (ForwardIterator *beg*, ForwardIterator *end*,
        UnaryPredicate *op*)

BidirectionalIterator
stable_partition (BidirectionalIterator *beg*, BidirectionalIterator *end*,
             UnaryPredicate *op*)

- Both algorithms move all elements in the range [*beg,end*) to the front, for which the unary predicate

  op(*elem*)

  yields true.
- Both algorithms return the first position for which *op*() yields false.
- The difference between partition() and stable_partition() is that the algorithm stable_partition() preserves the relative order of elements that match the criterion and those that do not.
- You could use this algorithm to split elements into two parts according to a sorting criterion. The nth_element() algorithm has a similar ability. See Section 11.2.2, page 514, for a discussion of the differences between these algorithms and nth_element().
- Note that *op* should not change its state during a function call. See Section 10.1.4, page 483, for details.
- Before C++11, partition() required bidirectional iterators instead of forward iterators and guaranteed at most *numElems*/2 swaps.
- Use partition_copy() (see Section 11.8.6, page 594) to copy elements into one destination range for fulfilling and one for not fulfilling a predicate (available since C++11).
- Complexity:
  - For partition(): linear (at most *numElems*/2 swaps and *numElems* calls of *op*() if bidirectional iterators or random-access iterators are used; at most *numElems* swaps if the iterators are only forward iterators).
  - For stable_partition(): linear if there is enough extra memory (*numElems* swaps and calls of *op*()); otherwise, n-log-n (*numElems* calls of *op*() but *numElems**log(*numElems*) swaps).

The following program demonstrates the use of and the difference between partition() and stable_partition():

```
// algo/partition1.cpp

#include "algostuff.hpp"
using namespace std;
```

```
int main()
{
    vector<int> coll1;
    vector<int> coll2;

    INSERT_ELEMENTS(coll1,1,9);
    INSERT_ELEMENTS(coll2,1,9);
    PRINT_ELEMENTS(coll1,"coll1: ");
    PRINT_ELEMENTS(coll2,"coll2: ");
    cout << endl;

    // move all even elements to the front
    vector<int>::iterator pos1, pos2;
    pos1 = partition(coll1.begin(), coll1.end(),        // range
                    [](int elem){                       // criterion
                        return elem%2==0;
                    });
    pos2 = stable_partition(coll2.begin(), coll2.end(),  // range
                    [](int elem){                        // criterion
                        return elem%2==0;
                    });

    // print collections and first odd element
    PRINT_ELEMENTS(coll1,"coll1: ");
    cout << "first odd element: " << *pos1 << endl;
    PRINT_ELEMENTS(coll2,"coll2: ");
    cout << "first odd element: " << *pos2 << endl;
}
```

The program has the following output:

```
coll1: 1 2 3 4 5 6 7 8 9
coll2: 1 2 3 4 5 6 7 8 9

coll1: 8 2 6 4 5 3 7 1 9
first odd element: 5
coll2: 2 4 6 8 1 3 5 7 9
first odd element: 1
```

As this example shows, stable_partition(), unlike partition(), preserves the relative order of the even and the odd elements.

11.8.6   Partition into Two Subranges

```
pair<OutputIterator1,OutputIterator2>
```
partition_copy (InputIterator *sourceBeg*, InputIterator *sourceEnd*,
                 OutputIterator1 *destTrueBeg*, OutputIterator2 *destFalseBeg*,
                 UnaryPredicate *op*)

- Splits all elements in the range [*beg,end*) according to the predicate *op*() into two subranges.
- All elements for which the unary predicate
    op(elem)
  yields true are copied into the range starting with *destTrueBeg*. All elements for which the predicate yields false are copied into the range starting with *destFalseBeg*.
- The algorithm returns a pair of the position after the last copied elements of the destination ranges (the first element that is not overwritten).
- Note that *op* should not change its state during a function call. See Section 10.1.4, page 483, for details.
- This algorithm is available since C++11.
- Use copy_if() (see Section 11.6.1, page 557) or remove_copy_if() (see Section 11.7.1, page 577) if you need only the elements that either fulfill or do not fulfill the predicate.
- Complexity: linear (at most *numElems* applications of *op*()).

The following program demonstrates the use of partition_copy():

```cpp
// algo/partitioncopy1.cpp

#include "algostuff.hpp"
using namespace std;

int main()
{
    vector<int> coll = { 1, 6, 33, 7, 22, 4, 11, 33, 2, 7, 0, 42, 5 };
    PRINT_ELEMENTS(coll,"coll: ");

    // destination collections:
    vector<int> evenColl;
    vector<int> oddColl;

    // copy all elements partitioned accordingly into even and odd elements
    partition_copy (coll.cbegin(),coll.cend(),  // source range
                    back_inserter(evenColl),    // destination for even elements
                    back_inserter(oddColl),     // destination for odd elements
                    [](int elem){               // predicate: check for even elements
                        return elem%2==0;
                    });
```

```
        PRINT_ELEMENTS(evenColl,"evenColl: ");
        PRINT_ELEMENTS(oddColl, "oddColl:  ");
    }
```

The program has the following output:

```
coll: 1 6 33 7 22 4 11 33 2 7 0 42 5
evenColl: 6 22 4 2 0 42
oddColl:  1 33 7 11 33 7 5
```

11.9   Sorting Algorithms

The STL provides several algorithms to sort elements of a range. In addition to full sorting, the STL provides variants of partial sorting. If their result is enough, you should prefer them because they usually have better performance.

Because (forward) lists and associative and unordered containers provide no random-access iterators, you can't use these containers (as a destination) for sorting algorithms. Instead, you might use associative containers to have elements sorted automatically. Note, however, that sorting all elements once is usually faster than keeping them always sorted (see Section 7.12, page 394, for details).

11.9.1   Sorting All Elements

```
void
sort (RandomAccessIterator beg, RandomAccessIterator end)
```

```
void
sort (RandomAccessIterator beg, RandomAccessIterator end, BinaryPredicate op)
```

```
void
stable_sort (RandomAccessIterator beg, RandomAccessIterator end)
```

```
void
stable_sort (RandomAccessIterator beg, RandomAccessIterator end,
             BinaryPredicate op)
```

- The first forms of sort() and stable_sort() sort all elements in the range [*beg,end*) with operator <.
- The second forms of sort() and stable_sort() sort all elements by using the binary predicate
    op(elem1,elem2)
  as the sorting criterion. It should return true if *elem1* is "less than" *elem2*.
- Note that *op* has to define a *strict weak ordering* for the values (see Section 7.7, page 314, for details).
- Note that *op* should not change its state during a function call. See Section 10.1.4, page 483, for details.
- The difference between sort() and stable_sort() is that stable_sort() guarantees that the order of equal elements remains stable.
- You can't call these algorithms for lists or forward lists, because both do not provide random-access iterators. However, they provide a special member function to sort elements: sort() (see Section 8.8.1, page 422).
- sort() guarantees a good performance (n-log-n) on average. However, if avoiding worst-case performance is important, you should use partial_sort() or stable_sort(). See the discussion about sorting algorithms in Section 11.2.2, page 511.

- Complexity:
  - For `sort()`: n-log-n on average (approximately *numElems**log(*numElems*) comparisons on average).
  - For `stable_sort()`: n-log-n if there is enough extra memory (*numElems**log(*numElems*) comparisons); otherwise, n-log-n*log-n (*numElems**log(*numElems*)^2 comparisons).

The following example demonstrates the use of `sort()`:

```
// algo/sort1.cpp

#include "algostuff.hpp"
using namespace std;

int main()
{
    deque<int> coll;

    INSERT_ELEMENTS(coll,1,9);
    INSERT_ELEMENTS(coll,1,9);

    PRINT_ELEMENTS(coll,"on entry: ");

    // sort elements
    sort (coll.begin(), coll.end());

    PRINT_ELEMENTS(coll,"sorted:    ");

    // sorted reverse
    sort (coll.begin(), coll.end(),      // range
          greater<int>());               // sorting criterion

    PRINT_ELEMENTS(coll,"sorted >: ");
}
```

The program has the following output:

```
on entry: 1 2 3 4 5 6 7 8 9 1 2 3 4 5 6 7 8 9
sorted:    1 1 2 2 3 3 4 4 5 5 6 6 7 7 8 8 9 9
sorted >: 9 9 8 8 7 7 6 6 5 5 4 4 3 3 2 2 1 1
```

See Section 6.8.2, page 228, for an example that demonstrates how to sort according to a member of a class.

The following program demonstrates how `sort()` and `stable_sort()` differ. The program uses both algorithms to sort strings only according to their number of characters by using the sorting criterion `lessLength()`:

```cpp
// algo/sort2.cpp

#include "algostuff.hpp"
using namespace std;

bool lessLength (const string& s1, const string& s2)
{
    return s1.length() < s2.length();
}

int main()
{
    // fill two collections with the same elements
    vector<string> coll1 = { "1xxx", "2x", "3x", "4x", "5xx", "6xxxx",
                             "7xx", "8xxx", "9xx", "10xxx", "11", "12",
                             "13", "14xx", "15", "16", "17" };
    vector<string> coll2(coll1);

    PRINT_ELEMENTS(coll1,"on entry:\n ");

    // sort (according to the length of the strings)
    sort (coll1.begin(), coll1.end(),            // range
          lessLength);                           // criterion
    stable_sort (coll2.begin(), coll2.end(),     // range
                 lessLength);                    // criterion

    PRINT_ELEMENTS(coll1,"\nwith sort():\n ");
    PRINT_ELEMENTS(coll2,"\nwith stable_sort():\n ");
}
```

The program has the following output:

```
on entry:
 1xxx 2x 3x 4x 5xx 6xxxx 7xx 8xxx 9xx 10xxx 11 12 13 14xx 15 16 17

with sort():
 2x 3x 4x 17 16 15 13 12 11 9xx 7xx 5xx 1xxx 8xxx 14xx 10xxx 6xxxx

with stable_sort():
 2x 3x 4x 11 12 13 15 16 17 5xx 7xx 9xx 1xxx 8xxx 14xx 6xxxx 10xxx
```

Only stable_sort() preserves the relative order of the elements (the leading numbers tag the order of the elements on entry).

11.9.2   Partial Sorting

```
void
partial_sort (RandomAccessIterator beg, RandomAccessIterator sortEnd,
              RandomAccessIterator end)

void
partial_sort (RandomAccessIterator beg, RandomAccessIterator sortEnd,
              RandomAccessIterator end, BinaryPredicate op)
```

- The first form sorts the elements in the range [*beg,end*) with operator <, so range [*beg,sortEnd*) contains the elements in sorted order.
- The second form sorts the elements by using the binary predicate
    op(*elem1* , *elem2*)
  as the sorting criterion, so range [*beg,sortEnd*) contains the elements in sorted order.
- Note that *op* has to define a *strict weak ordering* for the values (see Section 7.7, page 314, for details).
- Note that *op* should not change its state during a function call. See Section 10.1.4, page 483, for details.
- Unlike `sort()`, `partial_sort()` does not sort all elements but stops the sorting once the first elements up to *sortEnd* are sorted correctly. Thus, if, after sorting a sequence, you need only the first three elements, this algorithm saves time because it does not sort the remaining elements unnecessarily.
- If *sortEnd* is equal to *end*, `partial_sort()` sorts the full sequence. It has worse performance than `sort()` on average but better performance in the worst case. See the discussion about sorting algorithms in Section 11.2.2, page 511.
- Complexity: between linear and n-log-n (approximately *numElems*`*log`(*numSortedElems*) comparisons).

The following program demonstrates how to use `partial_sort()`:

```
// algo/partialsort1.cpp

#include "algostuff.hpp"
using namespace std;

int main()
{
    deque<int> coll;

    INSERT_ELEMENTS(coll,3,7);
    INSERT_ELEMENTS(coll,2,6);
    INSERT_ELEMENTS(coll,1,5);
    PRINT_ELEMENTS(coll);
```

```
// sort until the first five elements are sorted
partial_sort (coll.begin(),        // beginning of the range
              coll.begin()+5,      // end of sorted range
              coll.end());         // end of full range
PRINT_ELEMENTS(coll);

// sort inversely until the first five elements are sorted
partial_sort (coll.begin(),        // beginning of the range
              coll.begin()+5,      // end of sorted range
              coll.end(),          // end of full range
              greater<int>());     // sorting criterion
PRINT_ELEMENTS(coll);

// sort all elements
partial_sort (coll.begin(),        // beginning of the range
              coll.end(),          // end of sorted range
              coll.end());         // end of full range
PRINT_ELEMENTS(coll);
}
```

The program has the following output:

```
3 4 5 6 7 2 3 4 5 6 1 2 3 4 5
1 2 2 3 3 7 6 5 5 6 4 4 3 4 5
7 6 6 5 5 1 2 2 3 3 4 4 3 4 5
1 2 2 3 3 3 4 4 4 5 5 5 6 6 7
```

RandomAccessIterator
partial_sort_copy (InputIterator *sourceBeg*, InputIterator *sourceEnd*,
                 RandomAccessIterator *destBeg*, RandomAccessIterator *destEnd*)

RandomAccessIterator
partial_sort_copy (InputIterator *sourceBeg*, InputIterator *sourceEnd*,
                 RandomAccessIterator *destBeg*, RandomAccessIterator *destEnd*,
                 BinaryPredicate *op*)

- Both forms are a combination of copy() and partial_sort().
- They copy elements from the source range [*sourceBeg,sourceEnd*) sorted into the destination range [*destBeg,destEnd*).
- The number of elements that are sorted and copied is the minimum number of elements in the source range and in the destination range.
- Both forms return the position after the last copied element in the destination range (the first element that is not overwritten).

- If the size of the source range [*sourceBeg,sourceEnd*) is not smaller than the size of the destination range [*destBeg,destEnd*), all elements are copied and sorted. Thus, the behavior is a combination of copy() and sort().

- Note that *op* has to define a *strict weak ordering* for the values (see Section 7.7, page 314, for details).

- Complexity: between linear and n-log-n (approximately *numElems**log(*numSortedElems*) comparisons).

The following program demonstrates some examples of partial_sort_copy():

```cpp
// algo/partialsort2.cpp

#include "algostuff.hpp"
using namespace std;

int main()
{
    deque<int> coll1;
    vector<int> coll6(6);        // initialize with 6 elements
    vector<int> coll30(30);      // initialize with 30 elements

    INSERT_ELEMENTS(coll1,3,7);
    INSERT_ELEMENTS(coll1,2,6);
    INSERT_ELEMENTS(coll1,1,5);
    PRINT_ELEMENTS(coll1);

    // copy elements of coll1 sorted into coll6
    vector<int>::const_iterator pos6;
    pos6 = partial_sort_copy (coll1.cbegin(), coll1.cend(),
                              coll6.begin(), coll6.end());

    // print all copied elements
    copy (coll6.cbegin(), pos6,
          ostream_iterator<int>(cout," "));
    cout << endl;

    // copy elements of coll1 sorted into coll30
    vector<int>::const_iterator pos30;
    pos30 = partial_sort_copy (coll1.cbegin(), coll1.cend(),
                               coll30.begin(), coll30.end(),
                               greater<int>());

    // print all copied elements
    copy (coll30.cbegin(), pos30,
          ostream_iterator<int>(cout," "));
```

```
        cout << endl;
    }
```

The program has the following output:

```
3 4 5 6 7 2 3 4 5 6 1 2 3 4 5
1 2 2 3 3 3
7 6 6 5 5 5 4 4 4 3 3 3 2 2 1
```

The destination of the first call of `partial_sort_copy()` has only six elements, so the algorithm copies only six elements and returns the end of `col16`. The second call of `partial_sort_copy()` copies all elements of `col11` into `col130`, which has enough room for them, and thus all elements are copied and sorted.

11.9.3   Sorting According to the *n*th Element

```
void
nth_element (RandomAccessIterator beg, RandomAccessIterator nth,
             RandomAccessIterator end)
```

```
void
nth_element (RandomAccessIterator beg, RandomAccessIterator nth,
             RandomAccessIterator end, BinaryPredicate op)
```

- Both forms sort the elements in the range [*beg*,*end*), so the correct element is at the *n*th position, and all elements in front are less than or equal to this element, and all elements that follow are greater than or equal to it. Thus, you get two subsequences separated by the element at position *n*, whereby each element of the first subsequence is less than or equal to each element of the second subsequence. This is helpful if you need only the set of the *n* highest or lowest elements without having all the elements sorted.
- The first form uses operator < as the sorting criterion.
- The second form uses the binary predicate
    op(*elem1*,*elem2*)
  as the sorting criterion.
- Note that *op* has to define a *strict weak ordering* for the values (see Section 7.7, page 314, for details).
- Note that *op* should not change its state during a function call. See Section 10.1.4, page 483, for details.
- The `partition()` algorithm (see Section 11.8.5, page 592) is also provided to split elements of a sequence into two parts according to a sorting criterion. See Section 11.2.2, page 514, for a discussion of how `nth_element()` and `partition()` differ.
- Complexity: linear on average.

The following program demonstrates how to use `nth_element()`:

```
// algo/nthelement1.cpp

#include "algostuff.hpp"
using namespace std;

int main()
{
    deque<int> coll;

    INSERT_ELEMENTS(coll,3,7);
    INSERT_ELEMENTS(coll,2,6);
    INSERT_ELEMENTS(coll,1,5);
    PRINT_ELEMENTS(coll);

    // extract the four lowest elements
    nth_element (coll.begin(),          // beginning of range
                 coll.begin()+3,        // element that should be sorted correctly
                 coll.end());           // end of range

    // print them
    cout << "the four lowest elements are:  ";
    copy (coll.cbegin(), coll.cbegin()+4,
          ostream_iterator<int>(cout," "));
    cout << endl;

    // extract the four highest elements
    nth_element (coll.begin(),          // beginning of range
                 coll.end()-4,          // element that should be sorted correctly
                 coll.end());           // end of range

    // print them
    cout << "the four highest elements are: ";
    copy (coll.cend()-4, coll.cend(),
          ostream_iterator<int>(cout," "));
    cout << endl;

    // extract the four highest elements (second version)
    nth_element (coll.begin(),          // beginning of range
                 coll.begin()+3,        // element that should be sorted correctly
                 coll.end(),            // end of range
                 greater<int>());       // sorting criterion

    // print them
    cout << "the four highest elements are: ";
```

```
    copy (coll.cbegin(), coll.cbegin()+4,
          ostream_iterator<int>(cout," "));
    cout << endl;
}
```

The program has the following output:

```
3 4 5 6 7 2 3 4 5 6 1 2 3 4 5
the four lowest elements are:  2 1 2 3
the four highest elements are: 5 6 7 6
the four highest elements are: 6 7 6 5
```

11.9.4   Heap Algorithms

In the context of sorting, a *heap* is used as a particular way to sort elements. It is used by heapsort. A heap can be considered a binary tree that is implemented as a sequential collection. Heaps have two properties:

1. The first element is always (one of) the largest.

2. You can add or remove an element in logarithmic time.

A heap is the ideal way to implement a priority queue: a queue that sorts its elements automatically so that the "next" element always is (one of) the largest. Therefore, the heap algorithms are used by the `priority_queue` container (see Section 12.3, page 641). The STL provides four algorithms to handle a heap:

1. `make_heap()` converts a range of elements into a heap.

2. `push_heap()` adds one element to the heap.

3. `pop_heap()` removes the next element from the heap.

4. `sort_heap()` converts the heap into a sorted collection, after which it is no longer a heap.

In addition, since C++11, `is_heap()` and `is_heap_until()` are provided to check whether a collection is a heap or to return the first element that breaks the property of a collection to be a heap (see Section 11.5.5, page 554).

As usual, you can pass a binary predicate as the sorting criterion. The default sorting criterion is operator <.

Heap Algorithms in Detail

```
void
make_heap (RandomAccessIterator beg, RandomAccessIterator end)

void
make_heap (RandomAccessIterator beg, RandomAccessIterator end,
           BinaryPredicate op)
```

- Both forms convert the elements in the range [*beg*,*end*) into a heap.
- *op* is an optional binary predicate to be used as the sorting criterion:
  $op(elem1,elem2)$
- You need these functions only to start processing a heap for more than one element (one element automatically is a heap).
- Complexity: linear (at most, 3*numElems* comparisons).

```
void
push_heap (RandomAccessIterator beg, RandomAccessIterator end)

void
push_heap (RandomAccessIterator beg, RandomAccessIterator end,
           BinaryPredicate op)
```

- Both forms add the last element that is in front of *end* to the existing heap in the range [*beg*,*end*-1) so that the whole range [*beg*,*end*) becomes a heap.
- *op* is an optional binary predicate to be used as the sorting criterion:
  $op(elem1,elem2)$
- The caller has to ensure that, on entry, the elements in the range [*beg*,*end*-1) are a heap (according to the same sorting criterion) and that the new element immediately follows these elements.
- Complexity: logarithmic (at most, log(*numElems*) comparisons).

```
void
pop_heap (RandomAccessIterator beg, RandomAccessIterator end)

void
pop_heap (RandomAccessIterator beg, RandomAccessIterator end,
          BinaryPredicate op)
```

- Both forms move the highest element of the heap [*beg*,*end*), which is the first element, to the last position and create a new heap from the remaining elements in the range [*beg*,*end*-1).
- *op* is an optional binary predicate to be used as the sorting criterion:
  $op(elem1,elem2)$
- The caller has to ensure that, on entry, the elements in the range [*beg*,*end*) are a heap (according to the same sorting criterion).
- Complexity: logarithmic (at most, 2*log(*numElems*) comparisons).

```
void
sort_heap (RandomAccessIterator beg, RandomAccessIterator end)

void
sort_heap (RandomAccessIterator beg, RandomAccessIterator end,
           BinaryPredicate op)
```

- Both forms convert the heap [*beg,end*) into a sorted sequence.
- *op* is an optional binary predicate to be used as the sorting criterion:
    $$op(elem1, elem2)$$
- Note that after this call, the range is no longer a heap.
- The caller has to ensure that, on entry, the elements in the range [*beg,end*) are a heap (according to the same sorting criterion).
- Complexity: n-log-n (at most, *numElems**log(*numElems*) comparisons).

Example Using Heaps

The following program demonstrates how to use the different heap algorithms:

```
// algo/heap1.cpp

#include "algostuff.hpp"
using namespace std;

int main()
{
    vector<int> coll;

    INSERT_ELEMENTS(coll,3,7);
    INSERT_ELEMENTS(coll,5,9);
    INSERT_ELEMENTS(coll,1,4);

    PRINT_ELEMENTS (coll, "on entry:            ");

    // convert collection into a heap
    make_heap (coll.begin(), coll.end());

    PRINT_ELEMENTS (coll, "after make_heap(): ");

    // pop next element out of the heap
    pop_heap (coll.begin(), coll.end());
    coll.pop_back();

    PRINT_ELEMENTS (coll, "after pop_heap():  ");

    // push new element into the heap
    coll.push_back (17);
    push_heap (coll.begin(), coll.end());

    PRINT_ELEMENTS (coll, "after push_heap(): ");
```

```
// convert heap into a sorted collection
// - NOTE: after the call it is no longer a heap
sort_heap (coll.begin(), coll.end());

PRINT_ELEMENTS (coll, "after sort_heap():  ");
}
```

The program has the following output:

```
on entry:             3 4 5 6 7 5 6 7 8 9 1 2 3 4
after make_heap():    9 8 6 7 7 5 5 3 6 4 1 2 3 4
after pop_heap():     8 7 6 7 4 5 5 3 6 4 1 2 3
after push_heap():    17 7 8 7 4 5 6 3 6 4 1 2 3 5
after sort_heap():    1 2 3 3 4 4 5 5 6 6 7 7 8 17
```

After make_heap(), the elements are sorted as a heap:

```
9 8 6 7 7 5 5 3 6 4 1 2 3 4
```

Transform the elements into a binary tree, and you'll see that the value of each node is less than or equal to its parent node (Figure 11.1). Both push_heap() and pop_heap() change the elements so that the invariant of this binary tree structure — each node not greater than its parent node — remains stable.

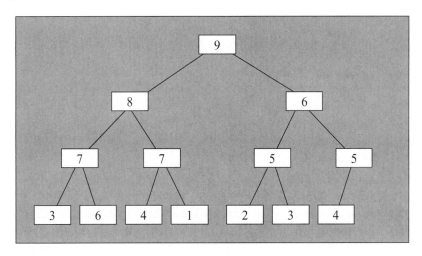

Figure 11.1. Elements of a Heap as a Binary Tree

11.10   Sorted-Range Algorithms

Sorted-range algorithms require that the source ranges have the elements sorted according to their sorting criterion. These algorithms may have significantly better performance than similar algorithms for unsorted ranges (usually logarithmic instead of linear complexity). You can use these algorithms with iterators that are not random-access iterators. However, in this case, the algorithms have linear complexity because they have to step through the sequence element-by-element. Nevertheless, the number of comparisons may still have logarithmic complexity.

According to the standard, calling these algorithms for sequences that are not sorted on entry results in undefined behavior. However, for most implementations, calling these algorithms also works for unsorted sequences. Nevertheless, to rely on this fact is not portable.

Associative and unordered containers provide special member functions for some of the searching algorithms presented here. When searching for a special value or key, you should use them.

11.10.1   Searching Elements

The following algorithms search certain values in sorted ranges.

Checking Whether One Element Is Present

```
bool
binary_search (ForwardIterator beg, ForwardIterator end, const T& value)
```

```
bool
binary_search (ForwardIterator beg, ForwardIterator end, const T& value,
               BinaryPredicate op)
```

- Both forms return whether the sorted range [*beg*,*end*) contains an element equal to *value*.
- *op* is an optional binary predicate to be used as the sorting criterion:
    op(*elem1*,*elem2*)
- To obtain the position of an element for which you are searching, use lower_bound(), upper_bound(), or equal_range() (see pages 611 and 613).
- The caller has to ensure that the ranges are sorted according to the sorting criterion on entry.
- Complexity: logarithmic for random-access iterators, linear otherwise (at most, $\log$(*numElems*) + 2 comparisons; but for other than random-access iterators, the number of operations to step through the elements is linear, making the total complexity linear).

The following program demonstrates how to use binary_search():

```
// algo/binarysearch1.cpp

#include "algostuff.hpp"
using namespace std;
```

```
int main()
{
    list<int> coll;

    INSERT_ELEMENTS(coll,1,9);
    PRINT_ELEMENTS(coll);

    // check existence of element with value 5
    if (binary_search(coll.cbegin(), coll.cend(), 5)) {
        cout << "5 is present" << endl;
    }
    else {
        cout << "5 is not present" << endl;
    }

    // check existence of element with value 42
    if (binary_search(coll.cbegin(), coll.cend(), 42)) {
        cout << "42 is present" << endl;
    }
    else {
        cout << "42 is not present" << endl;
    }
}
```

The program has the following output:

```
1 2 3 4 5 6 7 8 9
5 is present
42 is not present
```

Checking Whether Several Elements Are Present

bool
includes (InputIterator1 *beg*, InputIterator1 *end*,
          InputIterator2 *searchBeg*, InputIterator2 *searchEnd*)

bool
includes (InputIterator1 *beg*, InputIterator1 *end*,
          InputIterator2 *searchBeg*, InputIterator2 *searchEnd*,
          BinaryPredicate *op*)

- Both forms return whether the sorted range [*beg,end*) contains all elements in the sorted range [*searchBeg,searchEnd*). That is, for each element in [*searchBeg,searchEnd*), there must be an equal element in [*beg,end*). If elements in [*searchBeg,searchEnd*) are equal, [*beg,end*) must contain the same number of elements. Thus, [*searchBeg,searchEnd*) must be a subset of [*beg,end*).

- *op* is an optional binary predicate to be used as the sorting criterion:

  op(elem1, elem2)
- The caller has to ensure that both ranges are sorted according to the same sorting criterion on entry.
- Complexity: linear (at most, 2∗(*numElems*+*numSearchElems*) − 1 comparisons).

The following program demonstrates the usage of `includes()`:

```
// algo/includes1.cpp

#include "algostuff.hpp"
using namespace std;

int main()
{
    list<int> coll;
    vector<int> search;

    INSERT_ELEMENTS(coll,1,9);
    PRINT_ELEMENTS(coll,"coll:    ");

    search.push_back(3);
    search.push_back(4);
    search.push_back(7);
    PRINT_ELEMENTS(search,"search: ");

    // check whether all elements in search are also in coll
    if (includes (coll.cbegin(), coll.cend(),
                  search.cbegin(), search.cend())) {
        cout << "all elements of search are also in coll"
             << endl;
    }
    else {
        cout << "not all elements of search are also in coll"
             << endl;
    }
}
```

The program has the following output:

```
coll:    1 2 3 4 5 6 7 8 9
search: 3 4 7
all elements of search are also in coll
```

Searching First or Last Possible Position

```
ForwardIterator
lower_bound (ForwardIterator beg, ForwardIterator end, const T& value)

ForwardIterator
lower_bound (ForwardIterator beg, ForwardIterator end, const T& value,
             BinaryPredicate op)

ForwardIterator
upper_bound (ForwardIterator beg, ForwardIterator end, const T& value)

ForwardIterator
upper_bound (ForwardIterator beg, ForwardIterator end, const T& value,
             BinaryPredicate op)
```

- `lower_bound()` returns the position of the first element that has a value equal to or greater than *value*. This is the first position where an element with value *value* could get inserted without breaking the sorting of the range [*beg,end*].
- `upper_bound()` returns the position of the first element that has a value greater than *value*. This is the last position where an element with value *value* could get inserted without breaking the sorting of the range [*beg,end*].
- All algorithms return *end* if there is no such value.
- *op* is an optional binary predicate to be used as the sorting criterion:
  op(*elem1*,*elem2*)
- The caller has to ensure that the ranges are sorted according to the sorting criterion on entry.
- To obtain the result from both `lower_bound()` and `upper_bound()`, use `equal_range()`, which returns both (see the next algorithm).
- Associative containers provide equivalent member functions that provide better performance (see Section 8.3.3, page 405).
- Complexity: logarithmic for random-access iterators, linear otherwise (at most, log(*numElems*) + 1 comparisons; but for other than random-access iterators, the number of operations to step through the elements is linear, making the total complexity linear).

The following program demonstrates how to use `lower_bound()` and `upper_bound()`:

```
// algo/bounds1.cpp

#include "algostuff.hpp"
using namespace std;

int main()
{
    list<int> coll;
```

```
        INSERT_ELEMENTS(coll,1,9);
        INSERT_ELEMENTS(coll,1,9);
        coll.sort ();
        PRINT_ELEMENTS(coll);

        // print first and last position 5 could get inserted
        auto pos1 = lower_bound (coll.cbegin(), coll.cend(),
                                 5);
        auto pos2 = upper_bound (coll.cbegin(), coll.cend(),
                                 5);

        cout << "5 could get position "
             << distance(coll.cbegin(),pos1) + 1
             << " up to "
             << distance(coll.cbegin(),pos2) + 1
             << " without breaking the sorting" << endl;

        // insert 3 at the first possible position without breaking the sorting
        coll.insert (lower_bound(coll.begin(),coll.end(),
                                 3),
                     3);

        // insert 7 at the last possible position without breaking the sorting
        coll.insert (upper_bound(coll.begin(),coll.end(),
                                 7),
                     7);

        PRINT_ELEMENTS(coll);
    }
```

The program has the following output:

```
    1 1 2 2 3 3 4 4 5 5 6 6 7 7 8 8 9 9
    5 could get position 9 up to 11 without breaking the sorting
    1 1 2 2 3 3 3 4 4 5 5 6 6 7 7 7 8 8 9 9
```

pos1 and pos2 have type

```
    list<int>::const_iterator
```

Searching First and Last Possible Positions

```
pair<ForwardIterator,ForwardIterator>
```
equal_range (ForwardIterator *beg*, ForwardIterator *end*, const T& *value*)

```
pair<ForwardIterator,ForwardIterator>
```
equal_range (ForwardIterator *beg*, ForwardIterator *end*, const T& *value*,
          BinaryPredicate *op*)

- Both forms return the range of elements that is equal to *value*. The range comprises the first and the last position an element with value *value* could get inserted without breaking the sorting of the range [*beg,end*).
- This is equivalent to:
  ```
  make_pair(lower_bound(...),upper_bound(...))
  ```
- *op* is an optional binary predicate to be used as the sorting criterion:
  op(*elem1*,*elem2*)
- The caller has to ensure that the ranges are sorted according to the sorting criterion on entry.
- Associative and unordered containers provide an equivalent member function that has better performance (see Section 8.3.3, page 406).
- Complexity: logarithmic for random-access iterators, linear otherwise (at most, 2*log(*num-Elems*) + 1 comparisons; but for other than random-access iterators, the number of operations to step through the elements is linear, making the total complexity linear).

The following program demonstrates how to use equal_range():

```
// algo/equalrange1.cpp

#include "algostuff.hpp"
using namespace std;

int main()
{
    list<int> coll;

    INSERT_ELEMENTS(coll,1,9);
    INSERT_ELEMENTS(coll,1,9);
    coll.sort ();
    PRINT_ELEMENTS(coll);

    // print first and last position 5 could get inserted
    pair<list<int>::const_iterator,list<int>::const_iterator> range;
    range = equal_range (coll.cbegin(), coll.cend(),
                         5);
```

```
    cout << "5 could get position "
         << distance(coll.cbegin(),range.first) + 1
         << " up to "
         << distance(coll.cbegin(),range.second) + 1
         << " without breaking the sorting" << endl;
}
```

The program has the following output:

```
1 1 2 2 3 3 4 4 5 5 6 6 7 7 8 8 9 9
5 could get position 9 up to 11 without breaking the sorting
```

11.10.2   Merging Elements

The following algorithms merge elements of two ranges. The algorithms process the sum, the union, the intersection, and so on.

Processing the Sum of Two Sorted Sets

OutputIterator
merge (InputIterator *source1Beg*, InputIterator *source1End*,
       InputIterator *source2Beg*, InputIterator *source2End*,
       OutputIterator *destBeg*)

OutputIterator
merge (InputIterator *source1Beg*, InputIterator *source1End*,
       InputIterator *source2Beg*, InputIterator *source2End*,
       OutputIterator *destBeg*, BinaryPredicate *op*)

- Both forms merge the elements of the sorted source ranges [*source1Beg,source1End*) and [*source2Beg,source2End*) so that the destination range starting with destBeg contains all elements that are in the first source range plus those that are in the second source range. For example, calling merge() for
    ```
    1 2 2 4 6 7 7 9
    ```
  and
    ```
    2 2 2 3 6 6 8 9
    ```
  results in
    ```
    1 2 2 2 2 2 3 4 6 6 6 7 7 8 9 9
    ```
- All elements in the destination range are in sorted order.
- Both forms return the position after the last copied element in the destination range (the first element that is not overwritten).
- *op* is an optional binary predicate to be used as the sorting criterion:
    op(*elem1*,*elem2*)
- The source ranges are not modified.

- According to the standard, the caller has to ensure that both source ranges are sorted on entry. However, in most implementations, this algorithm also merges elements of two unsorted source ranges into an unsorted destination range. Nevertheless, for unsorted ranges, you should call copy() twice, instead of merge(), to be portable.
- The caller must ensure that the destination range is big enough or that insert iterators are used.
- The destination range should not overlap the source ranges.
- Lists and forward lists provide a special member function, merge(), to merge the elements of two lists (see Section 8.8.1, page 423).
- To ensure that elements that are in both source ranges end up in the destination range only once, use set_union() (see page 616).
- To process only the elements that are in both source ranges, use set_intersection() (see page 617).
- Complexity: linear (at most, *numElems1*+*numElems2*-1 comparisons).

The following example demonstrates how to use merge():

```
// algo/merge1.cpp

#include "algostuff.hpp"
using namespace std;

int main()
{
    list<int> coll1;
    set<int> coll2;

    // fill both collections with some sorted elements
    INSERT_ELEMENTS(coll1,1,6);
    INSERT_ELEMENTS(coll2,3,8);

    PRINT_ELEMENTS(coll1,"coll1:  ");
    PRINT_ELEMENTS(coll2,"coll2:  ");

    // print merged sequence
    cout << "merged: ";
    merge (coll1.cbegin(), coll1.cend(),
           coll2.cbegin(), coll2.cend(),
           ostream_iterator<int>(cout," "));
    cout << endl;
}
```

The program has the following output:

```
coll1:  1 2 3 4 5 6
coll2:  3 4 5 6 7 8
merged: 1 2 3 3 4 4 5 5 6 6 7 8
```

See page 620 for another example. It demonstrates how the various algorithms that are provided to combine sorted sequences differ.

Processing the Union of Two Sorted Sets

```
OutputIterator
set_union (InputIterator source1Beg, InputIterator source1End,
           InputIterator source2Beg, InputIterator source2End,
           OutputIterator destBeg)

OutputIterator
set_union (InputIterator source1Beg, InputIterator source1End,
           InputIterator source2Beg, InputIterator source2End,
           OutputIterator destBeg, BinaryPredicate op)
```

- Both forms merge the elements of the sorted source ranges [*source1Beg,source1End*) and [*source2Beg,source2End*) so that the destination range starting with destBeg contains all elements that are in the first source range, in the second source range, or in both. For example, calling set_union() for

    1 2 2 4 6 7 7 9

  and

    2 2 2 3 6 6 8 9

  results in

    1 2 2 2 3 4 6 6 7 7 8 9

- All elements in the destination range are in sorted order.
- Elements that are in both ranges are in the union range only once. However, duplicates are possible if elements occur more than once in one of the source ranges. The number of occurrences of equal elements in the destination range is the maximum of the number of their occurrences in both source ranges.
- Both forms return the position after the last copied element in the destination range (the first element that is not overwritten).
- *op* is an optional binary predicate to be used as the sorting criterion:
    op(*elem1*,*elem2*)
- The source ranges are not modified.
- The caller has to ensure that the ranges are sorted according to the sorting criterion on entry.
- The caller must ensure that the destination range is big enough or that insert iterators are used.
- The destination range should not overlap the source ranges.
- To obtain all elements of both source ranges without removing elements that are in both, use merge() (see page 614).
- Complexity: linear (at most, 2*(*numElems1+numElems2*) – 1 comparisons).

See page 620 for an example of the use of set_union(). This example also demonstrates how it differs from other algorithms that combine elements of two sorted sequences.

Processing the Intersection of Two Sorted Sets

```
OutputIterator
set_intersection (InputIterator source1Beg, InputIterator source1End,
                  InputIterator source2Beg, InputIterator source2End,
                  OutputIterator destBeg)

OutputIterator
set_intersection (InputIterator source1Beg, InputIterator source1End,
                  InputIterator source2Beg, InputIterator source2End,
                  OutputIterator destBeg, BinaryPredicate op)
```

- Both forms merge the elements of the sorted source ranges [*source1Beg,source1End*] and [*source2Beg,source2End*] so that the destination range starting with destBeg contains all elements that are in both source ranges. For example, calling set_intersection() for
  ```
  1 2 2 4 6 7 7 9
  ```
  and
  ```
  2 2 2 3 6 6 8 9
  ```
  results in
  ```
  2 2 6 9
  ```
- All elements in the destination range are in sorted order.
- Duplicates are possible if elements occur more than once in both source ranges. The number of occurrences of equal elements in the destination range is the minimum number of their occurrences in both source ranges.
- Both forms return the position after the last merged element in the destination range.
- *op* is an optional binary predicate to be used as the sorting criterion:
  op(elem1,elem2)
- The source ranges are not modified.
- The caller has to ensure that the ranges are sorted according to the sorting criterion on entry.
- The caller must ensure that the destination range is big enough or that insert iterators are used.
- The destination range should not overlap the source ranges.
- Complexity: linear (at most, 2*(*numElems1+numElems2*) – 1 comparisons).

See page 620 for an example of the use of set_intersection(). This example also demonstrates how it differs from other algorithms that combine elements of two sorted sequences.

Processing the Difference of Two Sorted Sets

```
OutputIterator
set_difference (InputIterator source1Beg, InputIterator source1End,
                InputIterator source2Beg, InputIterator source2End,
                OutputIterator destBeg)
```

```
OutputIterator
set_difference (InputIterator source1Beg, InputIterator source1End,
                InputIterator source2Beg, InputIterator source2End,
                OutputIterator destBeg, BinaryPredicate op)
```

- Both forms merge the elements of the sorted source ranges [*source1Beg*,*source1End*) and [*source2Beg*,*source2End*) so that the destination range starting with destBeg contains all elements that are in the first source range but not in the second source range. For example, calling set_difference() for
    ```
    1 2 2 4 6 7 7 9
    ```
  and
    ```
    2 2 2 3 6 6 8 9
    ```
  results in
    ```
    1 4 7 7
    ```
- All elements in the destination range are in sorted order.
- Duplicates are possible if elements occur more than once in the first source range. The number of occurrences of equal elements in the destination range is the difference between the number of their occurrences in the first source range less the number of occurrences in the second source range. If there are more occurrences in the second source range, the number of occurrences in the destination range is zero.
- Both forms return the position after the last merged element in the destination range.
- *op* is an optional binary predicate to be used as the sorting criterion:
    op(*elem1*,*elem2*)
- The source ranges are not modified.
- The caller has to ensure that the ranges are sorted according to the sorting criterion on entry.
- The caller must ensure that the destination range is big enough or that insert iterators are used.
- The destination range should not overlap the source ranges.
- Complexity: linear (at most, 2*(*numElems1*+*numElems2*) – 1 comparisons).

See page 620 for an example of the use of set_difference(). This example also demonstrates how it differs from other algorithms that combine elements of two sorted sequences.

OutputIterator
set_symmetric_difference (InputIterator *source1Beg*, InputIterator *source1End*,
                           InputIterator *source2Beg*, InputIterator *source2End*,
                           OutputIterator *destBeg*)

OutputIterator
set_symmetric_difference (InputIterator *source1Beg*, InputIterator *source1End*,
                           InputIterator *source2Beg*, InputIterator *source2End*,
                           OutputIterator *destBeg*, BinaryPredicate *op*)

- Both forms merge the elements of the sorted source ranges [*source1Beg,source1End*) and [*source2Beg,source2End*) so that the destination range starting with destBeg contains all elements that are either in the first source range or in the second source range but not in both. For example, calling set_symmetric_difference() for

    1 2 2 4 6 7 7 9

  and

    2 2 2 3 6 6 8 9

  results in

    1 2 3 4 6 7 7 8

- All elements in the destination range are in sorted order.
- Duplicates are possible if elements occur more than once in one of the source ranges. The number of occurrences of equal elements in the destination range is the difference between the number of their occurrences in the source ranges.
- Both forms return the position after the last merged element in the destination range.
- *op* is an optional binary predicate to be used as the sorting criterion:

  op(*elem1*,*elem2*)

- The source ranges are not modified.
- The caller has to ensure that the ranges are sorted according to the sorting criterion on entry.
- The caller must ensure that the destination range is big enough or that insert iterators are used.
- The destination range should not overlap the source ranges.
- Complexity: linear (at most, 2*(*numElems1*+*numElems2*) − 1 comparisons).

See the following subsection for an example of the use of set_symmetric_difference(). This example also demonstrates how it differs from other algorithms that combine elements of two sorted sequences.

Example of All Merging Algorithms

The following example compares the various algorithms that combine elements of two sorted source ranges, demonstrating how they work and differ:

```
// algo/sorted1.cpp

#include "algostuff.hpp"
using namespace std;

int main()
{
    vector<int> c1 = { 1, 2, 2, 4, 6, 7, 7, 9 };

    deque<int>  c2 = { 2, 2, 2, 3, 6, 6, 8, 9 };

    // print source ranges
    cout << "c1:                        " ;
    copy (c1.cbegin(), c1.cend(),
          ostream_iterator<int>(cout," "));
    cout << endl;
    cout << "c2:                        " ;
    copy (c2.cbegin(), c2.cend(),
          ostream_iterator<int>(cout," "));
    cout << '\n' << endl;

    // sum the ranges by using merge()
    cout << "merge():                  ";
    merge (c1.cbegin(), c1.cend(),
           c2.cbegin(), c2.cend(),
           ostream_iterator<int>(cout," "));
    cout << endl;

    // unite the ranges by using set_union()
    cout << "set_union():              ";
    set_union (c1.cbegin(), c1.cend(),
               c2.cbegin(), c2.cend(),
               ostream_iterator<int>(cout," "));
    cout << endl;

    // intersect the ranges by using set_intersection()
    cout << "set_intersection():       ";
```

```
        set_intersection (c1.cbegin(), c1.cend(),
                          c2.cbegin(), c2.cend(),
                          ostream_iterator<int>(cout," "));
    cout << endl;

    // determine elements of first range without elements of second range
    // by using set_difference()
    cout << "set_difference():              ";
    set_difference (c1.cbegin(), c1.cend(),
                    c2.cbegin(), c2.cend(),
                    ostream_iterator<int>(cout," "));
    cout << endl;

    // determine difference the ranges with set_symmetric_difference()
    cout << "set_symmetric_difference(): ";
    set_symmetric_difference (c1.cbegin(), c1.cend(),
                              c2.cbegin(), c2.cend(),
                              ostream_iterator<int>(cout," "));
    cout << endl;
}
```

The program has the following output:

```
c1:                          1 2 2 4 6 7 7 9
c2:                          2 2 2 3 6 6 8 9

merge():                     1 2 2 2 2 2 3 4 6 6 6 7 7 8 9 9
set_union():                 1 2 2 2 3 4 6 6 7 7 8 9
set_intersection():          2 2 6 9
set_difference():            1 4 7 7
set_symmetric_difference():  1 2 3 4 6 7 7 8
```

Merging Consecutive Sorted Ranges

```
void
inplace_merge (BidirectionalIterator beg1, BidirectionalIterator end1beg2,
               BidirectionalIterator end2)

void
inplace_merge (BidirectionalIterator beg1, BidirectionalIterator end1beg2,
               BidirectionalIterator end2, BinaryPredicate op)
```

- Both forms merge the consecutive sorted source ranges [*beg1*,*end1beg2*) and [*end1beg2*,*end2*) so that the range [*beg1*,*end2*) contains the elements as a sorted summary range.
- Complexity: linear (*numElems*-1 comparisons) if enough memory available, or n-log-n otherwise (*numElems**log(*numElems*) comparisons).

The following program demonstrates the use of `inplace_merge()`:

```
// algo/inplacemerge1.cpp

#include "algostuff.hpp"
using namespace std;

int main()
{
    list<int> coll;

    // insert two sorted sequences
    INSERT_ELEMENTS(coll,1,7);
    INSERT_ELEMENTS(coll,1,8);
    PRINT_ELEMENTS(coll);

    // find beginning of second part (element after 7)
    list<int>::iterator pos;
    pos = find (coll.begin(), coll.end(),     // range
                7);                           // value
    ++pos;

    // merge into one sorted range
    inplace_merge (coll.begin(), pos, coll.end());

    PRINT_ELEMENTS(coll);
}
```

The program has the following output:

```
1 2 3 4 5 6 7 1 2 3 4 5 6 7 8
1 1 2 2 3 3 4 4 5 5 6 6 7 7 8
```

11.11 Numeric Algorithms

This section presents the STL algorithms that are provided for numeric processing. However, you can process other than numeric values. For example, you can use `accumulate()` to process the sum of several strings. To use the numeric algorithms, you have to include the header file `<numeric>`:

```
#include <numeric>
```

11.11.1 Processing Results

Computing the Result of One Sequence

T
accumulate (InputIterator *beg*, InputIterator *end*,
          T *initValue*)

T
accumulate (InputIterator *beg*, InputIterator *end*,
          T *initValue*, BinaryFunc *op*)

- The first form computes and returns the sum of *initValue* and all elements in the range [*beg*,*end*). In particular, it calls the following for each element:
      initValue = *initValue* + *elem*

- The second form computes and returns the result of calling *op* for *initValue* and all elements in the range [*beg*,*end*). In particular, it calls the following for each element:
      initValue = *op*(*initValue* ,*elem*)

- Thus, for the values
      a1 a2 a3 a4 ...
  they compute and return either
      initValue + a1 + a2 + a3 + ...
  or
      initValue *op* a1 *op* a2 *op* a3 *op* ...
  respectively.
- If the range is empty (*beg*==*end*), both forms return *initValue*.
- *op* must not modify the passed arguments.
- Complexity: linear (*numElems* calls of operator + or *op*(), respectively).

The following program demonstrates how to use `accumulate()` to process the sum and the product of all elements of a range:

```
// algo/accumulate1.cpp

#include "algostuff.hpp"
using namespace std;
```

```cpp
int main()
{
    vector<int> coll;

    INSERT_ELEMENTS(coll,1,9);
    PRINT_ELEMENTS(coll);

    // process sum of elements
    cout << "sum: "
         << accumulate (coll.cbegin(), coll.cend(),   // range
                        0)                             // initial value
         << endl;

    // process sum of elements less 100
    cout << "sum: "
         << accumulate (coll.cbegin(), coll.cend(),   // range
                        -100)                          // initial value
         << endl;

    // process product of elements
    cout << "product: "
         << accumulate (coll.cbegin(), coll.cend(),   // range
                        1,                             // initial value
                        multiplies<int>())             // operation
         << endl;

    // process product of elements (use 0 as initial value)
    cout << "product: "
         << accumulate (coll.cbegin(), coll.cend(),   // range
                        0,                             // initial value
                        multiplies<int>())             // operation
         << endl;
}
```

The program has the following output:

```
1 2 3 4 5 6 7 8 9
sum: 45
sum: -55
product: 362880
product: 0
```

The last output is 0 because any value multiplied by zero is zero.

Computing the Inner Product of Two Sequences

T
inner_product (InputIterator1 *beg1*, InputIterator1 *end1*,
            InputIterator2 *beg2*, T *initValue*)

T
inner_product (InputIterator1 *beg1*, InputIterator1 *end1*,
            InputIterator2 *beg2*, T *initValue*,
            BinaryFunc *op1*, BinaryFunc *op2*)

- The first form computes and returns the inner product of *initValue* and all elements in the range [*beg,end*) combined with the elements in the range starting with *beg2*. In particular, it calls the following for all corresponding elements:

  initValue = *initValue* + *elem1* ∗ *elem2*

- The second form computes and returns the result of calling *op* for *initValue* and all elements in the range [*beg,end*) combined with the elements in the range starting with *beg2*. In particular, it calls the following for all corresponding elements:

  initValue = *op1*(*initValue*,*op2*(*elem1*,*elem2*))

- Thus, for the values

  ```
  a1 a2 a3 ...
  b1 b2 b3 ...
  ```

  they compute and return either

  initValue + (a1 ∗ b1) + (a2 ∗ b2) + (a3 ∗ b3) + ...

  or

  initValue *op1* (a1 *op2* b1) *op1* (a2 *op2* b2) *op1* (a3 *op2* b3) *op1* ...

  respectively.

- If the first range is empty (*beg1*==*end1*), both forms return *initValue*.
- The caller has to ensure that the range starting with *beg2* contains enough elements.
- *op1* and *op2* must not modify their arguments.
- Complexity: linear (*numElems* calls of operators + and ∗ or *numElems* calls of *op1*() and *op2*(), respectively).

The following program demonstrates how to use `inner_product()`. It processes the sum of products and the product of the sums for two sequences:

```
// algo/innerproduct1.cpp

#include "algostuff.hpp"
using namespace std;
```

```
int main()
{
    list<int> coll;

    INSERT_ELEMENTS(coll,1,6);
    PRINT_ELEMENTS(coll);

    // process sum of all products
    // (0 + 1*1 + 2*2 + 3*3 + 4*4 + 5*5 + 6*6)
    cout << "inner product: "
         << inner_product (coll.cbegin(), coll.cend(),   // first range
                           coll.cbegin(),                // second range
                           0)                            // initial value
         << endl;

    // process sum of 1*6 ... 6*1
    // (0 + 1*6 + 2*5 + 3*4 + 4*3 + 5*2 + 6*1)
    cout << "inner reverse product: "
         << inner_product (coll.cbegin(), coll.cend(),   // first range
                           coll.crbegin(),               // second range
                           0)                            // initial value
         << endl;

    // process product of all sums
    // (1 * 1+1 * 2+2 * 3+3 * 4+4 * 5+5 * 6+6)
    cout << "product of sums: "
         << inner_product (coll.cbegin(), coll.cend(),   // first range
                           coll.cbegin(),                // second range
                           1,                            // initial value
                           multiplies<int>(),            // outer operation
                           plus<int>())                  // inner operation
         << endl;
}
```

The program has the following output:

```
1 2 3 4 5 6
inner product: 91
inner reverse product: 56
product of sums: 46080
```

11.11.2   Converting Relative and Absolute Values

The following two algorithms enable you to convert a sequence of relative values into a sequence of absolute values, and vice versa.

Converting Relative Values into Absolute Values

```
OutputIterator
```
partial_sum (InputIterator *sourceBeg*, InputIterator *sourceEnd*,
            OutputIterator *destBeg*)

```
OutputIterator
```
partial_sum (InputIterator *sourceBeg*, InputIterator *sourceEnd*,
            OutputIterator *destBeg*, BinaryFunc *op*)

- The first form computes the partial sum for each element in the source range [*sourceBeg*, *sourceEnd*) and writes each result to the destination range starting with *destBeg*.
- The second form calls *op* for each element in the source range [*sourceBeg*,*sourceEnd*) combined with all previous values and writes each result to the destination range starting with *destBeg*.
- Thus, for the values
     a1 a2 a3 ...
  they compute either
     a1,   a1 + a2,   a1 + a2 + a3,   ...
  or
     a1,   a1 *op* a2,   a1 *op* a2 *op* a3,   ...
  respectively.
- Both forms return the position after the last written value in the destination range (the first element that is not overwritten).
- The first form is equivalent to the conversion of a sequence of relative values into a sequence of absolute values. In this regard, algorithm `partial_sum()` is the complement of algorithm `adjacent_difference()` (see page 628).
- The source and destination ranges may be identical.
- The caller must ensure that the destination range is big enough or that insert iterators are used.
- *op* should not modify the passed arguments.
- Complexity: linear (*numElems* calls of operator + or *op*(), respectively).

The following program demonstrates some examples of using `partial_sum()`:

```
// algo/partialsum1.cpp

#include "algostuff.hpp"
using namespace std;

int main()
{
    vector<int> coll;
```

```
    INSERT_ELEMENTS(coll,1,6);
    PRINT_ELEMENTS(coll);
```

```
    // print all partial sums
    partial_sum (coll.cbegin(), coll.cend(),        // source range
                 ostream_iterator<int>(cout," "));  // destination
    cout << endl;
```

```
    // print all partial products
    partial_sum (coll.cbegin(), coll.cend(),        // source range
                 ostream_iterator<int>(cout," "),   // destination
                 multiplies<int>());                // operation
    cout << endl;
}
```

The program has the following output:

```
1 2 3 4 5 6
1 3 6 10 15 21
1 2 6 24 120 720
```

See also the example of converting relative values into absolute values, and vice versa, on page 630.

Converting Absolute Values into Relative Values

```
OutputIterator
```
adjacent_difference (InputIterator *sourceBeg*, InputIterator *sourceEnd*,
                    OutputIterator *destBeg*)

```
OutputIterator
```
adjacent_difference (InputIterator *sourceBeg*, InputIterator *sourceEnd*,
                    OutputIterator *destBeg*, BinaryFunc *op*)

- The first form computes the difference of each element in the range [*sourceBeg*,*sourceEnd*) with its predecessor and writes the result to the destination range starting with *destBeg*.
- The second form calls *op* for each element in the range [*sourceBeg*,*sourceEnd*) with its predecessor and writes the result to the destination range starting with *destBeg*.
- The first element only is copied.
- Thus, for the values
      a1 a2 a3 a4 ...
  they compute and write either the values
      a1,   a2 - a1,   a3 - a2,   a4 - a3,   ...
  or the values
      a1,   a2 *op* a1,   a3 *op* a2,   a4 *op* a3,   ...
  respectively.

- Both forms return the position after the last written value in the destination range (the first element that is not overwritten).
- The first form is equivalent to the conversion of a sequence of absolute values into a sequence of relative values. In this regard, algorithm `adjacent_difference()` is the complement of algorithm `partial_sum()` (see page 627).
- The source and destination ranges may be identical.
- The caller must ensure that the destination range is big enough or that insert iterators are used.
- *op* should not modify the passed arguments.
- Complexity: linear (*numElems*-1 calls of operator - or *op*(), respectively).

The following program demonstrates some examples of using `adjacent_difference()`:

```
// algo/adjacentdiff1.cpp

#include "algostuff.hpp"
using namespace std;

int main()
{
    deque<int> coll;

    INSERT_ELEMENTS(coll,1,6);
    PRINT_ELEMENTS(coll);

    // print all differences between elements
    adjacent_difference (coll.cbegin(), coll.cend(),        // source
                         ostream_iterator<int>(cout," "));  // destination
    cout << endl;

    // print all sums with the predecessors
    adjacent_difference (coll.cbegin(), coll.cend(),        // source
                         ostream_iterator<int>(cout," "),   // destination
                         plus<int>());                      // operation
    cout << endl;

    // print all products between elements
    adjacent_difference (coll.cbegin(), coll.cend(),        // source
                         ostream_iterator<int>(cout," "),   // destination
                         multiplies<int>());                // operation
    cout << endl;
}
```

The program has the following output:

```
1 2 3 4 5 6
1 1 1 1 1 1
1 3 5 7 9 11
1 2 6 12 20 30
```

See also the example of converting relative values into absolute values, and vice versa, in the next subsection.

Example of Converting Relative Values into Absolute Values

The following example demonstrates how to use `partial_sum()` and `adjacent_difference()` to convert a sequence of relative values into a sequence of absolute values, and vice versa:

```cpp
// algo/relabs1.cpp

#include "algostuff.hpp"
using namespace std;

int main()
{
    vector<int> coll = { 17, -3, 22, 13, 13, -9 };
    PRINT_ELEMENTS(coll,"coll:     ");

    // convert into relative values
    adjacent_difference (coll.cbegin(), coll.cend(),   // source
                         coll.begin());                // destination
    PRINT_ELEMENTS(coll,"relative: ");

    // convert into absolute values
    partial_sum (coll.cbegin(), coll.cend(),           // source
                 coll.begin());                        // destination
    PRINT_ELEMENTS(coll,"absolute: ");
}
```

The program has the following output:

```
coll:     17 -3 22 13 13 -9
relative: 17 -20 25 -9 0 -22
absolute: 17 -3 22 13 13 -9
```

Chapter 12

Special Containers

The C++ standard library provides not only the containers for the STL framework but also some containers that fit some special needs and provide simple, almost self-explanatory, interfaces. You can group these containers into either the so-called *container adapters*, which adapt standard STL containers to fit special needs, or a bitset, which is a containers for bits or Boolean values.

There are three standard container adapters: stacks, queues, and priority queues. In priority queues, the elements are sorted automatically according to a sorting criterion. Thus, the "next" element of a priority queue is the element with the "highest" value.

A bitset is a bitfield with an arbitrary but fixed number of bits. Note that the C++ standard library also provides a special container with a variable size for Boolean values: `vector<bool>`. It is described in Section 7.3.6, page 281.

Recent Changes with C++11

C++98 specified almost all features of the container adapters. Here is a list of the most important features added with C++11:

- Container adapters now provide type definitions for `reference` and `const_reference` (see Section 12.4.1, page 645).
- Container adapters now support move semantics and rvalue references:
  - `push()` provides move semantics now (see Section 12.1.2, page 634, and Section 12.4.4, page 647).
  - Initial containers can be moved now (see Section 12.4.2, page 646).
- Container adapters provide the `emplace()` feature, which internally creates a new element initialized by the passed arguments (see Section 12.1.2, page 634, and Section 12.4.4, page 647).
- Container adapters now provide `swap()` (see Section 12.4.4, page 649).
- Constructor adapters now allow you to pass a specific allocator to their constructors (see Section 12.4.2, page 646).

12.1   Stacks

The class `stack<>` implements a stack (also known as LIFO). With `push()`, you can insert any number of elements into the stack (Figure 12.1). With `pop()`, you can remove the elements in the opposite order in which they were inserted ("last in, first out").

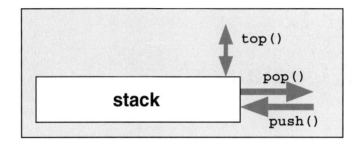

Figure 12.1. Interface of a Stack

To use a stack, you have to include the header file `<stack>`:

```
#include <stack>
```

In `<stack>`, the class stack is defined as follows:

```
namespace std {
    template <typename T,
              typename Container = deque<T>>
        class stack;
}
```

The first template parameter is the type of the elements. The optional second template parameter defines the container that the stack uses internally for its elements. The default container is a deque. It was chosen because, unlike vectors, deques free their memory when elements are removed and don't have to copy all elements on reallocation (see Section 7.12, page 392, for a discussion of when to use which container).

For example, the following declaration defines a stack of integers:

```
std::stack<int> st;        // integer stack
```

The stack implementation simply maps the operations into appropriate calls of the container that is used internally (Figure 12.2). You can use any sequence container class that provides the member functions `back()`, `push_back()`, and `pop_back()`. For example, you could also use a vector or a list as the container for the elements:

```
std::stack<int,std::vector<int>> st;        // integer stack that uses a vector
```

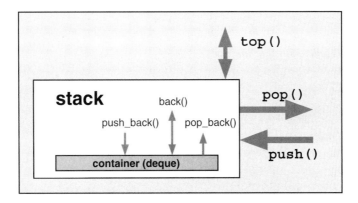

Figure 12.2. Internal Interface of a Stack

12.1.1   The Core Interface

The core interface of stacks is provided by the member functions push(), top(), and pop():

- **push()** inserts an element into the stack.
- **top()** returns the next element in the stack.
- **pop()** removes an element from the stack.

Note that pop() removes the next element but does not return it, whereas top() returns the next element without removing it. Thus, you must always call both functions to process and remove the next element from the stack. This interface is somewhat inconvenient, but it performs better if you want only to remove the next element without processing it. Note that the behavior of top() and pop() is undefined if the stack contains no elements. The member functions size() and empty() are provided to check whether the stack contains elements.

If you don't like the standard interface of stack<>, you can easily write a more convenient interface. See Section 12.1.3, page 635, for an example.

12.1.2   Example of Using Stacks

The following program demonstrates the use of class stack<>:

```
// contadapt/stack1.cpp

#include <iostream>
#include <stack>
using namespace std;

int main()
{
```

```
stack<int> st;

// push three elements into the stack
st.push(1);
st.push(2);
st.push(3);

// pop and print two elements from the stack
cout << st.top() << ' ';
st.pop();
cout << st.top() << ' ';
st.pop();

// modify top element
st.top() = 77;

// push two new elements
st.push(4);
st.push(5);

// pop one element without processing it
st.pop();

// pop and print remaining elements
while (!st.empty()) {
    cout << st.top() << ' ';
    st.pop();
}
cout << endl;
}
```

The output of the program is as follows:

```
3 2 4 77
```

Note that when using nontrivial element types, you might consider using `std::move()` to insert elements that are no longer used or `emplace()` to let the stack internally create the element (both available since C++11):

```
stack<pair<string,string>> st;

auto p = make_pair("hello","world");
st.push(move(p));    // OK, if p is not used any more

st.emplace("nico","josuttis");
```

12.1.3   A User-Defined Stack Class

The standard class `stack<>` prefers speed over convenience and safety. This is not what I usually prefer, so I have written my own stack class, which has the following two advantages:

1. `pop()` returns the next element.

2. `pop()` and `top()` throw exceptions when the stack is empty.

In addition, I have skipped the members that are not necessary for the ordinary stack user, such as the comparison operations. My stack class is defined as follows:

```
// contadapt/Stack.hpp

/* **************************************************************
 *  Stack.hpp
 *   - safer and more convenient stack class
 * *************************************************************/
#ifndef STACK_HPP
#define STACK_HPP

#include <deque>
#include <exception>

template <typename T>
class Stack {
  protected:
    std::deque<T> c;            // container for the elements

  public:
    // exception class for pop() and top() with empty stack
    class ReadEmptyStack : public std::exception {
      public:
        virtual const char* what() const throw() {
            return "read empty stack";
        }
    };

    // number of elements
    typename std::deque<T>::size_type size() const {
        return c.size();
    }

    // is stack empty?
    bool empty() const {
        return c.empty();
    }
```

```cpp
    // push element into the stack
    void push (const T& elem) {
        c.push_back(elem);
    }

    // pop element out of the stack and return its value
    T pop () {
        if (c.empty()) {
            throw ReadEmptyStack();
        }
        T elem(c.back());
        c.pop_back();
        return elem;
    }

    // return value of next element
    T& top () {
        if (c.empty()) {
            throw ReadEmptyStack();
        }
        return c.back();
    }
};

#endif /* STACK_HPP */
```

With this stack class, the previous stack example could be written as follows:

```cpp
// contadapt/stack2.cpp

#include <iostream>
#include <exception>
#include "Stack.hpp"         // use special stack class
using namespace std;

int main()
{
    try {
        Stack<int> st;

        // push three elements into the stack
        st.push(1);
        st.push(2);
        st.push(3);
```

```
        // pop and print two elements from the stack
        cout << st.pop() << ' ';
        cout << st.pop() << ' ';

        // modify top element
        st.top() = 77;

        // push two new elements
        st.push(4);
        st.push(5);

        // pop one element without processing it
        st.pop();

        // pop and print three elements
        // - ERROR: one element too many
        cout << st.pop() << ' ';
        cout << st.pop() << endl;
        cout << st.pop() << endl;
    }
    catch (const exception& e) {
        cerr << "EXCEPTION: " << e.what() << endl;
    }
}
```

The additional final call of pop() forces an error. Unlike the standard stack class, this one throws an exception rather than resulting in undefined behavior. The output of the program is as follows:

```
3 2 4 77
EXCEPTION: read empty stack
```

12.1.4 Class `stack<>` in Detail

The stack<> interface maps more or less directly to corresponding members of the container internally used. For example:

```
namespace std {
    template <typename T, typename Container = deque<T>>
    class stack {
      public:
        typedef typename Container::value_type      value_type;
        typedef typename Container::reference        reference;
        typedef typename Container::const_reference const_reference;
        typedef typename Container::size_type        size_type;
        typedef              Container                container_type;
```

```
    protected:
      Container c;         // container
    public:
      bool          empty() const              { return c.empty(); }
      size_type     size()  const              { return c.size(); }
      void          push(const value_type& x)  { c.push_back(x); }
      void          push(value_type&& x)       { c.push_back(move(x)); }
      void          pop()                      { c.pop_back(); }
      value_type& top()                        { return c.back(); }
      const value_type& top() const            { return c.back(); }
      template <typename... Args>
      void emplace(Args&&... args) {
            c.emplace_back(std::forward<Args>(args)...); }
      void swap (stack& s) ... { swap(c,s.c); }
      ...
  };
}
```

See Section 12.4, page 645, for details of the provided members and operations.

12.2 Queues

The class queue<> implements a queue (also known as FIFO). With push(), you can insert any number of elements (Figure 12.3). With pop(), you can remove the elements in the same order in which they were inserted ("first in, first out"). Thus, a queue serves as a classic data buffer.

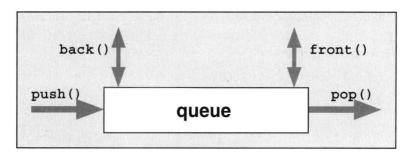

Figure 12.3. Interface of a Queue

To use a queue, you must include the header file <queue>:

```
    #include <queue>
```

In <queue>, the class queue is defined as follows:

```
namespace std {
    template <typename T,
              typename Container = deque<T>>
        class queue;
}
```

The first template parameter is the type of the elements. The optional second template parameter defines the container that the queue uses internally for its elements. The default container is a deque. For example, the following declaration defines a queue of strings:

```
std::queue<std::string> buffer;        // string queue
```

The queue implementation simply maps the operations into appropriate calls of the container that is used internally (Figure 12.4). You can use any sequence container class that provides the member functions front(), back(), push_back(), and pop_front(). For example, you could also use a list as the container for the elements:

```
std::queue<std::string,std::list<std::string>> buffer;
```

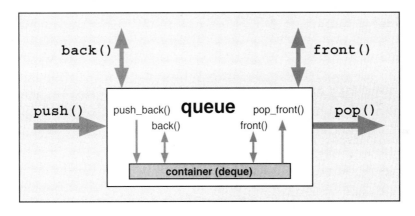

Figure 12.4. Internal Interface of a Queue

12.2.1 The Core Interface

The core interface of queues is provided by the member functions push(), front(), back() and pop():

- **push()** inserts an element into the queue.
- **front()** returns the next element in the queue (the element that was inserted first).
- **back()** returns the last element in the queue (the element that was inserted last).
- **pop()** removes an element from the queue.

Note that pop() removes the next element but does not return it, whereas front() and back() return the element without removing it. Thus, you must always call front() and pop() to process and remove the next element from the queue. This interface is somewhat inconvenient, but it performs better if you want to only remove the next element without processing it. Note that the behavior of front(), back(), and pop() is undefined if the queue contains no elements. The member functions size() and empty() are provided to check whether the queue contains elements.

If you don't like the standard interface of queue<>, you can easily write a more convenient interface. See Section 12.2.3, page 641, for an example.

12.2.2   Example of Using Queues

The following program demonstrates the use of class queue<>:

```
// contadapt/queue1.cpp

#include <iostream>
#include <queue>
#include <string>
using namespace std;

int main()
{
    queue<string> q;

    // insert three elements into the queue
    q.push("These ");
    q.push("are ");
    q.push("more than ");

    // read and print two elements from the queue
    cout << q.front();
    q.pop();
    cout << q.front();
    q.pop();

    // insert two new elements
    q.push("four ");
    q.push("words!");

    // skip one element
    q.pop();

    // read and print two elements
    cout << q.front();
```

```
        q.pop();
        cout << q.front() << endl;
        q.pop();

        // print number of elements in the queue
        cout << "number of elements in the queue: " << q.size()
             << endl;
}
```

The output of the program is as follows:

```
These are four words!
number of elements in the queue: 0
```

12.2.3   A User-Defined Queue Class

The standard class queue<> prefers speed over convenience and safety. This is not what programmers always prefer. But you can easily provide your own queue class as explained according to the user-defined stack class (see Section 12.1.3, page 635). An corresponding example is provided on the Web site of this book in files *contadapt/Queue.hpp* and *contadapt/queue2.cpp*.

12.2.4   Class `queue<>` in Detail

The queue<> interface maps more or less directly to corresponding container members (see Section 12.1.4, page 637, for the corresponding mapping of class stack<>). See Section 12.4, page 645, for details of the provided members and operations.

12.3   Priority Queues

The class priority_queue<> implements a queue from which elements are read according to their priority. The interface is similar to queues. That is, push() inserts an element into the queue, whereas top() and pop() access and remove the next element (Figure 12.5). However, the next element is not the first inserted element. Rather, it is the element that has the highest priority. Thus, elements are partially sorted according to their value. As usual, you can provide the sorting criterion as a template parameter. By default, the elements are sorted by using operator < in descending order. Thus, the next element is always the "highest" element. If more than one "highest" element exists, which element comes next is undefined.

Priority queues are defined in the same header file as ordinary queues, <queue>:

```
#include <queue>
```

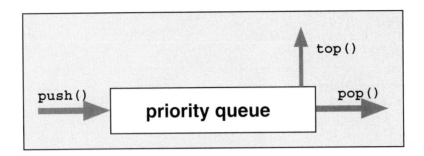

Figure 12.5. Interface of a Priority Queue

In <queue>, the class priority_queue is defined as follows:

```
namespace std {
    template <typename T,
              typename Container = vector<T>,
              typename Compare = less<typename Container::value_type>>
        class priority_queue;
}
```

The first template parameter is the type of the elements. The optional second template parameter defines the container that the priority queue uses internally for its elements. The default container is a vector. The optional third template parameter defines the sorting criterion used to find the next element with the highest priority. By default, this parameter compares the elements by using operator <. For example, the following declaration defines a priority queue of floats:

```
    std::priority_queue<float> pbuffer;        // priority queue for floats
```

The priority queue implementation simply maps the operations into appropriate calls of the container that is used internally. You can use any sequence container class that provides random-access iterators and the member functions front(), push_back(), and pop_back(). Random access is necessary for sorting the elements, which is performed by the heap algorithms of the STL (see Section 11.9.4, page 604). For example, you could also use a deque as the container for the elements:

```
    std::priority_queue<float,std::deque<float>> pbuffer;
```

To define your own sorting criterion, you must pass a function, a function object, or a lambda as a binary predicate that is used by the sorting algorithms to compare two elements (for more about sorting criteria, see Section 7.7.2, page 316, and Section 10.1.1, page 476). For example, the following declaration defines a priority queue with reverse sorting:

```
    std::priority_queue<float,std::vector<float>,
                        std::greater<float>> pbuffer;
```

In this priority queue, the next element is always one of the elements with the lowest value.

12.3.1 The Core Interface

The core interface of priority queues is provided by the member functions push(), top(), and pop():

- **push()** inserts an element into the priority queue.
- **top()** returns the next element in the priority queue.
- **pop()** removes an element from the priority queue.

As for the other container adapters, pop() removes the next element but does not return it, whereas top() returns the next element without removing it. Thus, you must always call both functions to process and remove the next element from the priority queue. And, as usual, the behavior of top() and pop() is undefined if the priority queue contains no elements. If in doubt, you must use the member functions size() and empty().

12.3.2 Example of Using Priority Queues

The following program demonstrates the use of class priority_queue<>:

```
// contadapt/priorityqueue1.cpp

#include <iostream>
#include <queue>
using namespace std;

int main()
{
    priority_queue<float> q;

    // insert three elements into the priority queue
    q.push(66.6);
    q.push(22.2);
    q.push(44.4);

    // read and print two elements
    cout << q.top() << ' ';
    q.pop();
    cout << q.top() << endl;
    q.pop();

    // insert three more elements
    q.push(11.1);
    q.push(55.5);
    q.push(33.3);
```

```
    // skip one element
    q.pop();

    // pop and print remaining elements
    while (!q.empty()) {
        cout << q.top() << ' ';
        q.pop();
    }
    cout << endl;
}
```

The output of the program is as follows:

```
66.6 44.4
33.3 22.2 11.1
```

As you can see, after 66.6, 22.2, and 44.4 are inserted, the program prints 66.6 and 44.4 as the
highest elements. After three other elements are inserted, the priority queue contains the elements
22.2, 11.1, 55.5, and 33.3 (in the order of insertion). The next element is skipped simply via a
call of pop(), so the final loop prints 33.3, 22.2, and 11.1 in that order.

12.3.3 Class `priority_queue<>` in Detail

The priority queue uses the STL's heap algorithms:

```
namespace std {
    template <typename T, typename Container = vector<T>,
              typename Compare = less<typename Container::value_type>>
    class priority_queue {
      protected:
        Compare comp;      // sorting criterion
        Container c;       // container
      public:
        // constructors
        explicit priority_queue(const Compare& cmp = Compare(),
                                const Container& cont = Container())
          : comp(cmp), c(cont) {
            make_heap(c.begin(),c.end(),comp);
        }
        void push(const value_type& x) {
            c.push_back(x);
            push_heap(c.begin(),c.end(),comp);
        }
        void pop() {
            pop_heap(c.begin(),c.end(),comp);
```

```
            c.pop_back();
        }
        bool               empty() const { return c.empty(); }
        size_type          size() const  { return c.size(); }
        const value_type& top() const   { return c.front(); }
        ...
    };
}
```

These algorithms are described in Section 11.9.4, page 604.

Note that, unlike other container adapters, no comparison operators are defined. See Section 12.4, page 645, for details of the provided members and operations.

12.4 Container Adapters in Detail

The following subsections describe the members and operations of the container adapters stack<>, queue<>, and priority_queue<> in detail.

12.4.1 Type Definitions

contadapt::**value_type**
- The type of the elements.
- It is equivalent to *container*::value_type.

contadapt::**reference**
- The type of element references.
- It is equivalent to *container*::reference.
- Available since C++11.

contadapt::**const_reference**
- The type of read-only element references.
- It is equivalent to *container*::const_reference.
- Available since C++11.

contadapt::**size_type**
- The unsigned integral type for size values.
- It is equivalent to *container*::size_type.

contadapt::**container_type**
- The type of the container.

12.4.2   Constructors

contadapt::**contadapt** ()

- The default constructor.
- Creates an empty stack or (priority) queue.

explicit *contadapt*::**contadapt** (const `Container&` *cont*)
explicit *contadapt*::**contadapt** (`Container&&` *cont*)

- Creates a stack or queue that is initialized by the elements of *cont*, which has to be an object of the container type of the container adapter.
- With the first form, all elements of *cont* are copied.
- With the second form, all elements of *cont* are moved if the passed container provides move semantics; otherwise, they are copied (available since C++11).
- Both forms are not provided for `priority_queue<>`.

Since C++11, all constructors allow you to pass an allocator as additional argument, which is used to initialize the allocator of the internal container.

12.4.3   Supplementary Constructors for Priority Queues

explicit *priority_queue*::**priority_queue** (const `CompFunc&` *op*)

- Creates an empty priority queue with *op* used as the sorting criterion.
- See Section 7.7.5, page 328, and Section 7.8.6, page 351, for examples that demonstrate how to pass a sorting criterion as a constructor argument.

priority_queue::**priority_queue** (const `CompFunc&` *op* const `Container&` *cont*)

- Creates a priority queue that is initialized by the elements of *cont* and that uses *op* as the sorting criterion.
- All elements of *cont* are copied.

priority_queue::**priority_queue** (`InputIterator` *beg*, `InputIterator` *end*)

- Creates a priority queue that is initialized by all elements of the range [*beg,end*).
- This function is a member template (see Section 3.2, page 34), so the elements of the source range might have any type that is convertible into the element type of the container.

priority_queue::**priority_queue** (InputIterator *beg*, InputIterator *end*,
                                 const CompFunc& *op*)

- Creates a priority queue that is initialized by all elements of the range [*beg*,*end*) and that uses *op* as the sorting criterion.
- This function is a member template (see Section 3.2, page 34), so the elements of the source range might have any type that is convertible into the element type of the container.
- See Section 7.7.5, page 328, and Section 7.8.6, page 351, for examples that demonstrate how to pass a sorting criterion as a constructor argument.

priority_queue::**priority_queue** (InputIterator *beg*, InputIterator *end*,
                                 const CompFunc& *op*, const Container& *cont*)

- Creates a priority queue that is initialized by all elements of the container *cont* plus all elements of the range [*beg*,*end*) and that uses *op* as the sorting criterion.
- This function is a member template (see Section 3.2, page 34), so the elements of the source range might have any type that is convertible into the element type of the container.

Since C++11, all constructors allow you to pass an allocator as additional argument, which is used to initialize the allocator of the internal container.

12.4.4 Operations

bool *contadapt*::**empty** () const

- Returns whether the container adapter is empty (contains no elements).
- It is equivalent to *contadapt*::size()==0 but might be faster.

size_type *contadapt*::**size** () const

- Returns the current number of elements.
- To check whether the container adapter is empty (contains no elements), use empty() because it might be faster.

void *contadapt*::**push** (const *value_type*& *elem*)
void *contadapt*::**push** (*value_type*&& *elem*)

- The first form inserts a copy of *elem*.
- The first form moves *elem* if move semantics are provided; otherwise, it copies *elem* (available since C++11).

void *contadapt*::**emplace** (*args*)

- Inserts a new element, which is initialized by the argument list *args*.
- Available since C++11.

reference contadapt::**top** ()

const_reference contadapt::**top** () const

reference contadapt::**front** ()

const_reference contadapt::**front** () const

- All forms, if provided, return the next element.
  - For a stack, both forms of top() are provided, which return the element that was inserted last.
  - For a queue, both forms of front() are provided, which return the element that was inserted first.
  - For a priority queue, only the second form of top() is provided, which yields the element with the maximum value. If more than one element has the maximum value, it is undefined which element it returns.
- The caller has to ensure that the container adapter contains an element (size()>0); otherwise, the behavior is undefined.
- The forms that return a nonconstant reference allow you to modify the next element while it is in the stack/queue. It is up to you to decide whether this is good style.
- Before C++11, the return type was (const) value_type&, which usually should be the same.

void contadapt::**pop** ()

- Removes the next element from the container adapter.
  - For a stack, the next element is the one that was inserted last.
  - For a queue, the next element is the one that was inserted first.
  - For a priority queue, the next element is the one with the maximum value. If more than one element has the maximum value, it is undefined which element it removes.
- This function has no return value. To process this next element, you must call top() or front() first.
- The caller must ensure that the container adapter contains an element (size()>0); otherwise, the behavior is undefined.

reference queue::**back** ()

const_reference queue::**back** () const

- Both forms return the last element of a queue. The last element is the one that was inserted after all other elements in the queue.
- The caller must ensure that the queue contains an element (size()>0); otherwise, the behavior is undefined.
- The first form for nonconstant queues returns a reference. Thus, you could modify the last element while it is in the queue. It is up to you to decide whether this is good style.
- Before C++11, the return type was (const) value_type&, which usually should be the same.
- Provided for queue<> only.

`bool` ***comparison*** (`const` *contadapt&* *stack1*, `const` *contadapt&* *stack2*)

- Returns the result of the comparison of two stacks or queues of the same type.
- ***comparison*** might be any of the following operators:
  operators `==` and `!=`
  operators `<`, `>`, `<=`, and `>=`
- Two stacks or queues are equal if they have the same number of elements and contain the same elements in the same order (all comparisons of two corresponding elements must yield `true`).
- To check whether a stack or queue is less than another, the container adapters are compared lexicographically (see Section 11.5.4, page 548).
- Not provided for `priority_queue<>`.

`void` *contadapt*::**swap** (*contadapt&* *c*)

`void` **swap** (*contadapt&* *c1*, *contadapt&* *c2*)

- Swaps the contents of `*this` with *c* or *c1* with *c2*, respectively. For priority queues, it also swaps the sorting criterion.
- Calls `swap()` for the corresponding container (see Section 8.4, page 407).
- Available since C++11.

12.5   Bitsets

Bitsets model fixed-sized arrays of bits or Boolean values. They are useful to manage sets of flags, where variables may represent any combination of flags. C and old C++ programs usually use type long for arrays of bits and manipulate them with the bit operators, such as &, |, and ~. The class bitset has the advantage that bitsets may contain any number of bits, and additional operations are provided. For example, you can assign single bits and can read and write bitsets as a sequence of 0s and 1s.

Note that you can't change the number of bits in a bitset. The number of bits is the template parameter. If you need a container for a variable number of bits or Boolean values, you can use the class vector<bool> (described in Section 7.3.6, page 281).

The class bitset is defined in the header file <bitset>:

```
#include <bitset>
```

In <bitset>, the class bitset is defined as a class template, with the number of bits as the template parameter:

```
namespace std {
    template <size_t Bits>
    class bitset;
}
```

In this case, the template parameter is not a type but an unsigned integral value (see Section 3.2, page 33, for details about this language feature).

Templates with different template arguments are different types. You can compare and combine bitsets only with the same number of bits.

Recent Changes with C++11

C++98 specified almost all features of bitsets. Here is a list of the most important features added with C++11:

- Bitsets now can be initialized by string literals (see Section 12.5.1, page 653).
- Conversions to and from numeric values now support type unsigned long long. For this, to_ullong() was introduced (see Section 12.5.1, page 653).
- Conversions to and from strings now allow you to specify the character interpreted as set and unset bit.
- Member all() is now provided to check whether all bits are set.
- To use bitsets in unordered containers, a default hash function is provided (see Section 7.9.2, page 363).

12.5.1 Examples of Using Bitsets

Using Bitsets as Sets of Flags

The first example demonstrates how to use bitsets to manage a set of flags. Each flag has a value that is defined by an enumeration type. The value of the enumeration type is used as the position of the bit in the bitset. In particular, the bits represent colors. Thus, each enumeration value defines one color. By using a bitset, you can manage variables that might contain any combination of colors:

```cpp
// contadapt/bitset1.cpp

#include <bitset>
#include <iostream>
using namespace std;

int main()
{
    // enumeration type for the bits
    // - each bit represents a color
    enum Color { red, yellow, green, blue, white, black, ...,
                 numColors };

    // create bitset for all bits/colors
    bitset<numColors> usedColors;

    // set bits for two colors
    usedColors.set(red);
    usedColors.set(blue);

    // print some bitset data
    cout << "bitfield of used colors:   " << usedColors << endl;
    cout << "number   of used colors:   " << usedColors.count() << endl;
    cout << "bitfield of unused colors: " << ~usedColors << endl;

    // if any color is used
    if (usedColors.any()) {
        // loop over all colors
        for (int c = 0; c < numColors; ++c) {
            // if the actual color is used
            if (usedColors[(Color)c]) {
                ...
            }
        }
    }
}
```

Using Bitsets for I/O with Binary Representation

A useful feature of bitsets is the ability to convert integral values into a sequence of bits, and vice versa. This is done simply by creating a temporary bitset:

```
// contadapt/bitset2.cpp

#include <bitset>
#include <iostream>
#include <string>
#include <limits>
using namespace std;

int main()
{
    // print some numbers in binary representation
    cout << "267 as binary short:    "
         << bitset<numeric_limits<unsigned short>::digits>(267)
         << endl;

    cout << "267 as binary long:     "
         << bitset<numeric_limits<unsigned long>::digits>(267)
         << endl;

    cout << "10,000,000 with 24 bits: "
         << bitset<24>(1e7) << endl;

    // write binary representation into string
    string s = bitset<42>(12345678).to_string();
    cout << "12,345,678 with 42 bits: " << s << endl;

    // transform binary representation into integral number
    cout << "\"1000101011\" as number:   "
         << bitset<100>("1000101011").to_ullong() << endl;
}
```

Depending on the number of bits for `short` and `long long`, the program might produce the following output:

```
267 as binary short:     0000000100001011
267 as binary long:      00000000000000000000000100001011
10,000,000 with 24 bits: 100110001001011010000000
12,345,678 with 42 bits: 000000000000000000010111100011000010101110
"1000101011" as number:  555
```

In this example, the following expression converts 267 into a bitset with the number of bits of type `unsigned short` (see Section 5.3, page 116, for a discussion of numeric limits):

```
bitset<numeric_limits<unsigned short>::digits>(267)
```

The output operator for `bitset` prints the bits as a sequence of characters 0 and 1.

You can output bitsets directly or use their value as a string:

```
string s = bitset<42>(12345678).to_string();
```

Note that before C++11, you had to write

```
string s = bitset<42>(12345678).to_string<char,char_traits<char>,
                                    allocator<char> >();
```

here because `to_string()` is a member template, and there were no default values for the template arguments defined.

Similarly, the following expression converts a sequence of binary characters into a bitset, for which `to_ullong()` yields the integral value:

```
bitset<100>("1000101011")
```

Note that the number of bits in the bitset should be smaller than `sizeof(unsigned long long)`. The reason is that you get an exception when the value of the bitset can't be represented as `unsigned long long`.[1]

Note also that before C++11, you had to convert the initial value to type `string` explicitly:

```
bitset<100>(string("1000101011"))
```

12.5.2 Class `bitset` in Detail

Due to the thickness of this book, the subsection that presents the members of class `bitset<>` in detail is provided as a supplementary chapter on the Web site of this book at http://www.cppstdlib.com.

---

[1] Before C++11, type `unsigned long` was not provided, so you could call only `to_ulong()` here. `to_ulong()` is still callable if the number of bits is smaller than `sizeof(unsigned long)`.

Chapter 13

Strings

This chapter presents the string types of the C++ standard library. It describes the basic class template `basic_string<>` and its standard specializations `string`, `wstring`, `u16string`, and `u32string`.

Strings can be a source of confusion because it is not clear what the term *string* means. Does it mean an ordinary character array of type `char*` (with or without the `const` qualifier)? Is it an instance of class `string<>`? Or is it a general name for objects that are kinds of strings? In this chapter, I use the term *string* for objects of one of the string types in the C++ standard library: `string`, `wstring`, `u16string`, or `u32string`. For "ordinary strings" of type `char*` or `const char*`, I use the term *C-string*.

Note that with C++98 the type of string literals (such as `"hello"`) was changed into `const char*`. However, to provide backward compatibility, there is an implicit but deprecated conversion to `char*` for them. Strictly speaking, the original type of a literal such as `"hello"` is `const char[6]`. But this type automatically converts (*decays*) to `const char*`, so you can almost always use (and see) `const char*` in declarations. Nevertheless, when working with templates, the difference might matter because for reference template parameters, decay doesn't occur unless type trait `std::decay()` is used (see Section 5.4.2, page 132).

Recent Changes with C++11

C++98 specified almost all features of the string classes. Here is a list of the most important features added with C++11:

- Strings now provide `front()` and `back()` to access the first or last element (see Section 13.2.6, page 671) and `shrink_to_fit()` to shrink capacity (see Section 13.2.5, page 670).
- Strings now provide convenience functions to convert strings to numeric values and vice versa (see Section 13.2.13, page 681).
- `data()` and `c_str()` no longer invalidate references, iterators, and pointers to strings (see Section 13.2.6, page 672).
- Strings now support move semantics (see Section 13.2.9, page 676) and initializer lists (see Section 13.2.8, page 675).

- Besides `string` and `wstring`, the `basic_string<>` specializations `u16string` and `u32string` are predefined now (see Section 13.2.1, page 664).
- Strings are now indirectly required to provide an *end-of-string* character (`'\0'` for `string`) because for a string s, `s[s.length()]` is always valid and `s.data()` returns the characters including a trailing *end-of-string* character (see Section 13.1.2, page 662).
- Reference-counted implementations of string classes are no longer supported (see Section 13.2.16, page 692).

13.1   Purpose of the String Classes

The string classes of the C++ standard library enable you to use strings as normal types that cause no problems for the user. Thus, you can copy, assign, and compare strings as fundamental types without worrying about whether there is enough memory or how long the internal memory is valid. You simply use operators, such as assignment by using =, comparison by using ==, and concatenation by using +. In short, the string types of the C++ standard library are designed to behave as if they were a kind of fundamental data type that does not cause any trouble (at least in principle). Modern data processing is mostly string processing, so this is an important step for programmers coming from C, Fortran, or similar languages in which strings are a source of trouble.

The following sections offer two examples that demonstrate the abilities and uses of the string classes.

13.1.1   A First Example: Extracting a Temporary Filename

The first example program uses command-line arguments to generate temporary filenames. For example, if you start the program as

```
string1 prog.dat mydir hello. oops.tmp end.dat
```

the output is

```
prog.dat => prog.tmp
mydir => mydir.tmp
hello. => hello.tmp
oops.tmp => oops.xxx
end.dat => end.tmp
```

Usually, the generated filename has the extension .tmp, whereas the temporary filename for a name with the extension .tmp is .xxx.

The program is written in the following way:

```
// string/string1.cpp

#include <iostream>
#include <string>
using namespace std;
```

```cpp
int main (int argc, char* argv[])
{
    string filename, basename, extname, tmpname;
    const string suffix("tmp");

    // for each command-line argument (which is an ordinary C-string)
    for (int i=1; i<argc; ++i) {
        // process argument as filename
        filename = argv[i];

        // search period in filename
        string::size_type idx = filename.find('.');
        if (idx == string::npos) {
            // filename does not contain any period
            tmpname = filename + '.' + suffix;
        }
        else {
            // split filename into base name and extension
            // - base name contains all characters before the period
            // - extension contains all characters after the period
            basename = filename.substr(0, idx);
            extname = filename.substr(idx+1);
            if (extname.empty()) {
                // contains period but no extension: append tmp
                tmpname = filename;
                tmpname += suffix;
            }
            else if (extname == suffix) {
                // replace extension tmp with xxx
                tmpname = filename;
                tmpname.replace (idx+1, extname.size(), "xxx");
            }
            else {
                // replace any extension with tmp
                tmpname = filename;
                tmpname.replace (idx+1, string::npos, suffix);
            }
        }

        // print filename and temporary name
        cout << filename << " => " << tmpname << endl;
    }
}
```

At first, the header file for the C++ standard string classes is included:

```
#include <string>
```

As usual, these classes are declared in namespace `std`.

The following declaration creates four string variables:

```
string filename, basename, extname, tmpname;
```

No argument is passed, so the default constructor for `string` is called for their initialization. The default constructor initializes them as empty strings.

The following declaration creates a constant string `suffix` that is used in the program as the normal suffix for temporary filenames:

```
const string suffix("tmp");
```

The string is initialized by an ordinary C-string, so it has the value `tmp`. Note that C-strings can be combined with objects of class `string` in almost any situation in which two `strings` can be combined. In particular, in the entire program, every occurrence of `suffix` could be replaced with `"tmp"` so that a C-string is used directly.

In each iteration of the `for` loop, the following statement assigns a new value to the string variable `filename`:

```
filename = argv[i];
```

In this case, the new value is an ordinary C-string. However, it could also be another object of class `string` or a single character that has type `char`.

The following statement searches for the first occurrence of a period inside the string `filename`:

```
string::size_type idx = filename.find('.');
```

The `find()` function is one of several functions that search for something inside strings. You could also search backward, for substrings, only in a part of a string, or for more than one character simultaneously. All these find functions return an index of the first matching position. Yes, the return value is an integer and not an iterator. The usual interface for strings is not based on the concept of the STL. However, some iterator support for strings is provided (see Section 13.2.14, page 684). The return type of all find functions is `string::size_type`, an unsigned integral type that is defined inside the string class.[1] As usual, the index of the first character is the value 0. The index of the last character is the value "*numberOfCharacters*-1."

If the search fails, a special value is needed to return the failure. That value is `npos`, which is also defined by the string class. Thus, the following line checks whether the search for the period failed:

```
if (idx == string::npos)
```

The type and value of `npos` are a big pitfall for the use of strings. Be very careful that you always use `string::size_type`, *not* int or unsigned, for the return type when you want to check the return value of a find function. Otherwise, the comparison with `string::npos` might not work. See Section 13.2.12, page 680, for details.

---

[1] In particular, the `size_type` of a string depends on the memory model of the string class. See Section 13.3.13, page 715, for details.

If the search for the period fails in this example, the filename has no extension. In this case, the temporary filename is the concatenation of the original filename, the period character, and the previously defined extension for temporary files:

```
tmpname = filename + '.' + suffix;
```

Thus, you can simply use operator + to concatenate two strings. It is also possible to concatenate strings with ordinary C-strings and single characters.

If the period is found, the `else` part is used. Here, the index of the period is used to split the filename into a base part and the extension. This is done by the `substr()` member function:

```
basename = filename.substr(0, idx);
extname = filename.substr(idx+1);
```

The first parameter of the `substr()` function is the starting index. The optional second argument is the number of characters, not the end index. If the second argument is not used, all remaining characters of the string are returned as a substring.

At all places where an index and a length are used as arguments, strings behave according to the following two rules:

1. An argument specifying the **index** must have a valid value. That value must be less than the number of characters of the string (as usual, the index of the first character is 0). In addition, the index of the position after the last character could be used to specify the end.

   In most cases, a use of an index greater than the number of characters throws `out_of_range`. However, all functions that search for a character or a position allow any index. If the index exceeds the number of characters, these functions simply return `string::npos` ("not found").

2. An argument specifying the **number of characters** could have any value. If the size is greater than the remaining number of characters, all remaining characters are used. In particular, `string::npos` always works as a synonym for "all remaining characters."

Thus, the following expression throws an exception if the period is not found:

```
filename.substr(filename.find('.'))
```

But the following expression does not throw an exception:

```
filename.substr(0, filename.find('.'))
```

If the period is not found, it results in the whole filename.

Even if the period is found, the extension that is returned by `substr()` might be empty because there are no more characters after the period. This is checked by

```
if (extname.empty())
```

If this condition yields `true`, the generated temporary filename becomes the ordinary filename that has the normal extension appended:

```
tmpname = filename;
tmpname += suffix;
```

Here, operator `+=` is used to append the extension.

The filename might already have the extension for temporary files. To check this, operator `==` is used to compare two strings:

```
if (extname == suffix)
```

If this comparison yields `true`, the normal extension for temporary files is replaced by the extension xxx:

```
tmpname = filename;
tmpname.replace (idx+1, extname.size(), "xxx");
```

Here, the number of characters of the string `extname` is returned by

```
extname.size()
```

Instead of `size()`, you could use `length()`, which does exactly the same thing. So, both `size()` and `length()` return the number of characters. In particular, `size()` has nothing to do with the memory that the string uses.[2]

Next, after all special conditions are considered, normal processing takes place. The program replaces the whole extension by the ordinary extension for temporary filenames:

```
tmpname = filename;
tmpname.replace (idx+1, string::npos, suffix);
```

Here, `string::npos` is used as a synonym for "all remaining characters." Thus, all remaining characters after the period are replaced with `suffix`. This replacement would also work if the filename contained a period but no extension. It would simply replace "nothing" with `suffix`.

The statement that writes the original filename and the generated temporary filename shows that you can print the strings by using the usual output operators of streams (surprise, surprise):

```
cout << filename << " => " << tmpname << endl;
```

13.1.2   A Second Example: Extracting Words and Printing Them Backward

The second example extracts single words from standard input and prints the characters of each word in reverse order. The words are separated by the usual whitespaces (newline, space, and tab) and by commas, periods, or semicolons:

```
// string/string2.cpp

#include <iostream>
#include <string>
using namespace std;

int main (int argc, char** argv)
{
    const string delims(" \t,.;");
    string line;
```

---

[2] In this case, two member functions do the same with respect to the two different design approaches that are merged here: `length()` returns the length of the string, just as `strlen()` does for ordinary C-strings, whereas `size()` is the common member function for the number of elements according to the concept of the STL.

```
        // for every line read successfully
        while (getline(cin,line)) {
            string::size_type begIdx, endIdx;

            // search beginning of the first word
            begIdx = line.find_first_not_of(delims);

            // while beginning of a word found
            while (begIdx != string::npos) {
                // search end of the actual word
                endIdx = line.find_first_of (delims, begIdx);
                if (endIdx == string::npos) {
                    // end of word is end of line
                    endIdx = line.length();
                }

                // print characters in reverse order
                for (int i=endIdx-1; i>=static_cast<int>(begIdx); --i) {
                    cout << line[i];
                }
                cout << ' ';

                // search beginning of the next word
                begIdx = line.find_first_not_of (delims, endIdx);
            }
            cout << endl;
        }
    }
```

In this program, all characters used as word separators are defined in a special string constant:

```
const string delims(" \t,.;");
```

The newline character is also used as a delimiter. However, no special processing is necessary for it because the program reads line by line.

The outer loop runs as far as a line can be read into the string `line`:

```
string line;
while (getline(cin,line)) {
    ...
}
```

The function `getline()` is a special function to read input from streams into a string. It reads every character up to the next end-of-line, which by default is the newline character. The line delimiter itself is extracted but not appended. By passing your special line delimiter as an optional third character argument, you can use `getline()` to read token by token, where the tokens are separated by that special delimiter.

Inside the outer loop, the individual words are searched and printed. The first statement searches for the beginning of the first word:

```
begIdx = line.find_first_not_of(delims);
```

The `find_first_not_of()` function returns the first index of a character that is not part of the passed string argument. Thus, this function returns the position of the first character that is not one of the separators in `delims`. As usual for find functions, if no matching index is found, `string::npos` is returned.

The inner loop iterates as long as the beginning of a word can be found:

```
while (begIdx != string::npos) {
    ...
}
```

The first statement of the inner loop searches for the end of the current word:

```
endIdx = line.find_first_of (delims, begIdx);
```

The `find_first_of()` function searches for the first occurrence of one of the characters passed as the first argument. In this case, an optional second argument is used that specifies where to start the search in the string. Thus, the first delimiter after the beginning of the word is searched. If no such character is found, the end-of-line is used:

```
if (endIdx == string::npos) {
    endIdx = line.length();
}
```

Here, `length()` is used, which does the same thing as `size()`: It returns the number of characters.

In the next statement, all characters of the word are printed in reverse order:

```
for (int i=endIdx-1; i>=static_cast<int>(begIdx); --i) {
    cout << line[i];
}
```

Accessing a single character of the string is done with operator `[]`. Note that this operator does *not* check whether the index of the string is valid. Thus, the programmer has to ensure that the index is valid, as was done here. A safer way to access a character is to use the `at()` member function. However, such a check costs runtime, so the check is not provided for the usual accessing of characters of a string.

Note that for operator `[]`, the number of characters is a valid index, returning a character representing the end of the string. This *end-of-string* character is initialized by the default constructor of the character type (`'\0'` for class `string`):[3]

```
string s;
s[s.length()]      // yields '\0'
```

---

[3] Before C++11, for the nonconstant version of operator `[]`, the current number of characters was an invalid index. Using it did result in undefined behavior.

Another nasty problem results from using the index of the string. That is, if you omit the cast of begIdx to int, this program might run in an endless loop or might crash. Similar to the first example program, the problem is that string::size_type is an unsigned integral type. Without the cast, the signed value i is converted automatically into an unsigned value because it is compared with a unsigned type. In this case, the following expression always yields true if the current word starts at the beginning of the line:

```
i>=begIdx
```

The reason is that begIdx is then 0, and any unsigned value is greater than or equal to 0. So, an endless loop results that might get stopped by a crash due to an illegal memory access. For this reason, I don't like the concept of string::size_type and string::npos. See Section 13.2.12, page 681, for a workaround that is safer, but not perfect.

The last statement of the inner loop reinitializes begIdx to the beginning of the next word, if any:

```
begIdx = line.find_first_not_of (delims, endIdx);
```

Here, unlike with the first call of find_first_not_of() in the example, the end of the previous word is passed as the starting index for the search. If the previous word was the rest of the line, endIdx is the index of the end of the line. This simply means that the search starts from the end of the string, which returns string::npos.

Let's try this "useful and important" program. Here is some possible input:[4]

```
pots & pans
I saw a reed
deliver no pets
nametag on diaper
```

The output for this input is as follows:

```
stop & snap
I was a deer
reviled on step
gateman no repaid
```

13.2 Description of the String Classes

13.2.1 String Types

Header File

All types and functions for strings are defined in the header file <string>:

```
#include <string>
```

As usual, it defines all identifiers in namespace std.

---

[4] Thanks to Sean Okeefe for providing the last two lines.

Class Template `basic_string<>`

Inside `<string>`, class `basic_string<>` is defined as a basic type for all string types:

```
namespace std {
    template <typename charT,
              typename traits = char_traits<charT>,
              typename Allocator = allocator<charT> >
        class basic_string;
}
```

This class is parametrized by the character type, the traits of the character type, and the memory model:

- The first parameter is the data type of a single character.
- The optional second parameter is a traits class, which provides all core operations for the characters of the string class. Such a traits class specifies how to copy or to compare characters (see Section 16.1.4, page 853, for details). If it is not specified, the default traits class according to the current character type is used. See Section 13.2.15, page 689, for a user-defined traits class that lets strings behave in a case-insensitive manner.
- The third optional argument defines the memory model that is used by the string class. As usual, the default value is the default memory model `allocator` (see Section 4.6, page 57, and Chapter 19 for details).

Concrete String Types

The C++ standard library provides a couple of specializations of class `basic_string<>`:

- Class `string` is the predefined specialization of that template for characters of type `char`:
```
namespace std {
    typedef basic_string<char> string;
}
```
- For strings that use wider character sets, such as Unicode or some Asian character sets, three other types are predefined (`u16string` and `u32string` are provided since C++11):
```
namespace std {
    typedef basic_string<wchar_t>  wstring;
    typedef basic_string<char16_t> u16string;
    typedef basic_string<char32_t> u32string;
}
```
See Chapter 16 for details about internationalization.

In the following sections, no distinction is made between these types of strings. The usage and the problems are the same because all string classes have the same interface. So, "string" means any string type: `string`, `wstring`, `u16string`, and `u32string`. The examples in this book usually use type `string` because the European and Anglo-American environments are the common environments for software development.

Operation	Effect
constructors	Create or copy a string
destructor	Destroys a string
`=`, `assign()`	Assign a new value
`swap()`	Swaps values between two strings
`+=`, `append()`, `push_back()`	Append characters
`insert()`	Inserts characters
`erase()`, `pop_back()`	Deletes characters (`pop_back()` since C++11)
`clear()`	Removes all characters (empties a string)
`resize()`	Changes the number of characters (deletes or appends characters at the end)
`replace()`	Replaces characters
`+`	Concatenates strings
`==`, `!=`, `<`, `<=`, `>`, `>=`, `compare()`	Compare strings
`empty()`	Returns whether the string is empty
`size()`, `length()`	Return the number of characters
`max_size()`	Returns the maximum possible number of characters
`capacity()`	Returns the number of characters that can be held without reallocation
`reserve()`	Reserves memory for a certain number of characters
`shrink_to_fit()`	Shrinks the memory for the current number of characters (since C++11)
`[]`, `at()`	Access a character
`front()`, `back()`	Access the first or last character (since C++11)
`>>`, `getline()`	Read the value from a stream
`<<`	Writes the value to a stream
`stoi()`, `stol()`, `stoll()`	Convert string to signed integral value (since C++11)
`stoul()`, `stoull()`	Convert string to unsigned integral value (since C++11)
`stof()`, `stod()`, `stold()`	Convert string to floating-point value (since C++11)
`to_string()`, `to_wstring()`	Convert integral/floating-point value to string (since C++11)
`copy()`	Copies or writes the contents to a character array
`data()`, `c_str()`	Returns the value as C-string or character array
`substr()`	Returns a certain substring
find functions	Search for a certain substring or character
`begin()`, `end()`	Provide normal iterator support
`cbegin()`, `cend()`	Provide constant iterator support (since C++11)
`rbegin()`, `rend()`	Provide reverse iterator support
`crbegin()`, `crend()`	Provide constant reverse iterator support (since C++11)
`get_allocator()`	Returns the allocator

Table 13.1. String Operations

13.2.2 Operation Overview

Table 13.1 (see previous page) lists all operations that are provided for strings.

String Operation Arguments

Many operations are provided to manipulate strings. In particular, the operations that manipulate the value of a string have several overloaded versions that specify the new value with one, two, or three arguments. All these operations use the argument scheme of Table 13.2.

Arguments	Interpretation
const *string&* *str*	The whole string *str*
const *string&* *str*, size_type *idx*, size_type *num*	At most, the first *num* characters of *str* starting with index *idx*
const *char** *cstr*	The whole C-string *cstr*
const *char** *chars*, size_type *len*	*len* characters of the character array *chars*
char *c*	The character *c*
size_type *num*, *char* *c*	*num* occurrences of character *c*
const_iterator *beg*, const_iterator *end*	All characters in range [*beg*,*end*)
initlist	All characters in *initlist* (since C++11)

Table 13.2. Scheme of String Operation Arguments

Note that only the single-argument version const char* handles the character '\0' as a special character that terminates the string. In all other cases, '\0' is *not* a special character:

```
std::string s1("nico");      // initializes s1 with: 'n' 'i' 'c' 'o'
std::string s2("nico",5);    // initializes s2 with: 'n' 'i' 'c' 'o' '\0'
std::string s3(5,'\0');      // initializes s3 with: '\0' '\0' '\0' '\0' '\0'

s1.length()                  // yields 4
s2.length()                  // yields 5
s3.length()                  // yields 5
```

Thus, in general a string might contain any character. In particular, a string might contain the contents of a binary file.

Passing a null pointer as *cstr* results in undefined behavior.

See Table 13.3 for an overview of which operation uses which kind of arguments. All operators can handle only objects as single values. Therefore, to assign, compare, or append a part of a string or C-string, you must use the function that has the corresponding name.

	Full String	Part of String	C-string (*char*)	*char* Array	Single char	*num* chars	Iterator Range	Init list
constructors	Yes	Yes	Yes	Yes	—	Yes	Yes	Yes
=	Yes	—	Yes	—	Yes	—	—	Yes
`assign()`	Yes	Yes	Yes	Yes	—	Yes	Yes	Yes
+=	Yes	—	Yes	—	Yes	—	—	Yes
`append()`	Yes	Yes	Yes	Yes	—	Yes	Yes	Yes
`push_back()`	—	—	—	—	Yes	—	—	—
`insert()` for idx	Yes	Yes	Yes	Yes	—	Yes	—	—
`insert()` for iter.	—	—	—	—	Yes	Yes	Yes	Yes
`replace()` for idx	Yes	Yes	Yes	Yes	Yes	Yes	—	—
`replace()` for iter.	Yes	—	Yes	Yes	—	Yes	Yes	Yes
find functions	Yes	—	Yes	Yes	Yes	—	—	—
+	Yes	—	Yes	—	Yes	—	—	—
==, !=, <, <=, >, >=	Yes	—	Yes	—	—	—	—	—
`compare()`	Yes	Yes	Yes	Yes	—	—	—	—

Table 13.3. Available Operations Having String Parameters

Operations Not Provided

The string classes of the C++ standard library do not solve every possible string problem. In fact, they do not provide direct solutions for regular expressions and text processing. Regular expressions, however, are covered by a separate library introduced with C++11 (see Chapter 14). For text processing (capitalization, case-insensitive comparisons), see Section 13.2.14, page 684, for some examples.

13.2.3 Constructors and Destructor

Table 13.4 lists all the constructors and the destructor for strings.

You can't initialize a string with a single character. Instead, you must use its address or an additional number of occurrences or the format of an initializer list (since C++11):

```
std::string s('x');      // ERROR
std::string s(1,'x');    // OK, creates a string that has one character 'x'
std::string s({'x'});    // OK, ditto (since C++11)
```

This means that there is an automatic type conversion from type `const char*` but not from type `char` to type `string`.

The initialization by a range that is specified by iterators is described in Section 13.2.14, page 684.

Expression	Effect
`string s`	Creates the empty string s
`string s(str)`	Copy constructor; creates a string as a copy of the existing string str
`string s(rvStr)`	Move constructor; creates a string and moves the contents of $rvStr$ to it ($rvStr$ has a valid state with undefined value afterward)
`string s(str,stridx)`	Creates a string s that is initialized by the characters of string str starting with index $stridx$
`string s(str,stridx,strlen)`	Creates a string s that is initialized by, at most, *strlen* characters of string str starting with index $stridx$
`string s(cstr)`	Creates a string s that is initialized by the C-string $cstr$
`string s(chars,charslen)`	Creates a string s that is initialized by $charslen$ characters of the character array $chars$
`string s(num,c)`	Creates a string that has *num* occurrences of character c
`string s(beg,end)`	Creates a string that is initialized by all characters of the range $[beg,end)$
`string s(initlist)`	Creates a string that is initialized by all characters in $initlist$ (since C++11)
`s.~string()`	Destroys all characters and frees the memory

Table 13.4. Constructors and Destructor of Strings

13.2.4   Strings and C-Strings

In standard C++, the type of string literals was changed from char* to const char*. However, to provide backward compatibility, there is an implicit but deprecated conversion to char* for them. Because string literals don't have type string, there is a strong relationship between string class objects and ordinary C-strings: You can use ordinary C-strings in almost every situation where strings are combined with other string-like objects (comparing, appending, inserting, etc.). In particular, there is an automatic type conversion from const char* into strings. However, there is *no* automatic type conversion from a string object to a C-string. This is for safety reasons. It prevents unintended type conversions that result in strange behavior (type char* often has strange behavior) and ambiguities. For example, in an expression that combines a string and a C-string, it would be possible to convert string into char* and vice versa. Instead, there are several ways to create or write/copy in a C-string. In particular, c_str() is provided to generate the value of a string as a C-string as a character array that has '\0' as its last character. By using copy(), you can copy or write the value to an existing C-string or character array.

Note that strings do *not* provide a special meaning for the character '\0', which is used as a special character in an ordinary C-string to mark the end of the string. The character '\0' may be part of a string just like every other character.

Note also that if you use an old-style null pointer (NULL) instead of nullptr (see Section 3.1.1, page 14) or a char* parameter, strange behavior results. The reason is that NULL has an integral type and is interpreted as the number 0 or the character with value 0 if the operation is overloaded for a single integral type. So you should always use `nullptr` or `char*` pointers.

There are three possible ways to convert the contents of the string into a raw array of characters or C-string:

1. **`data()`** and **`c_str()`** return the contents of the string as an array of characters. The array includes the *end-of-string* character at position [`size()`], so for `string`s, the result is a valid C-string including `'\0'`.

   Note that before C++11, the return type of `data()` was *not* a valid C-string, because no `'\0'` character was guaranteed to get appended.

2. **`copy()`** copies the contents of the string into a character array provided by the caller. An `'\0'` character is not appended.

Note that `data()` and `c_str()` return an array that is owned by the string. Thus, the caller must not modify or free the memory. For example:

```
std::string s("12345");
```

```
atoi(s.c_str())              // convert string into integer
f(s.data(),s.length())       // call function for a character array
                             // and the number of characters
```

```
char buffer[100];
s.copy(buffer,100);          // copy at most 100 characters of s into buffer
s.copy(buffer,100,2);        // copy at most 100 characters of s into buffer
                             // starting with the third character of s
```

You usually should use strings in the whole program and convert them into C-strings or character arrays only immediately before you need the contents as type `char*`. Note that the return value of `c_str()` and `data()` is valid only until the next call of a nonconstant member function for the same string:

```
std::string s;
...
foo(s.c_str());         // s.c_str() is valid during the whole statement
```

```
const char* p;
p = s.c_str();          // p refers to the contents of s as a C-string
foo(p);                 // OK (p is still valid)
s += "ext";             // invalidates p
foo(p);                 // ERROR: argument p is not valid
```

13.2.5 Size and Capacity

To use strings effectively and correctly, you need to understand how the size and capacity of strings cooperate. For strings, three "sizes" exist:

1. **size()** and **length()** are equivalent functions that return the current number of characters of the string.[5]

    The **empty()** member function is a shortcut for checking whether the number of characters is zero. Thus, it checks whether the string is empty. Because it might be faster, you should use empty() instead of length() or size().

2. **max_size()** returns the maximum number of characters a string may contain. A string typically contains all characters in a single block of memory, so there might be relevant restrictions on PCs. Otherwise, this value usually is the maximum value of the type of the index less one. It is "less one" for two reasons: (a) The maximum value itself is npos, and (b) an implementation might append '\0' internally at the end of the internal buffer so that it simply returns that buffer when the string is used as a C-string (for example, by c_str()). Whenever an operation results in a string that has a length greater than max_size(), the class throws length_error.

3. **capacity()** returns the number of characters a string could contain without having to reallocate its internal memory.

Having sufficient capacity is important for two reasons:

1. Reallocation invalidates all references, pointers, and iterators that refer to characters of the string.

2. Reallocation takes time.

Thus, the capacity must be taken into account if a program uses pointers, references, or iterators that refer to a string or to characters of a string, or if speed is a goal.

The member function reserve() is provided to avoid reallocations. reserve() lets you reserve a certain capacity before you really need it to ensure that references are valid as long as the capacity is not exceeded:

```
std::string s;        // create empty string
s.reserve(80);        // reserve memory for 80 characters
```

The concept of capacity for strings is, in principle, the same as for vector containers (see Section 7.3.1, page 270). However, there is one big difference: Unlike with vectors, calling reserve() for strings might be a call to shrink the capacity. Calling reserve() with an argument that is less than the current capacity is, in effect, a nonbinding shrink request. If the argument is less than the current number of characters, it is a nonbinding shrink-to-fit request. Thus, although you might *want* to shrink the capacity, it is not guaranteed to happen. The default value of reserve() for string is 0. So, a call of reserve() without any argument is always a nonbinding shrink-to-fit request:

```
s.reserve();          // "would like to shrink capacity to fit the current size"
```

Since C++11, shrink_to_fit() provides the same effect:

```
s.shrink_to_fit();    // "would like to shrink capacity to fit the current size" (C++11)
```

A call to shrink capacity is nonbinding because how to reach an optimal performance is implementation-defined. Implementations of the string class might have different design approaches with

---

[5] In this case, two member functions do the same thing because length() returns the length of the string, as strlen() does for ordinary C-strings, whereas size() is the common member function for the number of elements according to the concept of the STL.

respect to speed and memory usage. Therefore, implementations might increase capacity in larger steps and might never shrink the capacity.

The standard, however, specifies that capacity may shrink only because of a call of `reserve()` or `shrink_to_fit()`. Thus, it is guaranteed that references, pointers, and iterators remain valid even when characters are deleted or modified, provided that they refer to characters having a position that is before the manipulated characters.

13.2.6 Element Access

A string allows you to have read or write access to the characters it contains. You can access a single character via the subscript operator `[ ]` and the `at()` member function. Since C++11, `front()` and `back()` are provided to also access the first or last character, respectively.

All these operations return a reference to the character at the position of the passed index, which is a constant character if the string is constant. As usual, the first character has index `0`, and the last character has index `length()-1`. However, note the following differences:

- Operator `[ ]` does *not* check whether the index passed as an argument is valid; `at()` does. If called with an invalid index, `at()` throws an `out_of_range` exception. If operator `[ ]` is called with an invalid index, the behavior is undefined. The effect might be an illegal memory access that might then cause some nasty side effects or a crash (you're lucky if the result is a crash, because then you know that you did something wrong).
- In general, the position after the last character is valid. Thus, the current number of characters is a valid index. The operator returns the value that is generated by the default constructor of the character type. Thus, for objects of type `string` it returns the char `'\0'`.[6]
- `front()` is equivalent to `[0]`, which means that for empty strings the character representing the end of the string (`'\0'` for `strings`) is returned.
- For `at()`, the current number of characters is not a valid index.
- When called for an empty string, `back()` results in undefined behavior.

For example:

```
const std::string cs("nico");    // cs contains: 'n' 'i' 'c' 'o'
std::string s("abcde");          // s contains: 'a' 'b' 'c' 'd' 'e'
std::string t;                   // t contains no character (is empty)

s[2]                             // yields 'c' as char&
s.at(2)                          // yields 'c' as char&
s.front()                        // yields 'a' as char&
cs[2]                            // yields 'i' as const char&
cs.back()                        // yields 'o' as const char&
```

---

[6] Before C++11, for the nonconstant version of operator `[ ]`, the current number of characters was an invalid index. Using it did result in undefined behavior.

```
s[100]                          // ERROR: undefined behavior
s.at(100)                       // throws out_of_range
t.front()                       // yields '\0'
t.back()                        // ERROR: undefined behavior

s[s.length()]                   // yields '\0' (undefined behavior before C++11)
cs[cs.length()]                 // yields '\0'
s.at(s.length())                // throws out_of_range
cs.at(cs.length())              // throws out_of_range
```

To enable you to modify a character of a string, the nonconstant versions of [], at(), front(), and back() return a character reference. Note that this reference becomes invalid on reallocation:

```
std::string s("abcde");     // s contains: 'a' 'b' 'c' 'd' 'e'

char& r = s[2];             // reference to third character
char* p = &s[3];            // pointer to fourth character

r = 'X';                    // OK, s contains: 'a' 'b' 'X' 'd' 'e'
*p = 'Y';                   // OK, s contains: 'a' 'b' 'X' 'Y' 'e'

s = "new long value";       // reallocation invalidates r and p

r = 'X';                    // ERROR: undefined behavior
*p = 'Y';                   // ERROR: undefined behavior
```

Here, to avoid runtime errors, you would have had to reserve() enough capacity before r and p were initialized.

References, pointers, and iterators that refer to characters of a string may be invalidated by the following operations:[7]

- If the value is swapped with swap()
- If a new value is read by operator>>() or getline()
- If any nonconstant member function is called, except operator [], at(), begin(), end(), rbegin(), and rend()

See Section 13.2.14, page 684, for details about string iterators.

13.2.7   Comparisons

The usual comparison operators are provided for strings. The operands may be strings or C-strings:

```
std::string s1, s2;

...
```

---

[7] Before C++11, data() and c_str() also could invalidate references, iterators, and pointers to strings.

```
s1 == s2        // returns true if s1 and s2 contain the same characters
s1 < "hello"    // return whether s1 is less than the C-string "hello"
```

If strings are compared by <, <=, >, or >=, their characters are compared lexicographically according to the current character traits. For example, all of the following comparisons yield true:

```
std::string("aaaa") < std::string("bbbb")
std::string("aaaa") < std::string("abba")
std::string("aaaa") < std::string("aaaaaa")
```

By using the compare() member functions, you can compare substrings. The compare() member functions can process more than one argument for each string, so you can specify a substring by its index and its length. Note that compare() returns an integral value rather than a Boolean value. This return value has the following meaning: 0 means equal, a value less than 0 means less than, and a value greater than 0 means greater than. For example:

```
std::string s("abcd");
```

```
s.compare("abcd")        // returns 0
s.compare("dcba")        // returns a value < 0 (s is less)
s.compare("ab")          // returns a value > 0 (s is greater)

s.compare(s)             // returns 0 (s is equal to s)
s.compare(0,2,s,2,2)     // returns a value < 0 ("ab" is less than "cd")
s.compare(1,2,"bcx",2)   // returns 0 ("bc" is equal to "bc")
```

To use a different comparison criterion, you can define your own comparison criterion and use STL comparison algorithms (see Section 13.2.14, page 684, for an example), or you can use special character traits that make comparisons on a case-insensitive basis. However, because a string type that has a special traits class is a different data type, you cannot combine or process these strings with objects of type string. See Section 13.2.15, page 689, for an example.

In programs for the international market, it might be necessary to compare strings according to a specific locale. Class locale provides the parenthesis operator as a convenient way to do this (see Section 16.3, page 868). It uses the string collation facet, which is provided to compare strings for sorting according to some locale conventions. See Section 16.4.5, page 904, for details.

13.2.8 Modifiers

You can modify strings by using different member functions and operators.

Assignments

To modify a string, you can use operator = to assign a new value. The assigned value may be a string, a C-string, or a single character. In addition, you can use the assign() member functions to assign strings when more than one argument is needed to describe the new value. For example:

```
const std::string aString("othello");
std::string s;
```

```
s = aString;             // assign "othello"
s = "two\nlines";        // assign a C-string
s = ' ';                 // assign a single character

s.assign(aString);       // assign "othello" (equivalent to operator =)
s.assign(aString,1,3);   // assign "the"
s.assign(aString,2,std::string::npos);     // assign "hello"

s.assign("two\nlines");  // assign a C-string (equivalent to operator =)
s.assign("nico",5);      // assign the character array: 'n' 'i' 'c' 'o' '\0'
s.assign(5,'x');         // assign five characters: 'x' 'x' 'x' 'x' 'x'
```

You also can assign a range of characters that is defined by two iterators. See Section 13.2.14, page 684, for details.

Swapping Values

As with many nontrivial types, the string type provides a specialization of the swap() function, which swaps the contents of two strings (the global swap() function was introduced in Section 5.5.2, page 136). The specialization of swap() for strings guarantees constant complexity, so you should use it to swap the value of strings and to assign strings if you don't need the assigned string after the assignment.

Making Strings Empty

To remove all characters in a string, you have several possibilities. For example:

```
std::string s;

s = "";          // assign the empty string
s.clear();       // clear contents
s.erase();       // erase all characters
```

Inserting and Removing Characters

There are numerous member functions to insert, remove, replace, and erase characters of a string. To append characters, you can use operator +=, append(), and push_back(). For example:

```
const std::string aString("othello");
std::string s;

s += aString;            // append "othello"
s += "two\nlines";       // append C-string
s += '\n';               // append single character
s += { 'o', 'k' };       // append an initializer list of characters (since C++11)
```

```
s.append(aString);        // append "othello" (equivalent to operator +=)
s.append(aString,1,3);    // append "the"
s.append(aString,2,std::string::npos);      // append "hello"


s.append("two\nlines");   // append C-string (equivalent to operator +=)
s.append("nico",5);       // append character array: 'n' 'i' 'c' 'o' '\0'
s.append(5,'x');          // append five characters: 'x' 'x' 'x' 'x' 'x'


s.push_back('\n');        // append single character (equivalent to operator +=)
```

Operator += appends single-argument values, including initializer lists of characters since C++11. append() is overloaded for different arguments. One version of append() lets you append a range of characters specified by two iterators (see Section 13.2.14, page 684). The push_back() member function is provided for back inserters so that STL algorithms are able to append characters to a string (see Section 9.4.2, page 455, for details about back inserters and Section 13.2.14, page 688, for an example of their use with strings).

Similar to append(), several insert() member functions enable you to insert characters. These functions require the index of the character, after which the new characters are inserted:

```
const std::string aString("age");
std::string s("p");


s.insert(1,aString);      // s: page
s.insert(1,"ersifl");     // s: persiflage
```

Note that no insert() member function is provided to pass the index and a single character. Thus, you must pass a string or an additional number:

```
s.insert(0,' ');          // ERROR
s.insert(0," ");          // OK
```

You might also try

```
s.insert(0,1,' ');        // ERROR: ambiguous
```

However, this results in a nasty ambiguity because insert() is overloaded for the following signatures:

```
insert (size_type idx, size_type num, charT c);   // position is index
insert (iterator  pos, size_type num, charT c);   // position is iterator
```

For type string, size_type is usually defined as unsigned, and iterator is often defined as char*. In this case, the first argument 0 has two equivalent conversions. So, to get the correct behavior, you have to write:

```
s.insert((std::string::size_type)0,1,' ');   // OK
```

The second interpretation of the ambiguity described here is an example of the use of iterators to insert characters. If you wish to specify the insert position as an iterator, you can do it in three ways: insert a single character, insert a certain number of the same character, and insert a range of characters specified by two iterators (see Section 13.2.14, page 684).

Similar to `append()` and `insert()`, several `erase()` functions and `pop_back()` (since C++11) remove characters, and several `replace()` functions replace characters. For example:

```
std::string s = "i18n";                 // s: i18n
s.replace(1,2,"nternationalizatio");    // s: internationalization
s.erase(13);                            // s: international
s.erase(7,5);                           // s: internal
s.pop_back();                           // s: interna (since C++11)
s.replace(0,2,"ex");                    // s: externa
```

You can use `resize()` to change the number of characters. If the new size that is passed as an argument is less than the current number of characters, characters are removed from the end. If the new size is greater than the current number of characters, characters are appended at the end. You can pass the character that is appended if the size of the string grows. If you don't, the default constructor for the character type is used (which is the '\0' character for type `char`).

13.2.9   Substrings and String Concatenation

You can extract a substring from any string by using the `substr()` member function. For example:

```
std::string s("interchangeability");
```

```
s.substr()                // returns a copy of s
s.substr(11)              // returns string("ability")
s.substr(5,6)             // returns string("change")
s.substr(s.find('c'))     // returns string("changeability")
```

You can use operator + to concatenate two strings or C-strings or one of those with single characters For example, the statements

```
std::string s1("enter");
std::string s2("nation");
std::string i18n;

i18n = 'i' + s1.substr(1) + s2 + "aliz" + s2.substr(1);
std::cout << "i18n means: " + i18n << std::endl;
```

have the following output:

```
i18n means: internationalization
```

Since C++11, operator + is also overloaded for strings that are rvalue references to support the move semantics. Thus, if a string argument passed to operator + is no longer needed afterward, you should use `move()` to pass it to the operator. For example:

```
string foo()
{
    std::string s1("international");
    std::string s2("ization");
```

```
    std::string s = std::move(s1) + std::move(s2);   // OK
                     // s1 and s2 have valid state with unspecified value
    return s;
}
```

13.2.10 Input/Output Operators

The usual I/O operators are defined for strings:

- **Operator >>** reads a string from an input stream.
- **Operator <<** writes a string to an output stream.

These operators behave as they do for ordinary C-strings. In particular, operator >> operates as follows:

1. It skips leading whitespaces if the skipws flag (see Section 15.7.7, page 789) is set.
2. It reads all characters until any of the following happens:
   - The next character is a whitespace.
   - The stream is no longer in a good state (for example, due to end-of-file).
   - The current width() of the stream (see Section 15.7.3, page 781) is greater than 0, and width() characters are read.
   - max_size() characters are read.
3. It sets width() of the stream to 0.

Thus, in general, the input operator reads the next word while skipping leading whitespaces. A whitespace is any character for which isspace(c, *strm*.getloc()) is true (isspace() is explained in Section 16.4.4, page 895).

The output operator also takes the width() of the stream into consideration. That is, if width() is greater than 0, operator << writes at least width() characters.

Note also that since C++11, operators << and >> are declared to process rvalue references to streams. This, for example, allows you to use temporary string streams (see Section 15.10.2, page 806, for details).

getline()

The string classes also provide a special convenience function std::getline() for reading line by line: This function reads all characters, including leading whitespaces, until the line delimiter or end-of-file is reached. The line delimiter is extracted but not appended. By default, the line delimiter is the newline character, but you can pass your own "line" delimiter as an optional argument.[8] This way, you can read token by token, separated by any arbitrary character:

```
    std::string s;
```

---

[8] You don't have to qualify getline() with std:: because when calling a function *argument dependent lookup* (ADL, also known as *Koenig lookup*) will always consider the namespace where the class of an argument was defined.

```
while (getline(std::cin,s)) {        // for each line read from cin
    ...
}


while (getline(std::cin,s,':')) {  // for each token separated by ':'
    ...
}
```

Note that if you read token by token, the newline character is not a special character. In this case, the tokens might contain a newline character.

Note also that since C++11, `getline()` is overloaded for both lvalue and rvalue stream references, which allows using temporary string streams:

```
void process (const std::string& filecontents)
{
    // process first line of passed string:
    std::string firstLine;
    std::getline(std::stringstream(filecontents),     // OK since C++11
                 firstLine);
    ...
}
```

See Section 15.10, page 802, for details about string streams.

13.2.11 Searching and Finding

The C++ standard library provides many abilities to search and find characters or substrings in a string:[9]

- By using **member functions**, you can search
  - A single character, a character sequence (substring), or one of a certain set of characters
  - Forward and backward
  - Starting from any position at the beginning or inside the string
- By using the **regex library** (see Chapter 14), you can search for more complicated patterns of character sequences. See Section 13.2.14, page 687, for an example.
- By using **STL algorithms**, you can also search for single characters or specific character sequences (see Section 11.2.2, page 507). Note that these algorithms allow you to use your own comparison criterion (see Section 13.2.14, page 684, for an example).

---

[9] Don't be confused because I write about searching "and" finding. They are almost synonymous. The search functions use "find" in their names. However, unfortunately, they don't guarantee to find anything. In fact, they "search" for something or "try to find" something. So I use the term *search* for the behavior of these functions and *find* with respect to their names.

Member Functions for Searching and Finding

All search functions have the word *find* inside their name. They try to find a character position given a *value* that is passed as an argument. How the search proceeds depends on the exact name of the find function. Table 13.5 lists all the search functions for strings.

String Function	Effect
`find()`	Finds the first occurrence of *value*
`rfind()`	Finds the last occurrence of *value* (reverse find)
`find_first_of()`	Finds the first character that is part of *value*
`find_last_of()`	Finds the last character that is part of *value*
`find_first_not_of()`	Finds the first character that is not part of *value*
`find_last_not_of()`	Finds the last character that is not part of *value*

Table 13.5. Search Functions for Strings

All search functions return the index of the first character of the character sequence that matches the search. If the search fails, they return `npos`. The search functions use the following argument scheme:

- The first argument is always the value that is searched for.
- The second optional value indicates an index at which to start the search in the string.
- The optional third argument is the number of characters of the value to search.

Unfortunately, this argument scheme differs from that of the other string functions. With the other string functions, the starting index is the first argument, and the value and its length are adjacent arguments. In particular, each search function is overloaded with the following set of arguments:

- **const** *string& value*
  searches against the characters of the string *value*.
- **const** *string& value, size_type idx*
  searches against the characters of *value*, starting with index *idx* in *this.
- **const** *char* value*
  searches against the characters of the C-string *value*.
- **const** *char* value, size_type idx*
  searches against the characters of the C-string *value*, starting with index *idx* in *this.
- **const** *char* value, size_type idx, size_type value_len*
  searches against the *value_len* characters of the character array *value*, starting with index *idx* in *this. Thus, the null character (`'\0'`) has *no* special meaning here inside *value*.
- **const** *char value*
  searches against the character *value*.
- **const** *char value, size_type idx*
  searches against the characters *value*, starting with index *idx* in *this.

For example:

```
std::string s("Hi Bill, I'm ill, so please pay the bill");
```

`s.find("il")`	*// returns 4 (first substring* `"il"`*)*
`s.find("il",10)`	*// returns 13 (first substring* `"il"` *starting from* `s[10]`*)*
`s.rfind("il")`	*// returns 37 (last substring* `"il"`*)*
`s.find_first_of("il")`	*// returns 1 (first char* `'i'` *or* `'l'`*)*
`s.find_last_of("il")`	*// returns 39 (last char* `'i'` *or* `'l'`*)*
`s.find_first_not_of("il")`	*// returns 0 (first char neither* `'i'` *nor* `'l'`*)*
`s.find_last_not_of("il")`	*// returns 36 (last char neither* `'i'` *nor* `'l'`*)*
`s.find("hi")`	*// returns* npos

Note that the naming scheme of the STL search algorithms differs from that for string search functions (see Section 11.2.2, page 507, for details).

13.2.12   The Value `npos`

If a search function fails, it returns *string*`::npos`. Consider the following example:

```
std::string s;
std::string::size_type idx;        // be careful: don't use any other type!
...
idx = s.find("substring");
if (idx == std::string::npos) {
    ...
}
```

The condition of the `if` statement yields `true` if and only if `"substring"` is not part of string s.

Be very careful when using the string value npos and its type. When you want to check the return value, always use `string::size_type`, *not* `int` or `unsigned` for the type of the return value; otherwise, the comparison of the return value with `string::npos` might not work. This behavior is the result of the design decision that npos is defined as −1:

```
namespace std {
    template <typename charT,
              typename traits = char_traits<charT>,
              typename Allocator = allocator<charT> >
    class basic_string {
      public:
        typedef typename Allocator::size_type size_type;
        ...
        static const size_type npos = -1;
        ...
    };
}
```

Unfortunately, `size_type`, which is defined by the allocator of the string, must be an unsigned integral type. The default allocator, `allocator`, uses type `size_t` as `size_type`. Because −1 is converted into an unsigned integral type, npos is the maximum unsigned value of its type. However, the exact value depends on the exact definition of type `size_type`. Unfortunately, these maximum values differ. In fact, `(unsigned long)-1` *differs* from `(unsigned short)-1` if the size of the types differs. Thus, the comparison

```
idx == std::string::npos
```

might yield `false` if idx has the value −1 and idx and `string::npos` have different types:

```
std::string s;
...
int idx = s.find("not found");      // assume it returns npos
if (idx == std::string::npos) {     // ERROR: comparison might not work
    ...
}
```

One way to avoid this error is to check whether the search fails directly:

```
if (s.find("hi") == std::string::npos) {
    ...
}
```

However, often you need the index of the matching character position. Thus, another simple solution is to define your own signed value for npos:

```
const int NPOS = -1;
```

Now the comparison looks a bit different and even more convenient:

```
if (idx == NPOS) {        // works almost always
    ...
}
```

Unfortunately, this solution is not perfect, because the comparison fails if either idx has type `unsigned short` or the index is greater than the maximum value of int. Because of these problems, the standard did not define it that way. However, because both might happen very rarely, the solution works in most situations. To write portable code, however, you should always use *string*::`size_type` for any index of your string type. For a perfect solution, you'd need some overloaded functions that consider the exact type of `string::size_type`. I still hope the standard will provide a better solution in the future (although with C++11 nothing changed).

13.2.13 Numeric Conversions

Since C++11, the C++ standard library provides convenience functions to convert strings into numeric values or to convert numeric values to strings (see Table 13.6). Note, however, that these conversions are available only for types `string` and `wstring`, not `u16string` and `u32string`.

String Function	Effect
stoi(*str*, *idxRet*=nullptr, *base*=10)	Converts *str* to an int
stol(*str*, *idxRet*=nullptr, *base*=10)	Converts *str* to a long
stoul(*str*, *idxRet*=nullptr, *base*=10)	Converts *str* to an unsigned long
stoll(*str*, *idxRet*=nullptr, *base*=10)	Converts *str* to a long long
stoull(*str*, *idxRet*=nullptr, *base*=10)	Converts *str* to an unsigned long long
stof(*str*, *idxRet*=nullptr)	Converts *str* to a float
stod(*str*, *idxRet*=nullptr)	Converts *str* to a double
stold(*str*, *idxRet*=nullptr)	Converts *str* to a long double
to_string(*val*)	Converts *val* to a string
to_wstring(*val*)	Converts *val* to a wstring

Table 13.6. Numeric Conversions for Strings

For all function that convert strings to a numeric value, the following applies:

- They skip leading whitespaces.
- They allow you to return the index of the first character after the last processed character.
- They might throw std::invalid_argument if no conversion is possible and std::out_of_range if the converted value is outside the range of representable values for the return type.
- For integral values, you can optionally pass the number base to use.

For all functions that convert a numeric value to a string or wstring, *val* may be any of the following types: int, unsigned int, long, unsigned long, long long, unsigned long long, float, double, or long double.

For example, consider the following program:

```
// string/stringnumconv1.cpp

#include <string>
#include <iostream>
#include <limits>
#include <exception>

int main()
{
  try {
    // convert to numeric type
    std::cout << std::stoi ("  77") << std::endl;
    std::cout << std::stod ("  77.7") << std::endl;
    std::cout << std::stoi ("-0x77") << std::endl;

    // use index of characters not processed
    std::size_t idx;
```

```
      std::cout << std::stoi ("  42 is the truth", &idx) << std::endl;
      std::cout << " idx of first unprocessed char: " << idx << std::endl;

      // use bases 16 and 8
      std::cout << std::stoi ("  42", nullptr, 16) << std::endl;
      std::cout << std::stol ("789", &idx, 8) << std::endl;
      std::cout << " idx of first unprocessed char: " << idx << std::endl;

      // convert numeric value to string
      long long ll = std::numeric_limits<long long>::max();
      std::string s = std::to_string(ll);   // converts maximum long long to string
      std::cout << s << std::endl;

      // try to convert back
      std::cout << std::stoi(s) << std::endl;   // throws out_of_range
   }
   catch (const std::exception& e) {
      std::cout << e.what() << std::endl;
   }
}
```

The program has the following output:

```
77
77.7
0
42
 idx of first unprocessed char: 4
66
7
 idx of first unprocessed char: 1
9223372036854775807
stoi argument out of range
```

Note that `std::stoi("-0x77")` yields 0 because it parses only -0, interpreting the x as the end of the numeric value found. Note that `std::stol("789",&idx,8)` parses only the first character of the string because 8 is not a valid character for octal numbers.

13.2.14   Iterator Support for Strings

A string is an ordered collection of characters. As a consequence, the C++ standard library provides an interface for strings that lets you use them as STL containers.[10]

In particular, you can call the usual member functions to get iterators that iterate over the characters of a string. If you are not familiar with iterators, consider them as something that can refer to a single character inside a string, just as ordinary pointers do for C-strings. By using these objects, you can iterate over all characters of a string by calling several algorithms that either are provided by the C++ standard library or are user defined. For example, you can sort the characters of a string, reverse the order, or find the character that has the maximum value.

String iterators are random-access iterators. This means that they provide random access, and you can use all algorithms (see Section 6.3.2, page 198, and Section 9.2, page 433, for a discussion about iterator categories). As usual, the types of string iterators (`iterator`, `const_iterator`, and so on) are defined by the string class itself. The exact type is implementation defined, but string iterators are often defined simply as ordinary pointers. See Section 9.2.6, page 440, for a nasty difference between iterators that are implemented as pointers and iterators that are implemented as classes.

Iterators are invalidated when reallocation occurs or when certain changes are made to the values to which they refer. See Section 13.2.6, page 672, for details.

Iterator Functions for Strings

Table 13.7 shows all the member functions that strings provide for iterators. As usual, the range specified by beg and end is a half-open range that includes beg but excludes end, written as [beg,end) (see Section 6.3, page 188).

To support the use of back inserters for strings, the `push_back()` function is defined. See Section 9.4.2, page 455, for details about back inserters and page 688 for an example of their use with strings.

Example of Using String Iterators

A very useful thing that you can do with string iterators is to make all characters of a string lowercase or uppercase via a single statement. For example:

```
// string/stringiter1.cpp

#include <string>
#include <iostream>
#include <algorithm>
#include <cctype>
#include <regex>
using namespace std;
```

---

[10] The STL is introduced in Chapter 6.

Expression	Effect
s.begin(), s.cbegin()	Returns a random-access iterator for the first character
s.end(), s.cend()	Returns a random-access iterator for the position after the last character
s.rbegin(), s.crbegin()	Returns a reverse iterator for the first character of a reverse iteration (thus, for the last character)
s.rend(), crend()	Returns a reverse iterator for the position after the last character of a reverse iteration (thus, the position before the first character)
string s(*beg,end*)	Creates a string that is initialized by all characters of the range [*beg,end*)
s.append(*beg,end*)	Appends all characters of the range [*beg,end*)
s.assign(*beg,end*)	Assigns all characters of the range [*beg,end*)
s.insert(*pos,c*)	Inserts the character c at iterator position *pos* and returns the iterator position of the new character
s.insert(*pos,num,c*)	Inserts *num* occurrences of the character c at iterator position *pos* and returns the iterator position of the first new character
s.insert(*pos,beg,end*)	Inserts all characters of the range [*beg,end*) at iterator position *pos*
s.insert(*pos,initlist*)	Inserts all characters of the initializer list *initlist* at iterator position *pos* (since C++11)
s.erase(*pos*)	Deletes the character to which iterator *pos* refers and returns the position of the next character
s.erase(*beg,end*)	Deletes all characters of the range [*beg,end*) and returns the next position of the next character
s.replace(*beg,end,str*)	Replaces all characters of the range [*beg,end*) with the characters of string *str*
s.replace(*beg,end,cstr*)	Replaces all characters of the range [*beg,end*) with the characters of the C-string *cstr*
s.replace(*beg,end,cstr,len*)	Replaces all characters of the range [*beg,end*) with *len* characters of the character array *cstr*
s.replace(*beg,end,num,c*)	Replaces all characters of the range [*beg,end*) with *num* occurrences of the character c
s.replace(*beg,end, newBeg,newEnd*)	Replaces all characters of the range [*beg,end*) with all characters of the range [*newBeg,newEnd*)
s.replace(*beg,end, initlist*)	Replaces all characters of the range [*beg,end*) with the values of the initializer list *initlist* (since C++11)

Table 13.7. Iterator Operations of Strings

```cpp
int main()
{
    // create a string
    string s("The zip code of Braunschweig in Germany is 38100");
    cout << "original: " << s << endl;

    // lowercase all characters
    transform (s.cbegin(), s.cend(),    // source
               s.begin(),               // destination
               [] (char c) {            // operation
                   return tolower(c);
               });
    cout << "lowered:  " << s << endl;

    // uppercase all characters
    transform (s.cbegin(), s.cend(),    // source
               s.begin(),               // destination
               [] (char c) {            // operation
                   return toupper(c);
               });
    cout << "uppered:  " << s << endl;

    // search case-insensitive for Germany
    string g("Germany");
    string::const_iterator pos;
    pos = search (s.cbegin(),s.cend(),          // source string in which to search
                  g.cbegin(),g.cend(),          // substring to search
                  [] (char c1, char c2) {       // comparison criterion
                      return toupper(c1) == toupper(c2);
                  });
    if (pos != s.cend()) {
        cout << "substring \"" << g << "\" found at index "
             << pos - s.cbegin() << endl;
    }
}
```

Here, we twice use iterators provided by `cbegin()`, `cend()`, and `begin()` to pass them to the `transform()` algorithm, which transforms all elements of an input range to a destination range by using a transformation passed as fourth argument (see Section 6.8.1, page 225, and Section 11.6.3, page 563, for details).

The transformation is specified as a lambda (see Section 6.9, page 229), which converts the elements of the string (the characters) to lower- or uppercase. Note that `tolower()` and `toupper()` are old C functions that use the global locale. If you have a different locale or more than one locale in your program, you should use the new form of `tolower()` and `toupper()`. See Section 16.4.4, page 895, for details.

Finally, we use the search algorithm to search for a substring with our own search criterion. This criterion is a lambda that compares the characters in a case-insensitive way.

Alternatively, we could use the regex library:

```
// search case-insensitive for Germany
std::regex pat("Germany",                       // expression to search for
               regex_constants::icase);   // search case-insensitive
smatch m;
if (regex_search (s,m,pat)) {                   // search regex pattern in s
    cout << "substring \"Germany\" found at index "
         << m.position() << endl;
}
```

See Section 14.6, page 732, for details.

Thus, the output of the program is as follows:

```
original: The zip code of Braunschweig in Germany is 38100
lowered:  the zip code of braunschweig in germany is 38100
uppered:  THE ZIP CODE OF BRAUNSCHWEIG IN GERMANY IS 38100
substring "Germany" found at index 32
```

In the last output statement, you can process the difference of two string iterators to get the index of the character position:

```
pos - s.cbegin()
```

You can use operator − because string iterators are random-access iterators. Similar to transferring an index into the iterator position, you can simply add the value of the index.

If you use strings in sets or maps, you might need a special sorting criterion to let the collections sort the string in a case-insensitive way. See Section 7.8.6, page 351, for an example that demonstrates how to do this.

The following program demonstrates other examples of strings using iterator functions:

```
// string/stringiter2.cpp

#include <string>
#include <iostream>
#include <algorithm>
using namespace std;

int main()
{
    // create constant string
    const string hello("Hello, how are you?");

    // initialize string s with all characters of string hello
    string s(hello.cbegin(),hello.cend());
```

```
// ranged-based for loop that iterates through all the characters
for (char c : s) {
    cout << c;
}
cout << endl;

// reverse the order of all characters inside the string
reverse (s.begin(), s.end());
cout << "reverse:        " << s << endl;

// sort all characters inside the string
sort (s.begin(), s.end());
cout << "ordered:        " << s << endl;

// remove adjacent duplicates
// - unique() reorders and returns new end
// - erase() shrinks accordingly
s.erase (unique(s.begin(),
                s.end()),
         s.end());
cout << "no duplicates: " << s << endl;
}
```

The program has the following output:

```
Hello, how are you?
reverse:        ?uoy era woh ,olleH
ordered:           ,?Haeehlloooruwy
no duplicates:  ,?Haehloruwy
```

The following example uses back inserters to read the standard input into a string:

```
// string/string3.cpp

#include <string>
#include <iostream>
#include <algorithm>
#include <iterator>
#include <locale>
using namespace std;

int main()
{
    string input;
```

```
    // don't skip leading whitespaces
    cin.unsetf (ios::skipws);

    // read all characters while compressing whitespaces
    const locale& loc(cin.getloc());        // locale
    unique_copy(istream_iterator<char>(cin),     // beginning of source
                istream_iterator<char>(),        // end of source
                back_inserter(input),            // destination
                [=] (char c1, char c2) {         // criterion for adj. duplicates
                    return isspace(c1,loc) && isspace(c2,loc);
                });

    // process input
    // - here: write it to the standard output
    cout << input;
}
```

By using the `unique_copy()` algorithm (see Section 11.7.2, page 580), all characters are read from the input stream `cin` and inserted into the string `input`.

The passed lambda operation checks whether two characters are whitespaces. This criterion is taken by `unique_copy()` to detect adjacent "duplicates," where the second element can be removed. Thus, while reading the input, the algorithm compresses multiple whitespaces (see Section 16.4.4, page 895, for a discussion of `isspace()`).

The criterion itself takes the current local into account. To do this, `loc` is initialized by the locale of `cin` and passed by value to the lambda (see Section 15.8, page 790, for details of `getloc()`).

You can find a similar example in the reference section about `unique_copy()` in Section 11.7.2, page 582.

13.2.15 Internationalization

As mentioned in Section 13.2.1, page 664, the template string class `basic_string<>` is parametrized by the character type, the traits of the character type, and the memory model. Type `string` is the specializations for characters of type `char`, whereas types `wstring`, `u16string`, and `u32string` are the specializations for characters of type `wchar_t`, `char16_t`, and `char32_t`, respectively.

Note that you can specify the character sets used for string literals since C++11 (see Section 3.1.6, page 23).

To specify the details of how to deal with aspects depending on the representation of a character type, character traits are provided. An additional class is necessary because you can't change the interface of built-in types, such as `char` and `wchar_t`, and the same character type may have different traits. The details about the traits classes are described in Section 16.1.4, page 853.

The following code defines a special traits class for strings so that they operate in a case-insensitive way:

```cpp
// string/icstring.hpp

#ifndef ICSTRING_HPP
#define ICSTRING_HPP

#include <string>
#include <iostream>
#include <cctype>


// replace functions of the standard char_traits<char>
// so that strings behave in a case-insensitive way
struct ignorecase_traits : public std::char_traits<char> {
    // return whether c1 and c2 are equal
    static bool eq(const char& c1, const char& c2) {
        return std::toupper(c1)==std::toupper(c2);
    }
    // return whether c1 is less than c2
    static bool lt(const char& c1, const char& c2) {
        return std::toupper(c1)<std::toupper(c2);
    }
    // compare up to n characters of s1 and s2
    static int compare(const char* s1, const char* s2,
                       std::size_t n) {
        for (std::size_t i=0; i<n; ++i) {
            if (!eq(s1[i],s2[i])) {
                return lt(s1[i],s2[i])?-1:1;
            }
        }
        return 0;
    }
    // search c in s
    static const char* find(const char* s, std::size_t n,
                            const char& c) {
        for (std::size_t i=0; i<n; ++i) {
            if (eq(s[i],c)) {
                return &(s[i]);
            }
        }
        return 0;
    }
};

// define a special type for such strings
typedef std::basic_string<char,ignorecase_traits> icstring;
```

```
// define an output operator
// because the traits type is different from that for std::ostream
inline
std::ostream& operator << (std::ostream& strm, const icstring& s)
{
    // simply convert the icstring into a normal string
    return strm << std::string(s.data(),s.length());
}


#endif     // ICSTRING_HPP
```

The definition of the output operator is necessary because the standard defines I/O operators only for streams that use the same character and traits type. But here the traits type differs, so we have to define our own output operator. For input operators, the same problem occurs.

The following program demonstrates how to use these special kinds of strings:

```
// string/icstring1.cpp

#include "icstring.hpp"

int main()
{
    using std::cout;
    using std::endl;

    icstring s1("hallo");
    icstring s2("otto");
    icstring s3("hALLo");

    cout << std::boolalpha;
    cout << s1 << " == " << s2 << " : " << (s1==s2) << endl;
    cout << s1 << " == " << s3 << " : " << (s1==s3) << endl;

    icstring::size_type idx = s1.find("All");
    if (idx != icstring::npos) {
        cout << "index of \"All\" in \"" << s1 << "\": "
             << idx << endl;
    }
    else {
        cout << "\"All\" not found in \"" << s1 << endl;
    }
}
```

The program has the following output:

```
hallo == otto : false
hallo == hALLo : true
index of "All" in "hallo": 1
```

See Chapter 16 for more details about internationalization.

13.2.16   Performance

As usual, the standard does *not* specify *how* the string class is to be implemented but instead specifies only the interface. There may be important differences in speed and memory usage, depending on the concept and priorities of the implementation.

Note that since C++11, reference counted implementations are not permitted any longer. The reason is that an implementation that lets strings share internal buffers doesn't work in multithreaded contexts.

13.2.17   Strings and Vectors

Strings and vectors behave similarly. This is no surprise because both are containers that are typically implemented as dynamic arrays. Thus, you could consider a string as a special kind of a vector that has characters as elements. In fact, you can use a string as an STL container (see Section 13.2.14, page 684). However, considering a string as a special kind of vector is dangerous because there are many fundamental differences between the two. Chief among these are their two primary goals:

1. The primary goal of vectors is to handle and to manipulate the elements of the container, not the container as a whole. Thus, vector implementations are optimized to operate on elements inside the container.

2. The primary goal of strings is to handle and to manipulate the container (the string) as a whole. Thus, strings are optimized to reduce the costs of assigning and passing the whole container.

These different goals typically result in completely different implementations. For example, strings are often implemented by using reference counting; vectors never are. Nevertheless, you can also use vectors as ordinary C-strings. See Section 7.3.3, page 278, for details.

13.3   String Class in Detail

In this section, *string* stands for the corresponding string class: `string`, `wstring`, `u16string`, `u32string`, or any other specialization of class `basic_string<>`. Type *char* stands for the corresponding character type, which is `char` for `string`, `wchar_t` for `wstring`, `char16_t` for `u16string`, or `char32_t` for `u32string`. Other types and values in italic type have definitions that depend on individual definitions of the character type or traits class. The details about traits classes are provided in Section 16.1.4, page 853.

13.3.1   Type Definitions and Static Values

string::**traits_type**
- The type of the character traits.
- The second template parameter of class `basic_string`.
- For type `string`, it is equivalent to `char_traits<char>`.

string::**value_type**
- The type of the characters.
- It is equivalent to `traits_type::char_type`.
- For type `string`, it is equivalent to `char`.

string::**size_type**
- The unsigned integral type for size values and indices.
- It is equivalent to `allocator_type::size_type`.
- For type `string`, it is equivalent to `size_t`.

string::**difference_type**
- The signed integral type for difference values.
- It is equivalent to `allocator_type::difference_type`.
- For type `string`, it is equivalent to `ptrdiff_t`.

string::**reference**
- The type of character references.
- It is equivalent to `allocator_type::reference`.
- For type `string`, it is equivalent to `char&`.

string::**const_reference**
- The type of constant character references.
- It is equivalent to `allocator_type::const_reference`.
- For type `string`, it is equivalent to `const char&`.

string : :**pointer**

- The type of character pointers.
- It is equivalent to `allocator_type::pointer`.
- For type `string`, it is equivalent to `char*`.

string : :**const_pointer**

- The type of constant character pointers.
- It is equivalent to `allocator_type::const_pointer`.
- For type `string`, it is equivalent to `const char*`.

string : :**iterator**

- The type of iterators.
- The exact type is implementation defined.
- For type `string`, it is typically `char*`.

string : :**const_iterator**

- The type of constant iterators.
- The exact type is implementation defined.
- For type `string`, it is typically `const char*`.

string : :**reverse_iterator**

- The type of reverse iterators.
- It is equivalent to `reverse_iterator<iterator>`.

string : :**const_reverse_iterator**

- The type of constant reverse iterators.
- It is equivalent to `reverse_iterator<const_iterator>`.

`static const` *size_type* *string* : :**npos**

- A special value that indicates either "*not found*" or "*all remaining characters.*"
- It is an unsigned integral value that is initialized by `-1`.
- Be careful when you use npos. See Section 13.2.12, page 680, for details.

13.3.2 Create, Copy, and Destroy Operations

string : :**string** ( )

- The default constructor.
- Creates an empty string.

string : :**string** (const *string&* *str*)

- The copy constructor.
- Creates a new string as a copy of *str*.

string::**string** (*string&& str*)

- The move constructor.
- Creates a new string initialized with the elements of the existing string *str*.
- The contents of *str* is undefined afterward.
- Available since C++11.

string::**string** (const *string& str*, size_type *str_idx*)

string::**string** (const *string& str*, size_type *str_idx*, size_type *str_num*)

- Create a new string that is initialized by at most the first *str_num* characters of *str*, starting with index *str_idx*.
- If *str_num* is missing, all characters from *str_idx* to the end of *str* are used.
- Throws out_of_range if *str_idx* > *str*.size().

string::**string** (const *char* cstr*)

- Creates a string that is initialized by the C-string *cstr*.
- The string is initialized by all characters of *cstr* up to but not including '\0'.
- Note that passing a null pointer (nullptr or NULL) results in undefined behavior.
- Throws length_error if the resulting size exceeds the maximum number of characters.

string::**string** (const *char* chars*, size_type *chars_len*)

- Creates a string that is initialized by *chars_len* characters of the character array *chars*.
- Note that *chars* must have at least *chars_len* characters. The characters may have arbitrary values. Thus, '\0' has no special meaning.
- Throws length_error if *chars_len* is equal to *string*::npos.
- Throws length_error if the resulting size exceeds the maximum number of characters.

string::**string** (size_type *num*, *char* c)

- Creates a string that is initialized by *num* occurrences of character *c*.
- Throws length_error if *num* is equal to *string*::npos.
- Throws length_error if the resulting size exceeds the maximum number of characters.

string::**string** (InputIterator *beg*, InputIterator *end*)

- Creates a string that is initialized by all characters of the range [*beg,end*).
- Throws length_error if the resulting size exceeds the maximum number of characters.

string::**string** (InputIterator *beg*, InputIterator *end*)

- Creates a string that is initialized by all characters of the range [*beg,end*).
- Throws length_error if the resulting size exceeds the maximum number of characters.

string::**string** (*initializer-list*)

- Creates a new string that is initialized by the characters of *initializer-list*.
- Available since C++11.
- Throws `length_error` if the resulting size exceeds the maximum number of characters.

string::~**string** ()

- The destructor.
- Destroys all characters and frees the memory.

Most constructors allow you to pass an allocator as an additional argument (see Section 13.3.13, page 715).

13.3.3 Operations for Size and Capacity

Size Operations

`bool` *string*::**empty** () const

- Returns whether the string is empty (contains no characters).
- It is equivalent to *string*::`size()==0`, but it might be faster.

`size_type` *string*::**size** () const
`size_type` *string*::**length** () const

- Both functions return the current number of characters.
- They are equivalent.
- To check whether the string is empty, you should use `empty()` because it might be faster.

`size_type` *string*::**max_size** () const

- Returns the maximum number of characters a string could contain.
- Whenever an operation results in a string that has a length greater than `max_size()`, the class throws `length_error`.

Capacity Operations

`size_type` *string*::**capacity** () const

- Returns the number of characters the string could contain without reallocation.

void *string*::**reserve** ()

void *string*::**reserve** (size_type *num*)

- The first form is a nonbinding shrink-to-fit request.
- The second form reserves internal memory for at least *num* characters.
- If *num* is less than the current capacity, the call is taken as a nonbinding request to shrink the capacity.
- If *num* is less than the current number of characters, the call is taken as a nonbinding request to shrink the capacity to fit the current number of characters (equivalent to the first form).
- The capacity is never reduced below the current number of characters.
- This operation might invalidate references, pointers, and iterators to characters. However, it is guaranteed that no reallocation takes place during insertions that happen after a call to reserve() until the time when an insertion would make the size greater than num. Thus, reserve() can increase speed and help to keep references, pointers, and iterators valid (see Section 13.2.5, page 670, for details).

void *string*::**shrink_to_fit** ()

- Reduces the internal memory to fit the current numbers of characters.
- It has the same effect as reserve(0).
- The call is taken as a nonbinding request to allow latitude for implementation-specific optimizations.
- This operation might invalidate references, pointers, and iterators to characters.
- Available since C++11.

13.3.4 Comparisons

bool *comparison* (const *string&* *str1*, const *string&* *str2*)

bool *comparison* (const *string&* *str*, const *char** *cstr*)

bool *comparison* (const *char** *cstr*, const *string&* *str*)

- The first form returns the result of the comparison of two strings.
- The second and third forms return the result of the comparison of a string with a C-string.
- *comparison* might be any of the following:
  ```
  operator ==
  operator !=
  operator <
  operator >
  operator <=
  operator >=
  ```
- The values are compared lexicographically (see Section 13.2.7, page 673).

int *string*::**compare** (const *string&* *str*) const

- Compares the string *this with the string *str*.
- Returns
  - 0 if both strings are equal
  - A value < 0 if *this is lexicographically less than *str*
  - A value > 0 if *this is lexicographically greater than *str*
- For the comparison, traits::compare() is used (see Section 16.1.4, page 854).
- See Section 13.2.7, page 673, for details.

int *string*::**compare** (size_type *idx*, size_type *len*, const *string&* *str*) const

- Compares at most *len* characters of string *this, starting with index *idx* with the string *str*.
- Throws out_of_range if *idx* > size().
- The comparison is performed as just described for compare(*str*).

int *string*::**compare** (size_type *idx*, size_type *len*,
                        const *string&* *str*, size_type *str_idx*,
                        size_type *str_len*) const

- Compares at most *len* characters of string *this, starting with index *idx* with at most *str_len* characters of string *str*, starting with index *str_idx*.
- Throws out_of_range if *idx* > size().
- Throws out_of_range if *str_idx* > *str*.size().
- The comparison is performed as just described for compare(*str*).

int *string*::**compare** (const *char** *cstr*) const

- Compares the characters of string *this with the characters of the C-string *cstr*.
- The comparison is performed as just described for compare(*str*).

int *string*::**compare** (size_type *idx*, size_type *len*, const *char** *cstr*) const

- Compares at most *len* characters of string *this, starting with index *idx* with all characters of the C-string *cstr*.
- The comparison is performed as just described for compare(*str*).
- Note that passing a null pointer (nullptr or NULL) results in undefined behavior.

int *string*::**compare** (size_type *idx*, size_type *len*,
                        const *char** *chars*, size_type *chars_len*) const

- Compares at most *len* characters of string *this, starting with index *idx* with *chars_len* characters of the character array *chars*.
- The comparison is performed as just described for compare(*str*).
- Note that *chars* must have at least *chars_len* characters. The characters may have arbitrary values. Thus, '\0' has no special meaning.
- Throws length_error if *chars_len* is equal to *string*::npos.

13.3.5 Character Access

char& **string**::**operator [ ]** (size_type *idx*)

const *char&* **string**::**operator [ ]** (size_type *idx*) const

- Both forms return the character with the index *idx* (the first character has index 0).
- `length()` or `size()` is a valid index, and the operator returns the value generated by the default constructor of the character type (for `string`: `'\0'`). Before C++11, `length()` or `size()` was an invalid index value for nonconstant strings.
- Passing an invalid index results in undefined behavior.
- The reference returned for the nonconstant string may become invalidated due to string modifications or reallocations (see Section 13.2.6, page 672, for details).
- If the caller can't ensure that the index is valid, `at()` should be used.

char& **string**::**at** (size_type *idx*)

const *char&* **string**::**at** (size_type *idx*) const

- Both forms return the character that has the index *idx* (the first character has index 0).
- For all strings, an index with `length()` as value is invalid.
- Passing an invalid index — less than 0 or greater than or equal to `length()` or `size()` — throws an `out_of_range` exception.
- The reference returned for the nonconstant string may become invalidated due to string modifications or reallocations (see Section 13.2.6, page 672, for details).
- By ensuring that the index is valid, the caller can use operator [ ], which is faster.

char& **string**::**front** ()

const *char&* **string**::**front** () const

- Both forms return the first character.
- Calling `front()` for an empty string returns the value generated by the default constructor of the character type (for `string`: `'\0'`).
- The reference returned for the nonconstant string may become invalidated due to string modifications or reallocations (see Section 13.2.6, page 672, for details).

char& **string**::**back** ()

const *char&* **string**::**back** () const

- Both forms return the last character.
- Calling `back()` for an empty string results in undefined behavior.
- The reference returned for the nonconstant string may become invalidated due to string modifications or reallocations (see Section 13.2.6, page 672, for details).

13.3.6   Generating C-Strings and Character Arrays

const *char*∗ *string*::**c_str** () const

const *char*∗ *string*::**data** () const

- Returns the contents of the string as a character array, including a trailing end-of-string character '\0'. Thus, this is a valid C-string for strings.
- The return value is owned by the string. Thus, the caller must neither modify nor free or delete the return value.
- The return value is valid only as long as the string exists and as long as only constant functions are called for it.
- Before C++11, the return value of data() was guaranteed to contain all characters of the string without any trailing '\0' character. Thus, the return value of data() was *not* a valid C-string.

size_type *string*::**copy** (*char*∗ *buf*, size_type *buf_size*) const

size_type *string*::**copy** (*char*∗ *buf*, size_type *buf_size*, size_type *idx*) const

- Both forms copy at most *buf_size* characters of the string (beginning with index *idx*, if passed) into the character array *buf*.
- They return the number of characters copied.
- No null character is appended. Thus, the contents of *buf* might *not* be a valid C-string after the call.
- The caller must ensure that *buf* has enough memory; otherwise, the call results in undefined behavior.
- Throws out_of_range if *idx* > size().

13.3.7   Modifying Operations

Assignments

string& *string*::**operator =** (const *string*& *str*)

string& *string*::**assign** (const *string*& *str*)

- Copy assignment operator.
- Both operations assign the value of string *str*.
- They return *this.

string& *string*::**operator =** (*string*&& *str*)

string& *string*::**assign** (*string*&& *str*)

- Move assignment operator.
- Move the contents of *str* to *this.
- The contents of *str* are undefined afterward.
- Return *this.
- Available since C++11.

string& string::**assign** (const *string& str*, size_type *str_idx*, size_type *str_num*)

- Assigns at most *str_num* characters of *str*, starting with index *str_idx*.
- Returns *this.
- Throws out_of_range if *str_idx* > *str*.size().

string& string::**operator =** (const *char* cstr*)
string& string::**assign** (const *char* cstr*)

- Both operations assign the characters of the C-string *cstr*.
- They assign all characters of *cstr* up to but not including '\0'.
- Both operations return *this.
- Note that passing a null pointer (nullptr or NULL) results in undefined behavior.
- Both operations throw length_error if the resulting size exceeds the maximum number of characters.

string& string::**assign** (const *char* chars*, size_type *chars_len*)

- Assigns *chars_len* characters of the character array *chars*.
- Returns *this.
- Note that *chars* must have at least *chars_len* characters. The characters may have arbitrary values. Thus, '\0' has no special meaning.
- Throws length_error if the resulting size exceeds the maximum number of characters.

string& string::**operator =** (*char c*)

- Assigns character *c* as the new value.
- Returns *this.
- After this call, *this contains only this single character.

string& string::**assign** (size_type *num*, *char c*)

- Assigns *num* occurrences of character *c*.
- Returns *this.
- Throws length_error if *num* is equal to *string*::npos.
- Throws length_error if the resulting size exceeds the maximum number of characters.

string& string::**assign** (InputIterator *beg*, InputIterator *end*)

- Assigns all characters of the range [*beg*,*end*).
- Returns *this.
- Throws length_error if the resulting size exceeds the maximum number of characters.

string& string::**operator =** (*initializer-list*)
string& string::**assign** (*initializer-list*)

- Both operations assign the characters of *initializer-list*.

- Both operations return *this.
- Both operations throw length_error if the resulting size exceeds the maximum number of characters.
- Available since C++11.

void *string*::**swap** (*string& str*)

void **swap** (*string& str1, string& str2*)

- Both forms swap the value of two strings, either of *this and *str* or of *str1* and *str2*.
- You should prefer these functions over copy assignment, if possible, because they are faster. In fact, they are guaranteed to have constant complexity. See Section 13.2.8, page 674, for details.

Appending Characters

string& string::**operator +=** (const *string& str*)

string& string::**append** (const *string& str*)

- Both operations append the characters of *str*.
- They return *this.
- Both operations throw length_error if the resulting size exceeds the maximum number of characters.

string& string::**append** (const *string& str*, size_type *str_idx*, size_type *str_num*)

- Appends at most *str_num* characters of *str*, starting with index *str_idx*.
- Returns *this.
- Throws out_of_range if *str_idx* > *str*.size().
- Throws length_error if the resulting size exceeds the maximum number of characters.

string& string::**operator +=** (const *char* cstr*)

string& string::**append** (const *char* cstr*)

- Both operations append the characters of the C-string *cstr*.
- They return *this.
- Note that passing a null pointer (nullptr or NULL) results in undefined behavior.
- Both operations throw length_error if the resulting size exceeds the maximum number of characters.

string& string::**append** (const *char* chars*, size_type *chars_len*)

- Appends *chars_len* characters of the character array *chars*.
- Returns *this.
- Note that *chars* must have at least *chars_len* characters. The characters may have arbitrary values. Thus, '\0' has no special meaning.
- Throws length_error if the resulting size exceeds the maximum number of characters.

string& **string** : : **append** (size_type *num*, *char c*)

- Appends *num* occurrences of character *c*.
- Returns *this.
- Throws length_error if the resulting size exceeds the maximum number of characters.

string& **string** : : **operator +=** (*char c*)

void **string** : : **push_back** (*char c*)

- Both operations append character *c*.
- Operator += returns *this.
- Both operations throw length_error if the resulting size exceeds the maximum number of characters.

string& **string** : : **append** (InputIterator *beg*, InputIterator *end*)

- Appends all characters of the range [*beg,end*).
- Returns *this.
- Throws length_error if the resulting size exceeds the maximum number of characters.

string& **string** : : **operator +=** (*initializer-list*)

void **string** : : **append** (*initializer-list*)

- Both operations append all characters of *initializer-list*.
- Both operations return returns *this.
- Both operations throw length_error if the resulting size exceeds the maximum number of characters.
- Available since C++11.

Inserting Characters

string& **string** : : **insert** (size_type *idx*, const *string& str*)

- Inserts the characters of *str* so that the new characters start with index *idx*.
- Returns *this.
- Throws out_of_range if *idx* > size().
- Throws length_error if the resulting size exceeds the maximum number of characters.

string& **string** : : **insert** (size_type *idx*, const *string& str*,
                                size_type *str_idx*, size_type *str_num*)

- Inserts at most *str_num* characters of *str*, starting with index *str_idx*, so that the new characters start with index *idx*.
- Returns *this.
- Throws out_of_range if *idx* > size().
- Throws out_of_range if *str_idx* > *str*.size().
- Throws length_error if the resulting size exceeds the maximum number of characters.

string& string::insert (size_type *idx*, const *char* cstr*)

- Inserts the characters of the C-string *cstr* so that the new characters start with index *idx*.
- Returns *this.
- Note that passing a null pointer (nullptr or NULL) results in undefined behavior.
- Throws out_of_range if *idx* > size().
- Throws length_error if the resulting size exceeds the maximum number of characters.

string& string::insert (size_type *idx*, const *char* chars*, size_type *chars_len*)

- Inserts *chars_len* characters of the character array *chars* so that the new characters start with index *idx*.
- Returns *this.
- Note that *chars* must have at least *chars_len* characters. The characters may have arbitrary values. Thus, '\0' has no special meaning.
- Throws out_of_range if *idx* > size().
- Throws length_error if the resulting size exceeds the maximum number of characters.

string& string::insert (size_type *idx*, size_type *num*, *char c*)
iterator *string::insert* (const_iterator *pos*, size_type *num*, *char c*)

- Insert *num* occurrences of character *c* at the position specified by *idx* or *pos*, respectively.
- The first form inserts the new characters so that they start with index *idx*.
- The second form inserts the new characters before the character to which iterator *pos* refers.
- The first form returns *this.
- The second form returns the position of the first character inserted or *pos* if none was inserted.
- Note that the overloading of these two functions results in a possible ambiguity. If you pass 0 as the first argument, it can be interpreted as an index, which is typically a conversion to unsigned, or as an iterator, which is often a conversion to char*. In this case, you should pass an index with its the exact type. For example:
  ```
  std::string s;
  ...
  s.insert(0,1,' ');                      // ERROR: ambiguous
  s.insert((std::string::size_type)0,1,' ');  // OK
  ```
- Both forms throw out_of_range if *idx* > size().
- Both forms throw length_error if the resulting size exceeds the maximum number of characters.
- Before C++11, *pos* had type iterator, and the return type of the second form was void.

iterator *string::insert* (const_iterator *pos*, *char c*)

- Inserts a copy of character *c* before the character to which iterator *pos* refers.
- Returns the position of the character inserted.
- Throws length_error if the resulting size exceeds the maximum number of characters.
- Before C++11, *pos* had type iterator.

iterator *string*::**insert** (const_iterator *pos*,
InputIterator *beg*, InputIterator *end*)

- Inserts all characters of the range [*beg,end*) before the character to which iterator *pos* refers.
- Returns the position of the first character inserted or *pos* if none was inserted.
- Throws length_error if the resulting size exceeds the maximum number of characters.
- Before C++11, *pos* had type iterator, and the return type was void.

iterator *string*::**insert** (const_iterator *pos*, *initializer-list*)

- Inserts all characters of *initializer-list* before the character to which iterator *pos* refers.
- Returns the position of the first character inserted or *pos* if none was inserted.
- Throws length_error if the resulting size exceeds the maximum number of characters.

Erasing Characters

void *string*::**clear** ()
string& *string*::**erase** ()

- Both functions delete all characters of the string. Thus, the string is empty after the call.
- erase() returns *this.

string& *string*::**erase** (size_type *idx*)
string& *string*::**erase** (size_type *idx*, size_type *len*)

- Both forms erase at most *len* characters of *this, starting at index *idx*.
- They return *this.
- If *len* is missing, all remaining characters are removed.
- Both forms throw out_of_range if *idx* > size().

iterator *string*::**erase** (const_iterator *pos*)
iterator *string*::**erase** (const_iterator *beg*, const_iterator *end*)

- Both forms erase the single character at iterator position *pos* or all characters of the range [*beg,end*), respectively.
- They return the position of the first character after the last removed character (thus, the second form returns *end*).
- Before C++11, *pos*, *beg*, and *end* had type iterator.

void *string*::**pop_back** ()

- Erases the last character.
- Calling this for an empty string results in undefined behavior.
- Available since C++11.

Changing the Size

void *string*::**resize** (size_type *num*)

void *string*::**resize** (size_type *num*, *char c*)

- Both forms change the number of characters of *this to *num*. Thus, if *num* is not equal to size(), they append or remove characters at the end according to the new size.
- If the number of characters increases, the new characters are initialized by *c*. If *c* is missing, the characters are initialized by the default constructor of the character type (for string: '\0').
- Both forms throw length_error if *num* is equal to *string*::npos.
- Both forms throw length_error if the resulting size exceeds the maximum number of characters.

Replacing Characters

string& *string*::**replace** (size_type *idx*, size_type *len*, const *string*& *str*)

string& *string*::**replace** (begin_iterator *beg*, begin_iterator *end*,
                const *string*& *str*)

- The first form replaces at most *len* characters of *this, starting with index *idx*, with all characters of *str*.
- The second form replaces all characters of the range [*beg*,*end*) with all characters of *str*.
- Both forms return *this.
- Both forms throw out_of_range if *idx* > size().
- Both forms throw length_error if the resulting size exceeds the maximum number of characters.
- Before C++11, *beg* and *end* had type iterator.

string& *string*::**replace** (size_type *idx*, size_type *len*,
                const *string*& *str*, size_type *str_idx*, size_type *str_num*)

- Replaces at most *len* characters of *this, starting with index *idx*, with at most *str_num* characters of *str*, starting with index *str_idx*.
- Returns *this.
- Throws out_of_range if *idx* > size().
- Throws out_of_range if *str_idx* > *str*.size().
- Throws length_error if the resulting size exceeds the maximum number of characters.

string& *string*::**replace** (size_type *idx*, size_type *len*, const *char** *cstr*)

string& *string*::**replace** (const_iterator *beg*, const_iterator *end*,
                const *char** *cstr*)

- Both forms replace at most *len* characters of *this, starting with index *idx*, or all characters of the range [*beg*,*end*), respectively, with all characters of the C-string *cstr*.

- Both forms return *this.
- Note that passing a null pointer (nullptr or NULL) results in undefined behavior.
- Both forms throw out_of_range if *idx* > size().
- Both forms throw length_error if the resulting size exceeds the maximum number of characters.
- Before C++11, *beg* and *end* had type iterator.

string& **string**::**replace** (size_type *idx*, size_type *len*,
        const *char** *chars*, size_type *chars_len*)

string& **string**::**replace** (const_iterator *beg*, const_iterator *end*,
        const *char** *chars*, size_type *chars_len*)

- Both forms replace at most *len* characters of *this, starting with index *idx*, or all characters of the range [*beg*,*end*), respectively, with *chars_len* characters of the character array *chars*.
- They return *this.
- Note that *chars* must have at least *chars_len* characters. The characters may have arbitrary values. Thus, '\0' has no special meaning.
- Both forms throw out_of_range if *idx* > size().
- Both forms throw length_error if the resulting size exceeds the maximum number of characters.
- Before C++11, *beg* and *end* had type iterator.

string& **string**::**replace** (size_type *idx*, size_type *len*, size_type *num*, *char c*)

string& **string**::**replace** (const_iterator *beg*, const_iterator *end*,
        size_type *num*, *char c*)

- Both forms replace at most *len* characters of *this, starting with index *idx*, or all characters of the range [*beg*,*end*), respectively, with *num* occurrences of character *c*.
- They return *this.
- Both forms throw out_of_range if *idx* > size().
- Both forms throw length_error if the resulting size exceeds the maximum number of characters.
- Before C++11, *beg* and *end* had type iterator.

string& **string**::**replace** (const_iterator *beg*, const_iterator *end*,
        InputIterator *newBeg*, InputIterator *newEnd*)

- Replaces all characters of the range [*beg*,*end*) with all characters of the range [*newBeg*,*newEnd*).
- Returns *this.
- Throws length_error if the resulting size exceeds the maximum number of characters.
- Before C++11, *beg* and *end* had type iterator.

string& *string*::**replace** (const_iterator *beg*, const_iterator *end*,
                     initializer-list)

- Replaces all characters of the range [*beg,end*) with all characters of the *initializer-list*.
- Returns *this.
- Throws length_error if the resulting size exceeds the maximum number of characters.
- Available since C++11.

13.3.8   Searching and Finding

Find a Character

size_type *string*::**find** (*char c*) const

size_type *string*::**find** (*char c*, size_type *idx*) const

size_type *string*::**rfind** (*char c*) const

size_type *string*::**rfind** (*char c*, size_type *idx*) const

- These functions search for the first/last character *c* (starting at index *idx*).
- The find() functions search forward and return the first substring.
- The rfind() functions search backward and return the last substring.
- These functions return the index of the character when successful or *string*::npos if they fail.

Find a Substring

size_type *string*::**find** (const *string&* *str*) const

size_type *string*::**find** (const *string&* *str*, size_type *idx*) const

size_type *string*::**rfind** (const *string&* *str*) const

size_type *string*::**rfind** (const *string&* *str*, size_type *idx*) const

- These functions search for the first/last substring *str* (starting at index *idx*).
- The find() functions search forward and return the first substring.
- The rfind() functions search backward and return the last substring.
- These functions return the index of the first character of the substring when successful or *string*::npos if they fail.

size_type *string*::**find** (const *char** *cstr*) const

size_type *string*::**find** (const *char** *cstr*, size_type *idx*) const

size_type *string*::**rfind** (const *char** *cstr*) const

size_type *string*::**rfind** (const *char** *cstr*, size_type *idx*) const

- These functions search for the first/last substring that is equal to the characters of the C-string *cstr* (starting at index *idx*).

- The `find()` functions search forward and return the first substring.
- The `rfind()` functions search backward and return the last substring.
- These functions return the index of the first character of the substring when successful or *string*::npos if they fail.
- Note that passing a null pointer (`nullptr` or `NULL`) results in undefined behavior.

```
size_type string::find (const char* chars, size_type idx,
                        size_type chars_len) const
size_type string::rfind (const char* chars, size_type idx,
                         size_type chars_len) const
```

- These functions search for the first/last substring that is equal to *chars_len* characters of the character array *chars*, starting at index *idx*.
- `find()` searches forward and returns the first substring.
- `rfind()` searches backward and returns the last substring.
- These functions return the index of the first character of the substring when successful or *string*::npos if they fail.
- Note that *chars* must have at least *chars_len* characters. The characters may have arbitrary values. Thus, '\0' has no special meaning.

Find First of Different Characters

```
size_type string::find_first_of (const string& str) const
size_type string::find_first_of (const string& str, size_type idx) const
size_type string::find_first_not_of (const string& str) const
size_type string::find_first_not_of (const string& str, size_type idx) const
```

- These functions search for the first character that is or is not also an element of the string *str* (starting at index *idx*).
- These functions return the index of that character or substring when successful or *string*::npos if they fail.

```
size_type string::find_first_of (const char* cstr) const
size_type string::find_first_of (const char* cstr, size_type idx) const
size_type string::find_first_not_of (const char* cstr) const
size_type string::find_first_not_of (const char* cstr, size_type idx) const
```

- These functions search for the first character that is or is not also an element of the C-string *cstr* (starting at index *idx*).
- These functions return the index of that character when successful or *string*::npos if they fail.
- Note that passing a null pointer (`nullptr` or `NULL`) results in undefined behavior.

`size_type` *string*::**find_first_of** (const *char** *chars*, `size_type` *idx*,
                                    `size_type` *chars_len*) const

`size_type` *string*::**find_first_not_of** (const *char** *chars*, `size_type` *idx*,
                                    `size_type` *chars_len*) const

- These functions search for the first character that is or is not also an element of the *chars_len* characters of the character array *chars*, starting at index *idx*.
- These functions return the index of that character when successful or *string*::`npos` if they fail.
- Note that *chars* must have at least *chars_len* characters. The characters may have arbitrary values. Thus, '`\0`' has no special meaning.

`size_type` *string*::**find_first_of** (*char c*) const

`size_type` *string*::**find_first_of** (*char c*, `size_type` *idx*) const

`size_type` *string*::**find_first_not_of** (*char c*) const

`size_type` *string*::**find_first_not_of** (*char c*, `size_type` *idx*) const

- These functions search for the first character that has or does not have the value *c* (starting at index *idx*).
- These functions return the index of that character when successful or *string*::`npos` if they fail.

Find Last of Different Characters

`size_type` *string*::**find_last_of** (const *string&* *str*) const

`size_type` *string*::**find_last_of** (const *string&* *str*, `size_type` *idx*) const

`size_type` *string*::**find_last_not_of** (const *string&* *str*) const

`size_type` *string*::**find_last_not_of** (const *string&* *str*, `size_type` *idx*) const

- These functions search for the last character that is or is not also an element of the string *str* (starting at index *idx*).
- These functions return the index of that character or substring when successful or *string*::`npos` if they fail.

`size_type` *string*::**find_last_of** (const *char** *cstr*) const

`size_type` *string*::**find_last_of** (const *char** *cstr*, `size_type` *idx*) const

`size_type` *string*::**find_last_not_of** (const *char** *cstr*) const

`size_type` *string*::**find_last_not_of** (const *char** *cstr*, `size_type` *idx*) const

- These functions search for the last character that is or is not also an element of the C-string *cstr* (starting at index *idx*).
- These functions return the index of that character when successful or *string*::`npos` if they fail.
- Note that passing a null pointer (`nullptr` or `NULL`) results in undefined behavior.

size_type *string*::**find_last_of** (const *char* chars*, size_type *idx*,
                                    size_type *chars_len*) const

size_type *string*::**find_last_not_of** (const *char* chars*, size_type *idx*,
                                        size_type *chars_len*) const

- These functions search for the last character that is or is not also an element of the *chars_len* characters of the character array *chars*, starting at index *idx*.
- These functions return the index of that character when successful or *string*::npos if they fail.
- Note that *chars* must have at least *chars_len* characters. The characters may have arbitrary values. Thus, '\0' has no special meaning.

size_type *string*::**find_last_of** (*char c*) const

size_type *string*::**find_last_of** (*char c*, size_type *idx*) const

size_type *string*::**find_last_not_of** (*char c*) const

size_type *string*::**find_last_not_of** (*char c*, size_type *idx*) const

- These functions search for the last character that has or does not have the value *c* (starting at index *idx*).
- These functions return the index of that character when successful or *string*::npos if they fail.

13.3.9   Substrings and String Concatenation

string *string*::**substr** () const

string *string*::**substr** (size_type *idx*) const

string *string*::**substr** (size_type *idx*, size_type *len*) const

- All forms return a substring of at most *len* characters of the string *this (starting with index *idx*).
- If *len* is missing, all remaining characters are used.
- If *idx* and *len* are missing, a copy of the string is returned.
- All forms throw out_of_range if *idx* > size().

string **operator +** (const *string& str1*, const *string& str2*)

string **operator +** (*string&& str1*, *string&& str2*)

string **operator +** (*string&& str1*, const *string& str2*)

string **operator +** (const *string& str1*, *string&& str2*)

string **operator +** (const *string& str*, const *char* cstr*)

string **operator +** (*string&& str*, const *char* cstr*)

string **operator +** (const *char* cstr*, const *string& str*)

string **operator +** (const *char* cstr*, *string&& str*)

string **operator +** (const *string& str*, *char c*)

string **operator +** (*string&& str*, *char c*)

string **operator +** (*char c*, const *string& str*)

string **operator +** (*char c*, *string&& str*)

- All forms concatenate all characters of both operands and return the sum string.
- Whenever an argument is an rvalue reference, the move semantics are used, which means that the argument has an undefined value afterward.
- The operands may be any of the following:
  - A string
  - A C-string
  - A single character
- All forms throw `length_error` if the resulting size exceeds the maximum number of characters.

13.3.10   Input/Output Functions

ostream& **operator <<** (*ostream&& strm*, const *string& str*)

- Writes the characters of *str* to the stream *strm*.
- If *strm*.`width()` is greater than 0, at least `width()` characters are written, and `width()` is set to 0.
- *ostream* is the ostream type `basic_ostream<char>` according to the character type (see Section 15.2.1, page 748).
- Before C++11, the stream type was an lvalue reference.

istream& **operator >>** (*istream&& strm*, *string& str*)

- Reads the characters of the next word from *strm* into the string *str*.
- If the `skipws` flag is set for *strm*, leading whitespaces are ignored.
- Characters are extracted until any of the following happens:
  - *strm*.`width()` is greater than 0 and `width()` characters are stored
  - *strm*.`good()` is `false` (which might cause an appropriate exception)
  - `isspace`(*c*, *strm*.`getloc()`) is `true` for the next character *c*
  - *str*.`max_size()` characters are stored
- The internal memory is reallocated accordingly.
- *istream* is the istream type `basic_istream<char>` according to the character type (see Section 15.2.1, page 748).
- Before C++11, the stream type was an lvalue reference.

istream& **getline** (*istream& strm, string& str*)

istream& **getline** (*istream&& strm, string& str*)

istream& **getline** (*istream& strm, string& str, char delim*)

istream& **getline** (*istream&& strm, string& str, char delim*)

- Read the characters of the next line from *strm* into the string *str*.
- All characters, including leading whitespaces, are extracted until any of the following happens:
  - *strm*.good() is false (which might cause an appropriate exception)
  - *delim* or *strm*.widen('\n') is extracted
  - *str*.max_size() characters are stored
- The line delimiter is extracted but not appended.
- The internal memory is reallocated accordingly.
- *istream* is the istream type basic_istream<*char*> according to the character type (see Section 15.2.1, page 748).
- The overloads for rvalue references are available since C++11.

13.3.11 Numeric Conversions

int **stoi** (const *string& str*, size_t* *idxRet* = nullptr, int *base* = 10)

int **stol** (const *string& str*, size_t* *idxRet* = nullptr, int *base* = 10)

int **stoul** (const *string& str*, size_t* *idxRet* = nullptr, int *base* = 10)

int **stoll** (const *string& str*, size_t* *idxRet* = nullptr, int *base* = 10)

int **stoull** (const *string& str*, size_t* *idxRet* = nullptr, int *base* = 10)

int **stof** (const *string& str*, size_t* *idxRet* = nullptr, int *base* = 10)

int **stod** (const *string& str*, size_t* *idxRet* = nullptr, int *base* = 10)

int **stold** (const *string& str*, size_t* *idxRet* = nullptr, int *base* = 10)

- Convert *str* to the corresponding return type.
- *str* might be a string of type string or wstring.
- Skip leading whitespace.
- If *idxRet*!=nullptr, it returns the index of the first character not processed for the conversion.
- base allows you to specify a base number.
- Might throw std::invalid_argument if no conversion is possible and std::out_of_range if the converted value is outside the range of representable values for the return type.

string **to_string** (*Type val*)

wstring **to_wstring** (*Type val*)

- Converts *val* to a string or wstring.
- Valid types for *val* are int, unsigned int, long, unsigned long, long long, unsigned long long, float, double, or long double.

13.3.12   Generating Iterators

iterator *string*::**begin** ()

const_iterator *string*::**begin** () const

const_iterator *string*::**cbegin** ()

- All forms return a random-access iterator for the beginning of the string (the position of the first character).
- If the string is empty, the call is equivalent to end() or cend().

iterator *string*::**end** ()

const_iterator *string*::**end** () const

const_iterator *string*::**cend** ()

- All forms return a random-access iterator for the end of the string (the position after the last character).
- Note that the character at the end is not defined. Thus, $*s$.end() and $*s$.cend() result in undefined behavior.
- If the string is empty, the call is equivalent to begin() or cbegin().

reverse_iterator *string*::**rbegin** ()

const_reverse_iterator *string*::**rbegin** () const

const_reverse_iterator *string*::**crbegin** ()

- All forms return a random-access iterator for the beginning of a reverse iteration over the string (the position of the last character).
- If the string is empty, the call is equivalent to rend() or crend().
- For details about reverse iterators, see Section 9.4.1, page 448.

reverse_iterator *string*::**rend** ()

const_reverse_iterator *string*::**rend** () const

const_reverse_iterator *string*::**crend** ()

- All forms return a random-access iterator for the end of the reverse iteration over the string (the position before the first character).
- Note that the character at the reverse end is not defined. Thus, $*s$.rend() and $*s$.crend() result in undefined behavior.
- If the string is empty, the call is equivalent to rbegin() or crbegin().
- For details about reverse iterators, see Section 9.4.1, page 448.

13.3.13   Allocator Support

Strings provide the usual members of classes with allocator support.

string : :**allocator_type**
- The type of the allocator.
- Third template parameter of class `basic_string<>`.
- For type `string`, it is equivalent to `allocator<char>`.

`allocator_type` ***string*** : :**get_allocator** `() const`
- Returns the memory model of the string.

Strings also provide all constructors with optional allocator arguments. The following are all the string constructors, including their optional allocator arguments, according to the standard:[11]

```
namespace std {
    template <typename charT,
              typename traits = char_traits<charT>,
              typename Allocator = allocator<charT> >
    class basic_string {
      public:
        // default constructor
        explicit basic_string(const Allocator& a = Allocator());

        // copy and move constructor (with allocator)
        basic_string(const basic_string& str);
        basic_string(basic_string&& str);
        basic_string(const basic_string& str, const Allocator&);
        basic_string(basic_string&& str, const Allocator&);

        // constructor for substrings
        basic_string(const basic_string& str,
                     size_type str_idx = 0,
                     size_type str_num = npos,
                     const Allocator& a = Allocator());

        // constructor for C-strings
        basic_string(const charT* cstr,
                     const Allocator& a = Allocator());
```

---

[11] The copy constructor with allocator, the move constructors, and the constructor for initializer list are available since C++11.

```
// constructor for character arrays
basic_string(const charT* chars, size_type chars_len,
             const Allocator& a = Allocator());

// constructor for num occurrences of a character
basic_string(size_type num, charT c,
             const Allocator& a = Allocator());

// constructor for a range of characters
template <typename InputIterator>
basic_string(InputIterator beg, InputIterator end,
             const Allocator& a = Allocator());

// constructor for an initializer list
basic_string(initializer_list<charT>,
             const Allocator& a = Allocator());
...
};
}
```

These constructors behave as described in Section 13.3.2, page 694, with the additional ability that you can pass your own memory model object. If the string is initialized by another string, the allocator also gets copied.[12] See Chapter 19 for more details about allocators.

---

[12] The original standard states that the default allocator is used when a string gets copied. However, this does not make much sense, so this is the proposed resolution to fix this behavior.

Chapter 14

Regular Expressions

This chapter introduces the library for regular expressions. That library allows you to use wildcards and patterns to search and replace characters in strings.

In principle, you can do the following with regular expressions:

- **Match** the whole input against a regular expression
- **Search** for patterns that match a regular expression
- **Tokenize** a character according to a token separator specified as a regular expression
- **Replace** in the first or all subsequences that match a regular expression

For all these operations, you can use different grammars, which are used to define a regular expression.

I begin this chapter by introducing the various operations, then discussing different grammars, and finally listing the regex operations in detail.

14.1 The Regex Match and Search Interface

First, let's look at how we can check whether a sequence of characters matches or partially matches a specific regular expression:

```
// regex/regex1.cpp

#include <regex>
#include <iostream>
using namespace std;

void out (bool b)
{
    cout << ( b ? "found" : "not found") << endl;
}
```

```cpp
int main()
{
    // find XML/HTML-tagged value (using default syntax):
    regex reg1("<.*>.*</.*>");
    bool found = regex_match ("<tag>value</tag>",        // data
                              reg1);                     // regular expression
    out(found);

    // find XML/HTML-tagged value (tags before and after the value must match):
    regex reg2("<(.*)>.*</\\1>");
    found = regex_match ("<tag>value</tag>",             // data
                         reg2);                          // regular expression
    out(found);

    // find XML/HTML-tagged value (using grep syntax):
    regex reg3("<\\(.*\\)>.*</\\1>",regex_constants::grep);
    found = regex_match ("<tag>value</tag>",             // data
                         reg3);                          // regular expression
    out(found);

    // use C-string as regular expression (needs explicit cast to regex):
    found = regex_match ("<tag>value</tag>",             // data
                         regex("<(.*)>.*</\\1>"));       // regular expression
    out(found);
    cout << endl;

    // regex_match() versus regex_search():
    found = regex_match ("XML tag: <tag>value</tag>",
                         regex("<(.*)>.*</\\1>"));                   // fails to match
    out(found);
    found = regex_match ("XML tag: <tag>value</tag>",
                         regex(".*<(.*)>.*</\\1>.*"));               // matches
    out(found);
    found = regex_search ("XML tag: <tag>value</tag>",
                          regex("<(.*)>.*</\\1>"));                  // matches
    out(found);
    found = regex_search ("XML tag: <tag>value</tag>",
                          regex(".*<(.*)>.*</\\1>.*"));              // matches
    out(found);
}
```

First, we include the necessary header file and global identifiers in namespace std:

```cpp
#include <regex>
using namespace std;
```

Next, a first example demonstrates how a regular expression can be defined and used to check whether a character sequence matches a specific pattern. We declare and initialize `reg1` as a regular expression:

```
regex reg1("<.*>.*</.*>");
```

The type of the object representing the regular expression is `std::regex`. As with strings, this is a specialization of class `std::basic_regex<>` for the character type `char`. For the character type `wchar_t`, class `std::wregex` is provided.

`reg1` is initialized by the following regular expression:

```
<.*>.*</.*>
```

This regular expressions checks for "*<someChars>someChars</someChars>*" by using the syntax `.*`, where "`.`" stands for "any character except newline" and "`*`" stands for "zero or more times." Thus, we try to match the format of a tagged XML or HTML value. The character sequence `<tag>value</tag>` matches this pattern, so

```
regex_match ("<tag>value</tag>",     // data
             reg1);                   // regular expression
```

yields `true`.

We can even specify that the leading and the trailing tags have to be the same character sequence, which is what the next statements demonstrate:

```
regex reg2("<(.*)>.*</\\1>");
found = regex_match ("<tag>value</tag>",     // data
                     reg2);                   // regular expression
```

Again, `regex_match()` yields `true`.

Here, we use the concept of "grouping." We use "`(...)`" to define a so-called *capture group*, to which we refer later on with the regular expression "`\1`". Note, however, that we specify the regular expression as an ordinary character sequence, so we have to specify the "character \ followed by the character 1" as "`\\1`". Alternatively, we could use a *raw string*, which was introduced with C++11 (see Section 3.1.6, page 23):

```
R"(<(.*)>.*</\1>)"    // equivalent to: "<(.*)>.*</\\1>"
```

Such a raw string allows you to define a character sequence by writing exactly its contents as a raw character sequence. It starts with "`R"(`" and ends with "`)"`". To be able to have "`)"`" inside the raw string, you can use a delimiter. Thus, the complete syntax of raw strings is `R"delim(...)delim"`, where *delim* is a character sequence of at most 16 basic characters except the backslash, whitespaces, and parentheses.

What we introduce here as special characters for regular expressions is part of the grammar they have. Note that the C++ standard library supports various grammars. The default grammar is a "modified ECMAScript grammar," which is introduced in detail in Section 14.8, page 738. But the next statements show how a different grammar can be used:

```
regex reg3("<\\(.*\\)>.*</\\1>",regex_constants::grep);
found = regex_match ("<tag>value</tag>",     // data
                     reg3);                   // regular expression
```

Here, the optional second argument to the regex constructor `regex_constants::grep` specifies a grammar like the UNIX grep command, where, for example, you have to mask the grouping characters by additional backslashes (which have to be masked by backslashes in ordinary string literals). Section 14.9, page 739, discusses the differences of the various grammars supported.

All the previous examples used a separate object to specify the regular expression. This is not necessary; however, note that just passing a string or string literal as a regular expression is not enough. Although an implicit type conversion is declared, the resulting statement won't compile, because it is ambiguous. For example:

```
regex_match ("<tag>value</tag>",              // ERROR: ambiguous
             "<(.*)>.*</\\1>")
regex_match (string("<tag>value</tag>"),       // ERROR: ambiguous
             "<(.*)>.*</\\1>")
regex_match ("<tag>value</tag>",              // OK
             regex("<(.*)>.*</\\1>"))
```

Finally, we come to the difference of `regex_match()` and `regex_search`:

- `regex_match()` checks whether the *whole* character sequence matches a regular expression.
- `regex_search()` checks whether the character sequence *partially* matches a regular expression.

There is no other difference. Thus,

```
regex_search (data, regex(pattern))
```

is always equivalent to

```
regex_match (data, regex("(.|\n)*"+pattern+"(.|\n)*"))
```

where "`(.|\n)*`" stands for any number of any character ("`.`" stands for any character except the newline character and "`|`" stands for "or").

Now, you might say that these statements miss important information, at least for the function `regex_search()`: *where* a regular expression matches a given character sequence. For this and many more features, we have to introduce new versions of `regex_match()` and `regex_search()`, where a new parameter returns all necessary information about a match.

14.2   Dealing with Subexpressions

Consider the following example:

```
// regex/regex2.cpp

#include <string>
#include <regex>
#include <iostream>
#include <iomanip>
using namespace std;
```

```
int main()
{
    string data = "XML tag: <tag-name>the value</tag-name>.";
    cout << "data:              " << data << "\n\n";

    smatch m;    // for returned details of the match
    bool found = regex_search (data,
                               m,
                               regex("<(.*)>(.*)</(\\1)>"));

    // print match details:
    cout << "m.empty():         " << boolalpha << m.empty() << endl;
    cout << "m.size():          " << m.size() << endl;
    if (found) {
        cout << "m.str():          " << m.str() << endl;
        cout << "m.length():       " << m.length() << endl;
        cout << "m.position():     " << m.position() << endl;
        cout << "m.prefix().str(): " << m.prefix().str() << endl;
        cout << "m.suffix().str(): " << m.suffix().str() << endl;
        cout << endl;

        // iterating over all matches (using the match index):
        for (int i=0; i<m.size(); ++i) {
            cout << "m[" << i << "].str():      " << m[i].str() << endl;
            cout << "m.str(" << i << "):        " << m.str(i) << endl;
            cout << "m.position(" << i << "):   " << m.position(i)
                 << endl;
        }
        cout << endl;

        // iterating over all matches (using iterators):
        cout << "matches:" << endl;
        for (auto pos = m.begin(); pos != m.end(); ++pos) {
            cout << " " << *pos << " ";
            cout << "(length: " << pos->length() << ")" << endl;
        }
    }
}
```

In this example, we can demonstrate the use of `match_results` objects, which can be passed to `regex_match()` and `regex_search()` to get details of matches. Class `std::match_results<>` is a template that has to get instantiated by the iterator type of the characters processed. The C++ standard library provides some predefined instantiations:

- `smatch`: for details of matches in `strings`
- `cmatch`: for details of matches in C-strings (`const char*`)
- `wsmatch`: for details of matches in `wstrings`
- `wcmatch`: for details of matches in wide C-strings (`const wchar_t*`)

Thus, if we call `regex_match()` or `regex_search()` for C++ strings, type `smatch` has to be used; for ordinary string literals, type `cmatch` has to be used.

What a `match_results` object yields is shown in detail by the example, where we search for the regular expression

```
<(.*)>(.*)</(\1)>
```

in the string `data`, initialized by the following character sequence:

```
"XML tag: <tag-name>the value</tag-name>."
```

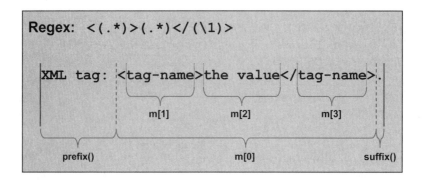

Figure 14.1. Regex Match Interface

After the call, the `match_results` object `m` has a state, which is visible in Figure 14.1 and provides the following interface:

- In general, the `match_results` object contains:
  - A `sub_match` object `m[0]` for all the matched characters
  - A `prefix()`, a `sub_match` object that represents all characters before the first matched character
  - A `suffix()`, a `sub_match` object that represents all characters after the last matched character
- In addition, for any capture group, you have access to a corresponding `sub_match` object `m[n]`. Because the regex specified here defines three capture groups, one for the introducing tag, one for the value, and one for the ending tag, these are available in `m[1]`, `m[2]`, and `m[3]`.
- `size()` yields the number of `sub_match` objects (including `m[0]`).
- All `sub_match` objects are derived from `pair<>` and have the position of the first character as member `first` and the position after the last character as member `second`. In addition, `str()` yields the characters as a string, `length()` yields the number of characters, operator `<<` writes the characters to a stream, and an implicit type conversion to a string is defined.

- In addition, the `match_results` object as a whole provides:
  - member function `str()` to yield the matched string as a whole (calling `str()` or `str(0)`) or the *n*th matched substring (calling `str(n)`), which is empty if no matched substring exists (thus, passing an *n* greater than `size()` is valid)
  - member function `length()` to yield the length of the matched string as a whole (calling `length()` or `length(0)`) or the length of the *n*th matched substring (calling `length(n)`), which is 0 if no matched substring exists (thus, passing an *n* greater than `size()` is valid)
  - member function `position()` to yield the position of the matched string as a whole (calling `position()` or `position(0)`) or the position of the *n*th matched substring (calling `length(n)`)
  - member functions `begin()`, `cbegin()`, `end()`, and `cend()` to iterate over the `sub_match` objects `m[0]` to `m[n]`

For this reason, the program has the following output:

```
data:              XML tag: <tag-name>the value</tag-name>.

m.empty():         false
m.size():          4
m.str():           <tag-name>the value</tag-name>
m.length():        30
m.position():      9
m.prefix().str():  XML tag:
m.suffix().str():  .

m[0].str():        <tag-name>the value</tag-name>
m.str(0):          <tag-name>the value</tag-name>
m.position(0):     9
m[1].str():        tag-name
m.str(1):          tag-name
m.position(1):     10
m[2].str():        the value
m.str(2):          the value
m.position(2):     19
m[3].str():        tag-name
m.str(3):          tag-name
m.position(3):     30

matches:
 <tag-name>the value</tag-name> (length: 30)
 tag-name (length: 8)
 the value (length: 9)
 tag-name (length: 8)
```

In other words, you have four ways to yield the whole matched string in a `match_result<>` m:

```
m.str()         // yields whole matches string
m.str(0)        // ditto
m[0].str()      // ditto
*(m.begin())    // ditto
```

and three ways to yield the *n*th matches substring, if any:

```
m.str(1)        // yields first matched substring, if any, or "" otherwise
m[1].str()      // ditto
*(m.begin()+1)  // yields first matched substring, if any, invalid otherwise
```

If you call `regex_match()` instead of `regex_search()`, the `match_results` interface is the same. However, because `regex_match()` always matches the whole character sequence, prefix and suffix will always be empty.

Now we have all the information we need to find *all* matches of a regular expression, as the following program demonstrates:

```
// regex/regex3.cpp

#include <string>
#include <regex>
#include <iostream>
using namespace std;

int main()
{
    string data = "<person>\n"
                  " <first>Nico</first>\n"
                  " <last>Josuttis</last>\n"
                  "</person>\n";

    regex reg("<(.*)>(.*)</(\\1)>");

    // iterate over all matches
    auto pos=data.cbegin();
    auto end=data.cend();
    smatch m;
    for ( ; regex_search(pos,end,m,reg); pos=m.suffix().first) {
        cout << "match:  " << m.str() << endl;
        cout << " tag:   " << m.str(1) << endl;
        cout << " value: " << m.str(2) << endl;
    }
}
```

Here, we use the regular expression (the backslash has to get escaped in the C++ string literal)

```
<(.*)>(.*)</(\1)>
```

to search for:

<anyNumberOfAnyChars1>anyNumberOfAnyChars2</anyNumberOfAnyChars1>

Thus, we search for XML tags (\1 means: *the same as the first matched substring*).

In this example, we use this regular expression by a different interface that iterates over matched character sequences. For this reason, instead of passing the character sequence as a whole, we pass a range of the corresponding elements. We start with the range of all characters, using cbegin() and cend() of the string we search in:

```
auto pos=data.cbegin();
auto end=data.cend();
```

Then, after each match, we continue the search with the beginning of the remaining characters:

```
smatch m;
for ( ; regex_search(pos,end,m,reg); pos=m.suffix().first) {
    ...
}
```

So, because the string data we parse has the following value:

```
<person>
 <first>Nico</first>
 <last>Josuttis</last>
</person>
```

the program has the following output:

```
match:  <first>Nico</first>
 tag:   first
 value: Nico
match:  <last>Josuttis</last>
 tag:   last
 value: Josuttis
```

To reinitialize pos, we could also pass m[0].second() (the end of the matched characters) instead of the expression m.suffix().first. Note that in both cases we have to use const_iterators. Thus, using begin() and end() to initialize pos and end would not compile here.

Note also that the output will be different if the tags in data were not separated by a newline character:

```
<person><first>Nico</first><last>Josuttis</last></person>
```

Then, the output would be:

```
match:  <person><first>Nico</first><last>Josuttis</last></person>
 tag:   person
 value: <first>Nico</first><last>Josuttis</last>
```

The reason is that regex functions try to operate in a *greedy* manner. That is, the longest match possible is returned. With newline characters, the tag opened with <person> could not match, because we were looking for ".*" as value, which means "any character except newline any times." Without newline characters, the whole tag opened with <person> now fulfills this pattern. To ensure that we still find the inner tags, we'd have to change the regular expression, for example, as follows:

```
"<(.*)>([^>]*)</(\\1)>"
```

For the value, we now look for "[^>]*", which means "all but character < any times." Therefore, subtags do not fit any longer as part of a value.

14.3   Regex Iterators

To iterate over all matches of a regular search, we can also use regex iterators. These iterators are of type regex_iterator<> and have the usual instantiations for strings and character sequences with prefixes s, c, ws, or wc. Consider the following example:

```
// regex/regexiter1.cpp

#include <string>
#include <regex>
#include <iostream>
#include <algorithm>
using namespace std;

int main()
{
    string data = "<person>\n"
                  " <first>Nico</first>\n"
                  " <last>Josuttis</last>\n"
                  "</person>\n";

    regex reg("<(.*)>(.*)</(\\1)>");

    // iterate over all matches (using a regex_iterator):
    sregex_iterator pos(data.cbegin(),data.cend(),reg);
    sregex_iterator end;
    for ( ; pos!=end ; ++pos ) {
        cout << "match:  " << pos->str() << endl;
        cout << " tag:   " << pos->str(1) << endl;
        cout << " value: " << pos->str(2) << endl;
    }

    // use a regex_iterator to process each matched substring as element in an algorithm:
    sregex_iterator beg(data.cbegin(),data.cend(),reg);
```

```
    for_each (beg,end,[](const smatch& m) {
                    cout << "match:  " << m.str() << endl;
                    cout << " tag:   " << m.str(1) << endl;
                    cout << " value: " << m.str(2) << endl;
                });
}
```

Here, with

```
sregex_iterator pos(data.cbegin(),data.cend(),reg);
```

we initialize a regex iterator, iterating over data to search for matches of reg. The default constructor of this type defines a past-the-end iterator:

```
sregex_iterator end;
```

We can now use this iterator as any other bidirectional iterator (see Section 9.2.4, page 437): Operator * yields the current match, while operators ++ and -- move to the next or previous match. Thus, the following prints all the matches, their tags, and their values (as in the previous example):

```
for ( ; pos!=end ; ++pos ) {
    cout << "match:  " << pos->str() << endl;
    cout << " tag:   " << pos->str(1) << endl;
    cout << " value: " << pos->str(2) << endl;
}
```

And, of course, you can use such an iterator in an algorithm. Thus, the following calls the lambda passed as third argument for each match (see Section 6.9, page 229, for details about lambdas and algorithms):

```
// use a regex_iterator to process each matched substring as element in an algorithm:
sregex_iterator beg(data.cbegin(),data.cend(),reg);
sregex_iterator end;
for_each (beg,end,[](const smatch& m) {
                    cout << "match:  " << m.str() << endl;
                    cout << " tag:   " << m.str(1) << endl;
                    cout << " value: " << m.str(2) << endl;
                });
```

14.4 Regex Token Iterators

A regex iterator helps to iterate over matched subsequences. However, sometimes you also want to process all the contents between matched expressions. That is especially the case if you want to split a string into separate tokens, separated by something, which might even be specified as a regular expression. Class regex_token_iterator<> having the usual instantiations for strings and character sequences with prefixes s, c, ws, or wc provides this functionality.

Again, to initialize it, you can pass the beginning and end of a character sequence and a regular expression. In addition, you can specify a list of integral values, which represent elements of a "tokenization":

- -1 means that you are interested in all the subsequences between matched regular expressions (token separators).
- 0 means that you are interested in all the matched regular expressions (token separators).
- Any other value *n* means that you are interested in the matched *n*th subexpression inside the regular expressions.

Now consider the following example:

```cpp
// regex/regextokeniter1.cpp

#include <string>
#include <regex>
#include <iostream>
#include <algorithm>
using namespace std;

int main()
{
    string data = "<person>\n"
                  " <first>Nico</first>\n"
                  " <last>Josuttis</last>\n"
                  "</person>\n";

    regex reg("<(.*)>(.*)</(\\1)>");

    // iterate over all matches (using a regex_token_iterator):
    sregex_token_iterator pos(data.cbegin(),data.cend(), // sequence
                              reg,                        // token separator
                              {0,2});        // 0: full match, 2: second substring
    sregex_token_iterator end;
    for ( ; pos!=end ; ++pos ) {
        cout << "match:  " << pos->str() << endl;
    }
    cout << endl;

    string names = "nico, jim, helmut, paul, tim, john paul, rita";
    regex sep("[ \t\n]*[,;.][ \t\n]*");  // separated by , ; or . and spaces
    sregex_token_iterator p(names.cbegin(),names.cend(), // sequence
                            sep,                          // separator
                            -1);        // -1: values between separators
    sregex_token_iterator e;
    for ( ; p!=e ; ++p ) {
```

```
                cout << "name:  " << *p << endl;
        }
    }
```

The program has the following output:

```
match:  <first>Nico</first>
match:  Nico
match:  <last>Josuttis</last>
match:  Josuttis

name:  nico
name:  jim
name:  helmut
name:  paul
name:  tim
name:  john paul
name:  rita
```

Here, a regex token iterator for `strings` (prefix s) is initialized by the character sequence *data*, the regular expression `reg`, and a list of two indexes (0 and 2):

```
sregex_token_iterator pos(data.cbegin(),data.cend(),  // sequence
                          reg,                         // token separator
                          {0,2});       // 0: full match, 2: second substring
```

The list of indexes we are interested in defines that we are interested in all matches and the second substring of each match.

The usual application of such a regex token iterator demonstrates the next iteration. Here, we have a list of names:

```
string names = "nico, jim, helmut, paul, tim, john paul, rita";
```

Now a regular expression defines what separates these names. Here, it is a comma or a semicolon or a period with optional whitespaces (spaces, tabs, and newlines) around:

```
regex sep("[ \t\n]*[,;.][ \t\n]*");   // separated by , ; or . and spaces
```

Alternatively, we could use the following regular expression (see Section 14.8, page 738):

```
regex sep("[[:space:]]*[,;.][[:space:]]*");   // separated by , ; or . and spaces
```

Because we are interested only in the values between these token separators, the program processes each name in this list (with spaces removed).

Note that the interface of `regex_token_iterator` allows you to specify the tokens of interest in various ways:

- You can pass a single integral value.
- You can pass an initializer list of integral values (see Section 3.1.3, page 15).
- You can pass a `vector` of integral values.
- You can pass an array of integral values.

14.5   Replacing Regular Expressions

Finally, let's look at the interface that allows you to replace character sequences that match a regular expression. Consider the following example:

```
// regex/regexreplace1.cpp

#include <string>
#include <regex>
#include <iostream>
#include <iterator>
using namespace std;

int main()
{
    string data = "<person>\n"
                  " <first>Nico</first>\n"
                  " <last>Josuttis</last>\n"
                  "</person>\n";

    regex reg("<(.*)>(.*)</(\\1)>");

    // print data with replacement for matched patterns
    cout << regex_replace (data,                        // data
                           reg,                         // regular expression
                           "<$1 value=\"$2\"/>")        // replacement
         << endl;

    // same using sed syntax
    cout << regex_replace (data,                        // data
                           reg,                         // regular expression
                           "<\\1 value=\"\\2\"/>",      // replacement
                           regex_constants::format_sed) // format flag
         << endl;

    // use iterator interface, and
    // - format_no_copy:    don't copy characters that don't match
    // - format_first_only: replace only the first match found
    string res2;
    regex_replace (back_inserter(res2),                 // destination
                   data.begin(), data.end(),            // source range
                   reg,                                 // regular expression
                   "<$1 value=\"$2\"/>",                // replacement
                   regex_constants::format_no_copy      // format flags
                    | regex_constants::format_first_only);
```

```
    cout << res2 << endl;
}
```

Here again, we use a regular expression to match XML/HTML-tagged values. But this time, we transform the input into the following output:

```
<person>
 <first value="Nico"/>
 <last value="Josuttis"/>
</person>

<person>
 <first value="Nico"/>
 <last value="Josuttis"/>
</person>

<first value="Nico"/>
```

To do this, we specify a replacement where we can use matched subexpressions with the character $ (see Table 14.1). Here, we use $1 and $2 to use the tag and the value found in the replacement:

```
"<$1 value=\"$2\"/>"      // replacement using default syntax
```

Again, we can avoid having to escape the quotes by using a raw string:

```
R"(<$1 value="$2"/>)"     // replacement using default syntax
```

By passing a regex constant `regex_constants::format_sed`, you can instead use the replacement syntax of the UNIX command sed (see the second column in Table 14.1):

```
"<\\1 value=\"\\2\"/>"        // replacement using sed syntax
```

Again, by using a raw string, we can avoid escaping backslashes:

```
R"(<\1 value="\2"/>)"         // replacement using sed syntax specified as raw string
```

Default Pattern	sed Pattern	Meaning
$&	&	The matched pattern
$*n*	*n*	The *n*th matched capture group
$'		The prefix of the matched pattern
$'		The suffix of the matched pattern
$$		The character $

Table 14.1. Regex Replacement Symbols

14.6   Regex Flags

We already introduced some regex constants you can use to influence the behavior of the regex interfaces:

```
regex reg3("<\\(.*\\)>.*</\\1>",regex_constants::grep);   // use grep grammar


regex_replace (data, reg,
               string("<\\1 value=\"\\2\"/>"),
               regex_constants::format_sed)     // use sed replacement syntax
```

But there is more. Table 14.2 lists all regex constants provided by the regex library and where they can be used. In principle, they can always be passed as the optional last argument to the regex constructor or to the regex functions.

Here is a small program that demonstrates the usage of some flags:

// regex/regex4.cpp

```cpp
#include <string>
#include <regex>
#include <iostream>
using namespace std;

int main()
{
    // case-insensitive find LaTeX index entries
    string pat1 = R"(\\.*index\{([^}]*)\})";        // first capture group
    string pat2 = R"(\\.*index\{(.*)\}\{(.*)\})";   // 2nd and 3rd capture group
    regex pat (pat1+"\n"+pat2,
               regex_constants::egrep|regex_constants::icase);

    // initialize string with characters from standard input:
    string data((istreambuf_iterator<char>(cin)),
                istreambuf_iterator<char>());

    // search and print matching index entries:
    smatch m;
    auto pos = data.cbegin();
    auto end = data.cend();
    for ( ; regex_search (pos,end,m,pat); pos=m.suffix().first) {
        cout << "match: " << m.str() << endl;
        cout << "  val: " << m.str(1)+m.str(2) << endl;
        cout << "  see: " << m.str(3) << endl;
    }
}
```

regex_constants	Meaning
Regex Grammar:	
ECMAScript	Use ECMAScript grammar (default).
basic	Use the basic regular expression (BRE) grammar of POSIX.
extended	Use the extended regular expression (ERE) grammar of POSIX.
awk	Use the grammar of the UNIX tool awk.
grep	Use the grammar of the UNIX tool grep.
egrep	Use the grammar of the UNIX tool egrep.
Other Creation Flags:	
icase	Ignore case-sensitivity.
nosubs	Don't store subsequences in match results.
optimize	Optimize for matching speed rather than for regex creation speed.
collate	Character ranges of the form [a-b] shall be locale sensitive.
Algorithm Flags:	
match_not_null	An empty sequence shall not match.
match_not_bol	The first character shall not match the *beginning-of-line* (pattern ^).
match_not_eol	The last character shall not match the *end-of-line* (pattern $).
match_not_bow	The first character shall not match the *beginning-of-word* (pattern \b).
match_not_eow	The last character shall not match the *end-of-word* (pattern \b).
match_continuous	The expression shall match only a subsequence that begins with the first character.
match_any	If more than one match is possible, any match is acceptable.
match_prev_avail	The positions before the first character is a valid positions (ignores match_not_bol and match_not_bow).
Replacement Flags:	
format_default	Use default (ECMAScript) replacement syntax.
format_sed	Use replacement syntax of the UNIX tool sed.
format_first_only	Replace the first match only.
format_no_copy	Don't copy characters that don't match.

Table 14.2. Regex Constants of Namespace std::regex_constants

The goal is to find LaTeX index entries that might have one or two arguments. In addition, the entries might use lowercase or uppercase mode. So, we have to search for either of the following:

- A backlash followed by some characters and index (lower- or uppercase) and then the index entry surrounded by braces for something like the following:

      \index{STL}%
      \MAININDEX{standard template library}%

- A backlash followed by some characters and index (lower- or uppercase), and then the index entry and a "see also" entry surrounded by braces for something like the following:

      \SEEINDEX{standard template library}{STL}%

Using the `egrep` grammar, we can put a newline character between these two regular expressions. (In fact, `grep` and `egrep` can search for multiple regular expressions at the same time, specified in separate lines.) However, we have to take *greediness* into account, which means that we have to ensure that the first regular expression does not also match the sequences that should match the second regular expression. So, instead of allowing any character inside the index entry, we have to ensure that no braces occur. As a result, we have the following regular expressions:

```
\\.*index\{([^}]*)\}
\\.*index\{(.*)\}\{(.*)\}
```

which can be specified as raw strings:

```
R"(\\.*index\{([^}]*)\})"
R"(\\.*index\{(.*)\}\{(.*)\})"
```

or as regular string literals:

```
"\\\\.*index\\{([^}]*)\\}"
"\\\\.*index\\{(.*)\\}\\{(.*)\\}"
```

We create the final regular expression by concatenating both expressions and passing the flags to use a grammar in which \n separates alternative patterns (see Section 14.9, page 739) and to ignore case sensitivity:

```
regex pat (pat1+"\n"+pat2,
           regex_constants::egrep|regex_constants::icase);
```

As input, we use all characters read from standard input. Here, we use a string `data`, which is initialized by begin and end of all characters read (see Section 7.1.2, page 256, and Section 15.13.2, page 830, for details):

```
string data((istreambuf_iterator<char>(cin)),
            istreambuf_iterator<char>());
```

Now note that the first regular expression has one capture group, whereas the second regular expression has two capture groups. Thus, if the first regex matches, we have the index value in the first subgroup. If the second regex matches, we have the index value in the second submatch and the "see also" value in the third submatch. For this reason, we output the contents of the first plus the contents of the second submatch (one has a value and the other is empty) as value found:

```
smatch m;
auto pos = data.begin();
auto end = data.end();
for ( ; regex_search (pos,end,m,pat); pos=m.suffix().first) {
    cout << "match: " << m.str() << endl;
    cout << "  val: " << m.str(1)+m.str(2) << endl;
    cout << "  see: " << m.str(3) << endl;
}
```

Note that calling `str(2)` and `str(3)` is valid even if no match exists. `str()` is guaranteed to yield an empty string in this case.

With the following input:

```
\chapter{The Standard Template Library}
\index{STL}%
\MAININDEX{standard template library}%
\SEEINDEX{standard template library}{STL}%
This is the basic chapter about the STL.
\section{STL Components}
\hauptindex{STL, introduction}%
The \stl{} is based on the cooperation of
...
```

the program has the following output:

```
match: \index{STL}
  val: STL
  see:
match: \MAININDEX{standard template library}
  val: standard template library
  see:
match: \SEEINDEX{standard template library}{STL}
  val: standard template library
  see: STL
match: \hauptindex{STL, introduction}
  val: STL, introduction
  see:
```

14.7 Regex Exceptions

When regular expressions are parsed, things can become very complicated. The C++ standard library provides a special exception class to deal with regular-expression exceptions. This class is derived from `std::runtime_error` (see Section 4.3.1, page 41) and provides an additional member `code()` to yield an error code. This might help to find out what's wrong if an exception is thrown when processing regular expressions.

Unfortunately, the error codes returned by `code()` are implementation specific, so it doesn't help to print them directly. Instead, you have to use something like the following header file to deal with regex exceptions in a reasonable way:

```
// regex/regexexception.hpp

#include <regex>
#include <string>

template <typename T>
std::string regexCode (T code)
{
```

```
switch (code) {
  case std::regex_constants::error_collate:
    return "error_collate: "
           "regex has invalid collating element name";
  case std::regex_constants::error_ctype:
    return "error_ctype: "
           "regex has invalid character class name";
  case std::regex_constants::error_escape:
    return "error_escape: "
           "regex has invalid escaped char. or trailing escape";
  case std::regex_constants::error_backref:
    return "error_backref: "
           "regex has invalid back reference";
  case std::regex_constants::error_brack:
    return "error_brack: "
           "regex has mismatched '[' and ']'";
  case std::regex_constants::error_paren:
    return "error_paren: "
           "regex has mismatched '(' and ')'";
  case std::regex_constants::error_brace:
    return "error_brace: "
           "regex has mismatched '{' and '}'";
  case std::regex_constants::error_badbrace:
    return "error_badbrace: "
           "regex has invalid range in {} expression";
  case std::regex_constants::error_range:
    return "error_range: "
           "regex has invalid character range, such as '[b-a]'";
  case std::regex_constants::error_space:
    return "error_space: "
           "insufficient memory to convert regex into finite state";
  case std::regex_constants::error_badrepeat:
    return "error_badrepeat: "
           "one of *?+{ not preceded by valid regex";
  case std::regex_constants::error_complexity:
    return "error_complexity: "
           "complexity of match against regex over pre-set level";
  case std::regex_constants::error_stack:
    return "error_stack: "
           "insufficient memory to determine regex match";
}
return "unknown/non-standard regex error code";
}
```

The detailed explanation written in parentheses after the name of the error code is taken directly from the specification of the C++ standard library. The following program demonstrates how to use it:

```
// regex/regex5.cpp

#include <regex>
#include <iostream>
#include "regexexception.hpp"
using namespace std;

int main()
{
  try {
    // initialize regular expression with invalid syntax:
    regex pat ("\\\\.*index\\{([^}]*)\\}",
               regex_constants::grep|regex_constants::icase);

    ...
  }
  catch (const regex_error& e) {
        cerr << "regex_error: \n"
             << " what(): " << e.what() << "\n"
             << " code(): " << regexCode(e.code()) << endl;
  }
}
```

Because we use the grep grammar here but do escape the characters { and }, the program might have an output such as the following:

```
regex_error:
 what(): regular expression error
 code(): error_badbrace: regex has invalid range in {} expression
```

14.8   The Regex ECMAScript Grammar

The default grammar of the regex library is a "modified ECMAScript" grammar (see [*ECMAScript*]), which is a much more powerful grammar than all the other grammars available. Table 14.3 lists the most important special expressions with their meanings.

Expression	Meaning
.	Any character except newline
[...]	One of the characters ... (may contain ranges)
[^...]	None of the characters ... (may contain ranges)
[[:*charclass*:]]	A character of the specified character class *charclass* (see Table 14.4)
\n, \t, \f, \r, \v	A newline, tabulator, form feed, carriage return, or vertical tab
\x*hh*, \u*hhhh*	A hexadecimal or Unicode character
\d, \D, \s, \S, \w, \W	A shortcut for a character of a character class (see Table 14.4)
*	The previous character or group any times
?	The previous character or group optional (none or one times)
+	The previous character or group at least one time
{*n*}	The previous character or group *n* times
{*n*,}	The previous character or group at least *n* times
{*n*,*m*}	The previous character or group at least *n* and at most *m* times
...|...	The pattern before or the pattern after |
(...)	Grouping
\1, \2, \3, ...	The *n*th group (first group has index 1)
\b	A positive word boundary (beginning or end of a word)
\B	A negative word boundary (no beginning or end of a word)
^	The beginning of a line (includes beginning of all characters)
$	The end of a line (includes end of all characters)

Table 14.3. Common Regex Expressions for the Default (ECMAScript) Grammar

Inside the bracket expressions, you can specify any combination of characters (including special characters), character ranges (for example, [0-9a-z]), and character classes (for example, [[:digit:]]). A leading ^ negates the whole expression, so the whole bracket expression means "any character except ...". Table 14.4 lists the possible character classes of regular expressions. Note that the basic classes correspond to the convenience functions for character classifications in Section 16.4.4, page 895. However, the one-letter shortcuts are supported only by regular expressions. The character class escape sequences are supported only by the ECMAScript grammar.

Here are some examples:

```
[_[:alpha:]][_[:alnum:]]*        // a C++ identifier
(.|\n)*                          // any number of any character (including newlines)
[123]?[0-9]\.1?[0-9]\.20[0-9]{2} // a date in the first century of 2000
                                 // (German format, for example 24.12.2010)
```

Character Class	Shortcut	Esc.	Effect
`[[:alnum:]]`			A letter or a digit (equivalent to `[[:alpha:][:digit:]]`)
`[[:alpha:]]`			A letter
`[[:blank:]]`			A space or a tab
`[[:cntrl:]]`			A control character
`[[:digit:]]`	`[[:d:]]`	`\d`	A digit
		`\D`	Not a digit (equivalent to `[^[:digit:]]`)
`[[:graph:]]`			A printable, nonspace character (equivalent to `[[:alnum:][:punct:]]`)
`[[:lower:]]`			A lowercase letter
`[[:print:]]`			A printable character (including whitespaces)
`[[:punct:]]`			A punctuation character (that is, it is printable but is not a space, digit, or letter)
`[[:space:]]`	`[[:s:]]`	`\s`	A space character
		`\S`	Not a space character (equivalent to `[^[:space:]]`)
`[[:upper:]]`			An uppercase letter
`[[:xdigit:]]`			A hexadecimal digit
	`[[:w:]]`	`\w`	A letter, digit, or underscore (equivalent to `[[:alpha:][:digit:]_]`)
		`\W`	Not a letter or a digit or an underscore (equivalent to `[^[:alpha:][:digit:]_]`)

Table 14.4. Character Classes and Corresponding Escape Sequences (ECMAScript)

14.9 Other Grammars

Beside the default ECMAScript grammar, the C++ standard library provides support for five other grammars, which you can specify by using the corresponding regex constants (see Section 14.6, page 732). So, you can choose from the following:

- `ECMAScript`: the default ECMAScript grammar
- `basic`: the basic regular expression (BRE) grammar of POSIX
- `extended`: the extended regular expression (ERE) grammar of POSIX
- `awk`: the grammar of the UNIX tool `awk`
- `grep`: the grammar of the UNIX tool `grep`
- `egrep`: the grammar of the UNIX tool `egrep`

Table 14.5 lists the major differences among those grammars. As you can see, the ECMAScript grammar is by far the most powerful one. The only feature it doesn't support is the use of newline characters to separate multiple patterns with "or," as `grep` and `egrep` provide, and the ability of `awk` to specify octal escape sequences.

Feature	ECMA-Script	basic	extended	awk	grep	egrep
Characters for grouping	( )	\(\)	( )	( )	\(\)	( )
Characters for repetitions	{ }	\{ \}	{ }	{ }	\{ \}	{ }
? means "zero or one"	Yes	-	Yes	Yes	-	Yes
+ means "at least one"	Yes	-	Yes	Yes	-	Yes
| means "or"	Yes	-	Yes	Yes	-	Yes
\n separates alternative patterns	-	-	-	-	Yes	Yes
\n refers to group n	Yes	Yes	-	-	Yes	-
Word boundaries (\b and \B)	Yes	-	-	-	-	-
Hex and Unicode escape sequ.	Yes	-	-	-	-	-
Character class escape sequences	Yes	-	-	-	-	-
\n, \t, \f, \r, \v	Yes	-	-	Yes	-	-
\a (alert) and \b (backspace)	-	-	-	Yes	-	-
\ooo for octal values	-	-	-	Yes	-	-

Table 14.5. Regex Grammar Differences

14.10   Basic Regex Signatures in Detail

Table 14.6 lists the signatures of the basic regex operations `regex_match()` (see Section 14.1, page 717), `regex_search()` (see Section 14.1, page 717), and `regex_replace()` (see Section 14.5, page 730). As you can see, there are always overloads to operate on strings, which can be both objects of class `basic_string<>` and ordinary C-strings, such as string literals, and iterators, which specify the begin and end of the character sequence to process. In addition, you can always pass format flags as an optional last argument.

Both `regex_match()` and `regex_search()` return `true` if a match was found. They also allow you to optionally pass an argument *matchRet* that returns details of the (sub)matches found. These arguments of type `std::match_results<>` (introduced in Section 14.2, page 721) must be instantiated for an iterator type that corresponds with the character type:

- For C++ strings, it is the corresponding `const` iterator. For types `string` and `wstring`, the corresponding types `smatch` and `wsmatch` are defined:

      typedef match_results<string::const_iterator> smatch;
      typedef match_results<wstring::const_iterator> wsmatch;

- For C-strings including string literals, it is the corresponding pointer type. For c-strings of `char` and `wchar_t` characters, the corresponding types `cmatch` and `wcmatch` are defined:

      typedef match_results<const char*>   cmatch;
      typedef match_results<const wchar_t*> wcmatch;

For `regex_replace()`, you have to pass the replacement specification *repl* as a string (again, it is overloaded for both objects of class `basic_string<>` and ordinary C-strings, such as string literals). The string version returns a new string with the corresponding replacements. The iterator

Signature	Effect
`bool regex_match(`*str*`,`*regex*`)`	Check full match of *regex*
`bool regex_match(`*str*`,`*regex*`,`*flags*`)`	
`bool regex_match(`*beg*`,`*end*`,`*regex*`)`	
`bool regex_match(`*beg*`,`*end*`,`*regex*`,`*flags*`)`	
`bool regex_match(`*str*`,`*matchRet*`,`*regex*`)`	Check and return full match
`bool regex_match(`*str*`,`*matchRet*`,`*regex*`,`*flags*`)`	of *regex*
`bool regex_match(`*beg*`,`*end*`,`*matchRet*`,`*regex*`)`	
`bool regex_match(`*beg*`,`*end*`,`*matchRet*`,`*regex*`,`*flags*`)`	
`bool regex_search(`*str*`,`*regex*`)`	Search match of *regex*
`bool regex_search(`*str*`,`*regex*`,`*flags*`)`	
`bool regex_search(`*beg*`,`*end*`,`*regex*`)`	
`bool regex_search(`*beg*`,`*end*`,`*regex*`,`*flags*`)`	
`bool regex_search(`*str*`,`*matchRet*`,`*regex*`)`	Search and return match
`bool regex_search(`*str*`,`*matchRet*`,`*regex*`,`*flags*`)`	of *regex*
`bool regex_search(`*beg*`,`*end*`,`*matchRet*`,`*regex*`)`	
`bool regex_search(`*beg*`,`*end*`,`*matchRet*`,`*regex*`,`*flags*`)`	
strRes `regex_replace(`*str*`,`*regex*`,`*repl*`)`	Replace match(es) according
strRes `regex_replace(`*str*`,`*regex*`,`*repl*`,`*flags*`)`	to *regex*
outPos `regex_replace(`*outPos*`,`*beg*`,`*end*`,`*regex*`,`*repl*`)`	
outPos `regex_replace(`*outPos*`,`*beg*`,`*end*`,`*regex*`,`*repl*`,`*flags*`)`	

Table 14.6. Regex Operation Signatures

version returns the first argument *outPos*, which has to be an output iterator specifying where the replacements are written to.

Finally, note that to avoid ambiguities no implicit type conversion from strings or string literals to type `regex` is provided. Thus, you always explicitly have to convert any string holding a regular expression to type `std::regex` (or `std::basic_regex<>`).

Chapter 15

Input/Output Using Stream Classes

The classes for I/O form an important part of the C++ standard library; a program without I/O is not of much use. The I/O classes from the C++ standard library are not restricted to files or to screen and keyboard but instead form an extensible framework for the formatting of arbitrary data and access to arbitrary "external representations."

The *IOStream library*, as the classes for I/O are called, is the only part of the C++ standard library that was widely used prior to the standardization of C++98. Early distributions of C++ systems came with a set of classes, developed at AT&T, that established a de facto standard for doing I/O. Although these classes have undergone several changes to fit consistently into the C++ standard library and to suit new needs, the basic principles of the IOStream library remain unchanged.

This chapter first presents a general overview of the most important components and techniques, and then demonstrates in detail how the IOStream library can be used in practice. Its use ranges from simple formatting to the integration of new external representations, a topic that is often addressed improperly.

This chapter does not attempt to discuss all aspects of the IOStream library in detail; to do that would take an entire book by itself. For details not found here, please consult one of the books that focus on the I/O stream library or the reference manual of the C++ standard library.

Many thanks to Dietmar Kühl, an expert on I/O and internationalization in the C++ standard library, who gave valuable feedback and wrote initial parts of this chapter.

Recent Changes with C++11

C++98 specified almost all features of the IOStream library. Here is a list of the most important features added with C++11:

- A few new manipulators were introduced: `hexfloat` and `defaultfloat` (see Section 15.7.6, page 788), as well as `get_time()` and `put_time()` (see Section 16.4.3, page 890) and `get_money()` and `put_money()` (see Section 16.4.2, page 882).
- In order to provide more information about an exception, the class for exceptions is now derived from `std::system_error` rather than directly from `std::exception` (see Section 15.4.4, page 762).

- String stream and file stream classes now support rvalue and move semantics, so you can move construct, move assign, and swap a string stream or a file stream. This also provides the ability to use temporary string or file streams for I/O. See Section 15.9.2, page 795, and Section 15.10.2, page 806,

- File streams now also allow you to pass a `std::string` for the filename rather than only a `const char*` (see Section 15.9.1, page 794).

- The output and input operators `<<` and `>>` are now also overloaded for `long long` and `unsigned long long`.

- I/O streams now partially support concurrency (see Section 15.2.2, page 752).

- Character traits are now also provided for types `char16_t` and `char32_t` (see Section 16.1.4, page 853).

- With the help of the new class `wbuffer_convert`, you can let streams read and write different character sets, such as UTF-8 (see Section 16.4.4, page 903).

15.1 Common Background of I/O Streams

Before going into details about stream classes, I briefly discuss the generally known aspects of streams to provide a common background. This section could be skipped by readers familiar with iostream basics.

15.1.1 Stream Objects

In C++, I/O is performed by using streams. A *stream* is a "*stream of data*" in which character sequences "*flow.*" Following the principles of object orientation, a stream is an object with properties that are defined by a class. *Output* is interpreted as data flowing into a stream; *input* is interpreted as data flowing out of a stream. Global objects are predefined for the standard I/O channels.

15.1.2 Stream Classes

Just as there are different kinds of I/O — for example, input, output, and file access — there are different classes depending on the type of I/O. The following are the most important stream classes:

- **Class `istream`** defines input streams that can be used to read data.
- **Class `ostream`** defines output streams that can be used to write data.

Both classes are instantiations of the class templates `basic_istream<>` or `basic_ostream<>`, respectively, using `char` as the character type. In fact, the whole IOStream library does not depend on a specific character type. Instead, the character type used is a template argument for most of the classes in the IOStream library. This parametrization corresponds to the string classes and is used for internationalization (see also Chapter 16).

This section concentrates on output to and input from "narrow streams": streams dealing with char as the character type. Later in this chapter, the discussion is extended to streams that have other character types.

15.1.3 Global Stream Objects

The IOStream library defines several global objects of type istream and ostream. These objects correspond to the standard I/O channels:

- **cin**, of class istream, is the standard input channel used for user input. This stream corresponds to C's stdin. Normally, this stream is connected to the keyboard by the operating system.
- **cout**, of class ostream, is the standard output channel used for program output. This stream corresponds to C's stdout. Normally, this stream is connected to the monitor by the operating system.
- **cerr**, of class ostream, is the standard error channel used for all kinds of error messages. This stream corresponds to C's stderr. Normally, this stream is also connected to the monitor by the operating system. By default, cerr is not buffered.
- **clog**, of class ostream, is the standard logging channel. It has no C equivalent. By default, this stream is connected to the same destination as cerr, with the difference that output to clog is buffered.

The separation of "normal" output and error messages makes it possible to treat these two kinds of output differently when executing a program. For example, the normal output of a program can be redirected into a file while the error messages are still appearing on the console. Of course, this requires that the operating system support redirection of the standard I/O channels (most operating systems do). This separation of standard channels originates from the UNIX concept of I/O redirection.

15.1.4 Stream Operators

The shift operators >> for input and << for output are overloaded for the corresponding stream classes. For this reason, the "shift operators" in C++ became the "I/O operators."[1] Using these operators, it is possible to chain multiple I/O operations.

For example, for each iteration, the following loop reads two integers from the standard input as long as only integers are entered and writes them to the standard output:

---

[1] Because these operators insert characters into a stream or extract characters from a stream, some people also call the I/O operators *inserters* and *extractors*.

```
int a, b;

// as long as input of a and b is successful
while (std::cin >> a >> b) {
    // output a and b
    std::cout << "a: " << a << " b: " << b << std::endl;
}
```

15.1.5   Manipulators

At the end of most output statements, a so-called manipulator is written:

```
std::cout << std::endl
```

Manipulators are special objects that are used to, guess what, manipulate a stream. Often, manipulators change only the way input is interpreted or output is formatted, like the manipulators for the numeric bases `dec`, `hex`, and `oct`. Thus, manipulators for `ostream`s do not necessarily create output, and manipulators for `istream`s do not necessary consume input. But some manipulators do trigger some immediate action. For example, a manipulator can be used to flush the output buffer or to skip whitespace in the input buffer.

The manipulator `endl` means "end line" and does two things:

1. Outputs a newline (that is, the character '\n')
2. Flushes the output buffer (forces a write of all buffered data for the given stream, using the stream method `flush()`)

The most important manipulators defined by the IOStream library are provided in Table 15.1. Section 15.6, page 774, discusses manipulators in more detail, including those that are defined in the IOStream library, and explains how to define your own manipulators.

Manipulator	Class	Meaning
endl	ostream	Outputs '\n' and flushes the output buffer
ends	ostream	Outputs '\0'
flush	ostream	Flushes the output buffer
ws	istream	Reads and discards whitespaces

Table 15.1. The IOStream Library's Most Important Manipulators

15.1.6   A Simple Example

The use of the stream classes is demonstrated by the following example. This program reads two floating-point values and outputs their product:

```cpp
// io/io1.cpp

#include <cstdlib>
#include <iostream>
using namespace std;

int main()
{
    double x, y;              // operands

    // print header string
    cout << "Multiplication of two floating point values" << endl;

    // read first operand
    cout << "first operand:   ";
    if (! (cin >> x)) {
        // input error
        // => error message and exit program with error status
        cerr << "error while reading the first floating value"
             << endl;
        return EXIT_FAILURE;
    }

    // read second operand
    cout << "second operand: ";
    if (! (cin >> y)) {
        // input error
        // => error message and exit program with error status
        cerr << "error while reading the second floating value"
             << endl;
        return EXIT_FAILURE;
    }

    // print operands and result
    cout << x << " times " << y << " equals " << x * y << endl;
}
```

15.2   Fundamental Stream Classes and Objects

15.2.1   Classes and Class Hierarchy

The stream classes of the IOStream library form a hierarchy, as shown in Figure 15.1. For class templates, the upper row shows the name of the class template, and the lower row presents the names of the instantiations for the character types `char` and `wchar_t`.

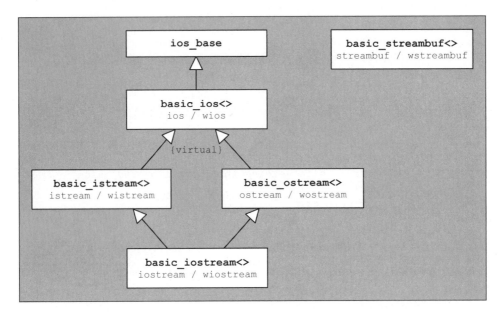

Figure 15.1. Class Hierarchy of the Fundamental Stream Classes

The classes in this class hierarchy play the following roles:

- The base class **ios_base** defines the properties of all stream classes independent of the character type and the corresponding character traits. Most of this class consists of components and functions for state and format flags.

- The class template **basic_ios<>** is derived from ios_base and defines the common properties of all stream classes that depend on the character types and the corresponding character traits. These properties include the definition of the buffer used by the stream. The buffer is an object of a class derived from the template class basic_streambuf<> with the corresponding template instantiation. It performs the actual reading and/or writing.

- The class templates **basic_istream<>** and **basic_ostream<>** derive virtually from basic_ios<> and define objects that can be used for reading or writing, respectively. Like basic_ios<>, these classes are templates that are parametrized with a character type and its traits. When internationalization does not matter, the corresponding instantiations for the character type char — istream and ostream — are used.

- The class template **basic_iostream<>** derives from both basic_istream<> and basic_ostream<>. This class template defines objects that can be used for both reading and writing.
- The class template **basic_streambuf<>** is the heart of the IOStream library. This class defines the interface to all representations that can be written to or read from by streams and is used by the other stream classes to perform the reading and writing of characters. For access to some external representation, classes are derived from basic_streambuf<>. See the following subsection for details.

Purpose of the Stream Buffer Classes

The IOStream library is designed with a rigid separation of responsibilities. The classes derived from basic_ios handle only *formatting* of the data.[2] The reading and writing of characters is performed by the stream buffers maintained by the basic_ios subobjects. The stream buffers supply character buffers for reading and writing. In addition, an abstraction from the external representation, such as files or strings, is formed by the stream buffers.

Thus, stream buffers play an important role when performing I/O with new external representations (such as sockets or graphical user interface components), redirecting streams, or combining streams to form pipelines (for example, to compress output before writing to another stream). Also, the stream buffer synchronizes the I/O when doing simultaneous I/O on the same external representation. The details about these techniques are explained in Section 15.12, page 819.

By using stream buffers, it is quite easy to define access to a new "external representation," such as a new storage device. All that has to be done is to derive a new stream buffer class from basic_streambuf<> or an appropriate specialization and to define functions for reading and/or writing characters for this new external representation. All options for formatted I/O are available automatically if a stream object is initialized to use an object of the new stream buffer class. See Section 15.13, page 826, for details of stream buffers and Section 15.13.3, page 832, for examples of how to define new stream buffers for access to special storage devices.

Detailed Class Definitions

Like all class templates in the IOStream library, the class template basic_ios<> is parametrized by two arguments and is defined as follows:

```
namespace std {
    template <typename charT,
              typename traits = char_traits<charT> >
        class basic_ios;
}
```

The template arguments are the character type used by the stream classes and a class describing the traits of the character type that are used by the stream classes.

---

[2] In fact, they don't even do the formatting! The formatting is delegated to corresponding facets in the locale library. See Section 16.2.2, page 864, and Section 16.4, page 869, for details on facets.

Examples of traits defined in the traits class are the value used to represent end-of-file[3] and the
instructions for how to copy or move a sequence of characters. Normally, the traits for a character
type are coupled with the character type, thereby making it reasonable to define a class template that
is specialized for specific character types. Hence, the traits class defaults to `char_traits<charT>`
if `charT` is the character type argument. The C++ standard library provides specializations of the
class `char_traits` for the character types `char`, `char16_t`, `char32_t`, and `wchar_t`.[4] For more
details about character traits, see Section 16.1.4, page 853.

There are two instantiations of the class `basic_ios<>` for the two character types used most
often:

```
namespace std {
    typedef basic_ios<char>    ios;
    typedef basic_ios<wchar_t> wios;
}
```

The type `ios` corresponds to the base class of the "old-fashioned" IOStream library from AT&T and
can be used for compatibility in older C++ programs.

The stream buffer class used by `basic_ios` is defined similarly:

```
namespace std {
    template <typename charT,
              typename traits = char_traits<charT> >
    class basic_streambuf;
    typedef basic_streambuf<char>    streambuf;
    typedef basic_streambuf<wchar_t> wstreambuf;
}
```

Of course, the class templates `basic_istream<>`, `basic_ostream<>`, and `basic_iostream<>`
are also parametrized with the character type and a traits class:

```
namespace std {
    template <typename charT,
              typename traits = char_traits<charT> >
    class basic_istream;

    template <typename charT,
              typename traits = char_traits<charT> >
    class basic_ostream;

    template <typename charT,
              typename traits = char_traits<charT> >
    class basic_iostream;
}
```

---

[3] I use the term *end-of-file* for the "end of input data." This corresponds with the constant EOF in C.

[4] Character traits for `char16_t` and `char32_t` are provided since C++11.

As for the other classes, there are also type definitions for the instantiations of the two most important character types:

```
namespace std {
    typedef basic_istream<char>     istream;
    typedef basic_istream<wchar_t>  wistream;

    typedef basic_ostream<char>     ostream;
    typedef basic_ostream<wchar_t>  wostream;

    typedef basic_iostream<char>    iostream;
    typedef basic_iostream<wchar_t> wiostream;
}
```

The types `istream` and `ostream` are the types normally used in the Western Hemisphere, where 8-bit character sets are enough.[5] `wchar_t` allow to use character sets with more than 8 bits (see Section 16.1, page 850). Note that for types `char16_t` and `char32_t`, no corresponding instantiations are provided by the C++ standard library.

The C++ standard library provides additional stream classes for formatted I/O with files (see Section 15.9, page 791) and strings (see Section 15.10, page 802).

15.2.2 Global Stream Objects

Several global stream objects are defined for the stream classes. These objects are for access to the standard I/O channels mentioned previously for streams, with `char` as the character type and a set of corresponding objects for the streams using `wchar_t` as the character type (see Table 15.2).

Type	Name	Purpose
istream	`cin`	Reads input from the standard input channel
ostream	`cout`	Writes "normal" output to the standard output channel
ostream	`cerr`	Writes error messages to the standard error channel
ostream	`clog`	Writes log messages to the standard logging channel
wistream	`wcin`	Reads wide-character input from the standard input channel
wostream	`wcout`	Writes "normal" wide-character output to the standard output channel
wostream	`wcerr`	Writes wide-character error messages to the standard error channel
wostream	`wclog`	Writes wide-character log messages to the standard logging channel

Table 15.2. Global Stream Objects

By default, these standard streams are synchronized with the standard streams of C. That is, the C++ standard library ensures that the order of mixed output with C++ streams and C streams

---

[5] The classes `istream_withassign`, `ostream_withassign`, and `iostream_withassign`, which are present in some older stream libraries (derived from `istream`, `ostream`, and `iostream`, respectively), are not supported by the standard. The corresponding functionality is achieved differently (see Section 15.12.3, page 822).

is preserved. Before it writes data, any buffer of standard C++ streams flushes the buffer of the corresponding C streams, and vice versa. Of course, this synchronization takes some time. If it isn't necessary, you can turn it off by calling `sync_with_stdio(false)` before any input or output is done (see Section 15.14.1, page 845).

Since C++11, some guarantees regarding concurrency are given for these stream objects: When synchronized with the standard streams of C, using them in multiple parallel threads does *not* cause undefined behavior. Thus, you can write from or read into multiple threads. Note, however, that this might result in interleaved characters, or the thread that gets a character read is undefined. For any other stream object or if these objects are not synchronized with C streams, concurrent reads or writes result in undefined behavior.

15.2.3 Header Files

The definitions of the stream classes are scattered among several header files:

- **`<iosfwd>`** contains forward declarations for the stream classes. This header file is necessary because it is no longer permissible to use a simple forward declaration, such as `class ostream`.
- **`<streambuf>`** contains the definitions for the stream buffer base class (`basic_streambuf<>`).
- **`<istream>`** contains the definitions for the classes that support input only (`basic_istream<>`) and for the classes that support both input and output (`basic_iostream<>`).[6]
- **`<ostream>`** contains the definitions for the output stream class (`basic_ostream<>`).
- **`<iostream>`** contains declarations of the global stream objects, such as `cin` and `cout`.

Most of the headers exist for the internal organization of the C++ standard library. For the application programmer, it should be sufficient to include `<iosfwd>` for the declaration of the stream classes and `<istream>` or `<ostream>` when using the input or output functions, respectively. The header `<iostream>` should be included only if the standard stream objects are to be used. For some implementations, some code is executed at start-up for each translation unit including this header. The code being executed is not that expensive, but it requires loading the corresponding pages of the executable, which might be expensive. In general, only those headers defining necessary "stuff" should be included. In particular, header files should include only `<iosfwd>`, and the corresponding implementation files should then include the header with the complete definition.

For special stream features, such as parametrized manipulators, file streams, or string streams, there are additional headers: `<iomanip>`, `<fstream>`, `<sstream>`, and `<strstream>`. The details about these headers are provided in the sections that introduce these special features.

---

[6] At first, `<istream>` might not appear to be a logical choice for declaration of the classes for input *and* output. However, because there may be some initialization overhead at start-up for every translation unit that includes `<iostream>` (see the following paragraph for details), the declarations for input *and* output were put into `<istream>`.

15.3   Standard Stream Operators << and >>

In C and C++, operators << and >> are used for shifting bits of an integer to the right or the left, respectively. The classes `basic_istream<>` and `basic_ostream<>` overload operators >> and << as the standard I/O operators. Thus, in C++, the "shift operators" became the "I/O operators."[7]

15.3.1   Output Operator <<

The class `basic_ostream` — and thus also the classes `ostream` and `wostream` — defines << as an output operator and overloads it for almost all fundamental types, excluding `void` and `nullptr_t`, as well as for `char*` and `void*`.

The output operators for streams are defined to send their second argument to the corresponding stream. Thus, the data is sent in the direction of the arrow:

```
int i = 7;
std::cout << i;            // outputs: 7

float f = 4.5;
std::cout << f;            // outputs: 4.5
```

Operator << can be overloaded such that the second argument is an arbitrary data type, thereby allowing the integration of your own data types into the I/O system. The compiler ensures that the correct function for outputting the second argument is called. Of course, this function should in fact transform the second argument into a sequence of characters sent to the stream.

The C++ standard library also uses this mechanism to provide output operators for specific types, such as strings (see Section 13.3.10, page 712), bitsets (see Section 12.5.1, page 652), and complex numbers (see Section 17.2.3, page 933):

```
std::string s("hello");
s += ", world";
std::cout << s;            // outputs: hello, world

std::bitset<10> flags(7);
std::cout << flags;        // outputs: 0000000111

std::complex<float> c(3.1,7.4);
std::cout << c;            // outputs: (3.1,7.4)
```

The details about writing output operators for your own data types are explained in Section 15.11, page 810.

The fact that the output mechanism can be extended to incorporate your own data types is a significant improvement over C's I/O mechanism, which uses `printf()`: It is not necessary to specify the type of an object to be printed. Instead, the overloading of different types ensures that

---

[7] Some people also call the I/O operators *inserters* and *extractors*.

the correct function for printing is deduced automatically. The mechanism is not limited to standard types. Thus, the user has only one mechanism, and it works for all types.

Operator << can also be used to print multiple objects in one statement. By convention, the output operators return their first argument. Thus, the result of an output operator is the output stream. This allows you to chain calls to output operators as follows:

```
std::cout << x << " times " << y << " is " << x * y << std::endl;
```

Operator << is evaluated from left to right. Thus,

```
std::cout << x
```

is executed first. Note that the evaluative order of the operator does not imply any specific order in which the arguments are evaluated; only the order in which the operators are executed is defined. This expression returns its first operand, std::cout. So,

```
std::cout << " times "
```

is executed next. The object y, the string literal " is ", and the result of x * y are printed accordingly. Note that the multiplication operator has a higher priority than operator <<, so you need no parentheses around x * y. However, there are operators that have lower priority, such as all logical operators. In this example, if x and y are floating-point numbers with the values 2.4 and 5.1, the following is printed:

```
2.4 times 5.1 is 12.24
```

Note that since C++11, concurrent output using the same stream object is possible but might result in interleaved characters (see Section 15.2.2, page 752).

15.3.2 Input Operator >>

The class basic_istream — and thus also the classes istream and wistream — defines >> as an input operator. Similar to basic_ostream, this operator is overloaded for almost all fundamental types, excluding void and nullptr_t, as well as for char* and void*. The input operators for streams are defined to store the value read in their second argument. As with operator <<, the data is sent in the direction of the arrow:

```
int i;
std::cin >> i;      // reads an int from standard input and stores it in i

float f;
std::cin >> f;      // reads a float from standard input and stores it in f
```

Note that the second argument is modified. To make this possible, the second argument is passed by nonconstant reference.

As with output operator <<, it is also possible to overload the input operator for arbitrary data types and to chain the calls:

```
float f;
std::complex<double> c;

std::cin >> f >> c;
```

To make this possible, leading whitespace is skipped by default. However, this automatic skipping of whitespace can be turned off (see Section 15.7.7, page 789).

Note that since C++11, concurrent input using the same stream object is possible but might result in characters where it is not defined which thread reads which character (see Section 15.2.2, page 752).

15.3.3 Input/Output of Special Types

The standard I/O operators are provided for almost all fundamental types (excluding `void` and `nullptr_t`) as well as for `char*`, and `void*`. However, special rules apply to some of these types and to user-defined types.

Numeric Types

When reading numeric values, the input must start with at least one digit. Otherwise, the numeric value will be set to 0 and the `failbit` (see Section 15.4.1, page 758) is set:

```
int x;
std::cin >> x;   // assigns 0 to x, if the next character does not fit
```

However, if there is no input or if the `failbit` is set already, calling the input operator will not modify x. This also applies to `bool`.

Type `bool`

By default, Boolean values are printed and read numerically: `false` is converted into and from 0, and `true` is converted into and from 1. When reading, values different from 0 and 1 are considered to be an error. In this case, the `ios::failbit` is set, which might throw a corresponding exception (see Section 15.4.4, page 762).

It is also possible to set up the formatting options of the stream to use character strings for the I/O of Boolean values (see Section 15.7.2, page 781). This touches on the topic of internationalization: Unless a special locale object is used, the strings `"true"` and `"false"` are used. In other locale objects, different strings might be used. For example, a German locale object would use the strings `"wahr"` and `"falsch"`. See Chapter 16, especially Section 16.2.2, page 865, for more details.

Types `char` and `wchar_t`

When a `char` or a `wchar_t` is being read with operator >>, leading whitespace is skipped by default. To read any character, including whitespace, you can either clear the flag `skipws` (see Section 15.7.7, page 789) or use the member function `get()` (see Section 15.5.1, page 768).

Type `char*`

A C-string (that is, a `char*`) is read wordwise. That is, when a C-string is being read, leading whitespace is skipped by default, and the string is read until another whitespace character or end-of-file is encountered. Whether leading whitespace is skipped automatically can be controlled with the flag `skipws` (see Section 15.7.7, page 789).

Note that this behavior means that the string you read can become arbitrarily long. It is already a common error in C programs to assume that a string can be a maximum of 80 characters long. There is no such restriction. Thus, you must arrange for a premature termination of the input when the string is too long. To do this, you should *always* set the maximum length of the string to be read. This normally looks something like the following:

```
char buffer[81];    // 80 characters and '\0'
std::cin >> std::setw(81) >> buffer;
```

The manipulator `setw()` and the corresponding stream parameter are described in detail in Section 15.7.3, page 781.

The type `string` from the C++ standard library (see Chapter 13) grows as needed to accommodate a lengthy string. Rather than using `char*`, this is much easier and less error prone. In addition, `strings` provide a convenient function `getline()` for line-by-line reading (see Section 13.2.10, page 677). So, whenever you can, avoid the use of C-strings and use strings.

Type `void*`

Operators `<<` and `>>` also provide the possibility of printing a pointer and reading it back in again. An address is printed in an implementation-dependent format if a parameter of type `void*` is passed to the output operator. For example, the following statement prints the contents of a C-string and its address:

```
char* cstring = "hello";

std::cout << "string \"" << cstring << "\" is located at address: "
          << static_cast<void*>(cstring) << std::endl;
```

The result of this statement might appear as follows:

```
string "hello" is located at address: 0x10000018
```

It is even possible to read an address again with the input operator. However, note that addresses are normally transient. The same object can get a different address in a newly started program. A possible application of printing and reading addresses may be programs that exchange addresses for object identification or programs that share memory.

Stream Buffers

You can use operators `>>` and `<<` to read directly into a stream buffer and to write directly out of a stream buffer respectively. This is probably the fastest way to copy files by using C++ I/O streams. See Section 15.14.3, page 846, for examples.

User-Defined Types

In principle, it is very easy to extend this technique to your own types. However, paying attention to all possible formatting data and error conditions takes more effort than you might think. See

Section 15.11, page 810, for a detailed discussion about extending the standard I/O mechanism for your own types.

Monetary and Time Values

Since C++11, it is possible to use manipulators to directly read or write monetary or time values. For example, the following program allows you to write the current date and time and reads a new date:

```cpp
// io/timemanipulator1.cpp

#include <iostream>
#include <iomanip>
#include <chrono>
#include <cstdlib>
using namespace std;

int main ()
{
    // process and print current date and time:
    auto now = chrono::system_clock::now();
    time_t t = chrono::system_clock::to_time_t(now);
    tm* nowTM = localtime(&t);
    cout << put_time(nowTM,"date: %x\ntime: %X\n") << endl;

    // read date:
    tm* date;
    cout << "new date: ";
    cin >> get_time(date,"%x");   // read date
    if (!cin) {
        cerr << "invalid format read" << endl;
    }
}
```

Before asking for a new date, the program might output:

```
date: 09/14/11
time: 11:08:52
```

The corresponding manipulators allow you to take international behavior into account. For details, see Section 16.4.3, page 890, for time manipulators; Section 16.4.2, page 882, for monetary manipulators; and Section 5.7, page 143, for the chrono library defining `std::chrono::system_time`.

15.4   State of Streams

Streams maintain a state. The state identifies whether I/O was successful and, if not, the reason for the failure.

15.4.1   Constants for the State of Streams

For the general state of streams, several constants of type `iostate` are defined to be used as flags (Table 15.3). The type `iostate` is a member of the class `ios_base`. The exact type of the constants is an implementation detail; in other words, it is not defined whether `iostate` is an enumeration, a type definition for an integral type, or an instantiation of the class `bitset`.

Constant	Meaning
goodbit	Everything is OK; none of the other bits is set
eofbit	End-of-file was encountered
failbit	Error; an I/O operation was not successful
badbit	Fatal error; undefined state

Table 15.3. Constants of Type `iostate`

The constant `goodbit` is defined to have the value 0. Thus, having `goodbit` set means that all other bits are cleared. The name `goodbit` may be somewhat confusing because it doesn't mean that any bit is set.

The difference between `failbit` and `badbit` is basically that `badbit` indicates a more fatal error:

- **failbit** is set if an operation was not processed correctly but the stream is generally OK. Normally, this flag is set as a result of a format error during reading. For example, this flag is set if an integer is to be read but the next character is a letter.

- **badbit** is set if the stream is somehow corrupted or if data is lost. For example, this flag is set when positioning a stream that refers to a file before the beginning of a file.

Note that `eofbit` normally happens with `failbit` because the end-of-file condition is checked and detected when an attempt is made to read beyond end-of-file. After reading the last character, the flag `eofbit` is not yet set. The next attempt to read a character sets `eofbit` *and* `failbit` because the read fails.

Some former implementations supported the flag `hardfail`. This flag is not supported in the standard.

These constants are not defined globally. Instead, they are defined within the class `ios_base`. Thus, you must always use them with the scope operator or with some object. For example:

```
std::ios_base::eofbit
```

Of course, it is also possible to use a class derived from `ios_base`. These constants were defined in the class `ios` in old implementations. Because `ios` is a type derived from `ios_base` and its use involves less typing, the use often looks like this:

```
std::ios::eofbit
```

These flags are maintained by the class `basic_ios` and are thus present in all objects of type `basic_istream` or `basic_ostream`. However, the stream buffers don't have state flags. One stream buffer can be shared by multiple stream objects, so the flags represent only the state of the stream as found in the last operation. Even this is the case only if `goodbit` was set prior to this operation. Otherwise, the flags may have been set by an earlier operation.

15.4.2 Member Functions Accessing the State of Streams

The current state of the flags can be determined by the member functions, as presented in Table 15.4.

Member Function	Meaning
`good()`	Returns `true` if the stream is OK (`goodbit` is "set")
`eof()`	Returns `true` if end-of-file was hit (`eofbit` is set)
`fail()`	Returns `true` if an error has occurred (`failbit` or `badbit` is set)
`bad()`	Returns `true` if a fatal error has occurred (`badbit` is set)
`rdstate()`	Returns the currently set flags
`clear()`	Clears all flags
`clear(`*state*`)`	Clears all and sets *state* flags
`setstate(`*state*`)`	Sets additional *state* flags

Table 15.4. Member Functions for Stream States

The first four member functions in Table 15.4 determine certain states and return a Boolean value. Note that `fail()` returns whether `failbit` or `badbit` is set. Although this is done mainly for historical reasons, it also has the advantage that one test suffices to determine whether an error has occurred.

In addition, the state of the flags can be determined and modified with the more general member functions. When `clear()` is called without parameters, all error flags, including `eofbit`, are cleared (this is the origin of the name *clear*):

```
// clear all error flags (including eofbit):
strm.clear();
```

If a parameter is given to `clear()`, the state of the stream is adjusted to be the state given by the parameter; that is, the flags set in the parameter are set for the stream, and the other flags are cleared. The only exception is that the `badbit` is always set if there is no stream buffer, which is the case if `rdbuf() == 0` (see Section 15.12.2, page 820, for details).

The following example checks whether `failbit` is set and clears it if necessary:

```
// check whether failbit is set
if (strm.rdstate() & std::ios::failbit) {
    std::cout << "failbit was set" << std::endl;

    // clear only failbit
    strm.clear (strm.rdstate() & ~std::ios::failbit);
}
```

This example uses the bit operators & and ~: Operator ~ returns the bitwise complement of its argument. Thus, the following expression returns a temporary value that has all bits set except `failbit`:

```
~ios::failbit
```

Operator & returns a bitwise "and" of its operands. Only the bits set in both operands remain set. Applying bitwise "and" to all currently set flags (`rdstate()`) and to all bits except `failbit` retains the value of all other bits while `failbit` is cleared.

Streams can be configured to throw exceptions if certain flags are set with `clear()` or `setstate()` (see Section 15.4.4, page 762). Such streams always throw an exception if the corresponding flag is set at the end of the method used to manipulate the flags.

Note that you always have to clear error bits explicitly. In C, it was possible to read characters after a format error. For example, if `scanf()` failed to read an integer, you could still read the remaining characters. Thus, the read operation failed, but the input stream was still in a good state. This is different in C++. If `failbit` is set, each following stream operation is a no-op until `failbit` is cleared explicitly.

In general, the set bits reflect only what happened sometime in the past: If a bit is set after an operation, this does not necessarily mean that this operation caused the flag to be set. Instead, the flag might have been set before the operation. Thus, if it not known whether an error bit is set, you should call `clear()` before an operation is executed to let the flags tell you what went wrong. Note however, that operations may have different effects after clearing the flags. For example, even if `eofbit` was set by an operation, this does not mean that after clearing `eofbit` the operation will set `eofbit` again. This can be the case, for example, if the accessed file grew between the two calls.

15.4.3   Stream State and Boolean Conditions

Two functions are defined for the use of streams in Boolean expressions (Table 15.5).

Member Function	Meaning
`operator bool ()`	Returns whether the stream has not run into an error (corresponds to `!fail()`)
`operator ! ()`	Returns whether the stream has run into an error (corresponds to `fail()`)

Table 15.5. Stream Operators for Boolean Expressions

With `operator bool()`,[8] streams can be tested in control structures in a short and idiomatic way for their current state:

---

[8] Before C++11, the operator was declared as `operator void*()`, which could cause problems such as those described in Section 15.10.1, page 805.

```
// while the standard input stream is OK
while (std::cin) {
    ...
}
```

For the Boolean condition in a control structure, the type does not need a direct conversion to bool. Instead, a unique conversion to an integral type, such as int or char, or to a pointer type is sufficient. The conversion to bool is often used to read objects and test for success in the same expression:

```
if (std::cin >> x) {
    // reading x was successful
    ...
}
```

As discussed earlier, the following expression returns cin:

```
std::cin >> x
```

So, after x is read, the statement is

```
if (std::cin) {
    ...
}
```

Because cin is being used in the context of a condition, its operator void* is called, which returns whether the stream has run into an error.

A typical application of this technique is a loop that reads and processes objects:

```
// as long as obj can be read
while (std::cin >> obj) {
    // process obj (in this case, simply output it)
    std::cout << obj << std::endl;
}
```

This is C's classic filter framework for C++ objects. The loop is terminated if the failbit or badbit is set. This happens when an error occurred or at end-of-file (the attempt to read at end-of-file results in setting eofbit *and* failbit; see Section 15.4.1, page 758). By default, operator >> skips leading whitespaces. This is normally exactly what is desired. However, if obj is of type char, whitespace is normally considered to be significant. In this case, you can use the put() and get() member functions of streams (see Section 15.5.3, page 772) or, even better, an istreambuf_iterator (see Section 15.13.2, page 831) to implement an I/O filter.

With operator !, the inverse test can be performed. The operator is defined to return whether a stream has run into an error; that is, the operator returns true if failbit or badbit is set. The operator can be used like this:

```
if (! std::cin) {
    // the stream cin is not OK
    ...
}
```

Like the implicit conversion to a Boolean value, this operator is often used to test for success in the same expression in which an object was read:

```
if (! (std::cin >> x)) {
    // the read failed
    ...
}
```

Here, the following expression returns `cin`, to which operator `!` is applied:

```
std::cin >> x
```

The expression after `!` must be placed within parentheses because of operator precedence rules: Without the parentheses, operator `!` would be evaluated first. In other words, the expression

```
!std::cin >> x
```

is equivalent to the expression

```
(!std::cin) >> x
```

This is probably not what is intended.

Although these operators are very convenient in Boolean expressions, one oddity has to be noted: Double "negation" does *not* yield the original object:

- `cin` is a stream object of class `istream`.
- `!!cin` is a Boolean value describing the state of `cin`.

As with other features of C++, it can be argued whether the use of the conversions to a Boolean value is good style. The use of member functions, such as `fail()`, normally yields a more readable program:

```
std::cin >> x;
if (std::cin.fail()) {
    ...
}
```

15.4.4   Stream State and Exceptions

Exception handling was introduced to C++ for the handling of errors and exceptions (see Section 4.3, page 41). However, this was done after streams were already in wide use. To stay backward compatible, by default, streams throw no exceptions. However, for the standardized streams, it is possible to define, for every state flag, whether setting that flag will trigger an exception. This definition is done by the `exceptions()` member function (Table 15.6).

Member Function	Meaning
`exceptions`(*flags*)	Sets flags that trigger exceptions
`exceptions()`	Returns the flags that trigger exceptions

Table 15.6. Stream Member Functions for Exceptions

Calling `exceptions()` without an argument yields the current flags for which exceptions are triggered. No exceptions are thrown if the function returns `goodbit`. This is the default, to maintain backward compatibility. When exceptions() is called with an argument, exceptions are thrown as soon as the corresponding state flags are set. If a state flag is already set when exceptions() is called with an argument, an exception is thrown if the corresponding flag is set in the argument.

The following example configures the stream so that, for all flags, an exception is thrown:

```
// throw exceptions for all "errors"
strm.exceptions (std::ios::eofbit | std::ios::failbit |
                    std::ios::badbit);
```

If 0 or goodbit is passed as an argument, no exceptions are generated:

```
// do not generate exceptions
strm.exceptions (std::ios::goodbit);
```

Exceptions are thrown when the corresponding state flags are set after calling clear() or setstate(). An exception is even thrown if the flag was already set and not cleared:

```
// this call throws an exception if failbit is set on entry
strm.exceptions (std::ios::failbit);
...
// throw an exception (even if failbit was already set)
strm.setstate (std::ios::failbit);
```

The exceptions thrown are objects of the class std::ios_base::failure. Since C++11, this class is derived from std::system_error (see Section 4.3.1, page 44).[9]

```
namespace std {
    class ios_base::failure : public system_error {
      public:
        explicit failure (const string& msg,
                              const error_code& ec = io_errc::stream);
        explicit failure (const char* msg,
                              const error_code& ec = io_errc::stream);
    };
}
```

Implementations are requested to provide an error_code object that provides the specific reason for the failure. In fact, an error caused by the operating system should have the category() "system" and the value() that was reported by the operating system. An error arising from within the I/O stream library should have the category() "iostream" and the value() std::io_errc::stream. See Section 4.3.2, page 45, for details about class error_code and how to deal with it.

Not throwing exceptions as default demonstrates that exception handling is intended to be used more for unexpected situations. It is called *exception handling* rather than *error handling*. Expected errors, such as format errors during input from the user, are considered to be "normal" and are usually better handled using the state flags.

The major area in which stream exceptions are useful is reading preformatted data, such as automatically written files. But even then, problems arise if exception handling is used. For example,

---

[9] Before C++11, class std::ios_base::failure was directly derived from class std::exception.

if it is desired to read data until end-of-file, you can't get exceptions for errors without getting an
exception for end-of-file. The reason is that the detection of end-of-file also sets the `failbit`,
meaning that reading an object was not successful. To distinguish end-of-file from an input error,
you have to check the state of the stream.

The next example demonstrates how this might look. It shows a function that reads floating-point
values from a stream until end-of-file is reached and returns the sum of the floating-point values read:

```cpp
// io/sum1a.cpp

#include <istream>

namespace MyLib {
    double readAndProcessSum (std::istream& strm)
    {
        using std::ios;
        double value, sum;

        // save current state of exception flags
        ios::iostate oldExceptions = strm.exceptions();

        // let failbit and badbit throw exceptions
        // - NOTE: failbit is also set at end-of-file
        strm.exceptions (ios::failbit | ios::badbit);

        try {
            // while stream is OK
            // - read value and add it to sum
            sum = 0;
            while (strm >> value) {
                sum += value;
            }
        }
        catch (...) {
            // if exception not caused by end-of-file
            // - restore old state of exception flags
            // - rethrow exception
            if (!strm.eof()) {
                strm.exceptions(oldExceptions);    // restore exception flags
                throw;                             // rethrow
            }
        }

        // restore old state of exception flags
        strm.exceptions (oldExceptions);
```

```
    // return sum
    return sum;
    }
}
```

First, the function stores the set stream exceptions in `oldExceptions` to restore them later. Then the stream is configured to throw an exception on certain conditions. In a loop, all values are read and added as long as the stream is OK. If end-of-file is reached, the stream is no longer OK, and a corresponding exception is thrown even though no exception is thrown for setting `eofbit`. This happens because end-of-file is detected on an unsuccessful attempt to read more data, which also sets the `failbit`. To avoid the behavior that end-of-file throws an exception, the exception is caught locally to check the state of the stream by using `eof()`. The exception is propagated only if `eof()` yields `false`.

Note that restoring the original exception flags may cause exceptions: `exceptions()` throws an exception if a corresponding flag is set in the stream already. Thus, if the state did throw exceptions for `eofbit`, `failbit`, or `badbit` on function entry, these exceptions are propagated to the caller.

This function can be called in the simplest case from the following main function:

```cpp
// io/summain.cpp

#include <iostream>
#include <exception>
#include <cstdlib>

namespace MyLib {
    double readAndProcessSum (std::istream&);
}

int main()
{
    using namespace std;
    double sum;

    try {
        sum = MyLib::readAndProcessSum(cin);
    }
    catch (const ios::failure& error) {
        cerr << "I/O exception: " << error.what() << endl;
        return EXIT_FAILURE;
    }
    catch (const exception& error) {
        cerr << "standard exception: " << error.what() << endl;
        return EXIT_FAILURE;
    }
```

```
        catch (...) {
            cerr << "unknown exception" << endl;
            return EXIT_FAILURE;
        }

        // print sum
        cout << "sum: " << sum << endl;
    }
```

The question arises whether this is worth the effort. It is also possible to work with streams not throwing an exception. In this case, an exception is thrown if an error is detected. This has the additional advantage that user-defined error messages and error classes can be used:

```
// io/sum2a.cpp

#include <istream>

namespace MyLib {
    double readAndProcessSum (std::istream& strm)
    {
        double value, sum;

        // while stream is OK
        // - read value and add it to sum
        sum = 0;
        while (strm >> value) {
            sum += value;
        }

        if (!strm.eof()) {
            throw std::ios::failure
                    ("input error in readAndProcessSum()");
        }

        // return sum
        return sum;
    }
}
```

This looks somewhat simpler, doesn't it?

I/O Exceptions before C++11

Before C++11, class `std::ios_base::failure` was directly derived from class `std::exception` and had only a constructor taking a `std::string` argument:

```
namespace std {
    class ios_base::failure : public exception {
      public:
        explicit failure (const string& msg);
        ...
    };
}
```

This caused the following limitations:

- For the generated exception object, it was possible to call `what()` only to get an implementation-specific string for the reason of the failure. No support for an exception category or value was provided.

- Because the constructor did take only a `std::string`, you had to include `<string>` when passing a string literal. (To enable the conversion to `std::string`, you need the declaration of the corresponding string constructor.)

15.5 Standard Input/Output Functions

Instead of using the standard operators for streams (operator << and operator >>), you can use the member functions presented in this section for reading and writing. These functions read or write "unformatted" data, unlike operators >> or <<, which read or write "formatted" data. When reading, the functions described in this section never skip leading whitespaces, which is different to operator >>, which, by default, skips leading whitespace. This is handled by a `sentry` object (see Section 15.5.4, page 772). Also, these functions handle exceptions differently from the formatted I/O operators: If an exception is thrown, either from a called function or as a result of setting a state flag (see Section 15.4.4, page 762), the `badbit` flag is set. The exception is then rethrown if the exception mask has `badbit` set.

The standard I/O functions use type `streamsize`, which is defined in `<ios>`, to specify counts:

```
namespace std {
    typedef ... streamsize;
    ...
}
```

The type `streamsize` usually is a signed version of `size_t`. It is signed because it is also used to specify negative values.

15.5.1 Member Functions for Input

In the following definitions, *istream* is a placeholder for the stream class used for reading. It can stand for `istream`, `wistream`, or other instantiation of the class template `basic_istream<>`. The type *char* is a placeholder for the corresponding character type, which is `char` for `istream` and `wchar_t` for `wistream`. Other types or values printed in italics depend on the exact definition of the character type or on the traits class associated with the stream.

For istreams, the C++ standard library provides several member functions to read character sequences. Table 15.7 compares their abilities (*s* refers to the character sequence the characters are read into).

Member Function	Reads Until	Number of Characters	Appends Terminator	Returns
`get(`*s*`,`*num*`)`	Excluding newline or end-of-file	Up to *num*−1	Yes	*istream*
`get(`*s*`,`*num*`,`*t*`)`	Excluding *t* or end-of-file	Up to *num*−1	Yes	*istream*
`getline(`*s*`,`*num*`)`	Including newline or end-of-file	Up to *num*−1	Yes	*istream*
`getline(`*s*`,`*num*`,`*t*`)`	Including t or end-of-file	Up to *num*−1	Yes	*istream*
`read(`*s*`,`*num*`)`	End-of-file	*num*	No	*istream*
`readsome(`*s*`,`*num*`)`	End-of-file	Up to *num*	No	Count

Table 15.7. Abilities of Stream Operators Reading Character Sequences

int *istream*::**get** ()

- Reads the next character.
- Returns the read character or *EOF*.
- In general, the return type is `traits::int_type`, and *EOF* is the value returned by `traits::eof()`. For `istream`, the return type is `int`, and *EOF* is the constant EOF. Hence, for `istream`, this function corresponds to C's `getchar()` or `getc()`.
- Note that the returned value is not necessarily of the character type but can be of a type with a larger range of values. Otherwise, it would be impossible to distinguish *EOF* from characters with the corresponding value.

istream& *istream*::**get** (*char& c*)

- Assigns the next character to the passed argument *c*.
- Returns the stream. The stream's state tells whether the read was successful.

istream& *istream*::**get** (*char* str*, `streamsize` *count*)
istream& *istream*::**get** (*char* str*, `streamsize` *count*, *char delim*)

- Both forms read up to *count*-1 characters into the character sequence pointed to by *str*.
- The first form terminates the reading if the next character to be read is the newline character of the corresponding character set. For `istream`, it is the character '\n', and for `wistream`,

it is `wchar_t('\n')` (see Section 16.1.5, page 857). In general, `widen('\n')` is used (see Section 15.8, page 790).
- The second form terminates the reading if the next character to be read is *delim*.
- Both forms return the stream. The stream's state tells whether the read was successful.
- The terminating character (*delim*) is not read.
- The read character sequence is terminated by a (terminating) null character.
- The caller must ensure that *str* is large enough for *count* characters.

istream& *istream*::**getline** (*char* str*, `streamsize` *count*)

istream& *istream*::**getline** (*char* str*, `streamsize` *count*, *char delim*)

- Both forms are identical to their previous counterparts of `get()`, except as follows:
  - They terminate the reading *including* but not before the newline character or *delim*, respectively. Thus, the newline character or *delim* is read if it occurs within *count*-1 characters, but it is *not* stored in *str*.
  - If they read lines with more than *count*-1 characters, they set `failbit`.

istream& *istream*::**read** (*char* str*, `streamsize` *count*)

- Reads *count* characters into the string *str*.
- Returns the stream. The stream's state tells whether the read was successful.
- The string in *str* is *not* terminated automatically with a (terminating) null character.
- The caller must ensure that *str* has sufficient space to store *count* characters.
- Encountering end-of-file during reading is considered an error, and `failbit` is set in addition to `eofbit`.

`streamsize` *istream*::**readsome** (*char* str*, `streamsize` *count*)

- Reads up to *count* characters into the string *str*.
- Returns the number of characters read.
- The string in *str* is *not* terminated automatically with a (terminating) null character.
- The caller must ensure that *str* has sufficient space to store *count* characters.
- In contrast to `read()`, `readsome()` reads all available characters of the stream buffer, using the `in_avail()` member function of the buffer (see Section 15.13.1, page 827). This is useful when it is undesirable to wait for the input because it comes from the keyboard or other processes. Encountering end-of-file is not considered an error and sets neither `eofbit` nor `failbit`.

`streamsize` *istream*::**gcount** () `const`

- Returns the number of characters read by the last *unformatted* read operation.

istream& istream::**ignore** ()

istream& istream::**ignore** (streamsize *count*)

istream& istream::**ignore** (streamsize *count*, int *delim*)

- All forms extract and discard characters.
- The first form ignores one character.
- The second form ignores up to *count* characters.
- The third form ignores up to *count* characters until *delim* is extracted and discarded.
- If *count* is std::numeric_limits<std::streamsize>::max() (the largest value of type std::streamsize; see Section 5.3, page 115), all characters are discarded until either *delim* or end-of-file is reached.
- All forms return the stream.
- Examples:
  - The following call discards the rest of the line:
        cin.ignore(numeric_limits<std::streamsize>::max(),'\n');
  - The following call discards the complete remainder of cin:
        cin.ignore(numeric_limits<std::streamsize>::max());

int istream::**peek** ()

- Returns the next character to be read from the stream without extracting it. The next read will read this character (unless the read position is modified).
- Returns *EOF* if no more characters can be read.
- *EOF* is the value returned from traits::eof(). For istream, this is the constant EOF.

istream& istream::**unget** ()

istream& istream::**putback** (*char c*)

- Both functions put the last character read back into the stream so that it is read again by the next read (unless the read position is modified).
- The difference between unget() and putback() is that for putback(), a check is made whether the character *c* passed is indeed the last character read.
- If the character cannot be put back or if the wrong character is put back with putback(), badbit is set, which may throw a corresponding exception (see Section 15.4.4, page 762).
- The maximum number of characters that can be put back with these functions is unspecified. Only one call of these functions between two reads is guaranteed to work by the standard and thus is portable.

When C-strings are read, it is safer to use the functions from this section than to use operator >>. The reason is that the maximum string size to be read must be passed explicitly as an argument. Although it is possible to limit the number of characters read when using operator >> (see Section 15.7.3, page 781), this is easily forgotten.

It is often better to use the stream buffer directly instead of using istream member functions. Stream buffers provide member functions that read single characters or character sequences efficiently, without overhead due to the construction of `sentry` objects (see Section 15.5.4, page 772, for more information on `sentry` objects). Section 15.13, page 826, explains the stream buffer interface in detail. Another alternative is to use the class template `istreambuf_iterator<>`, which provides an iterator interface to the stream buffer (see Section 15.13.2, page 828).

Two other functions for manipulating the read position are `tellg()` and `seekg()`, which are relevant mainly in conjunction with files. Their descriptions are deferred until Section 15.9.4, page 799.

15.5.2 Member Functions for Output

In the following definitions, *ostream* is a placeholder for the stream class used for writing. It can stand for `ostream`, `wostream`, or other instantiation of the class template `basic_ostream<>`. The type *char* is a placeholder for the corresponding character type, which is char for `ostream` and `wchar_t` for `wostream`. Other types or values printed in italics depend on the exact definition of the character type or on the traits class associated with the stream.

ostream& *ostream*::**put** (*char c*)

- Writes the argument *c* to the stream.
- Returns the stream. The stream's state tells whether the write was successful.

ostream& *ostream*::**write** (const *char** *str*, streamsize *count*)

- Writes *count* characters of the string *str* to the stream.
- Returns the stream. The stream's state tells whether the write was successful.
- The (terminating) null character does *not* terminate the write and will be written.
- The caller must ensure that *str* contains at least *count* characters; otherwise, the behavior is undefined.

ostream& *ostream*::**flush** ()

- Flushes the buffers of the stream: forces a write of all buffered data to the device or I/O channel to which it belongs.

Two other functions modify the write position: `tellp()` and `seekp()`, which are relevant mainly in conjunction with files. Their descriptions are deferred until Section 15.9.4, page 799.

As with the input functions, it may be reasonable to use the stream buffer directly (see Section 15.14.3, page 846) or to use the class template `ostreambuf_iterator<>` for unformatted writing (see Section 15.13.2, page 828). In fact, there is no point in using the unformatted output functions except that they use `sentry` objects (see Section 15.5.4, page 772), which, for example, synchronize tied output streams (see Section 15.12.1, page 819).

15.5.3   Example Uses

The classic C/UNIX filter framework that simply writes all read characters looks like this in C++:

```
// io/charcat1.cpp

#include <iostream>
using namespace std;

int main()
{
    char c;

    // while it is possible to read a character
    while (cin.get(c)) {
        // print it
        cout.put(c);
    }
}
```

With each call of the following expression, the next character is simply assigned to c, which is passed by reference:

```
cin.get(c)
```

The return value of get() is the stream; thus, while tests whether cin is still in a good state.[10]

For a better performance, you can operate directly on stream buffers. See Section 15.13.2, page 831, for a version of this example that uses stream buffer iterators for I/O and Section 15.14.3, page 846, for a version that copies the whole input in one statement.

15.5.4   `sentry` Objects

The I/O stream operators and functions use a common scheme for providing their functionality: First, some preprocessing prepares the stream for I/O. Then the actual I/O is done, followed by some postprocessing.

To implement this scheme, classes `basic_istream` and `basic_ostream` each define an auxiliary class `sentry`. The constructor of these classes does the preprocessing, and the destructor

---

[10] Note that this interface is better than the usual C interface for filters. In C, you have to use `getchar()` or `getc()`, which return both the next character or whether end-of-file was reached. This causes the problem that you have to process the return value as int to distinguish any char value from the value for end-of-file.

does the corresponding postprocessing.[11] Thus, all formatted and unformatted I/O operators and functions use a `sentry` object before they perform their actual processing and operate as follows:

```
sentry se(strm);        // indirect pre- and postprocessing
if (se) {
      ...               // the actual processing
}
```

The `sentry` object takes as the constructor argument the stream `strm`, on which the pre- and postprocessing should be done. The remaining processing then depends on the state of this object, which indicates whether the stream is OK. This state can be checked using the conversion of the `sentry` object to `bool`. For input streams, the `sentry` object can be constructed with an optional Boolean value that indicates whether skipping of whitespace should be avoided even though the flag `skipws` is set:

```
sentry se(strm,true);   // don't skip whitespaces during the additional processing
```

The pre- and postprocessing perform all general tasks of I/O using streams. These tasks include synchronizing several streams, checking whether the stream is OK, and skipping whitespaces, as well as possibly implementation-specific tasks. For example, in a multithreaded environment, the additional processing might be used for corresponding locking.

If an I/O operator operates directly on the stream buffer, a corresponding `sentry` object should be constructed first.

---

[11] These classes replace the member functions that were used in former implementations of the IOStream library (`ipfx()`, `isfx()`, `opfx()`, and `osfx()`). Using the new classes ensures that the postprocessing is invoked even if the I/O is aborted with an exception.

15.6 Manipulators

Manipulators for streams, introduced in Section 15.1.5, page 746, are objects that modify a stream when applied with the standard I/O operators. This does not necessarily mean that something is read or written. The basic manipulators defined in `<istream>` or `<ostream>` are presented in Table 15.8.

Manipulator	Class	Meaning
endl	basic_ostream	Inserts a newline character into the buffer and flushes the output buffer to its device
ends	basic_ostream	Inserts a (terminating) null character into the buffer
flush	basic_ostream	Flushes the output buffer to its device
ws	basic_istream	Reads and ignores whitespaces

Table 15.8. Manipulators Defined in `<istream>` or `<ostream>`

Manipulators with Arguments

Some of the manipulators process arguments. For example, you can use the following to set the minimum field width of the next output and the fill character:

```
std::cout << std::setw(6) << std::setfill('_');
```

The standard manipulators with arguments are defined in the header file `<iomanip>`, which must be included to work with the standard manipulators taking arguments:

```
#include <iomanip>
```

The standard manipulators taking arguments are all concerned with details of formatting, so they are described when general formatting options (see Section 15.7, page 779), time formatting (see Section 16.4.3, page 890), or monetary formatting (see Section 16.4.2, page 882) are introduced.

15.6.1 Overview of All Manipulators

Table 15.9 gives an overview of all manipulators provided by the C++ standard library, including the page where you can find details. `hexfloat`, `defaultfloat`, `put_time()`, `get_time()`, `put_money()`, and `get_money()` are provided since C++11.

Manipulator	Effect	Page
endl	Writes a newline character and flushes the output	776
ends	Writes a (terminating) null character	774
flush	Flushes the output	774
ws	Reads and ignores whitespaces	774
skipws	Skips leading whitespaces with operator >>	789
noskipws	Does not skip leading whitespaces with operator >>	789
unitbuf	Flushes the output buffer after each write operation	789
nounitbuf	Does not flush the output buffer after each write operation	789
setiosflags(*flags*)	Sets *flags* as format flags	780
resetiosflags(*m*)	Clears all flags of the group identified by mask *m*	780
setw(*val*)	Sets the field width of the next input and output to *val*	783
setfill(*c*)	Defines *c* as the fill character	783
left	Left-adjusts values	783
right	Right-adjusts values	783
internal	Left-adjusts signs and right-adjusts values	783
boolalpha	Forces textual representation for Boolean values	781
noboolalpha	Forces numeric representation for Boolean values	781
showpos	Forces writing a positive sign on positive numbers	784
noshowpos	Forces not writing a positive sign on positive numbers	784
uppercase	Forces uppercase letters for numeric values	784
nouppercase	Forces lowercase letters for numeric values	784
oct	Reads and writes integral values octal	785
dec	Reads and writes integral values decimal	785
hex	Reads and writes integral values hexadecimal	785
showbase	Indicates numeric base of numeric values	786
noshowbase	Does not indicate numeric base of numeric values	786
showpoint	Always writes a decimal point for floating-point values	788
noshowpoint	Does not require a decimal point for floating-point values	788
setprecision(*val*)	Sets *val* as the new value for the precision of floating-point values	788
fixed	Uses decimal notation for floating-point values	788
scientific	Uses scientific notation for floating-point values	788
hexfloat	Uses hexadecimal scientific notation for floating-point values	788
defaultfloat	Uses normal floating-point notation	788
put_time(*val*,*fmt*)	Writes a date/time value according to the format *fmt*	890
get_time(*val*,*fmt*)	Reads a time/date value according to the format *fmt*	890
put_money(*val*)	Writes a monetary value using the local currency symbol	882
put_money(*val*,*intl*)	Writes a monetary value using the currency symbol according to *intl*	882
get_money(*val*)	Reads a monetary value using the local currency symbol	882
get_money(*val*,*intl*)	Reads a monetary value using the currency symbol according to *intl*	882

Table 15.9. Manipulators Provided by the C++ Standard Library

15.6.2   How Manipulators Work

Manipulators are implemented using a very simple trick that not only enables the convenient manipulation of streams but also demonstrates the power provided by function overloading. Manipulators
are nothing more than functions passed to the I/O operators as arguments. The functions are then
called by the operator. For example, the output operator for class `ostream` is basically overloaded
like this:

ostream& ostream::operator << (*ostream&* (*op)(*ostream&*))
{
    // *call the function passed as parameter with this stream as the argument*
    return (*op)(*this);
}

The argument op is a pointer to a function that takes *ostream* as an argument and returns *ostream* (it
is assumed that the *ostream* given as the argument is returned). If the second operand of operator <<
is such a function, this function is called with the first operand of operator << as the argument.

    This may sound very complicated, but it is relatively simple. An example should make it clearer.
The manipulator — that is, the function — `endl()` for `ostream` is implemented basically like this:

```
std::ostream& std::endl (std::ostream& strm)
{
    // write newline
    strm.put('\n');

    // flush the output buffer
    strm.flush();

    // return strm to allow chaining
    return strm;
}
```

You can use this manipulator in an expression such as the following:

```
std::cout << std::endl
```

Here, operator << is called for stream `cout` with the `endl()` function as the second operand. The
implementation of operator << transforms this call into a call of the passed function with the stream
as the argument:

```
std::endl(std::cout)
```

The same effect as "writing" the manipulator can also be achieved by calling this expression directly.
An advantage to using the function notation is that it is not necessary to provide the namespace for
the manipulator:

```
endl(std::cout)
```

The reason is that, according to *ADL* (*argument-dependent lookup*, also known as *Koenig lookup*),
functions are looked up in the namespaces where their arguments are defined if they are not found
otherwise.

Because the stream classes are class templates parametrized with the character type, the real implementation of `endl()` looks like this:

```
template <typename charT, typename traits>
std::basic_ostream<charT,traits>&
std::endl (std::basic_ostream<charT,traits>& strm)
{
    strm.put(strm.widen('\n'));
    strm.flush();
    return strm;
}
```

The member function `widen()` is used to convert the newline character into the character set currently used by the stream. See Section 15.8, page 790, for more details.

How the manipulators with arguments work exactly is implementation dependent, and there is no standard way to implement user-defined manipulators with arguments (see the next section for an example).

15.6.3 User-Defined Manipulators

To define your own manipulator, you simply need to write a function such as `endl()`. For example, the following function defines a manipulator that ignores all characters until end-of-line:

```
// io/ignore1.hpp

#include <istream>
#include <limits>

template <typename charT, typename traits>
inline
std::basic_istream<charT,traits>&
ignoreLine (std::basic_istream<charT,traits>& strm)
{
    // skip until end-of-line
    strm.ignore(std::numeric_limits<std::streamsize>::max(),
                strm.widen('\n'));

    // return stream for concatenation
    return strm;
}
```

The manipulator simply delegates the work to the function `ignore()`, which in this case discards all characters until end-of-line (`ignore()` was introduced in Section 15.5.1, page 770).

The application of the manipulator is very simple:

```
// ignore the rest of the line
std::cin >> ignoreLine;
```

Applying this manipulator multiple times enables you to ignore multiple lines:

```
// ignore two lines
std::cin >> ignoreLine >> ignoreLine;
```

This works because a call to the function ignore(max,c) ignores all characters until the c is found
in the input stream, or max characters are read or the end of the stream was reached. However, this
character is discarded, too, before the function returns.

As written, there are multiple ways to define your own manipulator taking arguments. For example, the following code ignores n lines:

```
// io/ignore2.hpp

#include <istream>
#include <limits>

class ignoreLine
{
  private:
    int num;
  public:
    explicit ignoreLine (int n=1) : num(n) {
    }

    template <typename charT, typename traits>
    friend std::basic_istream<charT,traits>&
    operator>> (std::basic_istream<charT,traits>& strm,
                const ignoreLine& ign)
    {
        // skip until end-of-line num times
        for (int i=0; i<ign.num; ++i) {
            strm.ignore(std::numeric_limits<std::streamsize>::max(),
                        strm.widen('\n'));
        }

        // return stream for concatenation
        return strm;
    }
};
```

Here, the manipulator ignoreLine is a class, which takes the argument to get initialized, and the
input operator is overloaded for objects of this class.

15.7   Formatting

Two concepts influence the definition of I/O formats: Most obviously, there are format flags that define, for example, numeric precision, the fill character, or the numeric base. Apart from this, there exists the possibility of adjusting formats to meet special national conventions. This section introduces the format flags. Section 15.8, page 790, and Chapter 16 describe the aspects of internationalized formatting.

15.7.1   Format Flags

The classes `ios_base` and `basic_ios<>` have several members that are used for the definition of various I/O formats. For example, some members store the minimum field width or the precision of floating-point numbers or the fill character. A member of type `ios::fmtflags` stores configuration flags defining, for example, whether positive numbers should be preceded by a positive sign or whether Boolean values should be printed numerically or as words.

Some of the format flags form groups. For example, the flags for octal, decimal, and hexadecimal formats of integer numbers form a group. Special masks are defined to make dealing with such groups easier.

Member Function	Meaning
setf (*flags*)	Sets *flags* as additional flags and returns the previous state of all flags
setf (*flags, grp*)	Sets *flags* as the new flags of the group identified by *grp* and returns the previous state of all flags
unsetf (*flags*)	Clears *flags*
flags()	Returns all set format flags
flags (*flags*)	Sets *flags* as the new flags and returns the previous state of all flags
copyfmt (*stream*)	Copies *all* format definitions from *stream*

Table 15.10. Member Function to Access Format Flags

Several member functions can be used to handle all the format definitions of a stream (see Table 15.10). The functions `setf()` and `unsetf()` set or clear, respectively, one or more flags. You can manipulate multiple flags at once by combining them, using the "binary or" operator; that is, operator |. The function `setf()` can take a mask as the second argument to clear all flags in a group before setting the flags of the first argument, which are also limited to a group. This does not happen with the version of `setf()` that takes only one argument. For example:

```
// set flags showpos and uppercase
std::cout.setf (std::ios::showpos | std::ios::uppercase);
```

```
// set only the flag hex in the group basefield
std::cout.setf (std::ios::hex, std::ios::basefield);
```

```
// clear the flag uppercase
std::cout.unsetf (std::ios::uppercase);
```

Using `flags()`, you can manipulate all format flags at once. Calling `flags()` without an argument returns the current format flags. Calling `flags()` with an argument takes this argument as the new state of all format flags and returns the old state. Thus, `flags()` with an argument clears all flags and sets the flags that were passed. Using `flags()` is useful, for example, for saving the current state of the flags to restore the original state later. The following statements demonstrate an example:

```
using std::ios;
using std::cout;

// save current format flags
ios::fmtflags oldFlags = cout.flags();

// do some changes
cout.setf(ios::showpos | ios::showbase | ios::uppercase);
cout.setf(ios::internal, ios::adjustfield);
cout << std::hex << x << std::endl;

// restore saved format flags
cout.flags(oldFlags);
```

By using `copyfmt()` you can copy all the format information from one stream to another. See Section 15.11.1, page 811, for an example.

You can also use manipulators to set and clear format flags. These are presented in Table 15.11.

Manipulator	Effect
setiosflags (*flags*)	Sets *flags* as format flags (calls setf (*flags*) for the stream)
resetiosflags (*mask*)	Clears all flags of the group identified by *mask* (calls setf (0, *mask*) for the stream)

Table 15.11. Manipulators to Access Format Flags

The manipulators `setiosflags()` and `resetiosflags()` provide the possibility of setting or clearing, respectively, one or more flags in a write or read statement with operator `<<` or `>>`, respectively. To use one of these manipulators, you must include the header file `<iomanip>`. For example:

```
#include <iostream>
#include <iomanip>
...
std::cout << resetiosflags(std::ios::adjustfield) // clear adjustm. flags
          << setiosflags(std::ios::left);          // left-adjust values
```

Some flag manipulations are performed by specialized manipulators. These manipulators are used often because they are more convenient and more readable. They are discussed in the following subsections.

15.7.2 Input/Output Format of Boolean Values

The `boolalpha` flag defines the format used to read or to write Boolean values. It defines whether a numeric or a textual representation is used for Boolean values (Table 15.12).

Flag	Meaning
`boolalpha`	If set, specifies the use of textual representation; if not set, specifies the use of numeric representation

Table 15.12. Flag for Boolean Representation

If the flag is not set (the default), Boolean values are represented using numeric strings. In this case, the value 0 is always used for `false`, and the value 1 is always used for `true`. When reading a Boolean value as a numeric string, it is considered to be an error (setting `failbit` for the stream) if the value differs from 0 or 1.

If the flag is set, Boolean values are written using a textual representation. When a Boolean value is read, the string has to match the textual representation of either `true` or `false`. The stream's locale object is used to determine the strings used to represent `true` and `false` (see Section 15.8, page 790, and Section 16.2.2, page 865). The standard `"C"` locale object uses the strings `"true"` and `"false"` as representations of the Boolean values.

Special manipulators are defined for the convenient manipulation of this flag (Table 15.13).

Manipulator	Meaning
`boolalpha`	Forces textual representation (sets the flag `ios::boolalpha`)
`noboolalpha`	Forces numeric representation (clears the flag `ios::boolalpha`)

Table 15.13. Manipulators for Boolean Representation

For example, the following statements print b first in numeric and then in textual representation:

```
bool b;
...
std::cout << std::noboolalpha << b << " == "
          << std::boolalpha << b << std::endl;
```

15.7.3 Field Width, Fill Character, and Adjustment

Two member functions are used to define the field width and the fill character: `width()` and `fill()` (Table 15.14).

Member Function	Meaning
width()	Returns the current field width
width(*val*)	Sets the field width for the next formatted output to *val* and returns the previous field width
fill()	Returns the current fill character
fill(*c*)	Defines *c* as the fill character and returns the previous fill character

Table 15.14. Member Functions for the Field Width and the Fill Character

Using Field Width, Fill Character, and Adjustment for Output

For the output, width() defines a minimum field. This definition applies only to the next formatted field written. Calling width() without arguments returns the current field width. Calling width() with an integral argument changes the width and returns the former value. The default value for the minimum field width is 0, which means that the field may have any length. This is also the value to which the field width is set after a value was written.

Note that the field width is never used to truncate output. Thus, you can't specify a maximum field width. Instead, you have to program it. For example, you could write to a string and output only a certain number of characters.

The member function fill() defines the fill character that is used to fill the difference between the formatted representation of a value and the minimum field width. The default fill character is a space.

To adjust values within a field, three flags are defined, as shown in Table 15.15. These flags are defined in the class ios_base together with the corresponding mask.

Mask	Flag	Meaning
adjustfield	left	Left-adjusts the value
	right	Right-adjusts the value
	internal	Left-adjusts the sign and right-adjusts the value
	None	Right-adjusts the value (the default)

Table 15.15. Masks to Adjust Values within a Field

Table 15.16 presents the effect of the functions and the flags used for various values. The underscore is used as the fill character.

Adjustment	width()	-42	0.12	"Q"	'Q'
left	6	-42___	0.12__	Q_____	Q_____
right	6	___-42	__0.12	_____Q	_____Q
internal	6	-___42	__0.12	_____Q	_____Q

Table 15.16. Examples of Adjustments

After any formatted I/O operation is performed, the default field width is restored. The values of the fill character and the adjustment remain unchanged until they are modified explicitly.

Several manipulators are defined to handle the field width, the fill character, and the adjustment (Table 15.17).

Manipulator	Meaning
setw(*val*)	Sets the field width of the next input and output to *val* (corresponds to width())
setfill(*c*)	Defines *c* as the fill character (corresponds to fill())
left	Left-adjusts the value
right	Right-adjusts the value
internal	Left-adjusts the sign and right-adjusts the value

Table 15.17. Manipulators for Adjustment

The manipulators setw() and setfill() use an argument, so you must include the header file <iomanip> to use them. For example, the statements

```
#include <iostream>
#include <iomanip>
...
std::cout << std::setw(8) << std::setfill('_') << -3.14
          << ' ' << 42 << std::endl;
std::cout << std::setw(8) << "sum: "
          << std::setw(8) << 42 << std::endl;
```

produce this output:

```
___-3.14 42
___sum: _____42
```

Using Field Width for Input

You can also use the field width to define the maximum number of characters read when character sequences of type char* are read. If the value of width() is not 0, at most width()-1 characters are read.

Because ordinary C-strings can't grow while values are read, width() or setw() should always be used when reading them with operator >>. For example:

```
char buffer[81];
```

// read, at most, 80 characters:
```
cin >> setw(sizeof(buffer)) >> buffer;
```

This reads at most 80 characters, although sizeof(buffer) is 81 because one character is used for the (terminating) null character, which is appended automatically. Note that the following code is a common error:

```
char* s;
cin >> setw(sizeof(s)) >> s;      // RUNTIME ERROR
```

The reason is that s is declared only as a pointer without any storage for characters, and sizeof(s) is the size of the pointer instead of the size of the storage to which it points. This is a typical example of the problems you encounter if you use C-strings. By using strings, you won't run into these problems:

```
string buffer;
cin >> buffer;                          // OK
```

15.7.4   Positive Sign and Uppercase Letters

Two format flags are defined to influence the general appearance of numeric values: showpos and uppercase (Table 15.18).

Flag	Meaning
showpos	Writes a positive sign on positive numbers
uppercase	Uses uppercase letters

Table 15.18. Flags Affecting Sign and Letters of Numeric Values

Using ios::showpos dictates that a positive sign for positive numeric values be written. If the flag is not set, only negative values are written with a sign. Using ios::uppercase dictates that letters in numeric values be written using uppercase letters. This flag applies to integers using hexadecimal format and to floating-point numbers using scientific notation. By default, letters are written as lowercase, and no positive sign is written. For example, the statements

```
std::cout << 12345678.9 << std::endl;

std::cout.setf (std::ios::showpos | std::ios::uppercase);
std::cout << 12345678.9 << std::endl;
```

produce this output:

```
1.23457e+07
+1.23457E+07
```

Both flags can be set or cleared using the manipulators presented in Table 15.19.

Manipulator	Meaning
showpos	Forces writing a positive sign on positive numbers (sets the flag ios::showpos)
noshowpos	Forces not writing a positive sign (clears the flag ios::showpos)
uppercase	Forces uppercase letters (sets the flag ios::uppercase)
nouppercase	Forces lowercase letters (clears the flag ios::uppercase)

Table 15.19. Manipulators for Sign and Letters of Numeric Values

15.7.5 Numeric Base

A group of three flags defines which base is used for I/O of integer values. The flags are defined in the class `ios_base` with the corresponding mask (Table 15.20).

Mask	Flag	Meaning
basefield	oct	Writes and reads octal
	dec	Writes and reads decimal (default)
	hex	Writes and reads hexadecimal
	None	Writes decimal and reads according to the leading characters of the integral value

Table 15.20. Flags Defining the Base of Integral Values

A change in base applies to the processing of all integer numbers until the flags are reset. By default, decimal format is used. There is no support for binary notation. However, you can read and write integral values in binary by using class `bitset`. See Section 12.5.1, page 652, for details.

If none of the base flags is set, output uses a decimal base. If more than one flag is set, decimal is used as the base.

The flags for the numeric base also affect input. If one of the flags for the numeric base is set, all numbers are read using this base. If no flag for the base is set when numbers are read, the base is determined by the leading characters: A number starting with 0x or 0X is read as a hexadecimal number. A number starting with 0 is read as an octal number. In all other cases, the number is read as a decimal value.

There are two ways to switch these flags:

1. Clear one flag and set another:
   ```
   std::cout.unsetf (std::ios::dec);
   std::cout.setf (std::ios::hex);
   ```
2. Set one flag and clear all other flags in the group automatically:
   ```
   std::cout.setf (std::ios::hex, std::ios::basefield);
   ```

In addition, the C++ standard library provides manipulators that make handling these flags significantly simpler (Table 15.21).

Manipulator	Meaning
oct	Writes and reads octal
dec	Writes and reads decimal
hex	Writes and reads hexadecimal

Table 15.21. Manipulators Defining the Base of Integral Values

For example, the following statements write x and y in hexadecimal and z in decimal:

```
int x, y, z;
...
std::cout << std::hex << x << std::endl;
std::cout << y << ' ' << std::dec << z << std::endl;
```

An additional flag, showbase, lets you write numbers according to the usual C/C++ convention for indicating numeric bases of literal values (Table 15.22).

Flag	Meaning
showbase	If set, indicates the numeric base

Table 15.22. Flags to Indicate the Numeric Base

If ios::showbase is set, octal numbers are preceded by a 0, and hexadecimal numbers are preceded by 0x or, if ios::uppercase is set, by 0X. For example, the statements

```
std::cout << 127 << ' ' << 255 << std::endl;

std::cout << std::hex << 127 << ' ' << 255 << std::endl;

std::cout.setf(std::ios::showbase);
std::cout << 127 << ' ' << 255 << std::endl;

std::cout.setf(std::ios::uppercase);
std::cout << 127 << ' ' << 255 << std::endl;
```

produce this output:

```
127 255
7f ff
0x7f 0xff
0X7F 0XFF
```

Note that ios::showbase can also be manipulated using the manipulators presented in Table 15.23.

Manipulator	Meaning
showbase	Indicates numeric base (sets the flag ios::showbase)
noshowbase	Does not indicate numeric base (clears the flag ios::showbase)

Table 15.23. Manipulators to Indicate the Numeric Base

15.7.6 Floating-Point Notation

Several flags and members control the output of floating-point values. The flags, presented in Table 15.24, define whether output is written using decimal or scientific notation. These flags are defined in the class ios_base together with the corresponding mask. If ios::fixed is set, floating-point values are printed using decimal notation. If ios::scientific is set, scientific — that is, exponential — notation is used.

Mask	Flag(s)	Meaning
floatfield	fixed	Uses decimal notation
	scientific	Uses scientific notation
	None	Uses the "best" of these two notations (default)
	fixed|scientific	Hexadecimal scientific notation (since C++11)

Table 15.24. Flags for Floating-Point Notation

Before C++11, specifying fixed|scientific was not defined. Since C++11, this can be used to define a hexadecimal scientific notation, which also the format specifier %a provides for printf(): a hexadecimal value to the power of 2. For example, 234.5 is written as 0x1.d5p+7 (0x1.d5 times 2^7, which is $1*\frac{128}{1} + 13*\frac{128}{16} + 5*\frac{128}{256}$).

Using the flag showpoint, you can force the stream to write a decimal point and trailing zeros until places according to the current precision are written (Table 15.25).

Flag	Meaning
showpoint	Always writes a decimal point and fills up with trailing zeros

Table 15.25. Flag to Force Decimal Point

To define the precision, the member function precision() is provided (see Table 15.26).

Member Function	Meaning
precision()	Returns the current precision of floating-point values
precision(*val*)	Sets *val* as the new precision of floating-point values and returns the old

Table 15.26. Member Function for the Precision of Floating-Point Values

If scientific notation is used, precision() defines the number of decimal places in the fractional part. In all cases, the remainder is not cut off but rounded. Calling precision() without arguments returns the current precision. Calling it with an argument sets the precision to that value and returns the previous precision. The default precision is six decimal places.

By default, neither `ios::fixed` nor `ios::scientific` is set. In this case, the notation used depends on the value written. All meaningful but, at most, `precision()` decimal places are written as follows: A leading zero before the decimal point and/or all trailing zeros and potentially even the decimal point are removed. If `precision()` places are sufficient, decimal notation is used; otherwise, scientific notation is used.

Table 15.27 shows the somewhat complicated dependencies between flags and precision, using two concrete values as an example.

As for integral values, `ios::showpos` can be used to write a positive sign, and `ios::uppercase` can be used to dictate whether the scientific notations should use uppercase or lowercase letters.

	`precision()`	**421.0**	**0.0123456789**
Normal	2	4.2e+02	0.012
	6	421	0.0123457
With `showpoint`	2	4.2e+02	0.012
	6	421.000	0.0123457
`fixed`	2	421.00	0.01
	6	421.000000	0.012346
`scientific`	2	4.21e+02	1.23e-02
	6	4.210000e+02	1.234568e-02
`fixed|scientific`	2	0x1.a5p+8	0x1.95p-7
	6	0x1.a50000p+8	0x1.948b10p-7

Table 15.27. Example of Floating-Point Formatting

The flag `ios::showpoint`, the notation, and the precision can be configured using the manipulators presented in Table 15.28.

Manipulator	Meaning
`showpoint`	Always writes a decimal point (sets the flag `ios::showpoint`)
`noshowpoint`	Does not require a decimal point (clears the flag `showpoint`)
`setprecision(`*val*`)`	Sets *val* as the new value for the precision
`fixed`	Uses decimal notation
`scientific`	Uses scientific notation
`hexfloat`	Uses hexadecimal scientific notation (since C++11)
`defaultfloat`	Uses normal notation (clears the flag `floatfield`, since C++11)

Table 15.28. Manipulators for Floating-Point Values

For example, the statement

```
std::cout << std::scientific << std::showpoint
         << std::setprecision(8)
         << 0.123456789 << std::endl;
```

produces this output:

```
1.23456789e-01
```

Note that `setprecision()` is a manipulator with an argument, so you must include the header file `<iomanip>` to use it.

15.7.7 General Formatting Definitions

Two more format flags complete the list of formatting flags: `skipws` and `unitbuf` (Table 15.29).

Flag	Meaning
skipws	Skips leading whitespaces automatically when reading a value with operator >>
unitbuf	Flushes the output buffer after each write operation

Table 15.29. Other Formatting Flags

By default, `ios::skipws` is set, which means that leading whitespaces are skipped by operator >>. Often, it is useful to have this flag set. For example, with it set, reading the separating spaces between numbers explicitly is not necessary. However, this implies that reading space characters using operator >> is not possible because leading whitespaces are always skipped.

With `ios::unitbuf`, the buffering of the output is controlled. When it is set, output is unbuffered, which means that the output buffer is flushed after each write operation. By default, this flag is not set for most streams. However, for the streams `cerr` and `wcerr`, this flag is set initially.

Both flags can be manipulated using the manipulators presented in Table 15.30.

Manipulator	Meaning
skipws	Skips leading whitespaces with operator >> (sets the flag ios::skipws)
noskipws	Does not skip leading whitespaces with operator >> (clears the flag ios::skipws)
unitbuf	Flushes the output buffer after each write operation (sets the flag ios::unitbuf)
nounitbuf	Does not flush the output buffer after each write operation (clears the flag ios::unitbuf)

Table 15.30. Manipulators for Other Formatting Flags

15.8   Internationalization

You can adapt I/O formats to national conventions. To do so, the class `ios_base` defines the member functions presented in Table 15.31.

Member Function	Meaning
imbue(*loc*)	Sets the locale object
getloc()	Returns the current locale object

Table 15.31. Member Functions for Internationalization

Each stream uses an associated locale object. The initial default locale object is a copy of the global locale object at the construction time of the stream. The locale object defines, for example, details about numeric formatting, such as the character used as the decimal point or the strings used for the textual representation of Boolean values.

In contrast to the C localization facilities, you can configure each stream individually with a specific locale object. This capability can be used, for example, to read floating-point values according to American format and to write them using German format (in German, a comma is used as the "decimal point"). Section 16.2.1, page 860, presents an example and discusses the details.

Several characters, mainly special characters, are often needed in the character set of the stream. For this reason, some conversion functions are provided by streams (Table 15.32).

Member Function	Meaning
widen(*c*)	Converts the `char` character *c* to a character of the stream's character set
narrow(*c*,*def*)	Converts character *c* from the stream's character set to a `char`; if there is no such `char`, *def* is returned

Table 15.32. Stream Functions for the Internationalization of Characters

For example, to get the newline character from the character set of the stream `strm`, you can use a statement like

```
strm.widen('\n')
```

For additional details on locales and on internationalization in general, see Chapter 16.

15.9   File Access

Streams can be used to access files. This section discusses the corresponding features provided.

15.9.1   File Stream Classes

The C++ standard library provides four class templates for which the following standard specializations are predefined:

1. The class template `basic_ifstream<>` with the specializations `ifstream` and `wifstream` is for read access to files ("input file stream").
2. The class template `basic_ofstream<>` with the specializations `ofstream` and `wofstream` is for write access to files ("output file stream").
3. The class template `basic_fstream<>` with the specializations `fstream` and `wfstream` is for access to files that should be both read and written.
4. The class template `basic_filebuf<>` with the specializations `filebuf` and `wfilebuf` is used by the other file stream classes to perform the actual reading and writing of characters.

The classes are related to the stream base classes, as depicted in Figure 15.2, and are declared in the header file `<fstream>` as follows:

```
namespace std {
    template <typename charT,
              typename traits = char_traits<charT> >
            class basic_ifstream;
    typedef basic_ifstream<char>    ifstream;
    typedef basic_ifstream<wchar_t> wifstream;

    template <typename charT,
              typename traits = char_traits<charT> >
            class basic_ofstream;
    typedef basic_ofstream<char>    ofstream;
    typedef basic_ofstream<wchar_t> wofstream;

    template <typename charT,
              typename traits = char_traits<charT> >
            class basic_fstream;
    typedef basic_fstream<char>     fstream;
    typedef basic_fstream<wchar_t>  wfstream;

     template <typename charT,
               typename traits = char_traits<charT> >
            class basic_filebuf;
     typedef basic_filebuf<char>    filebuf;
     typedef basic_filebuf<wchar_t> wfilebuf;
}
```

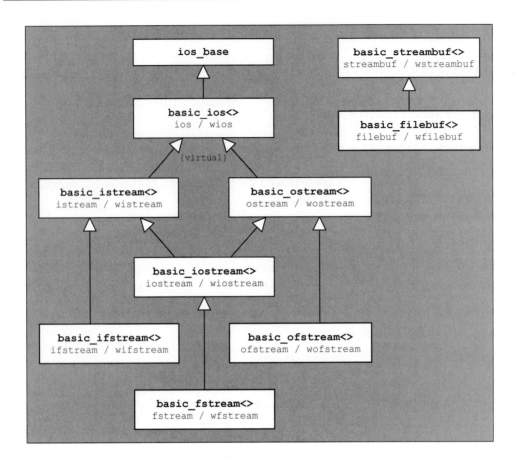

Figure 15.2. Class Hierarchy of the File Stream Classes

Compared with the mechanism of C, a major advantage of the file stream classes for file access is the automatic management of files. The files are automatically opened at construction time and closed at destruction time. This is possible, of course, through appropriate definitions of corresponding constructors and destructors.

For streams that are both read and written, it is important to note that it is *not* possible to switch arbitrarily between reading and writing.[12] Once you start to read or write a file you have to perform a seek operation, potentially to the current position, to switch from reading to writing or vice versa. The only exception to this rule is if you have read until end-of-file. In this case, you can continue writing characters immediately. Violating this rule can lead to all kinds of strange effects.

---

[12] This restriction is inherited from C. However, it is likely that implementations of the standard C++ library make use of this restriction.

If a file stream object is constructed with a string or C-string as an argument, opening the file for reading and/or writing is attempted automatically. Whether this attempt was successful is reflected in the stream's state. Thus, the state should be examined after construction.

The following program first opens the file `charset.out`, writes the current character set — all characters for the values between 32 and 255 — into this file, and outputs its contents:

```cpp
// io/fstream1.cpp

#include <string>       // for strings
#include <iostream>     // for I/O
#include <fstream>      // for file I/O
#include <iomanip>      // for setw()
#include <cstdlib>      // for exit()
using namespace std;

// forward declarations
void writeCharsetToFile (const string& filename);
void outputFile (const string& filename);

int main ()
{
    writeCharsetToFile("charset.out");
    outputFile("charset.out");
}

void writeCharsetToFile (const string& filename)
{
    // open output file
    ofstream file(filename);

    // file opened?
    if (! file) {
        // NO, abort program
        cerr << "can't open output file \"" << filename << "\""
             << endl;
        exit(EXIT_FAILURE);
    }

    // write character set
    for (int i=32; i<256; ++i) {
        file << "value: " << setw(3) << i << "    "
             << "char:  " << static_cast<char>(i) << endl;
    }

}   // closes file automatically
```

```
void outputFile (const string& filename)
{
    // open input file
    ifstream file(filename);

    // file opened?
    if (! file) {
        // NO, abort program
        cerr << "can't open input file \"" << filename << "\""
            << endl;
        exit(EXIT_FAILURE);
    }

    // copy file contents to cout
    char c;
    while (file.get(c)) {
        cout.put(c);
    }

}   // closes file automatically
```

In `writeCharsetToFile()`, the constructor of the class `ofstream` takes care of opening the file named by the given filename:

```
std::ofstream file(filename);   // open file for writing
```

Unfortunately, before C++11, the file stream classes did not provide a constructor taking a `string` as argument. So, before C++11, you had to write:

```
std::ofstream file(filename.c_str());   // open file for writing before C++11
```

After this declaration, it is determined whether the stream is in a good state:

```
if (! file) {
    ...
}
```

If opening the stream was not successful, this test will fail. After this check, a loop prints the values 32 to 255 together with the corresponding characters.

In the function `outputFile()`, the constructor of the class `ifstream` opens the file for reading. Then the contents of the file are read and output characterwise.

At the end of both functions, the file opened locally is closed automatically when the corresponding stream goes out of scope. The destructors of the classes `ifstream` and `ofstream` take care of closing the file if it is still open at destruction time.

Instead of copying the file contents character by character, you could also output the whole contents in one statement by passing a pointer to the stream buffer of the file as an argument to operator `<<`:

// copy file contents to `cout`
```
std::cout << file.rdbuf();
```
See Section 15.14.3, page 846, for details.

15.9.2   Rvalue and Move Semantics for File Streams

Since C++11, file streams provide rvalue and move semantics. In fact, ostreams provide an output
operator, and istreams provide an input iterator that accepts an rvalue reference for the stream. The
effect is that you can now use temporarily created stream objects, and they behave as expected. For
example, you can write to a temporarily created file stream:[13]

```
// io/fstream2.cpp

#include <iostream>
#include <fstream>
#include <string>

int main()
{
    // write string to a temporarily created file stream (since C++11)
    std::string s("hello");
    std::ofstream("fstream2.tmp") << s << std::endl;

    // write C-string to a temporarily created file stream
    // - NOTE: wrote a pointer value before C++11
    std::ofstream("fstream2.tmp", std::ios::app) << "world" << std::endl;
}
```

Since C++11, this writes `"hello"` and `"world"` to the file `"fstream2.tmp"`. Before C++11, in-
stead of the first output statement you had to write the following:
```
std::string s("hello");
std::ofstream os("fstream2.tmp");
os << s << std::endl;
```
Note that before C++11, the second output statement compiled but did something very unexpected:
It wrote a *pointer value* to `"fstream2.tmp"`. The reason for the old behavior was that the following
member function was called (see Section 15.3.3, page 756):
```
ostream& ostream::operator<< (const void* ptr);
```
In addition, file streams now have move and swap semantics providing a move constructor, a move
assignment operator, and `swap()`. So you can pass a file stream as argument or return a file stream
from a function. For example, if a file should be used longer than the scope in which it was created,

---

[13] Thanks to Daniel Krügler for providing this example.

you can return it as follows since C++11 (see Section 3.1.5, page 22, for details about returning values with move semantics):

```
std::ofstream openFile (const std::string& filename)
{
    std::ofstream file(filename);
    ...
    return file;
}
```

```
std::ofstream file;
file = openFile("xyz.tmp");              // use returned file stream (since C++11)
file << "hello, world" << std::endl;
```

Before C++11, you had to — and as an alternative you still can — allocate the file object on the heap and delete it later when it is no longer needed:

```
std::ofstream* filePtr = new std::ofstream("xyz.tmp");
...
delete filePtr;
```

For such a case, some smart pointer classes (see Section 5.2, page 76) should be used.

15.9.3 File Flags

A set of flags is defined in the class `ios_base` for precise control over the processing mode of a file (Table 15.33). These flags are of type `openmode`, which is a bitmask type similar to `fmtflags`.

Flag	Meaning
in	Opens for reading (default for `ifstream`)
out	Opens for writing (default for `ofstream`)
app	Always appends at the end when writing
ate	Positions at the end of the file after opening ("at end")
trunc	Removes the former file contents
binary	Does not replace special characters

Table 15.33. Flags for Opening Files

The flag `binary` configures the stream to suppress conversion of special characters or character sequences, such as end-of-line or end-of-file. In operating systems, such as Windows or OS/2, a line end in text files is represented by two characters (CR and LF). In normal text mode (`binary` is not set), newline characters are replaced by the two-character sequence, and vice versa, when reading or writing to avoid special processing. In binary mode (`binary` is set), none of these conversions take place.

The flag `binary` should always be used if the contents of a file do not consist of a character sequence but are processed as binary data. An example is the copying of files by reading the file to be copied character by character and writing those characters without modifying them. If the file is processed as text, the flag should not be set, because special handling of newlines would be required. For example, a newline would still consist of two characters.

Some implementations provide additional flags, such as `nocreate` (the file must exist when it is opened) and `noreplace` (the file must not exist). However, these flags are not standard and thus are not portable.

The flags can be combined by using operator `|`. The resulting `openmode` can be passed as an optional second argument to the constructor. For example, the following statement opens a file for appending text at the end:

```
std::ofstream file("xyz.out", std::ios::out|std::ios::app);
```

Table 15.34 correlates the various combinations of flags with the strings used in the interface of C's function for opening files: `fopen()`. The combinations with the `binary` and the `ate` flags set are not listed. A set `binary` corresponds to strings with `b` appended, and a set `ate` corresponds to a seek to the end of the file immediately after opening. Other combinations not listed in the table, such as `trunc|app`, are not allowed. Note that before C++11, `app`, `in|app`, and `in|out|app` were not specified.

`ios_base` Flags	Meaning	C Mode
`in`	Reads (file must exist)	`"r"`
`out`	Empties and writes (creates if necessary)	`"w"`
`out|trunc`	Empties and writes (creates if necessary)	`"w"`
`out|app`	Appends (creates if necessary)	`"a"`
`app`	Appends (creates if necessary)	`"a"`
`in|out`	Reads and writes; initial position is the start (file must exist)	`"r+"`
`in|out|trunc`	Empties, reads, and writes (creates if necessary)	`"w+"`
`in|app`	Updates at end (creates if necessary)	`"a+"`
`in|out|app`	Updates at end (creates if necessary)	`"a+"`

Table 15.34. Meaning of Open Modes in C++

Whether a file is opened for reading and/or for writing is independent of the corresponding stream object's class. The class determines only the default open mode if no second argument is used. This means that files used only by the class `ifstream` or the class `ofstream` can be opened for reading *and* writing. The open mode is passed to the corresponding stream buffer class, which opens the file. However, the operations possible for the object are determined by the stream's class.

The file owned by a file stream can also be opened or closed explicitly. For this, three member functions are defined (Table 15.35). These functions are useful mainly if a file stream is created without being initialized.

To demonstrate their use, the following example opens all files with names that are given as arguments to the program and writes their contents (this corresponds to the UNIX program `cat`).

Member Function	Meaning
open(*name*)	Opens a file for the stream, using the default mode
open(*name*, *flags*)	Opens a file for the stream, using *flags* as the mode
close()	Closes the streams file
is_open()	Returns whether the file is opened

Table 15.35. Member Functions to Open and Close Files

```cpp
// io/cat1.cpp

// header files for file I/O
#include <fstream>
#include <iostream>
using namespace std;

// for all filenames passed as command-line arguments
// - open, print contents, and close file
int main (int argc, char* argv[])
{
    ifstream file;

    // for all command-line arguments
    for (int i=1; i<argc; ++i) {

        // open file
        file.open(argv[i]);

        // write file contents to cout
        char c;
        while (file.get(c)) {
            cout.put(c);
        }

        // clear eofbit and failbit set due to end-of-file
        file.clear();

        // close file
        file.close();
    }
}
```

Note that after the processing of a file, clear() must be called to clear the state flags that are set at end-of-file. This is required because the stream object is used for multiple files. Note that open()

never clears any state flags. Thus, if a stream was not in a good state after closing and reopening it, you still have to call `clear()` to get to a good state. This is also the case if you open a different file.

Instead of processing character by character, you could also print the entire contents of the file in one statement by passing a pointer to the stream buffer of the file as an argument to operator `<<`:

```
// write file contents to cout
std::cout << file.rdbuf();
```

See Section 15.14.3, page 846, for details.

15.9.4 Random Access

Class	Member Function	Meaning
`basic_istream<>`	`tellg()`	Returns the read position
	`seekg(pos)`	Sets the read position as an absolute value
	`seekg(offset, rpos)`	Sets the read position as a relative value
`basic_ostream<>`	`tellp()`	Returns the write position
	`seekp(pos)`	Sets the write position as an absolute value
	`seekp(offset, rpos)`	Sets the write position as a relative value

Table 15.36. Member Functions for Stream Positions

Table 15.36 lists the member functions defined for positioning within C++ streams. These functions distinguish between read and write position (g stands for *get* and p stands for *put*). Read-position functions are defined in `basic_istream<>`, and write-position functions are defined in `basic_ostream<>`. However, not all stream classes support positioning. For example, positioning the streams `cin`, `cout`, and `cerr` is not defined. The positioning of files is defined in the base classes because, usually, references to objects of type `istream` and `ostream` are passed around.

The functions `seekg()` and `seekp()` can be called with absolute or relative positions. To handle absolute positions, you must use `tellg()` and `tellp()`, which return an absolute position as a value of type `pos_type`. This value is *not* an integral value or simply the position of the character as an index, because the logical position and the real position can differ. For example, in Windows text files, newline characters are represented by two characters in the file, even though it is logically only one character. Things are even worse if the file uses some multibyte representation for the characters.

The exact definition of `pos_type` is a bit complicated: The C++ standard library defines a global class template `fpos<>` for file positions. Class `fpos<>` is used to define types `streampos` for `char` and `wstreampos` for `wchar_t` streams. These types are used to define the `pos_type` of the corresponding character traits (see Section 16.1.4, page 855), and this `pos_type` member of the traits is used to define `pos_type` of the corresponding stream classes. Thus, you could also use `streampos` as the type for the stream positions. However, using `long` or `unsigned long` is wrong because `streampos` is *not* an integral type (anymore).[14] For example:

---

[14] Formerly, `streampos` was used for stream positions, and it was simply defined as `unsigned long`.

```
// save current file position
std::ios::pos_type pos = file.tellg();
...
// seek to file position saved in pos
file.seekg(pos);
```

Instead of

```
std::ios::pos_type pos;
```

you could also write:

```
std::streampos pos;
```

For relative values, the offset can be relative to three positions, for which corresponding constants are defined (Table 15.37). The constants are defined in class `ios_base` and are of type `seekdir`.

Constant	Meaning
beg	Position is relative to the beginning ("beginning")
cur	Position is relative to the current position ("current")
end	Position is relative to the end ("end")

Table 15.37. Constants for Relative Positions

The type for the offset is `off_type`, which is an indirect definition of `streamoff`. Similar to `pos_type`, `streamoff` is used to define `off_type` of the traits (see Section 16.1.4, page 855) and the stream classes. However, `streamoff` is a signed integral type, so you can use integral values as stream offsets. For example:

```
// seek to the beginning of the file
file.seekg (0, std::ios::beg);
...
// seek 20 characters forward
file.seekg (20, std::ios::cur);
...
// seek 10 characters before the end
file.seekg (-10, std::ios::end);
```

In all cases, care must be taken to position only within a file. If a position ends up before the beginning of a file or beyond the end, the behavior is undefined.

The following example demonstrates the use of `seekg()`. It uses a function that writes the contents of a file twice:

```
// io/cat2.cpp

// header files for file I/O
#include <iostream>
#include <fstream>
```

```
void printFileTwice (const char* filename)
{
    // open file
    std::ifstream file(filename);

    // print contents the first time
    std::cout << file.rdbuf();

    // seek to the beginning
    file.seekg(0);

    // print contents the second time
    std::cout << file.rdbuf();
}

int main (int argc, char* argv[])
{
    // print all files passed as a command-line argument twice
    for (int i=1; i<argc; ++i) {
        printFileTwice(argv[i]);
    }
}
```

Note that `file.rdbuf()` is used to print the contents of `file` (see Section 15.14.3, page 846). Thus, you operate directly on the stream buffer, which can't manipulate the state of the stream. If you print the contents of `file` by using the stream interface functions, such as `getline()` (see Section 15.5.1, page 768), you'd have to `clear()` the state of `file` before it could be manipulated in any way (including changes of the read position), because these functions set `ios::eofbit` and `ios::failbit` when end-of-file is reached.

Different functions are provided for the manipulation of the read and the write positions. However, for the standard streams, the same position is maintained for reading and writing in the same stream buffer. This is important if multiple streams use the same stream buffer (see Section 15.12.2, page 820, for details).

15.9.5 Using File Descriptors

Some implementations provide the possibility of attaching a stream to an already opened I/O channel. To do this, you initialize the file stream with a *file descriptor*.

File descriptors are integers that identify an open I/O channel. In UNIX-like systems, file descriptors are used in the low-level interface to the I/O functions of the operating system. The following file descriptors are predefined:

- 0 for the standard input channel
- 1 for the standard output channel
- 2 for the standard error channel

These channels may be connected to files, the console, other processes, or some other I/O facility.

Unfortunately, the C++ standard library does not provide the possibility of attaching a stream to an I/O channel using file descriptors. The reason is that the language is supposed to be independent of any operating system. In practice, though, the possibility probably still exists. The only drawback is that using it is not portable to all systems. What is missing at this point is a corresponding specification in a standard of operating system interfaces, such as POSIX or X/OPEN. However, such a standard is not yet planned, but at least `posix` is a reserved namespace since C++11.

Nevertheless, it is possible to initialize a stream by a file descriptor. See Section 15.13.3, page 835, for a description and implementation of a possible solution.

15.10 Stream Classes for Strings

The mechanisms of stream classes can also be used to read from strings or to write to strings. String streams provide a buffer but don't have an I/O channel. This buffer/string can be manipulated with special functions. A major use of this capability is the processing of I/O independent of the actual I/O. For example, text for output can be formatted in a string and then sent to an output channel sometime later. Another use is reading input line by line and processing each line by using string streams.

Before the standardization of C++98, the string stream classes used type `char*` to represent a string. Now, type `string` (or, in general, `basic_string<>`) is used. The old string stream classes are also part of the C++ standard library, but they are deprecated. Thus, they should not be used in new code and should be replaced in legacy code. Still, a brief description of these classes is found at the end of this section.

15.10.1 String Stream Classes

The following stream classes — corresponding to the stream classes for files — are defined for strings:

- The class template `basic_istringstream<>` with the specializations `istringstream` and `wistringstream` for reading from strings ("input string stream")
- The class template `basic_ostringstream<>` with the specializations `ostringstream` and `wostringstream` for writing to strings ("output string stream")
- The class template `basic_stringstream<>` with the specializations `stringstream` and `wstringstream` for reading from and writing to strings
- The class template `basic_stringbuf<>` with the specializations `stringbuf` and `wstringbuf`, used by the other string stream classes to perform the reading and writing of characters

These classes have a similar relationship to the stream base classes, as do the file stream classes. The class hierarchy is depicted in Figure 15.3.

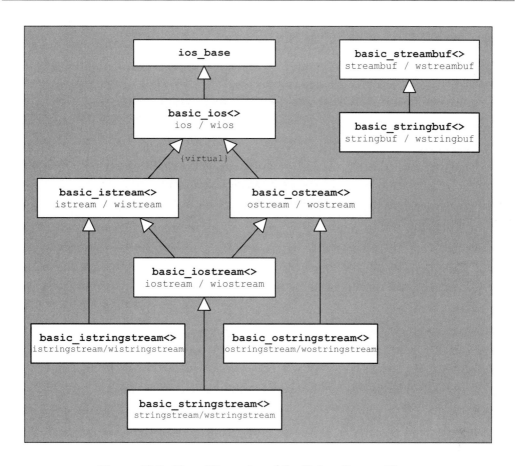

Figure 15.3. Class Hierarchy of the String Stream Classes

The classes are declared in the header file `<sstream>` like this:

```
namespace std {
    template <typename charT,
              typename traits = char_traits<charT>,
              typename Allocator = allocator<charT> >
        class basic_istringstream;
    typedef basic_istringstream<char>    istringstream;
    typedef basic_istringstream<wchar_t> wistringstream;

    template <typename charT,
              typename traits = char_traits<charT>,
              typename Allocator = allocator<charT> >
        class basic_ostringstream;
    typedef basic_ostringstream<char>    ostringstream;
    typedef basic_ostringstream<wchar_t> wostringstream;
```

```
template <typename charT,
          typename traits = char_traits<charT>,
          typename Allocator = allocator<charT> >
      class basic_stringstream;
typedef basic_stringstream<char>    stringstream;
typedef basic_stringstream<wchar_t> wstringstream;

template <typename charT,
          typename traits = char_traits<charT>,
          typename Allocator = allocator<charT> >
      class basic_stringbuf;
typedef basic_stringbuf<char>    stringbuf;
typedef basic_stringbuf<wchar_t> wstringbuf;
}
```

The major function in the interface of the string stream classes is the member function `str()`, which is used to manipulate the buffer of the string stream classes (Table 15.38).

Member Function	Meaning
str()	Returns the buffer as a string
str(*string*)	Sets the contents of the buffer to *string*

Table 15.38. Fundamental Operations for String Streams

The following program demonstrates the use of string streams:

```
// io/sstream1.cpp

#include <iostream>
#include <sstream>
#include <bitset>
using namespace std;

int main()
{
    ostringstream os;

    // decimal and hexadecimal value
    os << "dec: " << 15 << hex << " hex: " << 15 << endl;
    cout << os.str() << endl;

    // append floating value and bitset
    bitset<15> b(5789);
    os << "float: " << 4.67 << " bitset: " << b << endl;
```

```
    // overwrite with octal value
    os.seekp(0);
    os << "oct: " << oct << 15;
    cout << os.str() << endl;
}
```

The output of this program is as follows:

```
dec: 15 hex: f

oct: 17 hex: f
float: 4.67 bitset: 001011010011101
```

First, a decimal and a hexadecimal value are written to os. Next, a floating-point value and a bitset (written in binary) are appended. Using seekp(), the write position is moved to the beginning of the stream. So, the following call of operator << writes at the beginning of the string, thus overwriting the beginning of the existing string stream. However, the characters that are not overwritten remain valid. To remove the current contents from the stream, you can use the function str() to assign new contents to the buffer:

```
    strm.str("");
```

The first lines written to os are each terminated with endl. This means that the string ends with a newline character. Because the string is printed followed by endl, two adjacent newline characters are written. This explains the empty lines in the output.

Before C++11, a typical programming error when dealing with string streams was to forget to extract the string with the function str() and to write to the stream directly instead. This was, from a compiler's point of view, a possible and reasonable thing to do because there was an implicit conversion to void* (see Section 15.4.3, page 760). As a result, instead of its value the state of the stream was written in the form of an address (see Section 15.3.3, page 756). With C++11, this conversion was replaced by an explicit conversion to bool, so passing a string stream to the output operator << without calling str() is no longer possible.

A typical use for writing to an output string stream is to define output operators for user-defined types (see Section 15.11.1, page 810).

Input string streams are used mainly for formatted reading from existing strings. For example, it is often easier to read data line by line and then analyze each line individually. The following lines read the integer x with the value 3 and the floating-point f with the value 0.7 from the string s:

```
    int x;
    float f;
    std::string s = "3.7";

    std::istringstream is(s);
    is >> x >> f;
```

A string stream can be created with the flags for the file open modes (see Section 15.9.3, page 796) and/or an existing string. With the flag `ios::ate`, the characters written to a string stream can be appended to an existing string:[15]

```
std::string s("value: ");
...
std::ostringstream os (s, std::ios::out|std::ios::ate);
os << 77 << " " << std::hex << 77 << std::endl;
std::cout << os.str();   // writes: value: 77 4d
std::cout << s;          // writes: value:
```

As you can see, the string returned from `str()` is a copy of the string s, with a decimal and a hexadecimal version of 77 appended. The string s itself is not modified.

15.10.2 Move Semantics for String Streams

Since C++11, string streams provide rvalue and move semantics. In fact, ostreams provide an output operator, and istreams provide an input iterator that accepts an rvalue reference for the stream. The effect is that you can use temporarily created stream objects. For example, you can insert into a temporarily created string stream:[16]

```
// io/sstream2.cpp

#include <iostream>
#include <sstream>
#include <string>
#include <tuple>
#include <utility>
using namespace std;

tuple<string,string,string> parseName(string name)
{
    string s1, s2, s3;
    istringstream(name) >> s1 >> s2 >> s3;
    if (s3.empty()) {
        return tuple<string,string,string>(move(s1),"",move(s2));
    }
    else {
        return tuple<string,string,string>(move(s1),move(s2),move(s3));
    }
}
```

---

[15] Whether the flag `ios::app` has the same effect is currently not clear; so using it here instead is not portable.

[16] Thanks to Daniel Krügler for providing this example.

```
int main()
{
    auto t1 = parseName("Nicolai M. Josuttis");
    cout << "firstname: " << get<0>(t1) << endl;
    cout << "middle:    " << get<1>(t1) << endl;
    cout << "lastname:  " << get<2>(t1) << endl;
    auto t2 = parseName("Nico Josuttis");
    cout << "firstname: " << get<0>(t2) << endl;
    cout << "middle:    " << get<1>(t2) << endl;
    cout << "lastname:  " << get<2>(t2) << endl;
}
```

Before C++11, you had to implement

```
istringstream is(name);
is >> s1 >> s2 >> s3;
```

instead of

```
istringstream(name) >> s1 >> s2 >> s3;
```

In addition, string streams now have move and swap semantics, providing a move constructor, a move assignment operator, and swap(). So, you can pass a string stream as an argument or return a string stream from a function.

15.10.3 `char*` Stream Classes

The char* stream classes are retained only for backward compatibility. Their interface is error prone, and the classes are rarely used correctly. However, they are still in use and thus are described briefly here. Note that the standard version described here has slightly modified the old interface.

In this subsection, the term *character sequence* will be used instead of *string* because the character sequence maintained by the char* stream classes is not always terminated with the (terminating) null character and thus is not really a string.

The char* stream classes are defined only for the character type char. They include

- The class istrstream for reading from character sequences (input string stream)
- The class ostrstream for writing to character sequences (output string stream)
- The class strstream for reading from and writing to character sequences
- The class strstreambuf used as a stream buffer for char* streams

The char* stream classes are defined in the header file <strstream>.

An istrstream can be initialized with a character sequence (of type char*) that is either terminated with the (terminating) null character 0 or for which the number of characters is passed as the argument. A typical use is the reading and processing of whole lines:

```
char buffer[1000];        // buffer for at most 999 characters
```

```
// read line
std::cin.get(buffer,sizeof(buffer));
```

```
// read/process line as stream
std::istrstream input(buffer);
...
input >> x;
```

A char* stream for writing can either maintain a character sequence that grows as needed or be initialized with a buffer of fixed size. Using the flag ios::app or ios:ate, you can append the characters written to a character sequence that is already stored in the buffer.

Care must be taken when using char* stream as a string. In contrast to string streams, char* streams are not always responsible for the memory used to store the character sequence.

With the member function str(), the character sequence is made available to the caller together with the responsibility for the corresponding memory. Unless the stream is initialized with a buffer of fixed size — for which the stream is never responsible — the following three rules have to be obeyed:

1. Because ownership of the memory is transferred to the caller, the character sequence has to be released unless the stream was initialized with a buffer of fixed size. However, there is no guarantee how the memory was allocated,[17] so it is not always safe to release it by using delete[]. Your best bet is to return the memory to the stream by calling the member function freeze() with the argument false (the following paragraphs present an example).

2. With the call to str(), the stream is no longer allowed to modify the character sequence. It calls the member function freeze() implicitly, which freezes the character sequence. The reason for this is to avoid complications if the allocated buffer is not sufficiently large and new memory has to be allocated.

3. The member function str() does *not* append a (terminating) null character ('\0'). This character has to be appended explicitly to the stream to terminate the character sequence. This can be done by using the ends manipulator. Some implementations append a string (terminating) null character automatically, but this behavior is not portable.

The following example demonstrates the use of a char* stream:

```
float x;
...
// create and fill char* stream
// - don't forget ends or '\0' !!!
std::ostrstream buffer;        // dynamic stream buffer
buffer << "float x: " << x << std::ends;
```

---

[17] There is a constructor that takes two function pointers as an argument: a function to allocate memory and a function to release memory.

```
// pass resulting C-string to foo() and return memory to buffer
char* s = buffer.str();
foo(s);
buffer.freeze(false);
```

A frozen `char*` stream can be restored to its normal state for additional manipulation. To do so, the member function `freeze()` has to be called with the argument `false`. With this operation, ownership of the character sequence is returned to the stream object. This is the only safe way to release the memory for the character sequence. The next example demonstrates this:

```
float x;
...

std::ostrstream buffer;      // dynamic char* stream

// fill char* stream
buffer << "float x: " << x << std::ends;

// pass resulting C-string to foo()
// - freezes the char* stream
foo(buffer.str());

// unfreeze the char* stream
buffer.freeze(false);

// seek writing position to the beginning
buffer.seekp (0, ios::beg);

// refill char* stream
buffer << "once more float x: " << x << std::ends;

// pass resulting C-string to foo() again
// - freezes the char* stream
foo(buffer.str());

// return memory to buffer
buffer.freeze(false);
```

The problems related to freezing the stream are removed from the string stream classes, mainly because the strings are copied and because the string class takes care of the used memory.

15.11   Input/Output Operators for User-Defined Types

As mentioned earlier in this chapter, a major advantage of streams over the old I/O mechanism of C is the possibility that the stream mechanism can be extended to user-defined types. To do this, you must overload operators << and >>. This is demonstrated using a class for fractions in the following subsection.

15.11.1   Implementing Output Operators

In an expression with the output operator, the left operand is a stream and the right operand is the object to be written:

> *stream* << *object*

According to language rules, this can be interpreted in two ways:

1. As *stream*.operator<<(*object*)
2. As operator<<(*stream*,*object*)

The first way is used for built-in types. For user-defined types, you have to use the second way because the stream classes are closed for extensions. All you have to do is implement global operator << for your user-defined type. This is rather easy unless access to private members of the objects is necessary (which I cover later).

For example, to print an object of class `Fraction` with the format *numerator/denominator*, you can write the following function:

```
// io/frac1out.hpp

#include <iostream>

inline
std::ostream& operator << (std::ostream& strm, const Fraction& f)
{
    strm << f.numerator() << '/' << f.denominator();
    return strm;
}
```

The function writes the numerator and the denominator, separated by the character '/', to the stream that is passed as the argument. The stream can be a file stream, a string stream, or some other stream. To support the chaining of write operations or the access to the stream's state in the same statement, the stream is returned by the function.

This simple form has two drawbacks:

1. Because `ostream` is used in the signature, the function applies only to streams with the character type `char`. If the function is intended only for use in Western Europe or in North America, this

is no problem. On the other hand, a more general version requires only a little extra work, so it should at least be considered.

2. Another problem arises if a field width is set. In this case, the result is probably not what might be expected. The field width applies to the immediately following write; in this case, to the numerator. Thus, the statements

```
Fraction vat(19,100);    // I'm German and we have a uniform VAT of 19%
std::cout << "VAT: \"" << std::left << std::setw(8)
          << vat << '"' << std::endl;
```

result in this output:

```
VAT: "19      /100"
```

The next version solves both of these problems:

```
// io/frac2out.hpp

#include <iostream>
#include <sstream>

template <typename charT, typename traits>
inline
std::basic_ostream<charT,traits>&
operator << (std::basic_ostream<charT,traits>& strm,
             const Fraction& f)
{
    // string stream
    // - with same format
    // - without special field width
    std::basic_ostringstream<charT,traits> s;
    s.copyfmt(strm);
    s.width(0);

    // fill string stream
    s << f.numerator() << '/' << f.denominator();

    // print string stream
    strm << s.str();

    return strm;
}
```

The operator has become a function template that is parametrized to suit all kinds of streams. The problem with the field width is addressed by writing the fraction first to a string stream without setting any specific width. The constructed string is then sent to the stream passed as the argument. This results in the characters representing the fraction being written with only one write operation, to which the field width is applied.

As a result, the statements

```
Fraction vat(19,100);      // I'm German ...
std::cout << "VAT: \"" << std::left << std::setw(8)
          << vat << '"' << std::endl;
```

now produce the following output:

```
VAT: "19/100  "
```

Note that a user-defined overload of operator << for types of namespace std will have limitations. The reason is that it is not found in situations using *ADL* (*argument-dependent lookup*, also known as *Koenig lookup*). This, for example, is the case when ostream iterators are used. For example:

```
template <typename T1, typename T2>
std::ostream& operator << (std::ostream& strm, const std::pair<T1,T2>& p)
{
    return strm << "[" << p.first << "," << p.second << "]";
}

std::pair<int,long> p(42,77777);
std::cout << p << std::endl;     // OK

std::vector<std::pair<int,long>> v;
...
std::copy(v.begin(),v.end(),     // ERROR: doesn't compile:
          std::ostream_iterator<std::pair<int,long>>(std::cout,"\n"));
```

15.11.2 Implementing Input Operators

Input operators are implemented according to the same principle as output operators. However, input incurs the likely problem of read failures. Input functions normally need special handling of cases in which reading might fail.

When implementing a read function, you can choose between simple or flexible approaches. For example, the following function uses a simple approach, which reads a fraction without checking for error situations:

```
// io/frac1in.hpp

#include <iostream>

inline
std::istream& operator >> (std::istream& strm, Fraction& f)
{
    int n, d;

    strm >> n;        // read value of the numerator
```

```
    strm.ignore();    // skip '/'
    strm >> d;        // read value of the denominator

    f = Fraction(n,d);    // assign the whole fraction

    return strm;
}
```

The problem with this implementation is has that it can be used only for streams with the character type char. In addition, whether the character between the two numbers is indeed the character '/' is not checked.

Another problem arises when undefined values are read. When reading a zero for the denominator, the value of the read fraction is not well defined. This problem is detected in the constructor of the class Fraction that is invoked by the expression Fraction(n,d). However, handling inside class Fraction means that a format error automatically results in an error handling of the class Fraction. Because it is common practice to record format errors in the stream, it might be better to set ios_base::failbit in this case.

Finally, the fraction passed by reference might be modified even if the read operation is not successful. This can happen, for example, when the read of the numerator succeeds, but the read of the denominator fails. This behavior contradicts common conventions established by the predefined input operators and thus is best avoided. A read operation should be successful or have no effect.

The following implementation is improved to avoid these problems. It is also more flexible because it is parametrized to be applicable to all stream types:

```
// io/frac2in.hpp

#include <iostream>

template <typename charT, typename traits>
inline
std::basic_istream<charT,traits>&
operator >> (std::basic_istream<charT,traits>& strm, Fraction& f)
{
    int n, d;

    // read value of numerator
    strm >> n;

    // if available
    // - read '/' and value of demoninator
    if (strm.peek() == '/') {
        strm.ignore();
        strm >> d;
    }
```

```
else {
    d = 1;
}

// if denominator is zero
// - set failbit as I/O format error
if (d == 0) {
    strm.setstate(std::ios::failbit);
    return strm;
}

// if everything is fine so far
// - change the value of the fraction
if (strm) {
    f = Fraction(n,d);
}

return strm;
}
```

Here, the denominator is read only if the first number is followed by the character ' / '; otherwise,
a denominator of 1 is assumed, and the integer read is interpreted as the whole fraction. Hence, the
denominator is optional.

This implementation also tests whether a denominator with value 0 was read. In this case, the
`ios_base::failbit` is set, which might trigger a corresponding exception (see Section 15.4.4,
page 762). Of course, the behavior can be implemented differently if the denominator is zero. For
example, an exception could be thrown directly, or the check could be skipped so that the fraction is
initialized with zero, which would throw the appropriate exception by class `Fraction`.

Finally, the state of the stream is checked, and the new value is assigned to the fraction only if no
input error occurred. This final check should always be done to make sure that the value of an object
is changed only if the read was successful.

Of course, it can be argued whether it is reasonable to read integers as fractions. In addition,
there are other subtleties that may be improved. For example, the numerator must be followed by
the character ' / ' without separating whitespaces. But the denominator may be preceded by arbitrary
whitespaces because normally, these are skipped. This hints at the complexity involved in reading
nontrivial data structures.

15.11.3   Input/Output Using Auxiliary Functions

If the implementation of an I/O operator requires access to the private data of an object, the standard operators should delegate the work to auxiliary member functions. This technique also allows
polymorphic read and write functions, which might look as follows:

```
class Fraction {
  ...
  public:
    virtual void printOn (std::ostream& strm) const;  // output
    virtual void scanFrom (std::istream& strm);        // input
    ...
};

std::ostream& operator << (std::ostream& strm, const Fraction& f)
{
    f.printOn (strm);
    return strm;
}

std::istream& operator >> (std::istream& strm, Fraction& f)
{
    f.scanFrom (strm);
    return strm;
}
```

A typical example is the direct access to the numerator and denominator of a fraction during input:

```
void Fraction::scanFrom (std::istream& strm)
{
    ...
    // assign values directly to the components
    num = n;
    denom = d;
}
```

If a class is not intended to be used as a base class, the I/O operators can be made `friends` of the class. However, note that this approach reduces the possibilities significantly when inheritance is used. Friend functions cannot be virtual; as a result, the wrong function might be called. For example, if a reference to a base class refers to an object of a derived class and is used as an argument for the input operator, the operator for the base class is called. To avoid this problem, derived classes should not implement their own I/O operators. Thus, the implementation sketched previously is more general than the use of friend functions and should be used as a standard approach, although most examples use friend functions instead.

15.11.4   User-Defined Format Flags

When user-defined I/O operators are being written, it is often desirable to have formatting flags specific to these operators, probably set by using a corresponding manipulator. For example, it would be nice if the output operator for fractions, shown previously, could be configured to place spaces around the slash that separates numerator and denominator.

The stream objects support this by providing a mechanism to associate data with a stream. This mechanism can be used to associate corresponding data — for example, using a manipulator — and later retrieve the data. The class ios_base defines the two functions iword() and pword(), each taking an int argument as the index, to access a specific long& or void*&, respectively. The idea is that iword() and pword() access long or void* objects in an array of arbitrary size stored with a stream object. Formatting flags to be stored for a stream are then placed at the same index for all streams. The static member function xalloc() of the class ios_base is used to obtain an index that is not yet used for this purpose.

Initially, the objects accessed with iword() or pword() are set to 0. This value can be used to represent the default formatting or to indicate that the corresponding data was not yet accessed. Here is an example:

```
// get index for new ostream data
static const int iword_index = std::ios_base::xalloc();

// define manipulator that sets this data
std::ostream& fraction_spaces (std::ostream& strm)
{
    strm.iword(iword_index) = true;
    return strm;
}


std::ostream& operator<< (std::ostream& strm, const Fraction& f)
{
    // query the ostream data
    // - if true, use spaces between numerator and denominator
    // - if false, use no spaces between numerator and denominator
    if (strm.iword(iword_index)) {
        strm << f.numerator() << " / " << f.denominator();
    }
    else {
        strm << f.numerator() << "/" << f.denominator();
    }
    return strm;
}
```

This example uses a simple approach to the implementation of the output operator because the main feature to be exposed is the use of the function iword(). The format flag is considered to be a Boolean value that defines whether spaces between numerator and denominator should be written. In the first line, the function ios_base::xalloc() obtains an index that can be used to store the format flag. The result of this call is stored in a constant because it is never modified. The function fraction_spaces() is a manipulator that sets the int value that is stored at the index iword_index in the integer array associated with the stream strm to true. The output operator retrieves that value and writes the fraction according the value stored. If the value is false, the default formatting using no spaces is used. Otherwise, spaces are placed around the slash.

When `iword()` and `pword()` are used, references to `long` or `void*` objects are returned. These references stay valid only until the next call of `iword()` or `pword()` for the corresponding stream object, or until the stream object is destroyed. Normally, the results from `iword()` and `pword()` should not be saved.[18] It is assumed that the access is fast, although it is not required that the data be represented by using an array.

The function `copyfmt()` copies all format information (see Section 15.7.1, page 779), including the arrays accessed with `iword()` and `pword()`. This may pose a problem for the objects stored with a stream using `pword()`. For example, if a value is the address of an object, the address is copied instead of the object. If you copy only the address, it may happen that if the format of one stream is changed, the format of other streams would be affected. In addition, it may be desirable that an object associated with a stream using `pword()` be destroyed when the stream is destroyed. So, a deep copy rather than a shallow copy may be necessary for such an object.

A callback mechanism is defined by `ios_base` to support such behavior as making a deep copy if necessary or deleting an object when destroying a stream. The function `register_callback()` can be used to register a function that is called if certain operations are performed on the `ios_base` object. It is declared as follows:

```
namespace std {
  class ios_base {
    public:
      // kinds of callback events
      enum event { erase_event, imbue_event, copyfmt_event };
      // type of callbacks
      typedef void (*event_callback) (event e, ios_base& strm,
                                      int arg);
      // function to register callbacks
      void register_callback (event_callback cb, int arg);
      ...
  };
}
```

The function `register_callback()` takes a function pointer as the first argument and an `int` argument as the second. The `int` argument is passed as the third argument when a registered function is called and can, for example, be used to identify an index for `pword()` to signal which member of the array has to be processed. The argument `strm` that is passed to the callback function is the `ios_base` object that caused the call to the callback function. The argument `e` identifies the reason why the callback function was called. The reasons for calling the callback functions are listed in Table 15.39.

---

[18] In general, returned pointers and references should not be saved when it is not clear that the lifetime of the object they refer to is long enough.

Event	Reason
`ios_base::imbue_event`	A locale is set with `imbue()`
`ios_base::erase_event`	The stream is destroyed or `copyfmt()` is used
`ios_base::copy_event`	`copyfmt()` is used

Table 15.39. Reasons for Callback Events

If `copyfmt()` is used, the callbacks are called twice for the object on which `copyfmt()` is called. First, before anything is copied, the callbacks are invoked with the argument `erase_event` to do all the cleanup necessary, such as deleting objects stored in the `pword()` array. The callbacks called are those registered for the object. After the format flags are copied, which includes the list of callbacks from the argument stream, the callbacks are called again, this time with the argument `copy_event`. This pass can, for example, be used to arrange for deep copying of objects stored in the `pword()` array. Note that the callbacks are also copied and the original list of callbacks is removed. Thus, the callbacks invoked for the second pass are the callbacks just copied.

The callback mechanism is very primitive. It does not allow callback functions to be unregistered except by using `copyfmt()` with an argument that has no callbacks registered. Also, registering a callback function twice, even with the same argument, results in calling the callback function twice. It is, however, guaranteed that the callbacks are called in the opposite order of registration. Thus, a callback function registered from within another callback function is not called before the next time the callback functions are invoked.

15.11.5   Conventions for User-Defined Input/Output Operators

Several conventions that should be followed by the implementations of your own I/O operators have been presented. These conventions correspond to behavior that is typical for the predefined I/O operators. To summarize, these conventions are as follows:

- The output format should allow an input operator that can read the data without loss of information. Especially for strings, this is close to impossible because a problem with spaces arises. A space character in the string cannot be distinguished from a space character between two strings.
- The current formatting specification of the stream should be taken into account when doing I/O. This applies especially to the width for writing.
- If an error occurs, an appropriate state flag should be set.
- The objects should not be modified in case of an error. If multiple data is read, the data should first be stored in auxiliary objects before the value of the object passed to the read operator is set.
- Output should not be terminated with a newline character, mainly because it is otherwise impossible to write other objects on the same line.
- Even values that are too large should be read completely. After the read, a corresponding error flag should be set, and the value returned should be some meaningful value, such as the maximum value.
- If a format error is detected, no character should be read, if possible.

15.12   Connecting Input and Output Streams

Often, you need to connect two streams. For example, you may want to ensure that text asking for input is written on the screen before the input is read. Another example is reading from and writing to the same stream. This is of interest mainly regarding files. A third example is the need to manipulate the same stream using different formats. This section discusses all these techniques.

15.12.1   Loose Coupling Using `tie()`

You can *tie* a stream to an output stream. This means that the buffers of both streams are synchronized in a way that the buffer of the output stream is flushed before each input or output of the other stream. That is, for the output stream, the function `flush()` is called. Table 15.40 lists the member functions defined in `basic_ios` to tie one stream to another.

Member Function	Meaning
`tie()`	Returns a pointer to the output stream that is tied to the stream
`tie(`*ostream* strm*`)`	Ties the output stream to which the argument refers to the stream and returns a pointer to the previous output stream that was tied to the stream, if any

Table 15.40. Tieing One Stream to Another

Calling the function `tie()` without any argument returns a pointer to the output stream that is currently tied to a stream. To tie a new output stream to a stream, a pointer to that output stream must be passed as the argument to `tie()`. The argument is defined to be a pointer because you can also pass `nullptr` (or 0 or NULL) as an argument. This argument means "no tie" and unties any tied output stream. If no output stream is tied, `tie()` returns `nullptr` or 0. For each stream, you can have only one output stream that is tied to this stream. However, you can tie an output stream to different streams.

By default, the standard input is connected to the standard output by using this mechanism:

```
// predefined connections:
std::cin.tie (&std::cout);
std::wcin.tie (&std::wcout);
```

This ensures that a message asking for input is flushed before requesting the input. For example, during the statements

```
std::cout << "Please enter x: ";
std::cin >> x;
```

the function `flush()` is called implicitly for `cout` before reading `x`.

To remove the connection between two streams, you pass `nullptr` (or 0 or NULL) to `tie()`. For example:

```
// decouple cin from any output stream
std::cin.tie (nullptr);
```

This might improve the performance of a program by avoiding unnecessary additional flushing of streams (see Section 15.14.2, page 846, for a discussion of stream performance).

You can also tie one output stream to another output stream. For example, with the following statement, the normal output is flushed before something is written to the error stream:

```
// tieing cout to cerr
std::cerr.tie (&std::cout);
```

15.12.2 Tight Coupling Using Stream Buffers

Using the function rdbuf(), you can couple streams tightly by using a common stream buffer (Table 15.41). These functions suit several purposes, which are discussed in this and the following subsections.

Member Function	Meaning
rdbuf()	Returns a pointer to the stream buffer
rdbuf(*streambuf**)	Installs the stream buffer pointed to by the argument and returns a pointer to the previously used stream buffer

Table 15.41. Stream Buffer Access

The member function rdbuf() allows several stream objects to read from the same input channel or to write to the same output channel without garbling the order of the I/O. The use of multiple stream buffers does not work smoothly, because the I/O operations are buffered. Thus, when using different streams with different buffers for the same I/O channel, I/O may pass other I/O. An additional constructor of basic_istream and basic_ostream is used to initialize the stream with a stream buffer passed as the argument. For example:

```
// io/streambuffer1.cpp

#include <iostream>
#include <fstream>
using namespace std;

int main()
{
    // stream for hexadecimal standard output
    ostream hexout(cout.rdbuf());
    hexout.setf (ios::hex, ios::basefield);
    hexout.setf (ios::showbase);

    // switch between decimal and hexadecimal output
    hexout << "hexout: " << 177 << " ";
    cout   << "cout: "   << 177 << " ";
    hexout << "hexout: " << -49 << " ";
```

```
    cout    << "cout: "    << -49 << " ";
    hexout << endl;
}
```

Note that the destructor of the classes `basic_istream` and `basic_ostream` does *not* delete the corresponding stream buffer (it was not opened by these classes, anyway). Thus, you can pass a stream device by using a pointer instead of a stream reference to the stream buffer:

```
// io/streambuffer2.cpp

#include <iostream>
#include <fstream>

void hexMultiplicationTable (std::streambuf* buffer, int num)
{
    std::ostream hexout(buffer);
    hexout << std::hex << std::showbase;

    for (int i=1; i<=num; ++i) {
        for (int j=1; j<=10; ++j) {
            hexout << i*j << ' ';
        }
        hexout << std::endl;
    }

}   // does NOT close buffer

int main()
{
    using namespace std;
    int num = 5;

    cout << "We print " << num
         << " lines hexadecimal" << endl;

    hexMultiplicationTable(cout.rdbuf(),num);

    cout << "That was the output of " << num
         << " hexadecimal lines " << endl;
}
```

The advantage of this approach is that the format does not need to be restored to its original state after it is modified, because the format applies to the stream object, not to the stream buffer. Thus, the corresponding output of the program is as follows:

```
We print 5 lines hexadecimal
0x1 0x2 0x3 0x4 0x5 0x6 0x7 0x8 0x9 0xa
0x2 0x4 0x6 0x8 0xa 0xc 0xe 0x10 0x12 0x14
0x3 0x6 0x9 0xc 0xf 0x12 0x15 0x18 0x1b 0x1e
0x4 0x8 0xc 0x10 0x14 0x18 0x1c 0x20 0x24 0x28
0x5 0xa 0xf 0x14 0x19 0x1e 0x23 0x28 0x2d 0x32
That was the output of 5 hexadecimal lines
```

However, the disadvantage of this approach is that construction and destruction of a stream object involve more overhead than just setting and restoring some format flags. Also, note that the destruction of a stream object does not flush the buffer. To make sure that an output buffer is flushed, it has to be flushed manually.

The fact that the stream buffer is not destroyed applies only to `basic_istream` and `basic_ostream`. The other stream classes destroy the stream buffers they allocated originally, but they do not destroy stream buffers set with `rdbuf()`.

15.12.3 Redirecting Standard Streams

In the old implementation of the IOStream library, the global streams `cin`, `cout`, `cerr`, and `clog` were objects of the classes `istream_withassign` and `ostream_withassign`. It was therefore possible to redirect the streams by assigning streams to other streams. This possibility was removed from the C++ standard library. However, the possibility to redirect streams was retained and extended to apply to all streams. A stream can be redirected by setting a stream buffer.

The setting of stream buffers means the redirection of I/O streams controlled by the program without help from the operating system. For example, the following statements set things up such that output written to `cout` is not sent to the standard output channel but to the file `cout.txt`:

```
std::ofstream file ("cout.txt");
std::cout.rdbuf (file.rdbuf());
```

The function `copyfmt()` can be used to assign all format information of a given stream to another stream object:

```
std::ofstream file ("cout.txt");
file.copyfmt (std::cout);
std::cout.rdbuf (file.rdbuf());
```

Caution! The object `file` is local and is destroyed at the end of the block. This also destroys the corresponding stream buffer. This differs from the "normal" streams because file streams allocate their stream buffer objects at construction time and destroy them on destruction. Thus, in this example, `cout` can no longer be used for writing. In fact, it cannot even be destroyed safely at program termination. Thus, the old buffer should *always* be saved and restored later! The following example does this in the function `redirect()`:

```
// io/streamredirect1.cpp

#include <iostream>
#include <fstream>
#include <memory>
```

```
using namespace std;

void redirect(ostream&);

int main()
{
    cout << "the first row" << endl;

    redirect(cout);

    cout << "the last row" << endl;
}

void redirect (ostream& strm)
{
    // save output buffer of the stream
    // - use unique pointer with deleter that ensures to restore
    //   the original output buffer at the end of the function
    auto del = [&](streambuf* p) {
                    strm.rdbuf(p);
                };
    unique_ptr<streambuf,decltype(del)> origBuffer(strm.rdbuf(),del);

    // redirect ouput into the file redirect.txt
    ofstream file("redirect.txt");
    strm.rdbuf (file.rdbuf());

    file << "one row for the file" << endl;
    strm << "one row for the stream" << endl;
} // closes file AND its buffer automatically
```

By using a unique pointer (see Section 5.2.5, page 98), we can ensure that, even when resize() is left due to an exception, the original output buffer stored in origBuffer gets restored.[19]

The output of the program is this as follows:

```
the first row
the last row
```

The contents of the file redirect.txt are afterward:

```
one row for the file
one row for the stream
```

---

[19] Thanks to Daniel Krügler for pointing this out.

As you can see, the output written in redirect() to cout, using the parameter name strm, is sent to the file. The output written after the execution of redirect() in main() is sent to the restored output channel.

15.12.4   Streams for Reading and Writing

A final example of the connection between streams is the use of the same stream for reading and writing. Normally, a file can be opened for reading and writing by using the class fstream:

```
std::fstream file ("example.txt", std::ios::in | std::ios::out);
```

It is also possible to use two different stream objects, one for reading and one for writing. This can be done, for example, with the following declarations:

```
std::ofstream out ("example.txt", ios::in | ios::out);
std::istream  in (out.rdbuf());
```

The declaration of out opens the file. The declaration of in uses the stream buffer of out to read from it. Note that out must be opened for both reading and writing. If it is opened only for writing, reading from the stream will result in undefined behavior. Also note that in is not of type ifstream but only of type istream. The file is already opened and there is a corresponding stream buffer. All that is needed is a second stream object. As in previous examples, the file is closed when the file stream object out is destroyed.

It is also possible to create a file stream buffer and install it in both stream objects. The code looks like this:

```
std::filebuf buffer;
std::ostream out (&buffer);
std::istream in (&buffer);
buffer.open("example.txt", std::ios::in | std::ios::out);
```

filebuf is the usual specialization of the class basic_filebuf<> for the character type char. This class defines the stream buffer class used by file streams.

The following program is a complete example. In a loop, four lines are written to a file. After each writing of a line, the contents of the file are written to standard output:

```
// io/streamreadwrite1.cpp

#include <iostream>
#include <fstream>
using namespace std;

int main()
{
    // open file "example.dat" for reading and writing
    filebuf buffer;
    ostream output(&buffer);
    istream input(&buffer);
```

```
buffer.open ("example.dat", ios::in | ios::out | ios::trunc);

for (int i=1; i<=4; i++) {
    // write one line
    output << i << ". line" << endl;

    // print all file contents
    input.seekg(0);              // seek to the beginning
    char c;
    while (input.get(c)) {
        cout.put(c);
    }
    cout << endl;
    input.clear();               // clear eofbit and failbit
}
}
```

The output of the program is as follows:

```
1. line

1. line
2. line

1. line
2. line
3. line

1. line
2. line
3. line
4. line
```

Although two different stream objects are used for reading and writing, the read and write positions are tightly coupled. seekg() and seekp() call the same member function of the stream buffer.[20] Thus, the read position must always be set to the beginning of the file in order for the complete contents of the file to be written, after which the read/write position is again at the end of the file so that new lines written are appended.

---

[20] This function can distinguish whether the read position, the write position, or both positions are to be modified. Only the standard stream buffers maintain one position for reading and writing.

It is important to perform a seek between read and write operations to the same file unless you have reached the end of the file while reading. Without this seek, you are likely to end up with a garbled file or with even more fatal errors.

As mentioned before, instead of processing character by character, you could also print the entire contents in one statement by passing a pointer to the stream buffer of the file as an argument to operator << (see Section 15.14.3, page 846, for details):

```
std::cout << input.rdbuf();
```

15.13   The Stream Buffer Classes

As mentioned in Section 15.2.1, page 749, reading and writing are not done by the streams directly but are delegated to stream buffers.

The general interface to deal with stream buffers is pretty simple (see Section 15.12.2, page 820):

- `rdbuf()` yields a pointer to the stream buffer of a stream.
- The constructor and `rdbuf()` of streams allow setting a stream buffer at construction time or changing the stream buffer while the stream exists. In both cases, you have to pass a pointer to the stream buffer, which is what `rdbuf()` returns.

This ability can be used to let streams write to the same output device (see Section 15.12.2, page 820, to redirect streams (see Section 15.12.3, page 822), read from and write to the same buffer (see Section 15.12.4, page 824), or use other character encodings, such as UTF-8 or UTF-16/UCS-2, as input and output format (see Section 16.4.4, page 903).

This section describes how the stream buffer classes operate. The discussion not only gives a deeper understanding of what is going on when I/O streams are used but also provides the basis to define new I/O channels. Before going into the details of stream buffer operation, the public interface is presented for readers interested only in using stream buffers.

15.13.1   The Stream Buffer Interfaces

To the user of a stream buffer, the class `basic_streambuf<>` is not much more than something that characters can be sent to or extracted from. Table 15.42 lists the public function for writing characters.

Member Function	Meaning
sputc(c)	Sends the character c to the stream buffer
sputn(s, n)	Sends n characters from the sequence s to the stream buffer

Table 15.42. Public Members for Writing Characters

The function `sputc()` returns `traits_type::eof()` in case of an error, where `traits_type` is a type definition in the class `basic_streambuf`. The function `sputn()` writes the number of characters specified by the second argument unless the stream buffer cannot consume them. It does not care about (terminating) null characters. This function returns the number of characters written.

The interface to reading characters from a stream buffer is a little bit more complex (Table 15.43) because for input, it is necessary to have a look at a character without consuming it. Also, it is desirable that characters can be put back into the stream buffer when parsing. Thus, the stream buffer classes provide corresponding functions.

Member Function	Meaning
in_avail()	Returns a lower bound on the characters available
sgetc()	Returns the current character without consuming it
sbumpc()	Returns the current character and consumes it
snextc()	Consumes the current character and returns the next character
sgetn(b, n)	Reads n characters and stores them in the buffer b
sputbackc(c)	Returns the character c to the stream buffer
sungetc()	Moves one step back to the previous character

Table 15.43. Public Members for Reading Characters

The function in_avail() can be used to determine how many characters are at least available. This function can be used, for example, to make sure that reading does not block when reading from the keyboard. However, more characters can be available.

Until the stream buffer has reached the end of the stream, there is a current character. The function sgetc() is used to get the current character without moving on to the next character. The function sbumpc() reads the current character and moves on to next character, making this the new current character. The last function reading a single character, snextc() makes the next character the current one and then reads this character. All three functions return traits_type::eof() to indicate failure. The function sgetn() reads a sequence of characters into a buffer. The maximum number of characters to be read is passed as an argument. The function returns the number of characters read.

The two functions sputbackc() and sungetc() are used to move one step back, making the previous character the current one. The function sputbackc() can be used to replace the previous character by another character. These two functions should be used only with care. Often, only one character can be put back.

Finally, there are functions to access the imbued locale object, to change the position, and to influence buffering. Table 15.44 lists these functions.

Both pubimbue() and getloc() are used for internationalization (see Section 15.8, page 790): pubimbue() installs a new locale object in the stream buffer, returning the previously installed locale object; getloc() returns the currently installed locale object.

The function pubsetbuf() is intended to provide some control over the buffering strategy of stream buffers. However, whether it is honored depends on the concrete stream buffer class. For example, it makes no sense to use pubsetbuf() for string stream buffers. Even for file stream buffers, the use of this function is portable only if it is called before the first I/O operation is performed and

Member Function	Meaning
pubimbue(*loc*)	Imbues the stream buffer with the locale *loc*
getloc()	Returns the current locale
pubseekpos(*pos*)	Repositions the current position to an absolute position
pubseekpos(*pos, which*)	Same with specifying the I/O direction
pubseekoff(*offset, rpos*)	Repositions the current position relative to another position
pubseekoff(*offset, rpos, which*)	Same with specifying the I/O direction
pubsetbuf(*buf, n*)	Influences buffering

Table 15.44. Miscellaneous Public Stream Buffer Functions

if it is called as `pubsetbuf(nullptr,0)`, which means that no buffer is to be used. This function returns `nullptr` on failure and the stream buffer otherwise.

The functions `pubseekoff()` and `pubseekpos()` are used to manipulate the current position used for reading and/or writing. The position that is manipulated depends on the last argument, which is of type `ios_base::openmode` and which defaults to `ios_base::in|ios_base::out` if it is not specified. If `ios_base::in` is set, the read position is modified. Correspondingly, the write position is modified if `ios_base::out` is set. The function `pubseekpos()` moves the stream to an absolute position specified as the first argument, whereas the function `pubseekoff()` moves the stream relative to some other position. The offset is specified as the first argument. The position used as starting point is specified as the second argument and can be `ios_base::cur`, `ios_base::beg`, or `ios_base::end` (see Section 15.9.4, page 800, for details). Both functions return the position to which the stream was positioned or an invalid stream position. The invalid stream position can be detected by comparing the result with the object `pos_type(off_type(-1))` (`pos_type` and `off_type` are types for handling stream positions; see Section 15.9.4, page 799). The current position of a stream can be obtained by using `pubseekoff()`:

```
sbuf.pubseekoff(0, std::ios::cur)
```

15.13.2 Stream Buffer Iterators

An alternative way to use a member function for unformatted I/O is to use the stream buffer iterator classes. These classes provide iterators that conform to input iterator or output iterator requirements and read or write individual characters from stream buffers. This fits character-level I/O into the algorithm library of the C++ standard library.

The class templates `istreambuf_iterator<>` and `ostreambuf_iterator<>` are used to read or to write individual characters from or to objects of type `basic_streambuf<>`, respectively. The classes are defined in the header `<iterator>` like this:

```
namespace std {
    template <typename charT,
              typename traits = char_traits<charT> >
        class istreambuf_iterator;
```

```
        template <typename charT,
                typename traits = char_traits<charT> >
        class ostreambuf_iterator;
}
```

These iterators are special forms of stream iterators, which are described in Section 9.4.3, page 460. The only difference is that their elements are characters.

Output Stream Buffer Iterators

Here is how a string can be written to a stream buffer by using an `ostreambuf_iterator`:

```
// create iterator for buffer of output stream cout
std::ostreambuf_iterator<char> bufWriter(std::cout);

std::string hello("hello, world\n");
std::copy(hello.begin(), hello.end(),    // source: string
          bufWriter);                    // destination: output buffer of cout
```

The first line of this example constructs an output iterator of type `ostreambuf_iterator` from the object `cout`. Instead of passing the output stream, you could also pass a pointer to the stream buffer directly. The remainder constructs a `string` object and copies the characters in this object to the constructed output iterator.

Table 15.45 lists all operations of output stream buffer iterators. The implementation is similar to ostream iterators (see Section 9.4.3, page 460). In addition, you can initialize the iterator with a buffer, and you can call `failed()` to query whether the iterator is able to write. If any prior writing of a character failed, `failed()` yields `true`. In this case, any writing with operator = has no effect.

Expression	Effect
ostreambuf_iterator<*char*>(*ostream*)	Creates an output stream buffer iterator for *ostream*
ostreambuf_iterator<*char*>(*buffer_ptr*)	Creates an output stream buffer iterator for the buffer to which *buffer_ptr* refers
*iter	No-op (returns *iter*)
iter = *c*	Writes character *c* to the buffer by calling sputc(*c*) for it
++*iter*	No-op (returns *iter*)
iter++	No-op (returns *iter*)
failed()	Returns whether the output stream iterator is not able to write anymore

Table 15.45. Operations of Output Stream Buffer Iterators

Input Stream Buffer Iterators

Table 15.46 lists all operations of input stream buffer iterators. The implementation is similar to that for istream iterators (see Section 9.4.3, page 462). In addition, you can initialize the iterator with a buffer, and member function `equal()` is provided, which returns whether two input stream buffer iterators are equal. Two input stream buffer iterators are equal when they are both end-of-stream iterators or when neither is an end-of-stream iterator.

Expression	Effect
`istreambuf_iterator<`*char*`>()`	Creates an end-of-stream iterator
`istreambuf_iterator<`*char*`>(`*istream*`)`	Creates an input stream buffer iterator for *istream* and might read the first character using `sgetc()`
`istreambuf_iterator<`*char*`>(`*buffer_ptr*`)`	Creates an input stream buffer iterator for the buffer to which *buffer_ptr* refers and might read the first character using `sgetc()`
*iter	Returns the current character, read with `sgetc()` before (reads the first character if not done by the constructor)
++iter	Reads the next character with `sbumpc()` and returns its position
iter++	Reads the next character with `sbumpc()` but returns an iterator (proxy), where * yields the previous character
iter1`.equal(`*iter2*`)`	Returns whether both iterators are equal
iter1`==` *iter2*	Tests *iter1* and *iter2* for equality
iter1`!=` *iter2*	Tests *iter1* and *iter2* for inequality

Table 15.46. Operations of Input Stream Buffer Iterators

Somewhat obscure is what it means for two objects of type `istreambuf_iterator` to be equivalent: Two `istreambuf_iterator` objects are equivalent if both iterators are end-of-stream iterators or if neither of them is an end-of-stream iterator (whether the output buffer is the same doesn't matter). One possibility to get an end-of-stream iterator is to construct an iterator with the default constructor. In addition, an `istreambuf_iterator` becomes an end-of-stream iterator when an attempt is made to advance the iterator past the end of the stream (in other words, if `sbumpc()` returns `traits_type::eof()`. This behavior has two major implications:

1. A range from the current position in a stream to the end of the stream is defined by two iterators: `istreambuf_iterator<charT,traits>(`*stream*`)` for the current position and `istreambuf_iterator<charT,traits>()` for the end of the stream (*stream* is of type `basic_istream<charT,traits>` or `basic_streambuf<charT,traits>`).
2. It is not possible to create subranges using `istreambuf_iterators`.

Example Use of Stream Buffer Iterators

The following example is the classic filter framework that simply writes all read characters with stream buffer iterators. It is a modified version of the example in Section 15.5.3, page 772:

```
// io/charcat2.cpp

#include <iostream>
#include <iterator>
using namespace std;

int main()
{
    // input stream buffer iterator for cin
    istreambuf_iterator<char> inpos(cin);

    // end-of-stream iterator
    istreambuf_iterator<char> endpos;

    // output stream buffer iterator for cout
    ostreambuf_iterator<char> outpos(cout);

    // while input iterator is valid
    while (inpos != endpos) {
        *outpos = *inpos;        // assign its value to the output iterator
        ++inpos;
        ++outpos;
    }
}
```

You can also pass stream buffer iterators to algorithms to process all characters read from an input stream (see *io/countlines1.cpp* for a complete example):

```
int countLines (std::istream& in)
{
    return std::count(std::istreambuf_iterator<char>(in),
                      std::istreambuf_iterator<char>(),
                      '\n');
}
```

See Section 14.6, page 732, for an example using all characters read from standard input to initialize a string.

15.13.3   User-Defined Stream Buffers

Stream buffers are buffers for I/O. Their interface is defined by class `basic_streambuf<>`. For the character types `char` and `wchar_t`, the specializations `streambuf` and `wstreambuf`, respectively, are predefined. These classes are used as base classes when implementing the communication over special I/O channels. However, doing this requires an understanding of the stream buffer's operation.

The central interface to the buffers is formed by three pointers for each of the two buffers. The pointers returned from the functions `eback()`, `gptr()`, and `egptr()` form the interface to the read buffer. The pointers returned from the functions `pbase()`, `pptr()`, and `epptr()` form the interface to the write buffer. These pointers are manipulated by the read and write operations, which may result in corresponding reactions in the corresponding read or write channel. The exact operation is examined separately for reading and writing.

User-Defined Output Buffers

A buffer used to write characters is maintained with three pointers that can be accessed by the three functions `pbase()`, `pptr()`, and `epptr()` (Figure 15.4). Here is what these pointers represent:

1. `pbase()` ("put base") is the beginning of the output buffer.
2. `pptr()` ("put pointer") is the current write position.
3. `epptr()` ("end put pointer") is the end of the output buffer. This means that `epptr()` points to one past the last character that can be buffered.

The characters in the range from `pbase()` to `pptr()`, not including the character pointed to by `pptr()`, are already written but not yet transported, or flushed, to the corresponding output channel.

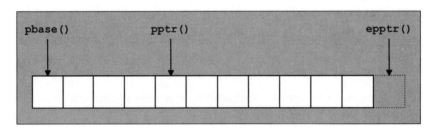

Figure 15.4. Interface to the Output Buffer

A character is written using the member function `sputc()`. This character is copied to the current write position if there is a spare write position. Then the pointer to the current write position is incremented. If the buffer is full (`pptr() == epptr()`), the contents of the output buffer are sent to the corresponding output channel by calling the virtual function `overflow()`. This function is responsible for sending the characters to some "external representation," which may be internal, as in the case of string streams. The implementation of `overflow()` in the base class `basic_streambuf` returns only end-of-file, which indicates that no more characters could be written.

The member function `sputn()` can be used to write multiple characters at once. This function delegates the work to the virtual function `xsputn()`, which can be implemented for more efficient writing of multiple characters. The implementation of `xsputn()` in class `basic_streambuf` calls `sputc()` for each character. Thus, overriding `xsputn()` is not necessary. Often, however, writing multiple characters can be implemented more efficiently than writing characters one at a time. Thus, this function can be used to optimize the processing of character sequences.

Writing to a stream buffer does not necessarily involve using the buffer. Instead, the characters can be written as soon as they are received. In this case, the value `nullptr` (or 0 or `NULL`) has to be assigned to the pointers that maintain the write buffer. The default constructor does this automatically.

With this information, the following example of a simple stream buffer can be implemented. This stream buffer does not use a buffer. Thus, the function `overflow()` is called for each character. Implementing this function is all that is necessary:

```cpp
// io/outbuf1.hpp

#include <streambuf>
#include <locale>
#include <cstdio>

class outbuf : public std::streambuf
{
  protected:
    // central output function
    // - print characters in uppercase mode
    virtual int_type overflow (int_type c) {
        if (c != EOF) {
            // convert lowercase to uppercase
            c = std::toupper(c,getloc());

            // and write the character to the standard output
            if (std::putchar(c) == EOF) {
                return EOF;
            }
        }
        return c;
    }
};
```

In this case, each character sent to the stream buffer is written using the C function `putchar()`. However, before the character is written, it is turned into an uppercase character using `toupper()` (see Section 16.4.4, page 895). The function `getloc()` is used to get the locale object associated with the stream buffer (see also Section 15.8, page 790).

In this example, the output buffer is implemented specifically for the character type `char` (`streambuf` is the specialization of `basic_streambuf<>` for the character type `char`). If other character types are used, you have to implement this function using character traits, which are introduced in Section 16.1.4, page 853. In this case, the comparison of c with end-of-file looks different: `traits::eof()` has to be returned instead of EOF and, if the argument c is EOF, the value `traits::not_eof(c)` should be returned, where `traits` is the second template argument to `basic_streambuf`. This might look as follows:

```
// io/outbuf1i18n.hpp

#include <streambuf>
#include <locale>
#include <cstdio>

template <typename charT,
          typename traits = std::char_traits<charT> >
class basic_outbuf : public std::basic_streambuf<charT,traits>
{
  protected:
    // central output function
    // - print characters in uppercase mode
    virtual typename traits::int_type
            overflow (typename traits::int_type c) {
        if (!traits::eq_int_type(c,traits::eof())) {
            // convert lowercase to uppercase
            c = std::toupper(c,this->getloc());

            // convert the character into a char (default: '?')
            char cc = std::use_facet<std::ctype<charT>>
                            (this->getloc()).narrow(c,'?');

            // and write the character to the standard output
            if (std::putchar(cc) == EOF) {
                return traits::eof();
            }
        }
        return traits::not_eof(c);
    }
};

typedef basic_outbuf<char>    outbuf;
typedef basic_outbuf<wchar_t> woutbuf;
```

Note that you have to qualify the call of `getloc()` by `this->` now because the base class depends on a template parameter. Also, we have to narrow the character before we pass it to `putchar()` because `putchar()` only accepts char only (see Section 16.4.4, page 891).

Using this stream buffer in the following program:

```
// io/outbuf1.cpp

#include <iostream>
#include "outbuf1.hpp"

int main()
{
    outbuf ob;                  // create special output buffer
    std::ostream out(&ob);      // initialize output stream with that output buffer

    out << "31 hexadecimal: " << std::hex << 31 << std::endl;
}
```

produces the following output:

```
31 HEXADECIMAL: 1F
```

The same approach can be used to write to other arbitrary destinations. For example, the constructor of a stream buffer may take a file descriptor, the name of a socket connection, or two other stream buffers used for simultaneous writing to initialize the object. Writing to the corresponding destination requires only that `overflow()` be implemented. In addition, the function `xsputn()` should be implemented to make writing to the stream buffer more efficient.

For convenient construction of the stream buffer, it is also reasonable to implement a special stream class that mainly passes the constructor argument to the corresponding stream buffer. The next example demonstrates this. It defines a stream buffer class initialized with a file descriptor to which characters are written with the function `write()`, a low-level I/O function used on UNIX-like operating systems. In addition, a class derived from `ostream` is defined that maintains such a stream buffer to which the file descriptor is passed:

```
// io/outbuf2.hpp

#include <iostream>
#include <streambuf>
#include <cstdio>

// for write():
#ifdef _MSC_VER
#include <io.h>
#else
#include <unistd.h>
#endif

class fdoutbuf : public std::streambuf {
  protected:
    int fd;       // file descriptor
```

```
    public:
      // constructor
      fdoutbuf (int _fd) : fd(_fd) {
      }
    protected:
      // write one character
      virtual int_type overflow (int_type c) {
          if (c != EOF) {
              char z = c;
              if (write (fd, &z, 1) != 1) {
                  return EOF;
              }
          }
          return c;
      }
      // write multiple characters
      virtual std::streamsize xsputn (const char* s,
                                        std::streamsize num) {
          return write(fd,s,num);
      }
};

class fdostream : public std::ostream {
  protected:
    fdoutbuf buf;
  public:
    fdostream (int fd) : std::ostream(0), buf(fd) {
        rdbuf(&buf);
    }
};
```

This stream buffer also implements the function xsputn() to avoid calling overflow() for each
character if a character sequence is sent to this stream buffer. This function writes the whole character
sequence with one call to the file identified by the file descriptor fd. The function xsputn() returns
the number of characters written successfully. Here is a sample application:

// io/outbuf2.cpp

```
#include <iostream>
#include "outbuf2.hpp"
```

```
int main()
{
    fdostream out(1);        // stream with buffer writing to file descriptor 1

    out << "31 hexadecimal: " << std::hex << 31 << std::endl;
}
```

This program creates an output stream that is initialized with the file descriptor 1. This file descriptor, by convention, identifies the standard output channel. Thus, in this example, the characters are simply printed. If some other file descriptor is available — for example, for a file or a socket — it also can be used as the constructor argument.

To implement a stream buffer that buffers, the write buffer has to be initialized using the function `setp()`. This is demonstrated by the next example:

```
// io/outbuf3.hpp

#include <cstdio>
#include <streambuf>

// for write():
#ifdef _MSC_VER
# include <io.h>
#else
# include <unistd.h>
#endif

class outbuf : public std::streambuf {
  protected:
    static const int bufferSize = 10;    // size of data buffer
    char buffer[bufferSize];             // data buffer

  public:
    // constructor
    // - initialize data buffer
    // - one character less to let the bufferSizeth character cause a call of overflow()
    outbuf() {
        setp (buffer, buffer+(bufferSize-1));
    }

    // destructor
    // - flush data buffer
    virtual ~outbuf() {
        sync();
    }
```

```
protected:
    // flush the characters in the buffer
    int flushBuffer () {
        int num = pptr()-pbase();
        if (write (1, buffer, num) != num) {
            return EOF;
        }
        pbump (-num);        // reset put pointer accordingly
        return num;
    }

    // buffer full
    // - write c and all previous characters
    virtual int_type overflow (int_type c) {
        if (c != EOF) {
            // insert character into the buffer
            *pptr() = c;
            pbump(1);
        }
        // flush the buffer
        if (flushBuffer() == EOF) {
            // ERROR
            return EOF;
        }
        return c;
    }

    // synchronize data with file/destination
    // - flush the data in the buffer
    virtual int sync () {
        if (flushBuffer() == EOF) {
            // ERROR
            return -1;
        }
        return 0;
    }
};
```

The constructor initializes the write buffer with setp():

```
setp (buffer, buffer+(size-1));
```

The write buffer is set up such that overflow() is already called when there is still room for one character. If overflow() is not called with EOF as the argument, the corresponding character can be written to the write position because the pointer to the write position is not increased beyond the end pointer. After the argument to `overflow()` is placed in the write position, the whole buffer can be emptied.

The member function `flushBuffer()` does exactly this. It writes the characters to the standard output channel (file descriptor 1) using the function `write()`. The stream buffer's member function `pbump()` is used to move the write position back to the beginning of the buffer.

The function `overflow()` inserts the character that caused the call of `overflow()` into the buffer if it is not EOF. Then, `pbump()` is used to advance the write position to reflect the new end of the buffered characters. This moves the write position beyond the end position (`epptr()`) temporarily.

This class also features the virtual function `sync()`, which is used to synchronize the current state of the stream buffer with the corresponding storage medium. Normally, all that needs to be done is to flush the buffer. For the unbuffered versions of the stream buffer, overriding this function was not necessary, because there was no buffer to be flushed.

The virtual destructor ensures that data is written that is still buffered when the stream buffer is destroyed.

These are the functions that are overridden for most stream buffers. If the external representation has some special structure, overriding additional functions may be useful. For example, the functions `seekoff()` and `seekpos()` may be overridden to allow manipulation of the write position.

User-Defined Input Buffers

The input mechanism works basically the same as the output mechanism. However, for input there is also the possibility of undoing the last read. The functions `sungetc()`, called by `unget()` of the input stream, or `sputbackc()`, called by `putback()` of the input stream, can be used to restore the stream buffer to its state before the last read. It is also possible to read the next character without moving the read position beyond this character. Thus, you must override more functions to implement reading from a stream buffer than is necessary to implement writing to a stream buffer.

A stream buffer maintains a read buffer with three pointers that can be accessed through the member functions `eback()`, `gptr()`, and `egptr()` (Figure 15.5):

1. `eback()` ("end back") is the beginning of the input buffer, or, as the name suggests, the end of the putback area. The character can only be put back up to this position without taking special action.
2. `gptr()` ("get pointer") is the current read position.
3. `egptr()` ("end get pointer") is the end of the input buffer.

The characters between the read position and the end position have been transported from the external representation to the program's memory, but they still await processing by the program.

Single characters can be read using the function `sgetc()` or `sbumpc()`. These two functions differ in that the read pointer is incremented by `sbumpc()` but not by `sgetc()`. If the buffer is read completely (`gptr() == egptr()`), no character is available, and the buffer has to be refilled by a call of the virtual function `underflow()`, which is responsible for the reading of data. If no characters are available, the function `sbumpc()` calls the virtual function `uflow()` instead. The

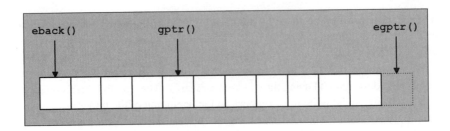

Figure 15.5. Interface for Reading from Stream Buffers

default implementation of uflow() is to call underflow() and then increment the read pointer. The default implementation of underflow() in the base class basic_streambuf is to return EOF. This means that it is impossible to read characters with the default implementation.

The function sgetn() is used for reading multiple characters at once. This function delegates the processing to the virtual function xsgetn(). The default implementation of xsgetn() simply extracts multiple characters by calling sbumpc() for each character. Like the function xsputn() for writing, xsgetn() can be implemented to optimize the reading of multiple characters.

For input, it is not sufficient simply to override one function, as it is in the case of output. Either a buffer has to be set up, or, at the very least, underflow() and uflow() have to implemented. The reason is that underflow() does not move past the current character, but underflow() may be called from sgetc(). Moving on to the next character has to be done using buffer manipulation or a call to uflow(). In any case, underflow() has to be implemented for any stream buffer capable of reading characters. If both underflow() and uflow() are implemented, there is no need to set up a buffer.

A read buffer is set up with the member function setg(), which takes three arguments in this order:

1. A pointer to the beginning of the buffer (eback())
2. A pointer to the current read position (gptr())
3. A pointer to the end of the buffer (egptr())

Unlike setp(), setg() takes three arguments in order to be able to define the room for storing characters that are put back into the stream. Thus, when the pointers to the read buffer are being set up, it is reasonable to have at least one character that is already read but still stored in the buffer.

As mentioned, characters can be put back into the read buffer by using the functions sputbackc() and sungetc(). sputbackc() gets the character to be put back as its argument and ensures that this character was indeed the character read. Both functions decrement the read pointer, if possible. Of course, this works only as long as the read pointer is not at the beginning of the read buffer. If you attempt to put a character back after the beginning of the buffer is reached, the virtual function pbackfail() is called. By overriding this function, you can implement a mechanism to restore the old read position even in this case. In the base class basic_streambuf, no corresponding behavior is defined. Thus, in practice, it is not possible to go back an arbitrary number of characters. For streams that do not use a buffer, the function pbackfail() should be implemented because it is generally assumed that at least one character can be put back into the stream.

If a new buffer was just read, another problem arises: Not even one character can be put back if the old data is not saved in the buffer. Thus, the implementation of `underflow()` often moves the last few characters (for example, four characters) of the current buffer to the beginning of the buffer and appends the newly read characters thereafter. This allows some characters to be moved back before `pbackfail()` is called.

The following example demonstrates how such an implementation might look. In the class inbuf, an input buffer with ten characters is implemented. This buffer is split into a maximum of four characters for the putback area and six characters for the "normal" input buffer:

```cpp
// io/inbuf1.hpp

#include <cstdio>
#include <cstring>
#include <streambuf>

// for read():
#ifdef _MSC_VER
# include <io.h>
#else
# include <unistd.h>
#endif

class inbuf : public std::streambuf {

  protected:
    // data buffer:
    // - at most, four characters in putback area plus
    // - at most, six characters in ordinary read buffer
    static const int bufferSize = 10;      // size of the data buffer
    char buffer[bufferSize];               // data buffer

  public:
    // constructor
    // - initialize empty data buffer
    // - no putback area
    // => force underflow()
    inbuf() {
        setg (buffer+4,      // beginning of putback area
              buffer+4,      // read position
              buffer+4);     // end position
    }
```

```
protected:
    // insert new characters into the buffer
    virtual int_type underflow () {
        // is read position before end of buffer?
        if (gptr() < egptr()) {
            return traits_type::to_int_type(*gptr());
        }


        // process size of putback area
        // - use number of characters read
        // - but at most four
        int numPutback;
        numPutback = gptr() - eback();
        if (numPutback > 4) {
            numPutback = 4;
        }


        // copy up to four characters previously read into
        // the putback buffer (area of first four characters)
        std::memmove (buffer+(4-numPutback), gptr()-numPutback,
                        numPutback);


        // read new characters
        int num;
        num = read (0, buffer+4, bufferSize-4);
        if (num <= 0) {
            // ERROR or EOF
            return EOF;
        }


        // reset buffer pointers
        setg (buffer+(4-numPutback),    // beginning of putback area
                buffer+4,               // read position
                buffer+4+num);          // end of buffer


        // return next character
        return traits_type::to_int_type(*gptr());
    }
};
```

The constructor initializes all pointers so that the buffer is completely empty (Figure 15.6). If a character is read from this stream buffer, the function underflow() is called. This function, always used by this stream buffer to read the next characters, starts by checking for read characters in the input buffer. If characters are present, they are moved to the putback area by using the function memcpy(). These are, at most, the last four characters of the input buffer. Then POSIX's low-level I/O function read() is used to read the next character from the standard input channel. After the buffer is adjusted to the new situation, the first character read is returned.

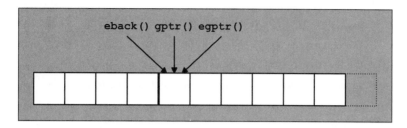

Figure 15.6. Get Buffer after Initialization

For example, if the characters 'H', 'a', 'l', 'l', 'o', and 'w' are read by the first call to read(), the state of the input buffer changes, as shown in Figure 15.7. The putback area is empty because the buffer was filled for the first time, and there are no characters yet that can be put back.

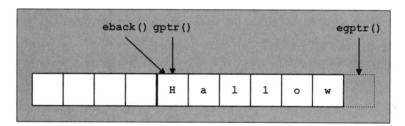

Figure 15.7. Get Buffer after Reading H a l l o w

After these characters are extracted, the last four characters are moved into the putback area, and new characters are read. For example, if the characters 'e', 'e', 'n', and '\n' are read by the next call of read(), the result is as shown in Figure 15.8.

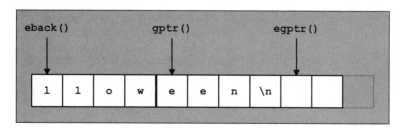

Figure 15.8. Get Buffer after Reading Four More Characters

Here is an example of the use of this stream buffer:

```cpp
// io/inbuf1.cpp

#include <iostream>
#include "inbuf1.hpp"

int main()
{
    inbuf ib;                   // create special stream buffer
    std::istream in(&ib);       // initialize input stream with that buffer

    char c;
    for (int i=1; i<=20; i++) {
        // read next character (out of the buffer)
        in.get(c);

        // print that character (and flush)
        std::cout << c << std::flush;

        // after eight characters, put two characters back into the stream
        if (i == 8) {
            in.unget();
            in.unget();
        }
    }
    std::cout << std::endl;
}
```

The program reads characters in a loop and writes them out. After the eighth character is read, two characters are put back. Thus, the seventh and eighth characters are printed twice.

15.14 Performance Issues

This section addresses issues that focus on performance. In general, the stream classes should be pretty efficient, but performance can be improved further in applications in which I/O is performance critical.

One performance issue was mentioned in Section 15.2.3, page 752, already: You should include only those headers that are necessary to compile your code. In particular, you should avoid including <iostream> if the standard stream objects are not used.

15.14.1 Synchronization with C's Standard Streams

By default, the eight C++ standard streams — the four narrow character streams `cin`, `cout`, `cerr`, and `clog`, and their wide-character counterparts — are synchronized with the corresponding files from the C standard library: `stdin`, `stdout`, and `stderr`. By default, `clog` and `wclog` use the same stream buffer as `cerr` and `wcerr`, respectively. Thus, they are also synchronized with `stderr` by default, although there is no direct counterpart in the C standard library.

Depending on the implementation, this synchronization might imply some often unnecessary overhead. For example, implementing the standard C++ streams using the standard C files inhibits buffering in the corresponding stream buffers. However, the buffer in the stream buffers is necessary for some optimizations, especially during formatted reading (see Section 15.14.2, page 845). To allow switching to a better implementation, the static member function `sync_with_stdio()` is defined for the class `ios_base` (Table 15.47).

Static Function	Meaning
`sync_with_stdio()`	Returns whether the standard stream objects are synchronized with standard C streams and concurrency is supported
`sync_with_stdio(false)`	Disables the synchronization of C++ and C streams (has to be called before any I/O)

Table 15.47. *Synchronizing Standard C++ and Standard C Streams*

`sync_with_stdio()` takes as argument an optional Boolean value that determines whether the synchronization with the standard C streams should be turned on. Thus, to turn the synchronization off, you have to pass `false` as the argument:

```
std::ios::sync_with_stdio(false);    // disable synchronization
```

Note that you have to disable the synchronization before any other I/O operation. Calling this function after any I/O has occurred results in implementation-defined behavior.

The function returns the previous value with which the function was called. If not called before, it always returns `true` to reflect the default setup of the standard streams.

Note that since C++11, disabling the synchronization with the standard C streams also disables the concurrency support, which allows you to use the standard stream object by multiple threads, although interleaved characters are possible (see Section 4.5, page 56).

15.14.2 Buffering in Stream Buffers

Buffering I/O is important for efficiency. One reason for this is that system calls are, in general, relatively expensive, and it pays to avoid them if possible. There is, however, another, more subtle reason in C++ for doing buffering in stream buffers, at least for input: The functions for formatted I/O use stream buffer iterators to access the streams, and operating on stream buffer iterators is slower than operating on pointers. The difference is not that big, but it is sufficient to justify improved implementations for frequently used operations, such as formatted reading of numeric values. However, for such improvements, it is essential that stream buffers are buffered.

Thus, all I/O is done using stream buffers, which implement a mechanism for buffering. However, it is not sufficient to rely solely on this buffering, because three aspects conflict with effective buffering:

1. It is often simpler to implement stream buffers without buffering. If the corresponding streams are not used frequently or are used only for output, buffering is probably not that important. (For output, the difference between stream buffer iterators and pointers is not as bad as for input; the main problem is comparing stream buffer iterators.) However, for stream buffers that are used extensively, buffering should definitely be implemented.

2. The flag `unitbuf` causes output streams to flush the stream after each output operation. Correspondingly, the manipulators `flush` and `endl` also flush the stream. For the best performance, all three should probably be avoided. However, when writing to the console, for example, it is probably still reasonable to flush the stream after writing complete lines. If you are stuck with a program that makes heavy use of `unitbuf`, `flush`, or `endl`, you might consider using a special stream buffer that does not use `sync()` to flush the stream buffer but uses another function that is called when appropriate.

3. Tieing streams with the `tie()` function (see Section 15.12.1, page 819) also results in additional flushing of streams. Thus, streams should be tied only if it is really necessary.

When implementing new stream buffers, it may be reasonable to implement them without buffering first. Then, if the stream buffer is identified as a bottleneck, it is still possible to implement buffering without affecting anything in the remainder of the application.

15.14.3   Using Stream Buffers Directly

All member functions of the class `basic_istream` and `basic_ostream` that read or write characters operate according to the same schema: First, a corresponding `sentry` object is constructed, and then the operation is performed. The construction of the `sentry` object results in flushing of potentially tied objects, skipping of whitespace for input, and such implementation-specific operations as locking in multithreaded environments (see Section 15.5.4, page 772).

For unformatted I/O, most of the operations are normally useless anyway. Only locking operation might be useful if the streams are used in multithreaded environments. Thus, when doing unformatted I/O, it may be better to use stream buffers directly.

To support this behavior, you can use operators `<<` and `>>` with stream buffers as follows:

- By passing a pointer to a stream buffer to operator `<<`, you can output all input of its device. This is probably the fastest way to copy files by using C++ I/O streams. For example:

    ```
    // io/copy1.cpp
    #include <iostream>
    ```

```
int main ()
{
    // copy all standard input to standard output
    std::cout << std::cin.rdbuf();
}
```

Here, `rdbuf()` yields the buffer of `cin` (see Section 15.12.2, page 820). Thus, the program copies all standard input to standard output.

- By passing a pointer to a stream buffer to operator `>>`, you can read directly into a stream buffer. For example, you could also copy all standard input to standard output in the following way:

```
// io/copy2.cpp

#include <iostream>

int main ()
{
    // copy all standard input to standard output
    std::cin >> std::noskipws >> std::cout.rdbuf();
}
```

Note that you have to clear the flag `skipws`. Otherwise, leading whitespace of the input is skipped (see Section 15.7.7, page 789).

Even for formatted I/O, it may be reasonable to use stream buffers directly. For example, if many numeric values are read in a loop, it is sufficient to construct just one `sentry` object that exists for the whole time the loop is executed. Then, within the loop, whitespace is skipped manually — using the `ws` manipulator would also construct a `sentry` object — and then the facet `num_get` (see Section 16.4.1, page 873) is used for reading the numeric values directly.

Note that a stream buffer has no error state of its own. It also has no knowledge of the input or output stream that might connect to it. So, calling

```
// copy contents of in to out
out << in.rdbuf();
```

can't change the error state of `in` due to a failure or end-of-file.

Chapter 16

Internationalization

As the global market has increased in importance, so too has *internationalization*, or *i18n* for short,[1] for software development. As a consequence, the C++ standard library provides concepts to write code for international programs. These concepts influence mainly the use of I/O and string processing. This chapter describes these concepts. Many thanks to Dietmar Kühl, who is an expert on I/O and internationalization in the C++ standard library and wrote major parts of this chapter.

The C++ standard library provides a general approach to support national conventions without being bound to specific conventions. This goes to the extent, for example, that strings are not bound to a specific character type to support 16-bit characters in Asia. For the internationalization of programs, two related aspects are important:

1. Different character sets have different properties, so flexible solutions are required for such problems as what is considered to be a letter or, worse, what type to use to represent characters. For character sets with more than 256 characters, type char is not sufficient as a representation.

2. The user of a program expects to see national or cultural conventions obeyed, such as the formatting of dates, monetary values, numbers, and Boolean values.

For both aspects, the C++ standard library provides related solutions.

The major approach toward internationalization is to use *locale objects* to represent an extensible collection of aspects to be adapted to specific local conventions. Locales are already used in C for this purpose. In the C++ standard, this mechanism was generalized and made more flexible. In fact, the C++ locale mechanism can be used to address all kinds of customization, depending on the user's environment or preferences. For example, it can be extended to deal with measurement systems, time zones, or paper size.

Most of the mechanisms of internationalization involve only minimal, if any, additional work for the programmer. For example, when doing I/O with the C++ stream mechanism, numeric values are formatted according to the rules of some locale. The only work for the programmer is to instruct the I/O stream classes to use the user's preferences. In addition to such automatic use, the programmer may use locale objects directly for formatting, collation, character classification, and so on.

---

[1] The common abbreviation for *internationalization*, *i18n*, stands for the letter *i*, followed by *18* characters, followed by the letter *n*.

Strings and streams use another concept for internationalization: *character traits*. They define fundamental properties and operations that differ for different character sets, such as the value of "end-of-file" as well as functions to compare, assign, and copy strings.

Recent Changes with C++11

C++98 specified most features of the localization library. Here is a list of the most important features added with C++11:

- For locales and facets, you can pass a `std::string` now, not only a `const char*` (see Section 16.2.1, page 863).
- A few new manipulators were introduced: `get_money()`, `put_money()`, `get_time()`, and `put_time()` (see Section 16.4.3, page 890, and Section 16.4.2, page 882).
- The `time_get<>` facet now provides a member function `get()` for a complete formatting string (see Section 16.4.3, page 887).
- The facets for numeric I/O now also support `long long` and `unsigned long long`.
- The new character class mask value `blank` and the corresponding convenience function `isblank()` were introduced (see Section 16.4.4, page 894, and Section 16.4.4, page 895).
- Character traits are now also provided for types `char16_t` and `char32_t` (see Section 16.1.4, page 853).
- The new classes `wstring_convert` and `wbuffer_convert` support additional conversions between different character sets (see Section 16.4.4, page 901, and Section 16.4.4, page 903).

16.1   Character Encodings and Character Sets

At the beginning of the age of computer science the character set of computers was limited to the characters of the English alphabet. Today in the area of globalization, there are character set standards of up to 32 bits, with more than 1 million different character values.[2] As a consequence, there are different standards and approaches to deal with characters in different countries and cultures.

16.1.1   Multibyte and Wide-Character Text

Two different approaches are common to address character sets that have more than 256 characters: multibyte representation and wide-character representation:

1. With *multibyte representation*, the number of bytes used for a character is variable. A 1-byte character, such as an ISO-Latin-1 character, can be followed by a 3-byte character, such as a Japanese ideogram.
2. With *wide-character representation*, the number of bytes used to represent a character is always the same, independent of the character being represented. Typical representations use 2 or 4

---

[2] Current 32-bit character sets use the values up to `0x10FFFF`, which are 1,114,111 values.

bytes. Conceptually, this does not differ from representations that use just 1 byte for locales where ISO-Latin-1 or even ASCII is sufficient.

Multibyte representation is more compact than wide-character representation. Thus, the multibyte representation is normally used to store data outside of programs. Conversely, it is much easier to process characters of fixed size, so the wide-character representation is usually used inside programs.

In a multibyte string, the same byte may represent a character or even just a part of the character. During iteration through a multibyte string, each byte is interpreted according to a current "shift state." Depending on the value of the byte and the current shift state, a byte may represent a certain character or a change of the current shift state. A multibyte string always starts in a defined initial shift state. For example, in the initial shift state, the bytes may represent ISO-Latin-1 characters until an escape character is encountered. The character following the escape character identifies the new shift state. For example, that character may switch to a shift state in which the bytes are interpreted as Arabic characters until the next escape character is encountered.

16.1.2 Different Character Sets

The most important character sets are:

- **US-ASCII**, a 7-bit character set standardized since 1963 for teleprinters and other devices, so that the first 16 values are "nonprintable characters," such as carriage-return, horizontal tab, backspace, or a bell. This character set serves as base for all other character sets, and usually the values between 0x20 and 0x7F have the same characters in all other character sets.

- **ISO-Latin-1** or **ISO-8859-1** (see [*ISOLatin1*]), an 8-bit character set, standardized since 1987 to provide all characters of the "Western Europe" languages. Also, this character set serves as base for all other character sets, and usually the values between 0x20 and 0x7F and from 0xA0 to 0xFF have the same characters in all other character sets.

- **ISO-Latin-9** or **ISO-8859-15** (see [*ISOLatin9*]), an 8-bit character set, standardized since 1999 to provide an improved version of all characters of the "Western Europe" languages by replacing some less common symbols with the euro sign and other special characters.

- **UCS-2**, a 16-bit fixed-sized character set, providing the 65,536 most important characters of the *Universal Character Set* and *Unicode* standards.

- **UTF-8** (see [*UTF8*]), a multibyte character-set using between one and four *octets* of 8 bits to represent all characters of the *Universal Character Set* and *Unicode* standards. It is widely used in the world of the World Wide Web.

- **UTF-16**, a multibyte character-set using between one and two *code units* of 16 bits to represent all characters of the *Universal Character Set* and *Unicode* standards.

- **UCS-4** or **UTF-32**, a 32-bit fixed-sized character set, providing all standardized characters of the *Universal Character Set* and *Unicode* standards.

Note that UTF-16 and UTF-32 might have a *byte order mark* (*BOM*) at the beginning of the whole character sequence to mark whether *big-endian* (default) or *little-endian* byte order is used. Alternatively, you can explicitly specify UTF-16BE, UTF-16LE, UTF-32BE, or UTF-32LE.

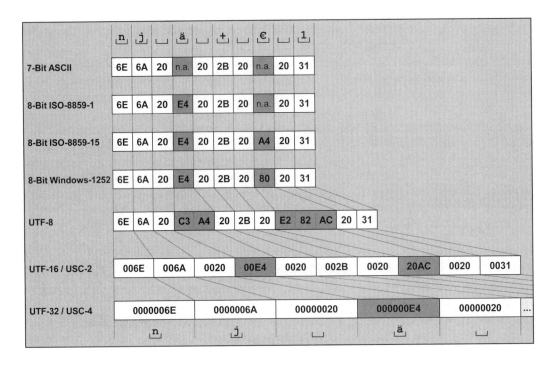

Figure 16.1. Hexadecimal Character Codes of Different Character Sets

Figure 16.1 shows the different hexadecimal encodings of an example character sequence, using ordinary ASCII characters, the German umlaut ä, and the euro symbol €. Here, UTF-16 and UTF-32 use no byte order marks. A byte order mark would have the value 0xFEFF.

Note that UTF-16 and UCS-2 almost match for the characters up to the value 0xFFFF. Only for very special characters not available in UCS-2, UTF-16 uses two code units of 16 bits given that UCS-2 is a multibyte character set.

16.1.3 Dealing with Character Sets in C++

C++ provides different character types to deal with these character sets:

- **char** can be used for all character sets up to 8 bits, such as US-ASCII, ISO-Latin-1, and ISO-Latin-9. In addition, it can be used for octets of UTF-8.
- **char16_t** (provided since C++11) can be used for UCS-2 and as code unit for UTF-16.
- **char32_t** (provided since C++11) can be used for UCS-4/UTF-32.
- **wchar_t** is the type for the values of the largest extended character set among all supported locales. Thus, it is usually equivalent to char16_t or char32_t.

All these types are keywords, so it is possible to overload functions with all these types. Note, however, that the support of char16_t and char32_t is limited. Although character traits provide the ability to deal with Unicode strings, no overloads for these types for I/O are provided.

Note that since C++11, you can specify string literals using different character encodings (see Section 3.1.6, page 24, for details).

To support character and code conversions, the C++ standard library provides the following features:

- To convert `strings` into `wstrings` and vice versa, you can use the member functions `widen()` and `narrow()` of the `ctype<>` facet (see Section 16.4.4, page 891). Note that they also can be used to convert characters of the native character set into characters of a locale's character set, both using the character type `char`.
- To convert multibyte sequences into `wstrings` and vice versa, you can use the class template `wstring_convert<>` and the corresponding `codecvt<>` facets (see Section 16.4.4, page 901).
- Class `codecvt<>` (see Section 16.4.4, page 897) is also used by class `basic_filebuf<>` (see Section 15.9.1, page 791) to convert between internal and external representations when reading or writing files.
- To read or write multibyte character sequences, you can use class `wbuffer_convert<>` and the corresponding `codecvt<>` facets (see Section 16.4.4, page 903).

16.1.4 Character Traits

The different representations of character sets imply variations that are relevant for the processing of strings and I/O. For example, the value used to represent "end-of-file" or the details of comparing characters may differ for representations.

The string and stream classes are intended to be instantiated with built-in types, especially with `char` and `wchar_t`, and, since C++11, maybe with `char16_t` and `char32_t`. The interface of built-in types cannot be changed. Thus, the details on how to deal with aspects that depend on the representation are factored into a separate class, a so-called *traits class*. Both the string and stream classes take a traits class as a template argument. This argument defaults to the class `char_traits`, parametrized with the template argument that defines the character type of the string or stream:

```
namespace std {
    template <typename charT,
              typename traits = char_traits<charT>,
              typename Allocator = allocator<charT>>
        class basic_string;
}

namespace std {
    template <typename charT,
              typename traits = char_traits<charT>>
        class basic_istream;
    template <typename charT,
              typename traits = char_traits<charT>>
        class basic_ostream;
    ...
}
```

The character traits have type `char_traits<>`. This type is defined in `<string>` and is parametrized on the specific character type:

```
namespace std {
    template <typename charT>
    struct char_traits {
        ...
    };
}
```

The traits classes define all fundamental properties of the character type and the corresponding operations necessary for the implementation of strings and streams as static components. Table 16.1 lists the members of `char_traits`.

Expression	Meaning
`char_type`	The character type (the template argument for `char_traits`)
`int_type`	A type large enough to represent an additional, otherwise unused value for end-of-file
`pos_type`	A type used to represent positions in streams
`off_type`	A type used to represent offsets between positions in streams
`state_type`	A type used to represent the current state in multibyte streams
`assign(c1,c2)`	Assigns character $c2$ to $c1$
`eq(c1,c2)`	Returns whether the characters $c1$ and $c2$ are equal
`lt(c1,c2)`	Returns whether character $c1$ is less than character $c2$
`length(s)`	Returns the length of the string s
`compare(s1,s2,n)`	Compares up to n characters of strings $s1$ and $s2$
`copy(s1,s2,n)`	Copies n characters of string $s2$ to string $s1$
`move(s1,s2,n)`	Copies n characters of string $s2$ to string $s1$, where $s1$ and $s2$ may overlap
`assign(s,n,c)`	Assigns the character c to n characters of string s
`find(s,n,c)`	Returns a pointer to the first character in string s that is equal to c or `nullptr` if no such character is among the first n characters
`eof()`	Returns the value of end-of-file
`to_int_type(c)`	Converts the character c into the corresponding representation as `int_type`
`to_char_type(i)`	Converts the representation i as `int_type` to a character (the result of converting EOF is undefined)
`not_eof(i)`	Returns the value i unless i is the value for EOF; in this case, an implementation-dependent value different from EOF is returned
`eq_int_type(i1,i2)`	Tests the equality of the two characters $i1$ and $i2$ represented as `int_type` (the characters may be EOF)

Table 16.1. Character Traits Members

The functions that process strings or character sequences are present for optimization only. They could also be implemented by using the functions that process single characters. For example, `copy()` can be implemented using `assign()`. However, there might be more efficient implementations when dealing with strings.

Note that counts used in the functions are exact counts, not maximum counts. That is, string-termination characters within these sequences are ignored.

The last group of functions concerns the special processing of the character that represents end-of-file (EOF). This character extends the character set by an artificial character to indicate special processing. For some representations, the character type may be insufficient to accommodate this special character because it has to have a value that differs from the values of all "normal" characters of the character set. C established the convention to return a character as `int` instead of as `char` from functions reading characters. This technique was extended in C++. The character traits define `char_type` as the type to represent all characters and `int_type` as the type to represent all characters plus EOF. The functions `to_char_type()`, `to_int_type()`, `not_eof()`, and `eq_int_type()` define the corresponding conversions and comparisons. It is possible that `char_type` and `int_type` are identical for some character traits. This can be the case if not all values of `char_type` are necessary to represent characters so that a spare value can be used for end-of-file.

`pos_type` and `off_type` are used to define file positions and offsets, respectively (see Section 15.9.4, page 799, for details).

The C++ standard library provides specializations of `char_traits<>` for types `char` and `wchar_t` and, since C++11, for `char16_t` and `char32_t`:

```
namespace std {
    template<> struct char_traits<char>;
    template<> struct char_traits<wchar_t>;
    template<> struct char_traits<char16_t>;
    template<> struct char_traits<char32>;
}
```

The specialization for `char` is usually implemented by using the global string functions of C that are defined in `<cstring>` or `<string.h>`. An implementation might look as follows:

```
namespace std {
    template<> struct char_traits<char> {
        // type definitions:
        typedef char       char_type;
        typedef int        int_type;
        typedef streampos  pos_type;
        typedef streamoff  off_type;
        typedef mbstate_t  state_type;

        // functions:
        static void assign(char& c1, const char& c2) {
            c1 = c2;
        }
    }
```

```
    static bool eq(const char& c1, const char& c2) {
        return c1 == c2;
    }
    static bool lt(const char& c1, const char& c2) {
        return c1 < c2;
    }
    static size_t length(const char* s) {
        return strlen(s);
    }
    static int compare(const char* s1, const char* s2, size_t n) {
        return memcmp(s1,s2,n);
    }
    static char* copy(char* s1, const char* s2, size_t n) {
        return (char*)memcpy(s1,s2,n);
    }
    static char* move(char* s1, const char* s2, size_t n) {
        return (char*)memmove(s1,s2,n);
    }
    static char* assign(char* s, size_t n, char c) {
        return (char*)memset(s,c,n);
    }
    static const char* find(const char* s, size_t n,
                            const char& c) {
        return (const char*)memchr(s,c,n);
    }
    static int eof() {
        return EOF;
    }
    static int to_int_type(const char& c) {
        return (int)(unsigned char)c;
    }
    static char to_char_type(const int& i) {
        return (char)i;
    }
    static int not_eof(const int& i) {
        return i!=EOF ? i : !EOF;
    }
    static bool eq_int_type(const int& i1, const int& i2) {
        return i1 == i2;
    }
};
}
```

See Section 13.2.15, page 689, for the implementation of a user-defined traits class that lets strings behave in a case-insensitive manner.

16.1.5 Internationalization of Special Characters

One issue with character encodings remains: How are special characters, such as the newline or the string termination character, internationalized? The class `basic_ios<>` has members `widen()` and `narrow()` that can be used for this purpose. Thus, the newline character in an encoding appropriate for the stream `strm` can be written as follows:

    strm.widen('\n')   // internationalized newline character

The string-termination character in the same encoding can be created like this:

    strm.widen('\0')   // internationalized string-termination character

See the implementation of the `endl` manipulator in Section 15.6.2, page 777, for an example use.

   The functions `widen()` and `narrow()` use a locale object: more precisely, the `ctype<>` facet of this object. This facet can be used to convert all characters between `char` and some other character representations. It is described in Section 16.4.4, page 891. For example, the following expression converts the character `c` of type `char` into an object of type `charType` by using the locale object `loc`:

    std::use_facet<std::ctype<charType>>(loc).widen(c)

The details of the use of locales and their facets are described in the following sections.

16.2   The Concept of Locales

A common approach to internationalization is to use environments, called *locales*, to encapsulate national or cultural conventions. The C community uses this approach. Thus, in the context of internationalization, a *locale* is a collection of parameters and functions used to support national or cultural conventions. According to X/Open conventions,[3] the environment variable LANG is used to define the locale to be used. Depending on this locale, different formats for floating-point numbers, dates, monetary values, and so on, are used.

   The format of the string defining a locale is normally this:

language[_*area*[.*code*]][@*modifier*]

where

- *language* represents the language, such as English or German. It is usually a string of two lower-case letters, such as en or de.

- *area* is the area, country, or culture where this language is used. It is usually a string of two uppercase letters, such as US or DE.

---

[3] POSIX and X/Open are standards for operating system interfaces.

- *code* defines the character encoding to be used. This, for example, is important in Asia, where different character encodings are used to represent the same character set. Examples are: `utf8`, `ISO-8859-1`, `eucJP`.

- *modifier* is allowed on some platforms to specify additional modifications, such as `@euro` for using the euro symbol or `@phone` for sorting according to the telephone directory.

Table 16.2 presents a selection of typical language strings, especially on POSIX systems. However, note that these strings are *not* portable. In fact, multiple standards are involved and proprietary values are used. For example, to use a German locale with an ISO-Latin1-like character set including the euro symbol, you might have to specify `de_DE.ISO-8859-15` or `de_DE@euro` or `deu_deu.1252` or `deu_germany` or just `german`. (Note that the euro symbol might have different integral values because different character sets are used.) The following references might help:

- For the *language*, ISO639 (see [*ISO639:LangCodes*]) defines two-letter acronyms, such as en or de, usually used by POSIX environments, and three-letter acronyms, such as eng and deu, usually supported by Windows platforms.

- For the *area*, ISO3166 (see [*ISO3166:CodeTab*]) defines two-letter acronyms, such as US or DE, usually used by POSIX environments. Note that Windows uses different codes here.

- See [*VisualC++Locales*] for the *language*, *area*, and *code* on Windows platforms, which use slightly different character sets.

For programs, that these names are not standardized is normally no problem because the locale information usually is provided by the user in some form. It is common that programs simply read environment variables or some similar database to determine which locales to use. Thus, the burden of finding the correct locale names is put on the users. Only if the program always uses a special locale does the name need to be hard-coded in the program. Normally, for this case, the C locale is sufficient, and is guaranteed to be supported by all implementations and to have the name C.

The next section presents the use of different locales in C++ programs. In particular, it introduces locale *facets*, which are used to deal with specific formatting details.

C also provides an approach to handle the problem of character sets with more than 256 characters. This approach is to first use the character types `wchar_t`, a type definition for one of the integral types with language support for wide-character constants and wide-character string literals. However, apart from this, only functions to convert between wide characters and narrow characters are supported. This approach was also incorporated into C++ with the character type `wchar_t`, which is, unlike the C approach, a distinct type in C++. However, C++ provides more library support than C, because everything available for `char` is also available for `wchar_t`, and any other type may be used as a character type.

Since C++11, types `char16_t` and `char32_t` also are supported. However, this is not done throughout the library. For example, there are no predefined I/O stream objects for these types, as `wcout` is provided in correspondence to `cout`.

16.2.1 Using Locales

Using translations of textual messages is normally not sufficient for true internationalization. For example, different conventions for numeric, monetary, or date formatting also have to be used. In

Locale	Meaning
C	Default: ANSI-C conventions (English, 7 bit)
de_DE	German in Germany
de_DE.ISO-8859-1	German in Germany with ISO-Latin-1 encoding
de_DE.utf8	German in Germany with UTF-8 encoding
de_AT	German in Austria
de_CH	German in Switzerland
en_US	English in the United States
en_GB	English in Great Britain
en_AU	English in Australia
en_CA	English in Canada
fr_FR	French in France
fr_CH	French in Switzerland
fr_CA	French in Canada
ja_JP.jis	Japanese in Japan with *Japanese Industrial Standard (JIS)* encoding
ja_JP.sjis	Japanese in Japan with *Shift JIS* encoding
ja_JP.ujis	Japanese in Japan with *UNIXized JIS* encoding
ja_JP.EUC	Japanese in Japan with *Extended UNIX Code* encoding
ko_KR	Korean in Korea
zh_CN	Chinese in China
zh_TW	Chinese in Taiwan
lt_LN.bit7	ISO-Latin, 7 bit
lt_LN.bit8	ISO-Latin, 8 bit
POSIX	POSIX conventions (English, 7 bit)

Table 16.2. Selection of Locale Names

addition, functions manipulating letters should depend on character encoding to ensure the correct handling of all characters that are letters in a given language.

According to the POSIX and X/Open standards, it is already possible in C programs to set a locale by using the function setlocale(). Changing the locale influences the results of character classification and manipulation functions, such as isupper() and toupper(), and the I/O functions, such as printf().

However, the C approach has several limitations. Because the locale is a global property, using more than one locale at the same time — for example, when reading floating-point numbers in English and writing them in German — is either not possible or is possible only with a relatively large effort. Also, locales cannot be extended. They provide only the facilities the implementation chooses to provide. If something the C locales do not provide must also be adapted to national conventions, a different mechanism has to be used to do this. Finally, it is not possible to define new locales to support special cultural conventions.

The C++ standard library addresses all these problems with an object-oriented approach. First, the details of a locale are encapsulated in an object of type locale. Doing this immediately provides the possibility of using multiple locales at the same time. Operations that depend on locales are

configured to use a corresponding locale object. For example, a locale object can be installed for
each I/O stream, which is then used by the different member functions to adapt to the corresponding
conventions. This is demonstrated by the following example:

```cpp
// i18n/loc1.cpp

#include <iostream>
#include <locale>
#include <exception>
#include <cstdlib>
using namespace std;

int main()
{
    try {
        // use classic C locale to read data from standard input
        cin.imbue(locale::classic());

        // use a German locale to write data to standard output
        // - use different locale names for Windows and POSIX
#ifdef _MSC_VER
        cout.imbue(locale("deu_deu.1252"));
#else
        cout.imbue(locale("de_DE"));
#endif

        // read and output floating-point values in a loop
        cout << "input floating-point values (classic notation): " << endl;
        double value;
        while (cin >> value) {
            cout << value << endl;
        }
    }
    catch (const std::exception& e) {
        cerr << "Exception: " << e.what() << endl;
        return EXIT_FAILURE;
    }
}
```

The first `imbue()` statement assigns the "classic" C locale to the standard input channel:

```cpp
cin.imbue(locale::classic());   // use classic C locale
```

For the classic C locale, formatting of numbers and dates, character classification, and so on, is
handled as it is in original C without any locales. The following expression obtains a corresponding
object of class `locale`:

```
std::locale::classic()
```

Using the following expression instead would yield the same result:

```
std::locale("C")
```

This last expression constructs a `locale` object from a given name. The name `"C"` is a special name and is the only one a C++ implementation is required to support. There is no requirement to support any other locale, although it is assumed that C++ implementations also support other locales.

Alternatively, you could use the default constructor of class `locale`, which initializes a locale according to the current global locale of the program, which by default is also the "classic" C locale:

```
cin.imbue(locale());     // use global locale (classic C locale by default)
```

Or you could use an empty string as locale name, which means that the "native" locale according to the environment of the program is used:

```
cin.imbue(locale(""));   // use native locale according to the environment
```

The next `imbue()` statements assign a German locale to the standard output channel using `de_DE` in a POSIX and `deu_deu.1252` in a Windows environment:[4]

```
#ifdef _MSC_VER
    cout.imbue(locale("deu_deu.1252"));
#else
    cout.imbue(locale("de_DE"));
#endif
```

This is, of course, successful only if the system supports this locale. If the name used to construct a locale object is unknown to the implementation, an exception of type `runtime_error` is thrown. For this reason, this call is surrounded by a `try-catch` clause.

If everything was successful, input is read according to the classic C conventions, and output is written according to the German conventions. The loop thus reads floating-point values in the classic English format:

```
47.11
```

and prints them using the German format:

```
47,11
```

(Yes, the Germans really use a comma as a "decimal point.")

Normally, a program does not predefine a specific locale except when writing and reading data in a fixed format. Instead, the locale is determined using the environment variable `LANG`. Another possibility is to read the name of the locale to be used. The following program demonstrates this:

```
// i18n/loc2.cpp

#include <iostream>
#include <locale>
#include <string>
```

---

[4] "de" and "deu" stand for "Deutschland," the German name of Germany.

```cpp
#include <cstdlib>
#include <exception>
using namespace std;

int main()
{
    try {
        // create the default locale from the user's environment
        locale langLocale("");

        // and assign it to the standard output channel
        cout.imbue(langLocale);

        // process the name of the locale to find out whether German is used
        cout << langLocale.name() << endl;
        bool isGerman = (langLocale.name().substr(0,2) == "de" ||
                         langLocale.name().substr(0,3) == "ger" ||
                         langLocale.name().substr(0,3) == "Ger");

        // read locale for the input
        cout << (isGerman ? "Sprachumgebung fuer Eingaben: "
                          : "Locale for input: ") << endl;
        string s;
        cin >> s;
        if (!cin) {
            if (isGerman) {
                cerr << "FEHLER beim Einlesen der Sprachumgebung"
                     << endl;
            }
            else {
                cerr << "ERROR while reading the locale" << endl;
            }
            return EXIT_FAILURE;
        }
        locale cinLocale(s);   // create locale by string (since C++11)

        // and assign it to the standard input channel
        cin.imbue(cinLocale);

        // read and output floating-point values in a loop
        cout << (isGerman ? "Gleitkommawerte: "
                          : "Floating-point values: ") << endl;
        double value;
```

```
            while (cin >> value) {
                cout << value << endl;
            }
        }
        catch (const std::exception& e) {
            cerr << "Exception: " << e.what() << endl;
            return EXIT_FAILURE;
        }
    }
```

In this example, the following statement creates an object of the class `locale`:

```
    locale langLocale("");
```

Passing an empty string as the name of the locale has a special meaning: The "native" locale from the user's environment is used, which is often determined by the environment variable LANG. This locale is assigned to the standard input stream with the statement

```
    cout.imbue(langLocale);
```

The following expression is used to retrieve the name of the default locale, which is returned as an object of type `string` (see Chapter 13):

```
    langLocale.name()
```

The following statements construct a locale from a name read from standard input:

```
    string s;
    cin >> s;
    ...
    locale cinLocale(s);   // create locale by string (since C++11)
```

To do this, a word is read from the standard input and used as the constructor's argument. Note that before C++11, the `locale` constructor accepted only type `const char*`, so before C++11, you had to write:

```
    locale cinLocale(s.c_str());   // create locale by string before C++11
```

If the read fails, the `ios_base::failbit` is set in the input stream, which is checked and handled in this program:

```
    if (!cin) {
        if (isGerman) {
            cerr << "FEHLER beim Einlesen der Sprachumgebung"
                << endl;
        }
        else {
            cerr << "ERROR while reading the locale" << endl;
        }
        return EXIT_FAILURE;
    }
```

Again, if the string is not a valid value for the construction of a locale, a `runtime_error` exception is thrown.

If a program wants to honor local conventions, it should use corresponding locale objects. The static member function `global()` of the class `std::locale` can be used to install a global locale object. This object is used as the default value for functions that take an optional locale object as an argument. If the locale object set with the `global()` function has a name, the C functions dealing with locales react correspondingly. If the locale set has no name, the consequences for the C functions depend on the implementation.

Here is an example of how to set the global locale object depending on the environment in which the program is running:

```
// create a locale object depending on the program's environment and
// set it as the global object
std::locale::global(std::locale(""));
```

Among other things, this arranges for the corresponding registration for the C functions to be executed. That is, the C functions are influenced as if the following call were made:

```
std::setlocale(LC_ALL,"")
```

However, setting the global locale does not replace locales already stored in objects. It modifies the locale object copied only when a locale is created with a default constructor. For example, the stream objects store locale objects that are not replaced by a call to `locale::global()`. If you want an existing stream to use a specific locale, you have to tell the stream to use this locale by using the `imbue()` function.

The global locale is used if a locale object is created with the default constructor. In this case, the new locale behaves as if it is a copy of the global locale at the time it was constructed. The following three lines install the default locale for the standard streams:

```
// register global locale object for streams
std::cin.imbue(std::locale());
std::cout.imbue(std::locale());
std::cerr.imbue(std::locale());
```

When using locales in C++, it is important to remember that the C++ locale mechanism is coupled only loosely to the C locale mechanism. There is only one relation to the C locale mechanism: The global C locale is modified if a named C++ locale object is set as the global locale. In general, you should not assume that the C and the C++ functions operate on the same locales.

16.2.2 Locale Facets

The dependencies on national conventions are separated into several aspects that are handled by corresponding objects. An object dealing with a specific aspect of internationalization is called a *facet*. A locale object is used as a container of different facets. To access an aspect of a locale, the type of the corresponding facet is used as the index. The type of the facet is passed explicitly as a template argument to the function template `use_facet()`, accessing the desired facet. For example, the following expression accesses the facet type `numpunct<>` specialized for the character type `char` of the locale object `loc`:

```
std::use_facet<std::numpunct<char>>(loc)
```

Each facet type is defined by a class that defines certain services. For example, the facet type numpunct<> provides services used with the formatting of numeric and Boolean values. For example, the following expression returns the string used to represent true in the locale loc:

```
std::use_facet<std::numpunct<char>>(loc).truename()
```

Note that use_facet() returns a reference to an object that is valid only as long as the locale object exists. Thus, the following statements result in undefined behavior because fac is no longer valid after the first expression:

```
const numpunct<char>& fac = use_facet<numpunct<char>>(locale("de"));
cout << "true in German: " << fac.truename() << endl;   // ERROR
```

Table 16.3 provides an overview of the facets predefined by the C++ standard library. Each facet is associated with a category. These categories are used by some of the constructors of locales to create new locales as the combination of other locales.

Category	Facet Type	Used for	Page
numeric	num_get<>()	Numeric input	873
	num_put<>()	Numeric output	871
	numpunct<>()	Symbols used for numeric I/O	870
monetary	money_get<>()	Monetary input	881
	money_put<>()	Monetary output	879
	moneypunct<>()	Symbols used for monetary I/O	874
time	time_get<>()	Time and date input	887
	time_put<>()	Time and date output	884
ctype	ctype<>()	Character information (toupper(), isupper())	891
	codecvt<>()	Conversion between different character encodings	897
collate	collate<>()	String collation	904
messages	messages<>()	Message string retrieval	905

Table 16.3. Facet Types Predefined by the C++ Standard Library

You can define your own versions of the facets to create specialized locales. The following example demonstrates how to do so. It defines a facet using German representations of the Boolean values:

```
class germanBoolNames : public std::numpunct_byname<char> {
  public:
    germanBoolNames (const std::string& name)
      : std::numpunct_byname<char>(name) {
    }
  protected:
    virtual std::string do_truename () const {
        return "wahr";
    }
```

```
        virtual std::string do_falsename () const {
            return "falsch";
        }
    };
```

Note that before C++11, the constructor had to declare name with type const char*.

The class germanBoolNames derives from the class numpunct_byname<>, which is defined by the C++ standard library. This class defines punctuation properties depending on the locale used for numeric formatting. Deriving from numpunct_byname<> instead of from numpunct<> lets you customize the members not overridden explicitly. The values returned from these members still depend on the name used as the argument to the constructor. If the class numpunct<> had been used as the base class, the behavior of the other functions would be fixed. However, the class germanBoolNames overrides the two functions used to determine the textual representation of true and false.

To use this facet in a locale, you need to create a new locale, using a special constructor of the class std::locale. This constructor takes a locale object as its first argument and a pointer to a facet as its second argument. The created locale is identical to the first argument except for the facet that is passed as the second argument. This facet is installed in the newly created locale after the first argument is copied:

```
    std::locale loc (std::locale(""), new germanBoolNames(""));
```

The new expression creates a facet that is installed in the new locale. Thus, it is registered in loc to create a variation of locale(""). Since locales are immutable, you have to create a new locale object if you want to install a new facet to a locale. This locale object can be used like any other locale object. For example,

```
    std::cout.imbue(loc);
    std::cout << std::boolalpha << true << std::endl;
```

would have the following output (see *i18n/germanbool.cpp* for the complete example):

```
    wahr
```

You also can create a completely new facet. In this case, the function has_facet() can be used to determine whether such a new facet is registered for a given locale object.

16.3 Locales in Detail

A C++ locale is an immutable container for facets. It is defined in the <locale> header file.

The strange thing about locales is how the objects stored in the container are accessed. A facet in a locale is accessed using the type of the facet as the index. Because each facet exposes a different interface and suits a different purpose, it is desirable to have the access function to locales return a type corresponding to the index. This is exactly what can be done with a type as the index. Using the facet's type as an index has the additional advantage of having a type-safe interface.

Locales are immutable. This means the facets stored in a locale cannot be changed except when locales are being assigned. Variations of locales are created by combining existing locales and facets to create a new locale. Table 16.4 lists the constructors for locales.

Expression	Effect
`locale()`	Default constructor; creates a copy of the current global locale
`locale("")`	Creates a "native" locale according to the environment
`locale(`*name*`)`	Creates a locale from the string *name*
`locale(`*loc*`)`	Copy constructor; creates a copy of locale *loc*
`locale(`*loc1,loc2,cat*`)`	Creates a copy of locale *loc1*, with all facets from category *cat* replaced with facets from locale *loc2*
`locale(`*loc,name,cat*`)`	Equivalent to `locale(`*loc*`,locale(`*name*`),`*cat*`)`
`locale(`*loc,fp*`)`	Creates a copy of locale *loc* and installs the facet to which *fp* refers
loc1`.combine<`*F*`>(`*loc2*`)`	Creates and yields a copy of locale *loc1* but with the facet of type *F* taken from *loc2*
loc1 `=` *loc2*	Assigns locale *loc2* to locale *loc1*

Table 16.4. Constructing and Assigning Locales

Almost all constructors create a copy of another locale. Merely copying a locale is considered to be a cheap operation, consisting of setting a pointer and increasing a reference count. Creating a modified locale is more expensive, because a reference count for each facet stored in the locale has to be adjusted. Although the standard makes no guarantees about such efficient behavior, it is likely that all implementations will be rather efficient for copying locales.

Two of the constructors listed in Table 16.4 take names of locales. The names accepted are not standardized, with the exception of the name C (see Section 16.2, page 857). Before C++11, *name* had to be a C-string.

The member function `combine()` needs some explanation because it uses a feature that is rarely used. It is a member function template with an explicitly specified template argument. This means that the template argument is not deduced implicitly from an argument, because there is no argument from which the type can be deduced. Instead, the template argument is specified explicitly (facet type *F* in this case).

The two functions that access facets in a locale object use the same technique (Table 16.5). The major difference is that these two functions are global function templates.

Expression	Effect
`has_facet<`*F*`>(`*loc*`)`	Returns `true` if a facet of type *F* is stored in locale *loc*
`use_facet<`*F*`>(`*loc*`)`	Returns a reference to the facet of type *F* stored in locale *loc*

Table 16.5. Accessing Facets

The function `use_facet()` returns a reference to a facet. The type of this reference is the type passed explicitly as the template argument. If the locale passed as the argument does not contain a corresponding facet, the function throws a `bad_cast` exception. The function `has_facet()` can be used to test whether a particular facet is present in a given locale.

The remaining operations of locales are listed in Table 16.6.

Expression	Effect
loc.name()	Returns the name of locale *loc* as string
loc1 == *loc2*	Returns true if *loc1* and *loc2* are identical locales
loc1 != *loc2*	Returns true if *loc1* and *loc2* are different locales
loc(*str1*,*str2*)	Returns the Boolean result of comparing strings *str1* and *str2* for ordering (whether *str1* is less than *str2*)
locale::classic()	Returns locale("C")
locale::global(*loc*)	Installs *loc* as the global locale and returns the previous global locale

Table 16.6. Operations of Locales

The name of a locale is maintained if the locale was constructed from a name or one or more named locales. If a locale has no name, name() returns the string "*". Again, the standard makes no guarantees about the construction of a name resulting from combining two locales. Two locales are considered to be identical if one is a copy of the other or if both locales have the same name. It is natural to consider two objects to be identical if one is a copy of the other. But what about the naming? The idea behind this is that the name of the locale reflects the names used to construct the named facets. For example, the locale's name might be constructed by joining the names of the facets in a particular order, separating the individual names by separation characters. Using this scheme, it would possible to identify two locale objects as identical if they are constructed by combining the same named facets into locale objects. In other words, the standard requires that two locales consisting of the same set of named facets be considered identical. Thus, the names will probably be constructed carefully to support this notion of equality.

The parentheses operator makes it possible to use a locale object as a comparator for strings. This operator uses the string comparison from the collate<> facet (see Section 16.4.5, page 904) to compare the strings passed as the argument for ordering. It returns true if *str1* is less than *str2* according to the local object. Thus, the locale object can be used as an STL function object (see Section 10.1, page 475) comparing strings. In fact, you can use a locale object as a sorting criterion for STL algorithms that operate on strings. For example, a vector of strings can be sorted according to the rules for string collation of the German locale as follows:

```
std::vector<std::string> v;

...

// sort strings according to the German locale
std::sort (v.begin(),v.end(),       // range
           locale("de_DE"));        // sorting criterion
```

16.4   Facets in Detail

The contained facets are the important aspect of locales. All locales are guaranteed to contain certain standard facets. The description of the individual facets in the following subsections explains which instantiations of the corresponding facet are guaranteed. In addition to these facets, an implementation of the C++ standard library may provide additional facets in the locales. What is important is that users can also install their own facets or replace standard ones.

Section 16.2.2, page 864, discussed how to install a facet in a locale. For example, the class `germanBoolNames` was derived from the class `numpunct_byname<char>`, one of the standard facets, and installed in a locale using the constructor, taking a locale and a facet as arguments. But what do you need to create your own facet? Every class F that conforms to the following two requirements can be used as a facet:

1. F derives publicly from class `std::locale::facet`. This base class mainly defines some mechanism for reference counting that is used internally by the locale objects. It also deletes the copy constructor and the assignment operator, thereby making it unfeasible to copy or to assign facets.

2. F has a publicly accessible static member named `id` of type `locale::id`. This member is used to look up a facet in a locale by using the facet's type. The whole issue of using a type as the index is to have a type-safe interface. Internally, a normal container with an integer as the index is used to maintain the facets.

The standard facets conform not only to these requirements but also to two special implementation guidelines. Although conforming to these guidelines is not required, doing so is useful. The guidelines are as follows:

1. All member functions are declared to be `const`. This is useful because `use_facet()` returns a reference to a constant facet. Member functions that are not declared to be `const` can't be invoked.

2. All public functions are nonvirtual and delegate each request to a protected virtual function. The protected function is named like the public one, with the addition of a leading `do_`. For example, `numpunct::truename()` calls `numpunct::do_truename()`. This style is used to avoid hiding member functions when overriding only one of several virtual member functions that has the same name. For example, the class `num_put` has several functions named `put()`. In addition, it gives the programmer of the base class the possibility of adding some extra code in the nonvirtual functions, which is executed even if the virtual function is overridden.

The following description of the standard facets concerns only the public functions. To modify the facet, you always have to override the corresponding protected functions. If you define functions with the same interface as the public facet functions, they would overload them only because these functions are not virtual.

For most standard facets, a "`_byname`" version is defined. This version derives from the standard facet and is used to create an instantiation for a corresponding locale name. For example, the class `numpunct_byname` is used to create the `numpunct` facet for a named locale. For example, a German `numpunct` facet can be created like this:

```
std::numpunct_byname("de_DE")
```

The _byname classes are used internally by the locale constructors that take a name as an argument. For each of the standard facets supporting a name, the corresponding _byname class is used to construct an instance of the facet.

16.4.1 Numeric Formatting

Numeric formatting converts between the internal representation of numbers and the corresponding textual representations. The iostream operators delegate the conversion to the facets of the locale::numeric category. This category is formed by three facets:

1. numpunct, which handles punctuation symbols used for numeric formatting and parsing
2. num_put, which handles numeric formatting
3. num_get, which handles numeric parsing

In short, the facet num_put does the numeric formatting described for iostreams in Section 15.7, page 779, and num_get parses the corresponding strings. Additional flexibility not directly accessible through the interface of the streams is provided by the numpunct facet.

Numeric Punctuation

The numpunct<> facet controls the symbol used as the decimal point, the insertion of optional thousands separators, and the strings used for the textual representation of Boolean values. Table 16.7 lists the members of numpunct<>.

Expression	Meaning
np.decimal_point()	Returns the character used as the decimal point
np.thousands_sep()	Returns the character used as the thousands separator
np.grouping()	Returns a string describing the positions of the thousands separators
np.truename()	Returns the textual representation of true
np.falsename()	Returns the textual representation of false

Table 16.7. Members of the numpunct<> Facet

The numpunct<> facet takes a character type charT as the template argument. The characters returned from decimal_point() and thousand_sep() are of this type, and the functions truename() and falsename() return a basic_string<charT>. The two instantiations numpunct<char> and numpunct<wchar_t> are required.

Because long numbers are hard to read without intervening characters, the standard facets for numeric formatting and numeric parsing support thousands separators. Often, the digits representing an integer are grouped into triples. For example, one million is written like this:

    1,000,000

Unfortunately, it is not used everywhere exactly like that. For example, a period is used instead of a comma in German. Thus, a German would write one million like this:

    1.000.000

This difference is covered by the `thousands_sep()` member. But this is not sufficient, because in some countries, digits are not put into triples. For example, people in Nepal would write

> `10.00.000`

using even different numbers of digits in the groups. This is where the string returned from the function `grouping()` comes in. The number stored at index *i* gives the number of digits in the *i*th group, where counting starts with zero for the rightmost group. If there are fewer characters in the string than groups, the size of the last specified group is repeated. To create unlimited groups, you can use the value `numeric_limits<char>::max()` or if there is no group at all, the empty string. Table 16.8 lists some examples of the formatting of one million. Note that the string is interpreted as a sequence of integral values. Thus, normal digits are usually not useful (for example, the string `"2"` would usually specify groups of 50 digits because the character '2' has the integer value 50 in the ASCII character set).

Value	As String	Result
`{ 0 }`	`""`	1000000 (default)
`{ 3, 0 }`	`"\3"`	1,000,000
`{ 3, 2, 3, 0 }`	`"\3\2\3"`	10,00,000
`{ 2, CHAR_MAX, 0 }`	n.a.	10000,00

Table 16.8. Examples of Numeric Punctuation of One Million

Note that `decimal_point()` and `thousands_sep()` might return '0' to sign no (special) defined character.

Numeric Formatting

The `num_put<>` facet is used for textual formatting of numbers. It is a class template that takes two template arguments: the type `charT` of the characters to be produced and the type `OutIt` of an output iterator to the location at which the produced characters are written. The output iterator defaults to `ostreambuf_iterator<charT>`. The `num_put` facet provides an overloaded set of functions, all called `put()` and differing only in the last argument, which specifies the value to format (see Table 16.9).

Expression	Meaning
`np.put`(*to*,*fs*,*fill*,*val*)	Writes *val* to *to*, using the format in *fs* and the fill character *fill*

Table 16.9. Members of the `num_put<>` Facet

The arguments `put()` processes are as follows:

- *to* is the output iterator the time is written to. `put()` returns a copy of this iterator with the position immediately after the last character written. Here, you can also pass a stream, which will be converted into a stream iterator.
- *fs* is a stream object of type `std::ios_base` that defines the formatting. It is usually a stream, imbued by the required locale and facets.

- *fill* is a character to use in case a filling character is needed.
- *val* is the value to format, overloaded for types `bool`, `long`, `long long`, `unsigned long`, `unsigned long long`, `double`, `long double`, and `const void*`.

The following program demonstrates how to use this facet:

```
// i18n/numput.cpp

#include <locale>
#include <chrono>
#include <ctime>
#include <iostream>
#include <exception>
#include <cstdlib>
using namespace std;

int main ()
{
    try {
        // print floating-point value with the global classic locale:
        locale locC;
        cout.imbue(locC);
        use_facet<num_put<char>>(locC).put (cout, cout, ' ',
                                                    1234.5678);
        cout << endl;

        // print floating-point value with German locale:
#ifdef _MSC_VER
        locale locG("deu_deu.1252");
#else
        locale locG("de_DE");
#endif
        cout.imbue(locG);
        use_facet<num_put<char>>(locG).put (cout, cout, ' ',
                                                    1234.5678);
        cout << endl;
    }
    catch (const std::exception& e) {
        cerr << "Exception: " << e.what() << endl;
        return EXIT_FAILURE;
    }
}
```

As you can see, you can simply pass the output stream with the corresponding locale and facets used for formatting as first two arguments:

```
locale locC;
cout.imbue(locC);
use_facet<num_put<char>>(locC).put (cout, cout, ' ',
                                     1234.5678);
```

On my machine, the program has the following output:

```
1234.57
1.234,57
```

As you can see, the put() statement produces different textual representations of the passed numeric value. In fact, with the German locale, the decimal point becomes ',' and the thousands separator becomes '.' used after each group of three digits.

The standard requires that the two instantiations num_put<char> and num_put<wchar_t> be stored in each locale. In addition, the C++ standard library supports all instantiations that take a character type as the first template argument and an output iterator type as the second.

Numeric Parsing

The num_get<> facet is used to parse textual representations of numbers. Corresponding to the facet num_put, it is a template that takes two template arguments: the character type charT and an input iterator type InIt, which defaults to istreambuf_iterator<charT>. It provides a set of overloaded get() functions that differ only in the last argument. The num_get<> facet provides an set of overloaded get() functions, differing only in the last argument, which specifies the type of the value to parse (see Table 16.10).

Expression	Meaning
ng.get(*beg*,*end*,*fs*,*err*,*valRet*)	Parses the character sequence [*beg*,*end*) according to the format in *fs* and the type of *valRet*

Table 16.10. Members of the num_get<> *Facet*

You can use the facet as follows (see *i18n/numget.cpp* for the complete example):

```
std::locale      loc;               // locale
InIt             beg = ...;         // beginning of input sequence
InIt             end = ...;         // end of input sequence
std::ios_base&   fs  = ...;         // stream that defines input format
std::ios_base::iostate err;         // state after call
T                val;               // value after successful call

// get numeric input facet of the loc locale
const std::num_get<charT>& ng
        = std::use_facet<std::num_get<charT,InIt>>(loc);

// read value with numeric input facet
ng.get (beg, end, fs, err, val);
```

These statements attempt to parse a numeric value corresponding to the type T from the sequence of characters between beg and end. The format of the expected numeric value is defined by the argument fs. If the parsing fails, err is modified to contain the value ios_base::failbit. Otherwise, ios_base::goodbit is stored in err and the parsed value in val. The value of val is modified only if the parsing is successful. get() returns the second parameter (end) if the sequence was used completely. Otherwise, it returns an iterator pointing to the first character that could not be parsed as part of the numeric value.

The num_get<> facet supports functions to read objects of the types bool, long, unsigned short, unsigned int, unsigned long, float, double, long double, and void*. There are some types for which there is no corresponding function in the num_put facet; for example, unsigned short. The reason is that writing a value of type unsigned short produces the same result as writing a value of type unsigned short promoted to an unsigned long. However, reading a value as type unsigned long and then converting it to unsigned short may yield a value different from reading it as type unsigned short directly.

The standard requires that the two instantiations num_get<char> and num_get<wchar_t> be stored in each locale. In addition, the C++ standard library supports all instantiations that take a character type as the first template argument and an input iterator type as the second.

16.4.2 Monetary Formatting

The category monetary consists of the facets moneypunct, money_get, and money_put. The moneypunct<> facet defines the format of monetary values. The other two facets use this information to format or to parse a monetary value.

Monetary Punctuation

How monetary values are printed depends on the context. The formats used in various cultural communities differ widely. Examples of the varying details are the placement of the currency symbol (if present at all), the notation for negative or positive values, the use of national or international currency symbols, and the use of thousands separators. To provide the necessary flexibility, the details of the format are factored into the facet moneypunct.

The moneypunct<> facet is a class template that takes as arguments a character type charT and a Boolean value that defaults to false. The Boolean value indicates whether local (false) or international (true) currency symbols are to be used. Table 16.11 lists the members of the facet moneypunct<>.

The following program demonstrates how these values might differ for various locales:

```
// i18n/moneypunct.cpp

#include <string>
#include <iostream>
#include <locale>
#include <exception>
#include <cstdlib>
```

Expression	Meaning
`mp.decimal_point()`	Returns a character to be used as the decimal point
`mp.thousands_sep()`	Returns a character to be used as the thousands separator
`mp.grouping()`	Returns a string specifying the placement of the thousands separators
`mp.curr_symbol()`	Returns a string with the currency symbol
`mp.positive_sign()`	Returns a string with the positive sign
`mp.negative_sign()`	Returns a string with the negative sign
`mp.frac_digits()`	Returns the number of fractional digits
`mp.pos_format()`	Returns the format to be used for non-negative values
`mp.neg_format()`	Returns the format to be used for negative values

Table 16.11. Members of the `moneypunct<>` *Facet*

```cpp
using namespace std;

// output operator for pos_format() and neg_format():
ostream& operator<< (ostream& strm, moneypunct<char>::pattern p)
{
    for (int i=0; i<4; ++i) {
        auto f = p.field[i];
        strm << (f==money_base::none ?   "none" :
                 f==money_base::space ?  "space" :
                 f==money_base::symbol ? "symbol" :
                 f==money_base::sign ?   "sign" :
                 f==money_base::value ?  "value" :
                 "???") << " ";
    }
    return strm;
}


template <bool intl>
void printMoneyPunct (const string& localeName)
{
    locale loc(localeName);
    const moneypunct<char,intl>& mp
            = use_facet<moneypunct<char,intl>>(loc);
    cout << "moneypunct in locale \"" << loc.name() << "\":" << endl;
    cout << " decimal_point: " << (mp.decimal_point()!='\0' ?
                                    mp.decimal_point() : ' ') << endl;
    cout << " thousands_sep: " << (mp.thousands_sep()!='\0' ?
                                    mp.thousands_sep() : ' ') << endl;
    cout << " grouping:        ";
```

```
        for (int i=0; i<mp.grouping().size(); ++i) {
            cout << static_cast<int>(mp.grouping()[i]) << ' ';
        }
        cout << endl;
        cout << " curr_symbol:   " << mp.curr_symbol() << endl;
        cout << " positive_sign: " << mp.positive_sign() << endl;
        cout << " negative_sign: " << mp.negative_sign() << endl;
        cout << " frac_digits:   " << mp.frac_digits() << endl;
        cout << " pos_format:    " << mp.pos_format() << endl;
        cout << " neg_format:    " << mp.neg_format() << endl;
    }

    int main ()
    {
        try {
            printMoneyPunct<false>("C");
            cout << endl;
            printMoneyPunct<false>("german");
            cout << endl;
            printMoneyPunct<true>("german");
        }
        catch (const std::exception& e) {
            cerr << "Exception: " << e.what() << endl;
            return EXIT_FAILURE;
        }
    }
```

On my Windows platform, the program has the following output:

```
    moneypunct in locale "C":
     decimal_point:
     thousands_sep:
     grouping:
     curr_symbol:
     positive_sign:
     negative_sign: -
     frac_digits:   0
     pos_format:    symbol sign none value
     neg_format:    symbol sign none value

    moneypunct in locale "German_Germany.1252":
     decimal_point: ,
     thousands_sep: .
     grouping:      3
```

```
curr_symbol:    €
positive_sign:
negative_sign: -
frac_digits:    2
pos_format:     sign value space symbol
neg_format:     sign value space symbol

moneypunct in locale "German_Germany.1252":
decimal_point: ,
thousands_sep: .
grouping:       3
curr_symbol:    EUR
positive_sign:
negative_sign: -
frac_digits:    2
pos_format:     symbol sign none value
neg_format:     symbol sign none value
```

As you can see, the German format changes the decimal point and the thousands separator (used to group three digits), and, depending on the second template parameter `intl`, the currency symbol is either the euro symbol or EUR. Note also that the German format differs in a way that the euro symbol is placed after the value, whereas EUR is placed before the value with no space. See page 880 for an application of these formats.

Monetary Punctuation in Detail

The `moneypunct<>` facet derives from the class `money_base`:

```
namespace std {
    class money_base {
      public:
        enum part { none, space, symbol, sign, value };
        struct pattern {
            char field[4];
        };
    }
};
```

Type `pattern` is used to store four values of type `part` that form a pattern describing the layout of a monetary value. Table 16.12 lists the five possible `parts` that can be placed in a pattern.

The `moneypunct<>` facet defines two functions that return patterns: the function `neg_format()` for negative values and the function `pos_format()` for non-negative values. In a pattern, each of the parts `sign`, `symbol`, and `value` is mandatory, and one of the parts `none` and `space` has to appear. This does not mean, however, that a sign or a currency symbol is printed. What is printed at the positions indicated by the parts depends on the values returned from other members of the facet and on the formatting flags passed to the functions for formatting.

Value	Meaning
none	At this position, spaces may appear but are not required.
space	At this position, at least one space is required.
sign	At this position, a sign may appear.
symbol	At this position, the currency symbol may appear.
value	At this position, the value appears.

Table 16.12. Parts of Monetary Layout Patterns

Only the value always appears. It is placed at the position where the part `value` is located in the pattern. The value has exactly `frac_digits()` fractional digits, with `decimal_point()` used as the decimal point unless there are no fractional digits, in which case no decimal point is used.

When reading monetary values, thousands separators are allowed but not required in the input. When present, they are checked for correct placements according to `grouping()`. If `grouping()` is empty, no thousands separators are allowed. The character used for the thousands separator is the one returned from `thousands_sep()`. The rules for the placement of the thousands separators are identical to the rules for numeric formatting (see Section 16.4.1, page 870). When monetary values are printed, thousands separators are always inserted according to the string returned from `grouping()`. When monetary values are read, thousands separators are optional unless the grouping string is empty. The correct placement of thousands separators is checked after all other parsing is successful.

Note that `decimal_point()` and `thousand_sep()` might return `'\0'` to signal no (special) defined character.

The parts `space` and `none` control the placement of spaces. The part `space` is used at a position where at least one space is required. During formatting, if `ios_base::internal` is specified in the format flags, fill characters are inserted at the position of the `space` or the `none` part. Of course, filling is done only if the minimum width specified is not used with other characters. The character used as the space character is passed as the argument to the functions for the formatting of monetary values. If the formatted value does not contain a space, `none` can be placed at the last position. The parts `space` and `none` may not appear as the first part in a pattern, and `space` may not be the last part in a pattern.

Signs for monetary values may consist of more than one character. For example, in certain contexts, parentheses around a value are used to indicate negative values. At the position where the `sign` part appears in the pattern, the first character of the sign appears. All other characters of the sign appear at the end after all other components. If the string for a sign is empty, no character indicating the sign appears. The character that is to be used as a sign is determined with the function `positive_sign()` for non-negative values and `negative_sign()` for negative values.

At the position of the `symbol` part, the currency symbol appears. The symbol is present only if the formatting flags used during formatting or parsing have the `ios_base::showbase` flag set. The string returned from the function `curr_symbol()` is used as the currency symbol, which is a local symbol to be used to indicate the currency if the second template argument is `false` (the default). Otherwise, an international currency symbol is used. In this example for the German locale, the international symbol EUR is used. With the second template argument to moneypunct<> being false, the euro symbol would be used instead.

Table 16.13 illustrates all this, using the value $-1234.56 as an example. Of course, this means that the showbase flag is set, frac_digits() returns 2, and a width of 0 is always used.

Pattern	Sign	Result
symbol none sign value		$1234.56
symbol none sign value	–	$-1234.56
symbol space sign value	–	$ -1234.56
symbol space sign value	()	$ (1234.56)
sign symbol space value	()	($ 1234.56)
sign value space symbol	()	(1234.56 $)
symbol space value sign	–	$ 1234.56-
sign value space symbol	–	-1234.56 $
sign value none symbol	–	-1234.56$

Table 16.13. Examples of Using the Monetary Pattern

The standard requires that the instantiations moneypunct<char>, moneypunct<wchar_t>, moneypunct<char,true>, and moneypunct<wchar_t,true> be stored in each locale.

Monetary Formatting

The money_put<> facet is used to format monetary values. It is a template that takes a character type charT as the first template argument and an output iterator OutIt as the second. The output iterator defaults to ostreambuf_iterator<charT>. The overloaded member function put() produces a sequence of characters corresponding to the specified format (see Table 16.14).

Expression	Meaning
tp.put(*to*,*intl*,*fs*,*fill*,*valAsDouble*)	Converts the monetary value passed as long double
tp.put(*to*,*intl*,*fs*,*fill*,*valAsString*)	Converts the monetary value passed as string

Table 16.14. Members of the money_put<> Facet

As you can see, both put() members of the money_put<> facet use the following arguments:

- *to* is the output iterator to which the monetary value is written. put() returns a copy of this iterator with the position immediately after the last character written. Here, you can also pass a stream, which will be converted into a stream iterator.
- *intl* is a Boolean value specifying whether the international currency symbol shall be used. Thus, it specifies the second template parameter of the moneypunct facet that is used.
- *fs* is a stream object of type std::ios_base that defines the formatting. It is usually a stream, imbued by the required locale, facets, and formatting state, such as the field width and showbase to force the currency symbol.

- *fill* is a character to use in case a filling character is needed.
- The last argument specifies the value that is formatted. You can either pass it as `long double` or as `std::string`. If the argument is a string, this string may consist only of decimal digits with an optional leading minus sign. If the first character of the string is a minus sign, the value is formatted as a negative value. After it is determined that the value is negative, the minus sign is discarded. The number of fractional digits in the string is determined from the member function `frac_digits()` of the `moneypunct` facet.

The following program demonstrates how to use the `money_put<>` facet:

```
// i18n/moneyput.cpp

#include <locale>
#include <iostream>
#include <exception>
#include <cstdlib>
using namespace std;

int main ()
{
    try {
        // use German locale:
#ifdef _MSC_VER
        locale locG("deu_deu.1252");
#else
        locale locG("de_DE");
#endif
        const money_put<char>& mpG = use_facet<money_put<char> >(locG);

        // ensure that the money_put<> facet impacts the output and currency is written:
        cout.imbue(locG);
        cout << showbase;

        // use double as monetary value (use local symbol)
        mpG.put (cout, false, cout, ' ', 12345.678);
        cout << endl;

        // use string as monetary value (use international symbol)
        mpG.put (cout, true, cout, ' ', "12345.678");
        cout << endl;
    }
    catch (const std::exception& e) {
        cerr << "EXCEPTION: " << e.what() << endl;
        return EXIT_FAILURE;
    }
}
```

The program has the following output:

```
123,46 €
EUR123,45
```

According to the format of the `moneypunct` facet for a German locale on my machine (see page 876), the first output format is "sign value space symbol," using the euro currency symbol. If the international currency symbol shall be used, it is "symbol sign none value," which means that there is no space between the currency symbol and the value.

Note that the unit used for the passed monetary value passed to `put()` is Cent in the United States or Eurocent in Europe. When passing a `long double` the fractional part of the value is rounded. When passing a string it is truncated.

The standard requires that the two instantiations `money_put<char>` and `money_put<wchar_t>` be stored in each locale. In addition, the C++ standard library supports all instantiations that take `char` or `wchar_t` as the first template argument and a corresponding output iterator as the second.

Monetary Parsing

The `money_get<>` facet is used for parsing monetary values. It is a class template that takes a character type `charT` as the first template argument and an input iterator type `InIt` as the second. The second template argument defaults to `istreambuf_iterator<charT>`. This class defines two member functions called `get()` that try to parse a character sequence and, if the parse is successful, store the result in a value of type `long double` or of type `basic_string<charT>` (see Table 16.15).

Expression	Meaning
`mg.get(`*beg*`,`*end*`,`*intl*`,`*fs*`,`*err*`,` *valAsDoubleRet*`)`	Parses the character sequence [*beg,end*) according to *intl* and the format in *fs* into the `long double` *valAsDoubleRet*
`mg.get(`*beg*`,`*end*`,`*intl*`,`*fs*`,`*err*`,` *valAsStringRet*`)`	Parses the character sequence [*beg,end*) according to *intl* and the format in *fs* into the string *valAsStringRet*

Table 16.15. Members of the `money_get<>` *Facet*

The character sequence to be parsed is defined by the sequence between *beg* and *end*. The parsing stops as soon as either all elements of the used pattern are read or an error is encountered. If an error is encountered, the `ios_base::failbit` is set in *err*, and nothing is stored in *valAsDoubleRet* or *valAsStringRet*. If parsing is successful, the result is stored in the value of type `long double` or `basic_string<>` that is passed by reference as the last argument. Note that a monetary value such as `$1234.56` would yield `123456` as `long double` and `"123456"` as string. Thus, the unit is Cent in the United States or Eurocent in Europe.

The argument *intl* is a Boolean value that selects a local or an international currency string. The `moneypunct<>` facet defining the format of the value to be parsed is retrieved using the locale object imbued by the argument *fs*. For parsing a monetary value, the pattern returned from the member `neg_format()` of the `moneypunct<>` facet is always used. At the position of `none` or `space`, the function that is parsing a monetary value consumes all available space, unless `none` is the last part in a pattern. Trailing spaces are not skipped.

The `get()` functions return an iterator that points to immediately after the last character consumed.

You can use the facet as follows:

```
// get monetary input facet of the loc locale
const std::money_get<charT>& mg
          = std::use_facet<std::money_get<charT>>(loc);


// read value with monetary input facet
long double val;
mg.get (beg, end, intl, fs, err, val);
```

The standard requires that the two instantiations `money_get<char>` and `money_get<wchar_t>` be stored in each locale. In addition, the C++ standard library supports all instantiations that take `char` or `wchar_t` as the first template argument and a corresponding input iterator as the second.

Using Monetary Manipulators

Since C++11, you can use manipulators, defined in `<iomanip>`, to read and write monetary values directly from or to a stream. These are presented in Table 16.16.

Manipulator	Effect
put_money(*val*)	Writes a monetary value *val*, using the local currency symbol (calls put (*strmBeg*, *strmEnd*, `false`, *strm*, *strm*.`fill()`, *val*) for the facet)
put_money(*val*, *intl*)	Writes a monetary value *val*, using the currency symbol according to *intl* (calls put (*strmBeg*, *strmEnd*, *intl*, *strm*, *strm*.`fill()`, *val*) for the facet)
get_money(*valRef*)	Reads a monetary value into *valRef*, using the local currency symbol (calls get (*strmBeg*, *strmEnd*, `false`, *strm*, *err*, *val*) for the facet)
get_money(*valRef*, *intl*)	Reads a monetary value into *valRef*, using the currency symbol according to *intl* (calls get (*strmBeg*, *strmEnd*, *intl*, *strm*, *err*, *val*) for the facet)

Table 16.16. Manipulators for Monetary Formatting

Again, the values can be (references to) `long doubles` or strings, and *intl* defines whether to use a local or international currency symbol, passed as second template argument to the `moneypunct` facet.

The following program demonstrates how to use these manipulators:

```cpp
// i18n/moneymanipulator.cpp

#include <locale>
#include <iostream>
#include <iomanip>
#include <exception>
#include <cstdlib>
using namespace std;

int main ()
{
    try {
        // use German locale:
#ifdef _MSC_VER
        locale locG("deu_deu.1252");
#else
        locale locG("de_DE");
#endif

        // use German locale and ensure that the currency is written:
        cin.imbue(locG);
        cout.imbue(locG);
        cout << showbase;

        // read monetary value into long double (use international symbol)
        long double val;
        cout << "monetary value: ";
        cin >> get_money(val,true);

        if (cin) {
            // write monetary value (use local symbol)
            cout << put_money(val,false) << endl;
        }
        else {
            cerr << "invalid format" << endl;
        }
    }
    catch (const std::exception& e) {
        cerr << "Exception: " << e.what() << endl;
        return EXIT_FAILURE;
    }
}
```

If I input

    EUR 1234,567

or just

    1234,567

the output would be

    1.234,56 €

16.4.3   Time and Date Formatting

The two facets `time_get<>` and `time_put<>` in the category `time` provide services for parsing and formatting of times and dates. This is done by the member functions that operate on objects of type `tm`. This type is defined in the header file `<ctime>`. The objects are not passed directly; rather, a pointer to them is used as the argument.

Both facets in the `time` category depend heavily on the behavior of the function `strftime()`, also defined in the header file `<ctime>`. This function uses a string with conversion specifiers to produce a string from a `tm` object. Table 16.17 provides a brief summary of the conversion specifiers. The same conversion specifiers are also used by the `time_put` facet.

Of course, the exact string produced by `strftime()` depends on the C locale in effect. The examples in the table are given for the `"C"` locale.

Time and Date Formatting

The `time_put<>` facet is used for formatting times and dates. It is a class template that takes as arguments a character type `charT` and an optional output iterator type `OutIt`. The latter defaults to type `ostreambuf_iterator` (see Section 15.13.2, page 828).

The `time_put<>` facet defines two functions called `put()`, which are used to convert the date information stored in an object of type `tm` into a sequence of characters written to an output iterator. Table 16.18 lists the members of the facet `time_put<>`.

As you can see, all `put()` members of the `time_put` facet use the following first four arguments:

- *to* is the output iterator to which the time is written. `put()` returns a copy of this iterator with the position immediately after the last character written. Here, you can also pass a stream, which will be converted into a stream iterator.
- *fs* is a stream object of type `std::ios_base` that defines the formatting. It is usually a stream, imbued by the required locale and facets.
- *fill* is a character to use in case a filling character is needed.
- *val* is the time value of type `tm*` storing the date to be formatted.

The first form of `put()` uses *cvt* to pass one of the conversion specifiers to `strftime()`, listed in Table 16.17, to define the requested formatting.

The second form of `put()` allows you to provide an optional modifier. The meaning of the argument *mod* is not defined by the standard. It is intended to be used as a modifier to the conversion as found in several implementations of the `strftime()` function.

Specifier	Meaning	Example
%a	Abbreviated weekday	Mon
%A	Full weekday	Monday
%b	Abbreviated month name	Jul
%B	Full month name	July
%c	Locale's preferred date and time representation	Jul 12 21:53:22 1998
%d	Day of the month	12
%H	Hour of the day using a 24-hour clock	21
%I	Hour of the day using a 12-hour clock	9
%j	Day of the year	193
%m	Month as decimal number	7
%M	Minutes	53
%p	Morning or evening (AM or PM)	PM
%S	Seconds	22
%U	Week number starting with the first Sunday	28
%W	Week number starting with the first Monday	28
%w	Weekday as a number (Sunday == 0)	0
%x	Locale's preferred date representation	Jul 12 1998
%X	Locale's preferred time representation	21:53:22
%y	The year without the century	98
%Y	The year with the century	1998
%Z	The time zone	MEST
%%	The literal %	%

Table 16.17. Conversion Specifiers for `strftime()`

Expression	Meaning
`tp.put`(*to*,*fs*,*fill*,*val*,*cvt*)	Converts, using the conversion specifier *cvt*
`tp.put`(*to*,*fs*,*fill*,*val*,*cvt*,*mod*)	Converts, using the conversion specifier *cvt* and modifier *mod*
`tp.put`(*to*,*fs*,*fill*,*val*,*cbeg*,*cend*)	Converts according to the format string [*cbeg*,*cend*)

Table 16.18. Members of the `time_put<>` *Facet*

The third form of put() uses the beginning and end of a character sequence [*cbeg*,*cend*) specifying the required format by using the conversion specifiers to strftime(). This character sequence guides the conversion very much like strftime(). It scans the string and writes every character that is not part of a conversion specification to the output iterator *to*. If it encounters a conversion specification introduced by the character %, it extracts an optional modifier and the conversion specifier and acts like the second form of put() for them. After that, put() continues to scan the string. Note that this form of put() is somewhat unusual because it does not call a corresponding virtual do_put() member function as introduced in Section 16.4, page 869. Instead, it calls the corresponding do_put() for the second form directly. Thus, the behavior of the third form can't be overwritten when deriving from time_put.

The following program demonstrates this for the default and for a German locale:

```
// i18n/timeput.cpp

#include <locale>
#include <chrono>
#include <ctime>
#include <iostream>
#include <exception>
#include <cstdlib>
using namespace std;

int main ()
{
    try {
        // query local time:
        auto now = chrono::system_clock::now();
        std::time_t t = chrono::system_clock::to_time_t(now);
        tm* nowTM = std::localtime(&t);

        // print local time with the global classic locale:
        locale locC;
        const time_put<char>& tpC = use_facet<time_put<char>>(locC);

        // use single conversion specifier
        tpC.put (cout, cout, ' ', nowTM, 'x');
        cout << endl;

        // use format string:
        string format = "%A %x %I%p\n";    // format: weekday date hour
        tpC.put (cout, cout, ' ', nowTM,
                 format.c_str(), format.c_str()+format.size() );

        // print local time with German locale:
#ifdef _MSC_VER
        locale locG("deu_deu.1252");
#else
        locale locG("de_DE");
#endif
        const time_put<char>& tpG = use_facet<time_put<char>>(locG);
        tpG.put (cout, cout, ' ', nowTM, 'x');
        cout << endl;
```

```
            tpG.put (cout, cout, ' ', nowTM,
                       format.c_str(), format.c_str()+format.size() );
        }
        catch (const std::exception& e) {
            cerr << "Exception: " << e.what() << endl;
            return EXIT_FAILURE;
        }
    }
```

First, we query the local time and convert it into a `struct tm*`, using the `std::system_clock` (see Section 5.7.3, page 149).[5] Next, we create two locales (a default classic locale and a German locale), create the `time_put` facets for them, and use these to output the current date and time.

The first call of `put()` uses `'x'` as conversion specifiers to `strftime()`, which means that the locale's preferred date representation is used:

```
    tpC.put (cout, cout, ' ', nowTM, 'x');
```

The second call of `put()` calls its third form, which uses the begin and end of a character sequence specifying the output format *"weekday date hour"*:

```
    string format = "%A %x %I%p\n";
    tpC.put (cout, cout, ' ', nowTM,
               format.c_str(), format.c_str()+format.size() );
```

On my machine, the program had the following output:

```
    09/13/11
    Tuesday 09/13/11 03PM
    13.09.2011
    Dienstag 13.09.2011 03
```

As you can see by the last line, in German we have no corresponding AM or PM specifier.

The standard requires that the two instantiations `time_put<char>` and `time_put<wchar_t>` be stored in each locale. In addition, the C++ standard library supports all instantiations that take `char` or `wchar_t` as the first template argument and a corresponding output iterator as the second.

Time and Date Parsing

The `time_get<>` facet is a class template that takes a character type `charT` and an input iterator type `InIt` as template arguments. The input iterator type defaults to `istreambuf_iterator<charT>`. Table 16.19 lists the members defined for the `time_get<>` facet. All these members, except `date_order()`, parse the string and store the results in the `tm` object pointed to by the argument `t`. If the string could not be parsed correctly, either an error is reported (for example, by modifying the argument `err`) or an unspecified value is stored. This means that a time produced by a program can

---

[5] `std::system_clock` was introduced with C++11. Before C++11, you had to declare a `std::time_t t` and call `std::time(&t);`

be parsed reliably, but user input cannot. With the argument fs, other facets used during parsing are determined. Whether other flags from fs have any influence on the parsing is not specified.

Expression	Meaning
tg.get(*beg*,*end*,*fs*,*err*,*t*,*fmtChar*)	Parses the character sequence [*beg*,*end*) according to the conversion specifier *fmtChar* (since C++11)
tg.get(*beg*,*end*,*fs*,*err*,*t*,*fmtChar*,*mod*)	Parses the character sequence [*beg*,*end*) according to the conversion specifier *fmtChar* and the modifier *mod* (since C++11)
tg.get(*beg*,*end*,*fs*,*err*,*t*,*fmtBeg*,*fmtEnd*)	Parses the character sequence [*beg*,*end*) according to the character sequence [*fmtBeg*,*fmtEnd*,)(since C++11)
tg.get_time(*beg*,*end*,*fs*,*err*,*t*)	Parses the character sequence [*beg*,*end*) as the time produced by the X specifier for strftime()
tg.get_date(*beg*,*end*,*fs*,*err*,*t*)	Parses the character sequence [*beg*,*end*) as the date produced by the x specifier for strftime()
tg.get_weekday(*beg*,*end*,*fs*,*err*,*t*)	Parses the character sequence [*beg*,*end*) as the name of the weekday
tg.get_monthname(*beg*,*end*,*fs*,*err*,*t*)	Parses the character sequence [*beg*,*end*) as the name of the month
tg.get_year(*beg*,*end*,*fs*,*err*,*t*)	Parses the character sequence [*beg*,*end*) as the year
tg.date_order()	Returns the date order used by the facet

Table 16.19. Members of the time_get<> *Facet*

All functions return an iterator that has the position immediately after the last character read. The parsing stops if parsing is complete or if an error occurs (for example, because a string could not be parsed as a date).

Available since C++11, get() reads the values according to the passed format, which is either a conversion character without the leading % plus optional modifier or a format string, passed as beginning and end of a character sequence.

Note the following:

- A function reading the name of a weekday or a month reads both abbreviated names and full names. If the abbreviation is followed by a letter, which would be legal for a full name, the function attempts to read the full name. If this fails, the parsing fails, even though an abbreviated name was already parsed successfully.

- Whether a function that is parsing a year allows two-digit years is unspecified. The year that is assumed for a two-digit year, if it is allowed, is also unspecified.

- `date_order()` returns the order in which the day, month, and year appear in a date string. This is necessary for some dates because the order cannot be determined from the string representing a date. For example, the first day in February in the year 2003 may be printed either as 3/2/1 or as 1/2/3. Class `time_base`, which is the base class of the facet `time_get`, defines an enumeration called `dateorder` for possible date-order values. Table 16.20 lists these values.

Value	Meaning
no_order	No particular order (for example, a date may be in Julian format)
dmy	The order is day, month, year
mdy	The order is month, day, year
ymd	The order is year, month, day
ydm	The order is year, day, month

Table 16.20. Members of the Enumeration `dateorder`

The following example demonstrates how to use the `time_get<>` facet:

```
// i18n/timeget.cpp

#include <locale>
#include <ctime>
#include <iterator>
#include <iostream>
#include <string>
#include <exception>
#include <cstdlib>
using namespace std;

int main ()
{
    try {
        // use German locale:
#ifdef _MSC_VER
        locale locG("deu_deu.1252");
#else
        locale locG("de_DE.ISO-8859-1");
#endif
        const time_get<char>& tgG = use_facet<time_get<char>>(locG);

        // print date order of German locale:
        typedef time_base TB;
        time_get<char>::dateorder d = tgG.date_order();
        cout << "dateorder: "
             << (d==TB::no_order||d==TB::mdy ? "mdy" :
```

```
                    d==TB::dmy ? "dmy" :
                    d==TB::ymd ? "ymd" :
                    d==TB::ydm ? "ydm" : "unknown") << endl;

            // read weekday (in German) and time (hh::mm))
            cout << "<wochentag> <hh>:<mm>: ";
            string format = "%A %H:%M";
            struct tm val;
            ios_base::iostate err = ios_base::goodbit;
            tgG.get (istreambuf_iterator<char>(cin),
                     istreambuf_iterator<char>(),
                     cin, err, &val,
                     format.c_str(), format.c_str()+format.size());
            if (err != ios_base::goodbit) {
                cerr << "invalid format" << endl;
            }
        }
        catch (const std::exception& e) {
            cerr << "Exception: " << e.what() << endl;
            return EXIT_FAILURE;
        }
    }
```

The program might print:

```
dateorder: dmy
<wochentag> <hh>:<mm>:
```

If I then input Dienstag 17:30, everything is fine. If I input Tuesday 17:30 or Dienstag 17:66, the program will output invalid format.

The standard requires that the two instantiations time_get<char> and time_get<wchar_t> are stored in each locale. In addition, the C++ standard library supports all instantiations that take char or wchar_t as the first template argument and a corresponding input iterator as the second.

Using Time Manipulators

Since C++11, you can use manipulators, defined in <iomanip>, to read and write time and date values directly from or to a stream. The manipulators use the get() or put() member of the corresponding facet. The manipulators are presented in Table 16.21. See Section 15.3.3, page 757, for an example of how to use these manipulators.

Manipulator	Effect
put_time(*valPtr*,*fmt*)	Writes the date/time value *valPtr* of type struct tm* according to the format *fmt*; calls for the facet: put(*strmBeg*,*strmEnd*,*strm*,*strm*.fill(),*val*,*fmtBeg*,*fmtEnd*)
get_time(*valPtr*,*fmt*)	Reads a time/date value into the struct tm* *valPtr* according to the format *fmt*; calls for the facet: get(*strmBeg*,*strmEnd*,*strm*,*err*,*val*,*fmtBeg*,*fmtEnd*)

Table 16.21. Manipulators for Time/Date Formatting

16.4.4 Character Classification and Conversion

The C++ standard library defines two facets to deal with characters: ctype<> and codecvt<>. Both belong to the category locale::ctype. The ctype<> facet is used mainly for character classification, such as testing whether a character is a letter. This facet also provides methods for conversion between lowercase and uppercase letters and for conversion between char and the character type for which the facet is instantiated. The codecvt<> facet is used to convert characters between different encodings and is used mainly by basic_filebuf to convert between external and internal representations.

Character Classification

The ctype<> facet is a class template parametrized by a character type. Three kinds of functions are provided by the class ctype<*charT*>:

1. Functions to convert between char and *charT*
2. Functions for character classification
3. Functions for conversion between uppercase and lowercase letters

Table 16.22 lists the members defined for the facet ctype.

The function is(*beg*,*end*,*vec*) is used to store a set of masks in an array. For each of the characters in the range between *beg* and *end*, a mask with the attributes corresponding to the character is stored in the array pointed to by *vec*. This is useful in order to avoid virtual function calls for the classification of characters if many characters are to be classified.

toupper() and tolower() can be used to set a string uppercase or lowercase. For example:

```
std::locale loc;
std::string s;

for (char& c : s) {
    c = std::use_facet<std::ctype<char>>(loc).toupper(c);
}
```

The function widen() can be used to convert a character of type char from the native character set to the corresponding character in the character set used by a locale. Thus, it makes sense to widen a character even if the result is also of type char. For the opposite direction, the function narrow() can be used to convert a character from the character set used by the locale to a corresponding char

Expression	Effect
ct.is(*m*,*c*)	Tests whether the character *c* matches the mask *m*
ct.is(*beg*,*end*,*vec*)	For each character in the range between *beg* and *end*, places a mask matched by the character in the corresponding location of *vec*
ct.scan_is(*m*,*beg*,*end*)	Returns a pointer to the first character in the range between *beg* and *end* that matches the mask *m* or *end* if there is no such character
ct.scan_not(*m*,*beg*,*end*)	Returns a pointer to the first character in the range between *beg* and *end* that does not match the mask *m* or *end* if all characters match the mask
ct.toupper(*c*)	Returns an uppercase letter corresponding to *c* if there is such a letter; otherwise, *c* is returned
ct.toupper(*beg*,*end*)	Converts each letter in the range between *beg* and *end* by replacing the letter with the result of toupper()
ct.tolower(*c*)	Returns a lowercase letter corresponding to *c* if there is such a letter; otherwise, *c* is returned
ct.tolower(*beg*,*end*)	Converts each letter in the range between *beg* and *end* by replacing the letter with the result of tolower()
ct.widen(*c*)	Returns the char converted into charT
ct.widen(*beg*,*end*,*dest*)	For each character in the range between *beg* and *end*, places the result of widen() at the corresponding location in *dest*
ct.narrow(*c*,*default*)	Returns the charT *c* converted into char, or the char *default* if there is no suitable character
ct.narrow(*beg*,*end*,*default*,*dest*)	For each character in the range between *beg* and *end*, places the result of narrow() at the corresponding location in *dest*

Table 16.22. Members of the ctype<> *Facet*

in the native character set, provided that there is such a char. For example, the following code converts the decimal digits from char to wchar_t:

```
std::locale loc;
char narrow[] = "0123456789";
wchar_t wide[10];

std::use_facet<std::ctype<wchar_t>>(loc).widen(narrow, narrow+10,
                                               wide);
```

Thus, the following convenience functions transform strings into wstrings and vice versa:

```
// i18n/wstring2string.hpp

#include <locale>
```

```
#include <string>
#include <vector>

// convert string to wstring
std::wstring to_wstring (const std::string& str,
                         const std::locale& loc = std::locale())
{
    std::vector<wchar_t> buf(str.size());
    std::use_facet<std::ctype<wchar_t>>(loc).widen(str.data(),
                                                   str.data()+str.size(),
                                                   buf.data());
    return std::wstring(buf.data(),buf.size());
}


// convert wstring to string with '?' as default character
std::string to_string (const std::wstring& str,
                       const std::locale& loc = std::locale())
{
    std::vector<char> buf(str.size());
    std::use_facet<std::ctype<wchar_t>>(loc).narrow(str.data(),
                                                    str.data()+str.size(),
                                                    '?', buf.data());
    return std::string(buf.data(),buf.size());
}
```

You can call these functions as follows:

```
// i18n/wstring2string.cpp

#include <string>
#include <iostream>
#include "wstring2string.hpp"

int main()
{
    std::string s = "hello, world\n";
    std::wstring ws = to_wstring(s);
    std::wcout << ws;
    std::cout << to_string(ws);
}
```

Class ctype derives from the class ctype_base. This class is used only to define an enumeration called mask. This enumeration defines values that can be combined to form a bitmask used for testing character properties. The values defined in ctype_base are shown in Table 16.23. The functions for character classification all take a bitmask as an argument, which is formed by combinations of the values defined in `ctype_base`. To create bitmasks as needed, you can use the operators for bit manipulation (`|`, `&`, `^`, and `~`). A character matches this mask if it is any of the characters identified by the mask.

Value	Meaning
`ctype_base::alnum`	Tests for letters and digits (equivalent to `alpha|digit`)
`ctype_base::alpha`	Tests for letters
`ctype_base::blank`	Tests for space or tabulator (since C++11)
`ctype_base::cntrl`	Tests for control characters
`ctype_base::digit`	Tests for decimal digits
`ctype_base::graph`	Tests for punctuation characters, letters, and digits (equivalent to `alnum|punct`)
`ctype_base::lower`	Tests for lowercase letters
`ctype_base::print`	Tests for printable characters
`ctype_base::punct`	Tests for punctuation characters
`ctype_base::space`	Tests for space characters
`ctype_base::upper`	Tests for uppercase letters
`ctype_base::xdigit`	Tests for hexadecimal digits

Table 16.23. Character Mask Values Used by `ctype<>`

Specialization of `ctype<>` for Type `char`

For better performance of the character classification functions, the facet `ctype` is specialized for the character type `char`. This specialization does not delegate the functions dealing with character classification (`is()`, `scan_is()`, and `scan_not()`) to corresponding virtual functions. Instead, these functions are implemented inline using a table lookup. For this case, additional members are provided (Table 16.24).[6]

Expression	Effect
`ctype<char>::table_size`	Returns the size of the table (>=256)
`ctype<char>::classic_table()`	Returns the table for the "classic" C locale
`ctype<char>(table,del=false)`	Creates the facet with table *table*
`ct.table()`	Returns the current table of facet *ct*

Table 16.24. Additional Members of `ctype<char>`

---

[6] Before C++11, `ctype<char>::table()` and `ctype<char>::classic_table()` were accidentally specified to be `protected` instead of `public` members.

Manipulating the behavior of these functions for specific locales is done with a corresponding table of masks that is passed as a constructor argument:

```
// create and initialize the table
std::ctype_base::mask mytable[std::ctype<char>::table_size] = {
    ...
};
```

```
// use the table for the ctype<char> facet ct
std::ctype<char> ct(mytable,false);
```

This code constructs a ctype<char> facet that uses the table mytable to determine the character class of a character. More precisely, the character class of the character c is determined by

```
mytable[static_cast<unsigned char>(c)]
```

The static member table_size is a constant defined by the library implementation and gives the size of the lookup table. This size is at least 256 characters. The second optional argument to the constructor of ctype<char> indicates whether the table should be deleted if the facet is destroyed. If it is true, the table passed to the constructor is released by using delete[] when the facet is no longer needed.

The member function table() is a protected member function that returns the table that is passed as the first argument to the constructor. The static protected member function classic_table() returns the table that is used for character classification in the classic C locale.

Global Convenience Functions for Character Classification

Convenient use of the ctype<> facets is provided by predefined global functions. Table 16.25 lists all the global functions. Note that for regular expressions, the same character classifications are possible (see Section 14.8, page 738).

For example, the following expression determines whether the character c is a lowercase letter in the locale loc:

```
std::islower(c,loc)
```

It returns a corresponding value of type bool.

The following expression returns the character c converted into an uppercase letter if c is a lowercase letter in the locale loc:

```
std::toupper(c,loc)
```

If c is not a lowercase letter, the first argument is returned unmodified.

The expression

```
std::islower(c,loc)
```

is equivalent to the following expression:

```
std::use_facet<std::ctype<char>>(loc).is(std::ctype_base::lower,c)
```

This expression calls the member function is() of the facet ctype<char>. is() determines whether the character c fulfills any of the character properties that are passed as the bitmask in the

Function	Effect
isalnum(*c*, *loc*)	Returns whether *c* is a letter or a digit (equivalent to `isalpha()||isdigit()`)
isalpha(*c*, *loc*)	Returns whether *c* is a letter
isblank(*c*, *loc*)	Returns whether *c* is a space or tabular (since C++11)
iscntrl(*c*, *loc*)	Returns whether *c* is a control character
isdigit(*c*, *loc*)	Returns whether *c* is a digit
isgraph(*c*, *loc*)	Returns whether *c* is a printable, nonspace character (equivalent to `isalnum()||ispunct()`)
islower(*c*, *loc*)	Returns whether *c* is a lowercase letter
isprint(*c*, *loc*)	Returns whether *c* is a printable character (including whitespaces)
ispunct(*c*, *loc*)	Returns whether *c* is a punctuation character (that is, it is printable but is not a space, digit, or letter)
isspace(*c*, *loc*)	Returns whether *c* is a space character
isupper(*c*, *loc*)	Returns whether *c* is an uppercase letter
isxdigit(*c*, *loc*)	Returns whether *c* is a hexadecimal digit
tolower(*c*, *loc*)	Converts *c* from an uppercase letter into a lowercase letter
toupper(*c*, *loc*)	Converts *c* from a lowercase letter into an uppercase letter

Table 16.25. Global Convenience Functions for Character Classification

first argument. The values for the bitmask are defined in the class `ctype_base`. See Section 13.2.14, page 688, and Section 15.13.3, page 833, for examples of the use of these convenience functions.

The global convenience functions for character classification correspond to C functions that have the same name but only the first argument. They are defined in `<cctype>` and `<ctype.h>` and always use the current global C locale.[7] Their use is even more convenient:

```
if (std::isdigit(c)) {
    ...
}
```

However, by using them, you can't use different locales in the same program. Also, you can't use a user-defined `ctype` facet using the C function. See Section 13.2.14, page 684, for an example that demonstrates how to use these C functions to convert all characters of a string to uppercase letters.

It is important to note that the C++ convenience functions should not be used in code sections where performance is crucial. It is much faster to obtain the corresponding facet from the locale and to use the functions on this object directly. If many characters are to be classified according to the same locale, this can be improved even more, at least for non-`char` characters. The function is(*beg*,*end*,*vec*) can be used to determine the masks for typical characters: This function determines for each character in the range [*beg*,*end*) a mask that describes the properties of the character.

---

[7] This locale is identical to the global C++ locale only if the last call to `locale::global()` was with a named locale and if there was no call to `setlocale()` since then. Otherwise, the locale used by the C functions is different from the global C++ locale.

The resulting mask is stored in *vec* at the position corresponding to the character's position. This vector can then be used for fast lookup of the characters.

Character Encoding Conversion

The `codecvt<>` facet is used to convert between internal and external character encoding. For example, it can be used to convert between Unicode and EUC (Extended UNIX Code), provided that the implementation of the C++ standard library supports a corresponding facet.

This facet is used by the class `basic_filebuf` to convert between the internal representation and the representation stored in a file. The class `basic_filebuf<charT,traits>` (see Section 15.9.1, page 791) uses the instantiation `codecvt<charT,char,typename traits::state_type>` to do so. The facet used is taken from the locale stored with `basic_filebuf`. This is the major application of the `codecvt` facet. Only rarely is it necessary to use this facet directly.

Section 16.1, page 850, introduced some basics of character encodings. To understand `codecvt`, you need to know that there are two approaches for the encoding of characters: One is character encodings that use a fixed number of bytes for each character (wide-character representation), and the other is character encodings that use a varying number of bytes per character (multibyte representation).

It is also necessary to know that multibyte representations use so-called *shift states* for space efficient representation of characters. The correct interpretation of a byte is possible only with the correct shift state at this position. This in turn can be determined only by walking through the whole sequence of multibyte characters (see Section 16.1, page 850, for more details).

The `codecvt<>` facet takes three template arguments:

1. The character type `internT` used for an internal representation
2. The type `externT` used to represent an external representation
3. The type `stateT` used to represent an intermediate state during the conversion

The intermediate state may consist of incomplete wide characters or the current shift state. The C++ standard makes no restriction about what is stored in the objects representing the state.

The internal representation always uses a representation with a fixed number of bytes per character. The two types `char` and `wchar_t` are intended mainly to be used within a program. The external representation may be a representation that uses a fixed size or a multibyte representation. When a multibyte representation is used, the second template argument is the type used to represent the basic units of the multibyte encoding. Each multibyte character is stored in one or more objects of this type. Normally, the type `char` is used for this.

The third argument is the type used to represent the current state of the conversion. It is necessary, for example, if one of the character encodings is a multibyte encoding. In this case, the processing of a multibyte character might be terminated because the source buffer is drained or the destination buffer is full while one character is being processed. If this happens, the current state of the conversion is stored in an object of this type.

As with the other facets, the standard requires support for very few conversions. Only the following two instantiations are supported by the C++ standard library:

1. `codecvt<char,char,mbstate_t>`, which converts the native character set to itself (this is a degenerated version of the `codecvt<>` facet)

2. `codecvt<wchar_t,char,mbstate_t>`, which converts between the native tiny character set (`char`) and the native wide-character set (`wchar_t`)

The C++ standard does not specify the exact semantics of the second conversion. The only natural thing to do, however, is to split each `wchar_t` into `sizeof(wchar_t)` objects of type `char` for the conversion from `wchar_t` to `char` and to assemble a `wchar_t` from the same number of `chars` when converting in the opposite direction. Note that this conversion is very different from the conversion between `char` and `wchar_t` done by the `widen()` and `narrow()` member functions of the `ctype` facet. The `codecvt` functions use the bits of multiple `chars` to form one `wchar_t` (or vice versa), whereas the `ctype` functions convert a character into one encoding to the corresponding character in another encoding (if there is such a character).

Like the `ctype` facet, `codecvt` derives from a base class used to define an enumeration type. This class is named `codecvt_base` and defines an enumeration called `result`. The values of this enumeration are used to indicate the results of `codecvt`'s members. The exact meanings of the values depend on the member function used. Table 16.26 lists the member functions of the `codecvt` facet.

Expression	Meaning
`cvt.in(s,fb,fe,fn,tb,te,tn)`	Converts external representation to internal representation
`cvt.out(s,fb,fe,fn,tb,te,tn)`	Converts internal representation to external representation
`cvt.unshift(s,tb,te,tn)`	Writes escape sequence to switch to initial shift state
`cvt.encoding()`	Returns information about the external encoding
`cvt.always_noconv()`	Returns `true` if no conversion will ever be done
`cvt.length(s,fb,fe,max)`	Returns the number of `externTs` from the sequence between *fb* and *fe* to produce *max* internal characters
`cvt.max_length()`	Returns the maximum number of `externTs` necessary to produce one `internT`

Table 16.26. Members of the `codecvt<>` Facet

The function `in()` converts an external representation into an internal representation. The argument *s* is a reference to a `stateT`. At the beginning, this argument represents the shift state used when the conversion is started. At the end, the final shift state is stored there. The shift state passed in can differ from the initial state if the input buffer to be converted is not the first buffer being converted. The arguments *fb* (from beginning) and *fe* (from end) are of type `const internT*` and represent the beginning and the end of the input buffer. The arguments *tb* (to begin) and *te* (to end) are of type `externT*` and represent the beginning and the end of the output buffer. The arguments *fn* (from next, of type `const externT*&`) and *tn* (to next, of type `internT*&`) are references used to return the end of the sequence converted in the input buffer and the output buffer, respectively. Either buffer may reach the end before the other buffer reaches the end. The function returns a value of type `codecvt_base::result`, as indicated in Table 16.27.

If ok is returned, the function made some progress. If `fn == fe` holds, the whole input buffer was processed, and the sequence between *tb* and *tn* contains the result of the conversion. The char-

Value	Meaning
ok	All source characters were converted successfully
partial	Not all source characters were converted, or more characters are needed to produce a destination character
error	A source character was encountered that cannot be converted
noconv	No conversion was necessary

Table 16.27. Return Values of the Conversion Functions

acters in this sequence represent the characters from the input sequence, potentially with a finished character from a previous conversion. If the argument *s* passed to in() was not the initial state, a partial character from a previous conversion that was not completed could have been stored there.

If partial is returned, either the output buffer was full before the input buffer could be drained, or the input buffer was drained when a character was not yet complete (for example, because the last byte in the input sequence was part of an escape sequence switching between shift states). If *fe==fn*, the input buffer was drained. In this case, the sequence between *tb* and *tn* contains all characters that were converted completely, but the input sequence terminated with a partially converted character. The necessary information to complete this character's conversion during a subsequent conversion is stored in the shift state *s*. If *fe!=fn*, the input buffer was not completely drained. In this case, *te==tn* holds; thus, the output buffer is full. The next time the conversion is continued, it should start with *fn*.

The return value noconv indicates a special situation. That is, no conversion was necessary to convert the external representation into the internal representation. In this case, *fn* is set to *fb*, and *tn* is set to *tb*. Nothing is stored in the destination sequence, because everything is already stored in the input sequence.

If error is returned, a source character that could not be converted was encountered. This can happen for several reasons. For example, the destination character set has no representation for a corresponding character, or the input sequence ends up with an illegal shift state. The C++ standard does not define any method that can be used to determine the cause of the error more precisely.

The function out() is equivalent to the function in() but converts in the opposite direction, converting an internal representation to an external representation. The meanings of the arguments and the values returned are the same; only the types of the arguments are swapped. That is, *tb* and *te* now have the type const internT*, and *fb* and *fe* now have the type const externT*. The same applies to *fn* and *tn*.

The function unshift() inserts characters necessary to complete a sequence when the current state of the conversion is passed as the argument *s*. This normally means that a shift state is switched to the initial switch state. Only the external representation is terminated. Thus, the arguments *tb* and *tf* are of type externT*, and *tn* is of type externT&*. The sequence between *tb* and *te* defines the output buffer in which the characters are stored. The end of the result sequence is stored in *tn*. unshift() returns a value as shown in Table 16.28.

The function encoding() returns some information about the encoding of the external representation. If encoding() returns −1, the conversion is state dependent. If encoding() returns 0, the number of externTs needed to produce an internal character is not constant. Otherwise, the number

Value	Meaning
ok	The sequence was completed successfully
partial	More characters need to be stored to complete the sequence
error	The state is invalid
noconv	No character was needed to complete the sequence

Table 16.28. Return Values of the Function unshift()

of externTs needed to produce an internT is returned. This information can be used to provide appropriate buffer sizes.

The function always_noconv() returns true if the functions in() and out() never perform a conversion. For example, the standard implementation of codecvt<char, char, mbstate_t> does no conversion, so always_noconv() returns true for this facet. However, this holds only for the codecvt facet from the "C" locale. Other instances of this facet may do a conversion.

The function length() returns the number of externTs from the sequence between *fb* and *fe* necessary to produce *max* characters of type internT. If there are fewer than *max* complete internT characters in the sequence between *fb* and *fe*, the number of externTs used to produce a maximum number of internTs from the sequence is returned.

Standard Code Conversion Facets

Since, C++11, the C++ standard library guarantees to provide three code conversion facets in <codecvt>, which are derived from codecvt<>:

- **codecvt_utf8<>** to convert between UTF-8 multibyte character sequences and UCS-2 sequences (if char16_t is used as character type) or UCS-4/UTF-32 sequences (if char32_t is used as character type)
- **codecvt_utf16<>** to convert between UTF-16 multibyte character sequences and UCS-2 sequences (if char16_t is used as character type) or UCS-4/UTF-32 sequences (if char32_t is used as character type)
- **codecvt_utf8_utf16<>** to convert between UTF-8 multibyte character sequences and UTF-16 multibyte character sequences

Their first template parameter is the wide-character type used (char16_t, char32_t, or wchar_t). The second template parameter is the maximum wide-character code allowed to convert without reporting an error (default: 0x10FFFF). The third template parameter is a flag of type std::codecvt_mode enabling reading or writing byte order marks or forcing little-endian mode.

For example, the following facet allows to convert between UTF-8 and wide-characters of type wchar_t consuming byte order marks, producing byte order marks, and using little-endian mode for the wide characters:

```
std::codecvt_utf8<wchar_t,
                  0x10FFFF,
                  std::consume_header
                    | std::generate_header
                    | std::little_endian>
            wchar2utf8facet;
```

The most convenient way to use these facets is provided by class `std::wstring_convert<>`.

Class `wstring_convert<>`

Since C++11, class `wstring_convert<>` allows convenient conversions between a wide-character string and a multibyte string. Template parameters are:

- a code conversion facet
- the type of the wide-character type (default: `wchar_t`)
- the allocator of the wide-character string (default: `allocator<wchar_t>`)
- the allocator of the multibyte string (default: `allocator<char>`)

With the members `to_bytes()` and `from_bytes()` you can create multibyte sequences out of a single character, a null-terminated sequence of characters, a corresponding string, or a range of characters and vice versa (see Table 16.29). The return type of `from_bytes()` is a string of the corresponding wide-character type (for example, `wstring` for `wchar_t`). The return type of `to_bytes()` is a `string` containing the multibyte sequence of `chars`.

Member Function	Meaning
`wc.from_bytes(`*c*`)`	Returns wide string for char *c*
`wc.from_bytes(`*cstr*`)`	Returns wide string for const char* *cstr*
`wc.from_bytes(`*str*`)`	Returns wide string for string *str*
`wc.from_bytes(`*cbeg*`,`*cend*`)`	Returns wide string for char range [*cbeg*,*cend*]
`wc.to_bytes(`*c*`)`	Returns multibyte sequence for wide character *c*
`wc.to_bytes(`*cstr*`)`	Returns multibyte sequence for const *truncated** *cstr*
`wc.to_bytes(`*str*`)`	Returns multibyte sequence for wide string *str*
`wc.to_bytes(`*cbeg*`,`*cend*`)`	Returns multibyte sequence for wide-character range [*cbeg*,*cend*]

Table 16.29. Members of Class `wstring_convert<>`

For example, the following convenience functions convert UTF-8 `strings` into `wstrings` and vice versa:

```
// i18n/wstring2utf8.hpp

#include <codecvt>
#include <string>

// convert UTF-8 string to wstring
std::wstring utf8_to_wstring (const std::string& str)
{
    std::wstring_convert<std::codecvt_utf8<wchar_t>> myconv;
    return myconv.from_bytes(str);
}
```

```cpp
// convert wstring to UTF-8 string
std::string wstring_to_utf8 (const std::wstring& str)
{
    std::wstring_convert<std::codecvt_utf8<wchar_t>> myconv;
    return myconv.to_bytes(str);
}
```

The following program demonstrates the application of these functions, converting a `string` into a `wstring` (using `to_wstring()`, introduced in Section 16.4.4, page 892) and transforming this `wstring` into a multibyte string, which is written to standard output:

```cpp
// i18n/wstring2utf8.cpp

#include <locale>
#include <string>
#include <iostream>
#include <exception>
#include <cstdlib>
#include "wstring2string.hpp"
#include "wstring2utf8.hpp"

int main()
{
    try {
#ifdef _MSC_VER
        // string with German umlaut and euro symbol (in Windows encoding):
        std::string s = "nj: ä + \x80 1";

        // convert to wide-character string (using Windows encoding):
        std::wstring ws = to_wstring(s,std::locale("deu_DEU.1252"));
#else
        // string with German umlaut and euro symbol (in ISO Latin-15 encoding):
        std::string s = "nj: ä + \xA4 1";

        // convert to wide-character string (using ISO Latin-15 encoding):
        std::wstring ws = to_wstring(s,std::locale("de_DE.ISO-8859-15"));
#endif

        // print string as UTF-8 sequence:
        std::cout << wstring_to_utf8(ws) << std::endl;
    }
    catch (const std::exception& e) {
        std::cerr << "Exception: " << e.what() << std::endl;
        return EXIT_FAILURE;
    }
}
```

String s has the format of the 8-bit Windows-1252 or ISO-8859-15 byte sequence shown in Figure 16.1 on page 852, which is written as the multibyte character sequence with the UTF-8 format in that figure.

Class `wstring_buffer`

Since C++11, class `wbuffer_convert<>` allows creation of a stream buffer (see Section 15.13, page 826) with underlying conversions from wide characters to multibyte characters. For example, the following program converts UTF-8 character sequences into UTF-16/UCS-2 character sequences:

```
// i18n/wbuffer.cpp

#include <string>
#include <iostream>
#include <codecvt>
using namespace std;

int main()
{
    // create input stream reading UTF-8 sequences:
    wbuffer_convert<codecvt_utf8<wchar_t>> utf8inBuf(cin.rdbuf());
    wistream utf8in(&utf8inBuf);

    // create output stream writing UTF-16 sequences:
    wbuffer_convert<codecvt_utf16<wchar_t,
                                  0xFFFF,
                                  generate_header>>
                utf16outBuf(cout.rdbuf());
    wostream utf16out(&utf16outBuf);

    // write each character read:
    wchar_t c;
    while (utf8in.get(c)) {
        utf16out.put(c);
    }
}
```

The program uses an input stream `utf8in` that reads UTF-8 multibyte character sequences into wide characters and an output stream `utf16out` that writes these wide characters as UTF-16 multibyte characters with leading byte order marks. That output almost matches a UCS-2 output because the character values are limited up to value 0xFFFF.

16.4.5   String Collation

The collate<> facet handles differences between conventions for the sorting of strings. For example, in German the letter *ü* is treated as being equivalent to the letter *u* or to the letters *ue* for the
purpose of sorting strings. For other languages, this letter is not even a letter and is treated as a special character, when it is treated at all. Other languages use slightly different sorting rules for certain
character sequences. The collate facet can be used to provide a sorting of strings that is familiar
to the user. Table 16.30 lists the member functions of this facet. In this table, col is an instantiation
of collate, and the arguments passed to the functions are iterators that are used to define strings.

Expression	Meaning
col.compare(*beg1*,*end1*,*beg2*,*end2*)	Returns 　1　if the first string is greater than the second 　0　if both strings are equal 　−1 if the first string is smaller than the second
col.transform(*beg*,*end*)	Returns a string to be compared with other trans- formed strings
col.hash(*beg*,*end*)	Returns a hash value (of type long) for the string

Table 16.30. Members of the collate<> *Facet*

The collate<> facet is a class template that takes a character type charT as its template argument. The strings passed to collate's members are specified using iterators of type const
charT*. This is somewhat unfortunate because there is no guarantee that the iterators used by the
type basic_string<charT> are also pointers. Thus, strings have to be compared as follows:

```
std::locale loc;
std::string s1, s2;
...
// get collate facet of the loc locale
const std::collate<char>& col = std::use_facet<std::collate<char>>(loc);

// compare strings by using the collate facet
int result = col.compare(s1.data(), s1.data()+s1.size(),
                         s2.data(), s2.data()+s2.size());
if (result == 0) {
    // s1 and s2 are equal
    ...
}
```

To check whether a string is less than another string according to a locale, you can use the function
call operator of the locale, which internally returns whether the call of compare() returns −1:

```
bool result = loc(s1,s2);   // check s1<s2 according to locale loc
```

This can be used to pass a locale as sorting criterion (see Section 16.3, page 868).

The `transform()` function returns an object of type `basic_string<charT>`. The lexicographical order of strings returned from `transform()` is the same as the order of the original strings using `collate()`. This ordering can be used for better performance if one string has to be compared with many other strings. Determining the lexicographical order of strings can be much faster than using `collate()` because the national sorting rules can be relatively complex.

The C++ standard library mandates support only for the two instantiations `collate<char>` and `collate<wchar_t>`. For other character types, users must write their own specializations, potentially using the standard instantiations.

16.4.6 Internationalized Messages

The `messages<>` facet is used to retrieve internationalized messages from a catalog of messages. This facet is intended primarily to provide a service similar to that of the function `perror()`. This function is used in POSIX systems to print a system error message for an error number stored in the global variable `errno`. Of course, the service provided by `messages` is more flexible. Unfortunately, it is not defined very precisely.

The `messages<>` facet is a class template that takes a character type `charT` as its template argument. The strings returned from this facet are of type `basic_string<charT>`. The basic use of this facet is to open a catalog, retrieve messages, and then close the catalog. The class `messages` derives from a class `messages_base`, which defines a type `catalog`, which is a type definition for `int`. An object of this type is used to identify the catalog on which the members of `messages` operate. Table 16.31 lists the member functions of the `messages` facet.

Expression	Meaning
`msg.open(`*name*`,`*loc*`)`	Opens a catalog and returns a corresponding ID
`msg.get(`*cat*`,`*set*`,`*msgid*`,`*def*`)`	Returns the message with ID *msgid* from catalog *cat*; if there is no such message, *def* is returned instead
`msg.close(`*cat*`)`	Closes the catalog *cat*

Table 16.31. Members of the `messages<>` Facet

The name passed as the argument to the `open()` function identifies the catalog in which the message strings are stored. This catalog can be, for example, the name of a file. The *loc* argument identifies a `locale` object that is used to access a `ctype` facet. This facet is used to convert the message to the desired character type.

The exact semantics of the `get()` member are not defined. An implementation for POSIX systems could, for example, return the string corresponding to the error message for error *msgid*, but this behavior is not required by the standard. The *set* argument is intended to create a substructure within the messages. For example, it might be used to distinguish between system errors and errors of the C++ standard library.

When a message catalog is no longer needed, it can be released by using the `close()` function. Although the interface using `open()` and `close()` suggests that the messages are retrieved from a file as needed, this is by no means required. It is more likely that `open()` reads a file and stores the messages in memory. A later call to `close()` would then release this memory.

The standard requires that the two instantiations `messages<char>` and `messages<wchar_t>` be stored in each locale. The C++ standard library does not support any other instantiations.

Chapter 17
Numerics

This chapter describes numeric components of the C++ standard library. In particular, it presents the components for random numbers and distributions, the classes for complex numbers, the global numeric functions that are inherited from the C library, and value arrays.

However, the C++ standard library provides more numeric components:

1. For all fundamental numeric data types, the implementation-specific aspects of their representation are specified by `numeric_limits`, as described in Section 5.3, page 115.

2. Class `ratio<>` provides fractional arithmetics especially as a base for durations and timepoints (see Section 5.6, page 140).

3. The STL contains some numeric algorithms, which are described in Section 11.11, page 623.

4. The C++ standard library provides a class `valarray` to deal with numeric arrays. However, in practice, this class plays almost no role; so besides a short introduction in Section 17.4, page 943, I provide details of valarrays in a supplementary chapter of the book, available at `http://www.cppstdlib.com`.

17.1 Random Numbers and Distributions

Since C++11, the C++ standard library provides a random-number library that offers a wide range of classes and types to address the needs of both novices and experts to deal with random numbers and distributions. The library is more complex than a naive programmer might expect. At first, the library provides many well-known *distributions*. But in addition, the C++ standard library provides multiple *engines*, which are the *sources of randomness*. These engines create random unsigned *values*, which are uniformly distributed between a predefined minimum and a maximum; the distributions transfer those values into random *numbers*, which are linearly or nonlinearly distributed according to user-supplied parameters.[1] Thus, you shouldn't use the values generated by the engines directly (see Section 17.1.1, page 912, for details). There are multiple engines because nothing in a computer is

---

[1] The correct technical term for what distributions provide is *random variants* rather than *random numbers*.

truly random and you might need much effort to provide good randomness, so the engines differ in quality, size, and speed.

Note that there is some confusion about the term *random-number generator* because it applies to two different things:

1. It might be a term for a source of randomness. In fact, according to the standard, each engine fulfills the requirements of a "uniform random-number generator."
2. It might be a term for the mechanism to generate random numbers, which is a combination of an engine and a distribution.

The latter is what we usually mean when we need random numbers in a program. Thus, you usually need an engine and a distribution, which is not a big deal, as we will see with the first example.

To use the random-number library, you have to include the header file `<random>`.

17.1.1   A First Example

Before going into details, I provide a first example for programmers who need random numbers or have to shuffle elements without caring in detail for the quality of the random numbers or the shuffling. The example is as follows:

```
// num/random1.cpp

#include <random>
#include <iostream>
#include <algorithm>
#include <vector>

int main()
{
    // create default engine as source of randomness
    std::default_random_engine dre;

    // use engine to generate integral numbers between 10 and 20 (both included)
    std::uniform_int_distribution<int> di(10,20);
    for (int i=0; i<20; ++i) {
        std::cout << di(dre) << " ";
    }
    std::cout << std::endl;

    // use engine to generate floating-point numbers between 10.0 and 20.0
    // (10.0 included, 20.0 not included)
    std::uniform_real_distribution<double> dr(10,20);
    for (int i=0; i<8; ++i) {
        std::cout << dr(dre) << " ";
    }
```

```
        std::cout << std::endl;

        // use engine to shuffle elements
        std::vector<int> v = { 1, 2, 3, 4, 5, 6, 7, 8, 9 };
        ...
        std::shuffle (v.begin(), v.end(),   // range
                        dre);               // source of randomness
        for (int i=0; i<v.size(); ++i) {
            std::cout << v[i] << " ";
        }
        std::cout << std::endl;
}
```

The program demonstrates the general approach of the random-numbers library. After including the header file for the random-number library:

```
#include <random>
```

we create random numbers by combining an *engine* dre with two *distributions* di and dr:

- **Engines** serve as a *stateful source of randomness*. They are function objects that are able to generate random unsigned *values* uniformly distributed according to a predefined minimum and maximum.

- **Distributions** serve as a way to specify how to use these random values to create random *numbers* that are distributed over a range of values according to user-supplied parameters.

The C++ standard library provides multiple engines because there are various approaches to generating random values (algorithms and implementations differ in quality and performance). In this case, we use a default engine for "relatively casual, inexpert, and/or lightweight use:"

```
std::default_random_engine dre;
```

According to the standard, this is "at least an acceptable engine ... on the basis of performance, size, quality, or any combination of such factors." But which engine is chosen here is implementation defined. For this reason, the output of the program might differ on different platforms.

The C++ standard library also provides various distributions for different value types: linear, normal/Gauss, exponential, gamma, Bernoulli, and so on. For the most common form, a linear distribution, where the numbers are equally distributed over a range defined by a given minimum and maximum value, two classes are provided, which we use here: one for integral and one for floating-point numbers.

First, we use uniform_int_distribution, which generates integral numbers. The type of these numbers has to be one of the types short, int, long, long long and their corresponding unsigned types. If no type is specified, int is the default. In the constructor, the first argument specifies the minimum value (default: 0), and the second argument specifies the maximum value (default: numeric_limits<*type*>::max(); see Section 5.3, page 115). Note that both minimum and maximum values can be generated, so this is *not* a half-open range. Thus, with the following statement we define that the random numbers of di are distributed over the values from 10 til 20 (both included):

```
std::uniform_int_distribution<int> di(10,20);
```

The way to generate a number is to call operator () for the distribution, with the engine passed as argument. Thus, to generate and yield the "next" random number in this distribution we simply call:

```
di(dre)
```

Note that the initial state of an engine is well defined and not random. Thus, the following statements will output the same value twice:

```
std::uniform_int_distribution<int> d;
std::default_random_engine dre1;
std::cout << d(dre1) << " ";
std::default_random_engine dre2;
std::cout << d(dre2) << " ";
```

If you need a nonpredictable random value, you have to set the state of the generator randomly by processing some behavior that you can't influence with your code, such as the number of milliseconds between two mouse clicks. That is, you have to pass a so-called *seed* to the constructor of the engine. For example:

```
unsigned int seed = ...                      // process some value really random
std::default_random_engine dre(seed);    // and use it for the initial engine state
```

Alternatively, you can use a *seed* to modify the state of an existing generator by using a member function.

In the same way, you can generate floating-point numbers. Note, however, that in this case the minimum and maximum passed indeed specify a half-open range. The default range is $[0.0, 1.0)$. The possible types are `float`, `double`, or `long double`, with `double` as the default type. Thus, the following statement defines a distribution `dr` that generates values from `10.0` until the highest number just below `20.0`:

```
std::uniform_real_distribution<double> dr(10,20);
```

By contrast, the following statement lets d generate `double` values from `0.0` until `0.9999...`, or whatever the largest double below `1.0` is:

```
std::uniform_real_distribution<> d;
```

Finally, the program demonstrates how to use a random-number generator to shuffle elements of a container or range. Since C++11, the algorithm `shuffle()` (see Section 11.8.4, page 589) is provided, which uses a uniform random-number generator, such as `std::default_random_engine`, to shuffle the elements:

```
std::default_random_engine dre;
...
std::shuffle (v.begin(), v.end(),   // range
              dre);                 // source of randomness
```

The output of the program might look as follows:[2]

---

[2] The term "might" is used because the exact definition of `default_random_engine` is implementation-defined. The values here match a definition of `default_random_engine` as `minstd_rand0`.

```
10 11 18 15 15 12 10 17 17 20 14 15 19 10 10 15 17 10 14 10
16.8677 19.3044 15.2693 16.5392 17.0119 17.622 10.4746 13.2823
1 6 3 4 2 8 9 5 7
```

Be Careful with Temporary Engines

Note that you can but should not pass an engine just temporarily created.[3] The reason is that each time you initialize an engine, its initial state is the same. Thus, if you program something like the following, the "shuffling" would happen twice in the same way:

```
std::shuffle(v.begin(),v.end(),               // range
            std::default_random_engine());    // random-number generator

...

std::shuffle(v.begin(),v.end(),               // range
            std::default_random_engine());    // random-number generator
```

That is, if the first element is shuffled to the end the first time, the first element will be shuffled to the end again the next time. Thus, with each call, shuffling modifies the positions of each element in the same way. For example:

```
1 2 3 4 5 6 7 8 9    // initial state
8 7 5 6 2 4 9 3 1    // after first shuffling
3 9 2 4 7 6 1 5 8    // after second shuffling with engine with equal state
```

Here, in this example, you can see why such shuffling is a problem, besides that the effect of shuffling is predictable after the first call. No matter how often you call shuffle(), the 4 would never get a position other than the fourth or sixth because, according to the current state, shuffle() simply swaps these two positions.

You should use the following code instead so that the shuffling will happen based on different states:

```
std::default_random_engine dre;

...

std::shuffle(v.begin(),v.end(),    // range
            dre);                  // random-number generator

...

std::shuffle(v.begin(),v.end(),    // range
            dre);                  // random-number generator
```

Now, each shuffling moves elements in a different way, which, for example, might look as follows:

```
1 2 3 4 5 6 7 8 9    // initial state
8 7 5 6 2 4 9 3 1    // after first shuffling
3 6 2 7 1 5 8 9 4    // after second shuffling with engine with different state
```

---

[3] Thanks to Walter E. Brown for pointing this out.

Don't Use Engines without Distributions

Now the naive programmer might ask: Why can't we just take an engine and use the value it produces as random numbers (if the range doesn't fit, I can simply use the modulo operator %)?

An important answer to this question is given in Section 7.4.4 of *Accelerated C++* by Andrew Koenig and Barbara E. Moo (see [*KoenigMoo:Accelerated*]). They explain why using `rand()`, the standard random-value generator of C, causes problems that engines in general have. The essence is as follows (words and phrases in *italics* are quoted literally):

> The technique to compute random numbers by using `rand()`%n *in practice fails for two reasons:*
>
> 1. *Many pseudo-random-number generator implementations give remainders that aren't very random, when the quotients* passed as n *are small integers. For example, it is not uncommon for successive results of* `rand()` *to be alternately even and odd. In that case, if* n *is 2, successive results of* `rand()`%n *will alternate between 0 and 1.*
>
> 2. On the other hand, *if the value of* n *is large, and the* generated maximum value *is not evenly divisible by* n, *some remainders will appear more often than others.* For example, if the maximum is 32767 and n is 2000, 17 generated values (500, 2500, ..., 30500, 32500) would map to 500, while only 16 generated values (1500, 3500, ..., 31500) would map to 1500. And this gets worse the larger n is.

Good linear generators take this into account when mapping values generated by engines to their range of generated numbers. Thus, to get random numbers of good quality, you should always use both an engine and a distribution.

17.1.2   Engines

The C++ standard library provides 16 random-number engines, which you can use to process random numbers by combining them with a distribution or for shuffling (see Figure 17.1).

As noted earlier, a random-number engine is a *stateful source of randomness*. Its state defines which sequence of random *values*, which are not random *numbers* (see Section 17.1.1, page 912), are generated. With each function call, using operator (), you yield a new random unsigned value, while the internal state is changed to be able to yield a new random value afterward.

Note that normally the state transitions and values generated are exactly specified. Thus, with the same state, a specific engine will create the same random values on any platform. The only exception is the `default_random_engine`, which represents an implementation-specific engine. It still creates predictable values, but the algorithms used can vary from platform to platform.

You might argue that each value an engine generates should always be random, but nothing is truly random on a computer. If you really need a nonpredictable value, you have to set the state of the generator randomly by processing some behavior that you can't influence with your code, for example, by processing the number of milliseconds between two mouse clicks.

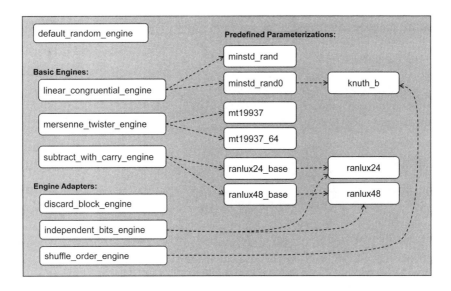

Figure 17.1. Predefined Random-Number Engines

On the other hand, the predictability of the random values has the advantage that you can run the same "random" scenarios based on random numbers, which helps, for example, for the purpose of testing.

The following program demonstrates this:

```
// num/random2.cpp

#include <random>
#include <iostream>
#include <sstream>

void printNumbers (std::default_random_engine& dre)
{
    for (int i=0; i<6; ++i) {
        std::cout << dre() << " ";
    }
    std::cout << std::endl;
}

int main()
{
    // create engine and generate numbers
    std::default_random_engine dre;
    printNumbers(dre);
```

```cpp
    // create equal engine and generate numbers
    std::default_random_engine dre2;   // same initial state as dre
    printNumbers(dre2);

    // create engine with initial state specified by a seed
    std::default_random_engine dre3(42);
    printNumbers(dre3);

    // save state of engine dre
    std::stringstream engineState;
    engineState << dre;

    // generate numbers according to current state of dre
    printNumbers(dre);

    // restore saved state of engine dre and create numbers again
    engineState >> dre;
    printNumbers(dre);

    // restore saved state of engine dre, skip 2 numbers and create numbers again
    engineState.clear();     // clear EOF bit
    engineState.seekg(0);    // and move read position to the beginning
    engineState >> dre;
    dre.discard(2);
    printNumbers(dre);
}
```

The program might have the following output:[4]

```
16807  282475249  1622650073  984943658  1144108930  470211272
16807  282475249  1622650073  984943658  1144108930  470211272
705894  1126542223  1579310009  565444343  807934826  421520601
101027544  1457850878  1458777923  2007237709  823564440  1115438165
101027544  1457850878  1458777923  2007237709  823564440  1115438165
1458777923  2007237709  823564440  1115438165  1784484492  74243042
```

After declaring a random-number engine (the default one in this case), we can use operator () to generate values:

```cpp
std::default_random_engine dre;
...
dre()
```

---

[4] The exact output differs because the `default_random_engine` is implementation-defined. The values here match a definition of `default_random_engine` as `minstd_rand0`.

Thus, an engine is a function object (an object that behaves like a function; see Section 6.10, page 233).

The generated values are unsigned integral values. The exact type can usually be specified except for `default_random_engine`, where the type is implementation defined. For each engine, `result_type` yields the type, and the static member functions `min()` and `max()` yield the minimum and maximum values that can be generated (both included).

If you declare an equal engine again, it will have the same initial state and therefore produce the same random values. To get the same state, you could also pass the engine by value to `printNumbers()` twice. Because `printNumbers()` would operate on a temporary copy of `dre` with each call, this would also generate the same numbers twice.

The next statement shows how to pass an initial seed value to change the initial state of the engine:

```
std::default_random_engine dre3(42);
```

Here, usually, you would pass a value coming from outside the program to start with a truly random value (for example, the duration between two clicks or a value processed out of a real-time clock).

The following statements demonstrate two other possibilities all engines have. You can use operators `<<` and `>>` to save and restore the state of an engine.[5] The following statements write the state into a string by using a string stream (see Section 15.10, page 802):

```
std::ostringstream engineState;
engineState << dre;
```

This state will be a sequence of values separated by spaces. (This is *not* a sequence of random numbers!) If we change the state of `dre` — for example, by generating numbers — and restore the state afterward, the engine will have the state it had when the state was saved and generate the same values again.

With the following statement we skip two states:

```
dre.discard(2);
```

Thus, afterward, `dre` is in the same state as if two values had been generated instead. However, `discard()` might be and often is faster than stepping through all states by calling operator `()`.

17.1.3 Engines in Detail

As Figure 17.1 (Section 17.1, page 913) demonstrates, we can put the engines provided by the C++ standard library into various categories:

- **Basic engines**, which provide various basic algorithms to generate random values:
    - Class std::**linear_congruential_engine**
    - Class std::**mersenne_twister_engine**
    - Class std::**subtract_with_carry_engine**

---

[5] This is probably the first and only serialization interface in the C++ standard library.

- **Engine adapters**, which can be initialized by a (basic) engine:
  - Class std::**discard_block_engine**, which adapts an engine by discarding a given number of generated values each time
  - Class std::**independent_bits_engine**, which adapts an engine to produce random values with a specified number of bits
  - Class std::**shuffle_order_engine**, which adapts an engine by permutation of the order of their generated values
- **Adapters with predefined parameters**:
  - std::**minstd_rand0**
  - std::**minstd_rand**
  - std::**mt19937**
  - std::**mt19937_64**
  - std::**ranlux24_base**
  - std::**ranlux48_base**
  - std::**ranlux24**
  - std::**ranlux48**
  - std::**knuth_b**

For example, type knuth_b is a shortcut for:

```
shuffle_order_engine<linear_congruential_engine<uint_fast32_t,
                                                 16807,
                                                 0,
                                                 2147483647>,
              256>
```

In addition, std::default_random_engine is an implementation-specific type definition. This is the only engine type that does not guarantee generation of identical value sequences on different platforms.

Operation	Effect
engine e	Default constructor; creates engine with default initial state
engine e(*seed*)	Creates engine with state according to *seed*
engine e(*e2*)	Copy constructor; copies engine (e and *e2* will have equal state)
e.seed()	Sets engine d to default initial state
e.seed(*seed*)	Sets engine d to state according to *seed*
e()	Returns next random value and advances its state
e.discard(*n*)	Advances to the *n*th next state (like *n* calls of e() but might be faster)
e1 == e2	Returns whether e1 and e2 have an equal state
e1 != e2	Returns whether e1 and e2 don't have an equal state
ostrm << e	Writes the state of e to the output stream *ostrm*
istrm >> e	Reads a new state from the input stream *istrm* into e

Table 17.1. Operations of Random-Number Engines

Table 17.1 lists the operations provided for random-number engines. All default-constructed engines of the same type initially have the same state, which means that operator == yields `true`, and both engines will produce an equal list of "random" values. Thus, you need a *seed* to produce different random values.

The state written by operator << is a list of decimal values separated by a space. Although this might look like a list of random values, it is *not*.

It is guaranteed that, when reading a written state by an engine of the same type, the engine becomes the same state (operator == yields `true` and equal values are generated).

17.1.4 Distributions

As written, distributions transform random *values* generated by an engine into real and useful random *numbers*. The probability of the numbers generated depends on the specific distribution used, which can be parametrized according to the programmer's needs. Table 17.2 gives an overview of all distributions provided by the C++ standard library.

Category	Name	Data Type
Uniform distributions	uniform_int_distribution	*IntType*
	uniform_real_distribution	*RealType*
Bernoulli distributions	bernoulli_distribution	bool
	binomial_distribution	*IntType*
	geometric_distribution	*IntType*
	negative_binomial_distribution	*IntType*
Poisson distributions	poisson_distribution	*IntType*
	exponential_distribution	*RealType*
	gamma_distribution	*RealType*
	weibull_distribution	*RealType*
	extreme_value_distribution	*RealType*
Normal distributions	normal_distribution	*RealType*
	lognormal_distribution	*RealType*
	chi_squared_distribution	*RealType*
	cauchy_distribution	*RealType*
	fisher_f_distribution	*RealType*
	student_t_distribution	*RealType*
Sampling distributions	discrete_distribution	*IntType*
	piecewise_constant_distribution	*RealType*
	piecewise_linear_distribution	*RealType*

Table 17.2. Distributions Provided by the C++ Standard Library

Almost all distributions are templates parametrized by the type of the generated values. The only exception is `bernoulli_distribution`, which is simply a class because it generates only `bools`. The default types are:

- `int` for *IntType*
- `double` for *RealType*

The C++ standard library guarantees that the following template instantiations are provided:

- For *IntType*: `short`, `int`, `long`, `long long`, and their corresponding unsigned types
- For *RealType*: `float`, `double`, `long double`

Table 17.3 lists the operations provided for distributions.

Operation	Effect
distr`::result_type`	The arithmetic type of the values generated
distr `d`	Default constructor; creates a distribution with default parameters
distr `d(`*args*`)`	Creates a distribution parametrized by *args*
`d(`*e*`)`	Returns the next value according to engine/generator *e* and advances the state of *e*
`d.min()`	Returns the minimum value
`d.max()`	Returns the maximum value
`d1 == d2`	Returns whether d1 and d2 have an equal state
`d1 != d2`	Returns whether d1 and d2 don't have an equal state
ostrm `<< d`	Writes the state of d to the output stream *ostrm*
istrm `>> d`	Reads a new state from the input stream *istrm* into d
distr`::param_type`	The type for the parametrization of *distr*
distr `d(`*pt*`)`	Creates a distribution parametrized by `param_type` *pt*
`d.param(`*pt*`)`	Sets the current parametrization to `param_type` *pt*
`d.param()`	Returns the current parametrization as type `param_type`
`d(`*e*`,`*pt*`)`	Returns the next value according to the engine/generator *e* and to the `param_type` *pt* and advances the state of *e*
`d.`*param*`()`	Returns the value of parameter *param*

Table 17.3. Types and Operations of Distributions

A distribution might be parametrized, so *args* and *pt* depend on the specific distribution. To deal with this parametrization, you can

- Pass these parameters as *args* to the constructor
- Use a member named according to the parameter to query its value
- Use its `param_type` to
    - Pass these parameters as one argument to the constructor
    - Pass these parameters to the next value generation
    - Query the value of these parameters

The `param_type` should itself provide a constructor to pass the parameter value(s) and named members to query their values.

For example, the uniform distributions have two parameters, a and b, which correspond with minimum and maximum (see Section 17.1.5, page 921). As a consequence, you can pass the arguments individually:

```
uniform_int_distribution<> d(0, 20);   // initialize parameters "a" and "b"
d.a()              // yields value of parameter "a"
d.b()              // yields value of parameter "b"
d.param().a()      // yields value of parameter "a"
d.param().b()      // yields value of parameter "b"
```

Or you can use a `param_type` to pass them as a whole:

```
uniform_int_distribution<>::param_type pt(100, 200);   // other parametrization
d(e,pt)              // generates one value according to parametrization pt
d.param(pt);         // let all generated values use parametrization pt
```

Only the sampling distributions use special constructors to pass `vectors` of values or a value generator.

Note that the maximum value passed as a parameter to distributions might sometimes be included and sometimes be excluded.

As for random engines, the state written by operator `<<` is a list of decimal values separated by a space. Although this might look like a list of random numbers, it is *not*.

The following program demonstrates how distributions can be used:

```
// num/dist1.cpp

#include <random>
#include <map>
#include <string>
#include <iostream>
#include <iomanip>

template <typename Distr, typename Eng>
void distr (Distr d, Eng e, const std::string& name)
{
    // print min, max and four example values
    std::cout << name << ":" << std::endl;
    std::cout << "- min():  " << d.min() << std::endl;
    std::cout << "- max():  " << d.max() << std::endl;
    std::cout << "- values: " << d(e) << ' ' << d(e) << ' '
              << d(e) << ' ' << d(e) << std::endl;

    // count the generated values (converted to integral values)
    std::map<long long,int> valuecounter;
    for (int i=0; i<200000; ++i) {
        valuecounter[d(e)]++;
    }
```

```
    // and print the resulting distribution
    std::cout << "====" << std::endl;
    for (auto elem : valuecounter) {
        std::cout << std::setw(3) << elem.first << ": "
                                  << elem.second << std::endl;
    }
    std::cout << "====" << std::endl;
    std::cout << std::endl;
}

int main()
{
    std::knuth_b e;

    std::uniform_real_distribution<> ud(0, 10);
    distr(ud,e,"uniform_real_distribution");

    std::normal_distribution<> nd;
    distr(nd,e,"normal_distribution");

    std::exponential_distribution<> ed;
    distr(ed,e,"exponential_distribution");

    std::gamma_distribution<> gd;
    distr(gd,e,"gamma_distribution");
}
```

On my machine, the program has the following output (distributed over two columns):

```
uniform_real_distribution:              normal_distribution:
- min():   0                            - min():   2.22507e-308
- max():   10                           - max():   1.79769e+308
- values: 8.30965 1.30427 9.47764 3.83416   - values: -0.131724 0.117963 -0.140331 0.538967
====                                    ====
  0: 20087                                -4: 9
  1: 20057                                -3: 245
  2: 19878                                -2: 4325
  3: 19877                                -1: 26843
  4: 20005                                 0: 136947
  5: 20118                                 1: 26987
  6: 20063                                 2: 4377
  7: 19886                                 3: 258
  8: 20003                                 4: 9
  9: 20026                               ====
====
```

```
exponential_distribution:                      gamma_distribution:
- min():   0                                    - min():   0
- max():   1.79769e+308                         - max():   1.79769e+308
- values: 0.185167 2.03694 0.0536495 0.958636   - values: 0.117964 1.60557 0.558526 1.21066
====                                            ====
   0: 126487                                       0: 126315
   1: 46436                                        1: 46477
   2: 17120                                        2: 17160
   3: 6294                                         3: 6271
   4: 2326                                         4: 2413
   5: 865                                          5: 866
   6: 283                                          6: 327
   7: 107                                          7: 109
   8: 52                                           8: 41
   9: 17                                           9: 12
  10: 6                                           10: 7
  11: 6                                           11: 1
  12: 1                                           12: 1
====                                            ====
```

17.1.5   Distributions in Detail

The distributions, their probability (density) functions, and their parameters are as follows:

uniform_int_distribution:

$$P(i \mid a, b) = 1/(b - a + 1)$$

Parameters:

IntType a (default: 0)

IntType b (default: $limits$::max())

uniform_real_distribution:

$$p(x \mid a, b) = 1/(b - a)$$

Parameters:

RealType **a** (default: 0.0)

RealType **b** (default: 1.0)

bernoulli_distribution:

$$P(b \mid p) = \begin{cases} p & \text{if} \quad b = \texttt{true} \\ 1 - p & \text{if} \quad b = \texttt{false} \end{cases}$$

Parameters:

double **p** (default: 0.5)

binomial_distribution:

$$P(i \mid t, p) = \binom{t}{i} \cdot p^i \cdot (1-p)^{t-i}$$

Parameters:
  IntType **t** (default: 1)
  double **p** (default: 0.5)

geometric_distribution:

$$P(i \mid p) = p \cdot (1-p)^i$$

Parameters:
  double **p** (default: 0.5)

negative_binomial_distribution:

$$P(i \mid k, p) = \binom{k+i-1}{i} \cdot p^k \cdot (1-p)^i$$

Parameters:
  IntType **k** (default: 1)
  double **p** (default: 0.5)

poisson_distribution:

$$P(i \mid \mu) = \frac{e^{-\mu}\mu^i}{i\,!}$$

Parameters:
  double **mean** (default: 1.0)

exponential_distribution:

$$p(x \mid \lambda) = \lambda e^{-\lambda x}$$

Parameters:
  RealType **lambda** (default: 1.0)

gamma_distribution:

$$p(x \mid \alpha, \beta) = \frac{e^{-x/\beta}}{\beta^\alpha \cdot \Gamma(\alpha)} \cdot x^{\alpha-1}$$

Parameters:
  RealType **alpha** (default: 1.0)
  RealType **beta** (default: 1.0)

weibull_distribution:

$$p(x \mid a, b) = \frac{a}{b} \cdot \left(\frac{x}{b}\right)^{a-1} \cdot \exp\left(-\left(\frac{x}{b}\right)^a\right)$$

Parameters:

RealType **a** (default: `1.0`)
RealType **b** (default: `1.0`)

extreme_value_distribution:

$$p(x \mid a, b) = \frac{1}{b} \cdot \exp\left(\frac{a - x}{b} - \exp\left(\frac{a - x}{b}\right)\right)$$

Parameters:

RealType **a** (default: `1.0`)
RealType **b** (default: `1.0`)

normal_distribution:

$$p(x \mid \mu, \sigma) = \frac{1}{\sigma\sqrt{2\pi}} \cdot \exp\left(-\frac{(x - \mu)^2}{2\sigma^2}\right)$$

Parameters:

RealType **mean** (default: `0.0`)
RealType **stddev** (default: `1.0`)

lognormal_distribution:

$$p(x \mid m, s) = \frac{1}{sx\sqrt{2\pi}} \cdot \exp\left(-\frac{(\ln x - m)^2}{2s^2}\right)$$

Parameters:

RealType **m** (default: `0.0`)
RealType **s** (default: `1.0`)

chi_squared_distribution:

$$p(x \mid n) = \frac{x^{(n/2)-1} \cdot e^{-x/2}}{\Gamma(n/2) \cdot 2^{n/2}}$$

Parameters:

RealType **n** (default: `1`)

cauchy_distribution:

$$p(x \mid a, b) = \left(\pi b\left(1 + \left(\frac{x - a}{b}\right)^2\right)\right)^{-1}$$

Parameters:

RealType **a** (default: `1.0`)
RealType **b** (default: `1.0`)

`fisher_f_distribution`:

$$p(x\,|\,m,n) = \frac{\Gamma\big((m+n)/2\big)}{\Gamma(m/2)\,\Gamma(n/2)} \cdot \left(\frac{m}{n}\right)^{m/2} \cdot x^{(m/2)-1} \cdot \left(1 + \frac{mx}{n}\right)^{-(m+n)/2}$$

Parameters:

RealType **m** (default: 1)

RealType **n** (default: 1)

`student_t_distribution`:

$$p(x\,|\,n) = \frac{1}{\sqrt{n\pi}} \cdot \frac{\Gamma\big((n+1)/2\big)}{\Gamma(n/2)} \cdot \left(1 + \frac{x^2}{n}\right)^{-(n+1)/2} .$$

Parameters:

RealType **n** (default: 1)

`discrete_distribution`:

$$P(i\,|\,p_0,\ldots,p_{n-1}) = p_i$$

Parameters:

vector<double> **probabilities**

For these parameters, the constructors take an initializer list of doubles, a range of doubles, and a function object that creates doubles.

`piecewise_constant_distribution`:

$$p(x\,|\,b_0,\ldots,b_n,\ \rho_0,\ldots,\rho_{n-1}) = \rho_i \text{ , for } b_i \leq x < b_{i+1}$$

Parameters:

vector<*RealType*> **intervals** (default: inconsistent)

vector<*RealType*> **densities** (default: inconsistent)

For these parameters, the constructors take a range of interval boundaries and weights, an initializer list of boundaries and a weight generator, as well as number, min, and max for boundaries and a weight generator.

`piecewise_linear_distribution`:

$$p(x\,|\,b_0,\ldots,b_n,\ \rho_0,\ldots,\rho_n) = \rho_i \cdot \frac{b_{i+1}-x}{b_{i+1}-b_i} + \rho_{i+1} \cdot \frac{x-b_i}{b_{i+1}-b_i} \text{ , for } b_i \leq x < b_{i+1}$$

Parameters:

vector<*RealType*> **intervals**

vector<*RealType*> **densities**

For these parameters, the constructors take a range of interval boundaries and weights, an initializer list of boundaries and a weight generator, as well as number, min, and max for boundaries and a weight generator.

Further details are given in the exact descriptions in the C++ standard library.

17.2   Complex Numbers

The C++ standard library provides the class template `complex<>` to operate on complex numbers. Complex numbers have two parts: real and imaginary. The imaginary part has the property that its square is a negative number. In other words, the imaginary part of a complex number is the factor i, which is the square root of -1.

Recent Changes with C++11

C++98 specified almost all features of the class `complex<>`. With the first standardization of C++, almost all features of class complex were specified. In fact, except for using `constexpr` where appropriate, none of the new language features of C++11 had an impact of class `complex<>` and its specializations. Only a few fixes and enhancements were added:

- The following operations taking a complex number as argument were added: `proj()`, `asin()`, `acos()`, `atan()`, `asin()`, `acosh()`, `atanh()`.

- With `real(`*val*`)` and `imag(`*val*`)`, you can now set the real and imaginary part directly.

17.2.1   Class `complex<>` in General

The class `complex<>` is declared in the header file `<complex>`:

```
#include <complex>
```

In `<complex>`, the class `complex<>` is defined as follows:

```
namespace std {
    template <typename T>
    class complex;
}
```

The template parameter T is used as the scalar type of both the real and the imaginary parts of the complex number.

In addition, the C++ standard library provides three specializations for `float`, `double`, and `long double`:

```
namespace std {
    template<> class complex<float>;
    template<> class complex<double>;
    template<> class complex<long double>;
}
```

These types are provided to allow certain optimizations and some safer conversions from one complex type to the other.

17.2.2   Examples Using Class `complex<>`

The following program demonstrates some of the abilities of class `complex<>` to create complex numbers, print different representations of complex numbers, and perform some common operations on complex numbers:

```cpp
// num/complex1.cpp

#include <iostream>
#include <complex>
using namespace std;

int main()
{
    // complex number with real and imaginary parts
    // - real part: 4.0
    // - imaginary part: 3.0
    complex<double> c1(4.0,3.0);

    // create complex number from polar coordinates
    // - magnitude: 5.0
    // - phase angle: 0.75
    complex<float> c2(polar(5.0,0.75));

    // print complex numbers with real and imaginary parts
    cout << "c1: " << c1 << endl;
    cout << "c2: " << c2 << endl;

    // print complex numbers as polar coordinates
    cout << "c1: magnitude: " << abs(c1)
         << " (squared magnitude: " << norm(c1) << ") "
         <<     " phase angle: " << arg(c1) << endl;
    cout << "c2: magnitude: " << abs(c2)
         << " (squared magnitude: " << norm(c2) << ") "
         <<     " phase angle: " << arg(c2) << endl;

    // print complex conjugates
    cout << "c1 conjugated:  " << conj(c1) << endl;
    cout << "c2 conjugated:  " << conj(c2) << endl;

    // print result of a computation
    cout << "4.4 + c1 * 1.8: " << 4.4 + c1 * 1.8 << endl;

    // print sum of c1 and c2:
```

```
                // - note: different types
                cout << "c1 + c2:          "
                     << c1 + complex<double>(c2.real(),c2.imag()) << endl;

                // add square root of c1 to c1 and print the result
                cout << "c1 += sqrt(c1): " << (c1 += sqrt(c1)) << endl;
        }
```

The program might have the following output (the exact output depends on the implementation-specific properties of the type `double`):

```
    c1: (4,3)
    c2: (3.65844,3.40819)
    c1: magnitude: 5 (squared magnitude: 25)  phase angle: 0.643501
    c2: magnitude: 5 (squared magnitude: 25)  phase angle: 0.75
    c1 conjugated:   (4,-3)
    c2 conjugated:   (3.65844,-3.40819)
    4.4 + c1 * 1.8: (11.6,5.4)
    c1 + c2:          (7.65844,6.40819)
    c1 += sqrt(c1): (6.12132,3.70711)
```

A second example contains a loop that reads two complex numbers and processes the first complex number raised to the power of the second complex number:

```
// num/complex2.cpp

#include <iostream>
#include <complex>
#include <cstdlib>
#include <limits>
using namespace std;

int main()
{
    complex<long double> c1, c2;

    while (cin.peek() != EOF) {

        // read first complex number
        cout << "complex number c1: ";
        cin >> c1;
        if (!cin) {
            cerr << "input error" << endl;
            return EXIT_FAILURE;
        }
```

```
// read second complex number
cout << "complex number c2: ";
cin >> c2;
if (!cin) {
    cerr << "input error" << endl;
    return EXIT_FAILURE;
}

if (c1 == c2) {
    cout << "c1 and c2 are equal !" << endl;
}

cout << "c1 raised to the c2: " << pow(c1,c2)
    << endl << endl;

// skip rest of line
cin.ignore(numeric_limits<int>::max(),'\n');
    }
}
```

Table 17.4 shows some possible input and output of this program. Note that you can input a complex number by passing only the real part as a single value with or without parentheses or by passing the real and imaginary parts separated by a comma in parentheses.

c1	c2	Output	
2	2	c1 raised to c2:	(4,0)
(16)	0.5	c1 raised to c2:	(4,0)
(8,0)	0.333333333	c1 raised to c2:	(2,0)
0.99	(5)	c1 raised to c2:	(0.95099,0)
(0,2)	2	c1 raised to c2:	(-4,4.89843e-16)
(1.7,0.3)	0	c1 raised to c2:	(1,0)
(3,4)	(-4,3)	c1 raised to c2:	(4.32424e-05,8.91396e-05)
(1.7,0.3)	(4.3,2.8)	c1 raised to c2:	(-4.17622,4.86871)

Table 17.4. Possible I/O of `complex2.cpp` *Example*

17.2.3   Operations for Complex Numbers

The class template `complex<>` provides the operations described in the following subsections.

Create, Copy, and Assign Operations

Table 17.5 lists the constructors and assignment operations for `complex`. The constructors provide the ability to pass the initial values of the real and the imaginary parts. If they are not passed, they are initialized by the default constructor of the value type.

Expression	Effect
`complex c`	Creates a complex number with 0 as the real part and 0 as the imaginary part $(0 + 0i)$
`complex c(1.3)`	Creates a complex number with `1.3` as the real part and 0 as the imaginary part $(1.3 + 0i)$
`complex c(1.3,4.2)`	Creates a complex number with `1.3` as the real part and `4.2` as the imaginary part $(1.3 + 4.2i)$
`complex c1(c2)`	Creates c1 as a copy of c2
`polar(4.2)`	Creates a temporary complex number from polar coordinates (`4.2` as magnitude rho and 0 as phase angle theta)
`polar(4.2,0.75)`	Creates a temporary complex number from polar coordinates (`4.2` as magnitude rho and `0.75` as phase angle theta)
`conj(c)`	Creates a temporary complex number that is the conjugated complex number of c (the complex number with the negated imaginary part)
`proj(c)`	Creates a temporary complex number from the projection of c onto the Riemann sphere (since C++11)
`c1 = c2`	Assigns the values of c2 to c1
`c1 += c2`	Adds the value of c2 to c1
`c1 -= c2`	Subtracts the value of c2 from c1
`c1 *= c2`	Multiplies the value of c2 by c1
`c1 /= c2`	Divides the value of c2 into c1

Table 17.5. Constructors and Assignment Operations of Class `complex<>`

The assignment operators are the only way to modify the value of an existing complex number. The computed assignment operators `+=`, `-=`, `*=`, and `/=` add, subtract, multiply, and divide the value of the second operand to, from, by, and into the first operand.

The auxiliary `polar()` function provides the ability to create a complex number that is initialized by polar coordinates (magnitude and phase angle in radians):

```
// create a complex number initialized from polar coordinates
std::complex<double> c2(std::polar(4.2,0.75));
```

A problem exists when you have an implicit type conversion during the creation. For example, this notation works:

```
std::complex<float> c2(std::polar(4.2,0.75));        // OK
```

However, the following notation with the equal sign does not:

```
std::complex<float> c2 = std::polar(4.2,0.75);       // ERROR
```

This problem is discussed in the next subsection.

The auxiliary `conj()` function provides the ability to create a complex number that is initialized by the conjugated complex value of another complex number (a conjugated complex value is the value with a negated imaginary part):

```
std::complex<double> c1(1.1,5.5);
std::complex<double> c2(conj(c1));    // initialize c2 with
                                      // complex<double>(1.1,-5.5)
```

Since C++11, the auxiliary `proj()` function is provided, which creates a complex number computed as a projection of another complex number onto the Riemann sphere.

Implicit Type Conversions

The constructors of the specializations for `float`, `double`, and `long double` are designed in such a way that safe conversions, such as `complex<float>` to `complex<double>`, are allowed to be implicit but less safe conversions, such as `complex<long double>` to `complex<double>`, must be explicit:

```
std::complex<float> cf;
std::complex<double> cd;
std::complex<long double> cld;

...

std::complex<double> cd1 = cf;     // OK: safe conversion
std::complex<double> cd2 = cld;    // ERROR: no implicit conversion
std::complex<double> cd3(cld);     // OK: explicit conversion
```

In addition, no constructors from any other complex type are defined. In particular, you can't convert a `complex` with an integral value type into a `complex` with value type `float`, `double`, or `long double`. However, you can convert the values by passing the real and imaginary parts as separate arguments:

```
std::complex<double> cd;
std::complex<int> ci;

...

std::complex<double> cd4 = ci;     // ERROR: no implicit conversion
std::complex<double> cd5(ci);      // ERROR: no explicit conversion
std::complex<double> cd6(ci.real(),ci.imag());  // OK
```

Unfortunately, the assignment operators allow less safe conversions. These operators are provided as function templates for all types. So, you can assign any complex type as long as the value types are convertible:[6]

```
std::complex<double> cd;
std::complex<long double> cld;
```

---

[6] The fact that constructors for the complex specializations allow only safe implicit conversions, whereas the assignment operations allow any implicit conversion, is probably a mistake in the standard.

```
std::complex<int> ci;
...
cd = ci;    // OK
cd = cld;   // OK
```

This problem also relates to `polar()`, `conj()`, and `proj()`. For example, the following notation works fine:

```
std::complex<float> c2(std::polar(4.2,0.75));    // OK
```

But the notation with the equal sign does not:

```
std::complex<float> c2 = std::polar(4.2,0.75);    // ERROR
```

The reason for this is that the expression

```
std::polar(4.2,0.75)
```

creates a temporary `complex<double>`, and the implicit conversion from `complex<double>` to `complex<float>` is not defined.[7]

Value Access

Table 17.6 shows the functions provided to access the attributes of complex numbers.

Expression	Effect
`real(c)`	Returns the value of the real part (as a global function)
`c.real()`	Returns the value of the real part (as a member function)
`c.real(1.7)`	Assigns 1.7 as new real part (since C++11)
`imag(c)`	Returns the value of the imaginary part (as a global function)
`c.imag()`	Returns the value of the imaginary part (as a member function)
`c.imag(1.7)`	Assigns 1.7 as new imaginary part (since C++11)
`abs(c)`	Returns the absolute value of c ($\sqrt{\texttt{c.real}()^2 + \texttt{c.imag}()^2}$)
`norm(c)`	Returns the squared absolute value of c ($\texttt{c.real}()^2 + \texttt{c.imag}()^2$)
`arg(c)`	Returns the angle of the polar representation of c (φ) (equivalent to `atan2(c.imag(),c.real())` as phase angle)

Table 17.6. Operations for Value Access of Class `complex<>`

Note that before C++11, `real()` and `imag()` provided only read access to the real and the imaginary parts. Changing only the real part or only the imaginary part required assigning a new complex number. For example, the following statement set the imaginary part of c to 3.7:

```
std::complex<double> c;
...
c = std::complex<double>(c.real(),3.7);    // since C++11: c.imag(3.7)
```

---

[7] In general, the initialization syntax with = requires that an implicit type conversion is provided.

Comparison Operations

To compare complex numbers, you can check only for equality (Table 17.7). The operators == and != are defined as global functions, so one of the operands may be a scalar value. If you use a scalar value as the operand, it is interpreted as the real part, with the imaginary part having the default value of its type, which is usually 0.

Expression	Effect
c1 == c2	Returns whether c1 is equal to c2
	(c1.real()==c2.real() && c1.imag()==c2.imag())
c == 1.7	Returns whether c is equal to 1.7
	(c.real()==1.7 && c.imag()==0.0)
1.7 == c	Returns whether c is equal to 1.7
	(c.real()==1.7 && c.imag()==0.0)
c1 != c2	Returns whether c1 differs from c2
	(c1.real()!=c2.real() || c1.imag()!=c2.imag())
c != 1.7	Returns whether c differs from 1.7
	(c.real()!=1.7 || c.imag()!=0.0)
1.7 != c	Returns whether c differs from 1.7
	(c.real()!=1.7 || c.imag()!=0.0)

Table 17.7. Comparison Operations of Class `complex<>`

Other comparison operations, such as operator <, are not defined. Although it is not impossible to define an ordering for complex values, such orderings are neither very intuitive nor very useful. Note, for example, that the magnitude of complex numbers by itself is not a good basis for ordering complex values, because two complex values can be very different and yet have identical magnitude (1 and −1 are two such numbers). An ad hoc criterion can be added to create a valid ordering. For example, given two complex values c1 and c2, you could deem c1 < c2 when |c1| < |c2| or, if both magnitudes are equal, when arg(c1) < arg(c2). However, such a criterion invariably has little or no mathematical meaning.[8]

As a consequence, you can't use complex<> as the element type of an associative container, provided you use no user-defined sorting criterion. The reason is that associative containers use the function object less<>, which calls operator <, to be able to sort the elements (see Section 6.11.1, page 244).

By implementing a user-defined operator <, you could sort complex numbers and use them in associative containers. Note that you should be very careful not to pollute the standard namespace. For example:

---

[8] Thanks to David Vandevoorde for pointing this out.

```
template <typename T>
bool operator< (const std::complex<T>& c1,
                const std::complex<T>& c2)
{
    return std::abs(c1)<std::abs(c2) ||
           (std::abs(c1)==std::abs(c2) &&
            std::arg(c1)<std::arg(c2));
}
```

Arithmetic Operations

Complex numbers provide the four basic arithmetic operations and the negative and positive signs (Table 17.8).

Expression	Effect
`c1 + c2`	Returns the sum of `c1` and `c2`
`c + 1.7`	Returns the sum of `c` and `1.7`
`1.7 + c`	Returns the sum of `1.7` and `c`
`c1 - c2`	Returns the difference between `c1` and `c2`
`c - 1.7`	Returns the difference between `c` and `1.7`
`1.7 - c`	Returns the difference between `1.7` and `c`
`c1 * c2`	Returns the product of `c1` and `c2`
`c * 1.7`	Returns the product of `c` and `1.7`
`1.7 * c`	Returns the product of `1.7` and `c`
`c1 / c2`	Returns the quotient of `c1` and `c2`
`c / 1.7`	Returns the quotient of `c` and `1.7`
`1.7 / c`	Returns the quotient of `1.7` and `c`
`- c`	Returns the negated value of `c`
`+ c`	Returns `c`
`c1 += c2`	Equivalent to `c1 = c1 + c2`
`c1 -= c2`	Equivalent to `c1 = c1 - c2`
`c1 *= c2`	Equivalent to `c1 = c1 * c2`
`c1 /= c2`	Equivalent to `c1 = c1 / c2`

Table 17.8. Arithmetic Operations of Class `complex<>`

Input/Output Operations

Class `complex` provides the common I/O operators `<<` and `>>` (Table 17.9).

The output operator writes the complex number with respect to the current stream state with the format:

(*realpart*, *imagpart*)

Expression	Effect
strm << c	Writes the complex number c to the output stream strm
strm >> c	Reads the complex number c from the input stream strm

Table 17.9. I/O Operations of Class complex<>

In particular, the output operator is defined as equivalent to the following implementation:

```
template <typename T, typename charT, typename traits>
std::basic_ostream<charT,traits>&
operator << (std::basic_ostream<charT,traits>& strm,
             const std::complex<T>& c)
{
    // temporary value string to do the output with one argument
    std::basic_ostringstream<charT,traits> s;

    s.flags(strm.flags());           // copy stream flags
    s.imbue(strm.getloc());          // copy stream locale
    s.precision(strm.precision());   // copy stream precision

    // prepare the value string
    s << '(' << c.real() << ',' << c.imag() << ')';

    // write the value string
    strm << s.str();

    return strm;
}
```

The input operator provides the ability to read a complex number with one of the following formats:

(*realpart,imagpart*)

(*realpart*)

realpart

If none of the formats fits according to the next characters in the input stream, the ios::failbit is set, which might throw a corresponding exception (see Section 15.4.4, page 762).

Unfortunately, you can't specify the separator of complex numbers between the real and the imaginary parts. So, if you have a comma as a "decimal point," as in German, I/O looks really strange. For example, a complex number with 4.6 as the real part and 2.7 as the imaginary part would be written as

(4,6,2,7)

See Section 17.2.2, page 927, for an example of how to use the I/O operations.

Transcendental Functions

Table 17.10 lists the transcendental functions (trigonometric, exponential, and so on) for `complex`.

Expression	Effect
`pow(c,3)`	Complex power c^3
`pow(c,1.7)`	Complex power $c^{1.7}$
`pow(c1,c2)`	Complex power $c1^{c2}$
`pow(1.7,c)`	Complex power 1.7^c
`exp(c)`	Base e exponential of c (e^c)
`sqrt(c)`	Square root of c ($\sqrt{c}$)
`log(c)`	Complex natural logarithm of c with base e ($\ln c$)
`log10(c)`	Complex common logarithm of c with base 10 ($\lg c$)
`sin(c)`	Sine of c ($\sin c$)
`cos(c)`	Cosine of c ($\cos c$)
`tan(c)`	Tangent of c ($\tan c$)
`sinh(c)`	Hyperbolic sine of c ($\sinh c$)
`cosh(c)`	Hyperbolic cosine of c ($\cosh c$)
`tanh(c)`	Hyperbolic tangent of c ($\tanh c$)
`asin(c)`	Arcus sine of c (since C++11)
`acos(c)`	Arcus cosine of c (since C++11)
`atan(c)`	Arcus tangent of c (since C++11)
`asinh(c)`	Arcus hyperbolic sine of c (since C++11)
`acosh(c)`	Arcus hyperbolic cosine of c (since C++11)
`atanh(c)`	Arcus hyperbolic tangent of c (since C++11)

Table 17.10. Transcendental Functions of Class `complex<>`

17.2.4 Class `complex<>` in Detail

This subsection describes all operations of class `complex<>` in detail. In the following definitions, T is the template parameter of class `complex<>`, which is the type of the real and the imaginary parts of the `complex` value.

Type Definitions

complex::**value_type**
- The type of the real and the imaginary parts.

Create, Copy, and Assign Operations

complex::**complex** ()

- The default constructor.
- Creates a complex value in which the real and the imaginary parts are initialized by an explicit call of their default constructor. Thus, for fundamental types, the initial value of the real and the imaginary parts is 0 (see Section 3.2.1, page 37, for the default value of fundamental types).

complex::**complex** (const T& *re*)

- Creates a complex value in which *re* is the value of the real part, and the imaginary part is initialized by an explicit call of its default constructor (0 for fundamental data types).
- This constructor also defines an automatic type conversion from T to `complex`.

complex::**complex** (const T& *re*, const T& *im*)

- Creates a complex value, with *re* as the real part and *im* as the imaginary part.

complex **polar** (const T& *rho*)
complex **polar** (const T& *rho*, const T& *theta*)

- Both forms create and return the complex number that is initialized by polar coordinates.
- *rho* is the magnitude.
- *theta* is the phase angle in radians (default: 0).

complex **conj** (const *complex*& *cmplx*)

- Creates and returns the complex number that is initialized by the conjugated complex value (the value with the negated imaginary part) of *cmplx*.

complex **proj** (const *complex*& *cmplx*)

- Creates and returns a temporary complex number from the projection of x onto the Riemann sphere.
- The behavior is equivalent to the C function `cproj()`.
- Available since C++11.

complex::**complex** (const *complex*& *cmplx*)

- The copy constructor.
- Creates a new complex as a copy of *cmplx*.
- Copies the real and imaginary parts.
- In general, this function is provided as both a nontemplate and a template function (see Section 3.2, page 34, for an introduction to member templates). Thus, in general, automatic type conversions of the element type are provided.
- However, the specializations for `float`, `double`, and `long double` restrict copy constructors, so less safe conversions — from `double` and `long double` to `float`, as well as from `long`

double to double — are not implicitly possible. See Section 17.2.3, page 930, for more information about the implications from this.

complex& ***complex*** : :**operator =** (const *complex& cmplx*)

- Assigns the value of complex *cmplx*.
- Returns *this.
- This function is provided as both a nontemplate and a template function (see Section 3.2, page 34, for an introduction to member templates). Thus, automatic type conversions of the element type are provided. (This is also the case for the specializations that are provided by the C++ standard library.)

complex& ***complex*** : :**operator +=** (const *complex& cmplx*)

complex& ***complex*** : :**operator -=** (const *complex& cmplx*)

complex& ***complex*** : :**operator *=** (const *complex& cmplx*)

complex& ***complex*** : :**operator /=** (const *complex& cmplx*)

- These operations add, subtract, multiply, and divide the value of *cmplx* to, from, by, and into *this, respectively, and store the result in *this.
- They return *this.
- These operations are provided as both a nontemplate and a template function (see Section 3.2, page 34, for an introduction to member templates). Thus, automatic type conversions of the element type are provided. (This is also the case for the specializations that are provided by the C++ standard library.)

Note that the assignment operators are the only functions that allow you to modify the value of an existing complex.

Element Access

T *complex* : :**real** () const

T **real** (const *complex& cmplx*)

T *complex* : :**imag** () const

T **imag** (const *complex& cmplx*)

- These functions return the real or the imaginary part, respectively.
- Note that the return value is not a reference. Thus, you can't use these functions to modify the real or the imaginary parts. To change only the real part or only the imaginary part, you must assign a new complex number (see Section 17.2.3, page 931).

T *complex* : :**real** (const T& *re*)

T *complex* : :**imag** (const T& *im*)

- These functions assign *re* or *im* as new real or imaginary part, respectively.
- Available since C++11. Before C++11, to modify only the real part or only the imaginary part, you had to assign a new complex number (see Section 17.2.3, page 931).

T **abs** (const *complex& cmplx*)

- Returns the absolute value (magnitude) of *cmplx*.
- The absolute value is $\sqrt{cmplx.\texttt{real}()^2 + cmplx.\texttt{imag}()^2}$.

T **norm** (const *complex& cmplx*)

- Returns the squared absolute value (squared magnitude) of *cmplx*.
- The squared absolute value is $cmplx.\texttt{real}()^2 + cmplx.\texttt{imag}()^2$.

T **arg** (const *complex& cmplx*)

- Returns the angle of the polar representation (φ) of *cmplx* in radians.
- It is equivalent to `atan2(`*cmplx*`.imag(),`*cmplx*`.real())` as the phase angle.

Input/Output Operations

ostream& **operator <<** (*ostream& strm*, const *complex& cmplx*)

- Writes the value of *cmplx* to the stream *strm* in the format
  (*realpart,imagpart*)
- Returns *strm*.
- See Section 17.2.3, page 933, for the exact behavior of this operation.

istream& **operator >>** (*istream& strm*, *complex& cmplx*)

- Reads a new value from *strm* into *cmplx*.
- Valid input formats are
  (*realpart,imagpart*)
  (*realpart*)
  realpart
- Returns *strm*.
- See Section 17.2.3, page 934, for the exact behavior of this operation.

Operators

complex **operator +** (const *complex& cmplx*)

- The positive sign.
- Returns *cmplx*.

complex **operator -** (const *complex& cmplx*)

- The negative sign.
- Returns the value of *cmplx* with the negated real and the negated imaginary parts.

complex **binary-op** (const *complex& cmplx1*, const *complex& cmplx2*)

complex **binary-op** (const *complex& cmplx*, const T& *value*)

complex **binary-op** (const T& *value*, const *complex& cmplx*)

- All forms return a complex number with the result of ***binary-op***.
- ***binary-op*** may be any of the following:
    ```
    operator +
    operator -
    operator *
    operator /
    ```
- If a scalar value of the element type is passed, it is interpreted as the real part, with the imaginary part having the default value of its type, which is 0 for fundamental types.

bool ***comparison*** (const *complex& cmplx1*, const *complex& cmplx2*)

bool ***comparison*** (const *complex& cmplx*, const T& *value*)

bool ***comparison*** (const T& *value*, const *complex& cmplx*)

- Returns the result of the comparison of two complex numbers or the result of the comparison of a complex number with a scalar value.
- ***comparison*** may be any of the following:
    ```
    operator ==
    operator !=
    ```
- If a scalar value of the element type is passed, it is interpreted as the real part, with the imaginary part having the default value of its type, which is 0 for fundamental types.
- Note that no operators <, <=, >, and >= are provided.

Transcendental Functions

complex **pow** (const *complex& base*, const T& *exp*)

complex **pow** (const *complex& base*, const *complex& exp*)

complex **pow** (const T& *base*, const *complex& exp*)

- All forms return the complex power of *base* raised to the *exp*th power, defined as:
    exp(*exp**log(*base*))
- The branch cuts are along the negative real axis.
- The value returned for pow(0,0) is implementation defined.

complex **exp** (const *complex& cmplx*)

- Returns the complex base *e* exponential of *cmplx*.

complex **sqrt** (const *complex& cmplx*)

- Returns the complex square root of *cmplx* in the range of the right-half plane.
- If the argument is a negative real number, the value returned lies on the positive imaginary axis.
- The branch cuts are along the negative real axis.

complex **log** (const *complex& cmplx*)

- Returns the complex natural base e logarithm of *cmplx*.
- When *cmplx* is a negative real number, imag(log(*cmplx*)) is pi.
- The branch cuts are along the negative real axis.

complex **log10** (const *complex& cmplx*)

- Returns the complex base 10 logarithm of *cmplx*.
- It is equivalent to log(*cmplx*)/log(10).
- The branch cuts are along the negative real axis.

complex **sin** (const *complex& cmplx*)
complex **cos** (const *complex& cmplx*)
complex **tan** (const *complex& cmplx*)
complex **sinh** (const *complex& cmplx*)
complex **cosh** (const *complex& cmplx*)
complex **tanh** (const *complex& cmplx*)
complex **asin** (const *complex& cmplx*)
complex **acos** (const *complex& cmplx*)
complex **atan** (const *complex& cmplx*)
complex **asinh** (const *complex& cmplx*)
complex **acosh** (const *complex& cmplx*)
complex **atanh** (const *complex& cmplx*)

- These operations return the corresponding complex trigonometric operation on *cmplx*.
- The arcus (inverse) operations (those that start with **a**) are available since C++11.

17.3 Global Numeric Functions

The header files `<cmath>` and `<cstdlib>` provide the global numeric functions that are inherited from C. Tables 17.11 and 17.12 list these functions.[9]

Function	Effect
`pow()`	Power function
`exp()`	Exponential function
`sqrt()`	Square root
`log()`	Natural logarithm
`log10()`	Base 10 logarithm
`sin()`	Sine
`cos()`	Cosine
`tan()`	Tangent
`sinh()`	Hyperbolic sine
`cosh()`	Hyperbolic cosine
`tanh()`	Hyperbolic tangent
`asin()`	Arcus sine
`acos()`	Arcus cosine
`atan()`	Arcus tangent
`atan2()`	Arcus tangent of a quotient
`asinh()`	Arcus hyperbolic sine (since C++11)
`acosh()`	Arcus hyperbolic cosine (since C++11)
`atanh()`	Arcus hyperbolic tangent (since C++11)
`ceil()`	Floating-point value rounded up to the next integral value
`floor()`	Floating-point value rounded down to the next integral value
`fabs()`	Absolute value of a floating-point value
`fmod()`	Remainder after division for floating-point value (modulo)
`frexp()`	Converts floating-point value to fractional and integral components
`ldexp()`	Multiplies floating-point value by integral power of 2
`modf()`	Extracts signed integral and fractional values from floating-point value

Table 17.11. Functions of the Header File `<cmath>`

In contrast to C, C++ overloads some operations for different types, which makes some numeric functions of C obsolete. For example, C provides `abs()`, `labs()`, `llabs()`, `fabs()`, `fabsf()`, and `fabsl()` to process the absolute value of `int`, `long`, `long long`, `double`, `float()`, and `long double`, respectively. In C++, `abs()` is overloaded so that you can use `abs()` for all these data types.

---

[9] For historical reasons, some numeric functions are defined in `<cstdlib>` rather than in `<cmath>`.

Function	Effect
abs()	Absolute value of an int value
labs()	Absolute value of a long
llabs()	Absolute value of a long long (since C++11)
div()	Quotient and remainder of int division
ldiv()	Quotient and remainder of long division
lldiv()	Quotient and remainder of long long division (since C++11)
srand()	Random-value generator (seed new sequence)
rand()	Random-value generator (next number of sequence)

Table 17.12. Numeric Functions of the Header File `<cstdlib>`

In particular, all numeric functions for integral values are overloaded for types int, long, and long long, whereas all numeric functions for floating-point values are overloaded for types float, double, and long double.

However, this has an important side effect: When you pass an integral value where only multiple floating-point overloads exist, the expression is ambiguous:[10]

```
std::sqrt(7)        // AMBIGUOUS: sqrt(float), sqrt(double), or
                    //            sqrt(long double)?
```

Instead, you have to write

```
std::sqrt(7.0)      // OK
```

or, if you use a variable, you must write

```
int x;
...
std::sqrt(float(x)) // OK
```

Library vendors handle this problem completely differently: Some don't provide the overloading, some provide standard conforming behavior (overload for all floating-point types), some overload for all numeric types, and some allow you to switch between different policies by using the preprocessor. Thus, in practice, the ambiguity might or might not occur. To write portable code, you should always write the code in a way that the arguments match exactly.

---

[10] Thanks to David Vandevoorde for pointing this out.

17.4 Valarrays

Since C++98, the C++ standard library has provided the class `valarray` for the processing of arrays of numeric values.

Purpose of Valarrays

A valarray is a representation of the mathematical concept of a linear sequence of values. It has one dimension, but you can get the illusion of higher dimensionality by special techniques of computed indices and powerful subsetting capabilities. Therefore, a valarray can be used as a base for both vector and matrix operations, as well as for the processing of mathematical systems of polynomial equations with good performance.

Technically, valarrays are one-dimensional arrays with elements numbered sequentially from zero. They provide the ability to do some numeric processing for all or a subset of the values in one or more value arrays. For example, you can process the statement

```
z = a*x*x + b*x + c
```

with a, b, c, x, and z being arrays that contain hundreds of numeric values. In doing this, you have the advantage of a simple notation.

Also, the processing is done with good performance because the classes provide some optimizations that avoid the creation of temporary objects while processing the whole statement. These are based on the fact that valarrays are guaranteed to be alias free. That is, any value of a nonconstant valarray is accessed through a unique path. Thus, operations on these values can get optimized better because the compiler does not have to take into account that the data could be accessed through another path.

In addition, special interfaces and auxiliary classes provide the ability to process only a certain subset of value arrays or to do some multidimensional processing. In this way, the valarray concept also helps to implement vector and matrix operations and classes.

The Problem of Valarrays

The valarray classes were not designed very well. In fact, nobody tried to determine whether the final specification worked. This happened because nobody felt "responsible" for these classes. The people who introduced valarrays to the C++ standard library left the committee long before the standard was finished. As a consequence, valarrays are rarely used.

For this reason and due to the thickness of this book, the section that presents class valarry is provided as a supplementary chapter at `http://www.cppstdlib.com`.

Chapter 18

Concurrency

Modern system architectures usually support running multiple tasks and multiple threads at the same time. Especially when multiple processor cores are provided, the execution time of programs can significantly improve when multiple threads are used.

However, executing things in parallel also introduces new challenges. Instead of doing one statement after the other, multiple statements can be performed simultaneously, which can result in such problems as concurrently accessing the same resources, so that creations, reads, writes, and deletions don't take place in an expected order and provide unexpected results. In fact, concurrent access to data from multiple threads easily can become a nightmare, with such problems as deadlocks, whereby threads wait for each other, belonging to the simple cases.

Before C++11, there was no support for concurrency in the language and the C++ standard library, although implementations were free to give some guarantees. With C++11, this has changed. Both the core language and the library were improved to support concurrent programming (see Section 4.5, page 55):

- The core language now defines a memory model that guarantees that updates on two different objects used by two different threads are independent of each other, and has introduced a new keyword `thread_local` for defining variables with thread-specific values.

- The library now provides support to start multiple threads, including passing arguments, return values, and exceptions across thread boundaries, as well as means to synchronize multiple threads, so we can synchronize both the control flow and data access.

The library provides its support on different levels. For example, a high-level interface allows you to start a thread including passing arguments and dealing with results and exceptions, which is based on a couple of low-level interfaces for each of these aspects. On the other hand, there are also low-level features, such as mutexes or even atomics dealing with relaxed memory orders.

This chapter introduces these library features. Note that the topic of concurrency and the description of the libraries provided for it can fill books. So, here, I introduce general concepts and typical examples for the average application programmer, with the main focus on the high-level interfaces.

For any details, especially of the tricky low-level problems and features, please refer to the specific books and articles mentioned. My first and major recommendation for this whole topic of concurrency is the book *C++ Concurrency in Action* by Anthony Williams (see [*Williams:C++Conc*]).

Anthony is one of the world key experts on this topic, and this chapter would not have been possible without him. Besides a preview of his book, he provided a first implementation of the standard concurrency library (see [*JustThread*]), wrote several articles, and gave valuable feedback, which all helped me to present this topic in what, hopefully, is a useful way. But in addition, I'd like to thank a few other concurrency experts who helped me to write this chapter: Hans Boehm, Scott Meyers, Bartosz Milewski, Lawrence Crowl, and Peter Sommerlad.

The chapter is organized as follows:

- First, I introduce various ways to start multiple threads. After both the high-level and the low-level interfaces are introduced, details of starting a thread are presented.
- Section 18.4, page 982, offers a detailed discussion of the problem of synchronizing threads. The main problem is concurrent data access.
- Finally, various features to synchronize threads and concurrent data access are discussed:
  - Mutexes and locks (see Section 18.5, page 989), including `call_once()` (see Section 18.5.3, page 1000)
  - Condition variables (see Section 18.6, page 1003)
  - Atomics (see Section 18.7, page 1012)

18.1   The High-Level Interface: `async()` and Futures

For novices, the best starting point to run your program with multiple threads is the high-level interface of the C++ standard library provided by `std::async()` and class `std::future<>`:

- `async()` provides an interface to let a piece of functionality, a *callable object* (see Section 4.4, page 54), run in the background as a separate thread, if possible.
- Class `future<>` allows you to wait for the thread to be finished and provides access to its outcome: return value or exception, if any.

This section introduces this high-level interface in detail, extended by an introduction to class `std::shared_future<>`, which allows you to wait for and process the outcome of a thread at multiple places.

18.1.1   A First Example Using `async()` and Futures

Suppose that we have to compute the sum of two operands returned by two function calls. The usual way to program that would be as follows:

```
func1() + func2()
```

This means that the processing of the operands happens sequentially. The program will first call `func1()` and then call `func2()` or the other way round (according to language rules, the order is undefined). In both cases, the overall processing takes the duration of `func1()` *plus* the duration of *func2()* plus computing the sum.

These days, using the multiprocessor hardware available almost everywhere, we can do better. We can at least try to run `func1()` and `func2()` in parallel so that the overall duration takes only the maximum of the duration of `func1()` and `func2()` plus processing the sum.

Here is a first program doing that:

```
// concurrency/async1.cpp

#include <future>
#include <thread>
#include <chrono>
#include <random>
#include <iostream>
#include <exception>
using namespace std;

int doSomething (char c)
{
    // random-number generator (use c as seed to get different sequences)
    std::default_random_engine dre(c);
    std::uniform_int_distribution<int> id(10,1000);

    // loop to print character after a random period of time
    for (int i=0; i<10; ++i) {
        this_thread::sleep_for(chrono::milliseconds(id(dre)));
        cout.put(c).flush();
    }

    return c;
}

int func1 ()
{
    return doSomething('.');
}

int func2 ()
{
    return doSomething('+');
}

int main()
{
    std::cout << "starting func1() in background"
              << " and func2() in foreground:" << std::endl;
```

```
// start func1() asynchronously (now or later or never):
std::future<int> result1(std::async(func1));

int result2 = func2();      // call func2() synchronously (here and now)

// print result (wait for func1() to finish and add its result to result2
int result = result1.get() + result2;

std::cout << "\nresult of func1()+func2(): " << result
          << std::endl;
}
```

To visualize what happens, we simulate the complex processings in func1() and func2() by calling doSomething(), which from time to time prints a character passed as argument[1] and finally returns the value of the passed character as int. "From time to time" is implemented using a random-number generator to specify intervals, which std::this_thread::sleep_for() uses as timeouts for the current thread (see Section 17.1, page 907, for details of random numbers, and Section 18.3.7, page 981, for details of sleep_for()). Note that we need a unique *seed* for the constructor of the random-number generator (here, we use the passed character c) to ensure that the generated random-number sequences differ.

Instead of calling:

```
int result = func1() + func2();
```

we call:

```
std::future<int> result1(std::async(func1));
int result2 = func2();
int result = result1.get() + result2;
```

So, first, we *try* to start func1() in the background, using std::async(), and assign the result to an object of class std::future:

```
std::future<int> result1(std::async(func1));
```

Here, async() *tries* to start the passed functionality immediately asynchronously in a separate thread. Thus, func1() ideally starts here without blocking the main() function. The returned *future* object is necessary for two reasons:

1. It allows access to the "future" outcome of the functionality passed to async(). This outcome might be either a return value or an exception. The future object has been specialized by the return type of the functionality started. If just a background task was started that returns nothing it has to be std::future<void>.

2. It is necessary to ensure that sooner or later, the passed functionality gets called. Note that I wrote that async() *tries* to start the passed functionality. If this didn't happen we need the future object to force a start when we need the result or want to ensure that the functionality was

---

[1] Output by concurrent threads is possible but might result in interleaved characters (see Section 4.5, page 56).

performed. Thus, you need the future object even if you are not interested in the outcome of a functionality started in the background.

To be able to exchange data between the place that starts and controls the functionality and the returned future object, both refer to a so-called *shared state* (see Section 18.3, page 973).

Of course, you can also, and usually will, use `auto` to declare the future (I explicitly wanted to demonstrate its type here):

```
auto result1(std::async(func1));
```

Second, we start `func2()` in the foreground. This is a normal synchronous function call so that the program blocks here:

```
int result2 = func2();
```

Thus, if `func1()` successfully was started by `async()` and didn't end already, we now have `func1()` and `func2()` running in parallel.

Third, we process the sum. This is the moment when we need the result of `func1()`. To get it, we call `get()` for the returned future:

```
int result = result1.get() + result2;
```

Here, with the call of `get()`, one of three things might happen:

1. If `func1()` was started with `async()` in a separate thread and has already finished, you immediately get its result.
2. If `func1()` was started but has not finished yet, `get()` blocks and waits for its end and yields the result.
3. If `func1()` was not started yet, it will be forced to start now and, like a synchronous function call, `get()` will block until it yields the result.

This behavior is important because it ensures that the program still works on a single-threaded environment or, if for any other reason, it was not possible for `async()` to start a new thread.

A call of `async()` does not guarantee that the passed functionality gets started and finished. If a thread is available, it will start, but if not — maybe your environment does not support multithreading or no more threads are available — the call will be deferred until you explicitly say that you need its outcome (calling `get()`) or just want the passed functionality to get done (calling `wait()`; see Section 18.1.1, page 953).

Thus, the combination of

```
std::future<int> result1(std::async(func1));
```

and

```
result1.get()
```

allows you to optimize a program in a way that, if possible, `func1()` runs in parallel while the next statements in the main thread are processed. If it is not possible to run it in parallel, it will be called sequentially when `get()` gets called. This means that, in any case, it is guaranteed that after `get()`, `func1()` was called either asynchronously or synchronously.

Accordingly, two kinds of outputs are possible for this program. If `async()` could successfully start `func1()`, the output might be something like the following:

```
starting func1() in background and func2() in foreground:
++..++++.++.+.+.....
result of func1()+func2(): 89
```

If `async()` couldn't start `func1()`, it will run after `func2()`, when `get()` gets called, so that the program will have the following output:

```
starting func1() in background and func2() in foreground:
++++++++++..........
result of func1()+func2(): 89
```

So, based on this first example, we can define a general way to make a program faster: You can modify the program so that it might benefit from parallelization, if the underlying platform supports it, but still works as before on single-threaded environments. For this, you have to do the following:

- `#include <future>`
- Pass some functionality that could run on its own in parallel as a *callable object* to `std::async()`
- Assign the result to a `future<ReturnType>` object
- Call `get()` for the `future<>` object when you need the result or want to ensure that the functionality that was started has finished

Note, however, that this applies only when no *data race* occurs, which means that two threads concurrently use the same data resulting in undefined behavior (see Section 18.4.1, page 982).

Note that without calling `get()`, there is no guarantee that `func1()` will ever be called. As written, if `async()` couldn't start the passed functionality immediately, it will *defer* the call so that it gets called only when the outcome of the passed functionality explicitly is requested with `get()` (or `wait()`; see page 953). But without such a request, the termination of `main()` will even terminate the program without ever calling the background thread.

Note also that you have to ensure that you ask for the result of a functionality started with `async()` no earlier than necessary. For example, the following "optimization" is probably not what you want:

```
std::future<int> result1(std::async(func1));
int result = func2() + result1.get();   // might call func2() after func1() ends
```

Because the evaluation order on the right side of the second statement is unspecified, `result1.get()` might be called before `func2()` so that you have sequential processing again.

To have the best effect, in general, your goal should be to maximize the distance between calling `async()` and calling `get()`. Or, to use the terms of [*N3194:Futures*]: *Call early* and *return late*.

If the operation passed to `async()` doesn't return anything, `async()` yields a `future<void>`, which is a partial specialization for `future<>`. In that case, `get()` returns nothing:

```
std::future<void> f(std::async(func));   // try to call func asynchronously
...
f.get();        // wait for func to be done (yields void)
```

Note, finally, that the object passed to `async()` may be any type of a *callable object*: function, member function, function object, or lambda (see Section 4.4, page 54). Thus, you can also pass the functionality that should run in its own thread inline as a lambda (see Section 3.1.10, page 28):

```
std::async([]{ ... })   // try to perform ... asynchronously
```

Using Launch Policies

You can force async() to not defer the passed functionality, by explicitly passing a *launch policy*[2] directing async() that it should definitely start the passed functionality asynchronously the moment it is called:

```
// force func1() to start asynchronously now or throw std::system_error
std::future<long> result1= std::async(std::launch::async, func1);
```

If the asynchronous call is not possible here, the program will throw a std::system_error exception (see Section 4.3.1, page 43) with the error code resource_unavailable_try_again, which is equivalent to the POSIX errno EAGAIN (see Section 4.3.2, page 45).

With the async launch policy, you don't necessarily have to call get() anymore because, if the lifetime of the returned future ends, the program will wait for func1() to finish. Thus, if you don't call get(), leaving the scope of the future object (here the end of main()) will wait for the background task to end. Nevertheless, also calling get() here before a program ends makes the behavior clearer.

If you don't assign the result of std::async(std::launch::async,...) anywhere, the caller will block until the passed functionality has finished, which would mean that this is nothing but a synchronous call.[3]

Likewise, you can force a deferred execution by passing std::launch:deferred as launch policy to async(). In fact, with the following you defer func1() until get() is called for f:

```
std::future<...> f(std::async(std::launch::deferred,
                              func1));    // defer func1 until get()
```

Here, it is guaranteed that func1() never gets called without get() (or wait(); see page 953). This policy especially allows to program *lazy evaluation*. For example:[4]

```
auto f1 = std::async( std::launch::deferred, task1 );
auto f2 = std::async( std::launch::deferred, task2 );
...
auto val = thisOrThatIsTheCase() ? f1.get() : f2.get();
```

In addition, explicitly requesting a deferred launch policy might help to simulate the behavior of async() on a single-threaded environment or simplify debugging (unless race conditions are the problem).

Dealing with Exceptions

So far, we have discussed only the case when threads and background tasks run successfully. However, what happens when an exception occurs?

---

[2] The launch policy is a *scoped enumeration*, so you have to qualify the values (enumerators) with std::launch or launch (see Section 3.1.13, page 32).

[3] Note that there was some controversial understanding and discussion in the standardization committee about how to interpret the current wording if the result of async() is not used. This was the result of the discussion and should be the behavior of all implementations.

[4] Thanks to Lawrence Crowl for pointing this out and providing an example.

The good news is: Nothing special; get() for futures also handles exceptions. In fact, when get() is called and the background operation was or gets terminated by an exception, which was/is not handled inside the thread, this exception gets propagated again. As a result, to deal with exceptions of background operations, just do the same with get() as you would do when calling the operation synchronously.

For example, let's start a background task with an endless loop allocating memory to insert a new list element:[5]

```
// concurrency/async2.cpp

#include <future>
#include <list>
#include <iostream>
#include <exception>
using namespace std;

void task1()
{
    // endless insertion and memory allocation
    // - will sooner or later raise an exception
    // - BEWARE: this is bad practice
    list<int> v;
    while (true) {
        for (int i=0; i<1000000; ++i) {
            v.push_back(i);
        }
        cout.put('.').flush();
    }
}

int main()
{
    cout << "starting 2 tasks" << endl;
    cout << "- task1: process endless loop of memory consumption" << endl;
    cout << "- task2: wait for <return> and then for task1" << endl;

    auto f1 = async(task1);   // start task1() asynchronously (now or later or never)

    cin.get();   // read a character (like getchar())

    cout << "\nwait for the end of task1: " << endl;
    try {
```

---

[5] Trying to consume memory until an exception occurs is bad practice, of course, which on some operating systems might cause trouble. So beware before trying this example out.

```
        f1.get();   // wait for task1() to finish (raises exception if any)
    }
    catch (const exception& e) {
        cerr << "EXCEPTION: " << e.what() << endl;
    }
}
```

Sooner or later, the endless loop will raise an exception (probably a bad_alloc exception; see Section 4.3.1, page 43). This exception will terminate the thread because it isn't caught. The future object will keep this state until get() is called. With get(), the exception gets further propagated inside main().

Now we can summarize the interface of async() and futures as follows: async() gives a programming environment the chance to start in parallel some processing that is used later (where get() is called). In other words, if you have some independent functionality f, you can benefit from parallelization, if possible, by passing f to async() the moment you have all you need to call f and replacing the expression where you need the result or outcome of f by a get() for the future returned by async(). Thus, you have the same behavior but the chance of better performance because f might run in parallel before the outcome of f is needed.

Waiting and Polling

You can call get() for a future<> only once. After get(), the future is in an invalid state, which can be checked only by calling valid() for the future. Any call other than destruction will result in undefined behavior (see Section 18.3.2, page 975, for details).

But futures also provide an interface to wait for a background operation to finish without processing its outcome. This interface is callable more than once and might be combined with a duration or timepoint to limit the amount of waiting time.

Just calling wait() forces the start of a thread a future represents and waits for the termination of the background operation:

```
std::future<...> f(std::async(func));   // try to call func asynchronously
...
f.wait();       // wait for func to be done (might start background task)
```

Two other wait() functions exist for futures, but those functions do *not* force the thread to get started, if it hasn't started yet:

1. With wait_for(), you can wait for a limited time for an asynchronously running operation by passing a duration:

   ```
   std::future<...> f(std::async(func));   // try to call func asynchronously
   ...
   f.wait_for(std::chrono::seconds(10));   // wait at most 10 seconds for func
   ```

2. With wait_until(), you can wait until a specific timepoint has reached:

   ```
   std::future<...> f(std::async(func));   // try to call func asynchronously
   ...
   f.wait_until(std::system_clock::now()+std::chrono::minutes(1));
   ```

Both `wait_for()` and `wait_until()` return one of the following:

- `std::future_status::deferred` if `async()` deferred the operation and no calls to `wait()` or `get()` have yet forced it to start (both function return immediately in this case)
- `std::future_status::timeout` if the operation was started asynchronously but hasn't finished yet (if the waiting expired due to the passed timeout)
- `std::future_status::ready` if the operation has finished

Using `wait_for()` or `wait_until()` especially allows to program so-called *speculative execution*. For example, consider a scenario where we must have a usable result of a computation within a certain time, and it would be nice to have an accurate answer:[6]

```cpp
int quickComputation();      // process result "quick and dirty"
int accurateComputation();   // process result "accurate but slow"

std::future<int> f;   // outside declared because lifetime of accurateComputation()
                      // might exceed lifetime of bestResultInTime()

int bestResultInTime()
{
    // define time slot to get the answer:
    auto tp = std::chrono::system_clock::now() + std::chrono::minutes(1);

    // start both a quick and an accurate computation:
    f = std::async (std::launch::async, accurateComputation);
    int guess = quickComputation();

    // give accurate computation the rest of the time slot:
    std::future_status s = f.wait_until(tp);

    // return the best computation result we have:
    if (s == std::future_status::ready) {
        return f.get();
    }
    else {
        return guess;   // accurateComputation() continues
    }
}
```

Note that the future `f` can't be a local object declared inside `bestResultInTime()` because when the time was too short to finish `accurateComputation()` the destructor of the future would block until that asynchronous task has finished.

By passing a zero duration or a timepoint that has passed, you can simply "poll" to see whether a background task has started and/or is (still) running:

```cpp
future<...> f(async(task));   // try to call task asynchronously
...
```

---

[6] Thanks to Lawrence Crowl for pointing this out and providing an example.

```
// do something while task has not finished (might never happen!)
while (f.wait_for(chrono::seconds(0) != future_status::ready)) {
    ...
}
```

Note, however, that such a loop might never end, because, for example, on single-threaded environments, the call will be deferred until get() is called. So you either should call async() with the std::launch::async launch policy passed as first argument or check explicitly whether wait_for() returns std::future_status::deferred:

```
future<...> f(async(task));    // try to call task asynchronously
...
// check whether task was deferred:
if (f.wait_for(chrono::seconds(0)) != future_status::deferred) {
    // do something while task has not finished
    while (f.wait_for(chrono::seconds(0) != future_status::ready)) {
        ...
    }
}
...
auto r = f.get();    // force execution of task and wait for result (or exception)
```

Another reason for an endless loop here might be that the thread executing the loop has the processor and the other threads are not getting any time to make the future ready. This can reduce the speed of programs dramatically. The quickest fix is to call yield() (see Section 18.3.7, page 981) inside the loop:

```
std::this_thread::yield();    // hint to reschedule to the next thread
```

and/or sleep for a short period of time.

See Section 5.7, page 143, for details of durations and timepoints, which can be passed as arguments to wait_for() and wait_until(). Note that wait_for() and wait_until() usually will differ when dealing with system-time adjustments (see Section 5.7.5, page 160, for details).

18.1.2 An Example of Waiting for Two Tasks

This third program demonstrates a few of the abilities just mentioned:

```
// concurrency/async3.cpp

#include <future>
#include <thread>
#include <chrono>
#include <random>
#include <iostream>
#include <exception>
using namespace std;
```

```cpp
void doSomething (char c)
{
    // random-number generator (use c as seed to get different sequences)
    default_random_engine dre(c);
    uniform_int_distribution<int> id(10,1000);

    // loop to print character after a random period of time
    for (int i=0; i<10; ++i) {
        this_thread::sleep_for(chrono::milliseconds(id(dre)));
        cout.put(c).flush();
    }
}

int main()
{
    cout << "starting 2 operations asynchronously" << endl;

    // start two loops in the background printing characters . or +
    auto f1 = async([]{ doSomething('.'); });
    auto f2 = async([]{ doSomething('+'); });

    // if at least one of the background tasks is running
    if (f1.wait_for(chrono::seconds(0)) != future_status::deferred ||
        f2.wait_for(chrono::seconds(0)) != future_status::deferred) {
        // poll until at least one of the loops finished
        while (f1.wait_for(chrono::seconds(0)) != future_status::ready &&
               f2.wait_for(chrono::seconds(0)) != future_status::ready) {
            ...;
            this_thread::yield();   // hint to reschedule to the next thread
        }
    }
    cout.put('\n').flush();

    // wait for all loops to be finished and process any exception
    try {
        f1.get();
        f2.get();
    }
    catch (const exception& e) {
        cout << "\nEXCEPTION: " << e.what() << endl;
    }
    cout << "\ndone" << endl;
}
```

Again, we have an operation doSomething() that from time to time prints a character passed as argument (see Section 18.1.1, page 948).

Now, with async(), we start doSomething() twice in the background, printing two different characters using different delays generated by the corresponding random-number sequences:

```
auto f1 = std::async([]{ doSomething('.'); });
auto f2 = std::async([]{ doSomething('+'); });
```

Again, in multithreading environments, there would now be two operations simultaneously running that "from time to time" print different characters.

Next, we "poll" to see whether one of the two operations has finished:[7]

```
while (f1.wait_for(chrono::seconds(0)) != future_status::ready &&
       f2.wait_for(chrono::seconds(0)) != future_status::ready) {
    ...
    this_thread::yield();    // hint to reschedule to the next thread
}
```

However, because this loop would never end if neither of the tasks were launched in the background when async() was called, we first have to check whether at least one operation was not deferred:

```
if (f1.wait_for(chrono::seconds(0)) != future_status::deferred ||
    f2.wait_for(chrono::seconds(0)) != future_status::deferred) {
    ...
}
```

Alternatively, we could call async() with the std::launch:async launch policy.

When at least one background operation has finished or none of them was started, we write a newline character and then wait for both loops to end:

```
f1.get();
f2.get();
```

We use get() here to process any exception that might have occurred.

In a multithreading environment, the program might, for example, have the following output:

```
starting 2 operations asynchronously
++.++..+.+..++.+.+
..
done
```

Note that regarding the order of all three characters ., +, and *newline*, nothing is guaranteed. It might be typical that the first character is a dot because this is the output from the first operation started — thus, started a little bit earlier — but as you can see here, a + might also come first. The characters . and + might be mixed, but this also is not guaranteed. In fact, if you remove the sleep_for() statement, which enforces the delay between each printing of the passed character, the first loop is done before the first context switch to the other thread, so the output might more likely become:

---

[7] Without doing something useful inside the loop, this would just be busy waiting, which means that the problem would be better solved with condition variables (see Section 18.6.1, page 1003).

```
starting 2 operations asynchronously
..........
++++++++++
done
```

This output will also result if the environment doesn't support multithreading, because in that case, both calls of doSomething() will be called synchronously with the calls of get().

Also, it is not clear when the newline character gets printed. This might happen before any other characters are written if the execution of both background tasks is deferred until get() is called. Then the deferred tasks will be called one after the other:

```
starting 2 operations asynchronously

..........++++++++++
done
```

The only thing we know is that newline won't be printed before one of the loops has finished. It is not even guaranteed that newline comes directly after the last character of one of the sequences, because it might take some time until the end of one of the loops is recorded in the corresponding future object and this recorded state is evaluated (note that this is not real-time processing). For this reason, you might have an output where a couple of + characters are written after the last dot and before the newline character:

```
starting 2 operations asynchronously
.+..+..+..+.+..++
+++
done
```

Passing Arguments

The previous example demonstrated one way to pass arguments to a background task: You simply use a lambda (see Section 3.1.10, page 28), which calls the background functionality:

```
auto f1 = std::async([]{ doSomething('.'); });
```

Of course, you can also pass arguments that existed before the async() statement. As usual, you can pass them by value or by reference:

```
char c = '@';
auto f = std::async([=]{        // =: can access objects in scope by value
                    doSomething(c);   // pass copy of c to doSomething()
                });
```

By defining the *capture* as [=], you pass a *copy* of c and all other visible objects to the lambda, so inside the lambda you can pass this copy of c to doSomething().

However, there are other ways to pass arguments to async() because async() provides the usual interface for *callable objects* (see Section 4.4, page 54). For example, if you pass a function pointer as the first argument to async(), you can pass multiple additional arguments, which are passed as parameters to the function called:

```
char c = '@';
auto f = std::async(doSomething,c);    // call doSomething(c) asynchronously
```

You can also pass arguments by reference, but the risk of doing so is that the values passed become invalid before the background task even starts. This applies to both lambdas and functions directly called:

```
char c = '@';
auto f = std::async([&]{ doSomething(c); });    // risky!
```

```
char c = '@';
auto f = std::async(doSomething,std::ref(c));    // risky!
```

If you control the lifetime of the argument passed so that it exceeds the background task, you can do it. For example:

```
void doSomething (const char& c);    // pass character by reference
...
char c = '@';
auto f = std::async([&]{ doSomething(c); });    // pass c by reference
...
f.get();    // needs lifetime of c until here
```

But beware: If you pass arguments by reference to be able to modify them from a separate thread, you can easily run into undefined behavior. Consider the following example where after trying to start an output loop for printing a character in the background you switch the character printed:

```
void doSomething (const char& c);    // pass character by reference
...
char c = '@';
auto f = std::async([&]{ doSomething(c); });    // pass c by reference
...
c = '_';    // switch output of doSomething() to underscores, if it still runs
f.get();    // needs lifetime of c until here
```

First, the order of accessing c here and in doSomething() is undefined. Thus, the switch of the output character might come before, in the middle of, or after the output loop. Even worse, because we modify c in one thread and another thread reads c, this is a nonsynchronized concurrent access to the same object (a so-called *data race*, see Section 18.4.1, page 982), which results in undefined behavior unless you protect the concurrent access by using mutexes (see Section 18.5, page 989) or atomics (see Section 18.7, page 1012).

So, let me make clear: **If you start to use** `async()`, **you should pass** *all* **objects necessary to process the passed functionality** *by value* **so that** `async()` **uses only** *local copies.* If copying is too expensive, ensure that the objects are passed as constant reference and that `mutable` is not used. In any other case, read Section 18.4, page 982, and make sure that you understand the implications of your approach.

You can also pass a pointer to a member function to *async()*. In that case, the first argument after the member function has to be a reference or a pointer to the object for which the member function gets called:

```
class X
{
  public:
    void mem (int num);
    ...
};
...


X x;
auto a = std::async(&X::mem, x, 42);   // try to call x.mem(42) asynchronously
...
```

18.1.3 Shared Futures

As we have seen, class `std::future` provides the ability to process the future outcome of a concurrent computation. However, you can process this outcome only once. A second call of `get()` results in undefined behavior (according to the C++ standard library, implementations are encouraged but not required to throw a `std::future_error`).

However, it sometimes makes sense to process the outcome of a concurrent computation more than once, especially when multiple other threads process this outcome. For this purpose, the C++ standard library provides class `std::shared_future`. Here, multiple `get()` calls are possible and yield the same result or throw the same exception.

Consider the following example:

// concurrency/sharedfuture1.cpp

```cpp
#include <future>
#include <thread>
#include <iostream>
#include <exception>
#include <stdexcept>
using namespace std;

int queryNumber ()
{
    // read number
    cout << "read number: ";
    int num;
    cin >> num;

    // throw exception if none
    if (!cin) {
        throw runtime_error("no number read");
```

```
    }

    return num;
}

void doSomething (char c, shared_future<int> f)
{
    try {
        // wait for number of characters to print
        int num = f.get();   // get result of queryNumber()

        for (int i=0; i<num; ++i) {
            this_thread::sleep_for(chrono::milliseconds(100));
            cout.put(c).flush();
        }
    }
    catch (const exception& e) {
        cerr << "EXCEPTION in thread " << this_thread::get_id()
                 << ": " << e.what() << endl;
    }
}

int main()
{
    try {
        // start one thread to query a number
        shared_future<int> f = async(queryNumber);

        // start three threads each processing this number in a loop
        auto f1 = async(launch::async,doSomething,'.',f);
        auto f2 = async(launch::async,doSomething,'+',f);
        auto f3 = async(launch::async,doSomething,'*',f);

        // wait for all loops to be finished
        f1.get();
        f2.get();
        f3.get();
    }
    catch (const exception& e) {
        cout << "\nEXCEPTION: " << e.what() << endl;
    }
    cout << "\ndone" << endl;
}
```

In this example, one thread calls queryNumber() to query an integral value, which is then used by other threads already running. To perform this task, the result of std::async(), which starts the query thread, gets assigned to a shared_future object, specialized for the return value:

```
shared_future<int> f = async(queryNumber);
```

Thus, a shared future can be initialized by an ordinary future, which moves the state from the future to the shared future. To be able to use auto for this declaration, you can, alternatively, use the share() member function:

```
auto f = async(queryNumber).share();
```

Internally, all shared future objects share the *shared state*, which async() creates to store the outcome of the passed functionality (and store the functionality itself if it is deferred).

The shared future is then passed to the other threads, starting doSomething() with the shared future as second argument:

```
auto f1 = async(launch::async,doSomething,'.',f);
auto f2 = async(launch::async,doSomething,'+',f);
auto f3 = async(launch::async,doSomething,'*',f);
```

Inside each call of doSomething(), we wait for and process the result of queryNumber() by calling get() for the shared future passed:

```
void doSomething (char c, shared_future<int> f)
{
    try {
        int num = f.get();   // get result of queryNumber()
        ...
    }
    catch (const exception& e) {
        cerr << "EXCEPTION in thread " << this_thread::get_id()
                  << ": " << e.what() << endl;
    }
}
```

If queryNumber() throws an exception, which happens if no integral value could be read, each call of doSomething() will get this exception with f.get(), so that the corresponding exception handling will occur.

Thus, after reading the value 5 as input, the output might be:

```
read number: 5
*+.*+.*.+*+.*.+
done
```

But if typing 'x' as input, the output might be:

```
read number: x
EXCEPTION in thread 3: no number read
EXCEPTION in thread 4: no number read
EXCEPTION in thread 2: no number read

done
```

Note that the order of the thread outputs and the ID values are undefined (see Section 18.2.1, page 967, for details about thread IDs).

Also note that there is a minor difference in the declaration of `get()` between `future` and `shared_future`:

- For class `future<>`, `get()` is provided as follows (T is the type of the returned value):

    ```
    T future<T>::get();              // general get()
    T& future<T&>::get();            // specialization for references
    void future<void>::get();        // specialization for void
    ```

    where the first form returns the moved result or a copy of the result.

- For class `shared_future<>`, `get()` is provided as follows:

    ```
    const T& shared_future<T>::get();   // general get()
    T& shared_future<T&>::get();        // specialization for references
    void shared_future<void>::get();    // specialization for void
    ```

    where the first form returns a reference to the result value stored in the shared *shared state*.

Or, as [*N3194:Futures*] states:

"The single-use value `get()` is move optimized (e.g., `std::vector<int> v = f.get()`). ...

 The const reference `get()` is access optimized (e.g., `int i = f.get()[3]`)."

This design introduces the risk of lifetime or data race issues if returned values are modified (see Section 18.3.3, page 977, for details).

You could also pass a shared future by reference (that is, declare it as reference and use `std::ref()` to pass it):

```
void doSomething (char c, const shared_future<int>& f)
auto f1 = async(launch::async,doSomething,'.',std::ref(f));
```

Now, instead of using multiple shared future objects all sharing the same *shared state*, you'd use one shared future object to perform multiple `get()`'s (one in each thread). However, this approach is more risky. As a programmer you have to ensure that the lifetime of `f` (yes, `f`, not the *shared state* it refers to) is not smaller than for the threads started. In addition, note that the member functions of shared futures do not synchronize with themselves, although the shared *shared state* is synchronized. So, if you do more than just read data, you might need external synchronization techniques (see Section 18.4, page 982) to avoid *data races*, which would result in undefined behavior. Or as Lawrence Crowl, one of the authors of the concurrency library, wrote in a private communication: "If the code stays tightly coordinated, passing by reference is fine. If the code may propagate into regions with an incomplete understanding of the purpose and restrictions, passing by value is better. Copying the shared future is expensive, but not so expensive as to justify a latent bug in a large system."

For further details of class `shared_future` see Section 18.3.3, page 976.

18.2   The Low-Level Interface: Threads and Promises

Besides the high-level interface of `async()` and (shared) futures, the C++ standard library provides a low-level interface to start threads and deal with them.

18.2.1   Class `std::thread`

To start a thread, you simply have to declare an object of class `std::thread` and pass the desired task as initial argument, and then either wait for its end or *detach* it:

```
void doSomething();

std::thread t(doSomething);   // start doSomething() in the background
...
t.join();   // wait for t to finish (block until doSomething() ends)
```

As for `async()`, you can pass anything that's a *callable object* (function, member function, function object, lambda; see Section 4.4, page 54) together with possible additional arguments. However, note again that unless you really know what you are doing, you should pass *all* objects necessary to process the passed functionality *by value* so that the `thread` uses only *local copies* (see Section 18.4, page 982, for some of the problems that might occur otherwise).

In addition, this is a low-level interface, so the interesting thing is what this interface does *not* provide compared to `async()` (see Section 18.1, page 946):

- Class `thread` doesn't have a launch policy. The C++ standard library always tries to start the passed functionality in a new thread. If this isn't possible, it throws a `std::system_error` (see Section 4.3.1, page 43) with the error code `resource_unavailable_try_again` (see Section 4.3.2, page 45).

- You have no interface to process the result or outcome of the thread. The only thing you can get is a unique thread ID (see Section 18.2.1, page 967).

- If an exception occurs that is not caught inside the thread, the program immediately aborts, calling `std::terminate()` (see Section 5.8.2, page 162). To pass exceptions to a context outside the thread `exception_ptrs` (see Section 4.3.3, page 52) have to be used.

- You have to declare whether, as a caller, you want to wait for the end of the thread (calling `join()`) or to *detach* from the thread started to let it run in the background without any control (calling `detach()`). If you don't do this before the lifetime of the thread object ends or a move assignment to it happens, the program aborts, calling `std::terminate()` (see Section 5.8.2, page 162).

- If you let the thread run in the background and `main()` ends, all threads are terminated abruptly.

Here is a first complete example:

```
// concurrency/thread1.cpp

#include <thread>
#include <chrono>
```

```
#include <random>
#include <iostream>
#include <exception>
using namespace std;

void doSomething (int num, char c)
{
    try {
        // random-number generator (use c as seed to get different sequences)
        default_random_engine dre(42*c);
        uniform_int_distribution<int> id(10,1000);
        for (int i=0; i<num; ++i) {
            this_thread::sleep_for(chrono::milliseconds(id(dre)));
            cout.put(c).flush();
            ...
        }
    }
    // make sure no exception leaves the thread and terminates the program
    catch (const exception& e) {
        cerr << "THREAD-EXCEPTION (thread "
            << this_thread::get_id() << "): " << e.what() << endl;
    }
    catch (...) {
        cerr << "THREAD-EXCEPTION (thread "
            << this_thread::get_id() << ")" << endl;
    }
}

int main()
{
    try {
        thread t1(doSomething,5,'.');   // print five dots in separate thread
        cout << "- started fg thread " << t1.get_id() << endl;

        // print other characters in other background threads
        for (int i=0; i<5; ++i) {
            thread t(doSomething,10,'a'+i); // print 10 chars in separate thread
            cout << "- detach started bg thread " << t.get_id() << endl;
            t.detach();   // detach thread into the background
        }

        cin.get();   // wait for any input (return)
```

```
        cout << "- join fg thread " << t1.get_id() << endl;
        t1.join();    // wait for t1 to finish
    }
    catch (const exception& e) {
        cerr << "EXCEPTION: " << e.what() << endl;
    }
}
```

Here, in `main()`, we start a couple of threads that perform the statements of `doSomething()`. Both `main()` and `doSomething()` have corresponding try-catch clauses for the following reasons:

- In `main()`, creating a thread might throw a `std::system_error` (see Section 4.3.1, page 43) with the error code `resource_unavailable_try_again`.
- In `doSomething()`, started as `std::thread`, any uncaught exception would cause the program to terminate.

For the first thread started in `main()`, we later wait for it to finish:

```
    thread t1(doSomething,5,'.');    // print five dots in separate thread
    ...
    t1.join();                        // wait for t1 to finish
```

The other threads are detached after they were started, so they still might be running at the end of `main()`:

```
    for (int i=0; i<5; ++i) {
        thread t(doSomething,10,'a'+i);    // print 10 chars in separate thread
        t.detach();                        // detach thread into the background
    }
```

As a consequence, the program would immediately terminate all background threads when `main()` ends, which is the case when, due to `cin.get()`, some input could be read, *and* due to `t1.join()`, the fifth dot as last character of the thread performing `doSomething(5,'.')` was written. Because the waiting for the input and the printing of the dots run in parallel, it doesn't matter what happens first.

For example, the program might have the following output if I press *Return* after the second dot was printed:

```
- started fg thread 1
- detach started bg thread 2
- detach started bg thread 3
- detach started bg thread 4
- detach started bg thread 5
- detach started bg thread 6
ecad.dbcebabd.a
- join fg thread 1
b.ceade.bbcadbe.
```

Beware of Detached Threads

Detached threads can easily become a problem if they use nonlocal resources. The problem is that you lose control of a detached thread and have no easy way to find out whether and how long it runs. Thus, make sure that a detached thread does not access any objects after their lifetime has ended. For this reason, passing variables and objects to a thread by reference is always a risk. Passing arguments by value is strongly recommended.

Note, however, that the lifetime problem also applies to global and static objects, because when the program exits, the detached thread might still run, which means that it might access global or static objects that are already destroyed or under destruction. Unfortunately, this would result in undefined behavior.[8]

So, as a general rule for detached threads, take into account the following:

- Detached threads should prefer to access local copies only.
- If a detached thread uses a global or static object, you should do one of the following:
  - Ensure that these global/static objects are not destroyed before all detached threads accessing them are finished (or finished accessing them). One approach to ensure this is to use condition variables (see Section 18.6, page 1003), which the detached threads use to signal that they have finished. Before leaving `main()` or calling `exit()`, you'd have to set these condition variables then to signal that a destruction is possible.[9]
  - End the program by calling `quick_exit()`, which was introduced exactly for this reason to end a program without calling the destructors for global and static objects (see Section 5.8.2, page 162).

Because `std::cin`, `std::cout`, and `std::cerr` and the other global stream objects (see Section 15.2.2, page 751) according to the standard "are not destroyed during program execution," access to these objects in detached threads should introduce no undefined behavior. However, other problems, such as interleaved characters, might occur.

Nevertheless, as a rule of thumb keep in mind that the only safe way to terminate a detached thread is with one of the "...`at_thread_exit()`" functions, which force the main thread to wait for the detached thread to truly finish. Or you can just ignore this feature, according to a reviewer who wrote: "Detached threads is one of those things that should be moved into the chapter on dangerous features that almost no one needs."

Thread IDs

As you can see, the program prints thread IDs provided either by the thread object or inside a thread, using namespace `this_thread` (also provided by `<thread>`):

```
void doSomething (int num, char c)
{
    ...
```

---

[8] Thanks to Hans Boehm and Anthony Williams for pointing out this problem.

[9] Ideally, you should use `notify_all_at_thread_exit()` (see Section 18.6.4, page 1011) to set the condition variable to ensure that all thread local variables are destructed.

```
        cerr << "THREAD-EXCEPTION (thread "
             << this_thread::get_id() << ")" << endl;
        ...
    }
```

```
    thread t(doSomething,5,'.');    // print five dots in separate thread
    cout << "- started fg thread " << t1.get_id() << endl;
```

This ID is a special type `std::thread::id`, which is guaranteed to be unique for each thread. In addition, class `id` has a default constructor that yields a unique ID representing "no thread":

```
    std::cout << "ID of \"no thread\": " << std::thread::id()
              << std::endl;
```

The only operations allowed for thread IDs are comparisons and calling the output operator for a stream. You should not make any further assumptions, such as that "no thread" has ID 0 or the main thread has ID 1. In fact, an implementation might generate these IDs on the fly when they are requested, not when the threads are started, so the number of the main thread depends on the number of requests for thread IDs before. So, the following code:

```
    std::thread t1(doSomething,5,'.');
    std::thread t2(doSomething,5,'+');
    std::thread t3(doSomething,5,'*');
    std::cout << "t3 ID:       " << t3.get_id() << std::endl;
    std::cout << "main ID:     " << std::this_thread::get_id() << std::endl;
    std::cout << "nothread ID: " << std::thread::id() << std::endl;
```

might print:

```
    t3 ID:        1
    main ID:      4
    nothread ID: 0
```

or:

```
    t3 ID:        3
    main ID:      4
    nothread ID: 0
```

or:

```
    t3 ID:        1
    main ID:      2
    nothread ID: 3
```

or even characters as thread IDs.

Thus, the only way to identify a thread, such as a master thread, is to compare it to its saved ID when it was started:

```
    std::thread::id masterThreadID;
```

```
void doSomething()
{
    if (std::this_thread::get_id() == masterThreadID) {
        ...
    }
    ...
}

std::thread master(doSomething);
masterThreadID = master.get_id();
...
std::thread slave(doSomething);
...
```

Note that IDs of terminated threads might be reused again.

For further details of class `thread`, see Section 18.3.6, page 979.

18.2.2 Promises

Now the question arises as to how you can pass parameters and handle exceptions between threads (which also explains how a high-level interface, such as `async()`, is implemented). Of course, to pass values to a thread, you can simply pass them as arguments. And if you need a result, you can pass *return arguments* by reference, just as described for `async()` (see Section 18.1.2, page 958).

However, another general mechanism is provided to pass result values and exceptions as outcomes of a thread: class `std::promise`. A promise object is the counterpart of a *future* object. Both are able to temporarily hold a *shared state*, representing a (result) value or an exception. While the future object allows you to retrieve the data (using `get()`), the promise object enables you to provide the data (by using one of its `set_...()` functions). The following example demonstrates this:

```
// concurrency/promise1.cpp

#include <thread>
#include <future>
#include <iostream>
#include <string>
#include <exception>
#include <stdexcept>
#include <functional>
#include <utility>

void doSomething (std::promise<std::string>& p)
{
    try {
        // read character and throw exceptiopn if 'x'
```

```cpp
        std::cout << "read char ('x' for exception): ";
        char c = std::cin.get();
        if (c == 'x') {
            throw std::runtime_error(std::string("char ")+c+" read");
        }
        ...
        std::string s = std::string("char ") + c + " processed";
        p.set_value(std::move(s));        // store result
    }
    catch (...) {
        p.set_exception(std::current_exception());   // store exception
    }
}


int main()
{
    try {
        // start thread using a promise to store the outcome
        std::promise<std::string> p;
        std::thread t(doSomething,std::ref(p));
        t.detach();
        ...

        // create a future to process the outcome
        std::future<std::string> f(p.get_future());

        // process the outcome
        std::cout << "result: " << f.get() << std::endl;
    }
    catch (const std::exception& e) {
        std::cerr << "EXCEPTION: " << e.what() << std::endl;
    }
    catch (...) {
        std::cerr << "EXCEPTION " << std::endl;
    }
}
```

After including `<future>`, where promises also are declared, you can declare a promise object, specialized for the value to hold or return (or `void` if none):

```cpp
    std::promise<std::string> p;   // hold string result or exception
```

The promise internally creates a *shared state* (see Section 18.3, page 973), which can be used here to store a value of the corresponding type or an exception, and can be used in a future object to retrieve this data as the outcome of the thread.

This promise is then passed to a task running as a separate thread:

```
std::thread t(doSomething,std::ref(p));
```

By using `std::ref()` (see Section 5.4.3, page 132), we ensure that the promise is passed by reference so that we can manipulate its state (copying is not possible for promises).

Now, inside the thread, we can store either a value or an exception by calling `set_value()` or `set_exception()`, respectively:

```
void doSomething (std::promise<std::string>& p)
{
    try {
        ...
        p.set_value(std::move(s));      // store result
    }
    catch (...) {
        p.set_exception(std::current_exception());   // store exception
    }
}
```

To store an exception, the convenience function `std::current_exception()`, which is defined in `<exception>`, is used (see Section 4.3.3, page 52). It yields the currently handled exception as type `std::exception_ptr` or `nullptr` if we currently do not handle an exception. The promise object stores this exception internally.

The moment we store a value or an exception in a *shared state*, it becomes *ready*. Thus, you can now retrieve its value somewhere else. But for the retrieval, we need a corresponding future object sharing the same *shared state*. For this reason, inside `main()`, by calling `get_future()` for the promise object we create a future object, which has the usual semantics introduced in Section 18.1, page 946. We could also have created the future object before starting the thread:

```
std::future<std::string> f(p.get_future());
```

Now, with `get()`, we either get the stored result or the stored exception gets rethrown (internally, calling `std::rethrow_exception()` for the stored `exception_ptr`):

```
f.get();   // process the outcome of the thread
```

Note that `get()` blocks until the *shared state* is *ready*, which is exactly the case when `set_value()` or `set_exception()` was performed for the promise. It does *not* mean that the thread setting the promise has ended. The thread might still perform other statements, such as even store additional outcomes into other promises.

If you want the *shared state* to become *ready* when the thread really ends — to ensure the cleanup of thread local objects and other stuff before the result gets processed — you have to call `set_value_at_thread_exit()` or `set_exception_at_thread_exit()` instead:

```
void doSomething (std::promise<std::string>& p)
{
```

```
        try {
            ...
            p.set_value_at_thread_exit(std::move(s));
        }
        catch (...) {
            p.set_exception_at_thread_exit(std::current_exception());
        }
    }
```

Note that using promises and futures is not limited to multithreading problems. Even in single-threaded applications, we could use a promise to hold a result/value or an exception that we want to process later by using a future.

Note also that we can't store both a value and an exception. Any attempt to do this would result in a `std::future_error` with the error code `std::future_errc::promise_already_satisfied` (see Section 4.3.1, page 43).

For further details of class `promise`, see Section 18.3.4, page 977.

18.2.3   Class `packaged_task<>`

`async()` gives you a handle to deal with the outcome of a task that you try to start immediately in the background. Sometimes, however, you need to process the outcome of a background task that you don't necessarily start immediately. For example, another instance, such as a thread pool, might control when and how many background tasks run simultaneously. In this case, instead of

```
    double compute (int x, int y);

    std::future<double> f = std::async(compute,7,5);   // try to start a background task
    ...
    double res = f.get();    // wait for its end and process result/exception
```

you can program:

```
    double compute (int x, int y);

    std::packaged_task<double(int,int)> task(compute);   // create a task
    std::future<double> f = task.get_future();            // get its future
    ...
    task(7,5);                 // start the task (typically in a separate thread)
    ...
    double res = f.get();    // wait for its end and process result/exception
```

where the task itself is usually, but not necessarily, started in a separate thread.

Thus, class `std::packaged_task<>`, also defined in `<future>`, holds both the functionality to perform and its possible outcome (the so-called *shared state* of the functionality; see Section 18.3, page 973).

For further details of class `packaged_task`, see Section 18.3.5, page 977.

18.3 Starting a Thread in Detail

Having introduced the high- and low-level interfaces to (possibly) start threads and deal with return values or exceptions, let's summarize the concepts and provide some details not mentioned yet.

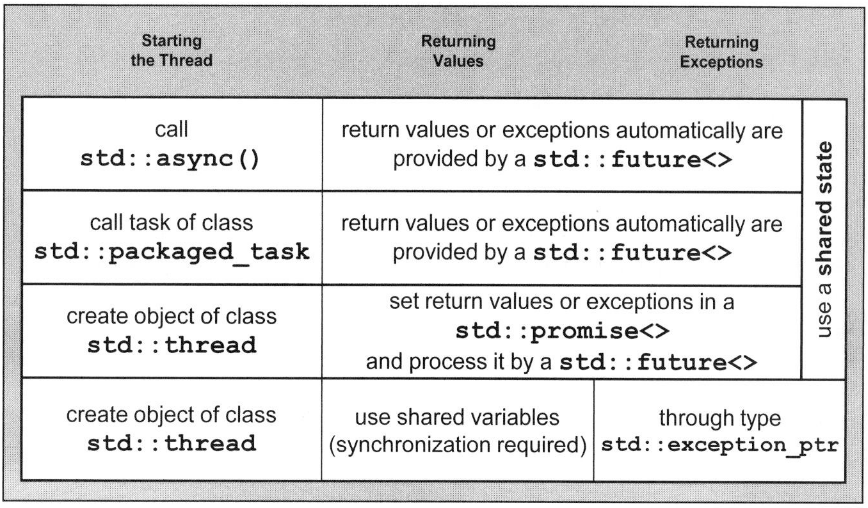

Starting the Thread	Returning Values	Returning Exceptions
call **std::async()**	return values or exceptions automatically are provided by a **std::future<>**	use a shared state
call task of class **std::packaged_task**	return values or exceptions automatically are provided by a **std::future<>**	
create object of class **std::thread**	set return values or exceptions in a **std::promise<>** and process it by a **std::future<>**	
create object of class **std::thread**	use shared variables (synchronization required)	through type **std::exception_ptr**

Figure 18.1. Layers of Thread Interfaces

Conceptionally, we have the following layers to start threads and deal with their return values or exceptions (see Figure 18.1):

- With the low-level interface of class `thread`, we can start a thread. To return data, we need shared variables (global or static or passed as argument). To return exceptions, we could use the type `std::exception_ptr`, which is returned by `std::current_exception()` and can be processed by `std::rethrow_exception()` (see Section 4.3.3, page 52).

- The concept of a *shared state* allows us to deal with return values or exceptions in a more convenient way. With the low-level interface of a `promise`, we can create such a *shared state*, which we can process by using a `future`.

- At a higher level, with class `packaged_task` or `async()`, the *shared state* is automatically created and set with a return statement or an uncaught exception.

- With `packaged_task`, we can create an object with a *shared state* where we explicitly have to program when to start the thread.

- With `std::async()`, we don't have to care when the thread exactly gets started. The only thing we know is that we have to call `get()` when we need the outcome.

Shared States

As you can see, a central concept used by almost all these features is a *shared state*. It allows the objects that start and control a background functionality (a promise, a packaged task, or `async()`) to communicate with the objects that process its outcome (a future or a shared future). Thus, a shared state is able to hold the functionality to start, some state information, and its outcome (a return value or an exception).

A *shared state* is *ready* when it holds the outcome of its functionality (when a value or an exception is ready for retrieval). A shared state is usually implemented as a reference-counted object that gets destroyed when the last object referring to it *releases* it.

18.3.1 `async()` in Detail

In general, as introduced in Section 18.1, page 946, `std::async()` is a convenience function to start some functionality in its own thread *if possible*. As a result, you can parallelize functionality if the underlying platform supports it but not lose any functionality if it doesn't.

However, the exact behavior of `async()` is complex and highly depends on the launch policy, which can be passed as the first optional argument. For this reason, each of the three standardized forms of how `async()` can be called as described here from an application programmer's point of view:

future **async** (`std::launch::async`, *F func*, *args...*)

- Tries to start *func* with *args* as an asynchronous task (parallel thread).
- If this is not possible, it throws an exception of type `std::system_error` with the error code `std::errc::resource_unavailable_try_again` (see Section 4.3.1, page 43).
- Unless the program aborts, the started thread is guaranteed to finish before the program ends.
- The thread will finish:
  - If `get()` or `wait()` is called for the returned future
  - If the last object that refers to the *shared state* represented by the returned future gets destructed
- This implies that the call of `async()` will block until *func* has finished if the return value of `async()` is not used.

future **async** (`std::launch::deferred`, *F func*, *args...*)

- Passes *func* with *args* as a "deferred" task, which gets synchronously called when `wait()` or `get()` for the returned future gets called.
- If neither `wait()` nor `get()` is called, the task will never start.

future **async** (*F func*, *args...*)

- Is a combination of calling `async()` with launch policies `std::launch:async` and `std::launch::deferred`. According to the current situation, one of the two forms gets chosen. Thus, `async()` will *defer* the call of *func* if an immediate call in `async` launch policy is not possible.
- Thus, if `async()` can start a new thread for *func*, it gets started. Otherwise, *func* is deferred until `get()` or `wait()` gets called for the returned future.

- The only guarantee this call gives is that after calling `get()` or `wait()` for the returned future, *func* will have been called and finished.

- Without calling `get()` or `wait()` for the returned future, *func* might never get called.

- Note that this form of `async()` will not throw a `system_error` exception if it can't call *func* asynchronously (it might throw a system error for other reasons, though).

For all these forms of `async()`, *func* might be a *callable object* (function, member function, function object, lambda; see Section 4.4, page 54). See Section 18.1.2, page 958, for some examples.

Passing a launch policy of `std::launch::async|std::launch::deferred` to `async()` results in the same behavior as passing no launching policy. Passing 0 as launch policy results in undefined behavior (this case is not covered by the C++ standard library, and different implementations behave differently).

18.3.2 Futures in Detail

Class `future<>`,[10] introduced in Section 18.1, page 946, represents the *outcome* of an operation. It can be a return value or an exception but not both. The outcome is managed in a *shared state*, which in general can be created by `std::async()`, a `std::packaged_task`, or a promise. The outcome might not exist yet; thus, the future might also hold everything necessary to generate the outcome.

If the future was returned by `async()` (see Section 18.3.1, page 974) and the associated task was *deferred*, `get()` or `wait()` will start it synchronously. Note that `wait_for()` and `wait_until()` do *not* start a deferred task.

The outcome can be retrieved only once. For this reason, a future might have a valid or invalid state: *valid* means that there is an associated operation for which the result or exception was not retrieved yet.

Table 18.1 lists the operations available for class `future<>`.

Note that the return value of `get()` depends on the type `future<>` is specialized with:

- If it is `void`, `get()` also has type `void` and returns nothing.

- If the future is parametrized with a reference type, `get()` returns a reference to the return value.

- Otherwise, `get()` returns a copy or move assigns the return value, depending on whether the return type supports move assignment semantics.

Note that you can call `get()` only once, because `get()` invalidates the future's state.

For a future that has an invalid state, calling anything else but the destructor, the move assignment operator, or `valid()` results in undefined behavior. For this case, the standard recommends throwing an exception of type `future_error` (see Section 4.3.1, page 43) with the code `std::future_errc::no_state`, but this is not required.

Note that neither a copy constructor nor a copy assignment operator is provided, ensuring that no two objects can share the state of a background operation. You can move the state to another future object only by calling the move constructor or the move assignment operator. However, the state

---

[10] Originally, the class was named `unique_future` in the standardization process.

Operation	Effect
future *f*	Default constructor; creates a future with an invalid state
future *f*(*rv*)	Move constructor; creates a new future, which gets the state of *rv*, and invalidates the state of *rv*
f.~*future*()	Destroys the state and destroys `*this`
f = *rv*	Move assignment; destroys the old state of *f*, gets the state of *rv*, and invalidates the state of *rv*
f.valid()	Yields `true` if *f* has a valid state, so you can call the following member functions
f.get()	Blocks until the background operation is done (forcing a *deferred* associated functionality to start synchronously), yields the result (if any) or raises any exception that occurred, and invalidates its state
f.wait()	Blocks until the background operation is done (forcing a *deferred* associated functionality to start synchronously)
f.wait_for(*dur*)	Blocks for duration *dur* or until the background operation is done (a *deferred* thread is *not* forced to start)
f.wait_until(*tp*)	Blocks until timepoint *tp* or until the background operation is done (a *deferred* thread is *not* forced to start)
f.share()	Yields a `shared_future` with the current state and invalidates the state of *f*

Table 18.1. Operations of Class `future<>`

of background tasks can be shared in multiple objects by using a `shared_future` object, which `share()` yields.

If the destructor is called for a future that is the last owner of a shared state and the associated task has started but not finished yet, the destructor blocks until the end of the task.

18.3.3   Shared Futures in Detail

Class `shared_future<>` (introduced in Section 18.1.3, page 960) provides the same semantics and interface as class `future` (see Section 18.3.2, page 975) with the following differences:

- Multiple calls of `get()` are allowed. Thus, `get()` does not invalidate its state.
- Copy semantics (copy constructor, copy assignment operator) are supported.
- `get()` is a *constant* member function returning a `const` reference to the value stored in the *shared state* (which means that you have to ensure that the lifetime of the returned reference is shorter than the *shared state*). For class `std::future`, `get()` is a *nonconstant* member function returning a move-assigned copy (or a copy if that's not supported), unless the class is specialized by a reference type.
- Member `share()` is not provided.

The fact that the return value of get() is not copied creates some risks. Besides lifetime issues, data races are possible. Data races occur with unclear order of conflicting actions on the same data, such as nonsynchronized reads and writes from multiple threads, and result in undefined behavior (see Section 18.4.1, page 982).

The same problem applies to exceptions. One example discussed during the standardization was when an exception was caught by reference and then modified:

```
try {
    shared_future<void> sp = async(f);
    sp.get();
}
catch (E& e) {
    e.modify();   // risk of undefined behavior due to a data race
}
```

This code introduces a data race if another thread processes the exception. To solve this issue, it was proposed to require that current_exception() and rethrow_exception(), which are used internally to pass exceptions between threads, create copies of the exceptions. However, the costs for this change were considered too high. As a result, programmers have to know what they're doing when dealing with nonconstant references used in different threads.

18.3.4 Class `std::promise` in Detail

An object of class std::promise, introduced in Section 18.2.2, page 969, is provided to temporarily hold a (return) value or an exception. Or, in general, a promise can hold a *shared state* (see Section 18.3, page 973). The *shared state* is said to be *ready* if it holds a value or an exception. Table 18.2 lists the operations available for class promise.

Note that you can call get_future() only once. A second call throws a std::future_error with the error code std::future_errc::future_already_retrieved. In general, if no *shared state* is associated, a std::future_error with the error code std::future_errc::no_state might be thrown.

All member functions that set the value or exception are thread safe. That is, they behave as if a mutex ensures that only one of them can update the *shared state* at a time.

18.3.5 Class `std::packaged_task` in Detail

Class std::packaged_task<> is provided to hold both some functionality to perform and its outcome (the so-called *shared state* of the functionality, see Section 18.3, page 973), which might be a return value or an exception raised by the functionality. You can initialize the packaged task with the associated functionality. Then, you can call this functionality by calling operator () for the packaged task. Finally, you can process the outcome by getting a future for the packaged task. Table 18.3 lists the operations available for class packaged_task.

Any exception caused by the constructor taking the task, such as if no memory is available, is also stored in its *shared state*.

Operation	Effect
promise *p*	Default constructor; creates a promise with shared state
promise *p*(allocator_arg,*alloc*)	Creates a promise with *shared state*, which uses *alloc* as allocator
promise *p*(*rv*)	Move constructor; creates a new promise object, which gets the state of *rv* and removes the *shared state* from *rv*
p.˜*promise*()	Releases the *shared state* and if it is not ready (no value or exception), stores a std::future_error exception with condition broken_promise
p = *rv*	Move assignment; move assigns the state of *rv* to *p* and if *p* was not ready, stores a std::future_error exception with condition broken_promise there
swap(*p1*,*p2*)	Swaps states of *p1* and *p2*
p1.swap(*p2*)	Swaps states of *p1* and *p2*
p.get_future()	Yields a future object to retrieve the *shared state* (outcome of a thread)
p.set_value(*val*)	Sets *val* as (return) value and makes the state *ready* (or throws std::future_error)
p.set_value_at_thread_exit(*val*)	Sets *val* as (return) value and makes the state *ready* at the end of the current thread (or throws std::future_error)
p.set_exception(*e*)	Sets *e* as exception and makes the state *ready* (or throws std::future_error)
p.set_exception_at_thread_exit(*e*)	Sets *e* as exception and makes the state *ready* at the end of the current thread (or throws std::future_error)

Table 18.2. Operations of Objects of Class promise

Trying to call the task or get_future() if no state is available throws a std::future_error (see Section 4.3.1, page 43) with the error code std::future_errc::no_state. Calling get_future() a second time throws an exception of type std::future_error with the error code std::future_errc::future_already_retrieved. Calling the task a second time throws a std::future_error with the error code std::future_errc::promise_already_satisfied.

The destructor and reset() *abandon* the *shared state*, which means that the packaged task releases the *shared state* and, if the *shared state* was not ready yet, makes the state ready with a std::future_error with error code std::future_errc::broken_promise stored as outcome.

As usual, the make_ready_at_thread_exit() function is provided to ensure the cleanup of local objects and other stuff of a thread ending the task before the result gets processed.

Operation	Effect
packaged_task pt	Default constructor; creates a packaged task with no *shared state* and no stored task
packaged_task pt(*f*)	Creates an object for the task *f*
packaged_task pt(*alloc*,*f*)	Creates an object for the task *f* using allocator *alloc*
packaged_task pt(*rv*)	Move constructor; moves the packaged task *rv* (task and state) to pt (*rv* has no *shared state* afterward)
pt.˜*packaged_task*()	Destroys *this (might make *shared state* ready)
pt = *rv*	Move assignment; move assigns the packaged task rv (task and state) to pt (*rv* has no *shared state* afterward)
swap(*pt1*,*pt2*)	Swaps packaged tasks
pt1.swap(*pt2*)	Swaps packaged tasks
pt.valid()	Yields true if pt has a *shared state*
pt.get_future()	Yields a future object to retrieve the *shared state* (outcome of the task)
pt(*args*)	Calls the task (with optional arguments) and makes the *shared state* ready
pt.make_ready_at_thread_exit(*args*)	Calls the task (with optional arguments) and at thread exit makes the *shared state* ready
pt.reset()	Creates a new *shared state* for pt (might make the old *shared state* ready)

Table 18.3. Operations of Class packaged_task<>

18.3.6 Class std::thread in Detail

An object of class std::thread, introduced in Section 18.2.1, page 964, is provided to start and represent a thread. These objects are intended to map one-to-one with threads provided by the operating system. Table 18.4 lists the operations available for class thread.

The association between a thread object and a thread starts by initializing (or move copy/assign) a *callable object* (see Section 4.4, page 54) to it with optional additional arguments. The association ends either with join() (waiting for the outcome of the thread) or with detach() (explicitly losing the association to the thread). One or the other must be called before the lifetime of a thread object ends or a new thread gets move assigned. Otherwise, the program aborts with std::terminate() (see Section 5.8.2, page 162).

If the thread object has an associated thread, it is said to be *joinable*. In that case, joinable() yields true, and get_id() yields a thread ID that differs from std::thread::id().

Thread IDs have their own type std::thread::id. Its default constructor yields a unique ID representing "no thread." thread::get_id() yields this value if no thread is associated or another unique ID if the thread object is associated with a thread (is *joinable*). The only supported operations

Operation	Effect
thread t	Default constructor; creates a *nonjoinable* thread object
thread t(f,...)	Creates a thread object, representing *f* started as thread (with additional args), or throws `std::system_error`
thread t(rv)	Move constructor; creates a new thread object, which gets the state of *rv*, and makes *rv nonjoinable*
t.~*thread*()	Destroys *this; calls `std::terminate()` if the object is *joinable*
t = rv	Move assignment; move assigns the state of *rv* to *t* or calls `std::terminate()` if *t* is *joinable*
t.joinable()	Yields `true` if *t* has an associated thread (is *joinable*)
t.join()	Waits for the associated thread to finish (throws `std::system_error` if the thread is not *joinable*) and makes the object *nonjoinable*
t.detach()	Releases the association of *t* to its thread while the thread continues (throws `std::system_error` if the thread is not *joinable*) and makes the object *nonjoinable*
t.get_id()	Returns a unique `std::thread::id` if *joinable* or `std::thread::id()` if not
t.native_handle()	Returns a platform-specific type `native_handle_type` for nonportable extensions

Table 18.4. Operations of Objects of Class `thread`

for thread IDs are to compare them or to write them to an output stream. In addition, a hash function is provided to manage thread IDs in unordered containers (see Section 7.9, page 356). A thread ID of a terminated thread might be reused again. Don't make any other assumptions about thread IDs other than that, especially regarding their values. See Section 18.2.1, page 968, for details.

Note that detached threads should not access objects whose lifetimes have ended. This implies the problem that when ending the program, you have to ensure that detached threads don't access global/static objects (see Section 18.2.1, page 967).

In addition, class `std::thread` provides a static member function to query a hint for the possible number of parallel threads:

unsigned int **std::thread::hardware_concurrency** ()

- Returns the number of possible threads.
- This value is just a hint and does not guarantee to be exact.
- Returns 0 if the number is not computable or well defined.

18.3.7 Namespace `this_thread`

For any thread, including the main thread, `<thread>` declares namespace `std::this_thread`, which provides the thread-specific global functions listed in Table 18.5.

Operation	Effect
`this_thread::get_id()`	Yields the ID of the current thread
`this_thread::sleep_for(`*dur*`)`	Blocks the thread for duration *dur*
`this_thread::sleep_until(`*tp*`)`	Blocks the thread until timepoint *tp*
`this_thread::yield()`	Hint to reschedule to the next thread

Table 18.5. Thread-Specific Operations of Namespace `std::this_thread`

Note that `sleep_for()` and `sleep_until()` usually will differ when dealing with system-time adjustments (see Section 5.7.5, page 160, for details).

The operation `this_thread::yield()` is provided to give a hint to the system that it is useful to give up the remainder of the current thread's time slice so that the runtime environment can reschedule to allow other threads to run. One typical example is to give up control when you wait or "poll" for another thread (see Section 18.1.1, page 955) or an atomic flag to be set by another thread (see Section 18.4.3, page 986):[11]

```
while (!readyFlag) {   // loop until data is ready
    std::this_thread::yield();
}
```

As another example, when you fail to get a lock or a mutex while locking multiple locks/mutexes at a time, you can make the application faster by using `yield()` prior to trying the locks/mutexes in a different order.[12]

---

[11] Thanks to Bartosz Milewski for this example.

[12] Thanks to Howard Hinnant for this example.

18.4   Synchronizing Threads, or the Problem of Concurrency

Using multiple threads is almost always combined with concurrent data access. Rarely are multiple threads run independently of one another. Threads might provide data processed by other threads or prepare preconditions necessary to start other processes.

This is where multithreading becomes tricky. Many things can go wrong. Or, put another way, many things can behave differently from what the naive (and even the experienced) programmer might expect.

So, before discussing different ways to synchronize threads and concurrent data access, we have to understand the problem. Then we can discuss the following techniques to synchronize threads:

- Mutexes and locks (see Section 18.5, page 989), including `call_once()` (see Section 18.5.3, page 1000)
- Condition variables (see Section 18.6, page 1003)
- Atomics (see Section 18.7, page 1012)

18.4.1   Beware of Concurrency!

Before discussing the details of the problems of concurrency, let me formulate a first rule just in case you want to start programming without going into the depth of this subsection. If you learn one rule about dealing with multiple threads, it should be the following:

> **The only safe way to concurrently access the same data by multiple threads without synchronization is when *ALL* threads only *READ* the data.**

By "the same data" I mean data that uses the same memory location. If different threads concurrently access *different* variables or objects or different members of them, there is no problem because, since C++11, each variable except a bitfield is guaranteed to have its own memory location.[13] The only exceptions are bitfields, because different bitfields might share a memory location so that accessing different bitfields means shared access of the same data.

However, when two or more threads concurrently access the *same* variable or object or member of it and at least one of the threads performs modifications, you can easily get into deep trouble if you don't synchronize that access. This is what is called a *data race* in C++. In the C++11 standard, a *data race* is defined as "two conflicting actions in different threads, at least one of which is not atomic, and neither happens before the other." A data race always results in undefined behavior.

As always with race conditions, the problem is that your code *might often* do what you intended, but it will not *always* work, which is one of the nastiest problems we can face in programming. Just by using other data, going into production mode, or switching a platform might suddenly break your code. So it's probably a good idea to care about concurrent data access if you use multiple threads.

---

[13] The guarantee of separate memory locations for different objects was not given before C++11. C++98/C++03 was a standard for single-threaded applications only. So, strictly speaking, before C++11 concurrent access to different objects resulted in undefined behavior, although in practice it usually caused no problems.

18.4.2 The Reason for the Problem of Concurrent Data Access

To understand the problems of concurrent data access, we have to understand which guarantees C++ gives regarding the usage of concurrency. Note that a programming language such as C++ always is an abstraction to support different platforms and hardware, which provide different abilities and interfaces according to their architecture and purpose. Thus, a standard such as C++ specifies the *effect* of statements and operations and not the corresponding generated assembler code. The standard describes the *what*, not the *how*.

In general, the behavior is not defined so precisely that there is only one way to implement it. In fact, behavior might even explicitly be undefined. For example, the order of argument evaluation of a function call is unspecified. A program expecting a specific evaluation order would result in undefined behavior.

Thus, the important question is: Which guarantees does a language give? Programmers should not expect more, even though the additional guarantees might be "obvious." In fact, according to the so-called *as-if rule*, each compiler can optimize code as long as the behavior of the program visible from the outside behaves the same. Thus, the generated code is a *black box* and can vary as long as the *observable behavior* remains stable. To quote the C++ standard:

> An implementation is free to disregard any requirement of this International Standard as long as the result is *as if* the requirement had been obeyed, as far as can be determined from the observable behavior of the program. For instance, an actual implementation need not evaluate part of an expression if it can deduce that its value is not used and that no side effects affecting the observable behavior of the program are produced.

Any undefined behavior is provided to give both compiler and hardware vendors the freedom and ability to generate the best code possible, whatever their criteria for "best" are. Yes, it applies to both: Compilers might unroll loops, reorder statements, eliminate dead code, prefetch data, and in modern architectures, for example, a hardware buffer might reorder loads or stores.

Reorderings can be useful to improve the speed of the program, but they might break the behavior. To be able to benefit from fast speed where useful, safety is not the default. Thus, especially for concurrent data access, we have to understand which guarantees are given.

18.4.3 What Exactly Can Go Wrong (the Extent of the Problem)

To give compilers and hardware enough freedom to optimize code, C++ does *not* in general give a couple of guarantees you might expect. The reason is that applying these guarantees in all cases, not only where useful, would cost too much in performance. In fact, in C++, we might have the following problems:

- **Unsynchronized data access**: When two threads running in parallel read and write the same data, it is open which statement comes first.

- **Half-written data**: When one thread reads data, which another thread modifies, the reading thread might even read the data in the *middle* of the write of the other thread, thus reading neither the old nor the new value.
- **Reordered statements:** Statements and operations might be reordered so that the behavior of each single thread is correct, but in combination of *all* threads, expected behavior is broken.

Unsynchronized Data Access

The following code ensures that `f()` is called for the absolute value of `val`, negating the argument `val` if it is negative:

```
if (val >= 0) {
    f(val);      // pass positive val
}
else {
    f(-val);     // pass negated negative val
}
```

In a single-threaded environment, this code works fine. However, in a multithreaded context, this code does not necessarily work. If multiple threads have access to `val`, the value of `val` might change between the `if` clause and the call of `f()` so that a negative value is passed to `f()`.

For the same reason, simple code such as:

```
std::vector<int> v;
...
if (!v.empty()) {
    std::cout << v.front() << std::endl;
}
```

can be a problem if `v` is shared between multiple threads, because between the call of `empty()` and the call of `front()`, `v` might become empty resulting in undefined behavior (see Section 7.3.2, page 275).

Note that this problem also applies to code implementing a function provided by the C++ standard library. For example, the guarantee that

`v.at(5)`   *// yield value of element with index* 5

throws an exception if `v` does not have enough elements no longer applies if another thread might modify `v` while `at()` is called. Thus, keep in mind the following:

> **Unless otherwise stated, C++ standard library functions usually don't support writes or reads concurrently performed with writes to the same data structure.**[14]

---

[14] As Hans Boehm points out, an approach to support concurrent access to library objects would not be useful in general because if I need synchronization around data structure accesses, it's usually not just the individual accesses I need to protect but larger sections of code. This means that programmers need to do their own locking anyway, and the library-provided locking would be at best redundant.

That is, unless otherwise stated, multiple calls on the same object from multiple threads will result in undefined behavior.

However, the C++ standard library provides some guarantees regarding thread safety (see Section 4.5, page 56). For example:

- Concurrent access to *different elements* of the same container is possible (except for class `vector<bool>`). Thus, different threads might concurrently read and/or write different elements of the same container. For example, each thread might process something and store the result in "its" element of a shared vector.

- Concurrent access to a string stream, file stream, or stream buffer results in undefined behavior. However, as we have seen in this chapter before, formatted input and output to a standard stream that is synchronized with C I/O (see Section 15.14.1, page 845) is possible, although it might result in interleaved characters.

Half-Written Data

Consider that we have a variable[15]

```
long long x = 0;
```

and one thread writing the data:

```
x = -1;
```

and one thread reading the data:

```
std::cout << x;
```

What is the output of the program; that is, which value does the second thread read when it outputs x? Well, the following answers are possible:

- 0 (the old value of x), if the first thread has not assigned -1 yet
- -1 (the new value of x), if the first thread assigned -1 already
- *Any other value*, if the second thread reads x during the assignment of -1 by the first thread

The last option — *any other value* — can, for example, easily happen if, on a 32-bit machine, the assignment results in two stores and the read by the second thread happens when the first store was done but the second store was not yet done.

And beware, this does not apply to `long long` only. Even for a fundamental data type, such as `int` or `bool`, the standard does *not* guarantee that a read or a write is *atomic*; that is, that a read or write is an exclusive noninterruptable data access. A data race might be less likely, but to eliminate the possibility, you have to take the steps.

The same applies to more complicated data structures, even if they are provided by the C++ standard library. For example, for a `std::list<>` (see Section 7.5, page 290), it's up to the programmer to ensure that it doesn't get modified by another thread while a thread inserts or deletes an element. Otherwise, the other thread might use an inconsistent state of the list, where, for example, the forward pointer is modified already but the backward pointer is not.

---

[15] This example is taken with permission from [*N2480:MemMod*].

Reordered Statements

Let's discuss another simple example.[16] Suppose we have two shared objects, an `int` to pass data from one thread to another and a Boolean `readyFlag`, which signals when the first thread has provided the data:

```
long data;
bool readyFlag = false;
```

A naive approach is to synchronize the setting of the `data` in one thread with the consumption of the `data` in another thread. Thus, the providing thread calls:

```
data = 42;
readyFlag = true;
```

and the consuming thread calls:

```
while (!readyFlag) {   // loop until data is ready
    ;
}
foo(data);
```

Without knowing any details, almost every programmer at first would suppose that the second thread calls `foo()` when `data` has the value 42, assuming that the call of `foo()` can be reached only if the `readyFlag` is `true`, which itself can be the case only after the first thread assigned 42 to `data`, because this happens before the `readyFlag` becomes `true`.

But this is not necessarily the case. In fact, the output of the second thread might be the value `data` had *before* the first thread assigned 42 (or even any other value, because the assignment of 42 might be half-done).

That is, the compiler and/or the hardware might reorder the statements so that effectively the following gets called:

```
readyFlag = true;
data = 42;
```

In general, such a reordering is allowed due to the rules of C++, which requires only that the *observable behavior inside a thread* of the generated code be correct. For the behavior of the first thread, it doesn't matter whether we first modify `readyFlag` or `data`; from the viewpoint of this thread, they are independent of each other. Thus, reorderings of statements are allowed as long as the visible effect to the outside of a single thread is the same.

For the same reason, even the second thread might reorder the statements, provided that the behavior of this thread is not affected:

```
foo(data);
while (!readyFlag) {   // loop until data is ready
    ;
}
```

---

[16] This example is taken from multiple articles in *Bartosz Milewski's Programming Cafe* (see [*Milewski:Multicore*] and [*Milewski:Atomics*] for details).

Note that the observable behavior might be affected by such a reordering if `foo()` throws. Thus, it depends on details whether such reorderings are allowed, but in principle, the problem applies.

Again, the reason to allow such modifications is that by default, C++ compilers shall be able to generate code that is highly optimized, and some optimizations might be to reorder statements. By default, these optimizations are not required to care about possible other threads, which makes these optimizations easier because local analyses are enough.

18.4.4 The Features to Solve the Problems

To solve the three major problems of concurrent data access, we need the following concepts:

- **Atomicity:** This means that read or write access to a variable or to a sequence of statements happens exclusively and without any interruption, so that one thread can't read intermediate states caused by another thread.
- **Order:** We need some ways to guarantee the order of specific statements or of a group of specific statements.

The C++ standard library provides very different ways to deal with these concepts, so that programs benefit from additional guarantees regarding concurrent access:

- You can use *futures* (see Section 18.1, page 946) and *promises* (see Section 18.2.2, page 969), which guarantee both atomicity and order: Setting the *outcome* (return value or exception) of a *shared state* is guaranteed to happen before the processing of this outcome, which implies that read and write access does not happen concurrently.
- You can use *mutexes and locks* (see Section 18.5, page 989) to deal with *critical sections*, or *protected zones*, whereby you can grant exclusive access so that, for example, nothing can happen between a check and an operation based on that check. Locks provide atomicity by blocking all access using a second lock until a first lock on the same resource gets released. More precisely: The release of a lock object acquired by one thread is guaranteed to happen before the acquisition of the same lock object by another thread is successful. However, if two threads use locked access to data, the order in which they access it may change from run to run.
- You can use *condition variables* (see Section 18.6, page 1003) to efficiently allow one thread to wait for some predicate controlled by another thread to become true. This helps to deal with the order of multiple threads by allowing one or more threads to process data or a status provided by one or more other threads.[17]
- You can use *atomic data types* (see Section 18.7, page 1012) to ensure that each access to a variable or object is atomic while the order of operations on the atomic types remains stable.
- You can use the *low-level interface of atomic data types* (see Section 18.7.4, page 1019), which allow experts to relax the order of atomic statements or to use manual barriers for memory access (so-called *fences*).

In principle, this list is sorted from high-level to low-level features. High-level features, such as futures and promises or mutexes and locks, are easy to use and provide little risk. Low-level fea-

---

[17] Concurrency experts won't consider condition variables to be a tool to deal with the problem of concurrent data access, because they're more a tool to improve performance than to provide correctness.

tures, such as atomics and especially their low-level interface, might provide better performance because they have lower latency and therefore higher scalability, but the risk of misuse grows significantly. Nevertheless, low-level features sometimes provide simple solutions for specific high-level problems.

With atomics, we go in the direction of *lock-free programming*, which even experts sometimes do wrong. To quote Herb Sutter from [*Sutter:LockFree*]: "[Lock-free code is] hard even for experts. It's easy to write lock-free code that appears to work, but it's very difficult to write lock-free code that is correct and performs well. Even good magazines and refereed journals have published a substantial amount of lock-free code that was actually broken in subtle ways and needed correction."

volatile and Concurrency

Note that I didn't mention `volatile` here as a feature for concurrent data access, although you might have expected that for the following reasons:

- `volatile` is known as a C++ keyword to prevent too much optimization.
- In Java, `volatile` provides some guarantees about atomicity and order.

In C++, `volatile` "only" specifies that access to external resources, such as shared memory, should not be optimized away. For example, without `volatile`, a compiler might eliminate redundant loads of the same shared memory segment because it can't see any modification of the segment throughout the whole program. But in C++, `volatile` provides neither atomicity nor a specific order.[18] Thus, the semantics of `volatile` between C++ and Java now differs.

See also Section 18.5.1, page 998, for a discussion, why `volatile` usually is not required when mutexes are used to read data in a loop.

---

[18] Thanks to Scott Meyers for pointing this out to me.

18.5 Mutexes and Locks

A mutex, or *mutual exclusion*, is an object that helps to control the concurrent access of a resource by providing exclusive access to it. The resource might be an object or a combination of multiple objects. To get exclusive access to the resource, the corresponding thread *locks* the mutex, which prevents other threads from locking that mutex until the first thread *unlocks* the mutex.

18.5.1 Using Mutexes and Locks

Consider that we want to protect concurrent access to an object `val` that is used at various places:

```
int val;
```

A naive approach to synchronize this concurrent access is to introduce a mutex, which is used to enable and control exclusive access:

```
int val;
std::mutex valMutex;   // control exclusive access to val
```

Then, each access has to lock this mutex to get exclusive access. For example, one thread might program the following (note that this is a poor solution, which we will improve):

```
valMutex.lock();   // request exclusive access to val
if (val >= 0) {
    f(val);        // val is positive
}
else {
    f(-val);       // pass negated negative val
}
valMutex.unlock();   // release exclusive access to val
```

Another thread might access the same resource as follows:

```
valMutex.lock();   // request exclusive access to val
++val;
valMutex.unlock();   // release exclusive access to val
```

It's important that all places where concurrent access is possible use the same mutex. This applies to both read and write accesses.

This simple approach can, however, become pretty complicated. For example, you should ensure that an exception, which ends an exclusive access, also unlocks the corresponding mutex. Otherwise, a resource might become locked forever. Also, deadlock scenarios are possible, with two threads waiting for a lock of the other thread before freeing their own lock.

The C++ standard library tries to deal with these problems but can't conceptionally solve them all. For example, to deal with exceptions, you should not lock and unlock a mutex yourself. You should use the RAII principle (*Resource Acquisition Is Initialization*), whereby the constructor acquires a resource so that the destructor, which is always called even when an exception causes the end of the lifetime, releases the resource automatically. For this purpose, the C++ standard library provides class `std::lock_guard`:

```
int val;
std::mutex valMutex;   // control exclusive access to val
...
std::lock_guard<std::mutex> lg(valMutex);   // lock and automatically unlock
if (val >= 0) {
    f(val);     // val is positive
}
else {
    f(-val);    // pass negated negative val
}
```

Note, however, that locks should be limited to the shortest period possible because they block other code from running in parallel. Because the destructor releases the lock, you might want to insert explicit braces so that the lock gets released before further statements are processed:

```
int val;
std::mutex valMutex;   // control exclusive access to val
...
{
    std::lock_guard<std::mutex> lg(valMutex);   // lock and automatically unlock
    if (val >= 0) {
        f(val);     // val is positive
    }
    else {
        f(-val);    // pass negated negative val
    }
} // ensure that lock gets released here
...
```

or just:

```
...
{
    std::lock_guard<std::mutex> lg(valMutex);   // lock and automatically unlock
    ++val;
} // ensure that lock gets released here
...
```

This is just a first simple example, but you can see that the whole topic can easily become pretty complicated. As usual, programmers should know what they program in concurrent mode. In addition, different mutexes and locks are provided, which are discussed in the upcoming subsections.

A First Complete Example for Using a Mutex and a Lock

Let's look at a first complete example:

```cpp
// concurrency/mutex1.cpp

#include <future>
#include <mutex>
#include <iostream>
#include <string>

std::mutex printMutex;   // enable synchronized output with print()

void print (const std::string& s)
{
    std::lock_guard<std::mutex> l(printMutex);
    for (char c : s) {
        std::cout.put(c);
    }
    std::cout << std::endl;
}

int main()
{
    auto f1 = std::async (std::launch::async,
                          print, "Hello from a first thread");
    auto f2 = std::async (std::launch::async,
                          print, "Hello from a second thread");
    print("Hello from the main thread");
}
```

Here, `print()` writes all characters of a passed string to the standard output. Thus, without a lock, the output might be:[19]

```
HHelHello from a second thread
ello from a first thread
lo from the main thread
```

or:

```
HelloHello fHello from a second ro from am th fthe main irrethreadstad
 thr
ead
```

---

[19] The fact that each character is written on its own with `put()` forces the behavior of getting interleaved characters when multiple parallel writes are performed. When writing each string as a whole, implementations often will not mix characters, but even this isn't guaranteed.

To synchronize the output in a way that each call of `print()` exclusively writes its characters, we introduce a mutex for the print operation and a lock guard, which locks the corresponding protected section:

```
std::mutex printMutex;    // enable synchronized output with print()
...
void print (const std::string& s)
{
    std::lock_guard<std::mutex> l(printMutex);
    ...
}
```

Now the output is simply something like this:

```
Hello from a first thread
Hello from the main thread
Hello from a second thread
```

This output also is possible (but not guaranteed) when no lock is used.

Here, the `lock()` of the mutex, called by the constructor of the lock guard, blocks if the resource is acquired already. It blocks until access to the protected section is available again. However, the order of locks is still undefined. Thus, the three outputs might still be written in arbitrary order.

Recursive Locks

Sometimes, the ability to lock recursively is required. Typical examples are active objects or monitors, which contain a mutex and take a lock inside every public method to protect data races corrupting the internal state of the object. For example, a database interface might look as follows:

```
class DatabaseAccess
{
  private:
    std::mutex dbMutex;
    ...  // state of database access
  public:
    void createTable (...)
    {
        std::lock_guard<std::mutex> lg(dbMutex);
        ...
    }
    void insertData (...)
    {
        std::lock_guard<std::mutex> lg(dbMutex);
        ...
    }
    ...
};
```

When we introduce a public member function that might call other public member functions, this can become complicated:

```
void createTableAndInsertData (...)
{
    std::lock_guard<std::mutex> lg(dbMutex);
    ...
    createTable(...);   // ERROR: deadlock because dbMutex is locked again
}
```

Calling `createTableAndInsertData()` will result in a deadlock because after locking dbMutex, the call of `createTable()` will try to lock dbMutex again, which will block until the lock of dbMutex is available, which will never happen because `createTableAndInsertData()` will block until `createTable()` is done.

The C++ standard library permits the second attempt to throw a `std::system_error` (see Section 4.3.1, page 43) with the error code `resource_deadlock_would_occur` (see Section 4.3.2, page 45) if the platform detects such a deadlock. But this is not required and is often not the case.

By using a `recursive_mutex`, this behavior is no problem. This mutex allows multiple locks by the same thread and releases the lock when the last corresponding `unlock()` call is called:

```
class DatabaseAccess
{
  private:
    std::recursive_mutex dbMutex;
    ...  // state of database access
  public:
    void insertData (...)
    {
        std::lock_guard<std::recursive_mutex> lg(dbMutex);
        ...
    }
    void insertData (...)
    {
        std::lock_guard<std::recursive_mutex> lg(dbMutex);
        ...
    }
    void createTableAndinsertData (...)
    {
        std::lock_guard<std::recursive_mutex> lg(dbMutex);
        ...
        createTable(...);   // OK: no deadlock
    }
    ...
};
```

Tried and Timed Locks

Sometimes a program wants to acquire a lock but doesn't want to block (forever) if this is not possible. For this situation, mutexes provide a try_lock() member function that *tries* to acquire a lock. If it succeeds, it returns true; if not, false.

To still be able to use a lock_guard so that any exit from the current scope unlocks the mutex, you can pass an additional argument adopt_lock to its constructor:

```
std::mutex m;

// try to acquire a lock and do other stuff while this isn't possible
while (m.try_lock() == false) {
    doSomeOtherStuff();
}
std::lock_guard<std::mutex> lg(m,std::adopt_lock);
...
```

Note that try_lock() might fail spuriously. That is, it might fail (return false) even if the lock is not taken.[20]

To wait only for a particular amount of time, you can use a timed mutex. The special mutex classes std::timed_mutex and std::recursive_timed_mutex additionally allow calling try_lock_for() or try_lock_until() to wait for at most a specified duration of time or until a specified point in time has arrived. This, for example, might help if you have real-time requirements or want to avoid possible deadlock situations. For example:

```
std::timed_mutex m;

// try for one second to acquire a lock
if (m.try_lock_for(std::chrono::seconds(1))) {
    std::lock_guard<std::timed_mutex> lg(m,std::adopt_lock);
    ...
}
else {
    couldNotGetTheLock();
}
```

Note that try_lock_for() and try_lock_until() usually will differ when dealing with system-time adjustments (see Section 5.7.5, page 160, for details).

Dealing with Multiple Locks

Usually a thread should lock only one mutex at a time. However, it is sometimes necessary to lock more than one mutex (for example, to transfer data from one protected resource to another). In that

---

[20] This behavior is provided for memory-ordering reasons but is not widely known. Thanks to Hans Boehm and Bartosz Milewski for pointing it out.

case, dealing with the lock mechanisms introduced so far can become complicated and risky: You might get the first but not the second lock, or deadlock situations may occur if you lock the same locks in a different order.

The C++ standard library, therefore, provides convenience functions to try to lock multiple mutexes. For example:

```
std::mutex m1;
std::mutex m2;
...
{
    std::lock (m1, m2);    // lock both mutexes (or none if not possible)
    std::lock_guard<std::mutex> lockM1(m1,std::adopt_lock);
    std::lock_guard<std::mutex> lockM2(m2,std::adopt_lock);
    ...
}   // automatically unlock all mutexes
```

The global `std::lock()` locks all mutexes passed as arguments, blocking until all mutexes are locked or until an exception is thrown. In the latter case, it unlocks mutexes already successfully locked. As usual, after successful locking, you can and should use a lock guard initialized with `adopt_lock` as second argument to ensure that, in any case, the mutexes are unlocked when leaving the scope. Note that this `lock()` provides a deadlock-avoidance mechanism, which, however, means that the order of locking inside a multiple lock is undefined.

In the same way, you can *try* to acquire multiple locks without blocking if not all locks are available. The global `std::try_lock()` returns -1 if all locks were possible. If not, the return value is the zero-based index of the first failed lock. In that case, all succeeded locks are unlocked again. For example:

```
std::mutex m1;
std::mutex m2;

int idx = std::try_lock (m1, m2);   // try to lock both mutexes
if (idx < 0) {   // both locks succeeded
    std::lock_guard<std::mutex> lockM1(m1,std::adopt_lock);
    std::lock_guard<std::mutex> lockM2(m2,std::adopt_lock);
    ...
}   // automatically unlock all mutexes
else {
    // idx has zero-based index of first failed lock
    std::cerr << "could not lock mutex m" << idx+1 << std::endl;
}
```

Note that this `try_lock()` does not provide a deadlock-avoidance mechanism. Instead, it guarantees that the locks are tried in the order of the passed arguments.

Note also that calling `lock()` or `try_lock()` without adopting the locks by a guard is usually not what was intended. Although the code looks like it creates locks that are released automatically when leaving the scope, this is not the case. The mutexes will remain locked:

```
std::mutex m1;
std::mutex m2;
...
{
    std::lock (m1, m2);    // lock both mutexes (or none if not possible)
    // no lock adopted
        ...
}
...    // OOPS: mutexes are still locked !!!
```

Class `unique_lock`

Besides class `lock_guard<>`, the C++ standard library provides class `unique_lock<>`, which is a lot more flexible when dealing with locks for mutexes. Class `unique_lock<>` provides the same interface as class `lock_guard<>`, plus the ability to program explicitly when and how to lock or unlock its mutex. Thus, this lock object may or may not have a mutex locked (also known as *owning* a mutex). This differs from a `lock_guard<>`, which always has an object locked throughout its lifetime.[21] In addition, for unique locks you can query whether the mutex is currently locked by calling `owns_lock()` or `operator bool()`.

The major advantage of this class still is that when the mutex is locked at destruction time, the destructor automatically calls `unlock()` for it. If no mutex is locked, the destructor does nothing.

Compared to class `lock_guard`, class `unique_lock` provides the following supplementary constructors:

- You can pass `try_to_lock` for a nonblocking attempt to lock a mutex:

  ```
  std::unique_lock<std::mutex> lock(mutex,std::try_to_lock);
  ...
  if (lock) {   // if lock was successful
      ...
  }
  ```

- You can pass a duration or timepoint to the constructor to try to lock for a specific period of time:

  ```
  std::unique_lock<std::timed_mutex> lock(mutex,
                                      std::chrono::seconds(1));
  ...
  ```

- You can pass `defer_lock` to initialize the lock without locking the mutex (yet):

  ```
  std::unique_lock<std::mutex> lock(mutex,std::defer_lock);
  ...
  lock.lock();   // or (timed) try_lock()
  ...
  ```

---

[21] The name *unique* lock explains where this behavior comes from. As with unique pointers (see Section 5.2.5, page 98), you can move locks between scopes, but it is guaranteed that only one lock at a time owns a mutex.

The `defer_lock` flag can, for example, be used to create one or multiple locks and lock them later:

```
std::mutex m1;
std::mutex m2;

std::unique_lock<std::mutex> lockM1(m1,std::defer_lock);
std::unique_lock<std::mutex> lockM2(m2,std::defer_lock);
...
std::lock (m1, m2);   // lock both mutexes (or none if not possible)
```

In addition, class `unique_lock` provides the ability to `release()` its mutex or to transfer the ownership of a mutex to another lock. See Section 18.5.2, page 1000, for details.

With both a `lock_guard` and a `unique_lock`, we can now implement a naive example, where one thread waits for another by polling a *ready flag*:

```
#include <mutex>
...
bool readyFlag;
std::mutex readyFlagMutex;

void thread1()
{
    // do something thread2 needs as preparation
    ...
    std::lock_guard<std::mutex> lg(readyFlagMutex);
    readyFlag = true;
}

void thread2()
{
    // wait until readyFlag is true (thread1 is done)
    {
        std::unique_lock<std::mutex> ul(readyFlagMutex);
        while (!readyFlag) {
            ul.unlock();
            std::this_thread::yield();   // hint to reschedule to the next thread
            std::this_thread::sleep_for(std::chrono::milliseconds(100));
            ul.lock();
        }
    } // release lock

    // do whatever shall happen after thread1 has prepared things
    ...
}
```

Two comments on typical questions this code might raise:

- If you wonder why we use a mutex to control the access to read and write the `readyFlag`, remember the rule introduced at the beginning of this chapter: Any concurrent access with at least one write should be synchronized. See Section 18.4, page 982, and Section 18.7, page 1012, for a detailed discussion about this.
- If you wonder that no `volatile` is necessary here to declare `readyFlag` to avoid that multiple attempts in `thread2()` to read it are not optimized away note the following: These attempts to read `readyFlag` happen inside a *critical section*, defined between the setting and releasing of a lock. Such code is not allowed to get optimized in a way that the read (or a write) is moved outside the critical section. So the reads of `readyFlag` must effectively happen here:
  - At the beginning of the loop, between the declaration of `ul` and the first call of `unlock()`
  - Inside the loop, between any call of `lock()` and `unlock()`
  - At the end of the loop, between the last call of `lock()` and the destruction of `ul`, which unlocks the mutex if locked

Nevertheless, such a *polling* for a fulfilled condition is usually not a good solution. A better approach is to use *condition variables*. See Section 18.6.1, page 1003, for details.

18.5.2   Mutexes and Locks in Detail

Mutexes in Detail

The C++ standard library provides the following mutex classes (see Table 18.6):

- Class `std::mutex` is a simple mutex that can be locked only once by one thread at a time. If it is locked, any other `lock()` will block until the mutex is available again and `try_lock()` will fail.
- Class `std::recursive_mutex` is a mutex that allows multiple locks at the same time by the same thread. The typical application of such a lock is where functions acquire a lock and internally call another function, which also acquires the same lock again.

Operation	mutex	recursive_ mutex	timed_mutex	recursive_ timed_mutex
lock()	Acquires mutex (blocks if not available)			
try_lock()	Acquires mutex (returns false if not available)			
unlock()	Unlocks locked mutex			
try_lock_for()	–	–	Tries to acquire a lock for a duration of time	
try_lock_until()	–	–	Tries to acquire a lock until a timepoint	
multiple locks	No	Yes (same thread)	No	Yes (same thread)

Table 18.6. Overview of Mutexes and Their Abilities

- Class std::**timed_mutex** is a simple mutex that additionally allows you to pass a duration or a timepoint that defines how long it tries to acquire a lock. For this, try_lock_for() and try_lock_until() are provided.
- Class std::**recursive_timed_mutex** is a mutex that allows multiple locks by the same thread with optional timeouts.

Table 18.7 lists the mutex operations, if available.

Operation	Effect
mutex m	Default constructor; creates an unlocked mutex
m. ~*mutex*()	Destroys the mutex (must not be locked)
m.lock()	Locks the mutex (blocks for lock; error if locked and not recursive)
m.try_lock()	Tries to lock the mutex (returns true if lock successful)
m.try_lock_for(*dur*)	Tries to lock for duration *dur* (returns true if lock successful)
m.try_lock_until(*tp*)	Tries to lock until timepoint *tp* (returns true if lock successful)
m.unlock()	Unlocks the mutex (undefined behavior if not locked)
m.native_handle()	Returns a platform-specific type native_handle_type for nonportable extensions

Table 18.7. Operations of Mutex Classes, If Available

lock() might throw a std::system_error (see Section 4.3.1, page 43) with the following error codes (see Section 4.3.2, page 45):

- operation_not_permitted, if the thread does not have the privilege to perform the operation
- resource_deadlock_would_occur, if the platform detects that a deadlock would occur
- device_or_resource_busy, if the mutex is already locked and blocking is not possible

The behavior of a program is undefined if it unlocks a mutex object it doesn't own, destroys a mutex object owned by any thread, or if a thread terminates while owning a mutex object.

Note that try_lock_for() and try_lock_until() usually will differ when dealing with system-time adjustments (see Section 5.7.5, page 160, for details).

Class lock_guard in Detail

Class std::lock_guard, introduced in Section 18.5.1, page 989, provides a very small interface to ensure that a locked mutex gets always freed when leaving the scope (see Table 18.8). Throughout its lifetime, it is always associated with a lock either explicitly requested or adopted at construction time.

Operation	Effect
lock_guard lg(*m*)	Creates a lock guard for the mutex *m* and locks it
lock_guard lg(*m*,adopt_lock)	Creates a lock guard for the already locked mutex *m*
lg.~*lock_guard*()	Unlocks the mutex and destroys the lock guard

Table 18.8. Operations of Class lock_guard

Class unique_lock in Detail

Class std::unique_lock, introduced in Section 18.5.1, page 996, provides a lock guard for a mutex that does not necessarily have to be locked (*owned*). It provides the interface listed in Table 18.9. If it locks/owns a mutex at destruction time, it will unlock() it. But you can control explicitly whether it has an associated mutex and whether this mutex is locked. You can also try to lock the mutex with or without timeouts.

lock() might throw a std::system_error (see Section 4.3.1, page 43) with the error codes listed for lock() for mutexes (see page 999). unlock() might throw a std::system_error with the error code operation_not_permitted if the unique lock isn't locked.

18.5.3   Calling Once for Multiple Threads

Sometimes multiple threads might not need some functionality that should get processed whenever the first thread needs it. A typical example is lazy initialization: The first time one of the threads needs something that has to get processed, you process it (but not before, because you want to save the time to process it if it is not needed).

The usual approach with single-threaded environments is simple: A Boolean flag signals whether the functionality was called already:

```
bool initialized = false;    // global flag
...
if (!initialized) {          // initialize if not initialized yet
    initialize();
    initialized = true;
}
```

or

```
static std::vector<std::string> staticData;

void foo()
{
    if (staticData.empty()) {
        staticData = initializeStaticData();
    }
    ...
}
```

Operation	Effect
unique_lock l	Default constructor; creates a lock not associated with a mutex
unique_lock l(m)	Creates a lock guard for the mutex m and locks it
unique_lock l(m,adopt_lock)	Creates a lock guard for the already locked mutex m
unique_lock l(m,defer_lock)	Creates a lock guard for the mutex m without locking it
unique_lock l(m,try_lock)	Creates a lock guard for the mutex m and tries to lock it
unique_lock l(m,dur)	Creates a lock guard for the mutex m and tries to lock it for duration dur
unique_lock l(m,tp)	Creates a lock guard for the mutex m and tries to lock it until timepoint tp
unique_lock l(rv)	Move constructor; moves lock state from rv to l (rv has no associated mutex anymore)
l.~*unique_lock*()	Unlocks the mutex, if any locked, and destroys the lock guard
unique_lock l = rv	Move assignment; moves the lock state from rv to l (rv has no associated mutex anymore)
swap(l1,l2)	Swaps locks
l1.swap(l2)	Swaps locks
l.release()	Returns a pointer to the associated mutex and releases it
l.owns_lock()	Returns true if an associated mutex is locked
if (l)	Checks whether an associated mutex is locked
l.mutex()	Returns a pointer to the associated mutex
l.lock()	Locks the associated mutex
l.try_lock()	Tries to lock the associated mutex (returns true if lock successful)
l.try_lock_for(dur)	Tries to lock the associated mutex for duration dur (returns true if lock successful)
l.try_lock_until(tp)	Tries to lock the associated mutex until timepoint tp (returns true if lock successful)
l.unlock()	Unlocks the associated mutex

Table 18.9. Operations of Class unique_lock

Such code doesn't work in a multithreaded context, because data races might occur if two or more threads check whether the initialization didn't happen yet and start the initialization then. Thus, you have to protect the area for the check and the initialization against concurrent access.

As usual, you can use mutexes for it, but the C++ standard library provides a special solution for this case. You simply use a std::once_flag and call std::call_once (also provided by <mutex>):

```
std::once_flag oc;               // global flag
...
std::call_once(oc,initialize);   // initialize if not initialized yet
```

or:

```
static std::vector<std::string> staticData;

void foo()
{
    static std::once_flag oc;
    std::call_once(oc,[]{
                         staticData = initializeStaticData();
                    });

    ...
}
```

As you can see, the first argument passed to call_once() must be the corresponding once_flag. The further arguments are the usual arguments for *callable objects*: function, member function, function object, or lambda, plus optional arguments for the function called (see Section 4.4, page 54). Thus, lazy initialization of an object used in multiple threads might look as follows:

```
class X {
  private:
    mutable std::once_flag initDataFlag;
    void initData() const;
  public:
    data getData () const {
        std::call_once(initDataFlag,&X::initData,this);

        ...
    }
};
```

In principle, you can call different functions for the same once flag. The once flag that is passed to call_once() as first argument is what ensures that the passed functionality is performed only once. So, if the first call was successful, further calls with the same once flag won't call the passed functionality even if that functionality is different.

Any exception caused by the called functionality is also thrown by call_once(). In that case, the "first" call is considered not to be successful, so the next call_once() might still execute the passed functionality.[22]

---

[22] The standard also specifies that call_once() might throw a std::system_error if the once_flag argument is no longer "valid" (i.e., destructed). However, this statement is considered to be a mistake because passing a destructed once flag anyway is either not possible or results in undefined behavior.

18.6   Condition Variables

Sometimes, tasks performed by different threads have to wait for each other. Thus, you sometimes have to synchronize concurrent operations for other reasons than to access the same data.

Now, you can argue that we have introduced such a mechanism already: Futures (see Section 18.1, page 946) allow you to block until data by another thread is provided or another thread is done. However, a future can pass data from one thread to another only once. In fact, a future's major purpose is to deal with return values or exceptions of threads.

Here we introduce and discuss condition variables, which can be used to synchronize logical dependencies in data flow between threads multiple times.

18.6.1   Purpose of Condition Variables

Section 18.5.1, page 997, introduced a naive approach to let one thread wait for another by using something like a *ready flag*, signaling when one thread has prepared or provided something for another thread. This usually means that the waiting thread *polls* to notice that its required data or precondition has arrived:

```
bool readyFlag;
std::mutex readyFlagMutex;

// wait until readyFlag is true:
{
    std::unique_lock<std::mutex> ul(readyFlagMutex);
    while (!readyFlag) {
        ul.unlock();
        std::this_thread::yield();   // hint to reschedule to the next thread
        std::this_thread::sleep_for(std::chrono::milliseconds(100));
        ul.lock();
    }
} // release lock
```

However, such a *polling* for a fulfilled condition is usually not a good solution.
Or as [*Williams:C++Conc*] points out:

> The waiting thread consumes valuable processing time repeatedly checking the flag and when it locks the mutex the thread setting the ready flag is blocked. ... In addition, it's hard to get the sleep period right: too short a sleep in between checks and the thread still wastes processing time checking, too long a sleep and the thread will carry on sleeping even when the task it is waiting for is complete, introducing a delay.

A better approach is to use *condition variables*, which the C++ standard library provides in `<condition_variable>`. A condition variable is a variable by which a thread can wake up one or multiple other waiting threads.

In principle, a condition variable works as follows:

- You have to include both `<mutex>` and `<condition_variable>` to declare a mutex and a condition variable:

  ```
  #include <mutex>
  #include <condition_variable>

  std::mutex readyMutex;
  std::condition_variable readyCondVar;
  ```
- The thread (or one of multiple threads) that signals the fulfillment of a condition has to call
  ```
  readyCondVar.notify_one();    // notify one of the waiting threads
  ```
  or
  ```
  readyCondVar.notify_all();    // notify all the waiting threads
  ```
- Any thread that waits for the condition has to call
  ```
  std::unique_lock<std::mutex> l(readyMutex);
  readyCondVar.wait(l);
  ```

Thus, the thread providing or preparing something simply calls `notify_one()` or `notify_all()` for the condition variable, which for one or all the waiting threads is the moment to wake up.

So far, so good. Sounds simple. But there's more. First, note that to wait for the condition variable, you need a mutex and a `unique_lock`, introduced in Section 18.5.1, page 996. A `lock_guard` is not enough, because the waiting function might lock and unlock the mutex.

In addition, condition variables in general might have so-called *spurious wakeups*. That is, a wait on a condition variable may return even if the condition variable has not been notified. To quote Anthony Williams from [*Williams:CondVar*]: "Spurious wakes cannot be predicted: they are essentially random from the user's point of view. However, they commonly occur when the thread library cannot reliably ensure that a waiting thread will not miss a notification. Since a missed notification would render the condition variable useless, the thread library wakes the thread from its wait rather than take the risk."

Thus, a wakeup does not necessarily mean that the required condition now holds. Rather, after a wakeup you still need some code to verify that the condition in fact has arrived. Therefore, for example, we have to check whether provided data is really available, or we still need something like a ready flag. To set and query this provided data or this ready flag, we can use the same mutex.

18.6.2   A First Complete Example for Condition Variables

The following code is a complete example that demonstrates how to use condition variables:

```
// concurrency/condvar1.cpp

#include <condition_variable>
#include <mutex>
#include <future>
#include <iostream>
```

```
bool readyFlag;
std::mutex readyMutex;
std::condition_variable readyCondVar;

void thread1()
{
    // do something thread2 needs as preparation
    std::cout << "<return>" << std::endl;
    std::cin.get();

    // signal that thread1 has prepared a condition
    {
        std::lock_guard<std::mutex> lg(readyMutex);
        readyFlag = true;
    } // release lock
    readyCondVar.notify_one();
}

void thread2()
{
    // wait until thread1 is ready (readyFlag is true)
    {
        std::unique_lock<std::mutex> ul(readyMutex);
        readyCondVar.wait(ul, []{ return readyFlag; });
    } // release lock

    // do whatever shall happen after thread1 has prepared things
    std::cout << "done" << std::endl;
}

int main()
{
    auto f1 = std::async(std::launch::async,thread1);
    auto f2 = std::async(std::launch::async,thread2);
}
```

After including the necessary header files, we need three things to communicate between threads:

1. An object for the data provided to process or a flag signaling that the condition is indeed satisfied (here: readyFlag))

2. A mutex (here: readyMutex)

3. A condition variable (here readyCondVar)

The providing thread `thread1()` locks the mutex `readyMutex`, updates the condition (the object for the data or for the ready flag), unlocks the mutex, and notifies the condition variable:

```
{
    std::lock_guard<std::mutex> lg(readyMutex);
    readyFlag = true;
} // release lock
readyCondVar.notify_one();
```

Note that the notification itself does not have to be inside the protected area of the lock.

A waiting (consuming/processing) thread locks the mutex with a `unique_lock` (Section 18.5.1, page 996), waits for the notification while checking the condition, and releases the lock:

```
{
    std::unique_lock<std::mutex> ul(readyMutex);
    readyCondVar.wait(ul, []{ return readyFlag; });
} // release lock
```

Here, a `wait()` member for condition variables is used as follows: You pass the lock `ul` for the mutex `readyMutex` as first argument and a lambda as *callable object* (see Section 4.4, page 54) double checking the condition as second argument. The effect is that `wait()` internally calls a loop until the passed callable returns `true`. Thus, the code has the same effect as the following code, where the loop necessary for dealing with spurious wakeups is explicitly visible:

```
{
    std::unique_lock<std::mutex> ul(readyMutex);
    while (!readyFlag) {
        readyCondVar.wait(ul);
    }
} // release lock
```

Again note that you have to use a `unique_lock` and can't use a `lock_guard` here, because internally, `wait()` explicitly unlocks and locks the mutex.

You can argue that this is a bad example for using condition variables, because futures can be used for blocking until some data arrives. So let's present a second example.

18.6.3   Using Condition Variables to Implement a Queue for Multiple Threads

In this example, three threads push values into a queue that two other threads read and process:

```
// concurrency/condvar2.cpp

#include <condition_variable>
#include <mutex>
#include <future>
#include <thread>
#include <iostream>
#include <queue>
```

```cpp
std::queue<int> queue;
std::mutex queueMutex;
std::condition_variable queueCondVar;

void provider (int val)
{
    // push different values (val til val+5 with timeouts of val milliseconds into the queue
    for (int i=0; i<6; ++i) {
        {
            std::lock_guard<std::mutex> lg(queueMutex);
            queue.push(val+i);
        } // release lock
        queueCondVar.notify_one();

        std::this_thread::sleep_for(std::chrono::milliseconds(val));
    }
}

void consumer (int num)
{
    // pop values if available (num identifies the consumer)
    while (true) {
        int val;
        {
            std::unique_lock<std::mutex> ul(queueMutex);
            queueCondVar.wait(ul,[]{ return !queue.empty(); });
            val = queue.front();
            queue.pop();
        } // release lock
        std::cout << "consumer " << num << ": " << val << std::endl;
    }
}

int main()
{
    // start three providers for values 100+, 300+, and 500+
    auto p1 = std::async(std::launch::async,provider,100);
    auto p2 = std::async(std::launch::async,provider,300);
    auto p3 = std::async(std::launch::async,provider,500);

    // start two consumers printing the values
    auto c1 = std::async(std::launch::async,consumer,1);
    auto c2 = std::async(std::launch::async,consumer,2);
}
```

Here, we have a global queue (see Section 12.2, page 638) concurrently used and protected by a mutex and a condition variable:

```
std::queue<int> queue;
std::mutex queueMutex;
std::condition_variable queueCondVar;
```

The mutex ensures that reads and writes are atomic, and the condition variable is to signal and wake up processing threads when new values are available.

Now, three threads provide data by pushing it into the queue:

```
{
    std::lock_guard<std::mutex> lg(queueMutex);
    queue.push(val+i);
} // release lock
queueCondVar.notify_one();
```

With `notify_one()`, they wake up one of the waiting threads to process the next value. Note again that this call does not have to be part of the protected section, so we close the block where the lock guard is declared before.

The threads waiting for new values to process operate as follows:

```
int val;
{
    std::unique_lock<std::mutex> ul(queueMutex);
    queueCondVar.wait(ul,[]{ return !queue.empty(); });
    val = queue.front();
    queue.pop();
} // release lock
    ...
```

Here, according to the interface of a queue (see Section 12.2, page 638), we need three calls to get the next value out of the queue: `empty()` checks whether a value is available. Calling `empty()` is the double-check to deal with spurious wakeups in `wait()`. `front()` queries the next value, and `pop()` removes it. All three are inside the protected region of the unique lock `ul`. However, the processing of the value returned by `front()` happens afterward to minimize the lock duration.

A possible output of this program is:

```
consumer 1: 300
consumer 1: 100
consumer 2: 500
consumer 1: 101
consumer 2: 102
consumer 1: 301
consumer 2: 103
consumer 1: 104
consumer consumer 1: 105
2: 501
```

```
consumer 1: 302
consumer 2: 303
consumer 1: 502
consumer 2: 304
consumer 1: 503
consumer 2: 305
consumer 1: 504
consumer 2: 505
```

Note that the output of the two consumers is not synchronized, so characters might interleave. Note also that the order in which concurrent waiting threads are notified is not defined.

In the same way, you can call `notify_all()` if multiple consumers will have to process the same data. A typical example would be an event-driven system, where an event has to get published to all registered consumers.

Also note that for condition variables, you have the interface of waiting for a maximum amount of time: `wait_for()` waits for a duration of time, whereas `wait_until()` waits until a timepoint has arrived.

18.6.4   Condition Variables in Detail

The header file `<condition_variable>` provides two classes for condition variables, class `condition_variable` and class `condition_variable_any`.

Class `condition_variable`

As introduced in Section 18.6, page 1003, class `std::condition_variable` is provided by the C++ standard library to be able to wake up one or multiple threads waiting for a specific condition (something necessary prepared or performed or some necessary data provided). Multiple threads can wait for the same condition variable. When a condition is fulfilled, a thread can notify one or all of the waiting threads.

Due to *spurious wakeups*, notifying a thread is not enough when a condition is fulfilled. Waiting threads have and need to use the ability to double-check that the condition holds after a wakeup.

Table 18.10 lists the interface the C++ standard library provides for class `condition_variable` in detail. Class `condition_variable_any` provides the same interface except `native_handle()` and `notify_all_at_thread_exit()`.

If it can't create a condition variable, the constructor might throw a `std::system_error` exception (see Section 4.3.1, page 43) with the error code `resource_unavailable_try_again`, which is equivalent to the POSIX errno `EAGAIN` (see Section 4.3.2, page 45). Copies and assignments are not allowed.

Operation	Effect
condvar cv	Default constructor; creates a condition variable
cv.~*condvar*()	Destroys the condition variable
cv.notify_one()	Wakes up one of the waiting threads, if any
cv.notify_all()	Wakes up all waiting threads
cv.wait(*ul*)	Waits for notification, using the unique lock *ul*
cv.wait(*ul*,*pred*)	Waits for notification, using the unique lock *ul*, until *pred* yields true after a wakeup
cv.wait_for(*ul*,*duration*)	Waits for a notification, using the unique lock *ul*, for *duration*
cv.wait_for(*ul*,*duration*,*pred*)	Waits for a notification, using the unique lock *ul*, for *duration* or until *pred* yields true after a wakeup
cv.wait_until(*ul*,*timepoint*)	Waits for a notification, using the unique lock *ul*, until *timepoint*
cv.wait_until(*ul*,*timepoint*,*pred*)	Waits for a notification, using the unique lock *ul*, until *timepoint* or until *pred* yields true after a wakeup
cv.native_handle()	Returns a platform-specific type native_handle_type for nonportable extensions
notify_all_at_thread_exit(*cv*,*ul*)	Wakes up all waiting threads of *cv*, using the unique lock *ul*, at the end of the calling thread

Table 18.10. Operations of Class condition_variable

Notifications are automatically synchronized so that concurrent calls of notify_one() and notify_all() cause no trouble.

All threads waiting for a condition variable have to use the same mutex, which has to be locked by a unique_lock when one of the wait() members is called. Otherwise, undefined behavior occurs.

Note that consumers of a condition variable always operate on mutexes that are usually locked. Only the waiting functions temporarily unlock the mutex performing the following three atomic steps:[23]

1. Unlocking the mutex and entering the waiting state
2. Unblocking the wait
3. Locking the mutex again

This implies that predicates passed to waiting functions are always called under the lock, so they may safely access the object(s) protected by the mutex.[24] The calls to lock and unlock the mutex might throw the corresponding exceptions (see Section 18.5.2, page 1000).

---

[23] The problem with a naive approach like "*lock, check state, unlock, wait*" is that notifications arising between *unlock* and *wait* would get lost.

[24] Thanks to Bartosz Milewski for pointing this out.

Called without the predicate, both `wait_for()` and `wait_until()` return the following *enumeration class* (see Section 3.1.13, page 32) values:

- `std::cv_status::timeout` if the absolute timeout happened
- `std::cv_status::no_timeout` if a notification happened

Called with a predicate as third argument, `wait_for()` and `wait_until()` return the result of the predicate (whether the condition holds).

The global function `notify_all_at_thread_exit(cv, l)` is provided to call `notify_all()` when the calling thread exits. For this, it temporarily locks the corresponding lock *l*, which must use the same mutex all waiting threads use. To avoid deadlocks, the thread should be exited directly after calling `notify_all_at_thread_exit()`. Thus, this call is only to cleanup before notifying waiting threads, and this cleanup should never block.[25]

Class `condition_variable_any`

Besides class `std::condition_variable`, the C++ standard library also provides a class `std::condition_variable_any`, which does not require using an object of class `std::unique_lock` as lock. As the C++ standard library notes: "If a lock type other than one of the standard mutex types or a `unique_lock` wrapper for a standard mutex type is used with `condition_variable_any`, the user must ensure that any necessary synchronization is in place with respect to the predicate associated with the `condition_variable_any` instance." In fact, the object has to fulfill the so-called *BasicLockable* requirements, which require providing synchronized `lock()` and `unlock()` member functions.

---

[25] A typical example would be to signal the end of a detached thread (see Section 18.2.1, page 967). By using `notify_all_at_thread_exit()`, you can ensure that thread local objects are destroyed before the main program (or master thread) processes the fact that the detached thread terminated.

18.7   Atomics

In the first example for condition variables (see Section 18.6.1, page 1003), we used a Boolean value `readyFlag` to let one thread signal that something is prepared or provided for another thread. Now, you might wonder why we still need a mutex here. If we have a Boolean value, why can't we concurrently let one thread change the value while another thread checks it? The moment the providing thread sets the Boolean to `true`, the observing thread should be able to see that and perform the consequential processing.

As introduced in Section 18.4, page 982, we have two problems here:

1. In general, reading and writing even for fundamental data types is not atomic. Thus, you might read a half-written Boolean, which according to the standard results in undefined behavior.
2. The generated code might change the order of operations, so the providing thread might set the ready flag before the data is provided, and the consuming thread might process the data before evaluating the ready flag.

With a mutex, both problems are solved, but a mutex might be a relatively expensive operation in both necessary resources and latency of the exclusive access. So, instead of using mutexes and lock, it might be worth using atomics instead.

In this section, I first introduce the *high-level interface* of atomics, which provides atomic operations using the default guarantee regarding the order of memory access. This default guarantee provides *sequential consistency*, which means that in a thread, atomic operations are guaranteed to happen in the order as programmed. Thus, problems of reordered statements as introduced in Section 18.4.3, page 986, do not apply. At the end of this section, I present the *low-level interface* of atomics: operations with relaxed order guarantees.

Note that the C++ standard library does not distinguish between a high-level and a low-level atomics interface. The term *low-level* was introduced by Hans Boehm, one of the authors of the library. Sometimes, it is also called the *weak*, or *relaxed*, atomic interface, and the high-level interface is sometimes also known as the *normal*, or *strong*, atomic interface.

18.7.1   Example of Using Atomics

Let's transfer the example from Section 18.6.1, page 1003, into a program using atomics:

```
#include <atomic>      // for atomic types
...
std::atomic<bool> readyFlag(false);

void thread1()
{
    // do something thread2 needs as preparation
    ...
    readyFlag.store(true);
}
```

```
void thread2()
{
    // wait until readyFlag is true (thread1 is done)
    while (!readyFlag.load()) {
        std::this_thread::sleep_for(std::chrono::milliseconds(100));
    }

    // do whatever shall happen after thread1 has prepared things
    ...
}
```

First, we include the header file `<atomic>`, where atomics are declared:

```
#include <atomic>
```

Then, we declare an atomic object, using the `std::atomic<>` class template:

```
std::atomic<bool> readyFlag(false);
```

In principle, you can use any trivial, integral, or pointer type as template parameter.

Note that you *always* should initialize atomic objects because the default constructor does not fully initialize it (it's not that the initial value is undefined, it is that the lock is uninitialized).[26] For static-duration atomic objects, you should use a constant to initialize them. If only the default constructor is used, the only operation allowed next is to call a global `atomic_init()` operation as follows:

```
std::atomic<bool> readyFlag;
...
std::atomic_init(&readyFlag,false);
```

This way of initialization is provided to be able to write code that also compiles in C (see Section 18.7.3, page 1019).

The two most important statements to deal with atomics are `store()` and `load()`:

- `store()` assigns a new value.
- `load()` yields the current value.

The important point is that these operations are guaranteed to be atomic, so we don't need a mutex to set the ready flag, as we had to without atomics. Thus, in the first thread, instead of

```
{
    std::lock_guard<std::mutex> lg(readyMutex);
    readyFlag = true;
} // release lock
```

we simply can program:

```
readyFlag.store(true);
```

---

[26] Thanks to Lawrence Crowl for pointing this out.

In the second thread, instead of

```
{
    std::unique_lock<std::mutex> l(readyFlagMutex);
    while (!readyFlag) {
        l.unlock();
        std::this_thread::sleep_for(std::chrono::milliseconds(100));
        l.lock();
    }
} // release lock
```

we have to implement only the following:

```
while (!readyFlag.load()) {
    std::this_thread::sleep_for(std::chrono::milliseconds(100));
}
```

However, when using condition variables, we still need the mutex for consuming the condition variable:

```
// wait until thread1 is ready (readyFlag is true)
{
    std::unique_lock<std::mutex> l(readyMutex);
    readyCondVar.wait(l, []{ return readyFlag.load(); });
} // release lock
```

For atomic types, you can still use the "useful," "ordinary" operations, such as assignments, automatic conversions to integral types, increments, decrements, and so on:

```
std::atomic<bool> ab(false);
ab = true;
if (ab) {
    ...
}

std::atomic<int> ai(0);
int x = ai;
ai = 10;
ai++;
ai-=17;
```

Note, however, that to provide atomicity, some usual behavior might be slightly different. For example, the assignment operator yields the assigned value instead of a reference to the atomic the value was assigned to. See Section 18.7.2, page 1016, for details.

Let's look at a complete example using atomics:

```
// concurrency/atomics1.cpp

#include <atomic>      // for atomics
#include <future>      // for async() and futures
```

```cpp
#include <thread>        // for this_thread
#include <chrono>        // for durations
#include <iostream>

long data;
std::atomic<bool> readyFlag(false);

void provider ()
{
    // after reading a character
    std::cout << "<return>" << std::endl;
    std::cin.get();

    // provide some data
    data = 42;

    // and signal readiness
    readyFlag.store(true);
}

void consumer ()
{
    // wait for readiness and do something else
    while (!readyFlag.load()) {
        std::cout.put('.').flush();
        std::this_thread::sleep_for(std::chrono::milliseconds(500));
    }

    // and process provided data
    std::cout << "\nvalue : " << data << std::endl;
}

int main()
{
    // start provider and consumer
    auto p = std::async(std::launch::async,provider);
    auto c = std::async(std::launch::async,consumer);
}
```

Here, thread `provider()` first provides some data and then uses a `store()` to signal that the data is provided:

```cpp
data = 42;              // provide some data
readyFlag.store(true);  // and signal readiness
```

The store() operation performs a so-called *release* operation on the affected memory location, which by default ensures that all prior memory operations, whether atomic or not, become visible to other threads before the effect of the store operation.

Accordingly, thread consumer() performs a loop of load()s and processes data then:

```
while (!readyFlag.load()) {        // loop until ready
    ...
}
std::cout << data << std::endl;    // and process provided data
```

The load() operation performs a so-called *acquire* operation on the affected memory location, which by default ensures that all following memory operations, whether atomic or not, become visible to other threads after the load operation.

As a consequence, because the setting of data *happens before* the provider() stores true in the readyFlag and the processing of data happens after the consumer() has loaded true as value of the readyFlag, the processing of data is guaranteed to happen after the data was provided.

This guarantee is provided because in all atomic operations, we use a default *memory order* named memory_order_seq_cst, which stands for *sequential consistent memory order*. With low-level atomics operations, we are able to relax this order guarantee (see Section 18.7.4, page 1019, for details).

18.7.2   Atomics and Their High-Level Interface in Detail

In <atomic>, the class template std::atomic<> provides the general abilities of atomic data types. It can be used for any trivial type. Specializations are provided for bool, all integral types, and pointers:

```
template<typename T> struct atomic;        // primary class template
template<> struct atomic<bool>;            // explicit specializations
template<> struct atomic<int>;

...

template<typename T> struct atomic<T*>;    // partial specialization for pointers
```

Table 18.11 lists the high-level operations provided for atomics. If possible, they map directly to corresponding CPU instructions. Column *triv* flags operations provided for std::atomic<bool> and atomics of other trivial types; column *int type* flags operations provided for std::atomic<>, if an integral type is used; and column *ptr type* flags operations provided for std::atomic<>, if a pointer type is used.

Note a couple of remarks regarding this table:

- In general, operations yield copies rather than references.
- The default constructor does not initialize a variable/object completely. The only legal operation after default construction is calling atomic_init() to initialize the object (see Section 18.7.1, page 1013).
- The constructor for a value of the corresponding type is not atomic.
- All functions except constructors are overloaded for volatile and *non*-volatile.

Operation	triv	int type	ptr type	Effect
atomic a=*val*	Yes	Yes	Yes	Initializes a with *val* (not an atomic operation)
atomic a; atomic_init(&a,*val*)	Yes	Yes	Yes	Ditto (without atomic_init(), a is not initialized)
a.is_lock_free()	Yes	Yes	Yes	true if type internally does not use locks
a.store(*val*)	Yes	Yes	Yes	Assigns *val* (returns void)
a.load()	Yes	Yes	Yes	Returns copy of the value of a
a.exchange(*val*)	Yes	Yes	Yes	Assigns *val* and returns copy of old value of a
a.compare_exchange_strong(*exp*, *des*)	Yes	Yes	Yes	CAS operation (see below)
a.compare_exchange_weak(*exp*, *des*)	Yes	Yes	Yes	Weak CAS operation
a = *val*	Yes	Yes	Yes	Assigns and returns copy of *val*
a.operator *atomic*()	Yes	Yes	Yes	Returns copy of the value of a
a.fetch_add(*val*)		Yes	Yes	Atomic t+=*val* (returns copy of new value)
a.fetch_sub(*val*)		Yes	Yes	Atomic t-=*val* (returns copy of new value)
a += *val*		Yes	Yes	Same as t.fetch_add(*val*)
a -= *val*		Yes	Yes	Same as t.fetch_sub(*val*)
++a, a++		Yes	Yes	Calls t.fetch_add(1) and returns copy of a or a+1
--a, a--		Yes	Yes	Calls t.fetch_sub(1) and returns copy of a or a-1
a.fetch_and(*val*)		Yes		Atomic a&=*val* (returns copy of new value)
a.fetch_or(*val*)		Yes		Atomic a|=*val* (returns copy of new value)
a.fetch_xor(*val*)		Yes		Atomic a^=*val* (returns copy of new value)
a &= *val*		Yes		Same as a.fetch_and(*val*)
a |= *val*		Yes		Same as a.fetch_or(*val*)
a ^= *val*		Yes		Same as a.fetch_xor(*val*)

Table 18.11. High-Level Operations of Atomics

For example, for `atomic<int>`, the following assignment operations are declared:

```
namespace std {
    // specialization of std::atomic<> for int:
    template<> struct atomic<int> {
      public:
        // ordinary assignment operators are not provided:
        atomic& operator=(const atomic&) = delete;
        atomic& operator=(const atomic&) volatile = delete;
        // but assignment of an int is provided, which yields the passed argument:
        int operator= (int) volatile noexcept;
        int operator= (int) noexcept;
        ...
    };
}
```

With `is_lock_free()`, you can check whether an atomic type internally uses locks to be atomic. If not, you have native hardware support for the atomic operations (which is a prerequisite for using atomics in signal handlers).

Both `compare_exchange_strong()` and `compare_exchange_weak()` are so-called *compare-and-swap* (*CAS*) operations. CPUs often provide this atomic operation to compare the contents of a memory location to a given value and, only if they are the same, modify the contents of that memory location to a given new value. This guarantees that the new value is calculated based on up-to-date information. The effect is something like the following pseudocode:

```
bool compare_exchange_strong (T& expected, T desired)
{
    if (this->load() == expected) {
        this->store(desired);
        return true;
    }
    else {
        expected = this->load();
        return false;
    }
}
```

Thus, if the value had been updated by another thread in the meantime, it returns `false` with the new value in `expected`.

The weak form may spuriously fail so that it returns `false` even when the expected value is present. But the weak form is sometimes more efficient than the strong version.

18.7.3   The C-Style Interface of Atomics

For the atomic proposal for C++, there was a corresponding proposal for C, which should provide the same semantics but could, of course, not use such specific C++ features as templates, references, and member functions. Therefore, the whole atomic interface has a C-style equivalent, which also was proposed as an extension to the C standard.

For example, you can also declare an `atomic<bool>` as `atomic_bool`, and instead of `store()` and `load()`, you can use global functions, which use a pointer to the object:

```
std::atomic_bool ab;          // equivalent to: std::atomic<bool> ab
std::atomic_init(&ab,false);  // see Section 18.7.1, page 1013
...
std::atomic_store(&ab,true);  // equivalent to: ab.store(true)
...
if (std::atomic_load(&ab)) {  // equivalent to: if (ab.load())
    ...
}
```

However, C added another interface, using `_Atomic` and `_Atomic()`, so the C-style interface in general is useful only for code that needs to be both C and C++ compilable in the nearer term.

However, using the C-style atomic types is pretty common in C++. Table 18.12 lists the most important atomic type names. There are more provided for less common types, such as `atomic_int_fast32_t` for `atomic<int_fast32_t>`.

Note that for shared pointers (see Section 5.2.1, page 76) special atomic operations are provided. The reason is that a declaration, such as `atomic<shared_ptr<T>>`, is not possible, because a shared pointer is not trivially copyable. The atomic operations follow the naming conventions of the C-style interface. See Section 5.2.4, page 96, for details.

18.7.4   The Low-Level Interface of Atomics

The *low-level interface* of atomics means using the atomic operations in a way that we have no guaranteed sequential consistency. Thus, compilers and hardware might (partially) reorder access on atomics (see Section 18.4.3, page 986).

Beware again: Although I give an example, this area is a minefield. You need a lot of expertise to know when memory reorderings are worth the effort, and even experts often make mistakes in this area.[27]

An expert using this feature should be familiar with the material mentioned in [*N2480:MemMod*] and [*BoehmAdve:MemMod*] or, in general, all material listed at [*Boehm:C++MM*].

---

[27] Special thanks to Hans Boehm and Bartosz Milewski for their support in letting me understand this and their help in providing the right wording. Any flaws are my fault.

Named Type	Corresponding Type
atomic_bool	atomic<bool>
atomic_char	atomic<char>
atomic_schar	atomic<signed char>
atomic_uchar	atomic<unsigned char>
atomic_short	atomic<short>
atomic_ushort	atomic<unsigned short>
atomic_int	atomic<int>
atomic_uint	atomic<unsigned int>
atomic_long	atomic<long>
atomic_ulong	atomic<unsigned long>
atomic_llong	atomic<long long>
atomic_ullong	atomic<unsigned long long>
atomic_char16_t	atomic<char16_t>
atomic_char32_t	atomic<char32_t>
atomic_wchar_t	atomic<wchar_t>
atomic_intptr_t	atomic<intptr_t>
atomic_uintptr_t	atomic<uintptr_t>
atomic_size_t	atomic<size_t>
atomic_ptrdiff_t	atomic<ptrdiff_t>
atomic_intmax_t	atomic<intmax_t>
atomic_uintmax_t	atomic<uintmax_t>

Table 18.12. Some Named Types of `std::atomic<>`

An Example for the Low-Level Interface of Atomics

Consider the second example for using atomics, introduced in Section 18.7.1, page 1014, where we declared an atomic flag to control access to some data:

```
long data;
std::atomic<bool> readyFlag(false);
```

and a thread providing the data:

```
data = 42;                  // provide some data
readyFlag.store(true);      // and signal readiness
```

and a thread consuming the data:

```
while (!readyFlag.load()) {       // loop until ready
    ...
}
std::cout << data << std::endl;   // and process provided data
```

Because we use the default memory order, which guarantees sequential consistency, this works as described in Section 18.7.1, page 1015. In fact, what we really call is:

```
data = 42;
readyFlag.store(true,std::memory_order_seq_cst);
```

and

```
while (!readyFlag.load(std::memory_order_seq_cst)) {
    ...
}
std::cout << data << std::endl;
```

Thus, each operation has an optional argument to pass the memory order, which by default is std::memory_order_seq_cst (*sequential consistent memory order*).

By passing other values as memory order, we can weaken the order guarantees. In our case, it is, for example, enough to require that the provider not delay operations past the atomic store and that the consumer not bring forward operations following the atomic load:

```
data = 42;
readyFlag.store(true,std::memory_order_release);
```

and

```
while (!readyFlag.load(std::memory_order_acquire)) {
    ...
}
std::cout << data << std::endl;
```

However, relaxing all constraints on the order of atomic operations would result in undefined behavior:

```
// ERROR: undefined behavior:
data = 42;
readyFlag.store(true,std::memory_order_relaxed);
```

The reason is that std::memory_order_relaxed doesn't guarantee that all prior memory operations become visible to other threads before the effect of the store operation. Thus, the provider might write data after setting the ready flag, so the consumer might read data while it gets written, which is a *data race*.

Note that you could also make data atomic and use std::memory_order_relaxed as memory order:

```
std::atomic<long> data(0);
std::atomic<bool> readyFlag(false);

// providing thread:
data.store(42,std::memory_order_relaxed);
readyFlag.store(true,std::memory_order_relaxed);

// consuming thread:
while (!readyFlag.load(std::memory_order_relaxed)) {
    ...
}
std::cout << data.load(std::memory_order_relaxed) << std::endl;
```

Strictly speaking, this is not *undefined behavior*, because we don't have a *data race*. However, this also would not work as expected, because the resulting value of data might not be 42 yet (the memory order is still not guaranteed). It's behavior that results in data having an *unspecified* value.

Using `memory_order_relaxed` would be useful only if we have atomic variables where reads and/or writes are independent of one another. An example would be a global counter, which different threads might increment or decrement and where we need only the final value after all threads ended.

Overview of Low-Level Operations

Table 18.13 lists the supplementary low-level operations provided for atomics. As you can see, the load, store, exchange, CAS, and fetch operations provide the supplementary ability to pass a memory order as an additional argument.

Operation	*triv*	*int type*	*ptr type*
`a.store(`*val*`,`*mo*`)`	Yes	Yes	Yes
`a.load(`*mo*`)`	Yes	Yes	Yes
`a.exchange(`*val*`,`*mo*`)`	Yes	Yes	Yes
`a.compare_exchange_strong(`*exp*`,`*des*`,`*mo*`)`	Yes	Yes	Yes
`a.compare_exchange_strong(`*exp*`,`*des*`,`*mo1*`,`*mo2*`)`	Yes	Yes	Yes
`a.compare_exchange_weak(`*exp*`,`*des*`,`*mo*`)`	Yes	Yes	Yes
`a.compare_exchange_weak(`*exp*`,`*des*`,`*mo1*`,`*mo2*`)`	Yes	Yes	Yes
`a.fetch_add(`*val*`,`*mo*`)`		Yes	Yes
`a.fetch_sub(`*val*`,`*mo*`)`		Yes	Yes
`a.fetch_and(`*val*`,`*mo*`)`		Yes	
`a.fetch_or(`*val*`,`*mo*`)`		Yes	
`a.fetch_xor(`*val*`,`*mo*`)`		Yes	

Table 18.13. Supplementary Low-Level Operations of Atomics

Some additional functions are provided to manually control memory access. For example, `atomic_thread_fence()` and `atomic_signal_fence()` are provided to manually program fences, which are barriers for memory-access reordering.

No More Details

I *don't* explain these low-level interfaces in more detail because this feature is for real concurrency experts or those who want to become experts. So, you should definitely use specific resources for that.

One good starting point is Anthony Williams book *C++ Concurrency in Action* (see [*Williams:C++Conc*]), especially Chapters 5 and 7. Another is Hans Boehm's list of URLs for material about memory models (see [*Boehm:C++MM*]).

Chapter 19

Allocators

Allocators, introduced in Section 4.6, page 57, represent a special memory model and are an abstraction used to translate the *need* to use memory into a raw *call* for memory. This chapter describes allocators and corresponding low-level features to deal with memory. Details are provided in a supplementary section of the book, available at the book's Web site: `http://www.cppstdlib.com`.

19.1 Using Allocators as an Application Programmer

For the application programmer, using different allocators should be no problem. You simply have to pass the allocator as a template argument. For example, the following statements create different containers and strings, using the special allocator `MyAlloc<>`:

```
// a vector with special allocator
std::vector<int,MyAlloc<int>> v;
```

```
// an int/float map with special allocator
std::map<int,float,std::less<int>,
         MyAlloc<std::pair<const int,float>>> m;
```

```
// a string with special allocator
std::basic_string<char,std::char_traits<char>,MyAlloc<char>> s;
```

If you use your own allocator, it probably is a good idea to make some type definitions. For example:

```
// special string type that uses special allocator
typedef std::basic_string<char,std::char_traits<char>,
                          MyAlloc<char>> MyString;
```

```
// special string/string map type that uses special allocator
typedef std::map<MyString,MyString,std::less<MyString>,
                 MyAlloc<std::pair<const MyString,MyString>>> MyMap;
```

```
// create object of this type
MyMap mymap;
```

Since C++11, you can use *alias templates* (template typedefs; see Section 3.1.9, page 27) to define the allocator type while leaving the element type open:

```
template <typename T>
using Vec = std::vector<T,MyAlloc<T>>;    // vector using own allocator

Vec<int> coll;    // equivalent to: std::vector<int,MyAlloc<int>>
```

When you use objects with other than the default allocator, you'll see no difference.

You can check whether two allocators use the same memory model by using operators == and !=. If it returns `true`, you can deallocate storage allocated from one allocator via the other. To access the allocator, all types that are parametrized by an allocator provide the member function `get_allocator()`. For example:

```
if (mymap.get_allocator() == s.get_allocator()) {
    // OK, mymap and s use the same or interchangeable allocators
    ...
}
```

In addition, since C++11, a type trait (see Section 5.4, page 122) is provided to check whether a type T has an `allocator_type`, which a passed allocator may be converted into:

```
std::uses_allocator<T,Alloc>::value    // true if Alloc is convertible
                                       //      into T::allocator_type
```

19.2 A User-Defined Allocator

Allocators provide an interface to allocate, create, destroy, and deallocate objects (Table 19.1). With allocators, containers and algorithms can be parametrized based on the way the elements are stored. For example, you could implement allocators that use shared memory or that map the elements to a persistent database.

Expression	Effect
`a.allocate(num)`	Allocates memory for num elements
`a.construct(p,val)`	Initializes the element to which p refers with val
`a.destroy(p)`	Destroys the element to which p refers
`a.deallocate(p,num)`	Deallocates memory for num elements to which p refers

Table 19.1. Fundamental Allocator Operations

Writing your own allocator is not very hard. The most important issue is how you allocate or deallocate the storage. For the rest, appropriate defaults are usually provided since C++11. (Before C++11, you had to implement the rest in a pretty obvious way.) As an example, let's look at an allocator that behaves just like the default allocator:

```cpp
// alloc/myalloc11.hpp

#include <cstddef>      // for size_t

template <typename T>
class MyAlloc {
  public:
    // type definitions
    typedef T value_type;

    // constructors
    // - nothing to do because the allocator has no state
    MyAlloc () noexcept {
    }
    template <typename U>
    MyAlloc (const MyAlloc<U>&) noexcept {
        // no state to copy
    }

    // allocate but don't initialize num elements of type T
    T* allocate (std::size_t num) {
        // allocate memory with global new
        return static_cast<T*>(::operator new(num*sizeof(T)));
    }

    // deallocate storage p of deleted elements
    void deallocate (T* p, std::size_t num) {
        // deallocate memory with global delete
        ::operator delete(p);
    }
};

// return that all specializations of this allocator are interchangeable
template <typename T1, typename T2>
bool operator== (const MyAlloc<T1>&,
                 const MyAlloc<T2>&) noexcept {
    return true;
}
template <typename T1, typename T2>
bool operator!= (const MyAlloc<T1>&,
                 const MyAlloc<T2>&) noexcept {
    return false;
}
```

As the example demonstrates, you have to provide the following features:

- A type definition of the `value_type`, which is nothing but the passed template parameter type.
- A constructor.
- A template constructor, which copies the internal state while changing the type. Note that a template constructor does not suppress the implicit declaration of the copy constructor (see Section 3.2, page 36).
- A member `allocate()`, which provides new memory.
- A member `deallocate()`, which releases memory that is no longer needed.
- Constructors and a destructor, if necessary, to initialize, copy, and clean up the internal state.
- Operators `==` and `!=`.

You don't have to provide `construct()` or `destroy()`, because their default implementations usually work fine (using *placement new* to initialize the memory and calling the destructor explicitly to clean it up).

Using this base implementation, you should find it easy to implement your own allocator. You can use the core functions `allocate()` and `deallocate()` to implement your own policy of memory allocation, such as reusing memory instead of freeing it immediately, using shared memory, mapping the memory to a segment of an object-oriented database, or just debugging memory allocations. In addition, you might provide corresponding constructors and a destructor to provide and release what `allocate()` and `deallocate()` need to fulfill their task.

Note that before C++11, you had to provide a lot more members, which, however, were easy to provide. See `alloc/myalloc03.hpp` for a corresponding complete example, which is also covered in the supplementary section about allocator details at `http://www.cppstdlib.com`.

19.3   Using Allocators as a Library Programmer

This section describes the use of allocators from the viewpoint of people who use allocators to implement containers and other components that are able to handle different allocators. This section is based, with permission, partly on Section 19.4 of Bjarne Stroustrup's *The C++ Programming Language*, 3rd edition (see [*Stroustrup:C++*]).

As an example, let's look at a naive implementation of a vector. A vector gets its allocator as a template or a constructor argument and stores it somewhere internally:

```
namespace std {
    template <typename T,
              typename Allocator = allocator<T> >
    class vector {
        ...
      private:
        Allocator alloc;       // allocator
        T*        elems;       // array of elements
        size_type numElems;    // number of elements
        size_type sizeElems;   // size of memory for the elements
        ...
```

```
    public:
        // constructors
        explicit vector(const Allocator& = Allocator());
        explicit vector(size_type num, const T& val = T(),
                        const Allocator& = Allocator());
        template <typename InputIterator>
        vector(InputIterator beg, InputIterator end,
               const Allocator& = Allocator());
        vector(const vector<T,Allocator>& v);
        ...
    };
}
```

The second constructor that initializes the vector by num elements of value val could be implemented as follows:

```
namespace std {
    template <typename T, typename Allocator>
    vector<T,Allocator>::vector(size_type num, const T& val,
                                const Allocator& a)
     : alloc(a)      // initialize allocator
    {
        // allocate memory
        sizeElems = numElems = num;
        elems = alloc.allocate(num);

        // initialize elements
        for (size_type i=0; i<num; ++i) {
            // initialize ith element
            alloc.construct(&elems[i],val);
        }
    }
}
```

Expression	Effect
uninitialized_fill(*beg*,*end*,*val*)	Initializes [*beg*,*end*) with *val*
uninitialized_fill_n(*beg*,*num*,*val*)	Initializes *num* elements starting from *beg* with *val*
uninitialized_copy(*beg*,*end*,*mem*)	Initialize the elements starting from *mem* with the elements of [*beg*,*end*)
uninitialized_copy_n(*beg*,*num*,*mem*)	Initialize *num* elements starting from *mem* with the elements starting from *beg* (since C++11)

Table 19.2. Convenience Functions for Uninitialized Memory

However, for the initialization of uninitialized memory, the C++ standard library provides some convenience functions (Table 19.2). The implementation of the constructor becomes even simpler using these functions:

```
namespace std {
    template <typename T, typename Allocator>
    vector<T,Allocator>::vector(size_type num, const T& val,
                                            const Allocator& a)
     : alloc(a)       // initialize allocator
    {
        // allocate memory
        sizeElems = numElems = num;
        elems = alloc.allocate(num);

        // initialize elements
        uninitialized_fill_n(elems, num, val);
    }
}
```

The member function `reserve()`, which reserves more memory without changing the number of elements (see Section 7.3.1, page 271), could be implemented as follows:

```
namespace std {
    template <typename T, typename Allocator>
    void vector<T,Allocator>::reserve(size_type size)
    {
        // reserve() never shrinks the memory
        if (size <= sizeElems) {
            return;
        }

        // allocate new memory for size elements
        T* newmem = alloc.allocate(size);

        // copy old elements into new memory
        uninitialized_copy(elems,elems+numElems,newmem);

        // destroy old elements
        for (size_type i=0; i<numElems; ++i) {
            alloc.destroy(&elems[i]);
        }

        // deallocate old memory
        alloc.deallocate(elems,sizeElems);
```

```
    // so, now we have our elements in the new memory
    sizeElems = size;
    elems = newmem;
  }
}
```

Raw Storage Iterators

In addition, class `raw_storage_iterator` is provided to iterate over uninitialized memory to initialize it. Therefore, you can use any algorithms with a `raw_storage_iterator` to initialize memory with the values that are the result of that algorithm.

For example, the following statement initializes the storage to which `elems` refers by the values in range [`x.begin()`,`x.end()`):

```
copy (x.begin(), x.end(),                        // source
      raw_storage_iterator<T*,T>(elems));        // destination
```

The first template argument (T*, here) has to be an output iterator for the type of the elements. The second template argument (T, here) has to be the type of the elements.

Temporary Buffers

In code, you might also find the `get_temporary_buffer()` and `return_temporary_buffer()`. They are provided to handle uninitialized memory that is provided for short, temporary use inside a function. Note that `get_temporary_buffer()` might return less memory than expected. Therefore, `get_temporary_buffer()` returns a pair containing the address of the memory and the size of the memory (in element units). Here is an example of how to use it:

```
void f()
{
    // allocate memory for num elements of type MyType
    pair<MyType*,std::ptrdiff_t> p
      = get_temporary_buffer<MyType>(num);
    if (p.second == 0) {
        // could not allocate any memory for elements
        ...
    }
    else if (p.second < num) {
        // could not allocate enough memory for num elements
        // however, don't forget to deallocate it
        ...
    }

    // do your processing
    ...
```

```
        // free temporarily allocated memory, if any
        if (p.first != 0) {
            return_temporary_buffer(p.first);
        }
    }
```

However, it is rather complicated to write exception-safe code with `get_temporary_buffer()` and `return_temporary_buffer()`, so they are usually no longer used in library implementations.

Bibliography

This bibliography lists the resources that were mentioned, adapted, or cited in this book. These days, many of the advancements in programming appear in electronic forums, which too are listed here.

Web sites are typically considerably more volatile than books and articles. The Internet links listed here may not be valid in the future, so I provide the list of links for this book at my Web site, which I expect to be stable: `http://www.cppstdlib.com`.

Newsgroups and Forums

The Internet also provides a diverse collection of forums or newsgroups about programming, C++, the C++ standard library, and the STL. Some of them are *moderated*, which improves the quality of the forum a lot because every submission is examined in some way for its appropriateness.

The most important newsgroups and forums are:

- Newsgroup **comp.lang.c++.moderated**, a moderated forum for technical discussions of C++ (see `http://groups.google.com/group/comp.lang.c++.moderated/about`)
- Newsgroup **comp.std.c++**, a moderated forum for discussions of the C++ standard (see `http://groups.google.com/group/comp.std.c++/about`)
- Forum **stackoverflow.com**, a moderated forum for discussions of programming, where you can use tags, such as c++ or c++11, for C++ specific topics (see `http://stackoverflow.com/tags/c++/info`)
- Newsgroup **comp.lang.c++**, an unmoderated forum for discussions of C++ (see `http://groups.google.com/group/comp.lang.c++/about`)
- Newsgroup **alt.comp.lang.learn.c-c++**, an unmoderated forum for beginners of C and C++ (see `http://groups.google.com/group/alt.comp.lang.learn.c-c++/about`)

Books and Web Sites

[*Abrahams:RValues*]
Dave Abrahams. **Move It With Rvalue References**
`http://cpp-next.com/archive/2009/09/move-it-with-rvalue-references/`

[*Austern:STL*]
Matthew H. Austern. **Generic Programming and the STL: Using and Extending the C++ Standard Template Library**. Reading, MA: Addison-Wesley, 1998

[*Becker:LibExt*]
Pete Becker. **The C++ Standard Library Extensions: A Tutorial and Reference**. Reading, MA: Addison-Wesley, 2007

[*Becker:RValues*]
Thomas Becker. **C++ Rvalue References Explained**
`http://thbecker.net/articles/rvalue_references/section_01.html`

[*Boehm:C++MM*]
Hans J. Boehm. **Threads and memory model for C++**
`http://www.hpl.hp.com/personal/Hans_Boehm/c++mm/`

[*BoehmAdve:MemMod*]
Hans J. Boehm and Sarita V. Adve. **Foundations of the C++ Concurrency Memory Model**
`http://www.hpl.hp.com/techreports/2008/HPL-2008-56.html`

[*Boost*]
Boost C++ Libraries
`http://www.boost.org/`

[*Breymann:STL*]
Ulrich Breymann. **Komponenten entwerfen mit der STL**. Bonn, Germany: Addison-Wesley, 1999

[*C++Std1998*]
ISO. **Information Technology—Programming Languages—C++**. Document Number ISO/IEC 14882-1998. ISO/IEC, 1998

[*C++Std2003*]
ISO. **Information Technology—Programming Languages—C++, Second Edition**. Document Number ISO/IEC 14882-2003. ISO/IEC, 2003

[*C++Std2011*]
ISO. **Information Technology—Programming Languages—C++, Third Edition**. Document Number ISO/IEC 14882-2011. ISO/IEC, 2011

[*C++Std2011Draft*]
Pete Becker, ed. ***Working Draft, Standard for Programming Language C++ (C++11)***
`http://www.open-std.org/jtc1/sc22/wg21/docs/papers/2011/n3242.pdf`

[*ECMAScript*]
Ecma International. ***ECMAScript Language Specification (ECMA-262)***
`http://www.ecma-international.org/publications/standards/Ecma-262.htm`

[*Eggink:C++IO*]
Bernd Eggink. ***Die C++ iostreams–Library***. München, Germany: Hanser Verlag, 1995

[*EllisStroustrup:ARM*]
Margaret A. Ellis and Bjarne Stroustrup. ***The Annotated C++ Reference Manual (ARM)***. Reading, MA: Addison-Wesley, 1990

[*HoadZobel:HashCombine*]
Timothy C. Hoad and Justin Zobel. ***Methods for Identifying Versioned and Plagiarised Documents***
`http://www.cs.rmit.edu.au/jz/fulltext/jasist-tch.pdf`

[*GlassSchuchert:STL*]
Graham Glass and Brett Schuchert. ***The STL <Primer>***. Englewood Cliffs, NJ: Prentice-Hall, 1996

[*GoF:DesignPatterns*]
Erich Gamma, Richard Helm, Ralph Johnson, and John Vlissides. ***Design Patterns: Elements of Reusable Object-Oriented Software***. Reading, MA: Addison-Wesley, 1994

[*ISO639:LangCodes*]
Codes for the Representation of Names of Languages
`http://www.loc.gov/standards/iso639-2/php/English_list.php`

[*ISO3166:CodeTab*]
ISO 3166-1 decoding table
`http://www.iso.org/iso/support/country_codes/iso_3166_code_lists/
        iso-3166-1_decoding_table.htm`

[*ISOLatin1*]
ISO/IEC 8859-1
`http://en.wikipedia.org/wiki/ISO_8859-1`

[*ISOLatin9*]
ISO/IEC 8859-15
`http://en.wikipedia.org/wiki/ISO_8859-15`

[*JustThread*]
Anthony Williams. ***C++ Standard Thread Library***
`http://www.stdthread.co.uk/`

[*Karlsson:Boost*]
Björn Karlsson. ***Beyond the C++ Standard Library: An Introduction to Boost***. Reading, MA: Addison-Wesley, 2006

[*KoenigMoo:Accelerated*]
Andrew Koenig and Barbara E. Moo. ***Accelerated C++: Practical Programming by Example***. Boston, MA: Addison-Wesley, 2000

[*Meyers:MoreEffective*]
Scott Meyers. ***More Effective C++: 35 New Ways to Improve Your Programs and Designs***. Reading, MA: Addison-Wesley, 1996

[*Milewski:Atomics*]
Bartosz Milewski. ***C++ atomics and memory ordering***
http://bartoszmilewski.wordpress.com/2008/12/01

[*Milewski:Multicore*]
Bartosz Milewski. ***Multicores and Publication Safety***
http://bartoszmilewski.wordpress.com/2008/08/04

[*MusserSaini:STL*]
David R. Musser and Atul Saini. ***STL Tutorial and Reference Guide: C++ Programming with the Standard Template Library***. Reading, MA: Addison-Wesley, 1996

[*N1456:HashTable*]
Matthew Austern. ***A Proposal to Add Hash Tables to the Standard Library (revision 4)***
http://www.open-std.org/jtc1/sc22/wg21/docs/papers/2003/n1456.html

[*N2351:SharedPtr*]
Peter Dimov and Beman Dawes. ***Improving shared_ptr for C++0x, Revision 2***
http://www.open-std.org/jtc1/sc22/wg21/docs/papers/2007/n2351.htm

[*N2480:MemMod*]
Hans-J. Boehm. ***A Less Formal Explanation of the Proposed C++ Concurrency Memory Model***
http://www.open-std.org/jtc1/sc22/wg21/docs/papers/2007/n2480.html

[*N2543:FwdList*]
Matt Austern. ***STL singly linked lists (revision 3)***
http://www.open-std.org/jtc1/sc22/wg21/docs/papers/2008/n2543.htm

[*N2661:Chrono*]
Howard E. Hinnant, Walter E. Brown, Jeff Garland, and Marc Paterno. ***A Foundation to Sleep On: Clocks, Points in Time, and Time Durations***
http://www.open-std.org/jtc1/sc22/wg21/docs/papers/2008/n2661.html

[*N3051:DeprExcSpec*]
Doug Gregor. ***Deprecating Exception Specifications***
http://www.open-std.org/jtc1/sc22/wg21/docs/papers/2010/n3051.html

[*N3194:Futures*]
Lawrence Crowl, Anthony Williams, and Howard Hinnant. ***Clarifying C++ Futures***
http://www.open-std.org/jtc1/sc22/wg21/docs/papers/2010/n3194.htm

[*N3198:DeprAdapt*]
Daniel Krügler. ***Deprecating unary_function and binary_function (Revision 1)***
http://www.open-std.org/jtc1/sc22/wg21/docs/papers/2010/n3198.htm

[*N3279:LibNoexcept*]
Alisdair Meredith and John Lakos. ***Conservative use of noexcept in the Library***
http://www.open-std.org/jtc1/sc22/wg21/docs/papers/2011/n3279.pdf

[*Nelson:C++*]
Mark Nelson. ***C++ Programmer's Guide to the Standard Template Library***. Foster City, CA: IDG
Books Worldwide, 1995

[*Plauger:C++Lib*]
P. J. Plauger. ***The Draft Standard C++ Library***. Englewood Cliffs, NJ: Prentice Hall, 1995

[*SafeSTL*]
Cay S. Horstmann. ***Safe STL***
http://www.horstmann.com/safestl.html

[*STLport*]
STLport
http://www.stlport.org/

[*Stroustrup:C++*]
Bjarne Stroustrup. ***The C++ Programming Language, Third Edition***. Reading, MA: Addison-
Wesley, 1997

[*Stroustrup:C++0x*]
Bjarne Stroustrup. ***What is C++0x?***
http://www2.research.att.com/b̃s/what-is-2009.pdf

[*Stroustrup:Design*]
Bjarne Stroustrup. ***The Design and Evolution of C++***. Reading, MA: Addison-Wesley, 1994

[*Stroustrup:FAQ*]
Bjarne Stroustrup. ***C++11 — the recently approved new ISO C++ standard***
http://www.research.att.com/b̃s/C++11FAQ.html

[*Sutter:LockFree*]
Herb Sutter. **Lock-Free Code: A False Sense of Security**
http://drdobbs.com/cpp/210600279

[*Teale:C++IO*]
Steve Teale. **C++ IOStreams Handbook**. Reading, MA: Addison-Wesley, 1993

[*UTF8*]
UTF-8
http://en.wikipedia.org/wiki/UTF-8

[*VisualC++Locales*]
Visual C++ Language and Country/Region Strings
http://msdn.microsoft.com/en-us/library/hzz3tw78.aspx

[*Williams:C++Conc*]
Anthony Williams. **C++ Concurrency in Action: Practical Multithreading**. Greenwich, CT: Manning, 2012

[*Williams:CondVar*]
Anthony Williams. **Multithreading and Concurrency: Condition Variable Spurious Wakes**
http://www.justsoftwaresolutions.co.uk/threading/?page=2

Index

Note: Page numbers in **bold** indicate the location of the definition of the item. Page numbers in the normal type face are other pages of interest. If the entry appears in source code the page numbers are in the *italic* type face.

F

M

N

O

T

W

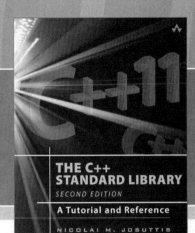

FREE
Online Edition

Safari
Books Online

Your purchase of **The C++ Standard Library, Second Edition,** includes access to a free online edition for 45 days through the **Safari Books Online** subscription service. Nearly every Addison-Wesley Professional book is available online through **Safari Books Online**, along with thousands of books and videos from publishers such as Cisco Press, Exam Cram, IBM Press, O'Reilly Media, Prentice Hall, Que, Sams, and VMware Press.

Safari Books Online is a digital library providing searchable, on-demand access to thousands of technology, digital media, and professional development books and videos from leading publishers. With one monthly or yearly subscription price, you get unlimited access to learning tools and information on topics including mobile app and software development, tips and tricks on using your favorite gadgets, networking, project management, graphic design, and much more.

Activate your FREE Online Edition at
informit.com/safarifree

STEP 1:   Enter the coupon code: ODFKGWH.

STEP 2:   New Safari users, complete the brief registration form.
Safari subscribers, just log in.

If you have difficulty registering on Safari or accessing the online edition,
please e-mail customer-service@safaribooksonline.com

  Adobe Press Cisco Press Press IBM Press Microsoft Press New Riders O'REILLY

 Peachpit Press PRENTICE HALL QUE Redbooks SAMS SAS Publishing  vmware PRESS WILEY WROX